Songs o

More praise for the book

"This collection is a tribute to the folk poetry and music that has enriched, and continues to enrich the culture of Eire and Northern Ireland. . . . This is an important work that belongs in every school and public library, not to collect dust in an obscure corner, but to be enjoyed again and again for generations. It certainly belongs on the shelf of every lover of poetry and music."
—Newsletter of the Folk Music Society of New York

"Although it will give people who want to sing the old songs of a place to find them, its greater purpose is to make available to scholars a wide selection of what the common people of Ireland were thinking and singing at the time."—*Eire-Ireland*

"It is not very often that a collection of this quality is published, and I am sure it will soon become a part of every standard, and indeed essential part of every traditional singer's library. Highly recommended."—*Folk North West*

"A treasure trove . . . A very significant contribution."—*Banjo Newsletter*

"An absolutely indispensable scholarly, yet lively collection of ballads, dirges, and humorous songs of the common people of Ireland."—*Martha's Vineyard Times*

Sam Henry's
Songs of the People

Edited, transcribed, and annotated by **Gale Huntington**

Revised, with additions and indexes by **Lani Herrmann**

Geographical index prepared with the aid of John Moulden

The University of Georgia Press Athens and London

Published in 1990 by The University of Georgia Press
Athens, Georgia 30602
www.ugapress.org

The collection copyright © by Olive Mary Craig

New material (including the introduction, transcriptions, Indexes, bibliography, discography, and melodic index) copyright © 1990 By Gale Huntington and
Lani Herrman

All rights reserved

Music Autography, book design, and production editing by Lani Herrman

Printed digitally in the United States of America

The Library of Congress has cataloged the hardcover edition of this book as follows:
Library of Congress Cataloging-in-Publication Data
LCCN Permalink: http://lccn.loc.gov/90036866

Sam Henry's Songs of the people / edited, transcribed, and annotated by Gale Huntington ; rev., with additions and indexes by Lani Herrmann ; geographical index prepared with the aid of John Moulden.
xxxix, 632 p. of music ; 29 cm.

ISBN 0-8203-1258-4 (alk. paper)
0820312592 (pbk. : alk. paper)

Ballads and songs of Ulster; unacc. melodies.
English words.
Collected by Sam Henry and originally published in tonic sol-fa notation in his regular column in the Northern constitution, of Coleraine, Northern Ireland, between 1923 and 1939.
Includes bibliographical references and indexes.

1. Folk music—Ulster (Northern Ireland and Ireland)
2. Folk songs, English—Ulster (Northern Ireland and Ireland) 3. Ballads, English—Ulster (Northern Ireland and Ireland) I. Henry, Sam, b. 1878. II. Huntington, Gale. III. Herrmann, Lani. IV. Title: Songs of the people.
M1745.3 .S35   1990   90-36866

Paperback reissue 2010 ISBN-13: 978-0-8203-3625-1
ISBN-10: 0-8203-3625-4

British Library Cataloging-in-Publication Data available

Preparation for this volume was made possible in part by a grant From the Program for Editions of the National Endowment for the Humanities, an independent federal agency.

Title page photo: Pay Kealey, fiddler and singer.
Copyright by Olive Mary Craig.

Contents

List of songs *vii*
Introduction *xvii*
Acknowledgments *xxxvii*
Abbreviations *xxxix*

A. Life in the old country
  1. Come let us all begin: Old choir rhymes *1*
  2. Rockin' the cradle is nae work, ava: Lullabies *5*
  3. I'll tell my ma: Children's games *9*
  4. Once I had a wee hen: Animals, hunting, racing *16*
  5. By the heat of my brow: Occupations, lifestyle *38*
  6. If you want a bit of fun: Celebrations *71*
  7. The Irish soldier boy: War *78*
  8. Bound away to the west'rd: Sea *95*
  9. A bold undaunted youth: Crime *118*
  10. Deep and dead water: Death, laments, ghosts *138*

B. The shamrock shore
  11. Erin, my country: Praise of home *155*
  12. The emigrant's farewell: Goodbye home *185*
  13. The call of home: Longing for home *206*

C. Personal relationships
  14. She's a lovely fair: Praise of a girl *224*
  15. Where's the lass to take my hand?: Courtship and dalliance *254*
  16. I will watch and pray: Faithful farewells *285*
  17. It's I am your Jamie: The returned lover *306*
  18. In man's array: Disguises *325*
  19. Youth and folly: Love uncertain *339*
  20. She will not condescend: Love unrequited *353*
  21. Content in the arms of another: Love unfaithful *382*
  22. When death was near: Deadly love *410*
  23. Cruel was my father: Despite relatives *426*
  24. To Hymen's car: Successful courtship *453*
  25. Wedlock's soft bondage: Domesticity *500*

Appendixes

Appendix A. Titles of songs in the original order (with dates) of their appearance in the *Northern Constitution* 522

Appendix B. Additional text, mainly by Sam Henry, from the original columns 532

Appendix C. Other relevant text, not by Sam Henry, but included by him in library copies of the columns 541

Indexes and reference aids

Glossary 543

Bibliography 546

Discography 566

Index of titles, including alternative titles, and first lines 584

Original sources of items in the columns as given by Sam Henry 605

Geographical index of sources 612

Melodic index 617

Sources of illustrations 631

Songs

A1. Come let us all begin: Old choir rhymes

Abbey *2*
Dublin/Coleshill *2*
Dundee *2*
French *2*
Mary's *2*

Martyrs *3*
York *3*
Newto[w]n *3*
Additional verses *3*
A1 References *4*

A2. Rockin' the cradle is nae work, ava: Lullabies

Heezh Ba *6*
Hush Alee *6*
Ballyeamon Cradle Song *6*
Irish Lullaby for the Christ-Child *7*

Lullaby for a Sailor's Child *7*
Raven-Locks *7*
A2 References *8*

A3. I'll tell my ma: Children's games

I am the Master *10*
Green Gravel *10*
Ring a Ring o' Roses *10*
Water, Water, Wallflowers *11*
I'll Tell My Ma *11*
Here's a Poor Widow *11*

Old Sally Walker *11*
Broken Bridges *11*
Fair Rosa/The Sleeping Beauty *12*
How Many Miles to Babyland? *12*
Cricketty Wee *12*
A3 References *13*

A4. Once I had a wee hen: Animals, hunting, racing

A Child's Lullaby *17*
The Little White Cat *17*
My Bonnie Wee Hen *17*
The Bonny Brown Hen *18*
Nell Flaherty's Drake *18*
The Duck from Drummuck *19*
The Lost Birdies/The Hobe and the Robin *20*
Robin Redbreast's Testament *20*
The Goat's Will *21*
Matty Broon's Soo *22*
The Moneygran Pig Hunt *22*
Bellaghy Fair *23*
Sport's Lament *23*
The Heifer *24*
The "Crummy" Cow *25*

The Mayogall Asses *26*
Seal Song *27*
The Crocodile *28*
The Fox and His Wife *29*
The Hunting Priest *29*
Squire Agnew's Hunt *30*
The Hare of Kilgrain *31*
The Hare's Dream *31*
The Clady River Water Bailiffs *32*
A Ballad of Master M'Gra[th] *32*
Cashel Green (II) *33*
Arthur Bond *34*
Spanking Maggie from the Ross *35*
A4 References *36*

A5. By the heat of my brow: Occupations, lifestyle

Waulking Song 39
The Tailor Boy 39
The Cobbler 40
Jim, the Carman Land 40
My Rattlin' Oul' Grey Mare 41
My Irish Jaunting Car 41
The Farmer 41
The Rocks of Bawn 42
The Charity Seed/We Never Died in the Winter Yet 43
The Lint Pullin' 43
The Jolly Thresher 44
As a King Went A-Hunting 44
Shanty Boy 45
The Shepherd Laddie 45
The Thatchers of Glenrea 46
The Dandy Chignon 47
Long Cookstown/Nancy Whiskey 47
The Jug of Punch 48
A Cup o' Tay 48
The Black Pipe 49
The Wee Cutty Pipe 49
The Rakes of Poverty 50
The Oul' Rigadoo 50
Old Rosin the Bow 51
Bryan O'Lynn 52
The State of Arkansaw 53
Denny Byrne, the Piper 53
The Sailor in the Alehouse 54
The Private Still 55
Mick Magee 56
My Grandfather Died 57
The Buttermilk Boy 57
O'Ryan 58
The Jolly Fisherman 59
Songs of Old Ireland 59
The Salutation 60
Fine Broom Besoms! 61
Better Bide a Wee 61
Gaol Song 62
The Bramble 62
The Leaves So Green 63
Dun Ceithern 63
Barossa/Oliver's Advice 64
The Yellow Bittern/An Bunnan Buidhe 64
The Parting Glass 65
A5 References 65

A6. If you want a bit of fun: Celebrations

Dan Murphy's Convoy 72
The Wedding at Ballyporeen 72
The Ballinderry Marriage 73
Coleraine Regatta 74
The Lammas Fair in Cargan 75
On the Road to Bethlehem 76
A6 References 77

A7. The Irish soldier boy: War

The Shepherd Boy 79
My Parents Reared Me Tenderly 79
The Black Horse 80
Pat Reilly 80
Pat Muldoney 81
You Broken-Hearted Heroes 81
Lovely Sally 82
The Deserter 83
Bonny Woodha' 84
My Son Ted 84
Lovely Jamie 85
The Hungry Army 86
The Plains of Waterloo (I) 87
The Plains of Waterloo (II) 87
The Drummer Boy at Waterloo 88
The Bonny Light Horseman 88
The Irish Soldier Boy 89
The Three Flowers of Chivalry 89
The Heights of Alma 90
Balaclava 91
Old Ireland Far Away 92
A7 References 92

A8. Bound away to the west'rd: Sea

Kishmul's Galley *96*
Sailors' Shanties *96*
It's Time for Us to Leave Her *96*
Tom's Gone to Ilo *96*
Santy Anna *96*
Paddy Doyle *97*
I'm Going Home *97*
The Girls of Valparaiso *97*
The S[team]s[hip] *Leinster Lass* *98*
The Cruise of the *Calabar* *98*
The *Zared* *99*
Yellow Meal *100*
The Shamrock Shore *101*
Patrick O'Neal *102*
The Sailor Boy *103*
Franklin the Brave *103*

The Loss of Seven Clergymen *104*
The Portrush Fishing Disaster (I) *105*
The Portrush Fishing Disaster (II) *105*
The Wreck of the *Enterprise* *106*
The *Falcon* *107*
The Wreck of the Fanad Boat *107*
The Wreck of the *Nimrod* *108*
The Loss of the *Royal Charter* *109*
The *Trader* *110*
The Wreck of the *Rebecca* *111*
The Good Ship *Mary Cochrane* *111*
The Banks of Newfoundland *112*
The French Privateer *112*
Captain Coulston *113*
A8 References *114*

A9. A bold undaunted youth: Crime

Botany Bay *119*
The Boston Burglar *119*
The Wild Colonial Boy *120*
Eight Mile Bridge *121*
Whiskey in the Jar *122*
Waltzing Matilda *122*
Heather Jock *123*
Jamie Raeburn's Farewell *124*
James Magee *125*
John Mitchel's Farewell to His Countrymen (a) *125*

John Mitchell (b) *126*
Hugh Hill, the Ramoan Smuggler *127*
The Three Huntsmen/Wilson, Gilmore and Johnson *128*
The Crafty Ploughboy *129*
Shane Crossagh *130*
The Breaking of Omagh Jail *131*
The Dreary Gallows *132*
Lambkin *133*
A9 References *134*

A10. Deep and dead water: Death, laments, ghosts

The Bard of Culnady/Charles O'Neill *139*
Finvola, the Gem of the Roe *139*
Heilan' Jane *140*
An Irish Mother's Lament *140*
The Cowboy of Loreto *141*
John McKeown and Margaret Deans *141*
Annie Moore *142*
Molly Bawn Lowry *143*
A Collier Lad *144*
My Lowlands, Away *144*
Mary's Dream *144*

The *Nightingale* (I) *145*
Willie Lennox *146*
Sloan Wellesley *147*
James Kennedy *147*
Miss Cochrane *148*
Rachel Dear/The Maine Water Side *148*
Polly Primrose *149*
Holland Is a Fine Place *149*
Susan on the Beach *150*
A10 References *151*

Sam Henry's Songs of the People

B11. Erin, my country: Praise of home

The Little Thatched Cabin 156
The Old Stone Wall 156
Old Arboe 157
The Hills o' Ballyboley 157
Ballycastle, O! 158
Ballymonan Brae 159
Benbradden Brae 159
The Braes of Carnanbane 160
Carnlough Shore 160
Beautiful Churchill 161
The Girls from [Dt,Wt: of] Coleraine 161
The Maids of Downhill 162
Dungiven Priory Church 162
Faughanvale 163
Bonny Garrydoo 164
Glenariffe 164
Glenelly 165
Lovely Glenshesk (I) 165
Old Inishowen 166
Kearney's Glen 166
The Shores of Sweet Kenbane 167
The Braes of Sweet Kilhoyle 167
Knocklayde 168
Lochaber Shore 168
Mountsandel 169
Mudion River 169

Oville 170
The Peistie Glen 170
Bonny Portrush 171
The River Roe (I) 171
The River Roe (II) 171
Slieve Gallen Brae 172
Fair Tyrone 173
Among the Green Bushes [Bp,Dp: in Sweet Tyrone] 174
Where Derry Meets Tyrone 174
The Land of the West 175
Old Ireland 175
Erin, My Country 176
The Enchanted Isle 176
The Mac's and the O's 177
The Connaught Man 177
The Rocky Road to Dublin 178
Dungiven Cricket Match 179
March of the Men of Garvagh 180
Ta Ra, Limavady 180
The Knights of Malta 180
The Bright Orange Stars of Coleraine 181
The Boys of Coleraine 182
Neuve Chappelle 182
B11 References 182

B12. The emigrant's farewell: Goodbye home

Lovely Armoy 186
Monk McClamont's "Farewell to Articlave" 186
Hannah M'Kay/The Pride of Artikelly 187
Farewell, Ballycastle 188
Carnanbane 188
Carntogher's Braes 189
The Flower of Craiganee 189
The Hills of Tandragee 190
My Girl from Donegal 190
The Flower of Sweet Dunmull 191
The Faughan Side 191
Finn Waterside 192
Gelvin Burn 192
Glenrannel's Plains 193
Farewell to Sweet Glenravel 193
The Glenshesk Waterside 194
Lovely Glenshesk (IIa) 194

In Praise of the Glen 195
The Brow of Sweet Knocklayd 196
Owenreagh's Banks 196
The Point Maid 197
Adieu to the Banks of the Roe 197
Farewell to Slieve Gallen 198
The Hills of Tyrone 199
Bonny, Bonny 199
Knox's Farewell 200
The Emigrant's Farewell 200
The Happy Shamrock Shore 201
The Brown-Haired Lass (a) 201
The Brown-Haired Lass (b) 202
Paddy's Green Countrie 203
The Shamrock Sod No More 203
B12 References 204

B13. The call of home: Longing for home

Norah McShane *207*
The Old Blacksmith's Shop *207*
The Little Old Mud Cabin on the Hill *207*
The Green Hills of Antrim *208*
Cloughwater/The Shamrock Shore *208*
The Coleraine Girl *209*
Oh, Derry, Derry, Dearie Me *209*
The Hills of Donegal *210*
Drumglassa Hill *210*
The Happy Green Shades of Duneane *211*
Oul' Dunloy *211*
Sweet Glenbush *212*
Glen O'Lee *212*
The Pretty Three-Leaved Shamrock from
    Glenore *213*
Juberlane *213*

Sweet Loughgiel *214*
Maguire's Brae *214*
Where Moyola Waters Flow *215*
Mullaghdoo *215*
The Maid of Mullaghmore *216*
Owenreagh *217*
The Banks of the Roe *217*
Farewell to the Banks of the Roe *218*
A Shamrock from Tiree *218*
The Call of Home *219*
Och, Och, Eire, O! *219*
There's a Dear Spot in Ireland *220*
Riding Herd at Night *220*
Charlie Jack's Dream *221*
The Irishman *221*
B13 References *222*

C14. She's a lovely fair: Praise of a girl

Happy 'Tis, Thou Blind, for Thee *225*
My Bonny Breeden *225*
O, Jeanie Dear *225*
Bonny Mary Hay *226*
So Like Your Song and You *226*
Not the Swan on the Lake *227*
Nancy, the Pride of the West *227*
The Maid of Erin's Isle *228*
Peggy of the Moor *228*
Mary M'Veagh *229*
The Holly Bough/The Pride of Altibrine *229*
The Maid of Burndennet (a) *230*
The Maid of Burndennett (b) *231*
Kate of Coleraine *231*
Kate of Glenkeen *231*
The Star of Glenamoyle *232*
The Flower of Glenleary *232*
The Flower of Gortade *233*
A Kintyre Love Song *234*
The Manchester Angel *234*
Mary Smith, the Maid of Mountain Plain *235*
Autumn Dusk/Coimfeasgar Fogmair *235*
The Dear-a-Wee Lass *236*
The Valley Below *236*
The Dark-Haired Girl *237*

Braiding Her Glossy Black Hair *237*
The Old Dun Cow *238*
Gragalmachree *238*
The Maid of Altaveedan *239*
Jean of Ballinagarvey *239*
The Flower of Benbrada *239*
The Beauty of the Braid *240*
The Maid from the Carn Brae *241*
Claudy Green (b) *241*
Maggie of Coleraine *242*
The Flower of Corby Mill *242*
The Flower of Magherally, O! *243*
Magilligan *244*
The Valleys of Screen *245*
Summer Hill *245*
The Maid from the County Tyrone *246*
Her Bonny Blue E'e *246*
Rosaleen Bawn *247*
The Blazing Star of Drim (a) *247*
The Blazing Star of Drung (b) *248*
Ann o' Drumcroon *248*
The Pride of Glenelly *249*
Mary, the Pride of Killowen *250*
Moorlough Mary *250*
C14 References *251*

Sam Henry's Songs of the People

C15. Where's the lass to take my hand?: Courtship and dalliance

Nae Bonnie Laddie tae Tak' Me Awa' 255
Maidens of Sixty-Three 255
The Black Chimney Sweeper 256
The Wee Article 257
Roger's Courtship 257
Grandma's Advice 258
The Nonsense o' Men 258
As I Go I Sing 259
The Strands of Magilligan 259
Green Grow the Rashes (a) 260
Green Grown the Rashes (b) 260
The Young Farmer's Offer 261
The Load of Kail Plants 261
An Irish Serenade 262
You're Welcome as the Flowers in May 262
Magherafelt Hiring Fair 263
The Roving Bachelor (a) 263
The Roving Bachelor (b) 264
The Whistling Thief 264
The Feckless Lover 265
The Ride in the Creel 265

I'm Seventeen 'gin Sunday 266
As I Gaed ower a Whinny Knowe 267
The Rambling Suiler 268
A Beggarman Cam' ower the Lea 269
The Galway Shawl 269
Where the Moorcocks Crow 269
The Maid of Seventeen 270
Cloughmills Fair 270
O'er the Moor amang the Heather 271
The Whinny Knowes 272
The Captain with the Whiskers 273
Youghall Harbour 273
The Cup of Gold 273
The Mountain Road 274
The Woods of Mountsandel 275
The Ould Lammas Fair 275
The Star of Moville 276
Mind Your Eye 277
The Basket of Oysters 278
Tumbling through the Hay 278
C15 References 279

C16. I will watch and pray: Faithful farewells

The Londonderry Air 286
Down in My Sally's Garden 286
Early, Early 287
The Green Banks of Banna 287
A Sweetheart's Appeal to Her Lover/[Dt:] Oh, It's down Where the Water Runs Muddy 288
My Sailor Boy 288
The Drinaun D[h]un 289
The Boatman/Fear a Bhàta 289
A Rathlin Song 290
Bring back My Barney to Me 290
Linton Lowrie 291
The Sea-Apprentice 291
My True Love's Gone A-Sailing 292
So Dear Is My Charlie to Me 292
The Jolly Roving Tar 293
Alt[i]mover Stream 293

Fare Ye Well, Enniskillen 294
My [Bt: The] Dear Irish Boy 294
The Banks of Sweet Lough Neagh 295
The Soldier Boy 295
The Banks of the Nile 296
Johnnie and Molly 297
The *Bold Privateer* 297
The Maid of Dunysheil 298
The Maid of Carrowclare 298
The Blooming Star of Eglintown 299
The Faithful Rambler 299
Love's Parting/Jamie and Mary 300
Dobbin's Flowery Vale 300
Londonderry Love Song 301
The Maids of Culmore 302
C16 References 302

Songs

C17. It's I am your Jamie: The returned lover

The Banished Lover 307
Learmount Grove 307
Mary Machree 308
James Reilly 309
Skerry's Blue-Eyed Jane 309
The Banks of the Clyde/One Fine Summer's Morning 310
Mary Doyle/The Wreck of the *Lady Shearbrooke* 310
Laurel Hill/Kyle's Flowery Braes 311
The *Lady of the Lake* 312
The Banks of Claudy 313
The Banks of [the] Dee 314

The Mantle So Green 314
Johnny Jarmin/The *Rainbow* 315
Mary and Willie 315
Lurgan Town 316
The Broken Ring 317
Green Garden 317
The Dark-Eyed Sailor 318
The Love Token 318
The Pride of Glencoe 319
The Banks of the River Ness 319
Jennie of the Moor 320
Bordon's Grove 320
C17 References 321

C18. In man's array: Disguises

The Drummer Maid 326
On Board of a Man-of-War 326
The Drum Major 327
The Female Highwayman 327
The Squire's Bride 328
Lovely Annie (II) 328
The Rich Merchant's Daughter 329
The Sailor on the Sea 330

The True Lovers' Departure 331
The Jolly Ploughboy 331
Blythe and Bonny Scotland/[*Dt:*] India's Burning Sands 332
Canada[,] Hi! Ho! 333
Willie Taylor (a) 334
Willie Taylor (b) 334
C18 References 335

C19. Youth and folly: Love uncertain

The Six Sweethearts 340
I've Two or Three Strings to My Bow (a) 340
I've Two or Three Strings to My Bow (b) 341
One Morning Clear 341
The Maid of Tardree 342
Dark-Eyed Molly 342
Farewell Ballymoney 343
The Sweet Bann Water 343
The Rejected Lover 344
The Banks of Mourne Strand 344

Fair Maid of Glasgow Town 345
The Ploughboy 345
The Blackbird and Thrush 346
Farewell He 347
The Cuckoo 347
If I Were a Fisher 348
The Star of Benbradden 348
I Am a Wee Laddie, Hard, Hard Is My Fate 349
C19 References 349

C20. She will not condescend: Love unrequited

John MacAnanty's Courtship 354
Paddy's Land 354
Claudy Green (a) 355
The Maid of Croaghmore 355
The Bonnie Wee Lass of the Glen 356
As I Walked Out 357

Farewell, Darling 357
Will Ye Pad the Road wi' Me? 358
The Maid of Craigienorn 359
Lurgan Stream (a) 360
Lurgan Stream (b) 360
Castleroe Mill 361

Sam Henry's Songs of the People

The Banks of Kilrea (II) 361
The True Lovers' Discussion 362
The Maid of the Sweet Brown Knowe 364
Cahan's Shade Glen 364
Fair Maid of Ballyagan 365
The Grey Mare 365
I'll Hang My Harp on a Willow Tree 366
The Bonnet sae Blue 367
Tarry Trousers 367
The Factory Girl 368
Campbell's Mill 368

The Maid of Faughan Vale 369
Wester Snow 369
Drummond's Land 370
My Charming Kate O'Neill 370
The Maid of Mourne Shore 371
The Girl from Turfahun 372
The Lass of Mohee 372
The Lakes of Ponchartrain 373
Am I the Doctor? 374
Barbara Allen 375
C20 References 376

C21. Content in the arms of another: Love unfaithful

The Ripest of Apples 383
The False Lover 383
The Bonny Bushes Bright 383
Willie Angler/The Banks of the Bann 384
Lovely Nancy 385
Under the Shade of a Bonny Green Tree 385
Must I Go Bound? (a) 386
Must I Go Bound? (b) 386
Phelimy Phil 386
Norah Magee 387
The Broken-Hearted Gardener 387
Gramachree 388
Belfast Mountains 389
My Love John 389
My Flora and I 390
The Flower of Sweet Strabane 390
Bring Me Back the Boy I Love (a) 391
Never Change the Old Love for the New 392
Oh, Johnny, Johnny 392

The Apron of Flowers 393
The Bonny, Bonny Boy 393
The Maid with the Bonny Brown Hair (a) 394
The Maid with the Bonny Brown Hair (b) 394
The Green Bushes 395
Out of the Window 395
My Bonny Brown Jane 396
The Slighted Suitor (a) 396
The Slighted Suitor (b) 397
Twenty-One 397
Polly Perkins of Paddington Green 398
My Darling Blue-Eyed Mary 399
My Bonnie Irish Boy 399
Sween Clonalee 400
An Old Lover's Wedding 400
The Laird's Wedding 401
The Girl I Left Behind 401
C21 References 403

C22. When death was near: Deadly love

The 'Prentice Boy 411
Blooming Caroline of Edinburgh Town 411
Ballindown Braes 412
The King o' Spain's Daughter 413
The Broomfield Hill 414
Lord Ronald 415
Susan Brown 415
Susan Carr 416

Flora, the Lily of the West 416
The Old Oak Tree 417
The Silver[y] Tide 418
The Willow Tree 419
Killeavy's Pride 420
The Pride of Newry Town 421
C22 References 422

C.23 Cruel was my father: Despite relatives

The Maid of Ballyhaunis *427*
The Banks of [*Wt:* the] Cloughwater *427*
Hibernia's Lovely Jane *428*
If I Were a Blackbird *428*
The Maid of Aghadowey *429*
The Slaney Side *429*
The Maid of Sweet Gorteen *430*
McClenahan's Jean *430*
We Met, 'Twas in a Crowd *431*
Johnny Doyle *431*
The Lover's Ghost *432*
Sweet William *433*
Young Edward Bold/The Lowlands Low *434*
The Constant Farmer's Son *434*
The Bonny Labouring Boy *435*
Willy Reilly *436*

Young Mary of Accland (a) *437*
Young Mary of Accland (b) *438*
Erin's Lovely Home *438*
Sweet Dunloy *439*
Henry Connor of Castledawson *440*
Sally Munro *441*
John Reilly the Sailor Lad *441*
Kellswater *442*
The Banks of the Bann *443*
Johnnie Hart *443*
Love Laughs at Locksmiths *444*
The *Lady Leroy* *445*
Eliza/When I Landed in Glasgow *446*
The Apprentice Boy/Covent Garden *446*
C23 References *447*

C24. To Hymen's car: Successful courtship

Our Wedding Day *454*
The Boy That Found a Bride *454*
The Swan *455*
The Tossing o' the Hay *455*
Pining Day and Daily *456*
The Pretty Blue Handkerchief (I) *456*
The Pretty Blue Handkerchief (II) *456*
The Gentle Shepherdess *457*
The Bonny Wee Lass *458*
Lovely Annie (I) *458*
I'm from over the Mountain (a) *459*
I'm from over the Mountain (b) *459*
The Bann Water Side *460*
Beardiville Planting *460*
Bess of Ballymoney *461*
The Blackwaterside *461*
Cashel Green (I) *462*
My Charming Coleraine Lass *462*
The Star of Donegal *463*
Glenarm Bay *464*
Greenmount Smiling Ann *464*
Gruig Hill *465*
Innishowen *465*
Kellswaterside *466*
The Banks of Kilrea (I) *466*
The Largy Line *467*

Sweet Londonderry *468*
The Lovely Banks of Mourne *468*
Wild Slieve Gallon Brae[s] *468*
Sandy's Wooing *469*
"Thank You, Ma'am," Says Dan *469*
The Yowe Lamb *470*
Petie Cam' ower the Glen *470*
The Navvy Boy *471*
One Penny Portion *472*
The Inniskilling Dragoon *472*
The Gallant Soldier *473*
Young Edward the Gallant Hussar *473*
Green Broom *474*
John Hunter (a) *475*
John Hunter (b)/[*Dt:*] The Wheelwright *476*
The Journeyman Tailor *476*
Lough Erne Shore *476*
Belfast Town *477*
Jamie and Nancy *478*
Molly, Lovely Molly *478*
When a Man's in Love *479*
Charming Mary O'Neill *479*
The County Tyrone *480*
My Father's Servant Boy *481*
Jamie, Lovely Jamie *482*
You Lovers All *483*

Mullinabrone *483*
Jamie's on the Stormy Sea *484*
Wait till the Ship Comes Home *484*
The Garden Gate *485*
Henry, the Sailor Boy *485*
The Lass of Glenshee *486*
The Hielan's o' Scotland *487*

The Glove and the Lions *488*
Johnny Scott *489*
The Keeper of the Game *490*
The Rich Ship Owner's Daughter *490*
Lord Beichan *491*
C24 References *492*

C25. Wedlock's soft bondage: Domesticity

The Married Man *501*
The Happy Pair *501*
The Day We Packed the Hamper for the Coast *501*
The Tay *502*
The Scolding Wife *503*
Upside Down *503*
The Single Days of Old *504*
The Wealthy Farmer *504*
Will the Weaver *505*
The Tailor in the Tea [*Dt*: Sea] Chest *505*

I Wish That You Were Dead, Goodman *506*
The Auld Man and the Churnstaff *507*
The Blin' Auld Man/The Covered Cavalier *508*
The Brown-Eyed Gypsies *509*
Fair Annie *510*
The Ship Carpenter's Wife *511*
Whisky Is My Name (a) *512*
Whiskey Is My Name (b)/The Blacksmith *512*
The Wee Wifukie *513*
Johnny, M' Man *514*
C25 References *515*

Introduction   A scholarly detective story

How a parochial feature series published in a Northern Irish weekly came to be a focus of scholarly interest over fifty years after its original publication is a long and convoluted story, but one worth the telling, for the tale of Sam Henry and "Songs of the People" has as many fascinating elements as a detective thriller.

The ballads and songs in "Songs of the People" were originally published as a regular weekly feature in the *Northern Constitution* between the years 1923 and 1939. The *Northern Constitution* is a provincial newspaper published in the market town of Coleraine on the banks of the river Bann in Northern Ireland. And, as might be expected, songs about both Coleraine and the Bann are well represented in the collection.

After the series came to an end with the beginning of World War II, Sam Henry, its principal editor and prime mover, attempted unsuccessfully to have his collection published as a book.[1] He eventually assembled three "official" sets of the collected "Songs of the People" and gave the first copy to the Belfast Free Library, then the second, on Alan Lomax's request, to the Library of Congress in Washington, D.C., and the third to the National Library of Ireland in Dublin.[2]

Twenty years after, in 1961, Gale Huntington, then recently retired from teaching history on Martha's Vineyard island off Cape Cod and the Massachusetts coast, was working on *Songs the Whalemen Sang* (1964), his own collection of songs from 19th-century whalermen's logbooks and journals. Seeking to identify some of the songs he had uncovered, he wrote to the National Library of Ireland. One song was "The County Tyrone," and the library's director, R. J. Hayes, responded that it was number 153 in Sam Henry's "Songs of the People" collection, and enclosed a copy.[3] Further correspondence established the size and content of the Henry collection. Intrigued by this apparently derelict body, Huntington pursued several leads by mail.

From Ivan M. Russell, then publisher of the *Northern Constitution*, he learned that some human magpie had made away with several of the paper's file copies of Henry's columns. Russell granted him permission to republish "Songs of the People" in exchange for some copies "for our files (which will this time be carefully preserved!)."[4]

From the Library of Congress, he learned that there were restrictions on Henry's gift set of two scrapbooks,[5] and that Helen Hartness

---

[1] Moulden 1979:9, introduction.
[2] Sam Henry to R. J. Hayes, 18 June 1941, transmitting the remainder of the Dublin set; the Dublin and Washington sets may have been prepared concurrently.
[3] R. J. Hayes to Gale Huntington, 17 April 1961.
[4] Ivan M. Russell to Gale Huntington, 22 May 1962.
[5] Edward N. Waters to Gale Huntington, 19 June 1962.

Flanders, the noted collector and wife of the U.S. senator from Vermont, had Henry's authorization as his literary agent in America.[6]

From Mrs Flanders, he learned that she had indeed carried on correspondence with Henry 20 years before. Anticipating a possible lecture tour of the United States, Sam Henry had formally authorized her to register his claim to United States copyright of his collection. However, because the U.S. copyright law then specified manufacture in the United States with copyright notice, and because neither Henry's nor Mrs Flanders' intentions extended to printing and distributing the requisite number of copies, she was not able to claim copyright on his collection for him. Sam Henry died in 1952 without having made the projected trip.

The existence of Sam Henry's collection was known to at least a few persons in Ireland besides Hayes. In the early 1950's Sam Hanna Bell, then a producer for the British Broadcasting Corporation (BBC), commissioned Seán O'Boyle, long-time collector of and expert on Ulster folksong, to examine the Henry collection and to prepare an index to be used by BBC producers in selecting program material for broadcast.[7]

According to Mrs O'Boyle (who helped compile the alphabetical section), the index, made from the Belfast set, was prepared "in a hurry" in about three weeks in the spring of 1954.[8] Besides the alphabetical title index, it included an indication of the county (or country) of origin and a thumbnail description for each song, sometimes with Seán O'Boyle's capsule evaluation. Additional indexes listed the songs by geographical origin and by theme. Some time after the BBC index had been typed and duplicated, Peter Kennedy made further notations, mainly adding titles and BBC recording references.[9]

But until recently few scholars seem to have recognized the importance of Sam Henry's work or even, indeed, to have known that it existed. The collection has in effect remained in library limbo: virtually inaccessible, substantially without publicity or circulation.[10] The few informed exceptions include Helen Flanders, though she was mainly interested in "ancient" ballads; Edith Fowke, who included several citations of the Henry collection in *Traditional Singers and Songs from Ontario* (1965); and Peter Kennedy, who cited the Henry collection among others in his extensive references for *Folksongs of Britain and Ireland* (1975).

In 1962, with the knowledge and assent of both Russell and Mrs Flanders, Gale Huntington purchased photostats of the Dublin copy and

---

[6] Helen Hartness Flanders to Gale Huntington, 25 July 1962; Sam Henry's authorization to Mrs Flanders was notarized and dated 1 August 1941.
[7] Sam Hanna Bell to Alan Reid of the BBC, 14 December 1979.
[8] Alice O'Boyle to Lani Herrmann, 1 July 1980.
[9] On the copy at the English Folk Dance and Song Society library only?
[10] A similar fate befell Gavin Greig's earlier series, "Folk Song of the North-East," which ran for four years, 1907-11, in the Buchan *Observer* and appeared in a limited edition soon after, but was not published as a book until 1963. It appears there is no simple substitute for the permanence of publication in book form.

Introduction

set to work, intending to prepare a scholarly edition. This occupied him, part time, for well over ten years. In 1970 he and his wife, on a visit to Ireland, called on Sam Henry's daughter, Olive Henry Craig, in County Derry, and obtained her blessing for his work.

In 1971 he submitted a completed manuscript of "Songs of the People" to the American Folklore Society. After lengthy scholarly review and extensive revision, the freshly re-revised manuscript was finally accepted in 1974, but by then the Society was no longer capable of subsidizing its publication. Gale Huntington then submitted his manuscript to a series of university presses, only to discover uniform discouragement: all agreed that, whatever the virtues of the collection, production costs would outweigh potential sales.

In 1975 a notice describing the prospective Huntington edition was printed in *Ceol Tire*, newsletter of the Folk Music Society of Ireland.

In 1977 there appeared two distinct articles describing and praising the Henry collection. The first, by Dave Kilkerr, appeared in the annual *Folk Music Journal* of the London-based English Folk Dance and Song Society. Intended mainly as an introduction to the collection and the collector, it included a sample of eleven songs transcribed and annotated by Kilkerr.[11]

A second article appeared in the same year, in the ephemeral (3 issues) *Slow Air* from Belfast. In it John Moulden described the collection and some results of his preliminary bibliographical research, and announced his intention to prepare an index of the non-Henry items[12] and to redact a selection of the songs, which has since been published.

Early in 1978 I heard about Gale Huntington's frustration, had a look at his manuscript, and offered to help him find a publisher. Eventually, with his approval, I applied for a grant from the National Endowment for the Humanities to complete his edition, bringing the references up to date and adding several indexes.

Purpose of the present edition

But recounting the tangled history of the Henry collection would be pointless if the collection itself were of little merit. To the contrary, "Songs of the People" has several unusual, worthwhile qualities.

First, foremost, and very unusual in such a series,[13] the tunes to the songs were printed in the paper, together with the texts in English.

---

11 This article has since been reprinted in *Treoir*, published in Dublin by Comhaltas Ceoltóirí Éireann.
12 Nos. 247-465; see Section 1 under "Procedures" below.
13 But not unique: see Alan Bruford's review of Moulden 1979 in *Tocher* 36&37, 1981-2:463.

They were written in a letter notation known as "tonic sol-fa," whose symbols, unlike standard staff notation, can be set in ordinary type or typewritten. Although basically simple, it is more than adequate to communicate the fundamental idea or matrix of a melody, and was thus ideal for the purposes of Henry's column.[14]

Another extraordinary asset was the Song Editor himself. Sam Henry was a career civil servant, an official of the Crown Customs and Excise service, a "gauger" or tax man. By his own self-description he was an ardent amateur naturalist, archaeologist, antiquarian, genealogist, and photographer.[15] He also "was a fair performer on the violin (a 'fiddler,' not a violinist)," according to his friend Jack McBride.[16] He is said to have been a well-known and popular lecturer, "able to communicate his enthusiasm and knowledge to other people" about his special hobbies, and he contributed many articles on such matters to the local papers.[17] But, unusual among editors of song columns, Henry actually went out into the countryside and collected most of the songs he printed. His efforts were conscientious: only a small handful of the items were repeated in the years he edited the columns.

Another special aspect of the series is its longevity, with its natural consequence in the proportions of the collection. Sixteen years and well over 800 song items imply a loyal readership of respectable numbers.[18] The printed columns frequently contained fragments or titles coupled with requests for more songs, readers' comments submitted with songs, and courteous acknowledgments of contributions received.[19] These are all time-honored and effective devices for mentioning readers' names and localities in print, thereby enticing and keeping their interest. They leave no doubt as to the column's popular appeal to its readership.

Considered as a whole, "Songs of the People" also has wider significance. It is by far the largest single collection of songs from Ulster between the World Wars. Thanks to Sam Henry's editorial hand, it is a generous sample of the "old songs" people wanted to remember and may well have been singing during that period.[20] These songs can be considered as a kind of time machine, a window into the concerns and interests, the pastimes and preoccupations of the northern Irish. They also reflect the history of the region, with representation from the immigrant Scots and English as well as the native Irish and a smattering from overseas. Even the few recently composed items tell something of the taste and expectations of Henry's readership. For example, in the time-honored manner of the broadside he prints new lyrics written to fit familiar tunes, rather than the reverse.

14 An example of an original printed column, with tonic sol-fa notation, is reproduced on p. xxxiii. The notation is discussed further in Section 4 below under "Procedure."
15 *Who's Who in Northern Ireland*, 1939 (Moulden 1979:6).
16 Jack McBride to Miss S. Jackson, Librarian of the EFDSS, 26 March 1954.
17 Kilkerr 1977:209; Moulden 1979:6.
18 Sam Henry was responsible for 618 columns over 13 of those years.
19 See Appendix B.
20 "The evidence is that the songs were largely sung at the time -- many still are" (John Moulden, 16 January 1983).

Introduction

As might be expected, many of the items have counterparts in other collections gathered in Ireland, Scotland, and England. Relatives of many also turn up in North American collections, particularly those from the Northeast. It is well known that immigrants bring their music as well as their customs and language with them as intangible, duty-free cultural baggage. And some of the less obvious effects of acculturation on immigrants, with baggage, are beginning to be recognized and studied. One example is the tendency for an immigrant group to become more typical and conservative of their culture than ever they were at home -- to "out-Irish the Irish" -- as if the new environment caused the group to define or to reaffirm the cultural interface between themselves and others.

Considering the obscurity which until recently was the fate of the Henry collection, these significant attributes would have been justification enough for any edition of "Songs of the People," except that one is now in preparation close to its home. Taking full advantage of being a native and resident of Northern Ireland, John Moulden has indefatigably investigated the repositories of the collection -- including Sam Henry's private papers, fortunately preserved in his daughter's house -- to produce *Songs of the People: Selections from the Sam Henry Collection*, Vol. 1, containing 100 songs, which was published by Blackstaff Press in 1979; he envisions more to follow. His stated purpose is to return "the songs" to "the people," thereby honoring Sam Henry and his informants in proper book publication and in context, after all these years. In the illuminating introduction and headnotes to his edition, Moulden deals competently with the context, as well as the column, the collection, and Henry.

But editions may politely differ in purpose and function. Thus, our edition is intended to be a guide to scholarly exploration of the Henry collection. Liberated by John Moulden of the obligation to provide *singable* versions, and perhaps better suited to long-distance scholarship, the purpose of the present edition is to facilitate access to the entire Henry collection published in "Songs of the People" -- texts and tunes together with Henry's commentary.

Editorial considerations

Of course, this editorial task is not as simple as it might appear. Sam Henry's editorial judgment and prerogative were constrained by his commitment to produce a regular weekly song column for his readers. This meant having at least one reasonably complete text, with suitable tune and appropriate commentary, in time for each deadline. Although he seems to have been aware of some value in preserving individual variants whenever possible, more frequently he collated them.

To his credit, Henry acknowledged his sources in some detail, and the resulting collations are virtually seamless. Furthermore, in preparing the later library sets he often brought his collection notes up to date and added variations later received. On the other hand, he seems to

Sam Henry's Songs of the People

have been less punctilious about preserving all the original copies, tunes and texts, for the record. Perhaps, as Moulden suggests, Henry felt he was restoring archetypes to their "original" or "ideal" form.[21] Or perhaps, in keeping with his role as a popularizer of folk songs in radio broadcasts,[22] he was preparing his own singer's notebook of songs to be learned or sung, or keeping a record of the adjustments made for broadcast timing.[23] Those aims are not necessarily incompatible.

Perhaps less defensible from a modern scholar's viewpoint is Henry's frequent, seemingly cavalier, practice of pairing one person's tune with another's text -- or with a collation from a committee of contributors, albeit chosen and coordinated by the Song Editor. However, Henry clearly considered this miscegenation to be permissible, at least in a good cause, such as to preserve a good tune with partisan or otherwise unprintable lyrics.[24] Or perhaps he understood that his tradition allowed and expected texts and tunes to be somewhat interchangeable -- though always "suitable."[25]

Sam Henry, collector and editor

In his original introduction to the collection, Gale Huntington writes that he had formed

> a mental picture of Sam Henry as a small, wiry individual pedaling a bicycle furiously all over Ulster collecting his songs.[26] That was not a true picture. He was not small, but a very large man, tall, broad and burly, who, according to his daughter, weighed over sixteen stone [225 pounds, over 100 kilograms]. He did ride a bicycle. But he also used a car in his travels about the northern counties, as well as the public transportation systems -- bus and train -- with which Northern Ireland is so well provided.

---

21 Moulden 1979:8, paragraph 5. In a letter to Mrs Flanders, 6 August 1939, he remarked: "I think it futile work to collect every slightest variation of the song. Childe [sic] overdoes it."
22 "Henry broadcast two series entitled 'Ulster's Heritage of Song' from Belfast and another series from Dublin apart from several single programmes" (John Moulden, 16 January 1983).
23 Henry's note prefacing the Belfast set: "Inserted ink amendments in the song were variations received after publication. In some instances verses are cancelled by lines drawn across. These verses are proper to the song and the lines merely indicate that when broadcast in the series "Ulster's Heritage of Song," only the uncancelled verses were sung."
24 E.g., H41 "Kate of Glenkeen," which he sets to the Orange air known as "Captain Black."
25 Sean O'Boyle asserts: "Equivalence in poetic metre between one song and another has always been the criterion for even 'illiterate' Irish people for finding an air for words presented to them without music. This explains why we sometimes find the same set of words sung to completely different airs in different parts of the country" (1977:28).
26 "Most of the songs were collected within 20 miles of Coleraine" (John Moulden, 1 April 1983).

Introduction

This editor had also thought of Sam Henry as one whose great and abiding passion from childhood had been folksong. It was indeed an abiding passion, but only one of several, for Sam Henry was a man of many interests. He was an antiquarian and genealogist of note, a Fellow of the Royal Society of Antiquaries of Ireland who thus could put F.R.S.A.I. after his name. He was a folklorist as well as a collector of folksong and wrote a fascinating little book on the folklore and humor of Northern Ireland.[27] He was an amateur ornithologist who was accepted as an authority on the birds of the north of Ireland.... He was also an enthusiastic amateur entomologist.

Thus, Sam Henry knew the Ulster countryside as perhaps only a scientist could know it, its byways, highways, streams, and hidden places. In his notes for the songs, Henry often gives us fascinating bits of information which have absolutely nothing to do with either the words or music, [such] as that the wolf had become extinct in Northern Ireland more than two hundred years earlier.

Sam Henry also had another abiding passion for which there is no exact scientific name -- he loved people. It was his love of people as well as his love of folksong that led him to begin his great collection. He began it while he was still active as a customs-and-excise officer, and continued it after his retirement. And one suspects, although he does not tell us directly, that many of the songs and ballads for which he does not give us his source were among those he had known from childhood.

The idea of trying to save as many as possible of the old songs, of collecting them, and finally of having them printed in the *Northern Constitution*, was stimulated[28] when to his official duties was added that of a Pension Officer, visiting the poor and aged of the area to see if they were eligible for old age pensions or relief. This duty led him into some of the most isolated parts of Northern Ireland, deep into the glens, and to lonely cottages and hamlets on the banks of small rivers and streams.

There is almost always a marked reticence about country folk whether they live in Northern Ireland or the Ozarks. To help break this down, Henry often took his fiddle with him on his visits, or his tin whistle. His daughter says that the latter was a gadget.[29] But it worked. He would play a tune, a jig tune perhaps, and then ask if anyone in the household knew any of the old songs, and often, very often, someone did. It seems as

---

27 "He [also] wrote several [other] booklets: 'A Hank of Yarns,' 'Dunluce and the Giant's Causeway,' 'St Patrick's Church, Coleraine,' 'Tales of the Antrim Seaboard'" (John Moulden, 1 April 1983).
28 "I'd substitute 'initiated'; ... he repeats the statement in later letters making it plain that his song collection had its *origin* in his contact with old people" (John Moulden, 1 April 1983).
29 Jack McBride to Miss S. Jackson, 26 March 1954.

though eventually collecting the old songs became quite as important to him as the official duty that had taken him to the cottage. And undoubtedly in that way he did save many songs ... that otherwise might have been irretrievably lost.

In those pretransistor days, Sam Henry's only recording devices were his musical ear and memory, and his knowledge of tonic sol-fa -- a notation which originated in Britain and was taught in Ulster schools and church choirs, so that many school children, and not a few of their parents, might have been able to decode a rudimentary melody written in tonic sol-fa. And, although it was developed and promulgated as a simpler alternative to staff notation and not for musicological accuracy, tonic sol-fa in the right hands has the potential to be as accurate, if perhaps not so elegant or graphic, as staff notation.[30] Certainly in Henry's hands the sol-fa notation served its purpose well, outlining the melody clearly enough so that the song he put with it might be sung. And, except for an occasional typographical slip, the notation printed in the paper seems legible and accurate enough for the purpose.[31]

Sam Henry's philosophy and practice as Song Editor is easy to document; several times in the column he printed specifications for what he wanted. He first telegraphed his intentions in the introduction to the very first column, on 17 November 1923:

Songs of the People

The ancient music of Ireland had three divisions -- the Gauntree, or merry music; the Golltree, or sorrowful music; and the Scontree, or sleep songs. Are they not indeed the counterpart in music of the charms of Irish landscapes -- the rustling corn, the laughing streams, the quiet, restful green fields, the sombre bogland where the curlew's cry is the only sound that breaks the stillness, the quiet moors where the sentinel hare strains his perpendicular ears to catch the sound of danger?

I need not expatiate on Irish scenery in order to convey its beauty. The titles of the old tunes are word pictures that save me that task. Let me lead you to this world of delight by naming some of the airs that take my fancy: "The Foggy Dew," "The Crows Are Coming Home," "The Field White with Daisies," "The Dance by the Old Mountains," "'Twas Pretty to Be in Ballinderry," "The Little Red Lark," "Down by the Sally Gardens," "The Pretty Girl Milking Her Cow," "Home across the Ford," and I could add a hundred more.

---

30 See text in Section 4 at n. 52 below.
31 It would, incidentally, be interesting to know how widely "Songs of the People" served as broadside/garland/songster to its readers, particularly with respect to the tunes. Did readers learn their melodies from the column, or did they primarily use the sol-fa as a reminder of how the tune, already known to them, went?

Introduction

A revival in a small way of Irish music has taken place, but its very enthusiasts mar the success by singing hackneyed songs. We want the songs to fit such tunes as "She Is the Blackberry's Fair Blossom," "Head of Curls," "Peggy O'Hara's Wedding," "John McAnanty's Welcome Home."

> The songs that through the valleys green
> Ring on from age to age
> Like his own river's voice have been
> The Peasant's heritage.

Let it be our joyful task to search out, conserve, and make known the treasures of the Songs of the People.

This series is a beginning, and the enterprise of the local typographer has, for the first time, made it possible to present the music with the songs.

The editor will welcome any songs of the people, and will try and rescue from oblivion the treasures that once made the glowing firesides of our native land reflect their brightness in the hearts of the people.

Much later, he summarizes his criteria for the "old songs" he desires:[32]

The Song Editor acknowledges his indebtedness to Mr Frank Thompson, of Priestland, Bushmills, for this excellent song in the true folk style. It conforms with the characteristics of the best folk song: it is very old; it is anonymous; it has a story in it; the metaphor of the cock is very striking and the promised reward to the "herald of the day" for postponing the break of day is paralleled in the very ancient ballads where a parrot is so rewarded.[33]

And, again, introducing his song contest, he comments on specific examples:

Song Competition

The Song Editor is of opinion that there are still many interesting old songs extant which have not been collected, and in order to ensure that these be not lost, we offer a weekly prize of a free copy of the Northern Constitution for six months for the best old song submitted. Address envelopes "Competition," Song Editor, Northern Constitution.

---

32 "This is a late view ... after Henry had absorbed the criteria of Cecil Sharp and others -- at first he had little idea of what constituted a folk song" (John Moulden, 16 January 1983).
33 H699 "The Bonny Bushes Bright."

xxv

This week's prize is awarded to "R. O. W." for the song, "Old Ireland and Norah McCheyne." This is an excellent song, and when the air is obtained will be published.

For guidance of future competitors, a few notes are appended on other songs received: --

'The Lady and the Fan.'-- Good old ballad type, but not Irish, and more suited for a recitation than for singing.
'When the Harvest Moon is Shining on the River.'-- Nice words, but not of the old type: too sentimental rather than real. Evidently an English song.
'Erin-go-Bragh.'-- Good verse, but hackneyed. As a rule the best old songs are anonymous. The sender is thanked for her kind remarks.
'The Banks of the Bann.'-- Good rhyme, hackneyed, and of political import. Not suitable for our columns. There are six different songs to this title.

Prize-winners will kindly oblige by furnishing names and addresses or nom-de-plume for publication.[34]

Finally, in a quotation from Allan Cunningham's introduction to David Herd's *Ancient and Modern Songs* (1769), he describes an admired collector:

Herd was at once a most successful and most faithful collector. The rough, the polished," says Allan Cunningham, "the rude, the courtly, the pure, the imperfect, and the complete were all welcome to honest and indiscriminating David -- he loved them all and he published them all. He seemed to have an art of his own in finding curious old songs; he was not a poet and could not create them; he was no wizard and could not evoke them from the dust; yet he had the good fortune to find them, and the courage to publish them without mitigation or abatement. Whatever contained a picture of old manners, whatever presented a lively image of other days, and whatever atoned for its freedom by its humour was dear to the good old Scotchman.[35]

Henry may have admired David Herd, but that does not mean that he sought to emulate the Scottish collector in his own column. More relevant and revealing are the topics that did not warrant space in "Songs of the

---

[34] H98b "Barossa." One of the few surviving mentions of the contest is in W: H113 "Young Edward Bold"; it repeats the address at the newspaper and announces the winner, Mrs Glenn for "Polly Perkins," which was printed as H132. "The Linenhall Library set ... has a note of the Song Competition and other prizewinners at H109" (John Moulden, 1 April 1983). Cf. report of another song competition, *JEFDSS* 9(5) 1964:269-73.
[35] H240 "Finn Waterside."

Introduction

People." Aside from some Presbyterian hymn tunes -- which must have been included for the novelty of their decidedly secular verses -- there are virtually no religious songs; no famine songs; almost no songs with political referents, colorful or not; and only the mildest of risqué "blue" songs.[36] This was, after all, a song column in a family newspaper in Ulster 60-odd years ago, and Henry's purpose was to inform and amuse, and to enhance the paper's circulation, not to trample tender issues.

In fact, John Moulden's preliminary report on the Henry papers suggests that self-censorship may have been operating very early in the collection process: it appears not only that Henry printed most of the items he collected, but also that there is not much in the way of "unprintable" material in the unpublished remainder.[37] Did Sam Henry hear such songs but simply not preserve them, or did his respectable position in the community and church prevent his informants from disclosing such material to him?

But, aside from topics deliberately excluded on account of their subject matter,[38] the collection covers eclectic ground. Combined with the numerous partial items and fragments printed in the hope of enticing more complete versions out from hiding, the collection list, by title or subject, is a rich and variegated sampler of the Ulster song repertoire of the time -- a bountiful garden where wildflowers and weeds, roses and herbs flourish side by side in colorful disarray.

Points of order

There is not the slightest order or logical continuity in "Songs of the People" as it appeared from week to week in the pages of the *Northern Constitution*. The original numerical-temporal sequence of songs might have been preserved in the present edition, but that would not have facilitated its use for reference. There are several instances of two or three versions of the same song under different titles which, if printed in strictly historical sequence, would have been widely separated in the result.[39] Similar problems are offered by presentation by titles in alphabetical order.[40]

Folksongs in collections have often been arranged or grouped according to their subject matter or theme, in categories based on verbal content. The language-oriented arrangements have worked well enough for the mainly literary purposes which have classically dominated folksong

---

[36] "There is a little evidence that Henry was not averse to a bit of bawdry -- but orally not written" (John Moulden, 16 January 1983).
[37] Moulden 1979:8, introduction.
[38] Shields 1981:21, introduction, section 5, and p. 36, n. 2.
[39] For the record, the original order and publication dates of the columns are preserved in Appendix A.
[40] This ordering principle is commonly used for smaller song collections (e.g., Moulden 1979, Shields 1981) and relatively handy for a hundred or so items; many more become unwieldy.

studies. Occasionally an editor has essayed organization by musical elements,[41] but the associated technical difficulties are considerable; musical literacy is relatively uncommon, and the attendant explanations are likely to be cumbersome.[42]

The underlying difficulty is inherent in the medium of book publication; using any single principle to determine the order in which the songs appear can be misleading. We currently lack simple means adequate to describe the multiple, organic relationships we may sense to exist among songs and song families, not to mention melodies. A good many scholars have been occupied with such problems for a very long time. In 1959 D. K. Wilgus presented comprehensive, constructively critical coverage of issues and scholars.[43] More recently he and Eleanor R. Long have been working on an index file of thousands of Irish narrative songs with the goal of developing a workable classification system. At the 1985 meetings of the American Folklore Society they presented a version of their system as part of the survey, "European ballad scholarship: Accomplishment and prospects"; and they are to preside over a forum on "The thematic index to European balladry" at the 1987 AFS meetings.

But whether or not a book is actually read page by page from beginning to end, its contents must be arranged in linear and, one may hope, logical sequence. Our present task is simply to arrange the songs in the Henry collection in some such sequence, so that the groupings that result are distinguishable and of manageable size. We might reasonably hope to establish neighborhoods for similar items, with ample provision for mutants and deviants, and to supply maps and signposts in the form of indexes and cross-references -- not pretending to systematic classification, but aspiring to supply a helpful guide for further study.

So it seems unnecessary to stray radically from a well-established and still serviceable order based on the topical content of the "Songs of the People." The collection numbers just under 690 items and falls into 25 thematic subject areas, with surprisingly little overlapping,[44] in three general fields: life in the old country (under 200 items); the Irish homeland (over 110); and (inter)personal relationships (380, over half the total). The largest topical group includes 66 items.

About half the items are narratives in the sense of classic "Child" ballads or broadside ballads. Nearly a score have recognizable counter-

---

[41] For an excellent summary of tune scholarship see D. K. Wilgus, *Anglo-American Folksong Scholarship since 1898* (New Brunswick, N.J.: Rutgers Univ. Press, 1959) pp. 326-36, esp. the discussion of melodic ordering and indexing, pp. 331-4; see also Bertrand H. Bronson, "Toward the comparative analysis of British-American folk-tunes" (JAF 72(#284)1959: 165-91, also pp. 172-201 in *The Ballad As Song* [Berkeley and Los Angeles: Univ. of California Press, 1969]).
[42] See, e.g., our melodic index, pp. 617-30.
[43] Wilgus 1959; see esp. pp. 256-7 for his discussion of criteria for a classification system.
[44] All the items belong to at least one real category (without need for a "miscellaneous" group), and fewer than a score of the song items (about 3 per cent of the total) prove problematic if confined to a single subject area.

Introduction

parts in Francis James Child's turn-of-the-century compilation,[45] and over a hundred more conform to one or another of Malcolm J. Laws's story types.[46] Perhaps thirty more ballads turn out to have relatives in more recent (i.e., post-Laws) collections, mostly from Canada and New England as well as from Ireland. Nearly two hundred more songs have apparently not survived traditionally, or at least have not yet been identified elsewhere in print or on recording.[47]

Procedure for this edition

The following editorial treatment has applied:

1. *Selection*

The three sets of collected columns prepared personally by Sam Henry are not identical. The Belfast and Washington sets contain a few songs not found in Dublin, and vice versa.

The three sets also vary in the physical nature of the items included. A large number are evidently printer's galley proofs provided when the column was originally prepared; only a few are clippings cut from the newspaper. Apparently Henry made up the sets with the proofs and cuttings on hand and then had the missing numbers typed. Accordingly, the Belfast set is the earliest and most carefully prepared, and has the greatest number of printed galley proofs, with 23 typed columns. There are quite a few carbon copies in both the Washington and Dublin sets, which were probably assembled at about the same time. In the Washington collection 472 columns are galleys, 3 are clippings, and 147 are typed or carbon copies; Dublin has 286 columns in typescript, with the rest printed proofs or clippings.

The quality of the typed copies also varies, especially the sol-fa notation. A fair number were prepared professionally on a pica machine, and the rest, in elite (small) type, was probably typed by Sam Henry himself.[48]

Other than the three sets at national libraries, Henry's daughter, Mrs Craig, has a partial set of the columns, as did Helen Flanders. In addition, John Moulden recently discovered an almost complete set of clippings of the column in eight scrapbooks at the Linenhall Library in Belfast. This set came as a bequest from A. A. Campbell, Sam Henry's

---

45 Child 1882-98(1965). Henry's columns (and the rest of the newspaper) were in English, the language imposed on the native Irish in the previous century, which may in part account for the relative scarcity of older ballads in the Henry collection.
46 Laws 1950(1964), 1957.
47 John Moulden suggests some reasons for their apparent decline may be "severe localizations, topicality, or personalizations. Many others ... are new and so bad I'm glad they haven't transmitted" (1 April 1983).
48 John Moulden, 1 April 1983. Most of his overseas correspondence was typed.

contemporary, correspondent, and fellow collector; it also includes clippings for the three-year period when Henry was not Song Editor.[49]

Unfortunately, as mentioned, the archive files of the *Northern Constitution* are incomplete. However, John Moulden reports the British Library in London has microfilm of its *Northern Constitution* files, which include the absent numbers of the column.

Several photocopies now also exist: of the Belfast set, at London's Cecil Sharp House (in the library of the English Folk Dance and Song Society), in the libraries of the British Broadcasting Corporation, and at the Center for Comparative Folklore and Mythology at the University of California, Los Angeles, where Gale Huntington's photostatic copy of the Dublin collection is also destined.

In all there are 836 numbers in "Songs of the People." Actually, there are more songs and ballads than that number indicates, for many columns, especially toward the beginning of the series, contain two or more songs. Of that total only numbers 1 through 246 and 464 through 836 -- a total of about 670 song items -- were contributed to the *Northern Constitution* by Sam Henry himself. The others were supplied by other editors[50] while Henry was incapacitated by a long illness. Henry did not include those items in his collection because, as he explained to the librarian Hayes in Dublin, they were "not confined to my idea of 'Songs of the People' in the sense of folk song."

Gale Huntington worked primarily from white-on-black photostats of the Dublin set. This is the most recent of the library sets and contains the latest information Henry wanted to preserve, but it also has the most typescript, that is, typed or carbon copies of the columns, which contain some uncorrected typist's errors in sol-fa and text and also some headnotes reworded or omitted.

Since both the Washington copy and the Belfast sets (in UCLA photocopy) were available for examination, I was able to compare the three in some detail (summarized in Appendix A). Exactly 20 columns exist only in typescript in all three library copies.[51] Where a copy of the printed column exists, it is taken to be the standard version; variations in text among the other copies are also identified and noted as such, except for obvious typographical burbles.

---

49 Moulden adds: "I've traced a set, virtually complete, Henry gave to Francis Collinson who presented it to the School of Scottish Studies who have handed it to the Ulster Folk and Transport Museum (through my agency). Boston Public Library have Sam Henry material presented them by C. K. Bolton of Shirley Hill, Massachusetts [Bolton is also mentioned in Mrs Flanders' correspondence]. Helen Hartness Flanders' set is at Middlebury College [Vermont]" (16 January 1983).

50 According to John Moulden (SA 1977), these were James Moore of Bushmills, William Devine of Coleraine, and William John Tweed of Bushmills; Moulden also says that column number 455 was never used.

51 John Moulden has kindly supplied photocopies of these from the other extant copies in the British Library microfilm and Linenhall Library.

2. Number, title

A "Henry number" is assigned to each *item*, corresponding to the number of the original column and preceded by an "H." If the column contains two or more items, the Henry number is followed by a lower-case letter of the alphabet in alphabetical order. A separate letter is assigned to each variant; for example, two texts that share a tune, or two tunes with the same text, are listed as two items. The purpose here is to give a unique differentiating label to each variant combination. (In some cases Henry labeled the *second* item with an "a." Rather than disturb an existing landmark, the *other* is designated "b"; multiple items are labeled in analogous manner.)

The main title of each item is that printed in the heading or subheading of the column in question; for a few items Henry gave two equivalent titles.

In numerous examples Henry also gave the name(s) of the tune (i.e., the title(s) of the song or songs commonly sung to the melody). Under "Other titles" the tune title joins other variant titles used in the references for the item, and all these variant titles appear in the index of titles and first lines.

3. *Texts and notes: Spelling, punctuation, glossary, more abbreviations*

For the texts of the songs Gale Huntington chose to preserve the British English spelling used in the original columns but to alter the punctuation where he felt the original, in full formal style, seemed unnatural -- principally, he substituted periods (full stops) for semicolons and omitted quotation marks entirely. The result seemed to me to contain too many full stops for fluent reading, and the absolute absence of quotation marks was sometimes confusing. For clarity and coherence, the texts were judiciously repopulated with commas, a few semicolons, and *single* quotation marks -- a discreet compromise, I hope.

But the spelling, especially of terms in dialect, has been left as it was in the original printed columns. Also, the *Northern Constitution* seems to have used a conventional apostrophe in "Mc" names ("M'Grath" for "McGrath"); since Henry's typed copies regularly restore the missing "c," the convention has been honored in all unpredictability. Numbers and dates have regularly been spelled out in the song texts.

Separate refrains ("choruses") meant to be repeated after each stanza are printed in *italics*, indented, only the first time they occur, with a blank line separating the refrain from the stanza. Refrains which change with the stanza are indented, but not italicized, directly after the stanza, without an intervening blank; but recurring internal lines which are the same for every stanza are italicized and indented in the first stanza. If, however, there is any deviation in the refrain pattern, the entire refrain is fully written out at each occurrence.

A glossary of dialect terms recurring in the song texts is included among the indexes. Explanations of terms that occur uniquely follow in footnotes to the individual items, each labeled with relevant stanza and line numbers.

Henry's notes, head and foot, are reproduced verbatim wherever appropriate, but I have not felt similarly obliged to preserve the spelling or, to a lesser extent, the punctuation. To distinguish among editors' comments, Henry's notes are labeled "s:" and Huntington's "g:"; my own interjections are preceded by an "l:" or inclosed in square brackets. The occasional titles and comments supplied by Sean O'Boyle (o:), John Moulden (m:), Hugh Shields (h:), and Peter Kennedy (k:) are so identified.

4. Music notation

Tonic sol-fa is a system of music notation developed by John Curwen around 1840 as an alternative that would be easier to teach and read than standard staff notation. Based on an earlier method which had its ultimate roots in the medieval names for the notes of the major scale and a "movable do," it enjoyed widespread pedagogical popularity in the British Isles and elsewhere.[52]

It is ironic that the very notation that made it possible to print the melodies in the *Northern Constitution* seems to have deterred later publication of the very same material in book form. Although earlier collectors such as Rev J. B. Duncan and Gavin Greig had used tonic sol-fa extensively for their field records,[53] apparently staff notation had enough snob value that its absence discouraged would-be publishers.[54] Henry was apparently able to write staff notation adequately, if it is indeed his notation preserved in two instances in the scrapbooks (H80 Phelimy Phil [W] and H162 Canada Hi! Ho! [D]). It is puzzling, though understandable in view of the size of the collection and wartime demands on his time and

---

[52] See Graham *EB* 1929 for explication of the fundamental notation and p. xxxiii in this edition for an example; also Hood 1982. Moulden adds: "Sol-fa was taught instead of staff in Ulster schools up to the 1940's and as recently as 1960 was used as an alternative and taught to students in training as teachers" (16 January 1983). The notation is employed in several Scottish Presbyterian hymnals; the Curwen vocal edition of Baring-Gould and Sharp's *English Folk-Songs for Schools* (1906) contains melodies in both staff and sol-fa. Both the notation and associated hand signals were taught at the Normal School for training teachers in Hawaii in the 1920's, and both were utilized in a school in California this past year.

[53] Greig/Duncan 1981:x; making one wish, parenthetically, that Greig's newspaper, the Buchan *Observer*, had a typesetter as inspired, or at least competent, as Henry's anonymous hero.

[54] This attitude provoked Sam Henry to remark in a letter to Francis Collinson: "Quite a number of eminent people have made overtures about these songs but partly because of the swank that despises 'sol-fa' notation they did not face the task of changing to staff notation" (Moulden 1979:9).

Concerning other methods of recording, Sam Henry wrote to Helen Flanders on 6 August 1939: "I do not think the dictaphone method would be of much use as the singers are so unmusical (especially the oldest and most valuable contributors) and it takes long experience to infer what they are trying to sing."

Introduction

SONGS OF THE PEOPLE.

No. 233.—THE GREEN BANKS OF BANNA.

From the collection of the late Mrs Houston, of the Academical Institution, Coleraine, who composed the words of the song to suit an old air learnt from her mother.

Key G

:l₁.l₁ | m₁ :l₁ :t | d :t₁ :l₁ | t₁.se₁ :– :m₁ | m₁ :– }

:de.t₁ | l₁ :ae :r | m :r.d :t₁ | l₁ :de :r | m :– }

:l₁.de | m :m :l | m :r :t₁ | l₁ :l₁ :l₁.m₁ | m₁ :– }

:m₁.fe₁ | s₁ :l₁ :t₁ | s :–.m :r | m.t₁ :– :l₁ | l₁ :– ‖

By the green banks of Banna I wander alone,
Where the river runs softly by sweet Portglenone,
And I think of that day in the Spring of the year
When he said " I must part from you, Molly, my dear."

O, many a tear I have shed since that day,
In grief for my true love so far, far away;
In the long nights of Winter I've trembled with fear
That I never might hear him say " Molly, my dear."

Fair river of Banna that flows to the sea,
Whisper soft to the waves to bring him back to me;
O, happy I'll be when his sweet voice I hear,
Saying, " I am come back to you Molly, my dear."

Above: A photocopy of H233 "The Green Banks of Banna" as it appears in the Belfast copy, very likely a printer's galley proof. The solfa is set in a pica-typewriter type, one of the three type styles utilized for the music in the column over the years; the other two were a boldface and bold condensed face related to the usual body type of the newspaper. *Right:* One of three pictures that appeared with Henry's column in the years he was Song Editor: H466 "My Parents Reared Me Tenderly," with the caption: "Air ... taken down from John M'Afee, who fiddles at the fairs in North Antrim, and is here seen at Dervock fair on Thursday last." (Of the others, one is uncaptioned, the likeness of a man, printed with H179 "John Mitchel's Farewell to His Countrymen," which John Moulden says is a picture of John Mitchel; he reports the other is a photograph of Portrush which appears with H775 "Bonny Portrush.")

xxxiii

energy, that he did not undertake to transcribe the tunes himself, especially after being disappointed by his potential publishers.

In his letter to R. J. Hayes dated 18 June 1941 accompanying the last installment of his gift set to the Dublin library, Henry described the limitations that newspaper printing had for sol-fa notation:

The column width prevented the full extension of the end bars and of any musical marks outside the ordinary fount [sic] of type.... Although the printing is a bit crude, the melodies are there and any competent musician can easily round off the tunes, completing the end-bars and inserting the proper bar divisions to indicate the strongly accented and less accented notes at the beginning of the bars; the half-bar of 4/4 times &c.

Gale Huntington wrote of his experience with the notation: "perhaps the proper word is transcribing, but it often has seemed like translating -- Henry's tonic sol-fa to regular musical notation...." One reason for Huntington's discomfort is that the typescript that makes up nearly the first half of the Dublin copy he used is of variable quality -- often photostats of carbon copies -- and some copies were prepared without great care to the sol-fa: octave marks and sometimes the bar divisions are missing or misplaced in the typed copies. The typeset sol-fa in the printed columns appears relatively accurate. Octave marks are the most frequent points of disagreement among the copies.

In verifying Gale Huntington's transcriptions I have attempted to follow the original printed sol-fa notation whenever possible, even to the grace notes, which are sometimes printed as if they were attached *following* the main melody notes. Parentheses placed around notes in the sol-fa (signifying optional notes) have been transferred directly to the staff notation. Where editorial intervention seemed necessary, brackets inclose small insertions or plausible corrections; in the few cases where significant disagreements exist among the copies, labels or alternative measures mark the discrepancies.

The key signature follows a modern convention in musicology and reflects not only the presumed mode but the notes actually present in the tune. Following tonic sol-fa practice I have used the note Henry specified as "do" as the basis for the key signature; this note may or may not be the tonal center of the tune.

Each tune is preceded by a treble-clef catch-signature which displays in order:

    the key signature;
    the actual tonal center as a whole note (or, if there is doubt, a
        question mark and two whole notes);
    the final note as an x;
    the range (compass) as black notes at the extremes, high and low;

Introduction

additional flat or sharp signs for temporarily inflected notes; and brackets inclosing notes absent within the range of the tune.

Thus, for example: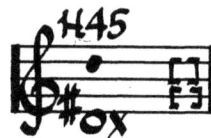

Although the sol-fa tunes as printed were sometimes divided, expanded, or compressed by typographical necessity to fit the available column width, after the first few numbers in the series some effort was evidently made to keep the melodies in lines conforming to the phrasing of the stanza lines. In redrawing the staff notation I have followed the same practice. The added commas (breath marks) represent arbitrary midline breaks which have to do with my analysis of the tune for indexing. The diagonal slashes delineate phrase-line breaks in the original sol-fa.

Two interrelated topics remain: time notation and the regularity of length of measures, especially of the end bars. I have approached these with a relatively relaxed attitude, and from a singer's viewpoint. Often Henry observed, for example, that the melody and words he printed were "difficult to adapt ... but suit admirably when sung by a traditional singer"[55] and: "The adaptation of the words to the air in this song is very difficult to convey. The traditional singer makes his own time and ignores bar lines. Yet to hear it so sung, it seems the most natural thing in the world"[56] and: "As is the manner of old ballads, the corresponding lines in the different verses do not always contain the same number of syllables. The difficulty is met by duplicating a note, or omitting one as the case may be."[57]

Tonic sol-fa notation implies the numerator but not the denominator of the time signature, indicating the number of pulses for each measure without specifying the time value assigned to those pulse divisions. The time signature supplied in this edition generally follows the original, with due notice given if it has been altered.[58] The denominator, based loosely on my presumption of the tempo at which the item might have been sung, is more arbitrary.[59] Parentheses enclose this time signature if there is any irregularity in the number of pulses per measure.

The few tunes for which Henry's sol-fa notation is irregular from measure to measure have required some judgment based primarily on the fit of the text and on the nature of other versions. However, when the odd end bars (the measures at the ends of phrases that are incompletely

---

55 H66 "Wester Snow."
56 H580 "Farewell, Darling."
57 H815 "Franklin the Brave."
58 The most common substitutions have been 3[/4] for 6[/8] or vice versa, and 4[/4] for 2.
59 Henry offered occasional verbal prescriptions -- "Slowly." "Tenderly." -- and only one numerical metronomic reference.

written in the sol-fa) seem consistent in the notation, they have been left as in the original, again with the corresponding time signatures inclosed in parentheses as warning that the time may not be absolutely regular.

5. References

The reference citations follow a modern short usage (general form *author date:page*); full citations are in the bibliography and discography. These brief citations are separated into rough categories, with the first reserved for standard classic printed references (e.g., Child, Laws); those that follow are labeled according to the country of origin, but other media (broadsides [BRS], recordings [REC], manuscripts) are not so segregated. References to tunes (MEL) are to items having the same title or the same melodic contour, or sometimes both. Each citation is followed by a variant title if that differs from the Henry title; an ellipsis indicates an echo of the wording of Henry's title.

We have preserved all citations of Irish references and recordings, indicating those already cited by others. Valuable sources of additional previous citations are marked "#."

Original introduction written by Gale Huntington, 1971-4
Revised by Lani Herrmann, 1987

Acknowledgments

Many people over several generations have helped produce this transatlantic edition of Sam Henry's song collection; we regret our present inability to acknowledge every one by name. We are particularly conscious of our debt to the first generation, now somewhat distant in time but not, we hope, in spirit: Sam Henry himself, the editors of the *Northern Constitution*, and his community which provided both the primary song material and the readership for his column. In the current generation, we are literally and morally indebted to the National Endowment for the Humanities for the generous grant which made feasible -- at long last -- the production of this edition, as well as to our families, friends, and colleagues, named and unnameable, who advised, guided, and supported us along the way.

We express special thanks to Olive Henry Craig of Kilrea, Co. Derry, Sam Henry's daughter, for her hospitality and for her generous permission to proceed with our edition; and to John Moulden of Portrush, Co. Antrim, educator and scholar, for his friendly and knowledgeable assistance and liberal abettance, for his wit, patience, and punctiliousness, and especially for his crash course in Irish geography.

We also offer our appreciation and gratitude over the years:

For useful information and many other courtesies: to R. J. Hayes, former Director of the National Library of Ireland; Ivan M. Russell, erstwhile editor of the *Northern Constitution*, Coleraine, Northern Ireland; Alice (Mrs Seán) O'Boyle of Armagh; Alan Reid of the British Broadcasting Corporation (BBC), Belfast; Sam Hanna Bell, novelist and retired BBC producer; Hugh Shields, respected Irish scholar and collector; Nicholas Carolan of the Folk Music Society of Ireland; and the librarians of the English Folk Dance and Song Society (EFDSS) in London.

For their helpful guidance through the riches in the collections in their charge: to Mrs Ruth Bleeker, Curator of Music at the Boston Public Library; Miss Caroline Elizabeth Jakeman, former Assistant Librarian for Reference in the Houghton Library of Harvard College Library; Joseph C. Hickerson and Gerald E. Parsons, Jr., of the Archive of Folk Culture and Alan Jabbour of the American Folklife Center, Washington, D.C.; and the reference librarians at the University of California, Los Angeles and Berkeley, and the Richmond (California) Public Library.

For precious gifts of friendship, example, and encouragement, and for special access to their private libraries: to the late Professor Bertrand H. Bronson of Berkeley, California, and the early Professor Kenneth S. Goldstein, University of Pennsylvania.

To Dr Emily B. Lyle of the School of Scottish Studies, Edinburgh, Scotland, for the loan of a sympathetic ear and twinkling eye, for valuable suggestions and other courtesies, and for proving true to her Celtic heritage.

To Professor Archie Green, now of San Francisco, folklorist and generator of ideas, for his illuminating suggestion about Irish broadsides, and for kindly advice and gentle reminders.

To Professor D. K. Wilgus and Dr Eleanor R. Long of UCLA for generously sharing preliminary versions of their Thematic Index scheme; and to Dr David Engle for his dissertation on the same subject in another country.

To Margaret MacArthur of Marlboro, Vermont, for access to Sam Henry's correspondence with the redoubtable Mrs Flanders of Vermont, and for a photograph of Sam Henry; to Helen Kivnick and Gary Gardner for sharing their collective books, records, and wisdom; and to Linda Morley, New Hampshire State Folklorist, for helpful critical reading and comments.

To Caroline and Sandy Paton and Lee Haggerty of Folk-Legacy Records, Sharon, Connecticut, for their warm hospitality and encouragement, for putting the editors' heads together, and for underwriting the working photocopy of Gale Huntington's manuscript.

To Mr Marion Welle of Newton, Iowa, for another photograph of Sam Henry, and for sharing his recollections of wartime visits with the Henry family in Ireland.

To the Huntingtons of Vineyard Haven, Massachusetts, for their cordial island welcome for a fiddling friend-of-a-friend (and suite), and for freely sharing ten years' manuscript labor.

Finally, to the Herrmanns, now mainly of California, for moral, spiritual, and palpable support, not solely during the long gestation of this edition: especially Cal, resident technical consultant, computer mechanic, symbiont, and wailing wall; our son Conrad for cheerfully producing usable, if quirky, computer programs on request and in time; and our daughter Alix for lending her steady hand, eye, and mind at the ultimate moment.

Gale Huntington
Lani Herrmann

Abbreviations

References to source copies of the Henry collection:

B = Belfast (Belfast Free Library, now Central Library, Royal Avenue, Belfast). Most of the earlier printed columns (H1-H246) used in this edition were taken from copies of this set.
D = Dublin (National Library of Ireland). The later printed columns (H464 --) mainly from this set.
W = Washington, D.C. (Library of Congress, Music Division; call number M 1744.H47).
BL = British Library, London; microfilm copy in the Ballymena Headquarters of the North Eastern Education and Library Board.
L = Linenhall Library, Belfast (clippings in scrapbooks, bequest of A. A. Campbell).

p = printed, either proof or clipping.
t = typescript.
(c) = carbon copy (of typescript).
written = handwriting, as distinguished from typing or printing.

(Thus, Bp indicates a printed copy in the Belfast set; Dt is a typed copy at Dublin; Dt=Wt(c) means the carbon copy in the Washington set is identical to the original typed copy at Dublin.)

w = text (of songs).
m = tune, melody.

In the headnotes and references (see also the bibliography):

= major source of previously published references.
? (preceding any entry) = something questionable or doubtful.

b: Brunnings 1981.	l: Lani Herrmann.
c: Cazden et al. 1982.	lc: AAFS Record List 1953.
cl: AAFS Check-List 1942.	m: John Moulden.
g: Gale Huntington.	o: Sean O'Boyle.
h: Hugh Shields.	s: Sam Henry.
k: Peter Kennedy.	

A1
Come let us all begin:
Old choir rhymes

Sam Henry's Songs of the People

Old Choir Rhymes

s: In olden days it was considered unseemly to use the words of the Psalms at the choir practices, or on occasions other than times of actual worship. Instead of the sacred songs of the psalmist, the words used were the composition of the local poet, and were often in praise of some fair damsel, whose presence inspired the muse.

The following tunes and words are from the music book of William Robb, which I have in my possession (by kind permission of Hugh Eccles, esq., J.P.). The book was begun "on Sunday between twelve and one of the clock, march the 30 day, 1729, the dominical letter A, the golden number, one, the epact 11, and the cicle of the sun 10, the moon's age 12 day, and the tide was going in at logh foyle, and onder the plennat jupiter."

In addition to these I add some verses which I took down in 1913 from an old lady, aged 91, at Urblereagh, Portrush, and also others which were used at Ballywillan choir practices.

The muse was exceedingly prolific in turning out this class of verse, and the selections given are from almost 100 examples.

Young love often found its expression in the Song of Solomon, and many of the rhymes are paraphrases of verses from that book. These simple rhymes were made by each member of the singing class in turn when challenged by the choir-master.

l: W includes a clipping of an article by John J. Marshall, M.A., M.R.S.A.I., "Collection of Rhymes by Classes when practising Presbyterian Psalmody in former days" (see Appendix C). The article includes all of the verses printed below, and supplies additional tune titles and notes (here enclosed in brackets and preceded by jm:), but mentions no sources. The publication in which the article appeared is also not identified; it is apparently a monthly periodical.

See also *Tocher* #31(Sum)1979:26 for 2 more stanzas with comment from Mrs Willie Mitchell (Campbeltown, Kintyre, Scotland).

Abbey   [H10a: 19 Jan 1924]

Source: William Robb ms.

Key G.

The Abbey tune is easy sung,
As I hear many say,
I'll summons you before the king
For leading me astray.

Dublin / Coleshill   [H10b: 19 Jan 1924]

Source: William Robb ms.

s: Note that the happy choristers ignored the sad wail of the minor key and fitted words that were bright and cheery.

Key C.

Hark how the cock, with sprightly note,
Crows loudly, shrill and gay,
And the brisk sounds that strain his voice
Foretell approaching day.

Dundee   [H10c: 19 Jan 1924]

Source: William Robb ms.

Key C.

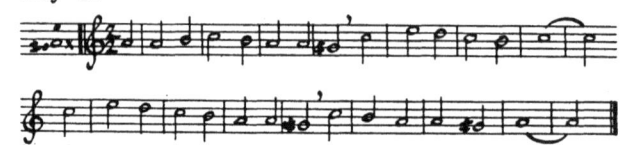

Dundee, it is a pretty place,
Surrounded by a wall,
Where brave Argyll did won the field
With sword and cannon ball.

French   [H10d: 19 Jan 1924]

Source: William Robb ms.

Key F.

Come let us all begin to 'French,'
The second measure low,
The third a little doth ascend,
The fourth doth downward go.

Mary's   [H10e: 19 Jan 1924]

Source: William Robb ms.

Key E flat.

Woman was taken out of man
His helper for to be,
She was made of a crooket rib,
And a crooket help made she.

Martyrs [H10f: 19 Jan 1924]

Source: William Robb ms.

s: The imagery is from the 8th chapter Song of Solomon.

Key G.

I'll marble wall thee round about,
Myself shall be the door,
And if your heart chance to break out,
I'll never leave thee more.

York [H10g: 19 Jan 1924]

Source: William Robb ms.

s: See Song of Solomon, 5th chapter, 2nd verse.

Key G.

My love, my dove, my undefiled,
My col-o do not slight.
My head is wat'red with the dew,
With dropings of the night.

.2: col-o = [?call-o].

Newto[w]n (as sung at Ballywillan) [H10h: 19 Jan 1924]

Source: William Robb ms.

s: Being in key F, the notes d1 d1 d1 [the 1's are superscripts] are the three high fas.

Key F.

O 'Newtown,' you are hard to sing,
Baith ill to time and place,
Your three high fa's strain a' my ja's
And wrinkle a' my face.

.2: baith = both.

A1 / Come let us all begin

Additional verses [H10i: 19 Jan 1924]

[s: Bp] Further verses without tunes, from William Robb's Book.
[Dt] From William Robb's tune book.

[jm: Tune -- Irish]

I wish my love was a [jm: red,] red rose
Beside yon garding wall,
And I myself a drop o' dew
Upon that rose to fall.

.2: garding = garden.
[jm: See more correct form of these lines in verse under "An Ulster Ploughman's Choir-Book."]

[jm: Tune -- Farrant]

My love she's fair and purty too,
She was in Coulrain bred,
Pleasant and yielding unto me,
Which makes my hert right gled.

.4: hert = heart; gled = glad.

[s: Bp] Sung to French. [Dt] Tune French.

This tune is 'French,' I tell to thee
Sure as the grass doth spring;
One word of French I cannot speak,
But yet the tune I'll sing.

[s: Bp] Sung to Newtown [jm: Tune -- Jackson]

The man yt stands on ye rock head
And vews [jm: views] Megilgan [jm: Magilligan] land,
He always thinks its in a flood,
And not like to Cinnan.

.1: yt = that.
.4: Cinnan = Canaan. The verse was completed before the dykes were made. [s: Bp]

[s: Bp] Sung (and rightly) to Dublin.
[Dt] Tune Dublin.

A man that climbs where nothing hings
And grips where nothing grows,
And loves a maid that loves not him,
Against the stream he rows.

Verses used in Ballywillan choir in the early 19th century.

Source: (w) [?some from] old lady, 91 (Urblereagh, Portrush)

[jm: Tune -- Belmont]

My love is fair, she's very fair,
She's Ballywillan bred;
Her skin it is a lily white,
Her cheeks a rosy red.

3

Sam Henry's Songs of the People

[jm: Tune -- Kilmarnock]

> My love she's in the school this nicht,
> She sings sae sweet sol-fa,
> She clods the brislocks in the fire
> And eats them skins and a'.

.3: clods = heaves.
.3: brislocks = toasted potatoes. In the choir practice this was the menu instead of tea. [s: Dt] [jm: potatoes roasted in turf (peat) ashes. W. H. Patterson, in "A Glossary of Words in Use in the Counties of Antrim and Down," gives -- "Brissle, to toast, to scorch. To *brissle* potatoes."]

[jm: Tune -- London (new)]

> As I cam' frae the school this nicht,
> A wunner did I see:
> A rabbit sittin' playin' the flute
> On John O'Gillian's lea.

.2: wunner = wonder.

[jm: Tune -- Tallis]

> A maiden's heed [jm: heart] is like a watch,
> It's easy set a glee [jm: agee];
> When the mainspring it is broke,
> It canna mended be.

.2: a glee [jm: agee] [adgee] = crooked, to one side.

[s: Bp] (The maiden's repartee at the poet's expense:)
[Dt] The maiden replies: [jm: Tune -- St. David]

> O' maiden's heeds you needna ta'k,
> O' them you hae nae skill,
> For you were [jm: You were six weeks] clock[-]ed in the pot
> Amang the grey wool.

.1: heeds = heads; ta'k = talk.
.3: clock-ed = hatched. [*The expression means*] a delicate child reared in a pot of grey wool. [s: Dt]

[jm: Tune -- Howard]

> My love and me does not agree
> Which I'm ashamed to tell:
> She blamed me wi' three barley scons
> Which she did eat hersel'.

.3: scons = scones.

[jm: Tune -- York]

> A blessin' on Glenmanus Mill,
> The happer and the stanes,
> For it puts beef upon our backs
> And marrow in our banes.

.2: happer = hopper; stanes = stones.
.4: banes = bones. [s]

More verses

Additional verses from Marshall article.

[jm: Tune -- Elgin]

> In Scotland fair a river runs,
> And Elgin is its name,
> And many a fruitful tree and bush
> Doth grow along the same.

[jm: Tune -- Martyrs]

> To 'Martyrs' always have regard
> To sing it very low,
> For if you chance to raise it high,
> Quite out of tune you'll go.

◆ A1 REFERENCES ◆

◆ Abbey *(H10a)* 2

REC Tangent TNGM 120 booklet, p. 6, "Abbay" from Hunt's 1634 Psalter, the same tune as Henry's.

◆ Dublin / Coleshill *(H10b)* 2

REC Murdina and Effie MacDonald, Tangent TNGM 120 (A2)

◆ Dundee *(H10c)* 2

Brunnings 1981: "... (O God of Bethel)"

REC Norman McLeod and group at Fidigarry, Isle of Lewis, Tangent TNGM 120 (B2); booklet, p. 6, photograph of Hunt's 1634 Psalter open to "Dundie," whose first three phrases are the same as, and the fourth is different from, Henry's.

◆ Martyrs *(H10f)* 3

Brunnings 1981: "I'll Marble Wall Thee Round About (Tune: Martyrs)"

REC Alasdair Graham and congregation, Tangent TNGM 120 (B4), a somewhat different tune in a minor mode.

◆ York *(H10g)* 3

Brunnings 1981: "My Love, My Dove, My Undefiled (Tune: York)"

◆ Newto[w]n *(H10h)* 3

REC Cf. group in Glasgow (Stornoway Free Church), Tangent TNGM 120 (B3) "London New" ("Newtoun," Hunt's 1635 Psalter)

A2
Rockin' the cradle
is nae work, ava:
Lullabies

Sam Henry's Songs of the People

Heezh Ba [H591a: "Two lullabies," 30 Mar 1935]

Source: Mrs Brownlow (Ballylaggan, Cloyfin, Coleraine).

1: The last 4 lines belong to "the best-known lullabye in England and America.... The age of both the rhyme and the melody is uncertain" (Opie/Opie 1951:61-2).

Key G.

When I was young I was airy and handsome,
A' my delight was in fiddlin' and dancin',
Noo I am auld and my joints are grown feeble,
Fittin' for nae thin' but rockin' the cradle.
Rockin' the cradle and singing heezh-ba,
Rockin' the cradle is nae work, ava,
I'll set my cradle on yon hill-top,
An' when the win' blows the cradle will rock,
An' when the win' staps the cradle will fa',
Doon comes the cradle, wee babbie an' a'.

1.9: staps = stops.
1.10: babbie = baby.

Hush Alee [H591b: "Two lullabies," 30 Mar 1935]

Source: Annie Patterson, from her mother (native, Loughan, Coleraine).

[Text is printed line for line under the sol-fa in the original column.]

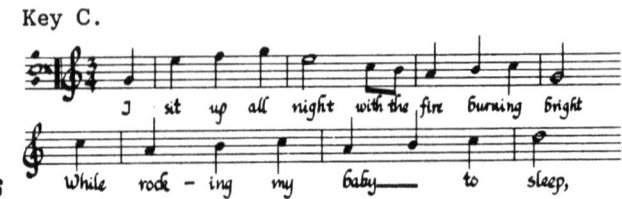

Key C.

I sit up all night with the fire burning bright
While rocking my baby to sleep,
Singing, Hush a-lee la lee, hush a-lo lee,
Your daddy will come by and by,
So close your eyes and go to sleep,
Your dear mother she is tired,
Singing, Hush alee lalee, hush a-lo,
Hush a-lee la lalee lo.

Ballyeamon Cradle Song [H596: 4 May 1935]

Source: J. Keevers Douglas (Ballycastle).

Key E [written in for D, crossed out].

Rest tired eyes awhile,
Sweet is thy baby smile,
Angels are guarding and watch o'er thee.
Sleep, Ian, grah me chree,
Here on your mother's knee,
Angels are guarding and watch o'er thee.

    The birdeens sing a fluting song,
    They sing for thee the whole day long,
    Wee fairies dance in dell and glade
    For very love of thee.
    The primrose in the sheltered nook,
    The crystal stream, the babbling brook,
    God gave you these his hands had made
    For very love of thee.

Dream, Ian, grah ma chree,
Here on your mother's knee,
Angels are guarding and watch o'er thee.
Twilight and shadows fall,
Peace to the childher small,
Angels are guarding and watch o'er thee.

1.4: grah me [ma] chree = dear of my heart.
2.5: childher = children.

Irish Lullaby for the Christ-Child
[H630: 28 Dec 1935]

o: (m) "The Old Man Rocking the Cradle."

Author Sam Henry based on Gaelic prose translation.

s: This lullaby is now first published in English. It was ... broadcast by [Sam Henry] from Belfast Station on 18th inst.

Key D.

Shoheen, shoho, my child is my treasure,
My jewel, my sinless, my share of the world,
Shoheen, shoho, how sweet is my pleasure,
My dark flag of sorrow for ever is furled.
Child of my bosom, may sleep ever thrive with
  you,
Luck and contentment be ever in store,
God and your mother will nothing deprive from
  you,
Sleep now, my baby, till dawn's at the door.

On the hill of the sidhe the fairies are dancing,
Playing their games by the fair moon of spring,
Here they come tip-toe, laughing and prancing,
To lure him away to the dun of their king.
They shall not entice you by dint of their
  charming,
They shall not allure you by the sound of their
  ceol,
I guard you by prayer from all that is harming,
And God with his warm wings will shelter your
  soul.

Bright as the branch of the red rowan berries,
Short are the years you are wrapped in my love;
Mo craoibhin, my child, close your eyes to the
  fairies,
And open your ears to the angels above.
God does not grudge me the love of my baby,
You are my toy and my plaything the while;
Toddle with me, for the day will come, may be,
When lonely you'll wander for mile after mile.

A2 / Rockin' the cradle is nae work, ava

Shoheen, shoho, my child is my treasure,
My jewel, my sinless, my share of the world,
Shoheen, shoho, how sweet is my pleasure,
My dark flag of sorrow for ever is furled.

2.1: sidhe = fairies. [s]
2.6: ceol = music. [s]
3.3: craoibhin = little branch. [s]

Lullaby for a Sailor's Child
[H517: 28 Oct 1933]

o: (m) "Shule Agra."

Source not given.

Key D.

Roar, roar, thunder of the sea,
Wild waves breaking on the sandy bar,
And my true love is sailing, sailing far
For his rosy little boy and Shena.

Sleep, sleep, lu la lo achree,
Billows blue and baby on my breast,
And sweet heaven guard my true love in the west
Toiling sore for his boy and Shena.

Wake, wake, sunshine on the sea,
Safe his boat rides the snowy foam,
And all the town will welcome Jamie home,
And so will his boy and Shena.

2.1: ... lu lo la achree. [Wt]

Raven-Locks
[H645: 4 Apr 1936]

s: (m) traditional Gaelic air.

Author Sam Henry.

Key G.

Sam Henry's Songs of the People

Horo, mo leanibh dhu, horo, mo leanibh dhu,
Ringlets as dark as the raven are thine,
Lovely thy cheek to me as is the apple tree,
Bud of my bosom, be love ever thine,
Sleep, little love, daddy's own dove.

Where the wild waves run free, daddy for you and me
Toils in the tempest to keep our bright home.
Soon may we see his face; hasten it, God of grace,
Bring our dear daddy safe over the foam,
Home to his dove, home to sweet love.

Shines the bright sun today, daddy is on the way,
Yonder his sail like the seagull's white wing,
Dance to your daddy, dear, dance now without a fear,
Dance to the blue waves where herring is king;
His step's at the door: our sorrows are o'er.

1.1: mo leanibh dhu [leanibh pronounced in two syllables, lyaniv] = my dark-haired baby. [s]

◊ A2 REFERENCES ◊

◊ **Heezh Ba** (*H591a*) 6

   Cf. Brunnings 1981: "Hishie Ba," somewhat allied in import and title, but not in form.

◊ **Lullaby for a Sailor's Child** (*H517*) 7

   Brunnings 1981: (m) "Shule Agra"

A3
I'll tell my ma:
Children's game songs

Sam Henry's Songs of the People

Children's Singing Games

s: In the introduction to *The Joyous Book of Singing Games*, by John Hornby (published by Messrs. E. J. Arnold & Son, Ltd.), the author, accounting for the sources of his rhymes and music, states: "One came from the smoky purlieus of Birmingham; one from a quiet vicarage in Westmoreland; one from the streets of Coleraine, and one from within the ken of the Broomielaw."

The children's singing games are the oldest folk-music in the world; some of them date back to the dawn of history, not merely Celtic but actually pre-Aryan. As our district is rich in this feature of folk-song we publish a short selection. Readers are invited to contribute others in use in the locality, especially such as are peculiar to North Ireland and hitherto unrecorded.

Acknowledgments are made to some Girl Guides who have already contributed interesting selections.

o: Ulster versions of several Children's Singing Games common to the British Isles.

I Am the Master
[H48a: "Children's singing games," 11 Oct 1924]

Other title: "Dusty Bluebells."

Source not given.

s: This singing game is a great favourite with the children of the Irish Society's School (Infant Department). No one knows where it came from. It is intimately connected with the curious custom in Devonshire and elsewhere of "crying the neck." The "Master of the Harvest" had his neck adorned with choice wheat grains, or, in this case, apples are supposed to be used, and evidently it was a festival when the little apples were on the trees and the bluebells were in bloom. These child games show that the roots of life are very deep. The figures on the brass of the harness on our horses are ancient Egyptian worship symbols. How slowly the old faiths die!

The game is played thus: A ring is formed, but the children do not catch hands, merely letting the arms hang by the side. A leader is chosen, who walks to the time of the music in and out through the others until the words "I am the master" are sung, when the leader stops and tips the shoulders of the nearest player. The person tipped follows the leader, and the game goes on until all have left the ring and are walking in single file to the music, and all tipping the shoulders of the player in front, when the second verse is being sung.

h: "Dusty Bluebells," children's game. Recorded from children in Magilligan, used for BBC-TV film as title and theme by David Hammond.

m: Very common in Ulster.

Key E.

In and out those dusty bluebells,
In and out those dusty bluebells,
In and out those dusty bluebells,
 I am the master.

Tip a little apple on my shoulder,
Tip a little apple on my shoulder,
Tip a little apple on my shoulder,
 I am the master.

Green Gravel
[H48b: "Children's singing games," 11 Oct 1924]

Other title: "...s."

Source not given.

s: This very quaint song may be explained by the "gravelle" -- diminutive of "grave" -- being of a brighter green from the fair maids buried there, whose beauty justified washing in milk, a winding sheet of silk, and immortal fame, written by a pen that could not rust.

Key G.

Green gravel, green gravel, your grass is so green,
And all you pretty fair maids are ashamed to be seen.
I'll wash you in milk and I'll roll you in silk,
And I'll write down your name with a glass pen and ink.
Green gravel, green gravel, your true love is dead.
He sends you a letter to turn about your head.

Ring a Ring o' Roses
[H48c: "Children's singing games," 11 Oct 1924]

Other title: "... around o' (the) Rosie(s)."

Source not given.

s: Some folklorists suggest that this singing game is a remnant of the old worship of the corn spirit. "A-tisha," generally regarded as a sneeze, may be the deity Attis, whose worship spread from Phrygia to Italy.

Key G.

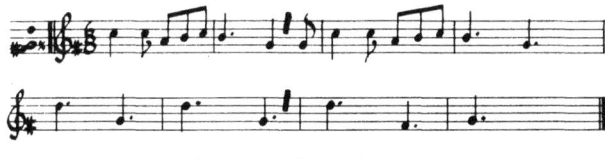

A ring, a ring o' roses,
A pocket full o' posies,
A-tisha! A-tisha!
All fall down.

Water, Water, Wallflowers
[H48d: "Children's singing games," 11 Oct 1924]

A ring game.

Other titles: "Wallflowers," "Water, Water, Wild Flower."

Source not given.

Key F.

Water, water, wallflower,
Growing up so high,
We are all made,
And we must all die,
All but Mary Johnston,
She's the youngest child,
She can dance and she can sing
And she can knock us all down.

Fie, fie, fie,
Shame, shame, shame,
Turn your back to the wall again.

I'll Tell My Ma
[H48e: "Children's singing games," 11 Oct 1924]

Source not given.

Key G.

I'll tell my ma when I go home,
The boys and girls won't let me alone,
They tossed my hair and broke my comb,
And I'll tell my ma when I go home.

Here's a Poor Widow
[H48f: "Children's singing games," 11 Oct 1924]

Other title: "Poor ...."

Source not given.

[Bp, Dt have 4 double-length lines.]

Key G.

Here's a poor widow, she lies her lone,
She lies her lone, she lies her lone,
Here's a poor widow, she lies her lone,
She wants a man and canny get none.

She may go round and choose her own,
And choose her own, and choose her own,
She may go round and choose her own
And choose a good one or else choose none.

Old Sally Walker
[H48g: "Children's singing games," 11 Oct 1924]

Other titles: "(Little) Sally ... (Saucer) Water(s)."

Source not given.

Key G.

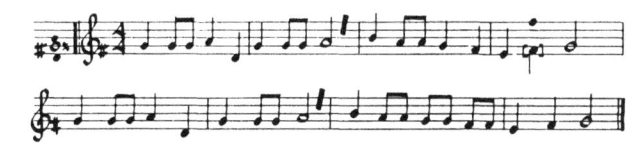

Old Sally Walker, old Sally Glenn,
Old Sally Walker, choose young men,
Choose to the east, choose to the west,
Choose to the very one you love best.

Now these couple are married with joy,
Every year a girl and a boy,
If that doesn't do, we wish them two,
Two pretty couple to kiss together.

Broken Bridges
[H48h: "Children's singing games," 11 Oct 1924]

s: (m) Gaelic "Gabhaid Sinn an Rathad Mor."
Other titles: "London Bridge Is Broken (Falling) Down."

Source not given.

s: A folk-song collector has heard the same air sung in the streets of Nicaragua in Central America. This singing game is supposed to hark back to the sacrificial acts accompanying the religious ceremonies connected with bridge-building.

Sam Henry's Songs of the People

It is noteworthy that the Pope's title, "The Supreme Pontiff," means chief bridge-builder.

Key E flat.

Broken bridges falling down, falling down, falling down,
Broken bridges falling down, my fair lady.

Here's a prisoner we have got ...

What's the prisoner done to you? ...

Broke our locks and stole our gold ...

What'll you take to set her free? ...

A chain of gold to set her free ...

A chain of gold you shall not get ...

Then off to the bridewell she must go ...

Fair Rosa / The Sleeping Beauty
[H599: 25 May 1935]

A singing game....

Other title: "Thorn Rosa."

Source: Park Street children (Coleraine).

Key G.

Fair Rosa was a lovely child,
    A lovely child, a lovely child,
Fair Rosa was a lovely child,
    A lovely child.

[*similarly:*]
Fair Rosa slept a hundred years.

A forest grew around her tower.

A wicked fairy found her there.

A noble prince came riding by.

And now she's happy as a bride.

How Many Miles to Babyland?
[H40a: "Three sleep songs," 16 Aug 1924]

Other titles: "... Babylon (Bethlehem)?"

Source not given.

s: The dialect pronunciation of the name of the word "Babyland" has led to its corruption to "Babylon," a meaningless title which spoils the theme.

Key F.

How many miles to Babyland?
Three score and ten.
Can we get there by candle light?
Yes, and back again.

How many miles to Babyland?
Anyone can tell:
Up one flight, to your right,
Please to ring the bell.

What do they do in Babyland?
Dream and wake and play,
Laugh and crow, shout and grow,
Jolly times have they.

What do they say in Babyland?
Why, the oddest things,
Might as well try to tell
What a birdie sings.

Who is the queen in Babyland?
Mother, kind and sweet,
And her love, born above,
Guides the little feet.

1.1 [*and throughout* Bp]: ... Baby Land?

Cricketty Wee
[H744: 26 Feb 1938]

Other titles: "Billy the Bob," "The Cutty Wren," "(S)Helg Yn Dreean," "(The) Hunt(ing of) the Wren," "I'm Goin' to the Woods," "'Let's Go A-Hunting,' (Says Richard to Robert)," "Let Us Go to the Woods," "O Where Are We Gannin?" "Richat and Robet," "Wise Willie," "The Wran"; cf. "Billy Barlow," "Poor Greeting Wilsie."

Source: (Co. Armagh).

s: This extraordinary child's rhyme ... evidently has some deeper meaning and is allied to the old morality plays as witness the reference to death in the last verse. The folk song collections in Belfast and in the National and Trinity College libraries, Dublin, have been searched and nothing comparable to this song has been found.

m: "Letter among Henry papers (23 February 1937, Rev. T. C. Topley, Rector of Ramoan, Ballycastle, to Sam Henry) reveals it to have been heard by Topley as a boy in Co. Armagh.... The notation of the air is not reliable.... I assume from another song (S of P 732) from the same source that the notation was by Mrs Topley" (1979:159-60).

Key D.

Where are ye goin'? says Arty Art,
Where are ye goin'? says Dandrum Dart,
Where are ye goin'? says Brother-in-Three,
I'm goin' to the fair, says Cricketty Wee.

[*similarly:*]
What will you do there?
I'll buy a wee pony.

But what will you do with it?
It's for my wife to ride on.

When will ye get married?
The day before the morrow.

Will there be any drink?
A glass and a half.

It'll not be all drunk.
I could drink it myself.

What'll you have to eat?
A loaf and a half.

It'll not get all ate.
I'll put it under my hat.

The mice will get at it.
I'll keep a good cat.

Will ye have any children?
Two, and two cripples.

I doubt they'll not work.
They'll work for death.

◇ A3 REFERENCES ◇

◇ I Am the Master *(H 48a) 10*

m: IREL Brady 1975:120 "Dusty Bluebells"
h: Daiken, p. 154
m: J. T. R. Ritchie 1964:24, 164 "Dusty Bluebells"
  Peirce 1979:10

REC Alison McMorland, Big Ben BBX 504 (B5f) "In and Out the Rushing Bluebells"

◇ Green Gravel *(H 48b) 10*

Dean-Smith 1954
Brunnings 1981: ?"... (See Green, Green, the Crab Apple Tree)," "Green Gravel, Green Gravel"

IREL Hammond 1978:10
  Peirce 1975:46

AMER Arnold 1950:129
  Bush 4,1977:7-8
  Ford 1940:256-7
  Justus 1957:54
  Linscott 1939:10-1

cl: REC Eva Grace Boone and children's group, AFS 3051 A1
cl: Samuel Clay Dixon, AFS 1749 A2
cl: Minnie Floyd, AFS 1300 A
cl: 4 children, AFS 2789 A2 "...s"
cl: Clarice Garland, AFS 2005 A2 & 3 (10") "...s"
cl: Group of children, AFS 4000 A4 "...s"
cl: Group of pupils, AFS 1450 A3 "...s"
  David Hammond, Tradition TLP 1028 (A3); Greenhays/Sruthán GR 702 (B4b)
    Jean Ritchie, Folkways FC 7054 (B7) "... Gravels"
    Ritchie Family, Folkways FA 2316 (A1) "... Gravels"
cl: Ray Wood, AFS 893 A5

◇ Ring a Ring o' Roses *(H 48c) 10*

Brunnings 1981: "Ring-a-Ring o' Roses - A Pocket Full of Posies," "... - Gloucestershire - Singing Game," "... - Somerset - Singing Game," "... - Singing Game (A Cup, A Cup o' Shell)"

BRIT Gomme 1894,2:108-11
  Opie/Opie 1951:364-5 (#443)

AMER Ford 1940:250-1
  Linscott 1939:49-50 "... around o' Rosies"
  Newell 1903:127-8 "Ring around the Rosie"

◇ Water, Water, Wallflowers *(H 48d) 11*

Brunnings 1981: "... - Growing up So High - Singing Game," "Wallflowers"

BRIT Gomme 1894,2:329-42 "Wallflowers"
  Greig 1907-11(1963): #152
  Polwarth/Polwarth 1969:33 "Wallflowers"

AMER Linscott 1939:54-6 "...Wild Flower"

REC Clancy Brothers, Tommy Makem, Tradition/Everest TR 2060 (B13) "Wallflower"
b: Clancy Brothers, Columbia CL 1950 "Wallflowers"
  Clancy Family, Tradition TLP 1034 (B1) "Wall Flowers"
cl: Celia Feldberg, AFS 3628 B3, 3631 A1 & 2 "Walter, Walter, Wildflower"
cl: Herbert Halpert, AFS 3641 B1 "Walter, Walter, Wildflower"
  Ewan MacColl, Folkways FW 8501 (A2,21)

◇ I'll Tell My Ma *(H 48e) 11*

Brunnings 1981: "... When I Get Home"

b: IREL Clancy Bros. 1964:12
b: Hammond 1978:18
  Loesberg 1,1980:47
  Peirce 1975:35, an extended version.

BRS Healy 1965:133-4, with a brief description of the game.
Songs and Recitations 4,1975:39-40

REC Peg, Bobby Clancy, Tradition TLP 1045 (B1)
b: Clancy Brothers, Columbia CL 1909 "... When I Get Home"

Sam Henry's Songs of the People

    Clancy Brothers, Tommy Makem, Tradition/Everest TR 2083 (B7)
    Elliot Family, Folkways FG 3565 (Transatlantic XTRA 1091) (A2)
    David Hammond, Tradition TLP 1028 (B4)

◊ **Here's a Poor Widow** *(H 48f)* 11

Brunnings 1981: "... from Sandiland - Singing Game," "... of Babylon," "... Who's Left Alone - Singing Game (Tune: Jin-Ga-Ring)"

BRIT Gomme 1894,2:62-3 "Poor Widow"

◊ **Old Sally Walker** *(H 48g)* 11

White/Dean-Smith 1951: "Sally Waters"
Brunnings 1981: "Sally, Sally Waters, Sprinkle in the Pan," "Little Sally Walker"

BRIT Greig 1907-11(1963): #152 "Sally ..."

AMER Arnold 1950:147 "Little Sally Waters"
    Hudson 1936:290-1 "Little Sally ..."
Jones/Hawes 1972:107-11 "Little Sally ...," 3 versions with game.
    Cf. Leadbelly 1962:92 "Little Sally ..."
    McIntosh 1974:86-7 "Little Sally ..."
    Rosenbaum 1983:50-1 "Little Sally ...," a black version.

cl: REC Josephine Alonzi and group of girls, AFS 3649 B4 "Little ... Saucer"
cl: Elizabeth Austin and group of women, AFS 420 A3 "Little Sally ..."
cl: Jessie Buchanan, Elgie Durr, AFS 3057 B2 "Little Sally ..."
    Eva Grace Boone and children's group, [cl:] AFS 3050 B1 "Little Sally ..."; AAFS L 9 (B7)
    Children of Lilly's Chapel School (AL), Folkways FE 4417 (A7) "Little Sally ..."
cl: Ruby Clifton, AFS 2970 A3 "Little Sally ..."
cl: Eight Negro girls, AFS 88 A2 "Little Sally ..."
cl: Wilford Jerome Fisher, Ruthie May Farr, AFS 2652 A2 "Little Sally ..."
cl: Four girls, AFS 2959 A1 "Little Sally ..."
cl: Hattie Godfrey, AFS 4017 B4 "Little Sally ..."
cl: Vera Hall, AFS 1323 B1 "Little Sally ..."
lc: Leadbelly, Stinson SLP 41
cl: Catharine Mason, AFS 3643 A1 "Little ... Water"
cl: Susie May Miller, group of five children, AFS 3074 A1 "Little Sally ..."
    Capt. Pearl R. Nye, [cl:] AFS 1009 B2 "Little ... Waters"; New World NW 291 (A2c) "Little Sally Water," a story.
    Pete Seeger, Folkways FC 7526 (A6) "Little Sally ..."
    Nettie May/Aleneda Turner, AAFS L 67 (B7) "Little Sally ..."

◊ **Broken Bridges** *(H 48h)* 11

Brunnings 1981: "... Falling Down - Singing Game (Tune: London Bridge Is Falling Down)," "London Bridge Is Broken/Falling Down (Tune of Broken Bridge's - Falling Down - Singing Game and See the Robbers Passing By - Singing Game)"

IREL Peirce 1975:11

BRIT Moffat/Kidson n.d.:13 "London Bridge Is Broken Down"

AMER Chase 1956:189
    Collins 1940:24-5
    Creighton 1971:173 "London Bridge"
Jones/Hawes 1972:179-81 "London Bridge"
Randolph 1946-50(1980)3:388-9 "London Bridge Is Falling Down"

cl: REC Emma Dusenbury, AFS 865 A1 "London Bridge"
cl: Four children of Heaton school, AFS 2859 A1 "London Bridge is Broken Down"
cl: Four girls, AFS 3648 A1 "London Bridge"
cl: Group of Negro children, AFS 2656 B3 "London Bridge"
cl: Mrs Birmah Hill Grissom, AFS 2965 B2 "London Bridge"
cl: Sam Harmon, AFS 2931 B3 "London Bridge Is a Burning Down"
cl: Audrey Hellums, Vivian Skinner, AFS 2982 A1 "London Bridge is Burning Down"
cl: Ina Jones, AFS 2994 A4 "London Bridge Is a Burning Down"
lc: Gene Kelly, Columbia JL 8001
    Alison McMorland, Big Ben BBX 504 (B5g) "London Bridge Is Falling Down"
cl: Mrs J. U. Newman, AFS 3775 B2 "London Bridge Is Breaking Down"
cl: Ethel Pharr, Ernestine High, AFS 3645 B4 "London Bridge Is Falling Down"
    Ritchie Family, Folkways FA 2316 (B3e) "London Bridge" with instructions.

◊ **Fair Rosa / The Sleeping Beauty** *(H 599)* 12

Brunnings 1981: "...," ?"Sleeping Beauty - Frank Luther," "Thorn Rosa"

b: IREL Hammond 1978:19

b: BRS *Come Let Us Sing* 1972:8-9 "Thorn Rosa"

REC David Hammond, Greenhays/Sruthan GR 702 (A1b)

[Instructions for the game, for corresponding stanzas:]
1. The children catch hands and dance round a child kneeling the center.
2. The child in the center sleeps.
3. The children gather closely round the center child and represent a forest -- the joined hands being uplifted.
4. One child detaches and enters the ring from outside and catches and shakes the child in the center, and both come out of the ring and run round outside.
5. The 'wicked fairy' resumes her place in the ring and the 'prince' detaches and offers his arm to the child in the center.
6. The 'prince' and the child run round outside the ring, arm in arm.

◊ **How Many Miles to Babyland?** *(H 40a)* 12

Brunnings 1981: "... Babyland? (See: To Baby Land)," "... Babylon?" "... Banbury?"

BRIT Gomme 1894,1:231-8 "How Many Miles to Babylon?" Gomme gives a number of other place names, such as Banbury Cross, Barney Bridge, Bethlehem, Burslem, etc.
    Opie/Opie 1951:63-4 (#26)

AMER McIntosh 1974:85 "... Bethlehem?" with game instructions.

◊ **Cricketty Wee** *(H 744)* 12

White/Dean-Smith 1951: "(The) Hunting of the Wren"
Dean-Smith 1954: "(The) Hunting of the Wren, Cutty Wren"
Brunnings 1981: "Billy Barlow," ?"Billy Barlow in Australia"

k: IREL Gill 1932
\# Moulden 1979:38
  McDonnell 1979:52

BRIT *Chapbook* 3(5):35 "Hunt the Wren (Shelg Yn Dreain)"
\# m: Kennedy 1975:188 (#78) "Helg yn Dreean [Hunt the Wren]" (in Manx Gaelic)
  See Lloyd 1967:96 concerning the possible significance of the "Cutty Wren."
  Palmer 1979b:233-4 (#143) "Hunting the Wren"
  Tocher #8(Win)1972:233 "Hunting the Wren"

AMER Darling 1983:93-4 (see Roberts/Barrand rec.)
  Fowke/Glazer 1960:175-7 "The Cutty Wren" quotes A. L. Lloyd on the background and symbolism; "Billy Barlow" is a descendant of this song.
  SO 1956:16-20 "Billy Barlow" and article on wren-hunting songs by Lewis L. Barnes.
  But not: b: Flanders/Olney 1953 "The Wran"

REC Joe, Winifred Woods, *FSB* 9 (B6) "Hunting the Wren"
  b: Bill Bonyun, Heirloom EP 501A (45 rpm) "Billy Barlow"
  ? b: Ian Campbell Folk Group, Topic TPS114 (TOP 82) "The Cutty Wren"
  cl: Dr. W. P. Davis, AFS 1349 B3 "Billy Barlow"
  m: Elliot Family, Folkways FG 3565 (= Transatlantic XTRA 1091) "Billy the Bob"
  b: Alan Lomax, Tradition TLP 1029 "Billy Barlow"
  ? b: *Pleasant and Delightful*, Vol. 2, Living Folk Records F-LFR 2 "The Cutty Wren"
  John Roberts, Tony Barrand, Front Hall FHR 026 (A1) "The Cutty Wren"
  Cf. Mike, Peggy Seeger, Rounder 8001 (B3) "Billy Barlow"
  Cf. Peggy Seeger, Prestige/Int. 13029 "Billy Barlow"; [b:] Prestige/Int. 13073
  Cf. Pete Seeger, Folkways FC 7601 (FTS 31501) (A6) "Billy Barlow"; [b:] Prestige 7375
  Cf. Tex-i-an Boys, Folkways FH 5328 (B5) "Billy Barlow"
  ? b: Ian, Sylvia Tyson, Vanguard VRS 9241 "The Cutty Wren"
  m: Bill Whiting, Topic 12T 254 (A5) "I'm Going to the Woods"
  cl: Bud Wiley, AFS 840 B "Billy Barlow"
  But not the Clancy family's "Wren Song," variously recorded on Tradition TLP 1004 (B3); Tradition 2060; Columbia CL 1950; Tradition TLP 1034

A4

Once I had a wee hen: Animals, hunting, racing

A Child's Lullaby

[H40b: "Three sleep songs," 16 Aug 1924]

Other title: cf. "Oor Cat's Deid."

Source: (w, m) old man (Killowen), from his mother.

s: I overheard an old man in Killowen singing a child to sleep with this little nonsense song. He told me he learnt it from his mother. [Bp only] I wonder how many generations has it hushed to sweet repose.

Key G.

Whirry, whirra, the cat she's deid,
And whirry, whirra, there's a sod on her heid,
And in a wee hole we'll bury them a',
And for wee puss we'll sing for a'.

1.2: ... sod at her ... [Dt]

The Little White Cat

[H510: 9 Sep 1933]

s: "An Caitin Ban"; o: "An Puisin Ban."

s: We re-publish, by request, the folk-song "The Little White Cat," for the convenience of competitors in class 28, Junior Folk Song (children under 16 years) at the Coleraine Musical Festival to be held in the last week of March, 1936.
This child's song is based on an old Gaelic Munster ditty, "An Caitin Ban." It should be sung slowly and with tender pity.

Key D flat.

The little white cat was walking along
When she found her wee kitten in danger,
And a week from that day she found him again,
Lying dead in the hay of a manger.

*The wee white cat, the wee white cat,
The wee white cat of Bridget,
The wee white kitten, snowy white,
The little white fluffy midget.*

A4 / Once I had a wee hen

The little mother rose up in her grief
When she saw her wee son lying,
She brought him home and made him a bed,
And then she started crying.

He never had broken a single thing
Nor butter of cow ever wasted,
And no one e'er spoke a word against him
Save the friends of the mice he had tasted.

His eye was grey and pretty his walk,
His footstep swift and lightsome,
It grieves me more, him under the clay,
Than the night all dark and frightsome.

My Bonnie Wee Hen

[H94: 29 Aug 1925]

Source: (Ballyhome district).

s: A child's nonsense song ... learnt [c. 1865], and at that time a very old song.

Key G.

Once I had a wee, wee hen and broon it was her tap,
She went oot tae seek her meat and ill it was her hap,
Ill it was her hap and bonnie was her care,
Every day she laid twa eggs and some days she laid mair.

I widna' for my seven sheep was smothered in the snaw,
Them that killed my bonny wee hen, I'll charge them at the law,
I'll charge them at the law and them I'll catechize,
I wasna half so sorry the night my husband died.

I opened up my bonny wee hen and viewed her a' within:
Four and twenty nice wee eggs a-hangin' on a string,
A-hangin' on a string and many's a wan forby,
The dear be with my bonny wee hen this night where she does lie.

To the funeral o' this bonny wee hen (she will lie at yon bog en')
Now I will invite you, both ladies and gentlemen,
Both ladies and gentlemen, and many's a wan forby,
The blessing be with the bonny wee hen this night where she does lie.

1.1: ... a wee hen ... [Dt]
.2: ... out to seek ... [Dt]

Sam Henry's Songs of the People

The Bonny Brown Hen [H88: 18 Jul 1925]

[Bp] A Magilligan song.

Source: (Magilligan, Co. Derry).

Key C.

You people so witty through country and city,
Give ear to my ditty, I won't keep you long.
In trouble I tell it, no grief can excel it,
My loss it is great, though my troubles are small.
I once had a chicken was well worth a keeping,
For eggs she was noble, as all the folks ken.
She's gone from me now and I canna tell how,
And it makes me lament for my bonny brown hen.

I called my hen Kitty, her tappin' was pretty,
It is a great pity if my hen should die.
In her neighbour's corn, when on foot or when growin',
She ne'er put her beak, but still flourished at home.
In Magilligan parish this chicken was cherished,
You need not me blame when I after her claim,
From the same place I came, William Balmer's my name,
And it makes me lament for my bonny brown hen.

For six eggs a week she brung home of the best,
Sure, my table was blessed when she entered my home,
She never would roam, but she would stay at home,
She never would trespass or o'er a wall fly.
If she had for to lay, she would keep it a day,
Till she'd bring her egg to her master. But then,
She's gone from me now and I canna tell how,
And still I lament for my bonny brown hen.

My hen was true game, from French Flanders she came,
And her breed was ne'er slain in cockpit or field.
In battle or combat she never was beaten,
But her haughty imposers she forced for to yield.
Her sire it was Black Neb, her dame it was White Leg,
Her grandfather came from the famed Johnny Glen,
She's of the same race and came from the same place,
That's why I lament for my bonny brown hen.

So now a reward to the clown or the bard:
Ten pound I will offer and will pay it down
For one sight again of my bonny brown hen,
Be she dead or alive or in city or town.
But the mark you must bring is a silver-tipped wing,
With a tap on the head, and if you see her then,
Fetch her and the villain; to pay I am willin'
And then I'll rejoice at receivin' my hen.

1.5: ... worth the keeping, [Dt]
2.7: ... William (Ban) ... * / * William Doherty (Ban) [Dt, *marginal note with asterisk in original.*]
4.7: ... and from the ... [Dt]

Nell Flaherty's Drake [H228b: 24 Mar 1928]

Other titles: "Ned ...," "... Flaugherty's ...," "The Wee Duck."

Source: (m) William Devine (Cross St, Coleraine).

s: A well-known humorous Irish song. Now first published to music....

o: Said to be symbolic reference to Robert Emmet.

Key F. Quick time.

My name it is Nell, right candid I tell,
And I live near a hill, I ne'er will deny;
I had a large drake, the truth for to spake,
My grandfather left me when going to die:
He was merry and sound and would weigh twenty pound,
The universe 'round would I rove for his sake;
Bad luck to the robber, be he drunk or sober,
That murdered Nell Flaherty's beautiful drake.

His neck it was green and rare to be seen,
He was fit for a queen of the highest degree,
His body so white it would you delight,
He was fat, plump and heavy, and brisk as a bee;
This dear little fellow, his legs they were yellow,
He could fly like a swallow or swim like a hake,
But some wicked baggage, to grease his white cabbage,
Has murdered Nell Flaherty's beautiful drake.

May his pig never grunt, may his cat never hunt,
That a ghost may him haunt in the dark of the night,

May his hens never lay, may his horse never
   neigh,
May his goat fly away like an old paper kite,
May his duck never quack, may his goose be
   turned black
And pull down the stack with her long yellow
   beak,
May the scurvy and itch never part from the
   britch
Of the wretch that has murdered Nell Flaherty's
   drake.

May his cock never crow, may his bellow ne'er
   blow,
Nor potatoes to grow -- may he never have
   none;
May his cradle not rock, may his chest have no
   lock,
May his wife have no frock for to shade her
   backbone,
That the bugs and the fleas may this wicked
   wretch tease
And a piercing north breeze make him tremble
   and shake,
May a four-year-old bug build a nest in the lug
Of the monster that murdered Nell Flaherty's
   drake.

May his pipe never smoke, may his teapot be
   broke,
And to add to the joke, may his kettle not boil,
May he be poorly fed till the hour he is dead,
May he always be fed upon lobsters and oil,
May he swell with the gout till his grinders fall
   out,
May he roar, howl and shout with a horrid
   toothache,
May his temple wear horns and his toes be all
   corns,
The wretch that has murdered Nell Flaherty's
   drake.

May his dog yelp and howl with both hunger
   and cold,
May his wife always scold till his brains go
   astray,
May the curse of each hag that e'er carried a
   bag
Light down on the wag till his head it turns
   gray,
May monkeys still bite him and mad dogs affright
   him
And everyone slight him, asleep or awake,
May the rats ever gnaw him and jackdaws still
   claw him,
The monster that murdered Nell Flaherty's
   drake.

But the only good news that I have to diffuse
Is of old Peter Hughes and young Paddy
   M'Quake,
And crooked Ned Manson, and big-nosed Bob
   Hanson --
Each one has a grandson of my beautiful drake,
Oh, the bird he has dozens of nephews and
   cousins,

And one I must have, or my heart it will break,
To keep my mind easy, or else I'll run crazy;
And so ends the song of my beautiful drake.

1.5: ... and round ... [Dt]
6.1: ... and coul', [Dt]

The Duck from Drummuck
[H228a: 24 Mar 1928]

A parody.

Other titles: "The Wee (Wonderful) Duck."

Source: Mrs Charles Moore [Dt: nee Annie White]
(Ballymacfin, Dervock).

[m = H228b]

I once had a duck when I lived in Drummuck,
I was quite in luck when I lived in that land,
Till some ugly thief took a greeding for beef
And for his relief he invented a plan:
At the head of the bed where the fine swaddy
   fed,
'By the hokey,' says Ned, 'I'll break open a
   hole.'
One morning in May by the break of the day,
She was out and away, my poor duck she was
   stole.

My duck, she's full blood, she waddles in mud,
She's as white as a crud when her wings she
   does shake,
She's grey on the back and green round her
   neck
And she's double related to Flaherty's drake,
Her eggs they are blue, each one big as two,
Believe me, it's true, I relate it with grief.
May the curse of the blind and the poor
   orphans nine
Together combine and lie down on the thief.

To curse him again I canna refrain --
You may all say 'Amen' when I finish my
   prayer --
May the weasels and rats build a nest in his
   hat,
And may a thousand long leeches on him make
   their lair,
May everything quit him and all the dogs bite
   him
And so to requite him that brought me bad
   luck,
When I'm in the street a-callin' 'Wheet, wheet,'
I may sigh and greet for my beautiful duck.

My poor duck she is stole, I suppose I must
   thole
And close up the hole at the end of the bed,
And see that the blaguard keeps oot o' oor
   haggard,
That murdering, beef-eating, duck-stealing
   Ned;
All the ducks in the town, they canna be found,
Every man is obliged to go out in the search.

Sam Henry's Songs of the People

In the year forty-nine, you may all bear in mind,
Mine had twelve dozen laid by the first day of March.

4.6: ... out on the ... [Dt]
2.2: crud = ?curd.
3.8: greet = cry.
4.1: thole = pin, peg.

The Lost Birdies
/ The Hobe and the Robin

[H40c: "Three sleep songs," 16 Aug 1924]

Source: coll. Maud Houston (Coleraine), from J[ames] Kennedy (Ratheane, Coleraine).

s: [Bp only] The only bird that builds "in the bog among the red fog," and which might be included in the category of crows, is the merlin hawk. [Bp, Dt] "Hobe," a dialect word for the young, is either derived from the French "hobe" to hover, or from the same root as hobble, indicative of awkwardness.
 ... This composition is more an old time musical monologue than a tune.

[Confused notation in Dt and Wt.]

Key G.

There was a wee crow bigg-ed down in yon bog amang the red fog,
She laid but ae egg, she brought out but ae bird,
The bird it came out an' it flew awa', and she gaed a' day
Crying, 'Hobe, hobe, hobe alane; hungry crap an' sorry wean,'
Quo' the wee crow for her bonny wee hobe.

A little redbreast built her nest in a wood where none could disturb;
She laid but ae egg, she brought out but ae bird,
The bird came out an' it flew awa', and she gaed a' day
Crying, 'Birdie, bird, ochone; hungry, sad and far from home,
Come back to your mother all alone.'

Robin Redbreast's Testament

[H527: 6 Jan 1934]

A song for the children.

s: (m) "Du, Du," or "The Lincolnshire Poachers"; l: resembles the tune used for "The Thing," American popular song c. 1950. Other titles: "Guid-Day Now, Bonnie Robin Lad," "Robin's Testament."

s: The verse form is as shown under the music. The note is duplicated where the syllables require it.

Key G.

Gude day, now, bonny Robin,
How lang have you been here?
'O, I've been bird about this bush
This mair than twenty year.'
 This mair than twenty year,
 This mair than twenty year,
 O, I've been bird about this bush
 This mair than twenty year.

But now I am the sickest bird
That ever sat on brier,
And I wad make my testament,
Goodman, if ye wad hear.
 Goodman, ...

'Gar tak' this bonny neb o' mine
That picks upon the corn,
And gie't to the Duke of Hamilton
To be a hunting horn.
 To be ...

'Gar tak' these bonny feathers o' mine,
The feathers o' my neb,
And gie to the Lady o' Hamilton
To fill a feather bed.
 To fill ...

'Gar tak' this gude right leg o' mine
And mend the brig o' Tay;
It'll be a post and pillar gude,
It will neither bow nor sway.
 It will ...

'And tak' this other leg o' mine
And mend the brig o' Weir,
It will be a post and pillar gude,
It'll neither bow nor steer.
 It'll neither ...

'Gar tak' these bonny feathers o' mine,
The feathers o' my tail,
And gie to the lads o' Hamilton
To be a barn-flail.
   To be ...

'And tak' these bonny feathers o' mine,
The feathers o' my breast,
And gie to ony bonny lad
That'll bring me to a priest.'
   That'll bring ...

Now in there came my lady Wren
With many a sigh and groan,
'What care I for a' the lads
If my wee lad be gone?'
   If my wee ...

Then Robin turned him round about,
E'en like a little king,
'Go pack ye out at my chamber door,
Ye little cutty quean.'
   Ye little ...

2.1: neb = beak, bill, nose.
4.2: brig = bridge.
10.4: cutty quean = an ill-tempered woman. [Moffat [1933]:32].

The Goat's Will [H119: 20 Feb 1926]

Larry's Old Goat, or Bessie (belled) and Mary (gray).

Source: Frank Magill (Mayogall, Knockloughrim, Co. Derry).

s: ... Magill ... writes:-- "This song was made about 1869 by an old mason, Hugh McCann, who lived in Gulladuff, assisted by others. Mary McCloy was taken to this place out of the Workhouse. She had left a plot and the goat went into them and true enough she killed the goat. The owner of the goat is dead long ago and left no friends behind him, so there is no one to be offended at this song."

1: The subtitle is a parody reference to Child ballad #201, "Bessy Bell and Mary Grey."

Key G.

Good people, pay attention, give ear unto my song,
These lines they are simple, although they may be long,
Concerning a battle took place in July
Between Larry's black goat and brave Mary McCloy.

'Oh Larry, you tethered me too near the crop
And then off my neighbours I got many a snap,
To infringe on my neighbours I ne'er did intend,
And this day I've come to an untimely end.

'While I am able, I will now make amends
To my good honest neighbours and well-wishing friends.
Boil my flesh all together, make dumpling and brose,
Divide with my neighbours as far as it goes.

'I won't trust you, Larry, your stomach's too wide,
You would eat all yourself and you would not divide,
So while I am able I will just make my will
In the presence of Michael and friend John Magill.

'Give my bells to Miss Martin on her bonnet to pin,
My beard to James Campbell to stick on his chin,
Give my lugs to Paddy's Biddy to cover her nose
From the hot summer sun and the cold winter snows.

'Give me teeth to old Neill, for I hear he has none,
My shin bones for drumsticks to wee Johnny Loan,
Give my horns to Larry to pick his old gooms,
My sinews to Kealy to tie up his looms.

'Give my tail to Paddy Conville to tie up his flail,
My skin for a drum to wee James O'Neill,
I bequeathe, too, a football for some little boy;
Make a rope of my puddings to hang Mary McCloy.

'Bad luck to you, Mary, your bonnets and bags,
Your trollops and wallops around you that wags,
May the fairies and witches your night walks annoy,
May the banshee soon cry for you, Mary McCloy.

'Oh, don't let Paddy Conville with his knife cut my throat,
But let me die here like an honest old goat,
You will think of my kindness when I'm dead and away,
How often you bribed me to cream your black tay.

'Sure, I was as good as e'er stood in a byre,
I gave my milk freely without borrow or hire,
And while I was able you ne'er wanted cream,
So I hope my two daughters will just be the same.

'Oh, tell my two daughters to be wise and beware,
And of this old damsel to be wise and take care,
If they see her coming, let them hasten away,
She could beat all the goats from here to Kilrea.

Sam Henry's Songs of the People

'Farewell to the fields and the meadows so green,
The hills, dales and valleys where I oftimes have been;
I had pastime and pleasure and sweet grass at will
In the fine summer days upon Annacramp Hill.'

9.4: ... to crame your ... [Dt]
10.3: ... wanted crame, [Dt]
12.2: ... where oftimes I've been; [Dt]

Matty Broon's Soo [H671: 3 Oct 1936]

Other title: "Tam Gibb and the Soo."

Source: James Bond (Termaquin, Limavady).

s: An old-time comic song with patter.... It is not so much a tune as a musical monologue.
　The second verse is sung to the last five lines of the tune, and the last verse to the last four lines.
　The song would seem to indicate that the settlers about Termaquin, Terrydoo, and Drumrammer came originally from Loch Ryan district.

Key G.

Quo' Nell, my wife, the tither night,
'Provision it is chape, man,
An' for the trifle it might tak',
A soo we well might keep, man.'
'Indeed,' quo' I, 'my dearest Nell,
I hae been thinking sae mysel',
An' since it's noo my notion,
I'll jaist go doon tae Matty Broon
This efternoon, an' very soon,
An' hae yin on a rape, man.'

It's when I entered Matty's dure,
She blithely met me on the flure,
Questions speyed me, half a score,
Some jokes befel, I cannot tell,
My herrin' they are scant, man.

[spoken:] Well, you may ken Mattie an' me was aul' sweethearts at yin time, but love jaist operates on me like medicine in an aul' wife's stomach.

Roon aboot aul' grumphy's legs,
The rope I quickly tied, man,
An' wi' a soople birchen twig
I driv' her frae the sty, man.
She might go east, I might go west,
An' ony road she liked the best,
At last she had my brain distressed;
I poked her 'neath and kicked her baith,
An' made her squeal alood, man.

[spoken:] Weel, I think I'd a-managed her if it hadnae been a big stane that was in the dyke sheugh that tuk my toe an' awa' I went my length and brenth in the glaur. Snap went the rape an' away she went, an' I ne'er sa' sicht o' her mair.

But while there's herrin' in Loch Ryan,
I'll ne'er want kitchen when I dine,
I bid adieu tae pig an' swine
An' Matty an' her soo, man.

1.2: chape = cheap, inexpensive.
 .3: soo = sow.
 .6: noo = now.
 .7: jaist = just.
 .8: rape = rope.
2.1: dure = door.
 .2: flure = floor.
 .3: speyed = ?asked.
 .4: befel = happened, befell.
3.3: jaist = just.
4.1: roon aboot = round about.
 .3: soople = supple.
 .6: ony = any.
 .7: baith = both.
 .8: alood = aloud.
5.3: stane = stone.
 .3: dyke sheugh = bank, dyke. [m: see H108b]
 .5: brenth = breadth.
 .5: glaur = mud.
 .6: sicht = sight.
 .7: mair = more.
7.2: kitchen = ?food.

The Moneygran Pig Hunt [H731: 27 Nov 1937]

s: (m) "The Bonnets o' Bonnie Dundee."

s: A song of Land League times.

[First published "by special permission," without music, in the *Northern Constitution* of 17 May 1924, signed Robert Stuart, with the following explanatory note: "In November, 1876, bailiffs and police were sent out to make seizures for rent on the Mercers' estate. The tenants let their pigs loose, and the ... poem describes the efforts of the officers of the law to capture them." No tune is prescribed.]

m: Current: Len Graham coll. from John M'Grath (Sam Henry's informant). For further information on the Land League (1879-81) [a popular agrarian movement which involved Charles Stewart Parnell and Michael Davitt] consult, e.g., pp. 285-8 in Moody/Martin 1967.

Key F. With spirit.

There was racing and chasing in old Moneygran,
And the fleet-footed porkers cried, 'Catch us who
    can,
We're the breed of the swine that the devil was
    in,
And our grandsires made rashers for Brian
    O'Lynn;
We're the boys pay the rent when the gale
    becomes due,
We're Home Rulers and Fenians and Orange pigs,
    too.
Don't you hear William's drum beating down by
    the Bann,
And the Ribbon-man's horn in old Moneygran?'

'Stand fast,' cried the war-hawks, 'we come from
    the queen.'
'Arrah, now,' says a porker, 'our bacon's not
    green!
Sure, you come from the sheriff, you rascally
    crew,
You shall never grab us -- we'll be hamm'd if you
    do!
We will run for our lives and our bacon we'll
    save,
You may follow and catch us, but not with our
    leave;
We will give you leg-bail, get the costs if you
    can --
We have raced you before, boys, in old
    Moneygran.'

Then away went the porkers, the bailiffs in
    chase,
Nor Epsom or Derby e'er saw such a race:
They flew over ditches like birds on the wing,
And each grunter's tail was a lovely round ring;
Through hedges they went -- over turf, bogs
    and whins,
They leapt a stone wall where the bums broke
    their shins,
Still racing and chasing, on, onwards they ran --
'Ten to one on the grunters of old Moneygran!'

The crowds on the hilltops stood watching the
    race,
Their eyes lit with fun and a glow on each face;
Wee Jackie cried out, 'We will feed them on tay
And cream it with whiskey from bonnie Kilrea.
See, see they are coming, oh look how they run!
They are at the last fence now, they're over --
    Well done!
Come cheer boys, hurrah! Let it ring o'er the
    Bann,
The pigs are the winners in old Moneygran.'

[*Differences in* Northern Constitution, *17 May 1924:*]
  1.4: ... our sires made ...
    .8: ... Ribbonmen's horns ...
  2.2: ... now, said a ...
    .4: You will never ... be hammed if ...
  3.4: And the tail of each grunter was ...
  4.3: Wee Jacky ... on tea,
    .7: ... hurrah! May it ...
  3.6: bums = bailiffs (of the meanest kind).
Land League (1879-81) = national Irish organization
    for agrarian reform, tenant protection, and famine
    relief.

Bellaghy Fair [H758: 4 Jun 1938]

Other titles: "I Went to the Fair at Bonlaghy,"
(m) "Just in the Height of Her Bloom," (m) "The
Swaggering Jig."

Source not given.

s: If any readers are aware of additional verses
to this popular ditty, they are invited to send
them to the Song Editor.
    Arms pronounced as two syllables, arr-ums.

Key E flat. Jig time.

I went to the fair in Bellaghy,
I bought a wee swad of a pig,
I got it up in my arms
And danced 'The Swaggering Jig.'
Then it's hi! for the top o' the heather,
And hi! for the root of the sprig,
And hi! for the bonny wee lassie
That danced 'The Swaggering Jig.'

As I went to the fair in Bellaghy,
I bought a wee slip o' a pig,
And as I was passing the poorhouse,
I whistled 'The Swaggering Jig.'
Then it's hi! for the cups and the saucers,
And hi! for the butter and bread,
And hi! for the bonny wee lassie
That danced 'The Swaggering Jig.'

As I being down by the poorhouse,
I whistled so loud and so shrill,
I made all the fairies to tremble
That live near Mccloughrim Hill,
Then it's hi! for the cups and the saucers,
And hi! for the butter and bread,
And hi! for the bonny wee lassie
That danced 'The Swaggering Jig.'

Sport's Lament [H772: 10 Sep 1938]

s: (m) "closely resembles 'Lamentation Air' used
by Alfred Percival Graves to set 'The Song of an
Island Fisherman' by Katherine Tynan (Hinkson)."

Sam Henry's Songs of the People

Source not given.

s: This is the only instance I know of a song supposed to be sung by a dog.

m: Written by Sam Henry?

Key F.

I am a poor forlorn dog and Sport it is my name,
My parents they were reared in Caw and kept the mountain game.
It's for my education, it's I got none at all,
And that's the very reason I was sent to Donegal.

It's when I went to Donegal, they used me very well
On a mash of Swedish turnips well mixed with oaten meal,
They shared their daily meals with me, all but the cup of tea,
And when they all retired to bed I licked the porker's tray.

But when the dog tax it came on, my master joined to frown
At paying of the licence and the loss of half a crown,
For paying tax and licence his purse it cannot stand;
Oh, master dear, take me, your dog; leave me in Carnanbane.

My curse upon their ignorance, the cause of all my woe,
If I'd been taught to heel or nip, or yet to scare the crows,
My master wouldn't part me for the loss of half a crown,
And that's the very reason that I range the world around.

Pat is my proprietor, I tell it with a sigh,
If I'd snatch a cold potato, I'd be sure of a black eye,
My neighboring dogs, they pity me because of my downfall,
I cannot bark until I get my tail against a wall.

I'll call on all my country dogs to witness my sad case,
I'll call on Mickey's Rover and on John M'Ginley's Bess,
There's Terry, Dash, and Tricky, I answer to their call,
I cannot bark until I get my tail against a wall.

In Carnanbane you'll find me, a tragedy to see:
I scarce can tell my master, for I served for two or three,
My coat is gray and shaggy, my equal can't be found,
And that's the very reason that I range the world around.

The Heifer [H675: 31 Oct 1936]

s: (m) "The Cuckoo's Nest."

Source: (w, m) James Bond (Termaquin).

s: Notes. -- Miller's donkey. James O'Kane, of Gortinure, the well-known author of the "Killelagh Cow" and many other songs, was known as the Miller.
Ballyhuone, a division of Coolcoscreaghan in Glenullin. The Cross of Ballinascreen, i.e., Draperstown.
Jarmy's Pound, near Dungiven, for impounding stray cattle.

Key D.

You have read of Tam O'Shanter, of Bobby Burns and all,
You have read of 'Miller's' donkey that came from Mayogall,
You have read about the two old mares that met at Matty's Row
And the gallant cow from Killelagh that conquered every foe,
But a story I am going to tell that happened here at home,
About three miles from Swateragh, not far from Ballyhoune,

It's all about a heifer that was bought at Newtown fair,
And when you hear her pedigree you'll think her very quare.

She was oul', she was boul', she was coloured like a mouse,
She was wee, she could see all the meal was in the house,
She had horns upon her heels and corns upon her toes,
And she was the greatest varmint to everything that grows.
She ate the blankets off my back as I lay in my bed,
She ate the very pillow from inunderneath my head,
She ate my coat and waistcoat, likewise my hat and shoes,
And she poutered up three acres of my early Skerry blues.

When you hear of her behaviour you needn't scratch your head:
She rumbled and she tumbled all the ditches I had made,
She ate the meal bag off my back and hunted me away;
If I canny sell her at the Cross I'll try her at Kilrea.
So be quick wi' the stick as she runs across the moss,
If she's tidy, agin Friday we will try her in the Cross,
We will sell her to Wee Harry, for he deals in things like thon,
And if he finds no buyer, he will put her in the pawn.

When Macaula' was done speaking, the heifer gien a roar,
Saying, 'Don't murder me, I pray, I've been murdered once before,
I'm the spirit of Lord Leitrim that was shot in Donegal,
When I got the devils all asleep, I crept across the wall.'
Macaula' then made answer, and this to her did say,
'From the grave there's no redemption, so how did you get away?
We read it in the scripture, likewise the book of prayer,
So we can't give you promotion to drive you to the fair.'

The heifer then made answer, 'Sure, they're all upon my back,
The night that I left Donegal, they drove me up to Glack,
They raffled me and baffled me from that unto the Glen,
And now I lie in Jarmy's Pound and ne'er has got a friend.'
Macaula' in amazement to hear she was the deil,
Wi' a splatter through the water, he run across the field,
Saying, 'We need not take this cow to market, town or fair,
We'll get three yards of dynamite and blow her in the air.'

2.4: varmint = noxious, objectionable animal, pest.
2.8: Skerry blues = (a variety of) potatoes.

The "Crummy" Cow [H501: 8 Jul 1933]

s: (m) "The *Bigler*."

Author native (West Bars, Co. Leitrim), c. 1855; source: (w) second cousin of author (Brooklyn, NY).

s: This humorous song was written about 80 years ago....
The air is a "stock" Irish air to which many old songs were sung, and, in particular, a song of the Great Lakes, about the sailing qualities of a timber drogher, called "The *Bigler*." Can any American reader supply the words of it?

Key E.

Now come all you good people, and I hope you'll lend an ear,
The travels of an old cow I mean to let you hear,
You could not get a match for her, and search through every fair,
She was reared by Pat O'Hurry, who lived at Ballinaglair.

He brought her out to Dowray and many another fair,
And then unto Drumkeerin and also Dromahaire,
Along to Knockarena, then on to Ballysadare
And then unto Drumshambo, but he couldn't sell her there.

He took her down near Sligo to a place called Ballinode,
When 'Crummy' she lay down there to die upon the road;
Pat went off for a butcher to ease her of her pain,
But 'Crummy' up and shook herself and took the road again.

He took her to Bundoran for to regain her health,
'If you don't bring me back,' says she, 'you'll have nothing but my pelt.'
He went on to Ballyshannon, I hear the people say,
And bargained with a grazer there for half a ton of hay.

Sam Henry's Songs of the People

'Ni racaid-se,' says Padraic, 'she won't eat it in a week,'
And then he drew his ticket and started for Belleek.
'In England if I was,' says she, 'it's there I would be sold.'
'Be damned to you,' says Padraic, 'your horns are far too old.'

'Ni racaid-se,' says she, 'you know I am strong.'
'Go Caiseal na mioga! Your horns are far too long!'
When in sight of Enniskillen at a place called Cork Macross,
Padraic he sat down there to reckon up his loss.

He had started out in high hopes a good sale for to make,
And if bad luck was to keep up, he felt his heart would break.
He had fifty shillings leaving home, had but a sixpence now.
'My curse I'll give, and while I live, unto the "Crummy" cow.'

One side of Enniskillen, it not being very far,
Padraic looked behind and saw the Opposition Car.
He spoke up to the driver, you may know he was no block,
'How much will you charge for "Crummy" and me as far as the Black Rock?'

On the other side of the car a gent was seated there,
When he saw 'Crummy' getting up, he fainted from the scare.
'Ni racaid-se,' says Padraic, 'you've fainted, to be sure,
Isn't my money and "Crummy's" money just as good as yours?'

Poor old Owen M'Sharry, who'd think he was so silly?
He ran down the road and threw his legs o'er 'Billy.'
He galloped on like thunder, as swift as any wind,
And when he met Hugh Haley he shouted, 'Mount behind!'

Philip Hart was lame, but when he heard the news,
He had corns on his big toes, but threw off both his shoes,
He galloped up the road, he did, as swift as e'er he could,
He sped until his legs gave out, up at Donnelly's wood.

My story is near ended, and I wish the cow no ill;
Jimmy Leonard bought her going up Camderry Hill.
Five goold pounds he paid for her, I heard some people say,
And Andy M'Sharry said the cow should have been given away.

Now, good people, in conclusion, I don't mean you all to laugh,
The last I heard of 'Crummy' was that she had had a calf;
She has a hump upon her back, but to the cow small blame,
For the man that has her now, like 'Crummy,' wears the same.

5.1: Ni racaid-se (pronounced "Nyee-raugha-sha") = I will not go. [s]
6.2: Go Caiseal na mioga = to Cashelnamega, may be an error for Cashelnavella, a village in Co. Leitrim. [s]

The Mayogall Asses [H130: 8 May 1926]

s: (m) "The Cuckoo's Nest."

Source: (w, m) George Millikan (Clonbullogue, Co. Kildare; from Co. Derry); author James O'Kane (Gortinure, Maghera).

s: George Millikan ... attributes the authorship to James O'Kane,... the writer of many songs which have passed into folk songs through their popular appeal. The best known is "The Killylagh Cow," an animal which, after veterinary inspection, may be presented some day to our readers [see Ó' Maoláin 1982:36-8].
Mr Milliken noted the air known as "The Cuckoo's Nest," of which he writes: "Between brushing up the tin whistle and blocking out the notes, I wasn't to say idle for a couple of hours. Though I am old -- 70 years -- and out of practice, "The Cuckoo's Nest," as here set forth by me is correct, and that to a note, and that note as I heard it long ago around the hills of Rocktown, Boragh, and sweet Drumard."
Mayogall is near Knochloughrim. The Editor has taken a slight liberty with the last line, which really intended a more terrible doom for the Jacks than a mild return to their native stables. The song is a humorous skit on an old rivalry that existed between the Glen parishioners and the "Sunburnt Laveys" or "Mayogallers."

m: see Hurl 1938; Ó Maoláin 1982:28-30 substitutes Sam Henry's version, but restores "what I hope was originally intended" as the subjects' destination.

Key D.

You've heard tell of the camels in the Asiatic land,
How they carry heavy burdens o'er the hot and burning sand,
You've heard tell of the asses in the ancient days of Saul,
And there's this tradition how they came from that to Mayogall.

They were there, I can swear, as they were among the Jews,
Some neglected, some dejected, some unshod and some with shoes.
They are used for various purposes for after death, they say,
Their hides are used by Ribbonmen to drum on Patrick's Day.

They were a cavalcade of donkeys by their masters neatly driven,
Heading west with cabbage plants to parts beyond Dungiven,
All ages and all qualities assembled into line:
I counted them both great and small: they numbered twenty-nine.

'I was young, I was strong, I was twice the age of you,
A courting boy, a sporting boy, without either sock or shoe.
I attended wakes and dances all over the old sod,
I was courting sweethearts right and left before that I was shod.

'So get up, my boy, and shake yourself and don't your master shame,
Before you get to Doorish's you'll not be half so lame,
In Carn they're fond of cabbage and they'll buy them as a rule,
I could sell a hundred loads of them in Cashel and Boviel.

'I can tell where to sell, for I know the road to go,
Tamniarn and the Carn and both sides of the Roe,
And away by Cluntygeeragh, where the greens are such a feast,
When they can't get them digested, they are calling for the priest.'

The donkey he got up and gave a very wicked pull;
Before they reached Pat Bradley's the fair was pretty full,
Going down at Harry (Oiney's) at a very lively trot,
He sold ass and all to Banin and got paid upon the spot.

He goes roaring and baloring, and I can't get words to pen
The awful consternation that arose throughout the Glen.
They've got half a ton of dynamite, they're swearing one and all
To blow those braying jacks across the hills to Mayogall.

12.3: [*Parentheses in original.*]
13.4: ... these braving jacks ... [Dt]
4.4: Ribbonmen = members of a 19th-century Irish Roman Catholic secret society.

Seal Song [H713: 24 Jul 1937]

Other title: ?cf. "Actual Song of the Seal," "Scotch Fisherman's Song for Attracting the Seals."

Source: (m) noted by "a lady"; author Sam Henry.

s: It is well known that seals are fond of music. They can be lured ashore by whistling softly to them. Strangest of all, they have a tune of their own, which has been heard by a native of the island of Jura and noted in musical notation by a lady to whom we are indebted for this extraordinary contribution to our columns.
To convey the air and the spirit of the scenes in which it is heard, the Song Editor has composed a song to suit the seal's music.

Key A flat.

Moan low, wild wave,
Drown not the seal's sad song.

Brown eyes love crave
Seal-kith and kin among.

Storm fiend, give place,
White babies helpless lie.

Great God, in grace
Hear the seal-mother's cry.

Storm-born, their babies
See first the winter sun.

Give them sweet life
Until their day be done.

Land-born, sea-reared,
Strenghthen their baby fins.

Lone lands, scenes weird,
Save from the hunter's sins.

Dark rock, blue sea,
A share of teeming fish.

Wide sky, life free:
These are the seal's deep wish.

Sam Henry's Songs of the People

Round heads, sleek necks,
Contented just to be.

God-made, why vex
These wonders of the sea?

The Crocodile [H231a: 14 Apr 1928]

A sailor's yarn.

Other titles: "... Song," "...'s Mouth," "The Great (Rummy) (Wonderful) ...," "Shipwrecked."

Source: William John M'Intyre (Craigtownmore, Portrush).

s: A version to a different air has been published in *English County Songs* [Broadwood/Maitland 1893]. This song is a type of a class of comic song of a hundred years ago, of which "The Derby Ram" is another well-known example....

Key A. Moderately quick.

[H231b: Dt=W(c)]

Source: (m) Hamilton Hemingway (Burnside, Coleraine).

Key G.

You landsmen all, on you I call; to tell the truth I'm bound,
Of what happened to me when I was at sea, and the wonders there I found:
Shipwrecked I once was off Peru, scarce half a league from the shore,
I landed and resolved to roam, the country to explore.

*To my tit falairo raddle diddle airo,
[T]it falairo whack.*

I had not ventured very far, when by the side of the ocean
I saw something there I could compare to the whole world in motion.

I quickly bore alongside of it and found 'twas a crocodile,
And from his nose to the tip of his tail he measured five hundred miles.

This crocodile, you may plainly see, was not of the common race,
I had to climb a very high tree to get a sight of his face,
My eye, when he did open his jaw, perhaps you'll think it's a lie,
It was above the clouds, nine mile four score, and his nose quite touched the sky.

I being aloft, the seas ran high, it blew a gale from the south,
I lost my hold and away did fly down into the crocodile's mouth,
He quickly clasped his jaws on me, thinking to grab a victim,
But I ran down his throat, d'ye see, feth, that's the way I tricked him.

I travelled for a month or two till I got into his maw,
Where I found of rum kegs not a few and plenty of bullocks and straw;
Of life I banished all my care, for grub I was not stinted,
In this crocodile ten years I lived, where I was well contented.

This crocodile being getting old, although one day he died,
He was six long years of getting cold, he being so large and wide,
His skin was six miles thick, I'm sure, or something there about,
It took me twelve long months and more tunnelling a hole to get out.

And now I'm once more on the earth, determined to roam no more;
On a ship that passed I got a berth, so you see me safe on shore,
And if my story you shall doubt, if ever you travel the Nile:
Right where he fell you'll find the shell of the royal crocodile.

3.3: ... think it a ... [Dt]
 .4: ... nine miles ... [Dt]

The Fox and His Wife

[H38: "Songs for the bairns," 2 Aug 1924]

Other titles: "The Black Duck," "The Fox," "(The) Fox and (the) (Grey) Goose (Geese)," "The Fox Traveled (Walked) Out," "A Fox Went out in Hungry Plight," "Old Daddy Fox," "Old Mother Hippletoe," "The Tod."

Source: (w) old native, 80+ (glens above Garvagh); (m) "The Fox and His Wife" (O'Neill 1903: #271).

s: The words were taken down by me from an old man, over 80, a native of the glens above Garvagh. He said, "You needny ask me to gie you the tune for I hae nether teeth nor lips for singin' and yet if I was lyin' in my bed wi' only a half wan in me I'd be tunin' it tae mysel'."

Key D.

The fox and his wife, they lived in great strife,
They never ate mustard in all of their life,
They never ate meat that was cut with a knife,
But they loved to be picking a bon-i-o.
   Bon-i-o, bon-i-o,
   They loved to be picking a bon-i-o.

It happened to be on a moonshiny night,
When the moon and stars filled the sky with their light,
'Aha,' says the fox, 'it would be a fine night
For me to go into thon little town-i-o.'
   Town-i-o, ...

He trotted along till he came to a stile,
He cocked up his lugs and he listened a while,
'Aha,' says the fox, 'it is but a short mile
From this unto thon little town-i-o.'
   Town-i-o, ...

And then he came to the farmer's back gate,
The ducks and the drakes they began for to quack,
Thought Reynard, 'I'll take you for your master's sake,
He's the honestest man in the town-i-o.'
   Town-i-o, ...

Then Reynard he caught a wee goose by the sleeve,
Saying, 'Madam, dear madam, it's now with your leave,
I think you have now got no longer to live,'
And her blood then came trinkling down-i-o.
   Down-i-o, ...

Then Reynard he caught a wee duck by the back,
Saying, 'Madam, dear madam, you feel very fat;
You'll dance on my back and you'll smile on my plate,
And I'll gallop you through thon wee town-i-o.'
   Town-i-o, ...

When Reynard, sly Reynard, came back near his den,
Where there he had young ones, yes, eight, nine or ten.
They all cried, 'Da, da, da, go back there again
For that was a lucky wee town-i-o.'
   Town-i-o, ...

1.1: ... lived at great ... [Dt]
2.2: ... and the stars ... [Dt]
7.3: ... cried, 'Da, da, go ... [Dt]

2.4: thon = yonder. [m/s]
a half one = a measure of whiskey, in Ireland a quarter gill.

The Hunting Priest

[H222: 11 Feb 1928]

A song of the good old days.

o: (m) "Tuirne Mhaire." Other titles: ?"Sing Tally Ho!" "Tally Ho the Hounds"; cf. "Parson Hogg."

[Dt] Source: Michael McCloskey ("Paul Beg") (Cluntygeragh, Dungiven) [Wp, same written in pen, spelled 'Beag' and 'Clintygeragh'].

[Dt] s: ... It is remarkable that this song has also been collected in Devon by Rev. Sabine Baring-Gould [/Sheppard 1895].

The last line of each verse is repeated in the second line of chorus following.

Key G.

A doctor's merit no more employs the burden of my song, sir,
I'll sing the life the priest enjoys with constitution strong, sir,
He laughs and winks at him who drinks, I dare lay fifty pounds, sir,

Sam Henry's Songs of the People

And in the morn he sounds his horn to 'Tally
  ho, the hounds, sir.'
Tally ho, tally ho, tally ho, the hounds, sir,
And in the morn he sounds his horn to 'Tally
  ho, the hounds, sir.'

Every morning when he rises he draws on his
  boots, sir,
And if the beagles call that way he'll join in the
  pursuit, sir;
On his well-groomed bay he leads the day at the
  head of all the town, sir,
O'er hedge and wall he'll risk a fall to 'Tally
  ho, the hounds, sir.' .
Tally ho, ...

Every day this priest affords to dine on boil
  and roast, sir,
And as great as any lord, he'll drink his
  favorite toast, sir,
It's his delight to drink at night, his care in
  punch to drown, sir,
And o'er each glass to let it pass to 'Tally ho,
  the hounds, sir.'
Tally ho, ...

St. Stephen's Day, that holy morn, the priest
  was going to mass, sir,
And heard the music of the horn and heard the
  bugle pass, sir,
He shut his book, his frock forsook, and he
  sought wider bounds, sir,
Set Orthodox to hunt the fox to 'Tally ho, the
  hounds, sir.'
Tally ho, ...

Next day there was a pair to wed and Puss
  appeared in view, sir,
He threw the surplice o'er his head and bid this
  pair adieu, sir,
They both did pray that he might stay, for
  they were but half-bound, sir,
But he said that they might go home that night
  and 'Tally ho, the hounds, sir.'
Tally ho, ...

This noble priest, he ne'er did wrong, nor
  ne'er knew fraud nor art, sir,
His life is worthy of my song, he had an honest
  heart, sir,
He ne'er distressed nor the poor oppressed, his
  praises I'll write down, sir,
Nor thought a crime at any time to 'Tally ho,
  the hounds, sir.'
Tally ho, ...

Squire Agnew's Hunt [H140: 17 Jul 1926]

s: "Princess Royal." Other title: "... Hall's
Watery Park."

Source: (w) John M'Fadden (Main St, Portrush);
(m) John H[enry] Macaulay (Ballycastle).

s: John McFadden ... remembers Squire Jones
Agnew driving his carriage and six up the Quay
Brae, Portrush.

Key G.

On the sixteenth of March in the year eighteen
  and nine,
My mind was transported with sentiments fine;
I took a walk down by Kellswater Park,
Where the small birds in chorus joined their notes
  with the lark.

Thinks I to myself, 'Eden's garden is near,'
When a number of small doves in my sight did
  appear;
Where the blackbird and thrush and the
  nightingale sing,
I saw the goose with green goslings, the teal on
  her wing.

The next thing I saw was more pleasant to view:
A large pack of dogs was laid on by Agnew.
I kept up on the dog that run hard on the deer,
'Spur your stews,' then says Agnew, 'my boys,
  never fear.'

Through the lowlands of Balan away we did pass
Till we came to Teague's mountain where the
  horses stood fast.
'Go round it,' says Agnew, 'go round it,' he
  calls,
'For the brae is so steep that our horses will
  fall.'

And while he went round it, the buck got his
  breath,
But old Jowler following after was the cause of
  his death;
The double he gave him was over Mount Hill,
Through the land of Balriggan, Ballygoudand,
  Hugh's Mill.

The next place we saw him was in Kellswater
  town,
Going o'er the domain of his old native ground;
Says the buck to himself, 'Is it here I'm to die?
For my limbs are so tired I'm scarce able to fly.'

The hunt it is over, we have no more to do:
We'll go and drink brandy with Squire Jones
  Agnew.
If his liquor is good, let our jogs never end,
And over each bottle we'll drink brother and
  friend.

The Hare of Kilgrain [H12: 2 Feb 1924]

Other title: "The Hare's Lament"; cf. "The Granemore Hare."

Source: (w) 3; (m) William Sloan (Dundooan formerly of Bushmills); author James Sloan (Topland, Ballyrock) c. 1770.

s: An 18th-century hunting song supposed to have been written by the hare.... The song must have been written about 1770. Its author['s] ... great grandchildren are still in the district.
   The version given is based on three renderings, and is, I believe, complete. It excludes later additions such as the drinking chorus, which would not have been written by a hare.
   Young's buildings referred to are now the homestead of Mr Samuel James Atchison, of Kilgrain.

[Refrain words written under sol-fa.]

Key G.

Come all you bold sportsmen of honour and fame,
That weekly appear on the braes of Kilgrain
With your servants and horses and dogs at
   command,
And young Richard Hunter to lead on their band.

Lol di dary hi ho,
Lol di dary hi ho,
Lol di dary tol lary,
Tol lary hi ho.

The praise of our huntsmen I mean for to sing,
Their cries make the woods and the valleys to
   ring.
Like old mighty Nimrod, that sportsman of fame,
Young Hunter goes on in pursuit of the game.

November fourteenth upon that fatal day,
As down from my dwelling I happened to stray
All alone past the side of yon whinny green hill
Where oftimes in plenty I sported at will.

As I wandered unhurtful to gather my food,
The hounds were uncoupled as I understood,
Neither wheat, corn or barley did I ever spoil
For I always took grass or the shamrock for soil.

In under a bush I did lurk for some time,
Till twenty around me and six did combine
My innocent life without pity to take,
But quick as the lightning away I did make.

Right over the mountains and away past Kilgrain,
Well buckled by Ringwood and Slasher by name,
And down past Young's buildings and away
   through Cloyfin.
That ould beagle Draper, my curse light on him.

All along by Drumadraw, for the bog once again,
Still thinking I there for some time might remain,
But Drummer and Borer down on me did rush
As I lay sore frightened in under a bush.

Once more for the braes I directed my course,
Right stoutly pursued by hounds, foot and horse,
And Hunter, still foremost of all for the prey,
With a voice like thunder cries loud, 'Harkaway.'

Of lady and fair maid I then took my leave,
While Hunter his hat by the stubble did wave,
To the sign of the trail they were bred to obey,
It was you, Richard Hunter, led my life away.

I then was discerned of moments but few,
Each eye was admiring while I kept in view,
And the cries of young Hunter so loud did he
   cheer,
Each beagle and beagles to Ringwood gave ear.

Right over my old course like lightning I flew,
To keep a good distance from that bloody crew,
But the hounds in full cry filled my heart with
   despair,
That bloodthirsty crew had my life in their care.

My race being run, I was forced to give o'er,
My innocent body in pieces they tore.
You may find other pastime and drink healths
   galore;
On the braes of Kilgrain you will hunt me no
   more.

The Hare's Dream [H172: 26 Feb 1927]

Other title: "The Hare's Lament"; cf. "Reynard the Fox."

Source: (w) Alexander Doey (Cashel, Macosquin); (m) Tom Black, fiddle (Croaghan, Macosquin).

s: ... The "70th year" mentioned in the song must mean 1770, as both these contributors knew the song since childhood, i.e., about 1850.

m: Variant air in Henry papers, quite close to that given.

[Absent is a direction to repeat half the tune once more, which would be necessary for the refrain.]

Key D.

Sam Henry's Songs of the People

On the twenty-sixth of January, and in the
  seventieth year,
The morning being beautiful, charming, bright
  and clear,
I being disturbed with dreams as I lay in my den,
I dreamed of heathery mountains, of high rock
  and low glen.

  With my hark, tally ho! hark over yon brow.
  'She's over,' says the huntsman, 'and yonder
    she'll go.'

As I sat in my form for to view the plains round,
I being trembling and shaking for fear of the
  hounds,
And seeing no danger appearing to me,
I quickly walked up to the top o' Sligue.

They hunted me up and they hunted me down,
At the loop of the burn they did me surround,
But up came the huntsman to end all the strife,
He says, 'Leave the hare down and give her play
  for her life.'

Bad luck to all sportsmen, to Bowman and
  Ringwood,
They sprinkled the plain with my innocent blood,
They let Reynard go free, that cunning old fox
That ate all the chickens, fat hens and game cocks.

It's now I'm for dying, and I know not the crime,
To the value of sixpence I ne'er wronged mankind.
I never was given to rob or to steal,
All the harm e'er I done was crap the heads o'
  green kale.

5.4: crap [crop] = to remove the upper or outer
  parts of, to clip.

The Clady River Water Bailiffs
[H764: 16 Jul 1938]

Author [unnamed] member of the police force.

s: Inveruadh (pronounced Inver Rue) [--] the red
river south. The Inveroe (as it is usually spelled) is a small tributary of the Bann rising in Kil-
lygullib, flowing through Hervey Hill, Lisnagrot,
Lislea, and entering the Bann about two miles
north of Portglenone.
  None of the persons mentioned in the song is
now alive. It was made about half a century
ago....

m: [This] Clady River runs through Upperlands,
which is a few miles south of Kilrea, where Mrs
Craig [Sam Henry's daughter] lives.

Key C.

Come all ye water bailiffs that round the Clady
  lie,
That watch upon the salmon as gently they float
  by,
I'm going to give you all a tip will be of use to
  you:
The salmon's left the Clady and gone up the
  Inveruadh.

Sammy and Willie M'Ateer are certain to be there,
The net was made in Staghan and with her none
  can compare,
On her there's a coghil tail an eel will not let
  through,
She'll be sure to net the salmon going up the
  Inveruadh.

There may be an odd one venture up upon the
  fords of Ruad,
But with gallant Willie Rankin no poacher dare
  intrude,
Then get your men in order, yes, David, get
  your crew
And sail away in the new boat to watch the
  Inveruadh.

'Whist, yonder's Shaw and Mooney coming up
  along the Bann,
I'll swear,' says Beattie, 'that I see a gaff in
  Mooney's hand.
We'll row across to the far shore and there we'll
  watch the two,
The night's too dark and stormy for to face the
  Inveruadh.

'Let Beattie come o'er from Glenone, McCartney
  from the Row,
John Boyd, go down along with them, M'Glamery
  also,
And David, get your waterproof and your
  sou'wester too,
You will need them all if there's a squall upon
  the Inveruadh.'

You poachers all, both great and small, that fish
  upon the Bann,
Don't use your boats this winter, boys, but keep
  on the dry land,
For if that you be got, boys, hot quarters they'll
  give you,
For the night's too dark and stormy for to face
  the Inveruadh.

A Ballad of Master M'Gra[th]
[H161c: 11 Dec 1926]

No source given.

s: Lord Lurgan's great greyhound, which won the
Waterloo Cup in 1868, 1869 and 1871. Lord Lurgan's family name is Brownlow. M'Grath is pronounced M'Gra'.

[Dt; Bp written, supplanting original G?] Key D.

Eighteen sixty-nine being the date of the year
When the Waterloo sportsmen once more did
   appear
To win the great prize and bear it awa'
From the champion of Ireland, our Master
   M'Grath.

On the twelfth of November, a day of renown,
M'Grath and his keeper they left Lurgan town,
A gale on the channel soon drove them o'er,
On the thirteenth they landed on fair England's
   shore.

When they arrived in big London town,
All the great English sportsmen were gathered
   around,
One of the gentlemen laughed a 'Ha ha!
Is that the great dog you call Master M'Grath?'

Then one of the gentlemen standing around
Said, 'What about you and your Irish greyhound?
For you and your greyhounds we don't care a
   straw,
And will humble the pride of your Master
   M'Grath.'

Lord Lurgan stepped forward and said,
   'Gentlemen,
If any amongst you have money to spend,
For your great English greyhounds I don't care a
   straw,
Here's five thousand to one upon Master
   M'Grath.'

M'Grath he looked up and he wagged his big tail,
Informing his lordship, 'I know you'll not fail;
So, noble Brownlow, don't fear them ava',
We'll tarnish their laurels,' said Master M'Grath.

Then Rose was uncovered -- the great English
   pride --
M'Grath and his keeper, they stood side by side;
The hare was let loose, the crowd cheered,
   'Hurrah!
There's the pride of old England against Master
   M'Grath.'

As Rose and the Master they both ran along,
Said Rose, 'I wonder what took you from home;
You should have stopped on your Irish domains
And not come to gain laurels on Albion's plains.'

A4 / Once I had a wee hen

Said M'Grath, 'I know we have wild heather bogs,
But you'll find in old Ireland both good men and
   dogs,
So, hold on, Britannia, give none of your jaw
And stick that up your nostrils,' said Master
   M'Grath.

The hare led off with a beautiful view,
And swift as the wind o'er the green fields she
   flew;
Rose gave the first turn according to law,
But the second was given by Master M'Grath.

M'Grath ran ahead as fast as the wind,
He was sometimes before and sometimes behind,
Then he jumped on the hare's back and held up
   his paw,
'Three cheers for ould Ireland,' said Master
   M'Grath.

["McGra" in Dt, except "McGrath" in the title.]
2.2: ... left London town, [Dt]
3.3: ... gentlemen gave ... [Dt]
4.: [Stanza in Dt only; not in Bp.]
11.4: ... Ireland and ... [Dt]

Cashel Green (II)   [H154: 23 Oct 1926]

A song of a horse race.

o: (m) "The White Hare of Creggan."

Source: author Francis Heaney, 81 (Magherabuoy,
Benady Glen).

s: ... Francis Heaney ... is of the same lineage
as Murrough O'Heaney, the founder of Banagher
Church in the 12th century. The mare mentioned
in the song was the dam of the famous foal, "Shane
Crotha," which was sold for 800 pounds, won the
Manchester Cup, and changed hands again at 6,000
pounds.
   Cashel Green, a lovely holm by a turn in the
Roe in the townland of Cashel, where once the
Ogilby family carried on a bleach-green. The
landlord in 1878 was named Campbell.

Key G.

In the year seventy-eight, on a Monday serene,
A race was appointed on sweet Cashel Green;
Permitted by Campbell, some thousands did go
For to view those swift steeds on the plains of
   the Roe.

Sam Henry's Songs of the People

A light-footed hunter from Derry came there
To erase the fame of McCloskey's brown mare,
And a steeple-trained rider selected had been
To oppose brave McCloskey, that youth of fifteen.

In coursing array the boys dressed for to ride,
The fish in the Roe all confounded did hide,
Saying, 'Oft to the angler we've shown action keen,
But there's something still greater this day on the green.'

As they mounted the saddle, the horns did resound;
Like a true bounding deer then the horse he went round,
But the trusty brown courser soon let them know
That she'd bear the plate from the plains of the Roe.

Like a train of bow arrows they centred the line,
When Campbell s good pony it was left behind,
McCloskey's brown courser her distance kept clear,
Yet Lynch's swift hunter close after did steer.

As they belted the circle just for the last round,
The echo of voices did ring on the mound,
Crying, 'Here comes M'Closkey dividing the air,'
For as bold as an eagle fast flew the brown mare.

When she passed to the pole that stood on the Roe plain,
The bettors assembled, their gold to obtain,
Well won by McCloskey, that youth of fifteen,
With his matchless brown courser on sweet Cashel Green.

Now the praise of those riders I'm not fit to tell,
They must come from Moscow that could him excel;
Long live young McCloskey, good health with him flow,
He made spectators wonder that day at the Roe.

Success unto Campbell, and long may he reign,
May no vile intruder usurp the Roe plain,
May each Easter Monday bring forth a new scene
With the matchless brown courser on sweet Cashel Green.

Arthur Bond [H783: 26 Nov 1938]

A hunting song.

s: (m) "Master Magrath."

Source not given.

s: In verse 5 repeat lines 3 and 4 of air for lines 5 and 6 of the verse.

Key D.

Come all ye young sportsmen, far off and near hand,
Till I sing the praises of brave Arthur Bond,
His weight's twelve stone two and his age is sixteen,
He's the nicest young horseman that e'er rode in green.

On the twelfth of October his course he did steer
To Armagh races without dread or fear.
Says Thompson to Filgate, 'It's what is the news?'
Says Filgate to Thompson, 'I fear you will lose.'

Here comes Arthur Bond with his bonny crop mare,
He'll take the cup from us, I vow and declare,
And if we will lose, we'll get nothing but blame,
We'll slip into Selloo and home into Slane.

The bugle was sounded for all to get on,
At the head of the hunt rode young Arthur Bond;
The first leap they came to, it puzzled them all,
The second they came to, two horses did fall.

Brave Arthur Bond gave one crack of his whip,
O'er hedges and ditches Kate Kearney did skip;
When the hunt had been going for near hand a mile,
Says Arthur to Kate, 'Ma'am, you go in great style,
I'll lift you up high and I'll set you down fair,
For there's none on the plain can run Arthur Bond's mare.'

When Arthur Bond rode into the winning post,
He called for a cup to drink the mare's toast;
Here's a health to Kate Kearney, and may she run still,
She brought the cup home to the shades of Bondville.

For there's Woodpark and Elmpark, likewise Fellows Hall,
There's sweet Tynan Abbey, the pride of them all,
There's sweet Tynan Abbey and Caledon Hill,
But there's none to compare with the shades of Bondville.

Spanking Maggie from the Ross

[H516: 21 Oct 1933]

Source not given.

s: Ross is a townland in the parish of Connor in the vicinity of Kells, near Ballymena.

Key G.

Come all ye young sports, for the muse I will court,
I ask your attention to listen to me:
It's of a grey mare whose quality rare
Through the strain of these few lines you will plainly see.

By Mr Montague a banter was made
To compete with his mare for one hundred a side;
By brave Campbell Miller, who had plenty of siller,
The wager was taken and the money soon tied.

On the eleventh of June, when the earth was in bloom
And the dawn of the morning was fair, fine and gay,
From the neat town of Larne to the Point of Glenarm
They met for their contest along that fine bay.

From the County Tyrone some hundreds had flown
To make up their fortune upon their fine mare,
Their great trusty luck had mettle and pluck,
And soon did the laurels of Antrim wear.

But Antrim's brave tars, at home from the wars,
Assembled to bet and on her confide,
They knew that her speed was swift, sure indeed,
And that her fine mettle could still be relied.

But once she competed and fairly defeated
A bay mare whose backers were deeply downcast,
Who in glory had come that the palm might be won
And borne with all honours from the town of Belfast.

From the standpoint they started and together departed,
Till Antrim's fair lassie, she fell in the rear,
Her friends had reliance and stood in defiance
While Tyrone's great boasters did lustily cheer.

But brave driver Bell, he knew fully well
The fox's fair game for to put on a bet,
His course to restrain by the bridle or rein
And as a sure dogging to keep her far back.

A4 / Once I had a wee hen

He still kept behind, some stakes more to bind,
And he said to the man who rode by his side,
'If your siller to stake a wager you'd make,
Then on my grey steed you can truly confide.

'I have trotted your mare till now I declare
Her spirit is fagged and almost outdone,
But let come what may, sure mine is the day
The palm of the chase by me must be won.'

He called then for road, as his filly soon showed
Her mettle by lifting her high head and tail,
And she seemed for to say to her friends by the way,
'The lassie of Antrim shall never say fail.'

Like an arrow from bow from her rivals did go,
Which caused her backers to laugh, cheer and smile,
Then she came to the goal, where greetings did roll,
A triumphant winner by near half a mile.

The wild fallow deer in speed does appear
To bound fast and swiftly along the green grass,
So in fastness she trod along the green road,
'Adieu to you all,' says the Antrim lass.

'The contest is o'er and I shall no more
Be bound to compete with the maid of Tyrone;
I have doubled her speed, so now she may feed
On the braes of Dungannon around her sweet home.'

And here's to the filly, be the road flat or hilly,
Who never was beaten, nor never shall be;
May fortune smile o'er her, while friends they adore her,
May great success meet her in every degree.

Likewise Campbell Miller, may he be kind till her,
May triumphs still meet him where'er he may go,
His friends are true blue and loyal sure, too,
Wherever his friendship and gallantry go.

And here's to her rider: long life for to drive her,
May pleasures and honesty round him still dwell,
May triumph's great star shine on that bold tar
Who swayed well his reins -- brave Hamilton Bell.

May he e'er be victorious, his day bright and glorious
As we drink to his health the full flowing glass,
While sure evermore our praises will pour
To Erin's great champion, the Antrim lass.

2.1: banter = challenge.
16.1: till = to.

Sam Henry's Songs of the People

◆ A4 REFERENCES ◆

◆ **A Child's Lullaby** *(H 40b)* 17

Brunnings 1981: "Oor Cat's Deid"

m: BRIT Cf. Buchan 1962:145 "Oor Cat's Deid"

◆ **The Little White Cat** *(H 510)* 17

IREL Costello 1923:87-8 "Ain Caitin Ban"

◆ **My Bonnie Wee Hen** *(H 94)* 17

IREL Moulden 1979:109

◆ **The Bonny Brown Hen** *(H 88)* 18

IREL Moulden 1979:23-4

◆ **Nell Flaherty's Drake** *(H 228b)* 18

Brunnings 1981: "...," "Ned ..."

IREL Galwey 1910:16, 34 (#17)
   Hayward 1925:68-9
b: O Lochlainn 1939:134-5

AMER Grover n.d.:190-1
   Milner/Kaplan 1983:132-3
   Welsh 1907,2:403-6

BRS BPL Irish: (n.i.)
   BPL Partridge: 1.274
   Harvard 1: 4.141 (Ross), 6.90 (Harkness), 9.146 (Bebbington), 11.123 (Such)
   UCLA 605: 4(Birmingham)
   Healy 1962(1968):71-3 "Ned ..."
   Healy 1978a "Ned ..."
   In Dublin's 1968:56-7
   617 [190-?]:26 "... Flaugherty's ..."
   Walton's New 1,1966:34-5

REC Clancy Brothers, Tommy Makem, Tradition/Everest TLP 1006; TR 2070
   "Songs of Cork and Kerry," Mercier, "Ned ..."

MEL O'Neill 1903:142 (#763)

◆ **The Duck from Drummuck** *(H 228a)* 19

IREL *JIFSS* 14,1914:27-30 "The Wee Duck"
   Shields/Shields *UF* 21,1975: #424 "(The) Wee Duck"

BRS Harvard 1: 4.65 (Gilbert) "The Wonderful Duck"

◆ **Robin Redbreast's Testament** *(H 527)* 20

BRIT Greig 1907-11(1963): #141 "Robin's Testament," 3 versions of this song and a fragment of another, from tradition; Greig also prints the song as found in Herd's collection of 1776, with which Henry's version is nearly identical. Greig also says the melody he collected is Dorian and differs from the one given by Chambers 1880:240-2.
   Mason 1878:41

◆ **Matty Broon's Soo** *(H 671)* 22

BRIT Greig 1906-7(1963):29, 1 stanza.
   Greig 1907-11(1963): #162 "Tam Gibb and the Soo"

◆ **Bellaghy Fair** *(H 758)* 23

IREL Moulden 1979:20

m: AMER Eddy 1939:316 "I Went to the Fair at Bonlaghy," a fragment

m: MEL Joyce 1909:61 (#122) "Just in the Height of Her Bloom"
   O'Neill 1903:211 (#1118) "The Swaggering Jig"

◆ **The "Crummy" Cow** *(H 501)* 25

Brunnings 1981: (m) "The *Bigler*"

◆ **Seal Song** *(H 713)* 27

? Cf. Brunnings 1981: "Actual Song of the Seal"

BRIT Cf. Smith 1883:103 "Scotch Fisherman's Song for Attracting the Seals"

◆ **The Crocodile** *(H 231)* 28

Dean-Smith 1954
Brunnings 1981

IREL Moulden 1979:39

BRIT Greig 1907-11(1963): #14
m: Kennedy 1975:646 (#292)

AUST Fahey 1977:18-9
   B. Scott, *Penguin 2* 1980:112-5

BRS Harvard 1: 2. (Livsey), 5.34 (Cadman)
   Harvard 3: (Such) (Catnach)

REC Dee Hicks, Tenn. Folklore Society TFS 104 (A1) "Crocodile's Mouth"
lc: Burl Ives, Encyclopedia Britannica Films 4 (78 rpm) B1 337 "... Song"

◆ **The Fox and His Wife** *(H 38)* 29

Dean-Smith 1954: "The Fox and the Grey Goose; Old Daddy Fox"
Brunnings 1981: "The Fox"

BRIT Kennedy 1975:656-7 (#301) "Old Daddy Fox"; lists 5 English and 2 Irish recorded versions.
   Moffat/Kidson n.d.:24 "A Fox Went out in Hungry Plight"
Sharp/Karpeles 1974,2:399-402 (#333) "The Fox and the Goose"

AMER Flanders/Brown 1931:119-20 "Fox and Goose"
   Hubbard 1961:385 "The Fox Traveled Out"
   Leach 1967:184-5
   Moore/Moore 1964:261-4 "The Fox Walked Out"
Randolph/Cohen (1982):135-7 "The Fox Walked Out"
   Stout 1936:42-4 "The Black Duck"

k: REC Cyril Biddick, *CWL* 3, Columbia KL 206 (A4,29) "Old Daddy Fox"
   J. D. Dillingham, New World NW 291 (A1b) "Old Mother Hippletoe"
   Mrs M. Heathman, Folkways FE 38553 (A3) "The Fox"
lc: Burl Ives, Encyclopedia Britannica Films 1 (78 rpm) B1 308 "The Fox"; Decca DL 5080; Stinson SLP 1
cl: Mary Glenn Jessee, AFS 2775 A3 "Fox Stepped out One Moonshiny Night"
cl: Naomi Nelson, AFS 3380 B1 "The Fox"
   Freda Palmer, Topic 12T 254 (A1) "... and the Grey Goose"
   Pete Seeger, Folkways FC 7611; Folkways FA 2321 (B8) "The Fox"
   Rosalie Sorrels, Folkways FH 5343 (B1) "The Fox"

Ellen Stekert, Folkways FA 2354 (B1) "The Fox"
Ivan Westaway, People's Stage Tapes cass. 04 (B7) "The Fox"

s: MEL O'Neill 1903:47 (#271)

◇ **The Hunting Priest** (H222) 29

Dean-Smith 1954: "Parson Hogg"
? Brunnings 1981: "Sing Tally Ho! (Squire Hogg)"

BRIT Cf. Baring-Gould/Sheppard 1892(1895):10-1 "Parson Hogg" [Dean-Smith]

REC Derek, Dorothy Elliott, Trailer LER 2033 (A3) "Tally Ho the Hounds"

◇ **Squire Agnew's Hunt** (H140) 30

IREL *UF* 13,1967:37 "... Hall's Watery Park"

◇ **The Hare of Kilgrain** (H12) 31

Brunnings 1981: cf. "The Granemore Hare"

IREL Cf. Morton 1970:73-4 "The Granemore Hare." Morton comments: "The fact that the 'puss' in this song can talk should be no surprise when you remember that certainly in Irish folk-lore the hare is a magic animal. It can change into human shape, and indeed I've heard it told that it can only be killed with a silver weapon" (pp. 74-5).

REC Len Graham, Topic 12TS 401 (B4) "The Hare's Lament"
b: Cf. David Hammond, Request RLP 8061, "The Granemore Hare"
 Cf. Mary Wall, Eagrán 0001 (A5) "The Granemore Hare"

◇ **The Hare's Dream** (H172) 31

IREL Moulden 1979:67-8 says Len Graham has collected 2 current versions in Co. Derry.

m: REC Len Graham, Topic 12TS 401 (B4) "The Hare's Lament"
 See Geordie Hanna, Eagrán MD 0002 (A8) for fragments of this song.
 Cf. Nic Jones, Trailer LER 2014 (B4) "Reynard the Fox," another, different song with the same theme and viewpoint.

◇ **A Ballad of Master M'Gra[th]** (H161c) 32

Brunnings 1981: "Master McGra'"

IREL Behan 1965: #49
 Hayward 1925:61-2
 Loesberg 3,n.d.:20-1 "Master ..."
b: O Lochlainn 1939:66-7

AMER Haskins n.d.:62

BRS *Ireland Calling* n.d.:17-8
 Irish Fireside n.d.:19
 O'Keeffe 1955(1968):48-9
 Songs and Recitations 4,1975:23
 Walton's New 2,1968:37

b: REC Dominic Behan, Topic TPS 145 "Master McGrath"
b: David Hammond, Request RLP 8059 "Master McGra'"
 Tom McClung, Outlet OAS 3027 (A2)

◇ **Cashel Green (II)** (H154) 33

IREL Moulden 1979:30

◇ **Arthur Bond** (H783) 34

Brunnings 1981: (m) "Master McGra'"

◇ **Spanking Maggie from the Ross** (H516) 35

IREL Moulden 1979:142-3
m: Shields/Shields *UF* 21,1975: #371 "Spanking Maggie"

A5

By the heat of my brow: Occupations, lifestyle

Waulking Song [H535(a): 3 Mar 1934]

From the Misty Isle of Skye.

Source: (m) coll. D. E. M. Smith, esq (Wandsworth Crescent, Belfast) at Uig, Loch Snizort, Isle of Skye; author Sam Henry.

Key G.

White the sheep that gave the wool,
Green the pastures where they fed,
Blue the skies above the pool
Where at noon they made their bed.

Sing the garden of the sea,
From whose flowers we won the dye;
Sing of sea-tang, wild and free,
From our misty Isle of Skye.

Light the hearts that love the sea,
Brown the face that seeks the sun,
Brown and happy, here are we,
Singing till our task is done.

Move the web towards the sun,
Round the table, thump and rub,
Stretch and clap till all is done,
Stretch and clap and thump and rub.

Now is waulked the web we spun,
Winter storms may rave in vain;
Bless the work by which we won
Comfort from the wind and rain.

The Tailor Boy [H199: 3 Sep 1927]

s: (m) "The Rocks of Bawn"; g: "The Weaver Lad."
Other title: "The Weaver and the Tailor."

[Bp] s: This song enjoyed widespread popularity when handloom weaving was in its heyday. It was sung in different districts to different "stock tunes": e.g., in Dungiven neighbourhood the air was "The River Roe"; in Ballymagarry district it was sung to the same air as "Will You Pad the Road Wi' Me?" It is here set to an air usually sung to "The Rocks of Bawn," as that song, to another air, has already been published in this series, and the tune is too good to lose.

Key A flat.

A5 / By the heat of my brow

As I walked out one evening down by yon shady grove,
I heard a couple talking and I knew it was of love;
One of them was a weaver lad, the tother a damsel coy,
And I knew right well by her discourse she loved the tailor boy.

'Did you ever see a tailor sitting at his work alone?
He would mind you on a skelington, just scarcely skin and bone,
Or a frog upon a napping stone with his two legs shot away,
While a weaver lad goes neat and trig among the ladies gay.'

'Oh, it's don't run down the tailor, for it is an ancient trade,
Adam was the first one in paradise,' she said.
'He sew-ed up the fig tree leaf and it looked very fine,
And ever since the tailor trade most brilliantlie does shine.'

'If you marry a tailor, girl, your misery's begun,
He'll make you set your praties and dig them every one,
He'll make you cut your turf and carry them in a creel,
While the puir bit silly tailor lad does wind his bar of steel.'

'Oh, it's love, it's to maintain you, my shuttle I'll make fly,
I'll wear my fingers to the bone some fine things for to buy,
And I'll dress you like a lady in your Spanish leather shoes,
And I'll buy you all the fine things you read of in the news.'

'Oh, it's love, it's you have won my heart,' the damsel did reply,
'I was only joking you, your temper for to try.
I wouldn't part my weaver lad for ony lord or peer,
So here's my hand in wedlock's band for the love of you, my dear.'

So this couple they got married, as we do understand,
He has got fifty pounds with her besides a farm of land,
The weaver makes his shuttle fly and the bride sits at her wheel,
And the tailor he may mourn his loss and wind his bar of steel.

1.3: ... the other ... [Dt]
3.3: ... fig leaf ... [Dt]
4.1: ... tailor, your ... [Dt]

2.2: skelington = skeleton.
2.3: napping stone = a stone on which whins were pounded [s: Bp] [Dt: as food for horses].

Sam Henry's Songs of the People

The Cobbler [H551: 23 Jun 1934]

k: "The Shoemaker"; m: (m) "The Rose Tree in Full Bearing." Other title: "...'s Boy."

Source not given.

s: This action song is known far and wide. One version was collected in Articlave district.

Key A flat.

I am a cobbler airy
That's lately gained my freedom-o,
I fell in love wi' a wee broon lass,
I'm afraid she will not hae me-o!

Whack de doo de dum,
Whack de doo de doody,
Whack de doo de dum,
Kate, you are my darling.

I am a shoemaker to trade,
I'll work in rainy weather,
O, I have made two pair today
From a side and a half of leather.

'If I consent to be your bride,
Pray, how for me will you provide?'
'I have twa coos and a heifer,
And I'll stay always by your side.'

I have five pounds of money
And a good store of leather,
And I've five pair o' auld shoon,
And I'll batter them all together.

Go hand me down my pegging awl,
I stuck it right up yonder,
Go hand me down my sewing awl,
To peg and sew my leather.

O, I have lost my ball of wax,
And where will I go find it-o,
It's enough to set an auld man mad,
O, here it's when I mind it-o.

My 'prentices and journeymen,
It's they are always mending-o,
And I'm a cobbler to my trade,
And I am always spending-o.

1.2: ... freedom, O. [Dp, *similarly throughout*]

1.1: airy = sprightly, vivacious; proud, lofty, buoyant.

Jim, the Carman Lad [H171: 19 Feb 1927]

s: (m) "Castles in the Air"; k: "Carter's Lad." Other titles: "Jim(my) (Joe) the Carter('s) (Carrier's) Lad," "Little ... Carter ...," "The Stage-Coach Driver's Lad"; cf. "The Country Carrier," "Rattling Irish Boy," "The Shanty Boys."

Source: (m) noted by A. E. Boyd (Cullycapple) from William Reid (Mayoughill, Garvagh); (w) Tommy Long (Brockagh, Garvagh).

s: ... Mr Reid has a different version of the words, but Mr Long's version is used because the song seems the older of the two.

Key D.

My name is Jim, the carman lad, a jolly chap am I
With my lot I am contented, be the weather wet or dry,
I snap my fingers at the snow, I whistle at the rain,
I breached the storm for many a year and can do so again.

Crack, crack, goes my whip, I whistle and I sing,
I sit upon my waggon, I'm as happy as a king,
My horse is always willing, and for me I'm never sad,
There's none can lead a happier life than Jim, the carman lad.

My father was a carman years before I was born,
He used to rise at the break of day and go his rounds each morn,
He used to take me with him, especially in the spring,
I loved to sit upon the car and hear my father sing.

The colleen that has won my heart, she serves
  behind the bar,
And for a drive I do contrive to take her on my
  car;
Next Sunday we'll be married and, boys, won't
  she be glad,
She will always live a happy life with Jim, the
  carman lad.

It's to conclude and finish, and time we were
  away,
My horse he will be wearied if I much longer stay;
We have travelled many a weary mile and happy
  days we had,
There's none can treat a horse more kind than
  Jim, the carman lad.

r.1: ... whistle as I ... [Dt]
 .2: ... waggon as happy ... [Dt]
 .3: ... for I'm ... [Dt]

My Rattlin' Oul' Grey Mare
[H664: 15 Aug 1936]

Other title: "The Country Carrier."

Source not given.

Key D.

I am a jolly carter and a jolly good soul am I,
I whistle and sing from morn till noon, all troubles
  I defy;
Round goes the world, my boys, all troubles I
  defy,
Jogging along together, my boys, my rattlin' mare
  and I.

She lifts her hoofs so splendid, she rattles o'er
  the stones,
So clear the road, here Joseph comes; crawlers
  shake your bones.
With a carrier's cart and a driver smart, all
  troubles I defy,
Jogging along together, my boys, my rattlin' mare
  and I.

For when she's heavy loadened or going up a hill,
She knows that I am by her side and goes with
  right good will,
She knows that I am well enough, because the
  whip I'll spare,
I haven't a trouble in all my life with my rattlin'
  oul' grey mare.

3.1: loadened = loaded.

My Irish Jaunting Car
[H592: 6 Apr 1935]

Other titles: "The ...," "I'm an Irish Boy," "Larry Doolan."

Source: John Henry Macaulay.

s: ... John Henry Macauley ... is the author of
"The Ould Lammas Fair" and "Riding Herd at
Night."
  Where extra syllables in the song occur they
are to be sung by duplication of the note.
  This song is published at the request of a correspondent in Argyllshire.

h: Noted 1955 in Annalong, Co. Down.

Key D.

I'm Larry M'Hugh, a boy so true, I belong to
  the Emerald Isle,
Fair attention I crave, I'll chant you a stave --
  perhaps it will cause you to smile;
I'm jolly and gay, the truth I'll say, and the
  girls both near and far
Think it a trate to take a sate and be drove on
  my jaunting car.

  Sarch oul' Ireland through and through,
    sarch it near and far,
  The divil a wan can aquail me at drivin' a
    jaunting car.

In Dublin town of great renown you'll find me on
  the stand,
On my car so nate just take a sate and we'll
  drive through streets so grand,
The sights so fine all others outshine no matter
  near or far,
The reins I'll grip, I'll crack my whip and off
  flies my jaunting car.

If you wish for sport, sure, I'm the sort can
  find you lots of fun,
I can sit in my yoke and crack a joke with any
  boy under the sun,
And I know well enough where they sell good stuff,
  and the girl behind the bar
Can tell by my wink what sort of a drink will
  grease the wheels of the car.

The Farmer
[H676: 7 Nov 1936]

Source: James Bond (Termaquin) from his father,
William Bond (Terrydoo), "who died in 1913, aged
103 years."

s: The last four lines of the song are sung to
the last half of the music.

Key C.

Sam Henry's Songs of the People

As I went out on a morning in May
To find myself some recreation,
I spied a wee lass, she was gallant and gay
And she talked of the pride of the nation.
She ne'er could find one, let her do as she can,
That looks so delightful and charming
As the lad of her heart -- he was lively and smart,
And he was the boy that kept farming.

The farmer gets up without watch or clock
Just as the bright day is at dawn,
It's all by the noise of the elegant cock
That tells him the dark night is gone,
And straight he prepares to market or fair
To sell of his corn and cattle,
And in triumph at night he brings cash to his wife,
And that is the fruits of his farming.

The kings that have crowns made of the pure gold,
In their lifetime they have little pleasure,
For when they are crowned they are daily in care
And they have not a moment of leisure,
But the farmer's not so, where he likes he can go
All around with his corn and his cattle,
With his bottle and glass he embraces his lass,
And the farm for him stands the battle.

If you be hungry or dry in the road passing by
And see a good haggard of corn, sir,
Go into that house, for there you'll carouse,
You'll be well entertained till the morn, sir.
There's no man on earth that ever drew breath
Should be as much praised as the farmer,
Horse, bullock and cow that is drawing the plough,
His lands cultivate in due order.

Ye nobles so fine that cannot well dine
Without a large loaf on the table,
Was it not for the farmer, we know very well
To provide one you scarce would be able,
But let us agree in sweet unity,
Since the words are in proper due order:
Here is a health and a full flowing glass
To the honest, industrious farmer.

The Rocks of Bawn   [H139: 10 Jul 1926]

Other titles: "...Baun (Bourne)."

Source: (w) Patrick Lagan (Park St, Coleraine); (m) Jim Doherty [Dt: Lafferty] (the Doaghs, Magilligan).

s: After two years search the words have been obtained.... Pat Magill, the famous author, told me that he heard the song in Strabane Fair, where, I am told, it and "Killeter Fair" are sold as a broadsheet. Bawn or Bawnboy is in Co. Cavan.

Key G.

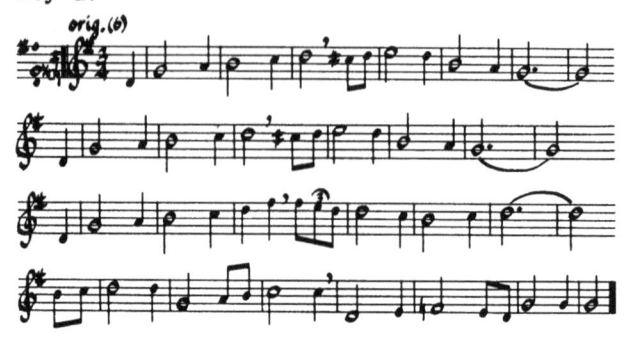

Come all you loyal heroes, wherever that you be,
Don't hire with any master till you know what
    your work will be,
For he will rise you early from clear daylight till
    dawn,
And you never will be able for to plough the
    rocks of Bawn.

Oh, rise up, lovely Sweeney, and give your horse
    some hay,
And give to him a feed of oats before you start
    the day;
Don't feed him on soft turnips, take him down to
    yon green lawn,
And then he will be able for to plough the rocks
    of Bawn.

Oh, my clothes they are all torn and my shoes
    they do let in,
And my socks they are all worn, I'm afraid
    they're wearing done,
And my heart is nearly broken from clear
    daylight till dawn,
And I never will be able for to plough the rocks
    of Bawn.

My curse upon you, Sweeney, you have me nearly
    robbed,
You are sitting by the fireside with the big pipe
    in your gub,
You're sitting by the fireside till clear daylight
    rolls on,
And you never will be able for to plough the
    rocks of Bawn.

O, I wish the queen of England had sent for me
    in time,
And placed me in some regiment all in my
    youthful prime;
I would fight for England's glory from clear
    daylight till dawn,
And I never would return again to plough the
    rocks of Bawn.

1.3: ... daylight to dawn, [Dt]
4.2: You're sitting ... [Dt]
4.2: gub [gob] = beak, mouth.

The Charity Seed
/ We Never Died in the Winter Yet
[H766: 30 Jul 1938]

s: (m) "Doran's Ass," "The Spanish Lady."

Source: (w) John M'Cluskey, per Teady M'Erlean (Clady, Portglenone); (m) James Kealey, fiddle (Union St, Ballymoney).

s: [Mr Kealey is] the well-known traditional fiddler.
   Two lines of verse to be sung to one line of music.

Key G.

To Strabane last Thursday I was walking
And quite early in the day,
I overheard two neighbours talking
Just before me on the way;
On the times they were discussing,
Wealthy people and their greed,
Farmers that had full and plenty,
All applying for the charity seed.

There's lots of food and prospects good,
Plenty of crops, my boys, don't fret,
Providence provides for all,
We never died in winter yet.

The people say near Ballintra,
When times were good, Richmond proved their
   cause;
Walter Black, the people say,
Got more than a strong horse could draw.
He got a ton of good potatoes,
And for them he had no need,
Believe me now, it's true you'll find,
You'll see a row about the seed.

Great distress was in the west,
Disraeli got a dreadful scare,
The land of Connaught, depend upon it,
It was near to be civil war;
Gladstone now will quell the row,
And I hope next year there will be no need,
Believe me now, it's true you'll find,
You'll see a row about the seed.

Now and then you will find men,
If the land was full from north to south
And a double price for their produce,
That poverty's still in their mouth.

A5 / By the heat of my brow

The Lint Pullin'
[H487: 1 Apr 1933]

Source: (m, w) John Elliot (Turfahun, Bushmills).

Key C.

When I was young and pulled at lint, I was
   handsome, spry and trig,
I always kept in temper wi' the lass was on my
   rig,
And if the pullers chanced to kemp, no matter wha
   was late,
I ay took special caution that my lass was never
   beat.

I once went down by Bushmills way, for they had a
   boon on there,
It's not for the greed of gear I went, but for
   the spree and tear,
For young ones then, I would have you ken,
   would fare jump at a chance
And they would work the lee-lang day, at night to
   get a dance.

The servant girl that was in the house, she was
   neat, genteel and fair,
She had twa bonny rosy cheeks and a head o'
   curly hair,
Besides she had that winnin' way that would your
   favour gain,
And I felt my heart a-warmin' for that maid called
   Mary Jane.

When we landed on the head rig, the maids they
   got their choice,
Each to pick their partner from among the men
   and boys,
And when we started at the foot my heart did
   jump wi' glee,
For Mary Jane was on the rig, for she had picked
   on me.

You see, I was the stranger there, I had no room
   to talk,
But them that has the knack can pull as fast as
   some can walk;
I looked across at Mary Jane, and says I, 'We've
   got to pull.'
She threw her bonnet down the field and
   answered back, 'We will.'

I did the sweeping cross the rig, she did the
   breakin' in,
And every time we pulled in front I made her
   tak' her win',

43

Sam Henry's Songs of the People

And though both right and left of us, they were pressing us very hard,
We were the first two at the head, we had beat them by a yard.

We had scarcely pulled the others out when the bell rung six o'clock,
We were a' fatigued and wearied and glad to hear the knock,
My comrade lingering at the gate, it's unto me did say,
'If they pull as hard the morrow, Rab, in the rig wi' you I'll stay.'

I helped her fill her creel that night, it was for the morning fire,
I asked her would she like for life with me to come and hire,
Says I, 'You'll have to work gye hard and your wages will no be big.'
Says she, 'We'll pull thegither, Rab, the way we pulled the rig.'

1.2: rig = ridge in a field.
1.3: kemp = to compete in labor. [s]
2.1: boon = ?unpaid service.
2.2: greed of gear = desire for wealth or goods.
2.2: spree = frolic, drinking bout.
2.2: tear = spree.

The Jolly Thresher [H622: 2 Nov 1935]

Other titles: "The Bold Thrasher," "The Honest Labourer," "... Thresherman," "... Reapers (Thrasher)," "The Labourer," "(The) Nobleman (Squire) and the Thra(e)sher(man)," "The Nobleman's Generous Gift (Kindness)," "The Thresherman (and the Squire)."

Source: John Millen (Fish Loughan, Coleraine), learned from James Moore, nicknamed "Cuckoo" or "The Three Wee Dears," travelling man, Waterloo veteran, c. 1875.

s: Where an extra syllable occurs in the verse, the note is duplicated to meet it.

Key G.

As I went a-walking one morning in May,
I met a jolly thresher upon the highway
With a flail on his shoulder and a bottle of good beer,
He was cheery as a lord with ten thousand a year.

Oh thresher, oh thresher, would you tell unto me
How do you support your poor famil-ee?
Your family is great and your wages they are small,
How then can you support your poor family at all?

Sometimes in summer we reap and mow,
At other times a-hedging and a-ditching we do go,
There's nothing comes amiss to us, neither harrow nor plough,
And we earn all our bread by the sweat of our brow.

And when we return home as tired as a bee,
The youngest of our family we dandle on our knee,
And the rest come all about us with a prattle and a noise,
And that's all the comfort that a poor man enjoys.

As a King Went A-Hunting [H117: 6 Feb 1926]

k: "The Nobleman and the Thresher," "Hunting Song."

Source: (w, m) coll. Maud Houston (Coleraine) in 1827 from Catherine Devlin, domestic servant (Cookstown, Co. Tyrone).

Key D.

As a king went a-hunting, a-hunting one day,
He met a jolly ploughman along the highway
With his flail upon his shoulder and a bottle of good beer,
He's as happy as a lord with ten thousand a year.

Says the rich man to the poor man, 'O, poor man,' says he,
'How do you maintain such a large family?
Your wages are but little and your children are small,
I don't know how you maintain them at all.'

'Oh, it's sometimes I labour and sometimes I sow,
Some days a-hedging and a-ditching I go,
Sometimes I thresh, sir, and other times I plough,
And I earn my bread by the heat of my brow.

'My wife and I together do join in one yoke,
Neither hardship nor poverty do ever us provoke,

We love one another though we are sometimes
   poor,
But we still incline to keep the bailiff far from
   the door.

'Oh, it's when I come home from work, it's tired
   I do be,
I take my youngest child and I set him on my
   knee,
While the oldest running round me with their
   little prattling noise,
This is all the happiness a poor man enjoys.'

'Since you are so industrious, both you and your
   wife,
There's thirty acres of good land I'll give you
   during life,
And if you be industrious and of it take good
   care,
I'll bestow it to your children and afterwards
   their heir.'

3.3: ... thresh and other ... [Dt, Wt]

Shanty Boy [H662: 1 Aug 1936]

[cf. H676 "The Farmer"]

Other titles: "The Farmer(s Son) and the ...,"
"... and the Farmer's Son," "The Shanty-Girl."

Source: (Drumtullagh district, Mosside, Co.
Antrim).

Key D.

As I roved out one evening
Just as the sun went down,
As carelessly I strayed along
Till I came to Trenton town,
I heard two maids conversing
As slowly I passed by;
One of them loved a farmer's son,
The other a shanty boy.

The one that loved the farmer's son
To the other one did say,
'The reason I love my farmer's son --
At home with me he'll stay,
He stays at home all winter,
When your shanty boy must go,
And when the springtime comes again,
His lands he'll plough and sow.'

A5 / By the heat of my brow

'For to plough and sow your land,'
The other one she did say,
'If your crops they don't grow well,
Your rent you have to pay,
If your crops they don't grow well
And your grain market's low,
The bailiff he will drive and sell
To pay the debt you owe.'

'For the bailiff selling it,
It does not me alarm,
There is no need to go in debt
If one has a good farm;
On the farm there grows your bread,
You need not work through storm or rain,
While your shanty boy every day must toil
His family to maintain.'

'The reason I love my shanty boy,
He goes out in the fall,
He is both stout and hardy
And fit to stand a squall,
With pleasure I'll receive him
In the spring when he comes home,
His money right free he'll share with me
When your farmer's son has none.'

'Dreadful are the hardships
Your shanty boy undergoes;
He's ordered out before daylight
To toil through frost and snows.
With pleasure and contentment
With my farmer's son I'll stay,
And he'll tell to me some tales of love
Till the storm it blows away.'

The one that loved the shanty boy
To the other one she did say,
'There's some of your farmers' sons
So green the cows might eat for hay;
It's easy knowing a farmer's son
When he comes into town,
The little lads will all cry out,
"Hi, Jack, how are you doin'?"'

'What you said of the shanty boy
I own that it is true,
And to wed this farmer's son
I fear I'm going to rue;
If ever I get the chance again,
With the shanty boy I'll go,
I'll leave him broken-hearted
Who has lands to plough and sow.'

The Shepherd Laddie [H617: 28 Sep 1935]

Other title: "The Crook and Plaid."

Source: Mrs H. Dinsmore (Stone Row, Coleraine).

1: The repetition of the penultimate line of the
refrain is evidently required, though not specified.

Key D.

Sam Henry's Songs of the People

Oh, I'll no hae the laddie
That drives the cart or ploo,
Although he may be tender,
Although he may be true,
But I will ha'e the laddie
That has my heart betrayed,
He's my bonny shepherd laddie,
And he wears the crook and plaid.

    And he's aye true to his lover,
    He's aye true to his lover,
    Aye true to me.

He climbs the mountains early,
His fleecy flock to view,
He spies the little laverock
Spring up frae 'mang the dew.
His faithful little doggie
Is so frolicsome and glad
He ventures wi' the laddie
That wears the crook and plaid.

For sic a faithful lover,
It's wha wid no comply?
For love's the purest pleasure
That's found beneath the sky,
And he's aye sae kindly
And he makes my heart right glad,
And he kens the way sae nicely
To fold me in his plaid.

r.2: [*Not in original Dp, but the sol-fa tune requires something of the sort.*]
2.3: laverock = (sky)lark.

The Thatchers of Glenrea [H186: 4 Jun 1927]

Source: (w) coll. Archie McEachran (Kilblaan, Southend, Argyleshire [Scotland]) from Hugh McMillan, neighbor, 79 (Kilbride, Southend), learned from the author, Hector (Hecky) McIlfatrick, thatcher (Ballycastle), died c. 1893.

[Bp] s: ... The close relationship between Kintyre and North Antrim is here proved, a relationship that began when the Picts pressed the Scots (then Irish) to take refuge in the peninsula across the Moyle over 1,500 years ago.... Mr McEachran was introduced to us [Dt: me] through the medium of the wireless from Belfast Broadcasting Station [Dt: of the radio (Belfast Station) by the kind offices of Mr Samuel Leighton, of Belfast, whose broadcasting of a folk recital led to the introduction.] Mr McEachran writes [Dt: He states] that the songs of Kintyre are mostly allied to North Antrim, and not to those of the mainland of Scotland.

Key G.

The first time I came to the shire of Argyle,
I went to Dalmore, where I wrought a good
    while;
My job being finished, big Jamie did say,
'Will ye gang and theek rashes twa days tae
    Glenrea?'

Now, when I crossed over the mountain so high,
I met an ould man with a patch on his eye
Who took me for a stranger, sayin', 'What
    brought you this way?'
'I was sent by big Jamie to thatch in Glenrea.'

The farmer spoke shyly, saying, 'I've little to
    do;
Thinks I, 'Perhaps you'd rather have Jamie or
    Hugh,'
And either to frighten or scare me away,
'Can you theek wi' ould rashes?' says McNeill o'
    Glenrea.

'I can theek wi' ould rashes, wi' heather or
    ling,
Bent, bracken or dockens or any wan thing.'
'Oh, you're just the man'll get plenty tae dae,
And I'll get you a ladder,' says McNeill o'
    Glenrea.

Then he brought out a ladder, 'twas like a slide
    car,
And an ould flail to mend it, all covered with
    tar;
While the ladder was mendin', we went in for
    our tay.
Troth, it's not a bad offer for to get at
    Glenrea.

I waited on there till I finished my job,
Then it's o'er yon wild mountains I had for to
    jog.
Should I stay in this country till my hair it
    turns gray,
Oh, I'll never go back for to thatch in Glenrea.

My wife's name's Ann Connell, she lives at the
    mill
In a nice little cot at the foot of the hill,
Och, and she does think long when I am away,
But I'll fetch her the money I earned at
    Glenrea.

As for big Hughie's wife, she's built up like a hut,
She takes a part from us both for to keep her well up,
She's as fond of the gillstoup as she's of the tay,
And she leaves us onable the rint for to pay.

So I took a notion it's home for to go,
I went to Ballycastle, the wages was low;
I went unto Hughie and this I did say,
'I'll go back to Kintyre, but not to Glenrea.'

So Hecky and Hughie and Felix and Dan,
With Ezekiel, Jamie and one other man,
All packed up our bundles and set out for say,
And the first place of landing was Cariskey Bay.

Then down comes McMillan, he gave a big roar,
'The big Irish thatchers have arrived on our shore,
My master he wants you without any delay
For to go an' theek rashes, but not to Glenrea.'

5.4: ... offer tae get ... [Dt]
8.4: ... unable the rent ... [Dt]

The Dandy Chignon [H227: 17 Mar 1928]

o: (m) "Bonnie Wee Widow." Other titles: "The Ladies' Bonnets and Chignons," "Oyster Shell Bonnet and ... (Chignauns).

Source: ? William Reid (Mayoghill, near Garvagh), (m) noted by A. E. Boyd, principal (Cullycapple P. E. School).

s: Collected on a memorable evening at the hospitable hearth of Mr William Reid....

Key B flat. Metronome 160.

Oh, of all the queer fashions you ever did see,
You will now hear of something, so listen to me:
It's of the proud lasses who ramble along
With a bundle of hair which they call a chignon.

A5 / By the heat of my brow

So twig your proud lasses as they walk along
With their oyster-shell bonnets and dandy chignon.

Such comical dresses and comical ways,
No such idea was in my grandmother's days,
They were homely and comely as they went along,
With sun bonnets hiding their sweet face from the sun.

Oh, there's a young damsel named Mary M'Call
Was invited the other night for to go to a ball,
In order to make her look handsome and fine,
She'd a chignon before and another behind.

There's an old cobbler's daughter lives over the way,
She wished for a chignon to make her look gay,
She so teased her old father and him did so vex,
He made her a chignon of birches and wax.

There's ould Katie Casey, she's late on in life,
The bridge of her nose is as sharp as a knife,
Her two legs are as stiff as if she had one,
She went to the barber and bought a chignon.

Long Cookstown / Nancy Whiskey [H745: 5 Mar 1938]

m: "The Calton Weaver," (m) "Youghal Harbour."
Other titles: "The Dublin Weaver," "Nancy's Whiskey," "Whiskey Nancy."

Source: Paddy M'Guckin (Orritor St, Cookstown).

Key G.

It's three long quarters I spent a-weaving,
And for my wages I was paid down,
And to buy a suit of new clothing,
I made my way in to long Cookstown.

As I was going up through long Cookstown,
Nancy Whiskey I chanced to smell;
Says I to myself, 'I'll go in and taste you,
For three long quarters I loved you well.'

I stepped in to an ale tavern,
I begged pardon for making free,
But Nancy met me in every corner,
'You're heartily welcome, young man,' says she.

When I awoke all in the morning,
I found myself in a strange bed,
I strove to rise but I was not able,
Nancy Whiskey run through my head.

Sam Henry's Songs of the People

Then I called on the landlady
To see what reckoning I had to pay;
There was fifteen shillings for ale and brandy,
And after that, 'You may go or stay.'

I put my hand into my pocket,
That was the money I did pay down;
On looking back into my small purse,
All that remained was one bare half-crown.

I put my head out of a window,
A smiling damsel I chanced to spy;
With her I spent my two and two pence,
Then all remained was the fourpenny boy.

So I'll go home and I'll join my weaving,
My little shuttle I'll steer awhile,
And I will earn more pocket money,
For Nancy Whiskey did me beguile.

The Jug of Punch [H490: 22 Apr 1933]

Other title: "Till I Be Full."

Source not given.

s: This song was sung about 1840 by Mrs Fitzwilliam, in Buckstone's drama "The Green Bushes." The song "The Green Bushes" was also sung by her from the same source. The song has been revived within recent years.

Key G.

As I was sitting in my room,
One pleasant evening in the month of June,
I heard a thrush singing in a bush,
And the tune he sang was 'The Jug of Punch.'

Too-ra-loo, too-ra-loo, too-ra-loo, too-ra-loo,
The jug of punch, the jug of punch,
And the tune he sang was 'The Jug of Punch.'

What more diversion might a man desire
Than to be sated by a nate turf fire,
And by his side a purty wench,
And on the table a jug of punch.

The muses twelve and Appollo fam'd
In Castilian pride drink pernicious strames,
But I would not grudge them ten times as much
As long as I had a jug of punch.

Sure the mortial gods drink their nectar wine,
And they tell me claret is very fine,
But I'd give them all just in a bunch
For a jolly pull at a jug of punch.

The doctor fails with all his art
To cure an impression on the heart,
But if life was gone within an inch,
What would bring it back like a jug of punch?

But when I'm dead and in my grave,
No costly tombstone will I ever crave,
But dig a grave both wide and deep
With a jug o' punch at my head and feet.

2.1: divarsion = diversion.
2.2: nate = neat; sated = seated.
3.2: strames = streams.
4.1: mortial = ?immortal.

The Cup o' Tay [H489: 15 Apr 1933]

Source: (m) Sam Dunlop, fiddler (Upper Main St, Bushmills).

Key D.

Och, prate about your wine,
Or poteen mighty fine,
There's no such draught as mine
From Ireland to Bombay,
And whether black or green
Or divil a shade between,
There's nothin' I have seen
Wid a gintale cup o' tay.

Whisht, hear the kettle sing
Like birds in early spring;
A sup for any king
Is the darlin' on the tray.
Ould cronies droppin' in,
The fat ones and the thin,
Since all their hearts I win
Wid a gintale cup o' tay.

Wid whiskey punch galore,
How many heads grow sore?
Shillelahs, to[o], a score
Most beautifully play.
With all their haithin ways,
Good luck to thim Chinaise
Who send us o'er the says
Such a gintale cup o' tay.

1.2: poteen = Irish moonshine (distilled liquor, usually illicit).
1.8: gintale = genteel.

The Black Pipe [H832a: 4 Nov 1939]

s: (m) "Paddy Kane."

Source: translated from Gaelic by Andy Doey (Ballymacaldrick, Dunloy), English verse by George Graham (Cross Lane, Coleraine).

Key C.

I am a woeful beggar as I go from door to door,
Seeking alms of those again that wouldn't give before,
Yet if I got the best of broth with helpings of cold tripe,
I would rather have an extra reek of my black pipe.

I never had much common sense or reason in my life,
But never was so foolish as to get myself a wife,
Nor with the pack can I be found, I never shoot the snipe,
My only fun is hunting up tobacco for my pipe.

Oh, would I be King Cormac buoyed up with royal joy?
Oh, would I be a Hector, who was once in famous Troy?
Or would I be a captain of an army in the fight?
No, I'd rather be a beggar with his own black pipe.

Suppose I was a bold Ardrigh with power to rule the land,
With wisdom great as Solomon, who had a king's command;
Yet all a kingdom ever meant, right off the slate I'd wipe
For my lonely mountain cabin and my own black pipe.

Now Orpheus upon his harp made music sweet and clear,
It charmed the rocks until they moved, the tides lay low to hear,
But all such tuneful melody would give me no delight
Unless I had a whiff or two of my own black pipe.

Not sweet to me the songs of birds throughout the countryside,
Nor yet the lonely silent swans that in the rivers glide,

The summer buds give no perfume when berried fields are ripe
Like the burning of tobacco in my own black pipe.

I'll say farewell forever to every kind of spree,
To making songs and stories and to vexing poetry;
I am afflicted sorely and my tears I will not wipe
Till they swim me to my coffin with my own black pipe.

The Wee Cutty Pipe [H465, 29 Oct 1932: Wt]

Other title: "The Derry Pipe."

Source: ? Frank Mullin (Draperstown) [see note to "Song Competition," H122]; author late James O'Kane (Gortinure, Maghera); (m) Denis Cassidy ([Wt: Fallalea,] Maghera).

[Not in B.]

Key A.

'Have you any tobacco?' says Sam unto Bill,
'Here's a wee cutty I want you to fill,
Not a tooth in my head but I think I will pull
Before they depart in a crowd from my skull.'

With a winkeltum, twinkletum, toor-ra-ra-a,
Lad da de, da di de, toor-ra-ra-a.

'My mother oft told me for me to take heed,
Beware of the boys who were using the weed;
You would know by their eyes and their noses and looks,
They paid little attention to scripture or books.'

'Did she read about Adam, that lonely old Jew?
When his apron was lost by the breezes that blew,
Or ere he saw Eve or the apple was ripe,
He consoled his misfortune wi' a wee Derry pipe.

'Did she read about Pharaoh when hunting the Jews,
Who ran into the Red Sea and lost his new shoes?
They say that the reason he chased with such spite
Was a chap o' the Kellys had stole his new pipe.

Sam Henry's Songs of the People

'Did she read about Jonah, when inside the whale,
When he went on a voyage to far Innisfail,
The whale being raging, through the ocean he
    ploughed,
And he called down to Jonah, 'No smoking
    allowed.'

'Did she read of Belshazzar, who sat in his hall
And saw the inscription was wrote on the wall,
And while the great prophet was reading to him,
He was cadging a chew from wee Larry McFlynn.

'Did she read about Noah when steering the ark?
He tried to cast anchor on Mount Ararat,
Being sick of the voyage, his brow he did wipe,
And he called for Pat Murphy to light him his pipe.

'Did she read ancient hist'ry? Did she read about
    Greece,
When Jason came searching for the golden fleece?
They begun on Slieve Gallion at the foot of the
    hill,
Where Micky Pat Roddy was running a still.

'I'm sure now the Greeks got the first of the pot
And then they sat down and they drank the whole
    lot,
They lit up their dudeens and talked about Greece
And set off for Broughderg in search of the
    fleece.'

'By the powers, then,' says Bill, 'sure your
    argument's grand.
The priest of the parish could not it withstand.
I'll smoke at my work and I'll smoke in my bed,
And I'll order a ton for my wake when I'm dead.'

Arrah, don't buy a meerschaum nor yet briar
    root,
But just a wee cutty as black as the soot,
For unless that your nose is as long as a snipe,
The shorter and blacker, the sweeter the pipe.

1.2: cutty = stumpy; cutty-peip = short, stumpy
    pipe.
9.3: dudeens = short clay pipes for tobacco.

The Rakes of Poverty [H741: 5 Feb 1938]

o: (m) "Winding Banks of Erne." Other titles:
cf. "The Son of a Gambolier," "The Ramble-eer."

Source: Valentine Crawford (Bushmills).

s: ... Popular in Killagan district.

Key G.

I am a rambling young man, from town to town I
    steer,
And like an honest fellow, I like my whiskey
    clear,
And like an honest fellow, I like my pint of beer,
I'm the rambling rakes of poverty, I'm the son of
    a gambaleer.

The old coat that is on my back I got in the pawn
    store,
And when it does get wet, my boys, I hang it on
    the floor,
And when it does get dry again, likewise I put it
    on;
You'd think I was some duke or earl, not the son
    of an honest man.

[repeat first stanza for refrain]

The old shoes that are on my feet, I got at the
    Crimee wars,
I got them from a soldier that died of wounds and
    scars,
The soles are leaving the uppers and the 'eels
    going back to sea,
The toes are burning me in the face with the
    relics of povertee.

[repeat first stanza]

I wish I had a keg of wine and sugar fifty pounds,
A great big tub to put it in and a stick to turn it
    round,
I would drink a health to all in the room and let
    myself go free,
So fill up your glass and let it pass with the relics
    of poverty.

[repeat first stanza]

The Oul' Rigadoo [H751: 16 Apr 1938]

Other titles: "The Beggarman's Song," "The Little Beggarman," "The Roving Journeyman"; cf. "The Colleen Dhas Rue."

Source: W. J. Lyons (Ballygan, Macfin, Ballymoney).

s: This song, sung at Coleraine Musical Festival by Mr W. J. Lyons ... won first prize (89 per cent) out of 14 entries in the Folk Song class and gained the Cup presented by Mrs Magee, of Dunedin Terrace, Coleraine.

Key G.

I am a little beggarman, a-begging I have been
For three score and more in this little isle of
  green;
I am known from the Liffey down to Segue,
Sure, I'm known by the name of oul' Johnny
  Hugh.
Of all the trades that's going, sure, begging is
  the best,
For when a man is tired he can sit down and rest,
He can beg for his dinner, he's got nothing else
  to do
But cut around the corner with his oul' rig-a-doo.

I slept in a barn down in Carrabawn,
A wet night in August, sure, I slept till the
  dawn,
With holes in the roof and the rain comin'
  through,
And the rats and the cats, they were playin' peek-
  a-boo;
Now whom did I waken but the woman of the
  house,
With her white-spotted apron and her calico
  blouse,
She began to frighten and I said, 'Ho,
It's don't be afraid, ma'am, it's only Johnny
  Hugh.'

I met a little flaxey-haired girl one day,
'Good morning, little flaxey-haired girl,' I did say;
'Good morning, little beggarman, and how do you
  do,
With your rags and your tags and your oul' rig-
  a-doo?'
'I'll buy a pair o' leggings, a collar and a tie,
And a nice young lady I'll marry by and by,
I'll buy a pair o' goggles and colour them blue,
And an old-fashioned lady I'll make her two.'

Over the road with my bag on by back,
Over the fields with my great heavy sack,
With holes in my shoes and my toes peeping
  through,
Singing, 'Skilly my rink a doodle, with my oul'
  rig-a-doo.'
I must be going to bed, it's getting late at night,
The fire's all raked and out goes the light,
So now you've heard the story of my oul' rig-a-
  doo,
So goodbye and good be with you, from oul'
  Johnny Hugh.

A5 / By the heat of my brow

Old Rosin the Bow [H698: 10 Apr 1937]

o: (m) "Gentle Maiden"; k: "Rosin the Beau."
Other title: "Rosin a-Beau."

Source: (m, part w) native (Foreglen, near Claudy); ("remainder" of w) Upper Valley of Thames [? by Williams 1923:93; all but one word in stanza 4 identical with Williams's version].

Key D.

I've travelled this wide world over,
And now to another I'll go,
For I know what good quarters are waiting
To welcome old 'Rosin the Bow.'
  To welcome old 'Rosin the Bow,'
  To welcome old 'Rosin the Bow,'
  For I know that good quarters are waiting
  To welcome old 'Rosin the Bow.'

When I'm dead and laid out on the counter,
A voice you will hear from below,
Crying out, 'Whiskey and water
To drink to old "Rosin the Bow."'
  To drink ...

And when I am dead, I reckon
The ladies will want to, I know,
Just lift off the lid of the coffin
And look at old 'Rosin the Bow.'
  And look ...

Then get a full dozen stout fellows
And stand them all round in a row,
And drink out of half-gallon bottles
To the name of old 'Rosin the Bow.'
  To the name ...

Then get half a dozen young fellows,
And let them all staggering go,
And dig a great hole in the meadow,
And in it toss 'Rosin the Bow.'
  And in it ...

Then get you a couple of tombstones,
Put one at my head and my toe,
And do not fail to scratch on it
The name of old 'Rosin the Bow.'
  The name ...

I feel that great tyrant approaching,
That cruel implacable foe
That spares neither age nor condition,
Not even old 'Rosin the Bow.'
  Not even ...

Sam Henry's Songs of the People

Bryan O'Lynn [H480a: 11 Feb 1933]

k: (m) "Laird o' Cockpen." Other titles: "Brian (Tommy) O'(A')Lin(n) (O'Flynn)," "Old Tombolin," "Tam o' the Lynn," "Tom Bolyn."

Source not given.

s: In the old records of the Manor of Cashel (Portglenone) we find under date 18th April, 1786, the name of Bryan O'Lynn as a Grand Juror, and on that same day he was appointed an "Apprizer." Under the signatures of the Grand Jurors is written:

   Bryan O'Lynn was a Scotchman born,
   His head it was bald and his beard it was shorn.

This hero of a comic song that has amused five generations was a real person. He was not a "Scotchman born," but of the ancient clan of the O'Lynns, of Hy Tuirtre, who were descended from Colla Ua.s [sic], king of Ireland about the third century.

Bryan was a popular and distinguished character of those days, at whose expense any Tom, Dick or Harry might add a verse to the song that had taken the people's fancy.

He is first recorded in the manorial records as an "apprizer" in 1770. On 17th October, 1775, it was decided that he was a proper person to serve as overseer of the market. On Tuesday, 15th October, 1782, he was appointed "pownkeeper for the ensuing year," and he was keeper of the pound for 14 years. On 10th October, 1786, Bryan was appointed to "view a march ditch." He was a grand juror from seven consecutive years from 1786 to 1793.

The innocent gibes at his expense he must have taken in good part. He seems to have been a happy-go-lucky man, easily contented and with a ready answer for all emergencies.

If any reader knows any verse that is not here included, it will be appreciated if it is sent to us to complete this amusing record of a side light on local history.

Key A flat.

[H480b: D(m)]

[2d tune: 1939 Coleraine Musical Festival version]

Class 29: Junior Folk Song.

Key G.

Bryan O'Lynn was a gentleman born,
He lived at a time when no clothes they were worn,
But as fashions went out, of course Bryan walked in:
'Whoo, I'll lead the fashions,' says Bryan O'Lynn.

Bryan O'Lynn had no breeches to wear,
He got him a sheepskin to make him a pair,
With the fleshy side out and the woolly side in,
'Whoo, they're pleasant and cool,' says Bryan O'Lynn.

Bryan O'Lynn had no shirt to his back,
He went to his neighbour's and borrowed a sack,
Then he puckered the meal bag up under his chin
'Whoo, they'll take them for ruffles,' says Bryan O'Lynn.

Bryan O'Lynn had no hat to his head,
He thought that the pot would do him instead,
Then he murdered a cod for the sake of its fin,
'Whoo, 'twill pass for a feather,' says Bryan O'Lynn.

Bryan O'Lynn was hard up for a coat,
He borrowed a skin of a neighbouring goat,
With the horns sticking out from his oxters, and then,
'Whoo, they'll take them for pistols,' says Bryan O'Lynn.

Bryan O'Lynn had no stockings to wear,
He bought him a rat's skin to make him a pair,
He then drew them on and they fitted his shin,
'Whoo, they're illegant wear,' says Bryan O'Lynn.

Bryan O'Lynn had no brogues to his toes,
He hopped on two crab shells to serve him for those,
Then he split up two oysters that matched just like twins,

'Whoo, they'll shine out like buckles,' says
   Bryan O'Lynn.

Bryan O'Lynn had no watch to put on,
He scooped out a turnip to make him a one,
Then he planted a cricket in under the skin,
'Whoo, they'll think it's a-tickin',' says Bryan
   O'Lynn.

Bryan O'Lynn to his house had no door,
He'd the sky for a roof and the bog for a floor,
He'd a way to jump out and a way to swim in,
'Whoo, it's very convanient,' says Bryan O'Lynn.

Bryan O'Lynn, his wife, and wife's mother,
They all went home o'er the bridge together,
The bridge it broke down and they all tumbled in,
'Whoo, we'll go home by water,' says Bryan
   O'Lynn.

[480b, *typed, has only stanzas 1, 3, 5, 7, 9.*]
9.3: oxters = armpits.

The State of Arkansaw   [H0: Wt; Laws H1]

Other titles: "... Arkansas," "The Arkansaw Navvy," "An Arkansas Traveller," "Bill Stafford (Staples)," "Old Arkansas," "The Rock Island Line," "Sanford Barney," "(When I Struck) Muskoka"; cf. "Hills of Mexico," "My Name Is John Johanna."

Source: (w, m) Jack McBride (Kilmore, Glenariff, Co. Antrim), learned from John McNeill, sailor (The Point, Carnlough, Co. Antrim).

1: Sam Henry sent a copy of this ballad to Alan Lomax, then at the Archive of Folk Song, Library of Congress, with a letter dated 5th November, 1941, discussing the deposit of a copy of the collected "Songs of the People" at the Archive. He said the song had been collected "a few weeks ago," and apparently intended it as a personal gift to Lomax; it is now in the Archive.

Key D.

Come all ye true-bred Irishmen and listen to my
   chant;
'Tis all the lamentation of an Irish emigrant
Who lately crossed the ocean, for a fortune
   thought he saw --
Five hundred men were wanted in the state of
   Arkansaw.

The first I met was Mr. Brown, who came up
   with a smiling face;
He said, 'Lad, come along with me; I keep a
   dacent place.'
He fed me on corn dodgers and his beef you
   couldn't chaw,
And he charged me fifty cents a day in the state
   of Arkansaw.

The next I met was Mr. Green and a different
   face had he;
He says, 'I keep a dacent place, just come along
   with me:
Give to me five dollars and a ticket you will
   draw,
That will put you to work on the railroad in the
   state of Arkansaw.'

I travelled along the railroad till I came to Little
   Rock,
And every depot I came to, my heart it got a
   shock,
For the divil a one I met that day extended me a
   paw,
Or says, 'Pat, you're very welcome to the state
   of Arkansaw.'

Well, now the railroad's finished, boys, and I am
   very glad;
I leave this part of the counteree, or else I will
   go mad.
I'll go to the Cherokee nation and there I'll
   marry a squaw,
And as sure as hell I'll bid farewell to the state
   of Arkansaw.

2.2: dacent = decent.
2.3: corn dodgers = cornmeal cakes.

Denny Byrne, the Piper
[H29: "A song from the south (serio-comic),"
   31 May 1924]

Other title: "The Cow (That) Ate the Piper."

Source: (w) Hamilton Hemingway, from an eminent K.C. in Dublin; (m) from his old schoolmaster (Kilmague, near the Curragh).

Key D.

Sam Henry's Songs of the People

In the year ninety-eight when troubles were great,
It was treason to be a Milesian,
But that black-whiskered set I will never forget
That history tells us were Hessians;
In those troublesome times how great were the crimes,
When at drinking they never were riper;
Nigh the town of Tralee, not an acre from me,
Lived one Denny Byrne, a piper.

Neither wedding or wake would be worth a burnt cake
If Denny he wasn't invited,
At the squeezing of bags or the emptying of kegs,
He astonished as well as delighted;
But those times poor Denny could not earn one penny,
Martial law had him stung like a viper,
Och, they kept him within till the bones in his shin
Did grin through the rags of the piper.

One night as poor Denny was straying away,
Coming home from the fair at Rathdangan,
On the branch of a tree, what there did he see
But the corpse of a Hessian there hanging;
The boots of the rogue shamed poor Denny's old brogues,
On the soger he laid such a griper,
And he pulled with such might and the boots were so tight
That legs and boots came with the piper.

Then Denny did run for fear he'd be hung,
Till he came to Tim Kennedy's cabin;
Tim shouts from within: 'Och, I can't let you in,
You'll be shot if you're found there a-rappin'.'
He went to the shed where the cow was in bed,
With a wisp he began for to wipe her,
So they lay down together in a seven-foot tether,
And the cow made it hot for the piper.

Then Denny did yawn as the day it did dawn
And he pulled off the boots of the Hessian,
The legs, by the law, he threw in the straw,
And gave them leg-bail for his mission.
When breakfast was done Tim sent out his son
To make Denny jump like a lamplighter,
When the legs there he saw, he roared like a daw,
'Arrah, daddy, the cow ate the piper!'

'Oh, bad luck to the beast, she's a musical taste
To eat such a musical chanter;
Arrah, Brian, avick, take this lump of a stick,
Drive off to Glasshealy and cant her.'
Biddy Kennedy bawled, and the neighbours all called,
They began for to humbug and jibe her,
To the graveyard they went with the legs in a box,
Sayin', 'The cow, she'll be hung for the piper.'

Brian Kennedy woke at the dawn of the day
And went off to the fair of Glasshealey,
Where the cow she was sold for four guineas in gold
To the clerk of the parish, Tim Daly.
They went into a tent, the luck penny was spent,
For the clerk was in a terrible swiper,
And who saw they there, playing "The Rakes of Kildare,"
But their friend, Denny Byrne the piper.

Tim then gave a bolt like a half-broken colt,
And at Denny he looked like a gommagh;
Says he, 'By the powers, I thought these eight hours
You were playing in Dhrimin Dhu's stomach!'
But Denny observed how the Hessian was served,
And they all wished Nick's cure for the viper;
Just for gra that they met, their whistles they wet
And like devils they danced round the piper.

1.2: Milesian = from Milesius, a fabulous Spanish king whose sons are supposed to have conquered Ireland c. 1300 B.C.; hence descendants of his sons, Irishmen.
1.4: Hessians = German mercenary soldiers.
5.4: gave leg bail = ran away.
6.2: avick = Irish *a mhic*, my son, an ironic term of endearment. [h]
6.4: cant = auction.
7.5: luck penny = portion of a price given back for luck.
7.6: swiper = person who drinks hastily and copiously, gulper.
8.2: gommagh [gomach] = fool, simpleton.
8.7: gra = love.

The Sailor in the Alehouse
[H779: 29 Oct 1938; Laws K36]

o: "The Green Beds." Other titles: "The Brisk Young Sailor Lad," "A Comical Dialogue between an Honest Sailor and a Deluding Landlady, etc." "The Green Bed Empty," "I'll Tell You of a Story," "Jack Tar," "Johnny the Sailor," "The Liverpool Landlady," "The Sailor (and the Landlady)," "(The) Wild Rover (No More)," "(You're Welcome Home,) Young Johnny."

Source: Jock Smylie (Leggyfat, Limavallaghan), 15 Oct 1938.

s: The curious word "green-beds" is a dialect term for a temporary couch, where a proper bed is not available. The word is used in the Channel Islands, but is very remarkable in an Antrim ballad.

Key C.

Oh, Johnny is a sailor, just newly come ashore,
He dressed himself up like a man that seem-ed to be poor,
He call-ed in an alehouse as he often did before,
He call-ed in the alehouse to pay up an old score.

'Landlady, oh landlady, trust us quarts two or three,
And bring your daughter Molly down and set her on my knee.'
'My daughter Molly, she's engaged and her you cannot see,
Nor neither will I trust you for quarts two or three.'

He call-ed for a candle to light him to his bed,
And likewise a napkin to tie upon his head;
'The beds are all bespoken and are since last week,
And for your lodging, for it you must go seek.'

'Oh landlady, oh landlady, what is there now to pay?
Tell me what is the score for what I drunk today?
There's a shilling of the new and there's twenty of the old.'
Then out of his pocket he pulled handfuls of gold.

When she saw the money she began for to relent,
And when she saw the money she began for to repent,
Saying, 'Johnny, lovely Johnny, all I said was in a jest,
For above all men breathing I count you to be the best.'

It was then her daughter Molly, she came tripping down the stairs,
It was then her daughter Molly came dressed in all her airs,
Saying, 'You're welcome, lovely Johnny, you're welcome, I declare,
The green beds are empty and you may lie there.'

'Before I would lie in your green bed, I would lie on the street,
For when I had no money, my lodgings was to seek,
But now I've money plenty, and enough to do my turn,
You and your ould mother can sit down and mourn.'

So come all you brisk sailor lads that plough the ocean wide,
And earn all your money by the cold and frosty tide,
Where the brown jugs and glasses come tumblin' in for fun,
There's no credit in an alehouse when all your money's done.

A5 / By the heat of my brow

The Private Still [H103: 31 Oct 1925]

Other title: "The Gauger's Song."

Source: (m, w) William Carton, retired N[ational] S[chools] T[eacher] [Dt: schoolteacher] (Garryduff, Ballymoney), from Daniel Moore c. 1885.

Key C.

A gauger once in Dublin town, the time that I was there,
He fancied that a private still was being wrought somewhere.
He met me out one morning, perhaps he fancied that I knew,
'Oh never mind,' he said, 'Pat, how do you do?'

With my fol-ol-dtha-di-do, fol-ol-dtha-dee.

'I'm pretty well, your honour, but allow me for to say
I don't know you at all, at all.' Said he, 'Perhaps you may.
I'm going to find a something out, assist me if you will,
Here's fifty pounds if you can tell where there's a private still.'

'Give me the fifty pounds,' said I, 'i' faith I surely can,
I'll keep my word, you may depend, as I'm an Irishman.'
The fifty pounds he then paid down, I pocketed the fee.
'Now button up your coat,' I said, 'and come along with me.'

Along the road we quickly walked for miles full half a score,
When by his gait 'twas evident his feet were getting sore.
'How far have we to go?' says he, 'for I am getting tired.'
'Let's hire a jaunting car,' says I, so then a car we hired.

As soon as we were on the car, said he, 'Now tell me, Pat,
Where is that blessed private still? Don't take me for a flat.'
'A flat, your honour, no,' said I, 'but hear me if you will,

55

Sam Henry's Songs of the People

And I at once will let you know where there's a
  private still.'

'In half a minute, now,' says I, 'the barrack's
  close at hand,
And if you look right through the gate, you'll
  see and hear the band.
And when the band's done playing, you will see
  the soldiers drill.'
'Oh, never mind the soldiers, Pat, but where's
  the private still?'

'In just a second now,' said I, 'I'll point him out
  to you.
See? There he is, that fat old chap standing
  between them two.'
'What's that you say?' says he. Says I, 'My
  brother Bill;
They won't make him a corporal, so he's a
  private still!'

The gauger swore and tore his hair to get his
  money back.
But I jumped onto the car myself and bolted in a
  crack,
And as he walked along the road, though sore
  against his will,
The people shout, 'Exciseman, have you got the
  private still?'

2.2: ... all, though me perhaps ... [Dt]
3.2: ... my faith, you ... [Dt]
4.: [Stanza in Dt only.]
5.4: Keep on your hair and very soon you'll find a
  ... [Dt]
6.2: If you ... [Dt]
 .3: ... you'll see ... [Dt]
8.2: ... on the car ... [Dt]
 .4: ... got a private ... [Dt]

Mick Magee [H740: 29 Jan 1938]

1: (m) resembles part of "The Rose Tree." Other
title: "... McGee."

Source: James M'Laughlin (Newhill, Ballymoney)
from Pat M'Closkey (Agivey) c. 1893.

s: This humorous Irish ballad has been supplied
by Mr James M'Laughlin, ... whose repertoire
includes many pantomime hits and comic songs of
half a century ago....

Key G.

Oh, nigh to Ardee lived Mick Magee,
Who once was a bold sailor-o,
But getting old, as I am told,
He turned out a walking dealer-o.

Tobacco, tay and poteen gay
He trudged through all the country-o,
To licence he would never agree,
Nor to the gauger's bounty-o.

One morning fair as Sol appeared,
It being in summer weather-o,
Poor Mick being quite void of fear,
He packed his wares together-o.

His wallet slung and off he sprung
To range the Irish nation-o,
When by mistake his course did take
Unto a police station-o.

The policemen being not within,
The taypot it was smoking-o,
The servant she was kind and free,
With Mick she fell a-joking-o.

Says she, 'My lad, pray what's your trade?
You look so gay and frisky-o.'
'Fair maid,' said he, 'I sell good tay,
Tobacco, rum and whiskey-o.'

'Sit down, my boy,' she did reply,
'I love the things you mention-o,
Perhaps that we may both agree,
To buy is my intention-o.'

Poor Mick, all slack, unloosed his pack
All for the dame's inspection-o,
When a fussee he chanced to see,
Which made him dread detection-o.

Behind his back there being a rack
Well thronged with police arms-o,
'Bedad,' says Mick, 'I cut my stick,
This fills me with alarms-o!'

'My lovely maid,' it's then he said,
'I can no longer wheedle-o,
But for a rag to help my bag,
I give a pin or needle-o.'

'You hoary vag, to ask a rag,'
Says she, 'you're only scheming-o.'
'Fair maid,' said he, 'you scold too free,
And me you are detaining-o.'

Then out he went, his course he bent
Straight forward in a splutter-o,
With a big stick would bang oul' Nick,
He ran like melted butter-o.

His heels did spin like the north wind
For three long miles and over-o;
He thought the crew did not pursue,
Says he, 'I am in clover-o.'

But looking back, his soul was racked,
Two police were pursuing-o,
'Those roving blades,' it's then he said,
'Will surely prove my ruin-o.'

A beggarman he called to stand,
Mick told him his condition-o,
'Your bag, pray then, come lend, my friend,
And don't work opposition-o.'

Nor loath was he for to agree,
The boon was freely granted-o,
And slipped away without delay,
Which was the thing was wanted-o.

To a bog hard by, bold Mick drew nigh
Unto a place that's hollow-o,
Where lay a hole where I am told
An elephant might wallow-o.

And very sly he did draw nigh
To the place that I did mention-o,
And sure as sin, the bog fell in,
It seemed without intention-o.

'Ha, ha, my boy,' the police said,
'It's now we'll surely catch you-o,
It's to Dundalk that you will walk
And we're the boys will fetch you-o.'

Up spoke Mick then, 'Pray gentlemen,
Have I at all offended-o?
If I've done ill, you are at will
My life, sure, for to end it-o."

And very sly they did draw nigh
Without the smallest leisure-o;
Their curses might you well affright
When they came at the treasure-o.

Some stirabout wrapped in a clout,
Some scraps of bread and bacon-o,
And meal and bones, about two stones,
A herring newly taken-o.

Of potatoes, too, there were a few,
And a torn ould pair of britches-o,
This is the whole, as I am told,
Of all the poor man's riches-o.

With heavy moans and cruel moans
And foaming with vexation-o,
Like tigers balked, it's off they stalked
Downhearted to the station-o.

The clever man who backed the plan,
Mick joined him in a hurry-o,
To hide his name would be a shame --
They called him Patrick Curry-o.

1.2 [and similarly at ends of even-numbered
 lines throughout:] ... sailor, O!
8.3: fussee [fusil] = light musket or firelock.

My Grandfather Died   [H732: 4 Dec 1937]

k: "The Foolish Boy," "Swapping Song." Other
titles: "The Bugle Played for Me," "My Father
(He) Died (a Month Ago)," "My Grandmother
Green," "Posey (Swappin') Boy," "Wing, Wang,
Waddle-O (Wobble-O)," "Wim-wam-waddles"; cf.
"The Lucan Dairy," "Me Grandfather Died."

Source: "esteemed contributor" (Ballycastle).

s: A song with the same theme has been collected
by the Rev. S. Baring-Gould and Cecil J. Sharp,
but this Ulster version is quite different both
in tune and words. It emanates originally from
Co. Armagh....

Key D.

A5 / By the heat of my brow

My grandfather died and I don't know how,
He left me six horses for to yoke in the plough.

*With a quing quang quaddle-um, jing jack
 traddle-um,
Mousie's in the barn and among the brew.*

Oh, I sold my horses and I bought a cow,
I never made a bargain but I knew well how.

Oh, I sold my cow and I bought a calf,
I never made a bargain but I lost the half.

Oh, I sold my calf and I bought a pig,
I set him in the doorway for to dance a jig.

Oh, I sold my pig and I bought a dog,
I put him on the hearthstone for to talk to a frog.

Oh, I sold my dog and I bought a cat,
But he went through the half-door after a rat.

My grandfather left me all he did own,
And I don't know how it is, but I'm here by my
 lone.

The Buttermilk Boy
[H57a: "Love and land -- two songs of aspiration,"
                                BLp, 13 Dec 1924]

Other titles: "A-Begging Buttermilk I Will Go,"
"A Song, To Curb Rising Thoughts."

s: Both of these songs were favourites in the
Carnglass (Ballybogey) district of Co. Antrim. I
am indebted for airs and words to W[illiam] Lyons,
esq., Dhu Varren, Portrush, retired Collector of
Customs and Excise, who often heard them sung
in the traditional style at the social fireside in
Ballyrashane parish.

Source: (w, m) William Lyons, customs collector
(Newcastle-on-Tyne, England; later Dhu Varren,
Portrush).

[BLp] s: The art of traditional folk song involves
the expert adaptation of the words to the air, or
vice versa. For example, in "The Buttermilk
Boy," in verses 3 and 5, for example, the word
"its" is sung to the note r[e], whereas the other
verses start on s[ol] with the first beat of the
bar. In the second line of the 1st verse, "pray"
is sung as a slur to the notes d[o]' d[o]' t[i]
l[a]. The word "down" in verse 7 is also phras-
ed in the same manner. In verse 2, line 2, "that"
is sung to the first beat of the bar (d[o]'), the
last note of line 1 being correspondingly extended by a beat. Other inequalities in the metre
are similarly adjusted.

m: This song was set for soloist and piano accompaniment by E. N. Hay and published by Curwen.

Sam Henry's Songs of the People

[Wt, Dt in 3.]

Key C.

There was an old woman and her son,
They lived together, as you may see;
Small was their names and small was their gains
Oh aye, and a landlord he would be.

'I'll go to some old woman, mother,
That has buttermilk in store,
And from her I'll get a sufficient reward,
It's I'll get half a gallon or more.

'It's I will sell the buttermilk, mother,
And for it I will get a penny,
And with my penny I will buy eggs,
And I'll get seven for a penny.

'I'll set them all in under a hen,
That seven cock chickens that they may be,
And the seven cock chickens will turn to be
  capons,
And that will be seven half crowns to me.

'It's I will go to the market, mother,
And none but gentlemen will see,
And with my money I will buy land,
Oh aye, and a landlord I will be.'

'Son, dear son, how will you know me
When you have gathered all your wealth?'
'Mother, dear mother, how will I know you?
For I will hardly know myself.'

There was one day he was going down the street,
He missed his foot against the wall,
Down come the buttermilk boy,
Oh aye, and his piggin and all did fall.

Come all ye young gentlemen far and near,
I pray be on your watch,
And don't be like the buttermilk boy
Who counted his chickens before they were
  hatched.

[Differences in Dt = Wt(c):]
1.3: ... their means and small their names,
1.4: Oh I ... [but cf. stanzas 5, 7]
2.1: ''Tis I will go ... woman
  .3: ... her get ...
  .4: And I will get ... gallon and more.
3.1: 'And I ...
  .4: And I will get ...
4.1: And I will set them in ...
  .2: ... chickens they ...
5.1: 'And I ...
6.1: 'Oh son, ...
  .3: Oh mother, ...
7.3: And down came the ...
8.2: I pray you be ...
  .3: And do not be ...

O'Ryan [H823: 2 Sep 1939]

A song of the stars.

s: (m) "The Girl I Left Behind Me." Other title:
"The Poacher."

No source given.

Key D.

O'Ryan was a man of might when Ireland was a
  nation,
And poachin' was his heart's delight and constant
  occupation,
He had an ould militia gun, and sartin sure his aim
  was,
He gave the keepers many a run and wouldn't mind
  the game laws.

St. Patrick once was passin' by O'Ryan's little
  houldin',
And as the saint felt wake and dry, he though
  he'd enter bould in,
'O'Ryan,' says the saint, 'avick, to praich at
  Thurles I'm goin',
So let me have a rasher quick and a drop of
  Innishowen.'

'No rasher will I cook for you while better is to
  spare, sir,
But here's a jug of mountain dew and there's a
  rattlin' hare, sir.'
St. Patrick, he looked mighty sweet and says,
  'Good luck attind you,
And it's whin you're in your windin' sheet, it's up
  to heaven I'll send you.'

O'Ryan gave his pipe a whiff -- 'Them tidin's is transportin',
But may I ax your saintship if there's any kind o' sportin'?'
St. Patrick said, 'A lion's there, two bears, a bull and cancer --'
'Bedad,' says Mick, 'the huntin's rare; St. Patrick, I'm your man, sir.'

So to conclude my song aright, for fear I'd tire your patience,
You'll see O'Ryan any night amid the constellations,
And Venus follows in his track, till Mars grows jealous rally,
But, faith, he fears the Irish knack of handling the shillelagh.

2.2: wake = ?weak.
3.2: mountain dew
4.3: cancer = the constellation of the Crab. [s]
5.2: O'Ryan = the constellation of Orion or the Hunter. His belt and his spear are easily distinguishable. [s]

The Jolly Fisherman [H639: 22 Feb 1936]

s: A popular song in 1800 A.D.

Key G.

I am a jolly fisherman, I catch what I can get,
Still going on my betters' plan, all's fish that comes to net.
Fish just like men I've often caught -- crabs, gudgeon, poor John Codfish,
And many a time to market brought a dev'lish sight of odd fish,
    A dev'lish sight of odd fish.
Thus all are fishermen through life with wary pains and labour:
This baits with gold and that, a wife, and all to catch his neighbour.

Then praise the jolly fisherman who takes what he can get,
Still going on his betters' plan, all's fish that comes to net.
    All's fish that comes to net,
    All's fish that comes to net,
Still going on his betters' plan, all's fish that comes to net.

The pike, to catch the little fly, extends his greedy jaw,
For all the world as you and I have seen the man at law.
He who laziness devotes his time is sure a numb fish,
And numbers who give silent votes may surely be call'd dumb fish,
    May surely be call'd dumb fish.
False friends to eels we may compare, the roach resembles true ones,
Like gold fish we find old ones rare; plenty as herrings, new ones.

Like fish, then, mortals are a trade, and trapp'd and sold and bought,
The old wife and the tender maid, with tickling both are caught.
Indeed, the fair are caught, 'tis said, if you but throw the line in,
With insects, flies, or something red, or anything that's shining,
    Or anything that's shining.
With small fish you must lie in wait for those of high condition,
But 'tis alone a golden bait can catch a high physician.

Songs of Old Ireland [H768: 13 Aug 1938]

Source: sung, accompanied on American organ, by Jane Doherty (Moneygran, Loughash, Co. Tyrone), who heard her grandmother, Catherine Donaghy (Lisglass, near Derry), sing it 50 years ago.

Key G.

Of fondest affection and sweet recollection
Of the days that are gone and the years long ago,
When we roamed in wild youth by the clear sunny fountain
By the banks of the Mourne where the Foyle waters flow.

Sam Henry's Songs of the People

Oh, sing me the songs that I do love the dearest,
The songs of old Ireland I heard long ago;
Oh, sing them again, I could listen forever
By the banks of the Mourne where the Foyle waters flow.

Oh, sing me a song of the bards of old Ireland,
I love the dear bards that to Erin belong,
For, sure, there is something more sweet and divine in
The music that thrills through an old Irish song.

Oh, sing me 'The Shamrock,' that oft in my childhood
My fond mother sang in sweet measures to me;
Oh, sing me 'The Coolin' or 'Kathleen Avourneen'
Or 'The Lark Singing High in the Blue Summer Sky.'

At the close of the day we roamed down to Derry,
Where Columbkille prayed at the stately oak trees,
And the vespers were ringing, how soft was their chiming,
The glorious music of Sancte Marie.

In the lovely green valleys the lambkins are sporting,
The thrushes are singing from groves and from trees,
And we sang together the songs of old Ireland
Where the Mourne joins the Foyle on its way to the sea.

Oh, happy remembrance; on the past I do ponder,
For youth it has gone, and forever, from me.
How happy was I and my schoolmates together
Where the Mourne joins the Foyle on its way to the sea.

The Salutation   [H756: 21 May 1938]

g: (m) "Tramp, Tramp, Tramp, the Boys Are Marching."

Author late James O'Kane, via his son Frank O'Kane (Gortinure, Maghera).

s: [The late James O'Kane's] songs have given delight to all Derry folk and are well known across the sea.

Key G. Marching time.

Aroun' Pat Murphy's hearth there was music, song and mirth,
And shanachies of fame assembled there;
Came a traveller to the door and the voice of Sheilah Mor --
Well they knew her by the fervour of her prayer.

'God save all here,' her salutation,
'God save you kindly,' they replied,
'For it's seldom that you call, so come in, take off your shawl,
For you're welcome to Pat Murphy's fireside.'

'Have you heard no news, agrah? Sure, you come from Maghera,
Or have you heard no tidings on the way?'
'Yes, the fairies all in green aroun' Beagh's raths were seen,
As I heard their fairy music on the brae.'

'God save all here,' their salutation,
'God save you kindly,' we replied, ...

'The fairy queen intends for to occupy the Glens
An' all the heathery mountains roun' Tiree;
Should these fairies here remain, then green Erin once again
Will inherit all her old prosperity.'

'God save all here,' her salutation,
'God save you kindly,' they replied, ...

So the Irishman may roam far from fields and native home,
He may sever all these ties without a fear,
From his mother's fond cares and his father's deep distress,
But ne'er again this greeting will he hear:

'God save all here,' their salutation,
'God save you kindly,' we replied, ...

60

Fine Broom Besoms! [H17a: BLp, 8 Mar 1924]

k: "Buy Broom ..."; g: "The Besom Maker," "Broom Besoms." Other titles: "(Buy) Broom Buzzems," "Green Besoms," "Green Broom ...."

Source not given.

o: Should be in 2/4 time.

g: All the versions cited below differ from one another and from Henry's version, except for the chorus.

l: Note the contrast in rhythmic-melodic feeling produced by a change in time; since the other copies are typed, but Dt shows signs of hasty preparation, it would be difficult to argue that Dt (in 2-time) is correct just because it may have been the last prepared.

[Print from British Library microfilm file of the *Northern Constitution* courtesy of John Moulden. In BLp stanza 1 is printed line for line under the sol-fa in 2 lines across double column width; the other stanzas are as given here.]

[BLp] Key E flat. [Bt, Dt] Key F.

Fine broom besoms, besoms fine and new,
Castleblayney heather, better never grew,
Besoms for a penny, scrubbers for a plack,
If you do not like them, tie them on back.

Fine broom besoms, besoms fine and new,
Castleblayney heather, better never grew.

Far I've wandered, wandered far and wide,
Gatherin' the heather on the mountain side.
When my mother's spinnin', Barney at the loom,
I am weavin' besoms of the yellow broom.

(Slow and sad:)
I've been dreamin', dreamin' I was young,
When I was wi' Barney, how we danced and sung,
Now the summer's over, hidin' from the blast
In the faded heather, I am tired at last.

So fine broom besoms, sweep away the snow,
Lay me in wi' Barney, I am glad to go.

1.2, r.2: Castleblaney ... [Bt]
1.4: ... on my back. [Bt, Dt]
r.1: And fine ... [Bt, Dt]
2.1: ... wander'd, wander'd ... [Bt, Dt]
3.2: ... was wid Barney ... [Dt]

1.3: plack = one third of 1 d. [s]; small copper coin current in 15th and 16th century Scotland, worth 4 pennies; a bit, a small value.

Better Bide a Wee [H598: 18 May 1935]

Other title: "We'd ...."

Source: "A Reader," anonymous, learned from her mother.

Key C.

Sam Henry's Songs of the People

The poor aul' folks at hame, ye min', are frail
    and ailin' sair,
An' weel I ken they'd miss me, lad, if I came
    hame nae mair.
The grist is oot, the times are hard, the kine
    are only three,
I canna' lea' the aul' folk, lad, we'd better bide
    a wee.

When first we told our story, lad, their blessing
    fell sae free,
They gave no thought to self at all, they only
    thought of me,
But, laddie, that's a time awa', an' mither's like
    tae dee,
I canna' lea' the aul' folk noo, we'd better bide
    a wee.

I fear me sair they're failin' baith, for when I
    sit apart,
They talk o' heaven sae earnestly it well nigh
    breaks my heart,
So, laddie, dinna sae nae mair, it surely winna'
    be,
I canna' lea' the aul' folks noo, we'd better bide
    a wee.

3.3: sae = say.

Gaol Song [H746: 12 Mar 1938]

Other titles: "Farewell to (Here's Adieu to All) Judges and Juries," "(Please) Meet Me Tonight (by the Moonlight)," "(The) (Old) Prisoner's Song," "Swansea Gaol," "Sweet Swansea (Jail)."

Source not given.

s: Composed by Kid Thomas, while serving a five-year sentence in the Eastern Penitentiary, Philadelphia. He was granted a reprieve on account of the song, or, as my informant put it, "he sung himself out o' gaol."

g: There are two other songs closely related to this one. The first is variously called "Farewell to Judges and Juries," "Here's Adieu to All Judges and Juries," "Sweet Swansea (Jail)"; the other is usually known as "Meet Me by Moonlight."

l: Evidently Sam Henry's informant gave him another of the many apocryphal tales about the authorship of this song; see esp. notes in Randolph/Cohen (1982) and Cazden et al. 1982 below.

Key D.

Oh, I wish I had someone to love me,
    Someone to call me their own,
Oh, I wish I had someone to live with,
    For I'm tired of living alone.

Please meet me tonight by the moonlight,
Please meet me tonight all alone,
I have got a sad story to tell you,
A tale I can never disown.

I go to my new cell tomorrow,
Leaving my darling alone,
With the cold prison bars all around me
And my head on a pillow of stone.

I have got a fine ship on the ocean,
All laden with silver and gold,
And before my poor darling will suffer,
This ship will be anchored and sold.

If I had the wings of an angel,
O'er these prison walls I would fly,
I would fly to the arms of my darling,
It's there I'd be willing to die.

The Bramble [H628: 14 Dec 1935]

Author Ebenezer Elliott (1781-1849), "The Corn-Law Rhymer" (Yorkshire), Sheffield iron merchant; source: [?Sam Henry].

s: Taught by the late Mr John Dallas to the "Fifth Class" in the Honourable the Irish Society's Boys' School, Coleraine, in the year 1880. This song has been a thing of beauty and a joy for ever and the memory has carried it unaided by book or script....

Key G.

Thy fruit full well the schoolboy knows,
Wild bramble of the brake,
So put forth thy small white rose,
I love thee for his sake.
Though woodbines flaunt and roses grow
O'er all the fragrant bowers,
Thou needst not be ashamed to show
Thy satin-threaded flowers.

For dull the eye, the heart is dull
That cannot feel how fair,
Amid all beauty beautiful,
Thy tender blossoms are.
The primrose to the grave is gone,
The hawthorn flower is dead,
The violet by the mossy stone
Has laid her weary head.

But thou, wild bramble, back dost bring
In all thy beauteous power
The fresh green days of life's fair spring
And boyhood's blossomy hour.
Scorn'd bramble of the brake! Once more
Thou bidst me be a boy
To gad with thee the woodlands o'er
In freedom and in joy.

The Leaves So Green [H719: 4 Sep 1937]

Source: (w, m) Dan MacAleese (Gortmacrane, Kilrea).

s: [The contributor's] script is a model of musical notation.

Key G.

When life has left the senseless clay,
By all but thee forgot,
O bear me, dearest, far away
To some green lonely spot,
Where none with careless steps shall tread
The grass upon my grave,
But gently o'er my narrow bed
The leave[s] so green may wave.

The flowers, too, I loved so well
Shall breathe their sweetness there;
With thrush and blackbird's music sweet
Amidst the fragrant air.
No noisy burst of joy or woe
Shall there disturb my rest,
But silent tears in secret flow
From those that love me best.

The crowded towns and haunts of men
I never loved to tread,
To sheltered vale or lonely glen
My weary spirit fled,
So bear me, dearest, far away,
By other eyes unseen,
Where gleams of sunshine rarely stray
Beneath the leaves so green.

Dun Ceithern [H523: 9 Dec 1933]

Source: (m) late Canon Armstrong (Castlerock), found in a waste paper basket in Trinity College, Dublin; author ? Sam Henry.

s: The song was inspired by the appreciation from Mr Andrew Doey, which appears in the Correspondence column in this issue.
 Dun Ceithern, commonly called "The Giant's Sconce," is the noble dun on the old Limavady road, five miles from Coleraine. It was the border fortress of the ancient kingdom of Uladh and guarded by the Red Branch Knights.
 ... Canon Armstrong ... was an ardent lover of folk music ... whose setting of the "Londonderry Air" retrieved that incomparable melody from oblivion.

Key G.

Standing by the margin of the northern sea,
Dreaming of the great days gone, the days that
  yet shall be,
Seeking from the past to build in dreams anew,
Land of ancient glory -- great and true;
Yonder from the hilltop
The noble red branch heroes won for Uladh's
  kingdom peace;
Hung their war shields up in Ceithern's royal dun --
Walked the terraced faha fearing none.

Bring us back the days of innocence and mirth
When a lovely maiden had nought to fear on earth,
Rode her prancing palfrey, pure and unafraid,
Dauntless in her robe that God had made;
Bring us back the coloured days,
When happy rainbowed life sped on in Erin's fields
  of peace;
Give in darkness faith that seeks the setting sun,
Strong as when the day had just begun.

Let us leave behind all quarrels of the past,
Build a land of comradeship whose walls will ever
  last,
Green our land and gracious, fair her hills and
  streams;
Let us build our Arcady of dreams,
Let us be led ever on,
Gael and Gall with love as when her saints made
  glad each hill and glen,
Conquered by the power that wields all hearts
  with love --
Foretaste of our cherished heaven above.

1.8: faha = the exercise green outside the royal dun.
  [s]
dun = ancient hill fortress or fortified eminence.

Sam Henry's Songs of the People

Barossa / Oliver's Advice

[H98a: "Two regimental songs," 26 Sep 1925]

Other titles: cf. "The Battle of Barossa (Trafalgar)," "Barossa's Plains," "Fare Ye Well, My Darlin'."

Source: (m) Jim Baxter, leader (Coleraine Fife and Drum Band); set by SH to text by William Blacker, lieut.-colonel (Carrickblacker, Co. Armagh), 1777-1855.

[Bp] s: Adapted for regimental use after the battle of Barossa, 5th March, 1811, in which the Regiment took a noble part.
... Musical conoisseurs have often been attracted by this air when played by ... [the Coleraine Fife and Drum Band] in the streets of Coleraine.
No. 839 Joyce's Old Irish Airs has a resemblance to this march.
In order that so good an air may not be lost for want of words I have set it to "Oliver's Advice." ... The song was founded on Cromwell's advice -- "Put your trust in God, but mind to keep your powder dry."
[Dt] The words were written by Lieutenant-Colonel William Blacker,... whose relatives have a mural tablet to their memory in St. Patrick's Church, Coleraine....
[Bp, Dt] The unequal battle of Barossa lasted only an hour and a half, in which time there were 50 officers, 60 sergeants, 1,100 British soldiers and more than 2,000 French killed and wounded. Six guns, an eagle, two generals (both mortally wounded) and 400 prisoners remained in the hands of the regiment. This eagle, the first captured in the Peninsula, was taken by Sergeant Masterton of the 87th Royal Irish Fusiliers and is figured in the colours of the regiment.

Key D.

The night is gathering gloomily, the day is closing fast,
The tempest flaps his raven wings in loud and angry blast,
The thunder clouds are driving athwart the lurid sky,
But put your trust in God, my boys, and keep your powder dry.

The power that led his chosen by pillared cloud and flame,
Through parted sea and desert waste -- that power is still the same;
He fails not, he, the loyal hearts that firm on him rely,
So put your trust in God, my boys, and keep your powder dry.

Then cheer, ye hearts of loyalty, nor sink in dark despair,
Our banner shall again unfold its glories to the air,
The storm that raves the wildest, the soonest passes by,
Then put your trust in God, my boys, and keep your powder dry.

For happy homes, for altars free, we grasp the ready sword,
For freedom, truth and God and his unmutilated word,
These, these the war cry of our march; our hope, the Lord on high,
Then put your trust in God, my boys, and keep your powder dry.

3.3: ... the loudest, the ... [Dt]

The Yellow Bittern / An Bunnan Buidhe

[H830: 21 Oct 1939]

Other titles: "(An) Buinnean (Bunnean) Buí (Buidhe)."

Author Cathal Buidhe MacGiolla Gunna; noted by "the well-known Gaelic scholar, Henry Morris, of the Ministry of Education, Eire" from Nancy Tracey (Greencastle, Co. Tyrone); translated by Andy Doey (Ballymacaldrick, Dunloy), versified in English by George Graham (Cross Lane, Coleraine).

s: This remarkable song was composed around the year 1700 by Cathal Buidhe MacGiolla Gunna, i.e., sallow-complexioned Charles M'Elgunn, of the barony of Tullyhaw, Co. Cavan. The M'Elgunns were common west of Enniskillen and Lough Erne. The author imbued with the old animistic ideas of the Gaelic race, calls himself, in verse 2, "brother Charles," implying that a common thirst made brothers of himself and the bird.
The bittern was a common bird in Goldsmith's time:--

The hollow sounding bittern guards its nest

but died out as a nesting species about 1850. A specimen, shot near Draperstown, was sent to me for identification a few years ago.
The poet finds the bittern lying dead by the shores of Lough Neasy, which is frozen, and moralizes that lack of drink killed the bird.
I heard this song in Gaelic at the hospitable hearth of Mr Andy Doey ... and was so taken with the air and the theme that I asked him to translate the song for me. Based on that translation, Mr George Graham ... has rendered the song in English verse and has kept very closely to the structure and internal rhymes of Gaelic poetry. The feature of such poetry is a similarity of vowel sounds rather than consonantal, as, for example, in the last verse where "time" rhymes with "wine."
Bunnan Buidhe is pronounced Bunawn Bwee.

A5 / By the heat of my brow

Key G.

O Bunnan Buidhe, 'tis my woe to see,
After all your spree, your bones stretched so;
Not want of food, but liquor good
By the frozen flood has laid you low,
Worse to relate than Troy's bitter fate
Is your sad state on the road so drear.
Your humble mind ne'er to ill inclined,
Nor preferred red wine to water clear.

O dear Bunnan, 'tis my heart is gone
To your corpse upon the roadway's bank;
Your 'grag' so gay I heard many a day
In the miry way where oft you drank.
This is what they of brother Charles say:
'Death will come this way.' 'Tis true, they think;
It is not so, for death's dark bow
Has laid you low for want of drink.

O my young Bunnan, my sad heart is gone
Out to you among the bushes laid;
The big rats quake to attend your wake,
Where fine sport they'll make and you upbraid.
Had you sent word, or could I have heard
Of your fate, poor bird, held in such pain,
Lough Neasy's frost I'd have cracked across,
From the frozen lough your drink to gain.

Not for all birds are these timely words;
I mourn not the blackbird, stork or thrush,
But my Bunnan Buidhe, so full of glee,
Is at heart like me or the swampy rush.
He was so gay that he drank all day,
And the people say that I am worse,
But good or ill I will drink my fill
Lest death should chill me through with thirst.

My wife wants me to leave off the spree --
'Or it's dead you'll be in a short time,'
But I replied that my wife has lied,
For this life will bide long years with wine.
Just think the cost, how the bird was lost
That died of thirst on an icy bed,
So, neighbours dear, go drink your beer,
There'll be none, I fear, when you are dead.

The Parting Glass [H769: 20 Aug 1938]

Other title: "Good Night and Joy Be with You All."

Source not given.

Key G.

A man may drink and not be drunk,
A man may fight and not be slain,
A man may court a pretty girl
And perhaps be welcomed back again,
And since it is so ordered,
By a time to rise and a time to fall,
Come fill to me the parting glass,
Goodnight and joy be with you all.

If I had money for to spend,
If I had time to waste away,
There is a fair maid in this town,
I fain would wile her heart away;
With her rosy cheeks and her dimpled chin,
My heart she has beguiled away,
So fill to me the parting glass,
Goodnight and joy be with you a'.

If I had money for to spend,
I'd spend it in her company,
And for all the harm that I have done,
I hope it's pardoned I will be;
What I've done for want of it,
To memory I can't recall,
So fill to me the parting glass,
Goodnight and joy be with you all.

My dearest dear, the time draws near
When here no longer can I stay;
There's not a comrade I leave behind
But is grieving that I'm going away,
But since it has so ordered been,
What is once past can't be recalled.
Now fill to me the parting glass,
Goodnight and joy be with you all.

◆ A5 REFERENCES ◆

◆ **Waulking Song** (H535a) 39

Not Brunnings 1981: "Waulking Song" (several listed)

◆ **The Tailor Boy** (H199) 39

BRS Logan 1869:407-9 "The Weaver and the Tailor"

◆ **The Cobbler** (H551) 40

Brunnings 1981: "... - I Am a Merry Cobbler," "Shoemaker's Song - I Am a Shoemaker by My Trade," ?"The Shoemaker - As I Was a-Walking the Other Day," ?"The Shoemaker - The Shoemaker Toils"

IREL Moulden 1979:32-3

Sam Henry's Songs of the People

AMER   Cf. Sharp/Campbell 1917:285 [Randolph]
Cf. Sharp/Karpeles 1932,2:75 (#100) "The Shoe-maker"

◇ Jim, the Carman Lad (H171) 40

Cazden et al. *Notes* 1982: #96 "The Stagecoach Driver's Lad"
Brunnings 1981: "Joe the Carter Lad," "The Country Carrier"

BRIT   Palmer 1979b:44-5 (#19) "Joe the Carrier's Lad" (see also Hinchcliffe rec.)

AMER   Cazden et al. 1982:357-60 "The Stage-Coach Driver's Lad"

BRS   BPL Partridge: 3.1226
UCLA 605: 4(Such) "Little ... Carter ..."

REC   Jack Goodfellow, *FSB* 3 (B9) "... Carter ..."
b: George Belton, EFDSS LP 1008 (B4) "... Carter ..."
Paul Clayton, Folkways FW 8708 (B1) "... Carter's ..."
Frank Hinchcliffe, Leader LEE 4058 (B3) "Joe the Carrier's Lad"
Bill 'Pop' Hingston, People's Stage Tapes cass. 03 (A3? or 7) "The Country Carrier"
Cf. Edward "Sandy" Ives, Folkways FH 5323 (B1) "The Shanty Boys," stanza 3.
Bob Mills, Peoples Stage Tapes cass. 05 (A4) "Jim ... Carter ..."
Cf. refrain sung by Bob Penfold, Topic 12TS 349 (B8) "Rattling Irish Boy"

◇ My Rattlin' Oul' Grey Mare (H664) 41

Brunnings 1981: "The Country Carrier"

◇ My Irish Jaunting Car (H592) 41

Brunnings 1981: "The ...," "The Knight of the Road"

IREL   Shields/Shields *UF* 21,1975: #208 "(The) Irish ..."

AMER   Dean [1922]:115-6 "The Irish ..."

BRS   UCLA 605: 3(Luckaway) "I'm an Irish Boy";
5(n.i.) "Larry Doolan"
b: Healy 1966:154-5 "The Irish ...," among other titles.
b: *The Shamrock* 1862 "The Irish ..."
Songs and Recitations 3,1976:26, a different song with the same title, would fit Henry's tune.

◇ The Farmer (H676) 41

? Brunnings 1981

IREL   Moulden 1979:52-3

◇ The Rocks of Bawn (H139) 42

Brunnings 1981

IREL   Behan 1965: #75
McDonnell 1979:53 (see also Heaney rec.)
b: O Lochlainn 1939:46-7 "A New Song on the Rocks of Baun"
Shields/Shields *UF* 21,1975: #339

BRS   *Songs & Recitations* 5,1978:24

REC   Seamus Ennis, *CWL* 1, Columbia AKL 4941 (A3, 11)

b: David Hammond, Request RLP 8061 "The Rocks of Bawn"
Joe Heaney, Topic 12T 91 (A1); Folkways FG 3575 (A3); Philo 2004 (B2)
b: Judy Mayhan, Horizon WP 1605 "Come All Ye Loyal Heroes"
b: *Pleasant and Delightful*, Vol. 2, Living Folk Records F-LFR 2 "The Rocks of Bawn"

MEL   Willie Clancy, Folkways FW 8781 (A3) "... Bourne," slow air.

◇ The Charity Seed / We Never Died in the Winter Yet (H766) 43

m: BRS NLI, P. J. McCall collection, "Extra volume" and Vol. 9-10

◇ The Lint Pullin' (H487) 43

Brunnings 1981: "... Pulling"

◇ The Jolly Thresher (H622) 44
As a King Went A-Hunting (H117) 44

White/Dean-Smith 1951: "(The) Jolly Thresherman or the Thresherman and the Squire or The Nobleman and the Thresherman"
Dean-Smith 1954 "(The) Nobleman and the Thresherman; The Nobleman's Generous Kindness/Gift; The Thresherman and the Squire; The Jolly Thresher"
Brunnings 1981: "The Thresher and the Squire"
Cazden et al. *Notes* 1982: #92 "... Thrasher"

c: BRIT Kennedy 1975:562 (#253); lists 2 other recorded English versions (see also Copper rec.).
Palmer 1979b:50-1 (#23) "The Jolly Thresherman"
TM #6,1977:21 (fragment of tune in a review)

AMER   Cf. Bush 2,1970:32 "Jolly Reapers"
Cazden et al. 1982:346-8
Warner 1984:336-8 (#146)

BRS   Harvard 1: 2.25 (Carrots), 3.184 (Forth) 6.79 (Durham), 10.66 (Bebbington)
UCLA 605: 4(Walker) "Squire and Thrasher"; 5 (Such) "The ..."

REC   Paul Clayton, Folkways FW 8708 (A5) "The Bold Thrasher"
Bob, Ron Copper, [b:] Folk-Legacy FSB 19 (B3) "The Honest Labourer"; [k:] EFDSS LP 1002
Frank Hinchcliffe, Topic 12TS 308 (A5) "The Nobleman and Thrasherman"
Sarah Makem, Topic 12T 182 (A6)

◇ Shanty Boy (H662) 45

Laws 1964:277 calls this a "ballad-like piece," not quite a ballad.
Brunnings 1981: "The Farmer and the Shanty Boy," "The ... and the Farmer's Son"

IREL   Moulden 1979:133

m: AMER Fowke 1970:183-6 "The Farmer's Son and the ..."
Peters 1977:88-9 "... and the Farmer"
Warner 1984:108-10 (#33) "..., Farmer Boy"
Not: b: Sandburg 1927:390 "The Shanty-Man's Life"

REC   Ellen Stekert, Folkways FA 2354 (B7) "... and the Farmer's Son"
b: *The Newport Folk Festival 1964*, Vol. 1, Vanguard VRS 9184 "The ... and the Farmer's Son"
cl: Lester Wells, AFS 2309A "The Farmer's Son and the ..."

◇ The Shepherd Laddie *(H617)* 45

Brunnings 1981: "Crook an' Plaid (True to His Love)"

BRIT Christie 2,1881:264-5 "The Crook and Plaid"
  Ford 1,1899:56-7 "The Crook and Plaid"
  Greig 1907-11(1963): #106 "The Crook and Plaid"
  Whitelaw 1844(1874):306 "The Crook and Plaid," the original version of the song by Rev. Henry S. Riddell, a former shepherd; quite different from Henry's fragment.

b: REC Marilynn Lovell, Jubilee JLP 1068 "Crook an' Plaid (True to His Love)"

◇ The Thatchers of Glenrea *(H186)* 46

BRIT *Tocher* #31(Sum)1979:4, set down by Willie Mitchell (Kintyre) in his notebook.

REC Dick Gaughan, Trailer LER 2072 (B1), Kintyre version.

◇ The Dandy Chignon *(H227)* 48

BRS BPL Irish: (n.i.) "Oyster Shell Bonnet and ..."
  Harvard 1: 14.48 (Disley) "The Ladies' Bonnets and Chignons"
  Harvard 3: (n.i.)
  UCLA 605: 4(Brereton) "Oyster Shell Bonnet and ... Chignauns"

◇ Long Cookstown / Nancy Whiskey *(H745)* 48

Brunnings 1981: "The Calton Weaver"

IREL Moulden 1979:91: "The late Joe Holmes of Ballymoney had this song and he and Len Graham sang it often together."
m: Shields/Shields *UF* 21,1975: #296 "Nancy's ..."

m: BRIT Kennedy 1975:611 (#279) "Nancy Whisky," a longer version, with London as the scene rather than Cookstown or Dublin.
  Tocher #31(Sum)1979:13 "Nancy's Whiskey"

BRS *Songs and Recitations* 5,1978:17 "The Callton Weaver (Whiskey Nancy)"

b: REC Theodore Bikel, Elektra EKS 7250 "The Calton Weaver"
b: *A Jug of Punch*, EMI Records CLP 1327 "Nancy Whisky"
  Ewan MacColl, Riverside S-2 (A4) "The Calton Weaver" (from RLP 12 605)

◇ The Jug of Punch *(H490)* 48

Brunnings 1981: "A ..."

b: IREL Clancy Bros. 1964:53
b: Graves 1897
  Loesberg 1,1980:13
  Shields/Shields *UF* 21,1975: #229

AMER Cf. Barbeau et al. 1947:32 "Till I Be Full"

BRS *617* [190-?]:37
  Healy 1965(1968):16-7
  Songs and Recitations 4,1975:33
h: *Walton's Treasury* n.d.:110

REC Edward Quinn, *FSB* 3 (A8)
  Clancy Brothers, Tommy Makem, [b:] Tradition/ Everest TLP 1042 (A7); Tradition/Everest TR 2050 (A4); [b:] Columbia CL 1950
cl: Eileen Curran, AFS 3653 A1

The Galliards, Monitor MFS 407 (A5)
b: *A Jug of Punch*, EMI CLP 1327
  A. L. Lloyd, Riverside RLP12 618
  McPeake Family, [b:] Prestige/Int. 13018; [b:] Topic TPS 114
b: Pete Seeger, Folkways FA 2451 (A2)
  Charlie Somers, EEOT *Shamrock* 2 cass. (B4)
b: *Songs from ABC Television's "Hallelujah,"* Fontana TL 5356

MEL Petrie/Stanford 1,1902:89 (#353) "... An air formed on that called Brigid astore. I spied a thrush on yonder bush, And the song she sang was a jug of punch."

◇ A Cup o' Tay *(H489)* 48

BRS O'Conor 1901:9
  617 [190-?]:112

◇ The Wee Cutty Pipe *(H465)* 49

m: IREL Ó Maoláin 1982:24-5 (Hurl) "The Derry Pipe"

◇ The Rakes of Poverty *(H741)* 50

Brunnings 1981: "The Son of a Gambolier," (m) "The Winding Banks of Erne"

IREL Shields 1981:135 (#60)
  Shields/Shields *UF* 21,1975: #327

b: AMER Cf. Sandburg 1927:44 "The Son of a Gambolier"

AUST Cf. Ward 1964:118 "The Ramble-eer"

◇ The Oul' Rigadoo *(H751)* 50

Brunnings 1981: "The Little Beggarman," "The Roving Journeyman"

IREL Joyce 1909:53-4 "The Colleen Dhas Rue," a related song.
  Loesberg 2,1980:16-7 "The Beggarman's Song"
  O Lochlainn 1965:52-3 "The Beggarman's Song"

b: BRIT Kennedy 1975:772-3 (#345) "The Little Beggarman," with tune "The Red-Haired Boy," "not unlike that of the Scots ballad 'Gilderoy'" (p. 796); 781 (#353) "The Roving Journeyman"

REC Paddy Doran, *FSB* 3 (A2) "The Roving Journeyman"
  Tommy Dempsey, Trailer LER 2096 (A1) "The Little Beggarman"
? Flanagan Brothers, Topic 12T 365 (A3)
b: *Irish Folk Night*, London LL 3414 "The Little Beggarman"
b: *The Lark in the Morning*, Tradition TLP 1004 "The Little Beggarman"
b: Tommy Makem, Tradition TLP 1044 "The Little Beggarman"
b: Ed McCurdy, Elektra EKL 205 "There Was an Old Soldier"
  Delia Murphy, EMI STAL 1055 (A4) "The Roving Journeyman"
b: *Songs and Sounds of the Sea*, National Geographic 705 "The Little Beggar Man"

MEL Moffat 1912:20

◇ Old Rosin the Bow *(H698)* 51

Dean-Smith 1954: "Rosin the Beau"

Sam Henry's Songs of the People

Brunnings 1981: "... Beau"

Spaeth 1948:82-3 says the song is "anonymous, but evidently of Scottish origin."

b: IREL   Clancy Bros. 1964:24-5 "Rosin the Bow"

BRIT   Sharp/Karpeles 1974,2:125 (#230)

AMER   Chappell 1939:97 "... Beau"
   Colorado FB 1(3,Nov)1962:24
   I. Ford 1940:56-7, 392-3, 127
Randolph/Cohen (1982):386-8
   Warner 1984:360-2 (#159)

BRS   Harvard 1: 7.241 (indecipherable imprint)
   Harvard 3: (Walker)
   UCLA 605: 4(Walker) (Such)
   Forget Me Not [1835]:224 "Rosen ..."

b: REC   Alf Edwards, Prestige/Int. 13060 (B10d) "Rosin the Bow"
  cl: George Vinton Graham, AFS 2274 A3
  cl: Jim Howard, AFS 1374 A2
  cl: Bascom Lamar Lunsford, AFS 1800 A2
  cl: Capt. Pearl R. Nye, AFS 1612 A1
  cl: Eliza Pace, AFS 1468 B2
   Walter Pardon, Home Made Music LP 301 "Rosin a-Beau"

MEL   Joyce 1909:162 (#352) [Sharp/Karpeles]
   O'Neill 1922:71

◇ **Bryan O'Lynn** *(H 480a)* 52

White/Dean-Smith 1951: "Brian ... or Tam o' the Lynn"
Dean-Smith 1954: "Brian ...; Tam o' the Lynn; Tom Boleyn"
Brunnings 1981: "Brian O'Linn," ?"Tom Bowline"

IREL   Loesberg 1,1908 "Brian O'Linn"
b: O Lochlainn 1939:30-1
   Shields/Shields *UF* 21,1975: #58

b: BRIT   Kennedy 1975:644 (#290) "Brian-o-Linn"; reports 2 other English versions and 1 Irish recorded.
   Richards/Stubbs 1979:61 "Brian O'Flynn"
   Spin 3(3):3 "Brian ..."; B. Davis n.d.:10

AMER   Belden 1940:501-2 "Tom Bo-lin," which "goes back at least to the sixteenth century ... [but] probably has no connection with the Child ballad [#39] of Tam Lane."
   Bush 2,1970:71-2
Hubbard 1961:322, "Brian O'Linn," a fragment.
   Hudson/Herzog 1937:20 "Jimmy"
   Kenedy 1890:393-4
   Leach 1965:272-3 "Brian O'Linn"
   Wells 1950:167 "Brian O' Lyn"
   Welsh 1907,2:365

BRS   Harvard 1: 10.175 (Bebbington), 12.113 (Such)
   In Dublin's 1968:62-3
   O'Conor 1901:64
   Popular Songs 1860:168 with a nonsense chorus.
   617 [190-?]:91
   Wehman's Irish 1937:70 [Randolph]

REC   Thomas Moran, *FSB* 10 (A2)
   Dick Cameron, Folkways FG 3516 (B2) "Brian O Linn"
   Paul Clayton, Folkways FW 8708 (B5)
  b: William Clauson, Capitol T 10158 "Brian O'Linn"
  cl: Eileen Curran, AFS 3653 B2 "Brian ..."
   Sam Hinton, Folkways FC 7548 (A2)
  b: *A Jug of Punch: Broadside Ballads Old and New*, EMI CLP 1327 "Brian O'Linn"
? b: Katie Lee, Horizon 1604 "Tom Bollyn"
b: Siobhan McKenna, Spoken Arts 707 "Brian O'Linn"
? cl: Lize Pace, AFS 1438 A2 "Tom Bolyn"
cl: Blaine Stubblefield, AFS 1848 A
? b: The Swagmen, Parkway SP 7105 "Tom Bollyn"
   Tony Wales, Folkways FG 3515 (B4) "Bryan O' Lynn"

◇ **Bryan O'Lynn** *(H 480b)* 52

MEL   O'Neill 1903:163 (#881)
   Vallely/Vallely 1973,3:2 (#2)

◇ **The State of Arkansaw** *(H0)* 53

Laws 1964:230 (H1) "An Arkansas Traveller"
Brunnings 1981: "... Arkansas"
Cazden et al. *Notes* 1982: #93 "The Rock Island Line"

AMER   Asch et al. 1973:44-5 (see Harrell rec.)
   Cf. Bush 3,1975:25-7 "Bill Stafford"
   Cf. Cazden et al. 1982:348-53 "The Rock Island Line"
   Darling 1983:227-8 "Old ..." (see Iron Mountain rec.)
Randolph/Cohen (1982):288-90
   Scofield 1981:97-8
   SO 10(2,Sum)1960:284 "When I Struck Muskoka" (see Brandon rec.)

c: REC   Cf. Kelly Harrell, *AAFM* 1, Folkways FP 251 (#14) "My Name Is John Johanna"; RCA Victor LPV 548 (A7)
c: Cf. Tom Brandon, Folk-Legacy FSC 10 (A4) "Muskoka," cf. (B2) "The Rock Island Line"
cl: Emma Dusenbury, AFS 865 B2 "... Arkansas"
   Jack Elliott, Derroll Adams, Topic 12T 104 (B4) "... Arkansas"
c: I. G. Greer, AAFS L 7 (B4) "Sanford Barney"
lc: Lee Hayes, Commodore FL 30,002 "... Arkansas"
c: Joe Hickerson, Folk-Legacy FSI 59 (A3) "... Arkansas"
   Dee Hicks, Tennessee Folklore TFS 104 (A5) "Bill Staples"
   Cf. Roscoe Holcomb, Folkways FA 2363 (A9) "Hills of Mexico"
cl: Theophilus G. Hoskins, AFS 1518 A2 "... Arkansas"
   Iron Mountain String Band, Folkways FA 2477 (A4) "Old Arkansas"
cl: Aunt Molly Jackson, AFS 827 A1 "... Arkansas"
lc: Jim Lackey, Mercury A 80 (78 rpm) "Old Arkansas"
cl: Elizabeth Minyard, AFS 1391 B1 "... Arkansas"
cl: Mrs Hallie May Preece, AFS 915 A2 "... Arkansas"
   Cf. parody sung by Pete Seeger, Folkways FH 5802 (D6b)
b: *The Soil and the Sea*, Mainstream S 16005
   Rosalie Sorrels, Green Linnet SIF 1024 (B5) "... Arkansas"
   Cf. Brian Stubblefield, AAFS L 61 (A6) "Way out in Idaho" [Hickerson]
b: The Weavers, Vanguard VRS 9043
cl: Mrs Ollie Womble, AFS 3031 A1 "... Arkansas"

MEL   Eddie Butcher, Outlet OAS 3007 (B2) "The Titanic"

◇ **Denny Byrne, the Piper** *(H 29)* 53

Brunnings 1981: "The Cow Ate the Piper"

IREL   O Lochlainn 1965:74-5 "The Cow Ate the Piper"

AMER   Kenedy 1890:36-7

BRS   O'Conor 1901:29 "The Cow That Ate the Piper"
   617 [190?]:6

◇ The Sailor in the Alehouse *(H779)* 54

White/Dean-Smith 1951: "(The) Green Bed"
Dean-Smith 1954: "(The) Green Bed"
Laws 1957:159-60 (K36) "Johnny the Sailor [Green Beds]"
Brunnings 1981: "Wild Rover No More"

IREL Loesberg 1,1980:43 "The Wild Rover"
Moulden 1979:128-9

BRIT Greig/Duncan 1,1981:100-4 (#48) "Johnnie and the Landlady," 6 vts. ("I'll Tell You of a Story," "The Brisk Young Sailor Lad," "The Sailor," "The Sailor and The Landlady")
b: Cf. Kennedy 1975:621 (#288) "Wild Rover"; notes 4 more English and 2 Irish versions recorded.

AMER Hudson 1936:156
Randolph/Cohen (1982):70-2 "Johnny the Sailor"
Warner 1984:142-3 (#49) "Captain John"

REC Paul Clayton, Folkways FA 2110 (A4) "Wild Rover"
Warde Ford, Folkways FE 4001 (B3) "Young Johnny"
? cl: George Vinton Graham, AFS 3816 B1 "Young Johnny the Sailor"
Cf. John Greenway, Folkways FW 8718 (B10) "Wild Rover No More"
Bill Hannaford, People's Stage Tapes cass. 03 (B5) "Wild Rover"
cl: Sam Harmon, AFS 2903 B1 "The Green Bed"
b: Rolf Harris, Epic LN 24110 "The Wild Rover"
b: Burl Ives, Decca DL 8125 "The Wild Rover"
Louis Killen, Fox Hollow FH 701 (A8) "The Wild Rover"
Cf. Sam Larner, Folkways FG 3507 (B3) "The Wild Rover"
Margaret MacArthur, Living Folk F-LFR 100 (B3) "You're Welcome Home, Young Johnny"
b: Peggy Seeger, Folk-Lyric FL 120 (A4) "Green Beds"
cl: Carrie Walker, AFS 3102 B2 "The Green Bed"

◇ The Private Still *(H103)* 55

Brunnings 1981: "The Gauger's Song"

b: Morton 1970:82-3 "The Gauger's Song"

BRIT Palmer 1980:27-8

BRS BPL Irish (n.i.)
O'Conor 1901:60 "A ..."
617 [190?]:66 "A ..."

MEL Petrie/Stanford 1,1902:111 (#442) "The Hornless Cow, or The Brown Ewe (a private still.)" does not seem to be related.

◇ Mick Magee *(H740)* 56

AMER Creighton 1971:160 "... McGee," a fragment from Angelo Dornan.

◇ My Grandfather Died *(H732)* 57

Dean-Smith 1954: "(The) Foolish Boy; Wing, Wang, Waddle-O; The Bugle Played for Me; Swapping Song"
Brunnings 1981: "The Swapping Song"

BRIT Cf. Davis n.d.:6 "Lucan Dairy," a list.
Goodman *JEFDSS* 1964:271 "The Foolish Boy"
b: Kennedy 1975:670 (#312) "Wim-wam-waddles"
Moffat/Kidson n.d.:5 "My Father He Died"
Sharp/Karpeles 1974,2:383-4 (#329) "The Foolish Boy, or The Swapping Song," 3 vts.

AMER Barrand *ED&S* 1981:23-4 "Posey Boy"
Bush 5,n.d.:25-6
CFMJ 3,1975:43 "The Swapping Song"
Cox 1939(1964):166-9 "The Foolish Boy," two very different versions.
Roberts 1974:100-1 "Swappin' Boy"
Sturgis/Hughes 1919:7-9 "Posey Boy"

BRS Cf. *Songs and Recitations* 5,1978:25 "The Lucan Dairy," another list.

REC Dorchester mummers, *FSB* 10 (A4) "Wim Wam Waddles"
b: *Authentic Folk Music and Dances of the World*, Murray Hill S 4195 (7 recs.)
Cf. Peg, Bobby Clancy, Tradition TLP 1045 (A7) "Me Grandfather Died," lists of things only, no swaps.
Paul Clayton, Tradition TLP 1011 (B4) "The Swapping Song"
lc: Richard Dyer-Bennet, Decca DL 5046 "Swapping Song"
b: *Folk Songs and Instrumental Music of the Southern Appalachians*, Murray Hill 927950
b: John Langstaff, HMV B.10369 (78 rpm) "The Swapping Song"
Maud Long, AAFS L21 (B11) "My Grandmother Green"
Cf. Ewan MacColl, Folkways FW 8501 (A4,41) [My father died a month ago], another list.
Troy Penfield, Folkways FE 38553 (A10) "Wim Wam Wobble O"
Jean Ritchie, Folkways FC 7054 (B2) "The Swapping Song"
b: Jean Ritchie, Paul Clayton, Tradition TLP 1011 "The Swapping Song"
b: Cyril Tawney, Argo ZFB 4 "The Foolish Boy"

◇ The Buttermilk Boy *(H57a)* 57

Dean-Smith 1954: "A-Begging Buttermilk I Will Go"

IREL Moulden 1979:29

◇ O'Ryan *(H823)* 58

Brunnings 1981: (m) "The Girl I Left Behind Me."

BRS *617* [190-?]:37 "The Poacher"

◇ The Salutation *(H756)* 60

Brunnings 1981: (m) "Tramp! Tramp! Tramp! The Boys Are Marching"

IREL Ó Maoláin 1982:64-5

◇ Fine Broom Besoms! *(H17a)* 61

Dean-Smith 1954: "Green ...; The Besom Maker," "Buy Broom Buzzems"
Brunnings 1981: "Buy ... /Buzzems," "Green Besoms -- I Am a Besom Maker"

BRIT Crawhall 1888(1965):24-7
Handle et al. 1972:8 "Broom Buzzems," a nonsense version (see also Ranters rec.)
Henderson et al. 1979:26-7 "The Besom Maker," a story!
Purslow 1974:4 "The Besom Maker"

AMER Milner/Kaplan 1983:61 "The Besom Maker," a story version.

BRS Harvard 1: 5.101 (n.i.), 9.51 (Bebbington)

b: REC Ian Campbell Folk Group, Topic TPS 145 "Buy Broom ..."

Sam Henry's Songs of the People

High Level Ranters, Trailer LER 2007 (B4) "Buy Broom ..."
Lou Killen, Prestige/Int. 13059 (A2) "Buy Broom Buzzems"

◊ **Better Bide a Wee** (*H598*) *61*

Brunnings 1981: "We'd ..."

b: AMER *Heart Songs* 1909:388-9 "We'd ..." credited to "Claribel": Charlotte A. Barnard.

MEL DeVille/Gould n.d.:66 "We'd ..."

◊ **Gaol Song** (*H746*) *62*

? White/Dean-Smith 1951
Not = same title in Brunnings 1981; but cf. "Prisoner's Song," "Seven Long Years in State Prison," "Sweet Swansea," "Meet Me By Moonlight," "Farewell to Judges and Juries"
Cazden et al. *Notes* 1982: #100 "The Prisoner's Song"

BRIT Cf. Purslow 1972:39, 125-6
 Cf. Sharp 1908-12(1961):226-8 "Farewell to Judges and Juries"

AMER Cazden et al. 1982:371-6 "The Prisoner's Song," with much information about this song's multiple relatives and ancestors.
 Cox 1939(1964):193-4
 Creighton 1932:309 "Prisoner's Song"
 Fuson 1931:143
 Peterson 1931:50
Randolph/Cohen (1982):489-91 "Meet Me Tonight," with informative notes on the song's origin, authorship, and copyright claims.
But not: b: Shellans 1968 "Within This Prison Cell"

BRS Cf. Ashton 1888:364-5 "Farewell to Judges and Juries"
 Cf. Harvard 1: 5.87 (Cadman) "Meet Me by Moonlight," 9.23 (Bebbington)
 Cf. UCLA 605: 4(Birt) "Meet Me by Moonlight"

REC Vernon Dalhart (Marion Try Slaughter), *Smithsonian Country* I (A5) "Prisoner's Song"
 Clarence Ashley, Folkways FA 2350 (B5) "The Prisoner's Song"; notes give references to early recordings.
 May Bradley, EFDSS LP 1006 (B2) "Sweet Swansea"
 Martin Carthy, Topic 12TS 345 (A9) "Here's Adieu to All Judges and Juries"
 Derek, Dorothy Elliott, Trailer LER 2033 (A6) "Adieu to All Judges and Juries"
? cl: George Vinton Graham, ARS 3814 A1 "The Prisoner's Song"
 Bobby Harrison, Folkways FS 3839 (A5) "Old Prisoner's Song"
 Ernest Helton, AFS L68 (A8) "Prisoner's Song"
 Estella Palmer, Shoestring Tape SGB 1 (A1) "Please Meet Me Tonight," text remarkably close to Henry's.

◊ **The Leaves So Green** (*H719*) *63*

g: MEL Joyce 1909:328 (#650) prints a melody entitled "The Leaves So Green" which could have been used with this song.

◊ **Barossa / Oliver's Advice** (*H98a*) *64*

Brunnings 1981: "Fare Ye Well, My Darlin'," "Oliver's Advice (Put Your Trust in God, Keep Your Powder Dry)"

IREL Duffy 1866:72-6
O Lochlainn 1965:241-3 "Oliver's Advice"
b: Sparling 1887 "Oliver's Advice"

BRS Healy 2,1969a:35-8 "Oliver's Advice"

MEL Cf. Greig/Duncan 1,1981:355-60 (#148) "The Battle of Barossa" ("The Battle of Trafalgar," "Barossa's Plains")
 Cf. Joyce 1909:406-7 (#839)

◊ **The Yellow Bittern / Bunnan Buidhe** (*H830*) *64*

IREL *JIFSS* 20,1923:46-8, "An Buinnean ..." a different version also translated from the Gaelic.
h: S. O Baoill 1944:6-7
 S. O'Boyle/M. O'Boyle 1975:83 "An Bunnan Bui"
 Shields/Shields *UF* 21,1975: #63 "Buinnean Bui (An)"
 Treoir 3(1)1972:23 "An Buinnean Bui"

AMER Milner/Kaplan 1983:216-7 "... Bui"

REC Seán 'ac Ḋonnċa, Claddagh CC 9 (B1) "An Buinneán Buí"
 Seán Mac Donnchadha (same singer, different spelling), Topic 12T 202 (B1) "An Buinneán Buí -- The Yellow Bittern"
 Joe Heaney (Seosamh Ó hÉanaí), Gael-Linn CEF 028 (B1) "An Buinneán Buí"; Philo 2004 (B6) "(The Yellow Bittern)"
 Tim Lyons, Trailer LER 3036
 Tom Pháidín Tom, Comhaltas Ceoltóirí Éireann CL 15 (A1) "An Bonnán Buí"
 Paddy Tunney, Green Linnet SIF 1037 (A5) "An Bunnan Bwee (The Yellow Bittern)"

MEL Bunting 1840:56 (#77)
 Bunting 1983:120-1 (#77) "An Bonnán Buidhe (The Yellow Bittern)"
 Hudson ms. 2:627 "Bunnean Buidhe"
 Joyce 1909:314 (#609)

◊ **The Parting Glass** (*H769*) *65*

Brunnings 1981: "... (Fill to Me ...; Tune of The American Wake)"

IREL Clancy Bros. 1964:64
O Lochlainn 1939:138-9

BRIT Greig 1906-7(1963):17 (no title)
b: *Spin* 4(2):31; Davis 1969

AMER Peacock 1965,2:573-4

BRS Healy 1965:140
Songs and Recitations 5,1978:20

REC *Ballads from the Pubs* ..., Mercier IRL 1
b: Clancy Brothers and Tommy Makem, Columbia CL 1950
 Joe Holmes, Len Graham, Topic 12TS 401 (B7)
b: (Ann) Mayo Muir, 20th Century-Fox TFS 4122

MEL Hudson ms. 2:602 "Good Night and Joy Be with You All"
 O'Neill 1903:10 (#58)

A6
If you want a bit of fun: Celebrations

Sam Henry's Songs of the People

Dan Murphy's Convoy [H663: 8 Aug 1936]

Source not given.

s: The names and place in this song are fictitious.

Key C.

Oh friends, pay attention to what I will mention,
My pen for a moment I now will employ;
I won't keep you late if you listen and wait
And hear what took place at Dan Murphy's convoy.

First comes young Ross and John Thompson no less,
And after that comes John Purdy's big boy
We stood there a wee wi' a man called Magee
And we all started down to Dan Murphy's convoy.

Young Thompson came in just as clean as a tin,
He took up the fiddle beside M'Ilroy,
First to luk roon her and then for tae tune her,
And the dancin' commenced at Dan Murphy's convoy.

We danced but wan set, for the kitchen was het,
Then the boys tuk the girls to a barn over-bye,
They were gye and content for tae dance on cement
The night that we gaen tae Dan Murphy's convoy.

Bob Fall got excited, some thought he would fight it,
I'm tellin' ye thon's a ferocious boy,
He cursed and he smoked, you'd a thought he'd a choked,
The night that we gaen tae Dan Murphy's convoy.

For meat, there was plenty, not a plate was left empty,
A cartload of whiskey came up frae Armoy,
The poteen was flyin' for them that was styin'
When we left for hame frae Dan Murphy's convoy.

The boys frae the mountain, they needed a huntin',
They run at the beans like a horse frae the Moy,
They were gye and ill aff for to riddle bean cauf
And fill themselves up at Dan Murphy's convoy.

And now pay attention, the poet I'll mention,
If you'd know who has wrote it, M'Michael's the boy;
When he's crossin' the ocean with waves in commotion,
He'll think of the spree at Dan Murphy's convoy.

1.4: convoy = escort (for honor, guard, or protection), accompany.
3.3: luk roon = look around.
4.1: wan = one; het = hot.
4.2: tuk = took; over-bye = ?alongside.
4.3: gye [gey] = considerable, worthy of notice; tolerable; middling. [m/s]
5.2: thon = that one.
5.4: gaen = went.
6.3: styin' = staying.
7.3: ill aff = badly off.

The Wedding at Ballyporeen [H93: 22 Aug 1925]

Other titles: "... of ..."; cf. "The Muntagh Wedding."

Source: William Sloan (Ballyrock), from his grandfather c. 1865.

[Bp] s: A rollicking old-time comic song, whose humour consists chiefly in absurd paradoxes....

Key C.

Descend, you chaste nine, to a true Irish bard,
You['re] old maids, to be sure, but he sends you his card.
He begs you'll assist a poor frolicsome elf
In a song ready-made (he composed it himself)
About boys, maids, a priest and a wedding,
A crowd you could scarce thrust your head in,
A supper, good cheer and a bedding,
That has happened at Ballyporeen.

One moonshining night, about twelve in the day,
When the birds fell to sing and the asses to bray,
When Patrick the bridegroom and Oona the bride,
With their best bibs and tuckers, set off side by side,
And the harpers went first in the rear, sirs,
The bride blushed, the groomsman did swear, sirs,
When they saw how the spalpeens did stare, sirs,
At the wedding at Ballyporeen.

There was Dion McDermott and Seaghan his brat,
Driscoll and Tyrus and Clattery's Pat,
There was Nora McCormick and Brian O'Linn,
And the big red-haired cook maid that lived at the inn,
There was Sheila and Larry the genius
And Pat's uncle, ould Darby Denis,
Black Thady and crooked McGuinness
Assembled at Ballyporeen.

They were soon tied together and home did return
To make merry the night at the sign of the churn
And when they assembled, that frolicsome troop,

A6 / If you want a bit of fun

The banks of old Shannon ne'er saw such a group
Of turf-cutters, thrashers and nailers,
Harpers and pipers and tailors,
Pedlars and smugglers and sailors
Assembled at Ballyporeen.

They sat down to meat, Father Murphy said grace,
Piping hot were the dishes and eager each face,
The knives and forks rattled, spoon and platter
  did play,
But they elbowed and jostled and walloped away.
Long sinews, fat sirloins did groan, sirs,
Large mountains of beef were cut down, sirs
We demolished all to the bare bone, sirs,
At the wedding at Ballyporeen.

There was greens and potatoes, the turkey was
  spoiled,
Potatoes cooked both ways, both roasted and
  boiled,
Ham knobs and red herring, the priest got the
  snipe,
Cod candles and dumplings, cow heel and tough
  tripe,
And we ate till we could eat no more, sirs,
The whiskey came pouring galore, sirs,
How Thady MacManus did roar, sirs,
Till he bothered all Ballyporeen.

Whiskey went round and the songsters did roar,
Tim sung 'Paddy O'Carroll'; Nell, 'Molly Asthore,'
Till a motion was made that their songs they'd
  forsake
And each lad take his sweetheart their trotters
  to shake.
Then harpers and couples advancing,
Brogues, pumps and bare feet fell a-prancing,
Such capering and figuring and dancing
Was ne'er seen at Ballyporeen.

Then the bride she got up and she made a low
  bow,
She tripped and she stuttered, I couldn't tell
  how,
She tripped and she faltered, a few words let fall
And she whispered so low that she bothered them
  all;
And her mother cried, 'What, are you dead, child?
For shame, can't you hold up your head, child?
Though I'm sixty, again I would wed, child,
I would rattle in Ballyporeen.'

Then the groom got up and he made an oration,
He charmed all their hearts with his kind
  botheration.
'You are welcome,' he said, and he invited them
  first,
'To eat while you're able and slacken your thirst.
The next party I have if I thrive, sirs,
I hope you'll all back again drive, sirs,
You'll be welcome all, dead or alive, sirs,
To the big night at Ballyporeen.'

Then the bride she got up and she made a low
  bow,
She tripped and she stuttered, I couldn't tell
  how,
She tripped and she faltered, a few words let fall
And she whispered so low that she bothered them
  all;
And her mother cried, 'What, are you dead, child?
For shame, can't you hold up your head, child?
Though I'm sixty, again I would wed, child,
I would rattle in Ballyporeen.'

Then the groom got up and he made an oration,
He charmed all their hearts with his kind
  botheration.
'You are welcome,' he said, and he invited them
  first,
'To eat while you're able and slacken your thirst.
The next party I have if I thrive, sirs,
I hope you'll all back again drive, sirs,
You'll be welcome all, dead or alive, sirs,
To the big night at Ballyporeen.'

Now to Patrick the bridegroom and Oona the bride
May the harp of old Erin be sounded with pride,
And to all the fair guests, old and young, grey
  and green,
That danced, sung and jigged it at Ballyporeen.
When Cupid does lend you his wherry
To cross o'er the conjugal ferry,
I wish you may be half as merry
As we were at Ballyporeen.

3.3: ... Bryan O'Lynn, [Dt]
 .4: ... cook that lived ... [Dt]
7.2: ... O'Carroll' and Nell, ... [Dt]
9.7: ... be all welcome, ... [Dt]
6.1: spoiled = despoiled, stripped.

The Ballinderry Marriage
[H805: 29 Apr 1939]

Source: John M'Closkey (Tyanee).

s: Sung to me by John M'Closkey at the midnight bonfire celebrations on St. John's Eve on Mullaghnamoyagh Hill, Clady, and now noted from him at Tyanee, where he stopped his horses and rested from harrowing, to whistle me the tune.
  Can any reader explain "ball-in-ramsey" in verse 1?

Key G.

Sam Henry's Songs of the People

It was in Balinderry near Ballinascreen,
Where this lovely wedding of late it has been;
I supped with the bride and I drank with the groom,
I ate ball-in-ramsey from morning to noon.

And you're welcome, all of you, heartily welcome,
Gramachree, welcome every one.

The priest of the parish rode his garran bawn
To see if ould Micky would marry Susanne;
MacDermott and Jeremy, twelve more beside,
With long rakes and pitchforks they welcomed the bride.

There was fine pratie pudding made in an ould still,
Where ladies and gentlemen might sup their fill;
Of barley-meal bannocks they had forty score,
And stocks of colcannon and butter galore.

This maid she was seated, both comely and fair,
She was small round the waist as a two-year-old mare,
She threw up her eyes like corncrakes' wings
And tore at the beef till she broke her eye strings.

This maid she was dressed in a bonny light gown,
The cloth it was new and her tails swept the ground,
Her petticoats silk and her stockings were blue,
Her handkerchief hemmed and her brocades were new.

The houseleek and garlic they had of their own,
And fine spotted herrings from dark Innishowen,
The scallions and onions, they come from afar,
The leeks they were brought up upon slide and slide car.

Their spirits were high, but the whiskey was low,
And at long and at last they got ready to go,
They searched for the bride, but not one could see her,
For Susanne trotted off with a shout, 'I'm not here!'

2.1: garran bawn = white horse. [s]
3.1: pratie = potato.
3.3: bannocks = flat bread cakes.
3.4: colcannon = a dish of meal and cabbage. [s]

Coleraine Regatta [H36: 19 Jul 1924]

Author James McCurry, blind fiddler (Myroe).

o: Tune should be a jig in 9/8 time.

Key C.

Good folks, I'll tell you true, now my song commences,
In the year of 'seventy-two, one day of my adventures:
The *Derry Standard* came to us, it bore the special motto
That on July the thirty-first comes off Coleraine Regatta.

Whack fal ol di da,
Whack fal ol di daddy,
Whack fal ol di da,
Right toorin intan addy.

The morning being fine as I prepared for starting,
I was led along the line by a man whose name was Martin,
In coming to the junction I heard two engines whistle,
The points were drawn together by a man called Frank M'Crystall.

The ladies shook their dress and stood there with compunction,
Until the guard expressed, 'Take seats at Newtown Junction,'
When I obtained my seat, my fiddle begun a-playing,
The engine she did beat, and the people fell hurraing.

Many a rosy cheek was there, and many an ugly bundle,
And many a lass received a smack as the train went through the tunnel.
One of the bandboys sat by me, I heard his name called Lowry,
The fifes and drums struck up a tune which we called 'Kate fa Gowrie.'

Then I arrived at sweet Coleraine, 'twas there my journey ended,
And also sweet Portrush to view each lad and lass intended,
As I stood on the platform amidst a vain oration,
But soon the din began to cease, the Portrush train left the station.

As we passed through the gates exposed to every danger,
Fearing to walk straight, and worse, I was a stranger,
The multitude was great, and thousands as they passed me,

When a female voice cried, 'Wake, play us
   "M'Donald's Strathspey."'

Crowd by crowd did strive as they passed one
   another,
Husbands lost their wives, and daughters lost
   their mothers,
Lads they lost their lasses, while pushing
   through they missed them,
And then I heard a voice shout out, 'Stop, stop!
   I've lost my sister!'

Some were selling matches there and others
   selling laces,
And some were crying, 'Who will buy a true list
   of the races?'
Lots o' lumps o' boys were there a-courting their
   young ladies,
John Harbison made me rejoice when he ta'en me
   up to Fadie's.

They conveyed me to the train, although my coat
   was duddy,
Whisky in my brain had made my senses muddy,
At Newtown Junction I stayed there till I had my
   slumber finished,
Then safely homeward I was ta'en by the sons o'
   Tom Miskimmin.

Now you've heard my song, which I have sung to
   please you,
Although I've kept you long, I did not mean to
   tease you,
But boys and girls beware, and keep this as your
   motto --
Never mix the rum and beer that they sell at the
   Regatta.

9.1: duddy = worn out. [m]

The Lammas Fair in Cargan
[H513: 30 Sep 1933]

o: (m) "The Girl I Left Behind Me."

Source not given.

s: The appropriate note should be duplicated,
where necessary, to conform with the metre.

Key C.

A6 / If you want a bit of fun

One fine harvest day as I happened for to stray
And I looked for some recreation,
I dandered for a while till I went about a mile,
When I reached my destination;
You may talk about shows and menageries,
But none of them's worth a farthin',
If you want a bit of fun, dress yourself and come
To the Lammas fair in Cargan.

There maybe you will see an oul' horny cow
On the hill beside William Gaston's,
If there's a dealer in the town, he'll be apt to come
   aroun'
And inquire what price is askin';
When the deal is finished out, he will stand all
   hands a stout
And there'll be a lot o' arguin',
And after it is past, it is sure to be the last
You will get that day in Cargan.

You will see a crowd of men, ay, maybe nine or
   ten,
Forby a lot of strangers,
All hurryin' to the fair, ay, but faith, when they
   come there,
O' hurry there will be no danger.
There'll be ladies in the fair, for I'm sure I saw a
   pair,
And an oul' stall wife ay brawlin',
And I wondered all along from what airt came the
   throng
To the Lammas fair in Cargan.

You'll get ginger nuts at call and a coconut big
   ball,
The police will be there with their commander,
And the chief of the police will be eatin' corned
   beef
With the Honourable John Alexander.
As I went up the street to get something for to eat
From an oul' wife who kept callin',
She struck me with her han' for eatin' off her
   stan',
And I could hardly keep from fallin'.

When I steadied on my feet, my teeth were on the
   street,
In my rage my gums were jergin',
And every here and there was a handful o' my
   hair
In the Lammas fair in Cargan.
When I was at large and the woman was in charge,
I went to get some porter,
A magistrate was there, she was sentenced then
   and there,
They agreed for to transport her.

And I came home half dead with a lump upon my
   head
And two black eyes into the bargain,
And a part o' my clothes and the skin off my nose
I left behind in Cargan.

3.7: airt = quarter of the compass, direction.
5.2: jergin' = ?jerking.

Sam Henry's Songs of the People

On the Road to Bethlehem
[H59: "A Christmas carol," 27 Dec 1924]

Author Robert Hugh Benson; composer Sir R. R. Terry.

Key E flat.

s: By kind courtesy of ... the composer and by special permission of the publishers, Messrs. J. Curwen & Sons, Ltd., whose edition, 80015, contains the staff and tonic sol-fa settings for soprano, alto, tenor and bass.

There went a merry company
  On the road to Bethlehem,
Going all to taxed be,
By the governor's decree,
  On the road to Bethlehem,
Would I had been there to see!

  Would I had been there to see!
  On the road to Bethlehem,
  Jesu, master, look on me.

[*similarly throughout:*]
Coldly blew the wind and snow,
Coldly blew the wind and snow,
Two there were that walked slow,
Would I had been there also.

One a maid of high degree,
Walking, walking wearily,
'Joseph, Joseph, wait for me.'
Would I had been there to see.

Thus they came the town within,
  To the town of Bethlehem,
Straight they sought the public inn
So they might a shelter win,
  In the town of Bethlehem.
See them tirling at the pin.

'Get you gone, the night is late.'
  In the town of Bethlehem,
Hear them chapping at the gate --
Richer folk both small and great,
  In the town of Bethlehem.
When they knock, the poor must wait.

Sought they straight the stable door,
Mary dropped upon the floor,
Wearied was she, wearied sore,
'Joseph dear, I can no more.'

What a lodging, cold and bare,
Bring me wrappings fine and fair,
Silk and satin rich and rare,
Lay our lady softly there.

Nay, no silk nor satin bright
Think ye on this wondrous sight,
Soon to see! The lord of light
Comes in lowliness tonight.

Ox and ass with patient face,
Mark the maiden full of grace
Lying in the manger place,
Lying in such sorry case.

Ere the night had past to morn,
Rose the sun on us forlorn,
In the manger old and worn,
Jesus Christ our lord was born.

Eastern kings are on their way
  To the town of Bethlehem,
Shepherds now, ere break of day,
At his feet their vows do pay
  In the town of Bethlehem,
Where a god incarnate lay.

Christian souls with one accord
  Come to holy Bethlehem,
Meet him at his holy board,
Praise the Saviour, praise the Lord,
  There in holy Bethlehem,
Who on us his glory poured.

r.1-3: [*Marked "Chorus--," but ambiguous as to which text lines are to be repeated in subsequent occurrences.*]
r.3: Jesus, ... [Dt]
4.6: tirling at the pin = rattling at the door latch.
5.3: chapping = rapping.

A6 / If you want a bit of fun

◆ A6 REFERENCES ◆

◆ **The Wedding at Ballyporeen** *(H93) 72*

Brunnings 1981: "... of ... (Tune of The Haswell Cages)"

IREL Cf. Shields *UF* 18,1972:60-1 "The Muntagh Wedding," "probably inspired by the text, and perhaps the air, of 'The Wedding at Ballyporeen.'"
  Leslie Shepard, *Ceol Tire* #26(Sep)1984:15-7, "... of ..." adds a contemporary footnote and several references to the record, including a traditional tune, "Ballymona Ora" (printed 1846), a broadsheet printed by A. Swindell in Manchester, and another produced in 1984 in the town of the title, Co. Tipperary.

BRIT Greig 1907-11 (1963): #47

AMER Mackenzie 1928:342-3 "... of ..."

BRS Harvard 1: 7.11 (n.i.)
  Healy 3,1969b:23-5 "... of ..."
  617 [190-?]:76 "... of ..."

REC Cf. Mary Ann Carolan, Topic 12TS 362 (B4) "The Wedding at [?of Sweet] Baltray," a parody of the same kind.

◆ **Coleraine Regatta** *(H36) 74*

IREL Moulden 1979:35-6
  Shields *UF* 27,1981: 11 (see Butcher rec.)

h: REC Paul Brady, Transatlantic TRA 185
m: Eddie Butcher, Free Reed FRR 003 (B5)

A7

The Irish soldier boy: War

The Shepherd Boy [H803: 15 Apr 1939]

g: "David and Goliath."

Source: (m) Andy Allen (Bridge Cottage, Coleraine); (w) "popular broadside of half a century ago."

o: A famous Masonic song. The time should be 6/8.

Key G.

One night as I lay on my bed I fell into a dream,
Some rugged paths I thought I trod until a
  sheepfold I came,
Down by a brook, with scrip and crook, a youth I
  did espy,
I asked his name, from whence he came, he said a
  shepherd boy.

The sheepfold being on a plain, near to a camp it
  lay,
The lovely lambs around their dams did fondly
  sport and play,
The fields were green, all things I seen to me did
  yield much joy,
But nothing there I could compare to the young
  shepherd's boy.

He got a pack placed on his back and a staff in his
  right hand;
'This very day I must obey my father's just
  command.'
I asked him were he was bound for, he made a
  quick reply,
'To yonder camp I must repair, although a
  shepherd's boy.

'My brethren I must go and see, they're fighting
  for the king,
This very hour their hearts I'll cheer, glad tidings
  I'll them bring.
I asked him how he could get there, or climb yon
  mount so high;
'A mark,' he said, 'was left to me to guide the
  shepherd boy.'

When we came into the camp I saw a terrible
  sight,
Two armies there they did prepare for to renew the
  fight;
A man six cubits and a span his brethren did
  defy,
None in that place that dare him face but the
  young shepherd's boy.

The king says, 'This Goliath does fill our camp
  with awe,
Whoever does this monster kill shall be my son-in-
  law.'
'Then I will go and lay him low,' the youth he did
  reply;
'Then go,' says he, 'Lord be with thee, my valiant
  shepherd boy.'

Then out of the brook five stone[s] he took and
  placed them in his scrip,
Undauntedly across the plain this gallant youth
  did trip,
At the first blow he laid him low, cut off his head
  forby,
He dropped his sling and they made a king of the
  young shepherd's boy.

Now for to conclude and finish this wondrous
  dream of mine,
There is none but he who is born free shall ever
  know the line;
So fill your glass, round let it pass, for I am
  getting dry,
And toast with me to the memory of the young
  shepherd's boy.

My Parents Reared Me Tenderly
[H466: 5 Nov 1932]

s: (m) "Willie Returned from Waterloo"; o: (m) "Bold Jack Donahoe." Other title: "The Soldier Boy."

Source: (m) John McAfee, fiddler (North Antrim fairs).

s: ... John M'Afee ... fiddles at the fairs in North Antrim, and is here seen at Dervock fair on Thursday last.

l: The photograph of fiddler McAfee is one of the few that ever appeared in the printed columns of the Henry collection. There are several unlikely interval jumps in the sol-fa notation of the melody as originally printed.

Key D.

My parents reared me tenderly, I being their only
  son,
But little they thought it would be my lot to follow
  the fife and drum,
They reared me up in fear of God, kept me from
  toiling sore,

Sam Henry's Songs of the People

Which makes me sigh and often say I wish that the wars were o'er.

For to improve my learning I went to school a while,
And my by own industry I went in decent style;
Strong liquor being in my head as I strolled through Glasgow green,
I with Joe Barber did enlist to go and serve the queen.

When I had learnt my exercises, 'twas then I did inquire
If I would have my liberty when five years would expire,
The answer that they gave to me, it grieved my heart full sore:
I would not have my liberty for twenty years or more.

I took the second bounty, I fear it is for life,
To cross the briny ocean, the gun to be my wife,
And since it's so that I must go and leave my native shore,
Oh, love, don't mourn, for I'll return when the cruel wars are o'er.

The Black Horse [H586: 23 Feb 1935]

s: (m) Hebridean "Cashelnagleanna." Other titles: "The Airy Bachelor," "Pat Reilly."

Source: (w) (Bushmills); (m) D. E. M. Smith, esq (Wandsworth Crescent, Belfast).

s: ... [I]n the town of Bushmills ... this song is an old favourite. "The Black Horse" was the name of the 7th Dragoon Guards (Princess Royal's), a regiment first raised in Derbyshire by William, first Duke of Devonshire at the time of the English Revolution to uphold the Protestant cause. It was originally known as the Tenth Regiment and subsequently as Schomberg's Horse. It fought at the Battle of the Boyne. The present name was given to the regiment in 1788. It fought at the Somme in July 1916, attached to the 18th Cavalry.

Key C.

Come all ye airy bachelors, a warning take by me,
I would have you shun night-walking, likewise bad companee,
For I lived as happy as a prince when I lived in the north,
For the first of my misfortunes was to 'list on the Black Horse.

It was on a certain Tuesday to Galway I did go,
And meeting a small officer, it proved my overthrow.
I met with Sergeant Ackeson in the market as I went down,
He says, 'Young man, would you enlist and be a light dragoon?'

'Oh no, kind sir, a soldier's life with me would not agree,
Nor neither would I bind myself down from my liberty,
For I lived happy as a prince, my mind does tell me so,
So fare you well, I'm just going down, my shuttle for to throw.'

'Oh, are you in a hurry, or are you going away?
Oh, won't you stop and listen to these words I'm going to say?
Perhaps now, cousin Charlie, you might do something worse
Than leave your native country and 'list on the Black Horse.'

Through all his kind persuasions with him I did agree,
I left my native country and fought for liberty;
Farewell to my old father, likewise my sisters three,
And farewell to you, dear mother, for your face I'll never see.
When I'm going through Armagh town you will run in my mind,
So fare you well, sweet Carlow town and the girl I left behind.

Pat Reilly [H574: 1 Dec 1934]

Other titles: "John(nie)(y) Collishaw (Coughlin) (Golicher) (Gallac(g)her)."

Source not given.

s: An old song from the heart, "spelt by the unlettered muse," preserved here for old time's sake. In verse four the air is repeated for lines five and six.

Key F.

It being on a Monday morning, it being our play day,
I met Sergeant Jenkins at our going away;
Says he to Pat Reilly, 'You're a handsome young man,
We'll go down to John Kelly's, where we'll get a dram.'

A7 / The Irish soldier boy

And while we sat boozing and drinking our dram,
He says to Pat Reilly, 'You're a handsome young
  man,
I'd have you take the bounty, come along with me
To the sweet County Longford, strange faces
  you'll see.'

Oh, it's I took the bounty, the reckoning was
  paid,
The ribbons were bought, I got up the cockade;
It's early the next morning we all had to stand
Before our grand general with our hats in our
  hand.

He says to Pat Reilly, 'You're a little too low,
With some other regiment I'm afraid you must go.'
I may go where I will, I have no one to mourn,
For my mother she's dead and will never return;
My father's twice married, brought a stepmother
  home,
And she fairly denies me and does me disown.

It's not in the morning that I sing my song,
But it's in the cold evening when I walk my lone,
With my gun o'er my shoulder I bitterly weep
When I think of my loved one that's now fast
  asleep.

My blessing on my mother, reared me neat and
  clean;
Bad luck to my father, made me serve the queen.
If he had been honest and learned me my trade,
I never would have listed or wore the cockade.

Pat Muldoney
[H832b: BLp, 4 Nov 1939; -m, 14 Oct 1939]

s: (m) "I'm off to Philadelphia in the Morning."

Author Frank O'Kane (Gortanure, Maghera, Co.
Derry).

s: [This] song was sung for the first time in
public at the entertainment given by the Rotary
Club of Coleraine to the officers and men of the
Light Anti-Aircraft Battery (R.A.) prior to their
departure from Coleraine. The words of the song
were published in the *Northern Constitution* in
our issue of 14th October [1939].

m: Although this song is in the same column as
H832a, Sam Henry's initials appear above it [im-
plying that he was not responsible for its pres-
ence]. Yet he had a broadside reprint in his
papers.
  [As Henry indicates,] the text also appears in
the [issue] of 14th October 1939, signed by Frank
O'Kane, with the added note: "The Song Editor
received this excellent war ballad and has pleasure in submitting it as most opportune and inspiring." The tune is indicated by title in this
printing also.

[Prints from British Library microfilm file of
Northern Constitution kindly furnished by
John Moulden.]

Key D.

My name is Pat Muldoney from a place called
  Munterloney,
I'm leaving now the cot where I was born in,
So I'll bid farewell to Erin and the lofty hills of
  Sperrin,
As I'm bound for France and freedom in the
  morning.

  *With my rifle o'er my shoulder, sure there's no
    boy could be bolder,*
  Let Hitler and Von Ribbentrop take warning,
  *For the Huns are loved in no land, so we'll pay
    them back for Poland,*
  *And I'm off to France and freedom in the
    morning.*

At the end of Casey's boreen, where I parted
  brown-haired Noreen,
For me all other lovers she was scorning,
But although I'm forced to leave her, sure I
  never will deceive her,
She'll be Mrs Pat Muldoney some fine morning.

There was grieving and vexation at the local
  railway station,
As the rising sun the heavens was adorning,
And my heart was sad, by jabers, to part with
  kind old neighbours
And to fight for France and freedom in the
  morning.

The hungry lords of Prussia and the Bolshevists
  of Russia
Across the plains of Poland may be swarming,
But the French and British forces will soon
  change the pirates' courses
And bring freedom back to Poland some fine
  morning.

So farewell unto my mother, to my sisters and my
  brother,
I'm bound for France where our brigade is
  forming,
And the Nazi institution that is used for
  persecution
Will meet with retribution some fine morning.

[In the *Northern Constitution*, 14 Oct 1939, the
name is "Muldooney" throughout.]

You Broken-Hearted Heroes
[H549: 9 Jun 1934]

o: "Winding Banks of Erne."

81

Sam Henry's Songs of the People

Source: (Lisnagogue district).

Key G.

You broken-hearted heroes that love your liberty,
I hope you'll pay attention and listen unto me:
It being of a bold militia man, did lately
  volunteer,
He has left his lovely Sally, the girl that he loved
  dear.

He was a proper tall young man, and few could
  him excel,
And for his regimentals, he does become them
  well;
He is forced to take the bounty and then to sail
  awa',
And leave his lovely Sally and the county of
  Armagh.

His Sally she convoyed her love as far as to
  Belfast,
And when no farther she could get, she had to
  part at last,
With a loud lamentation she cried out on the
  shore,
'Oh Jamie, lovely Jamie, will I never see you
  more?'

As they were these words discoursing, they heard
  the trumpet sound,
He kissed, shook hands and parted, saying, 'Love,
  away I'm bound.'
He with his pocket handkerchief his tears did wipe
  awa',
Saying, 'Go home, my lovely Sally, to the county
  of Armagh.'

When she heard these doleful news, she fell unto
  the ground,
Her lovely links of yellow hair and snow-white
  hands she [w]rung,
Saying, 'Jamie, lovely Jamie, for you I am
  undone,
I am banished from my parents, and how can I go
  home?'

It's Jamie's honoured father, he being standing
  by
To see this couple's parting, the tears fell from
  his eye,
Saying 'Sally, lovely Sally, come home and live
  with me,
Till Jamie does return again, I'll be father unto
  thee.'

It was all that long night over, Sally tossed and
  made great moan
To think of Jamie's pillow so cold and mortal lone;
'It's how can I contented be, and him so far awa'?
The boy I thought would live and die with me in
  sweet Armagh.'

It's to conclude and finish, I mean to drop my
  pen,
Here's a health to all militia men that lately
  crossed the main,
For they're the boys that fear no noise where the
  cannon loud does roar,
Like hearts of steel they'll stand the field on
  another foreign shore.

Lovely Sally [H724: 9 Oct 1937]

Source not given.

Key G.

You broken-hearted heroes that love your liberty,
I hope you pay attention and listen unto me:
It's of a bold militia man who did lately volunteer
And left his lovely Sally, the girl he once loved
  dear.

He was a proper tall young man, there's few could
  him excel,
And for his regimentals, he does become them
  well;
He is forced to take the bounty and for to sail
  awa'
And leave his lovely Sally in the county of
  Armagh.

It's Sally she convoyed her love as far as to
  Belfast,
And when no farther she could get, she had to
  turn at last,
With loud, loud lamentations she cried out on the
  shore,
'Oh Jamie, lovely Jamie, will I never see you
  more?'

As they these words discoursed, they heard the
  trumpet sound;
They kissed, shook hands and parted, saying,
  'Love, I must be bound,'
And with his pocket handkerchief the tears he
  wiped awa',
Saying, 'Go home, my lovely Sally, to the county
  of Armagh.'

Now when Sally heard this doleful news, she fell
   unto the ground,
Her golden links of golden hair with snow-white
   hand she wrung,
Saying, 'Jamie, lovely Jamie, for you I am
   undone,
I'm banished from home and parents, and how can
   I go home?'

It's Jamie's aged father, he had been standing by
To see these couple, the tears fell from his eye,
Saying, 'Come home, my lovely Sally, come home
   and live with me,
Till Jamie does return again, your father I will
   be.'

Oh, it's all that whole night over, Sally tossed
   and made great moan
To think of lovely Jamie out in the world alone,
Saying, 'How can I contented be with him so far
   awa'?
The boy I thought would live and die with me in
   sweet Armagh.'

Now to conclude and finish, I mean to end my
   song;
Here's a health to all militia men who proudly
   march along,
For they're the boys who fear no noise while loud
   the cannons roar,
Like hearts of steel they stand the field far from
   their native shore.

The Deserter [H223: 18 Feb 1928]

Other title: "Kelly's Lamentation."

Source: coll. Joseph F. M'Ginnis (339 Fifth St,
Brooklyn, NY), (m) from his cousin, Lawrence
M'Dermott (Brooklyn), (w) from M'Dermott's
grandfather (West Bars, Co. Leitrim) c. 1858,
completed by Hugh Murray (Managher), from his
mother c. 1865.

s: ... A version to a different air has been collected in the Dromore district of Co. Down [see
JIFSS ref. below]. The chorus is repeated at
the end of each verse.

Key G.

My parents and me could not agree,
On account of my nights' rambling,
I vowed a vow and a solemn vow
That I would leave their dwelling.

   Too-ri-ay, fol-de-diddle-day,
   Too-ri-ay, ri-ad-dy.

Then to a fair I did repair
In hopes to find a master;
To my sad grief I found one there,
Which makes me a deserter.

I had not been long in the town
Till the sergeant he came to me,
'What would you think, my lad,' said he,
'To pad the road with me, sir?'

'Oh no, oh no, kind sir,' I said,
'It's hiring I am bound for.'
'If you go with me, you'll be neat and clean,
See here now, take the shilling.'

'What would you think, my lad,' said he,
To go and get share of a noggin?'
'Oh no, oh no, the money is scarce,
To go I am unwilling.'

'There is a shilling I'll lend to you,
And we'll go sit and spend it,
Unto a tavern we will go
Where we'll get liquor plenty.'

Unto a tavern we did go,
Where we got liquor freely,
I scarce had paid a shot but two,
Daylight was disappearing.

The sergeant he came up to me,
He says, 'You're listed fairly,
Tomorrow you must march with me,
And that will be right early.'

When my mother heard tell of it,
That I was listed fairly,
Twenty guineas she did lay down
To buy me from the army.

'Oh no, oh no,' the sergeant said,
'For he has listed fairly,
Tomorrow morning he shall march,
And that will be right early.'

The time I was learning my exercise,
The weather it being warm,
I thought my heart would break in two
When I thought on sweet Lough Erne.

They put a black stock on my neck,
On my body a steel jacket,
And never a time I turned myself round
But the red blood it was flowing.

I climbed up to the sentry box,
I threw down gun and bayonet,
I thought to myself I would desert
While the guard house it was silent.

At twelve o'clock in the sentry box,
I threw down gun and bayonet,
I cleared the wall, made my way good,
And was bound for sweet Lough Erne.

Sam Henry's Songs of the People

I scarce had been a mile out of town
When I heard the drums a-beating,
I looked around and then I saw
One hundred men appearing.

I threw myself in a rampart deep,
And the green grass covered me over,
They passed me by and saw me not,
Nor they never spied poor Kelly.

When I came to my father's door,
'Who's that?' cries out my mother;
'It is your son, and your only son,'
Cries out my aged father.

My mother wrung her hands and cried,
And likewise did my father,
'If it be your son and your only son,
He's home as a deserter.'

He walked about his father's domain
For six long days and better,
And never a time his foot did lift
But his poor heart felt the fetter.

The seventh day he in sickness lay,
And the seventeenth day was buried,
His comrade boys took him away
And buried him in sweet Lough Erne.

3.3: ... me lad,' [Dt]
5.2: ... and share a noggin? [Dt]
7.2: ... liquor plenty, [Dt]
10.3: Tomorrow he ... [Dt]
16.3: ... and they saw ... [Dt]

Bonny Woodha' [H476: 14 Jan 1933]

o: (m) "The Green Bushes"; g: "Sweet Calder Burn."

Source not given.

Key G.

Down by yon green bushes, near Calder's clear
  stream,
Where I and my Annie sae often have been,
When the hours that flew past us, right happy
  were we,
It was little she thought that a sailor I'd be.

I said to my Annie, 'I now must away,
My country calls on me and I must obey,
But if heaven protect me until I return,
I will wed you, my Annie, near Calder's clear
  burn.'

On the fourteenth of August our regiment was
  lost,
When a ball from the enemy my line came across,
It struck me on the forehead, the blood trickled
  down,
I reeled and I staggered and I fell to the ground.

'Come here,' said our captain, 'come here with
  good speed,
For I fear by this bullet young Dinsmore lies
  dead.'
Two men with a stretcher did quickly prepare
And they carried me off to an hospital there.

Cold water and brandy they poured out so free,
And they turned me all over, my wounds for to
  see,
But if I had my Annie to bind up my wound,
One kiss from her sweet lips would deaden the
  stoun.

It's when I am weary and think on lang syne,
When I was a miner and wrought in yon mine,
The tears they do trickle and down they do fa'
Like the dew on the roses near bonny Woodha'.

5.4: stoun [stound] = pang, throb, pain. [m]

My Son Ted [H131: 15 May 1926]

A song of the peninsular wars.

o: "Mrs McGra[th]"; g: "Widow Magra," "Teddy McGraw." Other titles: "My Son Tim," "The Sergeant Said"; cf. "Felix the Soldier," "The Frenchman's Ball."

Source: Henry R. Browning (Redford, Moy, Co. Tyrone), [Dt] learned from a médical student in Belfast c. 1876.

[Dt] s: This song won first prize in the Folk Song section, Coleraine Festival....

[Alternative chorus and stanza 7 in Dt only, not in Bp.]

Key F.

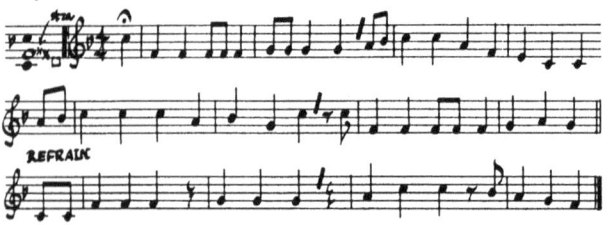

'Och, Misses Magra,' the sergeant said,
'Would you make a sojer of your son Ted?
Wid a big long sword an' a three-cock'd hat,
Och, Mrs Magra, how would you like that?'

  With a fal la la, fal la la,
  [F]al la la, fal la la la.

[Dt:] Alternative chorus:
With me ran-tan-ah, toor-an-ah,
My son was a Teddy McGra.

With his three-cock'd hat and his scarlet coat,
She bid Ted farewell at the dure o' the boat,
Saying, 'Farewell, Ted, when I see you again
It's mebbe you'll be marrit to the queen o' Spain.'

Now Mrs Magra's gone down to the shore
For the space of seven long years or more,
When a great big ship came across the say,
'Hooh! Whillabaloo, neighbours, clear the way.'

Now Mrs Magra to the captain said,
'Have ye just come over from Madrid?
It's have you heerd tell of my son Ted,
Is the crature alive or is he dead?'

Now Ted he has landed without any legs,
And instead of them he has two wooden pegs,
And after kisses, a dozen or two,
'Och, Ted, my jewel, sure this isn't you.

'Arrah, were you sleepin' or were you blind
When you left your darlin' legs behind?
Or were ye walkin' upon the sea
That you've worn them this way up to the knee?'

'Faith, I neither was asleep nor yet was I blind
When I left my own two legs behind,
But a thunderin' cannon ball came one day
And it shot your own son's legs away.'

'Now it's mighty wars I will proclaim
Agin Boneyparte an' the queen o' Spain,
And it's me that'll make them rue the time
That they ever shot the shins off a son o' mine.'

1.1: Och, Missus Magra ... [Dt]
4.2: Have you come ... [Dt]
6.3: ... you walkin' upon the say [Dt]
8.3: ... me that'd make ... [Dt]

Lovely Jamie [H618: 5 Oct 1935]

Source: (Dunloy district).

1: The refrain must be sung twice to fit the tune.
This is the same kind of bitter humor expressed
in "Mrs McGrath" (= H151 "My Son Ted").

Key F.

A7 / The Irish soldier boy

Come all you jolly mariners and listen unto me,
I'll sing you some good verses now that we are free,
All about two fine sons who are listed far from me,
Ay, and went to fight the Roosians away in the Crimee.

To my ring dou daw, fond the deedle day,
O Jamie, lovely Jamie, what made you go away?
To my ring dou daw, fond the deedle day,
O Jamie, lovely Jamie, what made you go away?

Well, I'll tell you why they 'listed and what it was about,
They soul' a load o' peats and they joined and drunk it out.
My brother Darby swore that he'd have revenge for that,
So he went to seek his fortune upon that very spot.

Then we blackened up our brogues and we started right away
And we never said 'Crank' till we came to Belfast Quay,
Where we spied two sergeants walking up the street,
And to take the shilling we went up the pair to meet.

O, it's when we landed there we bargained on the spot
To go to fight the Roosians, let us be killed or not;
They gave to us the shilling, these words to us did say:
'To the right about turn, boys, you're bound for the Crimee.'

O, when we landed there, sure, the war was raging hot,
We went off to take Sebastopool on the very spot,
Like divils we kept shooting at great big heaps of stones,
Till my brother Jamie lost his legs and lost the marrow bone.

But in a short time after, we got the thing complete,
We got a pair of wooden legs that fitted him so neat.
When I looked all around me, my brother Darby I spied
With his head hanging down and his knapsack by his side.

But who'll cut the turf and who'll mow the hay,
Or who'll shear the corn since Jamie went away?
Or ah, Jamie, lovely Jamie, but you were a mortal fool
For to go and dash your brains out against Sebastipool.

Or ah, what will my sweetheart Maggie think o' me,
Since I hae lost the twa legs out in the Crimee?

Sam Henry's Songs of the People

When I ask her hand in mine, she will say, 'You
  silly goose,
Sure a man without the legs is not the laste of
  use.'

But cheer up, my lads, for we're going to have
  good fun,
For all the oul' women are goin' to take the guns,
They shall be boldly coutered with large bustles
  on their backs
Before they fight the Russians or stand the
  grand attack.

r.3,4: [*Not in original Dp, but original sol-fa
  tune requires a repetition.*]

2.2: soul' = sold.
8.4: laste = least.
9.3: coutered = accoutered, furnished, equipped.
[en]['l]list, take the [king's] shilling = enlist in the
  army or navy.

The Hungry Army   [H92: 15 Aug 1925]

Source: Hamilton Hemingway (ex-constable,
R[oyal] I[rish] C[onstabulary], from John Doyle,
corporal, Kildare Rifles, c. 1885; from John Bailey, itinerant shoemaker, former soldier, "Third
Buffs" (Bog of Allen district).

s: A serio-comic of the old army days.... The
hero of the song was evidently in the Marine Artillery, whose headquarters was in Chatham, and
the pay was 4d a day.

Key E flat.

The wind in thundering gales did blow
As I left my home in black October,
The rain and hail in torrents came
And the world, I thought, was surely over.
The reason was my colleen dhas
And I fell out about cousin Barney,
So I bid farewell to hungry Kells
And I went into Dublin to join the army.

  *Rad le whack, fol ol the dol, ol the dol, ol the
    dol ay,
  Fol ol the dol, ol the dol addy.*

When I arrived in Dublin town,
I crossed the Liffey, that splendid river,
At the castle yard a big black guard
Asked me to enlist, the blacks to skiver.

I did agree, then he gave me
A gun, but the weight of it soon did warm me,
So I hired myself to the powers of Guelph
To go and smash China along with the army.

Next morning the corporal roars out, 'March!
In the barracks of Chatham you'll soon be
  quartered.'
'By the powers, I'll see that you won't quarter
  me,
For I didn't join you here to be slaughtered.'
The sergeant then said that I should be made,
But I knew that the colonel was tipping me
  blarney --
Och, the stripes I got on an awkward spot!
When my back was aching I cursed the army.

In a ship as big as a town we sailed,
In every hole and corner stuffing us,
To keep out the coul' I went into the houl'
By my sowl, it wouldn't hold half enough of us,
We were smothered to death for want of our
  breath,
And bursting with hunger, which didn't much
  charm me,
We were ordered to land and make a brave stand.
They might easy say 'Stand' to a hungry army.

On the field of battle I hadn't been long
Until I was wishing it all to be over;
To let a ball pass I sat down on the grass,
I didn't imagine myself in clover.
Och, that ball I can tell was a great bomb shell,
I got struck in the rere, but it didn't much harm
  me,
When to the next charge we got orders to march,
I'd a lame excuse for a halt in the army.

Unfit for the service, I got my discharge,
'Hook it, you cripple,' says uncle Toby,
'A pension you'll get, or if not, you'll be let
Go out to Kilmainham to be an old fogey.'
Och, should I live for four score years
With a fogey's fire all day to warm me,
I'll remember the day I got gunpowder tay
When I went up to Dublin to join the army.

1.8: And to Dublin went to ... [Dt]
2.3: ... big blackguard [Dt]
3.3: ... powers that be, you ... [Dt]
5.5: ... that bomb I ... [Dt]
5.7: ... we orders ... [Dt]
6.7: ... went to Dublin ... [Dt]
5.6: ... the rear ... [Dt]
5.7: ... we orders to ... [Dt]
6.8: ... went to Dublin ... [Dt]

[*Sam Henry's glossary:*]
1.5: colleen dhas = sweetheart. [Bp, Dt]
2.4: the blacks to skiver = to bayonet the foreign
  foe of the Ethiopian race [Bp]; to kill black men.
  [Dt]
2.7: powers of Guelph = the reigning royal family of
  England. [Bp]
6.2: Uncle Toby = an army phrase for the authorities
  in charge. [Bp]
6.4: old fogey = an old soldier. [Bp]
6.4: Kilmainham = in those days, Royal Hospital for
  old soldiers. [Bp]
6.7: gunpowder tay = military rations. [Bp]

The Plains of Waterloo (I) [H15: 23 Feb 1924]

A song of love and war.

Other title: "Waterloo."

Source: (m) R. R. Brownlow (Ballylagan, Cloyfin, Coleraine).

Key F.

Come all ye loyal lovers, I pray you to draw near,
Till I indite a verse or two I mean to let you hear,
In the praises of a worthy youth who was always just and true,
Who fought through Spain and Portugal and fell at Waterloo.

This young man that I sing about was proper, tall and trim,
His body like the waxwork, there were few could equal him,
His cheeks they were a rosy red, his eyes a dark, dark blue,
With my charming fair none could compare on the plains of Waterloo.

At the taking of Salamanca the Frenchmen topped the hill,
The small guns loud did rattle betwixt shot and shell did kill,
My love he fell a victim 'mongst thousands that lay slew,
Far from his own to hear his moan on the plains of Waterloo.

When the fight was at its fiercest they fought with and will
When guns did loudly rattle and shot and shell did kill.
My love he fell a victim 'mongst thousands that fate slew,
Far from his own to hear him moan on the plains of Waterloo.

My love he lay the whole night o'er, my love he lay in pain,
When the war was spread he raised his head and daylight came again,
When that his comrades found him 'mongst thousands that fate slew,
They discoursed my love an hour or more on the plains of Waterloo.

A7 / The Irish soldier boy

'Farewell, farewell my comrades dear, likewise to my sweetheart,'
They were the last words that he said and then he did depart.
They dug my love a silent grave, their tears they were not few,
They laid him away in the cold, cold clay on the plains of Waterloo.

The more he's gone and left me, no other will I take,
Through lonesome woods and shady groves I'll wander for his sake,
Through lonesome woods and shady groves I'll wander through and through,
And mourn for him that's dead and gone on the plains of Waterloo.

3.: [*Stanza not in* Bp.]
4.: [Bp; "or alternatively --" in Dt.]
4.3, 5.3: ... that lay slew, [Dt]

The Plains of Waterloo (II)
[H608: 27 Jul 1935]

Source: Kennedy Clinton (Coolderry, Coleraine).

Key C.

It bein' on the eighth of June, brave boys, eighteen hundred and fifteen,
With horse and foot we did advance, most glorious to be seen,
With horse and foot we did advance to the trumpet horn that blew,
And the sons of France, we made them dance on the plains of Waterloo.

Is yon Britannia's mountains I do see, yon place where I have been,
And likewise, too, my brown-haired girl, her fair face I have seen.
The very last words I spoke to her, it was, 'My love, adieu,
I must go and fight my foe, or fall at Waterloo.'

On the sixteenth day of June, brave boys, a letter I received
From off a mounted cavalry belonging to the Scots Greys,
And these few lines I will indite, and oftimes will renew,
Oh, when I think on my darling boy who's bound for Waterloo.

Sam Henry's Songs of the People

My love embarked from the Cove of Cork and
  crossed the stormy main,
And many's the battle he has fought through
  Portugal and Spain,
Many's the battle he has fought, ay, and oh, he
  had come through,
But alas, he lies to mould away on the plains of
  Waterloo.

The man who did my darling kill, no pardon
  need he crave,
Who left my darling boy to lie, alas, in that cold
  grave,
Oh, there to lie and mould away with many's a
  hero, too,
Oh, when I think on my darling boy, I dream of
  Waterloo.

The Drummer Boy at Waterloo
[H728: 6 Nov 1937; Laws J1]

Other titles: "... of ...," "... Edwin of Waterloo."

Source: (Bushmills).

Key G.

When England calls her warlike band,
Cannons roar and trumpets blow,
Young Edmond left his native land,
A drummer boy for Waterloo.

That dauntless youth was free from fears,
His knapsack o'er his shoulder drew,
Saying, 'Mother dear, dry up your tears,
For I'll return from Waterloo.'

His mother pressed him to her breast,
Her only son she bade adieu;
With wringing hands and heart distressed,
She saw him march for Waterloo.

And as he marched with sword and shield,
The enemy came into view;
A bullet on the battlefield
Soon laid him low at Waterloo.

They laid his head upon his drum,
All sprinkled o'er with midnight dew;
When night had passed and morning come,
They dug his grave at Waterloo.

The Bonny Light Horseman
[H122a: BLp, 13 Mar 1926]

A [BLp, Bt: Love] song of the Napoleonic Wars.

Other title: "Broken-Hearted I Wander."

Source: (m) John Parkhill (Railway Terrace, Coleraine), from his father.

s: This simple and haunting air is composed in the old Irish gapped scale in which the 4th and 7th notes of the modern scale do not occur. It is probably more than 400 years old. The song, adapted to this air, had widespread popularity in the days of Waterloo....
[Written at top of Bt] Waves of Torry -- College Lawn; Miss Lyons.

[The first two stanzas and new refrain appear only in Wt and Dt, the later copies which also include the second tune.]

[BLp] Key G. [Bt] Key F. [No key given for this tune on other copies.]

[H122b: D(c)=W(c)]

Source: (m) Valentine Crawford (Bushmills).

Key G.

Ye wise maids and widows, pray listen to me,
Unto this sad tale I rehearse unto thee:
A maid in distress who will now be a rover,
She relies upon George for the loss of her lover.

  Broken-hearted I'll wander for the loss of my
    lover,
  My bonny light horseman, in the wars he was
    slain.

Three years and six months since he left
  England's shore,
My bonny light horseman, will I ne'er see him
  more?
He's mounted on horseback, so gallant and gay,
And among the whole regiment respected was he.

When Boney commanded his armies to stand,
He levelled his cannon right over the land,
He levelled his cannons his victory to gain
And he slew my light horseman on the way
  coming hame.

The dove she laments for her mate as she flies;
'Oh where, tell me where is my darling?' she cries,
And where in this world is there one to compare
With my bonny light horseman who was slain in the war?'

1., 2.: [Not in BLp, Bt.]
r.: [substituted in BLp, Bt:]
Broken-hearted I'll wander, broken-hearted I'll remain
Since my bonny light horseman in the wars he was slain.
3.2: ... his cannons right ... [BLp, Bt]
4.3: ... fond wings I'd ... [BLp, Bt]

The Irish Soldier Boy

[H678: 21 Nov 1936; cf. Laws K13]

Source: Randal Hutchinson (the Aird, Giant's Causeway).

s: ... "Lochaber" district is very musical, which would point to the Highland origin of its folk.

Key D.

At a cottage door one winter night as the snow lay on the ground
Stood a woeful Irish soldier boy, to foreign lands was bound.
His mother stood beside him, saying, 'My boy, you'll win, don't fear.'
With loving arms around his waist she tied his bandoleer.

'Good-bye, God bless you, mother dear, I hope your heart won't pain,
But pray to God your soldier boy you soon will see again,
And when I'm out in the firing line, it will be a source of joy
To know that you're a mother proud of an Irish soldier boy.'

When the fighting it was over and the flag of hope was raised,
The leaders ordered the firing cease and the foe was sore dismayed,
His comrades came to the cottage door with a note from her pride and joy,
Containing the news and sad appeal of an Irish soldier boy:

'Good-bye, God bless you, mother dear, I'm dying a death so grand
Of wounds received in action trying to free my native land,
But I hope we'll meet in heaven above, in the land beyond the sky,
Where you'll always be in company with your Irish soldier boy.

'Then goodbye, farewell to Donegal, Kilkenny and Mayo,
Tipperary, Derry and Tyrone, where the bushes green do grow,
But when at night you'll kneel to pray, it will be a source of joy
To know that you're in memory still with your Irish soldier boy.'

The Three Flowers of Chivalry

[H99: 3 Oct 1925]

Source: (w) third textbook, National Schools, c. 1865; (m) A. E. Boyd [principal teacher, Cullycapple School] (Aghadowey).

m: author Andrew Orr, in *The Feast of Reason*.

Key E flat.

'Twas on the black Crimean shore, when midnight shadows met,
Around a camp fire, red and low, a warrior band was set,
But mute their tongues and bent their brows and gone the pulse aglee
As wild before them rose the sight tomorrow's sun should see.

'Cheer up!' cries out a gallant youth, 'let us drain a cup of wine
To Erin and to life, farewell: this parting pledge be mine.'
'And I am from green Erin, too,' a gallant youth replied,
'My boyhood spent in mirth and love on Brandon's heathery side.

'And my Mary there, with auburn hair, may comb and curl them now,
For she'll see me soon on Malin Bay with laurels on my brow.'
'There's a hand to each, my countrymen,' said a soldier stern and tall,
'My father sets his lines and nets on the coast of Donegal.'

Sam Henry's Songs of the People

'And Annie with her line-white locks and lips of
  magnet power
Blooms sweet among the heather bells, a matchless
  mountain flower;
Do you see that ring?   She placed it there the
  day our ship set sail,
I've borne it far o'er flood and field with a heart
  that scorns to fail.'

'Tis morn, but oh, the work of death has met the
  troubled eye,
It has flooded fire from spire to spire, it has
  flamed from sky to sky;
Cheers for the brave, the day is ours, our flag
  is floating fair,
But cold in death these gallant hearts who helped
  to place it there.

The banner of Britannia waves beside the flag of
  France,
The hero's death his country saves by ball and
  sword and lance;
The flowers they left so far away shall never see
  them more,
For they sleep beneath the reddened lower of
  Russia's fatal shore.

1.3: ... gone their pulse of glee [Dt]
2.1: ... let's drain ... [Dt]
 .3: ... I am sure from Erin, ... [Dt]
 .4: ... spent on mirth ... on Brendan's ... [Dt]
4.1: ... lint-white ... [Dt]

The Heights of Alma
                    [H123: 20 Mar 1926; Laws J10]

o: (m) "As I Walked Down the Road to Sligo."
Other titles: "The Battle of ...," "Bloody ...."

Author James Maxwell, schoolmaster (Dungiven).

[Dt] s: Composed by James Maxwell, ... who married Miss Scott of Tirmeel, Dungiven. He wrote many songs of which this is the best known. No. 245 in this series ["Adieu to the Banks of the Roe"] is also from his pen.

m: John J. Marshall, in *Popular Rhymes and Sayings of Ireland* [2d ed., 1931]:141, quotes Sir Charles Gavan Duffy (Sparling 1888:41): "Fag-an-Bealach vulgarly spelled Faugh-a-Ballach -- clear the way -- was the cry with which the clans of Connaught and Munster used in faction fights to come through a fair with high heart and smashing shillelaghs. The regiments raised in the South and West took their old shout with them to the Continental wars." Marshall goes on to say that it was the use of this *cri de guerre* by the old 87th (the Prince of Wales Irish) Regiment of Foot at the battle of Barossa, that caused the regiment, now the 1st Battalion Princess Victoria (Royal Irish Fusiliers) to be nicknamed 'The Old Fogs' or the 'Faugh-a-Ballagh Boys.'... The regimental gazette is named 'Faugh-a-Ballagh.'"
  The Royal Irish Fusiliers has fairly recently (1968) been amalgamated with various other Irish Regiments to form the Royal Irish Rangers.... I find that "Faugh-a-ballagh" was the unofficial motto of the Royal Irish Fusiliers itself.

o: Tune should be 6/8.

Key C.

Ye loyal Britons, pray give ear
Unto the news I bring you here,
While joy each Briton's heart doth cheer
For the vict'ry gained at Alma.
'Twas on September the eighteenth day,
In spite of dashing salt sea spray,
We landed safe in the Crimea
Upon our route for Alma.

All night we lay on the cold ground,
Neither tent or shelter to be found,
And with the rain were nearly drowned
To cheer us for the Alma.
Next morn a burning sun did rise
Above the darkling eastern skies,
Our gallant chief Lord Raglan cries,
'Prepare to march for Alma.'

But when the Alma came in view,
The stoutest heart it would subdue
To see that Russian motley crew
Upon the heights of Alma.
They were so strongly fortified
With batteries on the mountain side,
Our general viewed the forts and cried,
'There'll be hot work at Alma.'

The shot and shell it fell like rain
While we the batteries strove to gain,
And many a hero then was slain
Upon the heights of Alma.
The Thirty-thirds and Fusiliers,
They stormed the heights with rousing cheers,
While 'Faugh-a-ballagh' rent our ears
From Hibernia's sons at Alma.

The Highland lads wi' kilt and hose,
They were not last, you may suppose,
They boldly faced the Russian foes
And gained the heights of Alma,
And when the heights we did command,
We fought the Russians hand to hand,
But the Russian bear he could not stand
Our bayonet charge at Alma.

Their guns and knapsacks they threw down,
They ran like hares before the hound,
While 'Vive l'Empereur' did resound
From the sons of France at Alma,
But though the battle we have got
And gallantly our heroes fought,
Yet dearly was the victory bought,
For thousands died at Alma.

To Sebastopol our troops have gone,
And you shall hear it before long,
The fort will fall, were it twice as strong --
We'll have revenge at Alma.
From orphans' eyes the tears do roll,
And never a widow can control
Or staunch the streams of blood that stole
From thousands slain at Alma.

Many a purty girl may mourn
For her lover that will ne'er return,
By cruel war he's from her torn,
His body lies at Alma.
Then Britain's sons may well remember
Every twentieth of September
When we made the Russian bear surrender
And gained the heights of Alma.

[Dt *typed:* ("Additional lines:"); Wt *typed,* Bp *written:*]

Brave St. Arnold's now at rest,
Light be the turf upon his breast,
I hope his spirit now is blest,
Brave hero of the Alma.

[Bp, Wt *written;* Dt *typed*]

Prince Metchnikoff ran in dismay
And left his coach in Alma.

4.7: Faugh-a-ballagh = Clear the way! [m]

Balaclava [H829: 14 Oct 1939]

k: "Cardigan the Fearless," "The Charge of the Light Brigade."

Source: (w) John Love (formerly Limavady); (m) George Graham (Cross Lane, Coleraine), learned from his father, who learned it from Robert Farren, Crimean veteran (native of Ballymoney).

s: The charge of the Light Brigade at the battle of Balaclava took place on 25th October, 1854.
Nolan was Captain Lewis Edward Nolan of the 15th Hussars. He was killed by a Russian shell which penetrated his heart. The sword fell from his hand, but the hand still remained uplifted high in air and the grasp of the practised horseman still lingered on the bridle. From the erect form of the dying man there burst forth a cry so strange and appalling that it sounded unearthly to those who heard it. The cry was rather the result of those spasmodic forces which operate in death than the voice of a human will.
When the remnant of the Light Brigade formed up after the brilliant feat of arms, Earl Cardigan came forward and said, "Men! It is a mad-brained trick but no fault of mine." Someone had blundered in the orders given, but blundered to victory.

Key D.

Six hundred stalwart warriors, of England's pride the best,
Did grasp the lance and sabre on Balaclava's crest,
And with their trusty leader, Earl Cardigan the brave,
Dashed through the Russian valley to glory or a grave.

Oh, 'tis a famous story, proclaim it far and wide,
And let your children's children re-echo it with pride;
How Cardigan the fearless his name immortal made
When he crossed the Russian valley with his famous light brigade.

Their foemen stood in thousands, a dark and awful mass,
Beneath their famous strongholds resolved to guard the pass,
Their guns with fierce defiance belched thunders up the vale,
Where sat our English horsemen firm beneath their iron gale.

When Nolan brought the order, 'Great God, can it be true?'
Cried Cardigan the fearless, 'and my brigade so few?
To take these awful cannon from yonder teeming mass,
'Tis madness, sir. Where shall we charge? What guns bring from the pass?'

And they were but six hundred 'gainst two score thousand foes,
Hemmed in by furious cannon and crushed with savage blows,
Yet fought they there like heroes for our noble England's fame;
Oh, glorious charge, heroic deed, what glory crowns thy name!

Four hundred of those soldiers fell fighting where they stood,
And thus that fatal death vale they enriched with English blood;
Four hundred of those soldiers bequeathed their lives away
To the England they had fought for on that wild October day.

Sam Henry's Songs of the People

Old Ireland Far Away

[H816: 15 Jul 1939; Laws J7]

Other titles: "The Dying Soldier," "Old Erin ...."

Source: Frank Smith (Stitchville, 16 miles from Ottawa [Canada]), noted by a Bushmills man.

s: A song of the American Civil War.

Note [to H817]: -- In last week's song, "Old Ireland Far Away," the octave marks were inadvertently omitted on the following notes:
  1st and 4th lines, 6th note
  2d and 3d lines, 7th, 8th and 14th notes
These notes should read d [superscript]1 instead of d.

Key D.

As the sun went down o'er that eager sky and the terrible war was o'er,
Thousands lay on a battlefield that life could claim no more;
The pale moon shone o'er the battlefield where a wounded soldier lay,
And the rets of death upon him crept as his heart blood crept away.

'A lock of my hair I pray you bear to my mother far o'er the sea,
And every time she looks at it, she'll fondly think of me;
Tell them at home that no more I'll roam where in childhood I used to play,
In the merry green shades on the green grass blades of old Ireland far away.

Tell my sister long years have passed since I seen her fair fond face,
Her form lies promptly in my mind, her features I can trace,
Tell them at home that no more I'll roam where in childhood I used to play,
In the merry green shades on the green grass blades of old Ireland far away.

His comrades gathered round his grave to take their last farewell,
No braver, nobler soldier had e'er in battle fell,
And as they stood around his grave, a spirit seemed to say,
'Boys, I'll no more roam in my good old home in old Ireland far away.'

1.7: rets = ?[typographical error]

❖ A7 REFERENCES ❖

❖ **The Shepherd Boy** *(H 803)* 79

IREL Moulden 1979:134-5. "Initially it was a Masonic song, but the tune has been adopted as a march by Orange bands while the song is frequently heard at gatherings of Orangemen" (p. 134).

m: BRS BCL Biggar: J2:3 (Nicholson, Belfast)

REC Tom McClung, Outlet OAS 3027 (A4) "...'s ..."

❖ **My Parents Reared Me Tenderly** *(H 466)* 79

Probably not: Brunnings 1981: "The Soldier Boy"

AMER Peacock 1965,3:1018-9 "The Soldier Boy," very similar to Henry's.

❖ **The Black Horse** *(H 586)* 80

Brunnings 1981: "...," "The Airy Bachelor"

IREL Hayward 1925:58-60 "The Airy Bachelor"
b: Hughes 2,1915:14-21 "The Airy Bachelor"
  O Lochlainn 1939:34-5
  Planxty 1976:34 "Pat Reilly," a mixture of this and H574 "Pat Reilly" (see Planxty rec.)

AMER Milner/Kaplan 1983:87

BRS BPL Irish: (n.i.)
  Healy 1,1967b:92-3 "A New Song Called ..."

O'Keeffe 1955(1968): 60 "The Airy Bachelor"; the regiment is the "Light Horse."

REC Vin Garbutt, Leader LER 2081 [Milner/Kaplan]
  Kevin Mitchell, Topic 12TS 314 (B2) "The Light Horse"
  Planxty, Shanachie 79010 (A2) "Pat Reilly"

❖ **Pat Reilly** *(H 574)* 80

Brunnings 1981: "Johnny Gallagher"

IREL Shields 1981:132-3 (#58) (see Butcher rec.)
  Shields/Shields UF 21,1975: #315

BRIT Greig/Duncan 1,1981:186 (#80) "Johnnie Gallacher," 2 vts. ("John ...")
  MT #2,1984:38 "Johnny Golicher," NLI broadside.

BRS BPL H.80: (n.i.) "Johnny Golicher"
  Harvard 3: (Henson) "Johnny Golicher"
h: NLI (n.p.d.); McCall (supp. vol., n.p.d.)
  UCLA 605: 3(n.i.) "Johnny Gallagher"
h: Healy 1,1967b:91-2 "Johnny Golicher," from brs.

REC Eddie Butcher, EEOT *Shamrock* 3 cass. (A9)
  Mary Duffy, People's Stage Tapes cass. 09 (A2) "Johnny Gallagher"
  Planxty, Shanachie 79010 (A2), a mixture of "Pat Reilly" with H586 "The Black Horse."

MEL Hudson ms. 3:715

A7 / The Irish soldier boy

◊ You Broken-Hearted Heroes *(H549) 81*

Brunnings 1981: (m) "The Winding Banks of Erne"

◊ The Deserter *(H223) 83*

? Brunnings 1981

s: IREL *JIFSS* 4,1906:19 (Henry says to a different air); 19,1922:48 is not the same song.

BRIT   Cf. Greig/Duncan 1981:192-6
       Cf. Sharp/Karpeles 1974,2:127-9

BRS Healy 1,1967b:96-8 "Kelly's Lamentation," but there are at least 2 other ballads with the same title: see O Lochlainn 1939:136-7 "The Bold Deserter" (also in Healy 1,1967b:95-6 and Kidson/Moffat [1926]:62-3).

MEL *JIFSS* 13,1909:12

◊ Bonny Woodha' *(H476) 84*

IREL   Shields/Shields *UF* 21,1975: #53

BRIT   Greig 1907-11(1963): #82
       Lloyd 1952:43-4
       Ord 1930:310
       Palmer 1977:229-30

REC   Dick Gaughan, Topic 12TS 272 (B3)
       Andy Irvine, Green Linnet SIF 3006 (= Mulligan LUN 008) (A4) "... Woodhall"

◊ My Son Ted *(H131) 84*

Brunnings 1981: "Mrs McGrath"

IREL   Behan 1967:71-2 "Mrs McGrath"
       Loesberg 2,1980:6-7
b: O Lochlainn 1939:1142-3 "Mrs McGrath"

AMER   Creighton 1971:161, a fragment.
       Dean 1922:48-9 "Teddy McGraw"
       Cf. Flanders 1934:52-3 "The Frenchman's Ball"
       B. Ives 1955:79-81
       Cf. Lomax/Lomax 1941:198-9 "The Frenchman's Ball"
       Cf. Warner 1984:144-5 "Felix the Soldier"

AUST   Meredith/Anderson 1967:197-8
       B. Scott, *Penguin 2* 1980:120-3

BRS   Harvard 1: 10.176 (Bebbington)
b: Healy 1978 "The Widow McGrath"
       Healy 1962(1968):104-5 "The Widow McGrath"
In Dublin's 1968:66-8 "Mrs. McGrath (The Sergeant Said)"
       Songs and Recitations 5,1978:30-1 "Mrs. McGrath"
       Walton's New 1,1966:42-3

REC   Seamus Ennis, *CWL* 1, Columbia AKL 4941 (B3, 32) "Mrs. McGrath"
       Timothy Walsh, *FSB* 8 (B7) "... Tim"
b: Big Bill Broonzy and Pete Seeger in Concert, Verve/Folkways FV 9008 "Mrs McGrath"
       Peg Clancy Power, Folk-Legacy FSE 8 (B7) "Mrs. McGrath"
       Lori Holland, Folkways FG 3518 (B5) "Mrs. McGrath"
b: Ed McCurdy, Prestige/Int. 13002 "Mrs McGrath"
       Tommy Makem, Tradition TLP 1044 (B3) "Mrs. McGrath"
       John Millar, Folkways FH 5275 (A5)
b: Frank Ritchie, Request RLP 8057 "Mrs McGrath"
       Robin Roberts, Stinson SLP 63 [Bikel]; b: Prestige/Int. 13017 "Mrs McGrath"
       Pete Seeger, Folkways FTS 1018 (formerly FA 2455, FA 5233) (B4) "Mrs McGrath"

b: MEL Philharmonic Promenade Orchestra, Vanguard VRS 1093 "Mrs McGrath"

◊ The Hungry Army *(H92) 86*

BRIT   Lloyd 1967:200-1, partial text only.
     But not: Palmer 1977:79-81.

BRS Belfast Madden 24 (#743)

◊ The Plains of Waterloo (I) *(H15) 87*

White/Dean-Smith 1951
Dean-Smith 1954: "Waterloo"
Brunnings 1981

IREL   Moulden 1979:118 cites "Songs of the People" #270, published after Sam Henry left the column; collector not known.

AMER   Milner/Kaplan 1983:155-6

BRS   BPL H.80
       Harvard 1: 4.26 (Gilbert), 9.182 (Bebbington)

l: Both Henry's "Plains of Waterloo" ballads are similar in their broadside style, meter, and outcome, but otherwise differ quite a bit. His other version, H608, tells a much less coherent story than this one.
    For some of the other ballads, see Laws 1957:129-30, 219-20 (J3, J4, N32) and compare the following:

BRIT   Greig/Duncan 1,1981:373-9 (#152)
       Handle et al. 1972:28-9

AMER   Fowke 1965:54-6 (see also Abbott rec.)
       Fowke 1973:154-5 (also from O. J. Abbott)

BRS UCLA 605: 4(n.i.) a straight description of the battle.

REC   O. J. Abbott, Folkways FM 4051 (B2), Leader LEE 4057 (B2)
b: Shirley Collins, Import Records 1017
b: High Level Ranters, Trailer LER 2020
       Amos Jollimore, Folkways FE 4307 (A2)
       June Tabor, Topic 12TS 298 (A2)

◊ The Drummer Boy at Waterloo *(H728) 88*

Laws 1957:129 (J1) "... of ..."
Brunnings 1981: "... of ..."
Cazden et al. *Notes* 1982: #10 "... of ..."

AMER   Cazden et al. 1982:69-71

◊ The Bonny Light Horseman *(H122) 88*

Dean-Smith 1954

BRIT   Dallas 1972:92-3
       MacColl [1962?]:9, a fragment.
       Palmer 1977:252-3
       Cf. Seeger/MacColl 1960:5 "Broken-Hearted I Wander," a children's game song.

AMER   Creighton 1932:143-4, a different version.
       Grover n.d.:105 a fragment.
       Thompson 1958:74-5

BRS   Harvard 1: 3.1 (Forth), 5.145 (Catnach), 10.102 (Bebbington), 11.75 (Such)
       Harvard 3: (Batchelar) (Pitts)
       UCLA 605: 5(Such)
       Forget Me Not (1835):191-2

REC Mary Ann Carolan, Topic 12TS 362 (A6)

Sam Henry's Songs of the People

John Faulkner, Green Linnet SIF 3004 (Mulligan LUN 033) (B5)
Ewan MacColl, Folkways FW 8501 (A3,24) [Broken-hearted I wandered] rope-skipping game.
Tony Rose, Dingle's DIN 324 (A2)
Lal, Norma Waterson, Topic 12TS 331 (B2)

◆ The Irish Soldier Boy *(H678)* 89

Brunnings 1981

BRS   Jolliffe 1970:108-9 discusses the relationship of this ballad and H543 "The Sailor Boy."
All Ireland 1950 [Fowke]
Songs and Recitations 2,n.d.:20

REC   Tom Brandon, Folk-Legacy FSC 10 (A2)

◆ The Heights of Alma *(H123)* 90

Laws 1957:133 (J10)
Brunnings 1981: "...," "The Battle of Alma"

IREL   Shields/Shields *UF* 21,1975: #182

BRIT   Greig/Duncan 1,1981:387 (#58) "The Battle of ..."
  Palmer 1977:203-5 "Battle ..."

AMER   Dean [1922]:40-1
  Grover n.d.:106-7
  Leach 1965:150-1 "The Battle ... (Heights ...)"
  Manny/Wilson 1968:247

BRS   Healy 1,1967b:108-9 "Bloody ..."

REC   O. J. Abbott, Folkways FM 4051 (B9)
  Bob, Ron Copper, Leader LEA 4048 "The Battle of ..."
  Nic Jones, Pete and Chris Coe, Trailer LER 2105 (A6)
  Irish Country Four, Topic 12TS 209

◆ Balaclava *(H829)* 91

? Brunnings 1981: "... (See: The Two Soldiers)," "... - Six Hundred Stalwart Warriors

BRIT   Dallas 1972:218-9 (from Henry coll.)
  Palmer 1977:209-10

REC   Arky's Toast, Greenwich Village GVR 212 (B4) "The Balaclava Charge"
  Roy Harris, Fellside FE 017 (A1)
  Bob Mills, People's Stage Tapes cass. 05 (B4)
  Walter Pardon, Leader LED 2111 (B6)

◆ Old Ireland Far Away *(H816)* 92

Laws 1957:132 (J7) "The Dying Soldier [Erin Far Away II]"
Brunnings 1981: "Old Erin Far Away - The Sun Had Gone Down"

AMER   Wright 1975:470 (from Henry coll., BCL)

b: REC   Jerry Carey, Prestige/Int. 25014 (A5) "... Erin ..."

A8

Bound away to the west'rd: Sea

Sam Henry's Songs of the People

Kishmul's Galley [H535(b): Bt]

l: This song appears in Bt only. John Moulden reports that it was never published in Henry's column in the *Northern Constitution*, and is "in fact a copy of the original publication of this song in Marjory Kennedy-Fraser's [and Kenneth MacLeod's] *Songs of the Hebrides* [London: Boosey & Co., 1909].... I take it that this typescript of No. 535 and 'Kishmul's Galley' might have been prepared for a broadcast at some time." It is here omitted because it never appeared in Henry's column.

Sailors' Shanties [H53: BLp, 15 Nov 1924]

s: The days are almost gone when men collectively sang at their work. The sailors had a song for every task, when they were sailors, but steam -- that useful monster -- pitched Orpheus overboard.

An old sailor (T. W.) who spent most of his time under the white wings of ships (the *Rahany, Shandon, Lord Wolsley, Loch Carron, Star of Austria,* to name a few) has done his best to sing for me a few of the favourite shanties. He explained: "I can't do it away from the ship's crowd. I don't feel like shantying as when I was aboard ship." His songs were within my grasp, yet I only rescued a few. He had airs without words and words without airs, as for example:

> Some are bound for London
> And some are bound for France,
> And we are bound for Ireland,
> To give the girls a dance.

The first shanty he gave me I have not seen recorded elsewhere.

g: [My] experience in trying to get chanties from a chanteyman was much like Sam Henry's. Bill Tilton of Chilmark on Martha's Vineyard was a chanteyman on both American and British deepwater vessels for much of his active life; he was also [my] wife's great-uncle. He had a tremendous repertoire of songs and ballads which he would sing at the drop of a hat. But he would never sing a chantey. His excuse was that chanties were to be sung aboard ship to lighten the work, and they weren't really songs anyway. But more than that: there must have been a superstitious feeling that it was bad luck to sing them ashore or apart from the work.

It's Time for Us to Leave Her [H53b: BLp, 15 Nov 1924]

A hauling song.

Other titles: "Across the Western Ocean," "Leave Her, Johnnie(y)[, Leave Her]," "Time to Leave Her."

Source: T. W., old sailor.

[British Library microfilm print courtesy of John Moulden.]

[BLp] Key C. [Bt = Dt(c)] Key G.

O, the times are hard and the wages low,
  Leave her, Johnny, leave her,
I guess it's time for us to go,
  It's time for us to leave her.

O, don't you hear our old man say,
  Leave her, bullies, leave her,
Tomorrow you will get your pay,
  It's time for us to leave her.

Tom's Gone to Ilo [H53d: BLp, 15 Nov 1924]

A hauling song.

Key F.

O, Tom is gone, what shall I do?
  Ay, o ho, O ay ho,
Tom is gone and I'll go too.
  Tom's gone to Ilo.

Santy Anna [H496: 3 Jun 1933]

An American chantey.

Other titles: "(On) (the) Plains of Mexico," "Santa ... (Anno)," "Santianna."

Source not given.

s: General Taylor's force was now about 4,600 men; with this little army he resolved to hold the wild mountain pass of Buena Vista to the southwest of Monterey against the Mexican army, who were advancing to attack him. Santa Ana, the commander-in-chief of the Mexican army, surrounded Taylor with a force of 20,000 strong; he then sent the American general a dispatch telling him that he must surrender or be cut to pieces. "Old Rough and Ready," as his men called Zachary Taylor, determined to hold his ground, and the unequal contest began on 22d February 1847. Santa Ana retreated and Taylor had the victory at a cost of more than one-sixth of his entire force. General Zachary Taylor was elected President of the United States and was in office from 1849 until his death on 9 July 1850.

l: Note that Henry's version is historically accurate, while, e.g., Colcord (1938) remarks that the roles of the protagonists in her version are reversed.

Key D.

Oh, Zachary Taylor was his name,
  Hooray Santy Anna!
And Zachary Taylor gained great fame
  All on the plains of Mexico.

He fought the fight at Monterey,
He fought the fight and he gained the day.

Old Santy Anna fought that day,
An' he got licked an' he ran away.

He never stopped till he ran ten mile,
'Old Rough-and-Ready' had t' smile.

If he hadn't a stopped to ketch his breat',
The old boy'd bin a-runnin' yet.

Old Santy Anna's dead an' gone,
I hope he's moored in kingdom come.

For General Taylor, boys, hooray,
He licked old Santy good that day.

Paddy Doyle [H53c: BLp, 15 Nov 1924]

A furling chorus. [Wt: ... song.]

Other titles: "...'s Boots," "We'll Pay ... for His Boots."

Source: T. W., old sailor.

s: The shantyman improvised any phrase he fancied [BLp: instead of "We'll pay Paddy Doyle,"] and if it had imperishable merit (!) it was incorporated in the song [Wt: shanty].

[Print of British Library microfilm file supplied by John Moulden. Text printed line for line with the sol-fa.]

Key F.

To my way-a-ay ay ah,
We'll pay Paddy Doyle for his boots.

A8 / Bound away to the west'rd

I'm Going Home [H53a: BLp, 15 Nov 1924]

An unmooring song.

k: "Goodbye, Fare You (Ye) Well," "Homeward Bound."

Source: T. W., old sailor.

[Print of British Library microfilm of *Northern Constitution* files kindly provided by John Moulden. Text of this song is printed line for line with the sol-fa.]

Key F. Slow.

I'm going home no more to roam,
No more to sin and sorrow,
No more to wear the brow of care,
I'm going home tomorrow.
Goodbye, fare you well,
Hurrah, my boys, we're homeward bound.
Goodbye, fare you well.

1.6: ... boys, I'm ... [Bt, Dt]

The Girls of Valparaiso [H539: 31 Mar 1934]

g: "The Chile Girls." Other titles: "Around Cape Horn," "The Gals (Girls) around Cape Horn," "(The) Rounding the (of Cape) Horn."

Source: "an old salt."

s: ... [The] "old salt," ... when he retired from the sea, had to get his wife to throw buckets of water against the window at night to put him to sleep.
  Valparaiso, the second city of Chile (population 190,000) was founded in 1536. The name means "the valley of paradise."

Key C.

Sam Henry's Songs of the People

Our good ship's name's the *Hero*, the *Hero* of renown,
We're lying now in Plymouth, that far-famed lovely town,
We're waiting there for orders to carry us far from home:
It's first to Valparaiso and all around Cape Horn.

With skysails set and staysails, topgallant sails also,
In our white pants and jackets we cut a gallant show;
From ship to ship they saluted us as we did sail along,
All wishing us good weather at the rounding of the Horn.

And now we are around Cape Horn, where there's pleasure night and day,
And the first place we cast our anchor was Valparaiso Bay,
Where the Spanish girls came flocking down -- I avow and do declare,
They far exceed our English girls with their dark heads of hair.

They're like the Irish sailor when he goes on the spree,
For if they had one shilling, the half they'd share with thee,
They're not like those Glasgow girls, on you they won't impose,
For when the money is all done, they will not pawn your clothes.

Here's a health to Valparaiso, we drink it with a smile,
And to all around the borders of that fair Pacific isle,
And when our good ship it does come home, I'll sit and sing my song:
Here's a health to Valparaiso and the girls around Cape Horn.

The S[team]s[hip] Leinster Lass
[H808: 20 May 1939]

Source: John Lowe (formerly Limavady), learned from his brother c. 1889.

s: ... [F]ifty years ago [the song] was ... in great vogue.

1: Odd that this song is about a *steam*ship but stanza 4 urges the sailors to "reef and steer."

Key G.

One evening fair to take the air down by the banks o' Clyde,
I'll tell you true I stopped to view all nature in her pride,
I'll tell to you I stopped to view the ships as they did pass,
When a steamboat heaved all on the waves, the bonny *Leinster Lass*.

I'm told she is on new-found ground a-coursing up and down,
And round her docks of liberty she's seen by everyone,
A mermaid sits on yonder rock with her nice comb and glass,
And you're welcome home to Erin's isle, the bonny *Leinster Lass*.

'Twas on the seventeenth day of March, all on St. Patrick's Day,
I heard a band all on the strand, behold how it did play,
Her colours flew red, white and blue, and the birds sang round her mast,
And they welcomed her to Erin's isle, the bonny *Leinster Lass*.

Here's a health to her commander of honour and great fame,
Likewise to our brave captain, his name is Willie Kane,
Let every man on board of her toss up a flowing glass,
And reef and steer while danger's near, on board the *Leinster Lass*.

2.3: ... on younder ... [Dp]

The Cruise of the Calabar
[H502: 15 Jul 1933]

Other titles: "... *Calibar*," "The Good Ship *Calibar*," ?"The Manchester 'Angel,'" "The Strabane Fleet"; cf. "The Wreck of the *Mary Jane*."

Source not given.

Key C.

Come all ye dry-land sailors and listen to my song,
It has only forty verses, so I won't detain you long,
It's all about the history of this here British tar
Who sailed as a man before the mast on board of the *Calabar*.

Our vessel ploughed the waters of the Strabane Canal,
Being under close-reefed topsails, for the glass foretold a squall,
It was nor'east of the shipyard we were beating in the surf
On our way to the Carrigans Harbour with a cargo of good black turf.

The *Calabar* was a clipper flat, copper-fastened fore and aft,
Her rudder stuck out far behind, her wheel was a great big shaft,
With half a gale to swell each sail, she'd make two knots an hour,
Being the smartest craft on the whole canal, though only one horse-power.

Our captain was a strapping youth, his height was four feet two,
His eyes were black, his nose was red, his cheeks a Prussian blue,
He wore a leather medal that he'd won at the China war,
And his wife was pilot and passenger cook aboard of the *Calabar*.

We started with a fav'ring gale, the weather being sublime,
But just right under Derry Bridge, where you can't pass two at a time,
We were struck amidships by a scow that gave us a serious check,
For it stove in the larboard paddle box and shattered the hurricane deck.

Next day we ran short of buttermilk -- it was all the captain's fault --
So the crew were laid up with scurvy, for the herrings were terrible salt.
Our coloured cook said the meat was done, there wasn't a bap on the shelf;
'Then we'll eat the soap,' the captain cried, 'let no man wash himself.'

While hugging the shore near Sandy Brown's, a very dangerous part,
We ran bow on to a bank of mud that wasn't marked down on the chart,
Then to keep the vessel from sinking and save each precious life,
We heaved the cargo overboard, including the captain's wife.

Then all became confusion while the stormy winds did blow,
Our bo'sun slipped on an orange peel and fell in the hold below,

'A pirate ship,' our captain cried, 'and on us she does gain;
When next I go to Strabane, my boys, by Jove I'll go by train.'

We got our arms all ready to meet the coming foe,
Our grappling irons, boarding pikes and Armstrong guns also.
'Turn on full speed,' the captain said, 'for we are sorely pressed,'
But the engineer replied from the bank, 'The horse is doing his best.'

Oh, thick and fast the heroes fell, in streams the blood was spilt,
Great numbers fell before they were touched, to make sure they wouldn't be kilt,
At last when the enemy struck her flag, her crew being laid on their backs,
We found she was another scow with a cargo of cobbler's wax.

6.3: bap = roll of bread.

The Zared [H194: 30 Jul 1927; Laws D13]

Other titles: "The Banks of Newfoundland," "The (Clipper Ship) *Dreadnaught (Dreadnought)*," "The Flash (Fancy) Frigate," "Liverpool Packet," "La *Pique*"; cf. "Good bye, Fare Ye Well."

Source: (w, m) Hugh M'Daid (Shrove, Greencastle, Co. Donegal).

s: A Londonderry ship owned by Bartholomew M'Corkell, which sailed for Philadelphia in the winter of 1861 with 500 passengers. She was wrecked on her return voyage in January 1862, off the west coast of Ireland....

g: The *Zared* is also the vessel named in H518 "A Londonderry Love Song."

[Bp] Key G. [Dt] Key D.

You talk of fast packets, fast packets of fame;
She's a Londonderry packet, the *Zared*'s her name.
If you want to get in her, inquire down the Strand,
It's there you'll find M'Corkell and his office does stand.

Sam Henry's Songs of the People

It's now we're hauled out from Derry's old dock,
There the boys and the girls on the north quay
  do flock,
They gave us three cheers while the tears down
  did flow,
Bound away to the west'rd in the *Zared* we'll go.

It's now we are sailing on the old Irish Sea
With passengers five hundred and hearts full of
  glee,
While the sailors skylarking on the decks to and
  fro,
Bound away to the west'rd in the *Zared* we go.

It's now we are sailing on the Atlantic so wide,
Where the dark and green billows wash along our
  broad side,
With our sails neatly spread on each mast to and
  fro,
Bound away to the west'rd in the *Zared* we go.

It's now we are sailing on the banks of
  Newfoundland,
Where the water runs clear and the bottom's all
  sand,
Where the fish of the ocean do swim to and fro,
Bound away to the west'rd in the *Zared* we go.

It's now we are sailing down by Jersey shore,
Where the pilot he boards us as he oft did before.
'Back away your main topsail, board your
  foretack also,
The *Zared*'s a-holding, brave boys, let her go.'

Up steps our captain, on the deck he does stand
To see that the good ship was properly manned,
Saying, 'Give her more cloth, boys, and let her
  go free,
For the *Zared*'s a wild bird that ne'er feared the
  sea.'

It's now we're safe landed on Philadelphia Quay,
Where the passengers leave us and bid us
  good-bye.
We were turning around while the tears down did
  fall,
Bound away for Londonderry, may the Lord bless
  you all.

3.4: ... *Zared* would go. [Dt]

Yellow Meal [H827: 30 Sep 1939]

s: (m) "The Jessie Walker"; m: (m) closely related to Scottish "Musselburgh Fair." Other titles: "Tab Scott," "Tapscott," "We're All Bound to Go," "We're All away to Sea"; cf. "Heave Away (, My Johnny)."

Source: (w) part "known locally," remainder from American collection of "Come All Ye's" [?O'Conor, see references]; (m) George Graham (Cross Lane, Coleraine), learned as "The Jessie Walker" from his grandfather, Joseph Wilson (Roddenfoot, Ballymoney).

s: This song, sung by some very unlettered muse, was the means of tracing the ancestry of a lineal descendant of Captain Tapscott, now resident in New York....

From Lloyd's Registry of Shipping and from the Archives in Boston Free Library, I have been able to trace this little ship. By chance I also found in the *Derry Journal* for 1845 an account of the loss of the *Joshua A. Walker*. The malediction on the brig in verse five of the song was fulfilled. Here is an account of her loss, from "Virginia Patriot," published in Richmond, VA, on October 25th, 1815 (see page 3):

"The brig *Walker*, 180 tons, built in Sunderland in 1803 (Captain C. Speck), bound from Boston to Cork, with a cargo of tobacco, staves, &c., struck on a ledge of rocks off Seal Island (close to Cape Sable, the most southerly point of Nova Scotia) on the 19th inst., and was totally lost. All the information obtained respecting the brig is from a boy named Mathew Mortimore, who was picked up by a fishing vessel on Thursday, 21st inst., and carried into Yarmouth, Nova Scotia. He states that the brig sailed from Boston on 17th September and at 10 o'clock at night of the following Thursday she struck on a rock. The captain and three men jumped into the long boat; the remainder of the crew were on the wreck for about half an hour and disappeared. The long boat has since drifted ashore. There can be little doubt but the whole of the crew have perished."

The oldest dock in Liverpool was the Sligo Dock, now known as Collingwood Dock.

g: The cargo of tobacco and staves pretty well dates the song. The "yellow meal" -- corn meal -- seems not to have appealed to the Irish taste.

Key C.

As I walked out one morning down by the Sligo
  dock,
I overheard an Irishman conversing with
  Tapscott:
'Good morning, Mr Tapscott, would you be after
  telling me,
Have you ever a ship bound for New York in the
  state of Amerikee?

'Oh yes, my pretty Irish boy, I have a ship or
  two,
They're lying at the wharf there, waiting for a
  crew,
They all are New York packets and on Friday they
  will sail,
At present one is taking in a thousand bags of
  meal.

Straightway then I started, twas on the yellow-
  grog road,
Such roars of mille-murder, oh, the like was never
  knowed,
And there I paid my passage down in solid Irish
  gold,
And often I sat down and cried the way I had been
  sold.

The very day we started, 'twas on the first of
  May,
The captain he came on the deck and unto us did
  say,
'Cheer up, my hearty Irish blades, don't let your
  courage fail,
Today I'll serve you pork and beans, tomorrow
  yellow meal.'

One day as we were sailing in the channel of St.
  James,
A northwest wind came up to us and drove us back
  again;
Bad luck to the *Josh. A. Walker* and the day that
  she set sail,
Likewise to Captain Tapscott and his dirty yellow
  meal.

And then I went to Liverpool, walking through the
  street,
Not a penny in my pocket nor a mouthful for to
  eat;
Bad luck to the *Josh. A. Walker* and the day that
  she set sail,
For the dirty sailors broke open my chest and
  stole my yellow meal.

But now I'm in America and working upon the
  canal;
To cross the stream in one of these boats I know I
  never shall,
But I'll cross it in a great big ship that carries
  both meat and sail,
Where I'll get good lashings of corned meat and
  none of your yellow meal.

The Shamrock Shore   [H192: 16 Jul 1927]

Other titles: "Greencastle Shore," "Paddy's Green
...."

Source: (w) Henry Smyth (Mulkeragh South, Limavady), heard from Robert Smyth, 80, c. 1875,
learned from author M'Laughlin (Ballykelly).

s: ... Another version has been received from
the Articlave district, where the song was first
sung in 1827 by an Inishowen ploughman.

h: It is evidently a local composition which has
been adapted in recent times to general Irish
usage (1981, p. 88).

Key C.

A8 / Bound away to the west'rd

From Londonderry we set sail all on the eighth of
  May,
We had a sweet and pleasant gale going down to
  Moville Bay,
Fresh water there, near twenty tons, for
  passengers did store,
Lest we should want, going to St. Johns, far
  from the shamrock shore.

That evening at six o'clock our anchor we did
  weigh,
The sunbeams on Benevenagh rocks they
  splendidly did play,
Greencastle's ancient church fort and church,
  they made my sad heart sore,
Thinking of when Tyrconnell's court did grace
  the shamrock shore.

From scene to scene my fond eye roved o'er
  mountain, hill and dale,
Till resting on dear Walworth grove o'ertopped by
  Drumnameal,
My agonizing heart did swell, my soul was
  troubled sore,
Viewing those scenes I left behind upon the
  shamrock shore.

'Oh Ballykelly, much loved spot, and must we
  part?' I cried,
'Must I leave yon lovely cot where friends I love
  reside?
Friends of my heart, and must we part, perhaps
  to meet no more?
Your memory still will warm my heart far from the
  shamrock shore.'

At twelve o'clock we came in sight of famous Malin
  Head,
And Innistrahull far to the right rose out of
  ocean's bed,
A grander sight now met my eyes than e'er I saw
  before:
The sun going down 'twixt sea and sky far from
  the shamrock shore.

Next morning we were all seasick, not one of us
  was free.
Quite helpless on my berth I lay, no one to pity
  me,
No friends were near, but strangers drear, to
  lift my head when sore,
None of my own to hear me moan far from the
  shamrock shore.

Sam Henry's Songs of the People

Then lo, a dreadful storm arose, the seas like
  mountains roll,
Blue lightnings flash on every side and rush from
  pole to pole;
Regardless both of winds and waves and hoarse
  loud thunder's roar,
Our gallant crew the tempest braved far from the
  shamrock shore.

But now these scenes are past and gone and we
  are well once more,
In social parties we are joined, the whiskey flies
  galore,
In joking o'er our parting glass, lest we should
  meet no more,
A 'deuch an dhurrus' we will drined [drink?] far
  from the shamrock shore.

We landed on the other side in three and thirty
  days,
And drinking o'er a parting glass, we took our
  several ways,
We took each comrade by the hand, perhaps to
  meet no more,
And thought on all our absent friends and the
  lovely shamrock shore.

To Captain Harrison we owe our grateful thanks
  indeed,
Him and his crew were never slow to help us in
  our need.
In a full glass we'll drink his health and toast it
  o'er and o'er:
May he still in safety pass to and from the
  shamrock shore.

8.3: ... our parting glass, we took our several ways,
  [Dt]
8.4 - 9.2: [Bp, *not in* Dt; ?typing error]
8.4 [Dt] = 9.3 [Bp]; 8.5 [Dt] = 9.4 [Bp].

8.4: deuch an dhurrus = Gaelic phrase for a parting
  glass, spelt here phonetically, literally means "the
  drink of the door." [s]

Patrick O'Neal [H552: 30 Jun 1934]

Other title: (m) "The Fine Old Irish Gentleman";
cf. "The Press Gang."

Source: (w) *Northern Minstrel*, printed and sold
by Hugh Clark (Pottinger's Entry, Belfast, 1829);
(m) brothers M'Bride, fiddle (the Smiddy, Ballyvoy, Ballycastle).

Key A flat.

On April the first, I set off like a fool
From Kilkenny to Dublin to see Lawrence Toole,
My mother's third cousin, who often wrote down
For to come up and see how he flourished in town.
I had scarce set a foot in the terrible place
Before a spalpeen came and stared in my face --
He called to a press-gang, they came without fail,
And soon neck and crap carried Patrick O'Neal.

They scampered away, as they thought, with a
  prize,
Taking me for a sailor, you see, in disguise,
But a terrible blunder they made in their strife,
For I ne'er saw a ship nor the sea in my life.
Then straight to a tender they made me repair,
But of tenderness divil a morsel was there!
Och, I ramped and I cursed, but it did not avail,
Till a great swimming castle met Patrick O'Neal.

This big swimming thief rolled about in the tide,
Wid all her front teeth sticking fast by her side,
Where they bid me to mount and be sure for to
  keep
Fast hold with my trotters, for fear I should trip.
I let go my hands and stuck fast with my toes,
And (how it could happen, the lord above knows)
Fell plump in the water and splashed like a
  whale,
Till pretty well pickled was Patrick O'Neal.

Wid a great swell of laughter they hoisted me in
To this huge wooden world, full of riot and din:
What strings and what pulleys attracted my eye,
And how large were the sheets that were hung out
  to dry.
It seemed Noah's ark stuffed with different
  guests,
Hogs, pedlars, geese, sailors and all other beasts:
Some drank bladders of gin, some drank pitchers
  of ale,
While some sat and laughed at poor Patrick O'Neal.

Then to go down below I expressed a great wish,
Where they live under water, like so many fish;
I was clapt in a mess with some more of the crew,
They called it banyan day, so gave me burgoo.
For a bed I'd a sack swung as high as my chin,
They called it a hammock and bade me get in;
I took a great leap, but my footing was frail,
For clean over canted was Patrick O'Neal.

The divil a wink could I sleep all the night,
And awoke the next morn in a terrible fright:
'Up hammocks, down chests,' they began for to
  bawl,
'Here's a Frenchman in sight!' 'Sure,' says I, 'is
  that all?'
Then we hauled our large window shutters with
  speed,
And run out our bulldogs of true English breed;
While the creatures gave mouth, I held fast by
  the tail,
And they kicked me and run over poor Patrick
  O'Neal.

Thus we rattled away, by my sowl, hob or nob,
Till the Frenchman gave out, as he thought, a bad
  job;
To tie him behind, a large cord they did bring,
And we led him along like a pig in a string,
Then home to old England we dragged the French
  boy,
Och, the sight of the land made me seasick for
  joy.
They made up a peace, and (the war growing
  stale)
Set all hands adrift with poor Patrick O'Neal.

So, ye see, on dry land a safe course I can steer,
Neither cathead nor cat-block nor any cat fear,
While there's shot in the locker I'll sing, I'll be
  bound,
And Saturday night shall last all the week round,
But should king and country e'er call us amain,
By the piper of Leinster, I'll venture again --
Make another dry voyage, bring home a fresh tale,
And you'll laugh till you cry at poor Patrick
  O'Neal.

1.5: spalpeen = a low or mean fellow.
1.8: crap = gizzard, throat.
5.4: banyan day = a nautical expression for a day
  without meat ration. [s]
5.4: burgoo = a kind of gruel made on board ship;
  in army parlance, porridge and treacle. [s]
5.8: canted = turned.
6.5: bulldogs = guns. [s]
7.1: sowl = soul.
7.1: hob or nob = give or take. [s]
8.2: cathead = a timber projecting from the bow of a
  ship through which the ropes pass by which the
  anchor is raised. [s]
8.2: cat = a whip for flogging sailors. [s]

The Sailor Boy [H543: 28 Apr 1934; Laws K13]

[cf. H678 "The Irish Soldier Boy"]

Other titles: "The (Your) Faithful ...," "...'s
Farewell."

Source: (w) William Gault (Milltown, Dunseverick);
(m) James Wilkinson, "his colleague and neighbour," fiddler [Milltown, Dunseverick].

s: The words contributed by William Gault, ... at
whose hospitable hearth the song was taken down.
...

1: In notes to Cyril Poacher's record (q.v.),
Mike Yates and Keith Summers identify G. W.
Persley as the late 19th-century author.

Key C.

On a bitter cold, wild winter night
When the snow lay on the ground,
A sailor boy stood on the quay,
His course was outward bound.

A8 / Bound away to the west'rd

His sweetheart, she was standing by,
And shed a silent tear,
And as he clasped her to his breast
He whispered in her ear:

'Farewell, farewell, my own true love,
This parting gives me pain,
You'll be my own true guiding star
Till I return again.

'My thoughts will be on you, my love,
When the storms are raging high;
Farewell, farewell, remember me,
Your own true sailor boy.'

'Twas in a gale that ship set sail,
She bid her love goodbye,
And as she watched his ship from sight
A tear bedimmed her eye.

She prayed to him in heaven above
To guard him on his way,
Her lover's parting words that night
Re-echoed o'er the bay.

But, sad to say, that ship returned
Without her sailor boy,
He died while on that voyage at sea,
The flag was half-mast high.

And when his comrades came on shore,
They told her he was dead;
A letter then they gave to her
Whose last words sadly said:

'Farewell, farewell, my own true love,
On earth we'll meet no more,
But we will meet in heaven above
On that eternal shore.'

Franklin the Brave [H815: 8 Jul 1939; Laws K9]

Other titles: "Franklin's Crew," "The Franklin
Expedition," "(Lady) Franklin's Lament," "Lament
for Lord Franklin," "(Lord) Franklin (and His
Bold [Ship's] Crew)," "The Sailor's Dream."

Source: "old salt whose portly form is familiar at
the Quay Head, Portrush."

s: Sir John Franklin, an English Arctic explorer,
was born in Lincolnshire in 1786. He died near
Lancaster Sound on the north coast of Baffin Land
in 1847. His ill-fated expedition to find a waterway from the Atlantic to the Pacific set out in the
ships *Erebus* and *Terror*. It was not until twelve
years after his death that the whereabouts of the
tragedy of his icy death was discovered. In 1859
M'Lintock, leader of an expedition, discovered, at
Point Victory in King William's Land, a document
deposited in a cairn, which gave the details of the
last days of Sir John Franklin, who had died 18th
June 1847. After his death the crews, 105 in number, abandoned their ships and made overland to
Great Fish River, but none survived, although
their relics were found. Captain Parry, mentioned
in the song, gave his name to Parry's Islands in

Sam Henry's Songs of the People

the Arctic. Captain Ross was Sir John Ross, who led an expedition in 1829 to the Arctic and named King William's Land. He made a voyage in the *Felix* in 1850 in an endeavour to trace Franklin.

Key C.

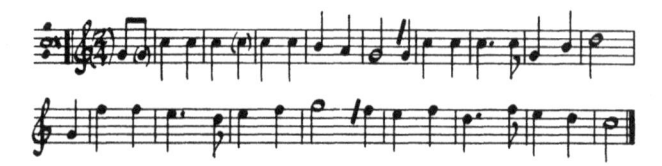

We were homeward bound all in the deep,
Alone in my hammock I fell asleep,
And I dreamt a dream which I thought was true,
All concerning Franklin and his bold crew.

As I was musing on yon foreign shore,
I heard a lady and she did deplore,
She wept aloud and to me did say,
'Oh, my loving husband, he stops long away.

'It is seven long years since three ships of fame
Caused my dear husband to cross the main,
And a hundred seamen of courage stout,
A northwest passage for to find out.

'They sail-ed east and they sail-ed west
To find their passage they knew not best.
Ten thousand pounds would I freely give,
If I only knew if my husband lived.

'There is Captain Parry of high renown,
There is Captain Hoggs of Seamore town,
There is Captain Ross and many more;
I'm afraid they are lost on yon foreign shore.

'In Baffin's Bay where the whalefish blows,
The fate of Franklin no one knows;
I'm afraid he is lost on yon foreign shore,
Where he left his home to return no more.'

Loss of Seven Clergymen [H742: 12 Feb 1938]

Other titles: cf. "Seven Priests."

Source: Dick Gilloway (Landscape Terrace, Coleraine) from James Kane (Aughill, Magilligan, Co. Derry).

s: This very curious song was collected by me.... The Magilligan airs are specially rich melodies.

o: The tune should be in 6/8.

m: Current, from Eddie Butcher.

Key E flat.

You feeling-hearted Christians, I pray you lend an ear
And listen to these doleful news that I have written here
Concerning seven clergymen whose loss we do deplore,
They were drowned all in the Nazen Lake, which grieves our hearts full sore.

Being fatigued by their oblations, I want to let you know,
Like the great apostle Peter, a-fishing they did go,
And amongst them was the vicar from St. Michael's Chapel came,
With the captain and the cabin boy to guide them on the stream.

Our boat she was in readiness, in favour blew the wind,
And to take some recreation for to refresh our mind,
We hoisted up our sheeting and for the lake did steer,
But little we expected that grim death he stood so near.

For to decoy the finny tribe, prepared with rod and line,
That day in hopes to catch some fish, it was our whole design;
Our baited hooks into those brooks each man of us then threw,
When the clouds with darkness overspread and the winds tremendous blew.

The storm arose, the thunder roared, the lightning it did flash,
The waves against our little boat in fury they did lash,
We gazed in silent agony in vain to see the land,
Upon that dark and dismal lake and no relief at hand.

But oh, that was an awful day, when these clergy in their prime
To each other gave a kiss of peace and their souls they did resign;
Next instant grim death swept the deep with a tremendous wave,
And alas, those seven clergymen all met a watery grave.

But when their flocks heard these sad news, which leaves them to deplore,
They quickly ran, their bodies found next morning on the shore;
They left their friends for to lament, their penitents to weep,

They left their church to mourn their loss while
   they lie in the deep.

But the captain and his cabin boy, they safely
   made their way,
And for those seven clergymen they mourn both
   night and day;
There were three of them belonged to France and
   four were Irishmen,
May the Lord have mercy on their souls; good
   Christians, say Amen.

The Portrush Fishing Disaster (I)

[H27b: [Bp] "Two songs of the Portrush fishing
          disaster of February 24, 1826," 17 May 1924]

s: (m) = H27a (H34b) "The Maids of Mourne
Shore," "Down by the Sally Gardens." Other
title: "The Portrush Fishermen."

Source: (w, m) Rev. J. R. Clinton.

[Bp] s: The air, ... to which the following words
were sung by Rev. J. R. Clinton at his recent
lecture on the sea, is one of the finest of all
the old Irish airs. The County Londonderry
setting is the most elaborate and beautiful of
all...."

[Dt is in 4-line stanzas, lines twice as long.]

Key E flat.

The sable curtains of the night
Were drawn up to the eastern sky,
And the hills were tinged with morning light
And a western breeze did gently fly,
When with bent sail before the gale
We to our destination steer,
We did disdain the foaming main
And sailed on without dread or fear.

But as we to Portrush returned,
Our sail being to the gunwale bound,
A stormy blast did sweep the deep
And stunned us with death's thund'ring sound;
Amidst the gale our strength did fail
And horror clouded every eye,
The ocean waves soon proved our graves,
And we beneath the billows lie.

When we were on the ocean wide,
A-tossing on the foaming main,
Oh, little thought when land we left
That we would ne'er return again.

A8 / Bound away to the west'rd

You boatmen good that stem the flood,
When you the spot do wander by
Where we lie low, as you do row,
Lean on your oars and heave a sigh.

Forbid, O muse, to name our names
Or our achievements to rehearse,
In any inspiring verse of fame
Our parents' sorrow to increase,
In verse or prose no number flows
That can describe their grief and pain,
With heartfelt sighs and watery eyes
They view our tomb, the widespread main.

Farewell, farewell to sweet Portrush,
Farewell to Ballywillan shore,
Your sandy banks and flowery braes,
We'll never see them any more.
Friends, cease to weep; at peace we sleep
Beneath the high and lofty waves,
The ocean bed beneath our head,
We calmly rest in a lonely grave.

So now, dear friends, yourselves prepare
To meet with us on yonder shore,
Where death-divided friends at last
Shall meet again to part no more,
No billows roll, no tempests growl,
But honey and new milk do flow
In that sweet scene, mild and serene,
So much unlike the world below.

4.6: ... grief or pain, [Dt]

The Portrush Fishing Disaster (II)

[H27c: [Bp] "Two songs of the Portrush fishing
          disaster of February 24, 1826," 17 May 1924]

Source: (m) William Sloan (Dundooan, Coleraine);
author Daniel McIlreavy, carpenter (Portstewart,
emigrant to Australian gold diggings).

[Bp] s: The song may also be sung to the air of
"The Banks of Cla[u]dy." ... The song was
written about 1826....

o: True folk composition, but set to a poor tune.

Key C.

Sam Henry's Songs of the People

Come all you jolly seamen bold who plough the
    raging main
And give me your attention till I relate the same,
Concerning four young heroes bold who were
    obliged to die,
And in the foaming ocean their bodies fair do
    lie.

Around the town of sweet Portrush much
    pleasure they had seen,
No more they'll roam the flowery hills where
    oftimes they have been.
Their sweethearts and their comrades dear, they
    bid them all adieu,
'Twas the raging seas and stormy waves that
    parted them from you.

The names of these four heroes you quickly now
    shall hear --
There was James and John Gillespie, they were
    two brothers dear,
Likewise young William Stewart, his equals were
    but few,
And Archie M'Ilvernock made up the jovial crew.

It was not for want of courage, or skill they did
    neglect,
A hard squall of wind came on, their boat it did
    upset;
The wind it blew tremendously and high did run
    the waves,
And soon the stormy ocean became their watery
    graves.

Oh, had you seen their doleful state, your
    tender hearts would sigh,
There was none to witness their distress but
    God who rules on high.
The mermaids of the ocean to their funeral did
    repair,
And on the banks of coral their bodies laid with
    care.

Oh, had it pleased Jehovah their bodies had
    been found,
Their parents had conveyed them safe to their
    own burying ground,
It would have eased their troubled hearts from
    sorrow, grief and pain,
But I hope they'll meet in heaven, where they'll
    never part again.

2.2: ... they had been ... [Dt]

The Wreck of the Enterprise

[H558: 11 Aug 1934]

Other title: "Machrihanish Bay."

Source: Alexander Horner, sr (Moycraig Hamilton,
Mosside, formerly Carnbore, Liscolman), learned
from his father, Alexander Horner, learned in
turn from his father, John Horner, fisherman
(Portballintrae); composed March 1837.

[No key indicated.]

It being on the fourth of March, brave boys, in
    the year of thirty-seven,
And dismal were our cries, brave boys, when by
    Glenarm driven,
The hail and sleet together met, and the spindrift
    it blew high
Together with a fall of snow, and dismal was the
    day.

The *Enterprise* of Lynn, brave boys, it was our
    good ship's name,
She was loaded with dollars and indigo, and from
    Peru she came,
She crossed the western ocean, where the foaming
    billows roar,
And she left her precious cargo all on the Largy
    shore.

It's for our captain's lady, as I do hear them tell,
She learned navigation and practised it right well,
She took an observation at ten o'clock that day,
Saying, 'I'll hold for fifty pounds, brave boys,
    we're off Glenarm Bay.'

When sailing east past by Black Rock, a light
    appeared in view,
'It's hold her off,' our captain cries, 'what the
    lady says is true.'
'It's hold her off,' our captain cries, 'some
    harbour we are near,'
But oh, alas, our joy soon fled, pale death did
    soon appear.

At three o'clock our good ship struck, unto our
    great surprise,
It's men, women and children, their cries rent the
    skies,
Our mainmast overboard it fell and our rigging
    tore away,
And our well-built ship in pieces split before the
    break of day.

Being early the next morning, before that it was
    clear,
The people ran from every part to get some of our
    gear;
Some got silver cup and plate, part of our gold
    beside,
While the captain and his seamen brave lay rolling
    in the tide.

Come all ye bold sea-captains that plough the
    raging main,

Be sure and steer your compass right and your
   helm never strain,
Be sure and steer your compass right and your
   helm never leave,
For if you strand on a bank of sand, for a
   wrecked ship you will grieve.

The Falcon [H95: 5 Sep 1925]

k: "Shipwreck."

Source: (w, m) (Magilligan district).

s: A song of a shipwreck which occurred on 5th
January 1868....

Key G.

Bound from Greenock to Derry, with hearts light
   and merry,
On Saturday evening she got on her way
With thirty-five passengers, crew and her cargo,
We put out to sea without fear or dismay.

We knew the danger we had to encounter
For stouter hearts never on shipboard did beat,
Expecting in a few hours in Lough Foyle to cast
   anchor,
With our wives and our friends with affection to
   greet.

But alas, before long that sweet hope proved
   elusive,
For in a few hours the wind did arise,
The unfortunate *Falcon* was tossed on the billows,
No help being at hand nor no moon in the skies.

Oftimes before she had faced the wild ocean,
Though she had a misfortune a long time before,
Yet even in that hour she was bold and
   undaunted
When the *Falcon* was drifting on a dark and lee
   shore.

Sorely they cried when they found that the
   engine
No longer could work and all hopes past and
   gone;
The water below, it was fast coming on us,
And none for to aid us but God here alone.

But think on the hour when our ship went in
   pieces,
The matchless waves over our vessel did roam,

A8 / Bound away to the west'rd

Think on Mrs Montgomery and her loving infant:
When the *Falcon* was sinking she jumped in the
   foam.

The widow may find a husband as tender,
The orphan's poor father lies under the wave,
And well may they weep for the wreck of the
   Falcon
That sent those poor creatures to a watery grave.

The Wreck of the Fanad Boat

[H602: 15 Jun 1935]

Source: Patrick Lynagh (Ballyshannagh, Fanad
peninsula, Co. Donegal).

Key D.

'Twas on the eighth of August,
Eighteen and forty-two,
Bound for the English harvest,
These boys they bid adieu.

Their hearts were light and merry,
No trouble on their mind,
Little they knew they ne'er would meet
The friends they left behind.

They launched the boat at Scroggy Bay,
Lies south of Fort Dunree,
They went to cross the Shinnan joint,
Runs from the Atlantic sea.

The boat was heavy loaded,
The wind it rose severe,
The seas began to roll so high
That death it did appear.

At last a wave had struck the boat,
There was no relief from shore,
And fifteen of brave Fanad boys
Had sunk to rise no more.

A boat was launched to their relief,
Came out from Urris shore,
All remained on their arrival
Was, of nineteen, only four.

There were fifteen could not be seen,
All sunk beneath the waves,
So as night processed and all at rest,
They came to watery graves.

It was a most appalling sight
To see their friends next day,
Crowding along Lough Swilly shore
From Stogger to Carr's Bay.

Sam Henry's Songs of the People

To hear the cries of orphans
And widows in despair
Distracted some old parents,
Who cried and tore their hair.

To keep those lads in memory,
Their names I will explain:
John Toland, first in order,
Then his cousin, James McLean.

John Duffy, Michael Toland,
Likewise the four M'Swines,
For loyalty and bravery
Their like you scarce could find.

There's a few lads to mention yet
That's worthy of reward,
Daniel Doherty, young Hugh Cannon,
And likewise brave James Carr.

Anton Friel we do bewail,
And Francis M'Ateer,
Danny Corran and young Breslin,
That's the number drowned, we hear.

It's sorrow, grief and mournin'
Through Fanad did prevail,
The mothers' tears, the withered locks,
The fathers they bewail.

Some sisters and some brothers cry,
Aloise! we're left alone,
And sweethearts they do mourn the boys
Their tender hearts had won.

Owen M'Swine we do lament,
Was a hero stout and true,
His widow and six children
Have reason for to rue.

There's many a cry and bitter sigh
Grieved all hearts full sore
The day his brother brought his corpse
In to Rathmullan shore.

Then, thanks be to kind Providence,
The corpses all were found,
And each of them was taken on
To consecrated ground.

May the mercy safe conduct their souls,
All hearts did earnest pray,
To the mercy of the glory
Where St. Peter keeps the key.

The Wreck of the Nimrod [H717: 21 Aug 1937]

Source: James Smyth, 80 (Knockmuir, Macosquin).

s: Contributed by Mr James Smyth, ... a veteran singer, with a memory which has served him well for eighty years.
Moreton Bay, on the east coast of Queensland, is formed inside the islands of Moreton and Stradbroke. The bay is 40 miles long by 17 broad. Brisbane is on one of the streams falling into it.

108 Key E flat.

Come all you jovial seamen bold, of high and low degree,
I hope you'll pay attention and listen unto me,
For the loss of the *Nimrod* steamship all Christians do deplore,
For she was engulfed all on the deep on the far Australian shore.

On the eighteenth day of January from Moreton we set sail,
Bound for the port of Liverpool, with a sweet and pleasant gale,
Our noble ship bore bravely, no danger could we spy,
Till on the twenty-fifth, my boys, most dismal grew the sky.

The lightning and the furious rain around our heads did fly
And darker every moment with thunder grew the sky;
Our captain cries, 'Look out, my boys, there's danger nigh at hand;
Unless by the mercy of the Lord, we'll never reach the land.'

Our noble ship was tossed about, all on the raging main,
All human help to aid us, alas, was all in vain,
The seas and winds they did combine, the lightning too did flash,
And o'er our heads the raging sea tumultuously did dash.

The dreadful storm continued on till darkness did appear,
But our gallant crew they grew so bold, no danger did they fear,
Till in the fury of the storm our ship was driven aground,
And nought could save us from the seas that tore the good ship round.

It was a dreadful sight to see as daylight did draw near,
The dead and dying mingled there with no assistance near,
Till a gallant bark she picked us up and brought us safe to shore;
May God protect all seamen bold and guide them evermore.

The Loss of the Royal Charter

[H623: 9 Nov 1935]

[cf. H565 "The Wreck of the *Rebecca*," H754 "The Good Ship *Mary Cochrane*"]

Other titles: "Royal ...."

Source: Dick Gilloway, bus driver, Northern Transport Board, learned "as a boy" from James Kane (Aughill, Magilligan).

Key G.

Ye inhabitants of Ireland, attention pray to me,
In grief I write the loss of life upon the raging sea,
This late and dismal storm, it leaves many to deplore,
And many met a watery grave close by their native shore.

On the thirtieth of August last, as plain as you may see,
We left the port of Melbourne with spirits light and free,
Four hundred souls we had on board, no danger did we fear,
Returning to our native home to friends and parents dear.

Our gallant ship the *Charter*, well manned with seamen bold,
With a rich and precious cargo and a heavy seam of gold,
Fifty-eight days our gallant ship did proudly cut the waves,
Which filled each heart with joy to see the speedy voyage she made.

When our gallant ship she come in sight of land just at Cape Clear,
Each Irish heart stood on the deck and gave a long loud cheer;
At Queenstown Harbour soon arrived and there made no delay,
We landed eleven passengers, to them a happy day.

Our ship was bound for Liverpool, our captain gave command,
Expecting the next morning in safety to land;
Great preparations there was made our goods for to receive,
But little we thought that all on board would meet a watery grave.

The storm it arose that night which filled our heart with fear,
At two o'clock upon that night when danger did appear,
The captain for to save our lives, he stayed the vessel's sail,
When all our crew for mercy called to calm that dismal gale.

The storm arose with violence and dreadful rolled the sea,
Our gallant ship she ran ashore nigh to the Red Wharf Bay.
A scene of terror there took place which proved death to all,
And to the God of heaven loud for mercy we did call.

When the ship was tumbling with the gale, one gallant seaman brave,
He swam ashore, made fast a rope, and twenty-five got saved;
Many more might have been saved but for an awful crash
That split our ship in pieces and it levelled down her masts.

Many by the swelling waves were washed from off the wreck,
And by the falling of her masts were killed upon the deck.
To see their bodies washed ashore, most dismal to behold,
All bruised and smashed by that sad crash, it would make your blood run cold.

Little we expected when leaving the Australian shore,
But God would guide us safe to see our home and friends once more;
Returning with our little store of hard industry
We earned on a foreign shore for our friends and families.

The violence of the storm in which our ship was lost
Caused loss of life and property round the Welsh and English coast.
Four hundred souls, we now may say, have suffered by the same,
They were hurried to eternity upon the raging main.

The violence of the storm in which our ship was lost
Caused loss of life and property round the Welsh and English coast.
Four hundred souls, we now may say, have suffered by the same,
They were hurried to eternity upon the raging main.

Now to conclude and finish, good Christians, let us pray

Sam Henry's Songs of the People

For all that perished on that night upon the raging sea.
Four hundred souls, I now may say, have sunk beneath the deep,
May the Lord have mercy on their souls and grant their friends relief.

The Trader [H11: 26 Jan 1924]

A broadsheet ballad of 1827.

s: (m) = H2 (Gow's *Second Collection of Strathspey Reels*, 1788) "Caledonian Hunt's Delight"; (O'Neill 1903: #311) "Banks of Lough Foyle"; (m) "Ye Banks and Braes [of Bonnie Doon]"; (m) "The Roving Baker of Milngavie."

Source: 2: old schoolmate of S. H.'s; old man, 80.

s: This ballad is a graphic description of a shipwreck at Downhill in November 1827. The *Trader* was a sailing vessel of 140 tons, bound from Galway to London with a cargo of foodstuffs.
[Bp only] ... Burns, in a letter to a friend, written about 1794, gives the history of the tune, to which he wrote "Ye Banks and Braes," as follows: -- James Miller, a Scotch patriot, who desired to compose a Scots tune on the advice of a musical friend, composed the rudiments of the tune by keeping to the black keys of the harpsichord, and the friend, Mr Clarke, polished the effort, which resulted in "The Caledonian Hunt's Delight." ...
Another version of the origin of the tune is, that a lady in Edinburgh heard a poor boy singing it in the street, and took it down from him. The lad had learnt it from his parents. It is interesting to speculate on the probable more distant origin from the tune given below, and as the name, derived from Lough Foyle, would indicate, this version, commonly sung in Magilligan, may be the parent tune. Its simplicity and Irish flavour bear this out.
I took it down from an old schoolmate, en route through Magilligan (accompanist, "Tin Lizzie" [Dt: (Ford's motor van)]) and had it corroborated by an old man of 80.
Another song is sung to it in Scotland, "The Roving Baker of Milngavie." It is also the proper tune for No. 2 ("Mullaghdoo"), and the old people always sing the song to that air.

[Bp: First stanza of "Ye Banks and Braes" is typed line for line under printed tune.]

Key G.

Come all ye seamen bold, I pray, and listen here a while to me,
And landsmen, too, while thus I do relate to you our sad ditt-ee.
It would melt each heart while I impart to sing these doleful lines all o'er:
A ship of fame, *Trader* by name, was lately wrecked upon our shore.

November on the twenty-first from Galway town our ship did sail;
The weather being calm and clear, we had a sweet and pleasant gale.
Our jovial crew, pleasant to view, no thoughts of danger did we fear,
For London town straight we were bound, our course intending there to steer.

Seven seamen bold, you may behold, it was our jovial companee,
Our numbers few but kind and true, we lived in great tranquilitee,
One hundred tons and forty more, it was our gallant vessel's load
Of corn and wheat as we thought fit, our gallant ship she was well stowed.

The night before in our cabin, as our brave captain sleeping were,
He thought a voice called him by name and these sad tidings did declare:
'Your ship and crew and cargo, too, shall in the storm be cast away,
Your family you ne'er shall see.' He dreamt it thrice e'er break of day.

Next morning straight, just by daylight, as our brave captain he arose,
He saw a storm a-gathering and in the north so fast did close.
He gave command to every hand to mind their post as they did before,
But oh, alas, the storm increased; we never reached that wished-for shore.

Soon did the waves like mountains rise; not knowing then well what to do,
Along the shore our course we bore till we came near the Point of Stroove.
Our ship was good and might have stood, although tempestuous winds did blow,
Till by a shock upon a rock which caused our helm off to go.

Now our sad fate who can relate, as we lay on the ocean wide,
In great distress, as you may guess, being tossed about by wind and tide,
The powers above we did implore the swelling billows for to still,
Death did appear as we drew near the lovely shores of the Downhill.

At five o'clock our vessel struck, just as daylight did disappear;
Our boat was gone, all hope was done, and pale death to us drawing near.

But oh, our cries would have rent the skies when
    overboard our mainmast fell;
With heartfelt sighs and watery eyes we bade our
    friends a long farewell.

All o'er our ship the waves did wash; we thought
    in triumph we would rise
To mansions high above the sky where us poor
    pilgrims there would dwell.
Our wives and all our children small on earth we
    never shall see more,
But hopes to meet, when God thinks fit, to join
    that bright celestial corps.

The people there from everywhere came flocking
    round the sight to see:
Seven heroes' corpse[s] upon the shore, the
    Trader's doleful companee.
It's in Dunboe they're lying low, and there you'll
    see their green, green grave.
No friends were near, but strangers there we
    buried them in sweet Articlave.

Now to conclude and make an end, no more at
    present will I speak,
But I'll lay down my tender quill, more learned
    than me it for to take,
And hope that they, like Shakespeare, may tell
    their distress to great and small
And have it rolled in high record the gallant
    Trader's sad downfall.

The Wreck of the Rebecca

[H565: 29 Sep 1934]

Source: Alexander Horner, sr (Moycraig Hamilton, Mosside).

s: ... The adaptation of the words is indicated in the first line of the air.

Key G.

When first I thought on Americay,
I got all things ready and fit for sea,
My parents' counsel I never would take,
But I boldly ventured for riches' sake.

We had fine weather two days or three,
We had fine weather all round the sea,
We had fine weather all round the head,
Till our maintop royals was almost spread.

On Sunday morning, as you shall hear,
A warning came to our sailors dear,
A cock on deck, he was heard to crow,
Which filled our sailors' brave hearts with woe.

On Monday morning before daybreak
Our cursed *Rebecca* she sprang a leak;
All hands were called, as you shall hear,
For to pump her dry and keep her clear.

Our cabin boy, he being up aloft,
He spied a vessel a great way off,
He says, 'Yonder's a vessel for our relief,
But the raging sea will soon end our grief.'

We hoisted a signal on our main-top high,
Thinking the sailors the same would spy.
Brave Captain Moore now the same did see,
And came bearing down quite courageously.

Said brave Captain Hall to Captain Moore,
'There's nothing approaching but death, I'm sure;
Take one half of my men, I crave,
Let the rest prepare for a watery grave.'

Now these poor passengers they stood in amaze
And at each other they all did gaze,
Lifting their heads to the heavens high,
Saying, 'Lord, have mercy on us ere we die.'

Says brave Captain Moore, 'Such things can't be
As to see poor passengers lie in the sea,
But come on board here along with me,
For the Lord can save by land and sea.'

Brave Captain Moore, your praise I'll sing
Through England, Ireland, France and Spain,
And you may live a long life to see,
And the Lord protect you by land and sea.

The Good Ship Mary Cochrane

[H754: 7 May 1938]

Source: James Smyth, 80 (Buckie Knowe, Knockmult).

s: Taken down from James Smyth ... whose 80 years have been brightened by song and laughter.

Key D.

Sam Henry's Songs of the People

When first I thought on Americay,
Straight to the ocean I took my way;
Americay it was my intent,
But, alas, sad fortune it did prevent.

We had scarce sail-ed three days off shore,
We had scarce sail-ed three days or four,
Till upon deck a cock did crow,
Which filled our sailors' hearts with woe.

On Tuesday morning, just as day did break,
Our gallant vessel she sprung a leak,
She sprung a leak and was hard to steer,
But all hands were ready without dread or fear.

On Wednesday morning at four o'clock,
Our cabin boy being on the main-top,
He spied a vessel just at full sail
With a favouring blast and a pleasant gale.

Down to his master he then did go,
Saying, 'Master, master, blow high, blow low,
Put up a signal for our relief;
Or the raging seas will soon end our grief.'

They hoist a signal on the main-top
In hopes the passing ship to stop;
It's Captain Moore, he did us see
And came tearing down immediately.

Says Captain Friar unto Captain Moore,
'We are all in danger, I'm very sure;
Take you half of my men, I crave,
Let the rest prepare for a watery grave.'

Says Captain Moore, 'That can never be,
But let them all come on board with me.'
We had scarce out of our own boat gone,
Till she turned around like any drunk man.

It's *Mary Cochrane* is our good ship's name,
Through England, Ireland, her praise is famed;
She is of a good and noble fame,
For she saved our lives on the raging main.

The Banks of Newfoundland
[H569: 27 Oct 1934]

Source: (w) John Henry Macaulay (Bog Oak Shop, Ballycastle).

Key G.

Oh, you may bless your happy lot, that lies secure on shore,
Free from the billows and the blast that round poor seamen roar,
It's little you know the dangers that we were forced to stand
For fourteen days and fourteen nights on the banks of Newfoundland.

Our good ship never crossed before the stormy western seas,
The raging waves came tumbling down, soon beat her into staves,
She being of green unseasoned wood, little could she stand,
For the hurricane had met us on the banks of Newfoundland.

We fasted for three days and nights when our provisions they ran out,
And on the morning of the fourth we sent the lots about.
The lot fell on the captain's son, and you may understand,
We spared him for another day on the banks of Newfoundland.

No sails appeared; reluctantly we ordered him prepare,
We gave him just another hour to offer up a prayer,
But providence was always kind, kept blood from every hand,
When an English vessel hove in sight on the banks of Newfoundland.

When we were taken off the wreck, we were more like ghosts than men,
They clothed us and they used us well and brought us home again,
But four of our brave Irish boys ne'er saw their native land,
And our captain lost his legs by frost on the banks of Newfoundland.

The French Privateer
[H560: 25 Aug 1934]

Other titles: "The Spanish ..."; cf. "The Neat Irish Girl," "The *Polly* Privateer," "The *Saucy Dolphin*."

Source: (w, m) Alexander Horner (Moycraig Hamilton, Mosside, Co. Antrim).

s: ... The Ulster dialect has been closely followed in the spelling. The remarkable word "snow" is a curious survival. It is from the Dutch "snaauw," a boat, and signifies a vessel equipped with two masts and a third small mast, close to the mainsail, to carry a trysail.
The three-lined verses are sung to the 1st, 2nd and 4th lines of the air.

Key C.

A8 / Bound away to the west'rd

On the eighteenth day of Aperile as we lay bound
  for sea,
Our goodly ship we launch-ed all on that very
  day,
Bound for the stormy ocean, where the
  thundering billows roar,
And we left our sweethearts m[o]urning all on
  their native shore.

We sailed the seas for three long days till part of
  the fourth noon,
When sailing round it's the French coasts, a
  Spanish snow we spied;
Stand to your guns, my brave boys, our noble
  captain cried.

We knock-ed down our caybins and we kept the
  decks quite clear,
We engag-ed them for four long hours, till the
  snow she ran away,
'That's nobly done,' our captain cries, 'we will
  soon make her stay.'

When that our bold commander saw that the snow
  was gone,
He hoisted every sail he had and after her did
  run,
We quick-lie did pursue her till early the next
  day,
When a loft-ie bold French privateer come bearing
  down our way.

Oh, they hail-ed us in French, brave boys, and
  asked us whence we came,
'Or what is your ship's company, or to where do
  you belong?'
The answer that we gave to them, it was a quick
  reply,
'If you be our foe, we'll let you know, we're true-
  bred Irish boys.'

When they heerd that we were Irishmen, they at
  us a gun let fly,
And we in opposition returned it instant-lie;
We both sailed down together where our
  thundering cannons roar,
And we sunk that bold French privateer all on
  their native shore.

It was in that very same action that our captain
  he was slain,
Likewise our warlike officers and many of our
  men;

If it hadn't been for that French privateer, the
  snow would have been our prize,
For neither French nor Spanish can fight our
  Irish boys.

2.2: ... it's they French ... [Dp]
4.3: ... early they next ... [Dp]
 .4: ... come beering down ... [Dp]

1.1: Aperile = April.
2.2: snow = from the Dutch 'snaauw,' a boat; signifies a vessel equipped with two masts and a
  third small mast, close to the mainsail, to carry a
  trysail. [s]

Captain Coulston [H562: 8 Sep 1934]

Other titles: "... Colstein (Colston) (Coulson)
(and the Pirate Ship)."

Source: (w, m) Alexander Horner (Moycraig Hamilton, Mosside); also a native (Alla, near Park,
Co. Derry).

Key B flat.

Oh, you heroes bold of Ireland that does intend to
  roam,
That does intend to stop your work and leave
  your native home,
Come join with Captain Coulston, that hero stout
  and bold,
Who fought his ways across the seas and never
  was controlled.

From the eleventh of June till the twenty-first we
  sail-ed on the sea,
With low, long days and merriment going to
  Americay,
The captain and his lady came up on deck each
  day
To crown our joys with merriment while sailing on
  the sea.

When merriment was over and going to bed one
  night,
The captain he came round the deck to see if all
  was right;
The captain says, 'Look out, brave boys, you need
  not think on sleep,
For it's in a few more hours you'll lie slumbering
  in the deep.

'There's a pirate ship approaching down from yon
  western sea
To rob us of our cargo going to Americay.'

Sam Henry's Songs of the People

When the pirate ship came up to us, she ordered us to stand:
'Your gold and precious loading this day I do demand.

'Your gold and precious loading resign to me this day,
For there's not one mortal soul of you shall reach Americay.'
It's out speaks Captain Coulston, that hero stout and bold,
Saying, 'It's in the deep we all shall sleep before we be controlled.'

The battle it commenced, while blood in streams did flow,
There was fifteen of our passengers proved the pirates' overthrow,
There was a lady on the deck and her true love by her side,
And she fought her way right manfully along the bulwark side.

She says to them, 'Hold on, brave boys, and I'll soon end the strife,'
And with a pistol bullet she took the pirate captain's life;
The cries of the poor passengers would have filled your heart with woe,
But the captain and brave sailor lads true Irishmen did show.

The battle it was over, still blood in streams did flow,
It was fifteen of our passengers proved the pirates' overthrow.
Now to conclude and finish, I mean to tell to you,
We did not lose one single soul excepting one or two.

The pirate ship surrendered just by the break of day,
And we took her as a prisoner, bound for Americay;
The pirate ship surrendered just by the break of day,
And our Irish lads gave three loud cheers, all for Americay.

❖ A8 REFERENCES ❖

❖ **Kishmul's Galley** *(H 535b)* 96

    Brunnings 1981: "Kishmul's Galley," "Beinn A' Cheathaich"

    b: REC Norman Kennedy, Folk-Legacy FSS 34 (B6) "Kishmul's Galley"

    Sailors' shanties, p. 96:
      Cf. the stanza Henry quotes with stanza 1 in Hugill 1961:141-2 "The Gals o' Dublin Town (b)," and *ibid.* "Heave and Bust Her."

❖ **It's Time for Us to Leave Her** *(H 53b)* 96

    White/Dean-Smith 1951: "Across the Western Ocean"
    Brunnings 1981: "Across the Western Ocean," "Leave Her, Johnny - Leave Her," "Leave Her, Johnny, Leave Her"

    IREL Meek 1978:18-9 "Across the Western Ocean"

    BRIT Davis/Tozer n.d.:11 "Leave Her Johnnie"
      Hugill 1961:292-8 "Leave Her, Johnny(, Leave Her)," 4+ vts.
        Hugill 1977b:58-9
        Nettel 1954:44

    AMER Scofield 1981:109 "Leave Her Johnny"

    BRS *A Broadside* 2(8,Jan)1910 "Leave Her, Johnny"

    lc: REC Sam Eskin, Folkways FP 19
      Leander Macumber, Folkways FM 4006 (B19c) "Leave Her, Johnny, Leave Her"
    b: Ed McCurdy, Elektra EKL 205
    cl: Capt. Richard Maitland, AFS 2533 B2 "Leave Her, Johnny, Leave Her"
      Bob Roberts, Topic 12TS 361 "Leave Her, Johnny"
      Hjalmar Rutzebeck, Folkways FSS 38554 (B3) "Leave Her, Johnnie"
    b: *Songs and Sounds of the Sea*, National Geographic 705 "Leave Her, Johnny, Leave Her"
    b: The Starboard List, Adelphi AD 1025 "Leave Her, Johnny, Leave Her"
      Tom Sullivan, Folkways FSS 37301 (B8) "Leave Her, Johnny"

❖ **Tom's Gone to Ilo** *(H 53d)* 96

    White/Dean-Smith 1951: (Chanties)
    Brunnings 1981: "... Hilo"

    BRIT Baker/Miall 1982:276-7 "... Hilo"
      Davis/Tozer n.d.:44-5
      Hugill 1961:261-4
      Smith 1888:33-4

    AMER Doerflinger 1951:30 "Tommy's ... Hilo"

    REC Stuart Frank, Folkways FTS 37300 (A8) "Tommy's ... Hilo"
    b: Ewan MacColl, A. L. Lloyd, Prestige/Int. 13043
    cl: Capt. Richard Maitland, AFS 2522B "Tommy's ... Hilo"

❖ **Santy Anna** *(H 496)* 96

    White/Dean-Smith 1951: (Chanties) "Santa ..."
    Brunnings 1981: "...," "Santa Anna," "... - Run Away"

    BRIT Davis/Tozer n.d.:34 "On the Plains of Mexico"
      Hugill 1977b:51-3 "Santiana"
      Whall (3d ed., 1913):89 "The Plains of Mexico"

    AMER Darling 1983:308-9 "Santy Anna"
    # Fowke 1981:27 "On the Plains of Mexico"

    AUST AT #19(Mar)1969:20-1

    REC Cf. Dan Aguiar, Folkways FTS 37311 (A2) "Santian[n]o"
    lc: Bill Bonyun, Folkways FP(FOL) 2 "... Anno"
      Garrett Brown, Al Dana, MGM E/SE 4153 "Santianno"
      Clancy Brothers, Tommy Makem, Columbia CS 9658 "... Anno (The Plains of Mexico)"
      Paul Clayton, Tradition TLP 1005
    cl: James M. Connolly, AFS 3627 B8, 3632 A1
    b: Meredydd Evans, Tradition TR 2078 "Santiana"
      Stuart M. Frank, Folkways FTS 37300 (A13) "... An[n]a"

A8 / Bound away to the west'rd

cl: John M. "Sailor Dad" Hunt, AFS 2839 B1, 2840 A1, 652 B "... Anno"
 Edward "Sandy" Ives, Folkways FH 5323 (A4)
cl: Capt. Richard Maitland, AFS 2519 B
 Hermes Nye, Folkways FH 2187 (A3) "Santa ..."; Folkways FH 5801 (E5)
 William Pint, Folkways FSS 38554 (B8) "Sana Anna," an unusual sad-love song text from Hjalmar Rutzebeck.
 Cf. The Watersons, Topic 12T 142 (B6) "The Plains of Mexico"
b: The Weavers, Vanguard FRS 9024 "Aweigh, Santy Ano"
b: X Seamans Institute, Folkways FTS 32419 "Santianno"

◆ Paddy Doyle *(H 53c)* 97

Brunnings 1981

BRIT Davis/Tozer n.d.:66
 Hugill 1977b:131
 Whall (3d ed. 1913):115

\# AMER Fowke 1981:28 "We'll Pay ... for His Boots"

b: REC Clancy Brothers, Tommy Makem, Tradition/ Everest TLP 1042 (A4); Tradition/Everest TR 2050 (B1) "...'s Boots"
b: Paul Clayton, Tradition TLP 1005 "...'s Boots"
lc: Sam Eskin, Folkways FP 19 "...'s Boots"
 A. L. Lloyd, Tradition TLP 1026 (A2)
b: A. L. Lloyd, Ewan MacColl, Stinson SLP 81
 Capt. Richard Maitland, [cl:] AFS 2532 A1, 2532 B1; AAFS L26 (B2) [Fowke]

◆ I'm Going Home *(H 53a)* 97

Brunnings 1981: "Goodbye, Fare You Well," "Goodbye Fare-Ye-Well - We're Homeward Bound to Liverpool Town," "Homeward Bound"

BRIT Greig/Duncan 1,1981:6 (#5) "Good-bye, Fare Ye Well," 2 vts.
 Hugill 1961:120 "Goodbye, Fare Ye Well"
 Hugill 1977b:56-7
 Whall (3d ed, 1913):17

AMER Fowke 1981:34 "Goodbye, Fare Ye Well"

REC Stanley Baby, Folkways 4018 (A7) "Homeward Bound" [Fowke]
 Clark Branson/Morrigan, Folkways FSS 38554 (D9) "Goodbye Fare Ye Well"
 Stuart Frank, Folkways FTS 37300 (A11) "Goodbye Fare Ye Well"
 Capt. Leighton Robinson, AAFS L 27 (B5) "Homeward Bound" [Fowke]

◆ The Girls of Valparaiso *(H 539)* 97

White/Dean-Smith 1951: "Rounding the Horn"
Brunnings 1981: "Around Cape Horn," ?"Around Cape Horn - Where Wild Winds Blow," "The Girls around Cape Horn," "The Gals around Cape Horn," "Round Cape Horn - The *Amphitrite*," "Round Cape Horn - Our Ship She Lay in Harbour," "Rounding the Horn"

IREL Moulden 1979:62

BRIT Baker/Niall 1982:165-7 "... around Cape Horn"
 Clements 1928:82-3 "Around Cape Horn"
 Hugill 1961:53-4, a related song.
 Richards/Stubbs 1979:36 "Rounding Cape Horn"
 Sharp/Karpeles 1974,2:290-1 "Cape Horn" (#290)

b: REC Paul Clayton, Tradition TLP 1005 "The Girls around Cape Horn"

b: Ewan MacColl, Peggy Seeger, Tradition 2059
 Tom Sullivan, Folkways FSS 37301 (A3) "Gals around Cape Horn"
b: Cyril Tawney, Argo ZFB 9 "Rounding the Horn"

◆ The Cruise of the Calabar *(H 502)* 98

White/Dean-Smith 1951: "(The) Manchester 'Angel' or ...; Farewell Manchester"
Brunnings 1981: "The Cruise of the *Calabar/Calibar*," "The Good Ship *Calabah*," "The Manchester Canal - Lancashire"; cf. "The Wreck of the *Mary Jane*"

b: IREL Hammond 1978:32-3 "... Calibar"
 Harte 1978:16-7
b: Cf. O Lochlainn 1939:40-1 "The Wreck of the *Mary Jane*"
b: O Lochlainn 1965:34-5

BRS *Derry Journal* [c. 1925],1:52 "The Strabane Fleet"; 2: a different version.
 Healy 1967a:121-3

REC Gary, Vera Aspey, Topic 12TS 407 (A5) "... Calibar"
 Clancy Brothers, Tommy Makem, Columbia CS 9658 "The Good Ship *Calibar*"
b: David Hammond, Tradition TLP 1028 (A10)
 Irish Folk Night, London LL 3414 "The Good Ship *Calabah*"
b: Cyril Tawney, Argo ZFB 9
b: Emma Vickers, EFDSS LP 1006 (A6)

◆ The Zared *(H 194)* 99

Laws 1964:167 (D13) "The *Dreadnaught*." g: Perhaps Laws is correct in including "The *Dreadnaught*" as American; however, it derives from a broadside ballad about a British naval vessel, "La *Pique*." Both "La *Pique*" and "The *Dreadnaught*" are printed by Whall and Hugill, see below. Cf. Smith 1888:56-8 "Goodbye, Fare Ye Well."
Brunnings 1981: "...," "The *Dreadnaught/Dreadnought*"

BRIT Hugill 1961:462-6 "The Flash Frigate [La *Pique*]," "The *Dreadnaught*"
 Spin 5(2)1966:14-5 "La *Pique* or the Fancy Frigate"
 Whall 1910(3d ed. 1913):17-21 "The *Dreadnaught*," "La *Pique*"

AMER Fowke 1981:19 "Liverpool Packet"
 Harlow 1962:101-4
 Milner/Kaplan 1983:107 "The *Dreadnaught*"

AUST *AT* #36(Dec)1974:11 "Goodbye Fare Ye Well (Capstan Song)"

REC Stanley Baby, Folkways FM 4018 (A3) "The *Dreadnaught*" [Fowke]
 Cliff Haslam, National Geographic 705 (A1b) "The *Dreadnought*"
 Gale Huntington, New World NW 239 (B3) "The *Dreadnaught*" [Fowke]
 Louis Killen, South Street Seaport SPT 102 [Milner/ Kaplan]
b: A. L. Lloyd, Ewan MacColl, Stinson SLP 81 "The *Dreadnaught*"
 Tom Sullivan, Folkways FS 3566 (B9) "The *Dreadnaught*"

◆ Yellow Meal *(H 827)* 100

Brunnings 1981: "... (See: We're All Bound to Go)," "We're All Bound to Go"

IREL Moulden 1979:153-4

AMER Beck 1957:182-3 "Tab Scott," with a 4-line nonsense chorus (= Wright 1975:530).
    Mackenzie 1928:259-61 "We're All away to Sea"
    Milner/Kaplan 1983:110-1 "Tabscott (We're All Bound to Go)"

BRS Healy 1967a:31-2 "We're All Bound to Go," a semi-chantey version.
m: O'Conor 1901:56, probably the collection to which Henry refers.

g: The chantey "We're All Bound to Go" came from this ballad. For some other versions of the chantey, see:
    Davis/Tozer n.d.:8-9,
    Harlow 1962:14-18,
    Hugill 1961:303-8,
    Hugill 1977b:46-8,
    Smith 1888:54-6,
    Whall (3d ed. 1913):79.

AUST AT #36(Dec)1974:3-4 "Heave away, My Johnny (Capstan Song)"

b: REC John Roberts, Tony Barrand, Swallowtail ST 4

◊ *The Shamrock Shore* (H192) 101

Probably not = the same title in Dean-Smith 1954
Brunnings 1981: "...," "Paddy's Green ... (Green ...)"

IREL Moulden 1979:131-2
m: Ranson 1948(1973):55
    Shields 1981:87-8 (#33) "Greencastle Shore"
m: Shields/Shields *UF* 1975: #177 "Greencastle Shore"
But not = the same title in O Lochlainn 1965:174-5, 246-7

And not: AMER Wright 1975 (from Kidson/Moffat [1926])

m: BRS O'Conor 1901:74

h: REC Paul Brady, Mulligan LUN 024 "Greencastle Shore"
m: Packie Byrne, EFDSS LP 1009 (B3) "Paddy's Green ..."
    Five Hand Reel, Topic 12TS 406 (B3) "Paddy's Green ..."; Topic TPSS 412 (B4)
    Dolores Keane, Green Linnet SIF 3003 (Mulligan LUN 043) (A1) "Paddy's Green ..."
    Joe McCafferty, EEOT *Ceolta agus* cass. (A8) "Paddy's Green ..."
h: Wolfe Tones, Dolphin TRL 1002 "Greencastle Shore"

◊ *Patrick O'Neal* (H552) 102

Brunnings 1981

IREL Moulden 1979:116-7

BRIT Cf. Dunstan 1932(1972):38-9 "The Press Gang"

REC Cf. Roy Harris, Fellside FE 017 (A2) "Muddley Barracks"

◊ *The Sailor Boy* (H543) 103

Laws 1957:147 (K13) "The Faithful Sailor Boy"
Brunnings 1981: "... - It Was a Dark and Stormy Night," "The Faithful Sailor Boy"

IREL Ranson 1948(1973):32-3

BRIT Dunn 1980:80-1 (cf. also Webb rec.)

    Greig 1907-11(1963): #64 "...'s Farewell"
    Greig/Duncan 1,1981:151-6 (#66) "The Faithful ...," 8 vts. ("The Sailor (Boy)('s Farewell)")
Munch 1970:58-60

AMER Cf. Fuson 1931:61-2 "The Soldier Boy" (see Jolliffe ref.)
    Haskins n.d.:116
    Manny/Wilson 1968:237-8 "The Faithful ..."

BRS Healy 1967a:24-5 "Your Faithful ..."
    Jolliffe 1970:108, 1 stanza quoted to show its relationship to "The Irish Soldier Boy."

cl: REC J. W. Green, AFS 3285 B
cl: Austin Harmon, AFS 2219 A2
cl: Samuel Harmon, AFS 2802 A1
? cl: Mrs L. L. McDowell, AFS 3182 B1 "...'s Request"
    Oak, Topic 12TS 212 (A5) "The Faithful ..."
    Cyril Poacher, Topic 12TS 252 (B6) "The Faithful ..."
    George Spicer, Topic 12T 235 (A4) "The Faithful ..."
    C. K., Dick Tillett, Folkways FS 3848 (B1)
    Percy Webb, Topic 12TS 243 "The Faithful ..."

◊ *Franklin the Brave* (H815) 103

Laws 1957:144-5 (K9) "Lady Franklin's Lament [The Sailor's Dream]"
Brunnings 1981: "Franklin's Crew," "Lord Franklin"

BRIT Greig/Duncan 1,1981:34-5 (#16) "(Lady) Franklin's Lament," 3 vts.
    Kelly 1964:17 "Lord Franklin"
    Sing 4(3,Aug-Sep)1957:41 "Lord Franklin"
    Spin 4(5):3 "Lord Franklin"

AMER Creighton 1971:202 "Franklin and His Bold Crew"

BRS BPL H.80

REC Martin Carthy, Topic 12TS 341 (A4) "Lord Franklin"
    Jerry Corcoran, Folkways FSS 38405 (A5) "Lord Franklin"
    Micheál Ó Domhnaill, Green Linnet SIF 3010 (= Mulligan) (A2) "Lord Franklin"
    Wade Hemsworth, Folkways FW 6821 (A6) "The Franklin Expedition"
b: A. L. Lloyd, Ewan MacColl, Stinson SLP 81 "Lord Franklin"
    Pentangle, Transatlantic XTRA 1172 (A3) "Lord Franklin"
    Alphonse Sutton, Folkways FE 4075 (B4) "Franklin"
    Mark Wittow, Folkways FES 34031 (A3b) "Lament for Lord Franklin"

◊ *Loss of Seven Clergymen* (H742) 104

IREL Cf. Shields 1981:191 (index) "Seven Priests"

◊ *The Portrush Fishing Disaster (I)* (H27b) 105

IREL Moulden 1979:120
    Cf. Shields/Shields *UF* 21, 1975: #322 "... Fishermen"

◊ *The Portrush Fishing Disaster (II)* (H27c) 105

m: IREL See 2 versions (1 m) in Lyle *IFMS* 1974-5: 18, also p. 16, n. 2, which includes a reference to Shields/Shields *UF* 1975: #322, "... Fishermen."
    Moulden 1979:120. "Len Graham believes this song is still sung in Portrush" (p. 164).

◇ The Wreck of the Enterprise *(H558)* 106

IREL Moulden 1979:152 describes the local tradition, which sets a precise date and location of the wreck (and description of the cargo), even though Lloyd's of London, the famous British insurance agency, informed Sam Henry nothing was found in its records. He also reports another version collected by Len Graham.

BRIT See *Tocher* #31(Sum)1979:7-8 "Macrihanish Bay," which Hamish Henderson says is a version Willie Mitchell learned from Alec McShannon.

◇ The Falcon *(H95)* 107

Not = same title in Brunnings 1981.

◇ The Loss of the Royal Charter *(H623)* 109

? Brunnings 1981: "The Wreck of the *Royal Charter*"

IREL Cf. Shields 1981:191 (Index) "Royal ...," with reference to fragments he collected.

Not: b: BRIT Palmer 1978 "The Wreck of the *Royal Charter*"

Not: b: REC Roy Harris, Topic 12TS 256 (B4) "The *Royal* ...," a different ballad entirely.

◇ The Trader *(H11)* 110

Brunnings 1981: (m) "Caledonian Hunt's Delight (Tune of The Banks o' Doon and Ye Banks and Braes o' Bonnie Doon)"

h: IREL Moulden 1979:146-7 says a version sung by Eddie Butcher is in Len Graham's collection.
  Shields 1981:150-2 (#68)
m: Shields/Shields *UF* 21,1975: #411

h: MEL O'Neill 1903 (1963):54 (#311) "The Banks of Lough Foyle"

◇ The Wreck of the Rebecca *(H565)* 111

AMER Wright 1975:329 (from Henry coll., BCL)

The Good Ship Mary Cochrane *(H754)* 111

IREL Moulden 1979:64

◇ The Banks of Newfoundland *(H569)* 112

l: Cf. also the French-language ballads "Sept ans sur mer" [Fowke] and "La courte paille."

Brunnings 1981: "... - Oh, Ye May Bless Your Happy Lots"; cf. "Sept Ans sur Mer (Seven Years at Sea)," "There Was Once a Little Ship - French"

IREL Ranson 1948(1973):118-9 [Fowke]
Shields 1981:46-7 (#6)
  Shields/Shields *UF* 21,1975: #29

BRIT *Tocher* #26(Aut)1977:93

AMER Fowke 1981:56-7 "... (On the ...)"; also lists another version in her collection.

BRS Harvard 1: 4.82 (Ross)
h: Healy 1967a:?98, 105-7

REC O. J. Abbott, Folkways FM 4051 (B7)
b: Margaret Christl, Ian Robb, Folk-Legacy FSC 62 (B5)
  LaRena Clark, Clark LCS 109 [Fowke]
? b: Bob, Louise De Cormier, Riverside/Wonderland RLP 1404 "The Little Sailors"
? Chris Foster, Topic 12TS 329
cl: Cf. Elida Hofpauir and sister, AAFS L5 (A8) "Sept Ans sur Mer"
  Cf. Ewan MacColl, Tradition TLP 1026 (B2)

A similar ballad with the same title is Laws 1957:153 (K25), which deals with the cold and hardships but not a shipwreck and rescue, e.g.:
b: Colcord 1938:173-4,
  Hugill 1977b:151-3,
  Vaughan Williams/Lloyd 1959:16-7,
  Warner 1984:327-9 (#141).

Creighton/Senior print 2 variants of "The *Dreadnought*" [= H194 The *Zared*] under this title. Yet another with the same title appears to be a native Newfoundland song: Peacock 1965,1:108-9

◇ The French Privateer *(H560)* 112

g: There are a number of what seem to be related songs. For some of them see:
  Creighton 1961:87 "The Neat Irish Girl",
  Greig 1907-11(1963): #125 "The *Saucy Dolphin*",
  Ashton 1891:84 "The *Polly* Privateer."

? Brunnings 1981: "The *Saucy Dolphin*," "The Neat Irish Girl"

IREL Moulden 1979:61; also lists a BBC Archive recording from Antrim.
m: Ranson 1948(1973):33-4 "The Spanish Privateer"

? b: AMER Rickaby 1926 "The *Saucy Dolphin*"

◇ Captain Coulston *(H562)* 113

Brunnings 1981: "... Colstein"

IREL Ranson 1948(1973):78-9, "one of the most popular ballads on the Wexford coast."

b: AMER Fowke 1965:22-3 "Captain Colstein" (see also Abbott rec.); she reports 2 more versions recorded for the BBC.
  Wright 1975:290-1 "Captain Colston" (from brs, Bebbington, BM)

BRS Harvard 1: 7.240 "Captain Coulston and the Pirate Ship"; 13.87 (Such), 9.128 (Bebbington)
  Healy 1967a:43-5

REC O. J. Abbott, Folkways FM 4051 (B5) "... Coldstein"
  Paddy Tunney, Topic 12TS 289 (A2) "... Coulson"

A bold undaunted youth: Crime

Botany Bay

[H691: 20 Feb 1937; Laws L16a]

Other titles: "The Transport('s Farewell)"; cf. "The Boston Burg(u)lar," "Frank James," "The Whitby Lad."

Source: Joe M'Conaghy (Main St, Bushmills) from a worker in Liscolman mill c. 1905.

Key G.

All you young men a warning, a warning take by me,
I'll advise you, stop nights walking, or else you'll rue the day,
I'll advise you, stop nights walking and shun bad company,
You'll be sent on transportation, my lads, you'll be sent to Botany Bay.

I was bred and born in sweet Belfast, a city you all know well,
Brought up by honest parents, the truth to you I'll tell,
Brought up by honest parents and reared right tenderly
Until I became a rakish blade through town and country.

My character was broken and I was sent to jail,
My parents strove to clear me, but the judge would take no bail,
My parents strove to clear me, but the judge to me did say,
'The jury has found you guilty, you must go to Botany Bay.'

Had you seen my tender father as he stood at the bar,
Likewise my aged mother, her old grey locks she tore,
And these my aged parents, they unto me did say,
'Oh son, dear son, what have you done that you're sent to Botany Bay?'

As we sailed down yon riverside on the twenty-first of May,
From every ship that we passed by, as we sped on our way,
From every ship that we passed by, we could hear the sailors say,
'Yonder goes a ship of clever young lads and they're bound for Botany Bay.'

A9 / A bold undaunted youth

The Boston Burglar

[H202: 24 Sep 1927; Laws L16b]

s: (m) "Bold Jack Donahoe." Other titles: "(The) ... Burgular (City) (Smuggler)," "Botany Bay," "Bound for Charlers (Sydney) Town," "Charlestown," "I Was Born in Boston," "Louisville Burglar"; cf. "The Colton Boy," "Frank James, the Roving Gambler," "Letcher County Burglar," "Market Square."

Source: (m) William Devine (Cross Lane, Coleraine).

[Bp] s: This song is repeatedly in request by correspondents in "The People's Journal" and other journals....

Key E flat.

I was born in Boston, a place you all know well,
Brought up by honest parents, the truth to you I'll tell,
Brought up by honest parents and reared most tenderly,
Till I became a sporting youth at the age of twenty-three.

My character was taken and I was sent to jail.
My friends combined together to get me out on bail,
But the jury found me guilty, the clerks they wrote it down,
The judge he passed my sentence: I was off for Charlestown.

Look at my aged father standing at the bar,
Likewise my dear old mother, her old grey locks she tore,
At the tearing of her old grey locks the tears came rolling down,
Crying, 'Son, dear son, what have you done? You're off for Charlestown.'

And now on board, a passenger in a dark December day,
At every station as I pass I hear the people say,
'Here comes the Boston burglar, with strong chains he is bound,
For some crime or another, he is off for Charlestown.'

Sam Henry's Songs of the People

There is a girl in Boston, a girl that I know
   well,
If e'er I have my liberty, with her I mean to
   dwell,
If e'er I have my liberty, bad company I'll
   shun,
Likewise my nights' rambling, likewise my
   drinking rum.

Come all you highwaymen, take a warning when
   you can,
To never tramp the streets at night nor break
   the laws of man,
For if you do you'll surely rue and then you'll
   be like me,
You'll be serving up your twenty-one years in a
   penitentiary.

4.4: ... off to Charlestown.' [Dt]
5.1: ... Boston, take a warning when you can, [Dt]
5.2-6.1: [Absent from Dt; ?typist's error.]
6.2-.4 [Dt] = 5.2-.4 [Bp].

The Wild Colonial Boy

[H750: 9 Apr 1938; Laws L20]

s: (m) "Bold Jack Donahoe." Other title: cf. "The Wild Montana Boy."

Source: composite "embodying the best in the several versions received" from contributors: Mrs David Browne (Lachute Mills, Quebec, Canada); John Anderson (Blenheim, Ontario, Canada); Albert Cole (Upperlands, Co. Derry); Alexander M'Elmoyle (Terrydoo Walker, Limavady); Bernard Walls (Annagh, Desertmartin); and "esteemed correspondent," letter quoted below.

s: An esteemed correspondent, a native of County Derry, writes from North Auckland, New Zealand, as follows:

I note in your issue of December 25th last a request for the accompanying song. Unfortunately, I cannot supply the musical notes, though I know the air well. Sixty years ago many of the ballads were set to it, though at the moment I can recall only a line of an old song:-- "To win' and dry your hay."
The "Wild Colonial Boy" was the most popular song in the Australian "Bush" when I landed in Victoria in 1880, the year in which the Kelly gang was stamped out, though the song itself is, of course, much older.
Another favourite song at that time was one descriptive of the famous Sayers and Heenan fight, the chorus of which, sung to a popular waltz tune, ran:

   Then shout hurrah! for Heenan and Sayers we
     will sing,
   For they are the best and bravest that fought
     in a British ring.

On both sides of the Atlantic the bout was of great international interest. Fifty years ago I listened to a graphic description of it by a man who witnessed the great combat. Its importance may be gauged by the fact that Parliament ceased its deliberations to attend the great battle, which ended in a draw, though the plucky little Sayers had an arm bone broken early in his fight with the much heavier American champion.

Castlemaine mentioned in the song is about ten miles south of Tralee in County Kerry. Castlemaine, in Victoria, Australia, 78 miles N.N.W. of Melbourne, one of the earliest of the gold diggings, is named from the Irish village. Beechworth is about 130 miles N.N.E. of Melbourne.

l: This song "has been distinguished [from "Bold Jack Donohue"] on the ground that [this] always has the names of the 3 pursuing officers and ["Donohue"] always has some reference to an escape from the jail at Sydney" (notes to Folkways FE 4001, booklet p. 8). John Greenway says that the related song "Bold Jack Donohue" "became an expression of political protest" and was banned by 19th-century Australian authorities. "Because of the official opposition, 'Bold Jack Donohue' was probably generalized into 'The Wild Colonial Boy'" (notes to Folkways FW 8718, booklet p. 6)."

Key E flat.

It's of a wild colonial boy, Jack Doolan was his
   name,
Of poor but honest parents he was born in
   Castlemaine,
He was his father's comfort, his mother's pride
   and joy,
And dearly did they always love their wild colonial
   boy.

   So now away, my hearties, that roam the
     mountain side,
   Together we will plunder, together we will ride,
   We'll wander over hills and we'll gallop over
     plains
   Before we'll work in slavery, bound down in
     iron chains.

At the tender age of sixteen years he left his
   native home
And to Australia's sunny land, a stranger he did
   roam;
He robbed the wealthy squires and their arms he
   did destroy,
And a terror to Australia was this wild colonial
   boy.

At the early age of eighteen years he began his
   wild career,
With a heart that knew no danger and a spirit
   knew no fear;

He stuck up Beechworth mail coach and robbed
   Judge M'Avoy,
Who trembling gave his money to the wild colonial
   boy.

He bade the judge good morning and told him to
   beware
And never lag a lantry cove that acted on the
   square,
And never part a mother from her son and only
   joy,
For fear he might turn robber like the wild colonial
   boy.

One morning as he gaily rode along the mountain
   side,
A-listening to the lyre-birds that pleasantly did
   chide,
When lo, three mounted troopers -- Evans, Kelly
   and Fitzroy --
Rode up and tried to capture the wild colonial
   boy.

'Surrender now, Jack Doolan, you see we're three
   to one,
Surrender in the king's name, you daring
   highwayman.'
Jack drew a pistol from his belt and shook the
   little toy,
'I'll die but not surrender,' cried the wild colonial
   boy.

He fired a shot at Kelly, which brought him to the
   ground,
Returning fire from Evans, he received a mortal
   wound,
But with his life fast ebbing, he kept firing at
   Fitzroy,
And that's the way they captured the wild colonial
   boy.

4.2: lag = term of transportation, penal servitude.
     cove = fellow, chap.
     on the square = without deceit, directly, openly.

Eight Mile Bridge [H486: 25 Mar 1933]

Other title: "Roger O Hehir."

Source: (m, w) John Elliot (Turfahun, Bushmills).

s: ... Turfahun, in Gaelic, is Tir-fo-thon (t silent -- pronounced exactly as the townland is locally named). It means "the land under waves," an apt description of Ireland as seen from the shores of the Scottish Highlands. The homesick Highlanders who settled in Antrim actually named a district near the Causeway, "Lochaber," after their own homeland.
  Turfahun and district is very rich in traditional folk music.
  Mr John Elliot is one of several excellent traditional fiddlers in the district named.

Key C.

A9 / A bold undaunted youth

At the Eight-Mile Bridge in the County Down,
I had honest parents of fame and renown,
Had I been obedient and kept their command,
I ne'er would have broken the laws of the land.

   Ladly fol ol dha dee.

My parents endeavoured to give me honest bread
And bound me apprentice unto the linen trade
To an honest weaver that lived hard by.
My mind being for rambling, it would not comply.

One beautiful creature, Jane Sharkey by name,
I gained her affections and I was to blame,
I own I enticed her and we ran away,
And my troubles began from that very same day.

That beautiful creature I then left forlorn,
And for fear of her parents I stepped up to
   Mourne,
But her cruel father pursued me with spite
And made me a prisoner that very same night.

Then it's off to Newry guard-house straightway I
   was sent,
For to whip me next morning it was their intent;
When I heard of this it put me in a fright,
And I broke Newry guard-house that very same
   night.

The guards they pursued me the very next day,
But the guards I beguiled and I soon got away;
Says the one to the other, 'He'll travel no more,'
And that very same night Newry Lough I swam o'er.

I rested myself for a day or two more,
I went to rob a bleach green where I ne'er was
   before,
They were strong of guards in the bleach green
   within,
They surrounded poor Roger and I taken was
   again.

Then back to Newry guard-house straightway I
   was sent,
For to hang me next morning it was their intent,
When I heard of this it put me in a fright
And I broke Newry guard-house that very same
   night.

The guards they pursued me the very same way,
But the guards I beguiled and I soon got away;
I went down to the shore where a vessel did lie,
I put my foot on shipboard and for England
   sailed I.

121

Sam Henry's Songs of the People

It's when that I landed in sweet Holyhead,
I had no honest way for to earn my bread,
I was loth for to beg but, alas, I did worse:
To make myself money I stole a grey horse.

It's when that I landed on sweet Irish ground,
I began my old tricks near fair Newry town.
For I stole a hat from one Thomas Wright,
And he made me his prisoner that very same night.

Now for to conclude and finish my wrath,
I never was occasion of any man's death,
But now I'm cut off in the height of my bloom
And an unworthy member of my father's old home.

Whiskey in the Jar

[H792: 28 Jan 1939; Laws L13a]

Other titles: "Captain Devin (Kelly)," "Gilgar(r)y Mountain," "The Highwayman," "The Irish Robber," "Sporting Hero," "There's ...," "... a Jar," "... Bar."

Source: John Laughlin, gardener (the Manse, Cumber-Claudy; native of Ervey).

Key C.

As I walked over Mulberry Mountain,
I met Captain Evans and his money he was
  counting;
I first drew my sword and then drew my rapier,
'Come stand and deliver, for I'm a bold desaver.'

Musha, rigga-do-a-da,
For there's whiskey in the jar.

I put my hand into his pocket, I fetch'd out fifty
  guineas,
I put it in my own; wasn't that a purty penny?
I fetch'd it home to Molly, not thinking she'd
  deceive me,
But the divil's in the weemen, for they never can
  be aisy.

I went to Molly's chamber to get a little slumber,
I lay down on the bed and I began to wonder;
I had not been lying long before I was awakened,
The press gang overtook me, and among them
  Captain Evans.

But Molly she was cunning, she knew what was the
  matter,
My pistols she disloadened and she filled them full
  of water,
She discharged my pistols that she had filled with
  water,
And a prisoner I was taken like a lamb to the
  slaughter.

I stood in the hall when the roll was a-calling,
I stood in the hall when the turnkey was a-
  bawling,
And by a metal ball I put the sentry down,
And I made my escape into Londonderry town.

[*spoken after last refrain:*]
And there's mair behind the bar.

1.4: desaver = deceiver.
2.4: weemen = women.
2.5: aisy [aizee] = easy, comfortable, unstrained.
4.2: disloadened = unloaded.

Waltzing Matilda [H566: 6 Oct 1934]

Source: Australian Boy Scouts at summer camp at Ganavan Sands, Oban.

s: This song should prove popular as a marching songs for Scouts, Boys' Brigades, Girl Guides....
    The second last line in each verse is repeated in the second last line of the chorus following.
    We are indebted to Oliver Paul, esq, J.P., for an interpretation of the Australian dialect....

g: Versions of this song will be found in many popular song books. Henry's setting of this melody [in 3/4 time!] leaves something to be desired.

l: Dyer-Bennet [1971:166] says the author is Andrew Barton "Banjo" Patterson (1864-1941) and the tune is a variant of a Scottish regimental march, "Craigielea." He cites a book by Sydney May, *The Story of 'Waltzing Matilda'* (1955), published in Australia.

Key D.

122

Once a jolly swaggie came to a bilabong
Under the shade of a coolibah tree,
And he sang as he sat and waited till his billy
   boiled,
'You'll come a-waltzing, Matilda, with me.'
   Waltzing Matilda, waltzing Matilda,
   You'll come a-waltzing, Matilda, with me,
   And he sang as he sat and waited till his billy
      boiled,
   'You'll come a-waltzing, Matilda, with me.'

Down came a jumbuk to drink at the bilabong,
Up jumped the swaggie and grabbed him with glee,
And he sang, as he put that jumbuk in his tucker-
   bag,
'You'll come a-waltzing, Matilda, with me.'
   Waltzing Matilda, ...

Down came the squatter mounted on his
   thoroughbred,
Down came the troopers, one, two, three,
'Whose that jolly jumbuk you've got in your
   tucker-bag?
You'll come a-waltzing, Matilda, with me.'
   Waltzing Matilda, ...

Up jumped the swaggie and jumped into the
   bilabong,
'You'll never catch me alive,' said he,
And his ghost may be heard as you pass by the
   bilabong,
'You'll come a-waltzing, Matilda, with me.'
   Waltzing Matilda, ...

Dialect interpretation from Oliver Paul, esq, J.P.:
1.1: swaggie (or swagman or sundowner) = a man
   who tramps the country in Australia and carries
   his swag, i.e., a blue blanket which he lays out
   on the ground, covers with a piece of canvas 8 feet
   by 4 feet in which he rolls all his belongings.
1.1: bilabong = an arm of the river running into the
   land for half a mile or more, which rises and falls
   according to the water in the river.
1.2: coolibah = coonibark, a tree, from the bark of
   which cut right round the base and also 6 or 7 feet
   up, a ready roof is made for the shack or hut.
1.3: billy = a can with a lid used for boiling water
   to make tea, etc.
1.4: waltzing Matilda = a name for a commercial traveller's bag of samples.

Heather Jock [H39: 9 Aug 1924]

s: (m) "Cameron's Got His Wife Again."

Source: (w) book on Scottish humor.

s: This song was traced by me from two lines
which had survived in the Cloyfin district:

> Swank and soople, sharp and thin;
> Fine for gaun against the win'.

Search for the remainder in the Coleraine neighbourhood was in vain, but a book on Scottish
humour, lent to me by a friend, contained the
song without the music. Further investigation
brought the tune and the history of this, one of
the most original and attractive of Scottish ballads. "Heather Jock" was John Ferguson, of
Dunblane, who, on 18th April, 1812, was transported for life for various acts of theft, especially stealing cows and black cattle.

Key C.

Heather Jock's noo awa',
Heather Jock's noo awa'.
The muircock noo may crousely craw
Since Heather Jock's noo awa'.

Heather Jock was stark and grim,
Faucht wi' a' would fecht wi' him,
Swank and supple, sharp and thin,
Fine for gaun against the win',
Tawnie face and tousie hair,
In his cleading unco bare,
Cursed and swore whene'er he spoke,
Nane could equal Heather Jock.

Jock kent ilka bore and bole,
Could creep through a wee bit hole,
Quietly pilfer eggs and cheese,
Dunts o' bacon, skeps o' bees,
Sip the kirn and steal the butter,
Nail the hens without a flutter.
Na! the watchfu' wily cock
Durstna craw for Heather Jock.

Eppie Blaikie lost her goun,
She coft sae dear at borough toun,
Sandy Tamson's Sunday wig
Left the hoose to run the rig,
Jenny Baxter's blankets a'
Took a thocht to slip awa',
And a' the weans bit printed frocks --
Who was thief but Heather Jock?

Jock was nae religious youth,
For at the priest he thrawed his mouth,
He wadna say a grace nor pray,
He played his pipes on Sabbath day,

Sam Henry's Songs of the People

Robbed the kirk o' bann and book,
Everything would lift, he took:
He didna lea' the weather cock,
Sic a thief was Heather Jock.

Nane wi' Jock could draw a tricker,
'Mang the moorfowl he was siccar:
He watched the wild ducks at the springs,
And hang'd the hares on hempen strings,
Blass'd the burns and spear'd the fish.
Jock had mony a dainty dish --
The best o' moorfowl and black cock
Aye graced the board o' Heather Jock.

Nane wi' Jock had ony say
At the nieve or cudgel play.
Jock for bolt nor bar e'er stayed
Till ance the jail his courage laid;
Then the judge, without delay,
Sent him aff to Botany Bay
And bade him mind the laws he broke,
And never mair play Heather Jock.

1.2: faucht = fought; fecht = fight.
1.4: gaun = going; win' = wind.
1.5: tawnie = tawny; tousie = rumpled, shaggy.
1.6: cleading = clothing; unco = unusual, strange.
r.3: muircock = moorcock; crousely = proudly, conceitedly, arrogantly, boldly.
2.1: kent = knew; ilka = each, every; bore = crevice, opening in wall. [g/d 2]
2.2: bit = tiny.
2.4: dunts = ?slabs [g/d 2: dauds = lumps]; skeps = beehives.
2.5: kirn = churn.
2.8: durstna = dares not; craw = crow.
3.1: goun = gown.
3.2: coft = bought; toun = town.
3.4: hoose = house; rig = ridge.
3.6: thocht = thought.
3.7: weans = young children; bit = tiny.
4.2: thrawed = twisted.
4.3: wadna = would not.
4.5: kirk = church; bann[s] = public announcement, especially in church, of a proposed marriage.
4.7: lea' = leave.
4.8: sic = such.
5.1: tricker = trigger.
5.2: siccar (sicker) = secure, assured, confident.
5.5: blass'd =
5.6: mony = many.
5.8: aye = ever, on all occasions.
6.1: ony = any.
6.2: nieve = fist, clenched hand.
6.4: ance = once.

Jamie Raeburn's Farewell [H151: 2 Oct 1926]

Other titles: "Farewell to Caledonia," "Jamie (Jimmy) (John) Raeburn."

Source: coll. Hubert Bradley, esq [Dt: Officer of Customs and Excise] (in Strabane district).

s: ... This was a Scottish street ballad of about 1840. The hero was Jamie Raeburn, a Glasgow baker, who was wrongfully convicted for theft. His sweetheart, Catherine Chandlier, protested his innocence, but in vain as her lover was tried and banished to Botany Bay. The song seems to have been adapted to other names, as in one version the name [Dt: of the hero] is given as Dave M'Williams.

o: Should be 6/8.

Key G.

Come all you brisk young fellows, wherever that you be,
I hope you'll pay attention and listen unto me,
I am a poor distracted youth, oppressed down by law
And forced to leave those hills and dales of Caledonia.

My name is Jamie Raeburn, in Glasgow I was born,
My home and habitation I'm forced to leave with scorn,
From my home and habitation I noo must gang awa'
Far from those bonny hills and dales of Caledonia.

It being on a Monday morning at the dawning of the day,
I overheard a turnkey who unto us did say,
'Arise ye hapless convicts, arise you one and a',
This day you'll leave the hills and dales of Caledonia.'

We all arose, pulled on our clothes, our hearts being filled with woe,
We all arose, pulled on our clothes, not knowing where to go;
The crowd had gathered round us, our hearts they rent in twa,
For to leave those bonny hills and dales of Caledonia.

Farewell to my old mother, she'll be sorry for what I've done,
I hope no one will upcast to her the mischief of her son,
I hope God will protect her, noo when I'm far awa',
Far from those bonny hills and dales of Caledonia.

Farewell to my old father, for he's the best of men,
And likewise to my sweetheart, it's Kathleen is her name;
No more we'll roam by Clyde's clear stream, nor by the Broomielaw,
For I must leave those hills and dales of Caledonia.

James Magee   [H136: 19 Jun 1926]

o: (m) "Henry Joy"; k: "... Maclean." Other title: "... McKee."

Source: coll. Maud Houston (Coleraine) from Charles Dempsey, rural postman.

[Bp] s: From Charles Dempsey, ... who learned most of his songs from hearing the old women sing who plucked feathers for his mother, a fowl merchant.... A version called "James Maclean" is current in Moneymore district.

The "green table" is an Ulster phrase [Dt: synonym] for the Court of Justice.... The [Ulster] custom of calling married women by their maiden names by those of close relationship is illustrated ... in the second [actually, third] to last verse.

Key F.

O, it's James Magee, it is my name, the same I will never deny,
It is from my native country I am obliged to fly,
All for my houses and free lands my aunt against me swore,
Now I must sail for New South Wales, far from my native shore.

My father died and left me, I was his only heir;
I lived with my grandmama, and of me she took great care:
Twelve years at Dublin I was taught at the Academy,
My learning might have served a knight or a lord of high degree.

When my father and my mother died, I had one aunt alive;
She was married to a young man which together did contrive
That she should swear my life away, that hang-ed I might be,
That she would become the only heir of all my property.

The morning of my trial, she at the green table stood:
'Gentlemen of the jury, give ear unto my word,
This is the man that did this wrong, on him you may lay hold,
Last Thursday night at ten o'clock, my husband's gun he stole.'

'Lord pardon you then, aunt,' I says, 'fully sorely you've wronged me,
Lord pardon you then, aunt,' I says, 'lest judged you might be,
But against that great tribunal day when Christ shall on us call,
Neither lawyers then nor jurymen -- one judge will judge us all.

'Tis not a penal yoke I dread, nor yet my far-off voyage,
But it is my little children that are not come of age;
May the curse of me and my poor wife and my three children small
Light down upon you, Kate Magee -- my aunt, I should you call.'

When the trial it was over, the judge to me did say,
'How can I befriend you? She swore so bitterly,
You must leave your native country in sorrow to bewail,
You must leave your wife and babes behind, you're bound for New South Wales.'

Now I have a house both large and wide, no room it could afford
To entertain a gentleman when they were in record,
But when I meet a nobleman, it is him I use right well;
Now they all walk past and never ask where James Magee did dwell.

5.1: ... says, 'sorely you've ... [Dt]

4.1: green table = Ulster phrase for the Court of Justice. [s]

John Mitchel's Farewell to His Countrymen (a)   [H179a: BLp, 16 Apr 1927]

Other title: "... Mitchel."

Source: (m) itinerant flute-player (Church St, Coleraine) from James Delaney, blind piper (Ballinasloe); (w) collation "based on the best of all the [8] versions sent in" (Ballycastle, Ballymena, Dungiven, Garvagh, Glenariffe, Knockloughrim, Newtowncrommelin, Portrush).

s: [The flute-player] was an ex-bandsman of the 88th Connaught Rangers.... It is a remarkable testimony to the memory of the people that in response to our request eight versions have reached us ... although the ballad is 80 years old. The readers who sent these versions are thanked for their kindness.... This ballad is published because of John Mitchel's connection with Dungiven, and also because it is deeper than its politics and belongs to the human sentiment that touches all.

[BLp print, provided by John Moulden, includes a photograph, presumably of the hero John Mitchel.]

Sam Henry's Songs of the People

[Bt is a hybrid version, with the title and sol-fa typed and the stanzas clipped from a newspaper or songster with narrow (2") columns. The name is typed "Mitchell" in the title, but the clipping is entitled "John Mitchel's Farewell to his Countrymen," as is BLp. Numerous small discrepancies between printed (BLp) and typed (B, Dt, Wt) tunes, primarily in notation of grace notes.]

1: This is the closest to an Irish political song in print in Henry's column, aside from the comic ones.

Key E flat.

I am a true-born Irishman, John Mitchel is my name,
When first I joined my countrymen, from Newry town I came;
I laboured hard both day and night to free my native land,
And for that I was transported unto Van Diemens Land.

When first I joined my countrymen, it was in forty-two,
And what did happen after that I'll quickly tell to you:
I raised the standard of Repeal, I gloried in the deed;
I vow'd to heaven I ne'er would rest till old Ireland would be freed.

Farewell, my gallant comrades, it grieves my heart full sore
To think that I must part from you, perhaps for evermore;
The love I bear my native land, I know no other crime,
That is the reason I must go unto a foreign clime.

As I lay in strong irons bound before my trial day,
My loving wife came to my cell and thus to me did say:
'Cheer up, my gallant husband, undaunted always be,
For 'tis better to die a thousand deaths than live in slavery.'

I said, 'My darling girl, it grieves my heart full sore,
To think it's from you that I must part, perhaps forevermore,
Also my friends and relatives will mourn my sad downfall,
But to part from you, my native land, it grieves me more than all.'

I was quickly placed in the dock, still in strong irons bound,
Whilst numbers of my countrymen were gathered all around;
I was offered then my liberty if I'd deny the cause,
But I'd rather die on the gallows high than submit to tyrant laws.

I was placed on board a convict ship without the least delay,
For Bermuda's isle our course was steered, I'll ne'er forget the day.
And as I stood upon the deck to take a farewell view,
I shed a tear, but not for fear; my native land, for you.

Adieu, adieu to sweet Belfast and likewise to Dublin too,
And to my young and tender babes: alas, what will they do?
But there's one request I ask of you when your liberty you gain:
Remember Mitchel far away, a convict o'er the main.

[Differences in B:]
1.2: And for to join my ...
 .3: I struggled hard ...
 .4: For which I ...
2.2: ... did follow after ... I now will tell ...
 .3: ... I glory in ...
 .4: ... till ould Ireland ...
4.1: When in the prison close confined before ...
 .2: ... wife, she came to me and ...
 .3: 'John, my dear, cheer up your heart, and daunted never be,
 .4: ... die for Ireland's rights than ...
5.1: ... grieves me to part with you,
 .2: Likewise my young and tender babes, alas, what will they do?
6.1: When I received my sentence, in irons I was bound,
 .2: ... were assembled all ...
 .3: ... I'd forsake the ...
 .4: ... die a thousand deaths than submit to slavish laws.
7.3: When on the deck I gazed around to ...
 .4: ... not through fear; it was, my ...
8.: [Substitute stanza:]
So cheer up your hearts, my gallant boys, the hour is near at hand.
For your success I always pray, though in a foreign land,
But one request I ask of you when your liberty you regain:
Remember John Mitchel that's far away, a convict o'er the main.

John Mitchell (b)   [H179b: Wt=D(c)]

[m = H179a "]

Source not given.

[Wt, Dt: Shorter, typed text under the same column number.]

I am a true-born Irishman, John Mitchell is my name,
To free my own brave countrymen from Newry town I came,
I struggled hard both night and day to free my native land,
For which I was transported, as you may understand.

When first I joined my countrymen, it was in forty-two,
And then what followed after, I'll quickly tell to you:
I raised the standard of Repeal and gloried in the deed,
And I vowed to heaven I'd never rest until Erin it was freed.

While here in prison close confined, waiting for my trial day,
My loving wife, she came to me and these words to me did say,
'Oh John, my dear, cheer up your heart and daunted do not be,
For it's better to die for Erin's rights than to live in slavery.'

When I received my sentence 'twas on a foreign ground,
Where hundreds of my comrades assembled all around,
My liberty was offered me if there I would forsake their cause,
But I'd rather die ten thousand deaths than forsake my Irish boys.

Farewell my true-born Irishmen, farewell my country, too,
But to leave my poor babes behind, it grieves me worse than all,
There is one request I ask of you when your liberty you gain:
Remember John Mitchell far away, though a convict bound in chains.

Hugh Hill, the Ramoan Smuggler
[H494: 20 May 1933]

s: (m) "Parting Glass"; m: (m) "Sweet Cootehill Town."

Source not given.

s: This song is of the smuggling days about the year 1800, when one might have heard:

Five and twenty ponies,
Trotting through the dark --
Brandy for the parson,
'Baccy for the Clerk;
Laces for a lady, letters for a spy,
And watch the wall, my darling, while 'the Gentlemen' go by.

For the parson! yes, even thirty years later, Hawker of Morwenstowe in Cornwall, the vicar of that parish, blessed the smugglers and gave his church to hide "the stuff."

The hero of our song, Hugh Hill, was a noted leader of the Antrim Coast smugglers. He was born at Carnately, near Ballycastle. The Hills of Carnately were people of substance. Fifty years ago, Father O'Laverty, in his history of the district, mentions Robert Hill, William Hill, John Hill, all farmers.

There were other noted smugglers in the district -- George Stewart, of Novally; James Baxter, of Ballycastle; George M'Nabb, of Drumavady -- but Hugh Hill was his country's pride. He was master of a ship which he used exclusively for smuggling.

The story behind the song is that Hugh Hill was betrayed by one Dixon to the authorities, his vessel being captured and brought to Greenock, but by some lucky chance no direct proof of smuggling was discovered, as the smuggled cargo was disposed of before the arrival of the Revenue cutter from Carrickfergus, with the result that Hill and his companions were set free.

According to tradition the famous smuggler ship was copper-bottomed and on a clear day shone like burnished gold.

The small "lean-to" or "grace" notes may be omitted if desired.

Key G.

Ye Ballycastles, now give ear
To these few lines which I have penned,
A doleful story you shall hear
Which caused our hero to lament:
We left New York to sail for Cork
And safely reached the Irish shore,
With a fresh gale that filled our sail
For Ballycastle straight we bore.

Soon as we rounded old Benmore,
Brave Hugh unto his men did say,
'Haul down your sheets, for we will meet
A hearty welcome at the quay.'
With flying jib we passed the Head,
But little did our hero know
That the man he thought would be his friend
Should prove his sad and mortal foe.

Oh, Dixon, you are much to blame,
The strangers' blood you caused to spill,
Our hero brave you did deceive --

Sam Henry's Songs of the People

The country's pride, our brave Hugh Hill.
So Dixon next day, without delay,
To Carrick went with due express
And information he gave there
Which proved our hero's sad distress.

A cutter then with forty men
From Carrick was rigged out in haste,
And along shore for Rathlin bore,
But we soon steered for the west.
The brave Agnew prevailed on Hugh,
For to outsail them was his thought,
But the wind did slack, we took a tack,
And unto Greenock we were brought.

At the 'green tables' Hugh was tried,
But his deeds were wrote on the salt sea,
Our country's pride the law defied
And we stepped out to liberty;
His sloop once more sailed o'er the main,
On the seven seas did safely hide,
The king's men she deceived again,
A phantom gleam on the heaving tide.

And now, thank God, like Aaron's rod,
He'll bud and flourish once again,
With due respect, we won't neglect
To drink his health while on the main.

The Three Huntsmen
/ Wilson, Gilmore and Johnson

[H185: 28 May 1927; Laws L4]

s: "The Three Butchers." Other titles: "The Battle of King's Mountain," "Bold (Brave) Johnston," "The Butchers Three," "Dixon and (Said to) Johnson," "The Jolly Butchermen," "... Boocher Lads," "... Butchers of England," "... Huntsmen's Tragedy," "Johnson," "... Jolly Butchers (Sportsmen)," "... Merry Butchers and Ten Highwaymen," "... Worthy Butchers of the North," "(The) Two (Three) (Jolly) (Jovial) Butchers (Huntsmen)," "Young Butcher Boy."

Source: Samuel A. Leighton (Islandmore).

[Bp] s: This song ... is the Irish version of a story, evidently founded on fact, which dates from the 17th century. In England it is known as "The Three Butchers" [Broadwood 1908] and the background is Norfolk, Northumberland, Sussex, Hampshire or Dorset, according to the place collected. In the English versions, Johnson is stabbed to death by the female "highwayman." The air given here differs from the English air and is one of the stock tunes to which many songs are sung.

l: The unusual outcome is unique to the version Henry prints.

Key G.

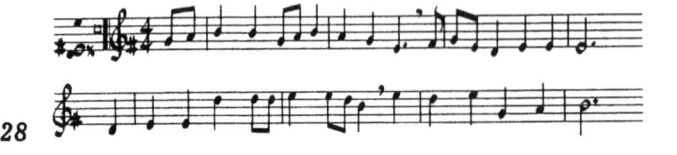

I'll sing you of three huntsmen brave, as plain as you may hear,
Brave Wilson, Gilmore and Johnson, remark these words I say,
Five hundred pounds of a wager laid upon their hunting day,
And they had got five hundred pounds to pay upon their way.

They rode high and they rode low o'er Wicklow mountains high;
'Hark, oh hark,' young Johnson says, 'I hear a woman's cry.'
Johnson being a valiant man, he searched the glens all round
Till he found a woman naked and her hair pinned to the ground.

'Are you an idle girl?' young Johnson he did say,
'Or a robber in disguise our lives for to betray?'
'A robber? No indeed, kind sir, that trade I will deny,
It was robbers stripped me naked and left me here to die.

'They took from me my gay gold watch, likewise five hundred pound,
And they left me here stripped naked and my hair pinned to the ground,
But I lay my life all in your hand; protect me, I do pray,
My father he's a wealthy man and your kindness he'll repay.'

Johnson being a feeling man, he took her on behind
And his red coat wrapped around her to save her from the wind.
It's they rode high and they rode low till they came unto a hill,
She put a whistle to her mouth and blew both loud and shrill.

She being the captain of the gang, they came at her command,
And eleven daring highwaymen caused our huntsmen for to stand,
Saying, 'Deliver up your gold to us and that without delay,
Or with our loaded pistols we'll take your life away.'

The huntsmen being well armed, then Wilson he let fly,
And three of those dandy robbers a-bleeding they did lie;
Gilmore peppered four of them with pistol balls of lead,
And Johnson with his blunderbuss the other four shot dead.

The captain mounted on Gilmore's horse and o'er
    the hills rode high,
The huntsmen followed after her and the balls
    made quickly fly,
Till a pistol caused her downfall and her blood
    did stain the lea,
'Hurrah, hurrah!' bold Johnson cried, 'we've
    gained the victory.'

For to see those robbers in their gore they came
    from far and near,
For years it has kept the countryside without
    either dread or fear,
Their cave lies in the mountainside and riches
    does retain,
And those highwaymen were buried in the
    ground where they were slain.

But those robbers they will rob no more,
    they've met their destiny,
Their number was eleven and the huntsmen only
    three:
Brave Wilson, Gilmore and Johnson, the truth I
    will proclaim,
So may all good luck protect them when they go to
    hunt again.

1.1: ... as brave as e'er you knew, [Dt]
2.1: ... rode along the greenwood side o'er ... [Dt]
5.3: They rode along the greenwood side beside a
     purling rill, [Dt]
9.2: They long had kept this country round in terror,
     dread and fear, [Dt]
   3: ... cave lay ..., rich treasures did contain, [Dt]
10.1: Those robbers ... [Dt]

The Crafty Ploughboy

[H51: 1 Nov 1924; Child #283, Laws L1]

[Bp] A song of a highway robbery.
[Dt] (Generally known in England as "The
Yorkshire Bite.")

s: "The Yorkshire Bite"; k: "Well Sold the Cow."
Other titles: "The Boy and the Cow (Coo) (High-
wayman)," "The Crafty Farmer," "The Farmer in
Leicester," "The Highway Robber," "Jack the
Cowboy (and the Robber)," "John and the Far-
mer," "The (Old) Spotted Cow," "The Oxford
Merchant," "The Silly Old Man," "There Was an
Old Man Lived in Yorkshire," "Well Sold the Cow,"
"The Yorkshire (Hampshire) (Lincolnshire) (Wise)
Farmer (Bite)"; cf. "The Rich Farmer's Daughter."

Source: 2: "respected ... resident" [Dt: Archie
Irwin], 96 (Coleraine) from his father, 1840;
Major J. Fairfax Blakeborough, folklorist coll.
(Yorkshire).

s: ... I have incorporated the Yorkshire version,
kindly supplied to me by Major J. Fairfax Blakeborough, the eminent Yorkshire folklorist.

[Bp typed at bottom] Corrections from Ballads
and Songs of Yorkshire. Ingledew...Bell and
Daldy...London...1860. The Irish version is
almost identical.

[Sam Henry's corrections, written on Bp, are
substitutions for words in his printed text.]

Key E.

Come all you good people, I pray lend an ear,
I'll tell you of a farmer that lived in Yorkshire;
A fine Yorkshire boy he had for his man,
To serve well his master, his name it was John.

   Fal da dee, fal da daddy,
   Fal da da dee-ing.

One morning right early he called for his man,
And when he came to him, thus he began:
Says he, 'Take this cow this day to the fair,
She is in good order, and her I can spare.'

Away went the boy with the cow in a band,
And he went to the fair, as you shall understand,
Before he had gone far he met with three men
And he sold them the cow for six pounds ten.

The boy and the merchant went in for a drink,
And the merchant he paid down the boy all his
    jink,
The boy to the landlady this he did say,
'Now what shall I do with this money, I pray?'

'Sew it in the lining of your coat,' she did say,
'For fear you be robbed alongst the highway.'
And there sat a highwayman drinking at wine,
Thought he to himself, 'All this money is mine.'

The boy took his leave and homeward did go,
The highwayman soon followed after also,
He soon overtook the boy on the highway,
And he asked him, 'How far are you going, I
    pray?

'Will you get up behind me?' the highwayman said,
'How far are you going?' replied the lad.
'Three or four miles, for aught that I know.'
So he up behind him and away they did go.

They rode till they came to a very dark lane.
'Now,' says the highwayman, 'I will tell you
    plain,
Deliver up your money without fear or strife,
Or this be the instant that you'll lose your
    life.'

The boy saw that there was no time to dispute,
And so he alighted without fear or doubt,
He tore his coat lining, the money pulled out,
And amongst the long grass he strewed it about.

Sam Henry's Songs of the People

The highwayman also jumped down from his horse,
And little he thought it would be to his loss,
But as he was putting the money into purse,
The boy jumped on horseback and off wi' the horse.

The highwayman shouted and begg'd him to stay,
The boy would not hear him, but kept on his way;
One of the maid servants saw Jack coming home,
And to acquaint his master she ran to his room.

The master he came to the door and said thus:
'Has the pox of a cow turned it into a horse?'
'Oh no, canny master, your cow I have sold,
But was robbed on the way by a highwayman bold.

'My money I strewed about on the ground;
For to take it up the rogue lighted down,
And as he was putting it into his purse,
I jumped up on horseback and off wi' his horse.'

The master did laugh and his sides he did hold.
He says, 'For a boy thou hast been very bold,
And as for this villain thou has served him right;
Thou hast put upon him a clean Yorkshire bite.'

He searched his bags, and quickly he told
Five thousand pounds in bright silver and gold
And two brace of pistols; the lad made a bow:
'I think, my good master, I well sold your cow.'

'It's now for your valour and courage so rare,
Three parts of the money you'll get for your share.
And since the bold robber has lost all his store,
He may go a-robbing till he gathers more.'

[*Written on Bp:*]
   1.2: ... in Hertfordshire.
    .4: ... was Dan.
   4.2: ... his chink.
   8.4: Or else I will certainly take your sweet life.
  11.3: And to his old master the whole he did bring:
    .4: Horse, saddle and bridle, a very fine thing.
  12.2: 'What the deuce! Has my ...
  15.2: Two hundred pounds ...
  16: [*Dt, Bp written at top:*] Add --

[*Incorporated in Dt:*]
  13.4: ... wi' the horse."
  15.1: He searched the saddle bags, as I hear it told,
    .2: And in it found five hundred pounds in bright gold,
    .3: Three brace ...
  16.4: ... he gets more.' [*Bp written*]

Shane Crossagh [H97: 19 Sep 1925]

[Bp] A song of Ulster's Robin Hood.

Source: (w) Patrick McNicholl (Cashel, Dungiven); (m, "the proper air") W[illiam] D[evine] (Foreglen, Dungiven, Co. Londonderry).

s: An excellent ballad....

Key G. Quick time.

It's up the heathery mountain and down the rushy glen,
Squire Staples has gone a-hunting Shane Crossagh and his men,
And forty mounted yeomen that galloped in a stream,
They swear they'll 'gin the gallows work when they come back again.

Shane Crossagh was a ploughboy that ploughed at Ballynascreen,
But now he is an outlaw for the wearing of the green,
For the wearing o' the green, oh, the wearing o' the green,
But now he is an outlaw today at Ballynascreen.

The squire rode a chestnut, his brother rode a grey,
Close behind Shane Crossagh they galloped all the day,
They galloped all the day and they hunted him by night,
They never let the outlaw one moment out of sight.

It was on the Sperrin Mountains far, far from Ballynascreen,
They kept the bloodhounds on his track, for the wearing of the green,
For the wearing of the green, for the wearing of the green,
They kept the bloodhounds on his track far, far from Ballynascreen.

Then said Torrens the farmer, 'We have him now, I know.
The bloodhounds now are on his track, he cannot leap the Roe.'
The river now was deep, its channel twelve yards wide,
The banks were high and steep, overhanging on each side.

The man he must be wearied, for a long chase this has been,
For three long days, and fasting since he left Ballynascreen,

Since he left Ballynascreen for the wearing of the green,
'We will hang him now for surely for the wearing of the green.'

Shane Crossagh had a wolf dog that never parted him,
And when the hounds they neared him, he tore them limb from limb,
'My dear friend,' said the outlaw when the tears began to flow,
'My gallant hound, we are both free if we can leap the Roe.'

Then up the hound he gave a bounce, 'Shane Crossagh, now I know,'
And with a shout they both leaped out and they have leaped the Roe,
And they have leaped the Roe and defied their every foe,
Ballynascreen will yet be seen by the man that leaped the Roe.

'A good leap,' said the squire, when he saw the chase was won.
'Not too great,' said the outlaw, 'for such a length of run,
But mark me, Squire Staples, when you come back again,
You might wish the river Roe between Shane Crossagh and his men.'

The squire and his yeomen came hurrying down Glenshane,
Right wearied and rejected, their chase was all in vain,
Their chase was all in vain and Shane Crossagh called amain,
'Right well we'll win, we'll meet the green before we cross Glenshane.'

Old Feeny Bridge was broken and on a search was seen
From them a fearful token, a bunch of holly green,
And from behind a grey rock a whistling ball had sped,
And Torrens, then, the farmer, fell from his charger, dead.

It's up the Squire Staples, 'Shane Crossagh, let me live,
And for your hounds a thousand pounds in yellow gold I'll give,
And bring your arms here singly, and bring them unto me,
For I must bind your yeomen, each man to a tree.'

It's bound is now Squire Staples, you'll find him in the glen.
The outlaw force consisted of seven gallant men,
Of seven gallant men, my boys, of seven gallant men,
And with despair he tore his hair and wept for Shane amain.

2.3: ... green, and all that it can mean, [Dt]
2.4: And now ... [Dt]
4.3: ... green, so plainly to be seen, [Dt]
13.1: [sic].

A9 / A bold undaunted youth

The Breaking of Omagh Jail
[H181: 30 Apr 1927]

Source: (w) 2: James Martin (Shell Hill, Coleraine), John M'Fadden (Main St, Portrush), and others; (m) John Thompson (Heatherlea Ave, Portstewart).

s: ... A correspondent writes -- "This song was the means of bringing together two men in the backwoods of Canada."
(Lines 3 and 4 of the air are repeated for lines 5 and 6 of verse 8.)

Key D.

I am a bold undaunted youth from the county of Tyrone,
Among the pretty fair maids in Cookstown I'm well known,
A curse a girl against me swore has caused me to bewail,
And now I am a prisoner and lodged in Omagh jail.

On Friday last, the twenty-first, the prisoners they were tried,
They were brought back to their cells their sentences to abide,
To sleep on such a night as that with me did not agree,
So fully bent to work we went to gain our liberty.

I had two comrades in my cell, to them I told my plan,
To see if they were willing to join me heart and hand,
They answered me quite manfully, their courage ne'er would fail,
So fully bent to work we went to break from Omagh jail.

The jailer came round to view the jail while I in a corner stood,
He shouted thrice, 'All things are well.' Says I, 'My boy, that's good,
Hold fast to that, there is no fear that I'll soon scale the wall,
Before that you be back again or shout, "All's well," or bawl.'

One of my comrades shook with fear when he heard the jailer shout,
He went into his cell again and never more looked out,

131

Sam Henry's Songs of the People

I laughed at him right heartily, for I knew I
  could prevail
To break the wall, both large and high, that did
  surround the jail.

With a shoemaker's knife I did ascend and moved
  the slates also,
Before we got the work complete, the cocks began
  to crow,
I made a rope of my blankets and likewise of my
  sheets,
I made a rope that I am sure would reach o'er
  forty feet.

I scaled the wall, as you may see, like a ship
  under full sail,
All danger past, I'm freed at last from being
  lodged in Omagh jail,
I took the road like a hunted deer, I never more
  looked round
Until seven miles had parted me from Omagh jail
  and town.

Farewell unto my comrades all round the shamrock
  shore,
Farewell ye jailers and police, I hope we'll meet no
  more,
Farewell fair maids of Cookstown, I'm sorry we
  part so soon,
All danger past, I'm freed at last, our ship sails
  this forenoon.
And from Derry Quay she bears away with a
  sweet and pleasant gale,
All dangers past, I'm freed at last from the cares
  of Omagh jail.

3.3: ... me right ... [Dt]

The Dreary Gallows

[H705: 29 May 1937; Laws L11]

o: "Derry Gaol." Other titles: "Brave (Sweet)
Ann O'Neill," "(The) Streets of Derry," "(The
Weary) ...."

Source: (w, m) Mrs James De Vine (Grosvenor
Road, Belfast), (m) noted by Maurice Craig (University Square, Belfast).

s: This song was asked for by the Rev. Walter
Pitchford, of Lamport Rectory, Northampton....
  In the six-line verses, the music of the third
and fourth lines of the tune is repeated.
  Where an extra syllable occurs the corresponding note is duplicated.
  The song may also be sung to the air of "The
True Lover's Discussion" or to "The Star of Glenamoyle."

Key F.

Source: (m) coll. Rev. Walter Pitchford (Lamport
Rectory, Northampton).

s: Alternative tune....

Key C.

My love is one of the finest young men
That nature formed or the sun shone on,
And how to gain him I do not know,
For he has got a sentence to be hung.

And as he walks the streets of Derry,
I'm sure he walks it right manfully,
He resembles more a commanding officer
Than one to die on the gallows tree.

The first step he went up the ladder,
His beloved father was standing by,
'Come here, come here, my beloved father,
And speak one word to me before I die.'

The second step he went up the ladder,
His beloved mother was standing by,
'Come here, come here, my beloved mother,
And speak one word to me before I die.'

The third step he went up the ladder,
His beloved sister was standing by,
'Come here, come here, my beloved sister,
And speak one word to me before I die.'

He pulled the gold ring off his mid-finger
And rolled it up in a napkin fine,
'Take this, take this, my beloved sister,
And bear me constantly in your mind.'

'O, hang him, hang him,' called the prosecutor;
With that, the clergy being standing by --
'I'll let you see, you dare not hang him
Till with me his confessions done,
And when that's over, you dare not hang him
Till within ten minutes of the setting sun.'

'Oh, what is keeping my love so long in coming,
Or what has detained her so long from me?
Or does she think it a great discredit
To see me die on the gallows tree?'

He looked around and saw his love coming,
She was dressed up in holland fine,
'Come down, come down from that dreary gallows,
I got your pardon from the queen,
I'll let them see we'll be united,
And I'll crown you, my Johnny, in the blooming
  spring.'

Lambkin [H735: 25 Dec 1937; Child #93]

Other titles: "Beaulampkin (Bolamkin) (Bolakin(s)) (Bolankin)," "Bold (Bo) (Bow) (Proud) (Young) Lamkin (Lankon)," "The Border Ruffian," "Cruel Lincoln," "False (Long) Lankin (Lankum) (Lanky)," "Lambert (Lambertkin) (Lammakin)," "Lambert Linkin," "... the (Wronged) Mason," "Lord Meanwell," "Orange."

Source: Alexander Crawford (Leck, Ballymoney), learned "when a boy at the Garry Bog from an old travelling woman" c. 1887.

s: [The woman] ... made the children's flesh creep with this sinister song.

It bears evidence of being a seventeenth-century ballad and may possibly be earlier. This is the most remarkable folk ballad yet discovered by the Song Editor. The name of the principal character in the ballad is variously spelt Lamkin, Lammikin, but the idea is to call so fierce a villain Lambkin, in mockery. The words can be adapted by duplication of notes where necessary.

Key C.

Lambkin, the finest mason that e'er laid a stone,
He built a lord's mansion and for payment got none;
He built it without and he sealed it within,
And he made a false window for himself to get in.

His lordship going to London once upon a time,
The Lambkin thought fit to commit his great crime.
'I fear the Lambkin,' the lady did say,
'I fear the Lambkin when your lordship's away.'

'I fear not the Lambkin nor any of his kind
When my gates are well barr'd and my windows pinned down.'
So in stepped the Lambkin in the middle of the night,
Without coal or candle to show him the light.

'Where is his lordship?' then said the Lambkin,
'He's in London buying pearls,' said the false nurse to him.
'Where's her ladyship?' said the Lambkin,
'She's in her chamber sleeping,' said the false nurse to him.

'How will I get at her?' says the Lambkin,
'Stab the baby in the cradle,' says the false nurse to him.

A9 / A bold undaunted youth

'It's a pity, it's a pity,' says the Lambkin,
'No pity, no pity,' says the false nurse to him.

So the Lambkin he rocked and the false nurse she sung,
And with a small pen-knife he dabbed now and then,
So the Lambkin he rocked and the false nurse she sung,
And the tearing of the cradle made the blood cold to run.

'Please my child, nurse, please him with the keys.'
'He won't be pleased, madam, you may do as you please.'
'Please my child, nurse, please him with the bell.'
'He won't be pleased, madam, till you come down yoursel'.'

'How can I come down, as my candle is out
And the room is so dark that I cannot move about?'
'You have three golden mantles as bright as the sun,
Throw one of them round you, it will show you light down.'

As soon as her ladyship entered the stairs,
So ready was the Lambkin to catch her with his snares;
'Good morrow, good morrow,' says the Lambkin,
'Good morrow,' says the lady to him.

'Where is his lordship?' ways the Lambkin,
'He's in London buying pearls for my lying-in.'
'You never will enjoy them,' says the Lambkin,
'The more is the pity,' says the lady to him.

'Spare my life, Lambkin, spare it but one day,
I will give you as much gold as you can carry away.'
'If you gave me as much gold as I could heap in a sack,
I could not keep my pen-knife from your lily-white neck.'

'Spare my life, Lambkin, spare it but one hour,
I'll give you my daughter Bessie, your bride for
   to be.'
'Bring down your daughter Bessie, she's both
   neat and trim,
With a silver bason to hold your life-blood in.'

'Oh no, no that, Lambkin, that would never do,
If you say that, then Bessie will never be for
   you.
Bessie, lovely Bessie, stay up in your room,
Watch for your father coming home, and that will
   be soon.'

Bessie sat watching that cold winter night,
With her father coming home with his men at
   daylight.
'Father, dear father, what kept you so long?
Your lady is murdered, and your own darling son.'

'There is blood in the kitchen, there is blood in
   the hall,
But the blood of my mamma is the worst blood of
   all,
For the Lambkin will be hung high up on a tree,
And the false nurse will be burned, such a villain
   was she.'

◆ A9 REFERENCES ◆

◆ **Botany Bay** *(H691)* 119

g: There is a ballad closely related to "Botany Bay," for which see Harvard 1:13.37, "The Transport's Farewell." H202 "The Boston Burglar" also derives from "Botany Bay."

White/Dean-Smith 1951
Dean-Smith 1954
Laws 1957:174-5 (L16A) "Botany Bay A"
Brunnings 1981
See also Cazden et al. *Notes* 1982: #114 "The Boston
   Burgular"

BRIT Morrison/Cologne 1981:10-2 "Bot'ny ..."
   Richards/Stubbs 1979:198-9

AMER Barrand *CD&S* 1981:32-3
   Darling 1983:111-2 (from London brs. c. 1800)

AUST Anderson 1955:18-20
   Edwards 1966:84 "... II"
   Ward 1964:24-5, 25-6
But not: Meredith/Anderson 1967:36-7, 113

BRS Harvard 3: (n.i.)

REC Paul Clayton, Folkways FA 2310 (A5)
b: Colyn Davies, Tradition TLP 1017
   John Greenway, Folkways FW 8718 (A1)
b: Rolf Harris, Epic LN 24110
   Derek Lamb, Folkways FW 8707 (A6), with some
different stanzas and a chorus.
b: Robin Roberts, Prestige/Int. 13017
   Cf. Joseph Able Trivett, Folk-Legacy FSA 2 (B3)
"Frank James"
   Cf. The Watersons, Topic 12T 167 (B7) "The Whitby Lad," including a refrain line.

◆ **The Boston Burglar** *(H202)* 229

Laws 1957:175 (L16B) "... (Botany Bay B)"
Brunnings 1981
Cazden et al. *Notes* 1982: #114 "... Burgular"

IREL Loesberg 2,1980:27 "Boston City"
   Meek 1978:54-5
   O Lochlainn 1939(1946):88-9, "Boston City" [Laws]
   Shields/Shields *UF* 21,1975: #54

BRIT Greig/Duncan 2,1983:266-7 (#260) "The Boston
Smuggler," 3 vts. ("I Was Born in Boston")
MacColl/Seeger 1977:284-6 (#92)

AMER Cf. Bethke 1981:67- "The Colton Boy"
   Cazden et al. 1982:427-9 "... Burgular"
   Darling 1983:112-3, B "Louisville Burglar" (see
Hickory Nuts rec.)

B. Ives 1955:56-7
Peterson 1931:62-3
c: Spaeth 1948:243-44 gives a possible formal publication date (1888); authorship credited to Michael G. Fitzpatrick, alias M. J. Fitzgerald, a printer: "At best he was probably no more than an arranger of traditional material, performing a trick that is still common in Tin Pan Alley" (p. 44).

BRS *Delaney's* #58:23
   In Dublin's 1968:16-7
   Walton's New 1,1966:12-3
c: Walton's 132:19
c: Wehman 2:29
c: Wehman's Universal #7:52

REC Pete Steele, *FMA* 12 (B6)
cl: Finley Adams, AFS 2796 A2
   Margaret Barry, Outlet SOLP 1029 (B1)
? cl: Cf. K. D. Begley, AFS 1454 B3 "Letcher County
Burglar"
   Cf. Fleming Brown, Folk-Legacy FSI 4 (A2) "Market Square"
cl: Mrs T. M. Bryant, AFS 1752
   Mrs C. H. Burke, *Sing Me a Song* cass. (A2)
(coll. Owens)
   Vernon Dalhart, Edison 51608-L [Randolph]
cl: William H. Dickinson, AFS 3671 A1
cl: Mrs Carlos Gallimore, AFS 1353 A1, 1353 B1
   Peggy Haine, Iron Mt. String Band, Folkways FA
2473 (A4) "Louisville Burgler"
cl: Louise Henson, AFS 662 B1
   The Hickory Nuts, County 522 "Louisville ..."
cl: Aunt Molly Jackson, AFS 826 A1
   Jimmy McBeath, Topic 12T 303 (B3) "... Smuggler"
cl: Mrs W. L. Martin, AFS 2747 B4
   Delia Murphy EMI 1055 (A6)
   Cf. New Lost City Ramblers, Folkways FA 2397 (A3)
"Louisville ..."
cl: Ben Rice, AFS 3224 A2
cl: Quartet of Negro convicts, AFS 232 A2
   L. D. Smith, AAFS L14 (A3) "Frank James, the
Roving Gambler"
   Carl T. Sprague, Victor 20534 [Randolph]
cl: Pete Steele, AFS 1704 A1
   Cf. Joseph Able Trivett, Folk-Legacy FSA 2 (B3)
"Frank James"
cl: Minnie Wilson, AAFS 1746 B1 & 2

◆ **The Wild Colonial Boy** *(H750)* 120

Laws 1957:177 (L20)
Brunnings 1981: "... I and II"
Cazden et al. *Notes* 1982: #113

c: IREL Clancy Bros. 1964:13
   Loesberg 2,1980:56
   Shields/Shields *UF* 21,1975: #433

BRIT   Dunn 1980:85-6

AMER   Cazden et al. 1982:422-7
   Darling 1983:113-4 (see Sorrels rec.)
   Grover n.d.:168

AUST   Ward 1964:74-5

c: BRS Jolliffe 1970:47-51 discusses some of the associated folklore.
c: *Songs & Recitations* 2,1950:50-1
c: *Walton's New* 2,1968:120-1 = *Walton's 132*:50-1

REC   Margaret Barry, Prestige/Irish 35001 (A3); Topic 12T 125 (B1)
b: Clancy Brothers, Columbia CL 1909 "The Wild Colonial Boy"
   Bob Davenport, Topic 12TS 530 (A1)
b: *The Folk Trailer*, Trailer LER 2019 "The Wild Colonial Boy"
   The Galliards, Monitor MFS 407
   John Greenway, Folkways FW 8718 (A10)
b: Rolf Harris, Epic LN 24110 "The Wild Colonial Boy"
   A. L. Lloyd, Topic 12TS 203 (A3)
   Kendall Morse, Folk-Legacy FSI 57 (A5)
cl: John Norman, AFS 2359A
   Rosalie Sorrels, Folkways FH 5343 (B6)
   Robert Walker, Folkways FE 4001 (A8)
b: Martin Wyndham-Read, Trailer LER 2009 "The Wild Colonial Boy"

◆ Eight Mile Bridge *(H486) 121*

REC   Planxty, Tara 3005 (A3) "Roger O Hehir"

◆ Whiskey in the Jar *(H792) 122*

Laws 1957:173 (L13A) "... [The Irish Robber A]"
Brunnings 1981

IREL   Galwey 1910:14, 31 "The Highwayman," an unusual version.
   Loesberg 1,1980:48
   O Lochlainn 1939:24-5 "There's ..." [MacColl/Seeger]

BRIT   MacColl/Seeger 1977:280-2 (#90)

AMER   Darling 1983:110-1 "Captain Devin" (see Gunning rec.)
   Warner 1984:145-6 (#51) "Gilgarrah Mountain"

AUST   Meredith/Anderson 1967:50-1 "Whisky ..."

BRS   Harvard 1: 7.50 (Ryle), 13.150 (Such)
   Healy 1965(1968):17-8
   Healy 1,1967:118-20
   Jolliffe 1970:34-6
   Popular Songs 1890:152-3
   Songs and Recitations 5,1978:28

REC   Seamus Ennis, *CWL* 1, Columbia AKL 4941 (B1,20)
   Ballads from the Pubs ...," Mercier IRL 1
   Bob Davenport, Topic 12TS 274 (A9)
b: *The Folk Scene*, Elektra SMP 6 "Gilgarry Mountain"
   Sarah Ogan Gunning, Folk-Legacy FSA 26 (B4) "Captain Devin"
   Cf. Max Hunter, Folk-Legacy FSA 11 (B2) "Sporting Molly"
b: *Irish Folk Night*, London LL 3414
   Irish Ramblers, Elektra EKL 9001 (A4)
   Tom Kines, Folkways FG 3522 (B6)
   Frank Warner, [b:] Elektra EKL 13 "Gilgarry Mountain"; [lc:] Elektra JH 504

MEL   Joyce 1909:345 (#686) "There's Whiskey in the Jar"

◆ Waltzing Matilda *(H566) 122*

Brunnings 1981: "...," ?"The Swagman"

AUST   Meredith/Anderson 1967:73-7
   Ward 1964:180-1, attributed to "Banjo" Patterson.

b: REC   Shirley Abicair, Columbia CL 1531
b: Jean Durand, Horizon WP 1607
b: Richard Dyer-Bennet, Tom Glazer, Mercury MG 20007 "The Swag Man"
   John Greenway, Folkways FW 8718 (B1), with a different tune, and in 2-time.
b: Rolf Harris, Epic LN 24110
b: Burl Ives, Decca DL 8125
b: Louis Killen, Front Hall FHR 013 (B3)
b: A. L. Lloyd, Topic 12TS 203
b: Josef, Miranda Marais, Decca DL 5106
b: The Wayfarers, RCA Victor LPM 1213
   Josh White, [lc:] Decca DL 5247; [b:] Decca A 611 (4 recs., 78 rpm)

◆ Heather Jock *(H39) 123*

BRIT   Ford 1,1899:143-7, longer but similar; he credits authorship to Dr. James Stirling of Perthshire.
   Greig/Duncan 2,1983:254-5 (#255)
   Palmer 1980:135-7
   Tocher #8(Win)1972:264-5; see also note by Ian A. Fraser, #36-7,1982:459.

◆ Jamie Raeburn's Farewell *(H151) 124*

White/Dean-Smith 1951: "John Raeburn"
Brunnings 1981: "Jamie Raeburn"

BRIT   Greig 1907-11(1963): #36 "Jamie Raeburn," "one of the most popular songs we have." Greig says that John Ord (superintendent of the Glasgow police) searched criminal records from 1833 without finding a record of Raeburn's conviction. [MacColl/Seeger]
   MacColl [1962?]:80
MacColl/Seeger 1977:288-90 (#94) "Jamie Raeburn"

AMER   Dean [1922]:90-1 "Farewell to Caledonia"

REC   Jessie Murray, *FSB* 7 (A2) "Jimmy Raeburn"
   Ian Manuel, Topic 12TS 301 (A5) "... Raeburn"
   Ewan MacColl, Riverside RLP 12 612 [Bikel]; Topic 12T 16
   Tom Scott, Folkways FW 8776 (A5) "Jimmy Raeburn"
   Willie Scott, Topic 12T 183 (A4) "... Raeburn"

BRS   Frank Kidson (*JFSS* 2(8)1906) reports "The Hills of Caledonia Oh" on "several broadsides."

◆ James Magee *(H136) 125*

Brunnings 1981

h: IREL   Morton 1970:70-2; Morton 1973:146-7 (the same version).
Shields 1981:104-5 (#42) "... McKee"
   Shields/Shields *UF* 21,1975: #219 "... McKee"

h: BRIT   Kilkerr *FMJ* 1977:217 (from Henry coll.); reprint, *Treoir* 12(1)1980:12

h: AMER   Grover n.d.:67-8, an interesting version.

h: REC   John Maguire, Mercier IRL 11-12; Leader LEE 4062

Sam Henry's Songs of the People

◆ John Mitchel[l]['s Farewell to His Countrymen] (*H179ab*) 125

Brunnings 1981: "... Mitchel"

IREL Galvin [1956?]:45
O Lochlainn 1965:54-5
Treoir 8,1976 "... Mitchel"

BRIT Shepheard n.d.:22

AMER Dean 1922:36
Haskins n.d.:54
Milner/Kaplan 1983:116-7 "... Mitchel"

BRS 617 [190-?]:17

REC Tommy Dempsey, Folkways FH 5415 (B1)
Roy Harris, Topic 12TS 217 (B5)
Joe Heaney, Topic 12T 91
McNulty Family, Copley COP 610
Paddy Tunney, Topic 12T 153 (B2) "... Mitchel"

◆ Hugh Hill, the Ramoan Smuggler (*H494*) 127

Brunnings 1981: *Not*: "Smuggler's Song"; ?"The Smuggler"

IREL Moulden 1979:72-3

REC "A Smuggler's Song" to the words Henry quotes is sung by Isla St. Clair on Isla 1 (A3).

m: MEL Joyce 1909:191 (#384) "Sweet Cootehill Town"

◆ The Three Huntsmen / Wilson, Gilmore and Johnson (*H185*) 128

White/Dean-Smith 1951: "(The) Three (Jovial or Worthy) Butchers or Gibson, Wilson and Johnson"
Dean-Smith 1954: "(The) Jovial/Jolly/Worthy Butchers; Gibson, Wilson and Johnson"
Laws 1965:166 (L4) "... Butchers [Dixon and Johnson]"
Brunnings 1981: "Johnson"
Cazden et al. *Notes* 1982: #111 "... Jolly Butchers"

BRIT Copper 1973:254-5 "Young Butcher Boy"
Greig/Duncan 2,1983:3-11 (#186) "The Three Jolly Butchers," 11 vts. ("The Butchers Three," "The Jolly Butchers (Three)," "The Three Butchers of England," "Bold (Brave) Johnston")
MacColl/Seeger 1977:118-21 (#24) "... Butchers"
Palmer 1979b:87-8 (#44) "The Three Butchers"

AMER Cazden et al. 1982:418-20 "... Jolly Butchers"
Randolph/Cohen (1982):74-5 "Dixon and Johnson," with refrain "I've been all around this world."

BRS BPL Irish: (Brereton) "... Huntsmen's Tragedy"
Harvard 1: 2.51 (Walker), 4.183 (Forth), 10.131 (Bebbington)
Harvard 2,51 (Walker)
Harvard 3,40 (Forth)
UCLA 605: 5(Brereton, 2 copies) "A New Song Call'd ... Huntsmen's Tragedy," (n.i., large sheet) "... Merry Butchers and Ten Highwaymen"
c: Healy 3,1969b:72-3 "A New Song Called ... Huntsmen's Tragedy"

REC Bob Scarce, *FSB* 7 (A10) "... Jolly Sportsmen"
Roy Bailey, Trailer LER 3021 (A1) "... Butchers"
cl: Troy Cambron, AFS 4138 B1 "Johnson-Jinkson"
Martin Carthy, Topic 12TS 341 (Fontana STL 5362) (A1) "Two Butchers"
Roy Harris, Topic 12TS 217 (A4) "... Butchers"
Nelson Penfold, Folkways FE 38553 (C1) #24 "The Two Butchers"
Obray Ramsey, Prestige 13020 (B2) "The Battle of King's Mountain"
c: Pete Seeger, Folkways FA 2319 (B2) "Johnson (The Three Butchers)"
? cl: Lena Bare Turbyfill, AFS 2850 B2 "Dixon and Jackson"
Nimrod Workman, Phyllis Workman Boyens, June Appal JA 001 (B7) "Dixon Said to Johnson"

◆ The Crafty Ploughboy (*H51*) 129

White/Dean-Smith 1951: "(The) Boy and the Highwayman or The Crafty Ploughboy; The Yorkshire Bite; The Yorkshire/Lincolnshire, etc., Farmer"
Dean-Smith 1954: "(The) Boy and the Highwayman; Crafty Ploughboy; Yorkshire Bite"
Child 1882-98(1965),5:128-31 (#283) "The Crafty Farmer," 5 vts.
Coffin/Renwick 1950(1977):151-2. In discussing the relationship of Child #283 to stories of the type Laws 1957:165 (L1) calls "The Yorkshire Bite," Coffin finds no justification for declaring them essentially different. Supplement, p. 277.
Bronson 4,1972:282-302, 511 "... Farmer"
Brunnings 1981: "The Crafty Farmer [Child 283]"
Cazden et al. *Notes* 1982: #117 "The Old Spotted Cow"

BRIT Greig/Duncan 2,1983:278-83 (#266) "The Yorkshire Farmer" ("The Boy and the Cow (Coo)," "The Yorkshire Bite," "The Highway Robber"), 8 vts.
Morrison/Cologne 1981:56-7
Cf. O'Shaughnessy 1971:22-3 "The Rich Farmer's Daughter"
Shepheard n.d.:20-1 "Jack and the Robber"
Tocher #4(Win)1971:106-7 "The Yorkshire Farmer"

AMER Cazden et al. 1982:437-44 "The Old Spotted Cow (The Yorkshire Farmer)"

BRS BPL Irish: (n.i.)
Harvard 1: 1.86 (Jacques), 3.49 (Kendrew), 4.153 (Walker), 12.64 (Such)
Harvard 9:113 (Bebbington), (n.i.) "The Crafty Ploughboy

REC Ewan MacColl, *Folkways CB*, FW 8755 (A3); *Riverside CB*, RPL 12 626 (A1) "The Crafty Farmer"; Topic 12T 16
Peggy Seeger, Ewan MacColl, *LH*, Argo ZDA 70, #5, 5 versions.
Amy Birch, Folkways FE 38553 (C4) #27 "There Was an Old Man Lived in Yorkshire"
Packie Manus Byrne, Topic 12TS 257 (A1) "John and the Farmer"
Cf. Margaret Christl, Ian Robb, Folk-Legacy FSC 62 (B1) "Jack the Cowboy"
Warde H. Ford, AAFS L58 (B3) "The Oxford Merchant" or "The Hampshire Bite" [Bronson]
cl: Sam Harmon, AFS 2905 A4 "Yorkshire Bite"
b: Ed McCurdy, Elektra EKL 205 "The Yorkshire Bite"
Nelson Penfold, Topic 12TS 349 (B3) "The Farmer in Leicester"
Harry Siemsen, Folkways FH 5311 (A5) "The Spotted Cow"

◆ Shane Crossagh (*H97*) 130

BRS *Derry Journal* [c. 1925],2:32 without the confusion of Henry's two last stanzas.

◆ The Breaking of Omagh Jail (*H181*) 131

IREL Moulden 1979:27-8

◆ The Dreary Gallows *(H705) 132*

Laws 1957:171-2 (L11) "Gallows." Laws says that, though related to Child #95 "The Maid Freed from the Gallows," this "is clearly a separate ballad"; he quotes Flanders et al. 1939:392 as to its Irish origin and the suggestion that it has "something to do with ... the rising of 1798."
Eleanor R. Long addresses most of the questions concerning this ballad in her article, "'Derry Gaol': From Formula to Narrative Theme in International Popular Tradition," *Jahrbuch fur Volksliedforschung* 20(1975): 61-85.
Brunnings 1981: "Derry Gaol"

IREL Shields *Ceol* 1970:110-1 "The Weary ..."
 Shields *YIFMC* 1971:112
 Shields/Shields *UF* 21,1975: #421 "(The) Weary ..."

b: BRIT Kennedy 1975:699 (#316) "Derry Gaol"; reports another version from Northern Ireland.
 Kilkerr *FMJ* 1977:227-8; reprint in *Treoir* 12(1) 1980:16

AMER *CBM* #23(Aug)1979:(4) "Brave Ann O'Neill"
 Leach 1965:90-1 "Sweet Ann O'Neill"

REC Sarah Makem, *FSB* 7 (B9) "Derry Gaol"; Mulligan LUN A 001 (B4)
 Bothy Band, Mulligan LUN 013 (A4) "The Streets of Derry"
 Peter Bellamy, Topic 12TS 400 (A6) "Derry Gaol"
 Shirley Collins, Topic 12T 170 (A7) "The Streets of Derry"
 Andy Irvine, Green Linnet SIF 3006 (Mulligan LUN 008) (B4) "Streets of Derry"
 Tim Lyons, Green Linnet SIF 1014 (B2) "The Streets of Derry"
 Susie Phaidi Oig, Leader LEA 4055 (A4) "The Weary ..."

◆ Lambkin *(H735) 133*

White/Dean-Smith 1951: "... (Lambert or Lambertkin) or The Border Ruffian; False Lankin; Lamkin the Wronged Mason; Lammakin; Long Lonkin; Orange; Proud Lamkin"
Dean-Smith 1954: "... [i.e. Lambertkin], False Lamkin"

Child 1882-98(1965),2:320-42 (#93) "Lamkin," 1 vt.; 513; 3:515; 4:480-1, 1 vt.; 5:229-31, 2 vts.; 295-6, 1 vt.
Bronson 2,1962:428-45; 4,1972:479-80
Brunnings 1981

See esp. Gilchrist *JEFDSS* 1932:1-17, a comparative study.

IREL Moulden 1979:81-3 also describes Henry's informant more fully and quotes one of his letters.
m: Munnelly *FMJ* 1975:15-7 "False Lankum"

BRIT Copper/Bell *JEFDSS* 1961:74-5 "Cruel Lincoln"
 Greig/Duncan 2,1983:12-3 (#187), 3 vts.
 Oxford Ballads 1969:313-7 (#82) "Lamkin"
 Palmer 1980:127-9

AMER Burton 1978:17-8 "Bolamkin"; 53-4 "Bolankin"; 103
 Darling 1983:64-5 "Bo Lankin" (see Proffitt rec.)
 Leach 1967:116-8
 Warner 1984:261-4 (#102) "Bolankin" (see Proffitt rec.)

m: REC Ben Butcher, *FSB* 4 (B9) "Cruel Lincoln"; Topic 12T 317 (A5)
 Peggy Seeger, Ewan MacColl, *LH*, Argo ZDA 68, #3 "Lamkin," 2 versions.
 A. L. Lloyd, *Riverside CB*, RLP 12 626, "Long Lankin"
 Martin Carthy, Topic 12TS 343 (B4) "Long Lankin"
 George Fosbury, Topic 12T 317 (A4) "False Lanky"
 Tom Gilfellon, Trailer LER 2037 (B4) "Long Lankin"
? cl: Mrs Sabra Bare Hampton, AFS 2869 A & D "Bolenkin"
? cl: Samuel Harmon AFS 2800 A, 2800 B1 "Boabkin"
cl: Mr, Mrs Nathan Hicks, AFS 2855 B1 "Bol' Lampkin"
b: High Level Ranters, Trailer LER 2037 "Long Lankin"
b: Ed McCurdy, Elektra EKL 108 "Lamkins"
 Frank Proffitt, Folkways FA 2360 (A3) "Bo Lamkin"
 John Reilly (the younger), EEOT *Irish Travellers* cass. (A6) "False Lankum"
 Lena Bare Turbyfill, AAFS L7 (B2) (AFS 2842 B2) "Bolakins" [Bronson]
 Hedy West, Topic 12T 163 (A2) "Beaulampkin"

A10

Deep and dead water:
Death, laments, ghosts

The Bard of Culnady / Charles O'Neill

[H50: 25 Oct 1924]

s: (m) "Savourneen Deelish"

Source not given.

Key C.

s: (Char-les pronounced in two syllables.)

Weep, weep, all who love the songs of dear Erin;
Let tears by her sons and her daughters be shed,
Since one -- whose sweet lays every land they
  appear in
Are hailed with applause -- mingles now with the
  dead.
No more, Maghera, shall thy minstrel awaken
With songs to thy praise, every mountain and
  vale,
Since he who first gave it to glory hath taken,
We hope, the pure spirit of Charles O'Neill.

Sweet bard of Culnady, so gifted by nature
With power of expression and thought most
  sublime:
Could I thy genius but show in each feature,
Or could my poor muse do thee justice in rhyme,
That friendship which I did through life for thee
  cherish
Would prompt me, with ardent devotion and zeal,
Thy praises to sing until memory would perish,
My ever true friend, dearest Charles O'Neill.

How oft for bestowing undue adulation
On vain, worthless greatness have scribes been
  caressed
And raised by their patrons to fortune and
  station,
Who never one tithe of thy genius possessed,
And while o'er the land the unmeaning effusions
Set forth by these rhymesters still float on the
  gale,

Productions of worth, unredeemed by seclusion,
Must rest in the grave with you, Charles O'Neill.

Though humble thy station, yet proud was thy
  spirit,
Unknown and unheeded by critics refined;
As few of thy friends rightly valued thy merits
Thou hast left no writings of moment behind,
But many an exile in far distant nations,
When asked for a song of beloved Innisfail,
Will draw from his hearers prolonged acclamations
When chanting thy verses, dear Charles O'Neill.

As thou upon earth wast beloved and respected
As father and husband, as neighbour and friend,
We hope that thy spirit, by angels protected,
To kingdoms celestial for ever ascend;
And as in deep anguish and disconsolation
Thy widow and children in tears do bewail,
Let each add 'Amen!' to my ejaculation,
A requiem eternal to Charles O'Neill.

Finvola, the Gem of the Roe

[H786: 17 Dec 1938]

Source not given.

h: "Songs of the People" No. 286 (4 May 1929)
"adopt[s] 'The Old Head of Dennis' (Moore's
'Meeting of the Waters').... [Sam Henry's version
(H786)] is otherwise an undistinguished air which
Henry seems to attribute to the late Alfred E.
Boyd of Garvagh" (Shields 1981:168).

Key D.

In the land of O'Cahan where bleak mountains rise
O'er whose brown ridgy tops now the dusky cloud
  flies,
Deep sunk in a valley a wild flower did grow,
And her name was Finvola, the gem of the Roe,
  And her name was Finvola, the gem of the Roe.

From the island of Islay appeared to our view
A youth clad in tartan, as strange as 'tis true,
With a star on his breast and unstrung was his
  bow,
And he sighed for Finvola, the gem of the Roe,
  And he sighed for Finvola, the gem of the Roe.

Sam Henry's Songs of the People

No more up the streamlets her maidens shall hie,
For wan the cold cheek and bedimmed the blue
  eye,
In silent affliction our sorrows shall flow
Since gone is Finvola, the gem of the Roe,
  Since gone is Finvola, the gem of the Roe.

Hielan' Jane   [H477: 21 Jan 1933]

Other titles: "(My Bonny Blooming) Highland ...."

Source: 2: Edward Armstrong (Slaughtmanus, Cross P.O., Co. Derry), J. M'K. (Ballyveeley, Pharis P.O., Ballymoney)

Key G.

As I roved out one morning clear,
Being in the pleasant month of June,
The river ran like crystal clear,
The rose and violet were in bloom.
In sad despair came to my ear
A voice across yon rural plain,
Crying, 'I have lost my bonny bride,
My bonny blooming hielan' Jane.

'She was the fairest of the fair,
Her eyes they shone like diamonds bright,
She was my joy, my only care,
My treasure, comfort and delight.
We lived alone like turtle doves
That sing in a melodious strain,
But now I'm left, poor bird, alone,
I've lost my bonnie hielan' Jane.

She was the pride of Scotland's isle,
All from the Tweed down to the Clyde,
No more again shall e'er I smile
Upon my handsome beauty bride.
Now through the dreary hours of night
I sit and sing a mournful strain
For the loss of her who shone so bright,
My bonnie blooming hielan' Jane.

She left behind one darling boy
Whose features fill me with amaze,
The more I look, the more I weep,
Still daily on him do I gaze.
She was like a flower sprung in an hour
And snatched from off yon level plain,
No bonny lass could e'er surpass
My bonnie blooming hielan' Jane.

It's cruel death, you were severe
To snatch so suddenly away
My lovely bride, just in her bloom,
To mix among the mouldering clay,
And now I'm doomed to sigh and weep
And wander o'er the dismal plain
Since I have lost my bonny bride,
My bonny blooming hielan' Jane.

My tears shall seek the mouldering clay
As I sit weeping o'er her grave,
And as the hours do flee away
From death I will one favour crave --
To take me to my rose that died,
Away from this dejected plain,
And leave me in the grave beside
My bonny blooming hielan' Jane.

An Irish Mother's Lament

[H600: 1 Jun 1935]

Source not given.

No key indicated.

Seated upon an Irish sward
  by a rustic grave in an old kirkyard,
An Irish mother nursed her child;
  her tears fell fast while the baby smiled.
'Won't you come back to your fond wife's arms?
  Have you no care for your sweet babe's charms?
Vain is my call, wilt thou never reply?
  Cushla mavourneen, why did you die?

  Why did you die, oh why did you die,
    and leave your poor Sheela to wail and to sigh
  My heart for you in the grave does lie,
    Cushla mavourneen, why did you die?

'The groves were green, the roses in bloom,
  the wild flowers wafted their sweet perfume,
The lambs did skip, the birds sang gay,
  but all would not tempt my love to stay.

I am left here alone to nurse my child,
   almost friendless, dark and wild,
Without one friend to care for me,
   my hopes are blighted like a withered tree.

'Who shall assuage my grief and care
   while I am sinking in deep despair?
Or who shall wipe the tear from my eye?
   Cushla mavourneen, why did you die?
Won't you come back to your fond wife's arms?
   Have you no care for your sweet babe's charms?
Vain is my call, wilt thou never reply?
   Cushla mavourneen, why did you die?'

The Cowboy of Loreto [H680: 5 Dec 1936]

Other titles: "...'s Lament," "... Song," "The Dying Cowboy (Ranger)," "St. James Hospital," "The Streets of La(o)redo," "Old Laredo," "Tom Sherman's Barroom"; cf. "The Bad Girl('s Lament)," "The Dying Stockman," "Let Her Go, Let Her Go, God Bless Her," "One Morning in May," "The Unfortunate Lass (Rake)," "(The) Young Sailor (Trooper) Cut down (in His Prime)," "The Whore's Lament."

Source: Bushmills man from Hammy M'Cafferty, former cowboy in Saskatchewan, from his uncle, Tom M'Cafferty, 83, former cowboy (Stitchfield, Ottawa).

s: ... Tom M'Cafferty ... in 1920 was a "wee oul' man wi' a bit o' a beard."
   Loreto (pronounced Lorayto) is a town in the ranching district of lower California.

l: More usually the town is "Laredo" and located in Texas.

Key D.

As I walked out on the streets of Loreto,
As I walked out on Loreto one day,
Who did I spy but a poor dying cowboy,
Wrapped up in white linen as cold as the clay.

'I see by your outfit that you are a cowboy,'
These words he did say as I gently passed by,
'Come sit down beside me and hear my sad story,
I got shot in the heart and I know I must die.

'Play the pipes slowly and play the drums lowly,
Play the Dead March as you carry me along,
Take me to yon graveyard and lay the sod o'er me,
For I'm a fool cowboy and I know I done wrong.

'Once in my saddle I used to go dashing,
Once in the saddle I used to ride gay,
First to the dram-house and then to the card-house;
I got shot in the breast and I'm dying today.

A10 / Deep and dead water

'Write me a letter to my grey-haired mother,
An answer the same to my sister so dear;
Not a word of this note now must you ever mention
When the boys gather round you my story to hear.

'Give me some water, a cup of cold water
To cool my poor lips,' then the cowboy he said,
But when I got to him, the spirit had left him,
Gone to his maker, the cowboy was dead.

We played the pipes slowly and played the drums lowly,
And bitterly wept as we bore him along;
We all loved our comrade so brave and so handsome,
We all loved our comrade although he done wrong.

John McKeown and Margaret Deans

[H129: 1 May 1926]

Source: (w, m) (Oughtymoyle, Bellarena).

s: ... The song was popular 50 years ago [Dt: in that district].

Key G.

John McKeown and Margaret Deans, they were a matchless pair:
He was manly, just and kind, and she was soft and fair,
He was like the lofty oak that stands the forest pride,
And she was like the tender rose had flourished by his side.

A long, a fond and mutual love had burn-ed in their breast,
In constancy they loved in hope to share each other's nest,
This honest love their friends approved, it was so true and pure
That happiness seemed made for both, should both their lives endure.

It happened on Whit Sunday morn, a most unlucky day,
When Johnny at her window tapped, these words to her did say,
'Awake, arise, my Margaret dear, and come along with me,
The fields are green, the sky is bright, but not as bright as thee.'

141

Sam Henry's Songs of the People

His Margaret well remembered, when parting John
  that night,
Along with him she said she'd go to climb the
  Cave Hill height;
A bright new gown she then put on, the first time
  it was wore,
John smiled and said she never looked one half so
  fair before.

She left her widowed mother's home and offered
  John her arm,
And yet three times she turn-ed back as if she
  dreaded harm.
John saw her eyes were wet with tears and that
  her cheeks seemed pale
And that some dark and hidden fear her bosom
  did conceal.

He caught her by the trembling hand and
  whispered in her ear,
'Oh, what strange trouble pains your breast, what
  danger do you fear?
So, Margaret dear, it's come with me and do not
  quit my side,
You know on this day week you will become my
  bonny bride.'

They walked along the dusty road and spent two
  happy hours,
When Margaret said, 'My sister Bess desired to
  bring her flowers,
And see below: there grows a bunch between
  two beetling banks,
Come pluck them quick and you shall get my
  smiles and warmest thanks.'

Poor Johnny stooped to pluck the flowers from
  that steep mountainside,
For he would go through earth and sea to please
  his promised bride.
He missed his foot, but grasped a rock before it
  was too late,
And shrill she cried and forward sprang to save
  him from his fate.

O'er rocks and shrubs her body fell, with many
  a bruise and blow,
And when a shepherd raised her up, her face
  you would not know,
For mangled was her angel face and torn her
  bosom fair,
The thorns and stones were covered with her
  brown and glossy hair.

The corpse of this once lovely maid was to her
  mother borne,
The flower of her widowed heart for ever crushed
  and torn.
Her morning fears had proved too true: far from
  the mountain top
Three hundred feet this maid was dashed, her fall
  no man could stop.

The shroud is now the bridal dress of this once
  lovely maid.
A simple hillock marks the spot where her
  remains are laid.

At close of day a robin sings his sweet sad song
  of rest,
Which seems to say how cold the clay lies softly
  on her breast.

1.4: ... rose that flourished ... [Dt]
2.2: ... they lived in ... [Dt]
6.4: ... my promised bride.' [Dt]

Annie Moore [H191: 9 Jul 1927]

A tragic song of the twelfth of '45.

Source: coll. Maud Houston (Coleraine).

Key C.

As I roved out one evening in the month of sweet
  July,
Through shady groves and valleys and streams as
  I passed by,
The small birds they sat mourning on each green
  shady grove;
They joined their notes all with that youth
  lamenting for his love.

He tore his hair distracted, oftimes his hands he
  wrung,
The tears ran down his rosy cheeks like an
  uneven stream,
But still he cried, 'My darling's gone, the maid
  that I adore,
By a sudden call to her long home, will I never
  see her more?

'She was a proper tall young girl, scarce
  seventeen years of age,
And in no riotous company was ever she engaged,
Her comrade girl she asked her out, a-walking
  for to go,
She took her to that fatal spot which proved her
  overthrow.

'It was on the twelfth day of July in the year of
  forty-five,
It ne'er shall be forgot by me as long as I'm alive,
It was that day, that very day, my love was torn
  from me;
She was the rose of Belfast town and the flower
  of the counter-ee.

'It was on the twelfth day of July, Orange arches
  we did form,
And Scully and his cavalry thought to cut them
  down by storm,

But all their efforts were in vain, for we could
not comply,
And so as we advanced, 'No surrender' was our
cry.

'When riding forth to cut them down, we received
a mortal blow:
You know a stone from David's sling did lay
Goliath low;
Then the Light Infantry got an order to fire a
round of ball,
It was at that fatal moment my true love she did
fall.

'A ball it entered in her breast and pierced her
body through,
She gently fell and waved her hand, she could
not bid adieu.
As I held her milk-white hand in mine, my breast
being filled with woe
To see those lips I oftimes kissed now whiter than
the snow.

'Annie Moore was my love's name, of credit and
renown,
She was the flower of the country and the rose of
Belfast town;
The protestant cause she dearly loved, William's
sons she did adore,
And round her neck even to the last an orange
ribbon wore.'

'The protestants of Belfast turned out like heroes
brave
To carry her remains to the cold and silent
grave,
And many of those heroes that day in tears were
found
At the leaving of her residence, convenient to the
town.

'Her dear friends and relations their lost one
now deplore,
Likewise her comrade girl was walking round the
shore,
And many hearts are merry while my poor heart
is dry,
For it makes me sigh when I think of the twelfth
day of July.'

3.2: ... company did ever she engage, [Dt]

Molly Bawn Lowry

[H114: 16 Jan 1926; Laws O36]

s: "The Shooting of His Dear," "Molly Bawn Aroo."
Other titles: "As Jimmie Went A-Hunting," "At the
Setting of the Sun," "The Fowler," "Jimmy Ran-
vul," "(Young) Mollie(y) (Peggy) (Polly) Ban
(Ba'n) (Bann) (Baum) (Bawn) (Bond) (Bonder)
(Van) (Vaughan) (Whan)," "Moll(e)y Bann (Baun)
Lavery."

Source: (m, "half the ballad") "Molly Bawn Aroo,"
coll. Maud Houston (Coleraine) from Peggy McGarry (Ballycastle, Co. Antrim); ("complete") Hugh
Clarke (Croaghan, Macosquin, Coleraine).

s: Versions of this song, under the title "The
Shooting of His Dear," have been collected by
Cecil Sharp at Hambridge (England), and in Kent.
Cecil Sharp was of [the] opinion that the ballad
was of Celtic origin because of the introduction
of the ghost.... After prolonged search I have
obtained the complete song.... The extra lines 5
and 6, verse 3, are sung to lines 1 and 2 of the
music.

Key C.

I will tell you a story that happened of late,
About Molly Bawn Lowry, that beautiful maid,
She being going to her uncle's when a shower
came on,
She went under a hawthorn the shower to shun.

*With her apron pinned around her, I took her
for a swan,
And oh and alas, it was my own Molly Bawn.*

It's when he ran up and found she was dead,
A well full of tears for his true love he shed.
He ran home to his father with his gun in his
hand,
Crying, 'Father, dear father, I have shot Molly
Bawn.'

His old father jumped up, his head being grey:
'Stay at home in your country, do not run away,
Stay at home in your country, let your trial come
on,
For before you be condemned I will lose all my
land.'
At the day of the trial Molly's ghost did appear,
Crying, 'Uncle, dear uncle, James Reynolds is
clear.'

Now the girls of this country they are all glad
for to hear
It's Molly Bawn Lowry the flower of Glenkeer,
For if all the young girls were placed in one row,
Molly Bawn she would appear as white as the
snow.

Now come all you sharp shooters that handle a
gun,
Beware of sharp shooting at the setting of the
sun,
For it might happen with you as it happened with
me,
For to shoot your own true love right under a
tree.

Sam Henry's Songs of the People

A Collier Lad [H110: 19 Dec 1925]

Other titles: "The Handsome ...," "Johnny Siddon," "Lament for John Sneddon."

Source: Sara Morrow (Drumcrow, Carnalbana, Broughshane, Co. Antrim).

Key C.

Come all ye pretty fair maids, I hope you'll lend an ear
To the grief and sorrow of my heart, you very soon shall hear,
For once I loved a collier lad and he loved me also,
But by a fatal accident he in a grave lies low.

My love he was a collier lad, he wrought beneath the ground.
His modest mild behaviour, his equal can't be found,
His two bright eyes and yellow hair, his cheeks a rosy red,
But alas, my handsome collier lad lies numbered with the dead.

Last night as I lay on my bed I fell into a dream,
I dreamt a voice came unto me and named me by name,
Saying, 'Jeannie, lovely Jeannie, for me you need not mourn,
My spirit's fled, I'm with the dead, I'll never more return.'

Early the next morning my dream was edified:
The neighbours all came rushing in, 'John Sneddon's dead,' they cried,
'As he was at his work last night the roof all on him fell,'
To the grief and sorrow of my heart no mortal tongue can tell.

The day was set, the bands were met and married we were to be,
My love and I we had agreed to sail to Americ-ee,
Or for to make a fortune all on some foreign shore,
But alas, my handsome collier lad shall now return no more.

Summer it will come again, all things they will seem gay,
And lovely lambs around their dams will fondly sport and play,
Other fair maids will have their joy, but in death I'll constant mourn
For alas, my handsome collier lad shall never more return.

2.2: For modest ... [Dt]
3.3: ... Jeanie, lovely Jeanie ... [Dt]
4.4: The grief ... [Dt]

4.1: edified = (verified?) [s: Dt]
5.1: bands were met = ?banns were posted.

My Lowlands, Away [H469: 26 Nov 1932]

Other titles: "Lowlands," "Lowlands Away."

Source not given.

Key C.

I dreamt I saw my own dear bride,
Lowlands, lowlands away, my John,
I dreamt I saw my own dear bride,
My lowlands away.

[*similarly:*]
And she was dressed in shimmering white.

All dressed in white, like some fair bride.

And then she smiled her sweetest smile.

She sang and made my heart rejoice.

The salt seaweed was in her hair.

It filled my heart with dark despair.

And then I knew that she was dead.

Then I awoke to hear the cry.

'All hands on deck! Oh, watch ahoy!'

Mary's Dream [H54: 22 Nov 1924; Laws K20]

s: (m) "The Coleraine Lass." Other titles: "Mary and Sandy," "Mary o' the Dee," "... Vision."

Source: (Fermoyle) [Dt: author John Lowe (Galloway)]; (m) J[ohn] M[urphy], SH's schoolmate (Railway Rd, Coleraine).

[Bp] s: The words usually sung to "The Coleraine Lass" are valueless. The air ... is too good to be lost. I have, therefore, wedded it to "Mary's Dream," a song which reached me from the Fermoyle district.
[Dt] The author was John Lowe, son of the gardener at Kenmure Castle, Galloway, and refers to Mary MacGhie, whose lover, Alexander Miller,

144

was drowned in 1772.... See Cromek's *Galloway Remains*, page 361, for the authorship.

[Dt] Key C. [Bp lacks key indication.]

The moon had climbed the highest hill
That rises o'er the source of Dee,
And from her eastern summit shed
Her silver light on tower and tree,
When Mary laid her down to sleep,
Her thoughts on Sandy far at sea;
When soft and low a voice she heard,
Saying, 'Mary, weep no more for me.'

She from her pillow gently raised
Her head to ask who there might be;
She saw young Sandy shivering stand
With visage pale and hollow e'e.
'O Mary dear, cold is my clay,
It lies beneath a stormy sea,
Far, far from thee I sleep in death,
So, Mary, weep no more for me.

'Three stormy nights and stormy days
We tossed upon the raging main,
And hard we strove our bark to save,
But all our striving was in vain.
Even then, when horror chilled my blood,
My heart was filled with love to thee.
The storm is past and I'm at rest,
So, Mary, weep no more for me.

'O maiden dear, thyself prepare,
We soon shall meet upon that shore
Where love is free from doubt and care,
And you and I shall part no more.'
Loud crowed the cock, the vision fled,
No more of Sandy could she see,
But soft the passing spirit said,
'Sweet Mary, weep no more for me.'

The Nightingale (I)

[H75a: [Bp]

"Two songs of the press gang," 18 Apr 1925]

Other titles: "The Loss of the ...," "The Sailor and His Love."

Source: (w) John H[enry] Macauley (Ballycastle); (stanza 1) William Sloan (Boghill); (m) W[illie] H[egarty] (Agivey district).

[Bp] s: ... A ship of this name, 251 tons, 24 guns, was taken by the French in August 1707 and re-taken by the *Ludlow Castle* in December 1707 and re-named *Fox*. Of the eight *Nightingales* in the Navy since 1651, this ship most nearly agrees with the ship in the song.
[Dt, also written on Bp] Another *Nightingale* sloop of 80 tons [Dt: is recorded] [Bp: for London] on 22d May 1783.

Key F.

Ye Christians all, where'er you be,
Give ear to my sad trag-ed-ee,
I'm lonely now, I here bewail
And mourn the fate of the *Nightingale*.

My love, he was a rich farmer's son
When first my tender young heart he won,
His love unto me he did reveal,
But little thought on the *Nightingale*.

The *Nightingale* was a vessel stout,
Well manned, well decked, well finished out
With thirty bright guns, the truth I'll tell,
But mark the fate of the *Nightingale*.

His cruel parents contrived it so
That my true love to the seas must go,
They bribed the press gang, who did not fail
To press my love on the *Nightingale*.

On the twenty-fifth of November last,
The wind it blew a most bitter blast,
My love stood under the lashing sail,
And to the bottom went on the *Nightingale*.

The very night that my love was lost,
He appeared to me in a frightful ghost
In sailor's clothing, his visage pale,
'Twas the clothes he wore on the *Nightingale*.

I lifted my head from my pillow high
And from the bedside the ghost did fly,
Saying, 'Molly, dear Molly, don't be in surprise,
In the Bay of Biscay my body lies.

'To become a prey to some shark or whale
It was my fate on the *Nightingale*,
To become a prey to some shark or whale
It was my fate on the *Nightingale*.'

1.: [*Typed on Bp, Wt*] "First verse ... William Sloan"
    [*Stanza 1 also typed on Bp.*]
    [*Typed on Dt:*] First verse from William Sloan, Boghill.
5.4: ... went the ... [Dt]

Willie Lennox [H176: 26 Mar 1927; Laws Q33]

s: "Willie Leonard" (Joyce); k: "The Lake of Cool Finn." Other titles: "Billy Henry," "The (Cruel) Lake(s) (Loch) of Col Fin (Col Flynn) (Cold Finn) (Cold Stream) (?Colefaine) (Cool Flynn) (Coolfin) (Colephin) (Coulfin) (Shallin) (Shellin) (Shilin) (Shillin) (Wolfrinn)," "(Lament for) Willie(y) Leonard," "Loughinsholin," "Poor (Young) Leonard," "Royal Comrade," "'Twas Early One Morning."

Source: (w, m) John Parker (Mayoghill, Garvagh); (w) "slightly amended to correspond with version sent by Joseph Reilly" (Moneycannon, Ballymoney).

s: ... It is a most interesting point in topography that the hero of the song was drowned in the lake (no longer on the map) which gives its name to the Barony of Loughinshollin -- "the lough of the island of the O'Lynns." The O'Lynns (originally O'Flynns -- the "F" being aspirated is not sounded) were a powerful sept who may have been the original builders of Dunluce Castle in the sixth century, and from 1121 a.d. onwards occupied Hy Tuirtre, a territory comprising the modern baronies of Lower Antrim, Lower Toome, Lower Glenarm, and Kilconway [Bp: on the east side of the Bann, and "two cantreds beyond the Bann." The lough was probably an expansion of the river not far north of Lough Beg. The accident described in the song probably took place on the 12th day of July (see last verse)].

o: The probable location of the tragedy was on the river Agivey at Inisholeen, north of Garvagh.

l: This song is unusual in that the repeated lines in the refrain sections are not always exact repetitions.

Key E flat. [Bp] Slowly and with pathos. (The music repeats for the repeated lines 5 and 6.)

It's early one morning Willie Lennox arose
And straight to his cousin's bedchamber he goes,
Saying, 'Arise, lovely cousin, and let no one know,
It's a fine summer morning, to the bathing we'll go.'
  Saying, 'Arise, lovely cousin, and let no one know,
  It's a fine summer morning, to the bathing we'll go.

Oh, as Willie and his cousin went down the long lane,
They met Sergeant Henry and Colonel O'Neill;
Says the colonel to Willie, 'Do not venture in,
For there's deep and dead water in Loughshollin.'
  Says the colonel, 'Do not venture in,
  For I saw a collin in the Loughshollin.'

Oh, Willie being stout-hearted, it's in he did go
And swam to an island which proved his o'erthrow;
He swam it twice over, was turning right round,
And in a few moments Willie Lennox went down.
  Small boats soon were lowered, long lines were let down,
  And in a few moments Willie Lennox was found.

Oh, there was an old woman being there standing by,
She ran to his mother and it's this she did cry:
'Bad news I have for you, which grieves my heart sore,
That your darling son Willie, his name is no more.'
  Saying, 'It's sorrowful news I have for you, I'm sure,
  For your darling son Willie, his name is no more.'

When she heard this, she ran to his father in despair,
By the wringing her hands and the tearing her hair,
Saying, 'I reared you a family of clever young sons,
But it's oh and alas, the flower of them's gone.'
  Saying, 'I reared you a family of clever young sons,
  But alas and anee, the flower of them's gone.'

Oh, it's for Willie's true love, she may mourn night and day
For the loss of her lover who lies cold in the clay,
For both morning and evening he did her salute
With the pink and the roses and all garden fruit.
  For both morning and evening he did her salute
  With the pink and red roses and all garden fruit.

All gathered together and stood in a ring
While the Orange and Purple around them did hing,
They all whispered slowly and raised up their hands,
Saying, 'Boys, while you[']r[e] living, beware of the Bann.'
  They all whispered slowly and raised up their hands,
  Saying, 'Boys, while you[']r[e] living, beware of the Bann.'

2.5: ... venture, do not venture in, [Dt]
 .6: For there's deep and dead water in Loughshollin.' [Dt]
3.4,6: ... few minutes ... [Dt]
5.2: To the ... [Dt]
 .3,.5: ... of eleven ... [Dt]
7.4,.6: ... while you're living ... [Dt]

Sloan Wellesley [H585: 16 Feb 1935]

Other titles: "The Dog and the Gun," "The Drowning of Young Robinson," "In the County of Innocent."

Source: (m) late John Parker (Mayoghill, Aghadowey); (w) Mrs. John Leighton (Ballyhome, Cloyfin, Coleraine).

s: ... The name is pronounced Walsley by the folk-singer. The song should be sung as a dirge.

Key D.

In the parish of Seagoe, near the town of
  Armagh,
Two men went a-fowling through frost and snow,
Each of them had with them their dog and their
  gun,
And alongst the Bann waters a-fowling begun.

A small boat had passed a few days ago,
And the ice it was broken, and they did not
  know;
They both step-ped forward and they plunged
  in,
To the bottom went Robertson; Sloan Walsley
  could swim.

Sloan Walsley ran home like a man in despair,
He was [w]ringing his hands and tearing his
  hair.
'Sloan Walsley, Sloan Walsley, where is my son
  gone?'
'He has gone to the bottom with dog, gun and
  all.'

With ropes his dear brother to the rescue did
  run,
But could reach him no further than the banks
  of the Bann;
'O brother, dear brother, your ropes are in
  vain,
I'm twice at the bottom and I'm going down
  again.

'Oh, tell my old mother to sorrow no more,
But it's awake me one night when she gets me
  ashore.'
'If the Lord has prepared you a watery tomb,
May the angels stand round you and guard you
  safe home.'

There were six hundred Orangemen all stood in
  one ring,
And from their left breast orange and purple did
  hing,
They all marched slowly and waving their hand,
Saying, 'Adieu, boys, forever, adieu to the
  Bann.'

James Kennedy [H633: 11 Jan 1936]

Source not given.

Key G.

One early Sunday morning James Kennedy arose,
And for to see his old sweetheart, light-heartedly
  he goes,
But when he came to Moyola bank he stripped into
  the skin,
He tried a place too deep for him; alas, he
  couldn't swim.

At last when he was drowning, for help he loud
  did call,
His friends they were faint-hearted and none did
  help at all,
The light then left his drowning eyes, his body
  went ashore,
Which made his friends and neighbours cry,
  'James Kennedy's no more.'

A message was sent off to the town where this
  young man did dwell,
His father heard it first and his father loved him
  well,
His mother cried, 'Oh, darling son, oh what took
  you away?
Or what took you to Moyola banks upon the
  Sabbath day?'

There was a proper tall young girl stood by the
  river side,
He had no other notion but to make of her his
  bride.
The clergy he came up to her and this to her did
  say,
'You'll meet your lover at the grave upon your
  wedding day.'

Sam Henry's Songs of the People

Miss Cochrane

[H42a: "Two Magilligan songs," 30 Aug 1924]

o: (m) "Eirigh Suas a Stoirin" (Donegal, coll. Seán O'Boyle).

Source: Charles Dempsey, postman (Coleraine) coll. Maud Houston (Coleraine).

Key G.

It was on an Easter Monday which happened of late,
Young Marg'ret got ready and set on her way,
The boat it was light, it blew hard on the sea,
And Miss Cochrane was drowned on Magilligan Bay.

A messenger unto her father was sent,
Saying, 'Margaret is lying and for you I am sent.'
He says to the little boy, 'The truth you may tell,
For Marg'ret is drownded, I know it right well.'

He mounted his horse and to Magilligan came,
Where numbers of boats he spied out on the main,
With boathooks and grapnels they were taking great pain
For to find out Miss Cochrane, but all was in vain.

Oh, it's fare you well, Marg'ret, now since you are gone;
Oftentimes have I warned you Lough Foyle for to shun,
But oh and alas, it has proved your overthrown,
Which makes you to lie on the bottom alone.

1.2: ... set out on ... [Dt]
2.1: ... father then went, [Dt]
 .4: ... it quite well, [Dt]
3.1: ... horse, to ... [Dt]
 .3: ... great pains [Dt]
4.2: Oftimes I have ... [Dt]
 .3: ... overthrow, [Dt]
 .4: It has caused you to sleep on the bottom below. [Dt]

Rachel Dear
/ The Maine Water Side [H62: 17 Jan 1925]

o: (m) "Roddy McCorley."

Source: William Murdoch (Olphert Place, Coleraine, native of Dunminning, Cullybackey), learned at a ceilidh c. 1865.

[Dt] s: ... Rachel MacLaughlin, who was drowned in the Maine, close to her home, went out to call her brother, who was fishing, in for his dinner, leaving her to hold the net. She fell into the river and was jammed between two rocks.

Key G.

On the twentieth of October last, that dark and dismal day,
It being on the morning my love was cast away,
The swelling waves they did prevail and heavy fell the rain
When lovely Rachel lost her life along the river Maine.

But when my love fell in the deep, the waters bore her down,
Like a milk-white swan she swimm-ed on through Cullybackey town,
And everyone as they passed by the doleful news did hear,
From every heart it drew a sigh, from every eye a tear.

Like a milk-white swan my love she swam through Cullybackey town,
The water bore her body on until it did her drown,
She struggled long in water deep in hopes to reach the shore,
But in death's cold arms she fell asleep, her troubles all were o'er.

Her cousin dear, who did live near, no peace nor rest could find,
And sore he was perplexed, dreams did disturb his mind,
He says, 'I will go look for her if providence will me guide,
And there he found his Rachel dear on the Maine water side.

If you had seen her mother, 'twould have made your heart relent,
Likewise her sweetheart Willie; unto her corpse he went,
He kissed her lips as cold as clay, he kissed them o'er and o'er,
Saying, 'Fare you well, my Rachel dear, we part to meet no more.'

Her cheeks they were a rosy red, her skin a clear milk white,
She was the fairest in my view, on her I took delight,

Her hair it was a lovely brown, most curious to
  behold,
And now fair Rachel is no more, she's in Ahoghill
  mould.

1.2: ... on that morning ... [Dt]
2.2: ... she floated on ... [Dt]
6.4: ... Ahoghill. [Dt]

Polly Primrose [H734: 18 Dec 1937]

Source: Tom Courtney (Drumearn, Cookstown)
from Willie Black (Aughless, Cookstown) c. 1887.

s: ... Willie Black [was] ... a man of many
trades, including that of ship's steward. He had
a large repertoire of songs he learnt at sea.

[The correction printed in the subsequent column,
H735, to the penultimate line of this melody ("bars
5 and 6 were superfluous") seems itself to be superfluous unless the corresponding words ("Oh!
my;") are also to be omitted.]

Key C.

Sweet Polly Primrose, a girl of nineteen
  summers-o,
Sure, I love my Polly better far than all the
  wealth I own,
For she was so very fond of me, it makes me wail
  and weep
That the girl I love's at present at the bottom of
  the deep.

   I wish I was a fish with a long, long tail,
   I wish I was a fish with a long, long tail,
   Any little tillibat, a winkle or a whale,
   At the bottom of the deep blue sea, oh my!
   At the bottom of the deep blue sea.

My love, she being on board a ship and bound for
  Carrick Cross,

And her cargo being firebrick, she began to pitch
  and toss,
My love being standing on the deck and the water
  rolling by,
Somehow she tumbled overboard and never said
  goodbye.

Since she's a sporty mermaid, I'm unhappy here
  above,
I think I'll take a trip and be a mermaid with my
  love;
Still, the praise of that locality I don't exactly
  know
Where I might find my Polly, so I think I will not
  go.

1.1: ... summers, O! [Bp]

Holland Is a Fine Place

[H180: 23 Apr 1927; Child #92a]

Other titles: "Abroad as I Was Walking," "The *Lily
of Arkansas*," "The Lowlands of Holland (Germany)," "The Low, Low Lands of Holland," "The
Maiden's Lament," "The Rocks of Giberaltar,"
"The Soldier Bride's Lament."

Source: (m, most w) John Henry Macaulay (Ballycastle), who heard a band play it in Ballycastle;
rest of text "reconstructed from other sources."

Key G.

The night that I was married and brought home
  my happy bride,
Up came a bold sea-captain and stood at my
  bedside,
Saying, 'Arise, young married man, and come
  along with me
To the lowlands of Holland to fight the enemy.'

Oh, Holland is a fine place and in it grows
  much green,
'Tis a wild inhabitation for my love to be in:
There the sugar cane grows plentiful and fruit
  on every tree,
But the lowlands of Holland have parted my love
  and me.

Says the mother to the daughter, 'Why do you
  so lament?
Is there ne'er a man in Ireland's ground to ease
  your discontent?'

Sam Henry's Songs of the People

'There are men enough in Ireland, but none at
    all for me,
For the lowlands of Holland are between my love
    and me.

'The love that I ha'e chosen, I'll therewith be
    content,
The salt sea shall be frozen before that I repent,
Repent it shall I never until the day I die,
But the lowlands of Holland they parted my love
    and me.

'My love lies in the saut sea and I am on the
    side,
Enough to break a young thing's heart wha
    lately was a bride,
Wha lately was a bonnie bride wi' pleasure in
    her e'e,
But the lowlands of Holland ha'e twined my love
    and me.

'My love he built a bonny ship and set her on
    the main,
With twenty-four brave mariners to sail her out
    and hame,
But the weary winds began to rise, the seas
    began to roar,
And my love and his bonny ship were lost when
    near the shore.

'There shall nae mantle cross my back, nae kame
    gie in my hair,
Neither shall coal or candlelight shine in my
    bower mair,
Nor shall I choose anither love until the day I
    dee,
Since the lowlands of Holland has parted my love
    and me.'

'Noo, haud your tongue, my daughter dear, be
    still and bide content,
There's ither lads in Gallawa, ye needna sae
    lament.'
'There's plenty o' lads in Gallawa, but there's
    nane o' them for me,
Since the ragin' seas and stormy waves has
    parted my love and me.'

1.1: ... my bonny bride, [Dt]
4.3: ... I dee. [Dt]
5.2: ... heart who ... [Dt]
7.1: ... kame gae ... [Dt]
 .4: ... Holland hae ... [Dt]
8.4: ... waves hae ... [Dt]

Susan on the Beach

[H774: 24 Sep 1938; Laws K19]

1: (m) "The River Roe" in 4; cf. others, in 6.
Other titles: "(As) Susan Strayed the Briny
Beach," "Sligo Shore."

Source not given.

Key G.

Poor Susan walked along the beach that skirted
    Sligo shore,
And as she walked she oftimes thought of the lad
    she did adore,
And often in soft accents would her tongue
    pronounce his name,
For to love a simple sailor lad she thought no sin
    or shame.

Her father was a gentleman of wealth and high
    degree,
And she, being kind in heart and mind, was
    beautiful to see;
Of lords and gentry many did her hand in
    marriage sue,
Which she rejected in her heart, still to her
    Willie true.

The night before, it blew a storm and still the
    waves ran high,
And as she viewed the swelling tide a tear stole
    to her eye;
Perhaps, she thought, while thus I stray, my
    Willie may be tossed
High upon some wicked wave or else entirely
    lost.

Now who would be a sailor lad, or care to be his
    bride,
When all his hope in life depends upon both wind
    and tide?
But happy are those landsmen's wives who live in
    houses warm,
Their husbands dear are ever near to shelter
    them from harm.

But yet I would not change my lot, although my
    Willie be
Guarded by one single plank from dark eternity,
For when he comes, no more we'll part, no more
    from me he'll roam;
All danger past, he'll share at last with me a
    happy home.

When thus she spoke, a longing look upon the
    sea she gave,
And she thought she saw like something dark
    approaching on the wave,
She watched it as it neared the shore, and then
    at length began
To see more clearly that it bore the semblance of
    a man.

A sickening fear crept through her heart when thus a closer view,
And as she watched the floating body dressed in navy blue,
She quickly marched along the beach, nor feared the ocean's roar,
Until a mountain wave then dashed the sailor on the shore

With more than woman's strength she bore the lifeless man on high,
And she laid him gently on the spot where all around was dry;
His manly neck was stripped clean, which showed his skin most fair,
And bits of seaweed were entangled in his nut-brown hair.

She placed her gold watch to his mouth to catch some sign of breath,
Its brightness never dimmed because his lips were closed in death.
With pain she gazed upon his face, it was all bruised and tore,
And something told her trembling heart she had seen that face before.

Sickening at the sight, she turned, assistance for to bring,
When on his finger she espied a dazzling diamond ring;
At one quick glance she knew it was the ring her Willie wore,
For she placed it on his finger when they parted on the shore.

Then she fell upon his mangled form and clasped him to her breast;
The sudden shock it broke her heart, her soul passed to its rest,
And thus in death's embrace they lay, until at length a crowd
That gathered round conveyed their bodies to her parents proud.

As they were carried to their grave it was a solemn sight:
There were twelve young sailors dressed in blue and twelve young girls in white,
And like two early flowers that were nipped in youthful bloom,
Their hearts that were both joined in love were buried in one tomb.

❖ A10 REFERENCES ❖

❖ The Bard of Culnady / Charles O'Neill (H50) 139

Brunnings 1981: (m) "Savourneen Deelish (Tune of The Exile of Erin and Green Were the Fields)"

❖ Finvola, the Gem of the Roe (H786) 139

IREL Shields 1981:81 (#29)

h: REC Anne, Francie Brolly, Homespun HRL 116

❖ Hielan' Jane (H477) 140

BRS Harvard 1: 4.18 (Walker) "Highland Jane," 4.126 (Ross), 5.165 (Catnach) "My Bonny Blooming Highland Jane," 6.46 (Watts), 9.124 (Bebbington), 11.126 (Such)

❖ The Cowboy of Loreto (H680) 141

Laws 1964:133 (B1) "The Cowboy's Lament (The Dying Cowboy)" traces the ancestry of this song to "The Bad Girl's Lament" (Laws Q25) and ultimately to "The Unfortunate Rake."
Brunnings 1981: "The Streets of Laredo"

Folkways FA 3805 is an entire album devoted to "The Unfortunate Rake" and its relatives, edited by Kenneth S. Goldstein: see esp. (A8) "The Cowboy's Lament" (Bruce Buckley); (A9) "The Streets of Loredo" (Harry Jackson).
D. K. Wilgus discusses thoroughly the Irish background of this song in "The Aisling and the Cowboy," WF 44(1985):255-300.
See also discussion in Chapter 1 of Darling 1983, esp. p. 9 "One Morning in May" (from Caroline Paton); pp. 9-10 "The Cowboy's Lament" (see Buckley rec. and Folkways FA 3805 above).

IREL Cf. Joyce 1909:249 (#442) "My Jewel, My Joy" [Belden]
Meek 1978:52-3 "The Dying Cowboy"

AMER Abrahams 1970:76-8 "Tom Sherman's Barroom"
Brumley 1970:36 "The Dying Cowboy"
Cox 1939(1964):141-2 "The Dying Cowboy"
Kincaid 2,1930:28-9 "The Streets of Laredo"
Randolph 1946-50(1980)2:179 (#182) "The Cowboy's Lament" [Laws]

BRS A Broadside 5(4,Sep)1912 "The Cowboy's Lament"

cl: REC Bill Atkins, AFS 1938 "The Dying Cowboy"
? cl: Vergis Bailey, AFS 1447 B1 "The Dying Cowgirl"
cl: E. A. Briggs, AFS 2637 A2 "The Cowboy's Lament"
  Bruce Buckley, Folkways FA 3805 (A8) "The Cowboy's Lament"
b: William Clauson, Capitol T 10158 "The Streets of Laredo"
b: Bob Cort Skiffle Group, London LL 1774 "The Streets of Laredo"
cl: Cowboy band, AFS 545 A "The Cowboy's Lament"
  Slim Critchlow, Arhoolie 5007 (B2) "The Cowboy's Lament"
  Dick Devall, RCA Victor LPV 548 (B5) "Tom Sherman's Barroom"; AAFS L20 (B6) "The Dying Cowboy"
b: Mark Dinning, MGM 3855 "The Streets of Laredo"
cl: Frank Goodwyn, AFS 2614 A3 & B2, 2621 B "The Dying Cowboy"
cl: Mrs G. A. Griffin, AFS 2695 B3 "The Dying Cowboy"
cl: Group of patients, Texas State Hospital, AFS 936 B2 "The Cowboy's Lament"
  Ewen Hall, Brunswick 141 [Randolph]
cl: Mrs Goldie Hamilton, AFS 2833 B1 "The Dying Cowboy"
b: Jim (Helms) and Art (Podell), Horizon WP 1603 "The Streets of Laredo"
cl: Mrs Lucile Henson, AFS 658 B2 "The Cowboy's Lament"
b: *Hootenanny at the Limelight*, Somerset SF 108 (5 recs) "The Streets of Laredo"
cl: Doc Hoppes, AFS 856 B2 "The Dying Cowboy"

b: Cisco Houston, Vanguard VRS 9107 "The Streets of Laredo"
Burl Ives, [lc:] Encyclopedia Britannica Films 6 (78 rpm) b1 351 "The Streets of Laredo"; [b:] Camay CA 3005; [b:] Decca A 431 (78 rpm); [b:] Columbia CL 628; Columbia CS 904 (A4) "Cowboy's Lament"
Harry Jackson, Folkways FH 3805 (A9) "Streets of Loredo"; Folkways FH 5723 (D2)
cl: Mrs Esco Kilgore, AFS 2832 B1 "The Dying Cowboy"
Bradley Kincaid, Supertone 9404 [Randolph]
Tom Lenihan, Topic 12TS 363 (A4) "St. James' Hospital"
b: A. L. Lloyd, Topic 12T 118 "St. James' Hospital"
b: Alan Lomax, Tradition TLP 1029 "The Dying Cowboy"
b: Ed McCurdy, Elektra EKL 108 "The Streets of Laredo"
Cf. Christy Moore, Tara 2008 (A4) "Lock Hospital"
b: Seraffyn Mork, Columbia CS 8957 "The Streets of Laredo"
New Century World of Song, Triton Record Productions (3 recs.) "The Streets of Laredo"
cl: Mrs J. U. Newman, AFS 3781 A2 & B1 "The Dying Cowboy"
Joan O'Bryant, Folkways FA 2338 (B8) "Tom Sherman's Barroom"
b: Stu Phillips, Rodeo RCW 1001 "The Streets of Laredo"
Johnny Prude, AAFS L28 (B3) "The Streets of Laredo"
Jean Ritchie, [lc:] Elektra EKLP 2 "One Morning in May," 2 versions; [b:] Prestige/Folklore 13003 (B7) "The Dying Cowboy"
Cf. Pete Seeger, [b:] Folkways FA 2319 (B5) "St. James Hospital"; [b:] Folkways FA 2452 (B1a) "Streets of Laredo," 1 stanza; [b:] Folkways FI 8354
cl: Francis Sullivan, AFS 1768 A2 & B1 "John Sherman's Barroom"
cl: Beale D. Taylor, AFS 3806 A2, 3808 A2 "The Cowboy's Lament"
Tex-i-an Boys, Folkways FH 5328 (A5) "The Streets of Laredo"
? cl: Capt. Asel Trueblood, AFS 2332 A & B1 "The Dying Ranger"
Cf. Doug Wallin, Home Made Music LP 003 "Let Her Go, Let Her Go, God Bless Her"
cl: Mrs Crockett Ward, Fields Ward, AFS 1372 B1 "The Cowboy's Lament"
cl: Mrs Susan Weddle, AFS 2235 A1 "The Dying Cowboy"
b: Cf. Alf Wildman, EFDSS LP 1006 (A4) "The Banks of the Clyde"
cl: Mrs Ollie Womble, AFS 3029 B1 "The Dying Cowboy"
Columbia 154 63-D [Randolph]

b: MEL *Hootenanny for Orchestra*, Liberty SLT 7332 "Laredo Lament"
b: *Liberty Hootenanny*, Liberty LL 5506 "Laredo Lament"

◆ Annie Moore (H191) 142

Brunnings 1981

b: IREL Morton 1970:68-9, with a brief description of the circumstances of the tragedy.

BRS BCL Biggar: J1.70 [Morton]

◆ Molly Bawn Lowry (H114) 143

White/Dean-Smith 1951: "(The) Shooting of His Dear or The Fowler"
Dean-Smith 1954: "(The) Shooting of His Dear; At the Setting of the Sun"
Laws 1957:243-4 (O36) "Molly Bawn (Shooting of His Dear)"
Brunnings 1981: "Molly Bawn"

See especially the articles by Barry (*BFSSNE* #10, 1935:12) and Gilchrist (*JFSS* 7(26)1922):17 "The Fowler [The Shooting of His Dear]." An important contribution to the discussion of whether the song is a local Irish production or a derivative of a Gaelic song based on the "swan maiden" motif is provided in notes to Flora MacNeill's recording, Tangent TGS 124.

IREL *JIFSS* 3(3&4)1905-6:25 "... Bawn Aroo" [Laws]
Joyce 1909:220 (#409) "Molly Bawn" [Laws]
Loesberg 1,1980:15 "... Ban"
Morton 1973:1-2
O Lochlainn 1939:58-9 "Young Molly Ba'n"
Shields *UF* 17,1971:21 "Molley Bann Lavery"; *UF* 18,1972:36-7
Shields/Shields *UF* 21,1975: #272 "Molly Bawn"

BRIT Kennedy 1975:716 (#330) "Polly Vaughan"; adds an Irish and an English version recorded.
Palmer 1980:55-6 "Molly Bawn"
Sharp/Karpeles 1974,1:235-6
Yates *FMJ* 1980:15-6 "Molly Van"

AMER Bush 1,1969:86-7 "Molly Bond"; 3,1975:79-80 "Polly Bond"
CD&S #10,1979:32 "Jimmy Ranvul"
Colorado FB 2,1963:6
Darling 1983:135-6, A "Molly Bawn" (see Cleveland rec.); B "... Bonder (see Buckley rec.)
Grover n.d.:104-5 "Mollie Bawn"
Kenedy 1890:80, 321, 2 versions
Leach 1967:176-7 "... Baum"
Milner/Kaplan 1983:51-2 "Polly Vaughan" (see Roberts/Barrand rec.)
Moore/Moore 1964:169-71 "Molly Bond"

BRS BPL Irish: (n.i.)

REC Seamus Ennis, *CWL* 1, Columbia AKL 4941 (B2,26) "... Bawn"
A. L. Lloyd, *CWL* 3, Columbia KL 206 (A2,23) "Polly Vaughan"; *Riverside CB*, RLP 12 629 (B5) "The Shooting of His Dear"
Harry Cox (Norfolk), *FSB* 7 (B3) "Polly Vaughan"
Louis Boutillier, Folkways FE 4307 (A5) "As Jimmie Went A-Hunting"
Bruce Buckley, Folkways FA 2025 (B4) "... Bonder"
Packie Manus Byrne, Topic 12TS 257 (A4) "... Bawn"; Mulligan LUN A 001; Green Linnet SIF 1005 (A5)
Martin Carthy, Topic 12TS 342 (Fontana STL 5434) (A2) "The Fowler or The Shooting of His Dear"
Paul Clayton, Folkways FA 2106 (B4) "Polly Van"
Sara Cleveland, Folk-Legacy FSA 33 (A3) "Molly Bawn"
Audrey Coppard, Folkways FP 917 (B4) "Polly Vaughan"
cl: Emma Dusenbury, AFS 3234 B2 "Polly Vaughan"
cl: Aunt Molly Jackson, AFS 2576 A & B1 "The Shooting of His Dear"
Flora MacNeil, Tangent TGS 124
John Maguire, Leader LEE 4062 (A1)
Joan O'Bryant, Folkways FA 2134 (B4) "... Bann"
John Roberts, Tony Barrand, Folk-Legacy FSI 65 (B5) "Polly Vaughan"
Tony Rose, Trailer LER 2101 (A4) "Polly Vaughan"
cl: Mrs J. H. Smith, AFS 990 B2 "Polly Vann"
Phoebe Smith, Topic 12T 193 (B1) "Molly Vaughan"
Dan Tate, Home Made Music LP 002 (A6b) "Molly Van"

MEL Hudson ms. 3:746

◆ A Collier Lad (H110) 144

Brunnings 1981: "Lament for John Sneddon"

IREL   Morton 1973:64-5 "The Handsome Collier Lad"

BRIT   Lloyd 1967:355-6 "Johnny Siddon"

◆ My Lowlands, Away *(H469)* 144

White/Dean-Smith 1951: (Chanties) "Lowlands"
Brunnings 1981: "Lowlands Away," "Lowlands,"
  "Lowlands - Lowland, Lowland, Hurrah My Boys"

BRIT   Davis/Tozer n.d.:20-1
  Hugill 1961:65-8
  Hugill 1977b:54-5 "Lowlands"
  Smith 1888:15

AMER   Harlow 1962:127-8
  Whall (3d ed. 1913):80

b: AMER   Joan Baez, Bill Wood, Theodore Alevizos,
Veritas Vol. 1, No. 1 "Lowlands"
b: Gordon Bok, Folk-Legacy FSI 40 (B3) "Lowlands"
  Bob Davenport, Topic 12TS 318 (B1b) "Lowlands"
lc: Richard Dyer-Bennet, Remington RLP 199-34
"Lowlands"
  Stan Hugill, Folkways FTS 37311 (A7) "Lowlands"
b: *The "Life" Treasury of American Folk Music*, Life
L 1001A, "Lowlands"
b: Leonard Mayoh, The Shanty Men, Rodeo/Int. RNT
2006, "Lowlands"
b: Odetta, Tradition TLP 1025 "Lowlands"

◆ Mary's Dream *(H54)* 144

Laws 1957:150 (K20) "[Mary o' the Dee]"
Brunnings 1981

BRIT   Aitkin 1874:56-7
  Buchan 1891:112-3
  Calliope 1788:16-7
  Gems 1894:206, with background information on
the author, John Lowe (1750-98). [Huntington]
  Greig/Duncan 2,1983:496 (#339)

AMER   Chappell 1939:72-3 "Mary and Sandy"
  Creighton 1971:143-4 "Mary's Vision"
  Grover n.d.:52-4

BRS   AS Thomas: (n.i.)
  Harvard 1: 3.193 (n.i.)
  Harvard 3: (Catnach) (Harkness)
  Delaney's Scotch 1910:14
  Forget Me Not [1835]:168

◆ The Nightingale (I) *(H75a)* 145

Dean-Smith 1954
Laws 1957:199 (M37)
Brunnings 1981: "... (My Love He Was a Farmer's
  Son)," "... - Name of Ship"

IREL   *JIFSS* 12,1912:26

BRIT   Greig/Duncan 1,1981:18 (#18), 2 vts. ("The Loss
of the ...," "The Sailor and His Love")
  Richards/Stubbs 1979:101
  Tocher #1(Spr)1971:3

AUST   AT #27 (Dec)1971:17

BRS   UCLA 605: 4 (Hill)

REC   Frankie Armstrong, Topic 12TS 232
? b: Judy Collins, Elektra EKS 75010
  Audrey Coppard, Folkways FP 917 (A5)
b: Helen Schneyer, Folk-Legacy FSI 50 (B4)

A10 / Deep and dead water

◆ Willie Lennox *(H176)* 146

Laws 1957:289-90 (Q33) "The Lake of Cool Finn (Willie
  Leonard)"
Brunnings 1981: "Lakes of Col Fin"
Cazden et al. *Notes* 1982: #72 "The Lakes of Col Flynn"

c: IREL   Graves 1895: #24
c: *JIFSS* 9,1911:15-6 "The Cruel Lake of Wolfrinn;
or, Lament for Willie Leonard"
k: Joyce 1873:103-4 (#100) "The Lake of Coolfin; or
Willy Leonard"
o: Joyce 1909:227-8 (#417) "The Lake of Coolfinn or
Willie Leonard"
  Moffat [1897]:290-1 "'Twas Early One Morning"
  Shields/Shields *UF* 21,1975: #435 "Willy Leonard"

BRIT   Greig/Duncan 2,1983:158-60 (#228) "The Loch
o' Shilin," 4 vts. ("Billy Henry")
  Palmer *FMJ* 1973:280 "Young Leonard (The Lakes of
Cold Stream)" (from George Dunn)

AMER   Cazden et al. 1982:264-6 "The Lakes of Col
Flynn"

BRS   BPL Irish: (n.i.)
  Harvard 3: (Catnach)
  Harvard 13,63 (Such #369) "The Lake of Cold
Finn" (Catnach)
  UCLA 605: 4(Such) "The Lakes of Cold Finn"
  A Broadside 1(12, May)1909 "Willy Leonard"
  Healy 1967a:115-6 "The Lake of Coolfin"
  Walton's New 2,1968:26
  Wehman's 1887,2:13

REC   Mary Reynolds, *FSB* 7 (A7) "The Lakes of Shel-
lin"
  Amy Birch, Topic 12TS 349 (B1) "Royal Comrade"
  Bob Davenport, Topic 12TS 530 (A5) "The Lakes of
Coolfin"
  Len Graham, Topic 12TS 401 (A2) "Loughinsholin"
? cl: J. W. Green, AFS 2296 A1 "The Lakes of Col-
faine"
  Mary Ann Haynes, Topic 12T 258 (A3) "Poor Leon-
ard"
  Nic Jones, Highway (Trailer) LTRA 507 (B3) "The
Lakes of Shilin"
  Tom Lenihan, Topic 12TS 363 (A6) "The Lake of
Coolfin"
  George Ling, Topic 12TS 292 "The Lakes of Coolfin"
  Oak, Topic 12TS 212 (A3) "The Lakes of Cool Flynn"
  Mrs Willie O'Donnell, EEOT *Irish Travellers* cass.
(B7) "... Leonard"
  Cathie Stewart, Topic 12T 138 "The Lakes of
Shillin"

MEL   Petrie/Stanford 2,1902:186 (#746) "Willy Leonard" [Sharp/Karpeles]

◆ Sloan Wellesley *(H585)* 147

Brunnings 1981: "The Dog and the Gun," "The
  Drowning of Young Robinson"

b: IREL   Morton 1970:14-5 "The Drowning of Young
Robinson"; he says it is an adaptation of H176 "Willie Lennox (The Lakes of Coolfin)."

◆ Miss Cochrane *(H42a)* 148

Brunnings 1981: (m) "Eirigh Suas a Stoirin (Rise up,
  My Darling)"

IREL   *JIFSS* 1(2&3):56
k: S. O Baoighill 1944:30, a tune written in the Dorian mode.

153

b: MEL Kennedy 1975:92 (#34) "Éirigh Suas a Stóirín (Rise up, My Darling)"; also reports another version recorded in Donegal.

◇ **Holland Is a Fine Place** (*H180*) 149

White/Dean-Smith 1951: "(The) Lowlands of Holland/ Germany"
Dean-Smith 1954: "(The) Low Low Lands of Holland"
Coffin/Renwick 1950(1977):89 indicates that this is not Child #92, "Bonny Bee Hom," but there is certainly a very close relationship between the two ballads. Also there are two types of this ballad, Scottish and Irish, but in the following references these have not been differentiated.
Bronson 2,1962:418 discusses the relationship of "The Lowlands of Holland" to Child #92; he includes the former as an Appendix to that ballad.
Brunnings 1981: "The Lowlands of Holland"

IREL *Ceol* 7(1&2,Dec)1984:6-7 "The Lowlands of Holland"
Hughes 2,1915:70 [Bronson]
JIFSS 2(1&2)1905:31-2
Joyce 1873:69-70 [Bronson]
Joyce 1909:214 (#404) "The Lowlands of Holland" [Bronson]
Loesberg 1,1980:49
Morton 1973:140-1 "The Rocks of Giberaltar," which Morton points out is a patchwork song but owes much to "The Lowlands of Holland."
b: O Lochlainn 1965:223 "The Lowlands of Holland," 4-stanza fragment.
Treoir 3(4)1971 "The Lowlands of Holland"

BRIT Chambers 1829,1:157-9
MacColl/Seeger 1977:78-81 (#12) "The Lowlands of Holland"
Oxford Ballads 1969:347-8 (#92) "The Lowlands of Holland"
Sing 4(4&5,Dec)1957:49 "The Lowlands o' Holland"
Slocombe *JEFDSS* 1955:242 "The Lowlands of Holland"

AMER Randolph/Cohen (1982):72-4 "The *Lily of Arkansas*"

BRS Harvard 1: 7.238 (Ryle), 9.24 (Bebbington), 12,82 (Such)
UCLA 605: 5(Disley) "The Lowlands of Holland"
Healy 1967a:75 "The Lowlands of Holland"
Jolliffe 1970:79 "The Lowlands of Holland"

REC Paddy Tunney, *FSB* 5 (A8) "The Lowlands of Holland"; Tradition TLP 1004 (B4), Topic 12T 165 (B2)
Peggy Seeger, Ewan MacColl, *LH*, Argo ZDA 75, #10 "The Lowlands of Holland," 3 versions.
b: Raphael Boguslav, Riverside RLP 12 638 "High Germany"
Marc Bridgham, Folkways FSS 37315 (A8) "The Lowlands of Holland"
Dick Cameron, Folkways FG 3516 (A2) "The Lowlands of Holland"
b: Isla Cameron, Murray Hill 920336 (5B6) "The Lowlands of Holland"
Martin Carthy, Topic 12TS 341 (= Fontana STL 5362) "Lowlands of Holland"
Peg Clancy Power, Folk-Legacy FSE 8 (A7) "The Lowlands of Holland"
b: Bud Dashiell, The Kinsmen, Warner W 1429 "Wars of Germany"
? cl: Minnie Floyd, AFS 1046 A2 "The Night That I Was Married"
b: *The Folk Scene*, Elektra SMP 6 "The Lowlands of Holland"
The Galliards, Monitor MFS 407 (B2) "Lowlands of Holland"
cl: George Vinton Graham, AFS 3812 A2 "The Lowlands of Holland"
Carrie Grover, AAFS L21 (B2) "The Lowlands of Holland"
Lori Holland, Folkways FG 3518 (B4) "The Lowlands of Holland"
b: *Hoot Tonight!* Warner Bros. 1512 "Wars of Germany"
Dolores Keane, Green Linnet SIF 3004 (Mulligan LUN 033) (B1) "The Low Low Lands of Holland"
Tim Lyons, Green Linnet SIF 1014 (B4) "The Lowlands of Holland"
b: Tommy Makem, Tradition TLP 1044 (A5) "The Lowlands of Holland"
Ian Manuel, Topic 12TS 220 (A4) "The Lowlands of Holland"
cl: Mrs L. L. McDowell, AFS 3183 A2 "The Lowlands of Holland"
Rory, Alex McEwen, Folkways FW 6390 (A4) "The Lowlands of Holland"
Des O'Halloran, Topic 12TS 305 (A3) "The Lowlands of Holland"
Jean Redpath, Folk-Legacy FSS 49 (A4) "The Wars o' High Germanie"
b: Robin Roberts, Prestige/Int. 13017 "The Lowlands of Holland"
b: Paddy Tunney, Tradition TLP 1004 (B4) "The Lowlands of Holland"

MEL O'Neill 1903:18
b: Philharmonic Ensemble Orchestra, Vanguard VRS 1093 "Folk Song Suite"
b: Vienna State Opera Orchestra, Westminster XWN 18928 "Folk Song Suite"

◇ **Susan on the Beach** (*H774*) 150

Laws 1957:149 (K19) "Susan Strayed the Briny Beach"
Brunnings 1981: (m) "The Winding Banks of Erne (Tune: The River Roe)"

IREL Ranson 1948(1973):70-1 "Sligo Shore," very different.

AMER Leach 1965:78-9 "Susan Strayed the Briny Beach"
Peacock 1965,3:646-7 "As Susan Strayed the Briny Beach"

B11

Erin, my country: Praise of home

Right well I remember that little thatched cabin
Where first shone the light of my life's early morn:
It stood on a hill in sight of a village,
And under that same roof my father was born.

I care not wherever through life I may wander,
I never could find it in palace or hall,
A place half so dear to my heart as that old home,
I found it to be the best home of all.

I grew up to manhood, I started life's journey,
Resolved that my fortune might rise and not fall,
But one thing I learned, I'll never forget it:
That little thatched cot was the best home of all.

'Twas there my poor mother first taught me in childhood
The duties of right and the errors of wrong,
'Twas there I first drove the cows home from pasture,
A bare-footed boy whilst I heard the birds' song.

I ploughed for my father, I mowed in the meadow,
I trained the young vine round the moss-covered wall,
But one thing I learned, though I talk not of pleasure:
That little thatched cot was the best home of all.

But now I'm grown old and kind fortune smiles on me,
And when I look back with a feeling of pain,
I would give all I could think of possessing
If I could live happy my boyhood again.

I sigh when I think of my father and mother,
In deathbed they sleep 'neath the old churchyard wall,
And all the kind friends I can call to my memory
Round that little thatched cottage, the best home of all.

1.1: ... that thatched little ... [Dt]
4.3: ... I talked not ... [Dt]

The Old Stone Wall [H83: 13 Jun 1925]

Source: (w, m) "Klondyke" Lyons, traveling showman (Portstewart), c. 1905.

Key D.

Outside Casey's cabin there is an old stone wall,
And it gave me joy in the days gone by to meet friends, foes and all,
Ah, many an Irish song was sung by colleen or gossoon,
Sure, the music there would rend the air at the rising of the moon.

When the nights would begin to fall, all the boys would assemble
With their colleens fresh and fair just to spend an hour there,
And the piper gay his tunes would play,
'twould make your old limbs tremble,
Sure, the roadside rang to the songs we sang on the top of the old stone wall.

Ah, many a merry meeting I've seen on summer nights,
Sure, it often was the rendezvous for sprees and faction fights;
I've seen a few of lovers, too, at night time give a call
Just to bill and coo, as lovers do, on top of the old stone wall.

If that old wall could tell a tale, 'twould often
   bring to mind
The pleasant scenes and fair colleens and the
   days we've left behind.
If I were king and had me fling, no throne I'd
   ask at all,
Sure, me crown I'd give all my days to live on
   top of the old stone wall.

1.3: And many ... [Dt]
3.1 ... old stone wall ... [Dt]
 .4: Sure, my crown ... [Dt]

1.3: colleen = cailin, Irish for girl; gossoon = Anglo-
   Irish for boy.

Old Arboe [H505: 5 Aug 1933]

o: (m) "County Antrim Air." Other title: "...
Ardboe."

Source: (m) coll. Mr Tobin, principal (Moortown
P.E.S.) from local singer; (w) Nancy Tassie
(Arboe); supposed author James Cairnes, teach-
er (Moortown School), assisted by Donald's Dan
Devlin, c. 1820.

s: ... The reference to 24th June and 2d August
in verse 3 refer[s] to the pattern day at Midsummer and the feast of Lammas in August.
   Similar celebrations are held at Cranfield, near
Randalstown, on June 29, and at Lissan and Mun-
derrydoe, near Pomero[illegible].
   The celebrations on 2d August, coinciding with
the feast of Lammas, were Franciscan in origin,
as Arboe was a Franciscan monastery in the Middle Ages. It is a great day for the children, as
stalls are erected at the Old Cross and sweet-
meats and other dainties are sold by vendors
from Ballymena, Draperstown and other centres.
   21st February is Saint's Day of Colman Mac
Aidhe -- the patron of Arboe.

Key B flat.

Ye gods, assist my poor wearied notion,
Ye inspired muses, lend me your hand
To help my endeavour both night and morning
To sing the praises of that lovely strand.

B11 / Erin, my country

Well situated in north of Ireland
All in the county of sweet Tyrone,
Along the banks of famed Lough Neagh
Is that ancient fabric of old Arboe.

Oh, stand awhile to view that harbour
Where purling streams roll to and fro,
Where fishes sporting both night and morning
Yield of their bounty to old Arboe;
No serpent lurks in our hallowed waters,
No odours poisoned infest the breeze,
While peace and plenty for sons and daughters
Abound around you, sweet Lough Neagh.

In the summer season for recreation
You can careless stray along the strands
Where Boreas' breezes are gently blowing
Along the shores where the fabric stands.
On the twenty-fourth [of] June and second of
   August
They do assemble from every part
For to petition the queen of heaven
To pardon sinners with contrite heart.

Humbly beseeching the queen of heaven
On her dear son for to prevail,
While on all occasions you'll be attended
By its dear loved pastor -- priest O'Neill.
It was St. Patrick that did adorn
That great cross he placed on high,
So that each spectator might well remember
How on the cross God's son did die.

I've travelled France and I've travelled Flanders
And all the countries beyond the Rhine,
But in all my rakings and undertakings,
Arboe, your equal I ne'er could find,
My course I've taken to Indian oceans
And the shores of Cana and Galilee,
But in all my rakings and undertakings,
Arboe, your equal I ne'er did see.

The Hills o' Ballyboley [H511: 16 Sep 1933]

s: (m) "The Bonnie Banks o' Loch Lomond."

Author William Hegan.

s: Ballyboley lies between Ballynure and Larne.
This original song ... captures the transient
joys of Tir-nan-og.

Key G. Moderately slow.

Sam Henry's Songs of the People

When morning dawns on the pleasant country
    round
And the sun sheds beams of beauty,
The lark is in the air and there's music
    everywhere
By the bonny green hills o' Ballyboley.

> *The bluebell's sweet that grows upon the hill,*
> *The heather and sweet-scented briar,*
> *But sweeter is the ling that in childhood I did*
>   *bring*
> *From the bonny green hills o' Ballyboley.*

The broom grows fresh on the bonny hillside,
The sloe and the sweet blaeberry,
But nowhere do I go where the wild flowers grow
Like the bloom on the hills o' Ballyboley.

The long summer's day with my schoolmates I did
    play
And roamed o'er the hills together,
Our steps were like the roe as bounding we did go
O'er the bonny green hills o' Ballyboley.

When the ripe golden grain spread[s] its wealth o'er
    the plain
And the blackberries lurked by the hedgerow,
To the glens I sped away on the smiling autumn
    day
By the bonny green hills o' Ballyboley.

My youthful days are gone, but fond memory
    ponders on
Those hills of fresh vernal beauty,
Where nature's kindest smile seems to linger all
    the while
On the bonny green hills o' Ballyboley.

Ballycastle, O!

[H28b: [Bp] "Two Ballycastle songs," 24 May 1924]

s: (m) "The Peacock"; o: (m) "The Parting
Glass."

Source: (w) [Bp] John Henry Macauley
(Ballycastle), from an old Mail Car driver; [Dt]
(m) Louie Barnes (L.R.A.M., Ballycastle).

s: ... The air is well known in Irish folk song,
and has been lost to many by its hitherto having
been associated with words of political import.

m: I have a ms. set collected by James Moore.

Key G.

The wintry winds away are fled and Flora does
    her mantle spread,
While balmy breezes round Knocklayde thro'
    flowery glens do rustle-o,
That place where early life I spent: on you my
    mind is ever bent,
Where first I lived in sweet content in dear old
    Ballycastle-o.

That place is ever dear to me, no matter when
    or where I be,
Though tossed upon the raging sea while wave
    'gainst wave do jostle-o,
I'll bear you always in my mind until my life I
    do resign;
May peace and plenty always shine around sweet
    Ballycastle-o.

The soldier who has been at war, in foreign
    climes anear and far,
Returning home a son of Mars from war's
    alarming bustle-o,
In latitudes of each degree, in all his travels,
    ne'er did see
A place of hospitality to equal Ballycastle-o.

Proud England of the rose may boast, that rears
    her head around her coast,
And Scotland heave a hearty toast to her majestic
    thistle-o,
To those emblems all we must comply, but none
    of them with ours can vie,
The shamrocks that around us lie in the vales of
    Ballycastle-o.

Ye hazel glens of Ballylig and whinny knowes of
    oul' Broombeg,
Returning home through sweet Kilcraig where
    blackbirds loudly whistle-o,
Ye balmy breezes milder blow; ye thick'ning
    wild-woods taller grow,
And groves that shade the streams that flow
    around old Ballycastle-o.

All they that were in different climes, in
    different parts at different times,
They sigh to think they ne'er can find a place
    like Ballycastle-o,
For there the sons of Granuaile make all their
    foes to know right well
That o'er them all they bear the bell -- the
    boys of Ballycastle-o.

1.2 [and similarly for every other line throughout:]
    ... rustle, O. [Bp]   ... rustle, O! [Dt, Wt]
[Extensive differences between Bp, above, and Dt,
Wt:]
    1.1: When wintry winds are o'er and fled...
    .2: While gentler ... do whistle-o,

.4: ... content around sweet Ballycastle-o.
2: [Stanza not in Bp.]
3.1: ... soldier that has been in war, in different parts both near ...
.2: ... home, the son of Mars, ...
.4: A place for ...
4.1: ... boast, who raised her head upon our coast,
.2: While Scotland gives a noble toast to the majestic
.3: Yet with these emblems we comply, we own there's none of them can vie
.4: With the shamrocks that do lovely lie around sweet ...
5.1: Ye lazy glens of Ballylig, ye broomy knowes around Broombeg,
.2: ... where the blackbird loudly whistles-o,
.3: Ye orient breezes ... ye thicket green-woods ...
.4: To shade the purling streams ... around sweet Ballycastle-o.
6: [Stanza not in Bp.]

Ballymonan Brae [H643: 21 Mar 1936]

Source: Mrs Frank Kealey (Ballysally, Coleraine).

s: This whimsical little song, with its concealed acrostic, is contributed by Mrs Frank Kealey,... whose store of songs of the Dungiven district is inexhaustible. Her love of music has been handed down to her son, Mr James Kealey, the well-known fiddler of Ballymoney.
Ballymonan -- "the townland of the little bog" -- is in the parish of Dungiven. It is full of little streams.

Key G.

Farewell to Ballymonan, where oftimes I have been,
Likewise the middle quarter that some call Curraghlane,
And likewise unto Kane's Brook, where the leaves are always green,
And where you'll see those purty maids, the rarest to be seen.

One summer of an evening it's pleasant to be there,
When nature shades those charming maids and life is free from care,
The young men follow after that their wishes might be seen,
And view the killing glances of their true loves on the green.

The beauty of this mountain foot is matchless in my sight,
In nature's shade the notes combine at evening, noon and night,

Down by the shade of yon green tree I oftimes took my way,
When the sultry beams were o'er us spread, to pass the time away.

The author of these verses I mean now to make clear,
In hopes there's none offended when the same do now appear.
His dwelling is convenient in a village down below
That is well situated upon the river Roe.

The alphabet being well pursued, the tenth letter it will tell,
The fifteenth following after, this young man's name will spell,
The eighth being joined in rotation, to aid your memory,
And the fourteenth being connected will spell his name to thee.

So now my pen I will leave down and my writing I'll give o'er,
In hopes the purty seasons to live and see once more,
And if I'm spared some time I'll spend round Ballymonan Brae
And drink success unto that place while the hours pass away.

Benbradden Brae [H572: 17 Nov 1934]

Source: Mrs Frank Kealey (Ballysally, Coleraine).

Key C.

As I traversed Benbradden Hill as Zephyr's breeze blew far,
The sheepbells they did circulate sweet echoes through the air,
The fox did bound with cunning pace, while huntsmen in array
With horse and hound pursued the chase upon Benbradden brae.

Delighted there I then sat down where pinks bloomed by my side;
The boiling spring of sweet Stroangall like silver streams did glide,
The green was clad around, beneath, with lads and lasses gay,
They all assembled in kind love to view that bonny brae.

Sam Henry's Songs of the People

Benbradden is sweet Erin's pride, old Graine
 loved its name,
The fair maids who traversed that brae in beauty
 decked its fame;
Would I go view old German-ee, my heart would
 sigh and say,
'Oh, bring me back to taste new joys upon
 Benbradden brae.'

There were cowslips, daisies, thyme and myrrh
 that strewed the path along,
The fair maids pulled blaeberries while youths
 conveyed a song,
The wine and brandy they went round to pass the
 time away,
We drank while love did press each heart upon
 Benbradden brae.

5.1: a-log = ?rocking, adrift.
1.4: brae = slope, hillside.
3.1: Graine =
4.2: blaeberry = bilberry, whortleberry, in America
 called blueberry, the fruit of a dwarf hardy shrub,
 genus Vaccinium.

The Braes of Carnanbane

[H651: 16 May 1936]

s: (m) "The Banks of Lough Foyle" (original air
of "Ye Banks and Braes").

Source: Pat Kealy, fiddler (Dungiven).

s: ... Pat Kealy, the well-known traditional fiddler,... loves the songs and airs of his native
mountains.

Key G.

It's now I'm going to take my leave
Of all ye woods and scented fields,
Where naught but pleasure ever smiles,
Nor paradise such joy e'er yields,
But when I'm sailing on the main
Or wandering through Columbia's land,
My absent time I'll still employ
To sing the praise of Carnanbane.

The dreary thoughts of joyless days
With midnight vapours fill my heart,
When thinking of those lovely dames
That shortly now I'll have to part;
In summertime oft have I strayed
Where trees and flowers were newly blown,
All for to view those lovely nymphs
Along the braes of Carnanbane.

Here Flora spreads her mantle wide
To deck each hill and valley round
With rarest flowers that nature yields
And nowhere else are to be found.
In beds of thyme the hares do course
Together with the blithesome lamb;
All for to breathe the evening air,
The lads and maids go hand in hand.

But cruel fate has signed my doom,
Those charming maids I leave with pain,
But still my ardent wish and prayer
Is still with them I should remain.
How can I leave those lovely scenes
Where beauty's empress rules our land?
In Erin's isle none can excel
The lovely maids of Carnanbane.

Its purling streams and winding rills
Are dwelling for a monarch meet,
There Venus in her lowly cot
A prince's heart would captivate.
The trout and salmon come and go,
How neatly glides the glittering swan,
The thrush and blackbird change their notes
In the shady bowers of Carnanbane.

Here's a health to every honest heart
Where social friendships smoothly glide
And run with ease in crystal streams
By virtue's never failing tide.
May peace and plenty flow with joy
And still on each industrial hand,
May love and blessing brightly smile
With golden rays on Carnanbane.

Carnlough Shore

[H686: 16 Jan 1937]

Source: (Dunloy district).

Key D.

Will you muses nine with me combine, assist me
 with my song,
Till I relate what was my fate as I did rove along;
Through the County Antrim I did go till I came to
 Ballinafore,
Then sweet Glencloy I did pass by and I reached
 the Carnlough shore.

With John M'Neill, lives in the vale, I spent ten
   days or more,
With John M'Neill, lives in the vale beside the
   Carnlough shore;
The people all seemed strange to me, but they
   were sweet and kind,
Which grieved me more at leaving home and all my
   friends behind.

With a farmer gay, lives near the sea, was the
   next place I did dwell,
No eloquence can teach me his praises for to tell,
Pat M'Gavrock was his name, he lives on Stony Hill,
And he feeds his sheep along both sides where the
   sea does ebb and fill.

When the summer time comes on again, to the sea
   I'll make my way,
And I'll take down my fiddle and right merrily I'll
   play,
The birds in chorus they will join, my music to
   adore,
And all the people will welcome me to Stony Hill
   once more.

Beautiful Churchill [H627: 7 Dec 1935]

Source: George M'Kay (Church St, Ballycastle).

Key G.

There's a spot in dear old Donegal is very full
   of cheer,
Where I love to walk and have a talk with my
   companions dear,
Where oftimes with my comrade boys I'd sit and
   drink my fill
And sing in praise of bygone times in beautiful
   Churchill.

This little town I boast of now shines white upon
   high land,
Green trees adorn it all around, the scenery is
   grand,
In its centre stands a factory where pretty girls
   do sew,
Its beauty shines through all my mind, no matter
   where I go.

Then Belven it lies on the left as you are
   walking through,
Plantations grand around it stand, most pleasant
   for to view,
Where laurels in their beauty bloom in the
   pleasant month of May:
This grand estate it lies quite neat to the banks
   of sweet Lough Veagh.

There is an island on this lake in memory I shall
   keep,
Where the snow-white seagull builds her nest in
   the middle of the deep,
Where oft I've sailed a little boat with my true
   love so gay,
But she has gone and left me to the shores of
   Americay.

Then Derryveagh and its lovely braes to the
   other side does lie,
Where four and forty families lived well in days
   gone by,
They were forced to leave their happy homes by
   the owner of the land,
And its lonely shore on a winter day is now the
   home of swans.

Then Gartan is a lovely place, I love to view its
   scenes,
Through its lovely groves fond sweethearts rove,
   and by its fields so green
There come gentry from everywhere to view its
   lakes and hills,
And Lacknacor, where once was born the great
   St. Columbkille.

'Tis a lovely place for fishing and its equal can't
   be found,
The anglers come from everywhere and some from
   London town,
There come gentlemen and ladies and every sort
   of swell
To spend their summer holidays in the grand
   Churchill Hotel.

Now to conclude and finish, one line I'll let you
   hear:
There is one little girl, and to me she's very dear;
If I could only win her, sure, my heart with joy
   would fill,
I would live content and my days be spent in
   beautiful Churchill.

The Girls from [Dt,Wt: of] Coleraine

[H64: BLp, 31 Jan 1925]

o: (m) "Taddy O'Neale."

Source: (w, m) John Murphy, Jr (Railway Rd,
Coleraine).

s: This simple and tuneful song has again become
a favourite in social gatherings....

[British Library microfilm print courtesy of John
Moulden. BLp sol-fa time notation is written as if
for 4/4, but units within the divisions are incon-
sistent with 4's.]

Key G.

Sam Henry's Songs of the People

There's a sweet little spot in the County of
    Derry,
If ever you go there you'll want to remain,
You can travel old Ireland from Antrim to Kerry
And not find a spot like the town of Coleraine.

The boys and the girls never seem there to
    alter,
It's go where you like, you'll find them always
    the same,
And if ever you're wanting a right hearty
    welcome,
Just come to the sweet little town of Coleraine.

The girls from Killarney sure fill you with
    blarney,
If ever you've been there they'd drive you
    insane,
The girls from the city all think they are pretty,
But none can compare with the girls of Coleraine.

The star of the north shining on yon Bann water,
I wonder if ever I'll see you again,
May fortune shine down on the sons and the
    daughters
That hail from the sweet little town of Coleraine.

1.2: ... you come there ... [Bt, Dt, Wt]
3.3: ... thinks themselves pretty, [Dt, Wt]

The Maids of Downhill [H809: 27 May 1939]

o: (m) "Love Song" (O'Friel's suite).

Source: (w) Pat Kealey (Dungiven); (m) Frank
Kealey, fiddle (Ballysally); author late Francis
Heaney (Magherabuoy, Dungiven)

Key G.

One evening as I chanced for to roam,
With a love and assiduous care,
To a place I would like to make known,
Its aspect my heart did ensnare.

It was down by Magilligan strand,
My mind with amusement did fill
As I travelled on that golden strand,
Till at length I arrived at Downhill.

To gaze on that murmuring tide,
The scene my hope does fulfill,
From Lough Foyle down to the Bann side
Surpasses man's nature and skill,
Where billows so loudly do roar
And the ships they do ride at full sail,
You can view them from that pleasant shore
As they sail along with the gale.

At a distance southwest of the sea,
On a green and commodious plain,
Stands the castle of splendour and sway
On Sir Hervey Bruce's demesne;
This building most spangled appears
When the proud eagle soars on gold wings;
Soft music does sound in my ears
While the joybell so gently rings.

Round the temple the lambs sport and play,
And the conies do sport on the green,
The groves and their sweet-scented trees;
There numberless songsters I've seen,
Their extra-sweet choir so strong,
Downhill they all seem to express
Harmoniously sound in their song,
With its humming accent of address.

The maids that traverse that gold strand,
No beauty with them can compare,
For the blooming rose of our land
Are not so effulgent and fair;
They're like goddesses sprung from the sea,
No manner or tongue can instill,
Fair Venus could not with them vie,
Sweet matchless fair maids of Downhill.

There were poets and bards tried their quill,
In praise were the poems that they wrote,
But their numbers in learning and skill,
Downhill they omitted to note,
For in Erin its equal's unfound
For tranquillity, friendship and love,
And its aspect is shining all round,
Which entices the fair turtle dove.

Had I the whole world at will,
It's there I would wish to reside,
And a full flowing glass I would fill
In love with those waves as they glide;
These verses I now must give o'er,
Unwilling for to drop my quill,
For want of being versed in the lore,
Exulting that place called Downhill.

Dungiven Priory Church [H187: 11 Jun 1927]

s: Ulster variant of "Savourneen Deelish."

Source: (w) 2: James Harper (the Castle, Dungiven) [Dt: (sexton of the Episcopal Church)];
James M'Gilligan (Cluntygeeragh, Dungiven);

B11 / Erin, my country

author James Maxwell, schoolteacher (native of
Armagh, taught at Dungiven); (m) coll. M. B.
(Antrim) from blind fiddler M'Kinley (Swateragh).

[Bp] s: ... James Maxwell ... was married to
Miss Sarah Anne Scott, of Termeil, Dungiven.
Maxwell was the author of several songs which
had a great vogue in their time, notably "The
Heights of Alma," which was the popular ballad
of the Crimean Wars.

The air given below is the Ulster variant of
"Savourneen Deelish," and may be an older form
than that generally sung....

Key B flat.

One fine summer's evening as Flora was flinging
  Her beautiful gems o'er the face of the ground,
Delighted I wandered to hear the birds singing
And gaze on the beauties of nature around.
I strayed to the old church not far from
  Dungiven,
Where beauteously grand the red river doth
  flow,
Possessed by the muses, 'mong tombs I was
  driven,
I stood on a grave and looked down on the Roe.

I gazed round in silence, confounded by
  grandeur,
Words cannot express the delight of my heart,
Inspired by Apollo, who reigns 'mid wild
  splendour,
I turned round to view the old ruin of art:
That sacred old fabric, would men only spare it,
The tempest may howl and the river may flow,
'Twas a noble conception for Christians to rear
  it
'Mong nature's wild charms on the banks of the
  Roe.

I love thee, dame nature, oh, how shall I woo
  thee?
Unveil thy fair bosom and come to my arms,
Thy powerful attraction has drawn my soul to
  thee,
E'en now let me feel the full force of thy
  charms.

The winter wind whistling around your high
  mountains,
The tempest's loud blast o'er the thick drifting
  snow,
Are dear to my heart as the soft murmuring
  fountains
Or wild mountain torrent that bounds to the Roe.

Around the old fabric the mighty are sleeping;
Tranquillity reigns in the city of death;
O man, fragile man, fellow worms are now
  creeping,
Our lives are a vapour, our years a mere
  breath.
Where, where now is rank? I hear some one
  replying:
The priest and the peasant, the high and the
  low,
The rich and the poor are promiscuously lying
In peace on the banks of the clear winding Roe.

Farewell, lovely spot, so romantic and splendid,
Where nature has lavished her beauties around.
In peace may I rest, when my days shall be
  ended,
Beside some ruin in hallow-ed ground,
But alas, as I wander, a poor cheerless
  stranger,
I'll think on Armagh, where the Callan doth
  flow.
Ah, little I thought I would e'er be a ranger
Or tune my rude harp on the banks of the Roe.

3.6: ... tempest's wild blast ... [Dt]

Faughanvale [H796: 25 Feb 1939]

Author Thomas Young (Killywill), written c. 1879;
sung by Mrs M'Cluskey (Minnegallagher), (m)
James O'Hara (Killywill).

s: This song, popular even today in Faughanvale
district, ... made a delightful song of the
people.

Key G.

As I roved out one evening down by a riverside,
The small birds sang melodiously, the streams did
  gently glide,
I roved along yon fountains clear, past scenes for
  to reveal,
Still thinking on the happy days I spent round
  Faughanvale.

Sam Henry's Songs of the People

Oh, Faughanvale's a village fair, convenient to the Foyle,
With seaweed in abundance for to enrich the soil,
Where every form of virtue reigns and friendships never fail;
Show me the spot throughout this land can equal Faughanvale.

As I sat meditating on a primrose bank so fine,
Past scenes and old acquaintances came rushing through my mind,
I thought upon those happy days and comrades true and leal,
And the youthful sports and pleasures that we had round Faughanvale.

If you would see that village on a twenty-ninth of June,
When all around looks beautiful and everything in bloom,
Where wheat and barley doth abide on every hill and dale;
Show me the spot throughout this land can equal Faughanvale.

Oh, I have roamed through Donegal, through Derry and Tyrone,
And round the coast of Antrim and likewise Inishowen,
All round the coast of Antrim, where beauty shines so real,
But none so fair as can compare with you, sweet Faughanvale.

Oh, if I had poetic skill, its praises I'd make known,
Or if I had Shakespeare's talents, its beauty I would own,
Or had I Tom Moore's eloquence, my tongue would never fail
For to describe the beauties that surround you, Faughanvale.

Bonny Garrydoo [H800: 25 Mar 1939]

Source not given.

g: "Farewell to Ireland" combined with a Masonic element.

Key G.

On March the first in 'forty-five I took my last adieu
From you, my loyal brethren who dwell in Garrydoo;
To part from friends so dear and true, it grieves my heart full sore
To leave you all in grief behind on Erin's northern shore.

From Belfast Quay we did set sail, bound for a foreign shore,
To leave that friendly vale of peace, perhaps to meet no more;
Thank providence we're safe arrived, though distant far from you,
But my heart will cleave for ever to bonny Garrydoo.

M'Cracken's master of our lodge, our number's thirty-one,
And in Ballymoney district it does ever proudly stand;
With honor he does fill his post, a man both leal and true,
And proudly shall his Orange flag wave o'er sweet Garrydoo.

Here's a health to our young heroines, for they are Orange flowers,
Their lives grow up in piety by wisdom's precious powers,
Kind providence protects their bloom and emblems of virtue,
And they will still be guarded by the boys of Garrydoo.

Prosperity to our grand lodge that now sits in Coleraine,
And may its district lodges in virtue ever reign,
May they maintain the glorious cause, stand to each other true;
Long may your crimson banners wave o'er bonny Garrydoo.

Glenariffe [H801: 1 Apr 1939]

Source: Jack M'Bride (Kilmore, Glenariffe), "who is now following a life on the ocean wave."

Key D.

A few lines of my native place with pleasure I enclose --
The vale of sweet Glenariffe, where the rippling water flows,
The beauty of our lovely glen is straight from God's own hand,

From the mountain ranges of Parkmore down to the Pebble Strand.

The river that runs down our glen speeds from our mountains tall,
Till on its course it tumbles o'er dark Ess-na-laragh Fall;
Adown the slopes of old Cloughcorr, where hazel coverts grew,
It glides to our Niagrara -- the fall of Ess-na-crub.

Below that mighty cataract the leaping rivers join
To shed more beauty on the glen, they seemingly combine;
Next, Toberwine and Discart are first to catch the eye,
Serene in lofty beauty, they almost reach the sky.

On Glassmullan and Clonreagh in my dreams I often gaze,
For in that valley I was born and spent my childhood's days;
Enchanting scenes of Tamlaght, I view them o'er and o'er,
And still my heart is captured by the beauty of Kilmore.

Kilmore, that hallowed ground, before I pass it by,
I think of all the heroes bold who in the grave there lie,
And Carrivemurphy Mountain, as it runs along the sea,
Enfolds me in its giant arms -- place ever dear to me.

Now to conclude these simple lines, let all join heart and hand
That God may send a blessing down upon our native land,
That all who dwell within the glen from wrong may aye be free;
For the dearest of the spots I've trod --
Glenariffe Glen for me.

Glenelly [H720: 11 Sep 1937]

Source: (Glenelly Valley, Co. Tyrone)

Key G.

There is no other spot in the land of the Gael
Where my young heart the full strains of pleasure could feel,
There is not a spot under heaven's crystal dome
So true to my heart as Glenelly, my home.

Glenelly, Glenelly, how lovely thou art,
Where pleasure and sunshine have shone in my heart,
Though far I may wander, far away may I roam,
I ne'er shall forget you, Glenelly, my home.

Though my cabin was poor, my affections were there,
'Twas dearer to me than a palace elsewhere,
But fortune unroofed its old walls made of clay,
Left me homeless and friendless as one cast away.

There the spirit of friendship shall be undefiled
Midst the valleys so fair and the mountains so wild,
There the chase of the hunter shall never find room,
But peace reign supreme in Glenelly, my home.

Oh, sweet were the dreams of my young boyhood's hours
When the summer fields round me were ardent with flowers,
'Twas little I thought that in manhood's first bloom
I should wander in grief from Glenelly, my home.

Accursed be the dark fate that bade me depart
From fields that were dear and the home of my heart,
Yet still shall my memory in sweet visions come
On a wing of delight to Glenelly, my home.

Adieu to the wild woods all clad in bright bloom
In valleys where the steps of my childhood have been;
Oh, hear me, oh, hear me, ere I sink in my tomb,
May I breathe my last prayer in Glenelly, my home.

Lovely Glenshesk (I) [H544: 5 May 1934]

[see H28a " (IIa), H547 "In Praise of the Glen [Lovely Glenshesk IIb]," very different]

Source not given.

Key C.

One fine summer's evening I was forced to my pen
To write down the praises of the top of the glen,
Where the small birds enchanted in every green tree,
Their songs of love practice to the highest degree.

Sam Henry's Songs of the People

Glenshesk, you're surrounded by hills dark and high,
And they who pass through say farewell with a sigh;
Fresh lakes and spring wells there, they shine calm and clear,
They were born to good fortune, had the luck to dwell here.

In you, sweet Glenshesk, I have dwelt since a boy,
Three miles from the Mairge and three from Armoy;
When Phoebus arises he there throws his beam,
It will grieve me far off for to mention your name.

My forefathers fought at the battle of Orra,
No wonder it grieves me to leave you tomorrow,
I'm leaving the country I love, without blame,
My fortune is nothing, M'Quillan's my name.

Old Inishowen [H824: 9 Sep 1939]

s: (m) old form of "The Old Head of Dennis,"
(m) "The Meeting of the Waters" (Thomas Moore).

Source: (m) Harry M'Anally (Clooney, Magilligan).

s: The air ... is the old form ... to which Tom Moore set his beautiful song, "The Meeting of the Waters."

Key G.

There is not in our island a vale or a lawn
Like that bosom of beauty -- the valley of Fahan,
Where Swilly's dark waves, when the winds are at rest,
Reflect in brown lustre the dark mountain's crest,
    Reflect in brown lustre the dark mountain's crest.

O'er the lake lies Tyrconnell to the west far away,
Where the valiant O'Donnell once held kindly sway,
And here in the annals of Erin well known
Are O'Doherty's realms of old Inishowen,
    Are O'Doherty's ...

To the north stands the castle of great Cahir, O,
He was a great hero and dared his proud foe;
He welcomed his friends with a hearty shake-hands
And a 'Cead-mile-failte' to Erin's proud lands,
    And a 'Cead-mile-failte' ...

But it's gone are the days of O'Donnell the brave,
And the valiant O'Doherty sleeps in his grave,
Yet the strong lines of beauty, by nature's hand drawn,
Shine blooming and fresh in the valley of Fahan,
    Shine blooming ...

Sweet valley of repose, may her inmates be blest
Both here and hereafter with comfort and rest;
May the blessings they wish in this world be their own,
And long may they flourish round old Inishowen,
    And long ...

1.2: fahan = bosom. [s]

Kearney's Glen [H715: 7 Aug 1937]

Source: "good offices" of Gerard Reid (Swateragh); (m) "a farmer."

s: This remote glen is in the townland of Granaghan. There are the ruins of an old Roman Catholic Church in the glen, in whose God's acre, lie the remains of Bishop Bradley and Friar Bradley. Not far away is St. Patrick's Well.
  I noted this air from a farmer who left his horses and plough in the capable charge of his wife and sang the song across the hedge to me.

m: By James O'Kane.

Key G.

Some poets sing of beauties rare that strew the verdant shore,
Killarney's lakes and mountain peaks, where the eagles love to soar,
But none of these my fancy please, or, could I wield a pen,
I would leave them all unheeded still and praise you, Kearney's Glen.

Go view that glen in springtime mild, when nature does adorn
Its landscape bright with daisies white beneath the spreading thorn;
It seems as if the thrush's note, some heavenly voice to gain,
Chants the sweet lays among the braes round Kearney's lovely glen.

On a Sunday summer evening when the weather it is fine,
The lads and lasses all flock there to pass away the time,

And there they sing and dance with joy till twilight hours extend,
Then homewards steer with mirthful cheer from Kearney's lovely glen.

There firmly stands within the glen an altar, old and grey,
Where in the dark and penal days the faithful knelt to pray.
All, all are gone to their reward and left this world of pain,
To join the rest, the true and blest, who dwelt round Kearney's Glen.

So now my song is at an end for want of classic lore,
Nor is it want of genius bright that I can say no more,
But still I'll pray that night and day God may his blessing send
To the kind and generous neighbours who dwell round Kearney's Glen.

The Shores of Sweet Kenbane

[H648: 25 Apr 1936]

Source: John Henry Macaulay (Bog Oak Shop, Ballycastle), from his old friend Thomas Harkin; author Dan White.

o: The time should be 6/8.

Key G.

One evening fair to take the air, alone I chanced to stray
In the month of June when flowers bloom and nature looked so gay,
Enraptured there with scenes so rare, strewn round by nature's hand,
I sat me down to gaze around the shores of sweet Kenbane.

My simple news I pray excuse, I haven't got much skill,
To tell those charms I'd think no harm, could I command my quill.
There in each bush, blackbird and thrush join in the chorus grand
While the nimble trout does sport about the shores of sweet Kenbane.

Close by the shore where billows roar, there grows a pleasant grove,
And lovers there do oft repair to breathe their tales of love,
And near that wood a castle stood where chief and warrior clan
In armour bright oft proved their might around by sweet Kenbane.

In days of yore there many a corps within those walls did shine,
Where lady bright and gallant knight in festive mirth did join,
But since that day the Gaul had sway in dear old Ireland,
And scarce a trace is in that place of the castle of Kenbane.

Round its rocky crest the wild birds' nest, far clear from all below;
On cliffs so steep above the deep, they fear no mortal foe;
The cuckoo's note around does float, while all the feathery band
Make the hills resound for miles around the castle of Kenbane.

In a lovely cot near that sweet spot there dwells a comely queen.
Though much inclined to tell my mind, I can't say who I mean,
But come what may, content I'd be, could I gain this fair maid's hand,
I'd bless the day I chanced to stray around by sweet Kenbane.

The Braes of Sweet Kilhoyle

[H464, 22 Oct 1932: Wt]

Source not given.

[Not in B.]

Key D.

Now one and all, both great and small, I hope you will incline
Till I sing to you a verse or two to pass away the time,
I'm here alone, not far from home, just at my daily toil,
Where many a pleasant day I spent on the braes of sweet Kilhoyle.

Sam Henry's Songs of the People

Kilhoyle it is a pleasant place in the lovely summer time,
Where the boys and girls to banish care along its braes do climb,
Where the primrose grows and the violet blows and clear spring wells do boil,
And the children sport the livelong day on the braes of sweet Kilhoyle.

Some times I work, more times I rest, just as I like to do,
And sometimes climb old Donald's hill to see the lovely view:
Newtown I see and all around, Magilligan braes also,
The Keady naps, Benbradagh taps, and all along the Roe.

Drumsurn it is now strikes my view as I lie on the grass,
If I was at O'Connor's I would drink a flowing glass,
I would drink a health to all my friends, Gortnaghy and the Glen,
If ever you're in trouble, they will surely stand a friend.

Knocklayde [H509: 2 Sep 1933]

o: (m) "Inniskilling Dragoon."

Source: (Dunloy district).

Key C.

I'll sing of a mountain, the pride of the north,
Its eminent qualities here to set forth,
To paint its true colours I'm almost afraid,
And it goes by the name of the famous Knocklayde.

Its base is extensive, its diameter wide,
And large its dimensions on every side,
It would take a surveyor and good at his trade
To count up the acres contained in Knocklayde.

The best of pure limestone is here to be seen,
And grazing for cattle both fertile and green,
And turf good as ever was cut with a spade,
Abound in great plenty all over Knocklayde.

Pure transparent water gushes down from its side,
From which the whole country for miles is supplied,
Its streamlets uniting form many a cascade,
Which add to the beauty and fame of Knocklayde.

The county of Antrim for mountains can boast,
From the falls near Belfast and for miles round the coast,
And from Ballycastle all round to the Braid,
There's none can compare with the famous Knocklayde.

At the foot of this mountain I'll sit down and sing
And call to remembrance one evening in spring,
Those days are long past, never more to return,
Those fine pleasant evenings that we did sojurn.

Lochaber Shore [H134: 5 Jun 1926]

[Bp] A song of Causeway side.

s: (m) "Murlough Shore."

Source: (w) James M'Caughan, carpenter (Bushmills; native of Lochaber), from his father; (m) Mrs Herd (Drumlee, Ballymoney).

s: ... "Lochaber" is a name given to the district of Aird, near the Giant's Causeway, and would seem to indicate that the settlers were from Lochaber in Scotland....

Key G.

Ye people all, both great and small, give ear unto my song,
And if you listen patiently I will not keep you long,
If I could write or yet indite, I would let you know far more
Of the story true I tell to you about sweet Lochaber shore.

To tell of all those noble men I have but little skill,
I'll mention one and then be done, and that's brave Mister Mill,
He was a noble Scotchman born, the same I'll tell you soon,
He lives along Lochaber shore, his dwelling place Portmoon.

I was sorry for that good man's loss he met last closing year,
Although his place I never saw, but only as I hear,
I trust his store will be doubled o'er and that he'll have ten times more,
Like Jacob's flocks, around the rocks of sweet Lochaber shore.

Lochaber is a purty place down by the Causeway
  side
But winter's day brings storm and spray where
  lofty vessels ride,
And in the time of dismal storms, when mighty
  billows roar,
It's many a splendid ship is wrecked along
  Lochaber shore.

The two winters past blew many a blast, right
  bitter off yon strand,
And ships and boats of every sort have lost full
  many a man,
And widows mourn, and babes forlorn their loved
  one's fate deplore;
And sobbings sound, for father's drowned along
  Lochaber shore.

In summer's breeze in levelled seas, when the
  skies are azure blue,
The fishermen launch out their boats, of them
  there's not a few;
Fish they catch of every sort, and gather a
  plentiful store;
May the Lord protect the fishermen around
  Lochaber shore.

Now to conclude, I won't be rude, I mean to end
  my song,
If I said much more about this shore, you'd maybe
  think it long,
But I hope your thoughts they will be set upon
  some greater store,
And you'll stay your mind on things divine when
  you leave Lochaber shore.

5.4, 6.1-3: [Missing from Dt.]

Mountsandel [H817: 22 Jul 1939]

s: (m) "The Braes of Glenbraon" (Hebrides).

Author George Graham (Cross Lane, Coleraine).

s: Words original, by Mr George Graham, ... who derived his inspiration for the scenes round the home of the Song Editor.

Key C.

Mountsandel, Mountsandel, I think long to be
By your soft sylvan splendour, my dreamland to
  see,
When your valleys are waking to April's bright
  sheen,
Or your trees are a mantle of rich summer green.

Alone I would wander by river and glen,
The scenes of my childhood to see once again,
With blackbirds a-fluting, as night breezes fan,
My dreams would come true by the cool sedgy Bann.

Coleraine is the jewel time set in your crown,
My corner of ferns and my own native town,
Where long-cherished friendships will ever
  increase
Like the slopes of Mountsandel in one grove of
  peace.

Mudion River [H108b: 5 Dec 1925]

An old song for Aghadowey readers.

s: (m) [H13] "The Star of Glenamoyle" or [H67] "The Fair Maid of Ballyagan"; m: (m) "Youghal Harbour."

Source: Sarah Crawford (Thorndale Cottages); author Master McMullan, "The Big Master," itinerant schoolteacher (reared at Castlerock), c. 1825.

s: Master Mullan ... was a lad o' parts, and the governess at Downhill had him educated although he was only a boy feeding the fowl at the Castle when she discovered his talent. The fun of the old song is, that in the words of an old Agivey man, Mudion's "nae mair than a good sheugh," yet he shows the white-winged argosies on its imaginary tide. Note the classical knowledge of the hedge schoolmaster coming out in the opening appeal to the Muses....

m: "Sheugh" means "ditch" in Ulster -- ditch means a dyke or bank! [Moulden 1979:107]

[Not in D, W, or B; print from British Library microfilm of *Northern Constitution* kindly provided by John Moulden. No tune given in original column.]

Ye gentle muses, it's pay attention
To these few verses I will indite,
Your noble aid I crave sincerely,
Your grand endeavours to set me right.
To sound the praises of Mudion River
It's my intention for to set forth:
It's well known through all the country,
It is the beauty of the whole North.

In Aghadowey you'll find this river,
It takes its rise in sweet Clarehill,
A clear stream is the first commencement,
The fountain head of this purling rill.
It eastward runs with most curious windings,
Oft delighting the eye of man,
Till it empties into the Agivey water,
Which lies convenient to the river Bann.

Mudion banks on a summer evening,
It would delight you if you were there,
The lads and lasses in couples walking
Along the banks of sweet Mudion fair;
The small birds singing, the flowers all springing,
The pink and daisy and primrose too,
And sweet May flowers along its borders,
To cheer its beauty, they do renew.

The Shannon water, it is proved worthy,
So, I believe, is the river Roe,

Sam Henry's Songs of the People

The sweet Bann water, how oft I've viewed it,
And oftimes also the sweet Barrow;
Of all its labours, I've speculated
Round Erin's courses, I do declare,
There's none compared to that sweet river,
The flowing banks of sweet Mudion fair.

If I had a fortune of fifteen thousand,
I would spend it all right cheerfully
Along that river, the pride of Erin,
And spend my days in tranquility;
A boat of pleasure I would have erected,
Each day to cruise on the silvery tide,
With a high topsail waving in the gale
To view the beauties on Mudion's side.

Oville [H666: 29 Aug 1936]

Source: James M'Closkey (the Hass, Dungiven), learned from his aunt, Mrs Kealey (Teeavin, Dungiven).

s: A townland in the parish of Dungiven, meaning "the place of rocks."

Key F.

The cot where I was born in, it stands upon a hill
Near to Altmover Fairy Glen in the townland of
  Oville,
To many foreign lands I've roamed, but my heart
  will still return
Back to Altmover's Fairy Glen and the cot where I
  was born.

I'll ne'er forget the Doo-an Rocks, nor yet the
  'Walls of Troy,'
For oftimes I have sported there when I was but a
  boy,
Seeking for the wild bird's nest and roaming
  through its dells,
Where in it grows the pale primrose and nods the
  proud bluebells.

My mind does oftimes wander back to the lowly
  rocks of Scall,
Where crystal streams have forced their track and
  o'er its rocks do fall;
Some would choose Dungiven Street, a pleasant
  hour to spend,
I'd rather view the Doo-an Rocks in sweet
  Altmover Glen.

The Peistie Glen [H654: 6 Jun 1936]

g: (m) "The Pretty Girl Milking Her Cow."

Source: Pat Kealey (Dungiven); author Francis Heaney (Magheraboy, Dungiven).

s: ... The Peist[i]e Glen is the beautiful portion of Banagher where the pool is located in which St. Murrough (Muiredhach) O'Heaney bound the serpent (peiste)....

Key G.

One evening as Zephyr was fanning
Each green shady bower so fair,
By Carnanbane's border I wandered,
The bright scenes of nature to share;
My mind did imbibe meditation,
Fond fancy implor-ed my pen
To write measured words eulogizing
The charms of the sweet Peistie Glen.

As I rambled the verge of this water
That murmurs beneath the Rockhead,
There the green mounds of Strieve elevated
Where the lustre of nature was spread.
Old Carnanbane lent its reflection,
O'er the Peistie its trees did extend
Where the eagle displayed its proud pinions
Aloft in the sweet Peistie Glen.

With perspective eye I stood gazing
As the Peistie cascade it did sound,
I thought on the patron saint Muiredhach:
A reptile right under he bound;
Convulsive it sunk at his powers,
While inspiring light did transcend
For St. Patrick's green emblem three-folded
Has power in the sweet Peistie Glen.

Where Erin's brave sons and fair daughters
In rapture do throng that bright vale,
The violets each path were perfuming,
And the primrose did scent the soft gale.
My heart with new joy was elated
Where friendship and love both did blend,
And the concord of voice emanated
In praise of the sweet Peistie Glen.

As I sat in the shade of that bower,
In fondness each bosom did glow,
And the hours of ecstacy vanished
As the sweet Peistie streams they did flow.
The songsters o'erhead they did hover,
While branches beneath them did bend,
Their soul-stirring strains rang vibrative,
Enchanting the sweet Peistie Glen.

Now the ship bells proclaim emigration,
I must leave this bright valley behind;
Old Carnanbane I abandon,
From Strieve's verdant braes I decline,
Farewell to this rural plantation,
Likewise to my love and each friend,
Adieu to those hours of enchantment
I spent in the sweet Peistie Glen.

Bonny Portrush [H775: 1 Oct 1938]

s: (m) "Bonny Portmore." Other title: "... Udny."

Author Sam Henry (Sandelford, Coleraine).

s: ... written by request....
The first verse is parodied on the old ballad, "Bonny Portmore."

Key G. Plaintively but moderately quick.

Oh, bonny Portrush, you shine where you stand,
And the more I think on you, the more my heart warms;
Were I near you now as I once was before,
All the gold of old England would ne'er part us more.

Ramore proudly rides like a ship on the sea,
With the isles of the Skerries away in the lee;
The sun and the sea bring blessing to all
As round thy bright borders we follow the ball.

One day on the links, kind fate came to me,
Her eyes lit with love as blue as the sea,
Her hair like the gold of your beautiful shore --
So now and forever my girl I adore.

Oh, bonny Portrush, I will ever be bound
To the hills of the pansy where heartsease I found;
You brought me all blessings that life has in store,
So good luck and goodbye to your wave-beaten shore.

The River Roe (I) [H649: 2 May 1936]

Source: Mrs Frank Kealey (Ballysally, Coleraine; native of Dungiven district).

s: ... The reference of Captain Moody reveals the fact that in 1782 there were two bleaching greens at Newtown Limavady owned by W. and J. Moody, respectively. The acreage under flax in Co. Derry in those times was 1,450, the bounty paid to encourage its growth 1,000 pounds annually, and the value of the annual production of linen 300,000 pounds.

Key G.

It was down by the banks of a large murmuring river
I wandered to take the fresh air,
The thrushes did sing and the blackbirds did whistle,
And all things of nature seemed charming.
The sky being serene and the morning being still,
Bright Phoebus his beams stretched o'er Donald's hill,
And now by this time we were at the Roe Mill,
Where brave Captain Moody goes on with his bleaching.
The boys in the green their white webs were stretching,
And the foreman among hands the white trout was catching
In the river Roe in the morning.

My business required me back into Newtown,
My fancy invited me farther;
I could not return there on any condition,
Unless it was love or for murder.
The cuckoo did sing till daylight did appear,
The woodlark and linnet with song filled my ear,
The valley with corncrakes did ring far and near.
Still onwards I doted, got drunk without drinking,
And to return homewards I soon forgot thinking
As I viewed the white trout in the streams that were jinking
In the river Roe in the morning.

The River Roe (II) [H629: 21 Dec 1935]

s: (m) "Cashlan Ui Neill."

Source not given.

s: An old song remodelled and set to the air "Cashlan Ui Neill."

Key E flat.

Sam Henry's Songs of the People

Through the land of O'Cahan a river in beauty
  doth flow
By mountain and valley; oh, where can you
  match the dark Roe?
On Glenshane's lone mountain it first has its
  infancy's source,
Through deep glen and meadow it follows its
  fanciful course.

By the church of Dungiven, where sleeps the
  brave Cooey na Gall,
Where the figures in stone his hero-deeds aye
  will recall:
A patron of learning, the friend of the friends
  of his land,
But a whirlwind of vengeance with his sword
  gleaming bright in his hand.

Now past the rude altar where warriors
  remembered their dead,
By the banks where the feet of the holy men
  often did tread,
Where the monks sang their matins on mornings
  long ages ago
In the grey roofless abbey that sleeps by the
  banks of the Roe.

Strangemore it encircles and then wanders
  onward again
Through Pellipar trees and Ogilby's splendid
  demesne;
John Mitchel of Scriggan, whose home was the
  cot on the hill,
In Van Dieman's island the scenes of his youth
  cherished still.

The river has sadness, and growing, it seems
  sore to mourn,
But awakes to the treble where rolls in the
  young Gelvin Burn.
Oh, they that loved dearly are dead or are gone
  far away,
On its banks now the toilers heed not the Roe's
  song of today.

Through Carrick it rushes under gorges majestic
  in height,
Past the rock where O'Cahan once stood in his
  serious plight:
When banned by the Saxon in a desperate mood
  to escape,
He cleared the wild waters defying grim death in
  his leap.

His glory is gone, and no more by the banks of
  the Roe
In his castle embattled shall the hearth shed its
  gladdening glow,
No longer the revels shall ring through the
  chieftain's bright hall,
And the embers are grey that were lighted by
  Cooey-na-Gall.

Like the voice of the wolf sounds the wind
  through the trees on its sides,
As tumbling and plunging the brown water
  sparkles and glides;
The cry of the banshee with sorrow the night air
  does fill,
And the hosts of the past haunt the mound of
  the Mullagh's green hill.

The bards and the chiefs once gathered on yon
  daisied hill,
And there from Iona had come the revered
  Columbkille;
At the court of Drumceatt kings and bards
  learned to love and agree,
And the calm of the dove brooded over the
  turbulent sea.

Now past Limavady in ripples the Roe sings its
  song,
It kisses the flowers of the meadows while flowing
  along,
It is joined by the wild birds as sweetly they
  warble their lays,
And music re-echoes as the Roe rounds the sweet
  Granagh braes.

A child of the mountains, now tamed, dark and
  silent doth flow,
Its banks clad with verdure, it winds through
  the plain of Myroe;
Its turbulence over, it seeks in the sea to find
  rest,
And Foyle, like a mother, will take the tired Roe
  to its breast.

1.1: O'Cahan [O Cathain]: land of O'Cahan = North
Derry. [h: 1981:6]

Slieve Gallen Brae [H784: 3 Dec 1938]

s: (m) "Rosaleen Bawn."

Author late James O'Kane (Gortanure, Maghera),
"composed just after 'Rosaleen Bawn' was written."

s: Rory Dall mentioned in verse four is Rory Dall
O'Cahan, who, in my reasoned opinion, was the
composer of the "Londonderry Air," a conclusion
arrived at before I knew of this song, and in
which my good friend, Mr Frank O'Kane, son of
the author of these words, concurs.

Key E flat.

Oh, come with me, my city friend,
From Leeds or London town,
And cross with me the Irish Sea
To hills with heather brown,
The Gray Man's path, the fairy rath,
Or dolmen old and gray:
A lonesome bed for chiefs long dead
On old Slieve Gallen Brae.

Then leave the city's smoky slums,
Where want and care abide,
And view the humble peasant homes
Along the mountain side;
While free from care, breathe God's pure air,
And hear the linnet's lay,
And see the hills and tiny rills
Around Slieve Gallon Brae.

In sun-kiss'd bowers, where nature's flowers
In wild profusion grow,
Where fairy bell with pimpernel
And sweet acacia blow,
The woodland charms of cottage farms
You'll pass along the way,
But call and see the vanathee
On old Slieve Gallon Brae.

Then come with me to Ullian's Glen,
The fairest glen of all,
Where sunlight gleams o'er mountain streams,
The home of Rory Dall;
We'll view the mound where oft the sound
Of music sweet did flow
Within this hall from Rory Dall,
The minstrel of the Roe.

From far and near the bards come here
To learn to play and sing,
He e'en went o'er to Albion's shore
To play before the king,
But here at hame and o'er the foam
The bard did sing and play;
Some of his lays were made in praise
Of wild Slieve Gallon Brae.

Ere close of day we'll haste away
Across Benbradagh crest,
And view the tomb where in the gloom
An Irish chief does rest;
That ruined hall of Cooey-na-gall,
The theme of many a lay,
On chiefs long dead and glories fled
And old Slieve Gallen Brae.

B11 / Erin, my country

Fair Tyrone [H189: BLp, 25 Jun 1927]

s: (m) "Youghal Harbour"; o: (m) "Eochaill."

Source: (w) James McNickle (Tyrone House, Portstewart).

s: The air is ... one of the stock tunes to which many folk songs are sung. The song can also be sung to "The Groves of Blarney" ("The Bells of Shandon").

m: The typed copies (Bt, Wt, and a typescript in the set Sam Henry gave to Francis Collinson [and now at the Ulster Folk and Transport Museum]) may represent a later singing version, whereas the 12 stanzas in the original column seem to be from a single source.

[Original column, intact on a print from BL microfilm kindly supplied by John Moulden, includes twelve 4-line stanzas but not stanza 7 below. Dp is also printed, but cut into 3 separate pieces: the title and headnotes ["Key E flat"], the text, and the tune ["Key D"]; stanza 7 is typed below the printed text, with an arrow drawn to indicate its position.
  BLp, Dp are in 4-line stanzas; Bt = Wt(c) is in 5 double (8-line) stanzas (which fit the tune), omitting stanzas 6, 10, and 13, but including stanza 7.]

[BLp] Key E flat. [Bt, in 2] Key D.

As oft I ponder, my thoughts do wander
On childhood's scenes now long since flown,
Fond memory stealing, again revealing
The hills and valleys in fair Tyrone.

There is Lough Attarrive, with its silvery surf:
Around it in childhood I oftimes roamed
And pulled wild flowers from the shady bowers
On Mountfield's braes in fair Tyrone.

There is Mullaghcarn in fell and tarn,
Its shadows cast in the moonlight lone
On the poteen dens in the fairy glens
That keep night vigils in fair Tyrone.

Rathmackin's fort with its fairy court
A-keeping watch on bush and stone
From Mullaghslin to Lower Cloughfin
And the Bantown braes in fair Tyrone.

Sam Henry's Songs of the People

There's Termon Rock, which rivals Knock,
In a crumbling ruin and bed of stone,
Where Patrick laid his hand and prayed
For God's own blessing on fair Tyrone.

I have seen the ocean in wild commotion,
With wreck and death in the wild wind's moan,
Niagara's fountains or in the Rocky Mountains,
But scenes far wilder in fair Tyrone.

There's Omagh town, in whose rivers brown
The salmon sport and bright pearls are strown,
Its tall church spires show the heart's desires
In the sacred plain of fair Tyrone.

There is Gortin Glen, with its romantic scenes,
Down their shaggy rocks bright streams are
  flowing,
With Seskinore and sweet Dromore
And the Booran Groves in fair Tyrone.

There's sweet Strabane with its fertile land;
Fair flowers there you will find grown,
No meadows greener or vale serener
Than those we find in fair Tyrone.

There's a place more rare, Greencastle fair,
With its romantic scenes and bright rivers
  flowing,
And Barness Glen with its deep black fen,
And the hawk's high nest in fair Tyrone.

I have seen flowers rarer, but none are fairer
Than the primrose sweets which were all our own,
In childhood's morning, the hills adorning
Owenreagh's banks in fair Tyrone.

What wild birds' chorus is more sonorous
In harmonic blending and wealth of tone
Than the song of the thrush from the hawthorn
  bush
With the larks and linnets of fair Tyrone?

But with all life's pleasures, fond memory
  treasures,
There is one among them that stands alone
To make life sweeter and far completer,
'Tis my schoolboy days in fair Tyrone.

1.2: ... childhood's memories ... [Bt]
2.2: Round it ... [Bt]
3.3: ... the piteen ... [Bt]
6.: [Dp, BLp only.]
7.: [Typed addition to Dp, also in Bt, but not BLp.]
10.: [Dp, BLp only]
11.2: ... sweets that are ... [Bt]
13.: [Dp, BLp only]

Among the Green Bushes [*Bp,Dp*: in Sweet Tyrone]

[H708: 19 Jun 1937]

Source: Mr Tobin, principal (Moortown P.E.S., Drumaney, Coagh).

174 Key F.

Oh, where is the man with a heart in his bosom
Who thrills not with fervent delight
Whenever he thinks of the land of his childhood,
The land where he first saw the light?
And I think with pride of a spot in old Ireland,
The dear place I'll never disown,
The darling old birthplace among the green
  bushes
In the sweet County Tyrone.

Among the green bushes in sweet Tyrone,
That is the place I will never disown.
Among the green bushes I drew my first breath,
Darling Tyrone, I will love you till death.

I see in my daydreams the darling old boreen
Where I used to play when a child;
Can I ever forget the dear friends of my
  childhood
With whom many hours I beguiled?
A man who would not love the home of his
  childhood --
His heart must be colder than stone,
But I'm proud to say I was born in old Ireland,
In the sweet County Tyrone.

Darling Tyrone, dearest home of my childhood,
Upon thee I never may gaze,
But still in my heart thy dear memory I'll cherish,
I always shall sing in thy praise.
There may be some lands where the scenery's
  fairer,
But to thee my heart beats alone,
And while I have life, I will love the green
  bushes
In the sweet County Tyrone.

Where Derry Meets Tyrone

[H601: 8 Jun 1935]

s: (m) "The Mountains High."

Source: (m) (Bond's Glen, Cumber parish); author Mrs M. S. Norris (Ballyboley, Greyabbey, Co. Down).

Key G.

B11 / Erin, my country

Have you ever been to Ireland where Derry meets
  Tyrone?
There are hills and glens and valleys with a
  beauty all their own.
Oh, to be there in springtime when the blossom's
  on the sloe
And the little wood-anemones bear blooms of pink-
  tipped snow,
When the birds are singing love songs and the
  fruit trees are in bloom,
There is little time for sorrow, there is none at
  all for gloom.

Have you ever been to Ireland where Derry meets
  Tyrone?
The queen of nature reigning there sits on her
  lovely throne,
She tinkles all the bluebells to call her subjects
  dear,
While the blackbird pipes his madrigal with fluty
  notes and clear;
There's a nutty fragrance stealing from the gold
  upon the whin,
And I feel I'm near to heaven with the peace of
  God within.

If you ever come to Ireland where Derry meets
  Tyrone,
You'll find a kindly welcome; what kinder hearts
  are known?
You'll see the glens and valleys, the hills that
  touch the sky,
And the little amber streamlets thread the
  meadows flowing by.
Oh, there's a wealth of beauty and a rapture all
  its own
In the valleys of the Sperrins where Derry meets
  Tyrone.

3.6: Sperrins = "the little sky." [s]

The Land of the West [H677: 14 Nov 1936]

Source: (w) Joseph Smith, 91 (Knockaduff,
Drumcroon) from Thomas Kelly (Knockaduff);
(m) Tom Smith, melodeon, learned from his father.

s: ... Joseph Smith ... in his 91st year is hale
and hearty and loves a song and a joke.

Key G.

Oh, come to the west, love, oh come there with me,
'Tis a sweet land of verdure that springs from the
  sea,
Where fair plenty smiles from her emerald throne,
Oh, come to the west and I'll make thee my own.
I'll guard thee, I'll tend thee, I'll love thee the
  best,
And you can say there's no land like the land of
  the west.

The south has its roses and bright skies of blue,
But ours are more sweet with love's own changeful
  hue,
Half sunshine, half tears, like the girl I love best,
Oh, what is the south to the beautiful west?
Then come there with me, and the rose of thy
  mouth
Will be sweeter to me than the flowers of the south.

The north hath its snow towers of dazzling array,
All sparkling with gems in the ne'er-setting day,
There the storm king may dwell in the place he
  loves best,
But the soft breathing zephyr, he plays in the
  west.
Then come to the west, where no cold wind doth
  blow,
And thy neck will seem fairer to me than the snow.

The sun in the gorgeous east chaseth the night,
Where he riseth refreshed in his glory and might,
But where does he go when he seeks his sweet
  rest?
Oh, doth he not haste to the beautiful west?
Then come there with me, 'tis the land I love best,
'Tis the land of my sires, 'tis my own darling west.

Old Ireland [H658: 4 Jul 1936]

Source: Mrs Frank Kealey (Ballysally); (m) noted by her son, James Kealey (Ballymoney).

Key G.

Sam Henry's Songs of the People

In the northwest of Europe there lies a green isle
Where the hills stand majestic and clad all fertile,
Where the orient breeze its valleys doth fan,
And its far-famed title is old Ireland.

I left fair Columbia to view this green isle,
Where freedom and friendship around me do smile,
Where honour and virtue go linked hand in hand
With the lads and fair lasses of old Ireland.

Instead of vile serpents, blithe lambkins do play,
No treacherous reptile dare obstruct my way;
Then I thought on St. Patrick, who raised his
   blest hand
And banished those monsters from old Ireland.

I rambled the banks where the Bann waters glide,
Where the song of the thrushes doth blend on each
   side,
Where the gay blooming flowers their leaves do
   expand
To array the fair shamrock of old Ireland.

Now farewell, lovely Erin, our ship hoists her sail
To yonder clear waters and the salt wintry gale.
To your sons and fair daughters I stretch forth
   my hand,
Though my heart lies enbosomed in old Ireland.

Erin, My Country [H478: 28 Jan 1933]

Other titles: "The Harp of Erin," "Oh ...," "The Sons of Fingal."

Source: J. H. M. [?John Henry Macauley] (Ballycastle), sung by Hugh Malone many years ago.

Key G.

Erin, my country, although thy harp slumbers
And lies in oblivion near Tara's old hall,
With scarce one kind hand to enliven its numbers
Or sound a lone dirge to the sons of Fin Gal.

The trophies of warfare they hang there
   neglected,
Since cold are the warriors to whom they were
   known,
But the harp of old Erin will still be respected
While there lives but one bard to enliven its tone.

Erin, my country, I love thy green bowers,
No music to me like thy murmuring rills,
The shamrock to me is the fairest of flowers
And naught is more dear than thy daisy-clad
   hills.

Then hail, fairest island of Neptune's old ocean,
The land of St. Patrick, my parents, agra!
Cold, cold must the heart be and void of emotion
That loves not the music of Erin-go-bragh.

The Enchanted Isle [H550: 16 Jun 1934]

s: (m) "The Little Red Lark."

Author Rev. Luke Aylmer Conolly (Ballycastle), 1806-33.

s: ... "There is a belief prevalent among the people of Rathlin that a green island rises every seventh year out of the sea between Bengore and their island. It is adorned with woods and lawns and crowded with people selling yarn and engaged in the common occupations of a fair." -- Dr. Drummond (1811). This is the phenomenon known as Fata Morgana, which has also been seen between Bushfoot and Skerries; between Torr and Cantyre; and between Sicily and Calabria.

Key E flat.

To Rathlin's isle I chanced to sail
When summer breezes softly blew,
And there I heard so sweet a tale
That oft I wished it could be true:
They said at eve, when rude winds sleep
And hushed is every turbid swell,
A mermaid rises from the deep
And sweetly tunes her magic shell.

And while she plays, rock, dell and cave
In dying falls the sounds retain
As if some choral spirits gave
Their aid to swell her witching strain.
Then, summoned by that dulcet note,
Uprising to th' admiring view,
A fairy island seems to float
With tints of many a gorgeous hue.

And glittering fanes and lofty towers
All on this fairy isle are seen,
And waving trees and shady bowers
With more-than-mortal verdure green,
And as it moves, the western sky
Glows with a thousand varying rays,
And the calm sea, tinged with each dye,
Seems like a golden flood of blaze.

They also say, if earth or stone
From verdant Erin's hallowed land
Were on this magic island thrown,
Forever fixed it then would stand,
But when for this some little boat
In silence ventures from the shore --
The mermaid sinks -- hushed is the note,
The fairy isle is seen no more.

The Mac's and the O's   [H484: 11 Mar 1933]

Source not given.

s: To mark the conclusion of our series of articles entitled, "What's in a Name?" we publish in our song column a rhymed list of the most outstanding names in Irish nomenclature.

Key C.

When Ireland was founded by Mac's and by O's
I never could learn, for nobody knows,
But hist'ry says they came over from Spain
To visit oul' Grania and there to remain.
Our fathers were heroes of wisdom and fame,
For multiplication, they practised the same;
Saint Patrick came over to heal their complaints
And very soon made them an island of saints.

The harp and the shamrock were carried before
Brave Roderick O'Connor and Rory O'Moore,
And the good and bad deeds of the Mac's and the O's
Are the tale that these verses are now to disclose.
Hugh O'Neill of Tyrone, O'Donnell, O'Moore,
O'Brien, O'Kelly, O'Connell galore,
All houses so royal, so loyal and old,
One drop of their blood was worth ounces of gold.

MacDonnell, MacDougal, O'Curran, O'Keeffe,
Sly Redmond O'Hanlon, the Rapparee chief,
O'Malley, MacNally, O'Sullivan rare,
O'Failey, O'Daly, O'Burns of Kildare,
O'Doherty, chief of the Isle Inishowen,
MacGuinness the prince of the valleys of Down,
The Collerans, Hollerans, everyone knows,
The Raffertys, Flahertys -- all of them O's.

One-eyed MacCormack and great Finn MacCool,
MacCarthy of Dermot and Tooley O'Toole,
Hugh Neill the grand, and Brian Boru,
Sir Tegan O'Regan and Con Donohue,
O'Hara, O'Meara, OConnor, O'Kane,
O'Carroll, O'Farrell, O'Brennan, O'Drane,
With Murtagh MacDermott, that wicked old Turk,
Who dared to make love to the wife of O'Rourke.

MacCrea and MacGrath, MacGill and MacKeown,
MacFadden, MacCadden, MacCarron, MacGlone,
MacGarren, MacFarren, MacClary, MacCoy,
MacHaley, MacClinch, MacIlrath, MacIlroy,
MacMillan, MacClellan, MacGillan, MacFinn,
MacCullagh, MacCunn, MacManus, MacGlynn,
MacGinlay, MacKinley, MacCaffrey, MacKay,
MacCarroll, MacFarrell, MacCurdy, MacVey.

O'Dillon, O'Dolan, O'Devlin, O'Doyle,
O'Mullan, O'Nolan, O'Bolan, O'Boyle,
O'Murray, O'Rooney, O'Conney, O'Kane,
O'Carey, O'Leary, O'Shea and O'Shane,
O'Brien, O'Rourke, O'Reilly, O'Neill,
O'Hagan, O'Regan, O'Fagan, O'Shiel,
O'Dennis, O'Dwyer, O'Blaney, O'Flynn,
O'Grady, O'Shaughnessy, Brian O'Lynn.

The daughters of Erin are Eileen Aroon
And Norah Acushla and Sheila MacClune,
With Kathleen Mavourneen and Molly Asthore,
The beautiful charmers we love and adore.
There is Donah MacCushla and widow Macree,
There is Molly Maguire and Biddy Magee,
There is dear Norah Creina and Sheila MacGrath,
And the mother of all is Erin-go-bragh!

The Connaught Man   [H219: 21 Jan 1928]

g: "The Boys of the West."

Source: (w) late Alexander Thompson (Park district, near Dungiven); (m) William Devine (Foreglen, Dungiven).

Key D.

Sam Henry's Songs of the People

I came from the west, from the province of
  Connaught,
To view the black north (may the devil light on
  it),
Sure, I shouldn't have worn the kilt and the
  bonnet,
The badge of my country, I love it the best.
The first place I landed was the sweet County
  Down, sir,
Those down-looking villains they did me
  surround, sir,
Sure I don't give a fig for country or town, sir,
They kept laughing and scoffing at me and my
  dress.

Up comes a big fellow, he says, 'Arrah, mister,
I'm sorry to see all your hooves in a blister,
I would have you go home or you'll frighten my
  sister,
Come flutter your wings and fly off to your
  nest.'
Then I gave a spring, sir, my stick gave a ring,
  sir,
Like that he fell flat on the broad of his back,
  sir.
'Oh, go home to your mother, I can batter your
  brother,
For we're mighty obliging that come from the
  west.'

The next place I landed was the sweet town of
  Belfast,
Where I thought that my troubles were over at
  last,
Not thinking of them or the time that was past,
I went into an alehouse the liquor to taste.
I called for a bumper, 'twas filled and I drank it.
'Your money,' they asked; 'Sure, I carry no
  pocket,
But if it's I had it, I'm sure you would get it.
It's seldom we need it at home in the west.'

Out steps a big fellow, he wanted to catch me,
Saying, 'Troth, if it wasn't for your stick I
  would match thee,
For there is not a toe in you fit for to scratch me,
Come on, my gay fellow, and show me your best.'
I put out my toe, sir, and kept the fist low, sir
I gave him a tip and away he did go, sir,
'If you come up to Connaught, we'll teach you a
  throw, sir.
Hurrah for the gay-hearted boys from the west.'

The battle commenced, the police came
  a-powering,
Those wicked black villians with batons came
  showering.
I fought like the divil that fight for an hour in,
Then they marched me to jail without bonnet or
  vest;
But now I'm at home, sir, I'll never more roam,
  sir,
I'll fight till I die for old Connaught again, sir.
I'll never deny my country or name, sir,
Hurrah for the gay-hearted boys of the west.

5.2: ... black villains ... [Dt]

The Rocky Road to Dublin

[H44: "A song of an Irish harvester," 13 Sep 1924]

Source: (w, m) Robert Morton (Ballytober,
Priestland), from Martin Smylie, itinerant
(Carnside, Giant's Causeway), c. 1885.

o: Tune is not the same as the slip jig of the
same name ... should be in 9/8.

Key C.

In the merry month o' June, boys, from my home
  I started,
Left the girls of Tuam nearly broken-hearted,
Saluted father dear, kissed my darling mother,
Drank a pint o' beer my grief and tears to
  smother;
Then off to reap the corn and leave where I was
  born,
I cut a stout blackthorn to banish ghost and
  goblin,
With a pair of bran' new brogues I rattled o'er
  the bogs,
And I scarred all the dogs on the rocky road to
  Dublin.

Whack fill ol da day.

In Mullingar that night I rested limbs so weary,
Started by daylight in the morning light and airy,
Took a drop o' the pure to keep my spirits from
  sinking,
That's an Irishman's cure whenever he's on for
  drinking.
To see the lasses smile and laughin' all the while
At my curious style, it would set your heart
  a-bubblin',
They asked me if I was hired, the wages I
  required,
Till I was almost tired on the rocky road to
  Dublin.

From there I got away, my spirits never failin',
Landed on the quay just as the ship was sailin',
Captain at me roared, said that no room had he,
When I jumped on board, no cabin found for
  Paddy;
Then down amongst the pigs, where we danced
  some funny jigs,

I didn't like the digs with the water round us
    bubblin',
When off to Holyhead I wished myself was dead
Or, better far instead, on the rocky road to
    Dublin.

When Dublin next arrived, I thought it such a
    pity
To be so soon deprived of a view of that fine
    city,
Then I took a stroll out amongst the quality,
My bundle I got stole in a neat locality:
Something crossed my mind, then I looked behind,
No bundle could I find upon my stick a-wobblin',
Inquiring for the rogue, they said the Connaught
    brogue
Wasn't much in vogue on the rocky road to
    Dublin.

The boys of Liverpool, when we safely landed,
Called myself a fool; I could no longer stand it,
Blood began to boil, temper I was losin',
Poor old Erin's isle she began a-buzzin';
'Hurra', my soul,' says I, my shillelagh I let
    fly,
Some Galway boys came by and they sees I was
    a-hobblin',
They joined in the affray, and 'Faugh a ballagh,'
    we quickly cleared the way,
And Connaught won the day on the rocky road to
    Dublin.

1.4: ... my griefs and ... [Dt]
 .8: And I scared ... [Dt]
5.4: Cf. O Lochlainn's "... isle they began abusin'"
 .7: ... 'Faugh a ballagh,' [Bp: *shouted*] ... we
    cleared the way, [Dt]

Dungiven Cricket Match [H669: 19 Sep 1936]

o: (m) "The Low-Backed Car."

Source not given; ?James Bond.

s: Leaving the Limavady-Garvagh bus at Ross's
Lane, and walking through the delectable country
of Glenkeen, Termaquin, Balleyrum, and Drumrammer, we reach the cottage across the burn where
James Bond lives. He has a wonderful repertoire
of old songs. A neighbour remarked to me, "I'd
rather hear Jamie Bond sing one of his oul' songs
than all the wireless and gramophones in the
world."
   The best music in the world is the simplest.
As a woman who was rearing her family close to
the foaming river replied, when we remarked,
"You have always the music of the water here,"
"Aye, and of the childher."
   Two lines of verse to be sung to each line of
music.

[Original printed in 4-line stanzas, each occupying half the sol-fa tune.]

Key C.

B11 / Erin, my country

You rantin' team of Derry boys
Who introduce my quill,
Listen to the praises
Of the cricket club and ball.
To challenge sweet Dungiven
The Derry boys consent,
We set a date to play them
And our challenge then we sent.

   With bat and ball we'll conquer all,
   Good action we can show,
   They think they'll match Dungiven,
   The Foyle against the Roe.

With horses placed and coasters traced
We enter-ed the town,
The ladies all admired us
Just as we lighted down,
With caps and colours glancing,
We were well set on our feet,
We called upon the ladies
Our challenge to uptake.

Dungiven men not fearing them,
They all came tripping down
To the demesnes of Pellipar,
A furlong out of town.
Undaunted cried brave Erwin,
'Draw nigh, we'll show them play;
We'll let them know before we go,
They'll never gain the day.'

   With bat and ball we'll conquer all,
   Good action we can show,
   We're a match for saucy Derry,
   We're Dungiven boys, you know.

The second heat was for the Plate,
Which was a hard contest,
Where each man did his utmost,
Dungiven proved the best.
Undaunted cries brave Erwin,
'No leisure time they'll get
For with jackets red we'll have them tried
Before the sun does set.'

From Derry round to Coleraine town,
Sure we have bate them all,
We'll try all parts of Europe
With our battin' and our ball,

179

Sam Henry's Songs of the People

And here is for a thousand
We'll play Derry o'er again,
So they pull-ed out their horses
And they went the road they came.

There was Davie Dunn and Mercer's son,
Young Fillis, too, beside,
Crampsie and the baker lad
Their valour did not hide,
O'Morrison, M'Closkey,
O'Kealey and O'Kane,
And likewise young George Wilkison,
They're worthy boys of fame.

With bat and ball we'll conquer all,
Good action we can show,
We're the sprigs of old Benbradden
And the champions of the Roe.

March of the Men of Garvagh

[H17b: 8 Mar 1924]

A marching song.

Source: coll. Maud Houston (Coleraine).

1: Not in D. Should probably be written with two pulses per measure. Stanza 1 and refrain are printed line for line beneath the sol-fa in Bp.

Key E flat.

We're marching, marching thro' Garvagh town,
We're ready to fight for queen and crown,
If any man won't we'll knock him down,
We're the gallant boys of Garvagh.

O, proudly, proudly the drums will beat
As we march down thro' Garvagh Street,
For the fifers' music is sounding sweet
In the ears of the men of Garvagh.

As I came over Garvagh Hill,
And by the race of my father's mill,
O, who came up but fighting Phil
With the gallant boys of Garvagh.

He was head and shoulders above the crowd,
His step was firm and his glance was proud;
I watched them pass and my heart beat loud
For the gallant boys of Garvagh.

Ta Ra, Limavady

[H706: 5 Jun 1937]

1: (m) resembles "Old Dan Tucker."

Source: (w) Leonard Donaghy (Protestant St, Limavady); (m) noted from John Taylor (Olphert Pl, Coleraine) from Leonard Donaghy, c. 1897.

Key A flat.

Let Derry boast her prentice boys,
Coleraine her boys both rough and ready,
But the boys that take the shine off both
Are the boys that come from Limavady.

Ta ra Limavady,
Ta ra Limavady,
Search Ireland round, there can't be found
Another town like Limavady.

Coleraine for Kitty justly proud,
Dungiven boasts her pretty Biddy,
But the girls that take the shine off both
Are the girls that come from Limavady.

Kilrea stands proudly on a hill
And overlooks the Bann, but had I
Five times twenty such Kilreas,
I'd give them all for Limavady.

Maghera has keen-set blades,
Garvagh men are cool and steady,
But the boys that take the shine off all
Are the boys that come from Limavady.

Moneymore has Quilley Glens,
Magherafelt has Killyvaddy,
But the Dog Leap on the River Roe
Is the pride and boast of Limavady.

Now may good luck attend her still,
And may her sons ne'er show a sad eye,
But every young man do his best
To raise the praise of Limavady.

The Knights of Malta

[H146: 28 Aug 1926]

o: (m) "Spanish Lady"; k: "Sons of Levi." Other titles: "Bright (and) Morning Star," "True Born Sons of Levi."

Source: (w) broadsheet printed by J. Nicholson, Cheapside Song House (Belfast); (m) Magilligan octogenarian, learned c. 1855.

Key G.

Come all you craftsmen that do wish
To propagate the grand design,
Come enter into our high temple
And learn the art that is divine.

For we are the true-born sons of Levi,
None on earth can with us compare,
We are the root and branch of David,
The bright and glorious morning star.

Come all ye knight templars of Malta,
Forth in glittering armour shine,
Assist your good and worthy master
To protect the ark divine.

With trembling steps I slowly advanced,
Some time I knocked both loud and shrill,
Till lo! a knight in armour bright
Demanded of me what was my will.

After some questions being asked,
To which I ahswered with some fear,
He told me neither Turk nor heathen
By any means could enter there.

With stars and shields placed on our breasts,
Its virtue guards our lines around,
We will remember the twelve stones
On Jordan's banks are to be found.

As Joshua and I passed over Jordan,
These twelve stones we bore along,
'Twas our high priest and our grand master
That moved the ark of God along.

There were seven trumpets of rams' horns
Sounded along before the ark;
Gilgal was our resting quarters,
There we left our holy mark.

Noah planted the first garden;
Moses planted Aaron's rod,
He smote the waters of the Egyptians
And turned the Jordan into blood.

Come all you brethren, join with me
And bear the ark as I have done.
Come, enter into our bright temple,
For it is a new Jerusalem.

B11 / Erin, my country

The Bright Orange Stars of Coleraine

[H87a: "Two songs by Robert Thompson," 11 Jul 1925]

o: (m) "Aghalee Heroes."

Source: H[arry] E[vans] (Past Master, L.O.L. 735, Coleraine); author Robert Thompson, d. 1885 (Coleraine).

s: [Bp: This poet, who][Dt: The author] was a leading member of the Orange Order and Black Preceptory [Bp: Institution, enjoyed a great celebrity in the Coleraine districts]. He died in 1885, at 80 years of age, and is buried in St. Patrick's Churchyard [Dt: Coleraine]. The strains of his songs might have been heard in "M'Murdy's," of Brook Street, Coleraine [Dt: an inn](the lodge meeting place) [Bp: in days long gone by]....

Key D.

On the glorious twelfth day of July our music it sweetly did play,
'The Protestant Boys' and 'Boyne Water' were the two tunes we played going away.
Like the sons of King William we marched till Coleraine town came in our view,
And O'Hara's church was decorated with the Orange, the Purple, the Blue.

Here, boys, we are banded together, determined to drain our last vein
To the memory of William for ever and the bright Orange stars of Coleraine.

Coleraine, you're a beautiful village where Bann's silvery stream does adorn,
Portraying each beautiful feature to hail that e'er glorious morn.
Your sons when they're proudly advancing regardless, all danger disdain,
As your thundering drums loud do rattle, well manned by the boys of Coleraine.

Shall e'er we forget that bright morning that brought to us such liberty,
When the banks of the Boyne were adorned from the flowers of the old Orange tree
Whose branches of purple extended their flowers over mountain and plain,
Each scene of the tyrant confounding, so inspiring the boys of Coleraine.

181

Sam Henry's Songs of the People

Now to conclude and to finish, and that now
   before we do go,
Let us toast all the true hearts in Derry with the
   stars that illumine the Roe,
Whose sons from their standard ne'er wandered,
   but determined to drain their last vein,
On whose hearts are inscribed 'No surrender,'
   like the bright Orange stars of Coleraine.

1.1: ... twelfth of July ... [Dt]

The Boys of Coleraine

[H87b: "Two songs by Robert Thompson," 11 Jul 1925]

[m = H87a]

Source: ?H[arry] E[vans] (Coleraine); author
Robert Thompson.

When Flora is decked in her roses, and fields are
   arrayed in their bloom,
And groves fully robed in their splendour, with
   meadows emitting perfume,
We'll spend Monday evening with pleasure,
   Portstewart we'll revisit again;
Come fill up your glasses good measure and drink
   to the boys of Coleraine.

We'll drink to those early companions who along
   with us rambled the shore,
Though they're exiled to foreign dominions, and
   the memory of them that's no more,
But such recollections do grieve me, then call up
   the waiter again,
From sorrow a glass will relieve me, then here's
   to the boys of Coleraine.

While viewing the great swelling ocean that washes
   the shores of the west,
There's a feeling of friendly devotion awakened
   anew in my breast,
It calls up emotions so frantic, brings back
   recollections again,
And swiftly glides o'er the Atlantic to greet our
   dear boys of Coleraine.

Yon flower-spangled braes, Port-na-happle, a
   place in my memory shall share,
There's no mosque, cathedral or chapel with thy
   bonny braes can compare.
If nature claims our adoration, can I in compliance
   restrain?
Each to his own celebration, then here's to the
   boys of Coleraine.

2.3: ... grieve us, ... [Dt]

Neuve Chappelle [H526: 30 Dec 1933]

s: (m) "The Rambling Irishman."

Source: street singer, ex-private, Royal Inniskilling Fusiliers (Long Commons, Coleraine); author sergeant, 27th Division.

s: The Battle of Neuve Chapelle, in the Great
War, was fought from 10th to 12th March, 1915.
   ... It was the favourite song of the Inniskillings or the Irish Rifles, and was commonly sung when leaving the trenches or in the estaminets....
[T]he 27th Division ... included the Inniskillings and Rifles....

Key G.

For when we landed in Belgium, the girls all
   danced with joy;
Says one unto the other, 'Here comes an Irish
   boy.'
Then it's fare thee well, dear mother, we'll do the
   best we can,
For you all know well that Neuve Chappelle was
   won by an Irishman.

   *Then here's good luck to the Rifles, the
      Inniskillings too,*
   *The Royal Irish Fusiliers and the Royal
      Artillery, too,*
   *For side by side they fought and died as noble
      heroes can,*
   *And you all know well that Neuve Chappelle was
      won by an Irishman.*

Said Von Kluck unto the Kaiser, 'What are we
   going to do?
We're going to meet those Irishmen -- the men we
   never knew.'
Says the Kaiser unto old Von Kluck, 'We'll do the
   best we can,
But I'm telling you true that Waterloo was won by
   an Irishman.'

◆ B11 REFERENCES ◆

◆ The Old Stone Wall *(H83) 156*

   BRS *In Dublin's* 1968:20-1
   Walton's 132 n.d.:22

◆ Old Arboe *(H505) 157*

   IREL *Treoir* 13(5)1981

   REC Geordie Hanna, Eagrán MD 0002 (A1)
      Paddy Tunney, Topic 12TS 289 (B2) "... Ardboe"

◊ Ballymonan Brae *(H643) 159*

   IREL Moulden 1979:15

◊ The Girls from [*Dt,Wt*: of] Coleraine *(H64) 161*

   Brunnings 1981: "... of ..."

   AMER Ives 1955:20-1, a longer version, source not given.

   BRS *Ireland Calling* n.d.:3

◊ Faughanvale *(H796) 163*

   IREL Moulden 1979:55

◊ Old Inishowen *(H824) 166*

   Brunnings 1981: (m) "The Meeting of the Waters (Tunes: The Old Head of Dennis and The Wild Geese)"

◊ Kearney's Glen *(H715) 166*

   IREL Ó Maoláin 1982:48

◊ Mudion River *(H108b) 169*

   IREL Moulden 1979:107-8

◊ Bonny Portrush *(H775) 171*

   REC Lizzie Higgins, Topic 12T 185 (A5) "Bonny Udny," especially stanza 1.

   MEL Bunting 1983:156-7 (#109) "... Portmore"

◊ The River Roe (I) *(H649) 171*

   ? Brunnings 1981: "The River Roe (Tune of The Winding Banks of Erne)," without references.

◊ Slieve Gallen Brae *(H784) 172*

   IREL Ó Maoláin 1982:14-5

   1: Not the same song as Wright 1975:191-2 (from Carl Hardebeck, *Gems of Melody*), O Lochlainn 1965:18, nor Meek 1978:58; which have the melody the McPeakes sing.
     The McPeakes' version (Topic 12T 87) has spread, e.g.:
     Bob Davenport, Topic 12TS 350 (B6)
     Dolores Keane, John Faulkner, Green Linnet SIF 3003 (= Mulligan LUN 043) (A5)
     Bill Meek, Folk-Legacy FSE 21 (B9)

◊ Where Derry Meets Tyrone *(H601) 174*

   Brunnings 1981: (m) "The Mountains High"

◊ The Land of the West *(H677) 175*

   AMER Kenedy 1890:281, credited to Samuel Lover.

   BRS Harvard 1: 4.179 (Forth), 6.99 (Pratt), 7.12 (Ryle), 9.101 (Bebbington), 12.137 (Such)
   Harvard 3: (Walker)
   Gems n.d.:128

◊ Erin, My Country *(H478) 176*

   Probably not: Brunnings 1981: "The Harp of Old Erin"

   IREL Joyce 1909:332-3 "Oh ...," tune and 2 lines.

   Shields *UF* 17,1971:6,22 "Oh ..."

   AMER Kenedy 1890:143

   BRS BPL H.80: (n.i.) "The Harp of Erin"
   Harvard 1: 11.84 (Such) "The Sons of Fingal"
   Emerald Isle 1904:51-2
   O'Conor 1901:42
   617 [190-?]:98

   MEL O'Neill 1903:22 (#124)

◊ The Enchanted Isle *(H550) 176*

   Brunnings 1981: ?"Enchanted Isle"; (m) "The Little Red Lark"

   AMER Welsh 1907:174-5

◊ The Mac's and the O's *(H484) 177*

   BRS O'Conor 1901:79
   617 [190-?]:21

◊ The Connaught Man *(H219) 177*

   BRS Cf. UCLA 605: 3(Haly) "The Connaughtman's Rambles to Dublin," another tale of a country lad's visit to the big city.

◊ The Rocky Road to Dublin *(H44) 178*

   Brunnings 1981: "... - Irish," "The Rocky Road"

   IREL Behan 1967:91-2
   O Lochlainn 1939:102-3

   AMER Kenedy 1890:279-80

   BRS BPL Partridge: 2.993 (Partridge)
   Healy 4,1969c:23-4
   Irish Fireside n.d.:130
   O'Conor 1901:19, with a 2(4)-line chorus.
   617 [190-?]:38
   Songs and Recitations 5,1978:14-5

   b: REC Ian Campbell Folk Group, Transatlantic TRA 110
   b: *The Folk Trailer*, Trailer LER 2019
   cl: Fred Fuco, AFS 2409 B3
   High Level Ranters, Trailer LER 2007
   Owen McBride, Fox Hollow FH 1968 R13053 (A5)

   b: MEL Alf Edwards, Prestige/Int. 13060 "The Rocky Road"
   Gallagher/Peroni 1936: #52
   O'Neill 1903:211 (#1116)
   Petrie 1855:175 "The Rocky Road"
   Scanlon 1923:74

◊ Dungiven Cricket Match *(H669) 179*

   IREL Moulden 1979:45-6 reports a version collected from Eddie Butcher.

◊ March of the Men of Garvagh *(H17b) 180*

   IREL *JIFSS* 13,1913:29

◊ Ta Ra, Limavady *(H706) 180*

   IREL Moulden 1979:144-5

◊ The Knights of Malta *(H146) 180*

   Dean-Smith 1954: "Sons of Levi"
   Brunnings 1981: "Sons of Levi"

Sam Henry's Songs of the People

BRIT Greig 1907-11(1963): #155 "The Sons of Levi"
  Ord 1930:392-3
  Cf. Sharp/Karpeles 1974,2:489-90 (#363) "The Sons of Levi"

AMER Fuson 1931:203 "The Sons of Levi," 3-stanza fragment with 4-line chorus.
  WPA Kentucky [1939?]:66 "True Born Sons of Levi"; (m) p. (8)

REC Mary Alice, Peter Amidon, Folk-Legacy FSI 86 (B5) "Bright Morning Star"
  Walker, Lola Caldwell, [cl:] AFS 294 B; New World NW 291 (B2) "Bright and Morning Star"
  Valley Folk, Topic 12T 192 (A6) "Sons of Levi"

◇ **The Bright Orange Stars of Coleraine** *(H 87a) 181*

l: For a documentary sample of Orange songs and processional Lambeg drumming, see Samuel Charters's recording, "The Orangemen of Ulster," Folkways FW 3003, 1961.

◇ **Neuve Chappelle** *(H 526) 182*

Brunnings 1981: "Neuve Chappelle"

g: This not only sings to the tune of "The Rambling Irishman" but seems to be a World War I version of that song; see Fowke 1965:92 and her notes for Folk-Legacy FSC 10 (A1), where "The Rambling Irishman" is sung by Tom Brandon (Ontario); see also Creighton 1971:43 "The Roving Journeyman."

B12

The emigrant's farewell: Goodbye home

Sam Henry's Songs of the People

Lovely Armoy [H9: 12 Jan 1924]

o: (m) "The Lover's Curse."

Source not given.

s: The last words in each verse of this beautiful song ... are hardly capable of being represented in musical notation. They sound, when sung by the traditional singer, like a descending quiver in the voice, and convey a tender sorrow which grief has shattered into words.

[Slight differences between printed (Bp) and typed copies: Bp in 6, Wt in 3, both in the key of C; Bt and Dt (different copies, though same typewriter), 2 stanzas only, set in 3 in the key of D.]

[Bp] Key C. [Bt, Dt] Key D. With tender feeling.

Draw near, my kind friends and relations,
I'm going to take my farewell
I'm bound for a far distant nation,
No longer in Armoy to dwell.
I'm leaving that sweet little village
Wherein I was reared as a boy,
And now for to leave you it grieves me,
And part from you, lovely Armoy.

By the banks of yon bonnie Bush water,
Where fishes swim neatly and fair,
By those banks I have oftentimes wandered
In an evening when free from all care,
By those banks I have oftentimes wandered
In the evening when free from employ;
No wonder it grieves me to leave you
And part with you, lovely Armoy.

I'm taking my leave off this evening
As bright Phoebus declines from my view;
I take my last walk round the garden
Where the flowers are all sparkled with dew,
With banks of blown roses all around me,
There the fair maid oft met me with joy;
No wonder it grieves me to leave you
And part from you, lovely Armoy.

We kissed and shook hands and then parted;
I started my course without fail
Till I came to the city of Belfast,
Where our good ship lay ready to sail.

Strict orders were given to board her,
My pen I no longer employ,
No wonder it grieves me to leave you,
I'll be far from you, lovely Armoy.

Monk McClamont's "Farewell to Articlave" [H65b: 7 Feb 1925]

s: (m) = H65a "Altimover Stream"; "The Shepherd's Boy," "Bathing in the Roe," "The Purple Man's Dream."

Author Monk McClamont (Articlave; emigrant to America c. 1860).

s: This song is the best of the compositions of Monk McClamont, ... who emigrated to America about 1860 and came back [a] poorer [man] than when he went. His remarkable name he derived from the occupier of Dartries House, Monk Eagleson, who came from Strabane district in the 1798 Rebellion times. The air is very popular and has been adapted to various songs....

Key G.

'Twas in the year of forty, and the year of forty, too,
The time I do remember when I bid my friends adieu,
Our noble ship *Provincial*, well fitted for the sea,
And commanded by our captain bold, bound for America.

'Twas on the fourth of April we sailed from Derry Quay,
Our vessel being well manned, bound for America,
Contrary to our wishes, our sails did scarcely fill,
And by our captain's orders we anchored at Moville.

But early the next morning when I on deck did stand
And looking all around me, I saw my native land,
'Twould mind you of a desert, your eyes with tears would fill
When I looked across sweet Articlave and the castle of Downhill.

When I looked by the Tower I saw my native strand,
Like Moses on Mount Nebo when he viewed the promised land,

My mind being bound for rambling, as I told you
  before,
I turned my back upon the scene I might behold
  no more.

Farewell unto sweet Articlave, where first my
  breath I drew,
Farewell my loyal comrades, a long farewell to
  you,
For now I'm on the ocean and all our sails are
  full
And so swiftly as she does pass by the isle of
  Innistrahull.

The names of our good officers I mean for to
  relate,
Our captain's name was William, and Primshaw
  was our mate,
He was as good a captain as e'er a ship did rule,
And the other was a seaman brave that came from
  Liverpool.

The second mate's Cabena, his station does well
  fill,
Like his father with Sir Hervey in the castle of
  Downhill,
When he was young and tender, he bound himself
  to sea,
And he gained that promotion before that he was
  free.

As for our commander, he is so good a man,
I am scarce fit to praise him when I do all I can,
But that God may be his pilot wherever he may
  be,
And keep him on the chosen path, from danger
  set him free.

I beg to be excused, I have no more to say,
The pilot he has come on board on the eighteenth
  day of May,
One hundred miles to the nearest port, he told
  our captain so,
Our orders were: 'Prepare yourselves, ye have
  several roads to go.'

1.4: ... Americee. [Dt]
8.4: ... path and from ... [Dt]
9.4: ... yourselves, you have ... [Dt]

Hannah M'Kay / The Pride of Artikelly

[H656: 20 Jun 1936]

Source: Frank Kealey (Ballysally, Coleraine).

s: ... from the full and liberal repertoire of Mr
Frank Kealey....

Key C.

B12 / The emigrant's farewell

Adieu, lovely Erin of sweet delectation,
Likewise to Magilligan where I did dwell,
The ship bells are warning for quick emigration,
I'll bid Grania's heroes and daughters farewell.
But how can I think for to leave this grand island,
Where love, peace and friendship beam bright in
  each eye,
Where young men are merry and maidens are
  smiling
And sympathy's glow in each bosom is nigh?

Artikelly I leave and its rural plantation,
Where the blackbird and linnet enchant every tree;
My heart oftimes beats with increased palpitation
As the thrushes in chorus sound sweet harmony,
Where Flora's gay mantle decks these shady bowers
And on the green pastures the lambkins do play,
Where once in my childhood I gathered wild flowers
And with my young schoolmates I loved for to
  stray.

On a mild summer's evening for soft recreation
I rambled the banks where the Curley streams
  flow,
Where young men and maidens in love's admiration
Encircled the verge where the primroses grow,
The small trout and salmon seem in consternation
As in this pleasant water they sport and they play,
Yet are vanished those pleasures; my heart with
  vexation
Is filled with the thought of sweet Hannah M'Kay.

Sweet were the hours in love's conversation
With this charming fair one to breathe the fresh
  air,
She was the object of my adoration,
My joy and my comfort, my pride and my care;
Oftimes I roamed from her father's grand dwelling,
And I thought by the Curley for life to reside.
My degree has expelled me to some foreign nation,
Which makes some new lover to make her his bride.

Near Drumachose church, where we oft made our
  station,
Where Laura O'Donnell's fond heart bled with love,
Young Hannah still shone like the north
  constellation,
With countenance magnetic and mild as a dove.
I ardently long to make her my relation
And I fain by the Curley would make time delay,
But now its streams downward in murmurs flow,
  telling
That gone is the lover of Hannah M'Kay.

Farewell, Artikelly, where I was excited,
Likewise unto Newtown where steam engines fly;
If I would return, I might well be delighted
With this pretty maiden to live and to die.
When I sail down Lough Foyle for Columbia's
  nation
I'll think on that bower where oft I did stray,
And heave a deep sigh for that nice habitation
When I think of that bonny lass, Hannah M'Kay.

187

Sam Henry's Songs of the People

Farewell, Ballycastle [H210: BLp, 19 Nov 1927]

Source: John Henry Macaulay (Bog Oak Shop, Ballycastle).

s: The words only appeared in our special Ballycastle issue of 1926 but are now republished to their appropriate air, in response to several requests.

[BLp appears in 4-line stanzas which fit half the tune; Bt is in 8-line stanzas with the same line length.]

Key D.

Farewell Ballycastle, farewell to thy bowers
That echo the note of the blackbird in spring,
Farewell to thy braes where the white hawthorn flowers,
Returning with summer, their sweet odours bring;
Away o'er the deep through the hurricane's danger
From friends who have eve[r] been kindly and true,
I go to a home in the land o[f] the stranger,
While sadly but fondly my heart beats adieu.

When morning appears, with an exile's devotion
My thoughts upon rising of Erin will be,
And with every zephyr that springs from the ocean
I'll waft back a sigh, Drumavoley, to thee.
When the evening stars shed their light on the billow
And seabirds are calling their mates to the shore,
I will turn away sadly and moisten my pillow
With tears for the friends I shall never see more.

In that land far away where the gold-laden fountains
From snow-covered Egmont roll proudly along,
I'll think of Knocklayde, and the far distant mountains
Shall ring with the strain of an old Irish song.
The gay round of pleasure will often remind me
Of scenes where young maidens their old story tell;
How often I'll sigh for the dear ones behind me,
To whom, with my loved one, I now bid farewell.

1.8: ... sadly and fondly ... [Dt]
2.5: ... star sheds its ... [Dt]
3.8: ... loved ones, I ... [Dt]

3.2: Egmont = a mountain in New Zealand. [s: BLp]

Carnanbane [H100a: Lp, 10 Oct 1925]

o: (m) "Star of the County Down."

Source: William Laverty (Drumafivey, Stranocum), from James Young (Drum, Dungiven) c. 1885.

[Lp, Dt] s: ... Carnanbane is situated [Dt: about] 2.5 miles from Park and 3.5 miles from Claudy, in the Glenrannel valley, and [Lp: about] 1.5 miles from the Tyrone border.

[Copy of printed column from Linenhall Library (Belfast) courtesy of John Moulden. Bt typed in 8-line stanzas; UCLA photocopy is somewhat indistinct. It differs slightly from Dt.]

[Lp, Dt] Key F. [Bt] Key G.

When I was young and foolish still, Americay ran in my head,
I from my native country strayed, which caused me many a tear to shed.
I left that place was nate, complete, where gently blossoms the hawthorn,
On the twenty-sixth of Ap-er-ile, it being on a Friday's morn.

My friends and comrades convoyed me to near a place called Claudy town,
And when our parting did draw near, the tears from them came trinkling down.
With courage stout I stepped out and down the Faughan took my way,
And in the space of two short hours my course I stopped on Derry Quay.

188

It's down the Foyle we then did steer and dropped our sails on Moville strand,
And as the sun was going down I lost the sight of Paddy's land.
Our seamen stout they stepped out while the headwinds did softly blow,
Still hoping for a pleasanter gale; next morning we to sea would go.

But when I'm landed in St. John's, I'll fill my glass and grieve no more,
Still hoping for the pleasant hours when I'll return to the Irish shore,
And when I'm in the fields alone or wandering o'er Columbia's land,
I'll often think of going home to the girl I left in Carnanbane.

1.2: And from my native land I strayed, [Dt]; ... many's the ... [Bt]
 .3: Where gentle blossoms ... [Bt]; Where gently blossomed ... [Dt]
 .4: ... of Aperile, ... [Bt]
2.1: ... me until we came to Claudy ... [Dt]
 .2: And then ... [Bt]
 .4: ... course was ... [Dt]
3.4: While hoping ... [Bt]
4.3: ... Columbia's strand, [Bt]

Carntogher's Braes [H237: 26 May 1928]

g: "Erin's Isle."

Source: Betty Kirkpatrick (Broad St, Magherafelt).

s: Carntogher pronounced as four syllables -- Car-an-togh-er.

Key G.

Above all the lands upon this earth there's none so dear to me
As that little spot called Erin's isle that lies beyond the sea,
And in that land there's not a place more worthy of my praise
Than where I spent my youthful days round Carntogher's braes.

How pleasant it was to roam those hills just at the early dawn,
Upon the north the Foyle flows free, to the east the river Bann,
And when the sun, his day's work done, far westward flings his rays,
His last bright beams do fall in streams round Carntogher's braes.

B12 / *The emigrant's farewell*

On a summer Sunday evening up to these hills we'd go,
The boys and girls would all flock there from the green plains below,
On Carn top we'd sit and sing some fine old Irish lays
Or dance until the sun went down on Carntogher's braes.

I little thought in those dear days that I would have to roam
And leave behind those heath-clad hills, likewise my native home,
But cruel fate has ordered it that I must sail the seas
And bid adieu, my love, to you and Carntogher's braes.

But when our fortune it is made and we're returning home,
Our former sports we will renew and we'll no longer roam;
When the good ship steers us back again for ever from our quay,
We'll dig for turf instead of gold round Carntogher's braes.

3.1: ... summer evening ... [Dt]

The Flower of Craiganee [H749: 2 Apr 1938]

g: "Johnny Hartin." Other title: "Craiganee."

Source not given.

s: Craiganee is two miles east of Ballintoy.

Key D.

Oh, come all ye sacred muses from high Knocksoghey hill
And give me your assistance while I use my slender quill,
For I'll go out to seek a home across the raging sea,
I'll bid farewell to all my friends and to old Craiganee.

When I rise up in the morning, I'll oil and comb my hair,
And dress myself in superfine and go to see my fair;
Her name I will not mention, lest offended she might be,

189

Sam Henry's Songs of the People

She is the fairest flower that ever bloomed in Craiganee.

When she rises in the morning, she walks along the quay
To watch the foaming billows as they roll o'er the sea;
She's watching for the small boat that bore her love away,
And she says, 'Young Johnny Harkin, boy, you're far from Craiganee.'

'Tis true I love old Erin's isle and her I do adore
Above other nations that stretch from shore to shore;
When I am on the ocean, neither home nor friends can see,
I'll still think on my old sweetheart I left in Craiganee.

Farewell unto you, Rathlin rocks that guard our native shore,
Likewise unto my old sweetheart, whom I may ne'er see more,
But if we chance to meet again and have our liberty,
We'll live and love each other as we did in Craiganee.

The Hills of Tandragee [H730: 20 Nov 1937]

Source: coll. James Carmichael (Waring St, Ballymena).

s: Another song from the collection of James Carmichael, ... whose enthusiasm is saving many old songs and dance airs in his district from oblivion.

Key C. Slow.

When my love wakes in the morning, she oils and combs her hair,
And dresses in her superfine all for to meet her dear;
Her name I will not mention, lest she should offended be,
For she is the fairest creature that dwells in Tandragee.

The time is drawing nigh, brave lads, when I must leave you here
And part with all my comrades, likewise my sweetheart dear,
For her beauty I admire above all that I can see,
And her killing glances bring the blush on the hills of Tandragee.

Farewell unto my native rocks, likewise you grand old shore,
Where with my daily comrades I've trod the sands all o'er,
And when I'm on the ocean wide, nor house nor home can see,
I'll be thinking on you, Rosie dear, that dwells in Tandragee.

When my love wakes in the morning, she walks down to the sea
To watch for the ship returning that bore her love away;
She'll watch the foaming billows as they roll in from the sea,
Saying, 'Oh, poor Johnny Hartin, you're far from Tandragee.'

My Girl from Donegal [H4: 8 Dec 1923]

Other titles: "Roisin Dubh."

Source not given.

s: Vocalists may make any little variations in time necessary to accommodate the rhythm of the words.

Key F. Slow and with rhythm.

Now, Derry boys, I wish you joys,
My eyes with big tears fill,
I'm bound today for Americay
In a big ship from Moville;
My time is brief, there's no relief,
And pride must have a fall,
And I'm leaving now my Aileen Oge,
My girl from Donegal.

For she has eyes like summer skies,
The sunlight's in her hair,
Her snow-white breast and slender waist,
And her face beyond compare;
From Derry Quay to Dublin Bay
None can compare at all
To my pretty little Aileen Oge,
My girl from Donegal.

I would be glad, but times are bad,
To work on Irish soil,
But pick and spade are poorly paid
From the Slaney to the Foyle.

B12 / The emigrant's farewell

I've wandered east, I've wandered west,
And my luck's gone to the wall,
And I'm leaving now my Aileen Oge,
My girl from Donegal.

And when out west I'll do my best
From morn till set of sun,
And when I tread the Irish sod
My fortune will be won;
With eyes so bright and step so light
I'll owe no one at all,
And I'll wed my pretty Aileen Oge,
My girl from Donegal.

1.7: Aileen Oge = young Eileen. [s: Bp]

The Flower of Sweet Dunmull

[H1: 17 Nov 1923]

s: (m) "The Top of Sweet Dunmull" (Petrie 1902: #560).

Source: (w, m) Nancy Harbison (Ballywillan, Portrush).

[Bp written] "The Flower" was Nancy Rankin of Slimague. Song at least 100 years old.

Key C.

It's in my native country, old Ireland, I do dwell.
Some days I spent in pleasure, far more than tongue can tell,
Till fate, that fickle mystery, my course pursued me still,
Which parted me from sweet Dunmull, that beautiful verdant hill.

Dunmull, it is a pretty place, most curious to be seen,
Its oval shape and lofty top all covered with shamrocks green,
From there the country you may view for twenty miles and more,
It's likewise situated just two miles from the shore.

The river Bann we have in view, and the town of sweet Coleraine,
The road that leads to the Causeway o'er the braes of sweet Kilgrain,
From the Malin Point to the Causeway Head the ship lies in our view;
I could part with all, my charming maid, but how can I part with you?

Last May eve so blithe we met, some pastime to pursue,
'Twas there sweet lovely Nancy, she first came in my view,
Her eyes did shine like the stars at night or the moon when she's in full,
And in my breast she still remains the flower of sweet Dunmull.

When I am in a far-off land where liberty does shine,
And the foaming billows 'twixt us boil, I hope I'll see the time
When I'll clasp you to my breast, my dear, saying all our joys are full,
And some evening fair we'll take the air on the top o' sweet Dunmull.

The Faughan Side

[H621: 26 Oct 1935]

Source: D. Ellis (Langford Lodge, Crumlin, Co. Antrim).

Key G.

A stream like crystal, it runs down
As plainly may be seen,
It's there you'll find the Irish oak
Trimmed with the ivy green,
The shamrock, rose and thistle,
The lily, too, beside:
All flourish there together, boys,
Along by the Faughan side.

Oh, could you see that lovely place
All in the summer time,
Each bush and tree, they look so gay,
Each meadow in its prime,
The blackbird and the golden thrush,
They tune their notes so gay,
But still I had the notion
Of going to Americ-ay.

Farewell unto this lonely place,
From it I mean to roam,
To leave my friends in Ireland
And my dear old Irish home;
Farewell unto my comrades
And the place where they reside,

Sam Henry's Songs of the People

For many a happy night we spent
Along the Faughan side.

It's about two miles from Derry
To the bridge of Drumahoe,
Where many a happy a night we spent
In the days of long ago,
Where lambs do sport and fair maids court
And the small fish gently glide,
In the blooming spring the small birds sing
Along the Faughan side.

The leaving of his lovely place
It grieves my heart full sore,
And the leaving of my own true love
It grieves me ten times more,
But if ever I return again
I will make her my bride,
And I'll take her in my arms, boys,
Along the Faughan side.

Finn Waterside [H240: 16 Jun 1928]

o: (m) "Jackets Green."

[Dt] Source: Alex. Thompson (Alla, near Park, Co. Derry).

[Written on Bp] Whistle also Claudy Green Black Bird of Carna[?] Armstrong[?]

Key D.

As I roved out one evening, being in the summer time,
I heard a voice made me rejoice, to wait I did incline,
I overheard my own true love, so sweet as he did sing,
'Come down along Finn waterside,' he made the woods to ring.

My parents thought all in my prime for to banish me away,
To dwell among the Indians and leave sweet Inver Bay,
But I'll let them know before I go, whatever may betide,
That I have a true love of my own, dwells nigh Finn waterside.

There is many a clever tall young man lives nigh Finn waterside,

But above them all, both great and small, I would rather be his bride,
I would rather hear my own true love sing in the month of May
Than all the herring fish or ling that swim round Inver Bay.

Farewell unto Finn waterside, where oftimes I have been,
Likewise unto sweet Inver Bay, adieu, you woods so green,
You lofty mountains I must cross, they do call Barnesmore,
Down by the rocks and yon rural well and along by the salt sea shore.

2.1: ... prime to banish ... [Dt]
 .4: ... dwells near Finn ... [Dt]
4.3: ... cross, the gap of Barnesmore [Dt]
 .4: ... and rural well and along the ... [Dt]

Gelvin Burn [H667: 5 Sep 1936]

s: (m) "Owenreagh's Banks."

Source: D. Nutt, sr (Feeny, Co. Derry).

Key E flat.

Ye banks and braes of Gelvin Burn, where oftimes I have roved,
And to ye maids of sweet Drumsurn and Pellipar's green groves:
From Templemoyle down to Kilhoyle, I take my leave of you,
For I must go far from the Roe, my fortune to pursue.

Benevenagh Braes and Donald's Hill and the Keady right between,
Where MacQuillan and his valiant men were nobly fighting seen,
The sweet bluebells of ferny dells no more shall meet my view,
For I must go far from the Roe, my fortune to pursue.

Dungiven with its lofty towers and ruined abbey grey,
Where O'Cahan and his valiant men once ruled with princely sway
From Loughermore down to the shore, I now must bid adieu,

For I must go far from the Roe, my fortune to
pursue.

There's Meenard, Dart and Sawell, and the high
hills of Tyrone,
And all their mountain gorges and away to
Innishowen,
From dark Glenshane to Carnanbane I take my
leave of you,
For I must go far from the Roe, my fortune to
pursue.

But when we reach Columbia's shore away far in
the west,
Our hearts will turn to Gelvin Burn, the spot that
we love best,
We hope that friends we'll meet once more and
former joys renew,
And no more go far from the Roe, our fortune to
pursue.

Glenrannel's Plains [H100b: Lp, 10 Oct 1925]

Source: Tilda Thorpe (Altibrian, Articlave); author James Devine (Lough Ash, Donemana) c. 1885.

[Absent from B, D, W. Copy of printed column from Linenhall Library (Belfast) by courtesy of John Moulden. Henry does not indicate the tune to which this is to be sung. It can be shoe-horned to fit the same melody as H100a, but the fit is rather lumpy.]

Farewell to sweet Glenrannel's plains and
streamlets winding clear,
Where on its banks the cheerful swains and lovely
maids appear,
To cross the wide Atlantic main is now their
destiny,
    *Farewell to sweet Glenrannel's plains, a long
farewell to thee.*

Farewell, my friends and neighbours all and
comrades dear, adieu,
My recollection will recall the hours I spent with
you,
My memory will still retain your friendship unto
me,
    Farewell ...

There's one that I do rank above all that I leave
behind,
My own sweetheart, the girl I love, she's ever in
my mind,
My bursting bosom heaves with pain her tearful
eye to see,
    Farewell ...

I fear not the Atlantic waves, nor yet the ocean's
roar,
I do not fear a foreign grave upon a distant
shore,
The ties of love may rend in twain, this is what
troubles me,
    Farewell ...

Now fill your glasses, comrades dear, we'll drink
before we go,
My love, dry up those falling tears, which like
pure crystal flow,
For my affection will remain when far across the
sea,
    Farewell ...

Farewell to Sweet Glenravel

[H727: 30 Oct 1937]

Source: Jim Carmichael (Waring St, Ballymena).

s: Kindly supplied by Mr Jim Carmichael,... whose repertoire includes the choicest airs of Ulster.

Key G.

Farewell to sweet Glenravel, its flowery banks and
braes,
Its heath-clad hills and sparkling rills where the
sporting minnow plays,
'Twas there I spent my childhood days and many a
playful scene,
I've sported light when daisies white were studded
o'er the green.

Oh, happy were those days, the brightest and the
best,
When I plucked the flowers among those bowers
and sought the wild bird's nest,
But childhood's days can't always last and
boyhood passes o'er,
And now I roam afar from home unto a distant
shore.

Wherever fate may bid me wait, my thoughts shall
e'er return
To the dear old glen that gave me birth and the
chatter of the burn,
But while blood flows within my veins and hope
lights up my breast,
I'll always dream of my island home -- of all the
world, the best.

I cross the deep blue ocean to toil with busy men,
Nor do I know my eyes shall e'er behold my native
glen;
If fortune only would be kind and succour me
awhile,
I'll steer away back o'er the ocean's track to the
land where the shamrocks smile.

Sam Henry's Songs of the People

Good-bye to friends and kindred all, to neighbours kind and true,
I will think of all when night shades fall upon the ocean blue,
I will think on the happy hallowed morn and the boom of the warning bell,
On bended knee, remember me in the land I love. Farewell!

The Glenshesk Waterside [H19a: 22 Mar 1924]

s: (m) "Star of the County Down" [only the second half of the tune].

Source: (w, m) coll. John H[enry] Macauley (Ballycastle); author P. C. J. McAuley, 80+ (Glenshesk, emigrant to America).

[Bp written] Time wrong. [over printed sol-fa:]
m / s : - : m / m : r : d / r : - : r / -
[where / are vertical measure marks].

l: Both original and corrected versions of Bp, in 3, are given here.

s: The author ... taught school in Glenshesk, and went to America. He wrote -- "On the third day of my voyage to New York we sailed along the northern coast of Rathlin, and as I came on deck I looked south and recognised Fair Head, and even the river as it flowed like a ribbon adown the glen into the sea, and the first line of the song at once burst from my lips."

Key F.

How often I have wandered forth along yon river side,
With mind elate and merry heart I oftimes did abide
In those sweet haunts of blissful hours with pleasure by my side,
But now I come to say farewell to the Glenshesk waterside.

My heart is sad because I see before me in review
The heathery braes and winding vales I oftimes have passed thro';
I onward look with cheerful hope o'er the billows safe to ride,
But still look back to the days I spent by the Glenshesk waterside.

Ye groves and woodlands that resound with merry songsters' voice,
I wish I could, as in former days, along with them rejoice,
But fate proposes I must go, in foreign lands abide,
And bid farewell to the friends so dear by the Glenshesk waterside.

Ye mountain tops that shine so bright as the orb of day ascends,
While from your elevated cliffs the holly bright depends,
And ye massive high projecting rocks that do the glen divide,
I'll think of ye when far away from the Glenshesk waterside.

Alas, no more shall I enjoy those quiet sequest[e]r'd hours
That I have spent 'mong Glenshesk's braes and her fragrant shady bowers,
No more I'll view the limpid streams where fishes nimbly glide,
No more, alas, shall I e'er see the Glenshesk waterside.

5.2: ... spent on Glenshesk braes and in her fragrant bowers, [Dt]

Lovely Glenshesk (IIa)

[H28a: [Bp] "Two Ballycastle songs," 24 May 1924]

[cf. H544 "Lovely Glenshesk (I)," a different song altogether]

Source: author John M'Cormick (Greenan, Culfeightrin); (m) John Henry Macauley (Ballycastle).

s: This fine air was taken down by me.... I am not aware that it has been recorded previously.
...
The air also suits the well-known song, "The Squire's Daughter, or Young Mary of Accland."

o: Tune written incorrectly.

l: Note the variety of words that presumably are intended to rhyme with "Glenshesk."

Key C.

B12 / *The emigrant's farewell*

This evening I take my departure from the lovely
  town where I was bred,
My friends and relations are round me, which
  cause me salt tears for to shed
When I think that I'm going to leave you, never
  more for to see the old place,
I grieve for my old tender parents and the
  parting of you, lovely Glenshesk.

I am come to the age of discerning, I am taught
  for to keep the commands,
Every one gets their own gift, and feeling sends
  me to a far foreign land.
Like the bee I will go gather honey, though I
  wander to many a strange place;
No wonder it grieves me to leave you and part
  with you, lovely Glenshesk.

The Israelites they were in bondage and they
  murmured at their going away,
They would rather turn back to their burthens
  and work at them both night and day,
But Moses gave them the bright promise; alas,
  they did grieve and transgress.
No wonder it grieves me to leave you and part
  from you, lovely Glenshesk.

Farewell to you, hills and green valleys and ye
  woods that spontaneously spring,
Where the feathered tribes of all species and th
  cuckoo melodious does sing,
All these beauties I'm parting this evening and
  my sorrow I think no disgrace,
No wonder it grieves me to leave you and part
  from you, lovely Glenshesk.

Only Adam and Eve's disobedience, we all would
  be happy and free,
The serpent tempted Eve in the garden to eat of
  the forbidden tree;
We would never have to work at hard labour, we
  all would be happy and blessed.
I hope we'll avoid all temptations when far, far
  from lovely Glenshesk.

1.2: ... which causes me salt tears to shed [Dt]
2.2: ... gift and feeling, and feeling ... [Dt]
3.1: ... bondage, and murmured at going ... [Dt]
4.2: ... cuckoo melodiously sings, [Dt]
5.3: ... have to sweat at ... [Dt]

In Praise of the Glen [H547: 26 May 1934]

[cf. H544 "Lovely Glenshesk (I)"]

o: (m) "The Lover's Curse."

Source not given.

Key C.

This evening I take my departure
From the lovely place where I was bred,
While my friends and relations flock round me,
Which causes my tears for to shed
When I think I am going to leave them
And never to stand in this place;
No wonder it grieves me to leave them
In the parting you, lovely Glenshesk.

I feel like the Hebrews in bondage
Who murmured at their going away,

Sam Henry's Songs of the People

And would rather turn back to their burdens
Which oppressed them by night and by day,
But Moses gave to them the promise
Of a land where their souls might find rest;
No wonder it grieves me to leave you
And part with you, lovely Glenshesk.

Farewell to you, Glenshesk sweet waters,
Sweet stream that does gently flow down,
And likewise to sweet Ballycastle,
A place of great fame and renown,
And to Knocklayde, the pride of old Ireland,
By nature a beautiful place;
No wonder it grieves me to leave you
In the parting you, lovely Glenshesk.

My full name it is John M'Cormick,
I have penned these few verses in rhyme,
And I hope that we'll all meet in glory,
In happiness ever to shine.
I hope that we all meet in glory.
Too much of your time I did waste,
So give me your blessing this evening,
And a long, long farewell to Glenshesk.

Brow of Sweet Knocklayd

[H19b: 22 Mar 1924]

s: Sung to the same air as "Glenshesk Waterside" [= H19a, "Star of the County Down"].

Source not given.

It was on a pleasant evening for pleasure as I
  stray'd
To view the pinks and primroses that bloom on
  sweet Knocklayd,
I came into a grove so green, I laid me down to
  rest,
I then beheld bright Phoebus, he was sinking in
  the west.

And such a charming prospect I'm sure I've
  never seen:
The small birds' notes were charming all in their
  groves of green,
They tuned their notes melodiously on the tree
  that was my shade,
And the lambkins fondly sport and play on the
  brow of sweet Knocklayd.

Now all those pleasures I must leave and bid a
  fond adieu,
Likewise unto my comrade boy: how can I part
  from you?
For many the pleasant evening together we have
  strayed
When we went to pull the blackberries on the
  brow of sweet Knocklayd.

Farewell to friends and parents dear, I leave you
  for awhile,
May providence protect you, kind fortune on you
  smile,
For I'm going to cross the ocean to some far-off
  foreign shore;
I'm going to cross the ocean where the foaming
  billows roar.

Then just as I was rising I was struck mute with
  surprise:
The moon was just appearing behind yon cloudy
  skies,
She was most glorious to behold, she was covered
  with a shade,
And she threw a deep reflection on the brow of
  sweet Knocklayd.

1.4: ... Phoebus, a-sinking ... [Dt]
2.4: ... fondly sported on ... [Dt]
4.3: ... to a far-off ... [Dt]

Owenreagh's Banks

[H225: 3 Mar 1928]

Source: (w) Edward Devlin (Drumsurn, Co. Derry); (m) Anna Devlin, fiddle (Kilhoyle, Drumsurn), from her father, John Devlin, from his father, also John Devlin, from his father, Edward Devlin (all from Kilhoyle).

s: ... This is a remarkable instance of the preservation of an old air in the verbal memory of the people, as it has not until now been recorded. The Owenreagh is one of the tributaries of the Roe and flows through the beautifully romantic glens south of Dungiven. The hold over the last note in each line is equivalent to five pulses.

Key E flat.

Farewell to sweet Owenreagh's banks and
  streamlets winding clear,
And those sweet glens where cheerful swains
  and maidens do appear,
To cross the broad Atlantic sea is now my
  destiny,
Farewell to sweet Owenreagh's banks and a long
  farewell to thee.

I do not fear the Atlantic waves, nor yet the
  ocean's roar,
I do not fear a foreign grave all on a foreign
  shore,
The ties of love now rent in two, it's that which
  troubles me,
Farewell to sweet Owenreagh's banks and a long
  farewell to thee.

There's one I rank above the rest of those I
  leave behind,
She is the darling of my heart and she's ever in
  my mind,

My bursting bosom throbs with pain her tearful
  eyes to see,
Farewell to sweet Owenreagh's banks and a long
  farewell to thee.

Come, comrades, fill the parting glass, we'll
  drink before we go,
And, love, dry up those fallen tears that like
  the crystal flow,
For my true love will be the same, though far
  across the sea,
Farewell to sweet Owenreagh's banks and a long
  farewell to thee.

The Point Maid

[H42b: "Two Magilligan songs," 30 Aug 1924]

g: "Edward Conn."

Source: former resident, 70 (Magilligan).

s: The air and words taken down by me from a [Dt:
former] resident [Dt: of Magilligan], over 70
years of age, who sang them in traditional style
in a manner which printer's ink cannot quite
capture.

h: Scraps of text recalled, not recorded, by
Eddie Butcher.

Key F. Slow, and with intense emotion.

My father is a farmer, his name is Edward Conn,
Through his hills I've oftimes ranged with my net
  in my hand,
But now it is all over, and sore against my will,
That I'll have to leave my old sweetheart and now
  bid her farewell.

The Point is it a purty place where boats they are
  hauled to,
I'll put my foot on shipboard and sail the ocean
  through,
And when that I'm safe landed all on the other
  side,
I will send you back a letter, love, whatever may
  betide.

I'll send you back a letter, love, and seal it with
  a kiss
In remembrance of the purty days and of our
  former bliss,
It's not forgetting the young man who thought to
  rival me,

B12 / The emigrant's farewell

Oh, so there, my purty Peggy, it's never you
  slight me.

As I went a-walking along the briny wave,
Still thinking on brave sailors who meet a watery
  grave,
But I'll put my dependence all on the God above
That he will send me back again to wed the girl I
  love.

It's not for the sake of friends or lands I'm
  grieved for going away,
But for sake of that fair charmer who did my heart
  betray,
But if she would restore to me my happy heart
  again,
I never would be grieved at the crossing o'er the
  main.

In leaving sight now of the Tower it makes my
  heart to bleed
When I think on the dangers in crossing o'er the
  deep,
But if I had purty Peggy all on ship aboard with
  me,
I never would return again unto this count-er-ee.

It's now to conclude and finish, I mean to make an
  end:
Farewell unto my neighbours, likewise unto my
  friends,
Farewell unto the Lower Doaghs, where I have
  oftimes strayed,
All for to meet that charmer that is call-ed the
  Point maid.

1.2: ... I've oftentimes ranged ... net stick in ...
  [Dt]
2.4: ... letter, whatever ... [Dt]
3.1: ... letter and ... [Dt]
5.1: ... friends nor lands ... [Dt]

1.2: The net is for rabbiting in the sand-hills. [s:
  Wp]
6.1: Tower = the Martello Tower at Magilligan Point.
  [s: Wp]

Adieu to the Banks of the Roe

[H245: 21 Jul 1928]

Author schoolteacher Maxwell (Dungiven) c. 1870.

[Bt] Key D. [Bp] Key E flat. Slowly and tenderly.

Adieu to the banks of the Roe,
My happiest moments are flown;
Must I leave the dear country I know
For scenes far remote and unknown?

Sam Henry's Songs of the People

On leaving old Erin I feel
Deep grief and unspeakable woe,
Farewell to the burn of Termeil,
Owenreagh, Owenbeg and the Roe.

Farewell to the church on the hill,
The pastor who taught me the truth,
I pray that Jehovah may still
Protect this dear guide of my youth.

Farewell to sweet Banagher Glen,
Benbradagh tops covered with show,
I'll never perhaps see again
The old church and the banks of the Roe.

Dear brothers and sisters, farewell,
Your tears at my absence may flow,
I feel as if bound by a spell
To you and the banks of the Roe.

As I climb up Australian hills
To dig for the gold buried low,
I'll think of my poor aged parents
And weep for the banks of the Roe.

Dungiven, sweet village, farewell,
Every object around thee is dear,
Every hill, every alley and dell
Where I rambled for many a year.

Necessity urges to roam,
But should fortune its favours bestow,
I'll return to Dungiven, my home,
And sleep near the banks of the Roe.

2.3: ... Termiel [Dt]
8.4: ... sleep by the ... [Dt]

Farewell to Slieve Gallen [H795: 18 Feb 1939]

Other title: "Wild Slieve Gallion Braes."

Source: Henry M'Daid (Ottawa St, Toronto [Canada]); author John Canavan (Lower Back, Stewartstown, Co. Tyrone).

s: A song of the Spanish-American War of 1898....

Key C.

To all intending emigrants I pen this simple lay:
Let one who lies in hospital, three thousand miles away,
Now warn you of the dangers that you may read and see,
And the fate of a young Irishman in the great land of the free.

I left my native country near to Slieve Gallen Brae,
Light-hearted as the moorcocks that among the heather play;
No hare on Carndaisy was then more fleet than I,
The day I left old Ireland and bid my last good-bye.

On board an ocean liner on the Foyle's black water's spray,
I went on board an emigrant bound for Americay,
And as I took my last fond look with heart both sad and sore,
I rued the day that drove me away from my lovely shamrock shore.

The morning that I landed I scaled two hundred pounds,
I feared not then brave Sullivan who wore the laurel crown;
Fresh from my native country with muscles strong as steel,
To no champion on Columbia's shore would I in fair play yield.

For six long months in search of work I wandered far and near,
Till at length I joined the army as an Irish volunteer;
No wonder on my wasting cheeks I felt the blush of shame,
To think I'd backed the Stars and Stripes against the sons of Spain.

I was put on board a battleship on that all fatal day,
When the Spanish fleet was captured and sent to Ego Bay;
A bombshell, fired that evening from out Fort Sanuwaile,
Left many a widow mourning and caused our hearts to fail.

Disabled now for life I am and never more to stray
By you, sweet Carndaisy or the banks of sweet Lough Fea;
Will e'er I see my parents there, who mourn my loss full sore,
Or my little Irish colleen from the town of Moneymore?

Ah, soon I'll not be dreaming of those happy days gone by,
For in a New York graveyard my wasting bones will lie;
Like thousands of my countrymen, I'll fill a nameless grave
Far, far from sweet Slieve Gallen Brae, where the blooming heather waves.

The Hills of Tyrone [H609: 3 Aug 1935]

Other titles: "Behind Yon Blue Mountain," "County ...."

Source: Mrs M'Elhinney (Chapel Rd Cottage, Dungiven).

Key A flat.

Above yon green mountains
Whose summit stands high,
I watched the sun rising
Out proud in the sky.
The grey clouds were drifting,
The sunbeams were thrown
On the lovely green hills that
Bedeck you, Tyrone.

The morning was bright,
But my heart is now low,
For far from those dear hills
I'll soon have to go
Across the wide ocean,
Forever to roam,
And leave far behind me
The hills of Tyrone.

My poor heart is breaking
With sorrow and pain
For friends and companions
I'll ne'er see again.
I'm bidding farewell
To the friends I have known,
And adieu to the wee lass
I leave in Tyrone.

When I'm far away
From the land of my birth,
I still will look on it
As the fairest on earth.
I will bless that dear land
That I now call my own
And the fair holy hills
Of the County Tyrone.

Bonny, Bonny [H75b:

[Bp] "Two songs of the press gang," 18 Apr 1925]

g: [The *Nightingale* (II)].

Source: (stanzas 1, 2, m) Peggy McGarry, 85 (Ballycastle) coll. Maud Houston (Coleraine); other stanzas by SH.

B12 / *The emigrant's farewell*

[Bp, Dt] s: This beautiful and pathetic air was taken down in 1909 .... The first two verses were obtained from the same source, the remainder are original [Bp: and anonymous] [Dt: and written by the Song Editor]. The *Nightingale* was one of his Majesty's ships used for the Press [Dt: gang.][Bp only: when the Navy's hungry maw was insatiable.]

Key C.

Bonny, bonny was my seat in yon red rosy yard,
And bonny was my portion in the town of
   Ballynagard:
Shade and shelter was for me till I began to fail,
Ye all may guess now my distress lies near the
   Nightingale.

While I go before these lords to let these nobles
   know
Our ship is in the ocean just ready for to go,
Surely all will get the call tomorrow or next day,
And my town boys will me convoy the day I go
   away.

Grief and woe that I must go to fight for
   England's king,
I neither know his friend nor foe, and war's a
   cruel thing;
The *Nightingale* is near at hand, my time at home
   is brief,
And Carey's streams and mountain land I part
   with bitter grief.

No more I'll walk the golden hills with Nancy by
   my side
Or dream along the sun-bright rills, or view my
   land with pride:
We sail away at dawn of day, the sails are ready
   set,
When old Benmore I see no more, I'll sigh with
   deep regret.

Now all must change and I must range across the
   ocean wide;
Our ship she may in Biscay's Bay lie low beneath
   the tide;
If I should fall by cannon ball, or sink beneath
   the sea,
Good people all, a tear let fall and mourn for
   mine and me.

If God should spare my graying hair and bring
   me back again,
I'd love far more my Antrim shore, its dark blue
   hills and rain,

Sam Henry's Songs of the People

Around its fires, my heart's desires, heaven
  grant till life shall fail,
And keep me far from cruel war and from the
  Nightingale.

Knox's Farewell [H49: 18 Oct 1924]

A Boveedy song.

s: (m) "My Love Nell"; l: (m) variant of "Star of the County Down."

Source: (w) 2: James H. Knox (Belfast), brother of the author, Samuel Knox (Boveedy, Co. Derry); (m) supplied by Sam Henry.

s: ... Mr Knox, in enclosing the song, informs us that he has been a reader of the *Constitution* since he got the first paper from the first parcel that ever reached Kilrea on the first day of publication. Some slight alterations of the two versions received were necessary to adapt the song to the only air which at once suited the metre and the mood of the writer.

Key G.

From old Carntogher's towering top
To the Bann's meandering stream,
From Coleraine's fair and flowery vale
To the cross at Ballynascreen,
Long have I wandered o'er the hills
In emerald mead and dell;
To all these scenes with melting heart
I now must bid farewell.

I now must cross the raging seas
And leave my native shore
To seek my fortune in the west
With comrades gone before.
You daughters fair and Erin's sons,
Whose praise no tongue can tell,
Stern fate has issued her decree
That I must say farewell.

Mourn not for me, my mother dear,
And, father, do not grieve,
Keep up your hearts, be of good cheer,
Though now my home I leave,
Keep up your hearts, be not dismayed;
God orders all things well;
It seems to me we'll meet again,
Though now I say farewell.

Adieu, farewell, Boveedy mine,
Where crystal fountains flow,
Far from your fair and fertile fields
O'er the ocean I must go
To wander far in foreign lands.
O'er Erin hangs a spell
Which causes me and many more
To bid our land farewell.

Farewell to Garvagh's sparkling streams
Where I met my comrades brave,
Some now are far from Erin's isle,
Some mould'ring in the grave.
To Aghadowey's lovely vale,
To the friends I love so well,
With tear-dimmed eye and heavy heart
I strive to say farewell.

Farewell, my brethren of Boveedy,
Ye valiant sons of light:
Oft have we met in social joy
And spent the festive night.
Each day your banner waves on high
And the sounds of music swell;
Still mind Sam Knox, though far away,
Whose pained heart sighed farewell.

The Emigrant's Farewell [H743: 19 Feb 1938]

Other titles: "... to Ireland," "... Love for His Native Land," "The Green Fields of (to) America(y) (Canada)."

Source: Dick Gilloway, learned "when a boy" from Jim Kane (Aughill, Magilligan).

s: ... Dick Gilloway's ... store [of songs] has often enriched this column....

Key G.

Farewell to old Ireland, the land of my childhood,
Which now and forever I am going to leave;
Farewell to the shores, the shamrock is growing,
It's the bright spot of beauty and home of the brave.
I will think on its valleys with fond admiration,
Though never again its green hills will I see,
I'm bound for to cross o'er that wide swelling ocean,
In search of fame, fortune and sweet liberty.

It's hard to be forced from the lands that we live in,
Our houses and farms obliged for to sell,

And to wander alone among Indians and strangers
To find some sweet spot where our children might
  dwell.
I've got a wee lassie I fain would take with me,
Her dwelling at present lies in County Down,
It would break my sad heart for to leave her
  behind me,
We will both roam together the wide world around.

So come away, Bessie, my own blue-eyed lassie,
Bid farewell to your mother and then come with
  me,
I'll do my endeavour to keep your mind cheery
Till we reach the green fields of Americay.
Our ship at the present lies below Londonderry,
To bear us away o'er the wide swelling sea;
May heaven be her pilot and grant her fair
  breezes
Till we reach the green fields of Americay.

Our farmers, our artists, our tradesmen are going
To seek for employment far over the sea,
Where they will get riches with care and industry;
There's nothing but hardship at home if you stay.
So cheer up your spirits, you lads and you
  lasses,
There's gold for the digging and lots of it, too,
And success to the hearts that have courage to
  venture,
And misfortune to him or to her that would rue.

There's brandy in Quebec at ten cents a quart,
  boys,
The ale in New Brunswick's a penny a glass,
There's rum in that sweet town they call Montreal,
  boys,
At inn after inn we will drink as we pass,
We'll call for a bumper of ale, wine and brandy,
And we'll drink to the health of those far away;
Our hearts will all warm at the thought of old
  Ireland
While we're in the green fields of Americay.

The Happy Shamrock Shore

[H69: 7 Mar 1925]

Other titles: "The Irishman's Farewell to His
Country," "The Shamrock ...."

Source not given.

Key D.

It was in our native country we might have lived
  well,
But times being bad and taxes high, our lands
  we were forced to sell,
To the wild woods of America it's we did venture
  o'er,
And the leaving of our native land and the happy
  shamrock shore.

It was on the fourth of April from Belfast we set
  sail,
And fortune did us favour with a sweet and
  pleasant gale,
And on the twenty-fourth of May we came to
  Baltimore,
Where full bumpers then we toasted round to the
  boys on the shamrock shore.

For six long weeks and better through the wild
  woods we strayed,
Sometimes the sky to cover us and the cold
  ground for a bed,
Wild beasts and venomous insects were ready to
  devour,
Sure, I could wish to be safe back on the happy
  shamrock shore.

Till at length my loving comrades and I had to
  divide,
We being four in number, three with great
  hardships died.
For the loss of my dear comrades, it grieved my
  heart full sore,
I could wish to live to leave their bones on the
  happy shamrock shore.

Ye sons of Erin, be advised and do not come
  away,
And do not come unto the lands they call America,
For I'll assure you it's not now as it was in the
  days of yore,
For there's numbers here that would like to be
  on the happy shamrock shore.

Ye sons of dear Hibernia, I now must bid adieu.
My mind was never easy since first I parted you,
But I'm in expectation to see you all once more,
And to live in splendour with the maids on the
  happy shamrock shore.

The Brown-Haired Lass (a)

[H116a: 30 Jan 1926]

o: (m) "Limerick Is Beautiful."

Source: (m) noted by James Adams, esq (Woodlands, Castlerock) learned in boyhood in Eglinton district; (w) multiple sources including (Lifford) (Stranocum).

s: The words of this old-time popular song have been obtained from places as far apart as Lifford and Stranocum....

m: Cf. "Songs of the People" #256, "The Black-Haired Girl" coll. James Moore.

Sam Henry's Songs of the People

l: The last line of the first stanza is reminiscent of "The Holy Ground (Fine Girl You Are)," which recently enjoyed pub-revival popularity; see, e.g., Behan 1967:51-2.

Key D.

Farewell to my native count-er-ee since I must bid adieu,
And likewise to my brown-haired girl since I must part with you,
Although it is against my mind that I'm crossing o'er the main,
Still I'm in hopes for to return to my brown-haired girl again.

My love's she's tall and handsome, her waist it is quite round,
Her cheeks they are like roses red, her hair a lovely brown,
Her teeth like polished ivory, her breath does smell like thyme,
It was her killing glances that stole this heart of mine.

Many's a pleasant evening on Manola's banks we spent,
With bonny woods and plantings which yield me much content,
It's there the thrush and blackbird do change their notes so gay;
It was never my intention, love, going to America.

One day as I stood musing, I thought my heart would break,
Still thinking of my brown-haired girl, not one word could I speak,
But as I took a notion of crossing o'er the main,
I went unto my brown-haired girl and told her so in plain.

'Oh Jamie, lovely Jamie, are you going to leave me here?
It was for your own sake, darling, that I shed many a tear.'
I clasped my darling to my breast while the crystal tears did flow,
Saying, 'There's not another breathing knows the pain we undergo.

'Our ship she is well manned, love, and we are bound for sea,
Our captain he gives orders, and him we must obey.'

'Aloft, aloft, my lively lads, without either fear or dread,
There is a south wind rising that will clear us round the head.'

Sailing down Lough Foyle, my boys, Magilligan we do pass,
I never will be happy till I wed my brown-haired lass,
And when we reach the far side, we'll drink a flowing glass,
And the toast will go right merrily round, here's a health to the brown-haired lass.

[2d tune]   [H116b: Wt=D(c)]

Source: (m) William Laverty, from his brother Sam Laverty (Dunaghy, Ballymoney).

s: ... The song to be sung as four-lined verse.

Key G.

[2d tune for both H116a and H116c; covers a half stanza.]

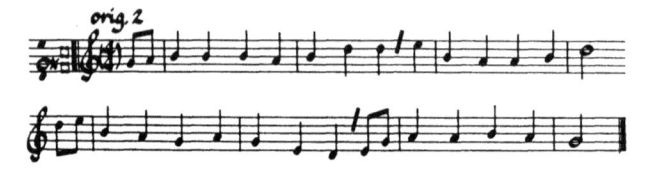

The Brown-Haired Lass (b) [H116c: Wt=D(c)]

Source not given. [Perhaps also William Laverty? Both tunes seem suitable.]

Oh, farewell to my native counterie,
For I must bid adieu,
And likewise to my brown-haired girl,
Since I must part from you.
It grieves me sore against my will
To cross the raging main,
But I live in hopes that I'll return
To my brown-haired girl again.

Oh, it's many a pleasant evening
Down by the grove I spent,
Where the lovely lambs around their dams
Did give me much content;
The blackbird and the comely thrush
Did change their notes so gay,
Oh, it never was my intention, love,
To sail for Americay.

We lifted our anchor and set sail
And soon were out of view,
We had a bold sea captain,
Likewise a jolly crew,
I thought my very heart would break
As Magilligan Point we passed,
And I'm sure it won't be whole again
Till I see my brown-haired lass.

Paddy's Green Countrie [H632: 4 Jan 1936]

Other title: "The Town of Antrim."

Author Mr Johnstone, c. 1835, according to James Kelly (Westmuir St, Glasgow); ?source: Hugh Kearney (Eden, Portglenone).

Key G.

Farewell unto old Ireland's isle since I left you behind,
It's now I'm going far away unto some foreign clime,
It's now I'm going far away, strange faces for to see,
For my mind is bent on rambling far from Paddy's green countrie.

In the County Antrim I was born, near to the river Bann,
It's the prettiest little river that runs through Ireland,
It's the nicest little river that e'er my eyes did see,
But my mind was bent on rambling far from Paddy's green countrie.

Around New Mills my thoughts will dwell when in some foreign land,
The sea may change the best of minds, but mine it never can,
When I'm away, far, far away, in the land of liberty,
My thoughts will dwell when far away on Paddy's green countrie.

Oh, cocks and cards, I love you dear as ever man has done,
You were the vice my mind ensnared, my thoughts still on you run,
But I will miss my comrades, my comrades they'll miss me,
But I will not forget them all far from Paddy's green countrie.

Farewell unto my comrade boys who meet me at Drumsoo,
Again next Easter Monday our minds we will renew.
If I'm alive upon that day, my mind will surely be
Along with you, my country girls, and Paddy's green countrie.

The Shamrock Sod No More

[H235: 12 May 1928]

s: (m) "Dear Old Derry Quay." Other titles: "Farewell to Ireland," "The Irish Emigrant's Lament."

Source: (w) Joseph Reilly (Millview Cottage, Moneycannon, Ballymoney); (m) James Lafferty (formerly Doaghs, Magilligan), [Bp] "who now often whistles it beneath the Southern Cross."

Key G.

I never will forget the sorrows of that day,
Being bound across the ocean, our grand ship sailed away,
I left my friends on Derry Quay, my love on Carrick shore,
For right well I knew I was doomed to tread the shamrock sod no more.

Right well knew when I left my home what my sad fate would be,
Still gazing on my comrade boys, they seemed to flee from me,
I watched them till my eyes grew dim and till my heart grew sore,
For right well I knew I was doomed to tread the shamrock sod no more.

Oh where, oh where is the trusty heart I once could call my own?
I took my last farewell of her, that day I sailed from home;
It was not her wealth that won my heart down by yon western main,
It's the constant smile of my favourite girl that filled my heart with pain.

Oh, if I was a little bird, I would light on my love's breast,
Or if I was a nightingale I would sing my love to rest,
Or had I the wings of an angel bright, my love I would guard on sea,
For the reason that I love my love is because my love loves me.

It's when I'm in my winding sheets, no one to pity me,
It's when I'm in my winding sheets, my thoughts will be on thee;
When I must eat the strangers' bread and bear the strangers' scorn,
It makes me sigh when I'm far away, sweet isle where I was born.

Sam Henry's Songs of the People

◆ B12 REFERENCES ◆

◆ **Lovely Armoy** *(H9)* 186

   Brunnings 1981: (m) "The Lover's Curse"

   IREL   *JIFSS* 1,1903:12
      Shields/Shields *UF* 21,1975: #251

   b: MEL   Kathleen Ferrier, London 5411

◆ **Hannah M'Kay / The Pride of Artikelly** *(H656)* 187

   Brunnings 1981: "... (Tune of The Collier Lass)," without references.

◆ **Carntogher's Braes** *(H237)* 189

   BRS   *Derry Journal* [c. 1925],1:16

◆ **The Flower of Craiganee** *(H749)* 189

   h: IREL   Hughes 4,1936:86-9
   h: *JIFSS* 3(2&3)1906:14, reprinted in Galwey 1910:12
      Shields 1981:63 (#18) "Craiganee"
      Shields/Shields *UF* 21,1975: #92 "Craiganee"

   REC   Bill Quigley, EEOT *Shamrock 2* cass. (A1) "Craiganee"

◆ **The Hills of Tandragee** *(H730)* 190

   Brunnings 1981: "... (Parody of The Hills of Glenswilly)"

   IREL   Cf. Morton 1970: 72-3, "an Orange standard," written by an old lady, former neighor in Ballyisle near Tandragee, "years ago." It is a parody of a song she had on an old 78 rpm record called "The Hills of Glensully," but resembles Henry's only in metre.

◆ **My Girl from Donegal** *(H4)* 190

   Brunnings 1981: (m) "Roisin Dubh -- Thomas Furlong (Little Black Rose; Roseen Duh)"

   BRS   *Derry Journal* [c. 1925],2:39 "Roisin Dubh"
      Walton's New 1,1966:138, a very different version.

◆ **The Flower of Sweet Dunmull** *(H1)* 191

   IREL   Moulden 1979:60 reports two current versions collected in Northern Ireland.

   m: MEL   Petrie/Stanford 2,1902:142 (#560) "The Top of Sweet Dunmul"

◆ **The Faughan Side** *(H621)* 191

   IREL   Moulden 1979:54
      Shields 1981:80 (#28)
   m: Shields/Shields *UF* 21,1975: #145

   REC   Eddie Butcher, EEOT *Shamrock 2* cass. (B7)
   h: Anne, Francie Brolly, Homespun HRL 116

◆ **The Finn Waterside** *(H240)* 192

   Brunnings 1981: (m) "Jackets Green (Patrick Sarsfield)"

◆ **Lovely Glenshesk** *(IIa)* *(H28a)* 194

   REC   Len Graham, Topic 12TS 401 (A5)

   MEL   *JIFSS* 2(1905):23, collected by Frederic Cairns Hughes "from the whistling of John Henry Macauley, a wood-carver of Ballycastle.... His mother, a native of Glenshesk, in the same county, had taught him these melodies, but they are now known only to the older people." A footnote explains the name: "Gleann-Seasg, the glen of the green sedge."

◆ **In Praise of the Glen** *(H547)* 195

   IREL   Moulden 1979:96-7 "Lovely Glenshesk (...)"

   m: REC   Joe Holmes, Len Graham, Topic 12TS 401 (A5) "Lovely Glenshesk"

   m: MEL   *JIFSS* 2(1&2)1905:23

◆ **The Point Maid** *(H42b)* 197

   IREL   Moulden 1979:119. "This song consists of localized lyrical local verses and was probably made by stringing together commonplace verses from other songs" (p. 164).

◆ **Farewell to Slieve Gallen** *(H795)* 198

   IREL   Morton 1970:44-5 "Wild Slieve Gallion Braes"

   AMER   Wright 1975:482 (from Henry coll., BCL)

◆ **The Hills of Tyrone** *(H609)* 199

   Not: Brunnings 1981: "The County of Tyrone"

   m: IREL   Morton 1973:6, 101 "Behind Yon Blue Mountain"
      Moulden 1979:71 reports two versions Robin Morton collected.

   m: BRS   *Songs and Recitations* 2,1960:46
      Walton's New 2,1968:59-60 "County Tyrone," a longer version.

◆ **Bonny, Bonny** *(H75b)* 199

   IREL   *JIFSS* 1(2&3):57, from the same source.

◆ **The Emigrant's Farewell** *(H743)* 200

   Brunnings 1981: "The Green Fields of America"

   h: IREL   Moulden 1979:48-9 reports 3 contemporary versions in Len Graham's collection.
      Shields 1981:85-6 (#32) "(The) Green Fields of America"
   m: Shields/Shields *UF* 21,1975: #172
   m: *Treoir* 8(3,May)1976 "The Green Fields of America" (see Graham rec.)
   h: Cf. Tunney 1979:156-8 "Green Fields of Canada," a "full" version.

   BRS   UCLA 605: 3(Brereton) "A New Song Called the Emigrant's Love for His Native Land. Revised by Edward O'Connor."
   m: Healy 4,1969b:92 "The Green Fields of America"

   b: REC   Beers Family, Columbia CS 9472 "The Green Fields of America"
   m: Len Graham, Topic 12TS 334 (A6) "The Green Fields of Amerikay"
      Paddy Tunney, Folk-Legacy FSE 7 (A6) "The Green Fields of Canada"; [h:] Sruthán LUN A 334

   MEL   Darley/McCall 1914:32 (#71) "The Green Fields to America. Reel."

B12 / The emigrant's farewell

◇ The Happy Shamrock Shore *(H69)* 201

? Brunnings 1981: "The Shamrock Shore"; "The Irishman's Farewell to His Country"

IREL Joyce 1873:44 "The Shamrock Shore," 1 double stanza and same tune.
But not: b: O Lochlainn 1965:246-7 "The Shamrock Shore"

BRS Harvard 1: 10.155 (Bebbington)
 Healy 4,1969c" A New and Admired Song: Called The Irishman's Farewell to his Country," a related song.

MEL O'Neill 1903:9 (#48) "The Shamrock Shore"
 Wright 1975:504 (from Henry coll., BCL)

◇ The Brown-Haired Lass *(H116)* 201

o: MEL O Lochlainn 1939:44

◇ Paddy's Green Countrie *(H632)* 203

Brunnings 1981: "The Town of Antrim (Tune: The Wreck of the "Mary Jane")"

IREL *JIFSS* 18,1921:26 "The Town of Antrim"
b: O Lochlainn 1939:206 "The Town of Antrim" from Cathal O'Byrne.
 Shields/Shields *UF* 21,1975: #410 "(The) Town of Antrim"

◇ The Shamrock Sod No More *(H235)* 203

Brunnings 1981: "Farewell to Ireland," ?"The Irish Emigrant's Lament," ?"The Lament of the Irish Emigrant"

? b: IREL Sparling 1887 "The Lament of the Irish Emigrant"

BRIT Ord 1930:352-3 "The Irish Emigrant's Lament," says the song was written by William Kennedy, "one of the Whistle-Binkie group of poets."

BRS *Gems* n.d.:145-6 "Farewell to Ireland," quite different.
b: *The Shamrock* 1962 "The Lament of the Irish Emigrant"

205

B13

The call of home: Longing for home

B13 / *The call of home*

Norah McShane [H157: 13 Nov 1926]

[Bp] By request.

Other titles: "Nora ..."; cf. "Lake Chemo."

Source: [Bp] (w, m) R. O. W.; (w) Lizzie M'Afee (Croftfoot Cottage, Gartcosh, Lanarkshire); [Dt] (Corndale, Limavady) and Mrs McAfee.

s: ... This favourite song has been printed (without the air) in *M'Glennon's Song Books*, No. 34. "Ballymornach" is the place named there, and in other versions "Londonderry" or other town is substituted.

l: According to Sam Hinton (see rec.), the English poetess Eliza Cook wrote the words to "Norah McShane," published in 1838, and the song was sung to several tunes in the American North Woods in the middle of the century.

Key B flat. [Bp] Slow and with swinging rhythm.

I left Ballymoney a long way behind me,
To better my fortune I crossed the wide sea,
I'm sadly alone, not a creature to mind me,
And in troth, I'm as wretched as wretched can be.

I sigh for the buttermilk, fresh as a daisy,
The beautiful hills and the emerald plain,
And oh, don't I oftentimes think myself crazy
About that young black-eyed rogue, Norah M'Shane.

I sigh for the peat fire, cheerfully burning,
When barefoot I trudged it from toiling afar,
When I tossed in the light the 'thirteen' I was earning
And whistled the old tune of 'Erin-go-bragh.'

In truth I believe I am half broken-hearted.
To my country and love I must get back again,
For I've never been happy at all since I parted
With sweet Ballymoney and Norah McShane.

How dear was the neat little cot I was born in,
Though the walls were of mud and the roof was but thatch,
How pleasant the grunt of the pigs in the morning
And the music in lifting the rusty old latch.

It was true I'd no money; well, then, I'd no sorrow;
If my pocket was light, sure, my heart had no pain.
And if God spares me health till the sun shines tomorrow,
I'll go back to ould Ireland and Norah McShane.

1.1: [Dt, *written*: "Some versions give Ballymornach."]
2.3: ... I often think ... [Dt]
5.2: ... was of thatch. [Dt]

The Old Blacksmith's Shop

[H541: 14 Apr 1934]

Source: John M'Quillan (Turfahun, Bushmills), learned from a songsheet in Scotland c. 1885.

Key F.

Some people ramble to lands far away,
And some visit Paris and Rome,
But the place I love best and am longing to see
Is my own darling sweet little home.
To me it is the dearest spot on earth,
And there forever I could stop
To watch the sparks fly from the fire to the sky
In the old village blacksmith's shop.

Bang, bang, bang goes the hammer on the anvil,
And all day long at the door I could stop
To watch the sparks fly from the fire to the sky
In the old village blacksmith's shop.

With pleasure I think on the days of my youth,
And to the old smiddy I would go;
To assist the old man, on a box I would stand,
And his bellows with pleasure I would blow.
The old man would lay down his hammer with a smile,
And from his work he would stop
And play with us all as if he were our dad
In the old village blacksmith's shop.

Now the old man's gone to his resting place,
And no more at the door I can stop
To watch the sparks fly from the fire to the sky
In the old village blacksmith's shop.

The Little Old Mud Cabin on the Hill

[H642: 14 Mar 1936]

Other titles: cf. "The Little Log Cabin by the Stream," "... Log Cabin in (down) the Lane," "Old Mud ...," "... Old Sod Shanty on the Claim."

Source: James Stewart, M.P.S.I. (High St, Ballymoney).

s: A favourite song at convoys....
The note is duplicated when the words require it.

Key G.

207

Sam Henry's Songs of the People

'I'll sell the cow and pig, agra, to send you far away,
For your dear old parents you must leave behind
To seek your fortune, darling, in the land beyond the sea,
For in Paddy's land but poverty you'll find.'
These were the words my father said when I left old Ireland,
And that sad farewell keeps on my memory still,
So I packed my bundle on my back and I left forevermore
That little old mud cabin on the hill.

For the roof was thatched with straw and the walls as white as snow,
And the big turf fire, I think I see it still.
Old Ireland's carven on my heart, it's the land where I was born
In that little old mud cabin on the hill.

I think I see the big turf fire, it attracts my father's gaze,
And my darling mother sitting by his side,
His pipe is lit, the smoke ascends, he's thinking on the time
When he sent his darling boy across the tide.
No more I'll dance the merry dance upon the cabin floor
To the music of the bagpipes loud and shrill,
No more I'll see the merry scenes I did in days of yore
From that little old mud cabin on the hill.

The Green Hills of Antrim

[H606: 13 Jul 1935]

s: (m) "The Mountains of Mourne."

Author late Canon Barnes (Ballycastle).

Key G.

O, dark was the day when I sailed from Cushleake
And crossed the wide ocean, my fortune to seek;
Sure my heart's wid' the hills o' my own native land
And the streams that go wanderin' down to the strand.
The place where I'm livin', the mountains are high
And lift their big heads far above to the sky,
But they'll never compare wid' the old place to me,
Where the green hills of Antrim sweep down to the sea.

The birds that I see here have plumage that's gay,
And the fields are all bright wid' the blossoms o' May,
But a lark from Knocknacarry'd be dearer than all,
Or the gorse that grows wild above sweet Cushendall.
The girls of this country are bonny and bright
And their ways and their dress are a wonderful sight,
But och, for one glimpse of my Molly Machree
Where the green hills of Antrim sweep down to the sea.

Cloughwater / The Shamrock Shore

[H610: 10 Aug 1935]

Source not given.

[Original Dp in 4-line stanzas = half the tune given.]

Key D.

My friends and comrades, pray pay attention
Till I sing to you so far away;
I left my friends and my aged parents
In 'fifty-six in the month of May.
To try my fortune I took a notion
To cross the ocean where billows roar,

Our topsails set sweetly, she glided neatly
And took me safe to Columbia's shore.

And when I landed, my friends received me
Like Irish men that's kind and true,
I'm now quite happy and contented
All o'er the billows and life's journey through.
But while I ponder, my mind does wander,
Though far away the Atlantic o'er,
To the fairest flower in nature's garden,
That happy place called the shamrock shore.

I oftimes think, while in Philadelphia,
Of the happy singings and scenes of fun,
And on the banks of the sweet Cloughwater,
Where I oftimes wandered with my dog and gun.
But while the ocean keeps in its motion
And the surges dark on its rocky shore,
I will still revere thee with fond emotion,
The land of my childhood, old Erin's shore.

So farewell, father, and farewell, mother,
And farewell, brother and sisters too,
And to my comrades, both lads and lasses,
I kindly send my respects to you.
Should fickle fortune to me prove kindly,
I might once more in old Erin dwell,
When I hope to meet with a kindly welcome.
I drop my pen with the word 'Farewell.'

The Coleraine Girl   [H646: 11 Apr 1936]

Source: Alex. Kane (Carnkirk Mountain, Bushmills).

s: Mr Alex. Kane ... is sincerely thanked for this song, which will appeal to many on account of its reference to Mount Sandy braes.

Key G.

Coleraine it is a purty place,
It's worthy of renown,
And likewise the Bann water,
Where the fish come rolling down.
I would rather hear my true love's voice,
So sweet as she would sing,
Coming down along Mount Sandy braes,
She would make the valleys ring.

In Coleraine town my love does dwell,
Which does disturb my mind
At the leaving of that country
And my wee girl behind,
But my constant mind will aye prove kind,
While I have breath to breathe,
To that wee girl I left behind
On yon Mount Sandy braes.

Coleraine it is a purty place
And likewise the Bann side;

If I was at my liberty,
'Tis there I would abide,
But lonesome mountains I must cross
By the gap of Barnesmore,
And all along Lough Swilly braes
And by the salt sea shore.

It's many's the lonesome night I spent
On the braes of Ballintrain;
I would rather spend an hour or two
In a tavern in Coleraine,
I would rather hear my true love's voice
Coming down Mount Sandy brae
As all the herring, fish or ling,
That swim in the salt sea.

Oh, Derry, Derry, Dearie Me

[H536: 10 Mar 1934]

Composer James Warnock (Knockantern, Coleraine).

Key B flat.

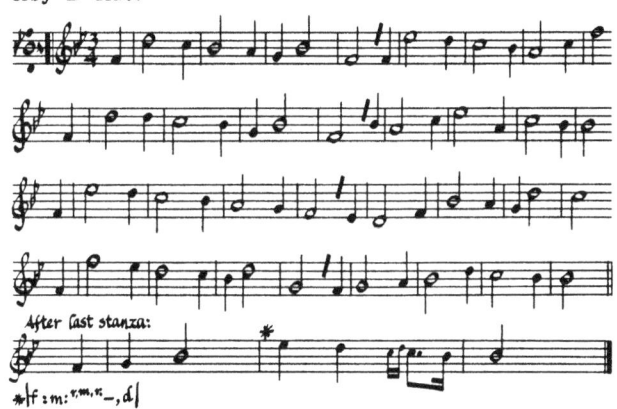

Oh, dearie me, in Derry all
The spring is yawning to awake,
And when the dales of Derry call,
I'd swim the Moyle for old sakes' sake.
And e'en were I in Antrim trim,
'Mid whitewashed farmsteads smoking blue,
My homing eyes would westward skim,
I'd climb Knocklayd to drink the view.

I soar in mem'ry's aeroplane
To find Coleraine astride the Bann,
And Limavady kissed by rain
That mourns for the O'Cahan clan,
To where the winds Slieve Gallion lash
I roam the bogs and top the brae,
But oh, I long to hear the wash
Of county-boundary'd Lough Neagh.

The staid folk down in County Down
Bepraise the Mourne and sing Dundrum,
But Derry, drowsy with renown,
Is fairyland and kingdom come,
And in the midst of London's thrall
I smell the peat, inhale the sea;
Must I be bound to Charing Cross?
Holy St. Pancras, set me free!

Oh, Derry, Derry, dearie me!
[Last line omitted in Dp.]

Sam Henry's Songs of the People

The Hills of Donegal [H196: 13 Aug 1927]

Source: (w, m) coll. Jim Moore (Ardeevin, Bushmills [Wt: Co. Antrim]) in Ramelton district.

[Bp] s: ... The air is old, but the words are modern.
  Verse 2: The van referred to in line 7 was Walsh's van, which plied between Letterkenny and Dunfanaghy about thirty years ago.
  Verse 5: "Tsuide" pronounced "Tee."

[D, W] Copyright claimed by James Moore, A.R.C.O....

Key C.

Oh! Donegal, the pride of all,
My heart still turns to thee
And my cottage home, where I oft did roam
When I was young and free.
Big houses grand in a foreign land
Can not compare at all
To my cottage bright on a winter's night
On the hills of Donegal.

Right well I mind in the harvest time
That dreary, doleful day
When leaving all in Donegal
To wander far away,
In Creeslough town my friends stood round,
I bade farewell to all,
And from the van I waved my hand
To the hills of Donegal.

When gazing back through Barnes Gap
At my own native hills,
I thought no shame, oh who could blame
While there I cried my fill?
My parents kind ran in my mind,
My friends and comrades all,
My heart did ache, I thought 'twould break
When leaving Donegal.

From Derry Quay we sailed away
On waters calm and still,
And down Lough Foyle our tug did toil
To the big ship at Moville.
Some loved to see each tower and tree
And ancient lordly hall;
My thoughts that day were far away
On the hills of Donegal.

Round Tory Isle we steamed in style,
On the mainland we could see
Tall Muckish grand with its glistening sand
Smile over Cruick-an-Tsuide,
While Errigal, much higher still,
Looked proudly over all.
I heaved a sigh and bid good-bye
To the hills of Donegal.

Oh gramachree! I long to see
My native hills again,
My heart is sore beyond the shore,
With an exile's longing pain.
Could I but see those mountains free,
'Twould compensate for all,
I'd live as my forefathers lived
On the hills of Donegal.

Drumglassa Hill [H703: 15 May 1937]

Source not given.

Key C.

Oh, be kind unto old Bellman
And don't you him neglect,
For I mean to make the valleys ring
When I return back;
No cry of hounds will her annoy,
While there she does remain,
Till young Johnston from America
Returns home again.

Here's a health to Mrs. Johnston,
Jane Lusket was her name,
And sirens sing her praises
As she rolls o'er the main,
And Cupid says to grumble,
While Neptune rules the waves;
She is the flower of all St. John
And till she lands in sweet Kilrea.

If ever I return back
Unto my native ground,
I'll charm all my comrades
With the cry, sure, of the hounds.
I'll gather all our sporting lads,
And sport we'll do our fill,
And we'll chase that bonny wee lassie
That feeds on Drumglassa Hill.

Here's a health unto Culnady, boys,
Likewise Dunglady braes,
Where often in my youthful days
I carelessly did stray;
Farewell unto yon purling streams,

Where the trout and salmon play,
And the hare that feeds without dismay
Upon Drumglassa braes.

The Happy Green Shades of Duneane

[H653: 30 May 1936]

Source: Andy Allen (Bann Bridge Cottages, Coleraine), learned from Joseph Hughes (Coleraine), learned from John MacLarnon (Staffordstown).

Key F.

You muses, I hope you'll assist me
And lend me your gracious aid
Till I sing of the praise of my country,
Likewise of my old comerade;
I will urge my affections sincerely,
Though my sentiments cannot explain,
While I sing of the praise of my country
And the happy green shades of Duneane.

Duneane was the home of my childhood
And that of my forefathers too,
Where oftimes in pleasure I sported
With no other changes in view,
But fate has ordained I must leave you,
And all my bright hopes they are slain.
Oh, am I no more to behold you,
You happy green shades of Duneane?

Your bowers, your hills and your valleys,
They seem so delightful and gay,
Your spontaneous productions of nature
That bloom in the sweet month of May,
But were I possessed of a kingdom,
I would ne'er be as happy again
As when I was with my old neighbours
In the happy green shades of Duneane.

Adieu, most respectful companions,
How dear was your friendship to me,
Though here I have now a new comrade,
There is none to compare unto thee.
Though I live in a country of grandeur,
Where everyone wealth can attain,
Yet what is it all when compared with
You happy green shades of Duneane?

Concluding, I hope you'll excuse me,
I wish you all well from my heart.
Such kindness I witnessed amongst you,
With sorrow, kind neighbours, I part,
But I hope that the day is advancing
When I'll see my old cottage again
And finish the last of my days in
The happy green shades of Duneane.

Oul' Dunloy

[H498: 17 Jun 1933]

s: (m) "Cailin deas Cruidthe na mbo" ("The Pretty Milking Girl").

Author Andrew Doey (Ballymacaldrick, Dunloy).

s: By special permission of the author ....

Key G.

I'm sick o' the brick-built city
An' its chimleys dark an' tall,
An' the smoke-cloud iver hingin'
Down over it like a pall.
Take me back to the lanes and hedges
Where I roamed a bare-foot boy,
Wi' the white clouds sailin' over
The green fields roun' Dunloy.

It's a moidherin' place, the city,
Wi' its dunner, night an' morn;
The clatter o' feet on the pavement,
The bell and the bizzin' horn.
Och dear, to be back in the counthry
Where a horn wud niver annoy,
Where ye'd sleep an' wake as it plaised ye,
Lak' they do in oul' Dunloy.

Shure, even the Sabbath stillness
Has a quareness in it here,
An' the chime o' thon gray oul' steeple
Falls lonesome-lak' on my ear,
An' I long for the wild lark's gloria,
Fillin' Sunday morn wi' joy,
When to mass bright childer scamper
'Cross the green fields roun' Dunloy.

We had niver a bell in Dunloy, boys,
At least, not when I was there,
It was Father Dan's 'Come on, boys,'
Used [to] gather us in to prayer,
An' faith to the fray we'd a' followed,
Had he led with his 'Shin-a-dhoy';
For min' ye, his word was heeded,
Them days in oul' Dunloy.

But I'm sick o' the smoky city
An' its drunkness, dirt and sin,
O' the faces pinched or bloated,
An' the hearts as hard as sin.
Och-an-nee! for the kin' oul' neighbours
That made life down there a joy,
An' the scent o' whins an' heather
Aff the hills aroun' Dunloy.

Sam Henry's Songs of the People

Sure, the hawthorn's white wi' blossom,
And the brairds are green down there,
While I pine in this drear oul' city
For a breath o' me native air.
Och, the ways o' the city weary
The heart o' a country boy,
An' the corncrake's voice keeps callin',
'Come back, come back to Dunloy.'

1.2: chimleys = chimneys.
2.2: dunner = thunder.
4.6: Shin-a-dhoy = a Gaelic phrase equivalent to the English "that's the style." [s]
2.7: plaised = pleased.
6.2: brairds = sprouts, shoots.

Sweet Glenbush [H573: 24 Nov 1934]

Source not given.

Key G.

Come all ye maidens now that pass,
I hope you'll place your hearts at last,
So listen to these verses truth
And pity every wandering youth.

When the sun's fierce rays on Orra blaze
And make his old brown head look young,
The scene's too bright for me to write,
Or to be sung in earthly song.

I think me of the day long past,
When I my fortune went to push,
And bid farewell to friends and foes,
And steered my course from sweet Glenbush.

The struggling moon beamed o'er the scene
And threw her light, now dim, now clear;
The winds came whistling down the glen
And filled the lonely hills with fear.

Now in my exiled pillow's dreams,
The scenes of old around me rush,
And wistfully they seem to say,
'Come back again to sweet Glenbush.'

Glen O'Lee [H672: 10 Oct 1936]

s: (m) "The River Roe"; o: "Ballyshanny." Other title: "The Hills of Glenswilly."

Source: Johnnie Deeney (Aughill, Magilligan, Co. Derry).

Key G.

Attention pay, my countrymen, and hear my native news,
I own my song is sorrowful, my name you will excuse.
I left my home in Donegal, a foreign land to see,
I bid farewell to all my friends and to sweet Glen O'Lee.

The summer sun was sinking fast behind the mountain gay
When I left my peaceful residence to wander far away,
And as I viewed the grand old glens, I grieved on leaving thee,
For all the happy days I spent around sweet Glen O'Lee.

Some tall men stood around me, my comrades kind and true,
And as I clasped each well-known hand to bid a last adieu,
I says, 'My gallant countrymen, it's soon you shall be free
To raise the sunburst proudly o'er the glens of Glen O'Lee.'

No more at balls or harvest-homes my fiddle I will play,
No more I'll dance the Irish jig among the girls so gay,
My treasured harp I left at home, the rest was dear to me;
It will keep my place when I am gone away from Glen O'Lee.

No more beside the sycamore I hear the blackbirds sing,
No more for me the bright cuckoo shall welcome back the spring,
No more I'll see the fertile fields across the Swilly sea,
On a foreign soil I'm bound to toil far, far from Glen O'Lee.

God bless you, dark old Donegal, my own, my native land,
In dreams I often see yon hill and towering mountains grand,
But alas! ten thousand miles now lie betwixt those hills and me,
I'm a poor forlorn exile away from Glen O'Lee.

May peace and sweet contentment reign around Lough Swilly shore,
May discord never enter its homesteads any more,
And may the happy time soon come when I return to thee,
And live where my forefathers lived, and die in Glen O'Lee.

The Pretty Three-Leaved Shamrock
from Glenore [H34: 5 Jul 1924]

Other titles: "My Little Four-Leaf ...," "... Four-Leaved ...."

Source: (w, m) coll. Maud Houston (Coleraine) from Lizzie Hassan (Irish Houses, Coleraine); [Dt] some variants from Andy Allen (Bann Bridge Cottages, Coleraine).

Key G.

[Appended to H34 is "The Maid of Mourne Shore," the lyrics to the "well-known" air of H27 to which the song of the Portrush Fishing Disaster was set; in Dt "The Maid ..." is numbered H27.]

It was on a bright and clear St. Patrick's morning
As I walked along the dark and dreary moor,
I shan't forget my dear old mother's warning
As she plucked the three-leaved shamrock from
  Glenore.

For it is the king of flowers from Killarney,
'Tis the prettiest you ever saw before,
It grows upon the shore of wildest grandeur,
'Tis the pretty three-leaved shamrock from
  Glenore.

But my mother she is getting old and feeble,
But still she sits outside our cottage door,
And while she sits, her sacred watch is keeping
On the pretty three-leaved shamrock from Glenore.

I have sailed across the wide Atlantic Ocean,
I have travelled through the sunny southern
  shore,
But there's nothing fills my heart with such
  devotion
As the pretty three-leaved shamrock from Glenore.

I will cherish still this precious little token
As the darling gem that grows upon our shore,
'Tis as fresh today as when its stem was broken,
'Tis the pretty three-leaved shamrock from
  Glenore.

[Dt, Wt include these changes:]
  1.3: Still thinking on my ...
  r.1: It's the king of all the flowers ...
   .2: The likes of it you never saw ...
  2.2: As she sits outside her lonely cabin door,
   .3: But while ... her vigil, watch she's keeping
  3.2: ... travelled o'er the ...
   .3: But nothing ...
  4.2: ... that comes from Erin's shore
   .3: It's as ...

Juberlane [H507: 19 Aug 1933]

o: (m) "When Irish Eyes Are Smiling."

Author Nellie Crowley, now Mrs Corrigan (native of Kilrush, Co. Clare; presently Knockera, Kilimore, Co. Clare), teacher (Magherahoney, Glenbush).

s: ... Juberlane is a lovely little wood on the banks of the river Bush, convenient to Magherahoney Roman Catholic Church and Schools.

Key C.

When the shades of eve are falling,
And I hear the wee birds calling,
My memory often wanders
To the happy days gone by,
And thou sitting in the gloaming,
Still in fancy I am roaming
Round the verdant glens of Antrim,
With its mountains blue and high.
I see the sweet Bush valley,
Where grows the fragrant bean,
Where the blackbird sings so sweetly,
And the thrush joins in the strain,
And enraptured I am listening
To the sweet melodious whistling
As they sing their little vespers
In the scroogs near Juberlane.

The spring is fast returning,
And my heart within is burning,
And I'd give the world could I review
Those beauty spots again,
But miles and miles divide me,
And duty here hath tied me;

Sam Henry's Songs of the People

'Tis but in dreams the beauty seems --
The scenes round Juberlane.
O, ye blackbirds and ye thrushes
That sing in yonder glen,
Had I your wings this evening,
'Twould ease my heart's deep pain.
For I'd fly to dear old Antrim
To hear the evening anthem
Of the feather'd tribe that always sing
The praise of Juberlane.

1.16: scroogs = ?scrogs, stunted bushes.

Sweet Loughgiel [H506: 12 Aug 1933]

s: (m) "Ye Banks and Braes" = H2 "[Hugh Fulton of] Mullaghdoo."

Author teacher M'Williams (Loughgiel School), c. 1885.

s: This song, of a district all too little known for its beauty of lake, mountain and river valley, was composed by ... a native of the parish....
The air is the original Irish form of the developed, ornate Scottish tune -- "Ye Banks and Braes."...

Key G.

A long time since, I bid adieu
To friends and comrades all at home
And went across the bounding deep
To a strange country for to roam;
I left my friends in Ireland,
Though sad and downcast I did feel
At parting with my native place,
My lovely home in sweet Loughgiel.

'Twas there I spent my early days
In brightest happiness and joy,
And o'er its verdant hills and dales
I sported, a light-hearted boy;
No wonder, then, it grieves me sore
When dark misfortune's cloud doth steal
All o'er the path that made me part
From my lovely home in sweet Loughgiel.

Oftimes when I do go to sleep,
Each well-known face I think I meet,
I think I see old friends again,
With smiling face again me greet,
But soon my dream comes to an end,
My waking thoughts too soon reveal
The parting with my native place,
My lovely home in sweet Loughgiel.

There's one kind word still fills my mind
Where'er I roam by land or sea,
And that is to return again,
My dear old native land, to thee.
In no place else in this wide world
Could I the same contentment feel,
Or spend my time so pleasantly
As among my friends in sweet Loughgiel.

Maguire's Brae [H747: 19 Mar 1938]

l: (m) "Star of the County Down."

Author late James O'Kane (Gortinure, Maghera).

s: This sweet song ... was from the pen of the late James O'Kane ... and is published by courtesy of his son, Mr Frank O'Kane, who resides in the old homestead. Maguire's Brae, near Swateragh, is famous for its fairy thorn.
Carn, as is the Gaelic idiom, is pronounced with a vowel sound between the consonants, Caran.

Key A.

Have you ever stood on the Carn crest
At the birth of the new-born day
And viewed those hills with their limpid rills
From the Foyle to the banks of Neagh?
There's the cromlech lone and the Ogam stone
And the dolmen, old and grey,
Where the fairy thorn greets the dawn of morn
On the slopes of Maguire's Brae.

I have travell'd east, I have travell'd west,
I have sailed o'er leagues of sea,
Yet the Carn hills with their raths and rills
Are the dearest hills to me.
In a shelter'd spot stands a whitewashed cot
Where the lark sings the livelong day,
And where'er I be, it is home to me,
That cot near Maguire's Brae.

With spirits light on a winter's night,
I have crossed the mountain path
O'er crag and cairn, through heath and fern
To my home near the fairy rath,
And my heart flies back o'er the ocean's track
At the close of this autumn day
To the comrades kind that I left behind
In their homes near Maguire's Brae.

Though here today in the U.S.A.
I toil on a foreign strand,

Yet where'er I roam, my thoughts fly home,
And I sigh for a friendly hand,
And I long for the sight of the turf fire bright
And the dance on the kitchen floor,
To the witching croon of the piper's tune
In a cot on my native shore.

1.5: cromlech = prehistoric stone structure, dolmen.
Ogam = writing in an ancient 20-character alphabet used by the British and Irish.

Where Moyola Waters Flow

[H787: 24 Dec 1938]

l: (m) resembles "When Irish Eyes Are Smiling."

Author late James O'Kane (Gortanure, Maghera), written when he was in the U.S.

Key D.

There's a little whitewashed cabin
Where in winter sings the robin,
And for it my heart is sobbin',
Little cot I've never seen;
There you'll hear the mavis singing,
Joy to the woodland bringing,
And the fairy bells are ringing
Where Moyola waters flow.

*Where Moyola's gently flowing
And the hollyhocks are blowing,
Lough Neagh like silver showing
'Neath the morn's refulgent glow;
Some may prize the hills of Kerry
Or the vales of Tipperary,
More dear to me is Derry
Where Moyola waters flow.*

*I'm here an exile toiling,
Far from my native island;*
I'm proud to call it my land,
Green emerald of the sea,
Whose fame on history's pages
Goes sounding down the ages;
The land of saints and sages
Is a dear old land to me.

From where Rio Grande is flowing
And the tall corn cobs are growing,
My thoughts keep ever soaring
O'er three thousand miles of sea,
Where a dear old mother's mourning
As she keeps the home fires burning
For the emigrants returning
From the land beyond the sea.

Where Moyola's water rushes
Through sedge and brake and bushes,
Where the linnets and the thrushes
Sweetly sing at even's close,
There, along with Kate and Noreen,
Oft I'd wander down the boreen
From that little whitewashed cabin
Where Moyola water flows.

Mullaghdoo

[H2: 24 Nov 1923]

s: (m) "Caledonian Hunt's Delight" (Scottish); "Ye Banks and Braes of Bonnie Doon" (author "the immortal ploughman" Robert Burns). Other titles: (m) "The Banks of Lough Foyle."

Source not given.

s: A townland situated in the sweetly sylvan district between Stranocum and Armoy.

[Note the differences between printed (Bp, in 3) and typed (Dt, in 6) variants of the tune, which also result in minor differences in position in the melodic index.]

Key G.

Sam Henry's Songs of the People

Hugh Fulton, once my comrade dear,
Pursuing fortune, left his home,
And through the lone sequestered plains
Of Nova Scotia now does roam.
He left his houses and fair lands
That lovely dwelling for to view;
The place that gave our hero birth
Was the wholesome braes of Mullaghdoo.

It grieves my heart, since we did part,
To view those planted groves and shades,
The covert of the feathered tribe
Where oft he courted blooming maids,
The goldspring, nightingale and thrush
That oftimes charmed our noble Hugh
Have dropped their wings with silent tongues
And say, 'We'll go frae Mullaghdoo.'

The generous lily, pink and rose
There oft with beauty smiled arrayed,
But now we see they are declined
Since away from them our hero strayed.
Their naked stem and leafless bower
No more require the morning dew,
Their summer robes they'll ne'er put on
Since Hugh's away from Mullaghdoo.

Thou silent moon and glittering orbs
That oftimes drew his image tall,
How can you light those immortal hills
Or cast a shadow on the wall?
How can ye peep out of the deep,
O'er lofty hills and mountains blue,
And o'er this place eclipse your face,
The midnight mourner, Mullaghdoo?

The night he took his last farewell
Of Chatham boys, his favoured few --
Our master's name was Dan McKay --
He says, 'A charge I leave wi' you:
Now, brave McKay, as you pass by
Wi' fifes and drums and colours blue,
The more my face you ne'er shall see;
Play "Auld Lang Syne" for Mullaghdoo.'

1.7: This lovely ... [Bp *written*]
2.5: The goldfinch, nightingale ... [Bp *written*]

The Maid of Mullaghmore

[H20a: "Two Aghadowey songs," 29 Mar 1924]

Other title: "The Shamrock Shore."

Source: (w, m) William Stewart (Park St, Coleraine)

g: More commonly known as "The Shamrock Shore"; all references below use that title.

o: Tune should be written in 6/8.

[Stanza 1 printed line for line below the sol-fa.]

Key F.

Ye muses nine, with me combine and grant me some relief,
I am here alone, making my moan, I'm overcome with grief
I am here alone, making my moan, far from her I adore,
My troubled mind no rest can find since I left Mullaghmore.

In spring you'll see on every lea the lambkins sport and play;
My way I took, my friends forsook, till I came to Derry Quay,
I entered as a passenger, for Scotland I sailed o'er
To leave behind that lovely maid alone in Mullaghmore.

Oh, Glasgow is a pretty place, in it I do reside,
It's a pretty place, I must confess, on the flowing banks o' Clyde,
Where the girls incline for to dress fine, they rich apparel wore,
But none were there I could compare to the maid of Mullaghmore.

When other boys go out to court, sure I must stay at home,
Both day and night I take delight in the making of my moan,
Both day and night I take delight, far from her I adore,
With a troubled mind no rest can find since I left Mullaghmore.

All ye young men that want a wife, ne'er do as I have done,
Never leave your sweetheart alone in grief to mourn,
For I can neither eat nor drink as I have done before,
For when I drink I always think on the maid of Mullaghmore.

Now to conclude and make an end, my pen is growing weak,
To mother dear: do not think long, nor trouble for my sake,
To father dear: do not think long, and mourn for me no more,
But when you think long, you can sing my song to the maid of Mullaghmore.

1.2, 1.3: I'm here ... [Bp *under sol-fa*, Dt]
6.3: ... long, nor mourn ... [Dt]
6.4: When you ... [Dt]

Owenreagh

[H542: 21 Apr 1934]

o: (m) "Green Bushes."

Author George Barnett (Owenreagh, Sixtowns, Draperstown).

Key F.

As I went a-walking one morning in June
Down by the lands where the wild roses bloom,
And by the meadows and over the brae
Where the wild whins were blooming by bonny
  Owenreagh,

My thoughts were of comrades long absent from
  home,
And of the paths were we used for to roam,
And of the causes which took them away
From the bonny wild roses which bloom at
  Owenreagh.

'Tis the soil which is barren and the climate is
  cold,
And there was but little of silver or gold
Their pockets to fill or their toil to repay,
Which caused them to wander from bonny
  Owenreagh.

I fancied them back where the green shamrocks
  grow,
I fancied them back in the meadows below,
But to the wild whins all abloom on the brae
They may never return to bonny Owenreagh.

Yet at the same place I still have my old home,
And by the same paths I delight for to roam,
And to think of the comrades so far, far away
From the bonny wild roses which bloom at
  Owenreagh.

Yet the roses may wither, but what of the gold?
It is only a moment we have it to hold.
Do riches give pleasure, does beauty cause pain?
I will wait for the bonny wild roses again.

The Banks of the Roe

[H24b: [Bp] "Two songs of the Roe valley,"
26 Apr 1924]

A song of pride of race.

Source: (w, m) M...
ligan, Co. Derry)

[Although this is ...
the unrepeated mel...

Key D.

Too long have I travelled the land of the
  stranger,
With little reward for the toils of the past,
Devoid of contentment and oftimes in danger,
My hopes for the best have been oft overcast.

Replace me again in the land of O'Cahan,
'Midst friendships and peace where I dwelt long
  ago,
My heart is at home by the hamlet or clachan,
I sigh for the scenes on the banks of the Roe.

As I strayed by the old church, that relic or
  ruin
That yet to my memory does visions recall,
Oft in youth have I pondered while sadly
  reviewing
The shrine-faded glory of Coey-na-Gall.

There he sleeps with his kindred in the garden
  of danger,
He long was the terror of Erin's proud foe,
His name lives to prove that he hunted the
  stranger,
His stronghold was once on the banks of the
  Roe.

Once his well-tested clan, of great might and
  number,
Came forth at his call from the mountains and
  glens,
But alas! they're now gone, and in peace they
  now slumber,
Yet forever will live the brave deeds of such
  men.

The name of O'Cahan resounded like thunder,
It routed the Danes and defied every foe,
No heartless invader could boast of their
  plunder,
They sank in defeat on the banks of the Roe.

Benbradden looms high with its breast to the
  ocean,
Reviewing at leisure the distant domains,
Like a garden of the peace in the depths of
  devotion,
Bestowing its bliss on its kindred plains.

...of the People

... I strayed by its murmuring
... its banks when youth's fancy did
... fond scenes shall dwell in my memory for
...er,
...ow I long to return to the banks of the Roe.

1.3: ... of content(i)ment ... [Dt]
3.3: ... I wander'd while ... [Dt]
4.2: Who long ... [Dt]
5.3: ... they are gone ... [Dt]

2.3: clachan = hamlet, village; inn.

Farewell to the Banks of the Roe

[H791: 21 Jan 1939]

l: (m) related to "Star of the County Down."

Source not given.

Key G.

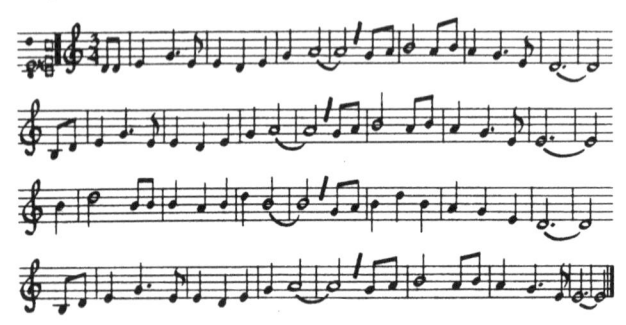

There's an isle on the verge of the ocean,
There's a land where the shamrock grows green,
There is Mary with snowy white bosom,
She's the fairest I ever have seen.
There's a stream that steals lone through the mountain,
Where my spirit's oft wandering, you know,
Inhaling pure draughts from that fountain,
And that crystalline stream is the Roe.

Then away with this sighing and crying,
Such feelings are followed by pain;
Though in far distant lands I am dying,
Yet in dream I oft creep back again:
There's a chair for the wand'rer at evening,
There's a bed where the weary repose,
For a friend there's a 'Cead mille failte,'
And 'Na baclish' for sorrows and woe.

There's a spirit to soothe you in trouble,
And a hand to protect you from wrong,
There's a heart with whom joys you may double,
And at night there's a cheery old song.
Then how can I leave you, old Erin?
Sure, my soul's in each mountain and rill;
Shall I never see white-bosom'd Mary,
Never list to her strains on the hill?

Round the green pole on May's hallowed morning,
How we've bounded with spirits of glee,

When nature the wilds was adorning
With the blackbird, the skylark and bee.
When I whispered the first tender breathing,
Dear Mary, how bright thy blue eye;
Can I call back the scene without grieving,
Or mention that name and not sigh?

Then farewell to those bright sunny valleys,
Dear Erin, I'll see you no more,
My heart whisper'd something of sorrow
When I took my last look at your shore.
There's a spirit of night breathes around me
And whispers of friends far away,
There's a spell that has oftentimes bound me
In the darkness as well as the day.

There's a soft sigh that's often heav'd near me
In a music that saddens the soul,
There's a shadow of light seems to cheer me
And to silence my woes to control,
Then farewell to the green banks of Erin,
To her mountains all shrouded in snow;
Farewell to you, soft-bosom'd Mary,
And adieu to the banks of the Roe.

2.8: na baclish = dry up your tears. [s]

A Shamrock from Tiree [H716: 14 Aug 1937]

l: (m) "The Rose of Tralee."

Author James O'Kane (Gortanure, Maghera).

s: Tiree, i.e., Tir Aodh, Hugh's Land, is the local name for Tirhugh, near Swateragh. The song was composed by James O'Kane when in New Jersey, on receiving shamrocks from Tiree, Swateragh, for St. Patrick's Day, 1858.

Key G.

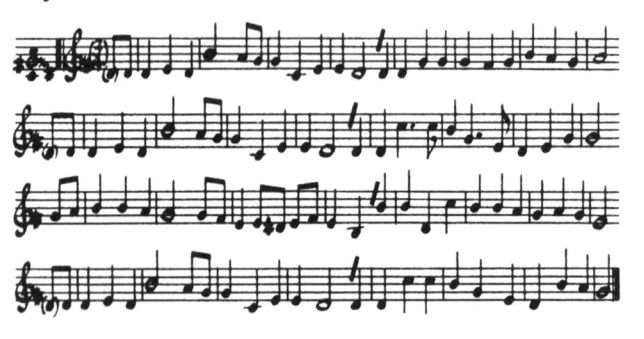

Green were the fields where I sported in childhood,
Red were the roses that hung round the door,
Sweet was the song of the thrush in the wildwood;
Erin, dear Erin, I'll see thee no more.
I love the old land with undying devotion,
My heart and my thoughts with her ever shall be,
In fancy tonight I'm back o'er the ocean
With comrades and friends and a cot in Tiree.

O Erin, loved Erin, the home of my childhood,
In dreams I revisit thy far-distant shore,

In fancy with playmates I roam through the
  wildwood
Or stand on the crest of Benbradden once more.
Behind looms the Carn, mighty monarch of
  mountains,
Below me the Bann flowing on to the sea,
The vale of Glenkeen with his clear crystal
  fountains
And the castle that stands near my home in Tiree.

In fancy I'm back in the mystical ages,
I'm one of the guests in O'Cahan's great hall,
I listen with chieftains, the bards and the sages
Entranced by the music of great Rory Dall.
Ah, the dear little shamrock, with petals so
  tended,
Sweet memories of boyhood you bring back to me,
When I roamed the green meadows at eve with the
  sender --
Sure, I know where she plucked you at home in
  Tiree.

The Call of Home [H674: 24 Oct 1936]

s: (m) "The Bonny Irish Boy."

Source: (m) Sarah M'Mullan (Upper Articlave).

m: Author said to be Mrs Jean Currie (Ballybogy,
Co. Antrim).

Key C.

Across the foaming ocean far o'er the rolling sea,
In a corner of old Ireland there's a place that's
  dear to me,
It's an old thatched cot so lonely, with tall weeds
  growing round,
And walls that I love dearly, fast crumbling to the
  ground.

'Twas in that old thatched cottage I first saw light
  of day,
There first I heard my mother's voice and on her
  bosom lay,
By the window peeped red roses that her hands
  had planted there,
In all the world I could not find a rural scene
  more fair.

When the early beams of morning shone slanting
  o'er the lea,
The blackbird trilled his matins from out the apple
  tree;

Upon the tall green hedges sang minstrels all the
  day,
From dawn until the evening's close they piped
  their tuneful lay.

I spent my happy boyhood's days amid those
  peaceful scenes,
I knew what love of parents and their devotion
  means,
But I heard the distant calling to brave the
  ocean's roar,
And youth found me forsaking the lowly cottage
  floor.

Here in the smoky city that with the millions teems
Come visions of my Irish home -- I see it in my
  dreams,
I'm sad to know it crumbles to ruin and decay,
I wish that time's fleet passage would lighter hold
  its sway.

Though fondest hopes here hold me, there's part
  of me that lies
Midst the ruins of that homestead beneath blue
  Irish skies,
Where roses bloom by the window and around the
  faded door
Of the cot which, save in memory, I never shall
  see more.

Och, Och, Eire, O! [H819: 5 Aug 1939]

A song of Glendun.

Source: Gaelic Journal 6(7)1895:108, taken down
from James M'Auley (Glenariff) and James M'Naughten (Cushendall), "composed by an emigrant
named M'Ambrois (M'Cambridge)"; translation by
Eleanor Hull.

s: This beautiful song and even lovelier air,
should be very popular in the Glens of Antrim.
It breathes the very spirit of that delectable
land. It describes the scenes round Ardacuan
(Cushendun)....
  I heard it sung in Gaelic by Michael M'Kernan,
of Straid, Knocknacarry, the last native Gaelic
singer in the Glens, when in his 90th year.

Key G.

Sam Henry's Songs of the People

Oh, were I again on my native bay
By the curving hills that are far away,
I scarcely would wander for half a day
From the Cuckoo's Glen of a Sunday.
    For och, och, Eire, O!
    Lone is the exile from Eire, O!
    'Tis my heart that is heavy and weary.

O, many a Christmas in Ireland
I would race with the boys on the pleasant strand,
With my hurling stick in my baby hand
And but little sense to guide me.
    And och, och, Eire, O!
    Sad is the exile from Eire, O!
    'Tis my heart that is heavy and weary.

Lonely and drear is this foreign plain
Where I hear but my own voice back again,
No call of the corncrake, cuckoo or crane
Now awakens me on a Sunday.
    Then och, och, Eire, O!
    Lost is the exile from Eire, O!
    'Tis my heart that is heavy and weary.

O, had I boat and single oar,
With the help of God I'd reach Erin's shore;
Nay, the very tide might drift me o'er
To die at home in Erin.
    Now och, och, Eire, O!
    Would I were back in Eire, O!
    'Tis my heart that is heavy and weary.

There's a Dear Spot in Ireland
[H821: 19 Aug 1939]

s: (m) "The Green Bushes."

Source: Willie Bradley (Cross Lane, Coleraine), learned in 1884 from companion-in-arms, Private Sam Smyrrell (Yorkshire Light Infantry, then stationed at Bombay).

Key G.

There's a dear spot in Ireland I'm longing to see,
It's the land of my childhood, it's heaven to me,
My dear aged mother lived there all alone,
And my brothers and sisters in a bright happy home.

She had not much money, my poor mother dear,
With a kiss on my brow she bid me never fear,
While the shadows of poverty darkened our door,
I left Ireland and mother because we were poor.

And well I remember that bright, holy morn,
On leaving old Ireland my poor heart did mourn,
My poor aged mother bid me be of good cheer,
Then, 'Goodbye, Danny darling; goodbye, Danny dear.'

My brothers and sisters took me by the hand,
They told me to write, as I left Ireland;
I bid them farewell at the old cabin door,
And left Ireland and mother because we were poor.

Since I left old Ireland, my poor mother's dead.
'God bless my dear son,' were the last words she said,
And the ring father gave her, she sent it to me;
'Twas a far brighter gem than the gems of the sea

My brothers and sisters, I wish they were here,
I'm longing to see them; they'll come, never fear,
I will make them a home in a far foreign shore
And live honest together, although we are poor.

Riding Herd at Night
[H588: Wp, 9 Mar 1935]

Author John Henry Macauley (Bog Oak Shop, Ballycastle).

s: To Jim, who got tossed by a wild steer on the ranch....
    Composed by John Henry Macauley ... (author of "The Ould Lammas Fair") on receiving a Christmas letter from Wyoming....
    Verses 1 and 4 are to be sung to the first half of the music; verses 2 and 3 to the second half.

Key C.

Riding herd at night, a lonely exile singing,
And through my waking dreams I can hear the
  joybells ringing;
Methinks I see the old Glenwater flowing
Past the cot where my love lies dreaming of me.

And here am I, away from home and kindred,
Riding in Wyoming thro' sleet and pelting hail,
Yet in my dreams I'm always back in dear old
  Ballycastle
With the little girl I left behind in the homeland
  of the Gael.

I'm now far away from the Glens I loved in
  boyhood,
I never thought I'd break a bronc or rope a
  plunging steer,
But Christmas time brings thoughts of home,
  and an Irish boy feels lonely
When thinking of the festive scenes to welcome
  the new year.

[repeat first stanza]

3.2: ... a bronk ... [Wp, Bt, Dt]

Charlie Jack's Dream [H799: 18 Mar 1939]

Source: John Bradley (Upper Main St, Garvagh).

s: ... This song has a great vogue in Glenullin.
The 14th June, 1886, was the opening date of St.
Joseph's Catholic Church, Glenullin. The Jubilee
of the opening was celebrated in 1936.

Key D.

One night as I lay slumbering in Philadelphia
  town,
I dreamt I was in Ireland with all my friends
  around,
I dreamt I stood on Carn braes when taking my
  last view
Of that sweet spot called Ullin's Glen, where first
  my breath I drew.

I dreamt I saw the ruins of the old church in the
  glen,
Where on its little altar stood the noblest of all
  men,
The Reverend John M'Laughlin, that great orator
  of fame,
And the Reverend James M'Laughlin were an
  honour to their name.

I saw the fourteenth day of June, when all
  Glenullin smiled;
The Reverend James M'Glinchy and also Father
  Boyle,
Father Walsh, from sweet Dungiven, cantata mass
  did sing,
The music of his heavenly voice still in my ears
  does ring.

I saw the Parnell family appearing in my view,
I saw old Dan O'Connell shaking hands with Brian
  Boru,
The Redmonds and O'Sullivans who gained such
  great applause,
And our valiant Tim O'Healey was holding forth
  our cause.

I saw Benbraddagh's tower and I think I see it
  still,
The little town of Carn and also Donald's hill,
The happy lands of Fanmile and also Ballyhuone,
And the little town of Essland that I used to call
  my own.

My scenery came to an end as Ellen tapped the
  door;
She says, 'Pray, Charlie, do get up; 'tis six
  o'clock and more.'
I raised my eyes, being in surprise, I found she
  was a friend,
I was three thousand miles and more from my dear
  native glen.

The Irishman [H712: 17 Jul 1937]

l: (m) "The Parting Glass."

Author James O'Kane (Gortinure).

s: Composed ... [after his] meeting with an old
Irish settler in the back woods [l: very likely
the "Pine Barrens" in the south] of New Jersey.
  By kind permission of Mr Frank O'Kane, son of
the author....

Key G.

When wandering o'er the woodlands wild
That hide New Jersey's soil of san',
An oasis in the desert smiled --
'Twas the home of an old Irishman.
His hair hung down in ringlets white
As I his features close did scan,
I found he was a splendid type
Of the bold and fearless Irishman.

Sam Henry's Songs of the People

The old man kindly asked my name
And when I left green Erin's shore,
He said no Irishman e'er came
That way for thirty years before;
Then at his hospitable board
I told him there where life began,
This touched a sympathetic chord
Within that kindly Irishman.

'I am an exile, sir,' said I,
'And oft had cause for to lament
I e'er bade Swateragh's hills goodbye,
Where youth and childhood's days were spent.'
No single word I heard him speak,
But silently he clasped my han';
Tear after tear coursed down the cheek
Of this old kindly Irishman.

'Oh, tell me, does the hawthorn tree
Still decorate Maguire's Glen,
Whose overspreading canopy
Would shield and shade five hundred men?
Or if old Carntogher's crest
Does still record the leaps of Shan?'
'Twas by those queries soon I guessed
The birthplace of that Irishman.

'Oh, tell me, does the Castle Rock
Still sentinel the church below?
Does one survive of that vast flock
Who worshipped there long years ago?
When the recording angel there
Sent down from heaven with golden pen
To mark each sigh, each tear, each prayer
That was sent up from Kearney's Glen?

'Does that rude altar still remain,
Memorial of a cruel blast
That swept with persecution's reign
Around those hills in ages past?
Or if each devious winding path
Is always trod by stalwart men,
Or if the colleen's lightsome laugh
Is ever heard round Kearney's Glen?

'Or are those wells among the hills
Saint Patrick blessed long years ago
Still sending forth their tiny rills
To hamlets in the vale below?
Or does each silver crystal stream
To Swateragh's river always trend,
Or if the sun, with golden beam,
Makes cheerful all round Kearney's Glen?

'Where's Beagh Quinns, the Walsh's girls,
Whose minstrelsy in every trill
Would lift your mind to higher worlds --
Raise or depress you at their will,
With Mick and Murt and Doherty,
Harry's James and Mooney's Dan,
Whose sweet unrivalled melody
Made dearer still my native land?

'Oh, is that grand old choir all gone
Whose name and fame went far and near?
Or, on poor Charlie's grave are none
To shed one lonely parting tear?'
And as the pearly teardrops fell
Down from his eyes, I clamped his han'
And bade a long and last farewell
To that old kindly Irishman.

◇ *B13 REFERENCES* ◇

◇ Norah McShane *(H157) 207*

Brunnings 1981

AMER Dean [1922]:105
   Haskins n.d.:62
   Wright 1975:406 (brs, Andrews)

BRS BPL Partridge: 1.160 (Wrigley)
   Clark n.d.:116
   40 n.d.:20
   O'Conor 1901:50 "Nora ..."
   120 n.d.:116
   Popular Songs 1860:186, very similar.
   617 [190-?]:88

REC Sam Hinton, Folkways FA 2401 (B5) "Lake Chemo," a direct parody of "Norah McShane," written by James Wilton Rowe of Maine in 1871, according to Barry's scholarly detective work reported in *BFSSNE* #7,1934:14-6.

◇ The Little Old Mud Cabin on the Hill *(H642) 207*

g: Directly or indirectly the American song "The Little Old Sod Shanty" derived from "The Little Old Mud Cabin on the Hill." For the shanty song, see Lomax 1960:397-8 with references. But Lomax says (p. 390) that the parent song of "The Little Old Sod Shanty" was an Irish music-hall song called "The Little Old Log Cabin in the Lane." The latter was actually a blackface minstrel song written by Will S. Hays (see Wier 1929:12-3). But the melodies of all three songs are very similar.

Brunnings 1981: Cf. "The Little Old Log Cabin in the Lane," "The Little Old Sod Shanty - I, II & III," "The Little Adobe Casa"

AMER Cf. *Colorado FB* 1(1,Jan)1962:5 "Little Old Sod Shanty on the Claim"; also 1(3,Nov)1962:14 "Little Ole Log Cabin in the Lane"; 2,1963:32
   Cf. Darling 1983:324-5 "Sod Shanty"
   Dean [1922]:100-1 "Old Mud ..."
   Cf. Peters 1977:122-3 "The Little Log Cabin by the Stream," which resembles "Mud Cabin" only in metrical pattern; 178 "Little Old Log Cabin in the Lane."
   Cf. Rosenbaum 1983:214 "Little ... Cabin in the Lane," a reworking.

BRS Cf. UCLA 605: 4(n.i.) "... Log Cabin down the Lane"
   Irish Fireside n.d.:20
   Walton's New 2,1968:38

REC Cf. Clarence Ashley, Folkways FA 2350 "... Mud Cabin in the Lane"
   Cf. Jimmy Denoon, AAFS L20 (A5) "... Sod Shanty"
b: Cf. Burl Ives, Decca DL 8125 "The Western Settler"
lc: Frank Luther, Decca DL 5035 "... Sod Shanty on the Plain"
b: Cf. *Our Singing Heritage*, Vol. 1, Elektra EKL 151 "The Little Old Log Cabin in the Lane"

◇ Cf. Ray Reed, Folkways FD 5329 (A4) "... Sod Shanty"
Cf. Roger Welsch, Folkways FH 5337 (A7) "... Sod Shanty"

c1: MEL Mr Miller (fiddle), AFS 3680 A3 "Sod Shanty on the Plains"

◇ **The Green Hills of Antrim** *(H606) 208*

Brunnings 1981: (m) "The Mountains of Morn/Mourne"

◇ **Cloughwater / The Shamrock Shore** *(H610) 208*

Probably not: Brunnings 1981: "The Shamrock Shore"

AMER Wright 1975:120-1 (from Henry coll., Belfast)

◇ **The Coleraine Girl** *(H646) 209*

? Brunnings 1981: "The Girls of Coleraine"

IREL Moulden 1979:34

◇ **The Hills of Donegal** *(H196) 210*

Brunnings 1981

BRS *Songs and Recitations* 2,n.d.:18

REC Margaret Barry, Riverside RLP 12 602 (A4); Outlet SOLP 1029 (A1)
b: *Everybody Sing!* Vol. 4, Riverside/Wonderland RLP 1421

MEL Cf. Archie Fisher, Folk-Legacy FSS 61 (A7) "The Echo Mocks the Corncrake"

◇ **Glen O'Lee** *(H672) 212*

m: IREL *Songs and Recitations* 2,1960:19 "The Hills of Glenswilly" [?old edition]

◇ **The Pretty Three-Leaved Shamrock from Glenore** *(H34) 213*

BRS *Ireland Calling* n.d.:11-2
Sing an Irish n.d.:9-10 "... Four-Leaved ..."
617 [190?]:57 "My Little Four-Leaf ..."
Walton's New 2,1968:18

◇ **Sweet Loughgiel** *(H506) 214*

m: Currently sung by John Watt, "Ireland's Singing Farmer."

◇ **Maguire's Brae** *(H747) 214*

IREL Ó Maoláin 1982:36

◇ **Where Moyola Waters Flow** *(H787) 215*

IREL Ó Maoláin 1982:68-9

◇ **Mullaghdoo** *(H2) 215*

Brunnings 1981: (m) "Caledonian Hunt's Delight (Tune of The Banks o' Doon and Ye Banks and Braes o' Bonnie Doon)"

MEL O'Neill 1903:54(#311) "The Banks of Lough Foyle"

◇ **The Maid of Mullaghmore** *(H20a) 216*

Brunnings 1981: "The Shamrock Shore"

IREL Joyce 1909:226-7, a 3-stanza fragment (from Joyce 1873)
b: O Lochlainn 1965:246-7

AMER Kenedy 1890:110-1

BRS BPL Irish: (n.i.)
Harvard 1: 6.236 (Cadman), 12.24 (Such)
Healy 1,1967b:77-8
O'Conor 1901:74
617 [190-?]:95

◇ **Owenreagh** *(H542) 217*

Brunnings 1981: (m) "Green Bushes"

◇ **Farewell to the Banks of the Roe** *(H791) 218*

Brunnings 1981: (m) "The Star of the County Down"

◇ **A Shamrock from Tiree** *(H716) 218*

IREL Ó Maoláin 1982:31

◇ **There's a Dear Spot in Ireland** *(H821) 220*

Brunnings 1981: (m) "The Green Bushes."

m: NLI, P. J. McCall coll. Vol. 10:66, cutting, origin unknown.

C14

She's a lovely fair:
Praise of a girl

Happy 'Tis, Thou Blind, for Thee

[H491: 29 Apr 1933]

s: (m) "Calen O Custure me" ("Colleen Oge Asthore"); o: "Colleen Og a Store." Other titles: "Caili'n O Chois tSiure," "Caleno Custure Me," "Callino Casturame."

Source not given.

o: The text printed here is a translation from the Gaelic by Douglas Hyde, set by Sam Henry to "Colleen Og a Store" and impossible as a song.

l: Under the title "Shakespeare and Irish Music" is a list compiled by Sam Henry of 10 references from Shakespeare's plays to Irish songs "current in his day." His comments are reprinted fully in Appendix B.

Key B flat.

Happy 'tis, thou blind, for thee,
That thou see'st not our star,
Couldst thou see but as we see her,
Thou would'st be but as we are.

Once I pitied sightless men,
I was then unscathed by sight,
Now I envy those who see not,
They can not be hurt by light.

Woe who once has seen her please
And then sees her not each hour,
Woe for him her love-mesh binding
Whose unwinding passes power.

My Bonny Breeden

[H512: 23 Sep 1933]

s: (m) "Cruchan na Feinne"; o: (m) "Avenging and Bright."

Author Andrew Doey (Ballymacaldrick, Dunloy).

s: Breeden is little Bridget or Bridie.

Key C.

She was born 'mong the wild flowers that bloom in our valley,
And like those same flowers she grew lovely and fair
And mild as the summer-eve zephyrs that dally
To play with the folds of her soft flaxen hair.
The morn of her birth all the Graces attended
And crowned her with garlands the valley's young queen,
While the rose and the lily their brightest tints blended
To paint the soft cheek of my bonnie Breeden.

And then while the Graces in beauty arrayed her,
Of soft glowing cheek and of fair flowing hair,
The heavens smiled pleased on the sweet face and made her
As gentle and good as she's lovely and fair.
So 'tis not that cheek's blush the roses excelling
Nor the beauty that crowns that young brow so serene,
But the calm light of truth in those blue eyes upwelling
That makes me the slave of my bonnie Breeden.

Ye angels of light in whose tenderest keeping
Alone maiden virtue can live undefiled,
On her journey thro' life, in her waking or sleeping,
Oh, fondly watch over M'Caffel's fair child,
And shield her young bloom 'neath your pinions of brightness
When rude breaths of winter come blighting and keen,
Nor let stain ever sully the virginal whiteness
Of that soul in the breast of my bonnie Breeden.

Breeden = little Bridget or Bridie. [s]

O, Jeanie Dear

[H545: 12 May 1934]

s: (m) Chicago vt. of "Londonderry Air" ("Rory's Lament").

Author Andrew Doey (Dunloy, Co. Antrim).

s: ... The air is a variant of the "Londonderry Air" ("Rory's Lament") collected in Chicago.
In a portfolio of Irish airs with settings by Beethoven and Haydn, published in 1814, there is the following interesting reference to Rory Dall O'Cahan: "The song 'O Harp of Erin' was composed on the death of O'Kain, the blind Irish harper, well known in Scotland by the admirable and feeling manner in which he played his native music; remarkable also for his independence of spirit, sarcastic wit, and conviviality."
A feature of Rory Dall O'Cahan's airs was the omission of the sub-dominant, *fa*, and analysis of the "Londonderry Air" points to him as the composer.

Key C.

Sam Henry's Songs of the People

O, Jeanie dear, the flow'rs, the flow'rs are
    springing,
Wee daisy, primrose shy, and violet blue,
All lovely things to my fond fancy bringing,
Ever avourneen, sweetest thoughts of you.
O, Jeanie dear, the lark, the lark is winging
His joyous flight aloft into the blue,
And to my ravished ear his wondrous singing,
Is all of love, asthore, of love -- and you.

O, Jeanie dear, your native vale rejoices
In life returning, life and light anew;
The spring is here with all its tuneful voices,
Speaking to me of love, of love -- and you.
O, Jeanie dear, sweet, sweet, the wild flowers
    springing,
The cuckoo's song, the lark's grand matin too,
But what to me are flow'rs or skylarks singing,
The cuckoo's song, or springtime, wanting you?

Bonny Mary Hay [H568: 20 Oct 1934]

Source: (Aberdeenshire, Scotland).

s: A charming traditional lyric....

Key F.

Bonny Mary Hay, I will lo'e thee yet,
For thine e'e is the slae and thy hair is the jet,
The snaw is thy skin and the rose is thy cheek,
Oh, bonny Mary Hay, I will lo'e thee yet.

Bonny Mary Hay, will ye gang wi' me,
When the sun's in the west, to the hawthorn tree?
To the hawthorn tree in the bonny Berrieden,
And I'll tell you, Mary Hay, how I lo'e thee then.

Bonny Mary Hay, it's haliday to me
When thou art sae couthie, kind-hearted and free;
There's nae clouds in the lift nor storms in the
    sky,
My bonny Mary Hay, when thou art nigh.

Bonny Mary Hay, thou mauna say me nay,
But come to the bow'r by the hawthorn tree,
But come to the bow'r and I'll tell you a' that's
    true,
How, Mary, I can ne'er lo'e ane but you.

1.2: slae = sloe.
1.3: snaw = snow.
3.1: haliday = a festive occasion.
3.2: couthie = kind, agreeable.
4.1: mauna = must not.
4.4: lo'e = love.
4.4: ane = one.

So Like Your Song and You

[H508: 26 Aug 1933]

s: (m) "My Singing Bird."

Author: Andrew Doey (Ballymacaldrick, Dunloy).

s: This beautiful song, to a well-known folk air, was composed by ... a singer whose songs are so vibrant with heart-chords that they become assimilated by the people as true folk songs.
    Mr Doey writes on the circumstances of the song's composition -- "A bonnie wee lassie, perched on a leafy bough, one summer evening, sang in a beautiful voice, swaying up and down to the music, the well-known song 'My Singing Bird.' The tune, the song and the vision of the singer haunted my mind all next day, with result in the song I send."
    On Saturday last Mr Doey and the Song Editor had the privilege of hearing "the bonnie wee lass" singing the song again and by her side were her husband and four bonnie children.

Key G. With slow swinging rhythm.

I wandered in the radiant dawn
O'er glistening fields of dew,
And listening to the lark's sweet song,
I thought, my love, of you.
The rosy morn, the music spilled
Adown the ether blue,
My listening soul with rapture filled --
'Twas like your song and you,
　　The lark's sweet song and rosy dawn
　　Were like your song and you,

　　Ah ... Ah ...,
　　So like your song and you,
　　Ah ... Ah ....

And while I turned the fragrant hay
That summer noontime, too,
I heard the brooklet chant its lay,
And thought, my love, of you.
Your voice was in the fairy croon
That sighed the tall grass through;
The streamlet's tune and sunlit noon
Were like your song and you,
　　The streamlet's croon and glowing noon
　　Were like your song and you.

And strolling at the sunset hour
Where tangled woodbines grew,
I paused beside the linnet's bower
And thought, my love, of you.
The smile that wreathed yon sunset sky,
The linnet's soft adieu,
Seemed to my raptured ear and eye
So like your song and you,
　　That linnet's lay and evening ray
　　Were like your song and you.

Not the Swan on the Lake

[H707: 12 Jun 1937]

Source: (Maghera); (w) translated from Irish by author Ewen MacLachlen, M.A. (Aberdeen), published in Whitelaw [1844 (1874)] [s: 1857].

Key C.

Not the swan on the lake or the foam on the shore
Can compare with the charms of the maid I adore;
Not so white is the new milk that flows o'er the
　pail,
Or the snow that is shower'd from the boughs of
　the vale.

As the cloud's yellow wreath on the mountain's
　high brow,
The locks of my fair one redundantly flow,
Her cheeks have the tint that the roses display
When they glitter with dews on the morning of
　May.

As the planet of Venus that gleams o'er the grove,
Her blue rolling eyes are the symbol of love,
Her pearl-circled bosom diffuses bright rays
Like the moon when the stars are bedimmed with
　her blaze.

The mavis and lark, when they welcome the dawn,
Make a chorus of joy to resound through the
　lawn,
But the mavis is tuneless, the lark strives in
　vain,
When my beautiful charmer renews her sweet
　strain.

When summer bespangles the landscape wi'
　flow'rs,
While the thrush and a cuckoo sing soft from the
　bowers,
Through the wood-shaded windings with Bella I'll
　rove
And feast unrestrained on the smiles of my love.

3.1: As the plant ... [Dp]

Nancy, the Pride of the West

[H495: 27 May 1933]

o: (m) "Love Song" (O'Friel's Suite).

Source not given.

s: A song with this title but with different words, metre and air, has been published by Joyce [1909:221 (#410)].

Key E.

Sam Henry's Songs of the People

We have dark lovely looks on the shores where the
    Spanish
From their gay ships came gallantly forth,
And the sweet shrinking violets sooner will vanish
Than modest blue eyes from our north,
But oh, if the fairest of fair-daughtered Erin
Gathered round at her golden request,
There's not one of them all that she'd think worth
    comparing
With Nancy, the pride of the west.

You'd suspect her the statue the Greek fell in
    love with,
If you chanced on her musing alone,
Or some goddess great Jove was offended above
    with
And chilled to a sculpture of stone,
But you'd think her no colourless classical statue
When she turned from her pensive repose,
With her glowing grey eyes glancing timidly at
    you,
And the blush of a beautiful rose.

Have you heard Nancy sigh? Then you've caught
    the sad echo
From the wind-harp enchantingly borne.
Have you heard the girl laugh? Then you've
    heard the first cuckoo
Chant summer's delightful return;
And the songs that the poor ignorant country-folk
    fancy,
The lark's liquid raptures on high,
Are just old Irish airs from the sweet lips of
    Nancy,
Flowing up and refreshing the sky.

And though her foot dances so soft from the
    heather
To the dew-twinkling tussocks of grass,
It but warms the bright drops to slip closer
    together
To image the exquisite lass.
We've no men left among us so lost to emotion
Or scornful or cold to her sex,
Who'd resist her if Nancy once took up the notion
To set that soft foot on their necks?

Yet for all that, the bee flies for honey-dew
    fragrant
To the half-opened flower of her lips,
And the butterfly pauses, the purple-eyed
    vagrant,
To play with her pink fingertips;
From all human lovers she locks up the treasure
A thousand are starving to taste,
And the fairies alone know the magical measure
Of the ravishing round of her waist.

The Maid of Erin's Isle

[H57b: "Love and land -- two songs of aspiration,"
                                    13 Dec 1924]

Source: (w, m) W[illiam] Lyons, former customs
collector (Newcastle-on-Tyne, England); later Dhu
Varren, Portrush), from childhood (Ballyrashane).

[Bp] Key B flat. [Dt] Key C.

Oh, the sun does set down in the west when his
    daily journey's o'er,
The little birds have sought their nests as night
    spreads o'er the shore;
With ruby wine I'll fill my glass, and I'll banish
    care awhile,
And I'll drink a health to my sweetheart, she's
    the maid of Erin's isle.

When I'm in my love's company, my mind does
    feel content,
And how to gain her favour my inclination's bent,
And if I chance to gain this maid, kind fortune
    would on me smile;
She's a lovely fair, none can compare with the
    maid of Erin's isle.

Her eyes they're as bright as any star that in
    the sky does shine,
Her lovely hair in ringlets folds, her form is all
    divine,
Her cheeks they are a rosy red, and her heart
    it knows no guile,
She's a lovely fair, none can compare with the
    maid of Erin's isle.

Oft have I roamed with you, Mary, o'er Boyden's
    flowery vale,
Where little lambs do sport and play through
    grove and quiet dale,
But look ye down, ye powers above, and on our
    union smile,
And while I've life I swear I love the maid of
    Erin's isle.

4.4: ... while I live ... [Dt]

Peggy of the Moor   [H761: 25 Jun 1938]

Source: Mary M'Keever (Balnamore) from her
mother, Jane Steele (Garvagh) c. 1888.

o: The tune should be in 6/8.

Key C.

C14 / She's a lovely fair

Come all ye sporting young men and listen unto me,
Come all ye loyal lovers that live in unity,
And we will join in chorus and lovingly we'll sing,
With a jug of punch before us to welcome in the spring.

Once I loved a fair maid when I was very young,
And oftentimes she told me I had a flattering tongue,
I slowly made her answer which did my love assure,
For I said I was enchanted by Peggy of the moor.

My love, she is admired by wealthy farmers' sons,
And they are daily running, her favour for to win,
But all their fond endeavours are useless, I am sure,
Since first the bold shoemaker sought Peggy of the moor.

Her eyes are like two diamonds shining in the vaulted sky,
Her cheeks they are a rosy red, her lips a coral dye,
Her breath so sweet would captivate the earl of Glenalure,
And the thrushes sing melodiously her praises through the moor.

So now I'll drop my pen and no more will I compose,
Here's a health to every bonny lass from sporting Ballyclose;
To kiss a pretty fair maid I never yet was coy,
Here's a health to every bonny wee lass that loves her 'prentice boy.

Mary M'Veagh [H773: 17 Sep 1938]

Source not given.

Key F.

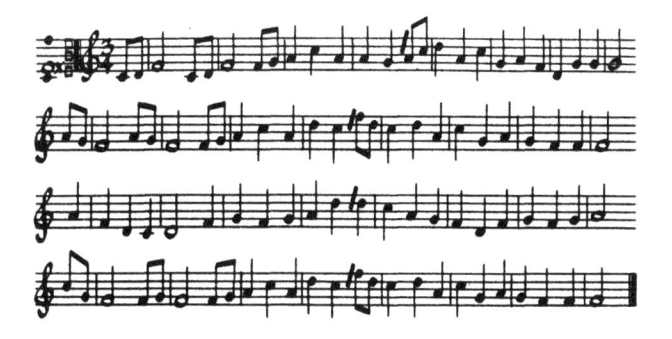

Long ago, when my hair was all curly,
There was many a colleen on me cast an eye;
Pretty girls, pretty girls going by late and early,
And they smiled as they passed, though I didn't know why;
But time, the old thief, with his mischievous fingers
Has stolen their names and their faces away,
Only one, only one in my memory lingers,
I've forgotten them all except Mary M'Veagh.

Nowadays, nowadays all my friends call me 'Tubby,'
And the few hairs I've got are as straight as a skewer,
Sorra girl, sorra girl would seek me for her hubby,
And I'd soon lose my breath if I tried to pursue her,
But when a man's rich he can take any notion
And go where he chooses, with none to say nay;
Back again, back again I came over the ocean
To the village where once lived Mary M'Veagh.

Very fine, very fine are these civilisations,
With their water laid on and six lamps down the street;
All the same, all the same I don't like alterations,
Nor their roofs of red iron and roads of concrete.
I turned to go back, with small gains for my trouble,
When there on the pavement just over the way,
There she stood, there she stood while my pulses beat double:
'Twas the spirit and image of Mary M'Veagh.

Just the same, just the same with her shawl and her basket,
And the same dear blue eyes looking up at my car;
When I said, 'Will you tell me one thing if I ask it,
Now isn't it Mary M'Veagh that you are?'
As the sun-gleam that runs across meadow and river
When white clouds of April blow over the brae,
Once again, once again that bright smile made me quiver
As she said, 'Sure, it's Granny was Mary M'Veagh.'

2.4: sorra = [*expression of the utter absence of*].

The Holly Bough / The Pride of Altibrine

[H111: 26 Dec 1925]

s: (m) "Cushendall."

Source: (m) coll. Maud Houston (Coleraine) from late Allan Mitchell (Coleraine).

229

Sam Henry's Songs of the People

s: The fair maid in the song was named Holly, hence its title, and the comparison with the evergreen is well sustained by the local muse....

Key C.

In Altibrine there lives a maid, a maid of beauty rare,
The violet or the primrose with her could ne'er compare,
The violet or the primrose with her could never show,
Nor any other flower that ever yet did grow.

To praise this fair beyond compare, it's more than I could do,
It would take the pen of Homer, likewise Apollo, too,
And when they would together meet, I'm sure they both would fail
Before half this fair maid's praises they ever could reveal.

Her eyes they are transparent, her skin as white as snow,
Her teeth they are like ivory set nicely in a row,
Her waist is round and slender, her fingers long and small,
And she's altogether handsome, yet not so very tall.

The beauty of this fair maid has so enticed me,
When I look to the mountains I think I do her see,
When I look to the mountains where the heather bells do blow
With the ivy fine and woodbine twine around the holly bough.

The holly is an evergreen grows by yon river side,
And from it I must have a sprig all for to be my bride,
And from it I must have a sprig, I care not for the toil,
I'll transplant it from the mountain unto a better soil.

It's young man, dearest young man, be witty and be wise:
Acquaint your aged parents and by them be advised,
Acquaint your aged parents and let them for to know
That they want a bigger fortune than we're able to bestow.

Now to conclude and finish, my pen can add no more,
The holly is an evergreen that young men should adore,
It's one of nature's choicest works and comely to be seen,
When other plants they do decay, the holly's evergreen.

5.2: And for it ... [Dt]
6.4: ... than they're able ... [Dt]

The Maid of Burndennet (a)

[H96a: 12 Sep 1925]

g: "The Rose of Tyrone."

Source: Frank Devine (Dunnaboe, Donemana); author James Devine (Lough Ash, Donemana).

s: Composed by the late James Devine ... who died about forty years ago. He was the author of many good songs such as "Farewell to Glenrannel," "Claudy Town" and probably "Moorlough Mary." Burndennet is a tributary of the Foyle and the valley through which it runs is one of the choicest pieces of [Bp: our Northern scenery] [Dt: scenery in North Ireland]....

l: In spite of the single author and source cited, the two texts, Bp and Dt, differ enough to justify printing both as variants. Wt is an identical copy of Bp.

[Bp pencil corr.] Key F. [orig. D crossed out]

Oh, fair all ye vales of our own native soil,
And clear all ye streams that do flow to Lough Foyle;
Above all the bright spots in the isle of the sea,
The banks of Burndennet are the dearest to me.

The home of my childhood, the home of my own,
She's the pride of Burndennet and the rose of Tyrone.

She's youthful and blooming, she's blithesome and gay,

Her smiles are more charming than the morning in
   May,
Like a queen in her beauty, she sits on her
   throne,
She's the flower of Burndennet and the rose of
   Tyrone.

We loved in the sunshine, we loved in all weather,
The storm could not part us, but bound us
   together;
Our rivals may sneer and the proud may complain,
But the love that once conquered will conquer
   again.

Blest is the bower that she claims as her own,
She's the pride of Burndennet and the rose of
   Tyrone,
She's my rare one, my fair one, my ain love
   alone,
She's the pride of Burndennet and the rose of
   Tyrone.

The Maid of Burndennett (b) [H96b: Dt]

Source: Frank Devine (Dunnaboe, Donemana);
author James Devine (Lough Ash, Donemana).

[Dt, tune identical to Bp]

Oh, fair are the vales of my own native soil
And clear are the streamlets that flow to the
   Foyle,
But of all the bright spots in this isle of the sea,
The banks of Burndennet are the dearest to me --
   The home of my childhood, the home of mine
      own,
   The pride of Burndennet, the rose of Tyrone.

She's youthful and blooming, she's modest and
   gay,
Her smile is more blithesome than morning in May,
Her accents are softer than notes of the dove,
Her blue eye is beaming with oceans of love;
   In the kingdom of beauty she sits on the
      throne,
   The pride of Burndennet, the rose of Tyrone.

I love her, for ripe is the flush of her cheeks,
I love her, for song is the language she speaks,
I love her, for virtue of highest degree,
O, I love her, the darling, because she loves me:
   My fair one, my rare one, my own love alone,
   The pride of Burndennet, the rose of Tyrone.

We loved in the sunshine, we loved in all weather,
The storms that would part us but bind us
   together,
The envious may sneer and the proud may
   complain,
But the love that has conquered will conquer
   again.
   Oh, blest shall the bower be that claims for its
      own
   The pride of Burndennet, the rose of Tyrone.

"Burndennett" in Dt title only.

Kate of Coleraine [H684: 2 Jan 1937]

s: (m) "Kitty of Coleraine."

Key G.

The maidens of France may be graceful and merry,
And stately and loving the damsels of Spain,
But match me, in either, the daughters of Derry,
The fairest among them, sweet Kate of Coleraine.
The flax that she dresses is shamed by her
   tresses,
So fair and so flowing -- no art to restrain;
The fates that we've read of, our lives spin the
   thread of;
Would that mine they had spun with sweet Kate's
   of Coleraine.

More bright is her smile than the Bann flowing by
   her,
More lustrous her soul than the blue eye it lights,
And if heaven the blessings of fortune deny her,
With blessings far better the loss it requites.
The white web she spreads on the green sward
   she treads on
Compares with the skin of her white foot in vain,
And oh, what a sin in the notion that linen
Could vie with the bosom of Kate of Coleraine.

Long, long on the banks of the Bann's sunny
   waters
Be maidens as blest and as beautiful seen,
May the sons of the soil show they're worthy her
   daughters
By loving and guarding their island of green.
May the fair and the tender proclaim 'No surrender'
To all who, contented, bear tyranny's chain,
And the breast of a helot, or dark scowling zealot
Ne'er pillow thy slumbers, sweet Kate of Coleraine.

Kate of Glenkeen

[H41: "A love song from Fagivey," 23 Aug 1924]

s: (m) "Captain Black"; o: (m) "Aghalee Heroes"
[cf. O'Neill 1903:8 (#44) "She's a Daughter of
Daniel O'Connell"].

Source: m: author Andrew Orr; s: (m) coll. Maud
Houston (Coleraine).

s: This fine air is sung to a well-known Orange
song.... I have used it for "Kate of Glenkeen,"
as the "Songs of the People" are intentionally

Sam Henry's Songs of the People

kept free from political bias, and yet so fine an air should not be lost.

Key C.

By the banks of the Barrow residing
Are girls of dark raven hair,
And where the Blackwater is gliding,
The maidens are faithful and fair,
But of all Erin's pure-hearted daughters,
I'll tell you the one that is queen,
She dwells by Agivey's bright waters --
She is lovely young Kate of Glenkeen.

She is pure as the snowdrops that cluster
Round the heath bell that blooms on Slievemore,
Her eye hath the diamond's lustre
That studs the grey breast of Benmore,
Than her voice the soft south is not sweeter
When breathing o'er spring's robe of green,
Or Errigal's fawn is not fleeter
Than lovely young Kate of Glenkeen.

The snow I have seen freshly falling
On Slemish's top as I stood,
The wild rose I've seen on Slievegallion
Just cleaving its emerald hood,
And the snow from the clouds newly driven,
The flower from the mountains o' Shean,
Are the colours that nature has given
The cheeks of young Kate of Glenkeen.

'Tis sweet when the sun is saluting
The heights of the misty Knocklayde,
'Tis sweet when the first ray is shooting
Through lovely Glenullin's green shade,
But oh, there's an hour that is sweeter,
When the star of the evening is seen,
And its bright twinkle tells me I'll meet her --
The lovely young Kate of Glenkeen.

The Star of Glenamoyle [H13: Wp, 9 Feb 1924]

Source: (w) (Cool, Cumber-Claudy); (m) native of the Tyrone border.

[Wp written at top] The Star was a daughter of Connolly the Landsteward.

[Wp] s: Glenamoyle is a lovely park land at the headstreams of the Faughan, standing amidst the guardian summits of Learmount, Sawell, Dart, Knockanbane, and Mullaghash....

[Bt is in 2/4 and G, but has no other substantial differences from Wp.]

[Wp] Key F.   [Bt, Dt] Key G.

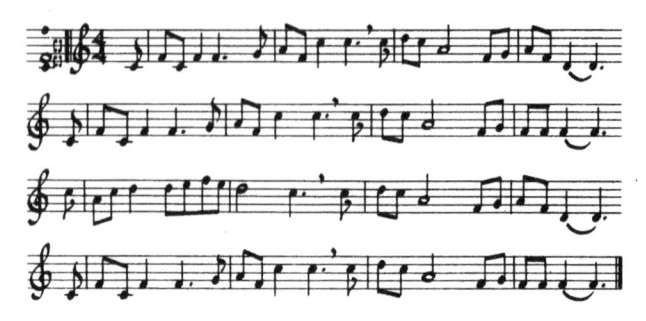

You gentle muse that will ne'er refuse
To sympathise with a rural swain,
To exercise on this composition
That has been sung on my night of fame.
Ye gentle breezes that blow from Sawell,
That lovely flower you could not spoil,
The darkest night you would find in winter,
Shines bright the star of sweet Glenamoyle.

Her cherry cheeks are as red as roses,
Her skin far whiter than the driven snow,
Her hair in ringlets its rolls are waving,
Like polished ivory her teeth doth show.
She has my very heart entangled,
I do declare, as she walks the soil;
I really thought that she was some goddess
That had descended to Glenamoyle.

The feathery train are all united
To pay her homage as she walks along,
The rabbits sporting and small birds courting,
To organise them the thrush does sing;
The whirring moorcock joins in the chorus,
The lark and linnet thought it no toil
To sing the praises of lovely Annie
Around the banks of sweet Glenamoyle.

Now to conclude these simple verses,
I'll stop my pen and no more I'll say,
But had young Joseph received this fair one,
Her golden glory would have decayed away;
But had young Joseph received this fair one,
To win his bride would have been no toil,
He would surely sail o'er the foaming billows
To wed the star of sweet Glenamoyle.

2.4: ... teeth does ... [Bt, Dt]

The Flower of Glenleary

[H22a, 12 Apr 1924: Dt]

s: (m) "Braes of Balquhidder."

Source: (w) Jackson Taggart (Carnalridge, Portrush); m: author Andrew Orr.

s: The poet and lover was evidently a stranger in Glenleary (possibly a schoolmaster, as his imagery is derived from the ancient kingdom of Desmond in Counties Cork and Kerry).

Key D.

Oh, Crossgar's sunny hills are bespangled with
  flowers,
And Drumcroon's sylvan braes fringed with
  blaeberry bowers,
Yet I sigh for the grove that encircles my Mary,
She's the queen of my heart and the flower of
  Glenleary.
    Yes, I sigh for the grove that encircles my
      Mary,
    She's the queen of my heart and the flower of
      Glenleary.

She's as pure as the snow on the Mangerton
  mountain,
She's as fleet as the roe by Lough Van's crystal
  fountain,
She is voiced like the lute and lipped like the
  rowan,
And she walks light o' foot as the breeze o'er
  the gowan.
    She is voiced ...

Her brow is as white as the foam on the Alla,
And her blue eyes as bright as the harebells o'
  Sallagh,
And her ringlets o' brown are a wild witching
  cluster,
And the sweep of her gown throws a sunshade
  of lustre.
    And her ringlets ...

Her neck's as the plume of the swan on Lough
  Barra,
And her cheeks have the bloom of the rosebud o'
  Clara;
She's mild as the dawn which in brightness
  reposes
O'er the dew on the lawn with its sunrise of
  roses.
    She's mild ...

Fair maid of my dreams, did we meet here to
  sever?
Yet I thirst for the stream that divides us
  forever.
May the sun ever shine, and may care never
  cumber

Till this bosom of mine be the couch for thy
  slumber.
    May the sun ...

The Flower of Gortade   [H178: 9 Apr 1927]

Source: Thomas H. Stewart, fiddle (Mayoghill,
Garvagh); author local blind poet Kane, in honor
of his sister.

s: ... The classical references were a feature of
songs of that period and may be traced to the influence of McCloskey's Academy at Tirgarvil from
which over 300 students graduated and obtained
degrees, including the renowned Dr. George Sigerson, the poet.
[Dt] Gortade, near Maghera, was the birthplace of
Charles Thomson, Secretary of Congress in Washington's time.
[Bp] (The last four words are spoken, not sung.)

o: The accidentals [E and B] should both be flattened [transforming the tune to the aeolian, natural minor, mode].

Key B flat.

Descend, ye chaste muses, ye bards and ye sages
With Orpheus, who tamed roaring beasts with his
  lyre;
You ancient historians that's dead many ages,
I hope you'll awake and my genius inspire;
You great men of learning, give your
  approbation,
Ye gods and philosophers, lend me your aid
In praise of a female who's leaving our nation:
She's the bright star of Erin and flower of
  Gortade.

Oh, was I as Homer, the prince of the writers,
Who sang of Athenians and Spartans so bold,
Could I paint with the skill of a Roman inditer,
The praise of this fair one can never be told.
Fair Penelope, Venus, Diana or Flora,
Whose beauty and chastity never can fade,

Sam Henry's Songs of the People

Fair Helen, Lucretia or famous Aurora:
All these could not equal the flower of Gortade.

Unrivalled she stands 'mongst the daughters of
   Erin,
For wit or for beauty, none can her excel;
On the third of September her vessel she's
   steering
Far, far from the place she did formerly dwell.
The consorts of Hector that's mentioned in story,
Susanna, whose virtues are still undecayed,
Queen Dido, who reigned with her sovereign in
   glory;
Even these do not equal the flower of Gortade.

Adieu to old Erin, the land of my childhood,
Where luxury, pomp and magnificence rove,
No more I'll traverse o'er the plains or the wild
   wood
Or listen to the mavis that sings in the grove;
No more by the creeks or promontories I'll wander
In search of the wild rose in beauty displayed,
No more in romances my memory shall ponder
Alongst with my comrades that dwell in Gortade.

Adieu to my mother, my sisters and brothers,
My cousins, my comrades and neighbours so kind;
When I'm far away from this old Irish nation,
They'll all join in chorus and bear me in mind,
And if to Columbia God sends me safe over,
I'll write a few lines to my dear comrade maid,
Who does constantly mourn with my friends and
   true lover
Since Margaret O'Kane has abandoned Gortade.

Since destined by fate to forsake Erin's nation,
I hope that my mother no longer will mourn,
I pray that the Lord may send her consolation
Till I to this island again do return,
For then will all sorrow and sadness be ended
And for all her trouble she'll then be repaid
When she in fond raptures with her arms
   extended
Will welcome her daughter once more to Gortade.

3.6: Susannah, ... [Dt]

A Kintyre Love Song [H195: 6 Aug 1927]

s: (m) "Ned of the Hill."

Source: (m) A[rchie] M'Eachran (Kilblaan, Southend, Argyleshire [Scotland]); author James
(Hamish Dall) Mactaggart, A.R.C.O. (High St,
Dalintober, Campbeltown, [Argyleshire, Scot-
land]).

[Bp] s: ... The air ... is ... "Ned of the Hill,"
of which George Moore, the novelist, says that,
played in a mist by someone unseen, it conveys
to the hearer the wistful spirit of the Celt in a
way that no other air can equal. It is interesting to find this air preserved in Kintyre, a
musical proof of the Irish origin of the Dalriadic
Scots. The beautiful words are ... well wedded
to the tune.

[D, W] Copyright reserved by Hamish Dall
McTaggart, ... who gave special permission for
its inclusion in the series.

m: A copy I have of a typescript made for S. H.
from the Belfast set is quite clear: all the even-
numbered lines start with *la* [= B].

Key D.

Like the vi'lets in spring, like the lark on the
   wing,
Like the sweet-scented lure in the breath of the
   moor,
Like the clear dancing rill, like the breeze on the
   hill,
Like the smile of April -- so, sweet is she.
Like the snowy white swan that the sun shimmers
   on,
Or the dimples we trace on the lake's clear face,
Like the sweet mountain fawn, like the faint flush
   of dawn,
Like the lilies on the lawn -- so, fair is she.

As when grey mists uprise to the sun-blazoned
   skies,
Or when silver starlight cheers the cold winter's
   night,
As a lull on the sea, as cool rain on the lea,
As the rose to the bee -- so, kind is she.
Like the stories they tell of St. Colum's green
   well,
Or the songs that are sung in the old mother
   tongue --
Dear as these, yes, and more, is the maid I
   adore,
Oh, it makes my heart sore -- so, dear is she.

The Manchester Angel [H711: 10 Jul 1937]

o: "The Irish Girl." Other titles: "As I Walked
Out," "The Country Girl," "The Irish Wash-Wo-

man," "Let the Wind Blow High or Low," "Molly Bawn," "My (The New) Irish Girl (Polly)," "Pretty Polly"; cf. "I Wish My Love Was a Red, Red Rose," "Love It Is a Killing Thing," "Mary from Dungloe."

Source: (w) James Currie (Pigtail Hill, Balnamore); (m) whistling of Valentine Crawford (Bushmills), from his father (Garry Bog, Ballymoney) c. 1877.

g: What Henry presents is actually a fragment of "The Irish Girl," and most of the references here are for that title.

Key G.

I wish I was in Manchester a-sitting on the grass,
And in my hand a flowing can and on my knee a lass;
I would call for liquor of the best and pay before I'd go,
I would kiss my true love's ruby lips, let the wind blow high or low.

I wish I was a butterfly, I would light on my love's breast,
Or if I was a nightingale, I would sing my love to rest,
Or if I was a mavis with the voice that's loud and clear,
I would sit and sing with you, Molly, for once I loved you dear.

I wish she was a red, red rose grows in yon garden fair,
Me to be the gardener, of her I would take care,
There's not a month in all the year but I would my love renew,
I would plant it round with posies -- sweet william, thyme and rue.

Mary Smith, the Maid of Mountain Plain

[H636: 1 Feb 1936]

Source: man (Bushmills), learned from Alex. Henderson in a lumber camp, Kippaway Lake, North Ontario, c. 1925.

Key C.

You maids of Columbia, wherever you be,
I beg your attention and now pity me,
My heart is surrounded by love's burning pain,
And this maid has got me wounded on sweet Mountain Plain.

The lands of Columbia I've travelled all o'er,
And a match for this fair one I ne'er saw before,
Two eyes like bubbles that glide o'er yon main,
Now in letters I'll mention this fair lady's name.

M says 'memory,' while A gives me 'aid,'
R says 'remember, you'll ne'er gain this maid,'
Y says 'she's youthful, and your love's in vain,
And she never shall wander from sweet Mountain Plain.'

S says 'surrender,' while M says 'don't mourn,'
I, 'feel inclined my fortune to turn,'
T tells me 'take her and cure all your pain,'
And H says to 'hold her in sweet Mountain Plain.'

I wish I was Adam and my love was Eve,
Some plan I would form, my love to receive,
In the garden of Eden not long would she stand,
I would take this fair damsel to her own native land.

If I don't gain her I'm forever undone,
The green fields I'll wander and frantic I'll run,
And when I think on her, I'll always exclaim,
'Fare you well, lovely Mary, on sweet Mountain Plain.'

Autumn Dusk / Coimfeasgar Fogmair

[H831: 28 Oct 1939]

Source: Gaelic sung by Anne Tracey (Greencastle, Co. Tyrone), coll. Henry Morris, translated by Andy Dooey [sic] (Ballymacaldrick, Dunloy), English verse by George Graham (Cross Lane, Coleraine).

s: This sweet song is from the Gaelic....

Key D.

Sam Henry's Songs of the People

It was on an autumn twilight,
I watched the seagulls glide,
When the fairest of all maidens
Stole softly by my side.

Her cheeks were red, golden her hair,
Her fingers soft and neat;
Such gentleness my heart beguiled,
Her voice was low and sweet.

I was wearily reclining
When this fair one came my way,
Her gentle arms embraced me
And she kissed me tenderly.

I thought she was a stranger,
She told to me her name,
Then in her native Gaelic tongue
She spoke it o'er again.

I have no words to utter
That would describe her grace,
Her radiant flowing tresses,
Her sweet and smiling face.

Oh, were we on Carnmullagh's side
At autumn's shadow time,
And in her eyes the love-light
Clear shining as in mine,

There would my heart be happy
Beneath the heaven above,
To wander with that maiden,
My first and only love.

The Dear-a-Wee Lass [H74: 11 Apr 1925]

Source: (w, m) coll. "North Antrim" [Dt: Robert MacMullan (Portballintrae)] from William Russell (Bushmills district), 1884.

[Bp] s: ... contributed by "North Antrim," who heard them on the Anchor Liner s.s. *Furnessia* at the saloon concert on her maiden trip of 12th July 1884. The singer ... received a great ovation on his traditional rendering of this simple song and air. The composition of this air is curious, repeating the first line of the music three times. The words are wedded to the tune in a remarkable way which I have tried to convey in the first verse. The striking feature is the singing of the first word of the third line at the end of the second line.
[Bp typed at bottom] A favorite song of the author -- "North Antrim."
[Dt] The song is included in the book *Rowlock Rhymes* by Robert McMullan [sic].

Key F.

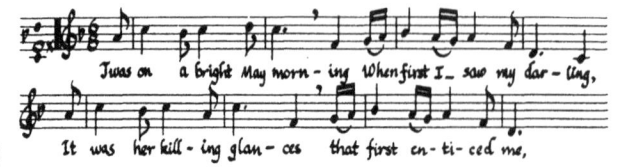

'Twas on a bright-a May morning when first I
   saw-w my darling,
It was her killing glances tha-at first en-ti-zed
   me, her
Eyes they were adorn-ed li-i-ke two bright
   sta-ars at mor-ning,
For ever I'll adore her, she's a dear-a-wee lass
   to me.

There were brewers, millers, bakers, aye, and
   journeymen shoemakers,
Sev'ral other tradesmen of a high and low-ow
   degree, in-
Sistin' for her favour, bu-ut theirs was useless
   labour,
For ev-er I'll adore her, she's a dear-a-wee lass
   to me.

If I had it in my pow-er, I'd go this blessed
   hour
And build my love a bower beneath some shady
   tree,
I'd marry her and love her and bless the God
   above her
Who moved me to adore her, she's a dear-a-wee
   lass to me.

The Valley Below

[H47: "A song from the English planters," 4 Oct 1924]

Other title: "She Lives in ...."

Source: (w, m) Mrs A[rchie] Hamill (Trooper's Hill, Kiltinney, Macosquin), from her father, principal (St. Johnston National School, Co. Donegal).

s: ... The reference to the nightingale and the turtle-dove, neither of which is found in Ireland, would indicate the origin of the song as having been in the English Home Counties.

l: The 16th notes in measures 2 and 6 should probably be 8ths; and one entire phrase, corresponding to one line of text (?line 7), is absent from the tune in Bp.

Key G.

C14 / She's a lovely fair

The broom bloomed so fresh and so fair,
The lambkins were sporting all round,
As I wandered to breathe the fresh air,
By chance a rich treasure I found:
A lass resting 'neath the green shade,
And whose smile the whole world did forego:
Oh, as blooming as May was the maid,

And she lives in the valley,
And she lives in the valley,
And she lives in the valley,
The valley below.

Her song struck my ear with surprise,
Her voice like the nightingale sweet,
But love took its seat in her eyes:
There beauty and innocence meet.
From that moment my heart was her own,
I lived but her wishes to know,
She's as blooming as roses new blown.

My cottage with woodbine's o'ergrown,
And the sweet turtle dove's cooing round;
My flocks and my herds are my own,
My pasture with hawthorn is bound.
All those riches I'd lay at her feet
If her heart in return she'd bestow;
She's as blooming as roses new blown.

3.7: As roses new blown she is sweet. [Dt]

The Dark-Haired Girl [H559: 18 Aug 1934]

Source: Michael M'Bride, 87 (East Torr), learned from his uncle Dan O'Hara; author Dan M'Glarry, stonecutter (Carey), "best man" at O'Hara's wedding.

Key D.

On the twentieth of July in the year of thirty-nine,
My com-er-ade and I to ramble did incline,
O'er lofty hills and mountains, not fearing any per'l,
It was then I first beheld my sweet dark-haired girl.

Her skin is like the lily and her cheeks a rosy red,
Her eyes they do sparkle like diamonds in her head,
Her teeth is far excelling either ivory or pearl,
And lightsome is the heart of my dark-haired girl.

Oh, my dark-haired girl, I do promise unto thee,
To keep the solemn oath we made 'twixt you and me,
My heart wouldn't change for the crown of an earl,
Oh, the pride of being in love with my dark-haired girl.

Though my love she was a servant, there is few I could compare
To this pretty little girl with the nice dark hair,
Although I've land and riches, from her hair a pretty curl,
Will be all I want as dower with my dark-haired girl.

Braiding Her Glossy Black Hair

[H493: 13 May 1933]

Author Andrew Doey (Ballymacaldrick); (m) whistled by James Brogan (Anticur).

s: The air taken down in the open field at Ballymacaldrick (Dunloy) from the whistling of ... James Brogan ...

Key G.

A bright April sun was adorning
The valley from Trostan's high brow,
The lark sang his welcome to morning
As I hied with my team to the plough,
When lo, like some mermaid or fairy,
Her white neck and shoulders all bare,
In the door of her cottage stood Mary
A-braiding her glossy black hair.

I paused for a moment to give her
Again the 'God save ye!' she gave,
When flashed from her eye's sparkling quiver
The arrow that made me her slave.
I passed to the ploughing, sore grieving,
My poor heart stuck fast in the snare
That Mary's fair fingers were weaving
As she braided her glossy black hair.

Ochone! for the boy that so gaily
Used [to] whistle along at the plough,

Sam Henry's Songs of the People

Grown dreamy and dreamier daily
Till weary's the look on his brow.
His steeds are grown wild and contrary,
His furrows are crooked and quare,
All bewitched by the eye of sweet Mary
As she braided her glossy black hair.

The Old Dun Cow [H492: 6 May 1933]

o: (m) "The Crocodile."

Source: Oliver Paul, J.P. (Coleraine), from a broadsheet sold at Powell & Clark's Circus (Fair Hill, Coleraine) c. 1880.

s: ... Oliver Paul['s] ... memory has retained the air ever since.

Key D.

Some miles from here in the County Clare there
   stands an old farm-house,
And in that house there lives the girl I would like
   to make my spouse.
Her name it is Dolly, a sort of a jolly good-looking
   girl, no doubt,
She is round and plump and my heart goes thump
   when I think how she served me out.

*For I'd roam many a mile over hedge and style
   to covet that girl, I vow,
And I'd stand like a fool while she sits upon a
   stool, milking her old dun cow.*

It was by a chance at a country dance that I first
   saw Dolly May,
She invited me to go and see her milk the old dun
   cow next day.
Next morning at five, I was up and all alive and
   went straight to the old barn,
The cocks were crowing and the cows were lowing,
   and her milking did me charm.

She had a dimpled chin and a purple skin and a
   sort of a dark green eye,
She had a knowing wink, and I really think to win
   that girl I'll try.
For a plain gold ring she'd sit and sing and
   likewise milk her cow,
I'll get married very soon, tomorrow afternoon,
   for I feel in the humour now.

Gragalmachree [H582: 26 Jan 1935; Laws M23]

(Gradh Geal mo Croidhe)

Other titles: "Down by the Fair River," "Gay Girl Marie," "Grá Mo Croí," "Griogal Cridhe," "Grogal McCree," "Groyle Machree," "Newry Mountain," "Sweet Gramachree."

Source: (m) James Kealey, fiddler (Ballymoney), learned in Dungiven district; (w) library, Royal Irish Academy.

s: This beautiful air, hitherto unrecorded, was played for the first time in public at the Ceilidh in connection with St. Malachy's Dramatic Club on Monday night....
   This song was broadcast from Belfast on Monday night by Sam Henry.

Key F.

At the foot of Newry mountain there runs a
   clear stream
Where I met my true love, sweet Molly by name,
She's slender in waist for young men to see,
And her name in plain Irish is Gragalmachree.

'Twas on a summer's morning as I walked along,
Down by a green valley I heard a fine song,
'Twas a fair damsel with her voice most clear,
Singing, 'Blest would I be if my darling was
   here.'

I then drew more near to a shade that was
   green,
Where the leaves grew about her and she scarce
   could be seen,
And it was her whole cry, 'My love, come away,
For without you, my Johnny, no more can I stay.

'The moon it may darken and may shew no light
And the bright stars of heaven may fall down
   quite,
The rocks they may melt and the mountains
   remove
If e'er I prove false to the fair one I love.

'O were I an empress, had care of a crown
And had all the money that's for it laid down,
I would freely remit it to the boy that I love
And my mind I'd resign to the great God above.'

Like a sheet of white paper is her neck and
  breast,
Her bosom's the swan's, and be it confest,
She's a pattern of virtue wherever she goes,
And her cheeks I compare to the red blushing
  rose.

The ships on the ocean may go without sails
And the smallest of fishes may turn into whales,
In the midst of the ocean grow an apple tree
If e'er I prove false to my Gragalmachree.

The Maid of Altaveedan [H603: 22 Jun 1935]

s: (m) "The Girl of the Golden Tresses."

Source not given.

Key D.

I met her on the brow of Altaveedan Hill,
The lambs were calling after her to stay there;
I gazed upon her beauty, but could not gaze my
  fill,
Her tresses matched the golden flowers of May
  there.
Oh, Altaveedan's hill leads up to Orra's crest,
And happy they who climb its purple heather
To see the god of day dying in the crimsoned west
To rise again at dawn in summer weather.

But there's a head of gold far lovelier than yon
  hill:
'Tis Shena's wealth of golden clustering tresses,
And I would climb each mountain and face life's
  every ill
To greet the dawn of love my heart that blesses.
See yonder on the hillside the wild bird knows no
  fear,
Yet in the snare he soon may be in danger;
Ten thousand golden hairs of her whom I love
  dear
Have captured me, and I'm no more a ranger.

1.5: Slieve-an-Orra = "the mountain of gold." [s]

Jean of Ballinagarvey [H822: 26 Aug 1939]

s: (m) "The Maid of Dunysheil"; g: "Lovely
Jean."

No source given.

[Original set in 2-line stanzas, but the tune fits
4 lines.]

Key C.

The first place that I saw my love was Ballymoney
  town,
I viewed her mild behaviour as she walked up and
  down.
She far exceeds Diana fair or any other queen,
She dwells in Ballinagarvey, and her name is lovely
  Jean.

Her ruby lips and her bright eyes, they so enticed
  me,
I wish and wish with all my heart she would with
  me agree.
Coming from her daily toil, no care upon her
  brow,
She's loved by all the young men who live around
  the Vow.

If I'd ten thousand pound in gold, or had ten
  thousand more,
I'd share them with the girl I love, who dwells on
  the Bann shore.
Her ringlets fair none can compare, she's fairer
  than the swan,
I took her for an angel when bathing in the Bann.

Oh, she's a lovely damsel, as fair as any queen,
With locks of wavy hair and dressed in emerald
  green.
I'll do my best endeavour to take her from her
  trade
And bid adieu for never more to this sweet lovely
  maid.

The Flower of Benbrada [H537: 17 Mar 1934]

Source: (w) Mrs Frank Kealey (Ballysally, Coleraine); (m) her son James Kealey (Union St, Ballymoney); author late Francey Heaney (Magheraboy [Dungiven]).

s: The Flower of Benbrada was Miss Lizzie Donaghy, of the Hass, on the slopes of Benbrada, near Dungiven, and this song was composed on the occasion of her leaving for America.
  ... Francey Heaney ... died about three years ago at the age of 90....

Key F.

Sam Henry's Songs of the People

One evening fair, to take the air,
By Curraghlane I chanced to stray,
I spied a maid -- her beauty swayed --
The fairest gem that blooms in May.
Her lovely form did nature charm
As o'er the lawn she roamed at will,
Perception smiled, she looked so mild,
That matchless flower of Benbrada Hill.

Sweet nature's face lit up with grace
Her features lovely and divine,
Sweet echoes there in chorus swell
Their mingling notes of every kind;
The feathered throng, convened in song,
Charm with their sweetly vocal skill,
Their heartfelt lays resound with praise
As she views the flowers of Benbrada Hill.

With sober mien she trod the green,
Fair as young Hebe of the hours,
The muses nine with Proserpine
Came there to strew her path with flowers;
The sylvan train bedecked the plain,
As ever did my bosom fill,
And Flora now bedecks her brow
With flowers bloomed on Benbrada Hill.

This lovely fair beyond compare,
She now intends to go away,
She was the beauty of our isle,
Fair as the goddess of the sea;
Till she returns, the rills will mourn,
With doleful notes their valleys fill;
The raging tide bore off with pride
The flower of sweet Benbrada Hill.

To tell her name might cause some blame
Hereafter on the mountain bard
For sake of she, and sever me
From one I fervently regard;
Could I like Homer or Virgil sing,
I ne'er would drop my rusted quill,
But I have tried and am still denied
To praise the flower of Benbrada Hill.

The Beauty of the Braid [H723: 2 Oct 1937]

Source: John Smylie (Leggyfat, Limavallaghan), from George Kielty, 80 (the Braid) c. 1907.

s: I obtained this lovely, very old and very interesting song ... in a quiet recess of the Cloughwater....

The song must be almost 200 years old as mention is made of the wolf, which is now extinct for close on two centuries.

The girl's name may have been Martha Martin, i.e., half a border (mar)gin; and half a bondage (thrall) -- tha. Irish bird -- martin. She may have lived at Knowehead (rising hill, near Broughshane). The expression of a name in a conundrum was a favourite artifice of songwriters.

Key C [Dp, written over crossed-out F].

I am a rover that roves strange nations
Through various stations of life to try,
Through town and country and corporations
I'm speculating most curiously.
No shield of Mars, nor no court of Venus
Could ever slay or my mind invade,
But my intellect is consummated
By the charming beauty lives in the Braid.

It was one morning for recreation
I chanced to walk o'er yon daisy hill,
Where the pinks and violets were decorated
All over the banks of a purling rill,
Where the feathered songsters they joined in chorus,
The lark and linnet their notes displayed,
The thrush and blackbird their bills did echo
To behold the beauty lives in the Braid.

I stood confounded in admiration,
My footsteps farther could not pursue,
By Cupid's armour I was entangled
When this lovely damsel appeared in view:
The raven ringlets hung o'er her shoulders,
Her neck the lily it did invade;
By nature's grandeur I must now surrender
To the charming beauty lives in the Braid.

Says I, 'My charmer, are you descended,
Or are you mortal? Pray tell to me,
If it's not treason, pray what's the reason
You're out so early in the dawn of day?
Your cherry cheeks are my heart enticing,
Your ruby lips have my mind mislaid;
If you don't relieve, I must die lamenting
For the charming beauty lives in the Braid.'

She says, 'Kind sir, do not tantalize me,
Your false delusion I do defy;
I'll let you know I'm a farmer's daughter
That rose this morning to let out the kye.

C14 / She's a lovely fair

The noise so great from the fold extended,
I heard the cries of a bleeding dam,
With my club in order I crossed the border
For fear the wolf had destroyed the lamb.'

Said I, 'My charmer, would you allow me,
Though I'm a stranger to you unknown,
To have the pleasure of some conversation,
To ask your name and convoy you home?'
'Oh, that's a thing, sir, I can't allow you,
For it's too early in the dawn of day;
I so respect you that I'll direct you
To call and see me some other day.

'When you find out my habitation,
There's one request you will bear in mind,
I so respect you that I'll direct you
To call and see me in time to dine.
Your modest countenance is so enticing
My mind forbids me to say you nay,
When you come hither, I'll acquaint my mother,
And I think she'll give you your evening tea.

'Take half a border in proper order,
And half a bondage, and that will do;
If you're acquaint['] with the Latin language,
My Christian name, sir, it will tell you.
A bird belongs to this Irish nation,
A beast enclosed near a rising hill:
If you're expert in your application,
That tells my name and the place I dwell.

'Walk on undaunted, your favour's granted,
To education you must apply,
At our next meeting we'll have more leisure,
All other rivals you do defy.
My business calls me, I cannot tarry,
I must attend to my mother's cry.'
With pleasing aspects in noblesse granted,
She dropped a courtesy and bid goodbye.

The Maid from the Carn Brae

[H704: 22 May 1937]

Author late James O'Kane (Gortinure, Maghera).

s: This beautiful song ... is published here by kind permission of [James O'Kane's] son, Mr Frank O'Kane, who hopes to give to the world in due course, the many fine songs composed by his father. James O'Kane was one of nature's poets. He sang with the same ease as the blackbird sings. He claimed an unbroken lineage from Cooey-na-Gall (1284 A.D.).
   Carn, as is the Gaelic idiom, is pronouced with a vowel sound between the consonants, Car-an.

l: Note the references in stanza 4 to other popular songs of the same genre.

Key A.

Sure, Fahy sung of the Galway maid,
He was captive in her thrall,
And the world stood by as he told them why
He was charmed by her old plaid shawl,
But I will try with the bard to vie
In a short but simple lay,
And I'll sing in praise of the girl who strays
By the slopes of the Carn Brae.

I saw this maid 'neath the sylvan shade
Of the hawthorn bushes, when
The sun's bright rays made a golden haze
Round the slopes of Maguire's Glen.
When I viewed the charm of her fairy form
An' her smile like the summer ray,
I was forced to own she was queen alone --
The maid from the Carn Brae.

As light as the fawn in the early dawn,
She trips o'er the dewy grass;
Demure and shy, she will pass you by
To the well on the mountain pass.
You may search in vain over France and Spain,
Yet homewards again you'll stray
In search of that pearl, that mountain girl
That resides near the Carn Brae.

They may sing of the maid from the County Down
And the star from Donegal,
An' the girl from Clare, an' God knows where
Is the girl with the old plaid shawl,
But I'll not roam from my mountain home,
An' the theme of my humble lay
Will arise for the girl with the nut-brown curls
That resides near the Carn Brae.

1.2: thrawl [Dp]

Claudy Green (b) [H115b. 23 Jan 1926: Dt]

[m = H115a.]

Source not given.

s: Alternative words.

Sam Henry's Songs of the People

One evening fair, for my recreation
Through Claudy borders I chanced to stray,
Where the wilds of nature set forth its praises
Through every valley and meadow gay,
Where the bird inhabitants of every species
Together chant their notes sublime,
Likewise the cuckoo on bending branches
To return in season she does incline.

I being free from all snares of Cupid,
With fond amusement my bosom filled
To see the leaves in the bowers wavering,
The Faughan water in clear streams ran still;
The little trout and the salmon sporting,
For to behold them I did draw near,
And from that moment I was eclipsed
By that lovely fair one who did appear.

I stepp-ed up to that matchless fair one,
Saying, 'Are you Flora, that goddess fair?
Or are you Venus sprung from the ocean
The hearts of young men to ensnare?'
'Oh no, kind sir, I am but a maiden
And through these valleys I've oftimes been;
For my amusement I am gathering flowers
That decorate sweet Claudy Green.'

Her skin was like to the olive paper,
Her breath as sweet as the scent of thyme,
And in my love's bosom my heart lies bleeding,
For all her actions they are divine.
I could serve like Jacob for fourteen seasons
Through burning sands or some distant clime;
All my vexations could bear with patience,
In my love's arms could I spend my time.

Maggie of Coleraine [H657: 27 Jun 1936]

s: (m) "The Girls of Coleraine," "Teddy O'Neill."

Source: Anthony Campbell (Levenside, Barrhead, Scotland), learned from James Kane (Clooney, Magilligan) c. 1896.

Key G.

Give me Coleraine where the lovely Bann river
Flows on in its splendour to meet the proud main,
For there lives the girl that is dear to my bosom,
And her I love dearly while life does remain.
Her cheeks like the roses in summer's due season,
When Flora with flowers decks mountain and plain,
She's the pride of the north and the beauty of Erin,
My Maggie who dwells in the town of Coleraine.

'Twas in the springtime when flowers were a-blooming,
And birds sweetly singing in each shady grove,
That I met sweet Maggie, my own blue-eyed maiden,
Along the Bann shore as she chanced for to rove.
Her hair like spun gold hung in curls down her shoulders,
And sweetly she tripped o'er the green mossy plain,
She's the pride of the north and the beauty of Erin,
My Maggie who dwells in the town of Coleraine.

It was in the evening when soft dews were falling,
Among the gay flowers I chanced for to stray
With Maggie, sweet Maggie, who smiled so enchanting,
She first charmed my heart and then stole it away.
Now, although far away from the lovely Bann water,
I hope soon to stray by its green banks again
With the pride of the north and the beauty of Erin,
My Maggie who dwells in the town of Coleraine.

The Flower of Corby Mill

[H612: 24 Aug 1935]

o: (m) "The Winding Banks of Erne"; g: "The Blooming Rose of Antrim." Other titles: "The Maid of the Colehill"; cf. "Swansea Barracks."

Source: John Smylie (Limavallaghan, Clough, Co. Antrim); m: according to a note found in Sam Henry's papers this song was made by John and William Brownlee of Clough, Co. Antrim [1979:57].

s: We are indebted to ... John Smylie ... for this typical song of the countryside.

Key G.

Come all you tender-hearted chaps, I hope you'll
  lend an ear
And likewise pay attention to these few lines I
  have here,
It's all in praise of a pretty maid I mean to use
  my quill,
She's the blooming rose of Antrim and the flower
  of Corby Mill.

It was on the first of Janu'ry last, I was going
  to Butler's Fair,
I spied this pretty fair maid, she was combing
  down her hair,
And as I gazed upon her, my heart with joy did
  fill,
She's the blooming rose of Antrim, the flower
  of Corby Mill.

It was all for recreation I went to the fair that
  day,
I didn't intend to tarry long when I crossed
  M'Mullan's Brae,
But meeting with some comrade lads when I
  arrived there,
Oh, kindly they saluted me, 'You're welcome to the
  fair.'

We went to Mrs Butler's where there we did sit
  down,
The jugs of punch came tumbling in, the toast
  went merrily round,
The silver it being plenty, we drunk with right
  good will,
As we toasted a glass to the bonny wee lass that
  works in Corby Mill.

This fair maid to make mention, I will not name
  her name,
Her parents might get angry and I myself get
  blame,
She is a mill-girl to her trade and has the best
  of skill,
She's the blooming rose of Antrim, the flower
  of Corby Mill.

I've travelled this country o'er and o'er, and
  part of Scotland, too,
I've travelled England far and near, believe me,
  friends it's true,
I've travelled Ireland o'er and o'er, crossed
  many a hollow and hill,
But an equal yet I ne'er could get to the flower
  of Corby Mill.

The Flower of Magherally, O!

[H220: BLp, 28 Jan 1928]

Source: Dominick Maguire, esq, principal (St
Malachy's Schools, Coleraine).

[BLp] s: ... A charming little song from Co.
Down. The exigencies of rhyme required the
humorous substitution of "the great titter-a-
tally O," the reference being in all probability
to Damer, of Shronill, near Tipperary, the richest man in Ireland about the year 1800, or it may
be a corruption of "the great Tetrarch Ali O!" as
the old song makers were very fond of learned
allusions.

[BLp, Dp in 4-line stanzas, but tune fits 8-line
stanza as in Bt. Also written at top of Dp:
"Hugh Bronte's bride."]

[Note to H221] Will collectors note that in song
no. 220, the first note in the third bar of line
1, the first and last notes of the second bar of
the third line, and the first note of the third bar
on the same line should be the higher octave.
[The corrections are made on Dp, evidently a
printer's first proof, not the final version
printed.]

Key C.

'Twas on a summer's morning,
The flowers were a-blooming-o,
Nature all adorning,
The wild birds sweetly singing-o,
I met my love near Banbridge town,
My charming blue-eyed Sally-o,
O, she's the pride of the County Down,
The flower of Magherally-o!

In admiration I did gaze
Upon that lovely maiden-o,
Adam was not more surprised
When he met Eve in Eden-o,
Her lovely hair in ringlets fell,
Her shoes of Spanish leather-o,
Her bonnet blue with ribbons strung,
Her scarlet scarf and feather-o.

An Irish boy although I be,
With neither wealth nor treasure-o,
She's the dearest of the dear,
My darling beyond measure-o.
If I'd all the wealth that is possessed
By the great titter-a-tally-o,
I'd give it to her that I love best,
The flower of Magherally-o.

But I hope the time will surely come
When we'll join hands together-o,

Sam Henry's Songs of the People

  It's then I'll take my darling home
  In spite of wind and weather-o.
  And let them all say what they will,
  And let them scowl and rally-o,
  For I shall marry the girl I love,
  The flower of Magherally-o.

1.2 [and similarly throughout all copies, including
 the title:] ... a-blooming, O!
1.7: ... of County Down, [Bt]
[Written on Dp, typed on Bt:]
 3.3: She is the ... [Bt]
 3.4: My darling and my treasure-o, [Bt: pleasure-o]
  .5: Had I the wealth ...
  .6: In Limerick's golden valley-o,
  .7: I'd share with her ...

4.: [Not in Dp or BLp.]

Magilligan
[H52a: "Two songs -- love lost and love won," 8 Nov 1924]

s: (m) "The Wearing of the Green." Other title: "The Shores of Sweet Benone."

Author Constable Fennell, R[oyal] I[rish] C[onstabulary] (Bellarena).

s: This song was composed for a concert about 30 years ago.... It at once attained popularity and is still a great favourite.

l: The tune, not included in the column, has been supplied from O'Neill 1903:81 (#467).

Kind friends, I've just come here tonight to sing to all of you
About the place, likewise my love: she lives down near the sea.
She was born in Magilligan with its mountains bold and grand,
And the first place that I spied her was down upon the strand.
Oh, Benvenue's rocks are lofty where the ravens build their nest,
I often took her for a walk and clasped her to my breast;
When we had been retiring from walking all that day,
Near old Duncrun I clasped her hand and hopefully did say --

 Oh, we'll never leave such scenery, my Mary dear and I,
 For if we leave Magilligan, I'm sure we would both die,
 We will comfort one another while there remains a stone
 Of that pretty seaside cottage in the hills of sweet Benone.

On a holiday up to the Bower I took my own asthore
And cut her name out on the bench as lovers did before,
Then looking through the bright red glass the sun was all aglow,
And turning to each other we beheld the winter snow.
We then retired outside awhile, the fresh breeze to inhale
And take a view from off that height of Nature's lovely vale,
Extending far beneath us and bounded by the sea.
I then sat down to rest myself with Mary on my knee.

I strolled one Sunday evening with my love to sweet Downhill,
I gently caught her by the hand when passing the limekiln,
We jogged along, but sadly, until we came in sight
Of Neilans's to get a drop to make our spirits light.
Poor Mary, she being temperate, had nought but ginger wine,
While I took something stronger to raise this heart of mine,
And when our thirsty throats were damped, we both sat by the sea
And starting by the swelling wave we both were forced to say --

On a New Year's day down by the Point I took my own dear pet,
The scenery we saw struck us, we never shall forget:
We saw a mighty, big large ship as she swiftly glided on
With thousands of fair daughters and sons with hearts so strong,
And as they waved their handkerchiefs, tears from their eyes did fall
When bidding adieu to Ireland and heading Donegal.
We both knelt down upon the strand and prayed most fervently
For God to guide that mighty ship safe o'er the deep blue sea.

*Oh, we'll never sail away like that, my Mary
   dear and I,
For if we leave Magilligan I'm sure we
   would both die,
We will comfort one another while there
   remains a stone
Of that pretty seaside cottage in the
   hills of sweet Benone.*

4.2: ... saw there, we ... [Dt]

The Valleys of Screen [H752: 23 Apr 1938]

o: (m) "The Aghalee Heroes"; g: "(The Banks of) Moyola," "The Flower of Sweet Ballinascreen."

Source: William Bradley (Tobermore) from Feddy M'Gonigal (Benady Glen, Dungiven) c. 1898.

Key G.

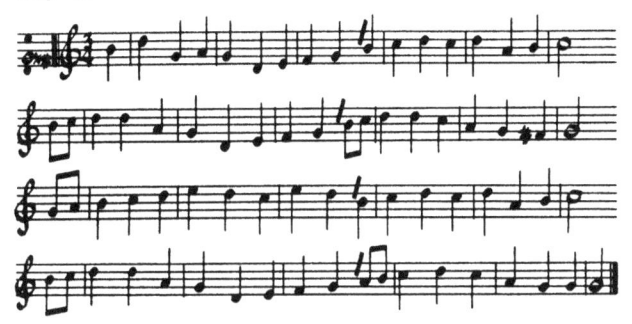

You people of every station,
Give ear to these lines I set forth,
Of a maiden, her pride of the nation
For virtue and beauty and worth.
She belongs to the famed County Derry,
Where many's a fair maid has been,
Where each lad and each lass sport together
In the lovely sweet valley of Screen.

All that do wish for to see her,
Give ear to these lines I pen down,
She lives in a townland quite near to
The village they call Draperstown.
She dwells on the banks of Moyola,
Where the trees and the meadows grow green;
She's my charming and sweet country girl
And she lives in the valleys of Screen.

Unto the astonished beholder,
Her eyes are most dazzling to view,
Her brown hair hangs down o'er her shoulder,
Her locks are most graceful, 'tis true;
She was dress-ed in clean, neat apparel,
No ornaments were to be seen
On that charming and plain country girl;
She's the flower of sweet Ballinascreen.

I first stepp-ed up and addressed her,
Saying, 'Pray tell me your dwelling and name,'
And when in my arms I pressed her,
My heart it was all in a flame.
'Kind sir, let my name be a secret,
My dwelling, it's plain to be seen,
I live in a neat little cottage
In the lovely sweet valleys of Screen.'

You have heard of some beautiful girls
Who lived in the great days of old,
Decorated with diamonds and pearls,
Ornamented with jewels and gold;
You have heard of fair Venus, the goddess,
And Helen, that Grecian queen,
But their faces were ne'er half so modest
As the flower of sweet Ballinascreen.

Summer Hill

[H20b: "Two Aghadowey songs," 29 Mar 1924]

Source: coll. Maud Houston

[Copy via Belfast Public Libraries from the Linenhall Library, Belfast, provided by John Moulden. Stanza 1 printed line for line beneath the sol-fa.]

Key E flat.

O, ye tender lovers, I pray draw near,
Of a rambling youth and you soon shall hear,
That took his way by yon purling rill
To view the beauty of Summer Hill.

I leaned me down for to muse awhile,
While I bein' quite happy on Erin's isle,
Where flowers bloom in yon bower still
To adorn the beauty of Summer Hill.

There cunning Cupid I chanced to spy,
His golden arrow at me let fly,
He pierced my breast and my heart did fill,
I'm a wounded lover on Summer Hill.

Her cheeks like roses that blow in June,
Her skin the snow that falls at noon,
Her teeth like ivory they do shine still,
She's the bloomin' beauty of Summer Hill.

But if I do get her, no more I'll mourn,
To the river Bann I will soon return,
To seek some pleasure along yon rill
And to bid adieu unto Summer Hill.

Now to conclude and to stop my pen,
To mention the poet I don't inten',
And here's to her and her true love still
An' she dwells contented on Summer Hill.

Sam Henry's Songs of the People

The Maid from the County Tyrone

[H528: 13 Jan 1934]

o: (m) "Rosin the Bow."

Source: (slopes of Mount Sawell).

s: Where the verse requires it the musical note should be duplicated.

Key G.

Many miles away in the country in a farmer's ancient home,
Where Michael Murphy bears the sway in the county of Tyrone,
He has one only daughter, as fair as the flowers in May,
And her looks they have decoyed me and stole my heart away.

And she's only a farmer's daughter, she is only a country maid,
She is only a simple Irish girl and she has my heart betrayed.
She is none of those saucy city folks, she does not pretend to be grand,
To me she's the fairest, dearest, rarest of all the young girls in the land.

Her eyes are bright as the stars above and her breath is fresh as the dew,
Her cheeks are red as two roses and her heart is loyal and true;
Could I but gain this fair one, all others I'd surely disown,
I'd wed with you, Maggie Murphy, the girl from the County Tyrone.

The first time that I saw my love, it was in the month of May,
The birds were sweetly singing and the lambs did sport and play,
And as we roved the meadows round, my love to her I made known,
And she stole this heart away from me, the girl from the County Tyrone.

Now I will cease my rambling and settle down in life,
I'll be her dear husband and she'll be my dear wife,
And I will cease my rambling and with her settle down,
Away out in the country, far from the noise of town.

Her Bonny Blue E'e

[H71: 21 Mar 1925]

A Scottish song popular in Ulster about 50 years ago.

o: (m) version of "Tanderagee."

Source: (m) coll. Maud Houston (Coleraine); (w) (Castleroe district).

Key B flat.

A wee bit awa' doon by the burn brae
There dwells 'mang the bushes a bonny wee fay,
And sleeping or wakin', by nicht or by day,
I never need try to forget her, I say.
She is queen o' my pleasure, she's the joy o' my cares,
She's uppermost always in a' my affairs,
And even the time I am saying my prayers,
I am thinking as much on her bonny blue e'e.

She comes in my dreams like a white summer cloud,
So graceful, so stately so artless and proud,
Wi' tresses a-cluster like tassels o' gowd,
And her footsteps as light as the lamb on the lea,
A lip o' the ruby, a brow o' the snaw,
A proud swelling bosom, a waist that is sma',
But sweetest and fairest and dearest o' a'
Is the blithesome wee blink o' her bonny blue e'e.

But noo I maun cross the rough ocean sae wide
And lea' her to be some ither a bride.
May a craven heart never win her to his side
Nor share the delight she is destined to gie;

May her home be a paradise, blooming and sweet,
Wi' sunshine around her and flowers at her feet;
May her bosom ne'er heave wi' a sigh o' regret
Nor a tear find its way to her bonny blue e'e.

Rosaleen Bawn

[H63: "A song of Barklie's Green," BLp, 24 Jan 1925]

Source: (w, m) Paul Mulholland, fiddle (Newmarket St, Coleraine, formerly of Tamneyrankin, Swateragh); [Bt] author Andrew Orr, linen lapper (Mullaghmore Bleach Green, emigrant to Australia); m: in *The Feast of Reason*.

s: ... The song was the heart's outpouring of a worker about 70 years ago [c. 1855] in Barklie's Green, Agivey, who loved a daughter of the employer and had nothing to offer her but the treasures of nature and his love.

[Bt] Robert Boyle, of Agivey, Aghadowey, states that the song was written ... in honour of Martha McKay of Mosside, who was reared with Miss Wilson of Mullaghmore.
    Andrew Orr became a poet of note in Australia.

[Print from British Library microfilm kindly provided by John Moulden. In Bt and Dt the first line of the sol-fa notation of the refrain is unnecessarily repeated. Bt, Dt in 3.]

Key D.

The midnight moon is beaming mild,
And flowers are glistening gay,
The fairy harps are warbling wild
Among the flowers of May;
Then leave Agivey's distant domes
Ere morn comes bright'ning on,
And seek with me my mountain home,
My own sweet Rosaleen Bawn.
    My own sweet Rosaleen Bawn,
    My own sweet Rosaleen Bawn,
    And seek with me my mountain home,
    My own sweet Rosaleen Bawn.

The heath shall strew its purple pearls
Around thy fairy feet,
Mild zephyr, with her flowing curls,
Shall tune thy silver lute,
And sweet as flow of syren's song,
And swifter than the dawn,
Our years of love shall glide along,
My own sweet Rosaleen Bawn.
    My own ...

You'll soon forget Agivey's towers
And gleaming halls of pride,
When seated in my mountain home,
My lovely mountain bride,
And maids more pure than mountain rills
Shall ever wait upon
The mandates of thy queenly will,
My own sweet Rosaleen Bawn.
    My own ...

Then come with me, my peerless queen,
And I with flowers shall deck
The clustering curls of silken sheen
That shade thy snow-white neck,
And round that angel form of thine,
Till life and light are gone,
These arms of love shall fondly twine
My own sweet Rosaleen Bawn.
    My own ...

Then haste, my love, the morning sky
Still bears the orbs of night,
All gleaming like thine own bright eyes
In floods of diamonds bright,
And ere the evening bells of dew
Bedeck the emerald lawn,
I'll waft thee to my hills of blue,
My own sweet Rosaleen Bawn.
    My own ...

1.2: The flowers ... [Bt, Dt]
2.5: ... of siren's song, [Bt, Dt]
4.6: Till light and life ... [Bt, Dt]

The Blazing Star of Drim (a)

[H197a: 20 Aug 1927]

Other title: "... Drum."

Source: A[rchie] MacEachran (Kilblaan, Southend, Kintyre, Argyleshire [Scotland]).

s: ... This song, to a different air, has been published in the journal of the Irish Folk Song Society of London. Readers are invited to send in any Ulster variants of the song.

Key A flat. Plaintive.

The first time that I saw my love, the stormy
  winds did blow,
The lofty hills and mountains were covered o'er
  with snow,
Where I being late a friend to treat, which caused
  me to stay,
There I beheld that lovely maid who stole my
  heart away.

The second time I saw my love, she smiled and
  passed me by;

Sam Henry's Songs of the People

Right earnestly I asked of her where did her
   dwelling lie.
Right modestly she answered me, and alluring
   was her tongue:
'As for my habitation, sir, I daily live in Drim.'

I stayed with her for that whole night and part
   of the next day,
Still wishing in my own mind that I had her o'er
   the sea,
But I asked her of her parents, and they said
   she was too young;
Till the day I die, I'll ne'er deny that I loved the
   star of Drim.

Oh, Peggy, you're my darling, my heart's
   delight, you know,
Your friends are got so saucy, love, they would
   not let you go,
But all their gold and riches I value not one pin,
Like a lady I would maintain you if I had you out
   of Drim.

My love is fair beyond compare and the aid of art
   does slight,
Her lovely neck and shoulders fair exceed the lily
   white,
Her eyes are bright as the stars at night and her
   hair is a light brown,
She is the darling of my heart, she's the blazing
   star of Drim.

Farewell to Letterkenny, where I was born and
   bred,
Likewise to ancient Derry, for 'twas there I
   learned my trade,
Farewell unto old comrades all, our ship waits
   neat and trim,
And twice farewell to my own true love, she's the
   blazing star of Drim.

The Blazing Star of Drung (b) [H197b: Dt]

[Dt] Source: Archie MacEachran; a version
contributed by Robert Clyde of Lensmore,
Bellarena.

[Dt] s: Drung is sometimes called Drum or Drim.

[Although Henry credits both H197a and b to the
same source, the two versions he prints are at
least different as are the spellings of the place
name in the title.]

The first time that I saw my love, the stormy
   winds did blow,
The hills and dales and valleys were covered o'er
   with snow,
It being too late a friend to treat, which caused
   me to stray,
Where I beheld that bonny wee lass that stole my
   heart away.

The next time that I saw my love, she smiled and
   passed me by.
Says I to her, 'My bonny wee lass, where does
   your dwelling lie?'

She answered me right modestly a mild and as
   mild a tongue,
'Kind sir, my habitation and my dwelling lie in
   Drung.'

I courted her the lee long night and part of the
   next day,
I could wish wi' all my heart I had her on the say.
I asked her of her brother John, [he] said she
   was too young;
Till the day that I die I'll ne'er deny that I loved
   the maid of Drung.

Oh, Nancy, you're my fancy, you're my only joy
   and care,
Your parents they were angry and would not let
   me near.
It's not your gold or silver that I would value a
   pin,
I'd maintain you like a lady if you were far from
   Drung.

My love, she's like the morning star, she dresses
   all by day,
Her lovely neck and shoulders they excel the lilies
   gay,
Her charming voice made me rejoice, she sung
   her notes so clear,
I would count it next to paradise to be with you,
   my dear.

It's farewell Londonderry, it was there I learned
   my trade,
And likewise to Dungiven where I was born and
   bred
Here's a health to my wee darling, our ship is
   going on,
And twice farewell to that bonny wee lass, she's
   the blazing star of Drung.

3.3: ... John, she said ... [Dt orig.]
6.4: ... the bleezing star ... [Dt]

Ann o' Drumcroon

[H26a: BLp "Two love songs to the same air,"
                                    10 May 1924; H246: 28 Jul 1928]

s: By the author of "The Flower of Glenleary"
[H22a; Andrew Orr].

[Print from British Library microfilm file of
Northern Constitution kindly sent by John
Moulden. H26 provides no music for this song.]

[Bp] ... Words republished by request. The air
now published for the first time.
[Dt] ... Andrew Orr ... afterwards became Editor of the *Ballarat Chronicle*, Australia.

Key C.

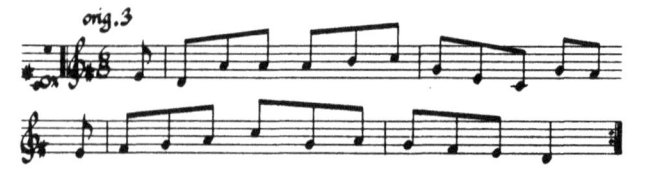

Ye maidens around me are lightsome and bonny,
But oh, for a sight of my own little queen,
Her brow is so snowy, her glance is so sunny,
Her footsteps of music so light on the green.
Her hair is a cluster of rich raven splendour,
Her cheeks are a fold of the rosebuds in June,
And the love and the graces, so sweet and so tender,
Unite in the beauties of Ann o' Drumcroon.

She's pure as the angels that guide her and guard her,
She's artless as nature and tender as love,
She's shy of the worship her beauty awards her,
Yet proud as the eagle and true as the dove.
She's sweet as the myrtle and bright as the Leven,
She's mild as the ray of the midsummer moon,
Oh, life would be rapture and home would be heaven
With love and the muses and Ann o' Drumcroon.

But why do I deepen my anguish of sorrow
While musing on visions of rapture and mirth?
Ere Phoebus encircles the round of the morrow,
My bark shall be far from the land of my birth.
I go with the weary regret of a lover,
I sigh that I part with my country so soon,
But the hopes and the pulses of freedom are over
That bind me to Erin and Ann o' Drumcroon.

Farewell then, for ever, thou home of my childhood,
The hope that awaits me I'm ready to brave,
Ere ocean of wildwood or city or desert
Will surely be able to yield me a grave,
But early the cypress or distant the roses,
The glory or infamy, cot or saloon,
My last weary sigh as my pilgrimage closes
Shall rise for my country and Ann o' Drumcroon.

4.3: ... ocean or wildwood ... [H26]

The Pride of Glenelly   [H607: 20 Jul 1935]

s: (m) "The Cottager's Daughter."

Source: (w) A. A. Campbell, F.R.S.A. (Drumnaferrie, Rosetta Park, Belfast); author James Devine (Loughash, Donemana).

Key F.

You followers of the nine, Apollo's tuneful line,
Residing in the valley of Glenelly,
The beauty of your hills, your vales and purling rills,
You needed not a stranger for to tell you.
The fair Italian grove where sylvans careless rove,
Or the Thracian pure crystalline fountains,
More pleasure can't afford to the natives, I'm assured,
Than the sight of your beloved native mountains.

No pencil can portray that luxuriant and gay
And wild romantic scenery of grandeur,
The landscape stretching wide on Glenelly's waterside
That in soft and silent majesty meanders.
In promiscuous order round, projecting cliffs abound,
Where Reynard in security is roving,
The distant mountains rear their summits that appear
To touch the azure canopy above them.

In that region of delight, where female beauty bright,
Most lovely of terrestrial creation,
Shines forth in all its pride, whilst virtue doth preside,
Must raise them in the poet's estimation.
A youthful nymph divine amongst the rest doth shine
Like Luna by the little stars surrounded;
I thought that it had been a vision I had seen
When her presence first my senses confounded.

Her hair, a golden hue, in silken tresses flew
In profusion on her lily neck and shoulders,
Her bright refulgent eyes with the clearest diamond vies,
But with soft and simple modest sweetness blended,
Her cheeks the rose in bloom, her breath the sweet perfume
Of Eden's odoriferous flowers,
Her lovely breast doth show like the purity of snow
Or the lily when refreshed by a shower.

Boast not of Helen's charms, who roused up Greece to arms,
Or Hero, the beloved of Leander,
Boast not of Dido fair, who died in deep despair
For Eneas, that accomplished commander.

Sam Henry's Songs of the People

These oriental dames gained most part of their fame
By their ornaments of jewels and brightest pearl,
But they ne'er could show a face adorned with every grace
Like this lovely modest simple country girl.

Farewell, ye sylvan shades where blushing rural maids
In guileless simplicity are sporting,
Farewell, you level strand, where young men hand in hand
In innocent amusement are resorting.
You poets, I beg leave your pardon here to crave
For directing your attention to this valley,
But in the Plumbridge Fair, when you're assembled there,
You will cry, 'Behold the pride of sweet Glenelly.'

Mary, the Pride of Killowen

[H26b: [Bp] "Two love songs to the same air," 10 May 1924]

o: (m) "Rose of Tralee."

Source: (w) Harry Evans (Chapel Square, Coleraine); m: author Andrew Orr.

s: ... This song may also be sung to the air "Burns and His Highland Mary," No. 8 in this series.

Key A flat.

The soft shades of evening o'er Coleraine were falling,
The green robes of summer adorned hill and dale,
The Bann's silvery tide to the ocean was rolling,
And the scent of the hawthorn was borne on the gale;
The flowers 'neath the hedgerows with dew drops were laden,
The birds to their places of slumber had flown,
When I sailed from Coleraine to the land of the stranger
And left bonnie Mary, the pride of Killowen.

On the Bann's lovely banks where we oft sat together,
Through Mountsandel's green groves we lingered for hours,
The sun was declining o'er Downhill's green mountains
And flung its last rays on the wild blooming flowers.
Every path where we trod in the gloaming together,
Every green grove and bower where we oft sat alone,
In memory's pages shall flourish for ever,
For the sake of sweet Mary, the pride of Killowen.

These scenes I'll remember where ever I wander,
I still love her dearly, though now far apart,
The last throb of life shall explode in my bosom
Ere the last look she gave me shall fade from my heart.
Sing on, you wild birds, your sweet strains I love dearly,
Bloom on, you wild flowers where we oft sat alone,
Flow on, bonnie Bann, through that green vale of splendour
Where first I met Mary, the pride of Killowen.

Moorlough Mary   [H173: 5 Mar 1927]

o: (m) "Anach Chuain" [Costello coll., 1923].
Other titles: "Moorlug ...," "A Tyrone Ballad."

Source: (w) Frank Devine (Dunnaboe, Donemana); (m) a grand-nephew of "Moorlough Mary," native (Foreglen, near Dungiven); author James Devine (Loughash, Donemana) c. 1876.

s: ... A version of this song has been collected by Mrs C. Milligan Fox [Bp: but the version here given differs slightly in words and materially in the air].

l: See Hugh Shields's review in *IFMS* 3,1976-8:68-9 for a hint as to the poet Devine's model.

Key E flat.

C14 / She's a lovely fair

When first I saw you, sweet Moorlough Mary,
  'twas in the market of sweet Strabane,
Your smiling countenance was so engaging, the
  hearts of young men you did trepan.
Your killing glances bereaved my senses of peace
  and comfort by night and day,
In my silent slumber I start with wonder -- och,
  Moorlough Mary, will you come away?

To see you, darling, on a summer's morning when
  Flora's fragrance bedecks the lawn,
Your neat deportment and manners courteous,
  around you sporting the lambs and fawn,
On you I ponder where'er I wander and will grow
  fonder, sweet maid, of thee,
By thy matchless charms I am enamoured -- och,
  Moorlough Mary, will you come away?

Were I a man of great education, or Erin's isle at
  my commands,
I'd lay my head on your snowy bosom, in
  wedlock's band, love, we'd join our hands,
I'd entertain you both night and morning, with
  robes I'd deck you both night and day,
With jewels rare, love, I would adorn you -- och,
  Moorlough Mary, will you come away?

Now I'll away to my situation, for recreation is all
  in vain,
On the river Mourne I'll sing your praises till the
  rocks re-echo my plaintive strain,
I'll press my cheese while my wool's a-teasing, my
  ewes I'll milk by the peep o' day,
When the whirrying moorcock and lark alarm me
  -- och, Moorlough Mary, will you come away?

On Moorlough banks I will never wander where
  heifers graze on a pleasant soil,
Where lambkins sporting, fair maids resorting,
  the timorous hare and blue heather bell
The thrush and blackbird all sing harmonious
  their notes melodious on Ruskey brae,
And pretty small birds all join in chorus -- och,
  Moorlough Mary, will you come away?

Farewell, my charming Moorlough Mary, ten
  thousand times I bid you adieu,
While life remains in my glowing bosom I'll never
  cease, love, to think of you.
Now I'll away to some lonesome valley, with tears
  lamenting both night and day,
To some silent arbour where none can hear me --
  och, Moorlough Mary, will you come away?

1.1: ... Murlough ... [Dt, *the only instance*]
1.2: ... men it did ... [Dt]
6.1: ... bid adieu, [Dt]

❖ C14 REFERENCES ❖

❖ **Happy 'Tis, Thou Blind, for Thee** *(H491)* 225

   Brunnings 1981

   IREL *Ceol* 2(4):94-5 "Cailín O Chois tSiure," also
   reference to the article about Shakespeare and Irish
   music by P. H. Curran in *Ceol* 1(4)
     See also Breathnach 1971:19-20
   b: Graves 1928

   MEL Fitzwilliam (1963)2:186-7 (#168) "Callino Casturame," by William Byrd.
     Tom Kines, Folkways FW 8767 (A6) "Caleno Custure
   Me"

❖ **My Bonny Breeden** *(H512)* 225

   Brunnings 1981: (m) "Cruachan na Feine," "Croo-
     ghan A Vence/Venee"

❖ **O, Jeanie Dear** *(H545)* 225

   Brunnings 1981: (m) "Londonderry Air"

❖ **Bonny Mary Hay** *(H568)* 226

   BRIT Buchan 1962:128
      Chambers 1829,2:610
      Whitelaw 1844(1874):7 "Bonnie ...," with some back-
      ground: attributed to Archibald Crawford.

❖ **So Like Your Song and You** *(H508)* 226

   MEL Clancy Bros. 1964:48 "Singin' Bird," attributed
   to Francis McPeake.
      Loesberg 1,1980:20 "My Singing Bird"
      McPeake Family, Topic 12T 87 (A5) "My Singing
   Bird"; Prestige/Int. 13018

❖ **Not the Swan on the Lake** *(H707)* 227

   Brunnings 1981: "Bonny Strathmore (...)"

❖ **Nancy, the Pride of the West** *(H495)* 227

   BRS O'Conor 1901:150, nearly identical to Henry's.

❖ **The Maid of Erin's Isle** *(H57b)* 228

   BRS Harvard 3: (Birt)

❖ **Kate of Coleraine** *(H684)* 231

   g: Not the song with the same title in the *Antihip-
   notic Songster* (Philadelphia) 1818:169.

❖ **The Star of Glenamoyle** *(H13)* 232

   Brunnings 1981: (Tune of Dreary Gallows; see:
      Derry Gaol)

Sam Henry's Songs of the People

◇ **The Flower of Glenleary** *(H22a)* 232

Brunnings 1981: "The Braes of Balquidder (Tune of The Roving Songster; see Wild Mountain Thyme)"

m: IREL *Derry Standard*, 6 Oct 1847

m: AUST Orr n.d.

◇ **The Flower of Gortade** *(H178)* 233

IREL   Moulden 1979:58-9
    Tunney 1979:120-1

m: REC Len Graham, Free Reed 007 (B6)

◇ **The Manchester Angel** *(H711)* 234

White/Dean-Smith 1951: "(The) Irish Girl"
Dean-Smith 1954: "(The) Irish Girl"
Brunnings 1981: "The Irish Girl"

IREL   *JIFSS* 3(3&4)1905-6:26-7 [Sharp/Karpeles]; 14, 1914:35 "I Would I Were Yon Red, Red Rose"; cf. 18, 1921:29 (#14) "Fare You Well, Sweet Donegal"
    Joyce 1909:190 (#382)
    Cf. Loesberg 1,1978 "Mary from Dungloe," esp. stanza 5.
    Cf. O Lochlainn 1939:148 (#75) "Mary from Dungloe" [Sharp/Karpeles]
    b: O Lochlainn 1965:4-5 "The New Irish Girl"

b: BRIT Sedley 1967:116-7; explains that his stanza 2 ("I went to church last Sunday") is from H625 "Dark-Eyed Molly," that Cecil Sharp found that "eclectic song" linked with "The Irish Girl" in the Southern Appalachians, "and in fact they fit well."
Sharp/Karpeles 1974,1:495-500 (#127), 4 vts.
    Shepheard n.d.:19-20

AMER Barry 1939:22-3
    Creighton/Senior 1950: 198-9 "Pretty Polly"
    Dean [1922]:109 "Molly Bawn," a fragment.
    Kenedy 1890:31-2
    Wright 1975:384 "The New Irish Girl" (from chap-book "The Merry Roundelay" [London: J. Evans])

BRS Harvard 1: 4.191 (Forth), 5.124 (Ryle), 11.28 (Such)
    Harvard 3: (Pitts)
    UCLA 605: 3(Pitts) "The Country Girl"; 5(n.i.) "The Irish Girl"
    A Broadside 5(7,Dec) 1912, 1 stanza; 7(5,Sep) 1914, "My Irish Girl"
    O'Keeffe 1955(1968):116, a very different version.
    617 [190-?]:98

REC Cf. Howie Bursen, Folk-Legacy FSI 74 (A4) "The New Irish Girl"
    Cf. Dick Cameron, Folkways FG 3516 (A4) "Love It Is a Killing Thing," esp. stanza 3 and metre.
    Bob, Ron Copper, Leader LEAB 404 (4047: B6) "As I Walked Out"
    David Hammond, Tradition TLP 1028 (B9) "The Irish Girl" ("Blackwaterside")
    Cf. Mick Hanly, Green Linnet SIF 3007 (B2) "I Wish My Love Was a Red, Red Rose"
    cl: Mrs Birmah Hill Grissom, AFS 2962 B3 "The Irish Girl"
    Tom Kines, Folkways FG 3522 (A7) "My Irish Polly"
    Walter Pardon, Leader LED 2063 (A2) "Let the Wind Blow High or Low"
    Levy Smith, Topic 12TS 304 (B7) "The Irish Girl"

MEL Petrie/Stanford 1,1902:118 (#469) "Oh Love It Is a Killing Thing"

◇ **Autumn Dusk / Coimfeasgar Fogmair** *(H831)* 235

IREL   H. Morris 1916 (?1935) ?1969

◇ **The Dear-a-Wee Lass** *(H74)* 236

IREL   Moulden 1979:43
    Cf. Joyce 1909:135 (#385) "She's the Dear Maid to Me," 1 stanza and tune of a gallows-side confession in the same metre although not at all in the same mood. Joyce adds: "The words of this rude, though very popular ballad were printed from a broadsheet in Duffy's *Ballad Poetry of Ireland* [1845? 1866]," and adds in a footnote that the title is an Irish idiom meaning "I have paid dearly for her" -- "she has cost me dearly."

◇ **The Valley Below** *(H47)* 236

Not = Brunnings 1981: "The Sweet Nightingale"

BRS Harvard 2: (Pitts) "She Lives in the Valley Below"
    AS Thomas: (n.i.)

◇ **The Dark-Haired Girl** *(H559)* 237

Not: Brunnings 1981

◇ **The Old Dun Cow** *(H492)* 238

Not: Brunnings 1981: "When the Old Dun Cow Caught Fire"

◇ **Gragalmachree** *(H582)* 238

Cf. Laws 1957:191 (M23) "Gay Girl Marie." Laws notes the relationship to the Irish song, and quotes Samuel P. Bayard about the title: "'My gay girl Marie' can reasonably be guessed to be a corruption of 'mo gradh geal mo chroidhe' (bright heart's love)."
Brunnings 1981: "Groyle Machree," "Newry Mountain," ?"Gra'-mo-chroi," ?"Gramachree"

l: Apparently another song entirely is in *Tocher* #13 (Spr)1974:192 "Gradh Geal Mo Cridh [Bheir Me O]," said to be a version of the "Eriskay Love Lilt."

IREL   Joyce 1909:103 (#209) "Newry Mountain"; 266-7 (#481) "Gradh Geal Mochroidhe: Gra Gal Machree, Fair Love of My Heart" [Fowke]
    O Lochlainn 1939:26-7 "Grá Geal Mo Chroí"

AMER Creighton/Senior 1950:150-1 "Down by the Fair River"
b: Fowke 1965:70-1 "Groyle Machree." Fowke also notes that "Gragalmachree" is related to the American "Gay Girl Marie."
    Leach 1965:324-5 "Grogal McCree"

BRS UCLA 605: 3(Pitts) "Grageral MacGree"

REC Joe Holmes, Topic 12TS 401 (B2) "Grá Mo Croí"
    Tom Kines, Folkways FG 3522 (B3) "Down by the Far River"
    Bill Meek, Folk-Legacy FSE 21 (B6) "Newry Mountain"
    ? Isabel Sutherland, Topic 12T 151 (A3) "Griogal Cridhe"

MEL Cf. Petrie/Stanford 3,1905:320 (#1273) "Grád Geal Mo Croíde", (#1274) "A slight variant of the preceding"; 324 (#1290) "Grád Geal Mo Croíde."

C14 / She's a lovely fair

◆ The Maid from the Carn Brae (H704) 241

m: IREL Ó Maoláin 1982:1

◆ Maggie of Coleraine (H657) 242

Brunnings 1981: (m) "The Girls of Coleraine," "Teddy O'Neal," "Teddy O'Neill"

◆ The Flower of Corby Mill (H612) 242

IREL Morton 1973:68 "The Maid of the Colehill," quite different and with two fewer stanzas.
Moulden 1979:57 disagrees with the notion that this is a parody or variant of Phil Tanner's "Swansea Barracks" (note, p. 161).

REC Cf. Phil Tanner, FSB 8 (A2) "Swansea Barracks"; [m:] EFDSS LP 1005
Eddie Butcher, Outlet OAS 3007 (A2)

◆ The Flower of Magherally, O! (H220) 243

Brunnings 1981

IREL JIFSS 1(2&3):57-8
S. O'Boyle 1977:62-3
O Lochlainn 1939:118-9

AMER Milner/Kaplan 1983:175-6 "... Magherally"

REC Frank Harte, Topic 12T 218 (A5) "... Magherally"
Cathal McConnell, Philo 1026 [Milner/Kaplan]

◆ Magilligan (H52a) 244

Brunnings 1981: (m) "The Wearing of the Green"

IREL Shields 1981:140-1 (#63) "The Shores of Sweet Benone"

◆ The Valleys of Screen (H752) 245

Brunnings 1981: "... (Tune of The Lasses' Resolution to Follow the Fashion)"

◆ The Blazing Star of Drim [Drung] (H197a,b) 247

s: IREL JIFSS 1(2&3)1903:65-6
Shields 1981:51

BRIT Tocher #31(Sum)1979:4 mentions 2 versions written by Willie Mitchell in his ms. book: "... Drum"

h: BRS O'Keeffe 1955(1968):123

REC Robert Butcher, EEOT Shamrock 2 cass. (A6)

◆ Ann o' Drumcroon (H26a, H246) 248

m: AUST Orr n.d.

◆ Mary, the Pride of Killowen (H26b) 250

m: IREL Derry Standard 6 Oct 1847

m: AUST Orr n.d.

◆ Moorlough Mary (H173) 250

Brunnings 1981: "Moorlug ..."

IREL Fox 1910:20-2
JIFSS 2(1&2)1905:21-2 "...: A Tyrone ballad"
S. O'Boyle 1977:74-5
h: O Lochlainn 1939:168-9 "Moorlug Mary"
Shields/Shields UF 21,1975: #274
Treoir 7,1975

AMER Milner/Kaplan 1983:172-3

BRS BPL H.80: (Poet's Box)
Derry Journal [c. 1925],1:64
O'Keeffe 1955(1968):93-4 calls this "A Tyrone Ballad."
Walton's New 2,1968:195

REC John Doherty, EFDSS LP 1003 (A4)
Paddy Tunney, Folk-Legacy FSE 7 (A2)
Peta Webb, Topic 12TS 223

o: MEL Costello 1923:98-101 "Anach-chuain (Annaghdown)"
JIFSS 9,1911:15
Seamus, Manus Maguire, Folk-Legacy FSE 78 (A3) "Anach Cuain"

C15

Where's the lass to take my hand?
Courtship, dalliance

Nae Bonnie Laddie tae Tak' Me Awa'

[H230: 7 Apr 1928]

k: "Sweet (Queen) Mary." Other titles: "The Aul' Maid," "Come along, Bonny Lassie, and Give Me a Waltz," "I Maun Gang tae the Garret," "... Wad Tak' Her Awa'," "Queen Mary(, Queen Mary)," "The Scotch Lassie."

Source: (w) 3; (m) Pat Hackett (Stone Row, Coleraine).

[Bp] s: This song dates from about the year 1800. The version here given contains the best of three versions received....

Key G.

My name it is Jean and my age is fifteen,
My father's a farmer, he leeves near the Green,
He has money in plenty, that mak's me sae
  braw,
And there's no bonnie laddie tae tak' me awa'.

When I rise in the morning my spirits is low,
The very first thing tae the taypot I go,
With my toes in the ashes I sit by the wa'
And sigh for a laddie tae tak' me awa'.

My shoes they are made o' the 'lastic so strong,
That they are admired by both old and young,
A sixpence would cover my heels, they're so sma',
Yet there's nae bonnie laddie tae tak' me awa'.

It's ten times a day I luk in the glass,
I think tae mysel' I'm a gye bonnie lass,
Wi' my hands on my hinches I gie a 'Ha, ha!'
Sayin', 'Is there nae bonnie laddie tae tak' me
  awa'?'

At church every Sunday I'm sure to be there,
But the clergy ne'er mentions in preachin' or
  prayer,
In preachin' or prayer there's nae word ava
Tae order young men tae tak' lasses awa'.

Each evening at duskis I mak' mysel' clean,
Wi' ruffles an' ribbons as gay as a queen,
Wi' the finest hair cushions and curls sae braw,
Yet there's nae bonnie laddie tae tak' me awa'.

And when I come hame then my mother does cry,
'For as braw as ye're dressed a' the lads pass ye
  by,

C15 / Where's the lass to take my hand?

Ere I was your age I had lads twenty-twa,
But I think ne'er a laddie will tak' ye awa'.

This speech o' my mother's it mak's me quite mad,
For tae think that I'm courted by never a lad,
Yet I hope the time's comin' when it will end a'
And some bonnie laddie will tak' me awa'.

Then be not offended at what I hae said,
For it's but the language o' every young maid,
It's the wish o' a' wishes o' yin and o' a'
That some bonnie laddie will tak' them awa'.

[*Stanzas 3 and 5 in Bp, not in Dt.*]
1.4: But there's ... [Dt]
4.4: ... nae laddie ... [Dt]
8.1: ... it made me ... [Dt]
8.2: ... think I was courted ... [Dt]
9.3: ... wishes of you and ... [Dt]

4.3: hinches = haunches, hips.

Maidens of Sixty-Three [H679: 28 Nov 1936]

s: (m) from Kinloch's *Ancient Ballads*, 1827.
Other title: "The Old Maid."

s: The last four-lined verse to be sung to the second half of the air.

Key G.

When I was a girl of eighteen years old,
Scornful as scornful could be,
I was taught to expect wit, wisdom, gold,
And nothing less would do for me.
Those were the days when my eyes beamed bright
And my cheeks were like the rose on the tree,
And my ringlets curled o'er my forehead so white,
And lovers came courting to me.

The first was a youth any girl might adore,
And as ardent as lover could be,
But my mother having heard that the young man
  was poor,
Why, he would not do for me.
Then came a duke with a coronet of gold
And his garter worn below his knee,
But his face, like his family, was wonderful old,
So he would not do for me.

The next was a baronet whose blood-red hand
Was emblazon'd in heraldry,
But having been known at a counter to stand,
Why, he would not do for me.

Sam Henry's Songs of the People

Then hobbled in, my favor to beg,
An admiral, a K.C.B.,
Though famous in arms, he wanted a leg,
And he would not do for me.

Then came a parson, burly and big,
Expecting a very rich see,
But I could not bear the thought of a horrid
   buzwig,
So he would not do for me.
Then came a lawyer, his claim to support
By precedents from chancery,
I told him I was judge in my own little court,
And he would not do for me.

The next was a dandy, had driven four in hand,
And he reduced to a tilbury,
In getting o'er the ground he ran through his land,
So he would not do for me.
Then came a nabob just landed six weeks,
Late Governer of Trincomalee,
His guineas were yellow and so were his cheeks,
And he would not do for me.

He was nearly the last, I was then forty-four,
I'm now only just sixty-three,
But I think that some I rejected before
Would do vastly well for me.
My ringlets I borrow, my roses I buy,
And I go about to vards and to tea,
But if ever I venture an ogle or sigh,
Why, nobody returns it to me.

Then all ye young ladies by me warning take,
Who scornful or cold chance to be,
Lest you from your silly dreams should awake
Old maidens of sixty-and-three.

6.6: vards = ?[typographical error]

The Black Chimney Sweeper

[H138: BLp, 3 Jul 1926]

Other titles: "(An) Auld (Old) Maid in a (the) Garret," "Chimney Sweepers Wedding," "Come All You True Lovers," "Don't Let Me Die a(n Old) Maid," "I Long to be Wedding," "I Was Told by My Aunt," "The Lovesick Maid," "(Marry) (Maids) (Some) at Eighteen," "The Old Maid's Lament (Song)," "Sister Sally," "The Spinster's Lament"; cf. "Time to be Made a Wife," "The Unmarried Maiden's Lament," "Young Men, Come Marry Me."

Source: (m, w) Mrs Sarah Crawford (Thorndale, Coleraine) from her mother, Matilda Shirley (the Rhee [Dt: Ree], Agivey, Co. Derry).

s: ... The Shirleys of the Ree are an old stock descended from the first linen bleacher who introduced the trade into the Aghadowey district at the beginning of the 18th century.

[Dt, handwritten on side] Published by Patersons Edinburgh (Lyric Colln 1534 - 4d)
[Bt includes sheet music: "The Black Chimney Sweeper" / Traditional Ulster Folk Song arranged by John Vine / Collected by Sam Henry, F.R.S.A., in Coleraine district. Copyright 19?37 in U.S.A. by Paterson's Publications Ltd.]

[Print from British Library microfilm courtesy of John Moulden.]

Key G. Quick time.

I was told by a prophet, I was told by my mother,
That going to a wedding would soon bring on
   another,
If I thought that, I would go without a bidding;
Dear knows in my heart how I long for a wedding.

Musha ring do a da, ring do a daddy.

There's my sister Ellen, she's younger far than I
   am,
She's got so many sweethearts she's going to deny
   'em;
As for myself, I haven't got so many,
Dear knows in my heart I would be thankful for
   any.

It's for my sister Annie, she never was forsaken,
At the age of sixteen for a bride she was taken,
At the age of eighteen she had both a son and
   daughter;
And now I'm forty-five and I never got an offer.

I would make a good wife, neither scold nor be
   jealous,
Give money to my husband to spend in the
   alehouse,
When he would be spending, sure I would be
   making,
Och, boys, look at that: am I no worth a
   taking?

Come hensman, come pensman, come brewer, come
   baker,
Come tinker, come tailor, come fiddler, come
   Quaker,
Come ragman, come madman, come foolish, come
   witty,
Don't let her die a maid, but marry her for pity.

It's now to conclude and to finish my ditty,
The chimney sweep has got her, he married her
   for pity,

And ever since he's got her, he vows that he'll keep her,
And now she's in the arms of her black chimney sweeper.

1.: [*In Bt, Wt this stanza is replaced by:*]
Come all ye pretty fair maids, so brisk and so merry,
From eighteen to twenty, that's now going to marry,
As for myself I'm afraid I must tarry,
For dear knows in my heart I'd be thankful for any.
[*But the original first stanza (as in BLp above) is used in the sheet music.*]
2.4: ... I'd ... [Bt, Dt]
3.3: ... of nineteen ... [Bt, Dt, Wt]
 .4: I'm sweet forty-five ... never had an ... [Bt, Dt]
4.4: ... worth the taking? [Bt, Wt]

The Wee Article [H833: 11 Nov 1939]

o: "Wee Daft Article."

Source: (Ballinascreen district).

Key G.

I'm a jolly servant lass, my name is Mary Ann,
I'm going to sing about a thing that calls itself a man;
He wanted me his wife to be, he's only four feet four,
And this is how I answered him when talking at the door.

　Orra, go wa', you daft wee article, you're nothing but a sham,
　Common sense is anything that constitutes a man;
　You're not the size of tuppence and your income isn't thrup[p]ence,
　You may find a lass to love you, but it won't be Mary Ann.

To see this little article, with laughter you'd explode:
His legs is like the letter K and his eyes look every road,

C15 / Where's the lass to take my hand?

But still he has the impudence to want a lass like me --
An article that you'd require a microscope to see.

If we went walking down the street I'd have him at command,
For I could take him up like suds and blow him off my hand;
He says he'll buy me dresses and treat me like a queen,
He cannot treat himself, poor man; such a sight you never seen.

Roger's Courtship [H820: 12 Aug 1939]

s: "Robin's Courtship," "William the Rose," "Poor Bob"; k: "Jan's Courtship." Other title: "Roger."

Source: "old worthy ... lately gone to his rest" (Moneysharvin, native of Aghadowey).

s: This song ... has been collected in Devon, Somerset and Cornwall by various collectors under such titles as "Robin's Courtship," "William the Rose," "Poor Bob."...
The only explanation I can offer as to this song being sung in Aghadowey is that the retainers of the Cunningham family brought it over from Warwickshire. I have collected another Warwickshire song, "The Mare and the Foal," in Aghadowey.

Key G.

Now Roger, my son, since thou art a man,
I'll gi'e the best counsel in life:
Sit down by me and I'll tell to thee
Of how thou must get thee a wife,
　Yis I will, man I will, Sure I will,
　I'll tell how to get thee a wife, yis I will.

You must put on your clothes and your new yellow hose;
They'll at first turn away and be shy,
But boldly step up and kiss each purty maid,
And they'll call thee their love bye and bye,
　Yis they will, man they will, Sure they will,
　They'll call thee their love by[e] and bye, yis they will.

So Roger put on his new holiday clothes,
They neither were ragged nor torn,
He put on his clothes and his new yellow hose,
You'd a-thought him a gentleman born, so you would,
　Yis you would, man you would, Sure you would,
　You'd a-thought him a gentleman born, yis you would.

Sam Henry's Songs of the People

The very first one that he came to court
Was a young farmer's daughter called Grace,
He'd scarce said, 'How do?' with a kind word or two
Till she hit him a slap in the face,
    Yis she did, man she did, Sure she did,
    She hit him a slap in the face, yis she did.

'Go on, you bold hussy, how dare you to slight such an offer as I?
Don't you see me new clothes and my new yellow hose?
You might live such a maid till you die,
    Yis you might, so you might, Sure you might,
    You might live such a maid till you die.'

If this be the way to get me a wife,
I never will look for another,
So I'll away now and here take a vow
I'll just live at home with my mother,
    Yis I will, so I will, Sure I will,
    I'll just live at home with my mother, yis I will.

4.5: yis = yes.

Grandma's Advice [H208: 5 Nov 1927]

o: (m) "Mrs McGrath; g: "Little Johnny Green."
Other titles: "Grandma Would Have Died an Old Maid," "(My) Grandma (Grandmother) (Lives on Winson) (Green) (Lived on Yonder Green)," "(My) Granny's (Grandma(w)'s) (Grandmother's) ...."

Source: (Raphoe district, Co. Donegal).

s: This [is a] jolly, tuneful little song.... (The notes in parentheses are for the excess syllable in some of the lines of the song.)

Key G.

My grandma lived in yonder village green,
The finest old lady that ever was seen,
And she often cautioned me with care
Of all false young men to beware,
    Timy i, timy i, ti timy imy a,
    Tum ti timy, timy i, my a,
    And she often cautioned me with care
    Of all false young men to beware.

The first that came to court me was young Johnny Green,
The finest young man that ever was seen,
But the words of my grandma kept ringing in my head
And I didn't hear a word of all he said.
    Timy i, ...

The next that came to court me was young Ellis Grove,
'Twas then that we met with a joyous love,
With a joyous love I couldn't be afraid:
Better get married than die an old maid.
    Timy i, ...

Says I to myself, there must be some mistake,
For to see what a fuss the old folks make,
If the girls of the boys had all been so afraid,
Then grandma herself would have died an old maid.
    Timy i, ...

2.4: ... heard a ... [Bp]
4.3: ... girls and the ... [Dt]

The Nonsense o' Men [H472: 17 Dec 1932]

[cf. H532 "Tarry Trousers," H641 "The Ripest of Apples"]

Source not given.

s: A suitable encore song for a lady singer.

o: Time should be 4/4.

Key G.

I hate to be teased by the nonsense o' men,
For my mammy has told me, again and again,
To do what she bid me, where'er I would go,
And if any man asked me, be sure and say No.
    To be sure and say No, to be sure and say No,
    And if any man asked me, to be sure and say No!

Young Donnelly looked steady, my heart for to gain,
He's the blithest young piper that pipes o'er the plain,

He told me love stories I took not amiss,
But I often said No when I'd fain have said Yes!
When I'd fain have said Yes, ...

Young Donnelly and I, as we walked through a
  grove,
He placed his arm round me and told me his love,
He modestly asked me to give him a kiss,
I was going to say No, but I mistook and said
  Yes!
I mistook and said Yes, ...

He ne'er was as pleased of a word in his life,
And I ne'er was so happy as since I am a wife,
So all you young maids, take a warning by this:
You will all die old maids if you do not say Yes!
If you do not say Yes, ...

As I Go I Sing [H661: 25 Jul 1936]

s: (m) "Cushleake."

Source not given; m: ?author Loui[?s]e Barnes
(Ballycastle).

s: Published by kind permission of Miss Louie
Barnes, L.R.A.M., Ballycastle.

Key G.

As I walk the hills my heart is light, and as I go I
  sing,
My brothers talk of land and gold and sorely do
  upbraid,
My mother says I'll rue my pride and die a lonely
  maid,
But I roam the hills, my heart is light, and as I go
  I sing.

There's people say that my heart is cold, and,
  troth, that same may be,
I tell them all I'll never wed, and sometimes think
  it's true,
For love brings care and marriage, pain -- I
  wonder what I'd do
If one wee lad from the leanin' end should come
  a-courtin' me.

As I walk the hills my heart is light, and as I go I
  sing,
My brothers had no land or gold, but found their
  sweethearts kind,;
My mother vowed she'd die a maid, but sure she
  changed her mind,
So I roam the hills and my heart is light, and as I
  go I sing.

C15 / Where's the lass to take my hand?

The Strands of Magilligan [H520: 18 Nov 1933]

o: (m) "Farewell Enniskillen"; g: "Faithful Emma," "Green Mountain," "Nellie," "The Streams of Lovely Nancy (Nant-si-an)"; cf. H780 "The Ploughboy." Other titles: "Come All You Little Streamers," "(O) the Sweet Dreams (Streams) of Nancy," "On Yonder Green Mountain," "The Sailor Boy"; cf. "Gragalmachree," "Newry Mountain," "The Soldier's Farewell to Manchester."

Source not given.

g: Versions of this song vary greatly; there are almost as many titles as versions.

Key D.

I'm a stranger in this country, from America I
  came,
There's few in it knows me or can tell my name,
And here among strangers I will stay for a while,
For the sake of my darling I'll go many a long
  mile.

The strands of Magilligan divide in two parts
Where young men and maidens they meet their
  sweethearts,
They will take no denial, we must frolic and sing,
And the sound of the fiddle, oh, it makes my
  heart ring.

On the top of a cliff where her castle does stand,
It is well built, with ivy down to the back strand,
It is well built, with ivy and diamonds so bright,
It's a pilot for sailors on a dark stormy night.

On Magilligan top where the wild birds do fly,
There is one amongst them that flies very high,
On eagle's wings soaring, I'll speed as the wind,
The wild deep exploring, my true love I'll find.

The strands of Magilligan divide in two parts
And rejoin, as in dancing do lads their
  sweethearts,
So the strands, bright and shining, tho' parted
  in twain,
Reunite like two lovers where the Foyle meets
  the Main.

Sam Henry's Songs of the People

Green Grow the Rashes (a)

[H165a: 8 Jan 1927]

g: "Green Grows the Laurel"; k: "The Orange and (the) Blue." Other titles: "(The) Green Laurel(s)," "... the Laurel(s) (Lilacs) (Rushes(-o) (O))," "... Grows the Laurels (Wild Isle)," "I Once Loved a Lass," "The Nightingale."

Source: coll. A. E. Boyd (Cullycapple, Aghadowey) from John Gilmore (Carnrallagh, Aghadowey), from James Duff (Carnrallagh) c. 1877.

[Bp] s: ... This song is quite different from Burns's song with the same title. An air with this title was known as early as 1628.... Two other versions have also come to hand, and our readers will understand from these variants why the songs as published in this column frequently differ from the versions known to them.
　The verse "Green Grow the rashes ..." is common to several old songs and must be very old. The use of the word "lee" -- shelter or warmth -- is peculiar, and the word "wellow," a derivative from the same root word as willow, meaning bending or drooping, is remarkable.
[Dt] It is suggested that the last verse should begin: Green grow the rashes in the top o' Glensma'. There is a highland glen by that name.

Key D.

Oh, if I were a clerk and could handle a pen,
I would write my love a letter and to her I
　would sen',
I would write her a letter and seal it with love;
If her heart's like yon mountain, I would make
　it remove.

If I were a fish and could swim yon salt sea,
And my love a trout would sport all around me,
I would clasp my fins round her and drag her
　to lee;
I am wounded in love, shall I never get free?

Green grow the rashes and the tops o' them sma',
Yet love is a thing that can conquer us a',
Oh, the tulip may wellow, it may fade and die
　soon,
But the red rose will flourish in the sweet month
　of June.

1.1: ... handle the pen, [Dt]

3.3: wellow = "a derivative from the same root word as willow, meaning bending or drooping" [s: Bp]

Green Grow the Rashes (b) [Green Grows the Laurel]

[H165b: 8 Jan 1927]

Source: (w) William Meighan (Drumneechy, Dungiven); (m) coll. Maud Houston (Coleraine) from Peggy M'Garry, 85 (Ballycastle), "the first song she ever learned."

s: Another song with the same title ...

Key C.

Green grows the laurel and so does the rue,
How sorry I am for the parting of you,
But at our next meeting our joys will renew,
We'll love one another as lovers should do.

Green grow the rushes and the tops of them
　small
For love is a thing that would conquer us all,
It would conquer us all, love, of a high and
　low degree,
Every one to their mind and fancy and my
　darling to me.

Little said is easy mended, and few words are
　best,
For those that speak seldom I count they are
　best,
I speak from experience and my mind tells me
　so,
If everyone had their own darling they would
　know where to go.

The frowns of my father I don't value a pin,
Nor the sighs of my mother for the losing of
　her son,
Since she is so hard-hearted and won't pity me,
I'll make myself happy in some strange country.

I'll go down to the lowlands where the small
　birds do sing,
Where no one shall hear me until I cry my fill;
Since notions provoke me for to take my own
　will,
My own rod is the sorest and does beat me still.

Over high hills and mountains, through hail,
　frost and snow,
I'll follow my darling where'er she may go,
Although she has not the clothes for to wear,
I'll work while I'm able and give my love share.

2.1: ... the rashes and ... [Dt]
 .4: Each one to his fancy and ... [Dt]
3.4: If each had his darling, he would ... [Dt]
4.4: ... counter-ee. [Dt]
5.4: ... rod's the ... [Dt]

The Young Farmer's Offer [H776: 8 Oct 1938]

Source: late James Stewart (Ballywatt), who died two years ago, aged 80.

m: Collected from Jim Minn (Hatt[i?]esburg, MS [USA]) 1980 at Conymeela, Co. Antrim. There is an 8-line fragment in Grieg [1907-11(1963):] #19.

Key C.

Now, friends, my heart is fu' o' glee,
I'll tell you all has happened me:
My father willed his wealth to me,
And I'm become a farmer.

My time was up but yesterday,
And I'm 'Welcome, Mr Farmer,'
My age it is but twenty-one,
And I'm become a farmer.

And where's the lass to take my hand
And be young Mrs Armour?
I have horses, carts and swine as well,
And I'm a wealthy farmer.

I've twarthree hunner in the bank
And we'll can live in wealth and rank;
She'll win a prize who weds the bank
And gets young William Armour.

There's a braw lassie sittin' there,
At me she tak's a homely stare;
I'll ask her when my song is done
To be young Mrs Armour.

My house it is but short and thick,
It is well furnished, front and back,
Of tables, chairs and stools nae lack
A' waiting Mrs Armour.

My granny's spinning wheel forbye,
And naethin' she will ha'e tae buy,
The very cradle, safe and dry
Awaits young Mrs Armour.

4.1: twarthree hunner = two or three hundred.

The Load of Kail Plants
[H25b: "Two old time comic songs," 3 May 1924]

A Ballymoney song.

Source: (w) ?Mary Clarke; author, man named Dempsey (Drumail).

C15 / Where's the lass to take my hand?

[Bp typed at bottom] Mary Clarke's version:
[followed by 7 alternative stanza lines]

m: Currently in tradition -- Len Graham.

Key C. [Written at top of Bp and at end of Wt:] Spoken at end.

O, sweet Ballymoney, of fame and renown,
I went to the fair, it being held in that town
On the fifth day of May in the year forty-five,
A very fine day for the bees for to hive.

I being young my fortune to advance,
I went to the fair with a load of kail plants,
And up the main street before Robinson's mart,
I lowered my cart with a proud beating heart.

The boys from Loughguile, likewise from Armoy,
They all gathered round me, my plants for to buy,
I addressed them with words both proper and plain,
When I said, 'For ever,' they all said, 'Amen.'

There were pamphrey and Dutch and curlies so sweet,
And rousing drumheads that grow up like a leek,
There were cow-kail, pull-early-boys, eat-while-your-able,
And pickle for dressing a gentleman's table.

Now my plants are all sold, I wish them long life,
I have nothing to do but look out for a wife;
The ladies I'll view, I'll mark all their points,
I won't take a wife that is stiff in the joints.

The first that I met, she wore a silk gown,
Her long yellow hair and her curls hingin' down,
Says I to myself, 'My girl, you're a swizzer,'
I stood her a tay where we got the big measure.

There we set off at a kind of a walk;
The boys and the girls they begun for to talk;
They himm'd and they ha'd, 'By my sang she's a fizzer,'
And there we popped in where we got the big measure.

And there I presumed for to kiss this young dame,
And there I presumed for to ask her her name,
'Well, indeed, then, kind sir, and my name is M'Cloy,
I'm the lame cadger's daughter from the town of Armoy.'

261

Sam Henry's Songs of the People

[Bp has some added typed lines labeled "Mary Clarke's version:" [B,MC]. Dt has 2 pairs of added alternative lines typed in parentheses after stanza 2, lines 3 and 4, and stanza 7, lines 3 and 4. Wt also has penciled corrections to 2.3 and 7.4.]
2.1: Being young and undaunted my fortune to advance, [B,MC]
 .3: ... before Lanigan's door, [also Wt]
 .4: I set down my cart and loosed out my mare. [Dt]
3.1: The Quinns from Loughguile and the Scotts from Armoy, [Dt]
 .2: All flocked round my cart ... [Dt]
 .4: When they cried, 'For ever,' sure I said ... [Dt]
4.1: There was ... [Dt]
 .3: There was cow-kale ... you're-able, [Dt]
5.1: Now my plants are all sold, and I wish ... [Dt]
6.2: Her long yellow hair in ringlets hung down,
 .3: Says I to myself, 'By my sang, she's a ...,' [Dt]
7.: [B,MC only]
7.3: 'Indeed then, kind sir, and you'll hear it just now:
 .4: I'm John Couter's daughter that lives in the Vow.' [Dt alternate; B,MC with "ye" for "you"]
 .4: I'm the peat ... [written on Bp and Wt]
[Wt written:] 3 words spoken at end of verse

An Irish Serenade [H82: 6 Jun 1925]

Other title: "Oh, Molly, I Can't Say That You're Honest."

Source: D[aniel] MacLaughlin, esq (Breezemount, Coleraine); author Samuel Lover.

s: ... One of Samuel Lover's songs in favour [Dt: vogue] thirty years ago.

Key C.

Oh, Molly, I can't say you're honest,
You've stolen my heart from my breast,
I feel like a bird that's astonished
When young vagabonds rob its nest.
My brightest of sunshine at night is,
'Tis just between midnight and dawn,
For then, Molly dear, my delight is
To sing you my little croonyawn.

Philaloo, wirrasthru, but I'm kilt,
May the quilt lie light on your beautiful form
When the weather is hot,
But my love, when 'tis not,
May it rowl you up cosy and warm, Philaloo.

I know that your father is stingy,
And likewise your mother the same,
'Tis mighty small change that you'll bring me
Exceptin' the change of your name,
But be quick with the change, dearest Molly,
Be the same, more or less, as it may,
And my own name I'll give you, sweet Molly,
The minute that you name the day.

Now, if you are sleepin', sweet Molly,
Ah, don't let me waken you, dear,
Some tender memorial I'll lave you
To just let you know I was here,
So I'll throw a big stone at your window,
An' if glass I should happen to break,
Sure, 'tis for love all the panes I am takin',
What w[o]uldn't I smash for your sake?

3.7: Sure, for ... [Dt]

1.8: croonyawn = cronan, Irish for humming; a song.
r.5: rowl = roll, wrap.

You're Welcome as the Flowers in May

[H804: 22 Apr 1939]

Author J. E. Carpenter, written c. 1889; (m) James Carmichael (Waring St, Ballymena).

s: I have included the song on account of the excellent air....

Key C.

'So, Katie dear, you've told your mother
That I'm a rogue by that and this;
We'll prove that same, somehow or other,
So first of all, I'll steal a kiss.'
'Och, Terry, dear, don't call it stealing,
A kiss you cannot take away,
The loss of that I'd not be feeling,
You're welcome as the flowers in May.'

'But, Katie dear, I'm growing bolder,
A great big thief I mean to start,
And before I am an hour older,
I'd like to steal away your heart.'
'Och, Terry dear, don't you call it robbin',
My heart you've owned this many a day,

But if you'd like to cease its throbbin',
You're welcome as the flowers in May.'

'But, Katie dear, I am not joking,
My wounded honour you must heal,
I'll not be called such names for nothing,
Sure, it's yourself away I'd steal.'
'Och, Terry dear, that would be housebreaking,
But if my mother won't say Nay,
It's to Father Tom you may be spaking,
You're welcome as the flowers in May.'

3.7: spaking = speaking.

Magherafelt Hiring Fair [H748: 26 Mar 1938]

g: "Tam Bo (Buie)." Other titles: "Bargain with Me," "O Faer Ye Gaun Will Boy?" "The Rigwiddy Carlin," "Tam Bo (Buie)," "The Wanton Widow."

Source: (Tobermore).

s: This song ... is at least 150 years old. The diet of sowans and eels would establish the locality. The first line of each verse, except the first, is spoken.

g: There are quite a few hiring-fair songs and ballads on broadsides in the Harvard collections, but this one was not located there.

Key G.

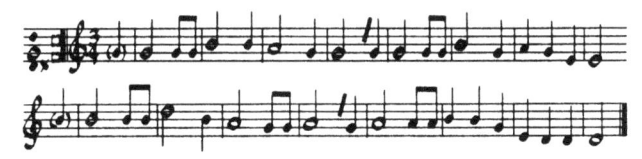

Would you hire with me, Tam Bo, Tam Bo?
Would you hire with me, my heart and my jo?
Would you hire with me, say you and say I,
    And what an' a rantin' young widow am I.

[*spoken*:] What wages, mistress?
    [*sung, as above*:]
Two pounds, five shillings, no pence.

Too little wages, mistress.
Then two pounds ten.

What diet, mistress?
Sowans and eels.

Too slippy diet, mistress.
Then potatoes and beef.

Where will I lie, mistress?
You'll lie in the laft.

The rats might eat me, mistress.
You'll lie wi' the weans.

The weans might kick me, mistress.
Well, then, we'll get married.

rugwiddie [rigwuddee] = "stubborn in disposition; deserving the 'widdie' or halter; ill-shaped, lean, bony." [Chambers, *Scots Dictionary*, quoted in Duncan 1967:17]
carlin = an old woman, a shrew, hag, a witch.

The Roving Bachelor (a) [H650a: 9 May 1936]

Other titles: "The Old ...," "... Journeyman."

Source: coll. Margaret Noble (Links Cottage, Cloughey, Co. Down) in Ards district, Co. Down.

s: [To the kindness of] Miss Margaret Noble ... we are indebted for the song.

g: The versions cited are quite different from Henry's two.

Key C.

I am a roving bachelor and have been all my life,
But now I am determined to gang and tak' a wife.

    With my rum-rum-row, a raddy rum-rum-row.

Now the sort of wife that I do want, she's no aisy
    to be fun',
She must be tall and handsome and worth a
    thoosan' pun'.

I strolled into the market place to see what a cud
    see,
When the bravest lass in a' the town begun tae
    wink at me.

I step-ped up beside her, said I, 'My maid sae shy
    ...'
The answer that she gaed me was, 'A'm nae sae
    shy as dry.'

The question then I axed her, what wud she hae
    tae drink?
The answer that she gaed me, 'Just onythin' ye
    think.'

The next question that I axed her, wud she no hae a
    gless?
And the answer that she gaed me, 'Ye couldna
    offer less.'

The next question that I axed her, did she ne'er
    lo'e a man?
The answer that she gaed me, 'I never loo'd but
    wan.'

Next question that I axed her, what like that
    might he be?
The answer that she gaed me was, 'The very
    image o' thee.'

Sam Henry's Songs of the People

Next question that I axed her, what way did she
  gang hame?
The answer that she gaed me, 'The very yin I
  came.'

So now we hae got married and the neighbours all
  can tell
That though she's tall and handsome she wears the
  breeks hersel'.

2.1: fun' = found.
2.2: pun' = pounds.
3.1: cud = could.
3.1: a = I.
4.2: gaed = gave.
9.2: yin = one.
10.2: breeks = britches.

The Roving Bachelor (b) [H650b: 9 May 1936]

[m = H650a]

A version collected in the Coleraine district
has the same theme, but elaborates the dialogue
between the lover and the lass. It runs --

As I went out one morning, being on the dewy
  grass,
'Twas by the will o' providence I met a bonny lass.

  *Dram-a-da, toor-an-addy, toor-al-oor-an-
    andy O.*

The first question that I axed her, what was her
  name?
And the answer that she geen tae me was, 'Bonny
  Jean, at hame.'

The next question that I axed her, could she milk
  a coo?
And the answer that she geen me was, 'Indeed, I
  could milk two.'

The next question that I axed her, was her
  fortune big?
And the answer that she geen me was, 'Ten
  shillings and a pig.'

The next question that I axed her, did her father
  deal in flax?
And the answer that she geen me, 'If you knowed,
  you widna ax.'

The next question that I axed her, was she good
  tae her mother?
And the answer that she gaen me, 'Times I shake
  her off her fother.'

'It's I am a gentleman and you're a country lass,
And all the fault I hae tae you, you hae ower
  muckle snash.'

'If you are a gentleman and I a country lass,
You might hae passed me by and geen me nane o'
  your snash.'

3.1: coo = cow.
6.2: fother = ?fodder, feed.
7.2: muckle = big, large, much.

The Whistling Thief [H710: 3 Jul 1937]

Other titles: "When Pat Came over the Hill."

Source: (w, m) Herbert Cunningham (Mullagh,
Maghera)

Key G.

When Pat came o'er the hill, his colleen fair to
  see,
His whistle loud and shrill the signal was to be,
  The signal was to be.

'Och, Mary,' the mother cried, "what noise is that
  I hear?'
'Och, mother, you know it's the wind that's
  whistling through the door,
  That's whistling through the door.'

'I've lived a long time, Mary, in this wide world,
  my dear,
And wind to whistle like that I never before
  did hear,
  I never before did hear.'

'Oh, mother, you know the fiddle hangs right
  behind the chink,
The wind upon the strings is playing a tune, I
  think,
  Is playing a tune, I think.'

'Och, Mary, I hear the pig uneasy in his mind.'
'But, mother, you know they say that pigs can see
  the wind,
  That pigs can see the wind.'

'It's all very well in the day, but I think you must
  remark
That pigs, no more than we, can see anything in
  the dark,
  Can see anything in the dark.'

'The dog is barking now and the fiddle can't play
  that tune.'
'But, mother, you know that dogs will bark when
  they see the moon,
  Will bark when they see the moon.'

'How can he see the moon, when you know the dog
  is blind?
Blind dogs can't bark at the moon, nor fiddles be
  played by the wind,
  Nor fiddles be played by the wind.

'I'm not such a fool as you think; I know very
  well it is Pat.
Get along, you whistling thief, and get along home
  out o' that,
    And get along home out o' that.

'And you'll be off to your bed, don't bother me
  with your tears,
For the more I've lost my eyes, I haven't lost my
  ears,
    I haven't lost my ears.'

Now, boys, too near the house don't courting go,
  d'ye mind,
Unless you're certain sure the ould woman's both
  deaf and blind,
    The ould woman's deaf and blind.

For the day when she was young, forget she never
  can,
She's sure to know the difference 'twixt a fiddle,
  pig, dog, or man,
    'Twixt a fiddle, pig, dog, or man.

The Feckless Lover [H216: 31 Dec 1927]

s: (m) "The Lothian Lassie."

Source: Maggie Kennedy (Blaugh).

Key F. Lively.

Last week as I sat wi' my wheel by the fire,
I heard our wee winnock play dirl;
Says I tae my mither, 'It's time for the byre,'
For weel I kent Johnny's love tirl,
  Love tirl,
  For weel I kent Johnny's love tirl.

I lifted my leglin and hied oot in haste,
Being laith that my lover should weary,
And swith ere I kent he'd his arm round my
  waist,
And kissed me and ca'd me his deary.

But before we had weel gotten time for a smack
My mither cam' oot in a hurry,
And wi' the graip shank ower his heid cam' a
  crack
Losh, guid, but she was in a flurry.

C15 / Where's the lass to take my hand?

She ca'd me a limmer, she ca'd me a slut,
She vowed she would cure me o' clockin',
She said that I neither had havers nor wit,
In my life I ne'er got sic a yokin'.

Next she flew at my lover wi' tongue like a sword,
Himsel' and his kindred misca'in,
While he, silly duffer, said never a word
But i' his cower'd cantle kept clawin'.

Dum-founded at length, he snooed oot o' the byre
As I aft seen a weel-threshen collie,
And trudged his way hameward through dub and
  through mire,
Nae doot lamentin' his folly.

An' ivir since syne, when we meet he looks blate,
As if we had ne'er been acquainted,
He ettels, it's plain, to lea' me to my fate,
But believe me, I'll no gang demented.

For the lover that's scared of an auld woman's
  tongue,
Though e'en like a dart it run through him,
Or yet by the weight o' her wrath or her rung,
Ill deserves that a lassie should lo'e him.

1.5,6: [*The refrain lines actually printed vary in
  pattern, but this seems to suit the music best.*]

1.2: winnock = window.
1.2: dirl = vibrate, tingle.
1.4: tirl = rattle, as at a door latch.
2.3: swith = quickly.
3.3: graip = a 3- or 4-pronged fork.
3.4: losh, guid = ?circumlocution for "Lord, God."
4.1: limmer = jade, hussy, minx.
4.2: clockin' = sitting, ?straggling.
4.3: havers = ?nonsense.
4.4: yokin' = subjugation, whipping into line.
5.4: cantle = corner.
6.1: snooed = ?slunk.
6.3: dub = pool, puddle.
7.1: blate = pale, void of feeling.
7.3: ettle [ettel] = plan, endeavor.
8.3: rung = a stout rounded stick.

The Ride in the Creel

[H201: 17 Sep 1927; Child #281]

s: "Wee Toun Clerk" [Ford 1899,1901]; k:
"Keach in the Creel," "Huroo-i-ah." Other titles:
"The (Auld) Wife and the (Peat) Creel," "The
Cetch ...," "The Coverin Blue," "The Creel,"
"The Cunning Clerk," "The Little Scotch Girl
(?Scotchee)," "Love Will Find a Way," "(The)
Newry Maid (Town)," "The Rock in the Same
Auld Creel."

Source: Sally Doherty (Oughtymoyle, Bellarena)
"with a few emendations" from David J. M'Googan
(Balnamore, Ballymoney).

[Bp] s: ... The song is 200 years old.... The
air here given is quite different from Ford's
[1904:277-80]. Some difficulty may be found in
adapting the words of the first verse to the tune.
I have indicated how this is overcome in the first
verse.

Sam Henry's Songs of the People

Key G.

[musical notation with lyrics: "Young Mol-ly she went up the street"]
REFRAIN

Young Molly she went up the street
Some fresh fish for to buy,
And a wee toun clerk he heard her feet
And followed her by and by.

To my right fol ol da daddy,
To my right fol ol da dee,
To my right fol ol da daddy,
To my raddy tan an ee.

Saying, 'Molly, lovely Molly,
For you I'm a'most dead.
Your oul' da locks the doors at night,
Keeps the keys inunder his head.

But I will get a 'lether' made
O' thirty step and three,
And put it to the chimley tap
An' come down in a creel to thee.

It's then he got the 'lether' made
O' thirty step and three,
And they tied the creel to the end of it,
And his comrades soon let him to she.

No rest, no rest could the auld wife get,
Her dreams she can't abide,
'I'll lay my life,' said the guid auld wife,
'There's a man by my daughter's side.'

It's up begot the guid auld man
To see if it was true;
She hid her lover from his sight,
And then the door shut to.

Saying, 'Father, dearest father,
What's rising you [so] soon?
You have disturbed my evening prayer
Which I should have said at noon.'

No rest, no rest could the auld wife get,
The dreams run in her mind,
'I'll lay my life,' quo' the guid auld wife,
'I'll rise and look mysel'.'

'Oh, the deil tak' you for a silly auld fool,
An' an ill death may you dee,
For she has the guid book in her arms,
An' she's prayin' for you an' me.'

It's up begot the guid auld wife
To see if it was true,
A wee peat clod it took her toe,
And in the creel she flew.

'Some help, some help, O guid auld man,
Some help I crave of thee;
You wished the deil he had my saul,
But he has me bodilie.'

'It's if the deil he has your soul,
That he may haud you fast,
For you gied me and my daughter
It was last night, little rest.'

The man that was on the chimley tap,
He gied the creel a haul,
He broke three ribs in the auld wife's side,
Knocked her head against the wall.

Know ye, ladies and gentlemen,
This is the end of my reel:
And any auld woman that is jealous of her
  daughter
Is welcome to a ride in the creel.

2.2: ... I'm a'maist dead. [Dt]
.3: Your aul' da ... [Dt]
7.2: ... you so soon? [Dt]
14.3: Any auld ... [Dt]

3.1: 'lether' = ladder.

I'm Seventeen 'gin Sunday

[H152: 9 Oct 1926; Laws O17]

[cf. H785 "My Darling Blue-Eyed Mary," H793 "As I Gaed ower a Whinny Knowe"]

g: "Seventeen Come Sunday." Other titles: "As I Roved (Walked) Out," "Hi Rinky Dum," "How Old Are You?" "I'll Be ... Come ...," "I'm Going to Get Married," "... Come (Cum) ...," "The Maid and the Soldier," "On a May Morning So Early," "The Modesty Answer," "Sixteen Come (Next) Sunday," "The Waukrife Minnie," "When Cockle Shells Make Silver Bells," "(Where Are You Going,) My Pretty (Fair) Maid?" "Yon High High Hill."

Source: (Ballycastle district).

[Bp] s: A song with this title, containing seven verses, was collected by the late Cecil J. Sharp in Somerset, England, and has been a very popular item in the wireless folk song concerts. The version here printed has a different air, a different plot and a different chorus, but is alike in structure and phraseology.... The tune is English, and contains what is uncommon in the folk airs of this district -- a change of key.
[Dt] Note the change of key in line 3, indicative of English origin.

1: But no such change is evident in Henry's tune, nor do key changes indicate English origin anyway.

Key F.

'Where are you going, my bonnie wee lass?
Where are you going, my honey?'
Right modestly she answered me,
'An errand for my mammy.'

    With my roor-ri-ra, Fond a doo a da,
    With my roo ri ranta mirandy.

'What's your age, my bonnie wee lass,
What's your age, my honey?'
Right modestly she answered me,
'I'm seventeen 'gin Sunday.'

'Would you tak' a man, my bonnie wee lass?
Would you tak' a man, my honey?'
Right modestly she answered me,
'If it wasny for my mammy.'

She had new shoes and stockin's too,
And her buckles shone like silver,
She had a dark and rolling eye,
And her hair hanging over her shoulders.

'If I would go doon to your wee hoose,
And the moon was shining clearly,
Would you open the do[o]r and let me in,
If the oul' wife widna hear me?'

I gaed doon to her wee hoose,
And the moon was shining clearly,
She opened the do[o]r and she let me in,
And the oul' wife didna hear me.

Canny slippin' aff my boots
In case that oul' thrush wid ken me,
But by my feth I wasn't long in
Till the oul' wife heard us talkin'.

Canny slippin' doon the stairs,
By the hair o' the heed she caught her
And with a great big hazel stick
She left her a well-bate daughter.

Throwing in the stool tae the fire
In case that oul' thrush wid ken me,
But by my feth I had tae tak'
The green fields tae defend me.

Come over the burn, my bonnie wee lass,
Come over the burn, my honey,
Till I get a kiss o' your sweet lips
To spite your aul' aul' mammy.

5.4: ... wife didna hear ... [Dt]
8.4: ... left a ... [Dt]
10.4: ... your dour auld ... [Dt]

7.1: aff = off.
7.3: feth = faith.

C15 / Where's the lass to take my hand?

As I Gaed ower a Whinny Knowe

[H793: 4 Feb 1939; Laws O17]

[cf. H785 "My Darling Blue-Eyed Mary"]

k: "Seventeen Come Sunday."

Source: Andy Allen (Bridge Cottage, Coleraine).

s: This excellent old song was noted from the singing of Mr Andy Allen....

Key G.

As I went ower a whinny knowe I met a bonny lassie,
She laughed at me, I winked at her, and oh, but I was sassie.

    Wi my ru rum ra, far an ta a na,
    [W]hack fal tar an addy.

Her shoes were black, her stockings white, her buckles shone like silver,
She had a dark and rolling eye and her hair hung ower her shoulder.

'Oh, where are you going, my bonny wee lass?
Oh, where are you going, my honey?'
Right modestly she answered me, 'Gaun a message for my mammy.'

'What is your age, my bonny wee lass? What is your age, my honey?'
Right cheerfully she answered me, 'I'll be seventeen come Sunday.'

'Would you give me a kiss, my bonny wee lass?
Would you give me a kiss, my bonny?'
Right bashfully she answered me, 'I dare not for my mammy.'

'Oh, where do you live, my bonny wee lass?
Oh, where do you live, my honey?'
Right joyfully she answered me, 'In a wee house wi' my mammy.'

So I went down to her wee house, the moon was shining clearly;
I rapped upon her window pane and the old wife didna hear me.

'Oh, open the door, my bonny wee lass, come open the door, my honey,
And I will give you a kiss or two, in spite of your old mammy.'

Sam Henry's Songs of the People

'Oh, soldier, would you marry me? For now's
  your time or never,
For if you do not marry me, my heart is broke
  for ever.'

So now she is the soldier's wife and sails across
  the brine-o,
The drum and fife is my delight, and a merry
  heart is mine-o.

10.1: ... brine, oh! [Dp]
  .2: ... mine, oh! [Dp]

1.2: sassie = saucy.

The Rambling Suiler [H183: 14 May 1927]

s: "The Gaberlunzie Man," "The Jolly Beggar."
Other titles: "... Shuler (Soldier)", "Trip with
the Roving Shooler"; cf. "The Gauger," "...
Sailor," "The Tarry Sailor."

Source: native (Castlewellan district, Co. Down).

s: (Dedicated to the three University men who
helped me to record the song.)
  The title means "the rambling beggarman," and
the song is a very close parallel to "The Gaberlunzie Man," "The Jolly Beggar," and other songs
alleged to have been composed by, or about, that
"merrie monarch," King James V of Scotland, who
used to wander among his people under the
disguise of the "Gudeman of Ballengeich," and
whose clandestine courtships are the theme of
these songs.
  A sea song, "The Rambling Sailor," evidently
modelled on this song, has just been published in
A Book of Shanties, by C. Fox Smith [1927].

[Dt] The last two words ... are spoken, not
sung.

Key D. Quick time.

Now the Hielan' Watch is come to town
And landed in headquarters,
The colonel fell in love with a pretty little girl,
A farmer's only daughter.
The general bet ten thousand pound
He'd dress the colonel in a beggar's gown
And travel the world go round, go round,
And she'll go with the rambling suiler.

The colonel dressed in a beggar's gown
And set out as a rambling suiler,
He travelled about the whole of the day
Till he came to the farmer's dwelling.

He said to the farmer, 'Will you entertain me
And keep me till I daylight see?
The dark of the night has overtaken me,
God help all rambling suilers.'

'As the night,' says the farmer, 'is dark and wet
You may sit by the kitchen fire.'
Says the beggar to the farmer's serving maid,
'It's you I do admire;
A gramachree and a cushla machree,
Will you lea' them all and come wi' me?
What a lusty fine beggar you would be,
Going off wi' the rambling suiler.'

The farmer and his servants all,
They fell into loud laughter,
When who came tripping down the stairs
But the farmer's only daughter;
As soon as the colonel did her spy,
She pleased the twinkling of his eye,
'She's a painted beauty from the top to the toe,
She'll be mine,' thought the rambling suiler.

The farmer and his servants all,
They went out to the byre;
He placed his arms around her waist
As they sat by the kitchen fire,
He placed his arms around her waist
And unto her gave kisses sweet,
'Houl' on,' says she, 'how dar' you make so free,
And you but a rambling suiler.'

When supper has been over-o,
They made his bed in the barn
Between two sacks and a winnow cloth
For fear he'd do any harm.
At twelve o'clock that very night
She came to the barn door-o,
He opened the door and let her in,
And says he, 'You are my jewel.'

O, he took off his beggar's gown
And threw it to the wa',
And stood the brawest gentleman
That was amang them a'.
'Would you look at my links o' yellow hair
In under the sooty ould hat I do wear:
I'm a colonel o' the army, I do declare,
Believe me, I'm no rambling suiler.

'I would not for two hundred pound
That you and I were found here,
Let us travel round the whole night round,'
She's away wi' the rambling suiler.
O, yonder is the colonel, I see he's come,
Great is the wager the general has won,
Salute the colonel with the fife and the drum
Since he took from them all his jewel.

6.1 [and similarly 6.6]: ... over, O, [Bp, Dt]

1.8: suiler = beggarman. [s]
3.5: a gramachree = O heart's love [s]

A Beggarman Cam' ower the Lea

[H810: 3 Jun 1939; Child #279]

k: "Gaberlunzie Man," "The Beggarman." Other titles: "The Auld (Dirty) (Ragged) Beggarman (Gaberlunzie)," "The Barley Straw," "The Beggar Laddie (Man)," "He Wadna Lie in Barn," "The Jolly Beggar."

Source: George Graham (Cross Lane, Coleraine) from his grandfather, Joe Wilson (Roddenfoot, Ballymoney) from his grandfather (Ballymoney).

Key G.

Oh, a beggarman cam' ower the lea,
An' he toul tidin's unto me,
He was luckin' for a help an' a charitee,
Wud ye lodge a beggarman?

Wae m' nantanoora-noora-nee,
Nanta-noora-noora-nee,
Wae m' nanta-noora-noora-nee,
Wud ye lodge a beggarman?

Oh, the oul' wife wudnae let me stay,
An' the young yin wudnae let me gae,
So Ah throwed m' meal-poke tae the wa',
And I began tae sing.

Early nixt mor[n]in' the oul wife rose,
She missed the beggar and his clothes,
First tae the cupboard an' then tae the chist,
Naethin' ava there could be missed,
Wasn't he the honest oul' man?

When the kettle was boiled an' the breakfast made,
She went to waken the young fair maid,
But ah! a shout the mither gaed,
She's awa' wi' the beggarman.

Now seven long years was passed an' gone,
The beggar he cam' back again,
He was luckin' for a help an' a charitee,
Wud ye lodge a beggarman?

Oh, beggar, Ah'l lodge nane ava,
The last Ah lodged taen mae dauchter awa',
The last Ah lodged taen mae dauchter awa',
On' Ah think you're the very oul' man.

1.2: toul = told.
1.3: luckin' = looking.
3.1: nixt = next.
3.3: chist = chest.
3.4: naethin' = nothing.

C15 / *Where's the lass to take my hand?*

The Galway Shawl [H652: 23 May 1936]

Source: Bridget Kealey (Termeil Cottages, Dungiven).

Key G.

Near Oranmore in the County Galway,
One evening in the month of May,
I spied a colleen who looked so charming,
Her beauty stole my heart away.
She wore no jewels, no costly diamonds,
No paint, no powder, ah, none at all,
She'd a pink sunbonnet with roses on it,
And around her shoulders a Galway shawl.

As we were walking she kept on talking
Until her cottage came in view,
She asked me in to meet her father
And, to please him, play 'The Foggy Dew.'
She sat me down beside the hearthstone
Fornenst her father, who was six foot tall,
And soon her mother had the kettle boiling,
While I kept thinking on the Galway shawl.

I played 'The Blackbird,' 'The Stack of Barley,'
'The Evening Glory' and 'The Foggy Dew,'
And she sang each note like an Irish linnet
While the tears filled up her eyes of blue.
I left it early the next morning
To walk the road to Donegal;
As she said good-bye, she cried and kissed me,
But my heart remains 'neath the Galway shawl.

2.6: fornenst = opposite.

Where the Moorcocks Crow

[H32: "A song of love and Letterloan," 21 Jun 1924]

k: "Mountain Streams." Other titles: "The Mountain Stream(s) ...(s)."

Source: (w) an old lady (Altibrian); (m) coll. Maud Houston, from Allan Mitchell (Coleraine).

s: The song was composed about 70 years ago by a roving sportsman in honour of a young lady of Letterloan....

Key C.

With my dog and gun o'er yon blooming heather
To seek for pastime I took my way,
Where I beheld that lovely creature,
Her charms invited me a while to stay.
Said I, 'My charmer, I find I love you,
Tell me your dwelling and your name also.'
'Excuse my name, and you'll find my dwelling
Near the mountain streams where the moorcocks crow.'

'If you'd consent and go with a rover,
My former roving I will leave aside,
I'm doomed to love you, so don't prove cruel,
But do consent and become my bride.'
'If my parents knew that I'd wed a rover,
Sure, deep reflections I would undergo;
I'm young and tender, but I might be courted
From the mountain streams where the moorcocks crow.'

Oh, it's crimson covered all her lovely features,
She stood a while but no answer made;
'Come to my arms, you fairest creature,
Don't stand to ponder or to be dismayed.
It's leave your parents and do come with me,
And I'll escort you to yon vale below
Where the linnet sings; it will yield more pleasure
Nor the mountain streams where the moorcocks crow.'

'If your love be true, then perhaps I'll see you,
So return again to your moorland dale,
If I find it's true, as you have declared it,
I'll pay attention to your lovesick tale,
But I'll go home and acquaint my parents,
Lest a hasty marriage should produce a foe;
As I'm young and tender, I will rest a season
Near the mountain streams where the moorcocks crow.'

3.8: nor = than.

The Maid of Seventeen [H144: 14 Aug 1926]

Source: (w, m) Willie Hegarty (Agivey district).

[Bp] s: ...In the old Irish airs, the air has two variants, the second being known as the "turn of the tune." In this air, the construction is unusual. The ordinary formula is a,b,b,a: sometimes we find a,b,a,b, but here we have a,a,a,b.

Key C.

Down by yon shady arbour I spied a handsome maid,
I stepp-ed up unto her and those words to her I said,
'Your rolling eye entices me, and your countenance serene,'
And the answer she made unto me: 'I'm only seventeen.'

'It's youth, my love, I'm wanting since I have met with you,
I'll court you one half hour if you to me be true;
On a pleasant summer evening all on the grass so green,
I long to be a-courting with a maid of seventeen.'

'You need not talk of courting, for I don't know the way,
Upon that tender subject not one word could I say.'
I taught my love a lesson, and for learning she seemed keen,
And I spent a pleasant evening with the maid of seventeen.

I said, 'I will go visit you.' 'Oh now, that would not do,
My mother would be angry, but I'll whisper, sir, to you,
Next Tuesday I'll be back this way, perhaps we'll meet again,'
And I know this maid admired me, although but seventeen.

My love's genteel and handsome, most rare for to be seen,
Her whole demeanour pleases me, she is so neat and clean;
If she consents to marry me, it's married we'll be soon,
For I long for to be married to the maid of seventeen.

1.2: ... to her said, [Dt]

Cloughmills Fair [H121: 6 Mar 1926]

Source: (w, m) coll. William Carton (Garryduff, Ballymoney) from Mrs Morrison (Drumlee, Ballymoney); (w) from her mother, Mrs R. Kirkpatrick (Maddykeel, Bendooragh, Ballymoney).

Key E flat.

It being on a pleasant morning in the cheerful
    month of June,
The feathered warbling songsters their tender
    notes did tune,
It chanced to be my fortune to Ballylig to go,
Where I met that charming fair one, and her skin
    was white as snow.

Her aspect was engaging, a sweet becoming air,
To make her still more graceful, in ringlets waved
    her hair,
So modest was her carriage, so handsome in my
    view,
My heart she captivated as she tripped it o'er the
    dew.

'Stop, stop, my charming fair one, one moment
    stop with me,
Till I disclose a secret which is unknown to thee:
I am become your lover and my heart is truly
    proved,
I am wounded by slight Cupid, the sovereign god
    of love.'

'The subject you're discoursing I have no wish to
    hear,
Besides, the theme of courtship stands coldly in
    my ear;
To Cloughmills I am going on an errand, as you
    see,
I'm not disposed to talk of love; good morning,
    sir, to thee.'

'If you have no objection, alongst with you I'll go.'
'Oh then,' she says, 'With pleasure, the road is
    free, you know.
Do not enforce the subject of courtship now, I
    pray,
I neither know nor want to know the dangers of
    the way.'

We chatted on together till we came unto the town,
I asked her in to have a glass, one moment to sit
    down.
'I have no time this morning, kind sir, I do
    declare,
But tomorrow is the ninth of June, and you'll find
    me in the fair.'

I bid her a good morning, when thus transported
    I
From that propitious moment I orderly did sigh;
At length the time arrived, and she whom I adore
In splendour dressed appeared far lovelier than
    before.

I bid her a good morning, she thus returned a
    smile,
From that propitious moment I gained her all the
    while,

C15 / Where's the lass to take my hand?

With modest intercession I see her home at night,
With modest conversation she fills me with delight.

So I have got permission with her to come and go,
And happy, happy are the hours, I now must let
    you know,
That pass between my love and me, congenial to
    her mind,
With raptures in her company; she's loving and
    she's kind.

Fair maidens seem reluctant when first they are
    addressed,
There is a gentle feeling prevails within their
    breast.
This is the end of courtship, you lovers may
    suppose,
And like to loyal lovers the bargain then we
    closed.

6.1: ... came to Cloughmills town, [Dt]
 .4: ... June, you'll ... [Dt]

O'er the Moor amang the Heather

[H177: 2 Apr 1927]

Other titles: "Among ...," "The Blooming ...,"
"Bonnie Lassie amang ...," "Doon (Down) the
Moor," "Heather on the Moor," "Herding Lambs
amongst ...," "The Lass amang ...," "O'er the
Muir;" cf. "Far up Yon Wide and Lofty Glens,"
"Queen amang ...," "Skippin Barfit thro the ...."

Source: John Parker (Mayoghill, Garvagh).

s: ... Burns, in his remarks on Scottish song,
quotes a version of "O'er the Moor amang the
Heather," which he states he obtained from Jean
Glover, a Kilmarnock lassie [Dt: born 31st October 1758, died Letterkenny, suddenly, in 1801],
who claimed it as her own composition. Jean [Bp:
from her moral delinquencies] had visited most of
the Houses of Correction in west Scotland [Dt:
and her claim to the authorship of this song
cannot be taken seriously].
[Bp: To her other faults, it would seem, must be
added unveracity, as clearly this old song was
composed long before her day. The version here
printed is fuller and more poetic.]

l: Gardner/Chickering and Morton suggest their
variants are related to Child #236, "The Laird o
Drum," although Bronson asserts: "The musical
record, it might be observed, lends no
corroboration to the assumption that the
secondary forms of the ballad have grown
traditionally from the earlier" (3,1966:395).

Key C.

Sam Henry's Songs of the People

One morning in May when fields were gay,
Serene and pleasant was the weather,
I happened to roam some miles from home
Amang the bonnie bloomin' heather.
  Doon the moor, roon amang the heather,
  O'er the moor and through the heather,
  I happened to roam some miles from home
  Amang the bonnie bloomin' heather,
  Doon the moor.

I trudged along with the lilt of a song,
My heart as light as any feather,
Until I met with a very bonnie lass,
She was brushing the dew frae amang the
  heather.
  Doon the moor, ...

'O,' said I, 'my fair lassie, where have you
  been?'
Her name and place I scarce could gather.
She answered me by the bonnie burn side,
'A-feeding of my flocks together.'
  Doon the moor, ...

Barefooted she was, and trig and clean,
Her cap as light as any feather,
With a tartan plaid hanging neatly round her
  waist,
She tripped through the bloomin' heather.
  Doon the moor, ...

We tigged and toyed from morn till e'en,
It being the langest day in summer,
Until the rays of the red settin' sun
Came trinklin' doon amang the heather.
  Doon the moor, ...

She charmed my heart and pleased my e'en,
I ne'er can think on ony ither,
If I was king she would be queen,
The lass I met amang the heather.
  Doon the moor, ...

4.3: And a tartain ... [Dt]

4.1: trig = trim or tight in dress; spruce, smart.
5.1: tig = a light but significant touch, a tap or pat.

272

The Whinny Knowes [H18b: 15 Mar 1924]

A song of our Scottish forebears ...

Other titles: "The Corncraik (Corncrake) amang
the ...," "The Echo Mocks the Corncrake."

Source: Robert Bacon (Coleraine).

o: Time should be 6/8.

[Bp has stanza 4 typed in, Wt has it added in
brackets.]

Key A flat.

Oh, the lass I had the first of all was handsome,
  young and fair,
With her I spent some happy days upon the banks
  of Ayr,
With her I spent some happy days where yonder
  burnie rows,
Where the echo mocks the corncrake amang the
  whinny knowes.

We loved each other dearly, disputes we seldom
  had,
As constant as the pendulum her heart beat always
  glad,
We sought for joy and found it where yonder
  burnie rows
Where the echo mocks the corncrake amang the
  whinny knowes.

Oh, the corncrake it is noo awa', the burn is to
  the brim,
The whinny knowes are clad wi' snaw that tops the
  highest whin,
But when cauld winter is awa' and summer clears
  the sky,
We'll welcome back the corncrake, that bird of
  rural joy.

Oh, maidens fair and pleasure dames, drive to the
  banks of Doon;
You'll dearly pay for every scent in barbers for
  perfume,
But rural joy is free to a' whaur scented clover
  grows,
And the echo mocks the corncraik amang the
  whinny knowes.

4.: [8-line stanza typed onto Bp, also in brackets in
  Wt; 4-line stanza in Dt.]
4.4: ... the corncrake ... [Dt]

2.3: burnie = diminutive of burn, brook.
4.3: whaur = where.

The Captain with the Whiskers

[H660: 18 Jul 1936]

Other title: "... with His ...."

Source: John Henry Macaulay (Ballycastle).

s: One more song from John Henry Macauley's repertoire, who as he carves his bog oak ... lilts these ditties of his youthful days.

Key D.

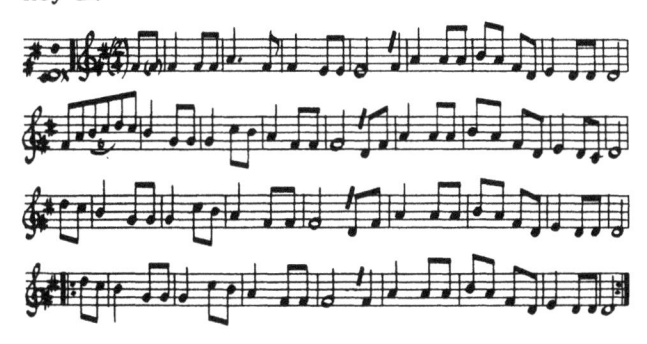

They marched through the town with their banners so gay,
I went to the window to hear the band play,
I peeped through the blind very cautiously then,
Lest the neighbours should say I was looking at the men,
I heard the drum beat and the music so sweet,
But my eyes just then had a much finer treat:
The troops were the finest that I ever yet did see,
And the captain with the whiskers took a sly glance at me.
    Took a sly glance at me, took a sly glance at me,
    The captain with the whiskers took a sly glance at me.

When we met at the ball, I of course thought I right
To pretend we had never met before that night,
But he knew me at once, I could see by his glance,
And I hung down my head when he asked me to dance.
He sat by my side at the end of the set,
And the sweet words he spoke I shall never forget,
My heart was enlisted and could not get free
When the captain with the whiskers took a sly glance at me.
    Took a sly glance ...

They marched from the town and I saw him no more,
But I think of him often and the whiskers that he wore.
I dream all the night and I talk all the day
Of the love of a captain who is gone far away,
And I keep in my mind how my heart would leap with glee
When the captain with the whiskers took a sly glance at me.
I remember with superabundant delight
How we met in the ball and danced all the night.
    Danced all the night, danced all the night,
    How we met in the ball and danced all the night.

C15 / Where's the lass to take my hand?

Youghall Harbour

[H503: 22 Jul 1933]

Other titles: "My Sunday Morning Maiden," "Youghal ..."; (m) "When First I Came to County Limerick."

Source: (m) Brieny Molloy, fiddler, 80+ (Meenaharvey, Glencolumbkille, Co. Donegal).

s: ... Brieny Molloy ... speaks Irish only, a Civic Guard acting as interpreter.... He played "Jackson's Jig," "The Pretty Milking Maid," and other airs. His play was very ornate, and for the sake of clarity the grace notes have been omitted from the accompanying air.

o: Surprisingly good translation of Gaelic.

Key G.

One Sunday morning, into Youghall walking,
I met a maiden upon the way,
Her little mouth sweet as fairy music,
Her soft cheeks blushing like dawn of day.

I laid my hand upon her shoulder
And asked a kiss, but she answered, 'No,
Fair sir, be gentle, let go my mantle,
'Tis none in Erin my grief can know.

"Tis but a little hour since I left Youghall,
And my love forbade me to return,
And now my weary way I wander
Into Cappoquin, a poor girl forlorn.

'Then do not tempt me, for, alas, I dread them
Who with artful offers teach girls to roam,
Who'd first deceive us, then, faithless, leave us
And send us heartsick and barefoot home.'

'My heart and hand here; I mean you marriage,
I have loved like you and known love's pain,
If you turn back now to Youghall Harbour,
You'll ne'er want house or home again.

'You shall have a lace cap like any lady,
Cloak and capuchin, too, to keep you warm,
And if God please, maybe a little baby
By and by, to nestle within your arm.'

The Cup of Gold

[H546: 19 May 1934]

A song of Movanagher hills.

s: (m) "The Cup of Gold."

Sam Henry's Songs of the People

Author Sam Henry.

Key C.

My love and I together lay
On Cuniberry Hill;
Of primroses and violets
We gathered there our fill,
Oh, blue the lowly violets
And blue my true love's eyes,
And blue the smiling skies above,
Lit by the spring's surprise,
The young year's surmise.

Oh, yellow was the primrose,
And yellow was her hair,
And yellow on the whinny knowe
The yorlin peeping there,
And yellow was the saffron
King Rory wore of old,
Who yonder on the King's Hill
Drank from his cup of gold
In great days of old.

Oh, were I king of Ireland
As Rory was of old,
The queen should be my Nora,
To share my lands and gold,
On Tully Hill I'd build her
A warm and cosy nest,
And through all the coloured years
With her I would be blest,
Her dear heart possessed.

Ah, lovely of the yellow bird,
Ah, lovely yellow flower,
We are but nature's children,
And beauty is our dower;
Then lo, the flashing sunlight
Finds in the dewy grass
A spangled gem of golden hue
That would adorn my lass --
Her bright curls surpass.

With bounding step I found the gem,
I clasped it to my breast,
'Twas good King Rory's golden cup,
Now mine by fate's behest,
An empty cup of other days
Now brims with happiness,
It brings us love and light and joy:
A home we now possess,
And King Rory bless.

The Mountain Road [H515: Dp, 14 Oct 1933]

[Bt, Wt] Source: (m) Archie [Bt: D. F.] McEachran (Kilblaan, Southend, Campbelltown); author Sam Henry.

[Dp is evidently a proof before correction: the refrain (see below) is crossed out and the replacement typed in, with no source given. Bt, Wt appear in 2-line stanzas with lines twice as long as Dp.]

Key G.

As I went up the mountain road
To cut my winter store,
I met a wee lassie coming down --
My heart was mine no more.

Hey rick-a-doo, rick-a-daddy,
Hey rick-a-doo, rick a day.

Her hair was dark as mountain turf,
Her eye the peat-fire flame,
That I should lose my heart to her,
On me there was small blame.

Her neck was white as canavan,
Her lips like rowans red;
As soon as I had told my love,
I asked when we might wed.

And now beneath my straw-winged cot
She shares the amber glow
Of turf we gathered on the hill
That now is clad with snow.

Sure I was bird-alone in troth
Who now am one of three,
I bless the day I found my rose
On the slopes of Slievanee.

[Dp *original refrain, crossed out and replaced by typed refrain as given above:*]

'God save you kindly,' she faltered,
'Blessings on you, asthore.'

r.1,2: *Hey rick a doo-oo, rick ...* [Wt, Bt]
4.3: ... hills [Wt, Bt]
.4: ... are now ... [Wt, Bt]

The Woods of Mountsandel

[H6: 22 Dec 1923, H567: 13 Oct 1934]

s: (m) "O, I Was in a Hurry."

Source: coll. Maud Houston (Coleraine).

s: In gently swinging time, fitting the words to the music as the spirit of the song suggests.

Key G.

Oh, there's no place so sweet, you may search where you can,
As the dear little town on the banks of the Bann,
Where the fields are so green and the skies are so blue,
And 'twas there, my sweet Kathleen, that first I met you.

*Singing Erin go bragh, tourin-in-a,
My blessin' go with you, sweet Erin-go-bragh.*

Oh, woods of Mountsandel, how often we strayed
Through thy cool summer meadows, and kissed in the shade,
With my arm round your waist as you sat on my knee,
While the river ran by on its way to the sea.

The summer is gone and the green trees are bare,
And the snows of the winter have whitened our hair,
But love in our hearts is as young as of yore,
When we wandered together along the Bann shore.

r.2: My blessing ... [H567 Dp]
2.3: With your arm round my waist [Dt]

The Ould Lammas Fair   [H101: 17 Oct 1925]

s: (m) "The Carver's Choice." Other title: "The Auld ...."

Author, composer: John Henry Macaulay (Bog Oak Shop, Ballycastle).

s: ... This song having won widespread popularity since it appeared in our columns in October 1925 ... is now reprinted in response to numerous requests. Mr Macauley has consummated the courtship of the original song by describing a happy marriage in an additional verse of tender sentiment.

m: Very popular song. For further information, see also Stanley Matchett, *Faces at the Fair: A photographic essay on the Ould Lammas Fair at Ballycastle, Co. Antrim* (Belfast: Blackstaff Press, 1975) and Theodora Fitzgibbon, *A Taste of Ireland* (London: J. M. Dent & Sons, 1968; London: Pan Books, 1970).

[Bp, Dp are identical, unnumbered, dateless reprints. Also included with Bp is a copy of Paterson's Publications edition of this song, arranged by John Vine, "from the People's Collection by Samuel Henry."]

Key A flat.

At the Ould Lammas Fair in Ballycastle long ago,
I met a little colleen who set my heart aglow,
She was smiling at her daddy buying lambs from Paddy Roe
At the Ould Lammas Fair in Ballycastle, oh.
I seen her home that night when the moon was shining bright
From the Ould Lammas Fair in Ballycastle, oh!

*At the Ould Lammas Fair, boys, were you ever there?
At the Ould Lammas Fair in Ballycastle, oh?
Did you treat your Mary Ann to dulse and 'yellow man'
At the Ould Lammas Fair in Ballycastle, oh?*

Sam Henry's Songs of the People

In Flanders fields afar, when resting from the war,
We drank 'Bon Sainte' to the Flemish lassies, oh,
But the scene that haunts my memory is kissing Mary Anne,
Her pouting lips all sticky from eating 'yellow man,'
As we crossed the silver Margey and walked along the strand
From the Ould Lammas Fair at Ballycastle, oh!

There's a nate little cabin on the slopes of ould Knocklayd
It's lit by love and sunshine where the heather honey's made
By the bees ever humming, and our childers' joyous call
Resounds across the valley when the shadows fall,
I take my fiddle down and my Mary smiling there
Brings back a happy memory of the Lammas Fair.

r.3: dulse = a red edible seaweed (*Rhodymenia palmata*), eaten dried (or in fish or vegetable soup) which grows in the sublittoral area inshore. See Fitzgibbon 1968(1970):103. [m]
r.3: 'yellow man' = a golden yellow homemade toffee, made in slabs and made amenable with a hammer. See Fitzgibbon 1968(1970):35, which quotes the song. [m]

The Star of Moville [H68: 28 Feb 1925]

Source: (w, m) M[atthew] Q[uinn], 84, fiddler (Bellarena); author, composer James McCurry, blind fiddler (Myroe).

[Bp, additions from Dt] s: Played on the fiddle by M[atthew] Q[uinn], ... who[se hands were twisted with rheumatism. He] learnt the air and words from the author and composer....

Key F.

You folk of this nation that hear my oration,
Come listen with patience and I won't keep you long,
There is no false pretension in what I here mention,
It is now my intention for to sing you a song.
I belong to a village where boatmen have knowledge
Of rowing and sailing, experience and skill,
They all took their places, as yearly the case is,
To witness the races this day at Moville.

My notion was bent, so to Blackburn's I went
To obtain his consent for a sail o'er Lough Foyle,
My friends and my neighbours had ceased from their labours
To obtain the day's pleasure, forsaking their toil.
My petition he granted, I got what I wanted,
He freely consented and said nothing ill,
He says, 'Get you ready and keep yourself steady,
Beware of your conduct this day at Moville.

Without further warning, for the morning was charming,
I set out on my journey, to the waters I strayed,
When I came to the Run, I found the boat it was gone;
Till another would come, with Montgomery I stayed.
I soon left the spot, when I got in a cot,
There I knew my conductor would drive her with skill,
Though the water was low, to the boat I did go
Where the crew had their frigate prepared for Moville.

I need not narrate, they began to debate;
For a damsel I waited, but she kept her word,
And when they viewed her, as soon as they knew her,
A party went to her and brought her on board.
No storm seemed to tease us, but all seemed to please us
With soft gentle breezes our sails for to fill,
From Blackburn's that morning, with Davis and Torrens
The fiddler and Margaret, set sail for Moville.

We did not sail free till we passed the Black Gwee,
When I thought I could see to the opposite shore,
Some sails at a distance in the sunbeams did glisten,
Which seemed to extend from the Point to Culmore.
As we drew nearer, the scene became clearer,
The lough with boats crowded like sheep on a hill,
As fast as a streamer we passed by the steamer,
And shortly our vessel was moored at Moville.

I profess not to show it, for indeed I don't know it,
To tell you in plain how the races were run,
Suffice it to say, about twelve in the day
The boats went away like the shot of a gun.
Some cheering for Allen and others for Blackburn,
Some for McCormick with cheers loud and shrill,
Surprised as by thunder, my heart leapt like wonder
When I met with Mary, the star of Moville.

My senses were frisky by means of some whiskey,
Says I, 'My fair lassie, how sweetly you sing.'
Some swaggering and roystering while others kept cursing,

Sly Cupid kept whispering, 'Slip round her your
    wing.'
Says I, 'Ma'am, excuse me and do not refuse me,
A wee drop of whiskey your sorrow would kill.'
She freely consented, so I was contented
When I had gained Mary, the star of Moville.

I says to my pet, 'Let us now have a wet,
Let us never forget that I play and you sing,
For that we'll not quarrel, for the poor of the
    world
Had always a winter before they have spring.'
She said, 'Sir, to cheer you, my name is called
    Mary,
From sweet Carndonagh I ramble at will.
Therefore excuse me my speech, don't abuse me,
I sing to gain pence on the streets of Moville.'

Then her I enlisted and of her requested
A promise of marriage to give me her hand.
'If on me you'll smile, we'll cross o'er Lough
    Foyle
And reside in the village called Ballymacran.'
She said, 'I've consented if that's all that's
    wanted.'
Says I, 'I'm contented for good or for ill;
In my heart I'd be willing to share the last
    shilling
And spend it with Mary, the star of Moville.'

I supplied her with pence to meet her expense,
And to taste we commenced, for her throttle was
    dry.
She entered a shop where she did not long stop
Till she came with a drop where I waited hard
    by.
She said, 'Sir, don't slight me and do not deride
    me,
Some people would slight me, of me would speak
    ill.'
She was brown as a berry, her lips like the
    cherry,
Then I kissed Mary, the star of Moville.

She was not neglected, but highly respected,
For a coach was erected to bear her away,
'Mid parlours and cellars, 'mid equals and fellows
She was requested some time for to stay.
To explain I'm not able how grand was the table,
Well covered with nothing her joys to fulfil.
With my senses afloat I went to the boat
To lament for my Mary, the star of Moville.

So now to conclude and to finish these verses,
I hope an offence I have given to none,
But I wish I could fly or the ground would rise
    high,
Or the waters would dry, I might reach
    Innishowen.
I'll promise you here, if you're over next year
At Elizabeth's or Jacob's your glasses to fill,
And like a canary I'll sing loud and cheery,
If you bring me Mary, the star of Moville.

1.8: ... this year at ... [Dt]
2.7: ... 'You get ready ... [Dt]
3.3: ... boat gone, [Dt]

C15 / Where's the lass to take my hand?

8.5: ... said, 'Love, to ... [Dt]
5.7: As fast as a steamer ... [Dt]
10.8: ... kissed my sweet Mary, ... [Dt]
12.4: ... I would reach ... [Dt]

Mind Your Eye [H700: 24 Apr 1937]

[cf. H725 "The Basket of Oysters"]

Other titles: "Bung ...," "Bungereye," "...,
Laddie," "(Quare) (Queer) Bungle (Bungo) Rye,"
"Young Bung-'er-Eye"; cf. "The Basket of Eggs,"
"Eggs in Her Basket."

Source: Frank Thompson (Priestland), learned in
Ballywatt district.

s: This [is a] humorous song ....

Key G.

One day as I was walking along a London street,
A pretty blue-eyed Irish girl I happened for to
    meet;
She had a basket on her arm and as she passed
    me by,
I asked her what she carried and she said, 'Mind
    your eye.'

Singing, down, down, a-dumps the darry dee.

'If you be a gentleman, as I take you to be,
I'll leave you now in charge of the basket,' said
    she,
'I'll go a-marketing, some custom for to find,'
So she left me in charge of the basket behind.

I waited for a moment to see what way she went,
To get the basket open, it was my whole intent,
When I opened the basket, a baby began to cry,
And into my arms jumped the young 'Mind your eye.'

To get the baby christened, it was my whole
    intent,
And off to the clergy straightway then I went;
'It's when will you christen the baby?' 'We'll
    christen it by-and-by.'
'What name shall we call it?' And I said, 'Mind
    your eye.'

'Mind your eye,' said the clergy, 'it's a very
    funny name.'

Sam Henry's Songs of the People

'In troth,' said the sailor, 'it's a funny way it came,
For when I opened the basket, the baby began to cry,
And into my arms jumped the young "Mind your eye."'

Come all you brisk young sailor lads, a warning take by me,
And never take a basket when you are on your way,
For if you do, you'll surely rue, you'll find it by and by,
When you become the daddy of a young 'Mind your eye.'

The Basket of Oysters

[H725: 16 Oct 1937; Laws Q13]

Other titles: "The Creel(ie) (Girlie) and the Oysters," "(The) Oyster Girl," "Oysters."

Source: (Ballyrashane district).

s: Where the duplicated note is not necessary, it should be omitted.

Key G.

As I walked up Manchester Street,
A pretty little oyster girl I happened for to meet,
And into her basket so neatly I did peep
To see if she had gotten any oysters.

'O, it's oysters, oysters, oysters,' quo' she,
'If you want any oysters, buy them a' frae me,
It's four for a penny, but five I'll gie to thee,
If you deal in my basket o' oysters.'

'We'll go down to yon tavern, yon tavern,' quo' she,
'And we'll get a bottle, it's one, two or three,
And then to the dance hall an hour, two or three,'
Where she laid down her basket o' oysters.

We danced till my noddle was all in a clew,
Then out of my pocket my treasure she drew,
And downstairs like lightning this oyster girl flew
And left me her basket o' oysters.

'O, it's landlord, landlord, landlord,' quo' he,
'Did you see the little oyster girl was dancing with me?

She has rifled my pockets and stolen my money,
And left me a basket o' oysters.'

'Oh ho,' says the landlord, 'that's a fine joke,
Since you have got no money, you must pop off your coat,
For the landlady says she has got it in her book
That she gave you bread and butter to your oysters.'

I've travelled through England, Ireland and France,
And in all my travels I ne'er met such a lass,
For the Manchester girls, they would learn you how to dance
If you deal in their basket of oysters.

3.1: noddle = head, pate.
3.1: clew = ?[from ball of thread: tight coil, knot].
1.5: gale = rent (periodical payment).

Tumbling through the Hay

[H697: 3 Apr 1937]

[cf. H631 "The Tossing o' the Hay," recounting an individual courtship]

k: "The Haymakers." Other titles: "Hayraking," "The Merry Haymakers," "(The) Merry (Pleasant) Month of May," "Pleasant Pastime between the Young-Men and Maids, in the Pleasant Meadows," "Raking the Hay," "Tumbling thru' the Hay."

Source not given.

Key C.

At the twelfth of July in the rosy time of year,
Down by yon flowery valleys the water does run clear.
The lambs and little fishes merrily sport and play
And lads and bonny lasses go tumbling through the hay.

Ladie fol dha da and ladie fol dha dee.

Up came lovely Johnny with a pitchfork and a rake,
And up came lovely Molly to help the hay to shake,
They tuned their notes so gaily as the nightingale did sing,
And from morning until evening they were at the haymaking.

C15 / Where's the lass to take my hand?

Up came the mowers, the hay for to cut down,
With the scythes upon their shoulders and their hair a dark, dark brown,
Up came the labourers, the hay for to shake out,
And when they had it all cut down, they taddled it about.

It was coming up to Saturday when all would get their pay,
And all the jolly haymakers were feeling blithe and gay.
The number of those haymakers as near as I can say
Was eight and forty boys and girls all tumbling through the hay.

Two short years and after, when all was past and gone,
There were four-and-twenty fair maids all making their sad moan,
Hushall an a ba and a babby, these fair maids they did say,
And they wished that they were free again to tumble through the hay.

❖ C15 REFERENCES ❖

❖ Nae Bonnie Laddie tae Tak' Me Awa' (H230) 255

White/Dean-Smith 1951: (Game Songs) "Sweet Mary or Queen Mary"
Brunnings 1981: "Queen Mary - Queen Mary - Singing Game," "Queen Mary, Queen Mary - My Age Is Sixteen - Singing Game"

IREL Moulden 1979:111: "It was originally written, according to Ford [1,1899], p. 208, by Thomas Scott of Falkirk on a young lady named Russell, the daughter of the farmer in the area.

BRIT Greig 1907-11(1963): #17 "The Aul' Maid"
Kerr's Cornkisters 1950:27-8 "I Maun Gang tae the Garret"
 Cf. *Tocher* #18(Sum)1975:75-6, the first of "Two Auld Maid's Laments"; #28(Spr-Sum)1978:240 "Queen Mary"

REC Ewan MacColl, Folkways FW 8501 (A2,17) [My name is sweet Jenny], singing game.

❖ Maidens of Sixty-Three (H679) 255

BRIT Greig 1907-11(1963): #17 (no title); the article includes 4 different songs about old maids.

BRS Harvard 1: 1.11 (n.i.) "The Old Maid"

❖ The Black Chimney Sweeper (H138) 256

Dean-Smith 1954: "Maids at Eighteen"
Brunnings 1981: "Old Maid's Song"

IREL Loesberg 1,1980:31 "Old Maid in the Garret"

BRIT Baring-Gould/Sheppard 1895:16-7 "Some at Eighteen," a quite different version.
 Henderson et al. 1979:19-21
 Cf. Purslow 1968:88, a related song in theme only.
 Cf. Sharp/Karpeles 1974,2:23 (#197) "The Unmarried Maiden's Lament"
Spin 2(8)[1964?]:13 "An Auld Maid in a Garret"; Davis n.d. 28

AMER Barrand *CD&S* 1981:24-5 "The Spinster's Lament (The Old Maid's Song)"
 Creighton 1971:52-3, much like Henry's version.
 # b: Fowke 1965:68-9 "Come All You True Lovers"
 Cf. Karpeles [1934]:55-8 "Time to Be Made a Wife"
 Cf. Karpeles 1970:235-6 "Young Men, Come Marry Me"

BRS AS Thomas: (n.i.)
BPL H.80: 2 broadsides, one "The Lovesick Maid," the other titled as Henry's.
BPL Irish: (Brereton) "Chimney Sweepers Wedding"
Harvard 1: 9.64 (Bebbington)
UCB Brereton
UCLA 605: (Brereton)

b: REC *America's Folk Heritage*, Murray Hill S4196 (6 recs.) "Old Maid's Song"
Dick Cameron, Folkways FG 3516 (A8) "I Was Told by My Aunt"
b: Isla Cameron, Tony Britton, Transatlantic TRA 105 "Take Me out of Pity"
 Cf. Lizzie Higgins, Lismor LIFL 7004 (A6) "An Old Maid in a Garret"
 Alan Mills, Folkways FW 6831 (A4) "Time to Be Made a Wife"
 Delia Murphy, EMI STAL 1055 (A3) "I Was Told by My Aunt"
b: Sandy Paton, Elektra 148 "An Auld Maid in a Garret"
 Peggy Seeger, Folkways FA 2049 (B5) "The Old Maid's Song"
b: Maxine Sellers, Prestige Folklore FL 14032 "The Old Maid's Lament"

❖ The Wee Article (H833) 257

Brunnings 1981: "... (Tune of New Dialogue and Song of the Times, The Rigs and Fun of Nottingham Goose Fair and Tally Man)"

IREL Moulden 1979:151

BRIT *Tocher* #22(Sum)1976:247 (no title)

m: REC Ewan MacColl, Folkways FW 8501 (= Topic 12T 41) (B6,85) [Awa' ye wee daft article]

❖ Roger's Courtship (H820) 257

Dean-Smith 1954: "Jan's ..."
Brunnings 1981: "Roger's Courtship (Roger and Nell"

BRIT Greig 1907-11(1963): #151 "Roger"
Sharp/Karpeles 1974,2:342-5 (#41) "Robin's Courtship," 3 vts.

❖ Grandma's Advice (H208) 258

Dean-Smith 1954
Brunnings 1981: "My ..."

IREL Moulden 1979:65-6

AMER Bush 4,1977:33-4 "My Grandma"
Father Kemp's 1917:76 "My Grandma's ..."
Peters 1977:157 "My Grandmother Lived on Yonder Green"
m: Randolph 1946-50(1980)1:383 "Grandmaw's ..."
Stout 1936:21-2 "Little Johnnie Green"

Sam Henry's Songs of the People

BRS   BPL Partridge: 2.675 (Partridge)

REC   John A. Bivens, Folkways FES 34151 (A9);   see also review in JEMFQ 65/66, 1982:92-3
Paul Clayton, Folkways FW 8708 (A6) "My Grandmother"
Maud Long, AAFS L 21 (B11) "My Grandmother Green"
cl: Mrs J. U. Newman, AFS 3779 "My Grandmother's ..."

◊ **The Strands of Magilligan** (H 520) 259

White/Dean-Smith 1951: "Come All You Little Streamers or Faithful Emma; The Streams of Lovely Nancy; The Streams of Nant-si-an"
Dean-Smith 1954: "(The) Streams of Lovely Nancy (Nant-si-an); Come All You Little Streamers; Faithful Emma"; a note (p. 107) explains "streamers = workers in tin-mines."
Brunnings 1981: "Streams of Lovely Nancy," "Nellie"

h: IREL   O Lochlainn 1939:94-5
Shields 1981:142-4 (#64); he also mentions another version in the column "Songs of the People" #397, 11 July 1931.
Shields/Shields UF 21,1975: #379

BRIT   Baring-Gould/Hitchcock 1976:80-1 "O the Sweet Dreams of Nancy"
Copper 1973:294 "The Streams of Lovely Nancy"
Henderson et al. 1979:44 "Come All You Little Streamers"
Cf. Hutchings 1976:44 "Come All You Little Streamers," esp. stanza 2.
Morrison/Cologne 1981:40-1 "The Streams of Lovely Nancy"

AMER   Gardner/Chickering 1939:95 "The Sailor Boy"
Grover n.d.:132-3 "On Yonder Green Mountain," esp. stanza 1.
Karpeles 1970:205-7 (#64) "The Streams of Lovely Nancy or The Dreams of Lovely Nancy"

BRS   Harvard 1: 10.137 (Bebbington), 11.32 (Such)
Harvard 3: (Pratt)
UCLA 605: 5(Such) "Streams of Lovely Nancy"
Songster's Museum 1803:111-2

REC   Victor "Turp" Brown, Topic 12T 317 (B7) "The Streams of Lovely Nancy"
Roy Harris, Topic 12TS 217
Mary Osborne, EEOT *Shamrock 2* cass. (B6)
Cf. John Reilly, EEOT *Irish Travellers* cass. (A5) "Newry Mountain"; cf. also H581 "Gragalmachree"
Cyril Tawney, Argo ZFB 87 (B7) "The Sweet Streams of Nancy"

◊ **Green Grow the Rashes** (H 165) 260

g: Many of the following songs cited are entitled "Green Grows the Laurel," but are essentially the same song. Cf. also stanzas in H479 "The Cuckoo" and H624 "I Am a Wee Laddie...."

White/Dean-Smith 1951: "(The) Orange and the Blue"
Dean-Smith 1954: "(The) Orange and the Blue"
Brunnings 1981: "..., O! - Burns," "Green Grow the Rushes O - The Sweetest Bed," "... O - In Sober Hours I Am a Priest - (A) - Burns," "... - O Wat Ye Ought o' Fisher Meg - (B) - Burns," "Green Grows the Laurel"

IREL   Hughes 4,1936:91-3
? k: Hughes 1909:91
h: Cf. JIFSS 13,1913:29

Meek 1978:34-5
Shields/Shields UF 21,1975: #175

BRIT   MacColl/Seeger 1977:212-5 (#62) "... Grows the Laurel," 2 vts.
Cf. Pinto/Rodway 1957(1965):346 (#119), an uninhibited version.
Sharp/Karpeles 1974,1:637 (#167) "The Orange and Blue, or Green Grows the Laurel" [MacColl/Seeger]

AMER   Bush 4,1977:63-4 "... Lilacs"
Manny/Wilson 1968:243-4 "... Rushes"
Randolph/Cohen (1982):118-21 "The Orange and Blue"
SO 12(3,Sum)1962:25 "... Lilacs"
Thompson 1939:386-7 "Green Laurel"

BRS   *Walton's* 132 n.d.:57

REC   Jeannie Robertson, FSB 1 (A1) "... Laurels"
LaRena Clark, Topic 12T 140 (B2) "I Once Loved a Lass"
Tommy Dempsey, Trailer LER 2096 (B1) "... Grow ..."
lc: Sam Eskin, Songs of Our Times 1020 "... Lilacs"
Louise Fuller, Topic 12TS 285 (A1) "... Laurels"
Marie Hare, Folk-Legacy FSC 9 (A2) "... Grows the Laurel"
Sue Harris, Free Reed FRR 020 (B4) "... Laurels"
Charlotte Higgins, Prestige/Int. 25016 (A8) "... Grows the Laurel"
Mike Kent, Folkways FE 4075 (A7) "The Nightingale"; in the notes MacEdward Leach mentions a possible connection with the "Bonnet of Blue" celebrating the bonnet of the Stuarts, of political import during the Rebellion of 1798.
lc: Tony Kraber, Mercury MG 20008 "... Lilacs"
cl: Bascom Lamar Lunsford, AFS 1809 B3 "... Laurels"
lc: Frank Luther, Decca DL 5035 "... Lilacs"
Ewan MacColl, Folkways FW 8501 (A3,28) [Green grows the laurel] rope-skipping game.
Artus Moser, Folkways FD 5331 (B4) "... Grows the Laurel"
cl: Lize Pace, AFS 1469 B2 "... Grows the Laurel"
lc: Tex Ritter, Capitol 112 (78 rpm) 1629 "... Lilacs"
b: Jo Stafford, Columbia CL 6274 "Green Grow the Rashes, O!"

MEL   John Doherty, Gael Linn CEF 072 (A6) "... Rushes-o," a schottische.
O'Neill 1922:126 (#s 234-5) "... Rushes O"

◊ **The Load of Kail Plants** (H 25b) 260

REC   Irish Country Four, Topic 12TS 209 "... Kale ..."

◊ **An Irish Serenade** (H 82) 262

BRS   617 [190-?]:36 "Oh, Molly, I Can't Say That You're Honest"

◊ **You're Welcome as the Flowers in May** (H 804) 262

BRS   617 [190-?]:31

◊ **Magherafelt Hiring Fair** (H 748) 263

Brunnings 1981: "The Rigwiddy Carlin," "Tam Booey"

b: BRIT   Kennedy 1975:450 (#194) "Bargain with Me"; quotes another contemporary recorded Scottish version ("Tam Buie") as well as Henry's.
Palmer 1980:201-2, from Henry coll.

REC   Irish Country Four, Topic 12TS 209

Duncan MacPhee, Prestige/Int. 25016 (A7) "Tam Booey"

◇ The Roving Bachelor *(H650) 263*

Brunnings 1981

BRIT Greig 1907-11(1963): #107 (no title, should be "The Roving Journeyman")
    Lyle 1975:175-6 "The Old Bachelor"

◇ The Whistling Thief *(H710) 264*

Brunnings 1981

AMER Kenedy 1890:102
    Welsh 1907,2:21 states that this is one of Samuel Lover's songs [*Songs and Ballads* (London 1839)]; his version differs from Henry's traditional one, and has two fewer stanzas.

BRS BPL Partridge: 2.712 (n.i.)
    Harvard 1: 14.23 (Andrews)
    UCLA 605: 5(Such)
    Healy 1,1967b:267-8
    Irish Fireside n.d.:14
    O'Conor 1901:154
    617 [190-?]:81
    Walton's New 2,1968:28-9

b: REC *Authentic Folk Music and Dances of the World*, Murray Hill S 4195 (7 recs.)
    Paul Clayton, Folkways FW 8708 (A8) "When Pat Came over the Hill"
    Seán 'ac Donnċa, Claddagh CC 9 (B6)
    Seán Mac Donnchadha (same singer, different spelling), Tradition TLP 1004 (A10)

◇ The Ride in the Creel *(H201) 265*

Dean-Smith 1954: "The Keach ..."
Child 1882-98(1965),5:121-5 (#281) "The Keach ...," 4 vts.
Coffin/Renwick 1950(1977):151
Bronson 4,1972:257-77, 511
Brunnings 1981: "The Keach ..."
Cazden et al. *Notes* 1982: #133 "The Little Scotch Girl"

IREL Moulden 1979:126-7 says a version from Joe Holmes is in Len Graham's collection.
c: C. O'Boyle 1979:32-3 "Newry Town"
m: Shields/Shields *UF* 21,1975: #93 "The Creel"
    Tunney 1979:92-3 "The Cetch ..."

BRIT Greig/Duncan 2,1983:431-44 (#317) "The Wee Toon Clerk," 22 vts. ("The Coverin Blue," "The Keach (in ...)," "The Cunning Clerk," "The Wife and ...," "The Rock in the Same Auld ...")
    Palmer 1980:223-4 "The Auld Wife and the Peat Creel"

AMER Cazden et al. 1982:492-4 "The Little Scotch Girl"

m: REC Michael Gallagher, *FSB* 5 (B10) "The Keach ..."
    Peggy Seeger, Ewan MacColl, *LH*, Argo ZDA 75, #10 "The Keach ...," 2 versions.
    Ewan MacColl, *Riverside CB*, RLP 12 624 (A1) "The Keach in ..."; Folkways FW 8759 (A1)
m: Alec Foster, Leader LEA 4055 (B5) "The Creel"
? cl: Aunt Molly Jackson, AFS 825 B3 "The Little Scotchee"
m: Jimmy MacBeath, Tangent TNGM 119/D (C4) "The Keach ..."
m: Packie Manus Byrne, Topic 12TS 257 (B5) "The Creel"

C15 / *Where's the lass to take my hand?*

Ian, Lorna Campbell, Transatlantic TRA SAM 17 (from XTRA 1061) (B4) "Keach ..."
Tom Gilfellon, Trailer LER 2079 (B1)
Jean Redpath, BBC 22293 (B9) "Keach in ..."

◇ I'm Seventeen 'gin Sunday *(H152) 266*
As I Gaed ower a Whinny Knowe *(H793) 267*

White/Dean-Smith 1951: "Seventeen Come ..."
Dean-Smith 1954: "Seventeen Come ...; On a May Morning So Early"
Laws 1957:234 (O17) "... Come ..."
Brunnings 1981: "Seventeen Come Sunday"
Cazden et al. *Notes* 1982: #128 "Where Are You Going, My Pretty Fair Maid?"

c: IREL Clancy Bros 1971:44-5
Loesberg 3,n.d.:2-3 "As I Roved Out"
Planxty 1976:8-9 "As I Roved Out" (see Moore rec.)
Shields/Shields *UF* 21,1975: #357

BRIT Kennedy 1975:297 (#121) "As I Roved Out" (see Ennis rec.); cites 5 more Irish and 4 English versions recorded.
    Palmer 1979b:138-9 (#77) "Seventeen Come ...,"
    Richards/Stubbs 1979:103-4 "Seventeen Come ..."
Sharp/Karpeles 1974,1:422-9 (#108) "Seventeen Come ...," 8 vts.

AMER Cazden et al. 1982:479-82 "Where Are You Going, My Pretty Fair Maid?"
    Creighton 1971:44, a fragment.
    Darling 1983:130, A "Seventeen Come Sunday" from Such brs.; 130-2, B "When Cockle Shells Make Silver Bells" (see Clayton rec.)
    Milner/Kaplan 1983:50-1 "The Maid and the Soldier"
    Warner 1984:148-9 (#52) "Hi Rinky Dum"

BRS Harvard 1: 7.212 (Catnach)
    Harvard 3: (Paul)
    UCLA 605: 5(Such) "Seventeen Come ..."

REC Seamus Ennis, *FSB* 1 (B1) "As I Roved Out"
Theo Bikel, Cynthia Gooding, Elektra EKL 109 "As I Roved Out"
The Broadside, Topic 12TS 228
b: Isla Cameron, Tony Britton, Transatlantic TRA 105 "As I Roved Out"
Clancy Brothers, Tommy Makem, Tradition TLP 2060 "As I Roved Out"; [b:] Columbia CL 1909
cl: W. E. Claunch, Christine Hayward, AFS 2974 B1 "How Old Are You, My Pretty Little Miss?"
Paul Clayton, Folkways FW 8708 (A1) "When Cockle Shells Make Silver Bells"
Harry Cox, Folk-Legacy FSE 20 (A1) "Seventeen Come ..."
Tommy Dempsey, Trailer LER 2096 (B4) "As I Roved Out"
Tríona ní Domhnaill, Green Linnet SIF 3005 (B1) "Sixteen Come Next ..."
b: Richard Dyer-Bennet, Mercury MG 20007 "Sixteen Come Sunday"
Mrs Edward Gallagher, Folkways FM 4006 (B22) "I'm Going to Get Married"
lc: Tom Glazer, Mercury Album A 58 (78 rpm) "Sixteen Come ..."
David Hammond, Tradition TLP 1028 (B1) "As I Roved Out"
Cliff Haslam, Folk-Legacy FSB 93 "Sixteen Come ..."
Bob Hart, Topic 12TS 243 (A2) "Seventeen Come ..."
Wallace House, Folkways FW 6823 (A1) "... Cum ..."
Norman Kennedy, Folk-Legacy FSS 34 (A2) "Sixteen Come ..."
Cf. Sarah Makem, Folkways FW 8872 (A1) "As I Roved Out"

Sam Henry's Songs of the People

    b: Cf. Tommy Makem, Tradition TLP 1044 "As I Roved Out"
    b: Alan Mills, Folkways FC 7009 "How Old Are You, My Pretty Little Miss?"
    cl: Ada Mooney, AFS 3018 B1 "Seventeen Next ..."
      Cf. Christy Moore, Shanachie 79010 (B4) "As I Roved Out"
      Ken Peacock, Folkways FG 3505 (B7) "I'll Be ... Come ..."
      Mike, Peggy Seeger, Rounder 8003 (A6) "How Old Are You?"
    So Early in the Morning, Tradition TLP 1034 "As I Roved Out"
      Steeleye Span, Chrysalis CHR 1151 (B4) "Seventeen Come ..."
      Cf. Joseph Able Trivett, Folk-Legacy FSA 2 (B6) "Black Jack David," stanza 2.
      Tony Wales, Folkways FG 3515 (A1) "Seventeen Come ..."
    b: Frank Warner, Elektra EKL 153 "Hi Rinky Dum"
    b: Stan Wilson, Clef MG 672 "Sixteen Come Sunday"
    But not: Rick, Lorraine Lee, Folk-Legacy FSI 55 "As I Walked Out"

    b: MEL Philharmonic Promenade Orchestra, Vanguard FRS 1093 "English Folk Song Suite"
    b: Vienna State Opera Orchestra, Westminster XWN 18928 "English Folk Song Suite"

◆ **The Rambling Suiler** *(H183)* 268

Cf. White/Dean-Smith 1951: "... Sailor"
Cf. Dean/Smith 1954: "... Sailor"
Cf. Brunnings 1981: "... Sailor," "The Beggar Man [Child 279]"

Alan Bruford says the Gaelic words "fear siubhail" mean "rover," and that Henry's tune resembles "The Minstrel Boy" and his text reflects "The Gaberlunzie-Man" (*Tocher* #36-7,1992:463).

m: IREL Lyle *IFMS* 1974-5:29 "Rambling Shuler"
   Moulden 1979:121-2; see p. 121 for description of another version set in World War II, and p. 164 for more about Henry's probable source.

BRIT Cf. Palmer 1977:276-7 "The Rambling Soldier"; the texts are not very similar, but the tunes are the same shape.
   Cf. Sharp/Karpeles 1974,2:305-10 (#298) "... Sailor," 6 vts.
   Cf. *Spin* 7(1)1969:27 "The Rambling Sailor"

BRS UCLA 605: 4(Such)
   Cf. Ashton 1891:139-40 "The Tarry Sailor"
   Forget Me Not [1835]:110 "... Soldier"

REC Cf. Norman Kennedy, Folk-Legacy FSS 34 (A4) "A Beggarman Cam' o'er Yon Lea"
   Cf. Martin Carthy, Topic 12TS 341 (Fontana STL 5362) (A5) "Ramblin' Sailor"
   Cf. Cilla Fisher, Artie Trezise, Folk-Legacy FSS 69 (A5) "The Jolly Beggar"
   Cf. Stuart Frank, Folkways FH 5256 (A2) "... Sailor"
   Cf. Roy Harris, Fellside FE 017 (A4) "... Soldier"
   b: Cf. The High Level Ranters, Trailer LER 2030 "The Jolly Beggar"
   Cf. A. L. Lloyd, Prestige/Int. 13043 (B1) "Trim-Rig Ducksie"
   Cf. Chris Willett, Topic 12T 84 (A5) "... Sailor"

m: MEL Joyce 1909:320 (#626) "Trip with the Roving Shooler"; Joyce writes: "(*Shooler*; a wanderer.)."

◆ **A Beggarman Cam' ower the Lea** *(H810)* 269

Dean-Smith 1954: "(The) Beggar-Man"
Child 1882-98(1965),5:109-16 (#279) "The Jolly Beg-
gar," 2 vts.; cf. 5:116-20 (#280) "The Beggar Laddie"; 305
Coffin/Renwick 1950(1977):150-1, 277
Bronson 4,1972:213-26 "The Jolly Beggar"; 227-49, (#279A) "The Gaberlunyie-Man," to which Henry's version seems to be related.
Brunnings 1981: "The Beggar Man [Child 279]"

IREL Joyce 1873:45 (#44)
   Loesberg 3,n.d.:30-1 "The Jolly Beggar"
   Planxty 1976:26 "The Jolly Beggar" (see Planxty rec.)

BRIT *Chapbook* 2(1):10, 15 "The Jolly Beggar"
   Greig/Duncan 2,1983:296-302 (#274) "The Jolly Beggar," 11 vts. ("He Wadna Lie in Barn," "The Beggar Man"); 303-18 (#275) "The Beggar Man," 27 vts. ("The Gaberlunzie Man, The Auld Gaberlunzie")
MacColl/Seeger 1977:102-4 (#18) "The Barley Straw"; 104-5 (#19) "(The Beggar Man)"
Oxford Ballads 1969:624-5 (#131) "The Jolly Beggar"
Palmer 1980:225-6 "The Ragged Beggarman"
Pinto/Rodway 1957(1965):297-8 "The Jolly Beggar"
Sharp/Karpeles 1974,1:201-8 (#43) "The Dirty Beggarman (The Jolly Beggar)"
Tocher #15(Aut)1974:278-80

AMER Milner/Kaplan 1983:45-6 "The Jolly Beggar"

BRS *Goose Hangs High* (DeWitt, Philadelphia, 1866)

REC Maggie and Sarah Chambers, *FSB* 5 (B9) "The Auld Beggarman"
   Jeannie Robertson, *FSB* 5 (B8) "The Jolly Beggar"
   Ewan MacColl, *Folkways CB*, FG 3510 (A1); *Riverside CB*, RLP 12 624 (A3) "The Jolly Beggar"; cf. Riverside RLP 12 626 (A5) "The Beggar Laddie"; Topic 12T 103 (B5) "The Beggar Man"
   The Exiles, Topic 12T 164 (A1)
   Cilla Fisher, Artie Trezise, Folk-Legacy FSS 69 (A5) "The Jolly Beggar"
   Lizzie Higgins, Tangent TNGM 119/D (B5) "The Jolly Beggar"; cf. Lismor LIFL 7004 (B4) "A Beggar, a Beggar"
   b: The High Level Ranters, Trailer LER 2030 "The Jolly Beggar"
   Jimmy Hutchinson, BBC 22293 (B3) "The Beggarman"
   Norman Kennedy, Folk-Legacy FSS 34 (= Topic 12T 178) (A4); (B5) "There Was a Jolly Beggarman"
   Enoch Kent, Topic 12T 128 (A4) "The Beggar Man"
   Planxty, Shanachie 79009 (B1); Polydor 2383 18b [Milner/Kaplan]
   Cf. Jean Redpath, Philo 1054 (A1) "Davy Faa"
   Peggy Seeger, Folkways FW 8731 (A2) "The Rambling Man"
   Davie Stewart, Topic 12T 293 (A2) "The Jolly Beggar"
   Lucy Stewart, Folkways FG 3519 (B2) "The Beggar King"
   Isabel Sutherland, Topic 12T 151 (B6) "The Beggin' Man"

MEL Bunting 1840:63 (#82) [Bronson]
   Bunting 1983:125-6 (#82) "An Deirchtheoir (The Beggar)"
   Petrie/Stanford 2,1902:170 (#678) "'It Was an Old Beggarman.' as sung in Donegal" (includes 2 stanzas and a chorus); (#679) "The Duke of Aberdeen' (see 'The Beggarman' in Bunting.)" [Bronson]

◆ **The Galway Shawl** *(H652)* 269

Brunnings 1981: "Galway Shwl" [sic]

REC Margaret Barry, Riverside RLP 12 602; Topic 12T 125 (A5); Outlet SOLP 1029 (B3)
   b: Jim McCann, Colonial ST LP 768

C15 / Where's the lass to take my hand?

◆ **Where the Moorcocks Crow** (H32) 269

Brunnings 1981: "The Mountain Stream/s (Where the Moorcocks Crow)"

IREL   S. O'Boyle 1977:76-7 "The Mountain Streams"
Shields 1981:125-6 (#54) "The Mountain Streams Where the Moorcock Crows"
Shields/Shields UF 21,1975: #276
Treoir 3(2)1971:17 "The Mountain Streams Where ..."
h: Tunney 1979:20-1 "The Mountain Streams Where ..."

BRIT   Brune 1965:38-9 "The Mountain Streams"
h: Kennedy 1975:313 (#136) "The Mountain Stream"; mentions 4 other recorded versions, including 1 from Scotland and a fiddle tune from Donegal.

h: REC   Paddy Tunney, *FSB* 1 (A11) "The Mountain Streams"; Mulligan LUN A 334; Topic 12T 264 (A1); Folk-Legacy FSI 7 (B1)
Eddie Butcher, Leader LED 2070 (A1) "The Mountain Streams ..."
Dolores Keane, Boot International ITB 4018 (A3) "The Mountain Streams"

◆ **The Maid of Seventeen** (H144) 270

IREL   Shields 1981:117 (#49)

◆ **O'er the Moor amang the Heather** (H177) 271

Brunnings 1981: "The Queen amang the Heather"

IREL   *JIFSS* 14,1914:26-7 "Among the Heather"
Morton 1970:5-6 "Heather on the Moor," very different.
h: O Lochlainn 1965:12-3 "Doon the Moor"
Shields/Shields UF 21,1975: #121 "Down the Moor"

BRIT   Aitkin 1874:4-5
b: Cf. Kennedy 1975:318 (#141) "The Queen among ..."; mentions 3 other versions recorded in Scotland.
Cf. Polwarth 1966(1967):18(#6) "The Blooming Heather"
Whitelaw 1853:356-7 "O'er the Muir," 2 versions, one collected by Robert Burns from Jean Glover, the other attributed to Stewart Lewis.

AMER   Cf. Gardner/Chickering 1939:149 "The Laird o' Drum (Child #236)" cites Chambers 1862 and his reference to Jean Glover.
Grover n.d.:20 "The Lass amang the Heather," perhaps only a related song.
Manny/Wilson 1968:248-9 "Herding Lambs amongst ..."
Milner/Kaplan 983:181-2 "Heather on the Moor"

REC   Paul Brady, Greenhays/Sruthan GR 705 (A1) "Heather on the Moor"
Eddie Butcher, Free Reed FRR 003 (A1) "Down the Moor"
Archie Fisher, Folk-Legacy FSS 61 (A4) "Queen amang ..."
Cf. Dick Gaughan, Topic 12TS 384 (A2) "Bonnie Lass amang ..."
b: Delia Murphy, Irish IR 35002 "Down the Moor"
Jean Redpath, Prestige/Int. 13041 "Skippin' Barfit thro' the Heather"
Belle Stewart, Topic 12TS 138 (A4) "Queen amang ..."; Topic 12TS 307 (A1)
June Tabor, Topic 12TS 298 (B4) "Queen amang ..."; Topic 12TS 410 (B1) "Heather down the Moor"; Topic TPSS 412 (A1)

◆ **The Whinny Knowes** (H18b) 272

Brunnings 1981: "The Corncrake among the Whinny Knowes (tune of 'The Shira Dam')," "The Echo Mocks the Corncrake"

BRIT   Ford 2,1901:244-6 "The Corncraik amang the ..."; he thinks the song is fairly recent.
Greig 1907-11(1963): #175 "The Corncrake amang the ...," says "this lilt is not a true folk-song, but ... composed."

b: REC   Archie Fisher, Folk-Legacy FSS 61 (A7) "The Echo Mocks the Corncrake"
Sheila Stewart, Topic 12T 138 "The Corncrake amang the ..."

◆ **The Captain with the Whiskers** (H660) 273

Brunnings 1981: "... with His ..."

BRIT   Greig/Duncan 1,1981:214 (#87) "... with His ..."

AMER   Randolph/Cohen (1982):214-6
Shoemaker 1931:58, 122
Warner 1984:171-3 (#69) "... with His ...," with reference to its 19th-century origin (author Thomas Haynes Bayly, composer Sidney Nelson).

BRS   BPL Partridge: 3.661 (Partridge)
Harvard 1: 12.119 (Such)
Walton's 132 n.d.:94-5

cl: REC   Walter Alderman, AFS 1359 B1
cl: Hubert Brady, AFS 3356 A1 "... with His ..."
cl: Bascom Lamar Lunsford, AFS 1837 A3, A4 "... with His ..."

◆ **Youghall Harbour** (H503) 273

Brunnings 1981: "Yougal/Youghall Harbour"

h: IREL   *Ceol* 3(1)1967:20
S. O'Boyle/M. O'Boyle 1975:45-6, in Irish.
h: O Lochlainn 1939:16
Shields/Shields UF 21,1975: #441
Shields 1981:163-4 (#74) "Youghal ..."

h: BRS   Healy 1967a:135-6, 245-7, 247-8 "My Sunday Morning Maiden"

REC   Eddie Butcher, Leader LED 2070 (B4) "Youghal ..."
h: Robert Cinnamond, Topic 12T 269 (A7)

MEL   Hudson ms. 1:37
Joyce 1909:340 (#680); cf. pp. 233-4 (#422) "When First I Came to County Limerick," which Joyce says is another setting.
O'Neill 1903:303 (#1633)
O'Neill 1922:37

◆ **The Mountain Road** (H515) 274

MEL   Petrie/Stanford 1,1902:104 (#412)

◆ **The Ould Lammas Fair** (H101) 275

BRS   *Songs and Recitations* 3,1976:5 "The Auld ..."

◆ **The Star of Moville** (H68) 276

IREL   Shields UF 27,1981:16-8

REC   Len Graham, Topic 12TS 334 (A5)

Sam Henry's Songs of the People

◊ Mind Your Eye *(H700) 277*

Brunnings 1981: "Queer Bungarey"

IREL Loesberg 1,1980:29 "Quare Bungle Rye"
Moulden 1979:105 says another version collected by Len Graham.
m: Shields/Shields *UF* 21,1975: #269

BRIT Greig/Duncan 2,1983:405-7 (#305) "Bung Your Eye," 3 vts.("The Exciseman," "Bangeria")
 Cf. Reeves 1958:73 "The Basket of Eggs"
 Cf. Reeves 1960:99-100 "Eggs in her Basket"
 Cf. Shuldham-Shaw *JEFDSS* 1949:16 "Eggs in Her Basket"

AMER Milner/Kaplan 1983:65 "Bung Your Eye"
 Peacock 1965,3:895-6 "Young Bung-'er-Eye"

BRS Harvard 1: 9.234 (Bebbington)
 Harvard 3: (Birt)

REC Bob Blake, Topic 12T 258 (A5) "The Basket of Eggs"
 Gordon Bok, Folk-Legacy FSI 54 (A4) "Queer Bungo Rye"; [b:] National Geographic 705 (B8a)
b: Peg, Bobby Clancy, Tradition TLP 1045 (B5) "Bungle Rye"
b: Clancy Brothers, Tommy Makem, Tradition/Everest TLP 1042 (B5) "Bungle Rye"
 The Dubliners, Fiesta FLPS 1627 [Milner/Kaplan]
 Tony Rose, Trailer LER 2024 (A6) "Basket of Eggs"
 Minty Smith, Topic 12TS 304 (A4) "The Basket of Eggs"
 Bernard Wrigley, Topic 12TS 211 (B2) "Bungereye"

◊ The Basket of Oysters *(H725) 278*

Dean-Smith 1954: "(The) Oyster Girl"
Laws 1957:279 (Q13) "The Oyster Girl"
Brunnings 1981: "The Oyster Girl"

BRIT Greig/Duncan 2,1983:399-404 (#304) "Oysters," 13 vts. ("The Creel(ie) (Girlie) and the Oysters")
MacColl/Seeger 1977:177-9
 Spin 7(2)1969:12 "The Oyster Girl"
 Tocher #36-7,1982:450-1 "The Oyster Girl"

BRS Harvard 1: 9.45 (Cadman)
 Harvard 3: (Selmerdine)
 UCLA 605: 4(Such) "The Oyster Girl"

REC Paul Clayton, Folkways FW 8708 (B3) "The Oyster Girl"
b: William Clauson, Capitol P 8539 "The Oyster Girl"
 Harold Covill, Topic 12TS 229 "The Oyster Girl"
 George Dunn, Leader LEE 4042 (A1) "The Oyster Girl"
 Hamish Imlach, Transatlantic TRA SAM 9 (A3) "The Oyster Girl"
 George Spicer, Topic 12T 235 (A3) "The Oyster Girl"
 Phil Tanner, EFDSS LP 1005 (A5) "The Oyster Girl"

MEL Hudson ms. 1:173
 O'Neill 1922:94

◊ Tumbling through the Hay *(H697) 278*

Dean-Smith 1954: "(The) Haymakers' Song; Merry Haymakers"
Brunnings 1981: "The Merry Haymakers"

b: BRIT Kennedy 1975:564 (#255) "The Merry Haymakers"; says another version recorded from Sam Larner.
 Palmer 1979b:29-30 (#9) "Pleasant Month of May"
 Cf. Pinto/Rodway 1957(1965):323-4 (#106) "The Merry Hay-Makers, or, Pleasant Pastime between the Young-men and Maids, in the Pleasant Meadows"
 Sing 6(9,May)1962:100 "Hayraking," combined with a form of "John Riley"

REC Bob, Ron Copper, *FSB* 3 (B11) "The Merry Haymakers"; Folk-Legacy FSB 19 (B2) "The Month of May"; Leader LEAB 404 (4046: (B1)); Leader LED 2067 (A1) "Pleasant Month of May"
 Cf. Arky's Toast, Greenwich Village GVR 212 (B1) "Merry Haymakers"
 Joe Holmes, Free Reed 007 (A3) "... thru' ..."
 Sam Larner, Topic 12T 244 (A2) "The Merry Month of May"
 Levi Smith, Topic 12T 253 (A12) "The Haymakers"

C16

I will watch and pray:
Faithful farewells

Sam Henry's Songs of the People

The Londonderry Air [H3: 1 Dec 1923]

Other titles: (m) "Londonderry Love Song," (m) "Danny Boy."

Source: (m) Petrie 1855:57, coll. Miss J. Ross (New Town, Limavady); author T. Wray Milnes (Beeston, Leeds).

s: ... This series of Songs for [sic] the People will render a signal service to the musical world if it elicits from our readers some old words or titles for this air, which surely can not, with its arresting beauty, have come down nameless and wordless through the ages.

l: As part of a long introduction to this air in his column (for complete text, see Appendix B), Sam Henry cites O'Neill 1903:33 (#188) "Londonderry Love Song" (in G, no source given) and Petrie 1855:57 (in E flat), among many others. Petrie says the air, without title or lyrics, was collected by Miss J. Ross in Limavady. Henry tells of his search for the "original" words, including a consultation with Frank Kidson of Leeds, "the foremost authority on folk song in the north of Great Britain. He told me that he could find none." At Kidson's request the lyrics Henry prints were produced by T. Wray Milnes, of Beeston, Leeds.

Probably the most widely known lyrics to this tune are "Danny Boy," written in 1913 by Fred E. Weatherly, according to Fuld 1966:279. (s: "What a pity that the air is chiefly linked in the popular mind with ... a song of such unreal sentiment that our credulity is overtaxed by its improbability.") Fuld also mentions Anne G. Gilchrist's article, "A New Light upon the Londonderry Air," *JEFDSS* 1(3)1934:115-21.

The air itself has been printed with a few startling variations: O'Neill's (O), which ends on L6, and Henry's own printed (Bo) and typed (Wo, D) versions, with added corrections (Bc, Wc), of which the corrected sol-fa notation may yet be faulty. Petrie's version (P) may be the one most familiar to modern readers.

m: [A]ccording to local tradition, [James McCurry, the blind fiddler of Myroe, Limavady] was the itinerant fiddler from whom Miss Anne Jane Ross of Limavady obtained the Londonderry Air.

Key D.

Flood tide that ebbs,
Dark waves in sullen motion,
Sad winds that sigh,
Take this, the heart of me,
To yonder ship,
White falcon of the ocean,
Bearing so swiftly my lost love across the sea.

Rain from gray skies,
Like tears of lamentation,
Beating across
Bleak sands and shoreland bare,
Weep with my soul
Alone in desolation,
Hopeless the grief and anguish of my sad
 despair.

Sweetest of all
My dream that, at the waking,
Swiftly was gone
And lost beyond recall,
Rose on the rood
That as the dawn was breaking,
So softly died as morning wept thy silent fall.

Sad wind and tide
That two fond hearts now sever,
Our faith proclaims
Triumphant over tears:
How still we love,
And shall do so for ever,
Who wait alone the secret of the coming years.

Down in My Sally's Garden

[H828: 7 Oct 1939]

Other titles: "(Down by the) Sally('s) Gardens"; cf. "The (You) Rambling Boys of Pleasure."

Source: George Graham (Cross Lane, Coleraine) from the late Willie M'Kay (Park St, Coleraine), who learned it in Toronto [Canada].

s: ... I have every reason to believe that this is the song of which W. B. Yeats founded his world-famous lyric, "Down by the Sally Gardens." Alternatively, Yeats may have founded this song on the first verse of another ballad called "The Rambling Boys of Pleasure":--

Down by yon valley gardens
One evening as I chanced to stray,
It's there I saw my darling,
I took her to be the queen of May.
She told me to take love easy,
Just as the leaves grow on the trees,
But I, being young and foolish,
Her then I did not agree.

This song has also been collected in Vermont, U.S.A.

l: This bears little enough resemblance to Yeats's well-known song (see, e.g., Moffat [1897]:47), set to an air in Petrie's collection, except perhaps for the meter and rueful mood. A parallel stanza is quoted in Flanders/Olney 1953:124 (from a copybook dated 1784, by Joseph Goffe of Bedford,

NH, in the Baker Memorial Library at Hanover, NH), which may be the song also "collected in Vermont" to which Henry refers. Seán O'Boyle concurs with Henry in thinking that "The Rambling Boys of Pleasure" may have provided "the matrix from which Yeats's poem eventually derived" (O'Boyle 1977:84-5).

Key G.

Down in my Sally's garden,
Upon an ivy bush,
At morning and at twilight,
There sings a sweet song thrush.

His notes come clearly ringing,
And tidings to me tell,
And oh, I know already
My Sally loves me well.

I kissed her milk-white features
One silv'ry eve of May;
She whispered, 'Won't you wander
Until the close of day?'

We wandered in her garden,
The flowers were wet with dew,
I saw the love-light beaming
In her fond eyes of blue.

Down in my Sally's garden,
Where snowy hawthorns blow,
My heart became love-weary
When I at last must go.

The bloom was on the hawthorn
That night I said farewell;
I left my Sally weeping
Down by an ivied dell.

Early, Early [H89: 25 Jul 1925]

o: "Died for Love"; k: "What a Voice"; g: "William and Mary."

Source: (w, m) Maria Doherty (Clooney, Magilligan).

s: Known in Magilligan as Ellen Lowry's song. Ellen Lowry was the only one who sang it. She brought it from Dungiven, of which district she was a native....

Key F.

Oh, it's early, early by the break of day,
Down by yon green fields I chanced to stray,
I heard a fair maid to sigh and say,
'The lad I love is gone far away.'

'He's gone and left me now in grief and woe,
And where to find him I do not know,
I'll search those green fields and valleys low,
Should the hills be clad, ay, with frost and snow.

'What voice, what voice now is yon I hear?
It's like the voice of my Willie dear.
Oh, had I the wings, love, I'd feel no fear,
But fly forever till I knew thee near.'

The Green Banks of Banna

[H233: 28 Apr 1928]

[Bp] Author Maud Houston (Coleraine); (m) from her mother.

o: Flatten all accidentals and air is beautiful.

g: Perhaps this pleasant little song, or fragment, is related to H204 "Gramachree."

Key G.

By the green banks of Banna I wander alone
Where the river runs softly by sweet
    Portglenone,
And I think of that day in the spring of the year
When he said, 'I must part from you, Molly, my
    dear.'

Sam Henry's Songs of the People

O, many a tear have I shed since that day
In grief for my true love so far, far away;
In the long nights of winter I've trembled with fear
That I never might hear him say, 'Molly, my dear.'

Fair river of Banna that flows to the sea,
Whisper soft to the waves to bring him back to me;
Oh, happy I'll be when his sweet voice I hear,
Saying, 'I am come back to you, Molly, my dear.'

A Sweetheart's Appeal to Her Lover / [Dt] Oh, It's down Where the Water Runs Muddy [H112: 2 Jan 1926]

[see H695 "Kellswater"]

s: (m) "Lovely Armoy"; o: (m) "An Saighdeur Treighthe" (coll. Sean O'Boyle); "The Lover's Curse" (Hughes [1,1909:60-3]).

Source: [Bp] (m) coll. Maud Houston (Coleraine); (w) 3: 3 stanzas coll. Maud Houston; Robert Morton (Ballytober, Priestland); H[?ugh] M[?urray], "learnt ... when he was a little boy" c. 1860.

s: [Bp] This song combines three imperfect versions which form here a perfect whole....

Key C.

Oh, it's down where the water runs muddy --
I'm afraid it will never run clear --
And when I begin for to study,
My mind lies with them that's not here.

My mind's like a ship on the ocean
That knows not what compass to steer,
From the east to the west, winds are blowing,
It minds me on the charms of my dear.

She slipped a gold ring off her finger,
Saying, 'Jamie, bear me in your mind,
And if ever you stray from old Ireland,
Don't go and leave me behind.'

But woe to the heart that confines me
Or keeps me from my heart's delight.
Strong walls and cold irons they bind me,
A stone for my pillow by night.

Oftimes I do wish that the eagle
Would lend me her wings for to fly,
I would fly o'er the seas to my Jamie,
To be with my love ere I die.

I wonder what's keeping my Jamie,
He was to be here in the spring,
And it's down in yon green grove I'll meet him,
Amongst the gay flowers we will sing.

O Jamie, don't prove a deceiver,
Or, if that you do, I'm undone;
My innocent heart, love, you gain-ed
When I was but foolish and young.

O, this one and that one will court you,
But if any one gains you but me,
It's daily and hourly I'll curse them
That steals lovely Jamie from me.

Once fare you well, dearest Jamie,
And twice fare you well, dearest joy,
Three times fare you well, dearest Jamie;
Will I ne'er see you more till I die?

My Sailor Boy [H759: 11 Jun 1938]

Source: (w, m) sung and fiddled by Mrs Delargey (Waterfoot, Glenariff) from her mother, Margaret M'Dade, nee Macauley (Titruan ["the house by the stream"], Glenariff).

Key C.

My boy he is a sailor,
A sailor boy in blue,
I know he has my heart,
And I hope he will prove true.
He's gone away to plough the sea,
To plough the raging main,
And soon he will return again
To his own dear Mary Jane.

My heart it is a-breaking
Until the day will come
When he and I will meet,
When he comes rambling home;
His cheeks are red and rosy
And his heart is ever true,
He is the darling of my heart,
My sailor boy in blue.

He promised he would bring me
A monkey and a bear,
And every sort of foreign toy,
And mats all made with hair,
Some flying fish and tortoise shells,
And shells from Timbuctoo,
And such a lot of presents from
My sailor boy in blue.

The Drinaun D[h]un [H206: 22 Oct 1927]

Other titles: "The Blackthorn (Tree)," "The Brown Thorn (Bush)," "An Dra(o)ighne'an Donn," "The (Drian Naun) (Dri(y)naun) (Drinan(e)) D(h)un (Donn)," "Ma Dimigh Tu," "My Dear, If You Left Me."

Source: John Thompson (Heatherlea Ave, Portstewart), learned from Patrick Lafferty ("Paddy the Poet") (Myroe), 1886.

s: The title of this song means the "brown thorn tree," i.e., the blackthorn, as contrasted with the hawthorn, or the whitethorn. It is used metaphorically for a young man -- a lover....
 Versions have been published by P. W. Joyce and A. P. Graves in this country and in America by Manus O'Conor in New York. The version given here is quite distinct both as to air and words. It has an expressive octave, l to l1 [subscript 1], which is absent in the other variants.

Key C. [Bp] Tenderly.

Of late I'm captivated by a handsome young boy,
I am daily complaining for my own darling joy,
All the day long I'll wander till the evening comes on,
I'll be sheltered by the green leaves of the drinaun dun.

My love he is away and no hopes of return,
And for his long absence I'll ne'er cease to mourn;
I'll join with the small birds when the springtime comes on,
I will welcome the blossom early on the drinaun dun.

My love he is as clear as the clear summer's day,
And his breath is as sweet as the new-mown hay,
His hair shines like the gold when exposed to the sun,
He's as fair as the blossom of the drinaun dun.

'Gin the fair I'll get fairings from that handsome young boy,
I'll get twenty sweet kisses from my own darling joy,

C16 / I will watch and pray

So confuse them, consume them that say I'm not true,
For over high hills and lofty mountains I'll wander for you.

So if I had a small boat for to row o'er thon main,
I would follow my own love where he is gane,
For I'd rather have my own boy to roll, sport and play,
As all the gold and silver lies betwixt the land and sea.

So come all ye purty fair maids, get married in time
Unto some proper young man that will keep up your prime,
But beware of the winter season when the cold breezes blow on
That will nip the blossom early from the drinaun dun.

1.4: ... drinaun dhun. [Dt, *the only time so spelled in text, although thus in both printed and typed titles.*]

The Boatman / Fear a Bhata

[H834: "A Rathlin song," 18 Nov 1939]

Source: noted from the Gaelic of Mrs James Glass (Rathlin Island) by Henry Morris, published in *Cead De Ceoltaib Ulad* (1915); literal translation by Andy Doey (Ballymacaldrick, Dunloy), English verse by George Graham (Cross Lane, Coleraine).

s: This world-famous song is generally regarded as of Scottish Highlands origin. As is the case with another beautiful song, "Ho Ro, My Nut-Brown Maiden," the oldest and fullest version is to be found in Rathlin Island.
 Fhir [sic] a bhata pronounced Far a vata. The words "na horo eile" are a call after the manner of yodeling.

Key A flat.

I climb the mountain, my heart is yearning
To see my boatman from sea returning;
When shall I greet him? Tonight? Tomorrow?
Who sailed and left me in bitter sorrow.

 Fhir a bhata na horo eile,
 Fhir a bhata na horo eile,

Sam Henry's Songs of the People

*Fhir a bhata na horo eile,
A thousand welcomes where'er you go.*

No sound I hear but the seabirds calling,
As thoughts of love bring the sad tears falling;
Shall I await here in expectation
Of one whose sailing was my vexation?

Of thee, my lover, I seek good tidings,
But passing boatmen have nought but chidings,
They say 'twas fickle to try and win you,
That I was foolish for trusting in you.

My boatman promised me fine silks for cotton,
A tartan plaid as my kinsmen fought in,
A golden ring of a bright reflection;
Alas, I fear for his recollection.

The people say that his love was fleeting,
Yet from my bosom I send him greeting,
When I am sleeping, I see him only,
And in the morning rise sad and lonely.

The love I gave him will never falter,
Nor can the seasons my visions alter;
Fond love I'll cherish within me ever,
There's nought but death can our young hearts sever.

The neighbours round me to pity waken,
They say my love must have me forsaken,
But I reply, though in lonely wailing,
'I love my boatman where he is sailing.'

In any village where thou art resting,
Oh, do not tarry at their requesting,
Lest thou should kindle a maid's affection
By singing songs of sweet recollection.

Henceforth shall I, till my love's returning,
Mourn as a swan in her death-gasp yearning;
O come, my boatman, in thy devotion,
Come home to Rathlin, the star of the ocean.

A Rathlin Song [H696: 27 Mar 1937]

Composer Miss Loui[?s]e Barnes, L.R.A.M., for the Notation Class, Coleraine Musical Festival; author Sam Henry.

s: ... the song sung by Mr James Moore, A.R.C.O., of Bushmills, at the Festival concert.

[Dp in 4-line stanzas, each occupying half the printed sol-fa tune.]

Key E.

Where the fulmar flies on Rathlin Head
O'er the lake on the cliff by the sea,
My love and I, in the days that are dead,
Watched the white clouds floating free.
The bird on the wing o'er the wide, wide foam
Can sport and call to his love,
But my love flew away from his island home,
And I sob like the mateless dove.

Och! When will Lauchlin come back to me?
Sure, the old folk on me died,
I lost their love that was full and free,
And I need him by my side.
Alone I dream in the whitewashed cot
Of the dear days yet to be
If God and Mary change my lot
And bring him back to me.

Bring back My Barney to Me

[H7: 29 Dec 1923]

Other titles: "... Johnny (...)," "My Johnny," "Send back ...."

Source: coll. Maud Houston (Coleraine) from Charles Dempsey, postman (Coleraine), "who remembered a soldier getting a prize for singing it at a Mess Concert."

s: ... not to be confused with the song of the same name to the Scotch tune, "Bring back My Bonnie to Me."

o: Time should be 6/8.

Key F.

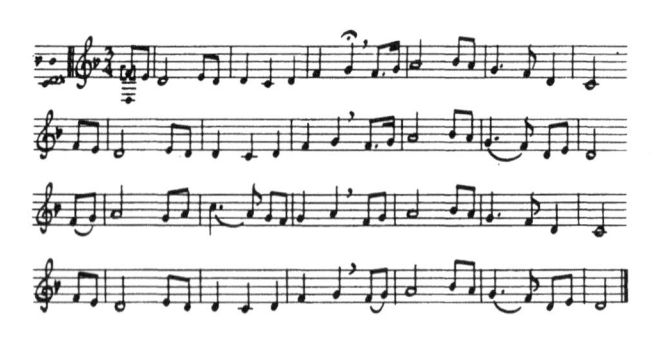

He is gone, and I'm now sad and lonely,
He has left me to cross the wide sea,
And I know that he thinks of me only,
And will soon be returning to me.
His eyes they were filled with emotion,
As my husband he said he'd soon be --
   O, blow gentle, sweet breeze of the ocean,
   And bring back my Barney to me.

When at night, as I rest on my pillow,
The wind blows a heave and a sigh
I think of the wild angry billow
And watch every cloud in the sky;
My bosom it fills with emotion,
And I pray for you over the sea,
  Then blow gentle, ...

He left me his fortune to better;
Sure, I know it was all for my sake.
I will soon be receiving a letter --
Or surely my poor heart will break --
To know he will soon be returning
To his dear native Ireland and me.
  Then blow gentle, ...

Linton Lowrie [H640: 29 Feb 1936]

Other titles: (m) "The Barnyards o' Delgaty," "Rhynie."

Source: Sam Henry, from his mother.

s: A song my mother sang to me.

Key B flat.

I tint my heart ae morn in May
When birdies sang on ilka tree,
When dew-draps hung on ilka spray
An' lammies played on ilka lea.
O, Linton Lowrie, Linton Lowrie,
Aye sae fond ye trowed to be,
I never wist sae bright a morn
Sae dark a night would bring tae me.

O, Linton's words sae saftly fell,
Sae pure the glimmer o' his e'e,
That I hae never been mysel'
Since e'er he spak and keekt to me.
O, Linton Lowrie, Linton Lowrie,
Come, dear Lowrie, back to me,
And siccan's love's I bear to you,
E'en your forgettin' will forgi'e.

His absence I'll nae langer bear,
My gried I canna langer dree;
I'll gang a thousand miles and mair
My Lowrie's comely face to see.
O, Linton Lowrie, Linton Lowrie,
Gin ye'll come to Logan lea,
I'll mak' ye laird o' Logan Ha',
And I your lovin' wife will be.

1.1: tint = lost. [s]
1.2: ilka = each. [s]
1.6: trowed = trusted, believed in.
1.7: wist = knew.
2.4: keekt = peeped, glimpsed.
2.7: siccan = such. [s]
3.2: gried = [? typographical error]
3.2: dree = suffer. [s]
3.6: gin = if.

The Sea-Apprentice [H739: 22 Jan 1938]

o: (m) "The Mill Doffin' Mistress"; k: "The Apprentice Boy"; g: Bonny Anne. Other titles: "The Apprentice Sailor," "By My Indenture," "A (The) Prentice Boy (in Love)," "The Sailor Boy."

Source: (w, m) from fiddling and singing of Mrs Margaret De Largy (Waterfoot, Glenariff); stanzas 2 and 5 from Alexander Crawford (Leck, Ballymoney).

s: A little ditty from Red Bay....

Key C.

When I first went a sea-apprentice bound,
I sailed the salt seas all round and round,
I had scarce sailed a voyage but one,
When I fell in love with my charming Anne.

  To my right fol-la, to my right fol-ay.

The captain says, 'You're a foolish boy
To court a girl you'll ne'er enjoy,
For she'll have sweethearts when you're at sea,
And she'll be married before you're free.'

'Well, I do not know, but I'll go and try,
For she might fancy an apprentice boy,
And she might alter her mind for me,
And wait on me till I be free.'

I went to my captain, both stout and bold,
And unto him all my secrets told,
Saying, 'I love yon lass as I love my life,
What would I give if she were my wife.'

I bought her ribbons, I bought her gloves,
By these to show a heart that loves;
She accepted all, she was not shy,
And vowed to wait for her 'prentice boy.

Sam Henry's Songs of the People

My True Love's Gone A-Sailing

[H160: 4 Dec 1926]

k: "The Maid on Shore."

Source: William Gamble (The Park, Armoy), from Lizzie Reynolds (Carnkirn, Armoy).

s: This tender little song was collected by me....

Key C.

My true love's gone a-sailing right o'er yon western main,
I wish him health and happiness till he returns again,
For should the seas prove my love's grave, till he returns to me,
A maid I'll always tarry and married ne'er will be.

Come all you purty fair maids whose love to sea will go,
Your mind will never be at ease while the stormy winds do blow,
For them that has no love at all are from care and trouble free,
Oh, I could wish frae a' my heart it was the case wi' me.

An old man came to court me with five hundred pounds a year,
He wanted me to marry him and to forsake my dear;
'Would you wed a tarry sailor lad or one brought up so mean?
And you a merchant's daughter of honour, birth and fame?'

'Oh, it's Willie I admire, and Willie I adore,
He's come of honest parents, although they are but poor,
For the sake of gold or riches would I inconstant prove?
I would rather live in poverty and wed the lad I love.'

I wish I was a blackbird, no danger would I fear,
For every night and morning I would go see my dear,
And as the ship would move along so gently, I would fly,
I would rest on my love's arms on the main topmast so high.

So Dear Is My Charlie to Me

[H533: 17 Feb 1934]

o: "Prince Charlie Stuart." Other titles: "Flora MacDonald's Lament," "The Lament of Flora Macdonald."

Source: (Dunloy district).

s: This [is a] curious Jacobite song and air....

Key D.

Come join in lamentation, ye queens and ye princes,
Ye lords and ye dukes o' a noble degree,
And pity the case o' a heartbroken lady
That's mourning for her darling night and day.
Although she was a lady of eight hundred pounds a year,
Both lords, dukes and earls to her they did draw near,
She disdained them all with silence and she bid them disappear,
For so dear is my Charlie to me.

If you had seen Charlie at the head of an army,
He was a gallant sight for to behold:
His buckles and his facings were all of fine valuables,
His buttons of the pure virgin gold.
The tartan my love wore, it was yellow and green silk,
His lovely legs inunder far whiter than the milk.
No wonder there were thousands of our Highland army killed
At restoring of my Charlie to me.

But if it be that my love and I be match-ed,
One object between us does stand:
My love he was brought up to the Catholic religion,
And I to the church of Scotland.
For what was betwixt us, I now will let it drop,
I will turn to my Charlie and worship on a rock,
I will then become a member of St. Peter's flock,
So dear is my Charlie to me.

The Jolly Roving Tar

[H670: 26 Sep 1936; Laws O27]

Other title: cf. "... Sailor."

Source: James Bond (Termaquin, Limavady) from his father, William Bond (Terrydoo Clyde, Limavady).

s: ... The Chinese War was in 1840-41.

Key G.

As down by yonder harbour I carelessly did stray,
There I beheld a sailor lad, likewise a lady gay,
She appeared to me like Venus bright or some superior star
As she walked the beach lamenting for her jolly roving tar.

It's had you seen her Willie when dressed in sailor's clothes,
Wi' cheeks as red as roses and eyes as black as sloes,
His hair hings down in ringlets fine; he's gone from her afar,
But her heart lies in the bosom of her jolly roving tar.

She put her foot in a small boat and they rowed her from the land,
And as the sailors rowed the boat she waved her lily-white hand,
Saying, 'Adieu, ye maids of Liverpool, from you I'm going afar
To sail the briny ocean for my jolly roving tar.'

She put her foot in a long boat and they rowed her from the shore,
And she's gone off to her father's ships to see if they're well stored,
To see if money be's plenty, or lots of grog in jar,
To sail the world all over with her jolly roving tar.

'Oh Willie, lovely Willie, what makes you go away?
When I arrive at twenty-one, sure I'm a lady gay,
I'll man one of my father's ships, go breeze the Chinese war,
And I'll sail the world all over with my jolly roving tar.

Alt[i]mover Stream [H65a: 7 Feb 1925]

[see H229a,b "Lurgan Stream" (a)(b)]

s: (m) = H65b "Farewell to Articlave"; "The Shepherd's Boy," "Bathing in the Roe," "The Purple Man's Dream."

Source: Patrick D. Hassan (Coolnamonan, Feeny, Co. Derry).

Key G.

It was on a summer evening, when my love by chance did meet,
I took her in my arms, and I gave her kisses sweet,
I asked her if she would marry me, or single would remain,
Or sail the seas along with me and leave Altimover Stream.

'Forbear, forbear, young man,' she said, 'give o'er your foolish talk,
It was for recreation sake that I came here to walk;
No Cupid dart will pierce my heart, or set it in a flame,
I'm free from love to range and rove around Altimover Stream.'

'Forbear, forbear, true love,' I said, 'your parents leave behind
And cross the sea along with me, you'll find me true and kind;
I'm bound for North America, you might never see me again,
It will break my heart to have to part you on Altimover Stream.

Was I possessed of noble skills, or had I Simpson's pen,
I'd join myself in harmony my love's praise to tell,
For since her mind has knocked me blind and undertakes my name,
I'm free from love to range and rove far from Altimover Stream.

Farewell unto sweet Dernaflaw, likewise Dungiven fair,
Where I spent many a happy day, I will never see them there,
And likewise to the White Hill, where often I have been,
Farewell to Ballyhargan, lies near Altimover Stream.

Come fill your glasses to the brim, let the toast now merrily pass,
Come fill a flowing bumper, drink a health to each bonnie lass,

Sam Henry's Songs of the People

May happy days shine on these braes till I return again,
And a true farewell to the maid that dwells near to Altimover Stream.

[*Title, text throughout Dt:*] Altmover ...
1.1: ... summer's ... love did chance to meet, [Dt]
1.3: ... if she'd marry ... [Dt]
2.2: ... for recreation's sake ... [Dt]
2.3: No Cupid's ... [Dt]
4.1: ... Simpson's quill, [Dt]

Fare Ye Well, Enniskillen [H631: 28 Dec 1935]

[see H98 "The Inniskilling Dragoon"]

Source: coll. Andrew Dooey (Ballymacaldrick, Dunloy) from his children. h: Graves 1894:54, author George Sigerson [1981:170 (#38)].

s: ... Andrew Dooey [sic] ... thinks it probably originated in the Dunloy district.

o: Probably the matrix of "The Inniskilling Dragoon" [H98].

Key D.

Farewell, Enniskillen, fare ye well for a while
To all your fair daughters and every green isle,
O, your green isles shall flourish and your fair waters flow,
While I from poor Ireland an exile must go.

Dark was her hair as the dark raven's wing,
Blue were her eyes as the bluebells in spring,
Light was her laugh as the sun on the sea,
Till the woes of the world came between her and me.

What can a man do when the world is his foe
And the looks of the people fall on him like snow,
But lift the brow bravely and sail away far
To seek out his fortune in Spain and the war?

My [Bt: The] Dear Irish Boy

[H142: Wp, 31 Jul 1926]

Other titles: "... Maid," (m) "My Conor His Cheeks are Like Roses."

Source: (w) Rev. John Troland (Norwich, CT, U.S.A.) heard in Ireland in 1867; (m) John Henry Macaulay (Bog Oak Shop, Ballycastle [Bp: Co. Antrim]), learned c. 1855 from Hugh Malone, c. 70, itinerant singer and orange-seller (Ballycastle).

s: Rev. Troland ... writes: "I am enclosing a copy of an old song, with a tender strain that I heard as late as 1867, when on a visit to the old country, thinking someone may recall the tune, which was plaintively sweet and musical."
... A. P. Graves has published a song, "My Connor," air "The Dear Irish Boy." It has the same chorus, but the words and air are different.

Key F.

My Connor, his cheeks are as ruddy as morning,
The brightest of pearl[s] but mimic his teeth,
And nature with ringlets his mild brow adorning,
His hair Cupid's bowstrings, and roses his breath.

Smiling, beguiling, cheering, endearing,
Together oft over the mountains we strayed,
By each other delighting and fondly uniting,
I've listened whole days to my dear Irish boy.

No roebuck more swift can flee over the mountains,
No veteran bolder in danger or scars,
He's sightly, he's sprightly and pure as the fountains,
His eye twinkles love and he's gone to the wars.

The wars are all over, and lonely I've waited,
I fear that some envious plot has been laid,
Or some cruel maid has him so captivated,
He'll never return to his dear Irish maid.

Alas for the love we so wondrously cherished,
All faded the visions that filled us with joy,
Throughout these deep shadows of hope that are perished,
I wander alone for my dear Irish boy.

Banks of Sweet Lough Neagh

[H158: 20 Nov 1926]

s: "... Rea." Other titles: "(On) ... Rae (Ray)."

Source: coll. Maud Houston

s: A counterpart of this song, called "The Banks of Sweet Lough Rea," in which the soldier is the narrator, has been received from Mr James Gamble (Culmore Hill, Rasharkin).

Key B flat.

A poor distressed fair maid as ever you did know,
In love I'm captivated, which proved my overthrow;
By the herding of my father's flock I carelessly did stray,
There I beheld a soldier lad on the banks of sweet Lough Neagh.

He boldly stepped unto me and unto me did say,
'What would you take, my pretty lass, and go along with me?
I'd clothe you like Queen Eleanor all in her golden pride,
When I do reach the town of Moy, I will make you my bride.'

Right modestly I answered him, 'Your suit must be denied,
For I'm in no way fitted to be a soldier's bride,
Far from my native country I never intend to stray,
It would break my heart with trouble in leaving sweet Lough Neagh.

He flew into her arms all with a kind embrace,
He says, 'I'll never ask you to leave your native place,
For we'll sit down and court awhile among these flowers so gay,
And we'll watch the sheep as they do feed on the banks of sweet Lough Neagh.'

Now my love has left me and he is crossing o'er the main
And I'll remain a single life till he returns again;
For there is no other young man that I love half so well,
But where to find my darling I'm sure I cannot tell.

C16 / I will watch and pray

Now my love has took his flight and the time steals slowly on,
But I will watch and pray for him until my love return,
A ring of gold I will put on and with him I will stray,
And I'll bid adieu to all my friends on the banks of sweet Lough Neagh.

2.1: ... stepp-ed up to me ... [Dt]
3.3: ... I ne'er intend ... [Dt]
4.3: ... flowers gay, [Dt]
5.1: ... and he's ... [Dt]
6.1: ... has taken ... [Dt]

The Soldier Boy [H244: 14 Jul 1928; Laws O31]

Other title: "The Irish ...."

Source not given.

Key E flat.

As I walked out one evening in the springtime of the year,
By the shady groves of sweet Glentarf I carelessly did steer,
Why, then I espied a soldier and a charming fair young maid,
A-gazing on each other, sequestered in the shade.

I was struck with great amazement when I saw this comely fair,
Her jet-black hair was hanging down over her shoulders bare,
Her fair form so majestic, it caused me to delay,
I stood a while in ambush to hear what they would say.

At length he broke the silence and unto her did say,
'Cheer up, my lovely Sally, cheer up and come away;
Right well you know that I must go, no longer can I stay,
For I hear the bugle sounding, yon call I must obey.'

She says, 'My dearest Johnny, how can you prove unkind,
To go off to the battlefield and leave me here behind,
For who would know but by the foe, my love, you might be slain,
Now left and stretched on those cold heaps all on the battle plain.'

295

Sam Henry's Songs of the People

He says, 'My dearest Sally, cheer up and banish woe,
The Irish boys were always brave wherever they did go,
At Trafalgar, Copenhagen, the Nile and Waterloo,
And on the plains of India they showed what they could do.'

She says, 'My dearest Johnny, since you cannot stay at home,
Along with you I'll venture, the wide world through to roam,
And if now by those Russians you might receive a ball,
To bandage up your bleeding wounds, my love, I'm at your call.'

He says, 'My dearest Sally, you cannot go with me,
For hardships in a foreign clime with you might not agree,
But I hope that I will soon return with lots of gold in store,
And God will be our union when the wars they all are o'er.'

As thus cold they were parting, they blushed and tears did flow,
Then they embraced each other with hearts oppressed with woe,
'My blessing go along with you and victory crown your joy,
My fervent prayer is your welfare, my fine young soldier boy.'

1.1: ... out evening ... [Dt]
 .2: ... sweet Clontarf ... [Dt]
 .3: Where I ... [Dt]
2.3: ... majestic caused ... [Dt]
7.4: ... wars will be all o'er.' [Dt]
8.1: As this couple they ... [Dt]

The Banks of the Nile

[H238a: 2 Jun 1928; Laws N9]

[cf. H561 "Lovely Annie (I)"]

o: (m) "Skibereen." Other titles: "Battle of the Nile," "Dixie's (Texas) Isle," "Men's Clothing I'll (Clothes I Will) Put On."

Source: (Vow district).

Key E flat.

[H238b (2d tune): Wp, Dt]

[typed on Wp] Source: Alexander Horner, Sr (Ballycraigach, Stranocum, Co. Antrim). [Dt: 'Ballycraigach' crossed out, and 'Moycraig' typed in.]

Key C.

'Oh hark, the drums are beating, love, no longer can I stay,
I hear the bugles sounding, that call we must obey,
We are ordered out from Portsmouth -- it's many a long mile --
To join the British army on the banks of the Nile.'

'Oh Willie, dearest Willie, do not leave me here to mourn,
You'll make me curse and rue the day that ever I was born,
For the parting with you, my love, is the parting of my life,
So stay at home, dear Willie, and I will be your wife.'

'Oh Nancy, lovely Nancy, that's a thing that can't be so,
Our colonel he gave orders, no women there can go,
We must forsake our old sweethearts, likewise our native soil,
And fight the blacks and negroes on the banks of the Nile.'

'Then I'll cut off my yellow locks and go along with you;
I'll dress myself in velvet gold, go see the captain, too,
I'll fight and bear your banner while fortune on us will smile,
And we'll comfort one another on the banks of the Nile.'

'Your waist it is too slender and your fingers are too small,
I fear you would not answer me when I would on you call,
Your delicate constitution would not bear the unwholesome clime
Of the burning sandy deserts on the banks of the Nile.'

'My curse attend the war and the hour that it began,

For it has robbed our country of many a gallant
  man,
It took from us our old sweethearts, protectors of
  our soil,
And their blood does steep the grass that's deep
  on the banks of the river Nile.'

'But when the war is over, it's home we'll all
  return
Unto our wives and sweethearts we left behind to
  mourn,
We will embrace them in our arms until the end of
  time,
And we'll go no more to battle on the banks of the
  Nile.'

1.4: ... army all on ... [Dt; Wp *written*]
1.4, 3.4, 4.4: ... of Nile. [Dt]
3.2: ... no woman ... [Dt]
 .4: And fights ... [Dt]
5.3: ... the foreign clime [Dt]

Johnnie and Molly [H755: 14 May 1938]

Other titles: "Johnny ...," "Jimmy and Nancy,"
"Lovely Mollie(y)"; cf. "... Mollie."

Source: William Johnston (West Burn St, Greenock) from his grandmother (Carnkirk, near Bushmills) c. 1888.

Key G.

Says Johnnie to Molly, 'Do not mourn for me,
Nor do not be grieved at my going away,
For the more we are parted, sure, we'll be true-
  hearted,
My dear, I'll return in the sweet month of May.'

Says Molly to Johnnie, 'Sure, I will mourn for
  you,
And I will be grieved at your going away,
It was your sweet company that I much admired,
I'm afraid you will die in some strange country.'

'Sure I'll dress myself up like a nice little sea-
  boy,
And I'll cut my hair short round my chin,
And when the stormy high winds are a-blowing,
My dear, I'll be with you to stand as your friend.'

'O, your nice little hands our tackle could not
  handle,
And your neat little feet up our shrouds could not
  go,

C16 / I will watch and pray

And the cold frosty weather, you ne'er could
  endure it,
So stay at home, darling, to the seas do not go.'

So the very next day the ship went a-sailing,
And Molly conveyed him as far as the shore,
And her lily-white hands on the shore she stood
  wringing,
Crying, 'O and alas, I will ne'er see you more.'

So come all you pretty maids, by me take a
  warning,
And don't trust to young men nor what they do
  say;
They will kiss you and court you and tell you false
  stories,
And then go and leave you as Johnnie left me.

The Bold Privateer

[H514: 7 Oct 1933; Laws O32]

Other titles: "Nancy Bell," "Our Captain Calls
All Hands"; cf. "Castle Hill Anthem," "Jimmy
and Nancy (the departure)," "Farewell Nancy,"
"Happy (Pleasant) and Delightful," "Pretty
Ploughboy," "A Sailor and His True Love."

Source not given.

s: The period of the song is after the French
Revolution.

g: There are a number of broadsides closely related to "The *Bold Privateer*," called "Adieu Lovely Nancy" or just "Lovely Nancy." For these see
Harvard 1 with index in Vol. 14.

Key C.

Fare you well, lovely Ellen, it is now we must
  part,
Must I leave you behind me, the true love of my
  heart?
I must leave you behind me, and all I hold dear,
Once more to go a-roving on the *Bold Privateer*,
  Once more to go a-roving on the *Bold
    Privateer*.

Sam Henry's Songs of the People

The French they are treacherous, right very well you know,
Did they not kill their own poor king not so very long ago?
You had better stay at home with the girl that loves you dear
Than to roam the wild ocean in the *Bold Privateer*.

Our boat lies on the strand and our ship lies in the bay,
Farewell, my dearest jewel, for I can no longer stay,
Our ship she lies a-waiting, so fare you well, my dear,
I must now go on board of the *Bold Privateer*.

There is now one can tell what hazards you may run,
So many have been slain since this cruel war's begun,
You had better not go and leave your Ellen here,
For I dread to see you leaving in the *Bold Privateer*.

Fear naught, lovely Ellen, I fain would with thee stay,
But gold I must gather for our wedding day,
We will soon beat down the pride of the lofty mounseer,
And will soon let them know she's the *Bold Privateer*.

Then since you are a-going, good luck attend to thee,
May kind heaven protect you on land and on sea,
May kind heaven protect you wherever you may steer
And send you safe back in the *Bold Privateer*.

Now the prizes we have taken are from France and from Spain,
And my true love at home, she shall share the gain,
And when the wars are over I'll return unto my dear
And go no more a-roving on the *Bold Privateer*.

5.3: mounseer = monsieur. [s]

The Maid of Dunysheil [H530: 27 Jan 1934]

g: ?"Rasharkin Fair."

Author Paddy M'Guckian, monumental sculptor.

s: Dunysheil ("the fort of the O'Sheils") is near Kilrea, on the east bank of the Bann, on the Gortreghy road. The song was taken down at the hospitable fireside of Mr Andrew Doey, of Ballymacaldrick, Dunloy.
   ... Paddy M'Guckian ... was not only a poet but a sculptor (monumental). He believed in phonetic spelling as evidenced by a headstone he erected in a local graveyard, at the bottom of which is cut the words: "Let no man brak this groun."
   The hero of the song was Tom M'Laughlin, "the last of the woollen weavers at Kilcreen," who did not win the heroine, nor did he ever reach Nova Scotia.

Key C.

O, Dunyshiel, it is the place where my true love does dwell,
That known place of beauty which admirers all can tell;
In that fragrant hawthorn bower where lovers tell their tale,
The joyful mind breathes in the wind in you, sweet Dunysheil.

The first place that I saw my love was in Rasharkin Fair,
Little I thought that I would meet one so exceeding fair:
His sparkling eyes, like diamonds bright, were comely to behold,
And her hair in ringlets wavering like the bright links of gold.

O, I stepped up to this fair maid with sentiments confined
For to admend my sorrow with nature's works combined.
Said I, 'Fair maid, your dwelling place from me do not conceal.'
She smiled and said, 'Sir, I was bred nigh to sweet Dunyshiel.'

Sweet Dunysheil, it is the place where this fair maid does dwell,
That chosen spot of nature where all the songsters dwell,
No charming note of bird afloat all in the morning gale
Could charm the grove like my true love -- dear maid of Dunysheil.

To sweet Kilcreen, where I have been, I must now bid adieu,
It grieves my heart all for to part with all my comrades too,
For Nova Scotia I am bound, tomorrow I'll set sail,
While o'er the sea, my heart shall be with the maid of Dunysheil.

The Maid of Carrowclare [H169: 5 Feb 1927]

Other titles: "Carrowclare," "Killyclare."

Source: (w, m) Joseph Allen (Drumavalley, Bellarena); author, composer James M'Curry, blind fiddler (Myroe).

[Bp][?] (This song held over since 5th February, 1927.)

s: James McCurry ... was a well-known figure in [Myroe] about 50 years ago. The young man in the song was named Moore and the young lady Peoples.

Key E flat.

Where Luna spreads her silver rays, disclosing many's the scene,
I overheard a youthful pair conversing on the green,
Where the skylark drops her evening notes and nature's quiet and still,
To hear their conversation I was forced to use my skill.

By the corncrake loudly calling, they my footsteps didn't hear
And the hawthorn proved my trustworthy friend as to them I drew near,
Till at length he says, 'I'm about to sail unto Columbia's shore
On board the ship *Britannia*, strange lands for to explore.'

When he spoke of his departure, she her arms around him drew,
And melting tears bedimmed her eyes, her locks were wet with dew;
It's when you reach Columbia's shore, some pretty fair maid you'll find,
Dressed in her country's fashion, will bear me from your mind.'

He placed his arm around her waist and whispered to his dear,
'I go to seek my fortune, so stay the falling tear.
Although I roam in foreign lands, the stranger's fate to share,
I'll ne'er forget the hours I spent with you in Carrowclare.'

2.1: ... footsteps did not hear, [Dt]
4.4: ... you at Carrowclare.' [Dt]

The Blooming Star of Eglintown

[H170: 12 Feb 1927]

o: (m) "The Parting Glass"; g: "Salthill."

Source: (m, whistled) Bernard Logue, tea merchant (Eglinton [Craigbrack]), met in the house of William M'Corriston (Ballyleighery, Magilligan).

Key F.

One morning as I went to walk, to take farewell of famed Salthill,
I met my darling on the way, with bursting joys my heart did fill.
I gently took her by the hand, on a mossy bank we both sat down,
And many's the loving look I took at the blooming star of Eglintown.

Sad I, 'My dear, it's come to pass that I must leave my native shore,
I'll break my heart with you to part, for you're the girl I do adore,
And if to me you do prove true till fortune does my favour crown,
I will return with gold in store and wed the maid of Eglintown.'

'Och, Pat,' says she, 'don't be afraid, for unto you I will prove kind,
No other man will get my hand, nor no other ways will change my mind,
May all goodness bless you, night and day, and keep you free from Neptune's frown,
Will be the prayer of Mary Ann till you return from Eglintown.'

We then shook hands, I went on board and parted with my heart's delight,
As on the deck I then did stand, I watched her while she was in sight
Till at length the night's dark cloud arose, the evening sun going gently down,
I bid farewell to all my friends and the blooming star of Eglintown.

The Faithful Rambler

[H825: 16 Sep 1939]

Source: (w) "here slightly varied" from James Currie (Pig Tail Hill, Balnamore); (m) George Graham (Cross Lane, Coleraine).

Key C.

I am a young man delights in sport;
To a strange country I mean to steer
And leave my home and boyhood's friends,
Also the girl that I love dear.

Sam Henry's Songs of the People

There is one among them I much admire,
And her I'll think on when far away;
May a pleasant gale ne'er blow on me
If I forget her in America.

Says she, 'My darling, since you must leave,
I wish you luck again and again;
If you return to Erin's shore,
Your true Eliza I'll remain.

'When you're boozing in a distant land,
The girl that's here you will never mind;
When you will sport and oftimes court,
You'll forget the girl you left behind.

He says, 'My darling, since I must go,
These vows I'll leave as a pledge with you,
That all I earn be lost to me,
And my life prove as slippery, too.'

Now to conclude and make an end,
May God be with this female fair,
From all divertments keep her free,
And make her his peculiar care.

Although the seas may separate,
And swelling seas may rise and fa',
In silent dreamland when we meet,
I'll court her still in America.

6.3: divertments = diversions (of path or way).

Love's Parting / Jamie and Mary

[H788: 31 Dec 1938]

Source: Jim Carmichael (Waring St, Ballymena).

Key C.

I am a youth that's inclined to ramble,
To some foreign country I mean to steer;
I am loth to part from friends and comrades
And my old sweetheart whom I love dear,
But there's one of those I do most admire,
On her I'll think when I'm far away,
For, since fate's decreed, I'm resolved to part her
And try my fortune in America.

'Now farewell, darling, since I must leave you
I put great dependence on your constancy,
That no other young man may gain your favour
Nor change your mind when I'm o'er the sea,
For although the seas do separate us,
And between us they may rise and fa',
If fortune favours me, you'll find your Jamie
Returning home from America.'

'Oh Jamie dear, do you remember
When I sat with you many an hour,
When my young fancy away was carried?
The bees hummed round us on each opening
  flower;
But when you're crossing the western ocean,
The maid that loved you, you'll ne'er mind ava,
You'll scarce e'er think on the maids of Erin,
You'll get strange sweethearts in America.'

'Oh Mary dear, I don't dissemble,
To all other fair maids I'll prove untrue,
And if you think that these are false promises,
I'll leave these vows as a pledge with you,
That what I have may prove unsuccessful,
And fortune prove to me a cliddery ba',
That a favouring gale it may ne'er blow on me,
If I forsake you in America.'

Now to conclude and end these verses,
May God protect this young female fair
And keep her from every wild embarrassment
And of my darling take the greatest care.
She's slow to anger, of kind disposition,
Her cheeks like roses in June do blaw,
In my nightly slumbers, when I think on her,
I could court her vision in America.

4.6: cliddery ba' = a slippery ball. [s]

Dobbin's Flowery Vale

[H85: 27 Jun 1925; Laws O29]

[cf. H242 "Mullinabrone"]

g: "Erin's Flowery Vale," "The Irish Girl's Lament." Other titles: "The Irish Maid," "Overn's ...."

Author: McGowan, shoemaker (Chapel Lane, Armagh).

s: This song ... had a great vogue....
"Dobbin's Flowery Vale," or "Dobbin's Walks," a large tract of land at Armagh, was the gift of the benevolent Leonard Dobbin for the use of the citizens of the city. The place, beautifully wooded, was a haunt of lovers on summer eves.
The young couple referred to in the song married and settled in the city of their nativity and carried on business in College Street, Armagh.

o: Tune given is not Hughes's version.

Key C.

One morning fair, when Phoebus bright his
  radiant smiles displayed,
When Flora in her verdant garb the fragrant
  plains arrayed,

As I did rove throughout each grove, no care
   did me assail,
A pair I spied by a riverside in Dobbin's flowery
   vale.

There I sat down for to behold, beneath a
   spreading tree,
The limpid streams that gently rolled conveyed
   their words to me:
'Farewell, sweet maid,' the youth he said, 'since
   I must now set sail
And bid adieu to Armagh, you and Dobbin's
   flowery vale.'

'Forbear the thought and word likewise that
   wound a bleeding heart,
It's true we both have met here now, but soon,
   alas, must part;
Must I alone here sigh and moan, to none the
   cause reveal,
But still lament my cause to vent in Dobbin's
   flowery vale?

'How many youths have left their homes to steer
   for freedom's shore
And lie beneath in silent tombs where foaming
   billows roar?
My advice take: don't me forsake, nor leave me
   here to wail,
But here remain with your fond dame in Dobbin's
   flowery vale.'

'Unwilling do I part from you, but here I cannot
   stay,
When love and freedom cry pursue, their words I
   must obey.
In foreign isles where fortune smiles, they're left
   by each concealed;
I will come home, no more to roam from Dobbin's
   flowery vale.'

'But when you reach Columbia's shore, some
   pretty maid you'll see,
It's then you'll think no more of love or the vows
   you made to me.
Hope may contain life's ending pain, but the
   thoughts will oft prevail
Of seeing no more the youth I adore in Dobbin's
   flowery vale.'

He said, 'Reflect not you're alone, or that I am
   untrue;
Wherever I may chance to roam, my thoughts will
   be of you,
There's not a flower or shady bower o'er verdant
   hill or dale
But will remind me of the maid behind in Dobbin's
   flowery vale.'

Their mutual love together drew both with a kind
   embrace,
While tears, like rosy drops of dew, did trinkle
   down her face.
She strove in vain him to detain, but while she
   did prevail,
He bade adieu, so I withdrew from Dobbin's
   flowery vale.

C16 / I will watch and pray

Londonderry Love Song [H518: 4 Nov 1933]

o: (m) "If I Were a Blackbird"; k: "Adieu,
Londonderry."

Source not given.

s: The *Zared* was a Londonderry ship owned by
Bartholomew M'Corkell, which sailed in the winter
of 1861 with 500 passengers. She was wrecked in
January 1862 off the west coast of Ireland on her
return voyage.

Key E flat.

As I roved out one evening in the sweet month of
   June
To view the green fields and to hear the lark's
   tune,
The blackbirds sang sweetly, purling streams on
   each side,
And the boys and girls courting down by the Bog
   Side.

My mind bent on rambling, I crossed Bishop's
   Grove,
Where me and my true love did oftentimes rove;
If she had proved constant and proved constant
   still,
We yet might be courting around Blue Bell Hill.

My love's tall and handsome, she lives by the Wall,
For beauty and daring she far exceeds all,
She gave me her hand that married we'd be,
Och, in sweet Londonderry, how happy we'd be.

Just two short months after, her father did say,
'Oh Mary, dear Mary, you must go away
To the fair land of promise, where stars always
   shine,
And leave Londonderry and your true love behind.'

On hearing this news she fell in despair,
To the wringing her hands and tearing her hair,
Saying, 'Father, dear father, it grieves my heart
   sore
To leave Londonderry and the boy I adore.'

On a ship called the *Zared* my love sailed away
On a bright Sunday morning to Americay,
Her banners were flying as she sailed by
   Culmore,
So adieu, Londonderry, I may ne'er see you
   more.

Sam Henry's Songs of the People

The Maids of Culmore [H687: 23 Jan 1937]

Other title: "... Maid ...."

Source: John Moore (Cloyfin), learned from James M'Mullan, itinerant farm laborer (Derry).

Key G.

From sweet Londonderry to fair London town,
There is no better harbour all round to be found,
Where the childer each evening go down to the shore
And join in the dance with the maids of Culmore.

The first time I saw her, my love passed me by,
The next time I saw her, she'd a tear in her eye,
The third time I saw her, her heart grieved full sore;
She sailed down Lough Foyle and away from Culmore.

If I had the power the storms for to rise,
I'd blow higher and higher and darken the skies,
I'd blow higher and higher and the seas cause to roar
For the day that my love sailed away from Culmore.

To the far lands of America my love I'll go see,
It's there I know no one and no one knows me;
If I do not find her, I'll return home no more,
Like a pilgrim I'll wander for the maid of Culmore.

◆ C16 REFERENCES ◆

◆ **The Londonderry Air** *(H3)* 286

Brunnings 1981: (Tune of Danny Boy; Emer's Farewell; In Derry Vale; Irish Love Song; Irish Tune from County Derry; My Gentle Harp; The Tender Apple Blossom; Would God I Were the Tender Apple Blossom.)

◆ **Down in My Sally's Garden** *(H828)* 286

Brunnings 1981: "Down by the Sally Gardens"

IREL   Loesberg 2,1980:62 "Sally Gardens"

BRIT   *Tocher* #11(Aut)1973:89-90 "Sally's ..."
  Cf. *TM* #6,1977:4 "You Rambling Boys of Pleasure" (see Cinnamond rec.)

AMER   Cf. Grover n.d.:12 "Sally's ..."

BRS   Cf. UCLA 605: 5(n.i.) "The Rambling Boys of Pleasure"
  Cf. *Forget Me Not* [1835]:96 "Rambling Boys of Pleasure"

REC   Cf. Robert Cinnamond, Topic 12T 269 (A1); Mulligan LUN A 001 (A6); Green Linnet SIF 1005 (A7) "You Rambling Boys of Pleasure"
b: Richard Dyer-Bennet Decca DLP 5046 "Oh Sally My Dear"
b: Kathleen Ferrier, London 5411 "Down by the Sally Gardens"
cl: J. W. Green, AFS 2276 A "... the Sally Gardens"
b: Jim McCann, Colonial ST-LP-768 "Sally Garden"
b: Robert Merrill, RCA MO 1306 (78 rpm)
  Mary O'Hara, Tradition/Everest 2115 (Emerald Gem, Belfast) (A6) "Down by the Sally Gardens"
  Cf. Paddy Tunney, Topic 12T 165 (B1) "The Rambling Boys of Pleasure"

MEL   Darley/McCall 1914:14 (#33) "Down by the Sally Gardens"

◆ **Early, Early** *(H89)* 287

Brunnings 1981: "Died for Love," "Died of Love"

BRS   Harvard 1: 7.143 (Ryle) "William and Mary," with some lines identical to Henry's.

REC   Isla Cameron, Tony Britton, Transatlantic TRA 105 "Died for Love"
Songs and Dances of Scotland, Murray Hill 920336

◆ **My Sailor Boy** *(H759)* 288

Not = Brunnings 1981

◆ **The Drinaun D[h]un** *(H206)* 289

Brunnings 1981: "An Draighnean Donn (The Blackthorn Tree)," "The Drinan Donn (The Brown Thorn, The Sloe-Tree)," "The Drynaun Dun"

IREL   Costello 1923:71-4 "An Droighnéan Donn (The Brown Thorn-Bush)"
  Duffy 1866:136
  Hughes 3,1934:26-9 "... Donn (The Brown Thorn)"
s: Joyce 1909:205-6 (#396) "The Drynaun ..."
  S. O'Boyle/M. O'Boyle 1978:46
b: O Lochlainn 1965:263-4 "The Drynaun Dun"
k: O'Sullivan 1960:49
k: O Tuama 8,1960:5
  Shields/Shields UF 21,1975: #123
  Sparling 1887:?8 "The Drinan Donn (The Brown Thorn; The Sloe-Tree)"
  Treoir 4(3)1972: f.p. 11 (English only)

BRIT   Kennedy 1975:89 (#32) "An Draighnean Donn (The Blackthorn Tree)"

AMER   Kenedy 1890:109

BRS   BPL Irish: 2 broadsides, neither with imprint.
  Harvard 1: 9.160 (Bebbington), 12.148 (Such)
  Harvard 3: (Catnach)
  UCB Brereton (for title see item below)
  UCLA 605: 3(Brereton) "A Much Admir'd Song Called the Drian Naun Don," (n.i.) "The Drinan Dhun"
  A Broadside, 6(5,Oct)1913 "... Donn"
  617 [190-?]:121 "Drinane Dhun"

302

REC Seán Dirrane, Folkways FE 4002 (B1) "An Droighnean Donn (The Blackthorn)"
 Seán Mac Donnchadha, Topic 12T 202 (A1) "An Droighneán Donn -- The Brown Thorn Bush"
 Sorcha ní Ghuairim, Folkways FW 6861 (B2) "An Draighnean Donn -- The Brown Thorn Bush"
 Joe Heaney, Philo 2004 (B3) "An Draighnéan Donn (The Blackthorn Bush)"
 Sarah, Rita Keane, Claddagh CC4 (B6) "An Droighnean Donn," in English.
 Ginny Phelps, Front Hall FHR 09 (A2) "The Blackthorn Tree"

MEL Hudson ms. 1:379, 2:548
 JIFSS 6,1908:24-5 "Ma Dimigh Tu (Droighnean Sun) / My Dear, If You Left Me" [from Bunting ms]
 O'Neill 1903:6 "The Brown Thorn," 3 melodies, all different from Henry's.
 Petrie/Stanford 1,1902:114 (#451) "The Brown Thorn, correctly set."

◆ The Boatman / Fear a Bhata *(H 834)* 289

Brunnings 1981: "... (Fear a Bhata)"

IREL S. O'Boyle/M. O'Boyle 1975:58

BRIT *Scottish Student's* 1891:152; [193?]:158
 Smith 1888:83-5

REC Gordon Bok, Ann Mayo Muir, Ed Trickett, Folk-Legacy FSI 96 (B6)

◆ Bring back My Barney to Me *(H 7)* 290

Brunnings 1981: "... Johnny"

BRIT Slocombe/Shuldham-Shaw *JEFDSS* 1953:96-105, article about Cecilia Costello (Birmingham; father from Roscommon), including transcription (p. 104) of "My Johnny," her version (see Costello rec.).

BRS UCLA 605: 3(n.i.) "Send back ..."
 617 [190-?]:51 "Send back ..."
 Walton's 132 n.d.:22

REC Isla Cameron, Prestige/Int. 13042 (B4) "... Johnny"
 Cecilia Costello, Leader LEE 4054 (A6) "My Johnny"
 Joe Hickerson, Folk-Legacy FSI 39 (A3) "... Johnny ..."

◆ Linton Lowrie *(H 640)* 291

g: Not located. In Ford 1,1899:255-6 there is a song called "Linton Lowrin" in the same meter, but which tells a different story.

MEL Cf. Bikel 1960:211-2 "The Barnyards o' Delgaty"
 Cf. Cilla Fisher, Artie Trezise, Folk-Legacy FSS 69 (A2) "Rhynie"

◆ The Sea-Apprentice *(H 739)* 291

? Brunnings 1981: "Sea Apprentice" appears as an alternate title for "The Doffin'/g Mistress," but all the references seem to be for the latter song.

b: IREL Hammond 1978:27 "The Doffing Mistress"

BRIT Greig 1907-11(1963): #64 "The Apprentice Sailor"
 Greig/Duncan 1,1981:123-8 (#54) "The Apprentice Sailor," 12 vts.(The Apprentice Boy," "The Sailor Boy," "By My Indenture")
 Purslow 1974:1 "The Apprentice Boy," said to be "one of the rarer British folk songs."

AMER Creighton 1932:304-5 "Prentice Boy"
 Greenleaf/Mansfield 1933:214-5 "The Prentice Boy"
 Peacock 1965,2:575-8 "A Prentice Boy in Love," 2 vts.

BRS (Haly, Cork) [Purslow]

b: REC Anne Briggs, Topic 12T 86 (= Elektra EKL 279) (B5) "The Doffing Mistress"
b: David Hammond, Request RLP 8059 "The Doffing Mistress"

◆ My True Love's Gone A-Sailing *(H 160)* 292

IREL Moulden 1979:110

◆ So Dear Is My Charlie to Me *(H 533)* 292

Brunnings 1981: "Prince Charlie," ?"Prince Charlie's Farewell," ?"Flora MacDonald's Lament"

? b: IREL Graves 1928 "The Lament of Flora Macdonald"
 Moulden 1979:138-9
 Tunney 1979:162 "Prince Charlie Stuart" (see Tunney rec.)

BRIT Hogg 2,1821:179 "The Lament of Flora Macdonald," a very different version translated from the Gaelic, if not an entirely different song; the last two lines are:
 Farewell my young hero the gallant and good
 The crown of thy fathers is torn from thy brow.

BRS Harvard 1: 10 (Bebbington) "Flora MacDonald's Lament," a longer and more coherent version which may also be a related song. [m:] The same broadside is in the Kidson collection at the Mitchell Library, Glasgow.

m: REC Brigid Tunney, *FSB* 8 (B6) "Prince Charlie Stuart"

◆ The Jolly Roving Tar *(H 670)* 293

? Dean-Smith 1954
Laws 1957:239 (O 27)
Probably not = Brunnings 1981

IREL Galwey 1910:11, 29 (#3)

BRIT Purslow 1968:83

AMER Cf. Burton/Manning 1967(1970):101-2 "The Jolly Sailor," a sadder story.
 Creighton 1971:37-8
But not: Warner 1984:175-7 (#71), a version of "Get up, Jack, John Sit Down"

BRS Ashton 1888:251-2
 Harvard 3: (Harkness)

◆ Fare Ye Well, Enniskillen *(H 631)* 294

Brunnings 1981: "... Thee ..."

b: IREL Clancy Bros. 1964 "Fare Thee Well, Enniskillen"

REC The Druids, Argo ZFB 22 (A9) "... Thee ..."

◆ My [Bt: The] Dear Irish Boy *(H 142)* 294

White/Dean-Smith 1951: "(The) Dear ..."
Brunnings 1981: "... (Tune of The Squatter's Man)"

303

IREL   Graves 1895
   Hughes 4,1936:39-40 "The ..."
o: Joyce 1909:207-8 (#398) "... or, The Dear Irish Maid"
   Sparling 1888:245

AMER   Haskins n.d.:121
   Kenedy 1890:28, 329
   Milner/Kaplan 1983:180-1 "The Dear ..."
   Welsh 1907,2:400-1

BRS   Harvard 1: 5.96, 9.55 (Bebbington), 12.37 (Such)
   Harvard 3: (Harkness)
   Emerald Isle 1904:74-5
   O'Conor 1901:57 "The Dear ..."
   617 [190-?]:109 "The Dear ..."
   Walton's New 1,1966:69

cl: REC   J. W. Green, AFS 2283 B1

MEL   Willie Clancy, Folkways FW 8782 (B5)
   Hudson ms. 2:677 "My Conor His Cheeks Are Like Roses"
   JIFSS 15,1915:28, 4 tunes.
   O'Neill 1903:13 (#73) "The ..."
   Scanlon 1923:53

◇ The Banks of Sweet Lough Neagh (*H158*) 295

Brunnings 1981: "... Sweet Loch Ray"

AMER   Flanders 1937:16-7 "On the Banks of Sweet Loch Rae"
   Flanders et al. 1939:203-5 "The Banks of Sweet Loch Ray"

◇ The Soldier Boy (*H244*) 295

Laws 1957:240 (O31)
Brunnings 1981: "The Irish ..."

IREL   Moulden 1979:140-1 mentions a version sung by Eddie Butcher.

BRS   BPL H.80: (n.i.) "The Irish Soldier Boy"
   BPL Irish: (n.i.) "The Irish Soldier"

b: REC   Tom Brandon, Folk-Legacy FSC 10 (A2) "The Irish ..."
cl: Emma Dusenbury, AFS 875 A2
cl: Mrs Callie Vaughan, AFS 2940 B2
? cl: Irvin David Williams, AFS 1023 B2

◇ The Banks of the Nile (*H238*) 296

Laws 1957:206-7 (N9) "... (Men's Clothing I'll Put On II), says this and Laws N8 are "clearly related ... but they are sufficiently different to be treated separately."
Brunnings 1981: "...," ?"The Banks of the Condamine (I and II)"

IREL   Morton 1973:139-40 "Texas Isle," essentially Henry's ballad except for the title; it is usually accepted as a different ballad.
   Cf. Mackenzie 1928:113-4 "Dixie's Isle," mentioned by Laws, and Peacock 1965,3:996-7 "Dixie's Isle," Fowke's reference; both appear to be the same except for the title.

BRIT   Greig/Duncan 1,1981:273-80 (#99), 14 vts.
   Palmer 1977:171-2

AMER   Fowke 1973:166-7 briefly surveys occurrences of this ballad (see Clark rec.).
   Milner/Kaplan 1983:84
Randolph/Cohen (1982):92-3 "Men's Clothes I Will Put On"

AUST   *AT* #29(Dec)1969:17

BRS   BPL Irish: (Brereton)
   Harvard 1: 8.47 (Andrews), 9.219 (Bebbington), 12.37 (Such)
   UCB Brereton
   UCLA 605: 3(Brereton)
   Healy 1,1967b:101-2

REC   Sidney Richards, *FSB* 8 (A5)
   Jumbo Brightwell, Topic 12TS 375 (A7)
   LaRena Clark, Topic 12T140 (B1)
   Sandy Denny, Island ILPS 9125
   Roy Harris, Fellside FE 017 (B5)
   A. L. Lloyd, Topic 12TS 232 (A2); cf. Topic 12TS 203 "The Banks of the Condamine"
   Ewan MacColl, Murray Hill 920336 (3A7)
   Tom Phaidin Tom, Comhaltas Ceoltoiri Eireann CL 15 (B3); -----, De Danann, Shanachie 79005 (A5)
   Young Tradition, Transatlantic TRA SAM 30 (= TRA 172)(A10)

MEL   O'Neill 1903:302 (#1625)

◇ Johnnie and Molly (*H755*) 297

Brunnings 1981: "Lovely Molly," but not "Johnny ... (Through the Groves)" or "Jimmy and Nancy - As Beautiful Nancy Was A-Walking One Day"

IREL   Hughes 4,1936:2-4 "Lovely Mollie"

AMER   Creighton 1971:101-2 "Jimmy and Nancy," a fragment that may be a very different version.
   Cf. Nye 1952:(16-7) "... Mollie"

REC   Seán Corcoran, Green Linnet SIF 1004 (A6) "Johnny ..."
   Joe Holmes, Len Graham, Topic 12TS 401 (B5)

◇ The Bold Privateer (*H514*) 297

1: Many songs cited below differ from Henry's version. Most of these are versions of "A Sailor and His True Love" ("Pleasant [Happy] and Delightful," "Farewell Dearest Nancy"), which share not only the metre but parallel thought if not direct common ancestry with Henry's (e.g., Greig/Duncan 1,1981:143-9). Cf. also Laws O30, "Jimmy and His Own True Love."

Dean-Smith 1954
Laws 1957:241 (O32): "Kittredge in *JAF* 35,1922:357-8 gives references to various American songsters."
Brunnings 1981: ?"...," "... - 'Tis Oh My Dearest Polly," ?"The Privateer"; cf. "Pleasant and Delightful"

BRIT   Cf. Dillon [1948?]:14 "Pleasant and Delightful"
   Cf. Greig/Duncan 1,1981:143-9 (#64) "A (The) Sailor and His True Love," 14 vts. ("(Charming) Mary Ann")
   Nettel 1954:194 "The *Privateer*"
   Cf. *Sing* 5(4,Aug)1961:73 "A Sailor and His True Love"

AMER   Cf. Peacock 1965,2:528-9 "Jimmy and Nancy (the departure)"; he suggests a possible precursor/progenitor of the class of returned-lover ballads may be the French "Germine" (p. 589).

BRS   BPL Partridge: 1.284 (Wrigley)
   UCLA 605: 3(Such)
   Cf. *A Broadside* 4(5,Oct)1911
   Popular Songs 1860:147

REC   Peter Bellamy, Trailer LER 2089 (B5)
   Tom Brandon, Folkways FM 4005 (B7)

C16 / I will watch and pray

Cf. Group at Stanhope Arms, Leader LEE 4058 (A2) "Castle Hill Anthem," a truncated version of "Pleasant and Delightful."
b: E. G. Huntington, Folkways FA 2032 (B7)
b: Cf. Lou, Sally Killen, Front Hall FHR 06 (B4) "Pleasant and Delightful"
b: Cf. Sam Larner, Folkways FG 3507 (B3) "Happy and Delightful"
Cf. A. L. Lloyd, Topic 12T 118 (B5) "Farewell Nancy"
Cf. John Millar, Folkways FH 5275 (A4) "Pleasant and Delightful"
? Kevin Mitchell, Topic 12TS 314 (A4) "Nancy Bell"
Cf. Cyril Poacher, Topic 12TS 252 "A Sailor and His True Love"
b: *Welcome to the Folk Festival*, Vol. 1, Ar-Co FB 12. 101 "Pleasant and Delightful"
Villagers of Hartland (Devonshire), People's Stage Tapes cass. 04 (?A14) "Pleasant and Delightful"

◇ The Maid of Carrowclare *(H169) 298*

IREL Shields *UF* 27, 1981:9-10 "Killyclare" (see E. Butcher rec.)
Shields 1981:56-7 (#13) "Carrowclare"
Shields/Shields *UF* 21, 1975: #76 "Carrowclare"

h: REC Eddie Butcher, Leader LED 2070 (A8) "Killyclare"
Robert Butcher, EEOT *Shamrock 2* cass. (A7) "Carrowclare"

◇ The Faithful Rambler *(H825) 299*

AMER Wright 1975:372 (from Henry coll., BCL)

◇ Love's Parting / Jamie and Mary *(H788) 300*

IREL Moulden 1979:98-9

m: REC Paul Brady, Mulligan LUN 024

◇ Dobbin's Flowery Vale *(H85) 300*

Laws 1957:240 (O 29) "Erin's Flowery Vale (The Irish Girl's Lament)"
Brunnings 1981: "...," "The Irish Girl's Lament (Erin's ...)"

b: IREL Hughes 2, 1915:6-11
b: Morton 1970:55-6
S. O'Boyle 1977:58-9
b: O Lochlainn 1939:162-3, 216

AMER Creighton 1971:39-40 "Overn's Flowery Vale"

REC Geordie Hanna, Eagrán 0002 (A7)
Mick Moloney, Green Linnet SIF 1010 (B7) "The Irish Maid"
Paddy Tunney, Topic 12TS 289 (B5)

MEL Joyce 1873:98

◇ A Londonderry Love Song *(H518) 301*

IREL Moulden 1979:90

m: MEL O Lochlainn 1939:92 "If I Was a Blackbird"

◇ The Maids of Culmore *(H687) 302*

Brunnings 1981

IREL Shields 1981:116 (#48) "... Maid ..."
Shields/Shields *UF* 21, 1975: #260

h: BRIT Kilkerr *FMJ* 1977:223-4; reprint, *Treoir* 12(1)1980:14

REC John Butcher, EEOT *Shamrock 2* cass. (A5) "The Maid ..."
Joe McCafferty, EEOT *Ceolta agus* cass. (A7) "... Maid ... Coolmore"

C17

It's I am your Jamie:
The returned lover

C17 / It's I am your Jamie

The Banished Lover [H23: 19 Apr 1924]

A Bannbrook song.

Other title: "The Parish of Dunboe."

Source: (w, m) John Sweeney (Benarees, Magilligan). [Sean O'Boyle suggests the author is the hero, John McCloskey (Dunboe).]

s: This song of the unlettered muse is a sincere effusion from the heart. It enjoyed a wide popularity from Aghadowey to Magilligan....

[Dt] Key G. [Bp illegible.]

I am a bold undaunted youth, I mean to let you know,
I was brought up in Bannbrook in the parish of Dunboe,
My aged parents banished me, I mean to let you hear,
I then set out for Eochaill in the pleasant time of year.

Oh, Eochaill is a purty place, it's all set round with trees,
And in the summer's evening, the honey feeds the bees,
And in the summer's evening a pleasure for to see,
For me to be with my true love and my true love with me.

I was coming in through Eochaill, it being late and after night,
The rain it fell and the wind it blew and the stars showed me no light,
I being among strangers, I knew not where to go,
I prayed to God to be my guide and keep me from my foe.

The people in this country, they bear me at a spite,
They give their tongues great liberty on me both day and night,
They say I am a stranger that knows not where to go,
And once a forlorn lover in the parish of Dunboe.

Walking on through Eochaill till I came to Mullagh Hill,
It's there I spied a pretty fair maid who sore lamented still,
I asked of her the reason why she lamented so,
It was parting from her own true love from the parish of Dunboe.

'What is your true love's name?' I says, 'Come tell to me in plain.'
'His name is John M'Closkey from the borders of Coleraine.
To me he was engaged and that not long ago,
For to wed the widow's daughter from the parish of Dunboe.'

'Dry up your tears, my charming maid, and weep no more for me,
In wedlock's bands we'll join our hands and married we will be,
You crossed the sea for love of me, you faced both friend and foe,
And I'm your wounded lover from the parish of Dunboe.'

Now to conclude and end these lines and leave all things aside:
There is a wee lass in this town whom I will make my bride,
To her I was engaged and that not long ago,
So I'll wed the widow's daughter from the parish of Dunboe.

3.3: ... strangers that knows not ... [Dt]

1.4: Eochaill, probably Aughill in Magilligan, means a yew wood. [s: Bp]

Learmount Grove

[H726: 23 Oct 1927; "The Banished Lover" (b)]

Source: Denis M'Gaughey (Aghafad, Ballinamallaght, Donemana).

Key G.

The first of my late rambling I mean to let you know:
When I had come to Claudy town, I knew not where to go.
I being tired walking, likewise I did think long,
I prayed to God to be my guide, I was so far from home.

Sam Henry's Songs of the People

When I came to Ballymullins, 'twas late on in the
   night,
The rain did rain excessively and the moon
   showed me no light.
I being tired of walking, likewise I did think
   long,
I thought my very heart would break, I was so
   far from home.

Learmount is a purty place, it's all grown o'er
   with trees,
And in the summer season the honey feeds the
   bees,
It's covered o'er with daisies, delightful for to
   see;
I wish I was with my true love and my true love
   with me.

The people of this country, they take a great
   delight
In giving their tongue liberty of me both day
   and night;
Because I am a stranger, and that right well
   they know,
I can find a loving sweetheart all roads that I
   do go.

When I quit my work at night, it's down the
   road I go
To see the pretty fair maids in yon little town
   below,
For I'm engaged already, and that not long ago,
Unto a widow's daughter along the banks of Roe.

Farewell to the Ballymullins, likewise to
   Learmount Hill,
And all around the borders where I did sport
   my fill.
The blessings I leave with them, you'll find they
   are not few,
And twice farewell to Learmount Grove, I now
   maun bid adieu.

Mary Machree [H485: 18 Mar 1933]

s: (m) "Reid-cnoc mna Duibe."

Source not given.

s: Note on the name of the air: -- Reid-cnoc mna
duibe, pronounced Ray-nyuck mna gyivvy, means
"the dark woman of the flat-topped hill."
   "Reid (d silent) is usually applied to a mountain
flat or a coarse, moory, level piece of land among
hills." -- Dr. O'Rorke's *History of Sligo*. Etymologists will find a clue in the word Reid, with its
variants Rea and Ree to the meanings of Knocknarea in Sligo, and Kilrea and Ree (Agivey district) in Co. Derry, all of which have the distinct
topographical feature of a Reid as defined by Dr.
O'Rorke.
   The air is not local, as an air with the same title and resembling it in some of its musical phrases, has been collected in Co. Tipperary.

308 Key D.

The flower of the valley was Mary Machree,
Her smiles all bewitching were lovely to see,
The bees round her humming when summer was
   gone,
When the roses were fled, might her lips take for
   one.

As oak leaves, when autumn is turning them sere,
Was the hue that bespangled her beautiful hair.
As light as young ash-sprays that droop in the
   grove
Were the ringlets that waved as the fetters of love.

Like stars that shine out from the calm summer
   sky
Were the glances that beamed from her melting
   blue eye,
Her lips red as poppies, her cheeks bright as
   morn,
And her bosom and neck like the bloom on the
   thorn.

Her laugh it was music, her breath it was balm,
Her heart like the lake was as pure and as calm,
Till love o'er it came like a breeze o'er the sea
And made the heart heave of sweet Mary Machree.

She loved and she wept, for was gladness e'er
   known
To dwell in the bosom that love makes his own?
His joys are but moments, his griefs are for years
He comes all in smiles, but he leaves all in tears.

Her lover was gone to a far distant land,
And Mary in sadness would pace the lone strand
And tearfully gaze on the dark rolling sea
That parted her soldier from Mary Machree.

Oh, pale grew her cheek when there came from
   afar
The tale of the battle and tidings of war,
Her eyes filled with tears when the clouds
   gathered dark,
For fancy would picture some tempest-tost bark.

But winter came on and the deep woods were bare
In the hall was a voice and a foot on the stair.
Oh, joy to the maiden, for o'er the blue sea
Her soldier returned to his Mary Machree.

James Reilly [H826: 23 Sep 1939; Laws N37]

Other titles: "John (George) (Young) Reily (Riley) (Rylie)," "When First I Came to the County Limerick"; cf. "As I Roved out from the County Cavan."

Source: (m) George Graham (Cross Lane, Coleraine) from his grandfather, Joseph Wilson (Roddenfoot, Ballymoney); (w) late John Henry Macaulay (Ballycastle), author of "The Ould Lammas Fair."

s: This song is not to be confused with No. 468, "John Reilly." ... The words [from] John Henry Macauley, from whom I received more than a score of traditional songs.... This is one of the very few instances in Irish folk tunes collected by me where a change of key occurs.

l: No such key change is detectible in this tune.

Key C.

As I went roving through the County Cavan
For to view the charms of life,
'Twas there I met with a lovely maiden,
She appeared to me like an angel bright.

Said I, 'Fair maid, it's would you marry,
Or would ye be a light horseman's wife?'
'Oh no, kind sir, I would rather tarry
I prefer to live a sweet single life.'

I asked this fair one, 'What is the reason
You differ far from all female kind?
You are so neat and so very handsome,
To wed with you I would be inclined.'

'Indeed, kind sir, the truth I'll tell you:
I might have been married seven long years ago
To one James Reilly who left this country,
It's he's the cause of my grief and woe.'

'Don't depend on Reilly, he might deceive you,
But come with me to some foreign shore,
We will both sail over to Pennsylvania,
Bid adieu to Reilly for evermore.'

'It's seven long years since my true love left me,
Seven long years since he sailed away,
And seven more I would wait upon him;
If he's alive, he'll come back to me.'

When he saw that this maid was constant,
The secret to her he did make known,
Saying, 'I'm your love and your long lost Reilly,
And since we've met, we will part no more.'

C17 / It's I am your Jamie

Skerry's Blue-Eyed Jane [H737: 8 Jan 1938]

Source: "veteran singer" (Burnquarter, Ballymoney).

s: ... M'William, the lover in the ballad, is the descendant of the Lord of Dunluce. The M'Quillans of Dunluce were dispossessed of their Antrim estate in 1608 -- the grandson of old M'Quillan (through his daughter, Ingeann Dhu) having been Randall M'Donnell, first Earl of Antrim. King James I, out of sympathy for old Edward M'Quillan, then blind and a centenarian, granted him Innishowen but his sentiment was against occupying it. An exchange was arranged and the family of Chichester (Marquis of Donegal) gave up part of his estate, i.e. Clanaghertie in Clandeboy in South Antrim, but in 1619 the M'Quillans were landless.

[Another returned, unrecognized lover. No indication is made of the tune for the refrain.]

Key C.

As I rode o'er by Skerry Tap
Alang the silvery Braid,
The sun was rising frae his nap
In crimson robes arrayed;
There I o'ertook a lovely maid,
Fair as the summer morn.
The dewdrop sparkled on the blade
And milk-white was the thorn.

*And still she sang, while caverns rang,
Re-echoing the strain,
'How sweet the days when o'er these braes
MacWilliam courted Jane.'*

'Dear lassie, would you go with me
And leave these hills and dales?
For thee I'll launch my bonny boat,
Unfurl her silken sails,
And when we reach old Rathlin's isle
Across the stormy tide,
You'll find brave men and maidens smile,
O'erjoyed to see my bride.'

'I would not leave these hills and dales,
Though wild they seem to thee,
By them I'll keep my fleecy sheep,
While wild fish swim the sea,
And for my bonny laddie's sake
I'll stay in this lone isle,
And if that he returns again,
I ne'er shall him beguile.'

Sam Henry's Songs of the People

'Dear lassie, he has left you now
Another maid to wed;
I saw him pledge his bridal vow
And laid in bridal bed.'
'You lie, false coward loon, you lie,
And were MacWilliam here,
Your blood would stain the daisied lea,
Red-reeking frae his spear.'

No longer could I be concealed
From one so true and kind,
Who often did her love reveal
To ease my troubled mind;
I pressed her fondly to my breast
And swore it o'er and o'er,
That she that night with me should rest
And ne'er see sorrow more.

I placed her on my milk-white steed
And scoured o'er hill and lea,
Blithe as the lamb we left to feed
Beneath its mother's e'e,
And e'er yon restless sun's gone doon
Beyond the dewy west,
I made this bonny lass my ain,
Her sorrow sank to rest.

*And many sang while clachans rang,
Enraptured with the strain --
'A sweeter maid ne'er left the Braid
Than Skerry's blue-eyed Jane.'*

6.5: ... e'er you ... [Dp etc.]

4.5: loon = boy, lad, fellow.
5.2: scoured = moved about hastily or energetically.
7.1: clachans = small Scottish Highland villages.

The Banks of the Clyde
/ One Fine Summer's Morning

[H812: 17 Jun 1939]

Other titles: "William and Jane on ...."

Source: Frank Kealy (Ballysally).

Key A flat.

One fine summer's morning as I went out walking
Along by the banks of a clear winding tide,
In ambush I lay while a couple were talking
By the side of a stream as it gently did glide;
A young man stood by, who to me was a stranger,
He says, 'Fairest creature, I've come from afar,
Then don't be afraid, love, or think it a danger
To walk by the side of a jolly young tar.'

'Kind sir, to tell you the truth most sincerely,
The colour you wear lies near to my heart,
Since faithful young Willie has gone and has left me,
He sails o'er the ocean to some foreign part;
Since that sad fortune has now separated,
Right constant I'll prove, should I ne'er see him more;
While yonder green hills are with flowers decorated,
My own dearest Willie I'll always adore.'

[?missing line]
'The flowers on yon hilltop will droop and will die;
Come, let us away from beneath these green bowers
And in Hymen's bonds join in sweet unity.
Your faithful young Willie, whom you love so dearly,
Is now joined in wedlock in some distant clime,
Since that is the case, you have lost him forever,
So give me your hand, love, and say you'll be mine.'

'I beg you'll excuse me, sir, I must retire,
And in this green shade I must bid you adieu;
It's a humble request that you seem to desire,
But my favour, kind sir, to another is due;
Should flowers decay in the dead stormy winter,
Yet spring's gentle breeze will again them renew,
This heart from my true love no friendship will sever,
Though he prove unconstant, I'll always prove true.'

'O Jane, what's the reason you seem not to know me?'
Then out of his pocket a small purse he drew,
Saying, 'Fifty bright guineas, my love, I'll bestow you,
Since you in my absence proved constant and true;
And since that kind fortune has brought us together,
Tomorrow, my darling, I'll make you my bride,
I'll love you forever and part we will never,
But dwell with my Jane on the banks of the Clyde.'

Mary Doyle
/ The Wreck of the Lady Shearbrooke

[H570: 3 Nov 1934]

Source not given.

Key G.

On the ship *Lady Shearbrooke* we left Londonderry
Bound for Quebec and Ameri-cay,
On the eighteenth of June from the Foyle we weighed anchor
With fine pleasant gale and hearts light and gay.

The captain and crew did share of our pleasures,
He was a good man with heart light and free,
He gained the affection of all who sailed with him,
And knew all the dangers in crossing the sea.

At midnight, it being the eighteenth of August,
We feared not the storm, but slumbered in bed,
When a dreadful shout from our dreams did alarm us,
The mate on our bows crying, 'Breakers ahead!'

And scarce had these words from his lips right proceeded,
When she struck on a rock with a sickening crash,
It would make your heart bleed for to see those poor voyagers,
When down through our hatchways the billows did dash.

It would make your heart bleed for to see the poor infants
O'erwhelmed in the deep before mothers' eyes,
While their fathers stood wringing their hands in despair,
Lured to their death by their babes' drowning cries.

Come all ye bold sea captains, I would have you take warning,
Keep clear of all danger in crossing the sea,
For who lived to see the next morning sunrise,
Of three-eighty-four remained thirty-three.

One evening long after, as daylight was closing,
I chanced for to stray by the banks of the Foyle,
Where I heard a fair maid making great lamentation,
Alas, I soon found it was poor Mary Doyle.

Her cries through the wild wind did sound through the valleys
And the tears from her eyes in large drops did flow
As she mourned for her love who lay low in the ocean,
A poor lonesome damsel to languish in woe.

I touched her fair shoulder and gently consoled her,
And said, 'Cry no more by the banks of the Foyle,
For I am your Willie returned o'er the ocean
To wed and live happy with you, Mary Doyle.'

Laurel Hill / Kyle's Flowery Braes

[H8: 5 Jan 1924]

s: (m) "Burns and His Highland Mary." Other titles: (m) "The Cot in the Corner," (m) "Far ower the Forth."

Source: (w) H. Evans; (m) 3: R. R. B[?rownlow], pennywhistle (Ballylagan, Cloyfin); W. J. Tweed, voice (Bushmills); native (Tyrone border).

s: The air is not the same as "Catherine Ogie," to which Burns wrote his song, "Highland Mary." It also was an Irish air, and was taken by the poet from the singing of Grey Robin Lyttle, of Lisnod, near Lisburn.

I have incorporated the best features of three versions of the tune known in Ulster as "Burns and His Highland Mary": one from R. R. B. of Ballylagan, Cloyfin, who played it on the tin whistle; one from Mr W. J. Tweed, who sang it over the telephone to me from Bushmills; and the third and most complete from a native of the Tyrone border. If preferred, the whole song can be sung to the first half of the music. The song, it should be remembered, was written about the time of the Battle of Waterloo, and before the Strand Road, Coleraine, was made.

It throws an interesting light on the life in nature in those days, as the fox and the otter were evidently common.

Key E flat.

When war had oppressed every nation with horror,
And Wellington ventured his life o'er the main
To pull down French tyrants and make them surrender,
For the sake of old Erin I ventured the same.
Then I left those green braes where I sported with Nancy;
She says, 'My dear Jamie, be true to me still.
Till you gain the victory and return from the slaughter,
I will mourn round these valleys of sweet Laurel Hill.'

When we landed in Spain we were almost exhausted,

Sam Henry's Songs of the People

Being tossed by the wind and the billows so high,
Pursuing our foes over yon snowy mountains,
Where many brave heroes were obliged for to die,
But at length we survived through the hottest of battle
And over yon mountains we fought with great skill,
While thousands lay bleeding in gore all around me,
I smiled at all danger far from Laurel Hill.

Our commander being brave and we being stout-hearted,
Sure, France, Spain and Holland know what we can do,
We pulled down their batteries with the great guns of Britain,
Caused orphans to mourn on distressed Waterloo.
So now the war's over and we all are returning,
From the dangers of war for to rest for awhile,
And we gave them three cheers as we sailed for old Erin,
The long-looked-for valley and beautiful isle.

Then at length I arrived on the banks of yon river,
Where I spied my dear maid by the side of yon mill,
Near the leap of Coleraine where I last parted with her
To gain British valour far from Laurel Hill.
She appeared unto me like one dressed in deep mourning;
I asked her the reason she roamed the Bann shore,
'My Jamie's a soldier, and all are returning,
But Jamie, alas, I will ne'er see him more.

'He has left me to wander these dark gloomy valleys,
Where the wild fox and otter do sport with free will
And the trout seeks its mate in the lovely Bann water,
But I can't find my Jamie around Laurel Hill.'
'Oh, it's I am your Jamie, your long-looked-for soldier,
Although my tongue's altered and I'm in disguise.
Don't you mind on old Kyle's flowery braes where we parted,
When the bugle's loud blast called me off in surprise?

'It was there we stood viewing the ships in yon harbour,
And the wild sporting angler whose aim was to kill,
And the trout as it played in yon lovely Bann water,
Still adding more beauty to grace Laurel Hill.'
She fell in my arms like one pale and silly,
The tears falling down like the dew from the thorn,
And her eyes were inviting each one that beheld her
To welcome her long-looked-for soldier's return.

Now the joybells of Erin may ring and be merry,
With great shouts of gladness fill valley and plain;
We'll never part more since we've joined together
In a neat little cottage near the town of Coleraine.
Now to conclude I'll sing Wellington's praises,
An undaunted hero and Irishman still,
His fame will be sounded when kings are forgotten,
And sung round those valleys of sweet Laurel Hill.

5.7: Do you ... [Dt]

The Lady of the Lake

[H765: 23 Jul 1938; Laws N41]

s: (m) "Bold Jack Donahoe." Other titles: "The Banks of Clyde," "... of Lak," "Liza Gray," "Loss of the ...."

Source: William Doey (Kilmoyangie, Kilraughts, Ballymoney).

[Yet another lost-lover-retrieved ballad.]

Key E flat.

One evening as I chanced to stray down by the banks of Clyde,
Near to the town of sweet Renfrew a bonny lass I spied,
She sobbed and sighed, and thus she cried, 'I well may rue the day
That my sailor lad left Belfast town to cross the raging sea.'

And being unperceived by her, it's quickly I drew near,
Not thinking that it was the voice of my Eliza dear,
Her doleful lamentations did greatly me surprise,
And the crystal streams in torrents flowed down from her tender eyes.

I stepp-ed up to this wee lass and thus to her did say,
'Why weep you here, my bonny lass, beneath this willow tree?'
And with a sigh she answered, 'Sir, I pray don't trouble me,
For when in grief I find relief beneath this willow tree.

'Once I loved a sailor, his name was William
   Brown,
And on the *Lady of the Lake* he sailed from
   Belfast town
With near three hundred emigrants bound for
   America,
And on the coast of Newfoundland his leave did
   take of me.'

When she made mention of my name, I to myself
   did say,
'Can this be her I longed to see, my dear Eliza
   Gray?
When tossing on the raging seas, four hundred
   miles from shore,
The nor'east wind in mountains high against our
   vessel bore.

'The *Lady of the Lake* that night was into pieces
   sent,
And all except but thirty-four down to the
   bottom went,
Young William Brown among the rest, alas, being
   cast away
Before our ship in pieces split, these loving
   words did say:

'"Farewell unto Eliza Gray, I fear her heart will
   break
When she hears that I am drown-ed on the *Lady
   of the Lake*,"
But providence was kind to him, and just as he
   went down,
A fishing lugger saved him, and I'm your William
   Brown.'

The Banks of Claudy

[H5: 15 Dec 1923, H693: 6 Mar 1937; Laws N40]

Other titles: "... Clady (Claudie) (Florida),"
"(The) Claudy Banks," "Dark and Stormy Night,"
"John Riley II."

Source: (Faughan vale).

s: This is the premier ballad of Ireland. It is
sung all over the Green Isle, and each district
has its own variations. This version ... though
sung in the cottage came to hand from the castle.

Key C.

As I roved out one morning, being in the month of
   May,
Down by the sally gardens I carelessly did stray,
I overheard a young maid in sorrow to complain
All for her absent lover, and Johnny was his
   name.

I stepp-ed up to this young maid, I took her by
   surprise,
I'll own she did not know me, I being in disguise,
Said I, 'My pretty fair maid, my joy and heart's
   delight,
Tell me how far you've travelled this dark and
   dreary night.'

'Kind sir, the road to Claudy would you be pleased
   to show?
Take pity on a fair one who knows not where to
   go.
I'm in search of a faithless young man and Johnny
   is his name,
Sure, it's on the banks of Claudy I'm told he does
   remain.'

'This is the banks of Claudy, the groun' whereon
   you stand,
Do not depend on Johnnny, for he's a false young
   man,
Do not depend on Johnny, he will not meet you
   here,
But tarry with me in these green woods; no
   danger need you fear.'

'Oh, if my Johnny were here this night, he'd keep
   me safe from harm,
But he's in the field of battle all in his uniform,
He's in the field of battle and his foes he does
   defy
Like a rolling prince of honour near to the walls of
   Troy.'

'It's about six months or better since Johnny left
   the shore,
He's sailing on the ocean, where foaming billows
   roar,
He's sailing on the ocean for honour and bright
   fame,
As I'm told, the ship was lost going round the
   coasts of Spain.'

Oh, when she heard this dreadful news, she could
   no longer stand;
To the tearing of her golden hair and wringing of
   her hand,
'Then, since my Johnny's drownded, no other man
   I'll take,
Through lonesome dales and valleys I'll wander for
   his sake.'

Then when he saw her loyalty, he could no longer
   stand,
He took her in his arms, saying, 'Betty, I'm the
   man,
I'm your true and constant Johnny, the cause of
   all your pain,
And since we met at Claudy banks, we'll never
   part again.'

Sam Henry's Songs of the People

The Banks of [the] Dee [H583: 2 Feb 1935]

Other title: cf. "The Banks of Champlain."

Source: (m, w) Maggie Brownlow (Hillview, Ballylagan, Cloyfin).

[Yet another rediscovered-lover ballad, sans token.]

Key C.

As daylight was appearing and the cloudy skies were clearing
And small birds' notes were cheering on the banks of the Dee,
There I heard a maid a-sighing, her watery eyes was drying,
And 'Johnny,' she was crying, 'oh, how could you leave me?'

'Twas on that spot we parted, I left her broken-hearted,
While crystal tears they started down from her eyes to flow,
Saying, 'Bid adieu for ever, since from you I must sever,
As you walk down by the river you'll remember me, I know.

'When I am on the ocean and billows are in motion,
When I am at devotion, I'll still repeat your name,
When drums they are a-beating, and we the foe are meeting,
From hence there's no retreating, I'll always be the same.'

I know right well what grieves her, but yet I won't relieve her:
When first I did receive her, I hid from her my name;
She appeared to me full sorry, I told her a mournful story:
'It was on a field so gory your youthful love was slain.'

When she heard those news she fainted, her cheeks like death were painted,
I from her heart relented and quickly told my name;
While on me she stood mazing, and on her I stood gazing,
With joy her hands upraising, said, 'Are you still the same?'

'Leave off your sobs and sighings, your fond heart I was trying,
Of all your sobs and sighings I was the whole to blame;
Here since we're met together, we'll walk down by yon river,
You and I'll be joined together, no more to part again.'

The Mantle So Green

[H76: 25 Apr 1925; Laws N38]

Other titles: "Famed Waterloo," "Her ...," "... of ...," "Round her ...," "(Young) Willie (O')Reilly."

Source: (w, m) native, 82 (Ballinrees, Macosquin), c. 1865 from young woman (Drumrammer, between Limavady and Ringsend).

s: ... Joyce [1909] has a variant of this tune, and one verse of the song, No. 325 Old Irish Airs. This version is of an older type than his, the formula of construction in the air, abba, a characteristic of Irish music, being more closely followed. It is remarkable that the flattened 7th, *ta*, was accurately preserved alike in Co. Limerick, where Joyce collected it, and here in Co. Derry.

Key G.

As I went a-walking one morning in June
To view the green fields and the valleys in bloom,
I spied lovely Nancy, she appeared like a queen
With her costly fine robes and her mantle so green.

I stepped up to her, put her in surprise,
I own she did not know me, I being in disguise,
Says I, 'Fairest creature, you appear like a queen
With your costly fine robes and your mantle so green.

'Now if you'll not marry, pray what's your love's name?
I have been in battle, I might know the same.'
'Draw near to my mantle where it's plain to be seen:
My love's name engraven on my mantle so green.'

At the rise of her mantle there I did behold
Her love's name and surname in letters of gold.

'Is it Willie O'Reilly appears in my view?
He was my chief comrade in famed Waterloo.

'Your love and I fought where the bullets do fly,
In the field of battle your true love does lie,
We fought for four days, till the fifth afternoon
He received his death summons on the eighteenth
    of June.'

When she heard these sad news she flew in
    despair,
To the wringing her hands and tearing her hair.
'To the green hills I'll wander to shun all men's
    view,
Since the lad I loved dearly is in famed Waterloo.'

'Oh Nancy, lovely Nancy, it was I won your
    heart
In your own father's garden the day we did part,
In your father's garden, it's plain to be seen,
I rolled you in my arms in your mantle so green.'

Now this couple's married, as we hear people say,
Great nobles attended on their wedding day,
He dressed her in silk, she appeared like a
    queen
With her costly fine robes and her mantle so
    green.

Johnny Jarmin / The Rainbow

[H156: 6 Nov 1926; Laws N43]

s: "Johnny Jarmer"; k: "Johnny German." Other
title: "Jack the German," "... Jarmanie."

Source: (m) Willie Hegarty, 74 (Ballydevitt,
Aghadowey), from his mother; (w) Annie Wilson
(Beagh, Maghera), from her grandfather, 85,
from his mother.

Key G.

As I walked down by Dublin town to hear some
    pleasant news,
I met with a brisk young sailor lad that seldom
    did refuse;
I met with a brisk young sailor, a tight and
    hardy lad,
He fell in love with a lady and her countenance
    was sad.

He says, 'Dear honoured lady, what makes you
    so cast down?'
Right modestly she answered without a tear or
    frown,
'My true love's gone and left me, he's sailing to
    and fro,
And he left me no true love token whether he
    would return or no.'

'Perhaps I saw your darling when I was last at
    sea,
And if I do describe him, the truth you'll tell
    to me;
And if I do describe him, I hope you'll tell me
    so,
That you'll agree and marry me, let him return
    or no.

'Your true love's tall and handsome, where'er he
    turns his back,
He's comely in his features and they call him
    handsome Jack,
He's away on board the Rainbow, he's sailing to
    and fro,
Your true love's Johnny Jarmin, is he the lad
    or no?'

'He's just the very sailor lad that you have
    mention-ed,
Pray tell to me, kind sir, is he alive or dead?'
'He was away on board the Rainbow and sailing
    to and fro,
Your true love John Jarmin is dead nine months
    ago.'

When she heard this doleful news, she fell in
    deep despair
To the wringing of her hands and the tearing of
    her hair,
She fled unto her chamber all for to make great
    moan,
It's expected any moment that death will claim
    its own.

He has dressed himself in scarlet red and is
    away to her again,
To ease her of her sorrows and cure her killing
    pain.
'Cheer up, cheer up, my Mary, for there's none
    so blithe as thee,
There's not two doves in all the world to equal
    you and me.

'The moon exceeds the sun, the sun exceeds
    the rose,
And upon your bosom, darling, that flower both
    buds and blows;
There's none shall e'er enjoy me but you that
    feels the smart
And I'll bid adieu to the Rainbow since Mary
    won my heart.'

1.3: ... sailor lad, a ... [Dt]
7.1: ... and's away ... [Dt]
 .2: ... and to cure ... [Dt]
8.1: ... sun and the ... [Dt]
 .2: ... and grows; [Dt]

Mary and Willie [H118: 13 Feb 1926; Laws N28]

Other titles: "The Beggarman," "As Willie and
Mary Strolled by the Seashore," "Little Mary(,
the Sailor's Bride)," "The Single Sailor," "Willie
(William) and Mary."

Source: (m) coll. Maud Houston (Coleraine); (w)
2: Mrs S. Warnock (Drumreagh Cottage, Bally-

Sam Henry's Songs of the People

money); George Loughrey (Gortnamoyagh, Garvagh).

s: ... The last two lines are sung to lines 3 and 4 of the music.

Key C.

As Willie and Mary stood by the seaside a long
  farewell for to take,
Says Mary to Willie, 'If you go away, I'm afraid
  my poor heart it will break.'
'Oh, don't be afraid, dearest Mary,' he said as
  he clasped his fond maid to his side,
'In my absence don't mourn, for when I return I
  will make you, sweet Mary, my bride.'

Seven long years had passed and no word at last,
  Mary stood in her own cottage door,
A beggar came by with a patch on his eye,
  'decripted' and ragged and tore.
'Your charity, fair maid, bestow upon me, your
  fortune I'll tell you beside:
Your lad which you mourn will never return to
  make little Mary his bride.'

She skipped and she started, saying, 'All that I
  have, it's freely to you I will give,
If you tell me true what I now ask of you: is
  my Willie dead or alive?'
'He's living,' said he, 'though in sad poverty,
  and shipwrecked he has been beside.
When he'd money untold and pockets of gold,
  he'd have made little Mary his bride.'

'Then if he is dead, no other I'll wed, no other
  I'll have by my side,
In riches though rolled or covered with gold,
  he'd have made his own Mary his bride.'
Then the patch off his eye the old beggar let fly,
  his old coat and crutches beside,
And in sailor's blue clothes and with cheeks like
  the rose, it was Willie who stood by her side.

'Oh, don't be afraid, dearest Mary,' he said, 'it
  was only your faith that I tried,
To the church we'll away by the break of the
  day, and I'll make little Mary my bride.'

2.2: decripted = decrepit [*quotation marks in original*].

Lurgan Town [H563: 15 Sep 1934]

316 Other title: "Sweet ...."

Source: (Ballymacaldrick district, Dunloy, Co. Antrim).

Key G.

As I walk-ed out one fine evening, bright Phoebus
  was just looking down,
I fell in with a farmer's young daughter convenient
  to sweet Lurgan town.
I instantly stepp-ed up to her and this unto her I
  did say,
'Are you a goddess descended, or tell your name
  to me, I pray.'

This maid then she quickly made answer, 'Your
  freedom, kind sir, I disdain;
I am no goddess descended, nor yet would I tell
  you my name,
For my heart I have give to a young man, the ring
  we have broke it in two,
Until that my Jamie returns home, to him I'll prove
  constant and true.'

'Oh, talk then no more about Jamie, in battle
  with me he did fall,
The very last battle in China, your Jamie was
  killed by a ball.
His last dying words, he lay bleeding, oh, Jamie,
  your lover, did say,
'If you take this gold ring home to Mary, content
  I would lie in the clay.'

When she saw the ring, then she fainted, the
  tears from her eyes down did fall,
She wrung her hands and lamented and on Jamie
  did bitterly call,
'Cruel, cruel were my parents who banished my
  love far away,
Through the valleys forever I'll wander, since
  Jamie lies cold in the clay.'

When he saw that his sweetheart was loyal, her
  true love he could not withstand,
He took this fair maid in his arms, saying, 'I am
  your Jamie returned,
I am your true lover Jamie, who has lately come
  over the sea,
Let us get married tomorrow and live, ay, in
  sweet unity.'

'Oh yes, we will marry tomorrow, since my
  Jamie's come over the sea,
And since you proved to me loyal, in unity we will
  agree.'
Now her father and mother's departed and left
  them full ten hundred pound,
And Jamie and Mary's got married and their home
  is in sweet Lurgan town.

The Broken Ring [H471: 10 Dec 1932; Laws N42]

k: "Young and Single Sailor." Other titles: "All in a Garden Green," "As I Walked Out One Summer's Morning," "The Brisk Young Sailor," "... Song," "(The) ... Token," "A Fair (Young) Maid (Miss) (Walking) (All) in (a) (Her) (the) Garden," "The Flowery Garden," "Her Sailor Boy," "In a Garden a Lady Walking," "(Young) John(ny) Riley," "A Lady Fair," "A Lady (Fair Maid) Walked (There Was a Lady) in Her Father's Garden," "Lover's Return," "The Maiden in the Garden," "(A) Pretty Fair (Little) Maid (Damsel) (Miss) (out) (in the (Her) Garden)," "Returning Soldier," "The Sailor and the Maid," "The Sailor's Return," "A Servant Maid in Her Father's Garden," "Seven (Long) Years (I Loved a Sailor) (Since I Had a Sweetheart)," "(A) Sweetheart in the Army," "The Young and Single Sailor," "A Young Maid (Stood in Her Father's) (in the) Garden"; cf. "The Dark-Eyed Sailor," "Lovely Jane from Enniskillen."

Source not given.

Key G. Rhythmically and rather slowly.

A lady standing in her father's garden,
A gentleman came a-riding by,
He stepped up to her and fain would woo her,
And he says, 'Fair lady, would you fancy I?'

'Oh no, kind sir, I am only a servant,
A servant girl of low degree,
I was ne'er to court, nor ne'er to marry,
For my true love is on the sea.'

'Oh, it's do you see yon fine, fine castle?
Or do you see yon lilies gay?
Or do you see yon ships on the ocean?
I'll leave you all if you marry me.'

'It's what care I for your fine, fine castle,
And what care I for your lilies gay,
Or what care I for your ships on the ocean,
That you'd leave to me if I'd marry thee?

'It's seven long years since I had a true love,
And seven more since I did him see,
And seven more will I wait upon him,
For if he's living he'll return to me.

'If he is living, I would wish to see him,
If he's dead, I wish him good rest,
And if he's married, I wish him happiness,
For he's the wee laddie that I love best.'

He pulled his hand out of his pocket,
His lily-white fingers were thin and small,
He showed her the ring was broke between them,
And when she saw it, down she did fall.

He stooped to her and his love he lifted,
And what he gave her was kisses three,
Saying, 'I'm your love and your single sailor
That has come home, love, for to marry thee.'

Now these pair they have got married
And a happy couple I'm sure they'll be,
For he spends his life with his loving wife
And has bid adieu to the rolling sea.

Green Garden [H818: 29 Jul 1939; ?Laws N42]

k: "Young and Single Sailor."

Source: (w) Joseph Derry (Sallowilly, Claudy, Co. Derry); (m) David Simpson (the Old Manse, Ballygrainey, Co. Down).

Key G.

As I went walking in yon green garden,
A pretty fair maid I chanced to spy,
I walked up to her all for to view her
And said, 'Fair maid, would you fancy I?'

'Indeed, kind sir, I had once a sweetheart,
It's seven long years since my love left me,
And although my love has proved a rambler,
His heart holds mine across the sea.

'If he is living, I love him daily,
If he is dead, I wish him rest;
No young man will e'er enjoy me,
For he is the boy I do love best.'

'If it's seven years since your love left you,
He surely is both dead and gone;
Come with me, I'll make you my lady,
And wait no longer on any man.'

When he saw she was so loyal,
He thought it a pity she should be crossed,
Saying, 'Here I am, your poor single sailor,
That the wide ocean has often crossed.'

He put his hand into his pocket,
His lily-white fingers were long and small,
And says, 'Here's the ring that was broke between us,'
And when she saw it, she down did fall.

Sam Henry's Songs of the People

Then in his arms he did enfold her,
And to the church went straight away,
And so this couple they got married
On a sweet and pleasant day.

The Dark-Eyed Sailor

[H232: 21 Apr 1928; Laws N35]

o: "Broken Token." Other titles: "The Brisk Young Sailor," "(Fair) Phoebe (Phoeby) and Her (the) ...," "The Sailor and His Love."

Source: (w) (Ballaghbeddy, Ballymoney); (m) Mrs Morrison (Moneycannon, Ballymoney).

s: ... A version, collected in Innishowen in 1846 by the late Miss Honoria Galway from a sailor's daughter, has been published in *Old Irish Croonauns* [Galwey 1910]. [Bp] The song appears under the title "The Broken Token" in *Songs of the West* (Rev. Sabine Baring-Gould [et al. 1905]), but to quite a different air.

Key F. [Bp] With feeling.

I'll tell you of a lady fair
Went out one evening to take the air,
She met a sailor lad along the way,
And I paid attention, and I paid attention
To hear what they would say.

Said Willie to her, 'Why walk alone?
The day's far spent and night's coming on.'
She said, while tears down her cheeks did fall,
'It's a dark-eyed sailor, it's a dark-eyed sailor,
That has proved my downfall.

'It's seven years since he left this land,
He took the gold ring all off my hand,
He broke it open, left the half with me,
While the other's rolling, the other's rolling
At the bottom of the sea.'

'If it's seven years since he left this land,
All by this time he's dead and gone,
Love turns aside and as cold does grow
As a winter's evening, as a winter's evening
When the hills are clad with snow.'

"Twas his rosy cheeks and his yellow hair
And his two dark eyes did my heart ensnare;

Genteel he was, he was no rake like you,
To advise a maiden, to advise a maiden
To slight a jacket blue.'

The half-ring then young Willie did show;
She fell half-distracted between joy and woe.
'You're welcome, Willie, I have lands and gold
For my dark-eyed sailor, for my dark-eyed sailor
Who was manly, true and bold.'

So these couple are married and they do agree,
They live in a cottage near to the sea,
So maids, be true when your love's away,
For a misty morning, for a misty morning
Oft turns out a pleasant day.

5.3: ... was, and no ... [Dt]

The Love Token [H581: 19 Jan 1935; Laws N29]

Other titles: "Down by the Seaside," "Jimmy and Nancy (the departure)," "The Nightingales of Spring," "A Seaman('s Happy Return to) (and) His Love," "The Welcome Sailor."

Source: Maggie Brownlow (Hillview, Ballylagan, Cloyfin).

Key C.

Down by the seaside I spied a ship sailing,
I spied a fair maid, she was weeping and
  wailing.
I stepped up and said, 'Fair maid, what is it
  grieves thee?'
And she answered and said, 'There's but one
  can relieve me.

'It's seven years and more since my love and I
  parted,
He parted and left me on shore broken-hearted,
He said he'd return if life would be spared him;
For his absence I'll mourn if death has deprived
  him.'

'Your love and I fought under one commander,
Fighting for George and the great Alexander,
Your love got a shot from a far higher power,
And there on the spot he died that same hour.

'Before your love died, ere his heart it was
  broken,
He pulled out this gold ring, saying, "Here's a
  love token,
Take this to her, I'm sure there's no fairer,
Tell her to prove true and her love give the
  bearer."'

'Begone, you false man, go look for your
   chances,
Since I'm left to mourn, I must please my own
   fancies,
If death has so served me, I'll ne'er wed a
   stranger,
Through the greenwood I'll go and become a
   wood ranger.'

He turned himself round; though she being
   surprised,
She knew her own love, though he being
   disguis-ed,
They sat down to sing, but she sang the
   clearest,
Like a sweet bird in spring, 'You're welcome, my
   dearest.'

The Pride of Glencoe

[H655: 13 Jun 1936; Laws N39]

Other titles: "The Banks of Glenco," "Donald of
...," "Glencoe," "(Mac)Donald's Return to ...";
cf. "The Lass o' ...."

Source: Mrs Frank Kealey (Ballysally, Coleraine).

s: ... This song is a general favorite and is
published by request.

Key D.

As I went a-walking one morning in May,
I spied a wee lassie, she was gallant and gay,
I asked her name and how far did she go,
And she answered, 'Kind sir, I am bound for
   Glencoe.'

Said I, 'My wee lassie, your enchanting smile
And comely sweet features my heart doth beguile,
And if your affection on me you'll bestow,
I would bless the sweet day that we met in Glencoe.'

'Young man,' she made answer, 'your suit I
   disdain,
I once had a sweetheart, M'Donnell's his name,
But he's gone to the war about ten years ago,
And a maid I'll remain till he returns to Glencoe.'

'Perhaps your M'Donnell regards not your name,
But has placed his affection on some other dame,
He may have forgotten, for all that you know,
The lovely wee lassie he left in Glencoe.'

'M'Donnell from his promise can never depart,
For love, truth and honour are found in his heart,
And if I ne'er see him, I single will go
For M'Donnell once called me the pride of Glencoe.'

Then, finding her constant, I pulled out a glove,
Which at our last parting was a token of love.
She hung on my breast while the tears they did
   flow,
Saying, 'Are you M'Donnell returned to Glencoe?'

'Cheer up, my dear Flora, your sorrows are o'er,
While life still remains, we will never part more.
The red storms of war at a distance may blow,
In peace and contentment we'll live in Glencoe.'

The Banks of the River Ness

[H205: 15 Oct 1927]

Other titles: "... Inverness," "Young William's Denial (Return)."

Source: John Thompson (Heatherlea Ave, Portstewart), learned from John Loughrey, hired servant of James Stewart (Kilgrain, Cloyfin, Coleraine) c. 1885.

Key C.

I am a brisk young sailor lad, just lately come
   ashore
To have some recreation and spend my gold in
   store,
Where there I spied a bonny wee lass all in a
   silken dress,
I heard her sigh as she passed by on the banks
   of the river Ness.

I stepp-ed up to this wee lass and unto her did
   say,
'Are you engaged to any young man? Come tell
   to me, I pray,
Are you engaged to any young man?' and she
   modestly answered, 'Yes,
To a sailor gay, but he's far away from the
   banks of the river Ness.'

'If you're engaged to this young man, come tell
   to me his name.'
'My true love's name is Willie, sure you all do
   know the same.
He has a mark on his left arm, besides a finger
   less,
And once he was a ploughboy gay on the banks
   of the river Ness.'

'If young Willie is your true love's name, it's him you'll ne'er see more,
For he is in cold irons bound upon thon western shore.'
'If he is in cold irons bound, I'll mourn for his distress,
And in deep despair she tore her hair on the banks of the river Ness.

It was when he saw her loyalty, he could no longer stand,
He showed the mark on his left arm, besides on his right hand,
She says, 'If you're my Willie dear, put off this tarry dress,
And put on your trousers and jacket blue on the banks of the river Ness.'

These couple they've got married, right well they do agree,
And since they are got married, he'll go no more to sea,
For they have money plenty for to relieve distress;
Blest be their lot in that sweet cot on the banks of the river Ness.

1.4: ... passed me by ... [Dt]
4.3: ... irons, I'll ... [Dt]

Jennie of the Moor

[H107: 28 Nov 1925; Laws N34]

Other titles: "(Sweet) Janie (Janey) (Jenny) (Ginny) ...."

Source: John Henry Macauley (Ballycastle), from a woman who learned it from a "basket woman" c. 1865.

Key G.

As I roved out for recreation down by the seaside,
The sun was gently rising, being decked in all his pride;
I espied a lovely fair one sitting by a cottage door
With roses blooming on her cheeks: 'twas Jennie of the moor.

I stood in contemplation as I viewed each charming scene,
Being filled with admiration as in some fairy dream,
Enchanted by this fair one as she walked along the shore,
She was gathering of the choice seaweed, was Jennie of the moor.

Says I, 'My fairest creature, how early do you rise?'
'I love to breathe the morning air when the lark soars in the skies.
Sweet's the spot to wander where breakers often roar
And wakes the bosom of the deep,' said Jennie of the moor.

We both sat down together by a pleasant shady side.
Says I, 'My dear, if you comply, I will make you my bride.
I have plenty at my own command brought from a foreign shore,
And proud the man that wins the hand of Jennie of the moor.'

'I have a true love of my own who long has been for me,
And true I'll be unto him while he is on the sea.'
The words were gently spoken as we walked along the shore,
'I'll wait on him till he returns,' said Jennie of the moor.

'If your true love's a sailor, come tell to me his name.'
'His name is Denis Reilly and from Newry town he came,
With laurels I'll entwine him when he returns on shore;
I will wait on him till he returns,' said Jennie of the moor.

'If Denis be your true love's name, I know him very well,
When fighting at the Alma, by an angry ball he fell,
Behold this true love token that upon his hand he wore.'
She fell and fainted in my arms, sweet Jennie of the moor.

'Since you have proved so true and kind, look up, dear girl,' he said,
'Behold, this is your Denis that is standing by your side,
Come, let us be united and live happy on the shore,
The bells will ring right merrily, I'll go to sea no more.'

Bordon's Grove

[H529: 20 Jan 1934]

Other titles: "Buren's ...," "Borland's Groves."

Source: (m, w) coll. J[ames] Moore, A.R.C.O. (Bushmills) from Andy M'Googan (Castlecatt), learned from his mother c. 1875.

[A broken-token ballad not noted by Laws.]

Key C.

It being down by Bordon's Grove, as I carelessly had strayed
For to hear the lamentation of a young and comely maid;
I boldly stepped up to her with compliments so kind,
'Och,' says I, 'my love and my beautiful dove, sure I wish that you were mine.'

'Hold off, hold off, young man,' she says, 'will you not me annoy?
Sure I mind the vow, I will stand it now, that I made my own dear boy,
To be true in Johnny's absence, right royal I'll remain,
For if ever we meet, we never will part on Bordon's Groves again.'

'What sort of lad was your Johnny, or what colour was his hair?''
'He's abroad in French Flanders, I'm sure you have been there,
He's abroad in French Flanders, where many's a youth did fall,
Och, my Johnny's got slightly wounded by the force of a cannon ball.'

Then she saw his true love's token that her Johnny always wore.
'You're welcome home, dear John,' she cried, 'with all your trials o'er;
You're welcome home, dear John,' she says, 'from all your grief and pain,
And since we have met we never will part from Bordon's Groves again.'

◆ C17 REFERENCES ◆

◆ The Banished Lover (H23) 307
Learmount Grove (H726) 307

IREL Shields 1981:130-1 (#57) "The Parish of Dunboe" cites another version in "Songs of the People" #287 (11 May 1929).

REC John, Eddie Butcher, EEOT *Shamrock* 2 cass. (A3) "The Parish of Dunboe"

◆ Mary Machree (H485) 308

BRS BPL H.80: (n.i.)

◆ James Reilly (H826) 309

Laws 1957:222 (N37) "John [George] Riley II [Young Riley]." Fowke 1973:210 suggests Laws's discussion of the various "Riley" ballads, pp. 172-83 in Beck 1962. Cazden 1958:115-6 mentions his classification in *Northern Junket* 4(7):29, (8):38, (9): 25; (10):31; and recommends (1982:107 and *Notes*) Robert H. Rennick's classification of 25 forms of the returned-lover ballad in *SFQ* 23,1960:215-32.

h: IREL Darley-McCall 1914:24
h: Joyce 1909:233-4 (#422) "When First I Came to the County Limerick"
h: "Songs of the People" No. 277 (2 March 1929)

h: BRIT Christie 2,1881:242-3
Greig 1907-11(1963): #138 "George Rylie"
Sing 5(4 Aug)1961:64 "John Riley"

AMER Cazden 1958,1:32-3
Grover n.d.:74 "George Riley," a fragmentary and much altered version.
Hubbard 1961:80-2 "John Riley I," 2 vts.
Kenedy 1890:103 with no happy ending
Thompson 1958:51-3 "George Reily"

BRS Harvard 1: 5.193 (Catnach), 6.182 (n.i.), 11.83 (Such)
Healy 4,1969:103-4 "Young Riley"
Come Let Us Sing 1974:54 "John Riley"

h: REC Cf. Eddie Butcher, Leader 2070 (B4) "Youghal Harbour," esp. stanzas 3-5.
Cf. Tríona ní Dhomhnaill, Gael Linn CEF 043 (B2) "As I Roved Out from the County Cavan"
Lucy Garrison, AFS 1504 B1 [Peggy Seeger]
Peggy Seeger, Folk-Lyric FL 114 [Peggy Seeger]
Pete Seeger, [lc:] Folkways FP 2 "John Riley"; [b:] Folkways FA 2003 (A1)

◆ The Banks of the Clyde
/ One Fine Summer's Morning (H812) 310

This does not seem to be related to either of the fragments in Sharp/Karpeles 1974,2:594-5 (#403).

White/Dean-Smith 1951
Cf. Laws 1957:219-20 (N32)
Brunnings 1981: "The Banks of the Clyde," "Faithful Nancy (One Fine Summer's Morning)"

IREL Moulden 1979:112-3

BRS BPL Irish: (Brereton)
BPL Libbie
Both BPL broadsides are called "William and Jane on the Banks of the Clyde."

◆ Mary Doyle
/ The Wreck of the Lady Shearbrooke (H570) 310

AMER Fowke 1981:79-81 "The Ship *Lady Sherbrooke* (... *Sherebrook*)"

REC Robert Walker, Folkways FE 4001 (B7) [Fowke]

◆ Laurel Hill / Kyle's Flowery Braes (H8) 311

h: IREL Moulden 1979:88-9 suggests this may be related to the Napoleonic ballads (e.g. Laws J3).
Shields 1981:112-3 (#46) (see also Butcher rec.)

h: REC Eddie Butcher, Outlet OAS 3007 (B6)

m: MEL Lizzie Higgins, Topic 12T 185 (A6)"Far ower the Forth," pipe tune from her father.

Sam Henry's Songs of the People

◊ **The Lady of the Lake** *(H765)* 312

  Laws 1957:224 (N41) "... [The Banks of Clyde]"
  Brunnings 1981: "... - Instrumentals," "... - One Evening as I Chanced to Stray"

  IREL Moulden 1979:79-80

  BRS UCLA 605: 4(n.i.) "... of Lak"

  ? cl: REC Emma Dusenbury, AFS 849 A1 "... o' ..."

  b: MEL Cazden 1955
     Hudson ms. 1:135

◊ **The Banks of Claudy** *(H5, H693)* 313

  White/Dean-Smith 1951: "(The) Claudy Banks"
  Dean-Smith 1954: "(The) Claudy Banks"
  Laws 1957:223-4 (N40)
  Brunnings 1981: "The Claudy Banks"

  IREL Bunting 1983:67-70 (#43), with text from the Henry collection.
  b: Morton 1970:3-4
     Morton 1973:134-5 "... Clady"
     O Lochlainn 1939:116-7 [Sharp/Karpeles]
     Shields/Shields *UF* 21,1975: #27

  BRIT Reeves 1958:70-1
  # Sharp/Karpeles 1974,1: 563-4 (#148)

  AMER Burton/Manning 1969:94 "Dark and Stormy Night"
     Creighton 1971:48-9 "... Claudie"
     Hubbard 1961:83 "John Riley II"
     Hudson/Herzog 1937:18 "... Claudie"
     Kenedy 1890:70

  BRS BPL H.80: (Pratt)
     BPL Irish: (n.i.)
     Harvard 1: 5.50 (Gilbert), 7.191 (Catnach), 9.20 (Bebbington)
     UCLA 605: 3(Such)
     Derry Journal [c. 1925],1:34
  b: *Guinness* n.d.
     Irish Fireside n.d.:15
     O'Conor 1901:38
     Songs and Recitations 3,1976:7
     Walton's New 2,1968:34
     Wehman's 1887,1:10

  REC Bob, Ron Copper, Leader LEAB 404 (4047, A3; LED 2067, A1) "Claudy Banks"
  cl: J. W. Green, AFS 2281 A2 "... Claudie"
     David Hammond, Donal Lunny, Greenhays/Sruthan GR 702 (B5)
     Fred Jordan, Topic 12TS 233 (A2)
     Margaret MacArthur, Living Folk F-LFR 100 (B5) "Banks of Florida"
     George Maynard, Topic 12T 286 (B4)
     Fred Redden, Folkways FM 4006 (A2)
  b: The Young Tradition, Transatlantic TRA 142 (B1)

  MEL Bunting 1840:33 (#43)
     O'Neill 1903:75 (#130)
     Petrie/Stanford 1,1902:107 (#s 422, 423) [Sharp/Karpeles]

◊ **The Banks of [the] Dee** *(H583)* 314

  g: This seems to be "The Banks of the Dee" from which the American ballad "The Banks of Champlain" (Huntington 1964:161-2) derived.
     There is another quite different song with the same title, for which see Johnson (1853)3: #516,
     Sturgis/Hughes 1919:14-5,
     Thompson 1939:337-8,
     Barrand *CD&S* 1981:25-7.

  l: It is also not the same song as "The Banks of the Dee" [The Old Miner] in, e.g., Lloyd 1967:265-6, of which the last refrain line is:

     "Aa can't get employment, for me hair it's turned grey."

  Brunnings 1981: "...," ?"Sands of Dee"

  BRS Harvard 1: 1.46 (n.i.), 4.53 (Gilbert)
     Harvard 3: (Walker)

◊ **The Mantle So Green** *(H76)* 314

  Laws 1957:222-3 (N38); for Laws's discussion of the various "Riley" ballads, Fowke (1973:210) cites pp. 172-83 in Beck 1962. Cazden (1958:115-6) also suggests his extended discussion in several issues of *Northern Junket* and (1982:107 and *Notes*) Robert H. Rennick's classification of 25 forms of the returned-lover ballad in *SFQ* 23,?1960:215-32.
  Brunnings 1981: "The Plains of Waterloo"
  Cazden et al. *Notes* 1982 #24 "Famed Waterloo"

  s: IREL Joyce 1909:151 (#325), 1 stanza and a similar melody.
     O Lochlainn 1939:14-5 [Sharp/Karpeles]

  # c: BRIT Sharp/Karpeles 1974,1: 565-8 (#149) "... of ..., or Famed Waterloo," 4 vts.

  AMER Cazden et al. 1982:112-3 "Famed Waterloo"
     E. Ives 1963:28-31
     Milner/Kaplan 1983:157-8

  BRS BPL Irish: (n.i.)
     Harvard 1: 7.40 (Ryle), 12.63 (Such)
     Harvard 3: (n.i.)
     UCLA 605: 3(Such) "... of ..."

  REC Robert Cinnamond, *FSB* 8 (B4) "Willie O'Reilly"; Topic 12T 269 (B6) "Young Willie Reilly"
  c: Ted Ashlaw, Philo 1022 (A1)
     Margaret Barry, Folkways FA 8729 (A1) "Her ..."; Topic 12T 123 (B5), Transatlantic XTRA 1090
  b: Paul Clayton, Tradition TLP 1005
     Marie Hare, Folk-Legacy FSC 9 (B5) "Round Her ..."; Folkways FM 4053 (A4)
     Cf. Barbara Moncure, Folkways FH 5311 (A3) "The Foggy Dew," which has a line about "her mantle of green."

  c: MEL Darley/McCall 1914:3 (#6)
     O'Neill 1903:62 (#357)

◊ **Johnny Jarmin / The Rainbow** *(H156)* 315

  Probably not: White/Dean-Smith 1951: "(The) *Rainbow*"
  Nor: Dean-Smith 1954: "(The) *Rainbow*"
  Laws 1957:225 (N43) "... German"
  Brunnings 1981: "Johnny Jarmanie"
  Cazden et al. *Notes* 1982: #23 "The *Rainbow*"

  AMER Cazden et al. 1982:110-11 "The *Rainbow*"

◊ **Mary and Willie** *(H118)* 315

  Dean-Smith 1954: "William and Mary"
  Laws 1957:217-8 (N28) "Willie and Mary (Little Mary; The Sailor's Bride)"
  Brunnings 1981: "...," "The Beggarman"

  BRIT Clements 1928:106-7
     TM #1, mid 1975:12 "William and Mary," "Little Mary the Sailor's Bride"

AMER Burton 1981:138-9 "As Willie and Mary Strolled by the Seashore"
  Grover n.d.:136-7 "William and Mary"
  Peters 1977:141-2 "Willie and Mary"

BRS Harvard 1: 1.98 (Jacques), 2.184 (Carbutt), 3.105 (Kendrew),
  4.36 (Walker), 7.44 (Catnach), 10.45 (Bebbington)
    Harvard 3: (Harkness)
    UCLA 605: 4(Such)

REC Freda Palmer, Topic 12T 254 (B8) "William and Mary"

◆ Lurgan Town (H563) 316

Not: the same title in Brunnings 1981

IREL Shields/Shields UF 21,1975: #383 "Sweet ..."
But not: O Lochlainn 1965:108-9

And not: REC Geordie Hanna, Eagrán MD 0002 (A3)

◆ The Broken Ring (H471) 317

White/Dean-Smith 1951: "(The) Young and Single Sailor"
Dean-Smith 1954: "... Token; The Young and Single Sailor; All in a Garden Green"
Laws 1957:224-5 (N42) "Pretty Fair Maid (The Maiden in the Garden; ... Token)"
Brunnings 1981: "John Riley"
Cazden et al. Notes 1982: #22 "Johnny Riley"

Fowke 1973:210 suggests Laws's discussion of the various "Riley" ballads, pp. 172-83 in Beck 1962. Cazden 1958:115-6 mentions his classification in Northern Junket 4(7):29, (8):38, (9):25; (10):31; and recommends (1982:107 and Notes) Robert H. Rennick's classification of 25 forms of the returned-lover ballad in SFQ 23,?1960:215-32.

h: IREL Hughes 4,1936:63-5 "A Young Maid Stood in Her Father's Garden"
  S. O'Boyle 1977:34 "A Lady Fair"
h: O Lochlainn 1939:4-5
Shields 1981:110-1 (#45) "A Lady Walked in Her Father's Garden"
  Shields/Shields UF 21,1975: #356 "Seven Years Since I Had a Sweetheart"

BRIT MacColl/Seeger 1977:128-33 (#27) "The Sailor's Return," 3 vts. ("The Brisk Young Sailor," "In a Garden a Lady Walking," "Seven Long Years")
  Cf. Palmer 1979b:180 "The Dark-Eyed Sailor"
Sharp/Karpeles 1974,1:552-5 (#144) "... Token, or The Young and Single Sailor" [MacColl/Seeger]

AMER Bush 3,1975:81-4 "A Pretty Fair Maid in the Garden," "A Pretty Fair Damsel"
  Cazden et al. 1982:108-9 "Johnny Riley"
  Cf. Cheney et al. 1976:123
  Milner/Kaplan 1983:101 "A Lady Fair"
  Peterson 1931:12
Randolph/Cohen (1982):97-9 "The Maiden in the Garden"
  Smith/Rufty 1930:65-6 "A Pretty Fair Miss"
  Vincent 1932:62-3

BRS Harvard 3: (Harkness)
  Songs and Recitations 5,1978:39-40 "A Fair Young Maid All in a Garden"

? cl: REC Evella Adams, AFS 2790 A2 "Neat Fair Girl"
? cl: Finley Adams, AFS 2774 A3 "Neat Fair Girl Walked in a Garden"

c: Joan Baez, Vanguard VRS 9078 "John Riley"
  Roy Bailey, Trailer LER 3021 (A6) "A Fair Maid Walking"
  John P. Baushears, Louisiana Folklore Society LFS 1201 [Fowke]
cl: Sewanee Begley, AFS 1455 A1 "Pretty Fair Lady Was Walking in Her Garden"
cl: G. W. Blevins, AFS 2763 A1 "Pretty Fair Damsel"
cl: Nancy Boggs, AFS 1382 A1 "Pretty Fair Maiden All in Her Garden"
cl: Mrs C. A. Burkett, AFS 838 B1 "Pretty Fair Maid"
cl: Mary Fuller Cain, AFS 2820 B2 "Pretty Fair Miss"
? b: William Clauson, Capitol P 8539 "The Sailor's Return"
  Elizabeth Cronin, Collector 1201 [Fowke]
cl: Rachel Davis, AFS 983 B2 "A Pretty Fair Miss in the Garden"
cl: Emma Dusenbury, AFS 863 B3 "Pretty Fair Miss in the Garden"
? Lester Flatt, Earl Scruggs, Harmony 30932 "The Sailor's Return"
  The Flying Cloud, Adelphi AD 1029 [Milner/Kaplan]
? Bob Gibson, Riverside RS 97542 "John Riley"
cl: Mrs G. A. Griffin, AFS 976 B2 "A Pretty Fair Miss"
  Sarah Hawkes, Asch 3831 (A2) "Returning Soldier"
  Roscoe Holcomb, Folkways FA 2368 (A7) "Fair Miss in the Garden"
? b: Burl Ives, Decca DL 8125 "The Sailor's Return"
cl: W. M. Keene, AFS 1472 "A Fair Young Lady Was Walking in Her Garden"
? John Langstaff, Tradition TLP 1009 "John Riley"
  Maud Long, AAFS L21 (B3) "... Token"
cl: Bascom Lamar Lunsford, AFS 1789 B1 "Pretty Fair Miss"
  Shanna Beth McGee, Folkways FW 8779 (B4) "John Riley"
Cf. John Maguire, Leader LEE 4062 (B6) "Lovely Jane from Enniskillen"
  Sarah Makem, Topic 12T 182 (B4) "A Servant Maid in Her Father's Garden" [she sings "master's garden"]
  New Lost City Ramblers with Cousin Emmy, Folkways FTS 31015 (A4) "Pretty Little Miss out in the Garden"
  Sarah Anne O'Neill, Topic 12TS 372 (B2) "A Fair Young Maid in Her Father's Garden"
? b: Our Singing Heritage, Vol. 1, EKL 151 "John Riley"
? b: Diane Oxner, Rodeo RLP 6 "The Broken Ring"
Cf. Hattie Presnell, Folk-Legacy FSA 23 (A6) "William Hall"
? b: Obray Ramsey, Prestige/Int. 13030 "Pretty Fair Miss"
? Jean Ritchie, Prestige/Folklore 13003 (A9) "A Pretty Fair Miss"; Collector 1201 [Fowke]
  Jeannie Robertson, Riverside RLP 12 6333 [Fowke]
? Peggy Seeger, [b:] Prestige/Int. 13061 "A Pretty Fair Maid"; Prestige 7375 (D6) "Pretty Fair Maid"
cl: Mary Sullivan, AFS 4115 B "Pretty Fair Maid"
cl: Hettie Swindel, AFS 2815 A1 "Pretty Fair Miss"
  Mrs William Towns, Folkways FM 4005 (B3) "A Fair Maid Walked in Her Father's Garden"
cl: Mrs Callie Vaughan, AFS 2940 B1 "Fair Maid All in the Garden"
  Doug Wallin, Home Made Music LP 003 "Pretty Fair Miss out in Her Garden"
  Rita Weill, Takoma A 1022 (A3) "Pretty Fair Damsel in the Garden"; cf. (A2) "William Hall"
cl: Mrs Ewart Wilson, AFS 2863 A2 "Pretty Fair Miss"

◆ Green Garden (H818) 317

Brunnings 1981: "The Young and Single Sailor (See: John Riley)"

Sam Henry's Songs of the People

◇ The Dark-Eyed Sailor *(H232) 318*

White/Dean-Smith 1951: "Fair Phoebe and Her ..."
Dean-Smith 1954: "...; Fair Phoebe and Her ..."
Laws 1957:221 (N35) "... (Fair Phoebe and Her ...)"
Brunnings 1981

s: IREL Galwey 1910:11, 28 (#1)
lw: O Lochlainn 1934 [1946]:10

BRIT MacColl/Seeger 1977:126-8 (#26) ("The Brisk Young Sailor")
Sing 9(2,Jun)1966(#55):26

AMER Darling 1983:127-9 (see Clayton rec.)
Grover n.d.:48-9
Huntington 1964:120-22
Manny/Wilson 1968:230-1

BRS BPL Partridge: 1.48 (Wrigley)
Harvard 1: 2.24 (Livsey), 2.177 (Jacques), 3.158 (Forth), 6.126 (Cadman), 7.92 (Catnach), 9.70 (Bebbington), 11.2 (Such)
UCLA 605: 4(Such) "Fair Phoebe and her ..."
Healy 1967a:17-9 "The Sailor and His Love"

b: REC George Belton, EFDSS LP 1008 (B3)
Paul Clayton, Folkways FW 8708 (A9)
cl: Pat Ford, AFS 4206 B1
Fred Jordan, Topic 12T 150 (A6)
b: Lou, Sally Killen, Front Hall FHR 06 (A2)
Christy Moore, Tara 2008 (A2)
Andy O'Brien, Green Linnet SIF 1016 (B3)
cl: Leon Ponce, AFS 3364 B2
Walter Pardon, Leader LED 2063 (B1)
Tony Rose, Dingle's DIN 324 (B5)
Peggy Seeger, [b:] Prestige/Int. 13061 "The Dark-Eyed Sailor"; [b:] Prestige 7375 (2 recs.) (C5) "The Dark-Eyed Sailor"
Phil Tanner, EFDSS LP 1005 (B1) "Fair Phoebe and the ..."

◇ The Love Token *(H581) 318*

Laws 1957:218 (N29) "A Seaman and His Love (The Welcome Sailor)"
Brunnings 1981: "The Welcome Sailor," "Down by the Seaside (Broken Ring Song)," "Down by the Seaside - A Maiden Sat Weeping"; cf. "Jimmy and Nancy - As Beautiful Nancy Was A-Walking One Day"

AMER Grover n.d.:80-1 "Down by the Seaside"
Peacock 1965,2:530-1 "Jimmy and Nancy (The return)," 2 vts.

BRS Harvard 1: 13.58 (Such)
Roxburghe, 2 versions: Laws notes one, 3:127-31 "A Seaman and His Love"; the other is 7:518-9 "A Seaman's Happy Return to His Love."
UCLA 605: 5(Pitts) "The Welcome Sailor"
Cf. Ashton 1891:214-5 "The Welcome Sailor"

REC Warde Ford, Folkways FE 4001 (A7) "The Nightingales of Spring"
Lal, Norma Waterson, Topic 12TS 331 (A4) "The Welcome Sailor"

◇ The Pride of Glencoe *(H655) 319*

Laws 1957:223 (N39) "MacDonald's Return to Glencoe"
Brunnings 1981: "The Banks of Glenco/e"
Cazden et al. *Notes* 1982: #25 "Glencoe"

IREL Shields/Shields *UF* 21,1975:#325

BRIT MacColl/Seeger 1977:133-6 "MacDonald's Return to ..."; cf. "The Lass o' ..."

AMER Cazden et al. 1982:113-5 "Glencoe"
Fowke 1981:67-8 "... (... Glenco)" also reports 4 other versions in her collection and 4 more in the Archives of the National Museum of Canada Centre for Folk Culture Studies.

BRS BPL Partridge: 2.470 (Partridge)
Harvard 1: 7.118 (Catnach), 9.119 (Bebbington), 11.108 (Such)
Harvard 3: (Hodges)
UCLA 605: 4(Walker) "Donald's Return to ..."; 5(Such) "Donald's Return to ..."
c: *Wehman's Irish* #2:21-2

cl: REC Louis Brideup, AFS 2306 A2, 2306 B1
Lotus Dickey, Audio Village cass. (B2)
cl: J. W. Green, AFS 2297 B2, 2298 A1 & A2
? cl: George Vinton Graham, AFS 3815 B1 & 2 "The Maid of ..."
Lizzie Higgins, Topic 12TS 260 (A5) "MacDonald of ..." [Fowke]
cl: Ben Rice, AFS 3223 A1 "McDonald of ..."
Sheila Stewart, Topic 12T 179 (B6) "Donald's Return to ..."
Peta Webb, Topic 12TS 223

MEL *JFSS* 2(7)[1905]:171 [Laws]
Petrie/Stanford 2,1902:170 (#677) "Glencoe" [Bronson]

◇ The Banks of the River Ness *(H205) 319*

Brunnings 1981: "... Inverness"

BRIT Greig 1907-11(1963): #153 "Young William's Denial," with a strange stanza in which the girl says that she took her uncle's life for her William's sake (perhaps an intrusion from "The Banks of Dundee [Laws M25].")

AMER Grover n.d.:54-5 "The Banks of the Inverness," quite a different version.

BRS Harvard 3: (Catnach) or "Young William's Return"

b: REC John Leahy, Prestige/Int. 25014 (A11) "... Inverness"

◇ Jennie of the Moor *(H107) 320*

Dean-Smith 1954: "Jenny of ..."
Laws 1957:220 (N34) "Janie of ..."
Brunnings 1981: "Sweet Jenny of ..."

IREL O Lochlainn 1965:116-7 "Sweet ..." [Fowke]

BRIT Reeves 1958:235 "Sweet Jenny of ...," "example of literary or sophisticated pieces adapted into the popular repertoire."

AMER Fowke 1981:70-1 "Sweet Jinny on the ... (... Mor)"

AUST *AT* #17(Sep)1968:9 "Ginny..." (see MacDonald rec.)

BRS BPL Partridge: 2.743 (Partridge)
617 [190-?]:49 "Sweet ..."

REC Simon MacDonald, Wattle Archives Series 2 [Fowke]

◇ Bordon's Grove *(H529) 320*

Brunnings 1981: "Borland's Groves"

AMER Creighton 1971:33 "Buren's Grove," a fragment "too short to say that it is the same with any certainty."

324

C18

In man's array: Disguises

Sam Henry's Songs of the People

The Drummer Maid [H497: 10 Jun 1933]

Other titles: "The Female Drummer (Soldier) (Warrior)," "I'll Beat the Drum Again," "The Pretty Drummer Boy," "The Soldier Maid," "When I Was a Fair Maid."

Source: Mrs Pat Hackett (Stone Row, Coleraine), learned in her girlhood (Ballywillan, near Portrush).

Key G.

When I was a maid about the age of sixteen,
I dressed as a man and took the shilling from the king,
I listed on the army and a drummer I became,
And I learned for to bate upon the rub-a-dub again.

My hat, cockade and feather, if you had them seen,
You would have cursed and swore that a man I had been,
The place that I went was to keep guard on a tower,
Where I might have been a maid to this very day and hour.

A young lady fell in love with me and told I was a maid,
And to my head officer my secret she betrayed,
My head officer sent for me to see if it was true,
'If that's what you ask of me, I can't deny of you.'

My officer he smiled and this to me he said,
'It's a pity we should lose such a drummer as you made,
It's now for human courage at the siege of Valenciennes,
A bounty we'll bestow on you, my girl, from the king.'

She got the king's bounty, and soon this charming maid
Was married to a young man whose heart on her was stayed,
And now she's got a husband and a drummer he's became,
And she's learned him to bate upon the rub-a-dub again.

326   1.4: bate = beat[en].

On Board of a Man-of-War [H556: 28 Jul 1934]

Other titles: cf. "The British ...," "Young Susan."

Source: (w, m) (in smiddy, Ballyvoy, Co. Antrim).

Key C.

As I roved out one evening in the springtime of the year,
I overheard a maid complain for the losing of her dear,
She says, 'I'm sore tormented and troubled in my mind,
Since my true love has gone to sea, no comfort can I find.

'My love's a gallant young man, dressed up in sailor's clothes,
My love's a gallant young man, his cheeks are like the rose,
He has two bright eyes like diamonds and they shine like any star,
And with my true love I'll sail the seas on board of a man-of-war.

''Twas on a Tuesday evening when we both went out to walk,
I really thought my heart would break when he began to talk,
He clasped his hands around my waist, so loving and so kind,
Says he, "Fair maid, be not afraid, for I won't leave you behind."'

Early the next morning this fair maid she arose,
She dressed herself in sailor's clothes from very top to toes
And bargained with the captain her passage to go free,
For seven years to sail the seas, a cabin boy to be.

We sailed the seas for seven years through stormy wind and cold,
But she dearly loved the sailor lad more better than land or gold,
But now she has returned to enjoy her darling swain,
And she bids adieu forevermore unto the raging main.

The Drum Major [H797: 4 Mar 1939]

Other titles: "(The) (Pretty) Drummer-Boy,"
"The Famous Woman Drummer."

Source: 2: Mrs Joseph Henry (Drumlee, Finvoy)
from her father "when he was weaving at the linen
trade"; James Carmichael (Waring St, Ballymena).

s: In response to advertised request, versions of
this very old song have been received from Mrs
[Henry and Mr Carmichael], both of whom are
cordially thanked.

Key G.

Come all you young fellows and bachelors too,
A comical story I'll tell unto you
Concerning a fair maid who carried a drum,
Who in search of her true love to Holland has gone.

Ladlie toor an ti a.

She enlisted voluntarily in a regiment of foot,
And being our drum major, great honour she got,
She acted so manly in every degree
That no one e'er took her a girl for to be.

She went down to bathe in a river so clear,
When a jolly young rifleman chanced to draw near,
He cried, as she parted the waves like a swan,
'Though your clothes are a soldier's, you are not a man.'

Then out of the water she quickly did run,
And with her small fingers her clothes she pinned on,
Saying, 'It's not for your gold, sir, that I listed here,
But for the sake of young Shelton, the bold grenadier.'

'Call on the sergeant and officers all,
Call on this fair maid'; they on her did call:
'You are a woman, this day we do hear,
And the cause of your listing we fain now would hear.'

'These seven long years in your regiment I've been,
Still hiding the face of a poor wounded dame;
It's not for your gold that I'm listed here,
I'm in search of young Shelton, the bold grenadier.'

'Call on the sergeant and officers all,
Call on young Shelton'; they on him did call,
They say, 'Here is a letter from your true love this day,
And to your drum major the postage you'll pay.'

'Give me the letter,' young Shelton did say,
'Give me the letter, the postage I'll pay.'
With a tear in her eye, the drum major did stand
Saying, 'Read me all over, for I'm just the one.'

Then he clasped her in his arms and embraced for a while,
Till at length this young damsel began for to smile,
And now they are married, the truth for to tell,
And our gallant drum major pleases young Shelton well.

The Female Highwayman

[H35: "A song from the English plantation of Ulster,"
12 Jun 1924]

k: "Silvy"; g: "Wexford City." Other titles:
"Gold Watch and Chain," "Nelly Ray," "Sovay(,
Sovay) ...," "Sovie, Sovie," "Sylvia's Request
and William's Denial," "(Pretty) Sylvia (Rode out
One Day)."

Source: (w, m) daughter of late Daniel Watton
(Ballyhome, Ballywillan).

s: [Dt] A song of English origin.... [Bp] It is
remarkable that this version is superior and more
complete than that collected by a folk-song
expert in England.

Key E. Slow.

Silvy, Silvy, all on a day,
She dressed herself in man's array,
With sword and pistol down by her side,
To meet her true love away did ride.

She met her true love all in the plain,
She stepped up to him and bid him stand:
'Stand and deliver unto me,' she said,
'Or in a moment your life I'll have.'

Sam Henry's Songs of the People

He gave her all his gold and store,
But still she said, 'There is one thing more:
A diamond ring, sir, I saw you wear,
Make haste and give it, and your life I'll spare.'

'This diamond ring is a pledge of love,
My life I'll lose before the ring I'll give.'
She being tender-hearted, just like a dove,
She turned round and left her love.

But one day after, these two were seen
Walking together in the garden green.
He spied the guard hang by her clothes,
Which made him blush like any rose.

'What makes you blush at so silly a thing?
I fain would have had your diamond ring;
It was I who robbed you down on the plain,
So here's your watch and gold again.

'And the reason why that I tried you so
Was to see whether you were a man or no,
But now I'm convinced all in my mind,
So heart and hand, love, are truly thine.'

2.4: ... your blood you'll shed.' [Dt]
3.1: ... gold in store, [Dt]
4.4: She turn-ed round ... [Dt]
5.2: Walking together on ... [Dt]

The Squire's Bride

[H524: 16 Dec 1933; Laws N20]

s: (m) "John McAnanty's Courtship"; k: "The Golden Glove." Other titles: "(The) (My) Dog and (the) (My) Gun," "The Farmer and His Bride," "Off She Went Hunting," "The Squire of Tamworth," "Waistcoat and Britches," "The Wealthy Squire," "With Her (My) Dog and (Her) (My) Gun."

Source: (w) man (Moyarget, Ballycastle), in his family for 3 generations.

s: [The contributor] said it was as old as "Methusalum".... He had no air for it, so it has been set to an appropriate old folk-air....

Key G.

The day was appointed, the knot to be tied,
The young farmer chosen to give him his bride,
But as soon as the lady the farmer did spy,
Her heart was inflamed: 'O, my heart!' she did cry.

Instead of being married, she went to her bed,
The thoughts of the farmer ran so in her head,
The thoughts of the farmer ran so in her mind,
A way for to get him she quickly did find.

She early next morning men's small-clothes put on
And she went a-hunting with her dog and gun,
She hunted all round where the farmer did dwell
Because in her heart she loved him so well.

Oftimes she did fire, but nothing did kill,
At length the young farmer came into the field,
And for to discourse him it was her intent,
With her dog and her gun to meet him she went.

'I thought you'd have been to the wedding,' she cried,
'To wait on the squire and give him his bride.'
'Oh, no,' said the farmer, 'since the truth I must tell,
I won't give her away, for I love her too well.'

'And what if the lady would grant you her love?
Ay, and the young squire your rival would prove?'
'Oh, no,' said the farmer, 'I'll take sword in hand,
If valour can gain her, quite fearless I'll stand.'

The lady was glad to hear him so bold,
She gave him a glove all clouded with gold
And told him she found it as she came along,
As she was a-hunting with her dog and gun.

The lady's gone home with her heart full of love,
She gave out a speech that she had lost her glove,
'And he that does find it and brings it to me,
The man that does find it, his bride I will be.'

The next morning early, the farmer arose
And dressed himself up in the finest of clothes;
He said, 'Honoured lady, I've picked up your glove,
Will you be so kind as to grant me your love?'

'It's already granted,' the lady replied,
'I love the sweet breath of a farmer,' she cried,
'I'll pride in my dairy and milking my cows
While my jolly farmer will sing as he ploughs.'

When the wedding was over, she told them the fun,
How the farmer she gained with her dog and her gun,
'And since I have got him so fast in my snare,
I'll love him forever, I vow and declare.'

3.1: small-clothes = knee-breeches. [s]

Lovely Annie (II)

[H166: 15 Jan 1927; Laws N14, "Polly Oliver"]

k: "Polly Oliver"; g: "Pretty Polly (Like a Trooper Did Ride)." Other titles: "(Pretty) Billy (Polly) Oliver's Rambles," "The Maids Resolution to Follow Her Love," "Young William."

Source: Alexander Wallace (Moneycannon, Ballymoney), learned from his brother William [Wallace], from his grandfather, William Wallace, known as "Dancing Wallace," born 1815 (Slaveney).

Key D.

Once in old England lovely Annie did dwell,
She was courted by a sea-captain who loved her
  right well,
But when that her parents they came for to
  hear,
They banished lovely Annie many miles from her
  dear.

One night as lovely Annie on her bed lay down,
The thoughts of her true love came into her
  mind,
Neither father nor mother to her mind doth
  adhere,
'I will dress like a soldier and go follow my
  dear.'

She went into the stable, viewed the horses all
  round,
She picked the one that was fit for the ground,
With a case of bright pistols, broad sword by
  her side,
In search of her true love, lovely Annie did
  ride.

She rode all alone to the bridge of renown,
She then pulled up at the cross of the town;
The first one came up was a bold English
  knight,
And the second came up was lovely Annie's
  delight.

She handed him a letter and then dropped him a
  tear,
Saying, 'This is a letter from Annie, your dear,
And under the sealing ten shillings you'll find,
That you and your true love might drink
  Annie's health round.'

The supper was over, he hung down his head,
He asked for a candle to light him to bed;
'My bed it is upstairs where I lie at my ease,
You can lie at my side, countryman, if you
  please.'

'To lie with a captain it would be a bold thing,
And me a poor soldier just serving my king,
Serving my king on sea, land or shore.'
'Here's a health to lovely Annie, she's the girl I
  adore.'

It being early the next morning, this fair maid
  arose,
And dressing herself in her own native clothes,
And going downstairs, she appeared like a
  dove:
'Here's a health to lovely Annie, she's the girl
  I do love.'

So these couple got married and now dwell at
  their ease,
Go out in the morning and come in when they
  please;
Now she has gone, left her old parents to
  mourn,
And five hundred is awaiting lovely Annie's
  return.

1.3: ... came to hear, [Dt]

The Rich Merchant's Daughter

[H108a: 5 Dec 1925; Laws N6]

Other titles: "The Constant Lovers," "Disguised
Sailor," "In Fair London City," "The Farmer's
Daughter," "It's of an Old Lord," "The Lady of
Riches," "In London Fair City," "The Merchant's
Daughter and Her Sailor," "The (Rich) Old Miser," "The Press Gang," "The (Rich) Merchant's
Daughter," "The Sailor's (Misfortune and) Happy
Marriage," "There Was a Rich Merchant."

Source: (m, w) "an octogenarian" (Magilligan).

Key C.

There was a rich merchant in London did dwell,
He had one fair daughter, few could her excel;
Rich lords came to court her, she slighted them
  all,
For she loved the sailor who was proper and tall.

Till at length was discovered by one of the men
That he saw a sailor of late coming in;
'Hold, hold,' said her father, 'we soon will them
  part,
And if she proves loyal it's not from my heart.'

He call-ed his daughter with an angry frown,
'Can you not get better matches of fame and
  renown?
Can you not get better matches, your arms to
  embrace
Than to wed with a sailor your friends to
  disgrace?'

'Oh no, my dear father, your pardon I crave,
There's none in this world but the sailor I'll
  have,

Sam Henry's Songs of the People

That sailor is Willie, the lad I adore,
Indeed, I'll go with him where the loud cannons
    roar.'

He says, 'My dearest daughter, since it's fell to
    your lot,
So wed with your sailor, I'll hinder you not.
Get married in private and talk not of me,
And when it is over we'll kindly agree.'

As this couple was walking down to the church
    door,
The press gang they met him, about half a score,
They took him a prisoner and they bore him
    away --
Instead of great joy it proved a sorrowful day.

This lady she dressed in a suit of men's clothes
And straight to the captain she instantly goes,
She agreed with the captain and it fell to her lot
To be a messmate of Willie's, though he knew her
    not.

As the lady and the sailor was crossing the deep,
Said the lady to the sailor, 'It's why do you
    weep?'
'I once had a sweetheart,' the sailor did say,
'And by her cruel parents I was sent away.'

'I am an extrolinger reared to my pen,
Extrolinger books I peruse now and then.
If you tell me your age, I will cast up your lot
To know if you gain this fair lady or not.'

He told her his age and the hour of his birth.
She says, 'You were born for great joy and
    mirth,
They done their endeavour to prove your
    downfall,
But I am your Polly in spite of them all.'

This couple's got married among the ship's crew.
You may say she proved loyal, both constant
    and true;
It's they are safe landed on famed Britain's
    shore,
Saying 'A fig for your father,' what could he do
    more?

11.3: If ... [Dt]

9.1: extrolinger = astrologer. [s]

The Sailor on the Sea [H203: 1 Oct 1927]

Other titles: "In London so Fair," "The Ship
That I Command," "Up in London Fair."

Source: John Thompson (Heatherlea Ave, Portstewart).

Key C.

It was in London fair that a lady, she lived
    there,
This lady was of beauty and delight;
When unto this lady gay I became a servant
    maid,
And in me she took great delight.

She has one only son, of beauty, birth was
    born,
Although he was a sailor on the sea,
And he courted this fair maid till he had her
    heart betrayed,
And then he was bound for the sea.

It happened to be in a bedroom where she lay,
That the tears from her cheeks at morn did
    flow,
Saying, 'Are you going away from me to ever
    stay
And leave me on the shores for to mourn?'

'Oh no, oh no,' says he, 'such things will
    never be
For as long as I'm a sailor on the sea,
And the ship that I command, may she never
    reach the land,
If ever I prove false, love, unto thee.'

Her long yellow hair, it hung down in ringlets
    fair,
To cut them off she thought no one would
    know;
The next morning she arose, dressed herself in
    sailor's clothes
And straightaway to the captain she over did
    go.

She was both neat and trim, complete in every
    limb,
And the clothes she wore, they fitted her so
    well,
As she gazed among the crew, then the captain
    near her drew,
And he says, 'Young man, have you ever been
    to sea?'

'Oh no, kind sir,' says she, 'I have never been
    to sea,
But take me as a young sailor bold,
For I do mean to go where the stormy winds do
    blow,
And it's neither for your money nor fine
    clothes.'

So it happened on a time when the crew was
    drinking wine
That the tears from the captain's eyes did flow,
Saying, 'You're like a lover of mine I remember
    many's a time
That I left upon the shore for to mourn.'

'Oh no, oh no,' says she, 'such things can never be
For as long as I'm a sailor on the sea,
And the ship that I command, may she never reach the land
If ever I prove false, love, unto thee.'

The captain knew his own dear words, for they still ran in his mind,
And he flew into her arms like a dove,
Saying, 'Since you have ventured here, love, all for the sake of me,
It's married then, oh, married we shall be.'

They called for a boy and they called for a girl,
And they called on a clergyman as well,
So their marriage lines were wrote and these couple married got,
And now they live happy on the sea.

4.4: ... love, to thee. [Dt]
5.3: Next morning ... [Dt]
 .4: ... straightway ... she did go. [Dt]
9.4: ... love, to thee. [Dt]

The True Lovers' Departure

[H584: 9 Feb 1935; Laws N15]

m: "The Simple Ploughboy" (coll. Baring-Gould). Other titles: "The Damsel Disguised," "The Noble Duke," "(The) Pretty Ploughboy."

Source: (w, m) John Wilkinson (employee, Old Bushmills Distillery; native, Liscolman).

s: ... The last two lines of verse six are sung to the last two lines of the air. Verse 5 describes a subterfuge by which the lovers eloped.

Key D.

Come all you loyal lovers that's locked in Cupid's chain,
Till I tell you of a couple that sported on yon plain,
She with her true love Willie as they did sport and play,
The press-guards came upon them and pressed her love away.

'I'll dress myself in a scarlet robe, put a broad star on my breast,'
She says, 'I'll kill the captain if he does me mislist,

My life I'll freely venture for this bold hero brave,
Intending to become his wife, or the seas to be my grave.'

But when she got unto the quay the ship was at full sail,
She waved unto the captain to turn her back again.
The captain came with heart and hand this noble youth to see,
Still thinking he was coming on board, commander for to be.

And when she got him to the quay, she locked him in a shed,
And she began to inquire at him if he knew such a maid;
When he heard his true love's name, the tears came down like rain,
She says, 'Hold your tongue, my darling, for I'm the very same.'

Betwixt her love and duty she dragg-ed him along;
She says, 'I will confine you in some prison strong,
You robbed me of my stores,' she said, 'I'll try you for your life.'
He says, 'Good my lord, I ne'er robbed in all my life.'

Then with ten thousand kisses and with ten thousand charms,
And with as many more he embraced her his arms.
'What brought you to the seas, my girl, to venture your sweet life?'
'I'll venture life and fortune all for to be your wife.'
'What brought you to the seas, my girl, to venture your sweet life?'
And off to church they marched and he made her his wife.

The Jolly Ploughboy

[H105: 14 Nov 1925; Laws M24]

g: "Little Ploughing Boy"; k: "The Pretty Ploughboy." Other titles: "As Jack the ..." "In Fair London City," "Ploughboys' Song," "The Ploughman's Glory," "The (Poor) (Pretty) (Simple) Ploughboy (Ploughing Boy) (Plowboy)"; cf. "Wounded Farmer's Son," "The Pretty Factory Boy."

s: This well-known song has been collected from many parts of the British Isles. The version printed here ... is worth recording for the sweetness of the air, and because it differs from the versions published by Joyce, Cecil Sharp, and others.

Key G.

Sam Henry's Songs of the People

There was a jolly ploughboy was ploughing up
  his land
With his horses in good order to keep,
He whistled and he sang as the plough she
  jogged along,
His intention was to court a pretty maid,
  A pretty maid,
  His intention was to court a pretty maid.

He ended his song as the plough she jogged
  along,
Saying, 'This fair maid's far above my degree,
If her parents they would know, they would
  prove my overthrow,
And the first place they would send me is the
  sea,
  To the sea, ...

When her old father knew she was courted on the
  plain,
He vowed he would send him o'er the sea,
A press gang then arose and he sent my love on
  board,
And he sent him to the war to be slain,
  To be slain, ...

She dressed herself up in a suit of men's clothes,
Her pockets well lined with bright gold,
As she walked up the street with her red rosy
  cheeks,
She acted as a young soldier bold,
  Soldier bold, ...

The first one she met was the captain of the ship,
And unto him she told all her woe,
Saying, 'They took from me my joy and my
  darling ploughboy,
And they sent him to the war to be slain,
  To be slain, ...'

She pulled out a purse of the bright shining
  gold:
'Here's fifty bright guineas and more,'
And she freely laid it down for her bonny
  ploughboy
And she got the young man she adored,
  She adored, ...

Now happy are these lovers whenever they do
  meet,
Their troubles will soon be all o'er,

And she taught the bells to ring and so sweetly
  she did sing
As she rowed him in her arms to the shore,
  To the shore, ...

Blythe and Bonny Scotland / [Dt] India's Burning Sands

[H120: 27 Feb 1926; Laws N2]

s: "Bonny Scottish Mary," "The New Recruit";
k: "The Village Pride." Other titles: "In Bonny
Scotland," "The Miracle Flower," "The Paisley Officer," "The Village Maid"; cf. "The Indian War."

Source: composite "best of" 6+: Mrs Thomas H.
Campbell (Drumlee, Finvoy); Mrs Tom Carmichael (Polintamney, Ballymoney); William Cassidy
(Vow, Bendooragh); Mrs James Fleming (Drumfin, Ballymena; Agnes M'Neill (Letterloan, Macosquin); James Spence (Portstewart).

Key G.

In blythe and bonny Scotland, where the
  bluebells sweetly grow,
There dwelt a fair and comely maid down in yon
  valley low,
And all day long she herded sheep down by the
  banks of Clyde,
And although her lot in life was low, she was
  called the village pride.

An officer from Paisley town went out to fowl one
  day
And wandered through these lonesome shades
  where Mary's cottage lay,
And often he came back that way, each time a
  visit paid,
His flattering tongue soon won the heart of that
  sweet village maid.

A long and loving look he took upon that form so
  fair,
And he wondered much so bright a flower should
  grow and flourish there,
And oft they would together walk through many
  a hill and dale,
Yet never deemed how love could steal those
  gentle hours away.

At length he came one morning fair, his face was
  dark with woe,
'Oh, Mary dear,' it's Henry says, 'from you I
  now must go,

The young recruits have got the rout, and I to
  duty yield,
I must forsake your lowland glens for India's
  burning field.'

'Oh Henry, lovely Henry, how can you from me
  part?
But take me as your wedded wife, you know
  you've won my heart,
Where green woods grow and valleys low, you
  were my heart's desire,
And as your servant I will go, disguised in man's
  attire.'

He brought her on to Paisley town, and much
  they wondered there
To see that young recruit that looked so gentle,
  slight and fair;
The ladies all admired her as she stood there on
  parade,
But little they knew a soldier's cloak concealed a
  lovely maid.

They soon crossed o'er the raging seas to India's
  burning lands,
No pen can tell what Mary bore through India's
  trackless sands,
But as she fought, her strength gave out, her
  woe she strove to hide
By smiling when she turned around to Henry by
  her side.

She saw her lover was cut down, a spear had
  pierced his side,
And from his post he never flinched, but where
  he stood he died;
She raised him from his bleeding gore and in her
  arms him pressed,
But as she strove to quench his wounds, a ball
  passed through her breast.

And as those couple lived in life, in death they
  loved the same,
And as their fond hearts' blood ran cold, it
  mixed in one red stream.
True love like this is hard to find, it is so true
  and strong,
She left her friends in the lowland glen, gone
  never to return.

Canada[,] Hi! Ho!

[H162: 18 Dec 1926; cf. Laws C17]

o: (m) "Skibbereen." Other titles: "Caledonia,"
"(The) Wearing of the Blue"; cf. "Canada(y)-i-o
(I.O.)," "Canadee-i-o (-I-O)," "Colley's Run-i-
o," "The Jolly Lumbermen," "Michigan-i-o."

[Bp] Source: (w, m) 2: Hugh Murray (Managher,
Drumcroon, Coleraine); Mary Ann Wilson, pensioner (Loguestown, Coleraine), learned when she
was "a wee thing herding" cattle (Bovevagh, Limavady [Co. Londonderry]).

[Dt: tune written neatly in staff notation in
S. H.'s hand.]

[Bp] Key G.

There was a merchant's daughter, being in her
  prime of years,
She fell in love with a sailor bold, it's true she
  loved him dear,
But how to get on board with him this fair maid
  did not know,
For she longed to see that bonny place called
  Canada-hi-ho.

She bargained with the sailors, all for a purse of
  gold,
Immediately they did comply to put her in the
  hold,
Saying, 'We'll dress you up in sailor's clothes,
  the captain will not know,
And soon you'll see that bonny place called
  Canada-hi-ho.'

When her true love heard of this, he flew into a
  rage
And with the crew and passengers a quarrel would
  engage,
Saying, 'I will tie her hand and foot and
  overboard she'll go,
She will never see that bonny place called
  Canada-hi-ho.'

When this fair maid heard of this, her heart was
  filled with woe,
Saying, 'You false-hearted young man, why do
  you say so?
I left my friends for love of you, not one of them
  did know,
And now you wish to drown me going to
  Canada-hi-ho.'

When the captain heard of this, he wept most
  bitterly,
Saying, 'If you drown this fair one, hang-ed you
  will be;
I will leave her in my cabin while the stormy
  winds do blow,
And soon we'll see that bonny place called
  Canada-hi-ho.'

After ploughing the raging main, the weather got
  calm and clear.
The captain fell in love with her and married her,
  we hear.
She's dressed in silk and satin and bears a
  gallant show,
And she's now a captain's lady gay in
  Canada-hi-ho.

Sam Henry's Songs of the People

Come all ye pretty fair maids, a warning take by me,
And always follow your true love when he goes out to sea,
For if the one prove false, some other will prove true,
And see what honour I have gained by the wearing of the blue.

[Dt and Bp have "Canada[,] Hi! Ho!" throughout.]
6.3: She dressed ... [Dt]

Willie Taylor (a) [H213: 10 Dec 1927; Laws N11]

Other titles: "(Bold) B(W)illy (William) ...,"
"Brisk Young Seamen"; cf. "Johnnie ...," "The Undaunted Female."

Source: 3: Mrs Campbell (Maghera St, Kilrea), John Thompson (Heatherlea Ave, Portstewart), William Devine (Cross Lane, Coleraine).

[Henry writes a sol-fa change of key at the refrain ("t = m"), but the F# is absent from the tune anyway, so the change is irrelevant.]

Key C. (Chorus.-- Key G).

Willie Taylor, a brisk young sailor,
Full of love and youthful air,
At length his mind he did discover
To a charming lady fair.

Fol da deedle, lairo, lairo, lairo,
Fol da deedle, lairo, lairo, lee,
Fol da deedle, lairo, lairo, lairo,
Fol da deedle, lairo, lairo, lee.

Then to the church for to get married,
Dressed they were in rich array,
But instead of getting married,
Pressed he was and sent to sea.

Now she has a mind to follow after,
First to England and France and Spain,
Should she live on bread and water
Until she returns again.

Now in shipboard she has entered
Under the name of Richard Kerr,
With her lily-white fingers small and slender
All now smeared by pitch and tar.

There was a scrimmage upon shipboard,
She was there among the rest,
Her silver buckles they flew open
And they spied she was a lady drest.

'Lady, lady,' says the captain,
'What misfortune brought you here?'
'Indeed, kind sir, it was my lover,
Pressed he was and sent to sea.'

'Lady, lady,' says the captain,
'What is your true lover's name?'
'Indeed, kind sir, it is Willie Taylor,
Pressed he was to the Isle of Man.'

'If Willie Taylor be your lover,
He's a boy I know right well,
And he has got married to a rich lady
In the Isle of Man where she does dwell.'

She wrung her hands and tore her hair
And overboard herself would throw,
Saying, 'My curse light upon you, Taylor,
You are the cause of all my woe.'

'Lady, lady,' says the captain,
Of your weeping now refrain,
You shall be a captain['s] lady
And Willie Taylor your servant's name.

'If you rise early in the morning
And walk down by the silvery strand,
You will see your true love, Taylor,
Walking his lady on the strand.'

She rose early in the morning,
Early by the break of day,
And there she spied her Willie Taylor
Walking with his lady gay.

'Willie, Willie, cruel Willie,
Think now of the deed you've done,
This very bride that you are enjoying,
Maybe it won't be for long.'

Then she called for sword and pistol,
Both of these being at command,
And she shot her false young Taylor
And left the new bride on the strand.

10.3: ... a captain's ... [Dt]

Willie Taylor (b) [H757: 28 May 1938; Laws N11]

Alternative version.

Source: (w) 7: Violet M'Afee (Ballybogey, Dervock), Alexander Boyd (Lismoyle, Swateragh), Mrs D. Cochrane (Dunseverick, Bushmills), John O'Hara (Shuttle Hill, Coleraine), Gladys Gilmour, 11 (Gortin, Kilrea), "who learnt it off her daddy"; Samuel Johnston (Moneysharvin, Maghera), David A. Forsythe (Seacon, Ballymoney); (m) Joe M'Conaghy (Upper Main St, Bushmills).

s: There are two versions of this very popular old ballad. One has already been published in this column (No. 213); the other, which we append, is quite different although the theme is the same. The air is also different. In response to our request for the words of the second version we have received replies from [the 7 contributors named above], all of whom we heartily thank. We are indebted to Mr Joe M'Conaghy ... for the air, which is very sweet.

Key G.

Willie Taylor, a brisk young sailor,
All alone by the shady grove,
Willie Taylor courted Nancy,
All his courtship to her was love.

Off to church this couple hurried,
Off to church without delay,
But instead of getting married,
Willie was pressed and sent away.

Soon this fair maid followed after,
Under the name of Richard Carr,
Her lily hands and snow-white fingers
Being smeared with pitch and tar.

On the sea there arose a scrimmage,
She being one amongst the rest,
Her silver buttons flew off her jacket
And they spied she was a lady drest.

'Oh lady, lady,' said the captain,
'What misfortune brought you here?'
'I'm in search of my true lover
Who was pressed the other year.'

'If you're in search of your true lover,
Tell to me what is his name.'
'Willie Taylor is my true lover,
And he was pressed in Hollin's Green.'

'If Willie Taylor is your true love,
He has proved false to thee;
He has married another lady
And left you lonely on the sea.

'If you rise early tomorrow morning,
Early, early by the break of day,
Then you'll see false Willie Taylor
Walking with his lady gay.'

She rose early the next morning
To look towards the Isle of Man,
There she saw false Willie Taylor
With his bride at his right hand.

'Oh, it's Willie, Willie, do you remember
The morning you were pressed in Hollin's Green?
Or in your mind does it ever enter
My fair face you have ever seen?'

'Oh, yes, I very well remember
When I was pressed from Hollin's Green,
But in my mind it never enters
That your fair face I've ever seen.'

'Oh Willie, Willie, cruel Willie,
Think on the deeds that you have done;
Think on the bright bride who enjoys you,
For your enjoyment won't be long.'

Sword and pistol she commanded,
Sword and pistol at her right hand,
She fired and shot false Willie Taylor
And left his young bride on the strand.

Then she called upon her servants,
She had servants more than one,
And they buried Willie Taylor
On the strands of the Isle of Man.

Then the captain did commend her
For the deed that she had done,
And he has made her his fair lady,
And in splendour they do shine.

◆ C18 REFERENCES ◆

◆ **The Drummer Maid** (H497) 326

Brunnings 1981: "The Female Drummer," "The Soldier Maid - When I Was a Fair Maid"

BRIT Greig 1907-11(1963): #104 "The Soldier Maid," comments that this song was well known.
  Greig/Duncan 1,1981:488-94 (#182) "The Soldier ...," 8 vts. ("The Drummer Girl," "The Drummer Maiden"); 494 (#183) "The Female Soldier"
  Ord 1930:311 "The Soldier Maid"
  Palmer 1977:163-4 "The Female Drummer"
  Shepheard n.d.:14-5 "... Girl"

AMER Peacock 1965,2:346-7
  SO 29(4,Oct-Dec)1983:34-5 "Female Drummer"

BRS Harvard 1: 1.132 (Spencer), 4.96 (Walker), 7.186 (Catnach)
  AS Thomas: (Coverly) (n.i.)

REC Frankie Armstrong, Topic 12TS 273 (B5) "The Female Drummer"; Sierra Briar SBR 4211 (B7)
  Ruby Beer, People's Stage Tapes cass. 04 (B4) "Female Drummer"
  Peter Bellamy, Topic 12T 200 (A3) "The Female Drummer"
  b: Harry Cox, Folk-Legacy FSB 20 (B2) "The Female Drummer," with a chorus.
  Tríona ní Dhomhnaill, Gael Linn CEF 043 (A1) "When I Was a Fair Maid"
  Mary Ann Haynes, Topic 12T 258 (A2) "The Female Drummer"; notes by Mike Yates mention broadsides by Pitts & Evans and Such, also the name of the real female drummer, who lived in the early 1800's.
  Walter Pardon, Leader LED 2111 (A3) "I'll Beat the Drum Again"
  Sally Rogers, Thrushwood 001 (B3) "When I Was a Fair Maid"
  Steeleye Span, B&C CAS 1029
  Tish Stubbs, People's Stage Tapes cass. 04 (B4) "Female Drummer"
  The Watersons, Topic 12T 167 (A3) "The Pretty Drummer Boy"

Sam Henry's Songs of the People

    Dick Wilder, Elektra EKL 129 (B4) "The Female Warrior"

◇ **On Board of a Man-of-War** *(H556)* 326

    Brunnings 1981: "Young Susan," "The British Man-of-War"

    BRIT Cf. Greig/Duncan 1,1981:479-81 (#179) "Young Susan," 4 vts.
        Kidson 1891:102-3, a ballad closely related to Henry's, and with the same title.
    ? *The Musical Gem* 1845 "Young Susan"

    For a related ballad called "The British Man-of-War," see [b:] Huntington 1964:108-10, where the girl does not go to sea, but waves goodbye to her man; cf. also Sharp/Karpeles 1974,1:526-8 (#136), *FR* 3(10,Aug) 1974:13.
    But Sharp/Karpeles 1974,2:299 (#294) "On Board of a Man of War O" is not related.

◇ **The Drum Major** *(H797)* 327

    Dean-Smith 1954: "(The) Drummer-Boy"
    Brunnings 1981: "... (The Female Drummer; Adapted Tune to General Monk's March)"

    IREL Moulden 1979:44

    BRIT Greig/Duncan 1,1981:495 (#184)

    BRS Roxburghe 7:730-2 "The Famous Woman Drummer," what seems to be a related ballad.

    REC Roy Harris, Fellside FE 017 (B3)
        The Watersons, Topic 12T 167 (A3) "The Pretty Drummer Boy"

◇ **The Female Highwayman** *(H35)* 327

    White/Dean-Smith 1951: "Sovie, Sovie (Sally, Sylvie, Silverie, Sylvia, Sovay, Shallo) or The Female Highwayman"
    Dean-Smith 1954: "Sovie, Sovie; The Female Highwayman/Robber; Sovie, Sovie All on One Day"
    Laws 1957:213 (N21)
    Brunnings 1981: "The Female Highwayman"

    IREL Moulden 1979:56

    # m: BRIT Kennedy 1975:722 (#334) "Sylvie"; says another English version recorded.
        Palmer 1980:191-2

    AMER Manny/Wilson 1968:201 "(Nelly Ray)"
        Milner/Kaplan 1983:73 "Sylvie"
        Warner 1984:157-8 (#58) "Pretty Sylvia"

    BRS Harvard 3: (Harkness)
        UCLA 605: 4(Such, 2 copies) "Sylvia's Request and William's Denial"

    m: REC Timothy Walsh, *FSB* 7 (A5) "Sylvia"
        Martin Carthy, Topic 12TS 340 (A3) "Sovay"
        Cliff Haslam, Folk-Legacy FSB 93 (A1) "Sovay"
        A. L. Lloyd, Topic 12T 118 (B3) "Sovay, the Female Highwayman"
        Isla St. Clair, Isla 1 (A1) "Sovay"
    b: Rosalie Sorrels, Prestige/Int. 13025 "The Female Highwayman"

◇ **The Squire's Bride** *(H524)* 328

    White/Dean-Smith 1951: "(The) Golden Glove"
    Dean-Smith 1954: "(The) Golden Glove"
    Laws 1957:212-3 (N 20) "The Golden Glove [Dog and Gun]"

    Brunnings 1981: "The Golden Glove"

    BRIT Greig/Duncan 1,1981:422-8 (#166) "The Golden Glove," 7 vts. ("(My) Dog and (My) Gun")
        Morrison/Cologne 1981:58-9 "The Golden Glove"
    # Sharp/Karpeles 1974,2:91-3 (#219) "The Golden Glove, or Dog and Gun"
        Shepheard n.d.:16-7 "The Golden Glove"

    AMER Bush 5,n.d.:70-3 "The Golden Glove"
        Colorado FB 1(3,Nov)1962:9
        Hudson/Herzog 1937:24
        Kincaid 1930:5
    # Randolph/Cohen (1982):95-7 "With Her Dog and Gun"
        Thompson 1958:71-3
        Warner 1984:335-6 (#145) "The Golden Glove (or, The Dog and the Gun"

    BRS BPL H.80: (n.i.)
        Harvard 1: 7.15 (Catnach), 12.11 (Such)
        Harvard 3: (Walker)
        UCLA 605: 3(Such)(Walker), 4(n.i.)

    REC O. J. Abbott, Folkways FM 4051 (A1) "The Dog and the Gun"
    cl: Robert L. Day, AFS 1696 A1 "The Dog and the Gun"
        Chris Foster, Topic 12T 329 "The Golden Glove"
        Besford Hicks, Tennessee Folklore Society TFS 104 (B6) "Boy and Gun (The Jolly Farmer)"
        Frank Hinchcliffe, Topic 12TS 308 (A2) "The Golden Glove"
    cl: Aunt Molly Jackson, AFS 2574 A & B "The Dog and Gun"
        Nic Jones, Shanachie 29003 (= Trailer ?)(A4) "The Golden Glove"
    cl: Mrs J. U. Newman, AFS 3769 A & B1 "Dog and Gun"
    cl: Alfred Osbourne, AFS 3401 B2 "The Dog and the Gun"
    cl: Harvey Porter, AFS 1555 B "The Golden Glove"

    MEL Petrie 1,1902:93 (#366) "With My Dog and My Gun," 96 (#380) "With Her Dog and Her Gun" [Sharp/Karpeles]

◇ **Lovely Annie (II)** *(H166)* 328

    Dean-Smith 1954: "Polly Oliver"
    Laws 1957:209-10 (N14) "Polly Oliver" [Pretty Polly]
    Brunnings 1981: "Polly Oliver's Rambles"

    IREL Moulden 1979:93: "This song was written by A. P. Graves, the Irish poet, and has been known to generations of school children as 'Pretty Polly Oliver.'"

    AMER Bush 3,1975:85-6 "Pretty Polly"
        Peters 1977:133-4 "Polly Oliver"

    BRS Harvard 1: 13.63 (Such)
        Harvard 3: (Catnach)
        UCLA 605: 4(Such, 2 c.) "Polly Oliver's Rambles", (n.i.)
        Holloway/Black 1975:174-5(#76) "The Maids Resolution to Follow Her Love"

    b: REC Leon Bibb, Liberty LRP 3358 "Polly Oliver"
    ? Barry Canham, Topic 12TS 219 "Billy Oliver's Rambles"
        Rita Weill, Takoma A 1022 (B6) "Polly Oliver's Rambles"

    m: MEL Joyce 1909:291 (#548) "Pretty Polly," 324-5 (#640) "Pretty Polly Like a Trooper Did Ride"

◇ The Rich Merchant's Daughter *(H108a)* 329

White/Dean-Smith 1951
Laws 1957:204 (N6) "Disguised Sailor [The Sailor's Misfortune and Happy Marriage; The Old Miser]"
Brunnings 1981: "The Disguised Sailor," "The Lady of Riches," "The Old Miser," ? "The Rich Merchant and Daughter," "The Sailor's Misfortune," "The Weaver Is Handsome"

m: IREL Allingham *Ceol* 1967
  Moulden 1979:123
Not O Lochlainn 1965 "The Merchant's Daughter"

BRIT Greig/Duncan 1,1981:463-6 (#174) "The Merchant's Daughter and Her Sailor" ("There Was a Rich Merchant," "The (Rich) Merchant's Daughter"), 4 vts.; 467-8 (#175) "In Fair London City"
  Lloyd 1967:223-5
  Munch 1970:79-80 "The Old Miser"
  Purslow 1968:63-4 "The Lady of Riches"
  Richards/Stubbs 1979:109 "The Old Miser," with a tragic end.
m: Sharp/Karpeles 1974,2:73-6 (#215) "The Press Gang, or In London Fair City," 3 vts.

BRS Cf. UCLA 605: 4(Birt) "The Old Miser"
  Holloway/Black 1975:239-41 (#106) "The Sailor's Happy Marriage"

REC Dave, Toni Arthur, Topic 12T 190 (B6) "The Press Gang"
  cl: Maude Clevenger, AFS 2937 A1
  ? cl: Mrs M. P. Daniels, AFS 3732 B1 "The Rich Old Miser"
  ? cl: Elmer George, AFS 3732 B2 "The Rich Old Miser"
  cl: J. W. Green, AFS 2275 B
  Roy Harris, Topic 12TS 232 "The Press-Gang"
  Mary Ann Haynes, Topic 12T 258 (A6) "The Old Miser"
  Ewan MacColl, Topic 12T 147
  b: Diane Oxner, Rodeo RLP 6 "The Disguised Sailor"
  Cf. Peggy Seeger, Prestige 13058 "The Weaver Is Handsome" [Peggy Seeger 1964]
  Chris Willett, Topic 12T 84 (B4) "The Old Miser"
  b: The Young Tradition, Vanguard VSD 79246 "The Old Miser"

◇ The Sailor on the Sea *(H203)* 330

BRIT Greig/Duncan 1,1981:475-8 (#178) "Up in London Fair," 5 vts. ("The Ship that I Command")

REC Mary Ann Carolan, Topic 12TS 362 (B1) "In London So Fair"
  Peta Webb, Topic 12TS 403 (A4) "In London So Fair"

◇ The True Lovers' Departure *(H584)* 331

Laws 1957:210 (N15) "The Noble Duke"
Brunnings 1981: "The Simple Ploughboy," "The Pretty Ploughboy"

IREL Moulden 1979:148

◇ The Jolly Ploughboy *(H105)* 331

White/Dean-Smith 1951: "(The) Pretty Ploughboy or The Ploughman's Glory"
Dean-Smith 1954: "(The) Pretty/Simple Plough-Boy; The Plough-Boy"
Laws 1957:191 (M24) "... (Little Plowing Boy; The Simple Plowboy)"

IREL Joyce 1909:223 (#412) "The Ploughboy" [Laws]

BRIT Baring-Gould/Hitchcock 1974:84-5 "Ploughboys' Song"

C18 / *In man's array*

Cf. Brocklebank/Kindersley 1948:2 "The Ploughboy"
Greig/Duncan 1,1981:442-51 (#170), 15 vts. ("The Poor ...," "The Ploughboy")
  Lloyd 1967:226-7
  Moffat [1897]:12 "As Jack ..." (from Bunting 1840)
  Palmer 1974b:160-1 (#94) "The Pretty Ploughboy"
  Purslow 1974:73 "The Pretty ..."
  Cf. Richards/Stubbs 1979:93-4 "The Pretty Factory Boy"
  Sharp 5,1909:20-3 "The Pretty Ploughing-Boy"
Sharp/Karpeles 1974,2:82-90 (#218) "The Simple ... or The Pretty ...," 8 vts.
  Shepheard n.d.:30 "The Pretty Ploughing Boy"
  Cf. Yates *FMJ* 1976:165 "Wounded Farmer's Son"

AMER Grover n.d.:13-4

BRS O'Keeffe 1955(1968):19 "The Ploughboy"

REC Packie Manus Byrne, Topic 12TS 257 (B1)
  Tish Stubbs, People's Stage Tapes cass. 01 (B2) "The Simple Ploughboy" [but she sings "Pretty ..."]

◇ Blythe and Bonny Scotland
 /[Dt:] India's Burning Sands *(H120)* 332

Laws 1957:202 (N2) "The Paisley Officer"
Brunnings 1981: "The Paisley Officer - I and II," ? "The Miracle Flower"

IREL Shields 1981:96-7 (#37)
  Shields/Shields *UF* 21,1975: #204

BRIT Greig/Duncan 1,1981:46 (#185) "The Paisley Officer," 2 vts. ("The Village Maid")
  Cf. Palmer 1977:196-7 "The Indian War," which ends happily.

REC Sara Cleveland, Folk-Legacy FSA 33 (B3) "In Bonny Scotland"

◇ Canada[,] Hi! Ho! *(H162)* 333

Dean-Smith 1984: "Canada I-O"
Cf. Laws 1950(1964):155 (C17) "Canaday-i-o (a), Michigan-i-o (b), Colley's Run-i-o (c)," a different ballad.
Brunnings 1981: "Canaday-I-O," "Canada I. O.," "Canadee-I-O - It Was of a Fair and Pretty Maid"

IREL Shields *UF* 10,1964:41-2 "Canada-i-o"
  Shields/Shields *UF* 21,1975: #74 "Canada-i-o"

BRIT Cf. Greig 1907-11(1963): #77 "Caledonia"
  Cf. Ord 1930:117-8 "Caledonia"
  Tocher #38(Spr)1983:62 "The Wearing of the Blue"

AMER Darling 1983:181-2 "Canaday-I-O"
  Eckstorm/Smyth 1927:22-3
  Cf. Eckstorm *BFSSNE* #6,1933:10-2 "Canaday I O," notes the relationship of this song to the lumberman's "Canada I O" and "The Buffalo Skinners," and prints a "woods" version.
  Cf. Fowke/Johnston 1954:68-9 "Canaday-i-o"
  Karpeles 1970:169-70 "Wearing of the Blue"
  Leach 1965:230-1 "Canadee-I-O"
  Thompson 1958:59-60 "Canada I O"

AUST B. Scott *Penguin 2* 1980:42-5 "Caledonia," 2 tunes and background.

BRS BPL H.80: (n.i).
  Harvard 1: 10.75 (Bebbington), 12.10 (Such)
  Forget Me Not [1835]:161-5

REC Nic Jones, Topic 12TS 411 "Canadee-i-o"; Topic TPSS 412 (B1)

337

◇ **Willie Taylor** *(H213, H757)* 334

k Cf. Vivien Richman, Folkways FG 3568 (A8) "The Jolly Lumbermen"
   Harry Upton, Topic 12T 258 (A1) "Canadee-I-O"
   Cf. Lester Wells, AAFS L56 (A2) "Michigan I-O"

◇ **Willie Taylor** *(H213, H757)* 334

White/Dean-Smith 1951: "William Taylor or Bold William Taylor; Billy Taylor; William Taylor and Sally Brown"
Dean-Smith 1954: "William ..."
Laws 1957:208 (N11) "William ..."
Brunnings 1981: "William Taylor - Was a Brisk Young Sailor," "Billy Taylor"

IREL Joyce 1909:235-6 (#424) [Laws]
h: Shields *UF* 10,1964:36
   Shields *Ceol* 2(3):62

BRIT Dawney 1977:45 "William ..."
   Firth 1908:326-8, 2 versions, 1 a burlesque.
   Greig/Duncan 1,1981:438-41 (#169) "Billy ...," 6 vts.
   Henderson et al. 1979:48-9 "William ..."
   Lyle 1975:53
\# Sharp/Karpeles 1974,2:63-72 (#214) "William ...," 10 vts.
   Tocher #26(Aut)1977:85-6 "Billy ..."

Not: the song with the same title about a poacher in, e.g., Stubbs (1963)1968:9.

AMER Bush 2,1970:80
   Manny/Wilson 1968:222-3 "Brisk Young Seamen (...)"
   Silverman 1971:118

BRS Harvard 3: (Hodges)
   Ashton 1891:256-61 (incl. "Bold William ...," brs.)

REC Harold Covill, *FSB* 8 (A8) "William ..."
   Frankie Armstrong, Bay 206 (A1) "William ..."
   Martin Carthy, Mooncrest Crest 25 (B2) "William ..."
   Cilla Fisher, Artie Trezise, Folk-Legacy FSS 69 (A6) "Billy ..."
cl: George Vinton Graham, AFS 3814 A3 "Willy ..."
cl: Pen McCready, AFS 3355 A2 "Willy ..."
cl: Jonathan Moses, AFS 3707 A2 & 3, 3708 A "Willy ..."
b: Joseph Taylor, Leader LEA 4050 (B1) "Bold William ..."
   Rob Watt, Topic 12T 180 (B1) "Billy ..."
   Hedy West, Fontana STL 5432

MEL Hudson ms. 1:266
   Cf. *JIFSS* 5:12 "Johnnie ..." [Sharp/Karpeles]
   O'Neill 1922:40 [not Henry's tune]
   Petrie/Stanford 2,1902:186 (#745) [Sharp/Karpeles]

C19

Youth and folly: Love uncertain

Sam Henry's Songs of the People

The Six Sweethearts [H605: 6 Jul 1935]

Other title: "Six Girls."

Source not given.

s: Lines 5 and 6 of the last verse are to be sung to lines 3 and 4 of the air.

Key D.

I've had a grand experience I'm going to tell you now,
By courting six girls all at once; they served me anyhow.
My mother said, 'You're wicked,' I laughed at her advice,
She said that I was naughty, but I was very nice.

> *So I fell in love with Mary Ann and then with Mary Jane,*
> *And then with pretty Miss M'Cann and then with Kate M'Clean,*
> *And then with Betty Hopsican and then with Nellie Small,*
> *I stayed at home on Sunday night for fear I'd meet them all.*

But oh dear me, I mixed their names, and at the garden gate
I bid good-night to Betty, but I called her darling Kate.
I wrote a note to Nellie, but I called her Mary Jane,
And then, to make the matter worse, addressed it 'Kate M'Clean.'

I never will forget the day I met the blessed six,
Mary Ann says, 'You will pay for all your little tricks,'
And then she caught me by the hair, and Mary Jane my coat,
And Miss M'Cann brought some young man who caught me by the throat.

Mary Jane she clawed my face until it ran with blood,
And as for Betty Hopsican, she smothered me with mud,
And then, to make the thing complete, sure, pretty Nellie Small
Bashed my hat till it was flat against the garden wall.

I tossed about in bed that night, I had such dreadful dreams,
I dreamt they were pursuing me with horrid scraighs and screams,
I dreamt they punched me black and blue and stuck me full of pins,
I dreamt they put on big nailed boots and kicked me on the shins,
I dreamt they roasted me alive and I was quite a-hot,
I dreamt that I became a Turk and married all the lot.

I've Two or Three Strings to My Bow (a) [H70a: 14 Mar 1925]

[Bp] A love song of a daring spirit in the early Victorian days.

Other title: "The Frugal Maid."

Source not given.

Key D.

[Lines 4 of original stanzas, and chorus (originally 2 lines, each twice as long) have been divided. The refrain, which appears to require repetition of a line from the particular stanza it follows, is not so specified in the original column (Bp, Dt) but instead is called "chorus."]

I am a fair maiden forsaken, but I have a contented mind,
Although my true love he has left me, I'll find another as kind,
I'll find another as kind as he, all this I would have him to know:
That I care no more for him that he cares for me,
I've two or three strings to my bow.
> I've two or three strings to my bow,
> All this I would have him to know,
> That I care no more for him than he cares for me,
> I've two or three strings to my bow.

So all you young maidens take warning, to your
   true lovers never be kind,
Young men are very deceitful, they are
   changeable as the wind,
A new face creates a new fancy, and this I would
   have him to know:
Be careless and free and take warning by me,
Keep two or three strings to your bow.
   Keep two ...

I own that once I did love him, but never to say
   I adore,
I loved him but to part with him; he left me,
   I'll love him no more,
He left me, I'll love him no more, and this I
   would have him to know:
That I care no more for him than he cares for me,
I've two or three strings to my bow.
   I've two ...

3.3: He left him ... [Dt]

I've Two or Three Strings to My Bow (b) [H70b: D(c)]

[m = H70a]

Source: Bobbie Johnston (Aughagash P.E.S., Glenarm).

Key G.

Oh, I'm a forsaken wee lassie, but ever
   contented in mind,
My true love from me has forsaken, but I have
   another as kind,
But I have another as kind, and this I would
   have you to know:

   Keep single and free, light-hearted like me,
   Keep two or three strings to your bow.

I own I did love this wee laddie, but never gave
   in to adore,
I loved him in this kind of fashion: when I left
   him I loved him no more,
When I left I loved him no more, and this I would
   have you to know:

Young men they are so deceiving, their mind it
   does change like the wind,
When they get a wee lassie to love them, sure
   they go and they leave her behind,
Sure they go and they leave her behind them,
   and this I would have you to know:

One Morning Clear [H548: 2 Jun 1934]

k: "Searching for Lambs."

Source not given.

Key F.

One morning clear, to meet my dear before the
   sun would rise,
Her cherry cheeks and ruby lips, they put me in
   surprise;
'Where are you going, my dear,' said I, 'your
   journey to pursue
Before bright Phoebus' golden beams dry up the
   morning dew?'
'I'm going to feed my father's flocks, his ewes and
   tender lambs
Down beneath yon forest where they're sporting
   with their dams.'
'Then, since together we are met, my love, let us
   agree,
I could wish that all true lovers were as happy
   met as we.'
My love's genteel and handsome, she's neat in
   every limb,
I courted her for four years and thought the time
   not long,
And thrice four years I'd a-courted her, if life
   that long would stay,
Not thrice four years but four hundred, and
   would count it all one day.
I love my love, there is no doubt, it's all for love
   again,
And if she says she loves me not, I laugh at her
   disdain;
If she is constant, I'll be true, and forever we'll
   agree,
But if ever I find she's changed her mind, I'll
   change mine as well as she.
The pleasantest month in all the year is the merry
   month of June,
When all the world is pleasant and all the flowers
   in bloom,
When all together sport and play, and birds sing
   every tune,
Where young women carry the key of love, young
   men may know their doom.

Sam Henry's Songs of the People

The Maid of Tardree [H733: 11 Dec 1937]

o: (m) "Lovely Willie."

Source: (Doagh district).

s: ... This song is stated to be 200 years old.

Key F.

Assist me, ye muses, and lend me your aid,
And with your dictation I'll not be afraid
For to sing a few verses, tho' the tear's in my e'e
When I think of the parting my friends in
    Tardree.

One night at a singing, dear comrades, you'll
    mind
I placed my affections on a female so kind,
She told me she loved me and that she would be
A loving, kind partner and live in Tardree.

As changes of faces, so changes the mind;
I placed my affections on another more kind,
I told her I loved her with a heart kind and true,
For the wiles of deception were unknown in
    Tardree.

Our first expectations were blighted, you know,
We sometimes had pleasure and other times, woe,
But now I'm resolved for to cross o'er the sea
To that land of freedom, far, far from Tardree.

Our ship has weighed anchor and ready to steer;
When I bid farewell I must do it with a tear,
When I think of the past time, the mirth and the
    glee,
And the social acquaintance I leave in Tardree.

Farewell, my dear parents, your care I must
    leave,
Likewise my dear brothers and sisters; I crave
To give me your blessing when I'm far from thee,
For perhaps we may ne'er meet again in Tardree.

Dark-Eyed Molly [H625: 23 Nov 1935]

k: "Going to Mass Last Sunday," "My Charming Molly." Other titles: "Black-Eyed (Handsome) (Lovely) Molly," "Courting is a Pleasure," "Down in Yonder Valley," "I Went to Mass on Sunday," "In Courtship There Lies (Meeting Is a) Pleasure"; cf. "The Irish Girl," "Lovin' Hannah."

Source: (w) 11: Edward Montgomery (Bushmills), John Corscadden (Bushmills), George Hutchinson (Ringsend, Garvagh), W. M'Ilreavy (Damhead), Mrs Morrison (Inchmearing, Coleraine), Teresa A. Henry (Ballynure, Draperstown), Mrs Purcell (Dartries), John J. Bradley (Aughacarnaghan, Toomebridge), Daniel M'Aleese (Gortmacrane, Kilrea), Daniel M'Kenna (Coolnasillagh, Maghera), James Steele (Carrichue); (m) "beautifully transcribed" by Daniel M'Aleese (Gortmacrane) from Valentine Crawford, fiddle (Bushmills).

Key D.

Oh, meeting is a pleasure betwixt my love and I,
I'll go down to yonder valley where I'll meet her
    bye and bye,
I'll go down to yonder valley where I'll meet my
    heart's delight,
And I'll stroll with my wee darling from morning
    until night.

So when you meet a bonny wee lass wi' a dark
    and rolling eye,
Kiss her and embrace her and tell her the reason
    why,
Kiss her and embrace her till you cause her
    heart to yield,
For a faint-hearted soldier will never gain the
    field.

I went to church last Sunday, my love she
    passed me by,
I knew her mind was changed by the rolling of
    her eye,
I knew her mind was altered to a lad of high
    degree,
Saying, 'Molly, lovely Molly, your love has
    wounded me.'

When up came her love Willie with a bottle in
    his hand,
Saying, 'Drink of this, dear Molly, our courtship
    ne'er will stand,'
Saying, 'Drink of this, dear Molly, let the bottle
    and glass go free,
For ten guineas lie in wagers that married we
    ne'er shall be.'

There's some court in earnest when others can
    court in fun,
And I can court the old sweetheart to draw the
    new one on,
Tell to her long stories to keep her mind at
    ease,
And when her back is turned I can court wi'
    whom I please.

Farewell to Londonderry, likewise the sweet
  Bann shore,
Farewell unto Macaskie braes, will I never see
  you more?
Americay lies far away, that land I will go see;
May all bad luck attend the lad that parted my
  love and me.

Farewell Ballymoney [H615: 14 Sep 1935]

g: "Lovely Molly"; (m) "Paddy's Green Country."

Source not given.

Key G.

Oh, meeting is a pleasure betwixt my love and I;
I'll go down to yon low valleys where she'll meet
  me by and by,
I'll go down to yon low valleys where stands my
  heart's delight,
And with you, lovely Molly, I'll spend till broad
  daylight.

Coming home from church last Sunday, my love
  she passed me by,
I saw her mind was chang-ed by the rolling of
  her eye,
I saw her mind was changed to one of higher
  degree,
And the small birds they sat murmuring, saying,
  'Farewell, malachree.'

Down come little Johnny with the bottle in his hand,
'Drink you of the top, my boys, and let the
  bottom stand,
Drink you of the top, my boys, and let the glass
  go free,
Ten guineas lie in wages, but wed we ne'er shall
  be.'

Some do court in fun and do not care a pin,
But I can court the old sweetheart and bring the
  new one in,
I can tell her loving stories to keep her mind at
  ease,
And when I get her back turned, I can court
  with whom I please.

Oh, never court a sweetheart with a dark and
  rolling eye,
Kiss her and embrace her, but don't tell her the
  reason why,
Kiss her and embrace her till you get her heart
  to yield,
For a faint-hearted soldier ne'er won the
  battlefield.

To the town of Ballymoney and to County Antrim,
  too,
Likewise my dearest Molly, I now must bid adieu;
America lies far away, the land I go to see,
But cursed may the day be that parts my love
  and me.

The Sweet Bann Water

[H722: 25 Sep 1937; Laws M34, ?Child 248]

[cf. H699 "The Bonny Bushes Bright"]

Other titles: "Arise, Arise (Awake, Awake) (Wake,
O Wake), You Drowsy Maiden (Sleeper)," "Awake,
Awake, My Old True Lover," "Awake, Arise (Wake
up), You Drowsy Sleeper(s)," "Bedroom Window,"
"The Cocks Are (Is) Crowing," "Death of William
and Mary," "The Drowsy Sleeper," "Father and
Daughter," "The Grey Cock," "(Here's) (A Health)
to All True Lovers," "I'll Go See My Love," "I'm
a Rover and Seldom Sober," "I Will Put My Ship
in Order," "Katie Dear," "Last Night as I Lay on
My Bed," "The Lover's Ghost," "Oh, Molly Dear,"
"The Night Visiting Song," "Our Ship She Lies in
Harbour," "Parents, Warning," "(The) Shining
(Silver) Dagger," "True Lover John," "Who Comes
Tapping to (Who's Taps at) (Who's That Knocking
at [under]) (My (Bedroom)) Window?" "Willie and
Minnie"; cf. "I'm Often Drunk and Seldom Sober,"
"One Night as I Lay on my Bed," "Who Is at My
Window Weeping," "Young Men and Maids."

Source: Valentine Crawford (Commercial Hotel,
Bushmills).

Key G.

I must away, I'll no longer tarry,
The sweet Bann water I mean to cross,
And over the mountains I'll roam with pleasure,
And spend one night with my own wee lass.

If the night was dark as a dungeon
And not a star ever to appear,
I would be guided without a stumble
To that sweet arbour where lies my dear.

When I came to my true love's window,
I kneel-ed low on a marble stone,
And through a pane I did whisper slowly,
Saying, 'Darling, darling, are you at home?'

Sam Henry's Songs of the People

She raised her head from her downy pillow,
And covered was her snow-white breast,
Saying, 'Who is that, that is at my window
Disturbing me quite of my night's rest?'

'It is I, it is I, your poor wounded lover,
So rise up, darling, and let me in,
For I am tired of my long journey,
Besides I'm wet, love, into the skin.'

When this long night was almost ended
And drawing nigh to the break of day,
She says, 'My darling, the cocks are crowing,
It's now full time you were going away.'

'Well, you may go, love, and ask your father
If he be willing you my bride may be,
And what he says, love, come back and tell me,
For this is the last night I'll trouble thee.'

'I need not go, love, to ask my father
For he is lying in his bed of ease
And in his hand he does hold a letter
Which leadeth much on to your dispraise.'

'Well, you may go, love, and ask your mother
If she be willing you my bride will be;
What she says, love, come back and tell me,
For this is the last night I'll trouble thee.'

'I need not go, love, to ask my mother,
For to love's silence she won't give ear,
But away, away, and court some other
That will consent without a fear.'

For after night, love, there comes a morning,
And after morning comes a new day,
And after one false love comes another,
It's hard to hold them that must sway.

The Rejected Lover [H589: 16 Mar 1935]

Other titles: "Alexander," (m) "I'll Travel to Mt. Nebo"; cf. "The Jilted Lover."

Source: native (Prolusk, near Straid, Co. Antrim) at Bushmills.

Key G.

For want of fine expressions to set forth my
 love's praise,
 I'll have to do it at one word, just as the wise
 man says:
My love is neat and handsome and from all
 faults she's free,
She is the maid of virtue and stole the heart
 from me.

She stole the heart right out of me, so I to her
 drew near,
Saying, 'Would you know the reason, love, this
 night that I come here?
Among all other fair ones, I could but fancy few,
So that's the very reason I place my mind on
 you.

'The night is drawing on, my love, now to the
 break of day,
So I require an answer: what have you now to
 say?'
'Well you know, my honourable young man, I
 live a happy life,
I never intend to marry, or be your wedded wife.

'For I have got a sweetheart and have thrown
 you aside,
So take this as your answer and for yourself
 provide.'
'You may have got a new sweetheart and have
 thrown me aside,
But providence is always kind and for me will
 provide.

'I'll go and court some other wee girl in hopes
 that she'll not rue,
And when I'm gone you may think long; so
 farewell, love, adieu,
I'll travel to Mount Nebo, where Moses viewed
 the ark,
And from that to Mount Ararat, where Noah did
 embark.

'I'll travel east, I'll travel west while I can wear
 a shoe,
And like a loyal lover I'll always think on you,
And if fortune only favours me to win your
 heart again,
I hope you will surrender and free my heart
 from pain.'

The Banks of Mourne Strand

[H564: 22 Sep 1934]

[cf. H18a "To Pad the Road"]

Source: (w, m) Alexander Thompson (Bushmills; native of Ballyhunsley, near Bushmills).

m: Current: Jackie Devening (Coleraine).

Key C.

C19 / Youth and folly

I am a rambling young man, I rambled up and
   down,
Still looking for my equal, but that was never
   found
Till I fell in love wi' a bonny wee girl, she's the
   girl that I adore,
She is the darling of my heart and she dwells on
   Mourne shore.

The first time that I saw my love, it was on
   Mourne strand,
I stepp-ed up unto her and offered her my hand,
I put my arm around her neck, I gave her kisses
   three,
Says I, 'My handsome Mourne's girl, will you pad
   the road wi' me?'

'To pad the road wi' you, kind sir, I'm a year far
   too young,
Besides, you are a Lurgan lad with a false and
   flattering tongue.'
The evening tide was coming in, she could no
   longer stand,
So I took her in my arms on the banks of Mourne
   strand.

She looked me in the eyes and she said, 'What will
   I do?
Will you marry me, my Lurgan lad, and make your
   promise true?
My father will his lands divide and share alongst
   with thee,
If you will but be willing to pad the road wi' me.'

'Oh, I'll tell you as you told me, I am a year far
   too young,
Besides, you are a Mourne's girl with a false and
   flattering tongue,
But if ever I come this road again, my vows I will
   make stand,
And I'll marry you, my Mourne girl, on the banks
   of Mourne strand.'

Fair Maid of Glasgow Town

[H579: 5 Jan 1935]

Source: (Bushmills).

o: Time 6/8.

Key G.

As I roved out one evening down by the banks of
   Clyde,
I spied a handsome fair one, I asked her for my
   bride.
Her hair was braided handsome with ringlets
   hanging down,
She stole the heart away from me, fair maid of
   Glasgow town.

She looked at me in modesty and then she made
   reply,
'Kind sir, you are a stranger, why should I then
   comply?
For young men they do flatter maids until they do
   prevail,
Unto some other fair one you can tell an equal
   tale.

'Mark what I say as candid, the truth I will tell
   you,
I am engaged to a young man, his age is twenty-
   two,
I'll be his bride whate'er betide, your company I
   refuse,
And on the lonesome banks of Clyde to walk alone
   I'll choose.'

I thanked her for her answer and slowly walked
   away,
When looking round behind me, she called me to
   stay:
'Come back, my honourable young man, you've
   won my heart,' cried she,
'And on the lonesome banks of Clyde your wedded
   bride I'll be.'

'Now you have consented my wedded bride to be,
But oh, alas, you are too late to make your vow to
   me,
Go wed that lad you mentioned first, when first I
   spoke to thee,
For if you be false to one true love, you could not
   be true to me.

'Of many's the bonny wee lass in Glasgow I could
   tell,
And oftimes I have won them by the ringing of the
   bell,
So adieu to you, my handsome maid, no more this
   way I'll pass,
And happyless through life I'll roam, my blue-
   eyed Glasgow lass.'

The Ploughboy [H780: 5 Nov 1938]

[cf. H520 "The Strands of Magilligan," ?cf. H637
"Lovely Nancy"]

k: "Johnny, Lovely Johnny"; g: "Lovely Molly."
Other titles: "I Am a Poor Stranger," "I Once
Was a ...."

345

Sam Henry's Songs of the People

Source: Jock Smylie (Leggyfat, Limavallaghan, Clough); (m) Jock Smylie from Margaret Curry (Islandstown, Clough).

g: This song is difficult to identify. It contains elements from a number of different songs. See in particular H520 "The Strands of Magilligan."

Key C.

I once was a ploughboy, but a soldier I'm now,
I courted lovely Molly, a milkmaid, I vow,
I courted lovely Molly, I delight in her charms,
And many's the long night I rolled in her arms.

'Adieu, lovely Molly, I am now going away,
There's great honour and promotion in crossing
  the sea,
And if e'er I return it will be in the spring,
When the lark and the linnet and the nightingale
  sing.

'I'll build my love a castle at the head of the
  town,
Where neither lord, duke or earl will e'er pull it
  down,
And if any one asks you where you are from,
You can tell them you're a stranger from the
  County Tyrone.

'You may go to all markets, all gatherings or
  fairs,
You may go to church on Sunday and choose
  your love there,
And if any one loves you as well as I do,
I'll ne'er ask to stop your wedding, so farewell,
  adieu.'

She sent me a posy of the red rose so fine,
I sent her another, it was rue mixed with thyme,
Saying, 'You keep your red rose and I'll keep
  my thyme,
You can drink a health to your love and I'll
  drink to mine.'

The Blackbird and Thrush

[H241: 23 Jun 1928]

k: "Farewell He." Other titles: "Single and Free."

Source: (Ballywindland district) learned in Skerry Glen c. 1865.

s: ... The words are hard to adapt to the air, but a slight knowledge of the traditional style of singing will overcome the difficulty.

g: This is a perfect example of how elements on one song cross over into another: here are phrases and lines found in "The Wagoner's Lad," H479 "The Cuckoo," H165 "Green Grows the Laurel (Green Grow the Rashes)," among other songs.

Key C. Slowly and tenderly.

As I walked down by the side of a bush,
I heard two birds whistling -- the blackbird and
  thrush,
I asked them the reason they so merry be,
And the answer they gave me, 'We are single and
  free.'

A meeting, a meeting, a meeting went I
For to meet lovely Johnny, he'll be here by and
  by;
To meet him in yon meadow it would be my delight,
Where I could be with him from morning till night.

A meeting's a pleasure, a parting's a grief,
An unconstant young man is worse than a thief,
For a thief can but rob you, take all that you
  have,
But an unconstant young man would send you to
  your grave.

I loved him, I loved him, I loved him, alas!
The gloves that I bought him was eight shillings
  in price,
But the dearer I loved him, the saucier he grew,
I loved a false young man and he caused me to
  rue.

He sent me a poesy of the rue mixt with thyme,
And in answer I sent back a red rose to him,
I bid him keep his red rose and I would keep
  mine
Till I find a young man more constant and kind.

Now since he is gone, he thinks for him I mourn,
But thanks to providence I can do my own turn,
I can work or sit idle as occasion calls me,
I can rest when I'm tired, so farewell he.

[*Italicized words written on Wp:*]
4.2: ... him, *no gloves could surpass,*

5.1: ... posy ... ['e' *crossed out*]
5.3: ... rose *until I would find*
.4: *Another a young man who'd prove to me constant and kind.*
6.4: ... farewell *to* he.

Farewell He [H504: 29 Jul 1933]

Other titles: "Adieu to Cold (Dark) Weather," "Black Frost," "... She," "Fare Thee Well Cold Winter," "The Independent Girl," "Let Him Go(, Let Him Tarry)," "(My Love Is Like a) Dewdrop," "My Love Is on the Ocean," "They Say He Courts Another," "To Cheer the Heart"; cf. "Goodbye to Old Winter and Adieu to Its Frost."

Source: (m) "old worthy" (Gortinmayoghill, Aghadowey), "who has since bade farewell to all."

s: In the last verse, the words "farewell he" are spoken, not sung.

Key A flat.

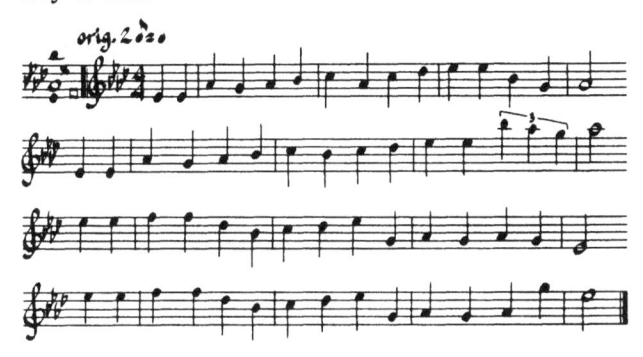

It is fare thee well, cold winter, it is fare thee well, cold frost:
There is nothing I have gained, but a lover I have lost,
I will sing and I'll be merry, and I'll clap my hands with glee,
And I'll rest me when I'm weary; let him go then, farewell he.

It was last fall that my lover gave to me a diamond ring,
O, I know not what he thought me but a vain and foolish thing,
If he prove to me unskilful, cannot win my heart from me,
I will prove a maiden wilful: let him go with -- farewell he.

If he has another sweetheart and tells me so in joke,
Why, I care not, be they twenty, he will never me provoke.
Well, and if he likes another and together they agree,
I can also find a lover, let him go with -- farewell he.

Add half a pound of reason, half an ounce of common sense,
Add a sprig of thyme in season and as much of sage prudence,

Prithee mix them well together, then I think you'll plainly see,
He's no lad for windy weather; let him go with -- farewell he.

The Cuckoo [H479: 4 Feb 1933]

[cf. H165 "Green Grow the Rashes," ?H755 "Johnny and Molly"]

Other titles: "A-Walkin' and A-Talkin'," "Brigg Fair," "The Coo Coo (Cuckoo) Bird," "A Forsaken Lover," "Go away from Me, Young Man," "If I Was a Blackbird," "I Once Had a True-Love," "Jimmy," "Lovely Willie," "Nancy and William," "Pretty Polly," "(The) (Maid of) (Streams of) Bunclody(, and the Lad She Loves So Dear)," "'Twas down in the Valley," "(The) Unconstant Lover"; cf. "The Wagoner's Lad."

Source not given.

g: Songs of this type are often difficult to identify because elements of one so easily cross over into another. Cf. H241 "The Blackbird and Thrush."

Key C.

The cuckoo is a purty bird, she sings as she flies,
She brings us glad tidings, she tells us no lies,
She drinks the rock water, her voice to keep clear
And she never calls Cuckoo till the summer draws near.

As I was a-walking and talking one day,
I met my own true love as he came that way,
Oh, to meet him was pleasure, but his courting was woe,
For I found him false-hearted, he would kiss me and go.

The next place I met my love was in a shady grove,
He modestly came up to me and offered me a rose,
I told him to keep his rose and I would keep my thyme,
He could write to his true love and I would write to mine.

I'll go down to yon valley where the small birds do sing,
There no one will hear me and I'll droop my wing,

Sam Henry's Songs of the People

My own notion provokes me, I took my own will,
My own rod's the sorest, it beats me more still.

I'll go down to yon meadow where streams do run still,
Where no one will see me and I'll cry my fill,
The more that my true love has no clothes to wear,
I'll work while I'm able and give him a share.

They say: Little said is the easiest mended,
And them that talk least, I think they talk best,
I know by experience, my mind tells me so,
Every lad has his sweetheart and knows where to go.

If I were a scholar and could handle the pen,
I would write to my true love and all roving men,
I would tell them the grief that attends on their lies,
I would wish them have pity on the flower when it dies.

She took a long sickness and she could not endure,
Neither father nor mother could give her a cure,
Neither sister nor brother could tell her disease,
But they're far from this country could set her at ease.

Oh, green grows the laurel and so does the rue,
And sorry was I for the parting of you,
But at our next meeting our joys we'll renew,
We'll embrace one another and vow to be true.

Oh, green grow the rashes and the tops of them small,
For love is a thing that will conquer us all,
It'll conquer us all, high or low our degree,
Every one to their fancy and my darlin' to me.

If I Were a Fisher [H709: 26 Jun 1937]

Source: James Kelly (Anectermore, Clontoe Richardson, Coagh, Moneymore).

s: Noted ... in his fishing boat on Lough Neagh.

Key F.

When I rise in the morning, to my garden I'll go,
For to pull my love flowers far whiter than snow;
Oh, some pull the red rose, leave the lily behind,
But I'll pull the flower that runs in my mind.

If I were a fisher around Lough Neagh strand
And Molly, a salmon, came rolling to land,
I'd cast out my draft net, catch her in a snare,
I'd bring home lovely Molly, I vow and declare.

If I were a scholar and could handle the pen,
I would write my love a letter and to her I would send,
I would write my love's praises, I would seal them with love:
If her heart was like a mountain, I'd have it remove.

It's not my long journey I value one straw,
Nor yet my expenses to the town of Carlow,
But there's one thing that grieves me and it troubles my mind,
Was the leaving of Molly and Carlow behind.

The cuckoo's a bonny bird, she sings as she flies,
She brings us good tidings, she tells us no lies,
She drinks the lough water to keep her voice clear,
And she never cries Cuckoo till the spring of the year.

So I'll build my love a castle in Strawberry Town,
Where neither lords, dukes or earls shall ever pull it down,
When instead of fine dresses, mourning suits I'll put on;
I'll become the woodranger since my darling is gone.

One Saturday night going to my bedroom,
When the stars showed me light, love, and so did the moon,
When a strange voice came to me for to let me know
That I lost lovely Molly by courting too slow.

6.2 [written on Dp]: Where ne'er lords, ... shall ... pull it ...

The Star of Benbradden

[H24a: [Bp] "Two songs of the Roe valley," 26 Apr 1924]

Source: (w, m) a native, 70 (Aghadowey), from his mother.

Key D.

At the foot of Benbradden clear waters do flow,
There dwells a wee damsel, her breast white as snow,
Her cheeks are like roses, her neck's like the swan,
She's the star of Benbradden, I would she were mine.

If I were a fisher down by yon burn side,
And my love a fish coming in with the tide,
I'd throw out my line and I'd draw her to me,
And I'd then have the prettiest gem of the sea.

If I were a clerk and could handle the pen,
I'd write her a letter, an answer to sen',
I'd write her a letter and seal it with love;
E'en her heart were a mountain, it surely would move.

Last night as I entered my lonely room door,
The stars gave me light and the moon gave me more,
A voice it spake to me sad tidings of woe,
I'd lost lovely Molly by courtin' too slow.

(It's woe unto yon mountains, but you be far away;
If I could see my wee darlin' but once every day,
While her looks they invite me and her tongue bids me go,
And I lost my wee darlin' by courting too slow.)

1.3: ... roses that I would entwine, [written on Bp]
3.2: ... write to her a letter again and [written on Bp]
.3: ... write to her a letter ... them [? Bp written]
5.: [written at bottom of Bp; typed as last stanza on Dt, in parentheses]
5.1 [Bp written as corr.]: ... woe to yon mountains, for you're ... woe to yon ... [Dt]
.2: ... darlin' for once ... [Dt]

I Am a Wee Laddie, Hard, Hard Is My Fate [H624: 16 Nov 1935]

[cf. H165a,b "Green Grow the Rashes," esp. stanza 5]

Source: John Millan, jr (Fish Loughan, Coleraine).

Key G.

I am a wee laddie, hard, hard is my fate,
I have travelled this country both early and late,
I courted a wee lass, I did her adore;
Though she has denied me, I'll try her once more.

At the late hour of midnight when souls are at rest,
I think of my true love with hope in my breast,
Saying, 'The time it is coming and that you will see,
When I'll be with my true love and she'll be with me.'

'Oh, it's Johnnie, dear Johnnie, such things cannot be,
As to be with your true love and you be with me,
For to leave father, mother, their poor hearts would break,
For to leave sisters, brothers, and follow a rake.'

'Oh, it's Molly, dear Molly, you're not much to blame,
When first I came courting, you scarce were eighteen,
Your parents did slight me because I loved so,
And for that very reason I love where you go.

'Oh, it's green grows the holly and so does the rue,
And I'm very sorry at parting with you,
But we'll have merry meetings, our joys to renew,
And we'll leave o'er the false love and start on the new.'

❖ C19 REFERENCES ❖

❖ The Six Sweethearts (H605) 340

Brunnings 1981: "Six Girls"

IREL Moulden 1975:136-7

❖ I've Two or Three Strings to My Bow (H70) 340

BRIT Ramsay 1768(15 ed):414-5 "The Frugal Maid," with no chorus.

❖ One Morning Clear (H548) 341

Dean-Smith 1954: "Searching for Lambs," "should not be confused with 'Searching for young lambs' encountered in MS collections and recordings, otherwise called 'The long and wishing -- i.e., languishing -- eye.' [p. 103]"
Brunnings 1981: ?"Searching for Lambs"

IREL Moulden 1979:114
k: Cf. Joyce 1909:180-1 (#375) "Searching for Young Lambs"

Sam Henry's Songs of the People

◇ **Dark-Eyed Molly** *(H625)* 342
Farewell Ballymoney *(H615)* 343

? Brunnings 1981: "Dark Eyed Molly," ?"The Irish Girl," "Courting Is a Pleasure," "Lovely Molly"; *not*: "Charming Molly"

IREL *JIFSS* 8,1910:12; 13,1913:28
   Joyce 1909:190 [Randolph]
   Shields *Ceol* 2(1):8 "Going to Mass Last Sunday"
   Shields/Shields *UF* 21,1975: #167

\# BRIT MacColl/Seeger 1977:216-7 (#63) "I Went to Mass on Sunday"

AMER Cohen/Seeger 1964:51 "Handsome Molly"
   Dean [1922]:111-2 "Down in Yonder Valley"
   Pete Seeger 1964:30 "Handsome Molly"

? b: REC Guy Carawan, Prestige/Int. 13013 "Hannah"
? b: *Folk Festival*, ABC Paramount ABC 408 "Loving Hannah"
   John McGettigan and His Irish Minstrels, Topic 12T 367 (B4) "Lovely Molly"
   Kevin Mitchell, Topic 12TS 314 (A6) "Going to Mass Last Sunday"
b: Tom Paley, Elektra EKL 217 (A6) "Handsome Molly"
b: Sandy, Caroline Paton, Folk-Legacy EGO 30 "Loving Hannah"
b: Frank Proffitt, Folk-Legacy FSA 1 "Handsome Molly"
b: Peggy Seeger, Folk-Lyric FL 114 "Handsome Molly"
   Paddy Tunney, Topic 12TS 289 (B6) "Going to Mass Last Sunday"
   Jackie Washington, Vanguard VRS 9172 "Loving Hannah"
   "Doc" Watson, Folkways FA 2355 (B4) "Handsome Molly"
b: Jeanie West, Archive AFM FS 208 "Handsome Molly"

◇ **The Sweet Bann Water** *(H722)* 343

Dean-Smith 1954: "Arise, Arise, You Drowsy Maiden," "Oh, Who is That..."; cf. "Father and Daughter," "Our Ship She Lies in Harbour"
Coffin/Renwick 1950(1977):139-40 briefly discusses the relationship of this ballad to Child #248 "The Grey Cock" or "Saw You My Father?" also pp. 267-71.
Laws 1957:181-2 (M4) "The Drowsy Sleeper"
Brunnings 1981: "... (Tune of The Grey Cock)," "... (See Love Is Pleasing)," cf. "The Grey Cock [Child 28]"
Cazden et al. *Notes* 1982: #51 "Awake, Awake Ye Drowsy Sleeper"

c: See C. R. Baskervill *PMLA* 36,1921:565-614, "English Songs of the Night Visit"

IREL Loesberg 2,1980:8 "I'm a Rover and Seldom Sober"
\# c: Shields *Ceol* 3(2)1968:44-5 "Who Comes Tapping to My Window?"
   Shields 1981:59-60 (#15) "The Cocks Is Crowing"
   Shields/Shields *UF* 21,1975: #86 "The Cocks Is Crowing"

BRIT Greig 1906-7(1963): #54
   Lloyd 1967:185-6
   Cf. Richards/Stubbs 1979:114-5 "Forty Miles"
   Vaughan Williams/Lloyd 1959:52-3 "The Grey Cock or The Lover's Ghost," which the editors say is Child #248. But it is close to Henry's ballad.

AMER Barrand *CD&S* 1981:31-2
   Cf. Barry et al. 1939:310
   Bush 2,1970:63-5 "The Silver Dagger"
   Cazden et al. 1982:195-9 "Awake, Awake Ye Drowsy Sleepers"
   Colorado FB 3,1964:37 "Willie and Minnie"
   Darling 1983:117:8, A "Awake, Awake, My Old True Lover" (see Presnell rec.); 118-9, B "Oh, Molly, Dear" (from B. F. Shelton (KY), rec. 1927); 119- "Who's That Knocking" ("similar to" Carter Family rec.); cf. also 223-4 "The Silver Dagger" (see Joines rec.)
   Joyner 1971:53
   Cf. Leach 1967:183-4
   Raim/Dunson 1968:86-7 "Who's That Knocking?"
\# Randolph/Cohen (1982):83-5 "The Drowsy Sleeper"
   Shellans 1968:86-7 "Parents, Warning"
   Solomon 1964:75-7 "Silver Dagger"
   Warner 1984:427-9 (#188) "Wake, O Wake, You Drowsy Sleeper"

BRS *Come Let Us Sing* 1974:52 "The Drowsy Sleeper"

REC Joan Baez, Vanguard VRS 9078 (A1) "Silver Dagger"
cl: Mrs T. M. Bryant, AFS 1753 A1 "The Drowsy Sleepers"
   Eddie Butcher, EEOT *Adam* cass. (B1) "The Cocks Are Crowing"
   John Butcher, EEOT *Shamrock 3* cass. (A1) "The Cocks Is Crowing"
   Carter Family (A. P., Maybelle, Sara), JEMF 101 (A2) "Who's That Knocking," with extensive notes and references.
   Dillard Chandler, Folkways FA 2309 (B1) "Awake, Awake,"
   LaRena Clark, Prestige/Int. 25014 (A3) "I'll Go See My Love"
   Lester A. Coffee, AAFS L55 (A4) "Awake, Arise, You Drowsy Sleeper"
   Cf. Triόna ní Dhomhnaill, Gael Linn CEF 043 (B5) "Here's to All True Lovers"
   Ray, Archie Fisher, Topic 12T 128 (B1) "The Night Visiting Song," a composite.
cl: Maggie Gant, AFS 66 B4 "Awake, Awake"
cl: Jim Garland, AFS 2008 A3 (10 in.)
cl: Mrs G. A. Griffin, AFS 981 A3 "Drowsy Sleepers"
cl: Mrs Birmah Hill Grissom, AFS 2963 A1 "Silver Dagger"
   Kelly Harrell, Victor 20280 [Randolph/Cohen]
   Joe Hickerson, Folk-Legacy FSI 39 (B6) "Last Night as I Lay on My Bed"
   Joe Holmes, Len Graham, Free Reed 007 (A1) "True Lover John"
cl: Aunt Molly Jackson, AFS 2540 A & B "The Silver Dagger"
   Cf. Paul Joines, Asch 3831 (A4) "Young Men and Maids," a double suicide.
cl: Mrs R. Jones, AFS 3426 A1 "Drowsy Sleeper"
   Norman Kennedy, Folk-Legacy FSS 34 (A1) "Night Visiting Song"
   Ewan MacColl, Tradition/Everest TR 2059 (A6) "One Night as I Lay on My Bed"
cl: Mrs J. U. Hewman, AFS 3769 B3, 3770 A1
   Cf. Ken Peacock, Folkways FG 3505 (A1) "Who Is at My Window Weeping," another double suicide.
   Lee Monroe Presnell, Folk-Legacy FSA 22 (A1) "Awake, Awake, My Old True Lover"
cl: Nellie Prewitt, Ina Jones, AFS 2995 A1 "Drowsy Sleeper"
   Belle Stewart, Topic 12TS 307 (A2) "Here's a Health to All True Lovers" with cocks crowing.
   Cf. Davie Stewart, Topic 12T 293 (A4) "I'm Often Drunk and Seldom Sober," which seems to be a recombinant ballad.
   Cf. Cyril Tawney, Argo ZFB 87 (B6) "One Night as I Lay on my Bed"
cl: Crockett Ward, AFS 1341 B "Silver Dagger"
cl: Clay Walters, AFS 1583 A "The Drowsy Sleepers"
lc: Harry, Jeanie West, Stinson 74
   Cf. Bob White, Front Hall FHR 011 (B4) "The Drowsy Sleeper"
cl: Mrs George L. White AFS 920 A2 "The Silver Dagger"

John Wright, Topic 12TS 348 (A1) "Awake, Awake, You Drowsy Sleeper"

h: MEL Hudson ms. 1:181
h: Joyce 1909:85-6 (#170) "When I Came to My True Love's Window"

◇ The Rejected Lover *(H589)* 344

? Cf. Laws 1957:253 (P10), which matches this metre better than does H159 "The Slighted Suitor," but is otherwise dissimilar.
? Brunnings 1981: "The Slighted Swain"

IREL Shields 1981:40 (#2) "Alexander"
Shields/Shields *UF* 21,1975: #12 "Alexander"
But not: Bunting 1983:85 (#55)

BRIT Cf. Greig 1907-11(1963): #159 "The Jilted Lover," which has the same stanza pattern but isn't the same otherwise.
Tocher #38(Spr)1983:61

? b: REC Joan Baez, Bill Wood, Theodore Alevizos, Veritas Vol. 1, No. 1 "The Rejected Lover"
Eddie Butcher, EEOT *Shamrock 2* cass. (A8) "Alexander"

h: MEL Joyce 1909:322 "I'll Travel to Mount Nebo"

◇ The Ploughboy *(H780)* 345

Not = Brunnings 1981: "Lovely Molly"

o: IREL Joyce 1873:73 (#72) "I'm a Poor Stranger and Far from My Own"

BRIT Cf. Purslow 1974:74 "Pretty Sally," esp. stanza 1.

REC John Faulkner, Green Linnet SIF 3004 (= Mulligan 033) (A1)
Jeannie Robertson, Prestige/Int. 13075 (A5) "I Once Was a ..."

◇ The Blackbird and Thrush *(H241)* 346

Brunnings 1981: ?"The Blackbird and the Thrush," "Farewell He!"

IREL Bunting 1983:5-6 (#3) "... and the ..."
Galwey 1910:12, 31 (#3)
? b: Graves 1897 "The Blackbird and the Thrush"
JIFSS 4,1906:33
Joyce 1909:104-5 (#213) "Single and Free"

BRS O'Keeffe 1955(1968):43-4

b: REC Shirley Abicair, Columbia CL 1531 "Let Him Go, Let Him Tarry"
b: Jean Redpath, Folk-Legacy FSS 49 (B6) "Farewell He!"

MEL Petrie 1855:148

◇ Farewell He *(H504)* 347

Dean-Smith 1954
Brunnings 1981: "...," "If He's Gone, Let Him Go," "Fare Thee Well, Cold Winter," ?"They Say," "My Love Is Like a Dewdrop"
Cazden et al. *Notes* 1982: #41 "My Love Is Like a Dewdrop"

BRIT Palmer 1979b:142 (#80) "Fare Thee Well, Cold Winter"
TM #1, mid 1975:13

AMER Cazden et al. 1982:165-8 "My Love Is Like a Dewdrop"
c: Randolph 4:236-41 (#751) reports that, according to Prof. Edwin Ford Piper, "a similar song was popular in Nebraska about 1877, under the title 'Goodbye to Old Winter and Adieu to Its Frost,' doubtless from [the] decade [1868]."
Randolph/Cohen (1982):491-3 "Adieu to Dark Weather"

BRS UCLA 605: 4(n.i.) "Fare-thee-well Cold Winter"
In Dublin's 1968:68-9 "Let Him Go, Let Him Tarry"
120 n.d.:110 "Let Him Go, Let Him Tarry"
c: *Walton's New* 1,1966:39 "Let Him Go Let Him Tarry"
c: *Walton's Treasury 7*

b: REC Shirley Abicair, Columbia CL 1531 "Let Him Go, Let Him Tarry"
b: Harry Belafonte, RCA Victor LSP 2957 "My Love Is Like a Dewdrop"
Margaret MacArthur, Philo 41001 (B3) "Dewdrop"
b: Howard W. Mitchell, Folk-Legacy FSI 29 (B2a) "If He's Gone, Let Him Go"
? cl: Alec Moore, AFS 576 A2 "Adieu to Damp Weather"
b: [Ann] Mayo Muir, 20th-Century Fox TFS 4122 "If He's Gone, Let Him Go"
Jean Redpath, Folk-Legacy FSS 49 (B6)
Cf. Cyril Tawney, Argo ZFB 87 (B8) "... She"
Cf. The Watersons, Topic 12TS 415 (A3) "Fare Thee Well, Cold Winter"

◇ The Cuckoo *(H479)* 347

White/Dean-Smith 1951
Dean-Smith 1954
Brunnings 1981: "...," "A-Walking and a-Talking - And a-Lonesome Go I," "The Cuckoo (The Cuckoo Is a Pretty Bird - Giddy Bird - Witty Bird)"
Cazden et al. *Notes* 1982: #34 "A-Walkin' and A-Talkin'"

IREL Healy 1977:61 "If I Was a Blackbird"
c: *JIFSS* 4,1906:21,33
m: Joyce 1909:316 (#614)
Cf. Loesberg 1,1980:18 "Bunclody"
Moulden 1979:40
Cf. O Lochlainn 1939:150-1 "The Maid of Bunclody, and the Lad She Loves So Dear"
Petrie 1855:95
Sparling 1888:224-5 "The Streams of Bunclody"
Tunney 1979:153 "I Once Had a True-Love"

BRIT MacColl/Seeger 1977:201-4 (#57)
Palmer 1979b:140 (#78)
Shepheard n.d.:13
Sing 8(1,Jan)1965:15

AMER Burton 1981:13 "The Coo-coo Bird (The Cuckoo Bird)"
Cazden et al. 1982:143-7 "A-Walking and A-Talking"
Hudson 1936:166 "Jimmy"
Hudson/Herzog 1937:20 "Jimmy (The Cuckoo)"
Randolph/Cohen (1982):117-8
Wells 1950:274

BRS Harvard 3: (Evans)
Healy 1967a:93-4 "The Streams of Bunclody"
c: Healy 1977:61 "If I Was a Blackbird"
Jolliffe 1970:21-2 "The Streams of Bunclody"

REC [T.] Clarence Ashley, *AAFM* 1, Folkways FP 251 (#57) "The Coo-Coo Bird"; Folkways FA 2359 (B1) [Randolph/Cohen]
Frankie Armstrong, Bay 206 (B5)
b: Hoyt Axton, Surrey SS 1005 "The Fifth Day of July"

Sam Henry's Songs of the People

cl: Charlie Black, AFS 1389 B1 "... Is a Pretty Bird"
   Fleming Brown, Folk-Legacy FSI 4 (B1) "The Coo-Coo"
c: Shirley Collins, Argo RG 150 (A8)
b: *English Garden*, Topic Sampler 8, Topic TPSS 221
cl: Mrs Joseph A. Gaines, AFS 832 A1
cl: Mrs Maggie Gant, AFS 66 A2
cl: Gant Family, AFS 72 B1
b: Carolyn Hester, Columbia 32 16 0264 "Coo, Coo"
cl: Aunt Molly Jackson, AFS AFS 823 B1 & 2
   Lou, Sally Killen, Front Hall FHR 06 (B3)
b: The Little Sisters, MGM E 4116
b: Alan Lomax, The Dupree Family, Kapp KS 3316 "A Pretty Girl is Like a Little Bird"
   Bob March, Riverside RLP12 641 (A7)
b: Judy Mayhan, Horizon WP 1605
cl: Mrs C. S. MacClellan, AFS 986 B2 "... Is a Pretty Bird"
cl: Jonathan Moses, AFS 3705 A2 "Cuckoo is a Fine Bird"
lc: John Jacob Niles, Boone-Tolliver LP, American Love Songs
cl: Mrs Lize Pace, AFS 1437 A1
   Edna Ritchie, Folk-Legacy FSA 3 (B1)
c: Jean Ritchie, [b:] Elektra EKLP 2; [lc:] Elektra EKL 125; Greenhays GR 701 (A3)
   Cf. Alastair Russell, Celtic Music CM 002 (A2) "Bunclody"
b: Sunny Schwartz, Cameo C 1030
b: Peggy Seeger, Folk-Lyric FL 114 "A-Walking and a-Talking - And a-Lonesome Go I"
b: Maxine Sellers, Prestige/Folklore FL 14037
cl: Vivian Skinner, AFS 2997 "Cuckoo is a May Bird"

Hobart Smith, Folk-Legacy FSA 17 (B4) "Cuckoo Bird"
b: *Songs of All Time* 1, World Around Songs N17
b: Pete Steele, Folkways FS 3828 (B3)
   Cyril Tawney, b: Argo ZFB 4; Argo ZFB 87 (B5)
   Joseph Able Trivett, Folk-Legacy FSA 2 "Go Away from Me, Young Man"
b: The Weavers, Vanguard VRS 9100 "A-Walkin' and A-Talkin'"
? cl: John Williams, AFS 4182 A2, B "Cuckoo Song"

MEL O'Neill 1922:26
cl: John Selleck, AFS 4219 A2

◊ If I Were a Fisher *(H709) 348*

Not = Brunnings 1981: "... (See: She Moved through the Fair)"

◊ The Star of Benbradden *(H24a) 348*

Brunnings 1981

◊ I Am a Wee Laddie, Hard, Hard Is My Fate *(H624) 349*

? Brunnings 1981: "I Am a Wee Laddie"

BRIT Greig 1907-11(1963): #61 gives an untitled song which may be a different version; it begins:

   I hae travelled this country both early and late.
   How hard's been my fortune, my sorrow's been great.

C20

She will not condescend: Love unrequited

Sam Henry's Songs of the People

John MacAnanty's Courtship

[H56: BLp, "A fairy song," 6 Dec 1924]

Other title: "The Fairy King's ...," "McAnanty's Welcome."

Source: (m) E. J. Bennett, esq (Coleraine), (w, m) from his mother (Adare district, Co. Limerick).

s: John MacAnanty, the Fairy King of Scrabo, whose palace was under the sepulchral mound at Scrabo, near Newtownards, did not confine his activities to the north, but in this song we find him wooing a maiden in Co. Limerick.

The air ... is much sweeter than that used by Joyce....

[Print from British Library microfilm from John Moulden. Bt, Dt in 3. Bt includes a copy of "A Fairy Song," Irish air arranged by John Vine (Oxford Descant Series, from The Oxford Choral Songs, General Editor, W. Gillies Whittaker.) No. D 23. Copyright 1934 by Oxford University Press, London.]

[BLp, Bt] Key F. [Dt] Key A flat.

On the first day of May at the close of the day,
As I stood in the shade of a green spreading tree,
A young lover a-courting a maiden I spied;
I drew very nigh them to hear and to see.

The dress that he wore was a velvet so green,
All trimmed with gold lace and as bright as the sea,
And he said, 'Love, I'll make you my own fairy queen
If you are but willing to ramble with me.

'Lisses and forts shall be at your command,
Mountains and valleys, the land and the sea,
And the billows that roar along the seashore,
Love, if you're willing to ramble with me.'

'To make me a queen, my birth is too mean,
And you will get ladies of higher degree;
I know not your name nor from whence you came,
So I am not willing to ramble with thee.'

'I will tell you my name, and I love you the same
As if you were a lady of higher degree.
MacAnanty's my name and from Scrabo I came,
And the queen of that country, my love, you shall be.'

'If I were to go with a man I don't know,
My parents and friends would be angry with me;
They'd bring me back again with shame and disdain,
So I am not willing to ramble with thee.'

'From your friends we will sail in a ship that won't fail,
With silken topsail and a wonderful flight,
From this to Coleraine, to France and to Spain
And home back again in a short summer's night.

'Many a mile I have roamed in my time
By sea and by land a-looking for thee,
And I never could find rest or peace to my mind
Until fortune proved kind and sent you to me.'

7.2: ... topmast and ... [Dt]
 .3: ... Coleraine and to ... [Dt]
 .4: ... summer night. [Bt, Dt]
8.1: 'Oh, many ... [Dt]

Paddy's Land

[H473: 24 Dec 1932]

Source: (w, m) Teady McErlean (Clady, Glenone, Portglenone), sung by John M'Donnell, fiddler (Kilrea).

[Aside from the repeat for the refrain, the tune would fit either a 16-measure jig in 6/8 time or an 11-bar jig in 9/8.]

Key C.

When I was young and in my prime, from care and trouble I was free,
I took a ramble o'er the Moyle, where Paisley lies beyond the sea,
It happened to be in harvest time when autumn winds did gently blaw,
And bonny lasses did combine to wile young laddies' hearts awa'.
  It happened to be in harvest time when autumn winds did gently blaw,
  And bonny lasses did combine to wile young laddies' hearts awa'.

In sweet content my time I spent amang the lasses kind and free,
But nane o' them could me beguile or rob me of my liberty,
Till I spied one amang the rest whose beauty far outshone them a',
And the glances o' her bonny e'e soon stole my tender heart awa'.
  Till I spied ...

C20 / She will not condescend

One day she said to me, 'My dear, do you belong
    to Scotland's soil?'
'Oh no, my dearest dear,' said I, 'my dwelling
    lies beyond the Moyle:
A city fair beyond compare, that on a lofty hill
    does stand,
Surrounded by the river Foyle that flows
    nor'west of Paddy's land.
    A city fair ...

'And now, my dear, if you'll agree to go across
    the Moyle with me,
My heart's best love I'll give to you and
    straightway we will married be.
In unity we will agree, in harmony joined hand in
    hand,
From hence I will conduct you safe to the
    charming shores of Paddy's land.'
    In unity we will ...

Tomorrow morn my ship sets sail; the object of
    my heart's desire,
When I am sailing down the Clyde, will set my
    tender heart on fire.
Tomorrow morn my ship sets sail, she's bound for
    Erin's blooming shore,
And when I'm sailing up the Foyle I'll sigh for
    the girl I'll see no more.
    Tomorrow morn ...

Claudy Green (a) [H115a: 23 Jan 1926]

Source not given.

[Dt] s: The last verse ... is sung to the second
half of the tune.

Key G.

One evening clear, for my amusement,
Near Claudy borders I chanced to stray,
Where the springs of nature sets forth their
    beauty
In every green field and meadow gay;
The wild inhabitants of every species
Do join the mavis with notes combined,
And the little cuckoo on bending branches
Returning seasons does still incline.

I being free from care and the snares of Cupid,
With soft amusement my heart did fill,
Viewing those flowers and bowers wavering,
From the Faughan water clear streams run still.
For to view the trout and salmon sporting,
For to behold them I did draw near,
And in a moment I was eclipsed
All by that fair maid that did appear.

I stepped forth to that matchless beauty,
Saying, 'Are you Diana, that goddess fair?
Or are you Venus, sprung from the ocean
The hearts of young men for to ensnare?'
'Well, indeed, kind sir, I am but a maiden,
These fragrant bowers I have oftimes seen,
And my inclination is in gathering flowers
That are decorating sweet Claudy Green.'

'I being free from care and the snares of Cupid,
To gain one part in your company,
In your snowy bosom my heart lies wavering,
Your smiles, my wee darling, would set me free,
I would serve you like Jacob for fourteen seasons
Through burning sand or some distant clime,
And all my vexations I would bear with patience
If with you, love, I could spend my time.'

'Well indeed, kind sir, I disdain those pleasures,
Nor in your company would I be seen.'
And those words she spoke have left me
    bewailing;
Adieu, you fair maid of Claudy Green.

The Maid of Croaghmore [H522: 2 Dec 1933]

Source not given.

s: Croaghmore is pronounced in three syllables,
Cro-agh-more. The Duke of Cumberland mentioned in verse 3 was William Augustus, second
son of George II, king of England. He was
known for his harsh methods in quelling the
rising of Bonnie Prince Charlie in 1745.

Key G.

Sam Henry's Songs of the People

I am a bold undaunted youth, I live in sweet Rarawn,
In Magheracastle born and bred, and there I am well known,
I fell in love with a pretty maid and her I do adore,
She's a daughter to James Anderson and lives in Croaghmore.

The first time I saw my love, I knew not what to do,
And to address this handsome maid, I straight did her pursue,
I asked her name and where she dwelt, some questions three or four,
She says, 'I'm Rachel Anderson and live in Croaghmore.'

My love's a sparkling tall young girl, her age is scarce nineteen.
If I was king of Erin's isle, sure she would be my queen,
Or was I Duke of Cumberland with whips of gold in store,
I'd freely share with that young dame who lives in Croaghmore.

Her teeth are like the ivory, her hair is a nut-brown,
For wit and good behaviour her equal can't be found,
Her eyes shine bright like stars by night, she has wounded me full sore,
I'm surely pained by that young maid who lives in Croaghmore.

Jacob served for seven years that Rachel he might own,
His father-in-law deceived him with Leah, 'tis well known,
And for the sake of Rachel, Jacob served for seven years more;
For that same name I'd serve the same, she's the pride of Croaghmore.

I courted her with compliments, her favour for to win,
The more I did pursue my love, the more she did me shun.
Was I to live a thousand years instead of a few score,
I ne'er would find one to my mind like the maid of Croaghmore.

Now to conclude and finish, I mean to end my song,
I asked her off her parents, they said she was too young;
If I don't gain this handsome maid, I'll leave my native shore
And bid farewell to all my friends that live round Croaghmore.

The Bonnie Wee Lass of the Glen

[H14a: 16 Feb 1924]

John Henry Macauley's air:

[Bp typed at top] Tune. The Maid with the Bonny Brown Hair. Corrections by Bridget Kealy, Termeil, Dungiven.

s: An old favourite in the Armoy and Ballycastle districts.... The air was taken down from ... an old schoolmate, whose friendship I have linked on again in the mutual love of the songs our mothers sang to us.

[Bp] Another air with this title, appeared in 1905 in Vol. 2 of the *Journal of the Irish Folk Song Society*, London. It was taken down from the whistling of Mr [John Henry] Macauley, who has now supplied the words. I have chosen the simpler air because it is the more easily sung and because of its characteristically Irish endings in lines 1 and 3.

[Bp written over printed sol-fa]
m s l s m r d r[? illegible] d

s: (m) "The Maid with the Bonny Brown Hair";
o: (m) "Aghalee Heroes."

Source: (w) J[ohn] H[enry] M[acauley] (Ballycastle); (m) J[ohn] M[urphy] (Coleraine), Sam Henry's old schoolmate.

Key B flat.

[H14b: Dt=W(c)]

Bridget Kealey's air ... :

Source: (m) Bridget Kealey (Tirmeil, Dungiven).

Key G.

C20 / She will not condescend

It being on a fine summer morning,
Alone as I carelessly strayed,
As Phoebus' bright beams were adorning
The beautiful brow of Knocklayd,
I went up to a neat little cottage,
A wee lassie bid me come ben;
I stood all amazed and said nothing,
But gazed on the lass o' the glen.

Her cheeks were as red as two roses,
The skin of this beautiful maid
Was whiter by far than the snow that
Blows over the brow of Knocklayd.
Her form was endowed with such beauty
I could not express with my pen,
So I long to be kissing and courting
The bonnie wee lass o' the glen.

She lives at the foot of Knocklayd
In a valley that's fertile and green,
By the side of a murmuring river
That flows through a town they call Breen,
Where the blackbird and thrush loudly whistle
And the cuckoo her notes does expen',
And with music the valley is ringing
To charm the wee lass o' the glen.

'Oh, Jamie,' she says, 'do not tease me,
Your talk I would have you give o'er;
Your flattering tongue does not please me,
It has deceived numbers before;
Besides, A[']m owre young for to marry,
My age it is scarce five and ten,'
And that was the answer I got frae
The bonny wee lass o' the glen.

So now to conclude these few verses
In praise of the dear girl I love,
May he who created all beauty
Shower blessings on her from above,
And if I can but gain her favour,
I will count myself blessed of all men,
And through life I will fondly endeavour
To please the wee lass o' the glen.

[Bp *typed at top*] Corrections by Bridget Kealy,
 Termeil, Dungiven:
[Alterations *written on Bp:*]
   3.6: ... cuckoo's clear notes do ascend,
   3.8: To cheer ...
   4.6: My age is scarce five years and ten,'
[Dt *incorporates Bp written alterations plus:*]
   1.5: I stepped up ...
   1.7: ... and said nothing, but gazed

1.8: On the bonnie wee lass of ...
2.3: ... the snow
2.4: That blows ...
3.1: ... foot of the mountain
3.4: ... town called the Breen,

1.6: ben = in.

As I Walked Out [H109: 12 Dec 1925]

Other title: cf. "A New Broom Sweeps Clean."

Source: William Carton (Garryduff, Ballymoney)
from his mother c. 1875.

Key D.

As I walked out on an evening so clear,
A young man lamented for the loss of his dear,
And as he lamented, full sore he did cry,
Saying, 'Alas, I'm tormented, for love I must
  die.'

'My dear and my jewel, my honey,' said he,
'Will you let me gang wi' you a sweetheart to be?
And my dear and my jewel, my honey,' said he,
'Will you let me gang wi' you a sweetheart to be?

'Were I to say yes, I would say 'gainst my mind,
And for to say no, you would think I was unkind.
For to sit and say nothing, you would say I was
  dumb,
So take that for your answer and go as you
  come.'

Oh, pox take you, Sally, for you are unkind,
You pulled the lily, left the red rose behind,
But the lily will yellow, and the time will come
  soon
When the red rose will flourish in the sweet
  month of June.

Oh, some court for beauty, but beauty soon
  fades,
Others marry for riches, get bold saucy jades,
But if I ever marry, as plain as you may see,
The wee lass that's loyal is the darling for me.

3.2: ... think 'twas ... [Dt]

Farewell, Darling [H580: 12 Jan 1935]

Other titles: "(O')Reil(l)y from the Co. Leitrim
(Kerry)," "The Phoenix of Erin's Green Isle,"

357

Sam Henry's Songs of the People

"When First I Came to County Limerick," "Young (O')R(e)il(l)y"; cf. "Youth and Folly."

Source: (Bushmills).

s: The adaptation of the words to the air in this song is very difficult to convey. The traditional singer makes his own time and ignores bar lines. Yet to hear it so sung, it seems the most natural thing in the world.

Key C.

As I roved out one summer's morning,
It was to view the green fields so gay,
I fell a-courting a pretty damsel,
She appeared to me like the queen of May.

Said I, 'My fair one, it's would you marry,
Or would you be a bright sailor's wife?'
'O it's no, kind sir, I would sooner tarry,
I would sooner choose a bright single life.'

'You are like the swan that swims on the ocean,
A-making motion with both her wings,
And your snow-white breast is a fit portion
For any lord or Irish king.

'If I had you in St. Finan's island,
A hundred miles from your native home,
Or in some valley between two mountains,
It's there, my darling, I'd call you my own.'

'It's no, kind sir, you'll have me in no island,
A hundred miles from my native home,
Nor in no valley between two mountains,
It's never there you will call me your own.

'It's do not tease me, for love won't please me,
It's along with you I don't intend to be,
For youth and folly make a young man marry,
And then they're as sorry as time does flee.'

'It's in the morning when I can't see you,
My heart will break for you all day,
And in the evening I'll still be grieving,
So farewell, darling, I'm going away.'

Will Ye Pad the Road wi' Me?

[H18a: 15 Mar 1924]

358 [cf. H564 "Banks of Mourne Strand"]

g: "To Pad the Road"; o: (m) "Winding Banks of Erne."

Source: (w) Pat Hackett (Stone Row, Coleraine).

s: This song may also be sung to the air of "The Whinny Knowes."

Key F.

Come draw your chair up to my loom and tell to me the time,
It's when will we be married, love, or when will you be mine?
Or when will we be married, love, that I may plainly see?
And it's ah, my bonnie lassie, will you pad the road wi' me?

For to pad the road wi' you, kind sir, the winter nights is lang,
And my ould aged parents has got ne'er a wean but wan,
And my ould aged parents has got nane but what you see,
And it's ah, my bonnie laddie, I'll no' pad the road wi' you.

I hae a laddie in my view, he's of a high renown,
He's proper, tall and handsome, and he dwells in Lurgan town,
There's not a fault in my true love, as far as I can see,
And it's ah, my bonnie laddie, I'll no' pad the road wi' you.

The lad that you hae in your view, he's but a silly clown,
He'll bate you and abuse you and he'll pull your courage down,
And he'll make you curse and rue the day that ever you did him see,
And it's ah, my bonnie lassie, will you pad the road wi' me?

It's naw a threed I'll bid you spin, but sit and drink your tay,
I'll tak' you in my arms, love, and I'll gee you kisses three,
I'll tak' you in my arms, love, and I'll gee you kisses three,
And it's ah, my bonnie lassie, will you pad the road wi' me?

When naw a threed you bid me spin, but sit and
   drink my tay,
And ye'll tak' me in your arms and you will gee me
   kisses three,
And ye'll tak' me in your arms and you will gee me
   kisses three,
And it's ah, my bonnie laddie, sure I'll pad the
   road wi' you.

When you hae nae better in your view that gars
   you slight at me,
You may light your can'le at Dymond's lamp wi' a
   lad o' your ain degree,
An' I'll light my can'le at Dymond's lamp wi' a lass
   o' my ain degree,
An' ye'll sit anither saison or you pad the road wi'
   me.

[Differences in Dt:]
1.4: ... will ye ...
2.2, 2.3: And my oul' ...
2.4, 3.4, 6.4: ... wi' thee.
4.3: ... that e'er ...
5.2, 5.3: ... I'll gie ...
6.2: And you'll tak ... you'll gie ...
6.3: ... you'll gie ...
7.2, 7.3: ... at Hymen's lamp ...
7.4: And you'll ...

2.2: wan = one.
5.1: naw = not; threed = thread.
7.1: gars = makes, causes.
7.2: light a can'le at Dymond's [Hymen's] lamp =
   marry.
7.4: saison = season; or = before, until.

The Maid of Craigienorn [H500: 1 Jul 1933]

Other title: cf. "The Maid of Island Moore."

Source: William Hegan (6 Claremont St, University Rd, Belfast).

Key F.

Ye muses nine with me combine, assist me with
   your aid
Until I sing the praises of a fair and comely maid
Whose dwelling's near Kilwaughter beneath a
   spreading thorn
On the bleak but lovely townland well known as
   Craigienorn.

She's five feet nine and figure fine, like waxwork
   is complete,
With rosy cheeks and ruby lips -- in fact, she's
   all that's neat,
She far exceeds fair Mary Stuart, who ruled the
   Scottish throne,
She's void of pride, and far from harm is the maid
   of Craigienorn.

One evening late, hard was my fate as I carelessly
   did stray,
The lovely lambs around their dames did freely
   sport and play,
Diana with her silvery rays each form did adorn,
'Twas there I spied this beauty bright, the star
   of Craigienorn.

And soon I fell in love with her, as you may
   understand,
I asked her if she would consent to join in
   wedlock's band,
Forsake her father's dwelling, yon cot beneath
   the thorn,
And she would be a lady gay, not far from
   Craigienorn.

'To leave my father's dwelling? 'Tis what I'll
   never do,
Nor for the sake of riches will I follow a rake like
   you,
I dearly love a young man, to leave him I would
   scorn,
I'm quite content with him I love to stay in
   Craigienorn.'

'Forsake the lad you dearly love and come along
   with me,
I'll take you to my father's cot -- no other heirs
   has he --
Mind, I am no pretender, love, my love for you is
   sure,
I've twenty acres of free land near the village of
   Ballynure.'

'Boast not to me of free lands, to them you may
   return,
And when from you I'm absent, I pray for me
   don't mourn,
You may go and court some other fair, and with
   your gold adorn;
I will not leave my father's home, nor yet sweet
   Craigienorn.'

'The young man that you dearly love has now gone
   far away
Unto the north of Ireland a long time for to stay,
To a place called Ballycastle, where he was born
   and bred,
And I'm afraid he'll soon forget his Craigienorn
   fair maid.'

Ye pretty maids of Craigienorn, a warning by me
   take,
And never give your hearts away to any false
   young rake,
He'll vow and swear he loves you dear and leave
   you here to mourn,
He'll break your tender heart like mine on the
   braes of Craigienorn.

Sam Henry's Songs of the People

The small birds of the forest do all their voices raise,
They all do join in chorus to sing this fair maid's praise.
The blackbird and the speckled thrush sit singing in yon thorn,
They seem to say, 'Ah, fair maid, stay and don't leave Craigienorn.'

This fair maid's name I will not tell, to name it I would scorn,
She is a Presbyterian and lives near Craigienorn
In a place called Bencubitt, where she was born and bred,
Her father a stone mason was and worked long at his trade.

Now to conclude and finish lest these verses I should rue,
The poet's name I fain would tell, but that would never do,
Old England's laws does me confine, of them I am afraid,
Success attend the shepherd's boy and his Craigienorn fair maid.

Lurgan Stream (a) [H229a: 31 Mar 1928]

[see H65a "Alt[i]mover Stream"]

o: "Largy (Leargaidh) Stream." Other titles: "(The) Lurgy Stream(s).

[Bp] Source: 2: Nellie M'Intyre (Mulkeragh South, Limavady), late Alexander Thompson (Alla, near Park).

1: Bp and Dt are different enough to justify printing both as variants.

Key F.

When to this country first I came, my mind from love being free,
It was the beauty of that female bright that so enticed me,
It was the beauty of that female bright that set my heart aflame;
To sing her praise I'll now set forth, she dwells near Lurgan Stream.

Her cheeks are like the roses red that's newly blown in June,
Her teeth like the polished ivory, and her breath a sweet perfume,
Her yellow hair waves in the air, most rare for to be seen,
And with a dart she pierced my heart and set it in a flame.

It was on a Monday evening my love I chanced to meet,
I took her in my arms and I gave her kisses sweet,
I asked her if she would marry me, or single would remain,
Or if she would cross o'er the seas with me and leave sweet Lurgan Stream.

'If I would cross o'er the seas with you, I am sure that would be known,
Or if I would cross o'er the seas with you, my friends would me disown;
If I would cross the seas with you, I would be much to blame,
So here at home I mean to roam and dwell near Lurgan Stream.'

'Oh, that the moon may be withdrawn, no more to rule the night,
Or that the sun may be withdrawn, no more to rule daylight,
The twinkling stars, they may fall down, no more for to be seen,
If ever, love, I prove false to you when far from Lurgan Stream.'

She says, 'Young man, from me withdraw; none of your foolish talk,
For it was for recreation sake that I came here to walk;
For Cupid's dart ne'er pierced my heart, nor set it in a flame,
When I would think on your false love when far from Lurgan Stream.'

My pen is getting feeble now, sure I can add no more;
Since she is too young to marry me, I will sail to a foreign shore,
I'll bid farewell to my old sweetheart, since her I can't redeem,
Likewise to you, old Ireland, when far from Lurgan Stream.

Farewell to Letterkenny town, lies near Glen Swilly shore,
Where I spent all my youthful days; will I never see you more?
And twice farewell to you, Argyle, where oftimes I have been,
Likewise to Kilmacrenan town, lies near sweet Lurgan Stream.

Lurgan Stream (b) [H229b: Wt=D(c)]

o: "Largy Stream."

No source given for this variant.

When into this country first I came, my mind from
    love being free,
The char-m of the female sex had not enticed me,
Until I beheld a charming maid who set my heart
    a-flame,
This lovely fair had nut-brown hair; she dwells
    near Lurgan Stream.

It was on a Sunday evening my love I chanced to
    meet,
I took her in my arms and gave her kisses sweet,
I asked her if she'd marry me, or single still
    remain,
Or if she'd cross the seas with me and leave sweet
    Lurgan Stream.

She says, 'Young man, be easy, no more of your
    foolish talk,
It wasn't for going away from here that I came
    here to walk;
King Cupid's dart ne'er pierced my heart nor set
    it in a flame,
I'm free from love and I'll always be, along sweet
    Lurgan's Stream.

'Besides, if I were to go with you I would be
    much to blame,
Likewise, kind sir, I being too young, my
    parents would me disown,
And if unfaithful you would prove, full sore
    would I complain
The hour that I'd forsake my friends along sweet
    Lurgan Stream.'

He says, 'My pretty fair maid, if you come along
    with me,
You'll find me always faithful and ever true to
    thee,
I'm bound for North Americay, you'll ne'er see me
    again,
My heart will break when I think to part with you
    and sweet Lurgan Stream.'

My lover's cheeks are like the rose blooms in the
    month of June,
Her teeth are like the ivory bright, and her
    breath like sweet perfume,
Her slender waist, her snow-white breast have set
    my heart aflame,
Her habitation it lies near unto sweet Lurgan
    Stream.

The sun shall cease to give its light, no more to
    rule the day,
And Luna in her twilight no more shall rule the
    night,
The twinkling star and dawn ne'er come, nor e'er
    be seen again,
The hour that I prove false to thee along sweet
    Lurgan Stream.

Farewell to Letterkenny town, likewise Lough
    Swilly shore,
Where many's the pleasant day I spent in scenes
    I'll ne'er see more,
And twice farewell to sweet Ardghais, where
    oftimes I have been,
Likewise to Kilmacrenan town that stands near
    Lurgan Stream.

C20 / She will not condescend

Castleroe Mill [H22b: 12 Apr 1924]

Source not given.

Key F.

As I went a-walking on last Lammas Day,
I met a wee lassie tripping lightly and gay,
The lilt of her song was like the lark's trill,
And she told me her dwelling was Castleroe Mill.

'No longer than Lammas the strangers I'll serve,
For I've got all my money laid up in reserve,
I'm off, love, to Canada if providence will:
Will you go along and leave Castleroe Mill?'

'Sir, my aged parents are on the decline,
And I can not leave yon poor dwelling of mine.'
Her eyes were as bright as the clear purling rill
That flows by yon valley by Castleroe Mill.

I am sailing the ocean, where billows do roar,
Oh, cruel the seas, I may ne'er see her more,
May goodness protect her from all that is ill,
And befriend the wee lassie from Castleroe Mill.

Farewell to Mountsandel, farewell to the Bann,
Where oft I have strayed with my love, hand in
    hand.
Where'er I may wander, where'er I may roam,
May sweet Castleroe at last be my home.

2.3: ... off o'er the ocean, if ... [Bp *written*; Dt]

The Banks of Kilrea (II)

[H150b: 25 Sep 1926]

[Dt] s: (m) "The Happy Green Shades of Duneane."

[Text is the second in Bp, presented as "another
song to this title and the same air...." However,
Dt includes a second tune specifically for this
song, and presents 10 4-line stanzas, each line
half the length of those in Bp.]

Source: 4: Mary M'Hugh, 96 (Baltytunn Hill,
Rasharkin), learned from a friend (Cushendall),
c. 1845; Patrick Brolly (Drum, Dungiven);
Francis M'Kenna (Ballymacpeake, Co. Derry);
William Ferguson (Craigbrack, Eglinton).

Key F.

One evening for my recreation, as I roved by the
  bonny Bann side,
A laddie was coaxing his lassie and fain would
  have made her his bride.
A young man was coaxing his darling, inviting her
  kindly away,
But she said, 'I'll not leave my parents alone on
  the banks of Kilrea.'

He says, 'Love, you're one of the fairest, my
  heart you have wounded full sore,
Would you leave the land of oppression and old
  Ireland we'll never see more?
'And if you consent to go with me, your passage
  I'm willing to pay,
And we'll reap the fruits of our labour far away
  from the banks of Kilrea.'

She said it was folly to flatter, she never would
  cross over the main,
'There's danger in crossing deep water, kind sir,
  all your coaxing's in vain.
'My parents are both old and feeble, their locks
  they are turning to gray,
And I never will leave them, no, never, alone on
  the banks of Kilrea.'

'Oh, darling, do you not well remember the
  promise you made unto me?
It was on the first day of November I told you I'd
  cross o'er the sea.
'You said I would leave you to mourn, you
  flattered me here for to stay,
But when that the spring would return, you would
  then leave the banks of Kilrea.'

Farewell to the bonny Bann water, for it's now I
  must leave down my pen;
Farewell to the bonny Bann water and the girls all
  around the Bridge End.
Farewell to my old friends and comrades, for now
  I am going away,
And you never will see me, no, never, on the
  lovely sweet banks of Kilrea.

1.2: ... and feign ... [Bp, Wt, Dt]

The True Lovers' Discussion

[H164: 1 Jan 1927]

s: (m) "Youghal Harbour," = H13 "The Star of
Glenamoyle," = H67 "The Fair Maid of Ballyagan";
o: (m) "One Harvest Morning." Other title: "...
Lovers' ...."

Source: (w, m) native, 75 (Ballyportery, Loughguile), learned from her mother c. 1860; author
schoolteacher M'Kittrick (Magheratimpan, near
Ballynahinch, Co. Down).

[Bp] s: This song is published in response to numerous requests from readers at home, and even
beneath the Southern Cross....
   The song, without an error [Dt: omission], was
sung to me by a native of Ballyportery....

[Dt is a hybrid copy: headnotes and sol-fa tune
typed, with the lyrics, in 8-line stanzas, evidently clipped from p. 77 of a book; there are
only 8 stanzas.]

m: The printed part comes from a copy of O'Conor
[1901], pp. 77-8. It was cut by Henry ... from
his copy....

Key G. [Bp, Wt] Slow with expression.

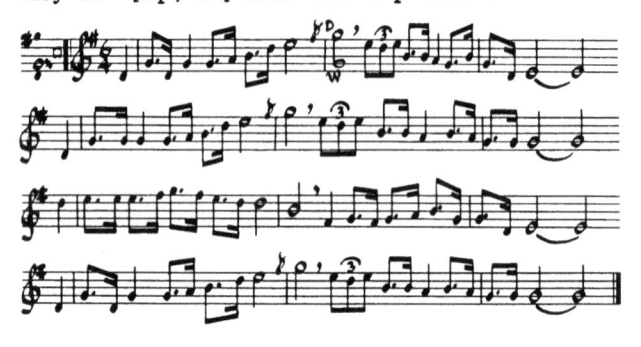

One pleasant evening, when pinks and daisies
  closed in their bosoms a drop of dew,
The feathered warblers of every species
  together chanted their notes so true,
As I did stray, rapt in meditation, it charmed
  my heart for to hear them sing,
Night's silent embers were just arising and the
  air with concert did sweetly ring.

With joy transported, each sight I courted while
  gazing round me with expecting eye;
Two youthful lovers, in conversation closely
  engaged, I chanced to spy.
The couple spoke with such force of reason,
  and their sentiments they expressed so clear,
That for to listen to their conversation, my
  inclination was to draw near.

He pressed her hand and he said, 'My darling,
  tell me the reason you changed your mind,
Or have I loved you to be degraded while youth
  and innocence are in their prime?
For I am slighted and ill requited for all the
  favours I did bestow,
You will surely tell me before I leave you why
  you're inclined to treat me so.'

With great acuteness she then made answer: 'If
  on your favours I would rely,
You might contrive to blast my glory, and our
  marriage day you might hover by.
Young men in general are fickle-minded and oh,
  to trust you I am afraid,
If for your favours I am indebted, both stock
  and interest you shall be paid.'

C20 / She will not condescend

'To blast your glory, love, I ne'er intended,
  nor fickle-minded will I ever be,
And as for my debts, you can never repay them
  except by true love and loyalty.
Remember, darling, our first engagement, when
  childish pastime was all we knew,
Be true and constant, and I'm thine forever, I'll
  brave all dangers and go with you.'

'Your proffer's good, and I thank you for it,
  but yet your offer I can't receive;
By soft persuasion and kind endearment the wily
  serpent beguiled Eve.
There's other reasons might be assigned: the
  highest tide, love, might ebb and fall,
Another fair maid might fit you better, therefore I
  can't obey your call.'

'Yes, I'll admit the tide in motion is always
  moving from shore to shore,
But still its substance is never changing, and
  never will, till time's no more.
I will sound the fame of all loyal lovers to fix
  their minds on whose love is pure,
Where no existence can ever change them, nor a
  physician prescribe a cure.'

She says, 'Young man, to tell you plainly, for to
  refrain you I am inclined,
Another young man of birth and honour has
  gained my favour and changed my mind.
My future welfare I have consulted, on fickle
  footing I'll never stand,
Besides my parents would be affronted to see
  you walking at my right hand.'

'What had you, darling, when you were born?
  What nature gave you, love, so had I.
Your haughty parents, I do defy them, and
  your ill-got riches I do deny.
An honest heart, love, is far superior; your
  gold and riches will fade away;
Sure, naked we came into this world, love, and
  much the same shall we go away.'

'You falsify when you say you love me, and
  slight my parents, whom I love dear;
I think it justice to degrade you when that's the
  course that you mean to steer.
By wealth or feature, or art, or nature, you're
  not my equal in any line;
Since I conjure you, insist no further, as to
  your wishes I'll not incline.'

'To falsify, love, I do deny it; your imputation
  is wrong, I swear,
And, like Eve, I find you a real deceiver with a
  heart as false as your face is fair.
For want of riches you meanly slight me, and
  my complexion you do disdain;
Our skins may differ, but true affection in black
  and white, love, is all the same.'

'Oh, curb your passion, sir,' she then
  exclaimed, 'it was not to quarrel that I
  brought you here,
But to discourse with you in moderation with a
  real intention to make appear.

I speak with candour: I will surrender to what
  is proper in every way,
If you submit to a fair discussion, and reason's
  dictates you will obey.'

'It is now too late to ask that question when you
  despised me before my friends;
Lebanon's plains, if you could command them,
  would not suffice to make amends;
There's not a tree in the Persian forest retains
  its colour excepting one,
And that the laurel that I will cherish and
  always carry in my right hand.'

'The blooming laurel, sir, you may admire
  because its virtue seems always new;
But there's another, you can't deny it, it's just
  as bright to the gardener's view.
It wisely resteth throughout the winter and
  blooms again when spring draws near,
The pen of Homer has wrote its praises, in June
  and July it doth appear.'

'You speak exceedingly, but not correctly, by
  words supporting your cause in vain;
Had you the tongue of a Siren goddess your
  exhortations I would disdain.
It was your love that I required, but since you
  placed it in a golden store,
I'll strike the string and my harp will murmur
  farewell, my darling, for evermore.'

She seemed distracted, her eyes affected, with
  exclamations she thus give way:
'Sir, my denial was but a trial -- ye gods, be
  witness to what I say --
But if, my darling, you don't forgive me and
  quite forget my incredulity,
A single virgin for your sake I'll wander, while
  a green leaf grows on yon laurel tree.'

So all young maidens, I pray take warning: let
  love and virtue be still your aim;
No worldly treasure should yield you pleasure,
  with those whose features you do disdain.
All loyal lovers will then respect you, and to
  your memory will heave a sigh;
The blooming rose and evergreen laurel will
  mark the spot where your bodies lie.

From Ballynahinch, about two miles distant,
  where blackbirds whistle and thrushes sing,
With hills surrounding and valley bounding a
  charming prospect in all the spring,
Where female beauty is never wanting, the
  lonely stranger a refuge finds,
In Magheratimpan, if you inquire, you will find
  the author of these simple lines.

[Differences in Dt (which has the first 8 stanzas
only, in 8-line stanzas half as long:]
  1.1: ... evening, as pinks ...
   .3: ... stray, wrapped in ... heart to hear ...
   .4: The silent orbs of night were ... air in
       concert ... sweetly sing.
  2.1: courted whilst gazing 'round with inspective
       eye,
   .3: Those couple ... reason, their ...

Sam Henry's Songs of the People

```
    .4: And just to ...
3.1: ... and said,
    .2: ... degraded, tho' ...
    .4: You'll surely ... inclined now to ...
4.1: ... she made him answer, saying, 'On your ...
    .2: But you ...
    .3: ... and to trust ...
5.2: As for ... never pay them but by ...
    .4: ... constant, I'm ...
6.1: ... good, sir, I ... your offers I ...
    .3: ... love, will ebb ...
    .4: Another female might suit you ...
7.2: ... changing, nor never ...
    .3: I'll sound your fame with all ... their love on
        whose mind is ...
    .4: ... change it, nor no physician ...
8.1: ... plainly, to refrain ...
    .2: ... and fortune has ...
    .3: ... have considered, on ...
    .4: ... be offended to ...
```

The Maid of the Sweet Brown Knowe

[H84: 20 Jun 1925, H688: 30 Jan 1937; Laws P7]

Republished by special request.

Other titles: "(At) The Foot (Maid) of the Mountain('s) Brow (Logan Bough)."

Key D.

Come all you lads and lasses and listen to me a
  while,
Till I sing to you a verse or two, 'twill cause you
  all to smile,
It's all about a young man I'm going to tell you
  now,
That lately went a-courting with the maid of the
  sweet brown knowe.

'Oh,' says he, 'my pretty fair maid, if you and I
  agree,
We will join our hands in wedlock banns and
  married we will be,
We will join our hands in wedlock banns by
  meeting with you now,
And I'll do all my endeavours for the maid of the
  sweet brown knowe.

This young and foolish fickle one, she knew not
  what to say,
Her eyes they shone like diamonds and merrily
  bright did play,
She says, 'Young man, you must excuse, I'm not
  just ready now,
I'll rest another season at the foot of the sweet
  brown knowe.'

Says he, 'My pretty fair maid, oh, why did you
  say no?
Look down in yonder valley where my crops do
  gently grow,
Look down in yonder valley at my horses and my
  plough,
Sure, they're at their daily labour for the maid of
  the sweet brown knowe.'

'If they're at their daily labour, kind sir, it's not
  for me;
I've heard of your behaviour, I have, kind sir,'
  said she.
'There is an inn where you call in, I hear the
  people say,
Where you rap and call and pay for all and go
  home at the break of day.'

'If I rap and call and pay for all, the money it is
  my own,
I'll not spend much of your fortune, for I hear
  you have got none;
You thought you had my poor heart won by
  meeting with you now,
But I'll leave you where I found you at the foot
  of the sweet brown knowe.'

5.4: ... at break ... [Dt]
6.3: ... heart broke by ... [Dt]

Cahan's Shaden Glen [H538: 24 Mar 1934]

Composer (w, m?) Francey Heaney (Magheraboy, Dungiven).

s: Cahan is pronounced Kane.

Key C.

In the land of O'Cahan, as I rambled at will
Where the songsters' sweet chorus had musical
  skill,
Where the herds were assembled their flocks for
  to pen,
I first spied Eliza of Cahan's shaden glen.

My mind was bewildered as this maiden drew near,
Her eyes showed like comets, effulgent and clear,
Her cheeks were like roses displayed on their stem
Which array the green bower of Cahan's shaden
  glen.

I kindly addressed her as she seemed to pass by,
With her voice emanating, she spoke in reply,

Some hours we rested, and I clearly saw then
That my love was envalleyed in Cahan's shaden
  glen.

In pure conversation we both tripped along
Through the heights of Benbraden where the
  sweet maidens throng,
In just competition, could my heart wield a pen,
I would first mark Eliza of Cahan's shaden glen.

She will not condescend, I have no gold in store,
For her sake I may wail where the wild billows
  roar,
For in gentle demeanour all virtues do blend
In sublime Eliza of Cahan's shaden glen.

Farewell, chosen flower, may your bloom ne'er
  decay,
Farewell, happy hours that our joys did portray,
In conjugal raptures my life I could spend
With courteous Eliza of Cahan's shaden glen.

Fair Maid of Ballyagan   [H67: 21 Feb 1925]

o: (m) "Youghal Harbour."

Source: (w, m) Mary Boyd (Aghadowey); author
Andrew Orr (Derrydoragh).

[Dt] s: ... Andrew Orr ... emigrated to Australia
and became editor of the *Ballarat Chronicle*. His
pen name was "The Ploughman Poet."

o: Tune should be in 2/4.

Key E flat.

In Aghadowey there stands a village,
Eastward from Garvagh a mile or more,
'Tis well inhabited by purty fair maids,
Among them one I did much adore.

Nigh yon purling stream lies my habitation,
It's well adorned by nature's shade,
Where I live content from the cares of Venus,
Working there at my weaving trade.

First when I viewed, I wished for riches
For to admit me to her companee,
And when she saw I so dearly loved her,
She condescended and was kind and free.

Till with passion void of dissimulation
I fond embraced her till my heart did glow,
And oftimes wished I had worldly treasure
That freely on her I would bestow.

Till at length she says, 'Sir, it's in my power
To advance my fortune, so your suit give o'er,
For I'm sure my friends would be much offended
If I'd wed a lad who'd no gold in store.'

Such a gross insult did much annoy me,
But from upbraiding I did refrain;
I parted from her without reluctance,
Intending never to meet again.

But the powers of love had such attraction,
They made me think on that charming she,
And curse the riches laid the foundation
To separate that sweet maid and me.

But since for gold she has proved inconstant,
No other fair maid shall hear my tale,
And in the evening when I quit my weaving
I'll sing these verses through some lonesome dale.

4.2: I embraced her fondly ... [Dt].

The Grey Mare   [H90: 1 Aug 1925; Laws P8]

k: "Young Roger, esq," "Young Roger the Mil-
ler." Other titles: "(Courting My) (Her) Father's
...," "Roger's ...," "Tip, the Gray," "(Young)
Roger(s) (Jimmy) (Johnny) the Miller."

Source: (w) (Knockaduff district); (w, m)
William Sloan (Ballyrock).

s: A widespread favourite old song of English
type but with Irish characteristics in the air.
The version given combines the best of two
renderings....

Key D.

Young Roger the miller came courting of late
To a rich merchant's daughter called beautiful
  Kate,
She had to her fortune fine jewels and rings,
Diamonds and rubies and costly fine things.
This caus-ed young Roger for to tell his mind,

Sam Henry's Songs of the People

If she would be constant, that he would be constant,
Both loving and kind.

When the match was made up and the money paid down,
Wasn't that a bright sight? About five thousand pound,
And yet and withal he did vow and declare
That he wouldn't take her without the grey mare,
Saying, 'Although that your daughter is charming and fair,
I won't take your daughter, I shan't take your daughter
Without the grey mare.'

Then out spoke her father and he spoke with speed,
Saying, 'I thought you'd have married my daughter instead,
But since it's no better, I'm glad it's no worse,
The money once more shall return to my purse,
For it's enough to drive a man into despair
To lose his own daughter, to lose his own daughter
For the sake of a mare.'

The money it then vanished out of his sight,
And so did Miss Katie, his joy and delight.
Young Roger was then shown the way to the door
Never again to come there any more,
Which caused him to tear his long yellow hair
And wish that he'd never, and wish that he'd never
Spoke of the grey mare.

About a year after or a little above,
Who did he meet but Miss Katie, his love.
Smiling, said Roger, 'O, don't you know me?'
'If I'm not mistaken, I saw you,' said she,
'Or a man in your apparel with long yellow hair
That once came a-courting, that once came a-courting
My father's grey mare.'

'My dear,' then said Roger, 'but you are mista'en,
It was to yourself that a-courting I came,
But I thought your father without any dispute
Would give me his daughter and grey mare to boot
Before he'd have lost such a charming young son,
But oh, I am sorry, but oh, I am sorry
For what I have done.'

'As for your sorrow, I value it not.
There is men eneu' in this world to be got.'
'It's enough to drive a man into despair
To lose his own darling for the sake of a mare.'
'The price of the grey mare it was not so great.
So fare you well Roger, fare you well Roger,
Go mourn for your Kate.'

    2.1: ... money paid, [Dt]
    5.5: ... apparel in long ... [Dt]
    6.3: ... though that your father without a dispute [Dt]
    7.2: eneu' = enough.

I'll Hang My Harp on a Willow Tree

[H155: 30 Oct 1926]

Source: (w, m) William Kennedy, retired guard, L.M.S.(N.C.[Dt: N.C.C.]) Railway (Railway Road, Coleraine).

Key A.

I'll hang my harp on a willow tree
And I'll off to the wars again;
My peaceful home has no charms for me,
The battlefield no pain.
The lady I love will soon be a bride
With a diadem on her brow,
Oh, why did she flatter my boyish pride?
She's going to leave me now.

She took me away from my warlike lord,
And gave a silken suit,
I thought no more of my master's sword
As I played on my lady's lute.
She seemed to think me a boy above
Her pages of low degree,
Oh, had I less loved with a boyish love,
It would have been better for me.

I'll hide in my breast ev'ry selfish care,
And I'll flush my pale cheek with wine,
When smiles await the bridal pair,
I'll hasten to give mine.
I'll laugh and I'll sing, though my heart may bleed,
And I'll walk in the festive train,
And if I survive it, I'll mount my steed
And I'll off to the wars again.

One lock of my lady's hair I'll twine
In my helmet's sable plume,
And then on the fields of Palestine
I'll seek an early doom,
And if by the Saracen's hand I fall
'Midst the noble and the brave,
One tear from my lady love is all
I'll ask o'er a warrior's grave.

1.8: She is going ... [Dt]

The Bonnet sae Blue [H644: 28 Mar 1936]

Other titles: "... o' ...," "The Bonny Sailor Lad," "A Company of Boatmen," "His Jacket of (Was) ...," "The Jacket Green," "The Jacket So ...," "The Wagoner."

Source: Mrs Frank Kealey (Ballysally, Coleraine).

Key G.

In Kingstown and Warwick and bonny Yorkshire,
Surrounded with riches and free frae all care,
Surrounded with riches, had sweethearts no few,
I was wounded by a lad wore a bonnet sae blue.

A regiment from Dublin to Kingstown had come,
And one was amongst them set my heart aflame,
There was one amongst them I wish I ne'er knew,
He's my bonny Scotch laddie wi' his bonnet sae blue.

It was then to parade they instantly came,
I stood there with patience to hear my love's name,
His name's Charles Stewart, my joys to renew;
Once a prince o' his name wore a bonnet sae blue.

She says, 'My dear jewel, I would buy your discharge,
I would get you your freedom and set you at large,
If that you'd love me and to me prove true,
I'd not leave one stain on your bonnet sae blue.

He says, 'My dear jewel, you would buy my discharge,
You would get me my freedom and set me at large
If that I would love you and to you prove true;
Oh, what would my own bonny Scotch lassie do?

'I have a wee lass in my ain counteree
And I'll never slight her for her poverty;
To the lass that I love I will always prove true,
And weel it becomes my bonnet sae blue.'

Tarry Trousers [H532: 10 Feb 1934]

[see also H641 "The Ripest of Apples," cf. H472 "The Nonsense o' Men," H790 "The False Lover"]

k: "Madam I Am Come to Court You," "Twenty Eighteen." Other titles: "All of Her Answers to Me Were No," "Come My Little Roving Sailor," "Kind Miss," "(Oh,) Madam, (Madam) (I'm [I Have] Come) (You Came) (A-)(Courting)," "Madam, I Have Gold and Silver," "My Man (Oh No,) John!" "No, Sir! (No!)" "Oh Dear Oh! If I Had a Sailor," "On the Mountain Stands a Lady," "Ripest Apples," "Sailor's Return," "Song on Courtship," "The Spanish Lady (Merchant's Daughter)," "There She Stands a Lovely (Once I Loved a Charming) Creature," "Yonder Hill There Is a Widow"; cf. "All You Boys Who Go A-Courting," "The Courting Case," "The Deil's Courtship," "(The Spanish Lady in) Dublin City," "Galway City," "I Went to See My Suzie," "The Keys of Canterbury (of Heaven)," "Oh, Miss, I Have a Very Fine Farm," "Paper of Pins," "The Quaker's Courtship (Wooing)," "A Sport Song," "Wheel of Fortune," "The Yankee Boys," "You Go to Old Harry!"

Source: (m) coll. J. Moore, A.R.C.O. (Bushmills); (w, m) "a reader" (Upperlands).

s: In the third and fourth verses the first two notes are duplicated to suit the metre.

Key C.

Yonder stands a pretty maiden,
Who she is I do not know,
I'll go court her for her beauty,
Let her answer yes or no.

'Pretty maid, I've come to court you,
If your favour I do gain
And you make me hearty welcome,
I will call this way again.'

'Sit you down, you're heart'ly welcome,
Sit you down and chat a while,
Sit you down, you're heart'ly welcome,
Suppose you do not call again?'

'Pretty little maid, I've gold and riches,
Pretty little maid, I've houses and lands,
Pretty little maid, I've worldly treasures,
And all will be at your command.'

'What do I care for your worldly treasures?
What do I care for your houses and lands?
What do I care for your gold and riches?
All that I want is a nice young man.'

'Why do you dive so deep in beauty?
It is a flower will soon decay,
It's like the rose that blooms in summer --
When winter comes, it fades away.'

'My love wears the tarry trousers,
My love wears the jacket blue,
My love ploughs the deep blue ocean,
So, young man, be off with you.'

Sam Henry's Songs of the People

The Factory Girl [H127: 17 Apr 1926]

Source: (w, m) Annie Wilson (Moneycannon) from her mother.

Key G. [Bp: Slowly and tenderly.]

Early one morning as the sun was adorning,
The birds on the bushes did warble and sing,
Gay lads and young lasses in couples were
    sporting
In yonder green valley, their work to begin.

I spied one among them, she was fairer than any,
Her cheeks like the red rose than none can excel,
Her skin like the lily that grows in yon valley,
And she's only a hard-working factory girl.

I stepped up to her, more closely to view her,
When on me she cast a look of disdain,
Saying, 'Young man, stand off me and do not
    come near me,
I work for my living and think it no shame.'

'It's not for to scorn you, fair maid, I adorn you,
But grant me one favour, love: where do you
    dwell?'
'Kind sir, you'll excuse me, for now I must leave
    you,
For yonder's the sound of my factory bell.'

'I have lands, I have houses adorned with ivy,
I have gold in my pocket and silver as well,
And if you'll go with me, a lady I'll make you,
So try and say yes, my dear factory girl.'

'Love and sensation rules many a nation,
To many a lady perhaps you'll do well;
For I am an orphan, neither friend nor relation,
I'm only a hard-working factory girl.'

It's true I did love her, but now she won't have
    me,
And all for her sake I'll go wander a while
Over high hills and valleys where no one shall
    know me,
I'll mourn for the sake of my factory girl.

Now this maid she's got married, become a great
    lady,
Became a rich lady of fame and renown,
She may bless the day and the bright summer's
    morning
She met with the squire and on him did frown.

It's now to conclude and to finish those verses:
It's may they live happy and may they do well,
Come fill up your glasses and drink to the lasses
That attend the sweet sound of the factory bell.

4.4: ... of the factory ... [Dt]
6.1: ... sensation rule many ... [Dt]

Campbell's Mill [H762: 2 Jul 1938]

Source: Mary Forsythe (Balnamore) from Mary Ann Young (Liscolman) c. 1888.

Key G.

As I roved out the other day,
When I had nothing else to do,
While walking down through Castle Street,
A lovely maid came in my view.

She had a nice pink cotton gown,
Bound with a light blue frill;
That moment Cupid stung my heart
For the maid of Campbell's Mill.

Said I, 'Fair maid, what is your name?
Be pleased to let me know,
Do you stray far along this way?
For along with you I'd like to go.'

'My name to you, sir, I won't tell,
But I reside in Carrick Hill.
A man like you, what would you do
With a girl that works in Campbell's Mill?'

'Your enchanting looks have won my heart,
One look of you is fit to kill,
So come with me no more to roam
So early to the spinning mill.'

'Oh no, kind sir, I'll mind my trade,
And I would have you understand
That I'm no equal match for you,
A fine well-looking gentleman.

'And I gave my hand to a young man
Whose charms to me my bosom fill;
He's a heckler lad and my delight,
And he works with me in Campbell's Mill.

'So fare ye well, I must away,
For the last whistle said its will,
I must go back to my young man
Who works with me in Campbell's Mill.'

7.3: heckler = operator of thread guides in a cloth mill.

The Maid of Faughan Vale

[H167: 22 Jan 1927]

o: (m) "The Mountains High." Other title: "Braes ...."

Source: Mary Ann Wilson (Bovevagh, Dungiven), learned at age 5 from her mother as she sat "drizzling and singing at her spinning wheel."

Key E flat.

As I roved out one morning to view the pleasant strand
Where Flora's flowery mantle bespangled all the land,
Where Flora's flowery mantle bespangled every dale,
I met a lovely fair maid not far from Faughan vale.

'Good morning to you, fair maid,' I unto her did say,
'Is this the road to Derry? Come tell to me, I pray.'
'This is the road to Derry, I'll give you honest bail,
And who are you acquainted with that lives in Faughan vale?'

'And indeed, miss, I may tell you, my acquaintances are few,
Your beauty's so enticing, I am ensnared by you,
Your beauty's so enticing and your graces are so real
That I must rue the morning I passed through Faughan vale.'

The small birds in the forest do join in harmony
In sounding my love's praises wherever that she be,
In sounding my love's praises through every hill and dale,
And the happy bells her praises tell on the banks of Faughan vale.

She modestly made answer, 'Kind sir, I'm not for you,
I'm engaged to another young man, my passage is paid through,
Our ship's for Philadelphia if it blows a pleasant gale,'
And her words left me lamenting on the shores of Faughan vale.

I will walk up to Derry, I'll call in at Sergeant Cole's,
I'll drink a health to Mary, she's the object of my soul,
And if she proves hard-hearted, till death I will bewail
Like a broken-hearted lover on the braes of Faughan vale.

["Faughanvale" *throughout* Dt.]
1.3: ... bespangled all the dale, [Dt]
3.3: ... enticing, your ... [Dt]
6.4: ... broken-hearted hero on ... [Dt]

2.3: give honest bail = deliver on trust.

Wester Snow

[H66: 14 Feb 1925]

g: "Easter Snow." Other title: "Estersnowe."

Source: (w) Mary McKendry (Carrowrragh, Mosside), learned in Glendun; (m) Denis McGreer, fiddle (Cushendun).

s: This beautiful air was taken down by me at Cushendun from Denis McGreer, who ... won the first prize for fiddling with this air at the Feis-na-nGleann (The Glens' Feis) held at Waterfoot, Glenariff, in June 1904.
 The words have been supplied by ... [Dt only: (an old sweetheart of Denis)] ... [Bp, Dt] who learnt them in Glendun. The words are difficult to adapt to the air but suit admirably when sung by a traditional singer. [Bp only] For example, the second syllable in 'twilight' (first line) is sung to all the notes in the second portion of the first complete bar (s, l, t, d1 [superscript], l).
 A folk tune, "Easter Snow," resembling this one in some respects, has been collected in Donegal.

o: Good ballad with fine air badly transcribed. Title is a folk rationalisation of the name of a Roscommon townland, Estersnowe.

Key D.

By the twilight of the morning, as I roved out upon the dew
With my morning cloak around me, intending all my flocks to view,
Then I behold that fair one, she was a charming beauty bright,

Sam Henry's Songs of the People

She far exceeds Diana or the evening star that shines by night.

As I approached this fair maid, said I, 'My joy and heart's delight,
My heart it is enamoured by your exceeding beauty bright.
To heal my lovesick passion, if you'll consent along with me to go,
I'll roll you in my morning cloak and bring you home to Wester Snow.'

Said I, 'My lovely Peggy, sit you down awhile by me
And cast your eye around you, some pastime you may see:
The gentle hares a-hunting, the fields are decorated so,
The valley sounds melodiously by the sporting plains of Wester Snow.'

Said I, 'My lovely Peggy, sit you down a while by me,
You'll see the fox a-hunting by the best nobility,
The gentlemen well mounted and the huntsmen crying Tallyho!
So glorious we'll pursue the chase from sweet Lough Gay to Wester Snow.'

She says, 'Young man, excuse a simple maiden of the moor,
Forbear such splendid eloquence for one who is so poor,
My heart is not my own to give, nor can I it bestow,
'Tis pledged to one who lives and loves far, far from Wester Snow.'

Drummond's Land [H212: 3 Dec 1927]

Other title: "David's Flowery Vale."

Source: 2: Mrs M. C. M'Keague (Tullaghans, Dunloy), Mrs Charles Moore (Ballymacfin, Stranocum).

s: ... Hamiltonsbawn is about six miles from Armagh on the Tandragee road. The song pictures the linen trade in its heyday.

Key G.

It was down by David's fountain where yon water does run calm,
Where yon purling stream does gently glide that divides my father's land,
All covered o'er with linen cloth and wrought most tenderly,
It was purchased by one Kennedy, a man of high degree.

As I walked out one morning to view my father's men,
The Armagh coach did pass me by, well loaded to the ground,
I put my spyglass to my eye, I viewed the coach all round,
And in the front a lady sat of honour and renown.

I quickly followed after to assist her from the coach;
I caught her by the milk-white hand, I led her round the coast,
I showed her all my father's ships that were bound for Chester fair,
'Had it not been for you, fair lady, I surely had been there.

'And now, my honoured lady, will you take the coach with me?
And we'll go down by Hamiltonsbawn, fair Drummond's land to see;
Five hundred pounds in ready gold on your father I'll bestow,
And I'll crown you queen of Drummond's land, fair lady, if you go.'

'Oh, I'm no honoured lady, although I wear fine clothes,
Nor for young men's company was ever I disposed.
I'm but a weaver's daughter lives nigh to Hamiltonsbawn,
And for further information, it is now called Drummond's land.

'Kind sir,' she says, 'your offer's good, but your suit must be denied,
For I have already promised to be another man's bride,
I am already promised for seven long years or more,
For to wed unto a weaver lad, he's the lad I do adore.'

2.3: ... put a spyglass ... [Dt]
6.2: For I've ... [Dt]

My Charming Kate O'Neill [H767: 6 Aug 1938]

A song of the glens of Antrim.

g: "Kate O'Neill"

Source: (w) Lieutenant James M'Dade (New York Police Department); (m) sung and fiddled by his sister, Mrs P. Delargey (Waterfoot, Glenariffe), from her late mother, 80, who died 6 years ago.

s: ... The heroine of the song was Kate O'Neill, of Gortaclea, near Cushenhall, a beautiful girl who captivated the hearts of the young Glensmen eighty years ago.

Key G.

The first place that I saw my love, 'twas on a summer's day,
She was going to her father's as I passed by Red Bay,
The little birds on every branch, their notes they did reveal.
May the powers above protect my love, my charming Kate O'Neill.

If you had seen my Katie all in her robes so dressed,
Amongst all other fair maids she far exceeds the best,
And her dwelling place, I hear them say, lies near to Cushendall,
Her beauty and her conduct do far exceed them all.

From Cushendall to Carnlough and twice as far away,
You would not find another one to equal this young fay,
She's related to Shane's Castle, as her state it does reveal,
Her name is known through Ireland as the charming Kate O'Neill.

I am a bold sea captain, my age is scarce nineteen,
I'm going to cross the ocean and leave old Erin's green,
Our ship she lies in readiness to sail the first of May,
I bid farewell to all my friends around Glenariffe Brae.

I'll sail along through Scotland and round the Scottish isles,
Where I and many a fair maid on each other had cast a smile,
But there's another young man, she intends his bride to be;
May they spend their days in pleasure that dwell around sweet Gortaclea.

C 20 / She will not condescend

The Maid of Mourne Shore

[H27a, orig. H34b: 5 Jul 1924]

m: (m) related to usual tune to Yeats's "Down by the Sally Gardens." Other titles: "The (Banks of) Moorlough Shore," "The (Maids of the) ...."

Source: (w) 2: resident (Magilligan); Annie White (Drumafivey, Stranocum); (m) Rev. J. R. Clinton (Co. Londonderry set).

s: ... These are the original words that give the title of the well-known air to which the song of the Portrush fishing disaster was set (No. 27). [This text was actually printed with column H34, a few weeks later.]

Key E flat.

Ye hills and dales and flowery vales that lie round Mourne shore,
Ye winds that blow o'er Martin's hills: will I never hear you more?
Where the primrose grows and the violet blows and the sporting trout there plays,
With line and hook, delight I took to spend my youthful days.

Last night I went to see my love to hear what she would say,
Thinking she would pity me, lest I should go away;
She said, 'I love a sailor, he's the lad that I adore,
And seven years I'll wait on him, so trouble me no more.'

'Perhaps your sailor may be lost when crossing o'er the main,
Or otherwise has fixed his mind upon some comely dame.'
'Well, if the sea proves false to me, no other I'll enjoy,
For ever since I saw his face I loved my sailor boy.'

Farewell now to Lord Edmund's groves, likewise the Bleaching Green,
Where the linen webs lie clean and white, pure flows the crystal stream,
Where many's the happy day I spent, but now, alas, they're o'er
Since the lass I love has banished me far, far from Mourne shore.

Sam Henry's Songs of the People

Our ship she lies off Warren's Point, just ready to set sail,
May all goodness now protect her with a sweet and pleasant gale.
Had I ten thousand pounds in gold, or had I ten times more,
I would freely share with the girl I love, the maid of Mourne shore.

4.4: ... Murlough shore. [Dt]

The Girl from Turfahun [H521: 25 Nov 1933]

o: (m) "Kate of Ballinamore."

Source: Alexander Thompson (Lurgan Row, Bushmills; formerly of Ballyhunsley, Bushmills).

Key G.

Ye bards may sing your sweetest lays
In praise of beauty's grace
And swell the part all round my heart
With maids of fonder face,
But if to me you lend an ear,
Before my song is done
I'll sing you of a bonny wee lass
Who lives in Turfahun.

It being on a Ballycastle fair
About the Lammas time,
When farming folks throw off all care
And hairst is in its prime,
Amang the lave and as for yet
My eye got fixed on one
Dismounting from a farmer's cart
That come from Turfahun.

I boldly stepp-ed up to her,
I helped her to alight,
She thanked me with her glancing eye
By token all was right.
My glance met hers, a vision passed,
And round my heart was spun
A web of love that bound me fast
To the girl from Turfahun.

I met her later, as by chance,
She yielded me her hand,
And in the middle of a dance
We entered fairyland.
I scarcely thought I touched the floor
When the jig had right begun;
I seemed to soar on music's wings
With the girl from Turfahun.

The dance being done, we both sat down,
I begged her name and place,
I praised the pattern of her gown
And the fairness of her face,
She gave her sunny curls a shake
When a cloud o'erswept my sun;
She says, 'My name is Mrs Ross
And I live in Turfahun.'

It's sweet to meet and hard to part;
It's years ago and yet
The memory of an old sweetheart
Is harder to forget.
Although I'm growing gray of hair
And the sands of life near done,
I mind that Ballycastle fair
And the girl from Turfahun.

2.4: hairst = harvest.
2.5: lave = rest, residue; as for yet = ?up to that time.

The Lass of Mohee [H836: BLp, 9 Dec 1939;

Bt=D(c),Wt, all labeled "No. 835"]

Other titles: "The Indian (Young Spanish) Lass," "The Lass of Mohea (Mowee)," "(My) (The) Little (Indian) (Pretty) Mohea (Mahmee) (Maumee) (Mawhee) (Mohee)(s) (Momie)," "?The Maumee Maid," "Old Smokey."

Source: George Graham (Cross Lane, Coleraine) from his mother [Bt: part of the words ... the rest from *The Flying Cloud*] [Wt: (an American song collection)] [Dean [1922]].

[Bt is numbered 835 and headed "Completion of the Series," although Dt, very likely a carbon copy, is not so labeled, and is in fact followed in D by No. "836," "Whisky Is My Name." There is no 836 in B.]

Key D.

As I went a-walking one morning in May
For fond recreation, the time passed away,
As I sat a-musing myself on the grass,
There chanced to come to me a fine Indian lass.

She sat down beside me, took hold of my hand,
Saying, 'Sir, you're a stranger and far from your land,
But I have free lodgings, if with me you'll stay,
You're welcome to sleep on the isle of Mohee.'

The sun was a-sinking down in the salt sea
When I went a-walking with the lass of Mohee,
We walked and we talked and the hills we did rove,
Till we came to her cot in a coc[o]anut grove.

A glass of good liquor she then gave to me,
Saying, 'Drink to the health of the lass of Mohee,
A stranger you are on a far foreign shore,
When you join your ship I may ne'er see you more.'

I tarried all night till it came to the dawn,
My ship being ready, I had to go on;
'Good morning, good morning, farewell, oh my dear,
My ship it is ready, for home I must steer.'

With fondest affection this fair one did say,
'Oh, stay, gallant sailor, and don't go away,
If you will but tarry and leave the salt sea,
I will teach you the ways of the isle of Mohee.'

I said, 'My fair creature, that never can be,
For I have a sweetheart far over the sea,
I will not forsake her for her povertee,
For her face is more fair than the lass of Mohee.'

And now I am home in my own native land,
And friends and relations around me do stand,
But of all that come near me, of all that I see,
There is none to compare with the lass of Mohee.

For this Indian lass, she was modest and kind,
As fair as a palm tree, as fleet as the wind,
When I was a stranger, she shared her snug home,
And I'll think on the Mohee as I wander alone.

And when I am smoking and drinking my glass,
My thoughts will go back to that dear Indian lass,
And when I am sporting on some foreign shore,
I'll think on the lass I may never see more.

The green tree of love grows in all lands I see,
But I plucked its flower on the isle of Mohee,
I left it to wither, the roots to decay,
Alas, my heart longs for it far, far away.

[Differences in Dt and Wt:]
1.3: ... myself by a pass,
 .4: ... come by a ...
2.2: Saying, You are a stranger far from your own land,
 .3: But if you'll go with me, you're welcome to come,
 .4: For I live by myself in a snug little home.'
3.3: ... talked till we came to her home,
 .4: And there stood her ...
4.1: ... liquor this maid gave ...
 .3: For you are a stranger on ...
5.1: ... till the day did appear,
 .2: ... ready, for home I must steer;
 .3: ... fare you well, ...
 .4: ... ready and for ...
6.1: With the fondest expressions this ...
 .2: 'If you will stay with me and not go away,
 .3: If you will stay with me and leave ...
 .4: ... the language of ...
7.1: ... fair lady, that ...
 .2: ... sweetheart in my own country, [Wt: countree]
 .3: And I would not ... poverty,
 .4: Her face ...
8.: [Stanza substituted:]
And when I'm sporting on some foreign shore,
I'll think on that pretty girl I may never see more,
And when I am smoking and drinking my glass,
My thoughts will go back to that sweet Indian lass.
9.1: ... lass was ...
 .2: She acted her part so beautiful and fine,
 .3: ... she took me to her home,
10.: [BLp only, not in Dt]
11.4: ... heart yearns for ...

The Lakes of Ponchartrain

[H619: 12 Oct 1935; Laws H9]

g: "The Creole Girl." Other titles: "On the ...," "On the Lakes of the Poncho Plains (Ponsreetain)," "Ponchartrain."

Source: Paddy M'Closkey (Carnamenagh, Corkey, Co. Antrim), learned from Frank M'Allister (Carnagall, Corkey) c. 1905, learned when a woodsman in America.

s: This [is a] very interesting song....
   Ponchartrain Lakes are five miles north of New Orleans in the state of Louisiana. These lakes are a constant menace to New Orleans, their waters having to be kept away by great earthen dykes. The land there is so waterlogged that no cellar can be built and all tombs are aboveground erections.
   A Creole is a native of Louisiana of French extraction.

Key G.

By swamps and alligators
I took my weary way,
Through railway lines and crossings
My weary steps did stray.

Until the dawn of evening,
Some higher grounds to gain,
Till I fell in love with a Creole girl
On the lakes of Ponchartrain.

'Good eve, good eve, fair lady,
My money does no good,
Were it not for alligators
I'd sleep all night in the wood.'

'You are welcome, welcome, stranger,
Our house is very plain,
But we never turned a stranger out
On the banks of Ponchartrain.'

She took me to her father's house
And treated me right well,
Her yellow hair and ringlets fair
Down o'er her shoulders fell.

Sam Henry's Songs of the People

I tried to paint her beauty,
But ah, I tried in vain,
So handsome was my Creole girl
On the banks of Ponchartrain.

I asked her if she'd marry me,
She said that ne'er could be,
For she had got a lover,
And he was far at sea.

She said she had a lover,
True to him would remain
Till he'd return to his Creole girl
On the lakes of Ponchartrain.

'Good-bye, good-bye, fair lady,
I may never see you more,
But I'll ne'er forget your kindness
In the cottage by the shore.'

And in each social gathering,
A flowing glass I'll drain,
And I'll drink a health to that Creole girl
On the lakes of Ponchartrain.

Am I the Doctor?

[H72: 28 Mar 1925; ?Child #295, Laws P9]

A song of slighted love.

g: "Pretty Sally," "A (The) Rich (Proud) Irish Lady," "Sailor from Dover." Other titles: "... You Wished for to See?" "The (Bonny) Brown Girl," "A (The) Brave Irish Lady," "Death of Queen Jane," "The Dover Sailor," "The Fair Damsel (Rich Lady) from London," "Fair (Fine) (Pretty) (Queen) Sally (of London)," "Proud Nancy," "A Royal Fair Damsel," "Sally (and Billy) (Sailsworth)."

Source: 3: resident (Killowen), from Alex Riddles (Cashel, Ringsend, Co. Derry) c. 1875 "while weaving at the loom"; (Portstewart district); also Joseph Reilly (Moneycannon, Ballymoney).

[Bp] s: This old song was obtained by me from two of the old stock.... Neither had the complete version as now given here....
[Bp written] Corrections by Joseph Reilly, Moneycannon.
[Dt] ... A version from Joseph Reilly, Moneycannon, Ballymoney, incorporated.
[Bp, written in another hand] The "corrections" are inferior to original. [indecipherable initials. Below, in same hand, with arrow pointing to written last stanza] Very bad add.

Key E flat.

A sailor from Dover, from Dover he came,
He courted lovely Sally and Sally was her name,
But still she walked so lofty and her fortune was
    so high
That she on a sailor would scarce cast an eye.

A few months being over and a few months being
    past,
This fair she began to grow sick at the last,
She grew sick at the last and she couldn't tell
    for why,
And she sent for the sailor that she oftimes did
    deny.

'Am I the doctor, that you sent for me?
Or am I the young man that you wished to see?'
'Oh yes, you're the doctor, you can either kill
    or cure,
The pain that I feel, dear, is hard to endure.'

'Where does the pain lie, does it lie in your
    head?
Or where does the pain lie, does it lie in your
    side?'
'Oh indeed, young man, you're not far off the
    guess,
The pain that I feel lies under my left breast.'

She took the gold rings off her fingers, by one,
    two or three,
Saying, 'Take you these, dear Willie, in
    remembrance of me,
In remembrance of me, my dear, when I am dead
    and gone,
And perhaps you'll be sorry then for what you
    have done.'

'Oh Sally, dearest Sally, oh Sally, dear,' said he,
'Don't you remember when you first slighted me?
You mocked me with cruelty and slighted me with
    scorn,
And now I'll reward you for what you have done.'

'Oh Willie, dearest Willie, forget and forgive,
And grant me a little while longer to live.'
'Oh no, dearest Sally, as long as I breathe,
I'll dance on your tomb while you lie underneath.'

(Now Sally's dead and got buried at last,
And Willie he's lamenting for all that is past,
Saying, 'Sally, lovely Sally, if you were yet alive,
It's you I would wed and all others deprive.')

[Written on Bp, Wt] "Corrections from Joseph Reilly,
    Moneycannon."
2.3: ... she knew the reason why, [written on both
    Bp, Wt]
    ... she couldn't tell why, [Dt]
6.4: ... reward you with an equal return.' [written,
    Bp and Wt]
    ... now you're rewarded with an equal return.' [Dt]

8.: [Written on Bp, typed in parentheses on Dt, in brackets on Wt.]

s: Moira O'Neill's poem, "A Late Wooing," is founded on the above song. Her rendering of the last verse is as follows:

> Oh, never be thinkin' you'll win me to rue,
> If you live or you die or whatever you do:
> You killed the young love that you cared not to save --
> I'll smile when the young grass is green on your grave.

Barbara Allen [H236: 19 May 1928; Child #84]

Other titles: "Barbro (Barb(a)ry) (Bav'ry) ... (Ellen)," "(Bonny) (Cruel) ... Allan (Ellen)," "Burber Helen," "Mary Alling."

Source: Alexander M'Ilmoyle (Ballymully, Limavady).

s: This favourite old ballad is here printed because the local version is different to that usually published, and the air, with its haunting pathos, is also peculiar to Ulster....
[Dt] The Ulster version of this universal ballad is different both as to air and words.

[Bp, Dt printed in 8-line stanzas, with the direction that the tune is to be repeated for the second half of the stanza.]

[Wp, penciled on back]   A. H I T L E (R)
                         6 2 5 1 4 3 (?)

Key E flat.

It was early, early in the spring,
When flowers began to blossom,
Young Johnny he lay sick in bed,
And he was just a-dying.

He sent a page to Barbara Allen,
A page unto her dwelliing,
Saying, 'My master wants one word with you
If you be Barbara Allen.'

'One word from me he ne'er shall get,
No, not if he was dying,
The better of me he ne'er will be
If I saw his heart's blood spilling.'

'Get up, her mother said, 'get up,
'Get up and go and see him.'
'O mother, don't you mind the time
You told me for to leave him?'

'Get up, get up,' her father replied,
'Get up and go and see him.'
'O father, don't you mind the time
You told me to deceive him?'

C20 / *She will not condescend*

Slowly, slowly she got up
And slowly she put on her,
And slowly she went to his bedside,
She says, 'Young man, you're dying.'

'Oh yes, indeed, I'm very bad,
And death shall be my dwelling.
One kiss from you would cure it all,
My charming Barbara Allen.'

'One kiss from me you ne'er shall get,
No, not if you are dying,
The better of me you ne'er will be,
If I saw your heart's blood spilling.

'O dear, O dear, don't you mind that time
When in yon garden walking,
You pulled a flower to all fair maids,
Pulled none to Barbara Allen.'

'O yes, love, yes, I mind the time
When in yon garden walking,
I pulled a flower to all fair maids,
A rose to Barbara Allen.'

'O dear, O dear, don't you mind the time,
When in yon tavern drinking,
You drank a health to all fair maids,
Drank none to Barbara Allen.'

'O yes, love, yes, I mind the time
When in yon tavern drinking,
I drank a health to all fair maids,
A toast to Barbara Allen.'

'Look up, look up at my bed head,
And there you'll see them hanging,
A gay gold watch and a diamond ring
Was bought for Barbara Allen.'

'Oh no, Oh no, I'll not look up,
Nor I'll not see them hanging,
A gay gold watch and a diamond ring
Was bought for Barbara Allen.'

He turned his pale face to the wall,
For death was drawing nearer,
'Adieu, adieu, dear mother,' he said,
'Be kind to Barbara Allen.'

As she went over her uncle's land,
She heard his death-bell tolling,
And every toll it seemed to say,
'Hard-hearted Barbara Allen.'

'Oh mother, mother, make my bed,
And make it long and narrow,
For my true love died for me today
And I'll die for him tomorrow.

'Oh father, father, dig my grave,
And dig it long and narrow,
For my true love died for me today,
And I'll die for him tomorrow.

They both were buried in the churchyard,
Down by yon shady bower,

Sam Henry's Songs of the People

Out of the one there grew a red, red rose
And out of the other a brier.

They grew so long and they grew so strong,
Till they could not grow no longer,
Till they both grew into a true lover's knot
And there remained forever.

2.3: ... with thee, [Dt]
4.1: 'Get up, get up,' her mother said, [Dt]
　.4: ... to shun him? [Dt: "leave" crossed out.]
8.1: ... shall forget, [Dt]
17.3: For the bell that tolls for him today [Dt]
　.4: Shall toll for me tomorrow. [Dt]
19.1: ... the same churchyard, [Dt]
　.3: ... one grew ... [Dt]
20.4: ... remain forever. [Dt]

❖ C20 REFERENCES ❖

❖ **John MacAnanty's Courtship** *(H 56)* *354*

IREL Joyce 1873:1-3 "The Fairy King's Courtship," text nearly identical to Henry's, tune not so similar.

REC Ginny Phelps, Front Hall FHR 09 (B2)

❖ **Paddy's Land** *(H 473)* *354*

Brunnings 1981: "... (Tune of The Lime Juice Tub and The Whaler's Rhyme)," without reference.

Not the same song as in *617* [190-?]:93.

❖ **The Bonnie Wee Lass of the Glen** *(H 14)* *356*

Brunnings 1981: (m) "The Maid with the Bonny Brown Hair"

IREL *JIFSS* 2(1&2)1905:23 is Macauley's other tune. See the same issue, pp. 14-5, for three versions of "The Lass [Maid] with the Bonny Brown Hair," including one from Mrs. Houston's collection.
Shields/Shields *UF* 21,1975: #51

b: MEL Hughes 2,1915:52-9
b: O Lochlainn 1939:12-3

❖ **As I Walked Out** *(H 109)* *357*

IREL Moulden 1979:14

AMER Creighton 1971:93-4 "A New Broom Sweeps Clean," a fragmentary and fairly different version.

❖ **Farewell, Darling** *(H 580)* *357*

Brunnings 1981: "...," "O'Reilly from the County Leitrim"; *but not* "Young Reilly"

IREL Joyce 1909:233-4 "When First I Came to County Limerick"
O Lochlainn 1939:186-7 "O'Reilly from the Co. Leitrim, or The Phoenix of Erin's Green Isle"
Treoir 8,1976: "Young O'Reilly"

AMER Cf. Cox 1925(1967):422-3 "Youth and Folly," esp. stanza 1, with stanza 6, "floating stanzas."
Leach 1965:308-9 "Young Riley"

BRS BPL Irish: (n.i.)
UCLA 605: 4(Brereton) "O'Reilly from the Co. Cavan or the Phoenix of Erin's Green Isle"; 5(Brereton) "Reily from the Co. Kerry"
A Broadside 7(8,Jan)1915: "O'Reilly from the County Kerry"
Healy 1,1967b: 248-50 "Reily from the Co. Kerry"; 4,1969:104-6 "O'Reilly from the Co. Kerry or The Phoenix of Erin's Green Isle"

❖ **Will Ye Pad the Road wi' Me?** *(H 18a)* *358*

BRIT Greig 1907-11(1963): #68 "To Pad the Road"
Ord 1930:78-9 "To Pad ..."

❖ **The Maid of Craigienorn** *(H 500)* *359*

g: Not located. In Barry 1939:44-5 there is a ballad called "The Maid of Island Moore," which seems vaguely related to Henry's; it also is confused.

❖ **Lurgan Stream** *(H 229)* *360*

BRS *Derry Journal* [c. 1925]1:7 "Lurgy Stream"

REC Geordie Hanna, Eagrán MD 0002 (B1) "The Leargaidh ..."
Kevin Mitchell, Topic 12TS 314 (A2) "The Lurgy Streams"

❖ **Castleroe Mill** *(H 22b)* *361*

Brunnings 1981: (Tune of The Collier)

IREL Moulden 1979:31

❖ **The Banks of Kilrea (II)** *(H 150b)* *361*

IREL Shields 1981:44-5 (#5) (see also Jimmy Butcher rec.)
Shields/Shields *UF* 21,1975: #28

m: BRIT Kilkerr *FMJ* 1977:219-20 (from Henry coll.): reprint, *Treoir* 12(1)1980:12-3.

h: BRS *Derry Journal* [c. 1925],1:14 ? 15-6?

REC Jimmy Butcher, EEOT *Shamrock 2* cass. (B3)

❖ **The True Lovers' Discussion** *(H 164)* *362*

? Brunnings 1981: "... (Tune of the Dreary Gallows)"

IREL C. O'Boyle 1979:26-9
Shields 1981: 153-5

BRS O'Conor 1901:77

REC Tom Dahill, Biscuit City BC 1318 (B2)
cl: J. W. Green, AFS 2295 A2
h: Jerry Hicks, BBC 28M

❖ **The Maid of the Sweet Brown Knowe** *(H 84, H 688)* *364*

Laws 1957:251 (P7) "The Foot of the Mountain Brow (The Maid of the Mountain Brow)"
Brunnings 1981: "... the Mountain Brow"
Cazden et al. *Notes* 1982: #26 "... on the Mountain Brow"

c: IREL Hayward 1925:85-6
b: Healy 1978b
O Lochlainn 1939:38-9 [Laws]
c: O'Keeffe 1968:112-3
Shields/Shields *UF* 21,1975:#259

BRIT MacColl/Seeger 1977:186-7

AMER Cazden et al. 1982:115-7 "... on the Mountain Brow"
Haskins n.d.:61

BRS UCLA 605: 4(Brereton) "A New Song Called the
... Broqwn Howe"
A Broadside 5(7,Dec)1912
Clark n.d.:104
Derry Journal [c. 1925]1:24
40 n.d.:13
c: Healy 1,1967b:256
   Healy 1977:65-6
   120 n.d.:104
   O'Keeffe 1955(1968):112-3
c: *Walton's New* 2,1968:117
c: *Walton's Treasury* :131

REC Tom Brandon, Folk-Legacy FSC 10 (A5) "...
of the Mountain Brow"
b: Frank Ritchie, Request RLP 8060

c: MEL *YIFMC* 3:75

◈ The Grey Mare *(H90) 365*

Dean-Smith 1954
Laws 1957:251-2 (P8)
Brunnings 1981

IREL Shields/Shields *UF* 21,1975: #179

b: BRIT Kennedy 1975:321 (#144) "Young Roger
Esquire"

AMER Bush 2,1970:59-62 "Young Jimmy, The Miller"
Colorado FB 1(2,Apr)1962:8 "Tip, the Gray ..."
Creighton 1971:169-70 "Roger the Miller"
Grover n.d.:32-33 "Her Father's Gray ..."
Hubbard 1961:106-7 "Courting My Father's Gray
..."
Manny/Wilson 1968:281-2 "Roger the Miller"
Vincent 1932:24-5

BRS Harvard 1: 4.179 (Forth)

REC Lena Armstrong, Etta Jones, Folk-Legacy FSA
23 (A7) "Roger's Gray Mare"
b: William Clauson, Victor LPM 1286 "Rogers the Miller"
cl: John Collier, AFS 1721 A "John Rogers, the Miller"
    Ollie Conway, Topic 12TS 369 (A2)
    Stanley MacDonald, Folkways FM 4053 (A3) "Roger
the Miller"
cl: Dr. Chapman J. Milling, AFS 3790 B "Young Rogers"
    Phil Tanner, EFDSS LP 1005 (B6) "Young Roger
Esquire"
b: Pick Temple, Prestige/Int. 13008 "Young Rogers
the Miller"

◈ I'll Hang My Harp on a Willow Tree *(H155) 366*

Brunnings 1981: "... on the ...," but apparently
   none of the other titles referred to under "When I
   Was a Maid"

BRIT Ord 1930:56-7

b: AMER Chapple 1909 "... on the ..."
   Johnson 1881:284-5

BRS BPL Partridge: 1.87 (Wrigley)
   Harvard 1: 7.213 (Ryle), 9.146 (Bebbington),
11.124 (Such)
   Harvard 3: (Marks) (Fortey) (Disley)

REC Walter Pardon, Leader LED 2111 (B2)
   Lotus Dickey, Audio Village cass. (B4) "... on the
..."

◈ The Bonnet sae Blue *(H644) 367*

Brunnings 1981: "Bonnets So Blue," "The Bonnet of
   Blue (The Bonny Scotch Lad)"
Cazden et al. *Notes* 1982: #43 "The Jacket So ..."

h: IREL Joyce 1909:153-4 "The Jacket So ..."
   Shields/Shields *UF* 21,1975: #218 "(The) Jacket So
..."

BRIT R. Ford 2,1901:1-3 "... o' ..."

AMER Cazden et al. 1982:170-2 "The Jacket So ..."

BRS Harvard 1: 5.209 (Catnach) 11.28 (Such)
   Harvard 3: (Harkness) (Fortey)
   UCB Brereton: (n.i.)
   UCLA 605: 4(n.i., ?Brereton) "The Jacket Green"
   Logan 1869:104-6 "... o' ..."

REC Jean Matthew, *FSB* 8 (A6) "... o' ..."
c: Nathan Hatt, Folkways FM 4006 (B24) "His Jacket
of ..."
cl: Ben Rice, AFS 3222 A3 "Jacket So ..."

◈ Tarry Trousers *(H532) 367*

g: There are several distinct versions of this song,
   of which "Tarry Trousers" is much the more rare.
     Also there is an entirely different song also called
   "The Tarry Trousers" [involving a mother-daughter
   conversation about marriage with a sailor], for which
   see, e.g.:
      Huntington 1964:96-9 for 2 versions,
      Butterworth 1974:24-5,
      Collinson/Dillon 1951:58-63,
      Creighton/Senior 1950:212,
      Sharp/Karpeles 1:547-9 (#142), 3 vts.

White/Dean-Smith 1951: "(The) Keys of Heaven or
   The Bells of Canterbury; Twenty Eighteen; Madam,
   I Have Come to Court You"
Dean-Smith 1954: "The Keys of Canterbury/Heaven,
   etc.; My Man John; Oh, No John; Twenty Eighteen,
   etc."
Brunnings 1981: "Madam, Madam, I'm Come a-Courtin'/g," "The Keys of Canterbury," ?"There Stands
   a Lady on the Mountain - Singing Game," ?"The
   Kirmington Plough-jags Play," ?"Madam, I Have
   a Very Fine Farm," ?"Madam, Madam - A Maiden
   Walking in Her Garden," "Oh, No John," ?"No,
   Sir! - No"
Cf. Cazden et al. *Notes* 1982: #36 "A Sport Song,"
   another related song more commonly known as "The
   Quaker's Courtship." The *Notes* differentiate the
   following as separate but related variants: "The
   Deil's Courtship," "The Keys of Canterbury," "The
   Keys of Heaven," "Madam, I Have Gold and Silver,"
   "My Man John," "No, Sir!" (by A. M. Wakefield),
   "Once I Loved a Charming Creature," "The Spanish
   Lady, or O, No, John."

h: IREL O Lochlainn 1965:243, much like Henry's.
   Shields/Shields *UF* 21,1975: #393

BRIT Butterworth 1974:4-5 "Yonder Stands a Lovely
Creature"
b: Kennedy 1975:315 (#138) "No Sir"; 135 (#135)
"Madam, Will You Walk?"
   Morrison/Cologne 1981:46-7 "No, Sir! No!"
   Cf. Polwarth/Polwarth 1970:41 "On the Mountain
Stands a Lady"

AMER Cf. Bikel 1960:55-6 "Wheel of Fortune"
   Cf. Bok 1977:54 "Dublin City"
   Bush 3,1975:43-4 "O, No, John"
   Cf. Cheney et al. 1976:170 (see Armstrong rec.)
   Colorado FB 1(3,Nov)1962:10 "No, Sir, No"

Sam Henry's Songs of the People

c: Cf. Randolph 3:40-5 (#354) "The Paper of Pins," 3 vts.; 53-5 (#361) "The Courting Cage"; 55-60 (#362) "The Courting Song," 4 vts.
  Cf. Silverman 1971:13 "You Go to Old Harry!"
  Wyman/Brockway [1920]:98-100 "No, Sir, No!"

AUST *AT* #20(Aug)1969:12-3 "The Spanish Merchant's Daughter"

REC Hattie, Ernest Stoneman, *AAFM* 1, Folkways FP 251 (#65) "The Spanish Merchant's Daughter"
  Bob, Ron Copper, *FSB* 1 (B9) "No, John, No"; Leader LEAB 404 (4047: B2); cf. Leader LEAB 404 (4046: A3) "All You Boys Who Go A-Courting"
  b: Helene Alter, private rec. "O No John"
    Cf. Frankie Armstrong, Topic 12TS 216 (A1)
  b: George, Gerry Armstrong, Folkways FA 2335 "Went to See My Suzie"
    Roy Bailey, Trailer LER 3021 (B3) "No Sir No"
    Cf. Theo Bikel, Elektra EKL 105, "Wheel of Fortune"
    Cf. Gordon Bok, Folk-Legacy FSI 54 (B3) "Dublin City"
    Cf. Dick Cameron, Folkways FG 3516 (A1) "Galway City"
  b: Clancy Bros., Tommy Makem, Tradition TLP 2060 "Paper of Pins"
  ? cl: Jennie Devlin, AFS 1775 A1
  c: Richard Dyer-Bennet, Vox 632.7.691
  b: *Elektra Folk Sampler*, Elektra SMP 2 "The Keys of Canterbury"
  b: *Everybody Sing!* Vol. 3 "Madam, I Have Come to Court You - Oh, Dear Me"
  b: *Folk Festival at Newport*, Vol. 3, Vanguard VRS 9064 "Paper of Pins"
  cl: Lucy Garrison, AFS 1504 A1, 1503 A1 "No, Sir, No"
  b: Julia Ann Gilman, ABC Paramount ABC 168 "Paper of Pins"
  cl: Mrs Goldie Hamilton, AFS 2783 A "Dublin City"
  b: *Greatest Folksingers of the Sixties*, Vanguard VSD 17 "Paper of Pins"
    Cf. Max Hunter, Folk-Legacy FSA 11 (A5) "Oh Miss, I Have a Very Fine Farm"
  lc: Burl Ives, Decca DL 5080 "Dublin City"
    The Johnstons, Pickwick PLD 8013 (A8) "The Spanish Lady"
    Sam Larner, Folkways FG 3507 (A2f) "No Sir, No Sir"
  cl: Mary Ila Long, AFS 2966 B2 "No, Sir"
  cl: Grace Lungino, AFS 2591 B1 "No, Sir, No"
    Cf. Alan Mills, Folkways FW 6831 (A3) "As I Roved Out"
  ? c: Milt Okun, Ellen Stekert, Riverside 12 634
  b: Cf. Lee Monroe Presnell, Folk-Legacy FSA 23 (A2) "I Went to See My Suzie"
  b: Jean Ritchie, Folkways FI 8352 "Went to See My Suzie"
  b: Jean Ritchie, Oscar Brand, Riverside RLP 12 646 "Paper of Pins"
  c: Paul Robeson, Vanguard VSD 57
    Peggy Seeger, Folkways FA 2049 (A5) "All of Her Answers to Me Were No"; [c:] Folkways FL 5401; [b:] Prestige/Int. 13061
    Pete Seeger, Folkways FA 2453 (A5) "No Sir No"
    Harry Siemsen, Folkways FH 5311 (B3) "Madam, I Have Gold and Silver"
  b: *So Early in the Morning*, Tradition TLP 1034 "Paper of Pins"
  b: *Songs of All Time* 1, World Around Songs N17 "Paper of Pins"
  b: Mrs Gail Stoddard Storm, New World NW 239 "My Man John"
  c: Andrew Rowan Summers, Folkways FP 21 "O No John, No!"
    Artie, Cilla Trezise, BBC 22293 (B2) "Wheel of Fortune"
  c: Hally Wood, Stinson SLP 73

◆ The Factory Girl *(H127)* 368

Brunnings 1981

h: IREL *Ceol* 1(3):8-9, and the man does not get the girl.
  Clifford 1957:16-7
h: Morton 1970:31-2
h: Morton 1973:129-30, notes (p. 171) that there are 2 types of this ballad: one in which the man gets the girl, and the other in which he does not.
  Shields/Shields *UF* 21,1975: #137
  Treoir 8,1976

BRIT Henderson et al. 1979:35-7 (see Armstrong rec.)
b: Kennedy 1975:50-1 (#221) mentions another Irish version and an English one recorded.
  Purslow 1972:29
  Not: Palmer 1974 "The Handsome ..."

b: AMER *And not*: Lomax 1934, an American complaint song.

BRS Harvard 1: 6.57 (Harkness), 10.119 (Bebbington)
  UCLA 605:3 (Sharp)

REC Frankie Armstrong, Sierra Briar SBR 4211 (A3)
m: Margaret Barry, Topic 12T 123 (B4)
   Bothy Band, Mulligan LUN 013 (B4)
   Alison McMorland, Peta Webb, Topic 12TS 403 (B1)
   Peg Clancy Power, Folk-Legacy FSE 8 (A3)
   Louis Killen, Collector 1932 (A5)
m: Sarah Makem, Topic 12T 182 (A5)

◆ The Maid of Faughan Vale *(H167)* 369

m: IREL "Songs of the People" #412 "Braes ..."

h: REC Eddie Butcher, coll. Hugh Shields c. 1975.

◆ Wester Snow *(H66)* 369

Brunnings 1981: "Easter Snow"

IREL S. O'Boyle 1977:60-1 "Estersnowe"
  Tunney 1979:29-30 (no title)

BRIT *Chapbook* 4(1):10-1 "Easter Snow" (from Tunney rec.)
  Kennedy 1975:304 (#128) "Easter Snow"

REC John Doherty, Gael Linn CEF 072 (B6) "Easter Snow"
  Tim Lyons, Green Linnet SIF 1014 (A5) "Easter Snow"
  Paddy Tunney, Topic 12T 139 (A5) "Easter Snow"

MEL *JIFSS* 5,1907:14 "Easter Snow"
  Galwey 1910:13 (#6)
  Petrie/Stanford 3,1905:284 (#1123) "Easter Snow, or, properly, Diseart Nuadhain; nó Sneachta Cásga," which Stanford says is the name of a place in Mayo.

◆ Drummond's Land *(H212)* 370

IREL Shields *UF* 18,1972:40; 21,1975: #109 "David's Flowery Vale"
  Shields 1981:68-9 (#21) "David's Flowery Vale" (see Butcher rec.)

h: REC Eddie Butcher, Leader LED 2070 (A4) "David's Flowery Vale"

◆ The Maid of Mourne Shore *(H27a)* 371

h: IREL Fitzpatrick 1963:31-4
h: Moulden 1979:102-3

Shields 1981:123-4 (#53) "The Moorlough Shore"
m: Shields/Shields UF 1975: #258

m: REC Joe Holmes, Topic 12TS 401 (A4)
m: Sarah, Rita Keane, Claddagh CC4 (B2) "The Banks of Moorlough Shore"
m: Kevin Mitchell, Topic 12T 314
m: John McGettigan and his Irish Minstrels, Topic 12TS 367 (A2), "... Moorlough Shore"
Bill, Tilly Quigley; John, Maria Butcher, EEOT Shamrock 3 cass. (A5) "The Moorlough Shore"
h: Peta Webb, Topic 12TS 273

m: MEL Graves 1895:55
JIFSS 5,1907:13 "The Maids of the ..."
Scanlon 1923:46
h: Joyce 1909:302 (#572) "Mourne Shore"
O'Neill 1903:9 (#49) "The Mourne Shore"
h: Petrie/Stanford 1,1902:75 (#302) "The Maids of ..."

◆ The Lass of Mohee (H836) 372

White/Dean-Smith 1951: "(The) Indian Lass"
Dean-Smith 1954: "(The) Indian Lass"
Laws 1964:233-4 (H8) "The Little Mohea"
Brunnings 1981: "The Little Mohee"

IREL Moulden 1979:86-7 also mentions a BBC archive recording.

BRIT Palmer 1980:183-4 "The Indian Lass"
Raven 1978:9 "The Indian Lass" (see Jones rec.)
Sing 7(1,Sep)1962:5 "The Indian Lass"

AMER Cox 1939(1964):147-50 "(The) Pretty ...," "The Pretty Mohea," "The Little Maumee"
Darling 1983:229-30 "The Little Mohea" (see Hall Brothers rec.)
Dean [1922]:17-8
m: Fowke 1965:148-9 "The Young Spanish Lass"; Fowke says this is related to "The Indian Lass" rather than "Mohee" (also in Fowke 1973:126).
Leach 1965:258-60
Leach 1967:173-4
Matteson/Henry 1936:30-1 "Little ..."
Randolph/Cohen (1982):484-6 "The Pretty ..."; also lists a goodly number of archive recordings.
Wetmore/Bartholemew 1926:16-23 "Little Mawhee"

cl: REC Finley Adams, AFS 2796 B2 "The Little Momie"
cl: Ray Bohannan, AFS 2878 B2 "Little Mohees"
b: Oscar Brand, Golden Wonderland GW 223 "The Little ..."
m: Jumbo Brightwell, Topic 12TS 261 "The Indian Lass"
cl: Mrs T. M. Bryant, AFS 1753 A2 & B1 "The Lassie Mawhee"
cl: Mrs W. R. Buchanan, AFS 2856 B1 "The Pretty ..."
cl: Kate Burkett, AFS 839 A2
Paul Clayton, Folkways FW 8708 (B10) "The Indian Lass"
cl: Alfred Caborne, AFS 3396 B1 "The Indian Lass"
cl: Mary, Cora Davis, AFS 1488 A2, "The Little ..."
cl: Capt. William T. Day, AFS 3821 A1 "The Little ..."
cl: Mrs M. P. Daniels, AFS 3738 B1 & 2
b: Everybody Sing! Vol. 2, Wonderland RLP 1419 "The Little ..."
cl: Mr, Mrs Carlos Gallimore, AFS 1345 A "The Little ..."
Hall Brothers (Roy, Jay Hugh), RCA Victor LPV 548 (A3) "Little ..."; Bluebird B 6843 [Randolph/Cohen]
cl: Doc W. Hoppes, AFS 840 A1 "The Little ..."
cl: Mrs A. J. Huff, AFS 2877 B1 "The Pretty ..."

Burl Ives, [lc:] Encyclopedia Britannica Films 1 (78 rpm) B1 301; [lc:] Columbia CL 6058 "Little ..."; [b:] Spinorama S 192 "The Little ..."; Columbia CS 9041 (B4) "Little ..."
cl: Aunt Molly Jackson, AFS 827 A2 "The Little ..."
Nic Jones, Shanachie 79003 (Trailer LER ?)(A5) "The Indian Lass"
cl: Lois Judd, Rosetta Spainhard, AFS 4092 A "My Little Mohee"
Buell Kazee, Brunswick 156 [Randolph/Cohen]
cl: Etta Kilgore, AFS 2762 A3 "The Little ..."
cl: Vera Kilgore, AFS 2093 B2 "The Little ..."
Bradley Kincaid, Gennett 6856 [Randolph/Cohen]
cl: Bascom Lamar Lunsford, AFS 1801 A1 "The Pretty ..."
cl: Mrs W. L. Martin, AFS 2756 B2 "The Little ..."
cl: Mrs Minta Morgan, AFS 922 B3 "The Little ... Girl"
John Jacob Niles, [lc:] American Folk Love Songs, Boone LP; [b:] RCA Camden CAL 245 "My Little ..."; Tradition/Everest S 2055 (B1) "Little ..."
Flora Noles, OKeh 45037 [Randolph/Cohen]
Bunk Pettyjohn, AFF 33-3 (B3) "Little Mohea"
Pie Plant Pete, ARC 35-10-14 [Randolph/Cohen]
Riley Puckett, Columbia 15277-D [Randolph/Cohen]
cl: James Rattery, AFS 3750 B
cl: George Roark, AFS 2015 B (10")
Roe Brothers, Columbia 15199-D [Randolph/Cohen]
Mr, Mrs Albert Simms, Leader LEE 4057 (A5) "The Young Spanish Lass"
b: Sing Out, Sweet Land! Selections from the Theatre Guild Musical Play, Decca A 404 (6 recs., 78 rpm) "The Little ..."
cl: Clyde Spencer, AFS 3294 B1
cl: Hettie Swindel, AFS 2816 A1 "The Little ..."
Joseph Able Trivett, Folk-Legacy FSA 2 (B2) "The Little ..."
cl: Mrs Callie Vaughan, AFS 2940 A3 "The Pretty ..."
? cl: Susan Weddle, AFS 2235 B2 "The Maumee Maid"
cl: Happy Jack Woodward, AFS 2411 A1 "The Little Mohea"
Bernard Wrigley, Topic 12TS 211 (A5) "The Indian Lass"

MEL WPA Kentucky [1939?] "Pretty ..." m only on unnumbered page.

◆ The Lakes of Ponchartrain (H619) 373

Laws 1964:234-5 (H9) "The Lake ..."; he quotes Flanders et al. 1939: "It is very probable that the author knew and imitated 'The Little Mohee.'"
Brunnings 1981: "...," "On the Lake of the Pancho Plains"

BRIT Planxty 1976:28

AMER Creighton 1932:299-300 "On the ..."
Manny/Wilson 1968:256-7
Peters 1977:134 "On the ..."

cl: REC Perry Allen, AFS 2264 B3 "The Lake of Poncytrain"
Sarah Anne Bartley, Folkways FE 4312 (A6) "... Ponchartraine"
cl: Pauline Fanine, Gladys Wilder, Don Reda Lewis, AFS 1562 A2 "The Lake of Poncytrain"
Hot Vultures, Sierra/Briar SBR 4212 (Plant Life) (A2) "Ponchartrain"
b: Our Singing Heritage, Vol. 1, Elektra EKL 151
Frances Perry, AAFS L55 (B7) "On the ..."
cl: Ben Rice, AFS 3224 B1 "The Lake Ponchartrain"
Ellen Stekert, Folkways FA 2354 (B4)
b: Mrs William Towns, Prestige/Int. 25014 (B4) "... Ponsreetain"

Sam Henry's *Songs of the People*

◇ **Am I the Doctor?** *(H72) 374*

White/Dean-Smith 1951: "(The) Brown Girl or Pretty Sally; The Sailor from Dover"
Dean-Smith 1954: "(The) Brown Girl, The Dover Sailor"
Cf. Child #295 "The Brown Girl"
Coffin/Renwick 1950(1977):159-61, 281-2
Bronson 4,1972: 402-22
Laws 1957: 252-3 (P9) "A Rich Irish Lady [The Fair Damsel from London; Sally and Billy; The Sailor from Dover; Pretty Sally; etc.]"
Brunnings 1981: "A Rich Irish Lady," "The Brown Girl [Child 295]," "The Dover Sailor"

m: IREL   Joyce 1909:78 (#153) "... You Wished for to See?"
Moulden 1979:12

BRIT   *Oxford Ballads* 1969:355-6 (#95) "The Bonny Brown Girl"

AMER   Bush 3,1975:45-6 "A Rich Irish Lady"
Darling 1983:138-9 "A Rich Irish Lady" (see West rec.)
Grover n.d.:35-6 "Fair Sally"
Karpeles [1934]:47-51 "Proud Nancy"
Randolph/Cohen (1982):104-7 "Pretty Sally of London"

REC   A. L. Lloyd, *Riverside CB*, RLP 12 625 (A2) "The Dover Sailor"
Kate Peters Sturgill, VT, BRI 002 (B5) "Queen Sally"
Frankie Armstrong, Topic 12TS 216 (B2) "The Brown Girl," which has the sexes reversed.
Loman D. Cansler, Folkways FH 5324 (A1) "Sally"
? cl: Emma Dusenbury, AFS 867 A1 "Sally"
Sarah Ogan Gunning, Folk-Legacy FSA 26 (B9) "Sally"
cl: Aunt Molly Jackson, AFS 2584 A & B1 "The Rich Irish Lady"
? cl: Theodosia Bonnett Long, AFS 2953 B "The Rich Lady from London"
Bascom Lamar Lunsford, AAFS L21 (B6) "Death of Queen Jane"
? cl: Capt. Pearl R. Nye, AFS 1608 B2, 1609 A1 "Pretty Sally"
Peggy Seeger, Folkways FA 2005 (A4) "The Rich Irish Lady"
Andrew Rowan Summers, Folkways FA 2364 (A3) "Pretty Sally" [Bronson]
Cass Wallin, Folkways FA 2309 (A2) "Fine Sally"
Hedy West, Folk-Legacy FSA 32 (B5) "The Rich Irish Lady"

◇ **Barbara Allen** *(H236) 375*

White/Dean-Smith "... Ellen or ..."
Dean-Smith 1954 "...; .../Barbry Ellen"
Child 1882-98(1965),2:276-9 (#84) "Bonny ...," 3 vts.; 3:514
Coffin/Renwick 1950(1977):82-4, 239-41
Bronson 2,1962:321-91; 4,1972:476-7
Brunnings 1981

See esp. Ed Cray, "Barbara Allen: Cheap Print and Reprint" (in Wilgus/Sommer 1967) and AAFS L 54: "Versions and Variants of the Tunes of Barbara Allen: As sung in traditional singing styles in the United States and recorded by field collectors who have deposited their discs and tapes in the Archive of American Folk Song in the Library of Congress, Washington, D.C.," ed. Charles Seeger. The accompanying booklet is a reprint from *Selected Reports of the Institute of Ethnomusicology* (University of California, Los Angeles), 1(1)1966:120-57. A crucial contribution to the history of the song is found in Eleanor R. Long, "'Young Man, I Think You're Dyin'': The Twining Branches Theme in the Tristan Legend and in English Tradition," *Fabula* 21 (1980):183-99.

IREL   Shields 1981:49-50 (#8) "Barbro ..."
Shields/Shields *UF* 21,1975: #35

AMER   Burton 1978:69-71, "Barbry Ellen" (see also Hicks rec.), 91-3, 94 (see also Harmon rec.)
Darling 1983:52-4 (Child #84B from Roxburghe Ballads); 54-5 "Barbro ..." (see West rec.)
Leach 1967:115-6
MacArthur *CD&S* 1981:9-10
Milner/Kaplan 1983:34-5
Randolph/Cohen 1982:41-4
Rosenbaum 1983:72
Warner 1984:128-30 (#40); 425-7 (#187)

BRIT   Copper 1973:278-9
MacColl/Seeger 1977:75-7 (#11) "Bonny ...," 2 vts. ("Barbry Ellen," "Barber Helen")
Munch 1970:88-90 "Bav'ry ... or ... Allan," a fragment.
Oxford Ballads 1969:35-54 (#94) "Bonny ..."
Palmer 1980:82-3
Shepheard n.d.:3-4

BRS   *Forget Me Not* [1835]:142-4
Ireland's Own, 2 Feb 1929:100
Songs and Recitations 5,1978:19-20 "... Allan"

REC   *Check-List* 1940 lists 64 recordings in the Archive of Folk Song under the title "Barbara Allen" and variations.
"Barbara Allen," *FSB* 4 (B7) composite: Jessie Murray, Fred Jordan, Charlie Wills, Mary Bennell, Thomas Moran, Phil Tanner
Ewan MacColl, *Folkways CB*, FG 3509 (B1) "Bawbee Allan"; *Riverside CB*, RLP 624 (B3); [b:] Tradition/Everest TR 2059 (A3); Topic 12T 147 (A3)
Peggy Seeger, Ewan MacColl, *LH*, Argo ZDA 69, #3 "Bonnie ...," 3 versions.
Dan Tate, VT, BRI 002 (A7)
Ted Ashlaw, Philo 1022 (A3)
lc: Bob Atcher, Columbia HL 9006
b: Joan Baez, Vanguard VSD 2097; Vanguard VRS 9094 "Barbara Allen"
Bertha Baird, TFS *Ballad* cass. (B8) "Barbry Ellen"
h: Thomas Baynes, Tradition TLP 1004 (B11) "... Ellen"
George Belton, EFDSS LP 1008 (A7)
Oscar Brand, National Geographic 00788 (A8)
h: Packie Byrne, EFDSS LP 1009 (A1) "... Ellen"
J. B. Cornett, Folkways FA 2317 (B7)
Mairéad ní Dhomhnaill, Gael Linn CEF 055 (B4); Green Linnet SIF 1004 (A4) 1977
Johnny Doughty, Topic 12TS 324
Richard Dyer-Bennet, Stinson SLP 35 (B1)
b: *Folk Festival*, ABC-Paramount ABC 408 "Barbara Allen"
Molly Galbraith, Folkways FE 4312 (A3)
b: Julia Ann Gilman, ABC Paramount ABC 168 "Barbara Allen"
Lena Harmon, TFS *Ballad* cass. (B1) "Barbry Ellen"
Bobby Harrison, Folkways FA 3830 (A8)
Bob Hart, Topic 12TS 243
b: Jim Helms, Art Podell, Horizon WP 1603
Seena Helms, Folkways FES 34152 (A4)
Buna Hicks, TFS Ballad cass. (A10) "Barbry Ellen"
Frank Hinchcliffe, Topic 12TS 308
lc: Burl Ives, Encyclopedia Britannica Films 1 (78 rpm) B1 303
Fred Jordan, Topic 12TS 233 (A4)
The Lark in the Morning, Tradition TLP 1004 "... Ellen"
Sam Larner, Topic 12T 244 (A6)
Lilly Bros., Don Stover, Folkways FA 2433
Gordeanna McCulloch, Topic 12TS 370 "Bawbie Allen"
Jon MacDonald, Topic 12TS 263 (A3)
Shanna Beth McGee, Folkways FW 8779 (A4)

C20 / She will not condescend

Sarah Makem, Folkways FW 8872 (A8); Topic 12T 182 (A5)
  I. N. (Nick) Marlor, New World NW 223 (A5) [from AAFS L 54]
b: Howie Mitchell, Folk-Legacy FSI 16 (B4) "... Ellen"
  Johnny Moynihan, Shanachie 79001 (B5)
  Glen Neaves and the Virginia Mountain Boys, Folkways 3830
  New Lost City Ramblers, Folkways FC 7064 (B2)
  Bill Nicholson, AAFS L14 (A1)
  John Jacob Niles, Tradition TLP 1046 (2 recs.) "Barbry Ellen"
  Granny Porter, Asch 3831 (A3) "Barbry ..."
  Mr Rew, Folkways FW 8871 (B6)
  Almeda Riddle, Minstrel JD 203 (A5)
  Jean Ritchie, Folkways FA 2301 (B4) "Barbry Ellen"; [b:] Folkways FI 8357 "Barbara Allen"
  George Roberts, Topic 12TS 349 (A5)
b: John Roberts, Tony Barrand, Front Hall FHR 04 (A3)

b: Pete Seeger, Folkways FA 2319 (B7); Folkways FI 8354
b: Jo Stafford, Capitol CC 75 (78 rpm); [lc:] Capitol H 75
  Lucy Stewart, Folkways FG 3519 (B4) "Barbry ..."
  Phoebe Smith, Topic 12T 253 (B1)
h: Charlie Somers, LEA 4055 (B4) "Barbro ..."
  Phil Tanner, EFDSS LP 1005 (A6)
  Rebecca Tarwater, AAFS L1 (A4)
  George Tucker, Rounder 0064 "... Ellen ..."
  Doug Wallin, Home Made Music LP 003
b: Hedy West, Folk-Legacy FSA 32 (A3)
b: Betty Vaiden Williams, Vanguard VRS 9028
  Charlie Wills, Leader LEA 4041 (A2)

MEL Roscoe Holcomb, Folkways FA 2368 (A5) "... Blues"
  Joyce 1873:79 (#78) [MacColl/Seeger]
h: *JIFSS* 1(2&3)1904:45
  Paddy Keenan, Gael Linn CEF 045 (A7)

C21

Content in the arms of another:
Love unfaithful

C21 / *Content in the arms of another*

The Ripest of Apples [H641: 7 Mar 1936]

[see H532 "Tarry Trousers"]

Other titles: "Tarry Trousers"; cf. "I Drew My Ship into a Harbour," "Love Is Pleasing," "Rattle on the Stovepipe."

Source not given.

Key G.

O, the ripest of apples, they must soon grow rotten,
And the warmest of love, it must soon grow cold,
And young men's vows, they must soon be forgotten,
Look out, pretty maiden, that you don't get controlled.

The seas they are deep and I cannot wade them,
Nor have I, nor ever, the wings for to fly.
I would that my love were a jolly boatman
To ferry me over, my love and I.

(repeat first stanza)

The False Lover [H790: 14 Jan 1939]

Other titles: "Love I(t')s Pleasing," "(The) Wheel of Fortune," "When I Was Young."

Source: Herbert Cunningham (Mullagh, Maghera) from his mother.

Key F.

When I was young, I was well beloved
By all young men in this counteree,
When I was blooming and in my blossom,
This false young man he deceived me.

I did not know he was going to leave me
Till the next morning when he came in;
When he sat down and began a-talking,
It was then my sorrows they did begin.

Turn you round, love, your wheel of fortune,
Turn you round, love, and smile on me,
For surely, surely there's a place of torment
For this young man, he deceiv-ed me.

When secret hearts, love, they shall be opened,
He can not deny what he told to me;
Against the day of the resurrection
This false young man's face I would like to see.

Against the day of the resurrection,
This false young man's face I would like to see;
When the secret hearts, love, they shall be opened,
He can not deny what he told to me.

The Bonny Bushes Bright

[H699: 17 Apr 1937; Child #248]

[cf. H722 "The Sweet Bann Water"]

k: "Grey Cock," "The Light of the Moon," "The Lover's Ghost." Other titles: "Biscayo," "Fly up, My Cock," "I'll Go See My Love," "I Must Away," "The Light of the Moon," "The Little Fishes," "My Willie-o," "Night Visit(ing) Song," "O Once I Loved a Lass," "Pretty Crowin(g) Chicken(s)," "Saw You My Father (True Love John?)," (m) "Song of the Ghost," "Willie's Ghost," "The Worrysome Woman"; cf. "Silver Dagger," "True Lovers."

Source: Frank Thompson (Priestland, Bushmills).

s: The Song Editor acknowledges his indebtedness ... for this excellent song in the true folk style. It conforms with the characteristics of the best folk song: it is very old; it is anonymous; it has a story in it; the metaphor of the cock is very striking and the promised reward to the "herald of the day" for postponing the break of day is paralleled in the very ancient ballads where a parrot is so rewarded.

Key C.

383

Sam Henry's Songs of the People

By the bonny bushes bright on a dark winter's night
I heard a fair maid making her moan,
She was sighing for her father, lamenting for her brother,
And grieving for her true lover John.

Oh, Johnny he was sweet and had promised her to meet,
But he tarried on the way an hour too long.
'He has met with some delay which has caused him to stay,
And I'm weary, weary waiting all alone.'

Johnny comes at last and he found the door was fast,
And he slowly, slowly tinkled to get in,
Then up this maid arose and she hurried on her clothes
In order to let young Johnny in.

His sweetheart gave consent and into the room they went,
And these lovers they sat talking of their plan:
'Oh John, my love,' said she, 'I wish this night to be
As long as when the world first began.

'Fly up, fly up, my pretty little cock,
And do not crow till the break of day,
And your cage shall become of the very brightest gold
And your wings of a silvery grey.'

This cunning little cock, so cruel as he was,
Flew down and crowed an hour to soon;
'You have sent my love away all before the break of day,
And it's all by the light of the moon.'

Then up this maid arose, and she hurried after him
Saying, 'When will you come back to me?'
'When the fishes they do fly and the seas they do run dry,
And seven moons shine briefly o'er the lee.'

'Once I thought my love was as constant unto me
As the stones that lie under the ground,
But now that I see that his mind has changed to me,
I would rather far live single than be bound.'

Willie Angler / The Banks of the Bann

[H614: 7 Sep 1935]

Other title: "Willie Archer."

Source: Andrew Allen (Bannbridge Cottages, Coleraine); author Johnny Spence, "a kind of a gentleman" (Castleroe), c. 1865.

s: There are four songs with this title. One has already been published as No. 86 in this series. The song now published was sung by Mr Andrew Allen, ... who states that it is the oldest of the songs so named and the air is the sweetest.
... Some singers give the lover's name as Ingram or Inglis.

Key D.

Down by yon harbour, near sweet Coleraine town,
With fountains, clear fountains and valleys all around,
I spied a pretty fair maid, as you may understand,
She was viewing fine fishes on the banks of the Bann.

The time, I remember, was the sweet month of May,
When Flora the goddess clothed the meadows so gay,
Where the fields were in bloom by nature's command,
I met with my darling by the banks of the Bann.

I stepped up to her and to her did say,
'Fair nature be with you, all art to betray,'
Saying, 'If you come with me, love, there is my hand,
And I'll be your true lover on the banks of the Bann.'

At length my persuasion seemed to take place,
I saw by the blushes that changed in her face,
I sat there love-making and squeezing her hand,
And I put my arm around her on the banks of the Bann.

'I cannot marry you, as an apprentice I'm bound
To be a linen weaver in sweet Coleraine town,
But when my time's ended, I will be your man,
And we both will get married on the banks of the Bann.'

'As you will not marry me, come tell me your name,
And where is your dwelling and from whence have you came?'
'My name is Willie Angler from sweet Mourne strand,
And my dwelling lies close to the banks of the Bann.'

Come all you fair maids, take a warning by me:
Don't go a-walking by one, two or three,
Don't go a-walking by twelve, two or one,
For fear of the Angler that roves by the Bann.

Lovely Nancy [H637: 8 Feb 1936]

[cf. H520 "The Strands of Magilligan," H780 "The Ploughboy"; cf. stanza 4 with the refrain of H114 "Molly Bawn Lowry"]

k: "Johnny, Lovely Johnny." Other titles: "The Cold (Dark) (Gonesome) (Lonesome) (Stormy) Scenes (Hours) (Winds) of Winter," "Flora," "Lovely Johnny," "The Lover's Lament."

Source not given.

Key C.

When first into this country a stranger I came,
I fell in love with Nancy, lovely Nancy by name,
Nancy was a wee girl that never was fond
Of young men's delusions or false flattering tongue.

One night as I was going, lovely Nancy to see,
She says, 'Tell me the reason you cannot love me.'
'Because there's a red rose, in yon garden grows fair,
I would love you, my darling, if it was not she's there.

'Sure I never courted you, no, never in my life,
That you might leave on me the cause of any strife.'
'Oh yes, sir, you courted me, and it is very well known,
In my own father's garden in the county of Tyrone,

'With my apron pinned around us to shade us from the sun,'
And ay, she cried, 'Jamie, you have my heart won,
And the next place you courted me was in yon green wood
Where the branches hung over us both where we stood.'

'If I ever courted you, it was only in jest,
I never intended to make you my best,
Nor I never intended to make you my wife,
Nor never shall I all the days of my life.'

'Oh yes, sir, you courted me and you know it is true,
You never felt happy unless I was in view.'
'But times are all altered and so is my mind,
So fare you well, darling, I must leave you behind.'

C21 / Content in the arms of another

'Fare you well, false love, it's all I can say,
But I hope you and I will be judged on one day,
And at that day of judgment, rewarded you will be
For the vows and false promises you made unto me.'

The mountains of Derry looked dismal that day,
And so did my Nancy at my going away,
But if providence spares my health to cross the main,
I'll wed lovely Nancy and cure all her pain.

Under the Shade of a Bonny Green Tree [H794: 11 Feb 1939; Laws P19]

Other titles: "As I Went out ae (One May) Morning," "(The) Bonny ...," "Down by the Woods and Shady Green Trees," "Tippling (Tripping) over the Lea (Plains)."

Source: James Carmichael (Waring St, Ballymena).

Key D.

As I went a-walking one fine summer morning,
One fine summer morning it happened to be,
I spied a wee lass, she appeared like an angel
In under the shade of a bonny green tree.

I stepped up to her and gently saluted,
Says I, 'My wee lassie, if you will agree,
I will make you a lady of high rank and honour,
If you give me a share of your bonny green tree.'

'Oh, I am no lady of high rank and honour,
I am a wee lassie of lower degree,
Your friends and your parents they would frown upon me
If you were to marry a poor girl like me.'

'Oh, what do I care for my friends or my parents?
My friends and my parents care nothing for me;
I am a wee laddie and you a wee lassie,
If I marry tomorrow, my bride you will be.'

The laddie sat down and she sat beside him,
He swore and he promised that married they'd be,
But when he arose, his mind it was altered,
And he said, 'If I marry, my bride you won't be.'

'Now I may go, I may go broken-hearted,
Ill bodes the day that I sat on his knee,
My first and my last was my false-hearted lover
Under the shade of a bonny green tree.

Sam Henry's Songs of the People

'Come all ye young lassies, pray now take a warning,
And ne'er court a young man above your degree,
For love is a blossom that quickly will wither,
And you will be left as my lover left me.'

Must I Go Bound? (a)   [H218a: 14 Jan 1928]

[cf. H482 "Bring Me Back the Boy I Love," H683 "The Apron of Flowers," ? H692 "Never Change the Old Love for the New"]

Other titles: "Deep in Love," "Down in Yon Meadows," "... I Be ...," "(Go Bring Me Back) My Blue-Eyed Boy," "(Yon) Green Valley; cf. "The Butcher's Boy," "That Fatal Courtship."

Source: 2: David A. Forsythe (Balnamore, Ballymoney), Joseph M'Callister (Broan, Killykergan, Coleraine).

s: This excellent folk song ... [has] two versions, one sung by the girl and the other by the lad. Evidently the girl's version was the original and the lad's a retaliatory plagiarism.

g: Some of the versions cited below differ so greatly from Henry's that it is difficult to decide whether or not to call them only related songs.

Key E flat.

The girl's version.

Must I go bound and you go free?
Should I love them that wouldn't love me?
Or should I act the childish part,
To follow the lad that would break my heart?

Once I heard a fair maid sing
That marriage was a pleasant thing,
But for myself I can't say so,
My wedding day cost me great woe.

The first thing that he bought me was a mantle to wear,
It was lined with sorrow and bound with care,
And the drink he gave me was vinegar and gall,
And the blows he gave me were worse than all.

The fields are green and the meadows gay,
The leaves are spreading on every tree,
The time will come and soon it will be,
He'll rue the day that he slighted me.

There is a bird sits on yon tree,
Some say it's blind and does not see;
Oh, I wish it had been the case with me
When first I fell into his companie.

I wish and I wish and I wish in vain,
I wish my sweetheart would come again.
He's far away now across the sea,
And my heart is breaking, och, anee!

Must I Go Bound? (b)   [H218b: 14 Jan 1928]

[m = H218a]

The lad's version.

Must I go bound and you go free?
Must I love them that wouldn't love me?
Or could I act a childish part,
And go with Martha that broke my heart?

One day I heard a shepherd sing
That marrying was a very fine thing,
But to my grief I found it so,
That my marriage day soon turned to woe.

The first thing that she brought me was a necktie to wear,
It was lined with sorrow and bound with care,
She brought me vinegar mixed with gall,
And she gave me blows far worse than all.

When I had money, she had part,
When I had none, she had my heart,
The more I wink, sure I am not blind,
When she had money, it was none of mine.

The fields are green and the meadows gay,
The leaves are spreading on every tree,
But the time will come, and that you'll see
She'll be tripping upstairs with gramachree.

Phelimy Phil   [H80: 23 May 1925]

g: "Balinderry." Other titles: "Balinderry and Cronan," "'Tis ('Twas) Pretty to Be in Balinderry."

Source: (m, stanza 1) coll. Maud Houston (Coleraine) from her mother; remainder written by Mrs Houston.

[Bp] s: This exquisite old song ... Mrs Houston learnt ... from her mother, who evidently knew but the first verse and the chorus. Her gifted daughter completed the song with admirable tenderness and simplicity. The scene is evidently Church Island in Lough Beg. The air is in the old pentatonic or gapped scale, which one eminent authority attributes to the eleventh or twelfth century.
[Dt only] The air is supposed to be a traditional [one] with a basis of a tune from the monastery of Bangor (8th century).
[Wt includes a copy of the tune in staff notation.]

Key D.

O, it's purty to be in the bonny Church Island,
Nobody there but Phelimy Diamond,
Phelim would whistle and I would sing
Until we would make the Church Island to ring.

O, Phelimy, Phelimy, why did you leave me?
Sure I could bake, I could card, I could spin,
Phelimy, Phelimy, why did you leave me?
I'll tell the priest on you, Phelimy Phil.

O, lonely I wander in bonny Church Island,
Far, far away from Phelimy Diamond,
The birds may whistle a merry tune,
But sorrowful May brought woeful June.

Och, cold in the furrow my Phelimy's lying,
Over his grave I am sobbing and sighing;
To lave him his lone, it would be a sin,
So take the sod off and lay me in.

3.3: lave = leave.

Norah Magee [H778: 22 Oct 1938]

Source: (m) Jock Smylie (Limavallaghan, Clough, Co. Antrim); (w) Smylie corroborates song from John Brennan (Kilfennan, Waterside, Londonderry).

s: This popular sentimental Irish song was in great vogue about 70 years ago....

Key G.

Oh Norah, dear Norah, I can't live without you;
Why did you leave me to cross the wild sea?
Oh Norah, dear Norah, oh why did you doubt me?
The world seems so dark and so weary to me.

Come back to old Ireland, the land of our
  childhood,
The old village well and the old willow tree,
Come back to the mountain, the valley and
  wildwood,
I can't live without you, Norah Magee.

Why from old Ireland have you been a ranger?
Or why have you chosen the wide world to
  roam?
Oh, why did you go to the land of the stranger
And leave your own Barney alone, all alone?

Why was I silent when I might have spoken
And told my dear Norah my heart was her own?
A true Irish heart that was tattered and broken,
Then why did you leave your own Barney alone?

I've wandered all day by the field and the farm,
I've wandered all night by the hill and the dale,
Now life's all a blank, has been robbed of its
  charm,
Oh, how I loved Norah, my tongue ne'er can
  tell.

Still must I wait while the cold pain is burning,
I'll watch and I'll pray while the wild billows
  roar,
That the ship may come safely with Norah
  returning
Back to old Ireland and Barney once more.

The Broken-Hearted Gardener

[H499: 24 Jun 1933]

o: (m) "Polly Perkins." Other title: cf. "The Broken-Hearted Fish Fag."

Source not given.

s: It has been wittily said that William Shakespeare, when in love, unburdens his soul in a sonnet, whereas plain John Smith, unable to express himself, takes the jaundice. In this old popular street ballad, the gardener, to ease his spirit, recites his flower list, another illustration of rare old Ben Jonson's "Every Man in His Humour."

The irregularities of the metre of the old ballad must be met by a duplication of the note where necessary.

Key E.

Sam Henry's Songs of the People

I'm a broken-hearted gardener and don't know
   what to do,
My love she's inconstant and a fickle jade, too;
One smile from her lips will ne'er be forgot,
It refreshes like a shower from a watering pot.

Oh, oh! she's as fickle as any wild rose,
A damask, a cabbage, a young China rose.

Oh, she is my myrtle, my ger-an-i-um,
She once was my sunflower, my sweet marjorum,
She's my tulip, my honeysuckle and my violet,
My hollyhock, my dahlia, my dear mignonette.

We grew up together like two apple trees
And clung to each other like double sweet peas,
They're going to trim her, plant her in a pot,
And I'm left to wither, neglected, forgot.

Oh, she is my snowdrop, my ranunculus,
My hyacinth, my gilliflower, my polyanthus,
My heartsease, my pink, my white water
   lily,
My buttercup, daisy and daffydowndilly.

I'm like a scarlet runner that has lost its stick
Or a cherry that's left for the dicky to pick,
Like a waterpot I weep, like a paviour sigh,
Like a mushroom I wither, like a cucumber, die.

I'm like a bumble bee that never can settle,
And she's a dandelion or else she's a nettle,
My heart's like a beetroot that's choked with
   chickweed,
My head's like a pumpkin a-running to seed.

I've a great mind to end as a felo-de-se
And finish my woes on the branch of a tree,
But I won't, for I know at my kicking you'd roar
And honor my death with a double encore.

Gramachree   [H204: 8 Oct 1927]

s: (m) resembles "Banks of Allan Water"; o:
(m) cf. "Molly My Treasure"; g: "Banna's Banks,"
"... Molly," "Molly Asthore." Other titles: "?Graih
My Chree! (Love of My Heart)," "Mailigh Mo Store."

Source: Gladys Moon (Ballydevitt), learned from
late David Simpson, Mus. Doc. Solicitor (Edinburgh), from his mother; author George Ogle.

[Bp] s: ... David Simpson ... son of the Minister
of Laurencekirk and cousin of J. T. Moon, esq,
Ballydevitt House, Aghadowey ... learned the air
from his mother, whose maiden name was Miss
Thomas of Ballydevitt, and who married first Dr.
M'Intyre of Coleraine and, on her widowhood, the
Rev. Mr Simpson of Laurencekirk. The air has
a similarity to "The Banks of Allan Water," the
composition of which is attributed by Burns to
Robert Crawford of Auchnames, but is marked
"traditional" in some collections. It is likely that
the air here printed is the original Irish air
which suggested "The Banks of Allan Water."
Burns states that the song was written by Mr
Poe, a counsellor-at-law in Dublin, and adds: "I
do not remember any single line in poetry that
has more true pathos than, 'How can she break
the honest heart that wears her in its core.'"
The author was, in reality, the Hon. George Ogle.

[Dt] The Banna is a small river in Co. Waterford.

Key F.

As down by Banna's banks I stray'd
One evening in May,
The little birds in blithesome notes
Made vocal ev'ry spray,
They sang their little tales of love,
They sang them o'er and o'er:

Ah, gramachree ma colleen oge,
Shee Molly mo store.

The daisy pied and all the sweets
The dawn of nature yields,
The primrose pale, the violet blue,
Lay scattered o'er the fields;
Such fragrance in the bosom lies
Of her whom I adore:

I laid me down upon a bank,
Bewailing my sad fate
That doomed me thus the slave of love
And cruel Molly's hate.
How can she break the honest heart
That wears her in its core?

You said you loved me, Molly dear,
Ah, why did I believe?
Yet who could think such tender words
Were meant but to deceive?
That love was all I ask'd on earth,
Nay, heaven could give no more.

O, had I all the flocks that graze
On yonder yellow hill,
Or lowed for me the numerous herds
That yon green pastures fill,
With her I love I'd gladly share
My kine and fleecy store.

Two turtle doves above my head
Sat courting on a bough,
I envied them their happiness
To see them bill and coo.
Such fondness once for me she show'd,
But now, alas, 'tis o'er.

Then fare thee well, my Molly dear,
Thy loss I still shall moan,
While life remains in Strephon's heart,
'Twill beat for thee alone.
Though thou art false, may heaven on thee
Its choicest blessings pour.

Strephon = a fond lover. [s]
r.1,2 translated means "Love of my heart, my little girl, Molly is my treasure." [s]

Belfast Mountains [H519: 11 Nov 1933]

Other title: "The Diamonds of Derry."

No source given.

s: This is a version of a street ballad popular in 1800. Another version was collected in 1893 by Miss Lucy Broadwood from Henry Burstow, a shoemaker in Horsham in Sussex and a bellringer known in most of the English belfries.
The Belfast Mountains (Cave Hill) were supposed to contain diamonds which shone at night. They were often referred to in the ballads of the period.
The first line of the version here printed is a local adaptation, as the scene of the original ballad was on the Belfast mountains and the sailor lad was from Cheshire, pointing to the frequent commerce between Belfast and Chester when the latter was an emigration port for America.
The Editor will feel obliged to any reader who will send a version of the ballad differing from that printed below.

g: Yet another song with confused viewpoint.

Key C.

Being on the banks of Claudy, I heard a maid complain,
Setting forth her lamentations down by yon purling stream,
Saying, 'Here I lie confined in the constant bands of love,
All by a British sailor lad that did inconstant prove.

'It's O, you Belfast mountains, can you bring me no relief?
Have you got no tongue to flatter with, or to ease me of my grief?

C21 / Content in the arms of another

Have you got no tongue to flatter with, or to ease me of my pain?
For it's hard to love an old sweetheart and not be loved again.'

She twined her arms around my neck just as we were going to part,
She twined her arms around my neck, saying, 'You're my old sweetheart,'
She twined her arms around my neck like the branches of yon vine,
Saying, 'Jamie, cruel Jamie, you have broke this heart of mine.'

'O, may you never prosper, nor may you never thrive
In any job you take in hand as long as you're alive,
On the very ground whereon you stand, may the grass refuse to grow,
For you're the whole occasion of my sad grief and woe.'

My Love John [H593: 13 Apr 1935]

o: Matrix of "The Verdant Braes of Skreen" (Hughes); k: "The False Young Man." Other titles: "As I Walked Out," "The Cottage [? r] D [? P]oor," "The Lover Proved False," "A Rose in the Garden," "T for Thomas," "Three Quarters of the Year."

Source: Edward Toal (Glascar, near Rathfriland).

s: ... Edward Toal ... left his team of horses, which were ploughing, to sing it.
The music is repeated for the second half of the verse. When an extra syllable requires it, the note is duplicated.

Key G.

As I rode out one bright May morning
For to hear the birds sing sweet,
I leaned myself against a rose-garden wall
For to see true lovers meet.
For to hear true lovers talk, my dear,
And to hear what they would say,
That I might know a little of their mind
Before I'd go away.

'It's sit you down, my dear,' he says,
'Upon this pleasant green,
For it's full three quarters of a year or more
Since together we have been.'
'I will not sit down, my dear,' she says,
'Neither now nor any other time,
For I'm told you're engaged with another young maid,
So your heart's no longer mine.

Sam Henry's Songs of the People

'For when your heart was mine, my dear,
Your head lay on my right breast,
You would make me believe what a false lover says,
That the sun rose and set in the west,
But I'll not believe what an old man says,
For his days they are not long,
Nor I'll not believe what a false lover says,
For they're sworn to many's a one.

'They are sworn to many's a one, they say,
And many's the false story they will tell,
But when they gain a pretty maid to their mind,
"Adieu, pretty maid, fare thee well."'
'Oh, I will climb up the highest tree
And rob a small bird's nest,
And I will come down safe again
To the one that I love best.'

'Oh, T it stands for Thomas, I suppose,
And it's J for my love John,
And it's W stands for you, false Willie,
But John, you're the only one,
But John, you're the only one, my dear,
But John, you're the only one,
And it's W stands for you, false Willie,
Och, it's John, you're the only one.'

My Flora and I [H30a: 7 Jun 1924]

o: "The Inconstant Lover." Other titles: "(My) Flora (and Me)," "Sheepcrook and Black Dog," "The Unkind Shepherdess," "(Young) Floro," "The Young Shepherd."

Source: coll. Maud Houston (Coleraine), (w, m) James Kennedy (formerly Ratheane), learned from an old man in a quarry.

Key G.

O, who is so happy, so happy as I,
As I and my Flora, my Flora and I?
I'll go down to my Flora and unto her say,
'When will we get married, love, when is the day?'

Out speaks the fair one, saying, 'The day is not come.
Besides, noble shepherd, to wed I'm too young;
I'll go first to service and then I'll return,
And then we'll get married if love carries on.'

According to promise, to service she went,
For to wait on this lady it was my intent,
For to wait on this fair one, this fair lady gay,
I call her my Flora and she calls me her ray.

In a month or two after, a letter I sent,
Two or three times for to show her intent.
She sent back an answer: she lived a happy life,
And she'd never intend to be a poor shepherd's wife.

Ye gates and gate stiles, now I bid you adieu,
My bottle and script I bestow unto you,
My hook, crook and whistle to you I'll resign,
Since this inconstant fair one has now changed her mind.

For when I was young I was red as a rose,
But now I'm as pale as the lily that grows,
Like the green leaves in winter I'm withered and gone;
Do you see what I'm come to by the loving too young?

5.1: ... stiles, I bid ... [Dt]
6.1: ... as the rose, [Dt]

The Flower of Sweet Strabane

[H224a: 25 Feb 1928]

g: "If I Was King of Ireland." Other titles: "Martha, the ...," "Sweet Straeban."

Source: (w) A. A. Campbell (Waring St, Belfast), (m) Roddy Kane (Glack, near Limavady).

[Bp] s: This popular ballad, which has been sung in our streets within the last few weeks, has the old theme of disappointed love. It tells of a draper's assistant named [Dt: whose name was] MacDonald, who sought in vain the hand of his employer's daughter, Miss Ramsay, of Strabane. The song is about 80 years old [Dt: was made about 1846]. It was first published in a Derry paper by Dan MacAnaw in 1909, but the air is now published for the first time. Ten versions have reached me, and it is evident that the song has two principal versions which differ considerably [Dt: and they divide into two categories], one beginning "If I was king of Erin's Isle [Dt: Ireland]," [and] the other we print below....

o: This is not the usual air.

Key C.

[H224b: Dt]

Source: (m) Lady Moore (Ballygawley Castle, Co. Antrim).

No key specified.

As I roved out one evening, being in the month of May,
Down by yon shady arbour I carelessly did stray,
I spied a lovely fair maid, as you can understand,
And they called her lovely Martha, the flower of sweet Strabane.

Were I the king of Ireland and had all things at my will,
I would roam for recreation, new comforts to find still,
But the comfort I would look for, you all may understand,
Is to win the heart of Martha, she's the flower of sweet Strabane.

Her cheeks are like the roses red, her hair a lovely brown,
And o'er her milk-white shoulders in ringlets it hangs down.
She's one of the fairest creatures in the whole Milesian clan,
And my heart lies captivated by the flower of sweet Strabane.

I wish I had my darling away down in Innishowen,
Or in some lonely valley in the wild woods of Tyrone,
I would do my whole endeavour, I would work the newest plan
To gain the heart of Martha, she's the flower of sweet Strabane.

I've often been in Phoenix Park and in Killarney Fair,
In blithe and bonny Scotland on the winding banks of Ayr,
But yet in all my travelling, I never met that one
That could compare with Martha, she's the flower of sweet Strabane.

But since I cannot win your love, no joy there is for me,
So I will seek forgetfulness in lands across the sea,
And unless you chance to follow me, I swear by my right hand,
MacDonald's face you'll never see, fair flower of sweet Strabane.

Farewell to bonny Lifford and Mourne's water side,
For now I'm for America, whatever may betide,
Sailing down Lough Foyle, brave boys, I will wave my bonny white hand
And I'll bid adieu to Martha, she's the flower of sweet Strabane.

First verse ... supplied by Tom Black, Croaghan, Macosquin. [s: Dt, *name and stanza number also written on Bp.*]
2.4: ... Martha, the ... [Dt]
4.1: ... Innishowen, [Dt]
5.2: ... the bonny banks ... [Dt]
 .4: ... Martha, the ... [Dt]
7.4: ... Martha, the ... [Dt]

Bring Me Back the Boy I Love (a)

[H482: 25 Feb 1933]

Other titles: "Adieu," "Bring back to Me (Go Bring Me Back) (My) (The) Blue-Eyed Boy," "The Girl I Love"; cf. "Died for Love."

Source not given.

Key E flat.

As I stood by my cabin door
To see my true love passing by,
He passed me with another girl,
And she was fairer still than I.

Oh, bring me back the boy I love,
Oh bring, oh bring him back to me,
If I only had the boy I love,
It's happy, happy would I be.

If my love's heart was made of glass,
That I could see it through and through,
I would read the lines of his dear heart
And see if he did love me true.

There is a tree I oftimes pass
That bears a leaf as green as grass,
But not so green as my heart's true,
When you love one you can't love two.

Sam Henry's Songs of the People

Never Change the Old Love for the New

[H692: 27 Feb 1937; "Bring Me back the Boy I Love" (b)]

Source not given.

Key E flat.

My love he's but a sailor lad
Who ploughs the ocean through and through,
And on his breast he wears a badge,
And on that badge his name in blue.

Oh, bring me back the boy I love,
Oh, bring him, bring him back to me;
If I only had the boy I love,
It's happy, happy would I be.

As I stood by my cabin door
To see my true love passing by,
He passed me with another girl,
And she was fairer still than I.

My love is like a little bird
That flits about from tree to tree,
For when he meets some other girl
He thinks, he thinks no more on me.

There is a tree I oftimes pass
That bears a leaf as green as grass,
Not half so green as my love's true
Who sails the ocean through and through.

I wish my love was made of glass
That I could see him through and through,
And read the lines of his dear heart,
To see if he'd prove false or true.

I wish my love was here this night,
He would keep me from all harm and fright,
He would roll me in his arms so gay,
And oh, how happy would I be.

Remember, love, and bear in mind,
A constant girl is hard to find;
If you find a lover kind and true,
Ne'er part the old love for the new.

Oh, Johnny, Johnny

[H16: BLp, 1 Mar 1924]

A song of disappointed love.

k: "Love Is Hot and Love Is Cold." Other titles: cf. "As (So) (A)broad as I Was Walking," "The Brisk Young Sailor," "Cockleshells," "The Colour of Amber," "The Constant Damsel," "(So) Deep in Love," "False Love," "I Wish(, I Wish) (I Was a Maid Again)," "Jamie Douglas," "Little Sparrow," "Love and Porter," "(O) Love Is Pleasing (a Sin) (Teasin')," "Maggie Goddon," "(?Sweet) Peggy Gordon," "A Ship Came Sailing," "(There Is a) Tavern in the Town," "Up the Green Meadows," "Waillie," "(O) Waly Waly(, gin Love Be Bonny) (up the Bank)," "The Water Is Wide," "What a Voice," "Will Ye Gang, Love," "Young Ladies," "Young (George) Riley," "('Tis) Youth and Folly (Make Young Men Merry)."

Source: (m) coll. Maud Houston.

s: The repetition of the word "fades" is to be imitated where the second word in the last line of the other verses is suitable.

[Print, from the British Library (BLp) microfilm files of the *Northern Constitution*, provided by John Moulden. In BLp stanza 1 is printed line for line beneath the sol-fa. Bt is typed in 2-line stanzas, each line twice as long as in BLp and Dt.]

m: [Stanza 9] does not ... appear in the paper. I have a 3-verse version ["Songs of the People" #401] collected by James Moore, where it or a similar verse is the first. Henry possibly used this verse or an adaptation in a singing version, for on 3 August 1943 Henrietta Byrne, who frequently broadcast on radio Henry songs under his direction, sent him an 8-verse set, of which this is verse 7, saying "Here are the words ... as we sang them."

Key F.

Oh, Johnny, Johnny, but love is bonny,
A little while when it is new,
But when it's old it groweth cold
And fades, fades away like the morning dew.

Oh, Johnny, Johnny, but you are nice, love,
In keeping company with me sae lang,
You are the first boy that e'er I had, love,
So kiss me, Johnny, before ye gang.

One kiss of my lips ye ne'er shall get, love,
For you have caused me sore to sigh,
Nor will I grant you that sweet request, love,
That oftentimes you did me deny.

If I would grant you that sweet request, love,
My heart on you I might then bestow,
But as good a lover as you may come, love,
So I'll not hinder you for to go.

For I have stepped the steps of love, dear,
And I have stepped a step too low;
Was it to be done that I have done,
It would never be done by me, I know.

It's ower the moss, love, you needna cross, love,
And ower the moor ye needna ride,
For I have gotten a new sweetheart, love,
And you may go get yourself a bride.

For love does come and love does go, love,
Like a little small bird unto its nest.
Was I to tell you, love, all I know, love,
They're far away that I love best.

It's had I known the first time I kissed you
That women's hearts were so ill to win,
I would have locked mine all in a chest, love,
And screwed, screwed it tight with a silver pin.

Oh, I wish my father had never whistled,
And I wish my mother had never sung,
And I wish the cradles had never rock-ed
When I was a boy and so very young.

1.3: ... groweth ["cold" omitted in Bt]
3.2: ... you hae caused ... [Dt]
6.1: ... moss you ... [Dt]
7.1: ... does go, [Dt]
8.2: ... were sae ill ... [Dt, Bt]
9: [Stanza absent from BLp, Bt.]

The Apron of Flowers

[H683: 26 Dec 1936; Laws P25]

g: "There Is an Alehouse in This Town." Other titles: "The Alehouse," "Betsy Watson," "A (The) Bold (Brisk) Young Cropper (Farmer) (Lover) (Sailor) (Courted Me)," "Dearest Billie," "The Deceased Maiden Lover," "Died for (of) Love," "Down in Yon Meadows," "I Wish, I Wish," "In Jessie's City (Tarrytown)," "(In) Sheffield (Yorkshire) Park," "Love Has Brought Me to Despair," "Love is Pleasing," "The Maiden's Lament," "My He'rt It Is Sair," "She's Like a (the) Swallow," "Slighted Love," "This Fair Maid to the Meadow's Gone"; cf. "The Butcher('s) Boy," "Deep in Love," "Morning Fair," "O Waly, Waly," "Railroad Boy," "A Rude and Rambling Boy," "A Sailor Coming Home on Leave," "The Tavern in the Town," "Through Lonesome Woods," "Up the Green Meadow."

Source: Mrs H. Dinsmore, sr (Stone Row, Coleraine).

g: "The Apron of Flowers" is surely ancestral to "The Butcher Boy."

Key D.

I loved a young man, I loved him well,
I loved him better than tongue can tell,
I loved him better than he loved me,
For he did not care for my companie.

Now I will tell you the reason why:
Because he had more gold than I,
But the gold will melt and the silver fly,
And perhaps he'll just be as poor as I.

There is an alehouse all in this town
Where he goes in and there sits down,
And he takes a strange girl on his knee
And he tells to her what he once told me.

But there's a flower grows in this place,
And some does call it the heart's ease,
And if I could but this flower find,
I would ease my heart and my troubled mind.

Into the green meadows there I'll go
And watch the flowers all as they grow,
And every flower I will pull
Until I have my apron full.

The Bonny, Bonny Boy [H215: 24 Dec 1927]

s: "I Will Walk with My Love" [Hughes 2,1915];
k: "Bonny Boy." Other titles: "Bonny Bird (Girl)," "Cupid's Trep(p)an," "I Built a Bower in My Breast," "I Once Loved a Boy (Girl)," "(My) Bonny (Irish) Boy," "Up the Green Forest"; cf. "The Grey Hawk," "Once I Courted a Bonny Little Girl."

Source: Thomas Thompson (Cappaghbeg, Portstewart), learned from his mother (Fox Dartries, Articlave); incomplete versions (Cloyfin) (Ballymoney).

s: ... A fragment (one verse) has been published by Herbert Hughes [2,1915] under the title "I Will Walk with My Love." It is set to a traditional air collected by him in Co. Dublin.

Key A flat.

Sam Henry's Songs of the People

I once loved a boy, and a bonny, bonny boy,
And a boy that I thought would be my own,
I loved him so well, and so very, very well,
He has taken his flight and he's gone,
  And he's gone,
  He has taken his flight and he's gone.

Now since he's gone, let him go, let him go,
For his absence I never will mourn,
Since he's got another he loves better than me,
For his love's sake I never will return.

I went up yon green bower and down by the glen,
The day it being sultry and warm,
And who did I spy but my own darling boy,
Wrapp-ed close in another fair maid's arms.

He gave me a sign with his lily-white hand,
Just as if I had been at his commands,
But I passed him by so shy, without lifting an
  eye,
The more I was bound in love's bands.

Now you that has my boy, and my bonny, bonny
  boy,
Be as kind to my boy as you can,
For the more he's none o' mine, he's a pleasure in
  my mind,
And I'll walk with him times now and then.

1,2.5: [Absent in Dt.]

The Maid with the Bonny Brown Hair (a) [H43: 6 Sep 1924]

o: (m) "Lough Erne's Shore." Other title: "The Lass ...."

Source: Lizzie Hassan (Irish Houses, Coleraine) from blacksmith's father, coll. Maud Houston (Coleraine).

[typed on Bp] Stated by Miss Kate Kane, of Cross Roads, Dreen, near Mount Sawell, to have been composed by Patrick McCloskey of Sawell.

Key F.

As I rode out very early
To view the green meadows in spring,
It was down by the side of a river
I spied a fair maid -- she did sing.
I stood in silent amazement
To gaze on that creature so fair,
She seemed to be brighter than Venus,
The maid with the bonny brown hair.

Her skin was as white as a lily
And her cheeks like the red rose in June,
Her eyes they were sparkling like diamonds
And her breath it did bear a perfume,
And a dress of the soft shining velvet
Was the dress this fair maiden did wear,
And chains of pure gold and bright silver
Were twined round her bonny brown hair.

For a long time we courted together,
Till at last we named the wedding day.
One day we were conversing together,
Very kindly to me she did say:
'I have another more kinder
My land and my fortune to share,
So farewell to you now and forever,'
Said the maid with the bonny brown hair.

Then I walked down by yon harbour,
I saw a ship for the proud land of Spain,
They were dancing and singing for pleasure,
But I had a heart full of pain.
As I saw the ship sail down the river,
I spied my old sweetheart so fair:
Quite content in the arms of another
Was the girl with the bonny brown hair.

Farewell to you, friends and relations,
It's a chance if I'll e'er see you more,
And when I'm in a far distant nation,
I'll sigh for my own native shore.
When I'm in a far distant nation,
I'll sigh for my lover so fair;
Quite content in the arms of another
Is the maid with the bonny brown hair.

1.6: ... that charmer so ... [written on Bp]
3.5: 'Oh, I have ... [written on Bp]

The Maid with the Bonny Brown Hair (b) [H575: 8 Dec 1934]

Source: John Leighton (Ballyhome, Cloyfin).

s: ... This song was published in this series eleven years ago, but the present version has differences that much enhance it and make it worthy of being reprinted. The air is in the ancient Irish gapped scale.

Key G.

As I walk-ed out very early
To view the green meadows in spring,
It's down by the side of a river
A charming wee darling did sing;
I stood in my silent amazement
And gazed on that wee lass so fair,
She appeared to me brighter than Venus,
The lass in her bonny brown hair.

Her eyes did sparkle like diamonds,
Her cheeks like the red rose in June,
Her skin was as white as the lily,
And her breath it did bear a perfume.
A dress of the rid-sprickled velvet
This charming wee darling did wear,
And a chain of the bright gold and jewels
Was warped round her bonny brown hair.

Oh, long had we talk-ed together
Till at length we set our wedding day,
And one day as we were talking,
How simply this wee girl did say,
'I've another wee laddie more tender,
My hand and my fortune to share,
So fare ye well, noo and forever,'
Said the lass in the bonny brown hair.

There were two ships lay down in yon river,
And one of them bound for proud Spain;
They were fifing and fiddling and dancing,
And I with my heart full of pain.
As we sail-ed down in yon river
I spied my wee darling so fair:
Content in the arms of another
Was the girl in the bonny brown hair.

Farewell to my friends and relations,
For them I will never see more,
When I'm in some far distant nation,
I'll sigh for my own native shore.
Farewell to my friends and relations,
For them I will never see more,
Farewell to my friends and relations,
I'll sigh for the girl I adore.

2.5: rid-sprickled = red-speckled.

The Green Bushes [H143: 7 Aug 1926; Laws P2]

Other titles: "Down by the ...," "The False Lovers."

Source: 2: Annie White (Drumafivey, Stranocum); Mary Patton (Ballylough, Bushmills).

[Wt, written in pencil] Barring?

k: "The song was sung by Mrs Fitzwilliam in Buckstone's play *The Green Bushes* (1845) and it was published in Duncombe's *Musical Casket* and other collections at the time. Since then the words have often been credited to J. B. Buckstone, with the music composed by E. F. Fitzwilliam, but we can presume that it was traditional long before it was used by Buckstone" (1975:378).

Key G.

C 21 / Content in the arms of another

As I went a-walking one evening in May
To hear the birds whistle and see the lambkins play,
I spied a fair damsel, so sweetly sang she
Down by the green bushes where she chanced to meet me.

'Why are you loitering here, pretty fair maid?'
'Oh, I'm waiting on my true love,' softly she said.
'Oh, will you be my true love, or will you agree
To forsake those green bushes and follow with me?

'Oh, I will buy you fine beavers and fine silken hose,
I will buy you swan petticoats flounced to the toes,
I will buy you fine jewels if you'll but agree
For to leave these green bushes and follow with me.'

'Oh, I want none of your beavers, your fine silken hose,
For I'm not so mean as to marry for clothes,
But if you will be constant and true unto me,
I will leave those green bushes and follow with thee.

'Come let us be going, kind sir, if you please,
Come let us be going from under those trees,
For it's yonder he's coming, my true love I see:
Down by yon green bushes he was to meet me.'

When he came there and saw she was gone,
He looked up and down and he cried all forlorn:
'She has gone with another and has deceived me,
And has left those green bushes where she vowed to meet me.

'I'll do as the schoolboy, spend my time at play;
I'll not let any false woman lead me astray,
I'll let a false woman delude me no more,
Farewell, faithless bushes, 'tis time to give o'er.'

6.1: When her lover came ... [Dt]

Out of the Window [H141: 24 Jul 1926]

[cf. H534 "Our Wedding Day"]

Other titles: "Our Wedding Day," "She Moved through the Fair"; cf. "I Once Had a True Love."

Source: (w, m) James Lafferty (Doaghs, Magilligan).

395

Sam Henry's Songs of the People

g: Stanza 2 of this song and stanza 3 of H534 "Our Wedding Day" are the same; stanza 5 is a floating verse found in a number of songs, e.g., H24a "The Star of Benbradden" (stanza 2), H709 "If I Were a Fisher" (stanza 2).

o: Tune should be 3/4.

Key C.

I once had a wee lass and I loved her well,
I loved her far better than my tongue can tell,
Her parents disliked me for my want of years,
So adieu to all pleasure since I lost my dear.

Then I dreamt last night that my love came in,
And she walked up so soft that her feet made no din.
I thought that she spoke and those words she did say,
'It won't be long now, love, till our wedding day.'

Then according to promise at midnight I rose
And found nothing there but the down-folded clothes,
The sheets they were empty, as plain as you see,
And out of the window with another went she.

Oh, it's Molly, lovely Molly, what's this that you have done?
You have pulled the thistle, left the red rose behind;
The thistle will wither and decay away soon,
But the red rose will flourish in the merry month of June.

Then if I was a fisherman down by the seaside
And Molly a salmon, coming in with the tide,
I would cast out my net and catch her in a snare,
I would have lovely Molly, I vow and declare.

Or if I was an eagle and had two wings to fly,
I would fly to my love's castle and it's there I would lie,
In a bed of green ivy I would leave myself down.
With my two folded wings I would my love surround.

My Bonny Brown Jane

[H613: BLp, 31 Aug 1935]

o: (m) "Lovely Willie"; g: "Courting Too Slow."

Source: Andrew Allen (Bannbridge Cottages, Coleraine).

s: [Andrew Allen] sang the song in true traditional style.

Key C.

I courted a wee lassie when I was but young,
Although she beguiled me with her false flattering tongue,
Although she beguiled me, I would have you to know
That I lost my wee lassie by courting too slow.

I loved her sincerely, as dear as my life,
I had no other intentions but to make her my wife,
Till a young man, a stranger, a-courting her came,
And he soon gained the faith of my bonny brown Jane.

Her eyes shone like stars on a clear frosty night,
And when I think on her, my head does get light,
Sometimes I think on her and at night I do dream
That I'm rolled in the arms of my bonny brown Jane.

I enlisted, took a shilling, a soldier to be,
To fight for my queen in a far country,
To roam among strangers it was my incline,
All for that wee lassie I'm leaving behind.

On a Saturday night men incline to their wives,
Young men to their sweethearts as dear as their lives.
When I'm left heartbroken for the girl I adore,
I'll pray for her welfare; what can I do more?

4.2: ... far counteree, [Dt, Bt]

The Slighted Suitor (a)

[H159a: 27 Nov 1926; ?Laws P10]

Other titles: "The Merchant's Daughter"; cf. "If One Won't, Another One Will," "Jenny Dear," "Lovely Nancy," "Once I Had a Love," "The Rejected Lover."

Source: John M'Laughlin (Mill St, Ballycastle, Co. Antrim), from his mother.

[Bp] s: ... It is very typical of the old unlettered ballads and enjoyed a widespread popularity. The last three words of the song are spoken, not sung. This sweet air has a very haunting rhythm.

[Bp] Key C.

Down in Dublin City there lives a merchant's
    daughter,
She had so many sweethearts to court her night
    and day,
At last there came a 'sut-i-or' from Clady banks
    to court her,
He took from thence the burning flame to melt her
    frozen heart.

She says, 'Young man, retire; your wealth I
    don't admire,
For I have no desire a single life to part.'
This young man being asham-ed, he went to be
    reliev-ed,
He went next Tuesday evening to one he had in
    view.

He's left disdainful Molly, he's gone a-courting
    Sally.
Here is some melancholy, I'll give you time to rue.
So just in six weeks after, she wrote to him a
    letter,
She wrote to him a letter saying for him to come
    back again.

So just in three weeks after, he wrote to her an
    answer;
He wrote to her an answer and sealed it with
    disdain,
Saying, 'When you could, you would not; now
    you would and shall not,
Read these lines and grieve not, you'll find my
    answer true.'

So come all ye fair maids, marry, that don't
    intend to tarry,
And never slight the young man that's master of
    your heart,
For when he goes a-roving, you'll find him long
    returning,
You'll spend your days in mourning -- it's I that
    feels the smart.

The Slighted Suitor (b)

[H159b: Dt; ?Laws P10]

No source given.

C21 / Content in the arms of another

[Dt] Key G.

In Coleraine town resided
A wealthy merchant's daughter,
Oh, she had sweethearts plenty
To court her night and day.

And when their love she gain-ed,
Their courtship she disdain-ed,
She did her whole endeavour
Their very hearts to break.

Till at length a wealthy suitor
From Claudy came to court her,
He brought with him the flames of love,
Her frozen heart to melt.

She says, 'Young man, retire,
Your suit I don't admire,
For I have no desire
A single life to part.'

In six months more or better,
She wrote to him a letter,
He wrote her back an answer
And sealed it with disdain.

Saying, 'When you could, you would not,
But now you would, you shall not.
Read these lines and grieve not,
You'll find my answer plain.'

So now he's courting Sally
And left deceitful Molly,
The tears of melancholy
He gave her time to rue.

Now all you maids of learning,
By Molly pray take warning:
Never slight the wee lad
That's master of your heart.

For when he goes a-roving,
You'll find him ne'er returning,
You'll spend your days in mourning,
It's me that feels the smart.

Twenty-One

[H33: 28 Jun 1924, H611: 17 Aug 1935]

Other title: "The Mullagh Lovers."

Source: (w, m) Thomas Cameron, coachman (from childhood, Ballinteer), coll. Maud Houston (Coleraine). [H611: No source given.]

1: This song originally appeared as H33; it was also reprinted as H611 with an additional last stanza and numerous revisions as given here.

Sam Henry's Songs of the People

Slurs are indicated only in Bp, which also has stanza 1 printed line for line under the sol-fa. Note the melodic changes in Dt and H611.

s: An incomplete version of this song was published as No. 33 in this series. The song is republished in response to many requests, one of which came from a soldier in Jerusalem.

[H33] Key F. [H611: Key G.]

At twenty-one I first begun to court a
  neighbour's child,
We both being young and full of fun, bright
  Phoebus on us smiled,
We courted away the livelong day, like angels
  did agree,
Full well I knew she would prove true and
  constant unto me.

At twenty-two no man could view what beauty
  she possessed,
Her yellow hair in ringlets fair hung down her
  snow-white breast,
The picture of her two blue eyes, my pencil
  could not tell,
Her effigy no man could draw, or paint her
  parallel.

At twenty-three she slighted me for the sake of
  another boy,
So jealousy got up in me this young man to
  destroy;
I fixed a plan for this young man, as plain as
  you may see,
Without sword or gun I made him run and shun
  her company.

My love is fair and will ensnare some young men
  in her time,
O'er all the rest I'll do my best to be her
  Valentine.
If God alone would hear me moan and help me as
  a friend,
I still have hopes she'd pity me and to me
  condescend,

On Claudy Hill I leave my quill to pen the naked
  truth,
My mind is bent on rambling, for I am a sporting
  youth,
The ground whereon my true love stands is
  strewed with rosemary,
Small birds in June may change their tune, so
  farewell, gramachree.

[The original column H33 (Bp, Dt) differs from H611 as follows:]
1.1: [Dt: At] Twenty-one ...
1.4: Until I found she would prove kind ...
2.1: ... view the beauty ... [Dt only]
 .2: Her dark brown hair and ringlets fair hung o'er ...
 .3: Her two black eyes rolled in her head; ...
 .4: Her effigy no more could view, nor ...
4.1: If goodness alone would hear my moan and help me as a friend
 .2: To see if she would pity me or make her [Dt: me] condescend;
 .3: My love is fair, she will ensnare some young men in her prime,
 .4: Above all the rest I'll do my best to [Dt: and] have her in her prime.
5: [Not in H33.]

Polly Perkins of Paddington Green

[H132: 22 May 1926]

g: "The Milkman." Other titles: "... Paddington's ...," "Pretty ...," "Sweet Pretty ...."

Source: Mrs E. Glenn (Mulkeragh South, Limavady), sung by her mother Margaret Smyth (Ballyhargin, Dungiven) c. 1855.

[Bp] s: (Chorus is sung to same air, lines 5 and 6 being sung to lines 1 and 2 of the music.)

[Bp has 6 lines labeled "chorus," including stanza 2; in Dt the same stanza is typed separately, and the directions for the refrain are simply "to the same air," with the remaining instructions, about lines 5 and 6, x'ed out.]

Key E.

I'm a broken-hearted milkman, in grief I'm
  arrayed
Through keeping of the company of a young
  servant maid
Who lived on bold wages to keep the house clean
In a gentleman's family near Paddington Green.

  *Oh, as pretty as a butterfly and as proud as a
    queen,*
  *Was pretty little Polly Perkins of Paddington
    Green.*

Her eyes were as black as the pips of a pear,
No rose in the garden with her cheeks could
  compare,
Her hair hung in ringlets so beautiful and long,
I thought that she loved me, but found I was
  wrong.

When I rattle in the morning and cry, 'Milk below,'
At the sound of my milk cans her face she would
  show,

With a smile upon her countenance and a laugh in
   her eye --
If I thought that she'd have loved me, I'd laid
   down to die.

When I asked her to marry me she said, 'Oh,
   what stuff,'
And told me to drop it, for she had quite enough
Of my nonsense; at the same time I'd been very
   kind,
But to marry a milkman she didn't feel inclined.

'Oh, the man that has me must have silver and
   gold,
A chariot to ride in and be handsome and bold,
His hair must be curly as any watch spring,
And his whiskers as big as a brush for clothing.'

The words that she uttered went straight through
   my heart,
I sobb'd and I sighed and straightway did depart
With a tear on my eyelid as big as a bean,
Bidding goodbye to Polly and Paddington Green.

In six months she married, this hard-hearted girl,
But it was not a Wicount nor was it a Hearl,
It was not a Baronite, but a shade or two worse,
'Twas a bow-legged conductor of a twopenny bus.

[*Differences in Dt:*]
   r.1: She's as ... butterfly; she's as ...
    .2: Is pretty ...
   2.3: ... ringlets, beautiful ...
    .4: ... but I found ...
   7.2: ... it an Hearl,

[*Corrections written on Bp:*]
   1.3: ... on what [?] wages ... [*writing unclear*]
   r.1: She's beautiful ...
   r.1,2: "The only repeat."
   3.4: ... laid me down ...
   4.3: ... been werry kind,
   7.3: ... a shide or ...

My Darling Blue-Eyed Mary

[H785: 10 Dec 1938]

[cf. H152 "I'm Seventeen 'gin Sunday"; H793
"As I Gaed ower a Whinny Knowe"]

s: (m) "original" of "The Boyne Water"; o: "Seventeen Come Sunday." Other title: "Blue-Eyed
...."

Source: John M'Neill from his grandfather, William
John Rankin (Knockmult).

Key C.

C21 / Content in the arms of another

As I walked out one summer's day
To view the flowers springing,
I met a maid upon the way,
And she was sweetly singing.

I stepped up and did salute,
She was both neat and airy,
She appeared to me like a diamond bright,
She's my charming blue-eyed Mary.

'Where are you going, my pretty fair maid?'
I asked her very kindly;
'To milk my cows, kind sir,' she said,
'And then to mind my dairy.'

'May I go along with you, fair maid?'
I asked her very kindly;
'Just as you say yourself,' replied
My charming blue-eyed Mary.

So we both hopped over the flowery fields
On a Monday morning early,
And on a primrose bank we sat,
As the skylark sang so rarely.

It was on a mossy bank we lay,
And she alone was near me,
And there I kissed those ruby lips
Of my charming blue-eyed Mary.

And as I took my leave of her,
These words by me were spoken,
'This diamond ring I give to you
To keep it as a token.'

So we both hopped over the flowery fields
On a Monday morning early;
Up stepped a young sea captain bold
And he says, 'Is this my Mary?

'Since I have sailed the seas so far
To seek your cows and dairy,
Will you come along with me this day,
My charming blue-eyed Mary?'

She gave consent and away they went,
She left her cows and dairy,
And now she's a young sea captain's wife,
And I lost my blue-eyed Mary.

My Bonnie Irish Boy

[H168: 29 Jan 1927; Laws P26]

g: "The Bonny Young Irish Boy." Other titles:
"The Bonny Boy," "The Bonny ...," (m) "Cupid's
Trappan or the Green Forest," "It Was in Dublin
City," (m) "My Own Bonny Boy."

Source: (w) Mary Beckett (Crocnamac, Portrush);
(m whistled) William Hemphill (Newmarket St, Coleraine).

o: Time should be 6/8.

Key D.

Sam Henry's Songs of the People

Oh, once I was courted by a bonnie Irish boy,
He called me his darling, his heart's delight and joy,
And oftimes he talked to me about getting wed,
But in a short time after, my bonnie boy was fled.

He bundled up his tools and to England took his flight,
I bundled up my clothes and followed him by night,
But when I arrived in a fair English town,
They told me he'd got wedded to a girl of high renown.

Farewell to the green fields where we used to walk,
Farewell to the meadows where we used to sit and talk,
The wee birds were singing and the lark sang loud and high,
And the song they were singing was 'My Bonnie Irish Boy.'

Come all you young fair maids, a warning take by me:
Never build your nest on the top of a high tree,
For the leaves they will wither and the roots will decay,
And the beauty of a bonnie boy will soon fade away.

Sweet Clonalee [H554: 14 Jul 1934]

Source: (Ballymoney).

s: This excellent little song was received anonymously ... and the sender is heartily invited to send others of the same type.

Key C.

When first from my country a stranger I went,
The thought of departing made me discontent,
But now to America I'm on the salt sea,
And I'm leaving forever my sweet Clonalee.

I loved a young damsel, her name was M'Hugh,
But alas, she was false, though I thought she was true,
For she married a man who did wrong against me,
Oh, it pains me to part from my sweet Clonalee.

The man was a farmer, was wealthy and old,
He got me in trouble by means of his gold,
He blamed me of stealing of sheep forty-three,
And that's why I'm leaving my sweet Clonalee.

Farewell to my parents, I was always their joy,
It grieves them to part from their own darling boy,
Bad luck and ill fortune be with you, James Magee,
For it's you that caused me to leave sweet Clonalee.

An Old Lover's Wedding

[H60a: "A song of sundered hearts," 3 Jan 1925]

s: "An (The) Old Farmer's Lover"; k: "The Nobleman's ..."; g: "Awful ...," "The Faultless Bride." Other titles: "All (a)round My Hat," "Another Man's ...," "The Bride's Death," "The Famous ...," "The Faultless (Penitent) Bride," "(The) (To Wear a) Green Willow (Tree)," "I Once Was a Guest at a Nobleman's ...," "Late(ly) Last Night," "The Love Token," "Once I Was [Invited to] [at] a Noble[man]'s ...," "(The) Orange and Blue," "The Wedding."

Source: [Dt] Joe Allen (Strand Terrace, Coleraine).

[Written on Bp, Wt] Corrections from Joseph Reilly, Moneycannon. [All, written under title] An Old Farmer's Lover.

Key G.

It happened to be at an old lover's wedding,
Everyone was to sing a song,
And who was there but the bride's best beloved,
And by him the first song was sung.

The old lover:
Saying, 'How can you sit at another man's table?
Or how can you drink of another man's wine?
Or how can you fly to another man's arms,
When you, my love, have been in mine?'

The bride, she'd been seated at the head of the table,
Every word she remarked right well,
And for to stand it no longer she was able,
And down at her new groom's feet she fell.

The old lover:
'Now lift up your bride, you false-hearted young man,
Lift up your bride and set her on your knee,
For once I thought she would be my bride;
False and inconstant she proved unto me.'

The bride:
'It's one request I ask of you, love,
The first and the last that ever it shall be:
To let me sleep this night with my mother,
And all the rest I will live with thee.'

[*The groom:*]
'That request I ne'er will grant you, love,
You might have thought of yourself in time,
That request I know right well,
The thoughts of your Johnnie still run in your mind.'

It's her request at length he granted,
Sighing and sobbing, she went to her bed,
Early, early the next morning
The groom he arose and found his young bride was dead.

He stooped down and he took her in his arms,
He carried her out to the garden green,
Fine sheets and pillows he did surround her,
Thinking his young bride would come to life again.

Saying, 'Mary, lovely Mary, cruel-hearted Mary,
I loved you better than you loved me,
I stole you from your lover Johnnie,
I went in between the bark and the tree.'

Saying, 'Come all ye young men that go a-courting,
This is a warning take by me,
If ever you go down between the grove and the valley,
Never venture in between the bark and the tree.'

2.1: How can ... [Dt]
3.1: ... she being seated ... [Dt]
6.3: ... well, love, [Dt]
6., 9.: [Bp, Wt, Dt *assign these to* "The old lover."]

The Laird's Wedding [H60b: Dt; Laws P31]

s: (m) = H60a "An Old Lover's Wedding."

Source not given.

C21 / Content in the arms of another

I being invited unto a laird's wedding,
All of a young maid who proved love unkind,
Oftimes she talked of her old former lover,
And the thoughts of her darling still run in her mind.

When supper was over and all things were ended,
It fell every man to sing a love song,
It happened to fall on her old former lover,
Which caused these verses, they were not so long:

'Many a one has been from their darling seven years,
And many a one has ne'er returned again,
But I have been from mine but one year,
And an inconstant lover to me she's became.'

The bride being sitting at the head of the table,
Not a word was said, but she knew it right well,
And to stand it any longer the bride was not able,
And down at the groom's feet she instantly fell.

Saying, 'Here's one request, love, that I will ask of you,
The first and the last if you grant it to me:
If you let me lie one night in my old mother's arms,
All the rest of my time, love, I'll spend it with thee.'

It was no sooner asked than unto her it was granted,
Sighing and sobbing, the bride went to bed,
But early the next morning the young groom awoke
And went into Sally's chamber, but oh! she was dead.

Oh Sally, lovely Sally, when you and I were courting,
Oftimes you said you loved no other one but me,
But them that depends on a young lady's folly,
Their heart will decay and will wither away.

I'll put on my hat and I'll wear the green and yellow,
All round my hat for a twelvemonth and a day,
And if anyone does ask me the reason I wear it,
I will tell them my Sally lies cold in the clay.

The Girl I Left Behind

[H188: 18 Jun 1927; Laws P1b]

o: (m) "Limerick Is Beautiful"; k: "My Parents Reared Me Tenderly." Other titles: "All Frolicking I'll Give Over," "... Gal ...," "Janie(ey) (Jennie) Ferguson," "Lacky Bill," "Maggie Walker (Blues) (, ...)," "(...) Maid ...," "My Parents Loved (Raised) (Treated) Me Tenderly," "Old George's Square," "Peggy Walker," "(The) Rambling (Roving) Cowboy (Lover)," "The Roveing (Roaming) Boy," "There Was a Wealthy (The Rich Old) Farmer," "The Wealthy Squire."

401

Sam Henry's Songs of the People

Source: (w) coll. G. B. Newe [Dt: esq, Prospect House, Cushendall] in Cushendall district; (m) John Henry Macaulay (Ballycastle), learned from his uncle, Patrick Macaulay, tailor (Greenans, Glenshesk).

[Bp] s: ... Patrick Macaulay ... used to "bang the goose" [Dt: (he was a tailor)] with great gusto at the words, "the girl I left behind."

o: No relation to the more widely known song of the same name ["... Me," popular song to the tune "Brighton Camp."].

[Bp has 8-line stanzas, each line half as long as those below, with directions for 2 lines to be sung to each line of music.]

Key E flat.

My parents reared me tenderly, had ne'er a child but me,
My mind being bent for rambling, with theirs would not agree,
So I became a courtier, it often grieved me sore,
I left my aged parents and never saw them more.

The first time I left Ireland, for Scotland I was bound,
And sailing up to Glasgow, we viewed that pleasant town:
Where trade and money was plenty and the girls to me proved kind,
But the chiefest object of my heart was the girl I left behind.

One evening when my work was done I walked by George's Square,
The mail coach it arrived and the postboy met me there,
He handed me a letter which let me understan'
That the girl I left behind me had wed another man.

If this be true you tell me, I wouldn't believe the fair,
For oftentimes she told me that she would prove sincere:
The Sunday before we parted, it was on the book she swore
That she would wed no one but me, and she vowed it o'er and o'er.

But as I perused it further I found the news too true,
I stood and looked all round me, I knew not what to do,
Said I, 'Hard labour I'll give o'er, to rambling I'll incline,
I'll think no more on the last farewell and the girl I left behind.'

I then set off for New York town, strange faces for to see,
Where handsome Peggy Walker fell deep in love with me,
My pocket it was empty and I thought it was full time
To stop with her and think no more on the girl I left behind.

One day as I sat condoling, she says, 'Don't grieve, my boy,
For I have money plenty to support both you and I,
Your pocket shall be loadened and hard labour you'll give o'er
If you consent to wed with me and you will rove no more.'

'If I would consent to wed with you, I would be much to blame,
My friends and my relations would look on me with shame;
I mean to see my parents before that they'll resign,
And to bid adieu and a last farewell to the girl I left behind.'

'If all that you reveal be true, our friendship's at an end.
Since first you came to this country I always proved your friend,
You had my money at your command when fortune seemed to frown,
And my boy's cause I still maintained when others run you down.'

It's then my heart it did relent, for what she said was true.
I promised for to marry her, what the d--l more could I do?
Now Peggy's mistress of my heart, she's loving and she's kind,
But the perjured vows I'll never forget of the girl I left behind.

7.3: loadened = loaded.

C21 REFERENCES

The Ripest of Apples (H641) 383

[for more references see H532 "Tarry Trousers"]

IREL JIFSS 9,1911:28, nearly identical.
  Cf. Loesberg 1,1980:26 "Love is Pleasing"

BRIT Cf. Bruce/Stokoe 1882(1965):93 "I Drew My Ship into a Harbour"
  ED&S 37(1,Spr)1975:15 "Ripest Apples"
  Sharp/Karpeles 1974,1:449 (#113) "Ripest Apples"
  Cf. Sharp/Karpeles 1975,1:71 "Tarry Trousers"
  Cf. Spin 2(8)[?1964]:17 "I Drew My Ship into a Harbour"

REC Cf. LaRena Clark, Topic 12T 140 (A1) "Rattle on the Stovepipe," esp. stanza 3.

The False Lover (H790) 383

Brunnings 1981: "Love Is Pleasing," "As I Walked through London City"

h: IREL Cf. Ceol 3(2)1968:467 "Love It's Pleasing"
  Shields 1981:156-7
  Shields/Shields UF 21,1975: #426 "(The) Wheel of Fortune"
h: "Songs of the People" (8 August 1931), no source given.

h: BRIT Christie 1,1876:260-1 "The Wheel of Fortune"
  Hamer 1967:45 "When I Was Young," a pretty 3-stanza fragment.

BRS Harvard 1: 1.111 (Stephenson), a longer version, but without Henry's last two stanzas.
h: Favourite Irish Songs, 1975:28

h: REC Ballads from the Pubs ..., Mercier IRL 1
h: Dolly McMahon, Claddagh CC3

The Bonny Bushes Bright (H699) 383

Dean-Smith 1954: "(The) Grey Cock; The Light of the Moon"
Child 1882-98(1965),4:61-74 (#248) "The Grey Cock" or "Saw You My Father?", 11 vts.; 5:252-3, 1 vt.; 301
Coffin/Renwick 1950(1977):139-40; see especially Renwick's analytical unraveling of the "Grey Cock" tangle of ballads, pp. 267-71. He concludes that much of the confusion stems from Cecilia Costello's composite text, which is "a unique integration made by a thoroughly competent and creative bearer of tradition, and not a prototype that became fragmented elsewhere" (p. 271).
Bronson 4,1972:15-23
Brunnings 1981: "Biscayo," "The Grey Cock [Child 248]"

IREL Joyce 1909:219 (#408) "The Lover's Ghost" [Karpeles]
  Hughes 2,1915:64-9 "The Light of the Moon" [Bronson]
  Morton 1973:5 "Willie's Ghost," a 2-stanza fragment. [Coffin/Renwick]

m: BRIT Kilkerr FMJ 1977:224-5; reprint in Treoir 12(1)1980:15
  Spin 7(1)1969:9-11 "The Lover's Ghost," 2 versions
  Tocher #19(Aut)1975:104-5

AMER Warner 1984:225-6 (#90) "Pretty Crowin' Chickens" (see Presnell rec.)

BRS Holloway/Black 1975:244-5 (#108) "Saw You My Father, a Favorite Scotch Song"

REC Peggy Seeger, B&R, Blackthorne ESB 81 (B2) "The Grey Cock"
  Cecilia Costello, FSB 5 (B2) "Willie's Ghost";
Leader LEE 4054 (B7) "The Lover's Ghost" [Fowke]
  Peggy Seeger, Ewan MacColl, LH, Argo ZDA 68, #5 "The Grey Cock," 5 versions.
  A. L. Lloyd, Riverside CB, RLP 12 628 (B4) "The Lover's Ghost" (male); [b:] Prestige/Int. 13066; [b:] Topic 12T 118 (A6) "The Lover's Ghost" (female)
  LaRena Clark, Prestige-Int. 25014 "I'll Go See My Love" [Fowke]
  Robert Cinnamond, Topic 12T 269 (B2) "Fly Up, My Cock"
b: Cf. Shirley Collins, Import 1917 "One Night as I Lay on My Bed"
  Cf. Ray, Archie Fisher, Topic TPS 145 "The Night Visiting Song"
b: Cynthia Gooding, Prestige/Int. 13010 "The Lover's Ghost"
  Len Graham, Topic 12TS 334 (B3) "My Willie-o"
  Cf. Bella Higgins, Andra Stewart, Prestige/Int. 25016 (A2) "I Must Away" [Fowke]
b: Cf. Norman Kennedy, Folk-Legacy FSS 34 "The Night Visiting Song"
  Cf. Louis Killen, Topic 12T 126 (B2) "The Cock"
  Lori Holland, Folkways FG 3518 (A6) "The Light of the Moon"
  Cf. Ewan MacColl, Riverside RLP 12 656 (A5) "O Once I Loved a Lass"; [b:] Tradition/Everest TR 2059 (A7) "The Grey Cock"
  Cf. Tommy Moore, Folkways FA 2355 (B7) "True Lovers"
  "Mr X," Leader LEA 4055 (A6) "Willy-o"
  Cf. Ken Peacock, Folkways FG 3505 (A1) "Who Is at My Window Weeping?"
  Hattie Presnell, Folk-Legacy FSA 22 (B6) "Pretty Crowing Chicken"
  Frank Proffitt, Rounder 0028 (A4) "Pretty Crowing Chicken"
  Virgie Wallin, Home Made Music LP 002 (B8) "The Worrysome Woman"

MEL Petrie/Stanford 2,1902:146 (#580) "The Song of the Ghost" [Bronson]

Willie Angler / The Banks of the Bann (H614) 384

Brunnings 1981: "Banks of the Bann"

IREL S. O'Boyle 1977:46-7; the hero's name is Willie Archer.
  C. O'Boyle 1979:14-5

AMER Milner/Kaplan 1983:197 "The Banks ... (Willie Archer)"

? b: REC A. L. Lloyd, Prestige/Int. 13066 "Banks of the Bann"
  Antoinette McKenna, Shanachie 29016
  Paddy Tunney, Green Linnet SIF 1037 (B4), a forthright version.

MEL Joyce 1909:295 (#556) "The Banks of the Bann," a slightly different setting of Henry's melody.

Lovely Nancy (H637) 385

l: Not close to either of the songs with similar title in Laws 1957:147 (K14) "Farewell, Charming ...," 220 (N33); nor Peacock 1965,2:477; nor Leach 1965:136 "... from England"; also dissimilar to Laws 1957:253-4 (P10-2).

Sam Henry's Songs of the People

Laws 1954:236 (H12) "The Lonesome (Stormy) Scenes of Winter"
Brunnings 1981: "...," "Lovely Johnny," "Chilly Scenes of Winter," ?"The Lover's Lament"

b: IREL Morton 1970:23-4 "Lovely Johnny," a very different version.

AMER Bush 4,1977:58-9 "Cold Scenes of Winter," with the lady's letter added from Laws P10 (cf. H159 "The Slighted Suitor")
    Dean [1922]:108-9 "Lonesome Hours of Winter"
b: Fowke 1973:134-5 (#57) "The Lonesome Scenes of Winter"; she suggests (p. 207) that this form is uniquely American. (Cf. also Leahy and Gladden recs.)
    Wyman/Brockway [1920]:94-7 "The Gonesome Scenes of Winter" also has elements of Laws P10 (see H159).

cl: REC Finley Adams, AFS 2791 A1 "Lonesome Scenes of Winter"
    Texas Gladden, Asch AA 4 (A5) "Dark Scenes of Winter"
    Addie Graham, June Appal JA 202 (A3) "The Lonesome Scenes of Winter"
cl: Mrs A. J. Huff, AFS 2876 A1 "Lonesome Scenes of Winter"
b: John Leahy, Prestige/Int. 25014 (A8) "The Lonesome Scenes of Winter"; Leader LEE 4057 (A6)
cl: Harvey Porter, AFS 1554 A "The Lonesome Scenes of Winter"
cl: Hattie Swindel, AFS 2814 A1 & 2 "Lonesome Scenes of Winter"
    Cf. Paddy Tunney, Topic 12T 165 (A3) "Johnny, Lovely Johnny"
cl: Molly Wylie, AFS 2814 A1 & 2 "The Lonesome Scenes of Winter"

◆ **Under the Shade of a Bonny Green Tree** (*H 794*) *385*

Laws 1957:258 (P19) "Tripping over the Lea"
Brunnings 1981: "The Bonny ..."

h: IREL *Ceol* 4(1)1972:5-6 "Bonny ..."
    O Lochlainn 1965:20-1 "The Bonny ..."
    Shields/Shields *UF* 21,1975: #46 "(The) Bonny ..."

BRIT Cf. Sharp/Karpeles 1974,1:661-2 (#174) "As I Walked out One May Morning, or Tippling over the Plains"

REC John Reilly, Topic 12T 359 (B1) "The Bonny ..."

◆ **Must I Go Bound?** (*H 218*) *386*

White/Dean-Smith 1951: "Deep in Love"
Brunnings 1981: "Must I Be Bound?" "Must I Go Bound?" "Deep in Love," "Down in Yon Meadows," "Green Valley," "Yon Green Valley," ?"Go Bring Me back My Blue-Eyed Boy"

IREL Hughes 1,1909:68-9

BRIT Henderson et al. 1979:34 "... I Be ... "

AMER Arnold 1950:33
    Brewster 1939:33 (#85) "Blue-Eyed Boy"
    Cf. Bush 2,1970:66-8 "The Butcher's Boy," especially the last stanza.
Randolph 1946-50(1980)4:260-2 "My Blue-Eyed Boy"

BRS Jolliffe 1970:68-9

b: REC Shirley Abicair, Columbia CL 1531
b: Frankie Armstrong, Topic 12TS 216 "Green Valley"
b: *Elektra Folk Sampler*, Elektra SMP 2
b: *Everybody Sing!* Vol. 3, Wonderland RLP 1420

    Marie Hare, Folk-Legacy FSC 9 (A1) "Green Valley"
cl: Bascom Lamar Lunsford, AFS 1784 A3
    Cf. Bud Reed, Rounder 0077 (B5) "The Butcher's Boy"; Heritage 18 (A5) "Butcher Boy"
b: Frank Ritchie, Request RLP 8060
    Cyril Tawney, Argo ZFB 87 (A4) "... I Be ..."
    Cf. Ephraim Woodie, "That Fatal Courtship," Old Timey LP 102 (A4), a version of "The Butcher Boy", esp. the refrain.

◆ **Phelimy Phil** (*H 80*) *386*

Brunnings 1981: "Tis Pretty to Be in Balinderry (See Balinderry)," "Balinderry"

IREL Bunting 1840:42 "Balinderry and Cronan"
    Bunting 1983:86-7 (#56) "Balinderry"
b: Clancy Bros. 1964:20
    Graves 1880:229-30 "'Twas Pretty to Be in Balinderry"
    Hayward 1925:3-4
    JIFSS 5,1907:37
    Moffat [1897]:283 "Tis Pretty to Be in Balinderry"
    Page 1935 "Tis Pretty to Be in Balinderry"

AMER Gallagher/Peroni 1936: #23

BRS Jolliffe 1970:20 "Balinderry"

REC Clancy Brothers, Tommy Makem, Tradition/Everest TLP 1042 (B4) "Balinderry"
b: David Hammond, Tradition TLP 1028 (A9) "'Tis Pretty to Be in Balinderry"
    Paddy Tunney, Topic 12TS 289 (A1) "'Tis Pretty to Be in Balinderry"

MEL Scanlon 1923:58

◆ **Norah Magee** (*H 778*) *387*

BRS 617 [190-?]:81

◆ **The Broken-Hearted Gardener** (*H 499*) *387*

Cf. also Child #219 "The Gardener"

Brunnings 1981

BRS BPL H.80: (n.i.)
    Harvard 1: 5.64 (n.i.)
    Cf. UCLA 605: 3(Brown) "The Broken-Hearted Fish Fag"

◆ **Gramachree** (*H 204*) *388*

? Dean-Smith 1954: "... (air) see (The) [Old] Auld Fisher's Farewell to Coquet" (in Stokoe/Reay [1899]).
Brunnings 1981: "...," "Gra'-mo-chroi'"

IREL Bunting 1983:95-7 (#62) "Molly Asthore (Molly, My Treasure" in 2; cf. pp 134-5 (#90) "Molly Bheag O'! (Little Molly O!), in 3.
    Croker 1839:135-6
b: Graves 1928 "Grai My Chree! (Love of My Heart)"
b: Sparling 1888:297-8 "Mailigh Mo Store"

BRIT Johnson (1853):1,47 (no title)

AMER *Songster's Museum* 1803:113-4 "... Molly"

BRS Harvard 1: 1.25 (Birt), 9.176 (Bebbington), 13.47 (Such)
    Derry Journal [c. 1925],1:26
    Emerald Isle 1904:80-1
    National and Historical n.d.:16
    O'Conor 1901:122 "Molly Asthore," 158 "... Molly"
    100 1857:20
    617 [190-?]:71 "... Molly"
    Walton's New 1,1966:173-4

C21 / Content in the arms of another

o: MEL Cf. Bunting 1840:46 (#62) "Molly My Treasure"
   Calliope 1788:259-60 "... Molly"
   Hudson ms. 1:543
   O'Neill 1903:91 (#524) "... Molly," a different tune.

◇ **Belfast Mountains** *(H519)* 389

White/Dean-Smith 1951
Dean-Smith 1954
Brunnings 1981: "... Mountain/s"

AMER Grover n.d.:71-2 "The Diamonds of Derry," which seems to be a version of "Belfast Mountains."

BRS Harvard 1: 5.100 (Bebbington)
   Harvard 2: (n.i.)
   Harvard 3: (Birt) (Catnach) (Toy & Marble)
g: In these broadsides, the story is told by the girl in the first person, and there is no curse.

cl: REC Elmer George, AFS 3711 B "The Diamonds of Derry"
b: David Hammond, Request RLP 8059 "Belfast Mountain/s"
   Margaret MacArthur, Philo 41001 (A5) "Diamonds of Derry"

◇ **My Love John** *(H593)* 389

Dean-Smith 1954: "Three Quarters of the Year"
Brunnings 1981: "The False Young Man"

IREL Hughes 1,1909:1 "The Verdant Braes of Skreen" [Fowke]
k: O Lochlainn 1965:16 (#8) "The Verdant Braes of Skreen"

b: BRIT Kennedy 1975:353 (#153) "The False Young Man"; mentions 2 other recordings, both from the McPeake family of Belfast (see McPeake rec.).

AMER Fowke 1973:136-7 "The False Young Man"

BRS Colum 1913:9

REC Frank, Francis McPeake, *FSB* 1 (B7) "The False Young Man"; [b:] Prestige/Int. 13018 "The Verdant Braes of Skreen"; Topic 12T 87
b: David Hammond, Request RLP 8061 "The Verdant Braes of Skreen"
   Colm Keane, BBC RPL 21911 [Fowke]
b: The Watersons, Topic 12TS 265 (B4) "T Stands for Thomas"

◇ **My Flora and I** *(H30a)* 390

White/Dean-Smith 1951: "Sheepcrook and Black Dog"
Dean-Smith 1954: "Sheepcrook and Black Dog"
Brunnings 1981: "Sheepcrook and Black Dog"

IREL *JIFSS* 4:23

BRIT MacColl/Seeger 1977:231 (#70) "Sheep-Crook and Black Dog"
   Palmer 1979b:144-5 (#83) "Sheepcrook and Black Dog"

BRS BPL H.80: "The Unkind Shepherdess"

REC Eddie Butcher, Free Reed FRR 003 (B2) "Flora"
   Ewan MacColl, Topic 12T 147 (= Tradition 2059) (A4) "Sheepcrook and Black Dog"
   Steeleye Span, Shanachie 79038 (A4) "Sheep-Crook and Black Dog"

◇ **The Flower of Sweet Strabane** *(H224)* 390

IREL Shields/Shields *UF* 21,1975: #149

BRIT Greig 1907-11(1963): #87 "Sweet Straeban," which Greig says "has the marks of the Irish love song -- sweetness and purity."

AMER Haskins n.d.:101
   Milner/Kaplan 1983:176-7

BRS *Derry Journal* [c. 1925],1:27
   Ireland Calling n.d.:11-2
   Songs and Recitations 4,1975:38

REC Margaret Barry, Riverside RLP 12 602 (B4); Topic 12T 123 (A3)
   David Hammond, Greenhays/Sruthan GR 702 (A6)
   Tom McClung, Outlet OAS 3027 (B5)
   John McGettigan and His Irish Minstrels, Topic 12T 367 (A1) "Martha, the ..."
   Johnny Moynihan, Shanachie 79001 (A5)
   Paddy Tunney, Topic 12T 139 (A3)

◇ **Bring Me Back the Boy I Love** (a) *(H482)* 391

AMER Arnold 1950:33 "Blue-Eyed Boy"
   Cf. Barbeau et al. 1947:45-6 "The Girl I Love"
   Brewster 1940:339 "The Blue-Eyed Boy"
? b: Brumley 1970 "Bring back to Me My Wandering Boy"
   Henry 1936:51 "The Blue-Eyed Boy"
   Matteson/Henry 1936:50-1 "The Blue-Eyed Boy"
Randolph 1946-50(1980)4:260-2 (#759) "My Blue-Eyed Boy," 3 vts.

REC Bill "Pop" Hingston, People's Stage Tapes cass. 03 (B3) "... One I ..."
   Cf. Jasper Smith, Topic 12TS 304 (B6) "Died for Love," stanzas 3, 4
cl: Woodrow Wilson (Woody) Guthrie, AFS 3412 A2 "Bring back to Me My Blue-Eyed Boy"

◇ **Never Change the Old Love for the New** *(H692)* 392

o: MEL Petrie 1905:293 (#1158).

◇ **Oh, Johnny, Johnny** *(H16)* 392

Most of the references below are at best cousins of Henry's version.

Dean-Smith 1954: "Deep in Love; O Waly Waly"
Brunnings 1981: "Jamie Douglas," "Love Is Pleasing," "(O) Waly Waly," "The Water Is Wide"

Cox 1925:419-20 (#140) "Young Ladies (Little Sparrow) notes the relationship of elements of this song (floating verses) to, e.g., "(O) Waly, Waly(, gin Love Be Bonny)," Child #204 "Jamie Douglas," "There Is a Tavern in the Town"; cf. Cox 1925: 422-3 "Youth and Folly," in which "the young man is the sufferer," with stanzas from "Maggie Goddon" ["Peggy Gordon"], "Young Riley" ["George Riley," "The Constant Damsel"].
See also Allen *JEFDSS* 1954:161-71 for further discussion and analysis of this complex of songs.

IREL *JIFSS* 8,1910:16, 1 stanza and tune. [Cox]
   Loesberg 2,1980:3 "Peggy Gordon"

BRIT Aitkin 1874:27-8
   Baring-Gould/Hitchcock 1974:96-7 "So Deep in Love"
   Copper 1973:290 "So Abroad as I Was Walking" (see Brown rec.)
   Johnson (1853):1,166 "Waly, Waly"; 3,458
   Kennedy 1975:349 (#149) "Deep in Love," with still more references.

Sam Henry's Songs of the People

   Oxford Book 1969:327-8 (#85b) "Waly, Waly"
   Palmer 1979b:143-4 (#82) "The Brisk Young Sailor"
   Raven 1978:6 "False Love"
   Ritson 1794,1:156-8 "Waly, Waly, gin Love Be Bonny"
   Ritson 1866:95-6 "Waly, Waly, gin Love Be Bonny"
   Sharp/Karpeles 1974,1:171-3 (#35) "Waly, Waly (Jamie Douglas)," 3 vts.
   Slocombe/Shuldham-Shaw *JEFDSS* 1953:103 "I Wish, I Wish"
   Spin 8(3)1972:3 "Love Is Teasing"
   Yates *FMJ* 1975:70 "The Colour of Amber" (see Haynes rec.)

AMER Bush 1,1969:70-1
   Folkways #3(Jan)1969:76 "O, Love Is Teasin'"
   Peggy Seeger 1964:62 "Peggy Gordon" (see Seeger rec.)
   SO 2(3,Sep)1951:13 "Waillie"; 18(1,Mar-Apr)1968:30 "Peggy Gordon" (see Seeger rec)

BRS *Delaney's Scotch* 1910:21
   Healy 1977:58 "Love Is a Sin"
   Songs and Recitations 5,1978:6-7 "Love Is Teasin'"
   Songs of All Time 1946,1957:2 "O Love Is Teasin'"

b: REC Tossi Aaron, Prestige/Int. 13027 "Waly, Waly"
b: Shirley Abicair, Columbia CL 1531 "Must I Go Bound?"
   Arthur Argo, Prestige-Int. PR-INT 13048 (A8) "Love Is Teasin'"
b: Joan Baez, Bill Wood, Theodore Alevizos, Veritas 1(1) "Waly, Waly"
b: Beers Family, Columbia MSC 705 "The Water Is Wide"
b: Robert H. Beers, Prestige/Int. 13047 "The Water Is Wide"
b: Leon Bibb, Vanguard VRS 9073 "The Water Is Wide"
   Amy Birch, Topic 12TS 349 (B7) "Up the Green Meadows"
lc: Bill Bonyun, Folkways FP 2 "Waly, Waly"; ? FOL 2 "'Tis Youth and Folly Make Young Men Merry"
b: Bill, Gene Bonyun, Heirloom HL 500 "Waly, Waly"
   Victor "Turp" Brown, Topic 12T 317 (B8) "As [So] Broad as I Was Walking"
   Peg, Bobby Clancy, Tradition TLP 1045 (B8) "Love and Porter"
   Mr Grace Clergy, Folkways FE 4307 (A7) "Peggy Gordon"
   Cecilia Costello, Leader LEE 4054 (A2) "I Wish, I Wish"
b: Richard Dyer-Bennet, Mercury MG 20007 "Waly, Waly"
b: *Elektra Folk Sampler*, SMP 2 "Must I Go Bound?"
b: *Everybody Sing!* Vol. 3 "Must I Go Bound?"
b: Kathleen Ferrier, London 5411 "The Water Is Wide"
   Archie Fisher, Topic 12TS 277 (A5) "Will Ye Gang, Love"
b: *Folk Songs and Instrumental Music of the Southern Appalachians*, Murray Hill 927950 "The Water Is Wide"
b: Isabella, Peter Gardner, Prestige/Int. 13032 "Cockleshells"
lc: Tom Glazer, Mercury Album A 58 (78 rpm)
b: Cynthia Gooding, Prestige/Int. 13010 "Arthur's Seat"
   David Hammond, Tradition TLP 1028 (B5) "I Wish I Was a Maid Again"
   Sarah Hawkes, Asch 3831 (A6) "Little Sparrow"
   Mary Ann Haynes, Topic 12TS 285 (B3) "The Colour of Amber"
b: The Heightsmen, 20th Century-Fox TFM 3108 "The Water Is Wide"
b: Carolyn Hester, Tradition TLP 1043 "The Water Is Wide"
b: Lou, Sally Killen, Front Hall FHR 06 "The Water Is Wide"

b: Lisa Kindred, Vanguard VRS 9196 "The Water Is Wide"
b: John Langstaff, Tradition TLP 1009 "The Water Is Wide"
   Ewan MacColl, Folkways FW 8755 (A1) "Waly, Waly"
   Shanna Beth McGee, Folkways FW 8779 (A2) "Love Is Teasing," (B2) "The Water Is Wide"
b: Kenneth McKellar, London SW 99384 "The Water Is Wide"
   Mechau Family, Stinson SLP 47 "Wailie, Wailie"
   Alan Mills, Folkways FG3532 (B3) "Peggy Gordon"
? cl: Mort Montonyea, AFS 3666 B1 "Sweet Peggy Gordon"
lc: John Jacob Niles, Boone-Tolliver LP *American Folk Love Songs*
   Dellie Norton, Home Made Music LP HMM 002 (A2) "Little Sparrow"
   Walter Pardon, Topic 12TS 392 "I Wish, I Wish"
   Obray Ramsey, Prestige 13030 (B2) "Little Sparrow"
   Jean Redpath, BBC 22293 (A1) "Love Is Teasin'"
b: Frank Ritchie, Request RLP 8060 "Must I Go Bound"
b: Sunny Schwartz, Cameo C 1030 "The Water Is Wide"
   Jeannie Robertson, Topic 12T 96 (A2) "What a Voice"
   Peggy Seeger, Prestige 13058 (B5) "Peggy Gordon"
b: *Songs and Dances of Scotland*, Murray Hill 920336 "The Water Is Wide"
   June Tabor, Topic 12TS 298 "Waly, Waly"
b: Jackie Washington, Vanguard VRS 9141 "The Water Is Wide"
b: The Weavers, Vanguard VRS 9010 "When Cockle Shells Turn Silver Bells"
b: Betty Vaiden Williams, Vanguard VRS 9028 "Wailie, Wailie"

◊ **The Apron of Flowers** *(H683)* 393

   White/Dean-Smith 1951: "Died for Love or The Alehouse; A Bold/Brisk Young Sailor/Farmer/Cropper, etc. Courted Me; I Wish, I Wish; In Jessie's City; In Yorkshire Park"
   Dean-Smith 1954: "Died of/for Love; The Bold/Brisk Young Sailor/Farmer"; cf. "Deep in Love," "O Waly, Waly"
   Laws 1957:261 (P25) "Love Has Brought Me to Despair"; cf. 260 (P24) "The Butcher Boy"
   Brunnings 1981: Cf. "The Butcher Boy," "Betsy Watson," "Down in Yon Meadows," "Love Is Pleasing," "She's Like the Swallow," "Waly, Waly," "The Water Is Wide"

b: IREL Cf. Graves 1928 "There Is a Tavern in the Town"
   Joyce 1909:134 (#283) "This Fair Maid to the Meadow's Gone"
   Cf. Loesberg 2,1980:60-1 "The Butcher Boy"
   Moulden 1979:13

BRIT Butterworth 1974:16-7 "A Brisk Young Sailor Courted Me"
   Cf. Copper 1973:218-9 "Love"; 250-1 "In Sheffield Park"
m: Cf. Kennedy 1975:349 (#149) "Deep in Love"; 360 (#160) "In Sheffield Park"; reports another version recorded in Hampshire.
   Lyle 1975:108 "Slighted Love"
   Polwarth 1966(1967):21 (#8) "Down in Yon Meadows," with a "Must I be bound" stanza.
   Cf. Richards/Stubbs 1979:110 "Through Lonesome Woods"
Sharp/Karpeles 1,1974:597-605 (#156) "A Brisk Young Lover," 10? vts; cf. 606-8 (#157) "Sheffield Park," 2 vts.
   Sing 7(1,Sep)1962:7 "She's Like the Swallow"

AMER Cf. *Colorado FB* 2,1963:10 "The Butcher Boy"
   Cf. Darling 1983:141-2,A "The Butcher Boy" (see Hinton rec.); 142, B "The Tavern in the Town" (see

Hinton rec.); 142-3,C "Morning Fair" (see Proffitt rec.)
   Fowke 1973:146-7 "She's Like the Swallow"
   Hubbard 1961:63-4 "Love Has Brought Me to Despair"
   Karpeles 1970:243 (#83) "She's Like the Swallow"
   Cf. Warner 1984:218-9 (#86) "A Rude and Rambling Boy"
   Wetmore/Bartholomew 1926:6-7 "Dearest Billie"
   Cf. WPA Kentucky [1939?]:76 "The Butcher Boy"

BRS Harvard 1: 9.187 (Bebbington) "Brisk Young Sailor"
   Roxburghe 1:295- "The Deceased Maiden Lover," which may be an ancestor of "The Apron of Flowers."
   UCLA 605: 5(Birt) "Sheffield Park"

REC Isla Cameron, *CWL* 3, Columbia KL 206 (A2,21) "Died for Love"
   -----, Tony Britton, [b:] Transatlantic TRA 105; [b:] Murray Hill 92036 (5B2)
b: Cf. Shirley Abicair, Columbia CL 1531, "Tarrytown"
b: Cf. Joan Baez, Vanguard VRS 9094 "Railroad Boy"
   Cf. Amy Birch, Topic 12TS 349 (B7) "Up the Green Meadow"
   Ben Butcher, Topic 12T 317 (B6) "In Sheffield Park"
   Campbell Family, Topic 12T 120 "I Wish, I Wish"
   Martin Carthy, Topic 12TS 344 (A5) "Died for Love"
   Audrey Coppard, Folkways FP 917 (A3) "Died of Love"
   Stuart Frank, Folkways FH 5626 (A8) "She's Like a Swallow"
   Cf. Lizzie Higgins, Lismor LIFL 7004 (A1) "What a Voice"
   Frank Hinchcliffe, 12TS 308 (B2) "Sheffield Park"
   Cf. 4 different versions sung by Sam Hinton, Folkways FA 2401 (A1) "The Butcher Boy," (A2) "The Tavern in the Town," (A3) "Grieve, Oh Grieve," (A4) "The Water is Wide"
   Roscoe Holcomb, Folkways FA 2374 (A6) "In London City"
   Hot Mud Family, Flying Fish 087 (A2) "Love Has Brought Me to Despair"
   Norman Kennedy, Topic 12T 178 "I Wish, I Wish"
   Cf. Enoch Kent, Topic 12T 128 "The Butcher Boy"
b: Cf. John Langstaff, Tradition TLP 1009 "She's Like the Swallow"
   Geoff Ling, 12TS 292 (A4) "Died for Love"
   Cf. Tommy Makem, [b:] GWP records ST 2006 "The Butcher Boy"; Tradition TLP 1044
b: Cf. Ed McCurdy, Tiara TST 537 "She's Like the Swallow"
   Alan Mills, Folkways FG 3532 (A4) "She's Like the Swallow"
b: Cf. Eric, Martha Nagler, Philo S 1010 "She Is Like a Swallow"
   Walter Pardon, Topic 12TS 392 (B5) "I Wish, I Wish"
b: *Pinewoods*: C.D.S. "She's Like the Swallow"
   Cf. Frank Proffitt, Folk-Legacy FSA 1 (A3) "Morning Fair"
   Bud Reed, Rounder 0077 (B5) "The Butcher's Boy," includes "Must I go bound" stanzas (cf. H218).
b: Cf. Jeannie Robertson, Prestige/Int. 13006 "The Butcher's Boy"
   Cf. Derek Sarjeant, Joy Special JS 5001 (A2) "A Sailor Coming Home on Leave"
b: Cf. Pete Seeger, Folkways FA 2412 "In Tarrytown"
   Cf. Jasper Smith, Topic 12TS 304 (B6) "Died for Love"
   Joseph Taylor, Leader LEA 4050 (A2) "Died for Love"
   Berzilla Wallin, Folkways FA 2309 (B3) "Love Has Brought Me to Despair"
   Tom Willett, Topic 12T 84 (A4) "Died for Love"

b: MEL Cf. *Hootenanny for Orchestra*, Liberty LST 7332 "Tarrytown"

◇ **The Bonny, Bonny Boy** (H215) 393

   White/Dean-Smith 1951: "Bonny Boy or Bonny Bird; Cupid's Treppan; My Bonny Boy; I Once Loved a Boy"
   Dean-Smith 1954: "... Bird/Girl; Bonny Irish Boy; Cupid's Trepan; I Once Loved a Boy"
   Brunnings 1981: "The Grey Hawk"
   Cazden et al. *Notes* 1982: #37 "The Bonny Boy"

IREL Cf. Graves 1880:205 "I Once Loved a Boy"
c: Graves 1901:127-9 (adapted)
b: Hughes 2,1914: "I Will Walk with My Love"
   Petrie 1855:79 (#389) "I Once Lov'd a Boy"
   (Walsh) Breathnach 2[191?]:198-9

c: BRIT Kidson/Moffat [1926]:108-9 "My ..."; Kidson says that the song is a survival of a 17th-century ballad called "Cupid's Trepan or Up the Green Forest"
   Cf. Palmer 1979b:177-8 (#106) "The Grey Hawk," with the sexes reversed (see Roberts rec.)

AMER Cazden et al. 1982:152-5 "The Bonny Boy"

BRS BPL Partridge: 2.592 (Wrigley)
   Harvard 1: 13.110 (Such)
   A Broadside 7(3,Aug)1914 "I Built a Bower in My Breast"
   Healy 1977:62 "I Once Loved a Boy"
c: *Hyland* 1901:172
c: *Ireland's Songs* 138-42
c: *Walton's New* 1,1966:163
c: *Walton's Treasury* n.d.:43
c: *Young Lady's Songster* ?183-

REC Battlefield Band, Topic 12TS 381
b: Anne Briggs, Topic TPS 114 "My Bonny Bonny Boy"
   Cf. Paul Clayton, Folkways FP 2007 (B3) "Once I Courted a Bonny Little Girl"
   Seán Mac Donnchadha, Tradition TLP 1004 (B8) "My Bonny Boy"
   Richard Dyer-Bennet, Stinson SLP 35 (A3) "I Once Loved a Girl"
b: Kathleen Ferrier, London 5411 "I Will Walk with My Love"
b: Lynn Gold, Warner Brothers W 1495 "I Once Loved a Boy"
   Cf. Charlie Hill, People's Stage Tapes cass. 04 (A7) "The Grey Hawk"
cl: Martin Montonyea, AFS 3669 A3 & B1
   Mary O'Hara, Tradition/Everest 2115 (= Emerald Gem, Belfast) (A8) "I Will Walk with My Love"
   Cf. Bob Roberts, Topic 12TS 361 (A2) "The Grey Hawk"
   Welcome to the Folk Festival, Vol. 1, Horsham Folk Music Festival 1962 "The Grey Hawk"

c: MEL Petrie/Stanford 1,1902:119 (#471) "I Once Loved a Boy"

◇ **The Maid with the Bonny Brown Hair** (H43, 575) 39

Brunnings 1981: "... (Tune of Erin's Green Shore)"

b: IREL Hughes 2,1915:52-9
   JIFSS 2(1&2)1905:14-6 "The Lass ..."
b: O Lochlainn 1939:12-3

BRS *Songs and Recitations* 4,1975:35

◇ **The Green Bushes** (H143) 395

White/Dean-Smith 1951
Dean-Smith 1954

Sam Henry's Songs of the People

Laws 1957:249 (P2)
Brunnings 1981

IREL Shields/Shields *UF* 21,1975: #171

BRIT Copper 1973:240-1 "Down by the ..."
  Dawney 1977:16
MacColl/Seeger 1977:221-4 (#66), 2 vts.
  Palmer 1979b:118-9 (#63)
  Polwarth 1966(1967):25 (#11)
  Shepheard n.d.:17-8

AMER Darling 1983:137-8 (see Christl rec.)

BRS UCLA 605: 4(Such) "Down by the ..."; 5(n.i.)
  Forget Me Not [1835]:246
  Songs and Recitations 4,1975:10

REC Margaret Christl, Folk-Legacy FSC 82 (A6)
  Joseph Leaning, Leader LEA 4050 (B3)
  Geoff Ling, Topic 12TS 292 (A1)
  Cyril Poacher, Topic 12TS 252 (A2)
  Phoebe Smith, Topic 12TS 304((A6)

o: MEL Joyce 1873:25 (#25)
  Petrie/Stanford 1,1902: 55 (#222), 56 (223), 93 (#s 368-70) "The Green Bushes," 152 (#603) "The Ploughboy," 169 (#674) "I Courted My Darling at the Age of 19," 193 (#771) "As a Soldier and a Sailor" [Sharp/Karpeles]
b: Philharmonic Promenade Orchestra, Vanguard VRS 1093
b: Vienna State Opera Orchestra, Westminster XWN 18928

◊ Out of the Window *(H141)* 395

Cf. Brunnings 1981: "She Moved Through the Fair,"
? cf. "I Once Had a True Love (Tune of Through Grief and through Danger)"

m: IREL *Ceol* 1(2)1963:8-9 "Our Wedding Day," from Eddie Butcher.
  Moulden 1979:115 mentions a version from Eddie Butcher in Len Graham's collection.
m: Shields/Shields *UF* 21,1975: #313 (see transcription in *Ceol* above)

m: BRIT Kennedy 1975:365 (#165) "Our Wedding Day"; reports 2 other Irish versions on record.

REC Paddy Tunney, Topic 12T 139 (A6) "I Once Had a True Love"; cf. Topic 12T 165 (A6)

◊ My Bonny Brown Jane *(H613)* 396

Brunnings 1981: (m) "Lovely Willie"

REC Joe Holmes, Len Graham, Free Reed 007 (A5)

◊ The Slighted Suitor *(H159)* 396

Laws 1957:253 (P10) "The Rejected Lover" may be related.
? Brunnings 1981: "... Swain," "The Rejected Lover," "Once I Knew a Pretty Girl"

Elements of this song may also appear in another (American?) song of uncertain love; see H637 "Lovely Nancy."

IREL O Lochlainn 1965:68-9 "The Merchant's Daughter"

AMER Cf. Burton/Manning 1969:50-1
  Cf. Manny/Wilson 1968:254-5 "Jenny Dear," which tells the same story.

AMER Cf. Carter Family, *FMA* 2 (A8) "If One Won't, Another One Will"
? b: Joan Baez, Bill Wood, Theodore Alevizos, Veritas Vol. 1, No. 1 "The Rejected Lover"
  Cf. Joan Baez, Vanguard VRS 9094 "Once I Knew a Pretty Girl"
  Mick Hanly, Green Linnet SIF 3017 (A2) "The Merchant's Daughter"
  Cf. Howie Mitchell, Folk-Legacy FSI 5 (B3) "The Rejected Lover"
  Cf. Derek Sarjeant, Joy Special JS 5001 (B3) "Once I Had a Love"

◊ Twenty-One *(H33, H611)* 397

IREL Moulden 1979:149

m: BRS CUL Madden "The Mullagh Lovers"

◊ Polly Perkins of Paddington Green *(H132)* 398

Brunnings 1981: "Polly Perkins," "Pretty Polly Perkins"; cf. "Cushie Butterfield," a parody.

BRIT Munch 1970:100-1 "Sweet Pretty ..."

BRS BPL Partridge: 3.897 (Partridge)
  Harvard 1: 13.148 (n.i.)
  Henderson 1938:65

REC Richard Carlin, Folkways FW 8846 (A3) "... Paddington's ..."
b: High Level Ranters, Trailer LER 2020 "Pretty Polly Perkins"
  Derek Lamb, Folkways FW 8707 (A5) "Pretty ..."
cl: Maude McShan Wesson, AFS 2950 B1, 2951 A1 "Pretty ... Perkins"

◊ My Darling Blue-Eyed Mary *(H785)* 399

BRS Harvard 1: 5.183 (Catnach) "Blue-Eyed Mary"

◊ My Bonnie Irish Boy *(H168)* 399

White/Dean-Smith 1951: "(The) Bonny (Irish) ..."
Dean-Smith 1954: "(The) Bonny Boy"
Laws 1957:261 (P26) "The Bonny Young Irish ..."

h: IREL *JIFSS* 17,1920:20-1 "The Bonny ..."
h: Joyce 1909:152 (#328) "My Lovely ..."
  Morton 1973:128-9 "The Bonny ...," very different, almost another song.
h: Petrie/Stanford 2,1902:189 (#755) "It Was in Dublin City," with 1 stanza.
  Shields 1981:52-3 (#10) "The ..."
  Shields/Shields *UF* 21,1975: #47

h: BRIT MacColl/Seeger 1977:217-9 (#64) "The Bonnie ..."

AMER Wright 1975:397-9 (from Peacock 1965)

BRS BPL H.80: "The Bonny Irish Boy"
  Harvard 1: 10.13
  O'Conor [1901]:54 "Bonny ...," with happy married ending.
  Cf. *617* [190-?]:95 "Bonny ...," ditto.
  Roxburghe 4:359-60 "Cupid's Trappan or the Green Forest," which may be a very early version if not the original.

REC O. J. Abbott, Folkways FM 4051 (A9) "The Bonnie ...," with 1 stanza from "The Bonny Laboring Boy" [Laws M14]
  John Maguire, Leader LEE 4062 (A3) "The Bonny ..."

MEL *JIFSS* 3(3&4)1905-6:21 "My Own Bonny Boy"

Sweet Clonalee *(H554) 400*

AMER Wright 1975:234 (from Henry coll., Belfast, type reset)

◇ An Old Lover's Wedding *(H60a) 400*
　The Laird's Wedding *(H60b) 401*

White/Dean-Smith 1951: "(The) Nobleman's Wedding or All Round My Hat"
Dean-Smith 1954: "All Round My Hat"
Laws 1957:264 (P31) "The Nobleman's ... [The Faultless Bride; The Love Token]"
Brunnings 1981: "The Nobleman's Wedding," "All 'Round My Hat - I Will Wear a Green Willow"

h: IREL Cf. *Ceol* 3(2)1968:44
　Shields *Hermathena* 1974:32-3
　Shields 1981:41-2 (#3) "Another Man's Wedding," 2 vts.
　Shields/Shields *UF* 21,1975: #302 "(The) Nobleman's ..."

h: BRIT Kennedy 1975:364 (#164) "The Nobleman's ..."; reports 2 Scottish and 1 other Irish versions recorded.
　Lyle 1975:56-7 "The Penitent Bride"
Sharp/Karpeles 1974,1:267 (#58) "The Nobleman's ..., or All around My Hat"

AMER Darling 1983:143-4 "To Wear a Green Willow" (see Cleveland rec.)
　Hubbard 1961:47-8 "The Bride's Death"
　Kenedy 1890:81-2
　Rosenbaum 1983:59 "The Famous Wedding"

h: BRS Colum 1913:5 "The Nobleman's ..."

REC Eddie Butcher, Leader LED 2070 (B6) "Another Man's Wedding"
　Sara Cleveland, Folk-Legacy FSA 33 (A1) "To Wear a Green Willow"
　Mairéad ní Dhomhnaill, Gael Linn CEF 055 (A4) "Lately Last Night"; Green Linnet SIF 1004 "Nobleman's Wedding"
cl: Maggie Gant, AFS 66 A4 "The Fatal Wedding"
cl: Helen Pischner, AFS 2290 B "The Fatal Wedding"
　Tony, Irene Saletan, Folk-Legacy FSI 37 (B2) "All Round My Hat"
　Belle Stewart, Topic 12TS 307 (B4) "Late Last Night"
　Cathie Stewart, Topic 12T 180 (B4) "Orange and Blue"

h: MEL Joyce 1909:224-5 (#413) "The Nobleman's ..."
h: Petrie 1855:178-80 "The Nobleman's ...," 3 sets
h: Petrie/Stanford 1,1902:124-5 (#s 491-5) "Once I Was [Invited to] [at] a Noble[man's] ..."

◇ The Girl I Left Behind *(H188) 401*

Laws 1957:248 (P1B) "(... Maid ...)"
Brunnings 1981: "... Me," "Peggy Walker"; cf. "The Rambling Cowboy," "The Roving Cowboy"
Cazden et al. *Notes* 1982: #39 (includes references for "... Me")

C21 / Content in the arms of another

c: IREL *JIFSS* 19,1922:46 (= Wright 1975:375-6)
　Cf. Shields *UF* 18,1972:42-4 "The Roveing Boy"
　Shields/Shields *UF* 21,1975: #158
Not: O Lochlainn 1939:36-7 "... Me"
And not: Bunting 1983:87-91 (#57) "An Spailin Fanach or the Girl I Left Behind Me"

BRIT MacColl/Seeger 1977:219-20 (#65)

AMER Burton/Manning 1967(1970):59-6 "Maggie Walker, the Girl I Left Behind"
　Cazden et al 1982:159-61
　Colorado FB 3,1964:6-7
　Creighton 1961:76-7
　Peters 1977:115 "There Was a Rich Old Farmer"
Randolph/Cohen (1982):101-4
　Warner 1984:340-2 (#148) "My Parents Raised Me Tenderly"

BRS Harvard 1: 2.102 (Walker)

REC Cf. Dick Reinhart, *FMA* 6 (A6) "Rambling Lover"
　Dave, Toni Arthur, Topic 12T 190 (A1) "All Frolicking I'll Give Over"
? cl: Jack Bailey, AFS 3293 A1 "My Parents Loved Me Tenderly"
　Pearl Borusky, AAFS L1 (A6) "The Rich Old Farmer"
　Dock Boggs, Asch AH 3903 (A8) "Peggy Walker"
　Eddie Butcher, Outlet OAS 3007 (A7)
cl: MacKinley Craft, AFS 1551 B1
? cl: Emma Dusenbury, AFS 3231 B1 "My Parents Raised Me Tenderly"
　Dave Frederickson, Folkways FH 5259 (B5)
cl: Munroe Gevedon, AFS 1558 A & B1 "My Parents Treated Me Tenderly"
cl: J. W. Green, AFS 2293 A4 & B1
cl: Mrs Audrey Hellums, AFS 2978 B2
　Delsie Hicks, Tenn. Folklore Society TFS 103 (A2) "My Parents Raised Me Tenderly"
　Hotmud Family, Flying Fish FF 251 (B4) "Country Blues / I've Always Been a Gambler"
　Clint Howard, Folkways FA 2355 (B2) "Maggie Walker Blues"
　Harry Jackson, Folkways FH 5723 (C6) "... Gal ..."
　Cf. Buell Kazee, Brunswick 156-A (78 rpm) "The Roving Cowboy" [Laws]
cl: Ed Larkin, AFS 3723 A1
　Pleaz Mobley, AAFS L12 (A5) "My Parents Raised Me Tenderly"
? cl: Alec Moore, AFS 3942 A3 "My Parents Treated Me Tenderly"
b: Spencer Moore, Prestige/Int. 25004 (A2)
cl: J. M. Mullins, AFS 1964 A2, 1595 B2
cl: Dizia Puckett, AFS 299 B2, 2990 A1
　Cf. Obray Ramsay, Prestige 13030 "The Roaming Boy"
b: Jim Ringer, Folk-Legacy FSI 47 (B5)
b: Jean Ritchie, Elektra EKL 25; Greenhays GR 701 (B3) "Old George's Square"
b: Jackie Washington, Vanguard VRS 9110
　Lal, Norma Waterson, Topic 12TS 331 (A7) "The Wealthy Squire"

C22

**When death was near:
Deadly love**

The 'Prentice Boy [H31: 14 Jun 1924; Laws O39]

g: "Sheffield Apprentice." Other titles: "The Apprentice ...," "Cupid's Garden," "Farewell Lovely Polly," "The Holland Song," "In Connaught I Was Reared," "In the Town of Oxford," "The (New York) (Sheffield) Prentice (Boy)," "Soefield," "Way up in Sofield."

Source: (w, m) J[ohn] H[enry] Macauley (Ballycastle).

Key E flat.

I was brought up in Connaught, not of a low degree,
My parents doted on me, had ne'er a child but me;
I roved about with pleasure, where'er my fancy led,
Until I was bound a 'prentice, and then my joys all fled.

My master and my mistress, I did not like them well
I formed a resolution not long with them to dwell,
Till, unknown to my aged parents, from them I stole away,
I steered my course to Dublin; I may curse that fatal day.

A lady out of Holland, she happened to be there,
She offered me great wages to serve her for a year,
To her deluding promises, with her I did agree
To go with her to Holland, which proved my destiny.

I was not long left Dublin, a year yet scarcely one,
Till my young and wealthy mistress of me got very fond,
Her gold and her silver, her houses and her lands,
And if I would wed with her, they should be at my command.

I said, 'My loving mistress, I cannot wed you now,
For I have made a promise, besides a solemn vow,
To wed no one but Molly, your only waiting maid,
So, madam dear, excuse me, she has my heart betrayed.'

One evening as I walked out all for to take the air,
My young and wealthy mistress was pulling flowers fair;
The gold ring off her finger, just as I passed her by,
She slipped it in my pocket, and for that same I die.

1.4: ... bound apprentice, ... [Dt]
4.4: If I ... her, should ... [Dt]

Blooming Caroline of Edinburgh Town

[H148: 11 Sep 1926; Laws P27]

[Dt] s: (m) "Flower of Sweet Strabane." Other titles: "... from Edinboro' ...," "... Edinborough ...," "Fair Caroline (Caroline ...)," "Lovely Caroline"; cf. "The Fate of Young Henry in Answer to Caroline of Edinboro ...."

Source: (w) 2+: John Thompson (Rockview, Portstewart), Miss Lily Williamson (Ballytunn, Rasharkin), and others; (m) William Gamble (Park, Armoy).

Key C.

Come all ye tender fair maids, give ear unto my rhyme,
I'll tell you of a fair maid, she was scarcely in her prime,
She beat the blooming roses, was admired all around,
This fair maid's name was Caroline of Edinburgh town.

Young Henry being a Highland lad, a-courting her he came,
And when her parents heard of it, they were angry at the same;
Young Henry being offended, he unto her did say,
'O, rise up, blooming Caroline, and we will go away.

'We will go to London, to London with great speed,
We will go to London, live happy there indeed.'
She bundled up her costly clothes, the stairs came tripping down,
And away goes blooming Caroline from Edinburgh town.

Sam Henry's Songs of the People

O'er lofty hills and mountains together they did roam,
O'er lofty hills and mountains and far away from home;
She says, 'True-hearted Henry, if ever you on me frown,
You'll break the heart of Caroline from Edinburgh town.'

They had not been in London, in London half a year
Till cruel-hearted Henry began to prove severe,
He says, 'Your friends and parents oftimes on me did frown,
Make no delay, but beg your way to Edinburgh town.'

Now she's in grief without relief, to the green wood she is gone
To gather meat that she can eat upon the bushes grown;
Some there are to pity her and some on her do frown,
And others say, 'What made you stray from Edinburgh town?'

She leaned her back up to an oak and she began to cry
To watch the little small boats and ships as they passed by;
Three sighs she gave for Henry and plunged her body down,
And away goes blooming Caroline of Edinburgh town.

A bonnet, cloak, likewise a note upon the shore was found,
And on the note these lines were wrote, 'Here Caroline lies drowned.
She's fast asleep all in the deep, the small fish wavering round,
She's no more the blooming Caroline of Edinburgh town.'

Come all ye tender parents and never hinder love,
For if you do, hard fortune will surely on you prove,
For if you do, hard fortune will surely on you frown,
For it broke the heart of Caroline of Edinburgh town.

7.2: And watch ... [Dt]

Ballindown Braes [H73: 4 Apr 1925; Laws P28]

k: "Betsy of Ballantown Brae"; g: "Bessie (Jessie) of Ballington Brae." Other titles: "Ballentown Brae," "Bessie of Ballydubray," "Sweet Ballenden Braes"; cf. "Answer to Betsy of Ballentine Bray."

Source: (w) H[ugh] M[urray] (Managher, Culcrow, Co. Derry), from his mother c. 1865.

412 Key B flat.

Come all you young fair maids, I pray lend an ear
Unto the sad fate of two lovers so dear,
Concerning young Bessie of Ballindown Brae
And the laird of yon moorland that led her to stray
From Ballindown Brae, sweet Ballindown Brae,
He courted young Bessie from Ballindown Brae.

One night in his slumber, as on his pillow he lay,
A vision came to him and this it did say,
'You are the young man that caused me to roam
Far, far from my own friends and my own native home,
And now my pale cheeks, alas, moulder away
Beneath the cold tomb in sweet Ballindown Brae.'

He arose from his slumber like one in surprise,
'Yes, yes, it's the voice of my Bessie,' he cries,
'And if she be dead as this vision does say,
I'll lie by her side in sweet Ballindown Brae,
Oh, Ballindown Brae, sweet Ballindown Brae,
I'll lie by her side in sweet Ballindown Brae.'

He ordered his servant to saddle his steed,
Over hills and high mountains he rode with great speed
Until he arrived at the noontide of day
At the cottage of Bessie of Ballindown Brae,
Oh, Ballindown Brae, sweet Ballindown Brae,
At the cot of young Bessie of Ballindown Brae.

Now Bessie's own father stood at his own gate
Like a man quite forlorn, bewailing his fate,
The young laird advanced to afford him relief
And begged he would tell him the cause of his grief.
'I had but one daughter,' the old man did say,
'But now she lies low in sweet Ballindown Brae.

'Her skin it was white as the lily or swan,
As bonnie a lassie as the sun e'er shone on,
But her heart it was broke and she died in despair.
Sometime she went frantic and tearing her hair,
All for a young man who caused her to stray
Far, far from her friends and sweet Ballindown Brae.'

'Yes, I was her lover,' the young laird replied,
'I certainly said I would make her my bride.'
And then from his scabbard a small sword he drew,
With a heart unrelenting he pierced his breast through,
And as he was dying these words he did say,
'Lay me down by young Bessie of Ballindown Brae.'

Now all things being ready, the grave it was made,
And down by young Bessie the young laird was laid.
All you young fair maids, from your cots do not stray,
But remember young Bessie of Ballindown Brae,
Oh, Ballindown Brae, sweet Ballindown Brae,
Remember young Bessie of Ballindown Brae.

2.4: ... my friends ... [Dt]
4.4: At the cot of young Bessie ... [Dt]
6.2: ... bonny ... [Dt]

The King o' Spain's Daughter

[H163: Dp, 25 Dec 1926; Child #4]

Other titles: "The Castle by the Sea," "The Dapple(dy) (Dapherd) Grey," "Don't Prittle Nor Prattle," "Elfin Knight," "The False-Hearted Knight (and Pretty Carol Lynn)," "False Sir John," "The Gates (Doors) of Ivory," "The King's (Seven) Daughter(s)," "Lady Isabel(le) (and the Elf Knight)," "The Lord from the West," "May Collen (Colvin) (Colyean) (and the Knight)," "The North Strand," "Old Notchy Road," "An (The) Outlandish Knight (Robber) (Rover)," "The Parrot Song," "Pretty Polly (Ann) (and False William)," "Rich Nobleman," "Six King's Daughters (Pretty Maids)," "Sweet William," "The Young Officer"; cf. "The Cruel Youth."

Source: Willie Hegarty (Ballydevitt), learned when he was a young man from the girls in the "stove" at Mullamore Bleach Green (Barklie's).

s: ...This is the Ulster version of the very old ballad, "May Colvin."

l: The stanza (which would be the sixth here) in which the false lover asks her to remove her robe is missing, although its sequel is not only present but apparently uncensored.

Key G.

False-hearted Johnny came to court
A king's daughter in Spain,
He courted her up and he courted her down
Till at length her favour did gain.

'Steal some of your mamma's gold,
Some of your daddy's fees,
Two of the best steeds in your father's stable,
Where there stand thirty and three.'

She stole some of her mammy's gold,
Some of her daddy's fees,
Two of the best steeds in her father's stable,
Where there stand thirty and three.

Pretty Gold Ann got on the one,
And Johnny got on the other,
And they rode up to North Hambleton water,
Where there he lighted down.

'Light ye down, my pretty Gold Ann,
No further you'll go with me,
For seven king's daughters I have drowned here,
And the eighth one you shall be.'

'Turn ye round, false-hearted John,
And view the green leaves on the tree,
It never became a laird or a knight
A naked woman to see.'

Just as he turned himself around
To view the green leaves on the trees,
She threw her arms around him
And tumbled him into the sea.

'Lie you there, false-hearted John,
You may as well lie there as me,
You thought you would drown me just as I was born,
But my ghost it will go with thee.'

'Take my hand, my pretty Gold Ann,
Take my hand,' said he,
'In all the vows that ever I made thee,
I'll double them all in a ban'.'

So pretty Gold Ann got on again,
Took Johnnie's in her hand,
And she rode up to her father's castle,
Where there they lighted down.

Out spoke the pretty parrot
In the cage just where it lay,
'I told you, I told you, my pretty Gold Ann,
You would rue your going away.'

'Hold your tongue, my pretty parrot,
And tell no tidings on me;
Your cage shall be made of the beaten gold
Instead of a briar tree.'

Out bespoke the king himself
In the chamber just where he lay,
'What ailed you, what ailed you, my pretty parrot?
You have prattled so long before day.'

Sam Henry's Songs of the People

'Two wild cats came to my cage door,
I thought they had worried me,
And I was calling my pretty Gold Ann
To frighten those cats away.

'This maid being young and she slept sound,
She wouldn't be wakened by me,
But me and my little prattling tongue
Has frightened those cats away.'

[Written on Dp and Bt:]
1.4: And he courted her over again.
4.1: ... the grey,
 .2: ... the brown,

The Broomfield Hill

[H135: 12 Jun 1926; Child #43]

Other titles: "The Bonny (Merry) Broomfields," "The Bonny Green Woods," "... Wager," "A Wager, A Wager," "West Country Wager," "The Young Squire"; cf. "Jock Sheep," "The Sea Captain."

Source: (m, incomplete w) John M'Laughlin (Mill St, Ballycastle), learned at 10 years of age from his mother; (remaining w) *Oxford Book of Ballads*, No. 24.

s: ... It is most remarkable that this ballad, dating from the days of falconry, should have persisted to the present day in the Ballycastle district, and that the air should have been preserved here, although lost in Great Britain.

l: The stanzas borrowed from the *Oxford Book* were omitted by Mr Huntington; they are printed below in italics.

Key D.

There was a knight and a lady bright
Set trysts amang the broom,
The ane to come at morning ear,
The other at afternoon.

*I'll wager, I'll wager, I'll wager wi' you
Five hundred merks and ten
That a maid shanna gae to the merry broom fields
And a maid return again.*

I'll wager, I'll wager, I'll wager wi' you
Five hundred merks and ten
That a maid shall gae to the merry broom fields
And a maid return again.

The maid she sat at her mother's bower door
And aye she made her moan:
'O, whether should I gang to the Broomfield Hill
Or should I stay at home?'

Up then spake an auld witch-wife
Sat in the bower abune,
'O, ye may gang to the Broomfield Hill
And safe return again.

'For when ye gang to the Broomfield Hill
Ye'll find your love asleep,
Wi' a silver belt above his head
And a broom branch at his feet.

'Tak' ye the bloom frae aff the broom,
Strew't at his head and feet,
And aye the thicker that ye do strew,
The sounder he will sleep.

'Tak' ye the rings aff your fingers
And put them on his own
To let him know when he does wake
His love had been and gone.'

*Lord John has ta'en his milk-white steed
And his hawk wi' his bells sae bright,
And he's ridden swift to the Broomfield Hill,
Was never a bolder knight.*

*She kilted up her petticoats,
Likewise her silken gown,
Until she came to the merry broom fields
She never let them down.*

When she came to the Broomfield Hill,
She found her true love asleep
With his gay goshawk and his silk-string bows
And a green broom under his feet.

She's pu'ed the blossom off the broom,
Saying, 'O, but it smells sweet,'
She put the broom in under his head
She's ta'en from under his feet.

When she did what the auld witch-wife had told,
She cunningly stole away,
And derned herself behind the broom
To hear what her true love would say.

'My curse light on you, gay goshawk,
And an ill death may you dee,
That wadna watch and waken
When my true love was with me.'

'I clapped wi' my wings, master,
And aye my bells I rang,
And aye cried, "Waken, waken, master,
Before the ladye gang."'

*'But haste, but haste, my gude white steed,
To come the maiden till,
Or a' the birds of the gude greenwood
O your flesh shall have their fill.*

*'Ye needna burst your gude white steed
Wi' racing o'er the howm.'
Nae bird flies faster thro' the wood
Than she fled frae the broom.*

5.2: abune [aboon] = above, overhead.
13.3: derned = concealed, hidden.
17.2: howm = holm.

414

Lord Ronald [H814: 1 Jul 1939; Child #92]

s: "King Henry, My Son" (England); "Grandmother Adder-cook" (Germany); o: (m) "Villikins [and His Dinah]." Other titles: "Dirandel," "Henry (Willy) My Son," "... Donald (Randal)(l) (Rendal) (Ronald)(, My Son)," "Jimmie(y) (Johnny) Random (Ransom) (Randal)(l)(, My Son)," "My (Bonny Brown [Bon]) (Own Darling) Boy," "My Bonny Tammy," "My Ramboling Son," "Oh, Mak' My Bed Easy," "Le Testament du Garçon Empoisonné," "An Tiarna (Tighearna) Randall"; cf. "Billy Boy," "Croodlin Dow," "Ennery My Son," "Green and Yellow," "My Boy Tommy," "Willie Doo."

Source: John M'Neill (Jubilee Terrace, Coleraine) from his mother, "who heard it sung by the late John F. M'Laughlin, the last of an old family of Cromwellian settlers in Glenleary."

s: This is the most widespread song in Europe. In England it is entitled "King Henry, My Son"; in Germany it is entitled "Grandmother Addercook," and there are versions in Italian, Swedish, Dutch, Magyar and Wendish.
 The version here printed is the Scottish version. Each country has its characteristics embodied in the ballad. For example, the South Irish version contains the stanza:

> What was in the dinner you got, my fair-haired heart-pulse and my treasure?
> What was in the dinner you got, thou flower of young men?
> An eel that Nuala gave me with deadly poison in it,
> Oh, my head it is paining me, and I want to lie down.

 In the version in the *Oxford Book of Ballads* [1910], page 292, the ballad ends at the verse about the poisoning and does not include the various bequests as in the version below.

o: This is world-famous "Lord Randal" set by Philistine to "Villikins."

Key C.

Where have you been, Lord Ronald, my son?
Where have you been, my jolly young man?
Oh, mother, I was out courting, so make my bed soon,
I'm sick to the heart and fain would lie doon.

[*similarly:*]
'Will I make you some supper, ...'
'Mother, I've had my supper, ...'

'What had you for supper, ...'
'I had fish flukes in plenty, ...'
'For I'm ...'

'I doubt you are poisoned, ...'
'Oh, mother, I'm poisoned, ...'
'I'm ...'

'What will you leave to your father, ...'
'I will leave him my horses, ...'

'What will you leave to your mother, ...'
'I will leave you my money, ...'

'What will you leave to your sweetheart, Lord Ronald, my son?
What will you leave to your sweetheart, my jolly young man?'
'I will leave her yon high hills and yon gallows tree,
For it's there she'll be hung for the poisoning of me.'

Susan Brown [H771: 3 Sep 1938]

Source: Bob Greer (Ballinaloob, Knockahollet), originally sung c. 1868 by old Scottish traveller, William Irvine (Stewart St, Bellshill, Lanarkshire).

Key G.

Come hear the last words of young Susan Brown,
The pride of her parents from fair Armagh town,
The fairest of creatures by the clear Callan side,
Now dying an outcast on the banks of the Clyde.

In my eighteenth year my charms were in bloom,
And few of the fair maids with me could presume,
My sweethearts oft told me my skin was like snow,
My teeth like the pearls and my eyes like the sloe.

Like many's a young girl, my thoughts were in vain,
I loved to keep all my admirers in pain,
I made them believe that I favoured them all,
And my folly at last on my own head did fall.

Sam Henry's Songs of the People

The lad I adored was a rich farmer's son,
Oftimes I pretended his company to shun,
Till I lost the affections of this comely youth,
Though I was trying his fondness and truth.

To the milking I went as I journeyed along,
The sun had gone down and the birds ceased
  their song,
I spied my lost sweetheart -- he did not see
  me --
Beside his intended beneath a green tree.

I crept up behind them, down softly I lay
To hear the sweet words that these lovers would
  say,
I heard that the day of their marriage was near,
And something was whispering revenge in my
  ear.

Then up I arose and quietly I went,
And round by the Callan my steps they were
  bent,
A dose of strong laudanum from my doctor got I,
I fully determined my lost love should die.

His face bore a smile as together we met,
In yon shady nook together we sat,
He bade me adieu, as soon married he'd be,
When of poisoned new milk a long draft took he.

Lest I be suspected, the seas I crossed o'er
And tried to find work on the far Scottish
  shore,
But the curse being on me, no rest could I find,
Till at length in a prison they had me confined.

At last in a heavy consumption I fell;
The hard-hearted keepers kept me by mysel'
Till the doctor concluded I'd die if confined,
And he sent me, some far kinder shelter to find.

Now I'm dying, and I'm far away from my home,
Few days are left me, my sins to atone;
I disgraced my own parents by the clear Callan
  side,
And now I'm dying by the banks of the Clyde.

Susan Carr [H690: 13 Feb 1937; ?Laws P33]

A murder ballad.

Other title: cf. "Susannah Clargy."

Key D.

When Billy Green was but a boy,
With Susan Carr he did kiss and toy;
Susan was young, and being fond to wed,
She dropped her courtship, from Green has fled.

'Very well,' said Green, 'then reveng'd I'll be
All on young Thompson, or him on me.'
Green being walking down the street,
Who but young Thompson did he chance to meet.

They both went in to an inn to drink,
When death was near, but they didn't think.
Said Green to Thompson, 'Susan's mine by right.'
'Come, come,' said Thompson, 'for her we'll fight.'

Green struck Thompson once o'er the head,
With a single blow he has killed him dead.
When Billy Green saw what he had done,
Out of the room he did quickly run.

Down to the quay where the boats they lay,
Some of the workmen did hear him say,
'Susan Carr, you are much to blame,'
And he plunged into the rolling strame.

The word went up and the word went down
That Green killed Thompson and he was drowned.
What a shocking sight for the parents dear,
What a dreadful news for the maid to hear.

With shaking bones she has gone to bed,
And three days after, Susan Carr was dead;
The three was buried in St. John's churchyard,
And on the tombstone it may be read --

'Here lies young Thompson and Susan Carr,
Whose killing smile did his heart ensnare.
The body of Green in the tower below,
Who killed young Thompson with a single blow.'

5.4: strame = stream.

Flora, the Lily of the West

[H578: 29 Dec 1934; Laws P29]

Other titles: "Flora," "(The) ...."

Source: Maggie Brownlow (Ballylaggan, Cloyfin).

s: ... This ballad was widespread, versions having been collected in Devonshire, Yorkshire and elsewhere.
  Rev. S. Baring-Gould in The Songs of the West states: "The ballad has clearly an Irish origin but what air is used for it in Ireland I am unable to say. This song was sung annually at the Revel at St. Breward's on the Bodmin Moors and can be traced back there to 1839."

o: Tune should be 6/8.

Key C.

When first I came to Ireland some pleasures for to
   find,
There I espied a damsel most pleasing to my mind:
Her curly hair and ringlets fair like arrows
   pierced my breast,
Her name was lovely Flora, the lily of the west.

Her cheeks they are like roses red, her dress is
   spangled o'er,
She had rings on every finger, brought from a
   foreign shore,
She'd entice both kings and princes, so costly
   was she dressed,
She far exceeds Diana, she's the lily of the west.

As I roved out one evening down by yon shady
   grove,
I spied a lord of high degree conversing with my
   love,
She sang a song most beautiful, while I was sore
   oppressed,
I was then deceived by Flora, the lily of the west.

I stepped up to my rival with dagger in my hand,
I dragged him from my false love and boldly bid
   him stand,
Being mad with desperation, I pierced my rival's
   breast,
For I was betrayed by Flora, the lily of the west.

I had to stand my trial and boldly did I plead
The cause in my indictment that shortly had me
   freed.
This beauty bright I did adore, the judge did her
   address,
Saying, 'Go, you faithless Flora, the lily of the
   west.'

It's now I am at liberty, a-roving I will go,
I'll ramble Ireland over and travel Scotland thro';
She tried to swear my life away and still disturbs
   my rest,
I roam for sake of Flora, the lily of the west.

6.2: I'll travel ... [Dt]

The Old Oak Tree

[H207: 29 Oct 1927; Laws P37]

s: (m) variant of "My Love Nell"; [W, penciled]
"My Lovely Nell"; o: (m) slow "Star of the
County Down"; g: "Squire Nathaniel and Betsy."
Other title: "Eliza Long"; cf. "Poor Murdered
Woman."

Source: 3: (w, m) Harry Evans (Chapel Square,
Coleraine), learned in his boyhood; also Patrick
M'Mullan (Tullybane, Cloughmills), learned from
John Stewart (Kilmandel, Culcrum, Co. Antrim) c.
1875; John Parker (Mayoghill, Moneydig).

s: ... These three contributors sang it to different
airs. The air here published is that supplied
by Mr Evans. It is a variant of the air to
which is sung the song, "My Love Nell." Note
that the air is in the old Irish gapped scale, having
neither the note "*fa*" nor "*t*".

Key A.

Dark was the night, cold blew the wind and
   thickly fell the rain
When Eliza left her own dear home, ne'er to
   return again.
She left her widowed mother's side, not fearing
   rain nor cold,
She was young and fair to look upon, but love
   had made her bold.

That very night at ten o'clock beneath the old
   oak tree,
She promised James, her own true love, that
   with him she would be,
She heeded not the drenching rain nor yet the
   thunder's roar,
But threw her cloak around her head, walked
   quickly from the door.

When night had passed and morning came and
   she did not return,
It sadly grieved her friends to think that Eliza
   thus did roam.
At length her mother started off with cries and
   actions wild,
Saying, 'I will ramble the kingdom through till I
   find my only child.'

For three long weary weeks she spent in
   searching the country round,
Her journeys proved of no avail, Eliza ne'er was
   found,
And now to reach her lonely cot this grief-worn
   widow tried,
Oppressed with grief, she there lay down --
   with broken heart she died.

Near to the scene of all this woe, the owner of
   these grounds,
Young Squire Cowan went to hunt that way and
   with him all his hounds.

Sam Henry's Songs of the People

Up hill, down dale he haughtily rode with a
  gallant company,
Till, as if by chance, the fox they lost beneath
  the old oak tree.

The dogs began to sniff and yelp and to tear
  up the clay,
All that horn or whip could do could not drive
  those hounds away,
The gentlemen all gathered round, they called
  for pick and spade,
They dug the ground and there they found the
  long-lost murdered maid.

The cheeks that once were rosy red were black
  with wounds and blows,
And from her side fresh blood gushed forth and
  sprinkled Cowan's clothes,
And in her breast a knife was found, and to
  his grief and shame,
The gentlemen upon the heft read young Squire
  Cowan's name.

'I've done the deed,' young Cowan cried, 'my soul
  is fit for hell,
Pray hide her cold corpse from my sight and I
  the truth will tell,
It's true I loved Eliza long, but with a villain's
  art,
I won her by my evil ways till triumph made us
  part.

'With the knife I cut my dinner, with it I
  pierced her breast,
'Twas with the heft I knocked her down, I need
  not tell the rest;
From that unlucky hour to this, she stands
  before my sight,
I think I see her bleeding ghost and view her
  dying plight.

'But I am sentenced, I must die a death of sin
  and shame.'
He drew a pistol from his breast and fired it
  through his brain,
And he was buried where he fell, no Christian
  grave got he,
None could be found to bless the ground
  beneath the old oak tree.

2.4: She threw ... [Dt]
5.2: ... hunt and with ... [Dt]
6.2: ... do would not ... [Dt]
  .3: ... gathered, they ... [Dt]
10.4: Nor could ... [Dt]

The Silver[y] Tide

[H77: 2 May 1925; Laws O37]

g: "Mary of the Silvery Tide." Other title: "Poor Mary in the ...."

Source: (w, m) (slopes of Carntogher); also Lizzie MacMullan (the Station, Rathlin Island)

s: ... Carntogher [is] a country which was, in the past, a veritable home of song. [The song] ... bears the mark of the genuine old ballad type, in which the sailor's name is Henry, and the romance hangs round an identifying ring.
[Bp, written at bottom] Corrections from Miss Lizzie M'Mullen....
[Dt] A version from Miss Lizzie MacMullan ... incorporated.
[Bp title has "y" added in writing.]

Key G.

There was a nice young lady lived near to the
  seaside,
She was proper, tall and handsome, she was
  called the village pride,
She was courted by a sailor lad and she vowed to
  be his bride,
And true she was to Henry when on the silver
  tide.

In young Henry's absence a nobleman there came
To court this pretty fair maid, but she refused
  the same:
'Your vows are vain, he's on the main, the boy I
  love,' she cried,
'So go, begone, I love but one and he's on the
  silver tide.'

This nobleman was walking one day all in his
  pride,
When he spied this pretty fair maid down by the
  seaside,
Then said this hateful villain, 'Consent and be
  my bride,
Or you'll sink or swim far, far from him that's on
  the silver tide.'

With trembling lips said Mary, 'My vows I ne'er
  shall break,
I love young Henry dearly and I'll die for his
  sweet sake.'
With a handkerchief he bound her hands and he
  threw her on her side,
And floating went young Mary upon the silver
  tide.

Now in a few days after, young Henry came from
  sea,
Still thinking to be happy and to fix the wedding
  day.
'I'm afraid your true love's murdered,' her aged
  parents cried,
'For she proved her own destruction down by the
  silvery tide.'

Young Henry on his pillow no comfort could he find,
The thoughts of darling Mary disturbed his wounded mind.
One day as he was walking down on the ocean side,
He saw young Mary floating upon the silver tide.

He knew it was his Mary by his own ring on her hand,
He soon unbound the handkerchief which put him to a stand,
The name of the beastly murderer it's there he soon espied,
Which proved he ended Mary upon the silvery tide.

The nobleman was taken, the gallows was his doom
For ending pretty Mary, who had scarce obtained her bloom,
And Henry, sad and dejected, he wandered till he died
And his last words were of Mary, died on the silver tide.

[Bp has the following written "corrections" from Lizzie McMullan, typed on Dt as original text:]
  1.1: ... a lovely lady ...
    .4: Henry upon the silvery ....
  2.1: Being in young ...
    .3: 'The boy I love is on the main, I'm pledged to him,' she cried,'
  3.3: 'Come,' said ...
  4.1: With trembling lips poor Mary said, ...

[Additional changes only on Dt:]
  2.4: So pray, be gone ...
  3.2: ... maid along by ...
  7.3: ... of Mary's murderer ...
  6.4: ... floating down by the ...
  8.3: ... sad, dejected ...

The Willow Tree [H789: 7 Jan 1939]

An Irish Enoch Arden.

Source: ?Sam Lamont (Cloyfin district).

s: ... This is one of Sam Lamont's songs. He learnt it from his mother, a native of Ballymena.

Key E flat.

The night was dark and the hour late,
Cold blew the winter air,

And as four farmers homeward walked
Down through Lifford Fair,
And as they passed an old churchyard,
They thought they heard a cry,
Both sad and sharp it struck their ear,
Although the winds blew high.

They climbed the wall and searched the tombs
That thickly filled the ground,
And, spreading on a new-made grave,
A sorrowful youth they found;
His wild moans filled the chilly air,
For he looked pale and wild,
His loud cries would have pierced your heart,
For he wept like a child.

They roused him from the cold wet earth,
Inviting him away,
He says, 'Move me not from this sad spot,
For here I mean to stay;
This is my true-love's grassy bed,
And here all night I'll lie,
All by the side of my long-lost bride,
I will remain and die.

'In early life we both were joined
In love both fond and true,
There's not a care but touched my heart
But touched my Fanny's, too;
The times were bad and I was poor,
It was then I went away,
To make my fortune in strange lands,
I crossed the roaring sea.

'Scarce before I went away,
In wedlock's bands we joined,
It was then I left my tender bride,
So lonely, young and fond;
For three long years I stayed away
And I won gold in store,
Then I came home to claim my own
And part with her no more.

But oh, alas, begins my grief,
My woe it then begun;
When I came home they had her wed
Unto another one,
And with false letters they imposed
All in her heartless ear,
And told her I had died abroad
All in a second year.

'It being on a summer evening,
Calm and fragrant was the air
She sat before her father's door
And never looked more fair;
I stood before her suddenly,
And when I caught her eye,
She clasped her hands before her face
And gave a piercing cry.

'The sudden shock had reached her heart;
The story soon was told:
When I came home her father gave
His hands to ancient gold,
But all the gold that e'er was shown
Did fail to ease her mind,

Sam Henry's Songs of the People

And like a tender flower crushed,
Away she drooped and pined.

'Mark what followed after this --
I need not stop to tell --
In that day month, sure I could hear
The tolling funeral bell.
Now I have done all with this earth,
And it has done with me:
My love lies dead in her cold clay bed
Beneath yon willow tree.'

They stooped, but neither force nor word
Could raise him from the ground,
All night he lay on the cold clay,
And the next day was found,
And when they touched him he was dead,
For where he lay he died;
They dug his grave and, side by side,
They laid him with his bride.

9.3: that day month = that same day a month later.

Killeavy's Pride [H190: 2 Jul 1927]

o: (m) "Skibereen."

Source: (w) John Henry Macaulay (Bog Oak Shop, Ballycastle, Co. Antrim); also Patrick Hegarty (Railway Cottage, Faughanvale), learned from Edward Carlin (Killywill, Greysteel), died c. 1905; (m) whistled by plowman (Armoy).

s: ... John Henry Macaulay ... writes: -- "This old ditty was a great favourite with old Francis McBride, who was a sailor in his early days and afterwards taught school in Glenshesk. He died in 1910, aged 80." ... The air was collected ... from a ploughman who stopped his team to whistle it to me....

Key C.

How beautiful young Mary looked, she was
 Killeavy's pride,
Her parents dwelt near Newry town all on the
 Armagh side,
She and William promised were, all from their
 early youth,
True love between them early sprang all in the
 bloom of youth.

When young, their parents they both died, and
 homeless they were cast,
But he that rules the seas and waves against the
 fatal blast
Raised up a friend who said he'd never see them
 homeless roam --
A neighbour man who pitied them and brought
 these orphans home.

And so, in kind humility, in peace they did
 reside,
Not knowing the want of parents until this good
 man died,
But then again these faithful pair were doomed to
 parted be:
Young Mary went to service, young Willie went to
 sea.

And when they were about to part, they broke a
 ring in two,
And each of them they took a part and vowed
 they would be true,
Through life and death they promised were,
 whatever would befall,
That steadfastly they'd keep their vows and live
 through changes all.

But when the months rolled into years and when
 the years rolled by,
No word of Willie coming home, her faith began to
 die;
At length a rich farmer's son, he won her love off
 hand,
He says, 'Your William now lies dead all in a
 foreign land.'

Young Mary lent an ear to him and she did her
 promise break,
Oh yes, she said, all in a week she would her
 farmer take,
He won her by his flattering tongue, his presence
 fond and dear,
But still and all throughout their joy her heart
 felt some strange fear.

So well she might, for Willie lived and high
 promotion got,
He won it in the stormy cold and in the battle
 hot,
Through stormy cold and battle hot did this poor
 sailor roam
Till the captain he gave orders to turn and sail
 for home.

They sailed the seas most gallantly, in peace they
 did abide
And crossing the Atlantic waves, dropped on the
 evening tide
Till they reached the bay at Warrenpoint and
 sailed the channel down
And came unto their own dear home, long-wished-
 for Newry town.

They moored the ship, young Willie sprang with
 three shipmates ashore,
Saying, 'Come on, boys, and you will see the girl
 that I adore;

The years have passed and I have sailed with you the world around,
But for youth and beauty none like Mary ever can be found.'

The well-known path they quickly trod and to the house drew near,
The lumination caught their eye while music caught their ear,
He thought it strange when in he dashed to see Killeavy's pride,
For Mary sat in bridal white and her husband by her side.

'Oh Mary, dear, have you proved false?' young Willie loud did cry,
And Mary, looking up to see, she caught his flashing eye.
'Oh Willie, dear, they said you died,' she cried with a loud moan,
And fainting fell upon the floor as lifeless as a stone.

Her new-made husband he jumped up and aimed at Willie a blow;
Despair gave Willie so much strength he soon put down his foe,
They fell upon him, he near was killed when his three friends dashed in
To his rescue; they caught him and the four made out again.

Young Willie's heart it being broke, he went to sea once more,
He says he'll ne'er in all his life return to Newry shore.
Young Mary's conscience being struck, she went quite mad at last
And died a victim to false love in that asylum near Belfast.

Come all ye men and maidens, a warning take by me,
Be true to your promises whatever they may be,
For when you have your tender joy, your sweetheart by your side,
Still think on her who once was called Killeavy's only pride.

3.1: ... humility and peace ... [Dt]
9.2: ... on, my boys, ... [Dt]
12.1: ... jumped and ... [Dt]

The Pride of Newry Town

[H798: 11 Mar 1939]

Source: Willie Bradley (Cross Lane, Coleraine), learned 60 years ago from a soldier pal (Bombay, India).

s: [Willie Bradley's] memory, in his 79th year, is still unimpaired.

Key D.

C22 / When death was near

How beautiful young Mary looked, she was young Fleming's pride,
Their parents dwelt in Newry town, being on the Armagh side;
Young Mary and William Fleming were pledged in solemn truth,
For love between those two had sprung all in their blooming youth.

Their parents died when they were young and they were homeless cast,
But he who rules both sea and land and calms the stormy blast
Found them a friend who said he would not see them homeless roam --
A neighbour man who pitied them and took these orphans home.

Contented did these couple live and in sweet love confide;
They never knew the want of friends until this poor man died,
And when it was this couple's fate that parted they should be,
Young Mary went to service and young William went to sea.

And when they were about to part they cut a ring in two,
And each of them that took a half vowed that they would be true,
True to life and liberty, whatever be their fate,
They said they'd keep their promise and remain in single state.

Now months rolled into years and years went passing by,
And William not returning back, her faith began to die;
She was courted by a farmer's son who gained her willing hand,
He said, 'Your William, he is dead all in some foreign land.'

But still withal in Mary's heart there was a strange fear dwelt,
And so there might, for in her heart she still the old love felt;
Though absent long, still William lived and high promotion got,
He won it on the stormy seas and in strange battles fought.

421

Sam Henry's Songs of the People

In battles and in breezes this seaman he did roam
Until his ship got orders to return and sail for home.
Young William's vessel sprung a leak and brought them all to shore,
He said, 'My comrades, come with me and see her I adore.

'For seven long years I've sailed the seas the whole world round and round,
For love and beauty there is none like Mary I have found.'
They travelled o'er the well-known road and to the house came near,
And it was lighted up and strains of music met their ear.

Young William was the first dashed in to see his love and pride,
And Mary sat in bridal white, her husband by her side,
'Oh Mary dear, have you proved false?' aloud young William cried,
And turning round she knew his voice and saw his flashing eyes.

From her pale lips they only heard a bitter sigh and moan,
She fainted then unto the floor as lifeless as a stone;
Mary's husband he got up, at William aimed a blow,
But William picked up courage and left him lying low.

Friends and neighbours gathered in to see what did begin,
And by their means their lives were saved and the boys got out again;
Young William, broken-hearted, lost the girl he did adore,
And never more in all his life was seen on Newry shore.

2.4: ... who pitted them ... [Dp]

◊ C22 REFERENCES ◊

◊ **The 'Prentice Boy** *(H31) 411*

White/Dean-Smith 1951: "(The) Sheffield Apprentice"
Dean-Smith 1954: "(The) Sheffield Apprentice"
Laws 1957:245 (O39) "The Sheffield Apprentice"
Brunnings 1981: "The Apprentice Boy (The Prentice Boy)," "The Sheffield Apprentice," "The Sheffield 'Prentice Boy (Farewell, Lovely Nancy)"
Cazden et al. *Notes* 1982: #55 "The Holland Song"

IREL Shields/Shields *UF* 21,1975: #202 "In Connaught I Was Reared"

BRIT Holloway/Black 1975:251-2(#111) "The Sheffield Prentice"
  Palmer 1980:93-4 "The Sheffield Apprentice"
Sharp/Karpeles 1974,2:571-4 (#388) "The Sheffield Apprentice," 4 vts. [Laws]

AMER Burton/Manning 1969:56-7 "Soefield"
  Cazden et al. 1982:209-12 (#55) "The Holland Song"
  Warner 1984:208-9 (#80) "Way up in Sofield (or, The Sheffield Apprentice)"; 347-9 (#152) "The Sheffield 'Prentice"

BRS Harvard 1: 10.62 (Bebbington), 13.26 (Such)
  UCLA 605: 5(Walker) "The Sheffield Apprentice," (Disley)
  Forget Me Not (NY) [1835]: 244

cl: REC Mrs T. M. Bryant, AFS 1751 B "The Sheffield Apprentice"
cl: Mrs M. P. Daniels, AFS 3724 B "The Sheffield Apprentice"
  June Lazare, Folkways FH 5276 (A9) "The New York 'Prentice Boy"
  Joseph Leaning, Leader LEA 4050 (B4) "The Sheffield Apprentice"
  Hedy West, Topic 12T 163 "Sheffield Apprentice"
  But not: "The London Prentice Boy" sung by Dick Woolnough, Topic 12TS 375 (A5)

◊ **Blooming Caroline of Edinburgh Town** *(H148) 411*

Laws 1957:262 (P27) "Caroline ..."
Brunnings 1981: "Caroline .../Town"

IREL Morton 1973:70-1 "... from ..."

BRIT MacColl/Seeger 1977:184-5

AMER Cox 1939(1964):81-2 "Fair Caroline (Caroline ...)"
  Dean [1922]:53

BRS BPL Libbie: (n.i.)
  BPL Partridge: 1.36
  Harvard 1: 5.153 (Catnach), 10.132 (Bebbington)
  Harvard 3: (Pearson)
  UCLA 605:3 (Brereton)(Such); see also (Batchelar) "The Fate of Young Henry in Answer to Caroline of Edinboro Town," which continues Henry's story to a soggy end: he drowns. [Laws says Kittredge (*JAF* 35,1922) reports a broadside by Pitts with the same story.]

REC Packie Byrne, EFDSS LP 1009 (B1) "... Caroline"
cl: J. W. Green, AFS 2298 A3 "Caroline of Edinborough ..."
  Geordie Hanna, Comhaltas Ceoltóirí Eireann CL 14 (A3) "Caroline ..."; Eagrán MD 0002 (B7) "Caroline from ..."
  Charles Ingenthron, AAFS L14 (A4) "Caroline ..."
  Belle Stewart, Topic 12T 138 (A2) "Caroline ...";
Topic 12TS 307

◊ **Ballindown Braes** *(H73) 412*

Laws 1957:262 (P28) "Bessie of Ballington Brae"
Brunnings 1981: "Bessie of Ballydubray"

IREL Joyce 1909:150 "Ballindown Braes" [Laws]

BRS BPL Irish: (n.i.)

REC Nora Cleary, Topic 12TS 369 (B4) "Bessie of Ballantown Brae"
  Cecilia Costello, Leader LEE 4054 (B2) "Betsy of Ballantown Brae"

◆ The King o' Spain's Daughter *(H163)* 413

White/Dean-Smith 1951: "(The) Outlandish Knight or May Colvin; An Outlandish Rover; The Highway Robber"
Dean-Smith 1954: "(The) Outlandish Knight; The Robber Knight; May Colvin"
Child 1882-98(1965),1:22-62 (#4) "Lady Isabel and the Elf Knight," 6 vts.; 485-9; 2:496-7, 1 vt.; 3:496-7, 1 vt.; 4:440-2, 1 vt.; 5:206-7
Coffin/Renwick 1950(1977):25-28, 211-2
Bronson 1,1959:39-100; 4,1972:442-3
Brunnings 1981: "Lady Isabel and the Elf-Knight [Child 4]"

Nygard 1958 presents a detailed international study of this ballad. See also *JAF* 65,1952:1-12 and 68, 1955:141-52; Grundtvig, *DgF* 4; and Iivar Kemppinen, "The Ballad of Lady Isabel and the False Knight" (Helsinki, 1954); also Lajos Vargyas, *Hungarian Ballads and the European Tradition* (Budapest, 1983), II #3; and David D. Buchan, "Lady Isabel and the Whipping Boy," *SFQ* 34,1970:62-70, on versions given by Peter Buchan [Coffin/Renwick 1977].

IREL Morton 1970:21-3 "The Parrot Song" [MacColl/Seeger]

BRIT *FR* 2(5,Mar)1973:15 "The Outlandish Knight"
Greig/Duncan 2,1983:146-7 (#225) "May Colvin," 2 vts.
Lloyd "Meaning" 1978:15-6 "Six Pretty Maids" (see Jordan rec.)
Lyle 1975:83-6 "May Colyean"
MacColl/Seeger 1977:50-1 (#2) "Lady Isabel and the Elf Knight" ("Don't Prittle Nor Prattle")
Morrison/Cologne 1981:48-50 "The Outlandish Knight"
Oxford Ballads 1969:49-51 (#12) "May Colven"
Palmer 1979b:109-11 (#58) "The False-Hearted Knight" (see Brightwell rec.)
Sing 8(3,Apr)1965:2 "The Outlandish Knight"
Spin 4(2):14-5 "Six Pretty Maids (The Outlandish Knight)"

AMER Darling 1983:23-4, A "Lady Isabel and the Elf-Knight; 24-5, B "Six Pretty Maids (The Outlandish Knight)" (see Mills rec.)
Leach 1967:15-20 "May Collen and the Knight"
Randolph/Cohen (1982):16-8 "Pretty Polly Ann"
Cf. Silverman 1971:117 "The Cruel Youth"
SO 29(1,Jan-Feb)1981:10-1 "Lady Isabelle and the Elf Knight"
Warner 1984:130-2 (#41) "The Castle by the Sea"

BRS UCLA 605: 4(n.i.), (Such)

REC Jumbo Brightwell, *CWL* 3, Columbia KL 206 (A4, 28) "The False-Hearted Knight"; Topic 12TS 261
m: Fred Jordan, *FSB* 4 (A4) "Six Pretty Maids"; Topic 12TS 233 (A1)
Peggy Seeger, Ewan MacColl, *LH*, Argo ZDA 71, #6 "Lady Isabel and the Elf Knight," 5 versions.
A. L. Lloyd, *Riverside CB*, RLP 12 622 (B2) "The Outlandish Knight"
Frankie Armstrong, Sierra Briar SBR 4211 (A1) "The Outlandish Knight"
b: May Bradley, EFDSS LP 1006 (B1) "The Dappledy Grey"
cl: Mrs T. M. Bryant, AFS 1735 A "Lady Isabel and the Elf Knight"
The Broadside, Topic 12TS 228 "The Outlandish Knight"
Martin Carthy, Mooncrest Crest 25 (A4) "Outlandish Knight"
LaRena Clark, Topic 12T 140 (B3) "The Dapple Gray"
Paul Clayton, Folkways FP 2007 (B2) "Pretty Polly and False William"; Folkways FW 8708 (B9) "The False-Hearted Knight"

cl: Mrs M. P. Daniels, AFS 3730 A "Six Kings' Daughters"
b: Richard Dyer-Bennet, Decca DLP 5046 "The Willow Tree"
Tom Gilfellon, Trailer LER 2079 (A2) "The Outlandish Knight"
cl: Mrs Haden, AFS 1746 A2 "Lady Isabel and the Elf Knight"
cl: Mrs A. M. Harris, AFS 1415 B "Lady Isabel and the Elf Knight"
Clara Hawkes, Folkways FE 4001 (B7) "Pretty Polly (The False-Hearted Knight)"
Mary Ann Haynes, Topic 12T 253 (A4) "The Young Officer"
Joe Hickerson, Folk-Legacy FSI 59 (B2) "Lady Isabel and the Elf Knight"
Dee Hicks, Tenn. Folklore Society TFS 104 (A10) "Pretty Polly (Six King's Daughters)"
cl: Mrs Boyd Hoskins, AFS 1495 B "Six Kings' Daughters"
Nic Jones, Trailer LER 2014 (B3) "The Outlandish Knight"; Trailer LER 2027 (A5), another version.
Pat Kuchwara, Troubador TR 3 (A4) "Lady Isabel and the Elf-Knight"
Sam Larner, Topic 12T 244 (B3) "The Outlandish Knight"
Tim Laycock, Greenwich Village GVR 216 (B1) "The Outlandish Knight"
cl: Theodosia Bonnett Long, AFS 2954 B1 "The King's Seven Daughters"
cl: Dr. David McIntosh, AFS 3250 A1 "Lady Isabel and the Elf Knight"
cl: Myra Barnett Miller, AFS 845 A2 "Lady Isabel and the Elf Knight"
Alan Mills, Folkways FG 3532 (A6) "Lady Isabel"
cl: Mrs J. U. Newman, AFS 3786 B3 "Lady Isabel and the Elf Knight"
Jean Ritchie, Folkways FA 2301 (A2) "False Sir John"
Peggy Seeger, Folk-Lyric FL 120 (A1) "Lady Isabel and the Elf Knight"
cl: Marion Stoggill, AFS 1725 B1 "Lady Isabel and the Elf Knight"
cl: Carrie Walker, AFS 3064 A1 "Lady Isabel and the Elf Knight"

MEL Petrie/Stanford 2,1902:199 (#795) "Tune of the Old English Ballad 'Lord Robert and Fair Ellen.'" [Coffin/Renwick]

◆ The Broomfield Hill *(H135)* 414

White/Dean-Smith 1951: "... or The Bonny Broomfields; Bonny Green Woods; Broomfield Wager; Merry Broomfields; West Country Wager; The Young Squire"
Dean-Smith 1954: "... Wager"
Child 1882-98(1965),1:390-9 (#43), 6 vts.; 508; 2:506; 3:506; 4:458; 5:290
Coffin/Renwick 1950(1977):51-2, 223
Bronson 1,1959:336-47; 4,1972:460
Brunnings 1981

IREL Cf. Joyce 1909:152 (#327) "The Mermaid" [Bronson]

BRIT Dawney 1972:29 "Merry Broomfield"
Greig/Duncan 2,1983:458 (#322) "The Bonnie Broomfields," 2 vts. ("Broomfield Hills"); also cf. stanza 1 of Greig/Duncan 2,1983:392 "Jock Sheep"
MacColl/Seeger 1977:63-6 (#7) [untitled]
O'Shaughnessy 1971:4-5
Oxford Ballads 1969:72-4 (#21)
Palmer 1979b:121-3 (#65)
Palmer *FMJ* 1973:288-9
Richards/Stubbs 1979:82-3

REC Cyril Poacher, *FSB* 4 (A10) "... Wager," Topic 12TS 252 (A1)

Ewan MacColl, *Folkways CB*, FG 3510 (B4); *Riverside CB*, RLP 12 623 (A1)
Peggy Seeger, Ewan MacColl, *LH*, Argo ZDA 68 #3, "The Broomfield Hill," 2 versions.
Martin Carthy, Topic 12TS 340 (A6), Topic 12TS 345 (B4)
Roy Harris, Topic 12TS 217 (A2) "The Bonny Green Woods"; b: Topic TPSS 221
George Maynard, Topic 12T 286 (B7) "A Wager, A Wager"
Walter Pardon, Topic 12TS 392
John Roberts, Tony Barrand, Folk-Legacy FSI 65 (A2) "... Wager"

◆ **Lord Ronald** *(H 814)* 415

White/Dean-Smith 1951: "... Rendal or King Henry My Son; Little Wee Croodlin' Doo; ... Rendal/ Ronald; Three Drops of Poison"
Dean-Smith 1954: "... Rendal/Randal/Ronald; King Henry My Son; Jacky My Son"
Child 1882-98(1965),1:151-66 (#12) "... Randal," 15 vts.; 498-501, 4 vts.; 2:498-9; 3:499; 4:449-50, 1 vt.; 5:208-9, 286-7
Coffin/Renwick 1950(1977):36-9, 216-7 "... Randal"
Bronson 1,1959:191-225 "... Randal"; 4,1972:451
Brunnings 1981: "... Randall"

For a comparative study of Canadian French versions of this ballad which are apparently literal translations of the English, see Paquin *CFMJ* 1979.

IREL Behan 1965: #60 "My Bonny Brown Boy," a very different version.
Harte 1978:30-1
JIFSS 18,1921:33-4 "My Boy Tommy, O!"
Joyce 1909:394-5 (#812) "Where Were You All the Day, My Own Pretty Boy?" [Bronson]
Loesberg 3,n.d.:26 "Henry My Son"

BRIT *Chapbook* 2(2):22 "... Donald"
Greig/Duncan 2,1983:60-5 (#209) "Lord Ronald," 11 vts. ("Henry My Son," "Oh Mak' My Bed Easy," "Lord Donald")
Hall *FMJ* 1975:42
MacColl [1962]:3-4 "... Randall"
MacColl/Seeger 1977:54-7 (#4) "Lord Randal" ("... Ronald," "Henry, My Son")
Oxford Ballads 1969:243-4 (#63) "Lord Ronald"
Palmer 1979b:105-6 (#55) "Henry, My Son" (see Dunn rec.)
Palmer 1980:98-9 "Green and Yellow," a music-hall parody.
Sharp/Karpeles 1974,1:17-26 (#4) "... Randal," 11 vts.
Sing 7(4 Jan/Feb)1963:46 "Henry My Son"
Tocher #14(Sum)1974:202-3

AMER Bush 5,n.d.:89-91 "Willy, My Son"
Darling 1983:45-6, A "... Randall" (see MacColl rec.); 46, B "Johnny Randall" (see Older rec.)
Grover n.d.:199-200 "My Own Darling Boy"
Leach 1967:3-4 "... Randal," also 5-6 "Croodlin Dow," 6 "Billy Boy"
Cf. Milner/Kaplan 1983:17 "My Boy Tommy, O!"
Paquin *CFMJ* 7,1979:4,5 "Le testament du garçon empoisonné," "... Randal"
Peters 1972:195 "Dirandel"
Warner 1984:271-3 (#107) "Lord Randall," (#108) "Jimmy Ransome"

BRS *Come Let Us Sing* 1974:64-5 "... Rendal"

REC "... Randall," *FSB* 4 (A6) composite: Jeannie Robertson, Elizabeth Cronin, Thomas Moran, Colm McDonagh, Eirlys, Edis Thomas
Ewan MacColl, *Folkways CB*, FG 3509 (A3) "... Randall"; *Riverside CB*, RLP 12 621 (A1); [b:] Riverside S 2 (B5); Topic 12T 103 (A4) "... Randal"
Peggy Seeger, Ewan MacColl, *LH*, Argo ZDA 66, #1 "... Randal," 6 versions.
Bob "Fiddler" Beers, Evelyne Beers, Folkways FS 2376 (B3) "... Randall"
b: Tossi Aaron, Prestige/Int. 13027 "John Randolph"
b: Harry Belafonte, RCA Victor LPM 1022 "... Randall"
Oscar Brand, Jean Ritchie, Folkways FA 2428 (B2) "... Randall My Son"
Alison Bricknell, Folkways FE 38553 (A8) "Henry My Son"
Isla Cameron, Murray Hill 920336 (5A6) "... Randall"
Grace Carr, Folkways FE 4312 (A5) "Henry, My Son"
Martin Carthy, Mooncrest Crest 25 (B1) "... Randall"; Topic 12TS 389 (A4) "... Randall"; Rounder 3020 [Milner/Kaplan]
b: William Clauson, Capitol P 8539 ... Randall
Sara Cleveland, Folk-Legacy FSA 33 (A4) "My Bonny Bon Boy"
Max Dunbar, Folkways FP 30006 (A2) "... Randal"
George Dunn, Leader LEE 4042 (B4) "Henry My Son"
lc: Richard Dyer-Bennet, Remington RLP 199-34 "... Randall"
Elliot Family, Folkways FG 3565 (Transatlantic XTRA 1091) (A2) "Henry, My Son"
Cf. Sam Eskin, Sierra FMI 7 "Croodlin' Doo" [Bronson]
cl: Celia Fenton, AFS 3631 A4 & 5, 3634 A3, 3635 A1 "Johnny Randal (My Son)"
b: Julia Ann Gilman, ABC-Paramount ABC 168 "... Randall"
lc: Shep Ginandes, Elektra JH 508 "... Randal"
George Vinton Graham, AFS 3814 B2, B3 "Dear Adel My Son" [Bronson]
cl: Mrs G. A. Griffin, AFS 954 B2 "Jimmy Ransom"
cl: Mrs Goldie Hamilton, AFS 2780 B "Make My Bed Soon"
cl: Edith Harmon, AFS 2932 A4 & B1 "Jimmy Randal"
cl: Sam Harmon, AFS 2899 A1 "Jimmy Randal"
Cf. Frank Harte, Topic 12T 172 "Henry My Son," a street song.
Joe Heaney, Topic 12T 91 (B3) "An Tighearna Randall"; (Seosamh Ó hÉanaí) Gael-Linn CEF 028 (B2) "An Tiarna Randall"
cl: Sarah Isom, AFS 2809 A2 "Randal, My Son"
cl: Aunt Molly Jackson, AFS 2545 B1, 2456 A "Johnny Randal"
Burl Ives, [lc:] Encyclopedia Britannica Films 1 (78 rpm) B1 305 "... Randall"; Columbia CL 6058
Tom Kines, Fox Hollow FH 1969 R13054 (A2) "... Randall"
cl: Joseph Kling, AFS 3659 B "Henry, My Son"
b: John Langstaff, Tradition TLP 1009 "Croodin Doo," "Lord Rendal"
John MacDonald, Topic 12TS 263 (A3)
b: Ed McCurdy, Elektra EKL 205 "Lord Randal"
Howie Mitchell, Folk-Legacy FSI 5 (B7) "... Randall"
? cl: Mort. Montonyea, AFS 3668 B "Ranzel, My Son"
cl: Alec Moore, AFS 665 B1 "Mama, Make My Bed Soon"
Artus Moser, Folkways FA 2112 (B4) "... Randal"
b: *The Music of Scotland*, National Geographic Society 707 "Wee Croodin' Doo"
cl: Mrs J. U. Newman, AFS 3788 B1 "... Randall"
John Jacob Niles, [b:] Tradition TLP 1046 "Jimmy Randal/1"; [b:] RCA/Victor Vintage Series LPV 513 "Jimmy Randal/1"
Lawrence Older, Folk-Legacy FSA 15 (B2) "Johnny Randall"
b: Sandy Paton, Elektra 148 "Wee Croodlin' Doo"
Frank Proffitt, Folk-Legacy FSA 1 (A5) "... Randall"
b: Gene, Francesca Raskin ? Love & War "... Randall"
Jean Ritchie, Folkways FA 2302 (B4) "... Randall";

Folkways FA 2428 (B3) "Ennery My Son"
  Tony Rose, Trailer LER 2101 (B2) "... Rendal"
b: Pete Seeger, Columbia Harmony H 30899 "Henry, My Son"
b: Tom Smith, Pennywise PW 123 "Henry M' Son"
b: *Songs and Dances of Scotland*, Murray Hill 920336 "Croodin Doo"
  George Spicer, Topic 12T 235 (B3) "Henry My Son"
  Christina Stewart, Topic 12T 179 (B1) "My Bonny Tammy"
cl: Lena Bare Turbyfill, AFS 2842 A2 & B1 "Jimmy Ransom"
cl: Mrs George A. Webb, AFS 577 A "... Randal"
  Harry, Jeanie West, Stinson SLP 36 (A2) "Jimmy Randall"
  Josh White, Decca A 611 (78 rpm, 4 recs.) "Lord Randall, My Son"; [lc:] Decca DLS 247

MEL Petrie/Stanford 1,1902:83 "(#330) "Where Were You All the Day My Own Pretty Boy"; 2,1902:198 (#794) "Air to an Old English Ballad. Learnt in Mayo." [Bronson]

◇ Susan Brown *(H771) 415*

Not = same title in Brunnings 1981

◇ Susan Carr *(H690) 416*

g: Not located, but it may be related to Laws 1957: 265 (P33) "Susannah Clargy." Laws's only reference is Sharp/Karpeles 1932,2:261.

◇ Flora, the Lily of the West *(H578) 416*

Dean-Smith 1954
Laws 1957:263 (P29) "The ..."
Brunnings 1981: "The ..."

IREL O Lochlainn 1939:184-5

BRIT *ED&S* 27(3,Apr)1965:81
  Spin 2(8)[1964?]:15 "Lily ..."

AMER Grover n.d.:153-4 "The ..."
  Milner/Kaplan 1983:184 "The ..."
Moore/Moore 1964:191-2 "The ..."
  Peacock 1965,2:473-4 "The ..."
  Rosenbaum 1983:135 "The ..."
  Sandburg 1950:61

BRS BPL Partridge: 1.312 (Wrigley), with Louisville instead of Ireland as the locale.
  Harvard 1: 1.122 (Spencer), 2.180 (n.i.), 3.65 (Forth), 4.54 (Gilbert), 5.201 (Catnach), 10.87 (Bebbington), 11.35 (Such)
    Harvard 3: (Barr) (Taylor)
    UCLA 605: 4(Such)

b: REC Joan Baez, Vanguard VRS 9094 (?VSD 2097) "The ..."

cl: Mrs Mary Fuller Cain, AFS 2823 A2 "The ..."
  Bascom Lamar Lunsford, Rounder 0065 [Yates]
cl: H. L. Maxey, AFS 2744 B4 "The ..."
  Joan O'Bryant, Folkways FA 2328 (A7) "The ..."
cl: Lize Pace, AFS 1440 A "Handsome Mary, The ..."
  Peter, Paul and Mary, Warner Bros. W 1473 (A3) "Flora"
  Evelyn Ramsey, Home Made Music LP 001 (B8) "The ..."
  Vivien Richman, Folkways FG 3568 (B6) "Handsome Mary, the ..."

◇ The Old Oak Tree *(H207) 417*

Laws 1957:270 (P37)
Brunnings 1981

b: IREL Morton 1970:24-5
  Morton 1973:141-3

AMER Leach 1965:52-6
  Manny/Wilson 1968:232-4 "Eliza Long (...)"
  Peacock 1965,2:628-9

BRS BPL Irish: (n.i.), probably the same broadside noted by Flanders et al. 1939:74 as evidence of the Irish origin of the ballad, and referred to by Laws.

b: REC Boys of the Lough, Trailer LER 2086
  Mary Ann Carolan, Topic 12TS 362 (A4)
cl: J. W. Green, AFS 2992 B
  Paddy Tunney, Topic 12TS 264 (B3)

◇ The Silver[y] Tide *(H77) 418*

White/Dean-Smith 1951: "Poor Mary in the ..."
Dean-Smith 1954: "Mary in the ..."
Laws 1957:244 (O37)
Brunnings 1981

BRIT Sharp/Karpeles 1974,1:304-7 (#68) "Mary in the ..."

AMER Grover n.d.:9-10
  Manny/Wilson 1968:289-91 (see also Jagoe rec.)

BRS Harvard 1: 9.37 (Bebbington)

cl: REC J. W. Green, AFS 2276 B, 2281 A1
  Sam Jagoe, Folkways FM 4053 (B1) "... Silvery ..."
cl: Mrs J. U. Newman, AFS 3786 B2

◇ Killeavy's Pride *(H190) 420*
  The Pride of Newry Town *(H798) 421*

IREL Hayward 1925:103-6
  Shields/Shields *UF* 21,1975: #231

◇ The Willow Tree *(H789) 419*

Not = Brunnings 1981 [several listings of this title].

C23

**Cruel was my father:
Despite relatives**

C23 / Cruel was my father

The Maid of Ballyhaunis [H483: 4 Mar 1933]

s: (m) "Port [jig] Gordon."

Source not given.

Key G. Tenderly.

My Mary dear, for thee I'd die,
O, place your hand in mine, love --
My fathers here were chieftains high,
Then to my plaints incline, love.
O plaited-hair! that now we were
In wedlock's bond united,
For, maiden mine, in grief I'll pine
Until our vows are plighted.

But thy *cuilin ban* I marked one day
Where the blooms of the bean-field cluster,
Thy bosom white, like ocean's spray,
Thy cheek like rowan's lustre,
Thy tones that shame the wild bird's fame
Which sings in summer weather --
And O, I sigh, that thou and I
Steal not from this world together.

Thou rowan bloom, since thus I rove,
All worn and faint to greet thee,
Come to these arms, my constant love,
With love as true to meet me.
Alas, my head -- my wits are fled,
I've failed in filial duty --
My sire did say, 'Shun, shun for aye
That Ballyhaunis beauty.'

If with thy lover thou depart
To the land of ships, my fair love,
No weary pain of head or heart
Shall haunt our slumbers there, love.
O, haste away ere, cold death's prey,
My soul from thee withdrawn is,
And my hope's reward, the churchyard
In the town of Ballyhaunis.

The Banks of [Wt: the] Cloughwater

[H777: 15 Oct 1938]

Other title: cf. "The Moon Shined on My Bed Last Night."

Source: (w, m) Jock Smylie (Leggyfat, Limavallaghan, Clough, Co. Antrim); [Wt] "a version" from Joseph Russell, now deceased (Priestland) from Robert Orr (Novally, Ballycastle) c. 1913.

Key C.

On the banks of the Cloughwater, where the
  streams do gently glide,
As my love and I sat talking down by the river
  side,
It was of her modest countenance I oftimes stole
  a look
Where the lofty trout and salmon sport down by
  yon crystal brook.

On my bed last night, the moon was bright,
  when I no rest could find,
Still thinking of the company that I had left
  behind,
They are modest, tall and neat young men, fair
  maidens just and free;
If I had my will, wouldn't I be still in my love's
  company?

Oh, Ellen, do you remember when first I courted
  you?
Your parents they were angry, kept you out of
  my view;
Your parents they were angry, swore venge[a]nce
  against me,
Which makes me stand on guard this night to
  shun your companee.

Many, many was the night and many, many was
  the day
You stood before my father's door showing your
  silly play;
With heavy sighs and downcast eyes I'll go unto
  my bed,
Instead of sleep, I'll sigh and weep and many a
  tear I'll shed.

Ellen, but you're handsome, you have a slender
  waist,
Above all women breathing I do count you the
  best;
There's no doubt at all we'll get a call tomorrow
  or next day,
And our town boys will convoy us just as we're
  going away.

427

Sam Henry's Songs of the People

But Ellen dear, if I had you ten hundred miles from home,
In spite of friends and parents I would still make you my own,
For I'm a clever fellow, I care not where I go;
I have gold in every pocket, I regard neither friend or foe.

[Wt *begins with 1 additional stanza and contains other changes:*]

> Oh, I have a wee girl in my mind and she enticed me,
> And her cheeks are like the blooming rose new blown in Germany,
> Her dwelling lies convenient to the little town below;
> She is the darling of my heart, she's the flower of all I know.

1.1: ... stream does gently ...
 .2: My love ...
 .3: ... I oft would steal ...
 .4: ... sported in the crystal ...
2.1: ... moon shone bright ...
4.: [*stanza substituted in Wt:*]

> Oh Ellen dear, you need never fear, though angry my friends be,
> My parents hold an angry pact which oft disturb-ed me,
> But I'm a clever tall young man, I don't care where I go,
> I have gold in every pocket, I regard neither friend nor foe.

5.4: ... will us convoy just ...
6.1: Oh Ellen, if ...
 .2: ... I would make ...
 .3: 'Tis not for cursed riches that I'd inconstant prove,
 .4: I would rather live in poverty and wed the girl I love.

Hibernia's Lovely Jane [H467: 12 Nov 1932]

s: (m) resembles "O' A' the Airts the Win' Can Blaw." Other title: "... Jean.

Source: (Ballycastle).

s: Jessie, the Flower of Dunblane, mentioned in verse 2, is the heroine of Robert Tannahill's (1774-1810) song of that title. Proserpine (i.e. Persephone) [is] a beautiful goddess in Roman mythology. The song dates from the time of the Peninsular Wars [1808-14].

Key G.

We parted from the Scottish shores, those high and mossy banks,
And to fair Spain we did sail o'er to join the hostile ranks.
In Ireland we once more arrived after a long campaign,
Where a bonny maid my heart betrayed -- Hibernia's lovely Jane.

Her cheeks were like the red, red rose, and the bright blinks o' her e'en,
They sparkled as the drops o' dew bedeck yon meadows green;
Jane Cameron ne'er was half so fair, nor Jessie o' Dunblane,
And Proserpine could ne'er outshine Hibernia's lovely Jane.

This bonny Irish lassie braw, she being o' high degree,
Her parents said a soldier's bride their daughter ne'er would be;
O'ercome with care, grief and despair, no hope can now remain
Since that nymph divine can ne'er be mine -- Hibernia's lovely Jane.

If I Were a Blackbird [H79: 16 May 1925]

(Republished by request.)

Other titles: "The ...," "I Am a Young Maiden," "I'm a Young Bonnie Lassie," "... Was ...."

Source not given.

l: All three library copies are printed and include the subheading "republished by request," but give no clue to the date of the reprinting.

Key F sharp. Slow with tenderness.

When I was a young maid, my fortune was told
That I'd fall in love with a young sailor bold,
He courted me fondly by night and by day,
But he's gone and he's left me, he's gone far away.

> *If I were a blackbird, I'd whistle and sing,*
> *I'd follow the vessel my true love was in,*
> *And on the top riggin' I'd there build my nest*
> *And lie the night long on its lily-white crest.*

My love's tall and handsome in every degree,
But my parents despise him because he loves me,
But let them despise him and say as they will,
While there's breath in my body I will love him
  still.

My parents despised him because he was poor,
But I loved him better, I loved him the more,
But now he has left me and gone far away,
My heart it is breaking for my own sailor boy.

He promised to buy me at the bonny bright fair
A bunch of blue ribbons to bind round my hair,
But he's gone and he's left me, he's gone far
  away,
And I'm breaking my heart for my own sailor boy.

The Maid of Aghadowey

[H673: 17 Oct 1936; ?Laws O2]

[g: see H86 "The Banks of the Bann"]

s: (m) "Youghal Harbour."

Source not given.

Key D.

Come all ye young men inclined to ramble
To some strange country your friends to see,
Come pay attention to what I mention,
And soon you'll hear what has happened me.
I left the parish called Aghadowey,
Which causes me here in grief to stand
And ponder deeply on the days I sported
Down by the banks of the bonny Bann.

I oftimes sported but seldom courted,
  a fair one I chanced to spy;
She being a stranger and I a ranger,
I deemed no danger to wink my eye.

Then I stepped up to her, not to pursue her,
But my heart to cure of a sudden ache,
But I knew not how to congratulate her,
I feared she'd think I was a rake.

'I hear your parents are dead against me,
Oh, pray don't let their counsel stand,
They would insist that you quite deny me
And wed some young man possessed of land,
But was I as rich as olden Dives,
Or yet a monarch to wear a crown,
My dear, it would be my daily study
To place upon you fame and renown.

'But I'll away to yon high mountains,
Down by the banks of the bright Bann side,
And I'll look back unto Mourne's water,
'Tis there the clear streams do gently glide.
My heart rejoices to see my country,
Its rugged mountains so wild to view,
And was I keeper of India's treasure,
I'd bestow it all, love, for sake of you.'

The Slaney Side

[H52b: "Two songs --
love lost and love won," 8 Nov 1924]

g: "(Down by) the Tan-Yard Side."

Source: (w, m) native [Dt: William Devine],
(Foreglen, Co. Derry).

Key D.

I am a rambling hero, by love I am ensnared;
Near to the town of Milford there dwells a comely
  maid,
She is fairer than Diana and free from earthly
  pride,
This comely maid, her dwelling place lies near
  the Slaney side.

The first time that I saw my love was in the
  month of May,
As I roved for recreation's sake, I carelessly did
  stray,
The small birds joined in chorus, the stream did
  gently glide,
I stood amazed, on her I gazed down by the
  Slaney side.

I stood in meditation and viewed this maid all
  round,

Sam Henry's Songs of the People

I thought she was an angel from heaven had come down;
'Oh no, kind sir, I'm a country girl,' she modestly replied,
'I'm daily labouring for my bread down by the Slaney side.'

For six long months we courted, in love we did agree
To acquaint our friends and parents, and married we would be,
But at length her cruel father, to me he proved unkind,
Which makes me for to sail the seas and leave my love behind.

Farewell to friends and parents, I now must bid adieu,
I am crossing the main ocean in sorrow, dear, for you,
But if ever I return again I will make you my bride,
I will take you in my arms down by the Slaney side.

The Maid of Sweet Gorteen

[H594: 20 Apr 1935]

Other titles: "... Gartheen (Gartine) (Gurteen).

Source not given.

Key D.

Come all ye gentle muses, combine and lend an ear
While I set forth the praises of a charming maiden fair;
It's the curling of her yellow locks that stole away my heart,
And death, I'm sure, must be the cure if she and I must part.

The praises of this lovely maid I mean for to unfold:
Her hair hangs o'er her shoulders like lovely links of gold,
Her carriage neat, her limbs complete, which fractured quite my brain,
Her skin is whiter than the swan that swims the purling stream.

Her eyes are like the diamonds bright that shine in crystal stream,
So modest and so tender she's fit to be a queen,
Many pleasant hours I spent behind the hedgerow green
In hopes to get another sight of the maid of sweet Gorteen.

It was my cruel father that caused my grief and woe,
He locked her in a room and would not let her go;
Her windows I have daily watched, thinking she might be seen,
In hopes to get another sight of the maid of sweet Gorteen.

My father rose one morning and thus to me did say,
'Oh, my dear son, be warned by me, don't throw yourself away
To marry a poor servant girl whose parents are so mean,
So stay at home and do not roam and with me still remain.'

'O father, dearest father, don't part me from my dear,
I would not lose my darling for a thousand pounds a year,
Was I possessed of England's crown I would make her my queen,
In high renown I'd wear the crown with the maid of sweet Gorteen.'

My father in a passion flew and thus to me did say,
'Since that's the case, within this place no longer shall she stay,
Mark what I say, from this very day you ne'er shall see her face,
For I will send her far away unto some lonesome place.'

'Twas in a few days after, a horse he did prepare
And sent my darling far away to a place I know not where.
I may go view my darling's room where she oftimes has been,
Thinking to get another sight of the maid of sweet Gorteen.

Now to conclude and make an end, I take my pen in hand,
John O'Brien is my name and Kerry is my land,
Many happy days I spent when I my darling seen,
Now her abode is on the road that runs through sweet Gorteen.

McClenahan's Jean

[H81: 30 May 1925]

Source: (w) (Blackhill district, Coleraine); (m) supplied by S. H. (Ballywillan district).

s: ... I could not trace the air, but I have used a tune ... to a song which is not suitable for pub-

lication on account of the personal names therein being identifiable.
[penciled on Wp] By David Herbison.

[No key given.]

There's few but has heard of McClenahan's dochter,
Her beauty enlivened the paths where she strayed,
I wandered those valleys oftimes for to see her
And couldn't help loving that beautiful maid.

Her cheeks they appeared like twa bonny roses
When first on the dew-drookit bushes they're seen.
Nae charm was a-wantin' tae mak' her enchantin',
Sae lovely and fair was McClenahan's Jean.

But when her auld faither he heard we were courtin',
He swore by the blood that did a' sin redeem
That in merriage we ne'er should be buckled thegither,
The lad that was poor would ne'er meet his esteem.

'For I hae for Jeanie a laird that is wealthy,
His kilt and his braw hoose she's never yet seen.
Wi' him she'll sit smilin', the moments beguilin',
Sae dearly he loves his beloved wee Jean.'

'Contentment has left you, McClenahan's dochter,
[*spoken by the jilted lover, evidently in derision to Jean's husband standing by:*]
Ye auld doatin' boady, ye auld crazy boady,
He's ne'er made to wed wi' a maid o' sixteen;
Away wi' your treasure, for ae moment's pleasure
Is better by far tae McClenahan's Jean.'

5.2: [?For 'husband' read 'father.']

2.2: drookit = drenched, wet.
5.2: doatin' = doting, weak-minded from old age; boady = body.

We Met, 'Twas in a Crowd

[H638: 15 Feb 1936]

Source: (m, w) Mrs Simpson (Dervock), learned from Mrs Thomas Boyd (Ballyhamage, Doagh, Co. Antrim); (similar m but more ornate) Mrs J. W. M'Kierahan (Home Bank, Portstewart); also Mrs Katie Glass (Ouig, Rathlin Island), Mrs Clarke (Long Commons, Coleraine), and others.

s: ... Versions also sent by ... others, all of whom are thanked for their interest in "The Songs of the People."
In John Masefield's classic sea-story, "The Bird of Dawning," when the men of the Black Gauntlet, one of the China tea-clippers, had to abandon their ship and take to the open boats, 700 miles from the Azores, they sang old songs to keep their hearts up and pass the time. The above song was the favourite, the sailors all joining with great gusto in the line, "Thou hast been the cause of this anguish, my mother."

Key G.

We met, 'twas in a crowd, and I thought he would shun me,
He came, I could not breathe, for his eyes were upon me,
He spoke, his words were few, but his voice was unaltered,
I knew how much he felt, for his deep-toned voice faltered.

I wore my bridal wreath, how I rivalled its whiteness,
Bright gems were in my hair, how I hated their brightness.
He called me by my name as the bride of another;
Thou art the cause of this anguish, my mother.

I saw him once again and a fair girl was near him,
He smiled and whispered low, as I oftimes did hear him.
She leaned on his arm, once mine and mine only,
I wept, for I deserved to feel wretched and lonely.

And he'll make her his bride, at the altar he will give her
That love that was too pure for a heartless deceiver.
The world may think me gay, for my feelings I'll smother;
Thou hast been the cause of this anguish, my mother.

Johnny Doyle [H137: 26 Jun 1926; Laws M2]

o: (m) "Farewell to Enniskillen." Other titles: "I'd Cross the World for (over with) You, ...," "It's of a Tender Maiden," "Johney ...," "... Dial," "Young Johnnie."

Source not given.

s: A favourite. Versions have been received from Coleraine, Articlave and Bellarena districts.

Sam Henry's Songs of the People

[Stanza 2 is added, typed on Bp and enclosed in brackets in Dt. For a clipping included with W, see Appendix C.]

Key G.

There's one thing that grieves me that I will confess,
That I go to meeting and my true love goes to mass,
But if it was so ordered, I would bear it with the toil,
Through the world I would wander with you, Johnny Doyle.

I am a fair maiden all tangled in love,
My case I'll make known to the great God above;
I thought it a credit and I thought it no toil
Through the wide world to wandure with you, Johnny Doyle.

It happened to be on a Saturday night
When Johnny Doyle and I, we were going to take our flight,
My waiting maid being standing by, as plain as you may see,
She went unto my mother and she told upon me.

My mother she locked me in a room that was high,
Where no one could hear me nor no one could me spy,
She bundled up my clothes and she told me to begone,
So slyly and so slowly I put them on.

Five hundred bright guineas my father did provide
The day that I was to be Sammy Moore's bride,
And six double horsemen to ride to Ballintown
Unto one Mr Gordon's, where we lighted down.

We rode together till we came to the town,
Until Mr Gordon's we all dismounted down;
If theirs was the pleasure, mine was the toil,
For my heart I left behind me with young Johnny Doyle.

Soon as the minister he opened the door,
My earrings they bursted and fell till the floor,
And to fifty-five pieces my laces all flew,
I thought that my poor heart was going to break in two.

So behind my old brother I was then carried home,
And by my old mother conveyed unto my room,
And on my own bedside I leaned myself down,
And both sick, sore and weary my body I found.

'I'll send for Johnny Doyle, mother, if that he will come.'
'To send for Johnny Doyle, child, the way is far too long.'
'The journey is far and death will be my fate,
To send for Johnny Doyle, mother, it is far too late.

'So mother, dear mother, make you fast the room door;
Till the breaking of the day, don't let in Sammy Moore.'
Early the next morning when young Sammy Moore arose,
And straight to his mistress' bedchamber he goes.

Folding down the clothes, he found she was dead,
And Johnny Doyle's handkerchief tied round her head,
Folding down the clothes, he found she was dead;
And a fountain of tears over her he did shed.

2.: [Typed on Bp, included in brackets in Dt.]
4.4: ... I then put ... [Bp, written]
5.2: The day I was ... [Dt]

The Lover's Ghost

[H217: 7 Jan 1928; Child #272]

k: "The Suffolk Miracle." Other titles: "The Farmer's Daughter," "His Heart's Delight," "The Holland Handkerchief," "The Lady near New York Town," "There Was an Old and Wealthy Man."

Source: William Davidson (Drumnakeel, Ballyvoy, Co. Antrim).

[Bp] s: ... The construction of the air in the formula a,a,a,b is unusual.
A song with this title has been published by Joyce and by Hughes, in which the ghost is the lady.

Key D.

There was a squire lived in this town,
He was a man of high renown,
He had a daughter, a beauty bright,
And the name he called her was his 'heart's delight.'

Lords, dukes and earls to court her came,
But none of them could her favour gain.
There came a lad of low degree,
And above them all she fancied he.

Then when her father came this to know
That she was in love with this young man so,
Full fifty miles he sent her away,
To disappoint her on her wedding day.

One night as she lay in her bed bound,
And loosing off her morning gown,
She heard a voice of a deadly sound,
Saying, 'Loose off these bonds, love, they're too
  long bound.'

Then looking out of her window high,
Her father's steed she chanced to spy;
'It's your father's steed, love, has come for you,
And your mother's mantle to make it true.'

Her father's steed she right well did know,
And her mother's mantle she knew also,
She dressed herself up in rich attire
And she is away with her heart's desire.

Then when he got her fixed on behind,
He rode full swifter than the wind,
He rode a mile and a little more,
And he says, 'My darling, my head is sore.'

A Holland handkerchief she then pulled out
And with the same bound his head about;
She kissed his lips and these words did say,
'My love, you're colder far than the clay.'

They rode along to her father's gate.
'Leap off, my love, and go to your bed,
Leap off, my love, and go to your bed,
For your steed in the stable I will see fed.'

Then when she went to her father's hall,
'Who's that? Who's that?' did the old man call.
'It's I, dear father, didn't you send for me
With such a young man?' and she mentioned he.

The old man knew this young man was dead,
He tore the grey hairs out of his head,
He wrung his hands and he cried full sore,
But this young man's darling cried more and
  more.

Then early, early by the break of day,
They rode away where this young man lay,
Although this young man being nine months dead,
Sure, this Holland handkerchief was round his
  head.

Take warning, fathers and mothers too,
Who cause their children oftimes to rue;
When their troth is plighted and the promise
  give,
In wedlock bands you should let them live.

1.4: ... was 'heart's ... [Dt]
6.4: ... she's away ... [Dt]
8.1: ... Holland kerchief ... [Dt]
 .4: ... colder than ... [Dt]
9.2: ... love, for the hour is late, [Dt]
10.3: ... father, you sent ... [Dt]
12.3: Although her lover was nine ... [Dt]
 .4: Sure, her ... [Dt]
13.4: In wedlock's ... [Dt]

C23 / Cruel was my father

Sweet William [H587: 2 Mar 1935; Laws M35]

o: "Lovely Willie"; k: "Lament for Willie." Other titles: "The Father in Ambush," "Lovely Jimmie(y) (Willie)."

Source: native (Prolusk, near Straid) at Bushmills.

Key C.

One fine summer's evening at the playing of ball,
My love passed by me, she was proper and tall,
I knew by her looks and her dark rolling eye
That I was the young man she styl-ed so high.

I stepp-ed up to her and unto her did say,
'My pretty fair maid, do you go far this way?'
'Come along with me a piece down the road,
I will show you my dwelling and place of abode.'

'There's a tree in my father's garden, lovely
  Willie,' said she,
'Where young men and maidens do all wait on me,
And when they are sleeping and at their silent
  rest,
I'll wait on you, Willie, you're the lad I love
  best.'

Her father being listening to all that did pass,
And with a sharp reaper he pierced Willie's
  breast.
'O father, cruel father, if that be's your will,
The blood of my innocent lover don't spill.'

A grave being made ready and Willie left in,
This far maid walked around it from morning till
  noon,
Crying, 'This is the place where my Willie does
  lie,
God's blessing be on him, he's my darling boy.

'I will go away to some strange counteree
Where I will know no one, nor no one know me,
And if ever I return, as I know not the time,
I will plant my love's grave with sweet roses and
  thyme.

'O, I'll go away to some strange count-er-ee,
Where I will know no one, nor no one know me,
And if e'er I return, I know not the time,
I'll plant my love's grave with sweet william and
  thyme.'

Sam Henry's Songs of the People

Young Edward Bold / The Lowlands Low

[H113: 9 Jan 1926; Laws M34]

k: "Young Edwin." Other titles: "Come All Young Men and Maidens," "Lowlands (So) Low," "My Father Keeps a Public House," "Ploughman Boy," "Young Edmund (Edmondale) (Edward) (Emsley) (Was a Sailor Boy)," "Young Amy (Emma) (Emily) (Emly)," "(Young) Edwin (Edmund) (Edward) in (of) the Lowlands (Low)"; cf. "The Ploughboy of the Lowlands."

Source: (m) coll. Maud Houston from Charles Dempsey, [Dt: rural] postman [Dt: Coleraine]; (w) Mrs Scally (Town Head, Ballycastle), learned c. 1865, via John Henry Macauley (Bog Oak Shop, Ballycastle).

s: ... Where the verse has six lines repeat the music of lines 3 and 4. It is not an unusual feature for these old songs to vary in the length of the verses.

Key C.

Young Emily was a servant maid, her love a sailor bold,
He ploughed the main, much gold to gain for Emily, as we're told,
When six long years were over, young Edward he came home,
He bade adieu to the main seas, for he no more would roam.
Inquiring for his Emily, he to her the gold did show
Which he had gained upon the main and above the lowlands low.

Her father kept a tavern that stood down by the sea,
Said Emily, 'You may enter in and there this night can stay,
I'll meet you in the morning, don't let my parents know
That your name it is young Edward bold that ploughed the lowlands low.'

Young Edward he sat drinking till time to go to bed,
But little was his thinking such sorrow crowned his head,
Now Edward he had gone to bed and scarce had fell asleep

When Emily's cruel father unto the room did creep.
He stabbed and dragged him out of bed, unto the beach did go,
And he sent his body sinking down into the lowlands low.

As Emily lay sleeping she dreamt a frightful dream,
She dreamed she saw her true love, and blood from him did stream,
She started by the break of day, unto her home did go
Because she loved him dearly that ploughed the lowlands low.

Saying, 'Father, where's the stranger came here last night to lie?'
'It's he is dead, no tales he'll tell,' her father did reply.
'Oh father, cruel father, you'll die a public show
For the murder of young Edward bold that ploughed the lowlands low.'

Said Emily, 'I will wander down by yon stormy wave,
Where my dear love lies under that ploughed the seas so brave.
The fish that's in the ocean swim over my love's breast,
His body lies in motion, I hope his soul's at rest.
Cruel was my father that proved my overthrow,
He took the gold from him so bold who ploughed the lowlands low.'

Now Emily's cruel father neither day nor night could rest;
For the deed that he had done, his guilt he soon confessed.
Now he is cast and sentence passed to die a public show
For the murder of young Edward bold that ploughed the lowlands low.

1.2: ... main, rich gold ... Emily, we are told, [Dt]
3.2: ... was he thinking ... [Dt]

The Constant Farmer's Son

[H806: 6 May 1939; Laws M33]

Other titles: "Bruton Town," "... Contented ...," "In Zepo Town," "The Jealous Brothers," "Late One Evening," "The Merchant's Daughter"; cf. "The Bramble Briar."

Source: (w) 3: May Logan (Drumrammer, Limavady); Frank Kealey (Ballysally, Coleraine); Mary M'Guigan (Newlands Road, Newlands, Glasgow); (m) Frank Kealey.

s: This song is a universal favorite. I received a version some years ago ... but it is only now that I have got the tune.... All of these contributors are thanked for their kindness in the matter.

Key G.

C23 / *Cruel was my father*

There was once a farmer's daughter near Limerick
  town did dwell,
She was modest, tall and handsome and her
  parents loved her well,
Admired by lord and squires, but all their hopes
  were vain,
There was but one, a farmer's son, young Mary's
  heart could gain.

A long time they had courted till at length they
  fixed the day,
Her loving parents gave consent; her brothers
  they did say,
'There is a lord has pledged his word and him you
  must not shun,
For we'll delay and we will slay your constant
  farmer's son.'

The fair being held all in the town, her brothers
  went straightway
And asked young William's company with them to
  spend the day;
The day was gone and night came on, her lover's
  race was run,
For with a stick the life they took of her constant
  farmer's son.

While Mary on her pillow lay, she fell into a dream;
She dreamt she saw her true love dead down by
  yon crystal stream.
The young maid rose, put on her clothes, to seek
  her love did run,
And dead and cold she did behold her constant
  farmer's son.

The tears upon her rosy cheeks were mingled with
  his gore,
And to relieve her broken heart she kissed him
  o'er and o'er,
She gathered green leaves from the tree to shade
  him from the sun,
A night and day she passed away with her
  constant farmer's son.

Hunger came on this poor girl, she wept with grief
  and woe,
To find out the murderers, she straightway home
  did go;
'Oh parents dear, and did you hear the dreadful
  deed was done?
In yonder vale lies cold and pale my constant
  farmer's son.'

Up rose the oldest brother and swore, 'It was not
  me,'
Up rose the youngest brother and swore most
  bitterly,
Young Mary says, 'You need not swear or try the
  law to shun,
Yours was the deed and you must bleed for my
  constant farmer's son.'

These villains then did own their guilt and for the
  same must die,
The doctors got their bodies for to practice by and
  by,
But Mary's thoughts both day and night did on her
  lover run:
In grief she sighed and in sorrow died for her
  constant farmer's son.

The Bonny Labouring Boy

[H576: 15 Dec 1934; Laws M14]

Other titles: "My ..."; cf. "The Railroad Boy."

Source: (w, m) Mrs Brownlow (Hillview, Ballylagan, Cloyfin).

s: Three versions of this song were obtained --
one from Ballylaggan, one from Ballymulderg,
Magherafelt; and a third from Downhill. In one
version Plymouth is the place from which they
took their flight.
  In verses 3 and 4 the additional half verses
are sung to the last two lines of the music.

Key D.

As I roved out one evening, all in the blooming
  spring,
I overheard a fair maid most grievously to sing:
Oh, cruel was my father, who did me sore annoy
And would not let me tarry with my bonny
  labouring boy.

Young Johnny was my true love's name, as you
  may plainly see;
My parents they employed him, their labouring
  boy to be,
To harrow, reap and sow the seed and plough my
  father's land,
But soon I fell in love with him, as you may
  understand.

My father watched us closely down in yon shady
  grove,

435

Where we pledged our vows together in the
   constant bands of love;
My father stepped up to me and seized me by the
   hand,
He swore he'd banish Johnny into some foreign
   land.

He locked me in my bedroom, my comforts to
   annoy,
And he left me there to weep and mourn for my
   bonny labouring boy.
Earl-ie the next morning my mother came to me,
Saying, 'Your father has determined to appoint
   your wedding day.'

Right nobly she made answer, 'To him I'll ne'er
   comply,
For single I will still remain for my bonny
   labouring boy.'
'Oh daughter, dearest daughter, why do you talk
   so strange,
To marry a poor labouring boy the wide world for
   to range?

'Some noble duke might fancy you, great riches to
   enjoy,
So do not throw yourself away upon a labouring
   boy.'
'Oh mother, dearest mother, your talk is all in
   vain,
And for rich lords, dukes or nobles, their
   promise I disdain.

'I would rather live a humble life and all my time
   employ
Increasing nature's prospects with my bonny
   labouring boy.'
Five hundred pounds with all my clothes I took
   that very night,
And with the wee lad I adore to Belfast took my
   flight.

So fill your glasses to the brim, let the toast go
   merrily round,
Here's a health to every labouring boy that
   ploughs and tills the ground,
For when his day's work is over, to his girl he
   steers with joy,
And happy is the girl who gets a bonny labouring
   boy.

Willy Reilly [H234: 5 May 1928; Laws M10]

An Ulster ballad of the early nineteenth century.
Founded on fact.

k: "Loving Reilly"; g: "Riley's (Reilly's) Trial."
Other titles: "Fair Julian Bond," "Liam O' Raghal-
laigh," "Reily's Jailed," "(William) Riley and
Colinband," "(Trial of) Willy Reil(l)y," "Will(ie)
(O')Riley," "William (Willy) ... (and His Dear
Colleen Bawn)."

Source: (w) (orig. Drumsurn district); (m) coll.
Maud Houston.

s: This ballad is well known, but is here published for the first time to this air.... This song
must have made a deep impression, as all the
versions are word perfect....

o: Early 19th century ballad based on historical
fact. The unusual tune given here is very good.

Key G.

'O rise up, Willy Reilly, and come along with me,
I mean for to go with you and leave this
   counterie,
To leave my father's dwelling, his houses and
   free land,
And away goes Willy Reilly and his dear Cooleen
   Bawn.

They go by hills and mountains and by yon
   lonesome plain,
Through shady groves and valleys, all dangers
   to refrain,
But her father followed after with a well-armed
   band,
And taken was poor Reilly and his dear Cooleen
   Bawn.

It's home then she was taken and in her closet
   bound,
Poor Reilly all in Sligo jail lay on the stony
   ground,
Till at the bar of justice before the judge he'd
   stand
For nothing but the stealing of his dear Cooleen
   Bawn.

'Now in the cold, cold iron my hands and feet are
   bound,
I'm handcuffed like a murderer and tied unto the
   ground,
But all the toil and slavery I'm willing for to
   stand,
Still hoping to be succoured by my dear Cooleen
   Bawn.'

The jailor's son to Reilly goes and thus to him
   did say,
'O, get up, Willy Reilly, you must appear this
   day,
For great Squire Foillard's anger you never can
   withstand,
I'm afear'd you'll suffer sorely for your dear
   Cooleen Bawn.

'This is the news, young Reilly, last night that I
   did hear,
The lady's oath will hang you, or else will set
   you clear.'
'If that be so,' says Reilly, 'her pleasure I will
   stand,
Still hoping to be succoured by my dear Cooleen
   Bawn.'

Now Willy's drest from top to toe all in a suit of
   green,
His hair hangs o'er his shoulders, most glorious
   to be seen,
He's tall and straight and comely as any could be
   found,
He's fit for Foillard's daughter, was she heiress
   to a crown.

The judge he said, 'This lady being in her tender
   youth,
If Reilly has deluded her, she will declare the
   truth.'
Then like a moving beauty bright, before him she
   did stand,
'You're welcome there, my heart's delight and
   dear Cooleen Bawn.'

'O gentlemen,' Squire Foillard said, 'with pity
   look on me,
This villain came amongst us to disgrace our
   family,
And by his base contrivances this villainy was
   planned,
If I don't get satisfaction I'll quit this Irish
   land.'

The lady with a tear began, and thus replied
   she,
'The fault is none of Reilly's, the blame lies all
   on me,
I forced him for to leave his place and come along
   with me,
I loved him out of measure, which wrought our
   destiny.'

Out bespoke the noble Fox, at the table he stood
   by,
'O gentlemen, consider on this extremity:
To hang a man for love is murder, you may see,
So spare the life of Reilly, let him leave this
   counterie.'

'Good my lord, he stole from her her diamonds
   and her rings,
Gold watch and silver buckles and many precious
   things,
Which cost me in bright guineas more than five
   hundred pounds;
I'll have the life of Reilly, should I lose ten
   thousand pounds.'

'Good my lord, I gave them as tokens of true
   love,
And when we are a-parting, I will them all
   remove,
If you have got them, Reilly, pray send them
   home to me.'

'I will, my loving lady, with many thanks to
   thee.'

'There is a ring among them I allow yourself to
   wear,
With thirty locket diamonds well set in silver
   fair,
And as a true love token, wear it on your right
   hand,
That you'll think on my poor broken heart when
   you're in foreign lands.'

Then out spoke noble Fox, 'You may let the
   prisoner go,
The lady's oath has cleared him, as the jury all
   may know,
She has released her own true love, she has
   renewed his name,
May her honour bright gain high estate and her
   offspring rise to fame.'

1.1: ... Willie Reilly ... [Dt]
 .4 [and throughout]: ... Colleen Bawn. [Dt]
14.4: ... poor heart ... [Dt]

Young Mary of Accland (a)

[H30b: BLp, 7 Jun 1924; Laws M16]

No source given.

s: This old song may be sung to the air "Lovely
Armoy" [H9] ... or to ... "Lovely Glenshesk"
[H28].

[No sol-fa notation. Print from British Library
microfilm files of *Northern Constitution*
courtesy of John Moulden.]

Come all ye young lovers, draw nigh me, the
   truth unto you I'll unfold:
I was loved by a lady of honour much better than
   silver or gold;
When Venus discovered her beauty, false Cupid
   he did me annoy,
So now for the squire's young daughter in the
   cold chains of prison I lie.

When her father saw that she did love me,
   concealed close in ambush he lay,
Convenient to me and my darling to hear the soft
   words we would say;
A gold ring she slipped on my finger, saying,
   'Jamie, keep me in your mind,
And if ever you roam from this island, I hope
   you'll not leave me behind.'

We kissed and shook hands and then parted, we
   promised to meet there next noon,
But hard was the heart of her father, he bound
   my love close in a room;
A guard of police he commanded and swore to her
   ring on my hand,
And for the squire's young daughter I fear a
   hard trial I'll stand.

But Mary was constant and loyal and straight to
   my trial did come,

Sam Henry's Songs of the People

My parents being weeping and forlorn, she says,
  'I'll protect your dear son.'
She was dressed like a lady of honour, the best
  of silk robes she did wear,
And at her the judge looked surprised, and all
  the grand jury did stare.

She proudly saluted those nobles, and this to the
  judge she did say:
'In case that you loved a young damsel, why
  should you be banished away?
For seven long years we have courted, I own that
  I gave him my heart,
And nothing but death can relieve me if my
  Jamie and I have to part.'

And now to conclude and to finish, and thanks to
  the powers above,
Likewise to young Mary of Accland, she wore the
  true armour of love;
Her father he thought to transport me away from
  my own countrie,
But Mary, you freed me from bondage and set me
  at sweet liberty.

Young Mary of Accland (b)

[H721: 18 Sep 1937; Laws M16]

s: (m) "beautiful variant" of "Lovely Armoy"; k: "Mary Acklin," "The Squire's Young Daughter." Other titles: "Mary Riley," "Sweet Mary Ackland."

Source: Valentine Crawford (Commercial Hotel, Bushmills).

Key C.

You tender young lovers, draw near me,
The truth unto you I'll unfold:
I was loved by a lady of honour,
Much better than silver or gold;
When Venus discovered her beauty,
False Cupid he did me annoy,
So now for the squire's young daughter
In the cold chains of prison I lie.

One evening to pass my vacation
In viewing the flowers so rare,
I roved for a while's recreation,
Not thinking I would meet her there;
Her parents they knew that she loved me,
In silence in ambush they lay
Convenient to me and my darling
For to hear the soft words we would say.

A gold ring she slipped on my finger,
Saying, 'Jamie, bear me in your mind,
And if ever you roam from this island,
I hope you won't leave me behind.'
We kissed and shook hands and then parted,
We promised to meet there next noon,
But hard was the heart of her father,
He bound my love close in a room.

A guard of police he commanded
And swore to her ring on my hand,
And for young Mary of Accland
I fear a hard trial I'll stand.
She dressed like a lady of honour,
And the best of silk robes she did wear,
And at her the judge looked surpris-ed,
And all the grand jury did stare.

She proudly saluted those nobles,
And this to the judge she did say,
'In case that he loved a young damsel,
Why should he be banished away?
For seven long years we have courted,
I own that I gave him my heart,
And nothing but death can relieve me
If my Jamie and I have to part.'

And now to conclude and to finish,
And thanks to the powers above,
Likewise to young Mary of Accland,
She wore the true armour of love.
Her father he thought to transport me
Away from my own countrie,
But Mary proved constant and loyal
And set me at sweet liberty.

Erin's Lovely Home

[H46: 27 Sep 1924; Laws M6]

Other titles: "Aran's Lonely ...," "Old Erin's Lovely Vale," "(Seven Links on My Chain)."

Source: (Stranocum district).

s: This well-known song was sent to me.... It is interesting to note that a version has been collected by Cecil Sharp at Bishop's Nympton, N. Devon.

l: Another ballad with the same title appears in Shields 1981:76 (also rec. Mary Ellen Butcher, EEOT *Shamrock* 2); it describes another hazard to emigrants en route: disease.

Key G.

All you young men I pray draw near that have your liberty,
A sad and dismal story I mean to let you know,
While in a foreign country I now must sigh and moan
When I think on the days I spent round Erin's lovely home.

When I was young and in my prime, my age was twenty-one,
I then became a servant to a noble gentleman,
I served him too, in honesty and very well, it's known,
Till cruel fate has banished me from Erin's lovely home.

The reason that he banished me I mean to let you know,
It's true I loved his daughter and she loved me also,
She had a princely fortune; of riches I had none,
So that is why he banished me from Erin's lovely home.

'Twas in her father's garden all in the month of June,
When everything was silent and nature in full bloom,
She said, 'My dearest Willie, if along with me you'll roam,
You need not fret for those you left round Erin's lovely home.'

That very day I gave consent that proved my overthrow,
And far from her father's dwelling along with her did go;
The night was bright with the moonlight as we set out alone,
We thought we had got safe away from Erin's lovely home.

When we arrived in Belfast all by the break of day,
She said, 'Prepare, my jewel, our passage for to pay.'
Five hundred pounds she counted down, saying, 'That will be your own,
So never fret for those you left round Erin's lovely home.'

Now to my great misfortune, I mean to let you hear,
It was in three days after, He brought me back to Omagh of Tyrone,
From that I was transported from home.

When I received my sentence, it grieved my full sore,
The parting from my own true love, it grieved me ten times more.
There are seven links upon my chain and every link a year,
Before I can return again to the arms of my dear.

When the coach came to the jail yard to take us all away,
My true love she came to me and thus to me did say,
'Cheer up, my dearest Willie, for you I'll not disown,
Until you do return again to Erin's lovely home.'

1.2: ... let you see, [Dt]
3.3: ... fortune, and of ... [Dt]
6.2: ... jewel, my passage ... [Dt]
7.4: And from that ... [Dt]

Sweet Dunloy [H577: 22 Dec 1934]

Source: (w, m) John Elliott (Turfahun), learned from Mrs Henry Scally (Cairney Hill, Dervock; nee Ellen M'Camphill, Dunloy) c. 1895.

Key F.

On the twelfth day of November last, I hope you'll bear in mind,
My love and I, we did agree to leave our friends behind.
We bid farewell to Galdanagh, likewise to sweet Dunloy,
We were bound for bonny Scotland, our fortune for to try.

To Londonderry we set out without the least delay,
A vessel bound for Glasgow town, she at the harbour lay,
Our passage paid, we stepped on board to leave the Irish soil,
The moon shone bright, she gave us light as we sailed down Lough Foyle.

The captain on the deck did stand, the ocean for to view,

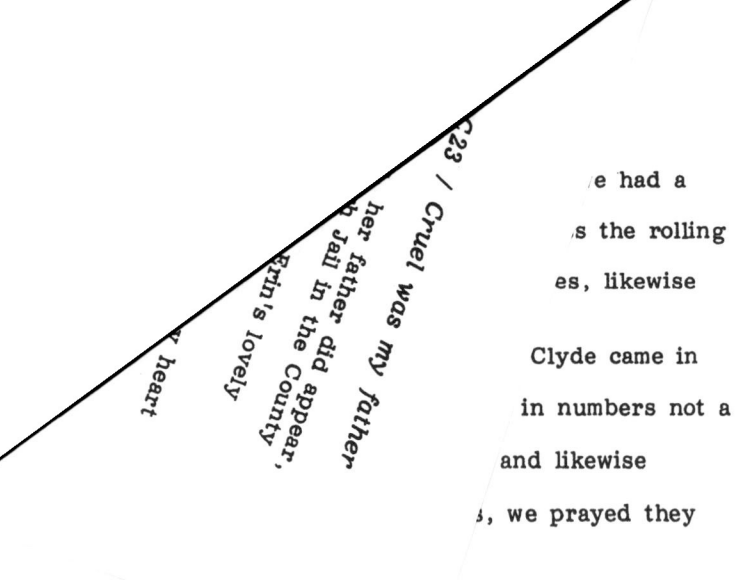

The [...] reach when we thought [...]
And vowed we'd [...] llock's bands when on the Scottish shore,
But her father followed after us, it grieves me here to tell,
And he swore an oath that got us both placed in a prison cell.

Then back again he did us bring, as you shall quickly hear,
And vowed I would transported be for enloping with his dear;
Two bailsmen then I had to find, the sum being forty pounds,
To stand the next assizes to be held in Omagh town.

July the sixth the law came on; young Lizzie proved my friend,
She says, 'I did enlope with him, on this you may depend,
I left my home and country and with him I did go,
And forever I'll prove constant to my own young darling Joe.'

Her father from the witness box at me he cast a frown,
He says, 'The young man's guilty, his name is Joseph Brown.'
When the jury heard the evidence, it did not favour me,
For the judge says, 'Brown, you're guilty, and imprisoned you must be.'

It's when I heard my sentence, it grieved my heart full sore,
Twelve months to lie in Belfast jail my fate for to deplore,
Still thinking of my own true love, young Lizzie is her name,
But when I get my liberty I will enlope again.

Now to conclude and finish, I mean to drop my pen,
These lines to all young lovers I'm determined for to send;
I am at the law's defiance, but once I do get free,
We'll sail to Philadelphy, the land of liberty.

440   6.2: enloping = eloping.

Henry Connor of Castledawson

[H128: 24 Apr 1926; Laws M5]

Other title: "... Connors."

Source: (w) 3+: John M. O'Keenan (Tulnaveagh, Leitrim Nursery, Castledawson), James Murphy (Creagh, Toomebridge), William Moran (Bellarena), and others; (m) (Drumavalley, Bellarena).

s: The episode commemorated in the ballad occurred about 100 years ago....

Key A.

My name's Henry Connor from sweet Castledawson,
That neat village I'll ne'er set my eyes on again,
Transported for life in the bloom of my vigour,
Which leaves my old parents to blush for my shame.

Oh, had they but known the hard lot was before me,
They could wish in their hearts that I ne'er had been born,
To the grave I have brought their grey hairs down with sorrow,
To think their one son from their arms would be torn.

But what is the crime that they're imputing to me --
Was it for murder or base perjury at the bar,
Or shedding the blood of my own fellow creature,
That this hard-hearted judge gives me this sentence for?

Oh, no, 'twas the father of her I loved dearly,
A robbery he swore 'gainst his daughter and me,
For fear a poor servant would gain such a treasure,
I being poor and mean and below her degree.

He tried many plans to tempt and betray me
By leaving his money without lock or key,
And to hasten my ruin he brought to my chamber
His gold and his bank notes in secret convey.

The keys of his drawer he put under his pillow,
And a note well marked in my purse did conceal,
And as that very night we were bound for eloping,
The house was surrounded and I sent to jail.

Still finding me honest through every temptation,
And knowing his daughter would die for my sake,
He hired a spy to watch our correspondence,
He studied this plan, on us vengeance to take.

This false, deluding woman, she brought us together
While poor Mary's father lay listening hard by,
She made us consent to get married in secret
And sail o'er to Scotland, our fortune to try.

But what was the use of my protestations
When none was nearby, my innocence to prove?
And though a harsh sentence 'gainst me was recorded,
The one, only crime I committed was love.

Hard is my lot, yet it will be more happy
To drag my chains after thro' heat and thro' cold
Than to die with a dark load of guilt on his conscience,
By base persecution my liberty sold.

Better fate had consigned me to death on my pillow
Or to yield up my life on the high gallows tree
Than to wear cruel fetters like a beast that is burthen'd
Till kind death shall come to set poor Connor free.

The sentence was passed and no room for exception,
The sentence which I also now must abide:
To be leaving old Ireland and my kind relations
And to cross o'er the ocean so stormy and wide.

Now the order has come and I'm bound for Kingston,
It's an order that I can not help but obey,
And when I'll be leaving the jail in the morning,
Few friends will be waiting to see me away.

Adieu to you, Mary, for you've been my ruin,
We might have lived happy had you been my wife,
But your father has put the wide ocean between us,
And sent your Connor a convict for life.

3.1: ... imputing me -- [Dt]
4.4: ... mean below ... [Dt]
11.3: ... to cruel ... [Dt]
12.2: ... which also ... [Dt]

Sally Munro [H571: 10 Nov 1934; Laws K11]

Other titles: "(Young) ... Munro(e)."

Source: (m, w) John Elliott (Turfahun, near Bushmills).

s: ... The extra lines in verse four are to be sung to the last two lines of the air. This is a common feature of Ulster folk song.

Key C.

My name it is James Dickson, a blacksmith to trade,
I'm from the County Antrim along the banks of Braid;
Away unto Belfast a-roving I did go,
Where I fell in love with young Sally Munro.

I wrote my love a letter and to her it did send,
I sent it by a com-er-ade I took to be a friend,
Instead of being a friend, he turn-ed out a foe,
And he never gave my letter to young Sally Munro.

But went unto her mother and told lies upon me,
That I had a wife in my ane counteree.
Her mother she replied, 'Then, if that be so,
He will never enjoy his young Sally Munro.'

Till one day as I was walking, it's down by Sandy Row,
It was there I fell in with young Sally Munro,
Saying, 'Here is my hand, love, and here is my heart,
Till death separate us, we never more shall part.'
She says, 'I've no objections along with you to go,'
And that day I set sail with young Sally Munro.

We were not long set sail till our good ship lay a-log
In the middle of the ocean surrounded by fog,
There were six hundred passengers all smothered down below,
And amongst all the rest went young Sally Munro.

It was from her aged parents I stole my love away,
Which will always check my conscience until my dying day;
It was not for to harm her I asked her for to go,
And I sigh when I think on young Sally Munro.

John Reilly the Sailor Lad

[H468: 19 Nov 1932; Laws M8]

o: (m) "With Kitty I'll Go for a Ramble"; k: (m) "Willy Reilly." Other titles: "As I Roved out One Morning," "Billy (John)(ny) (Will)(ie) (O')Reilly (Rally) (Riley) (Rylie)," "One Evening Fair," "Riley's Farewell," "Riley (Sent) to America," "(Young) (O')Reilly (Riley) (the Fisherman)."

Source: (Gortcorbries, Limavady), (Moneycannon, Ballymoney).

o: Time 6/8.

Key F. Rather slow.

Sam Henry's Songs of the People

As I roved out one evening down by a riverside,
I heard a lovely maid complain as the tears fell from her eyes;
'This is a dark and stormy night,' she unto me did say,
'For my love to sail the raging sea bound for America.'

'My love he is a sailor lad, his age is scarce sixteen,
He is as fine a young man as ever yet was seen;
My father he has riches great, but Reilly he is poor;
Because I love my sailor lad, he cannot him endure.

'Then up stepped my mother and caught me by the hand,
Saying, "If you love John Reilly, you must quit your native land."
Saying, "If you love John Reilly, though handsome he may be,
You cannot be his wedded wife, so shun his company."'

'Oh, mother dear, don't be severe, where can I send my love?
My very heart lies on his breast as constant as a dove.'
'Oh, daughter dear, I'm not severe, here is a thousand pounds,
Send Reilly to America to purchase you some grounds.'

When she had got the money, quick to Reilly she did run,
'My father swears he'll have your life, last night he charged his gun,
Here is a thousand pounds in gold my mother sent to you,
So be off now to America and I will follow you.'

Oh, when the money he had got, next day he sailed away,
And as he put his foot on board these words to her did say,
'Here is a token of true love' -- a ring he broke in two --
'You have my heart, you have half my ring till I come back to you.'

It was scarcely three years after as she walked by the sea,
John Reilly had come back again to take his love away,
The ship was wrecked, all hands were lost, a father grieved full sore
To see John Reilly in her arms lie drown-ed on the shore.

They got a letter in her breast and it was wrote with blood,
Saying, 'Cruel was my father, who tried to shoot my love.'
Then let this be a warning to all fair maids, I pray,
For to never let the lad they love sail to America.

Kellswater [H695: 20 Mar 1937]

[cf. H112 "A Sweetheart's Appeal to Her Lover [Oh, It's down Where the Water Runs Muddy]"]

o: (m) "The Lover's Curse." Other titles: "(Lovely) Jimmie(y) (and I Will Get Married)," "Bonnie ...."

Source: (m, w) J. Carmichael (Waring St, Ballymena).

Key E flat.

Here's a health unto bonnie Kellswater,
Where you get all the pleasures of life,
Where you get all the fishing and fowling
And a bonnie wee lass for your wife,
For it's down where yon waters run muddy,
I'm afraid it will never run clear,
And when I begin for to study,
My mind is on them that's not here.

For it's this one and that one may court him,
But if anyone gets him but me,
It's early and late I will curse them
That stole lovely Willie from me;
For the father he called on his daughter,
'Two choices I'll give unto thee:
Would you rather see Willie's ship sailing,
As be shot like a dog at yon tree?'

'Oh father, dear father, I love him,
I can hide it no longer from thee;
Thro' an acre of fire I'd travel
Along with my Willie to be.'
It was hard was the heart that confined her
And took her from her heart's delight;

May the chains of old Ireland bind round them,
And soft be their pillows at night.

Oh, yonder's a ship on the ocean
And she does not know what way to steer,
From the east to the west she's a-blowing,
It reminds me on the charms of my dear.
It's yonder my Willie he's coming,
He said he'd be here in the spring,
And down by yon green shades I'll meet him
And amongst the wild roses we'll sing.

He placed a gold ring on her finger,
Saying, 'Love, bear this in your mind,
If ever I sail from old Ireland,
I'll mind not to leave you behind.'
Here's a health unto ye, bonnie Kellswater,
Where you get all the pleasures of life,
Where you get all the fishing and fowling
And a bonnie wee lass for your wife.

The Banks of the Bann

[H86: 4 Jul 1925; Laws O2]

[see H673 "The Maid of Aghadowey"]
[not = H614 "Willie Archer"]

Other titles: "... Band," "The (Bonny) Brown Girl," "Lovely Bann Water," "The Maid of Aghadowey."

Source not given.

[Bp] s: There are four songs called by this title, and all with different airs. This one is the most select.

Key C.

When first to this counteree a stranger I came,
I placed my affection on a maid that was young;
She being young and tender, her waist small and slender,
Kind nature had formed her for my overthrow.

On the banks of the Bann when first I beheld her,
She appeared like fair Juno of the Gratian queen,
Her eyes shone like diamonds or stars brightly shining,
Her cheeks bloomed like roses or blood drops on snow.

'Twas her cruel parents that first caused our variance,
All because she was rich and above my degree,
But I'll do my endeavour to gain my love's favour,
Although she is come of a rich fam-ilee.

'Oh Johnny, dear Johnny, be not melancholy,
For if you prove faithful, sure I will prove true,
For there's no other inferior will e'er gain my favour,
On the banks of the Bann I will ramble with you.'

Had I all the money that's in the East or West Indies,
Or had I all the riches that's in the queen's store,
I would spend it on pearls on you, my brown girl,
For there's no other charmer on this earth I adore.

Now since I have gained her I'm contented for ever,
I'll put rings on her fingers and gold in her ears,
We will live on the banks of the lovely Bann river
And in all sort of splendour I will style her my dear.

4.3: ... other lover will ... [Dt]
5.1: ... money in the ... [Dt]

Johnnie Hart

[H106: 21 Nov 1925]

Other titles: "Johnny Harte."

Source: (w) Mrs Tom Carmichael (Polintamney, Ballymoney); (m) daughter and granddaughter of Margaret Morrow, 86 (Park, Priestland).

s: The words of this song of the unlettered muse were supplied by Mrs Tom Carmichael.... The air was taken down ... from the daughter and granddaughter of Margaret Morrow ... whose memory is a treasure house of old songs.
  Note that the second verse has six lines. The music for lines 3 and 4 is repeated for lines 5 and 6. (The words "lives on the Slaney side" are spoken, not sung.)

Key G.

It's of a farmer's daughter lived near the town of Ross,
She's courting a private soldier, his name is Johnny Hart,

Sam Henry's Songs of the People

And for six long months they courted, and her
    parents they knew not,
Yet he was her darling soldier, dressed in his
    Highland plaid.

Says the mother to the daughter, 'I shall go
    distracted mad
If you marry a private soldier dressed in his
    Highland plaid.'
'Oh mother dear, do not despise my love, nor
    run him down,
Sure, many's the farmer's son,' she says,
    'belongs unto the crown,
And many's the farmer's daughter, too, perhaps
    has more than I,
When the bugle sounds before them, it fills their
    hearts with joy.'

It was early next morning her mother went to
    Ross
And to the colonel's quarters was gently shown
    across.
'Be quick, my decent woman, to hear you I'm
    inclined,
And if I find your case is fair I'll see you
    justified.'

'I have one only daughter and she is a foolish
    lass,
She is courting a private soldier, his name is
    Johnnie Hart,
And to wed with a private soldier is below my
    child's degree,
And if you run him out of Ross, my blessing I'll
    give thee.'

The bugle sounded for parade, young Hart he
    did appear.
The colonel he stepped up to him all on the
    barrack square,
'If you court this woman's daughter, that I may
    find it out,
I'll send you on detachment till the regiment
    gets the rout.'

'It's hard enough,' young Hart did say, 'for
    courting an Irish lass
To send me on detachment and leave my dear in
    Ross.
But I'll court this woman's daugher, for me she
    is inclined;
I would court your honored daughter, sir, could
    I but gain her mind.'

'That's well done, my gallant soldier, I like your
    courage well,
And you shall be promoted for these words you
    boldly tell.
I'll put top-lace on your shoulders and then
    you'll be the match
For the richest farmer's daughter comes into the
    town of Ross.'

This couple they are got married, the colonel
    gave consent.
Her parents paid her portion, so now they are
    content.
Young Hart's become an officer, the nearest to
    Captain Bright,
And he is joined to the richest farmer lives on
    the Slaney side.

5.2: ... barracks square, [Dt]
6.1: 'Oh, hard ... [Dt]
8.1: ... Captain Blight, [Dt]

Love Laughs at Locksmiths

[H668: 12 Sep 1936; Laws M15]

k: "Daughter in the Dungeon," "The Iron Door."
Other titles: "The Affectionate Lover," "The
Banks of Shannon," "The Cruel Father (and Affectionate Lover(s))," "Mary Ann and Her Servant Man," "Since Love Can Enter an Iron Door,"
"The Two Affectionate Lovers," "The (Young)
(Her) Servant-Man"; cf. "(Down) in the Town
of Marlborough," "The Handsome Young Servant-
man," "Young Ellender."

Source not given.

[Henry prints 13 four-line stanzas; each occu-
pies half the length of the tune.]

Key D.

It's of a damsel both neat and handsome,
These lines are true that I'm going to tell,
In the Isle of Arran there's a lofty mountain
Where this noble princess was known to dwell.
Her hair was black as the raven's feather,
Her form and features describe who can,
But as love's folly belongs to nature,
She fell in love with a servant man.

One day as Edward and his love were walking,
Her old father he did draw nigh
To hear two lovers in conversation;
It was in great anger he then did fly.
To build a dungeon was his intention,
To part true lovers he fixed a plan,
He swore an oath, too wild to mention,
He'd part his daughter and the servant man.

With bricks and mortar he built a dungeon,
Three flights of stairs down inunder ground,
And bread and water was her whole feeding,
The only comfort for her was found.
Three times a day he severely beat her,
Till at last one day this maid gave in,

Saying, 'Father, dear father, since I've
  transgress-ed,
I'm willing to die for my servant man.'

When Edward found out her habitation,
It was with great anger an oath he swore,
He swore in spite of that whole nation,
He would have her releasement, or be no more,
And at the ground stone het ready,
A pick and crowbar he did ge[t], then began,
And at his leisure he toiled with pleasure,
She cries, 'My faithful young servant man.'

A suit of clothing he did get ready
And her old clothing he did put on,
'Indeed,' says Edward, 'I'll surprise your father
When to this dungeon he does come in.
Her father came with bread and water,
He loudly called on Mary Ann;
'Indeed,' says Edward, 'I have freed your
  daughter
Out of this dungeon. Do all you can.'

When the old man saw he had freed his daughter,
With great anger an oath he swore,
Saying, 'It's out of Scotland I'll have you
  banished,
Or with my broadsword I'll spill you gore.'
Young Edward, he being young and active,
Caused him to fall on the dungeon floor,
And he says, 'True love, aye, laughs at
  locksmiths,
Since love has broken through an iron door.'

So now this couple they've got married
And they are joined both heart and hand;
Young Mary Ann she lives quite happy
With faithful Edward her servant man.

4.5: het = ?[typographical error].

The Lady Leroy [H214: 17 Dec 1927; Laws N5]

Other titles: "Brave Annie and Her Young Sailor
Boy," "The *Lady LeRoy* (*Uri*)," "The Sailor Boy,"
"Sally and Her Lover."

Source: Willie Hegarty, 74 (Agivey), learned in
youth from James Catherwood (Carclinty, Cullybackey); also William Hugh Graham (Culnady,
Upperlands), learned from his mother, 75, from
her mother; [Bp] and (Ballaghbeddy, Ballymoney).

s: ... The song has been printed in U.S.A. without music, and a song with the same plot, but
different as to air and words, has been published
by Cecil Sharp, the well-known English folklorist.

Key A.

As I went walking one evening in June
To view the green fields and meadows in bloom,
I spied a lovely couple on Erin's green shore,
They were viewing the ocean where the loud
  billows roar.

'O Sally, lovely Sally, you're the maid I adore,
To be parted from you, it would grieve my heart
  sore,
But your parents are rich, love, and angry with
  me,
And for me to enforce you my ruin might be.'

Sally dressed herself up in a suit of men's clothes
And down to her father she instantly goes,
She purchased a vessel, paying down his demand,
But little he knew 'twas from his own daughter's
  hand.

She wrote her love a letter and this she did say,
'Be quick and make ready, there's no time to
  delay.'
They hoisted their topsails with signs of great
  joy,
And over the ocean sailed the *Lady Leroy*.

When Sally's old father came this for to know,
Like a man in distraction to a captain he did go,
He bid him go find them and her lover destroy,
For he ne'er will enjoy the fair *Lady Leroy*.

With bold indiscretion this sea captain did go,
And quickly made ready like some daring foe,
He spied a large vessel with her colours let fly,
And he hailed her and found her, the *Lady
  Leroy*.

'Return, you young couple, to Erin's green
  shore,
Or a broadside of grapeshot on your lives I will
  pour.'
But Sally's true lover he made this reply,
'I'll never surrender, I'll conquer or die.'

Then broadside to broadside they on other did
  pour,
Far louder than thunder their cannons did roar,
But Sally's true lover gained the victorie,
And he sunk the proud captain in the dark raging
  sea.

We landed in Boston, that city of fame,
With a bold chief commander, I'll not mention his
  name;
Drink a health to lovely Sally and the *Lady Leroy*,
She's the source of all comfort and my only joy.

Write home to your father and this let him know:
That I would not be conquered by friend or by
  foe,

Sam Henry's Songs of the People

We wish him good fortune, long life to enjoy,
But he lost all his prospects on the *Lady Leroy*.

1.1: ... went a-walking ... [Dt]
8.1: ... broadside on broadside they on other pour, [Dt]

Eliza / When I Landed in Glasgow

[H58: 20 Dec 1924]

A song of Cupid and a conscript.

g: "The Inconstant Lover," "Lovely Willie."
Other title: "The Young Maid's Love."

Source: (w, m) native (Ardverness, Macosquin), from her father c. 1850.

s: ... The reference to the Spanish ships would seem to point to the last half of the 16th century as the date of the song [Bp:], and probably to an engagement in British waters with the Spanish armada.

[typed on Bp] Corrections by Tom Black, of Croaghan, Macosquin --4/1/26

Key E flat.

Farewell Ballymena, farewell darling swain,
And to all purty fair maids that walk by the Main,
For I'm with my darling, most rare to be seen,
She exceeds all the fair maids that walk Glasgow Green.

Her father was a rich merchant of fame and renown,
He possessed five hundred acres of land near the town,
And I a poor weaver of a low degree,
I courted his daughter and she loved me.

When that her father he came for to know
That any poor weaver loved his daughter so,
He took me a prisoner and sent me to jail,
Confined in strong irons, no man to find bail.

Then I got a letter for to go afar,
For to go a sailor on a man-of-war,
For to go a sailor to plough the rough main;
Fare ye well, dear Eliza, will we ne'er meet again?

For six weeks and better we had a calm sea,
Till a man from the topmast aloud he did say,
'Ye sons of Britannia, your valours ne'er fail,
Twenty-two sail of Spaniards appear in the gale.'

We gave them a broadside, we made them to yield,
We gave them another and soon gained the field,
We brought them from Britain to East Port's fair shore,
And each man's divide was five hundred pounds and more.

Then off to old Scotland I straight took my way,
Where I landed in Glasgow one fine summer's day,
Where I landed in Glasgow in the afternoon,
Where I met dear Eliza a mile out of town.

I stepp-ed up to her, I made myself known,
She wondered to see me, how rich I was grown,
I says, 'Dear Eliza, a weaver ne'er fear,
Good luck will attend us, it does now appear.'

Then off to her father I instantly went
For to ask Eliza, likewise his consent.
'You shall have Eliza and my blessing also,
Five hundred pounds portion on her I'll bestow.'

Now to conclude and to finish my song,
I mean to be married and that before long,
For I have a spirit above my degree,
I would scorn to love anyone who would not love me.

[*Written on Wt, typed on Bp:*] corrections by Tom Black, of Croaghan, Macosquin, 4/1/26
[*Typed on Bp, Dt, Wt*] Verse 2 added from Tom Black, Croaghan.
2.1 [*Written on Bp, Wt with caret*]: back
[*Originally written as corrections on Bp and Wt, and typed as the original on Dt:*]
 5.2: ... topmast a strange sail did see,
 .4: Twenty-six sail ...
 .3 [*Written correction on all 3*]: ... to Portsmouth's fair shore,
[Not on Dt:]
 7.1: I being dressed like a gentleman airy and free,
 .2: Then off to old Scotland I straight took my way,
2.3: ... Glasgow one fine afternoon, [Dt]
8.1: ... her and made ... [Dt]

The Apprentice Boy / Covent Garden

[H729: 13 Nov 1937; Laws M12]

k: "The Lady and the Apprentice Boy." Other titles: "Covent's Garden," "Down in Cupid's Garden," "The Prentice ...."

Source: Charles M'Ilreavy (Circular Rd, Coleraine) from his grandmother, Ruth M'Ilreavy (Loughan Hill, Coleraine) c. 1897.

Key D.

C23 / Cruel was my father

It was down by Covent Garden as I one day did walk,
I heard two loyal lovers that lovingly did talk:
One was an honoured lady, the other an apprentice boy,
And privately they courted and he was all her joy.

He says, 'Right honoured lady, I'm but an apprentice boy,
And how could a poor apprentice think a lady to enjoy?'
Her cheeks did blush like roses, her humour was kind and free,
She says, 'If ever I marry, I'll surely marry thee.'

It's when her aged parents, they came to understand,
They banished this apprentice to a far-off foreign land,
While she lay broken-hearted, lamenting she did cry,
'For my bonny, handsome 'prentice boy, a maid I'll live and die.'

This young man being an apprentice, to a merchantman was bound,
And by his good behaviour, great favour there he found,
He soon became a bo'sun, promoted to great fame,
And by his good behaviour, a mate he then became.

This young man in a lottery his fortune he put down,
And when he drew his ticket, he had thirty thousand pound;
He had gold and silver plenty, his clothes were laced indeed,
And he returned to England to see his love with speed.

He offered her kind embraces, she still flew from his arms,
'Neither lord nor duke nor noble knight shall e'er enjoy my charms;
I hate the gold that glittereth and riches I despise;
For my handsome young apprentice boy, a maid I'll live and die.'

He said, 'Right honoured lady, I have been in your arms,
For here's the ring you gave me for kissing of your charms;
You told me if ever you'd marry, my love you would enjoy;
Your father did me banish, and I'm your apprentice boy.'

When she beheld his features, she fell into his arms,
Saying, 'Lord nor duke nor noble knight shall e'er enjoy my charms.'
It's down through Covent Garden a road to church they found,
And now they're joined in happiness -- together they are bound.

◇ *C23 REFERENCES* ◇

◇ **The Maid of Ballyhaunis** *(H483)* 427

IREL O Lochlainn 1965:90-1

BRS *A Broadside* 7(9, Feb)1915
 Emerald Isle 1904:9-10
 O'Conor 1901:157
 617 [190-?]:37

◇ **The Banks of** [*Wt:* the] **Cloughwater** *(H777)* 427

m: REC Cf. Jeannie Robertson, Transatlantic XTRA 5041 "The Moon Shined on My Bed Last Night," which contains echoes although thematically different.

◇ **Hibernia's Lovely Jane** *(H467)* 428

Brunnings 1981: "... Jean"

AMER Kenedy 1890:138

BRS Harvard 3: (n.i.)
 Delaney's Scotch 1910:8
 b: *The Shamrock* 1862 "... Jean"
 617 [190-?]:75 "... Jean"
 Wehman's 1887,2:81

MEL Joyce 1909:101 (#205), nearly identical to Henry's.

◇ **If I Were a Blackbird** *(H79)* 429

Brunnings 1981: "If I Was/Were a Blackbird," "The Blackbird," "If I Were a Blackbird (See: The Blackbird)"

h: IREL O Lochlainn 1939:92
 Shields/Shields UF 21,1975: #200 "If I Was ..."

BRIT Collinson/Dillon 1946:24-5
MacColl/Seeger 1977:139-41 "If I Was ... "
 Sharp/Karpeles 1974,1:493-4 (#126) "The Blackbird," 2 vts.

AMER Cazden et al. 1982:155-9 "I Am a Young Maiden"

BRS O'Keeffe 1955(1968):109 "... Was ..."
 Sing an Irish n.d.:2
 Walton's New 2,1968:45
 Walton's 132 n.d.:82, quite a different version.

447

Sam Henry's Songs of the People

REC Blanche Wood, *FSB* 1 (B8) "I'm a Young Bonnie Lassie"
b: Omar Blondahl, ARC 567
  May Bradley, EFDSS LP 1006 (B3) "The Blackbird" ("My Love")
  Delia Murphy, EMI STAL 1055 (A2)

MEL Bunting 1840:72 (#98) "The Blackbird" is an entirely different tune; cf. O'Neill 1903:336 (#1793).

◊ **The Maid of Aghadowey** *(H673) 429*

? White/Dean-Smith 1951: "(The) Brown Girl or Pretty Sally; The Sailor from Dover"
? Dean-Smith 1954: "(The) Brown Girl; The Dover Sailor"
? Cf. Laws 1957:227 (O2)

IREL Moulden 1979:100-1

m: BRS *Derry Journal*:26

m: MEL O Lochlainn 1939:16 "Youghal Harbour"
m: *JIFSS* 8,1910:13 "In Aghadowey," a related tune.

◊ **The Slaney Side** *(H52b) 429*

Laws 1957:194 (M28) "The Tan-Yard Side"
Brunnings 1981: "The Slaney Side," "Down by the Tanyard Side (Tune of Fish and Chips)"

IREL Hughes 2,1915:37-44
b: O Lochlainn 1939:82-3 "Down by the Tanyard Side"

AMER Haskins n.d.:116
  Peacock 1965,2:592-3

BRS UCLA 605: 5(Such) "The Tan-Yard Side"
  A Broadside 6(10,Mar)1914 "The Tan-Yard Side"
  Healy 1977:68 "Down by the Tanyard Side"
  O'Keeffe 1955(1968):84 "Down by the Tanyard Side"
  617 [190-?]:38 "The Tan-Yard Side"
  Songs and Recitations 1,1974:7 "Down by the Tanyard Side"
  Walton's 132 n.d. "Down by the Tanyard Side" (also Wright 1975:349)
  Walton's New 2,1968:77

REC Phoebe Smith, Topic 12T 193 (B2) "The Tanyard ..."

◊ **The Maid of Sweet Gorteen** *(H594) 430*

Brunnings 1981: "... Gurteen"

h: IREL *Ceol* 3(1)1967:19
h: O Lochlainn 1939:44-5 "... Gurteen"
  Shields/Shields *UF* 21,1975: #257 "... Gurteen"

AMER *CFB* 3(5/6)1980:46-7 "... Gurteen," with notes by Edith Fowke.
  Kenedy 1890:64-5
  Manny/Wilson 1968:272-3 "... Gartine"
  Peacock 1965,2:375-6 "... Gartheen"

BRS Harvard 1: 4.42 (Walker), 6.174 (Cadman), 9.34 (Such)
  Derry Journal [c. 1925],1:26
  Healy 1977:53-4
  O'Conor 1901:31
  617 [190-?]:7
  Songs and Recitations 4,1975:31 "... Gurteen"

MEL Hudson ms. 1:339 (also in O'Neill 1922:35)
  Petrie/Stanford 1,1902:47 (#185), 83 (#328, 329) "The Maid of Sweet Gurteen"

◊ **We Met, 'Twas in a Crowd** *(H638) 431*

Brunnings 1981: "... -- 'Twas ...," ?"We Met - From 'Songs of the Boudoir'"

BRS BPL Partridge: 1.241 (Wrigley)
  Harvard 1: 1.107 (Harkness), 2.90 (Walker), 9.68 (Bebbington), 11.59 (Such)
  UCLA 605: 5(n.i.) "We Met"

◊ **Johnny Doyle** *(H137) 431*

White/Dean-Smith 1951
Cf. Child #239 "Lord Saltoun and Auchanachie"
Laws 1957:180-1 (M2)
Brunnings 1981
Cazden et al. *Notes* 1982: #54

IREL Hughes 4,1935:72-5
  O' Néill/MacCathmeoil 1904:42
  Shields *UF* 17,1971:8, 20 "Johney Doyle"; 8,1972:52-4
  Shields 1981:106-7 (#43)
  Shields/Shields *UF* 21,1975: #224

c: BRIT Sharp/Karpeles 1974,1:340-2 (#82), 2 vts.

AMER Cazden et al. 1982:207-9
  Colorado FB 2,1963:9
Randolph/Cohen (1982):80-1
  Warner 1984:209-11 (#81) "Young Johnnie"

BRS BPL Partridge: 2.549 (Wrigley)
  Wehman's 1887,2:107

cl: REC G. W. Blevins, AFS 2764 A1
cl: Mrs G. A. Griffin, AFS 976 A1
cl: Sam Harmon, AFS 2899 A2
  Frank Harte, Topic 12T 218 (A2)
c: Buna Hicks, Folk-Legacy FSA 22 (B3)
cl: Mrs Nathan Hicks, AFS 2855 "Young ..."
cl: Theodosia Bonnett Long, AFS 2967 B
cl: Mrs J. H. Smith, AFS 990 A
  Berzilla Wallin, Folkways FA 2309 (B4) "... Dial"

MEL Hudson ms. ?.436 "I'd Cross the World for You, Johnny Doyle"
h: *JIFSS* 1(2&3)1904:66
h: O'Neill 1903:83 (#476)
c: Petrie/Stanford 1,1902:112 (#443) "I'd Cross the World over with You Johnny Doyle"; h: 2,1952:158 (#629, 630) "I'd Range the World over with You, ..."

◊ **The Lover's Ghost** *(H217) 432*

Child 1882-98(1965),5:58-67 (#272) "The Suffolk Miracle," 1 vt.; 5:302
Coffin/Renwick 1950(1977):142-3, 271-2
Bronson 4,1972:84-91
Brunnings 1981: "The Suffolk Miracle [Child 272]"

IREL Shields/Shields *UF* 21,1975: #186 "His Heart's Delight"

BRIT Dawney 1977:22-3
  Palmer 1980:51-2 "The Holland Handkerchief"

REC Peggy Seeger, *B&R*, Blackthorne ESB 79 (A2) "The Suffolk Miracle"
  Packie Manus Byrne, Topic 12TS 257 (A3) "The Holland Handkerchief"
b: Dean Gitter, Riverside RLP 636 "The Suffolk Miracle"
? cl: J. W. Green, AFS 2294 A3 & B1 "White Holland Handkerchief"
  Tom Lenihan, Topic 12TS 363 (B3) "The Holland Handkerchief"
  Dol Small, AAFS L58 (B1) "There Was an Old and Wealthy Man"

MEL Darley/McCall 1914:14 (#34) "The Holland Handkerchief"

◆ Sweet William *(H587)* 433

Not: the same title in Dean-Smith 1954
Laws 1957:198 (M35) "Lovely Willie"
Brunnings 1981: "Lovely Willie," "Lovely Jimmy";
but not "Sweet William"

IREL Hughes 4,1936:72 [Karpeles]
O Lochlainn 1939:110 Lovely Willie [Laws]
Tunney 1979:138-9 "Lovely Willie"

AMER Grover n.d.:101 "Willie"
Karpeles 1970:210-1 (#66) "The Father in Ambush," a different version which includes a "green grows" stanza, and the hero is "Lovely Jimmy."
Milner/Kaplan 1983:171-2 "Lovely Willie"

REC Dáithí Sproule, Shanachie 29015 (A4) "Lovely Willie"
Paddy Tunney, Green Linnet SIF 1005 (B2) "Lovely Willie"

◆ Young Edward Bold / The Lowlands Low *(H113)* 434

White/Dean-Smith 1951: "... Edwin in the Lowlands Low"'
Dean-Smith 1954: "... Edwin in the Lowlands Low"
Laws 1957:197-8 (M34) "Edwin (Edmund, Edward, etc.) in the Lowlands Low"
Brunnings 1981: "Young Edwin in the Lowlands Low," "Young Emma"
Cazden et al. *Notes* 1982: #49

IREL JIFSS 3(3&4)1905-6:24 "The Lowlands Low (Irish version)" [Sharp/Karpeles]
Morton 1970:53-4 "Young Edwin in the Lowlands Low"
Shields/Shields UF 21,1975: #253 "(The) Lowlands ..."

BRIT Greig/Duncan 2,1983:14-21 (#189) "Young Emma," 13 vts. ("Young Amy (Emly) (Emily)," "Ploughman Boy," "The Lowlands Low")
c: Sharp/Karpeles 1974,1:290-1 (#63) "Edwin in the Lowlands Low," 2 vts.

AMER Cazden et al. 1982:190-1 "The Lowlands ..."
Darling 1983:123-4 "Young Emily" (see Wallin rec.)
Peters 1977:194 "My Father Keeps a Public House" (see Borusky rec.)
Cf. Warner 1984:154-5 (#56) "The Ploughboy of the Lowlands," "a most unusual version."

BRS BPL H.80: (n.i.)
Harvard 1: 7.243 (Catnach), 10.160 (Bebbington)
Harvard 3: (Toy & Marble)
UCLA 605:4 (Such) "Young Edwin in the Lowlands Low"

cl: REC Finley Adams, AFS 2797 B1 "The Lowlands So Low"
cl: Mrs James T. Adams, AFS 2778 B1 "The Lowlands Low"
Peter Bellamy, Topic 12TS 400 (B4) "Edmund in the Lowlands"
cl: Pearl Jacobs Borusky, AFS 4174 A1 "My Father Keeps a Public House"
cl: Warde H. Ford, AFS 4194 A2, A3 "The Lowlands Low"
cl: George Vinton Graham, AFS 3818 B3 "Edwin in the Lowlands Low"; AFS 3377 B1 "The Lowlands Low"
cl: Mrs Haden, AFS 1745 B2, 1746 A1 "Edwin in the Lowlands Low"
George Hanna, Topic 12TS 372 (A5) "Young Edmund in the Lowlands Low"

Lizzie Higgins, Topic 12T 185 (A4) "Young Emsley"
? cl: Joe Hubbard, AFS 2824 B2 "Young Edward Was a Sailor Boy"
cl: Myra E. Hull, AFS 1871 B1 (10")
? cl: Sarah Ison, AFS 2811 B "Young Edward"
Louis Killen, Topic 12T 126 (A1) "Young Edwin in the Lowlands"
cl: Jonathon Moses, AFS 3703 B1 "The Lowlands Low"
Dellie Norton, Rounder 0028 (B2) "Young Emily"
Peggy Seeger, Folk-Lyric FL 114 (A7) "Edwin in the Lowlands"
Betty Smith, Folk-Legacy FSA 53 (A1) "Young Emily"
cl: Blaine Stubblefield, AFS 2506 A, 2506 B "The Lowlands Low"
? cl: Mary Sullivan, AFS 4144 A2 "Young Emily"
? cl: Capt. Asel Trueblood, AFS 2326 A2, 2326 B "Young Edwin"
Doug Wallin, Folkways FA 2418 (B7) "Young Emily"
cl: Dora Ward, AFS 1742 A2 "Young Edward in the Lowland Low"

◆ The Constant Farmer's Son *(H806)* 434

White/Dean-Smith 1951: "... or The Merchant's Daughter"
Dean-Smith 1954: "...; The Merchant's Daughter"
Laws 1957:197 (M33); cf. Laws M32, "The Bramble Briar," which has a different metrical form.
Brunnings 1981: "The Jealous Brothers"
Cazden et al. *Notes* 1982: #47

c: IREL Morton 1973:40-1, 108

BRIT Greig/Duncan 2,1983:131 (#221), 2 vts.
Richards/Stubbs 1979:94-5 "Strawberry Town"
Sharp/Karpeles 1974,1:283-9 (#62), 4 vts.; cf. 280-2 (#6) "Bruton Town," 2 vts.

AMER Bush 3,1975:89-94 "The Jealous Brothers"
Darling 1983:122-3 "In Zepo Town" (see Shelton rec.)

BRS Harvard 1:10.112 (Bebbington), 12.14 (Such)

b: AMER George, Gerry Armstrong, Folkways FA 2335 "The Jealous Brothers"
George Belton, EFDSS LP 1008 (B5)
b: Oscar Brand, Wonderland RLP 1438 "The Jealous Brothers"
Cf. Logan English, Folkways FA 2136 (B2) "Bruton Town"
cl: Sam Harmon, AFS 2915 A1 "The Bramble Briar"
b: Louis Killen, Topic 12T 126 "Bramble Briar"
A. L. Lloyd, Riverside RLP 12 629 (A3) "The Bramble Briar"
Ewan MacColl, Topic 12T 147 (A5) "Bramble Briar"; Tradition 2059 (A5)
John Maguire, Leader LEE 4062 (B1)
Pentangle, Pickwick PLD 8013 (B1) "Bruton Town" a fragment.
Hattie Presnell, Folk-Legacy FSA 22 (B4) "The Jealous Brothers"
Lisha Shelton, Folkways FA 2309 (A8) "In Zepo Town"
b: Molly Scott, Prestige/Int. 13022 "Seaport Town"
Tish Stubbs, People's Stage Tapes cass. 01 (A6); 02 (B5)
Barry Sutterfield, New World 223 (A6) "Late One Evening"
cl: Dora Ward, AFS 1744 A "The Bramble Briar"

◆ The Bonny Labouring Boy *(H576)* 435

White/Dean-Smith 1951
Dean-Smith 1954
Laws 1957:187 (M14)
Brunnings 1981: "... Labouring/Laboring ..."
Cazden et al. *Notes* 1982: #52

IREL Hughes 4,1936:59-62 "My ..." [Fowke]
   O Lochlainn 1939:18, from brs. [Laws]
   Treoir 3(5)1971:18

c: BRIT Kennedy 1975:347 (#147); also reports
another version recorded in Antrim.
   Palmer 1979b:161-3 (#95)

AMER Cazden et al. 1982:199-202
c: Fowke 1973:160-1
   SO 13(3,Sum)1963:4

BRS UCLA 605: 4(Such)
   A Broadside 5(5, Oct)1912: "My ..."
   O'Conor [1901]:84 [Laws]

REC Bob Blake, Topic 12T 258 (B4). Notes by Mike
Yates refer to 19th-century broadsides including publications by Catnach, Ryle, Fortey, Such (all of London), and Cadman (Manchester).
   c: Shirley Collins, Argo RG 150
   c: Harry Cox, Folk-Legacy FSE 20 (B1)
   c: Robert, Louise De Cormier, Stinson SLP 72
      George Edwards, Asch AA 4 (A9); [c:] Asch 560
   b: Kenneth McKellar, London SW 99389 "The Bonnie
Labouring ..."
      Derek Sarjeant, Joy Special JS 5001 (A4)
      Cf. Martin Sullivan, Folkways FM 4005 (A6) "The
Railroad Boy"

MEL O'Neill 1903:34 (#195)
   Petrie/Stanford 1,1902:126 (#498) "The Maid of
Timahoe"; 2,1902:165 (#657) "As I Roved out One
Morning" [O Lochlainn]

◇ Willy Reilly *(H234)* 436

l: This is not the same song as "John (George) Riley
[II] (Young Riley)" (H826 "James Reilly") [Laws N37],
"Will[y] O'Reilly" (H76 "The Mantle So Green") [Laws
N38], or "Will O'Riley (John Riley, Young Riley the
Fisherman)" (H468 "John Reilly The Sailor Lad") [Laws
M8]. Fowke 1973:210 suggests Laws's discussion of
the various "Riley" ballads, pp. 172-83 in Beck 1962.
Cazden 1958:115-6 mentions his classification in
Northern Junket 4(7):29, (8):38, (9):25; (10):31;
and recommends (1982:107 and *Notes*) Robert H.
Rennick's classification of 25 forms of the returned-
lover ballad in *SFQ* 23,1960:215-32.

Laws 1957:184-5 (M10) "William (Willie) Riley (Riley's
Trial)"
Brunnings 1981: "...," "Fair Julian Bond," "Willie
Reilly (Cooleen Bawn)," "Willie Riley (Sweet
Riley)," "Reily's Jailed"
Cazden et al. *Notes* 1982: #53 "Fair Julian Bond"

c: IREL Carleton 1855,1:viii-ix
   Hayward 1925:96-7
   Joyce 1909:230-3 (#420)
m: Shields *UF* 17,1971:8-9, 24
   Shields/Shields *UF* 21,1975: #437
b: Sparling 1887?8:382-4 "Willie Reilly (Cooleen
Bawn)"
   Tunney 1979:40-2 "... and His Dear Colleen Bawn"
c: Walsh 1,1918:47-9

AMER Cazden et al. 1982:202-6 "Fair Julian Bond"
   Haskins n.d.:106
   Kenedy 1890:90-1
   Leach 1965:328-9 "Willie Riley"
   Thompson 1958:50-1

BRS BPL H.80
   Harvard 1: 2.22 (Livsey), 5.154 (Catnach), 11.101
(Such)
   Harvard 3: (Hodges) (Harkness)
   UCLA 605: 5(n.i.) "Trial of Willy Reilly," (Brereton)
"Willy Reilly and His Dear Colleen Bawn"

Delaney's Irish #3:12 [Laws]
Derry Journal [c. 1925],1:6
Holloway/Black 1975:230-2 (#102) "Riley and Colinband"
c: O'Conor 1901:86
   617 [190-?]:70
c: *Walton's New* 1,1966:156-7

cl: REC George Vinton Graham, AFS 3817 A & B
"... and His Dear Coolin Bawn"
cl: Capt. Pearl R. Nye, AFS 1008 B1
   Padráic Ó Catháin, Topic 12T 202 "Liam O' Raghal-
laigh" (Willie Reilly)
cl: Gus Schaffer, AFS 2413 B1 & 2

MEL Jackie Daly, Topic 12TS 358 (B7)
   DeVille/Gould n.d.:79 "Willie Reily"
   Hudson ms. 1:275
   O'Neill 1903:26 (#150) (also O'Neill 1922:40)

◇ Young Mary of Accland *(H30b, H721)* 437

White/Dean-Smith 1951: "Mary Acklin or (The)
Squire's Young Daughter"
Laws 1957:188 (M16) "Mary Acklin [The Squire's
Young Daughter]"

IREL Hayward 1925:110 "Mary Acklin" [Laws]

◇ Erin's Lovely Home *(H46)* 438

l: Another ballad with the same title appears in
Shields 1981:76 (#25) (also rec. Mary Ellen Butcher,
EEOT *Shamrock 2* cass.); it describes another hazard
to emigrants en route: disease.

White/Dean-Smith 1951
Dean-Smith 1954
Laws 1957:183 (M6)
Brunnings 1981

IREL *Ceol* 3:47-8
   JIFSS 1,1903:11-2 [Laws]
   O Lochlainn 1939:202-3 [MacColl/Seeger]

BRIT MacColl/Seeger 1977:250 (#77) "Old ... Vale"
   Morrison/Cologne 1981:20-1
Sharp/Karpeles 1974,1:349-51 (#80), 3 vts.
[MacColl/Seeger]

AMER Grover n.d.:102-3
   Thompson 1958:81-2 "Erins Lovly Home"
   Wright 1975:358-9

BRS BPL Partridge: 1.59
   Harvard 1: 4.95 (Bebbington), 6.73 (Cadman),
11.31 (Such)
   Harvard 3: (Harkness)
   UCLA 605: 3(Birmingham) (Brereton) "A New Song
Call'd ..."

REC Mary Ann Haynes, Topic 12T 253 (B4)
But not: George Hanna, Topic 12TS 372 (A4)

MEL Hudson ms. 1:340

◇ Sweet Dunloy *(H577)* 439

AMER Wright 1975:422 (from Henry coll., Belfast)

◇ Henry Connor of Castledawson *(H128)* 440

Laws 1957:182 (M5) "Henry Connors"; cf. Laws M6
(H46) "Erin's Lovely Home"

cl: REC ? J. W. Green, AFS 2297 B1 "... Conners"

◆ Sally Munro *(H571)* 441

Laws 1957:145-6 (K11) "Sally Monroe"
Brunnings 1981

IREL   C. O'Boyle 1979:34-5 "... Munroe"

BRIT   Greig/Duncan 1,1981:53-60 (#23) "Sally Munro," 11 vts.
   Shepheard n.d.:33
   Tocher #9(Spr)1973:8-9

AMER   Leach 1965:108-9 "... Monroe" (= Wright 1975:419)
   Peacock 1965,2:488-9 "Young ... Monro"

BRS   BPL H.80

◆ John Reilly the Sailor Lad *(H468)* 441

White/Dean-Smith 1951: "John Reilly or Young Riley the Fisherman"
Dean-Smith 1954: "John Reilly or Young Riley the Fisherman"
Laws 1957:183-4 (M8) "Riley's Farewell (Riley to America, John Riley)"
Brunnings 1981: "John Riley," "John Riley (Riley to Ameriky)," "Young Riley"

Fowke 1973:210 suggests Laws's discussion of the various "Riley" ballads, pp. 172-83 in Beck 1962. Cazden 1958:115-6 mentions his classification in *Northern Junket* 4(7):29, (8):38, (9):25, (10):31; and recommends (1982:107 and *Notes*) Robert H. Rennick's classification of 25 forms of the returned-lover ballad in *SFQ* 23,?1960:215-32.

IREL   *JIFSS* 1,1903:5 "One Evening Fair" [Laws]
   Joyce 1909:29 (#53) "One Evening Fair" [Sharp/Karpeles]
   O Lochlainn 1965:14-5 "Reilly the Fisherman" [Sharp/Karpeles]
   Petrie/Stanford 1,1902:88 (#349) "I thought my heart ...," 89 (#351) "John O'Reilly"
   Shields/Shields *UF* 21,1975: #223 "... Reilly"

BRIT   Greig/Duncan 1,1981:49-52 (#22)"John Riley," 6 vts. ("... Rally," "... Rylie," "Willie or Billy Riley," "Reilly")
   Nettel 1954:146
Sharp/Karpeles 1974,1:357-60 (#88) "Reilly Sent to America"

AMER   Fowke 1973:156-7 "Will O'Riley"
   Warner 1984:338-40 (#147) "... Reilly"
   Wright 1975:271-2

BRS   BPL Partridge: 3.131 (n.i.)
   Harvard 1: 4.17 (Walker) [Laws], 6.192 (Cadman), 7.32 (Ryle), 9.22 (Bebbington), 11.21 (Such)
   Delaney's Irish #3 [Laws]
   De Marsan [Laws]
   O'Conor [1901]:49 [Laws]
   617 [190-?]:121 "O'Reilly the Fisherman"

REC   George Dunn, Leader LEE 4042 (B3) "... Riley"
   Mrs Edward Gallagher, Folkways FE 4307 (A10) "Young Riley"
   Sarah Anne O'Neill, Topic 12TS 372 (B3) "... Reilly"
   John Reilly, EEOT *Irish Travellers* cass. (A4) "... Reilly"
? cl: Margaret Sullivan, AFS 3745 A3 "Reilly, The Fisherman" (spoken)

◆ Kellswater *(H695)* 442

Brunnings 1981: "The Lover's Curse."

m: IREL   Hughes 1,1909:60-3 "The Lover's Curse," in which the lover is Willie and he has been taken to fight in "the lowlands of Holland."
m: *JIFSS* 3(3&4)1905-6:21, from Houston coll. Moulden 1979:76-7 reports a version from Ballymoney collected by Len Graham.

BRIT   Clifford 1957:10-1 "Lovely Jimmy"

AMER   Creighton 1961:45 "Jimmy and I Will Get Married," a fragment.

b: REC   Kathleen Ferrier, London 5411 "The Lover's Curse"
   The Irish Rovers, Decca DL 74951 (A2) "Bonnie ..."
   Planxty, Tara 3005 (A5)

◆ The Banks of the Bann *(H86)* 443

Laws 1957:227 (O2) "The Brown Girl"
Brunnings 1981: "...," "The Brown Girl - When First to This Country I Came as a Stranger"

IREL   Shields 1981:48 (#7)
   Shields/Shields *UF* 21, 1975: #32
h: "Songs of the People" #461 (1 Oct 1932)

AMER   Milner/Kaplan 1983:169-70 "... (The Brown Girl)"

BRS   Harvard 2: (Such) "Brown Girl"
   UCLA 605: 3 (Birt) "... Band"
   Derry Journal [c. 1925],1:55 "The Maid of Aghadowey"
   Forget Me Not [1835]:127-8
   Ireland Calling n.d.:14

REC   Eddie Butcher, Outlet OAS 3007 (A6) "Lovely Bann Water"
   Hom Bru, Celtic Music CM 009 (B6)
h: Richard Hayward, HMV (Ireland) IM 668 (78 rpm)
   Tom Kines, Folkways FG 3522 (A3) "The Brown Girl"
   A. L. Lloyd, Prestige INT 13066 [Milner/Kaplan]

h: MEL   Joyce 1909:295

◆ Johnnie Hart *(H106)* 443

Brunnings 1981: "Johnny Harte"

h: IREL   *Ceol* 1(4)1964:10-1
   Morton 1973:84-5
h: O Lochlainn 1939:174-5
   Shields/Shields *UF* 21,1975: #225 "Johnny ..."

REC   Teresa Maguire, *FSB* 8 (A9) "Johnny Harte"

◆ Love Laughs at Locksmiths *(H668)* 444

White/Dean-Smith 1951: "(The) Young Servant-Man, or The Cruel Father and Affectionate Lovers; The Daughter in the Dungeon; The Two Affectionate Lovers"
Dean-Smith 1954: "(The) Daughter in the Dungeon; The Two Affectionate Lovers"
Laws 1957:187-8 (M15) "The Iron Door"
Brunnings 1981: "The Cruel Father and Affectionate Lovers"

k: IREL   O Lochlainn 1965:122-3 "The Young Serving Man"

BRIT   Copper 1973:220-1 "Her Servant Man"
b: Kennedy 1975:361 (#161) "The Iron Door"; also notes another English version recorded for the BBC.
   Cf. Morrison/Cologne 1981:60-1 "In the Town of

Marlborough," which contains elements of "The Iron Door."
   Cf. Purslow *FMJ* 1967:155-6 "Down in the Town of Marlborough (The Handsome Young Servantman)"
   Sharp/Karpeles 1974,1:343-5 (#83) "Daughter in the Dungeon," 3 vts.

AMER Grover n.d.:112-3 "The Servant Man"

BRS Harvard 1: 10.102 (Bebbington)
   Healy 1,1967b:311-2 "The Cruel Father, or The Affectionate Lover"

REC Cf. Phoebe Smith, Topic 12T 193 (A3) "Young Ellender"
   Gladys Stone, Topic 12T 317 (B3) "Her Servant Man"

◇ **The Lady Leroy** *(H214)* 445

White/Dean-Smith 1951
Laws 1957:204 (N5)
Brunnings 1981
Cazden et al. *Notes* 1982: #58

IREL Moulden 1979:78

m: BRIT Kilkerr *FMJ* 1977:220-1; reprint, *Treoir* 12(1)1980:13

AMER Cazden et al. 1982:220-3
m: Fowke 1965:96-7 (see Brandon rec.). Among Fowke's references is Leach 1965:86-7, who states that this song had been collected only in America. However, Henry's discussion clearly indicates that "The *Lady Leroy*" was known in Northern Ireland, and may even have originated there.

c: REC Tom Brandon, Folk-Legacy FSC 10 (A6)
cl: Warde H. Ford, AFS 4205 A2, B
cl: Mrs McNamara, AFS 1484 B1 & 2 "Ladle Leroy"

cl: Alfred Osborne, AFS 3401 A1

c: MEL Petrie/Stanford 1,1902:99 (#389) "The Merchant's Daughter"

◇ **Eliza / When I Landed in Glasgow** *(H58)* 446

Brunnings 1981: "The Young Maid's Love"

m: IREL Galwey 1910:15 (#12)
m: Joyce 1909:153 (#329) with the same titles as Henry gives, and 1 stanza very similar to Henry's.
   Moulden 1979:47
m: O Lochlainn 1939:90-1 "A New Song Called The Young Maid's Love," a confused version of what is apparently this song.

◇ **The Apprentice Boy / Covent Garden** *(H729)* 446

White/Dean-Smith 1951: "Covent Garden"
Dean-Smith 1959: "Cupid's Garden; Love's Tale; I Love a Sailor Bold"
Laws 1957:186 (M12)
Brunnings 1981: "The Apprentice Boy (The Prentice Boy)," "Cupid's Garden," probably not "The Prentice Boy (See The Jealous Lover)"

BRIT Greig 1907-11(1963): #151 "Covent's Garden," #155 (no title)

AMER *Colorado FB* 3,1964:38 "Down in Cupid's Garden (The Prentice ...)"
   Creighton 1961:52
   Creighton 1971:61-2 "Cupid's Garden"
   Grover n.d.:5 "The Prentice ..."
   Manny/Wilson 1968:276-8 "The Prentice ..."
   Thompson 1958:55-6 "The 'Prentice ..."

BRS BPL Partridge: 1.446

MEL Hudson ms. 2:706
   O'Neill 1903:73 (#421)

C24

To Hymen's car: Successful courtship

Sam Henry's Songs of the People

Our Wedding Day [H534: 24 Feb 1934]

[cf. H141 "Out of the Window"]

o: "She Moved through the Fair"; k: "Lovely Molly."

Source not given.

s: This simple little song is the expression of one happy thought. It should be sung slowly and with wistful happiness.

l: Text reworked by Padraic Colum from an "old ballad" to a Donegal air collected by Herbert Hughes (1,1909). James Healy says "This is one of the few cases where the now, more scholarly edition could be considered better than the old" (1977:79). But Healy himself prints a version somewhat transformed by "folk process," with a different 2d stanza and the 3d in transition ("my dear love came in") between Colum's original, ghostless stanza ("she came softly in") and Margaret Barry's haunting one ("my dead love came in").

Henry's is the only version among those cited that substitutes "kine" (cattle) for Colum's "kind" (standing or property inherent by birth).

Key C.

My young love said to me, 'My mother won't min',
And my father won't slight you for your lack of kine.'
She laid a hand on me and this she did say,
'It will not be long, love, till our wedding day.'

She went away from me, she moved through the fair,
And fondly I watched her move here and move there,
And then she went homeward with one star awake,
As the swan in the evening moves over the lake.

Last night she came to me, she came softly in,
So softly she came that her feet made no din,
She put her arms round me, and this she did say,
'It will not be long, love, till our wedding day.'

The Boy That Found a Bride [H665: 22 Aug 1936]

s: (m) "The River Roe"; k: "Fair Gallowa'."

Source not given.

Key G.

'Twas in the month of August, when yellow waved the corn,
And a' the hills were covered ower wi' flowers that scent the morn,
I roved about frae toon tae toon amang the lasses braw,
Although my tender parents leeved in fair Gallawa'.

It's down by Glasgow city there is a pleasant green,
Where hundreds of bra' lasses is there for to be seen,
But I spied one amang the rest, the flower of them a',
And as sweet's my life she'll be my wife in far Gallawa'.

I stepped up to this wee lass as I went on my way,
Enquirin' for a town I kent, to hear what she would say,
'You seem to be a stranger, lad, so wi' me come awa',
And I'll show you the road,' she said, 'down by the Broomiela'.'

And so wi' this wee lassie I took my chance to go
Down by Clyde's green bonny banks where purling streams do flow;
She seemed to be a nice wee lass, her name was Lenie La',
And as sweet's my life she'll be my wife in far Gallawa'.

I courted this wee lassie the leelong night and day
Until the time was coming on that I must go away,
'So take your will, my bonny wee lass, stay or come awa',
Or pad the road alang wi' me to far Gallawa'.

'The road it is baith braid and lang and the hills, tae, they are high,
An' neither friends nor relatives have I for to come nigh.
Perhaps you'll rue it, my bonnie wee lass, when I am far awa',
When you're in bonny Glasgow green and me in Gallawa'.'

Just as we were parting, to me she thus did say,
'Stay at home, my bonny lad, at least this ae yin
  day;
As quick as we get married, we'll leave them yin
  and a','
And noo we live a happy life in far Gallawa'.

1.3: toon = town.
1.4: leeved = lived.
1.4: Gallawa' = Galloway.
3.2: kent = knew.
5.1: leelong = livelong.
5.4: alang = along.
6.1: baith = both; braid = broad.

The Swan [H475: 7 Jan 1933]

Source not given.

Key A.

On the lovely banks of Bann as we watched the
  gliding swan,
My darling Mary by my side,
I whispered, 'For your sake, these scenes I
  would forsake
And seek my fortune far across the tide.

'Though it grieves my heart to go and leave the
  friends I know,
Yet, Mary, you are all to me,
I care not if I roam if at last I build a home
Where we'll forever live and happy be.'

Mary's eyes looked up in mine, 'Jamie, dear, why
  cross the brine?
A crust is sweeter on this soil
Than all that you can gain, exiled o'er the bitter
  main,
Sure, love will flavour all the fruits of toil.

'See the swan upon the stream like a vision in a
  dream,
His wings would bear him o'er the sea --
He has no thought to roam, the Bann's his chosen
  home;
Then let us, like him, at home contented be.'

I held her to my breast and whispered, 'Here our
  nest
We'll build among the scenes we love,
Oh Mary, you're my pride, and soon you'll be my
  bride,
On the banks of Bann you'll be my homing dove.'

The Tossing o' the Hay [H635: 25 Jan 1936]

[cf. H697 "Tumbling through the Hay"]

Other titles: "Raking the (of) ...," "Tossing
the ..."; cf. "The Bonny Bunch of Rushes Green,"
"Haymaking Courtship," "Joy after Sorrow," "The
New Mown ...."

Source: Andrew Allen (Bann Bridge Cottages,
Coleraine), learned from Pat M'Loone (Long Commons, Coleraine; native of Dungiven), learned
from his wife's uncle, John Carr (Derry).

Key G.

It being on a summer evening, abroad as I did
  rove,
I sauntered out for pleasure down by yon shady
  grove,
Down by yon spicy meadows I carelessly did stray,
Where I saw a maid quite busy at the tossing of
  the hay.

Through a close hedge I watched my love, to her I
  was unseen,
Her beauty it did far outshine that Catherine
  Jane, your queen,
And all around her ivory neck the amber locks did
  play,
And the diamond glances of her eye at the tossing
  of the hay.

I stepp-ed up to this fair maid; she unto me did
  say,
'I'm afraid we'll have a fall of rain, we have a
  gloomy sky.'
'No, ma'am,' said I, 'those weighty clouds will
  shortly pass away,
There will be no rain for to detain the tossing of
  the hay.'

I asked her the reason why she was left alone;
'My brother he as left me, to the turf bog he has
  gone
To lay the turf in winnow-rows while he has light
  of day,
And he left me here, a bird alone, to toss and dry
  the hay.'

I took her in my arms and we sat down on the
  green,
Then I began to kiss the maid and she began to
  scream,

Sam Henry's Songs of the People

And I being in a merry mood, with her did sport and play,
Saying, 'The day is long, there's time enough to toss and dry the hay.'

I said, 'My pretty fair maid, if you come along with me,
We'll join our hands in wedlock bands and married we will be,
We'll join our hands in wedlock bands before the break of day,
And we'll combine together for to toss and dry the hay.'

Pining Day and Daily [H149: 18 Sep 1926]

k: "Lovely Molly."

Source: (w, m) Kate Kane (Crossroads, Dreen (Park), near Sawell).

[Sam Henry refers to a descriptive article "Towards the Mists of Sawell" in the current issue of the *Northern Constitution*.]

Key G.

I am pining day and daily this twelve months and above,
I am pining day and daily, and all about my love,
My beauty it is fading like the leaves on thon green tree,
And I wish I was with my true love and my true love with me.

I hear my true love coming, right well I know his walk,
Yonder my true love's coming, right well I know his talk;
His cheeks are like the roses, his skin is white as snow,
He'd the darling of my heart wherever he may go.

'Love, do you not remember when we were gathering flowers?
Love, do you not remember, when in thon shady bowers,
The tales of love you told me? I thought they were all true,
I never thought you would exchange the old love for the new.'

'Oh, Molly, lovely Molly, these words have won my heart,
Come, let us have a wedding, and that before we part;
Let your father keep his gold in store till I return again,
For when we're young and in our prime, we'll plough the raging main.'

The Pretty Blue Handkerchief (I)

[H161a: 11 Dec 1926]

s: (m) = H161c "Master McGra[th]." Other titles: "The Blue Kerchief," "Bonny Blue ...," "The Hanky."

Source: (w) late William Shaw, 80, bathing attendant (Herring Pond, Portstewart).

s: A little love song ...

As I went a-walking one morning in May,
I met a wee lassie come tripping this way,
Her cheeks were like roses, so sweetly she sang
With her bonnie blue kerchief tied under her chin.

Said I, 'My wee darling, what brought you this way?'
'I'm going to my work, kind sir,' she did say,
'I'm going down to yon cottage my wool for to spin,
With my bonnie blue kerchief tied under my chin.'

'Why do you wear it all on the one side?'
'It's my country fashion, kind sir,' she replied,
'The fashion you know I should like to be in
With my bonnie blue kerchief tied under my chin.'

This couple got married, as I hear them say,
The drums they do beat and the music doth play,
She's no more the poor spinner, but wears a gold ring
And he the blue handkerchief under his chin.

The Pretty Blue Handkerchief (II)

[H161b: Dt]

English version.
[(m) = H161c "Master McGra[th]"]

Source: arranged by E. K. Sweeting; sung at Coleraine Musical Festival.

C24 / To Hymen's car

As I was a-walking one morning in May,
A bonny young lass came a-tripping that way;
With cheeks red as roses, she cheerfully did
  sing,
And a bonny blue handkerchief tied under her
  chin.

'Where so quickly?' I asked her, and caught her
  slim waist;
'To my work, sir, I'm walking all in a great
  haste:
To work in yon factory where cotton they spin,'
With a bonny blue handkerchief tied under her
  chin.

'Why wear you the kerchief that covers your
  head?'
'It's the fashion they keep in the country,' she
  said,
'And you know that the fashion we like to be in,
With a bonny blue handkerchief tied under my
  chin.'

'Why wear you the colour that glows in your veil?'
'Because it's true blue, sir, that never shall fail,
Like a sailor's blue jacket that fights for the
  king,
With a bonny blue handkerchief tied under my
  chin.'

When I found her so charming, how could I
  forbear?
I flew to her side, I called her my dear,
'My own dearest jewel, come take the gold ring,
With a bonny blue handkerchief tied under your
  chin.

'To church we will go and be married with speed,
A loving young couple and happy indeed;
When the day's work is over so cheerfully you'll
  sing
With a bonny blue kerchief tied under you[r]
  chin.'

The Gentle Shepherdess

[H104: 7 Nov 1925; Laws O8]

s: "A Farmer's Son So Sweet" coll. Cecil Sharp,
Somerset. Other titles: "The Handsome ...," "The
Pretty Young ...," "The (Sailor and the) Shepherdess," "The Sailor's Courtship," "The Shepherdess and the Sailor."

Source: (m, w) William Carton, retired N. S. T.
[schoolteacher] (Garryduff, Ballymoney), from his
father c. 1875.

s: ... A folk song from Somerset, entitled "A Farmer's Son So Sweet," collected by Cecil Sharp, is
the counterpart of the song here printed. In the
Somerset song it is the young man who is asleep
and the maiden kisses him.

Key D.

There was a gentle shepherdess was herding her
  flock
On a rock that was nigh the seaside,
And a bonnie little sailor lad by chance came that
  way,
And he fain would have made her his bride.

The weather being warm, as she lay fast asleep
Whilst the lambs round her did sport and play,
He stole a sweet kiss as she lay fast asleep,,
Saying, 'Alas, you have stole my heart away.'

She wakened with surprise when she opened her
  eyes
And saw the young sailor standing by.
'Oh sailor dear,' said she, 'how came you here
  by me?
And alas, she began for to cry.

'Oh dear,' said he, 'I came from yon ship you
  see,
I was tossed on these rocks here alone,
And I came to you, my dear, for to find some
  comfort here;
If I don't, I'm forever undone.'

'Oh sailor dear,' said she, 'you need never come
  to me,
For I never could give my consent,
For when you should be on the seas I should
  never be at ease,
You would leave me for to sigh and lament.'

'Oh dear,' said he, 'if you could but fancy me,
I have plenty of gold laid in store.
The seas I would forsake and a promise I would
  make
That I'd be true to you for evermore.'

She gave her consent and married they were,
And now this couple's blest for evermore,
And they do live in peace and their joys still do
  increase,
And the sailor does his shepherdess adore.

2.3: ... kiss from this maiden so sweet, [Dt]
5.1: ... 'you may never ... [Dt]
 .3: ... I would never ... [Dt]
7.1: ... were soon, [Dt]
 .3: ... joys do still ... [Dt]

457

Sam Henry's Songs of the People

The Bonny Wee Lass [H763: 9 Jul 1938]

Other title: "... Wee Trampin' ...."

Source: Mrs Rutherford (Rectory, Carrickfergus).

s: ... This song, which is truly racy of the soil, is widely known. I have collected versions at Balnamore and at Limavady.

Key A flat.

As I gaed oot one summer day tae tak' a wee bit stroll,
I dandered on along the road till I gaed by the toll,
I hadnae gone sae far that way till Jeremy's Bridge I did pass,
And there I met upon the road a wee bit country lass.

'Where are ye goin'? How are ye doin'? Give me your han',' sez I,
'Hold up your head, my bonny wee lass, and dinna look sae shy.
'Whaur dae ye bide? Whaur dae ye stay? Come tell tae me your name;
'Dae ye think would your fether be angry noo if I was tae see you hame?'

She tel't me whaur it was she worked: doun in the Milltoun fiel',
Trampin', trampin' hanks o' yarn and liked it unco' weel;
Her earnings were ten bob a week when she was on full time.
'What about that, my bonny wee lass, when you will soon be mine?'

We talkit on a little while aboot the thing ca'd love,
Till everything grew quate aboot and the sky grew dark above;
She drew her shawl aboot her heid and this she did exclaim,
'Are ye gaun' tae keep your bargain noo? Are ye gaun tae lee me hame?'

And noo we have got married, we're as happy as can be,
Twa bits o' bairnies at my feet and anither at my knee;
Oftimes I stroll doon by the toll an' think o' days gone by,
When first I met my bonny wee lass an' she was awful shy.

3.2: quate = quiet.

Lovely Annie (I) [H561: 1 Sep 1934; Laws N8]

[cf. H166 " (II) (Polly Oliver's Rambles)]

k: "Lisbon"; g: "Farewell Charming Nancy."
Other titles: "Farewell My Dear(est) Nancy," "It Was Early One ('Twas on a) Monday Morning," "Jimmy (William) (The Sailor) and Nancy (Polly) (on the Sea)," "Johnnie," "Men's Clothing I'll Put On," "Molly and William," "The Youthful Damsel"; cf. "I'm Going to Join the Army," "Jack Munro (Went a-Sailing)," "Lily, Lily, Oh," "William and Nancy's Parting."

Source: (w, m) Alex. Horner (Moycraig Hamilton, Mosside, Co. Antrim), learned from David M'Candless (Derrykeighan) on board ship off Banks of Newfoundland c. 1880.

Key G.

It being on a Monday morning, before the cock crew day,
'All hands aloft,' our captain cries, 'brave boys, we must away.
The wind it blew from the southwest, for Melbourne we were bound,
And the hills and dales were garnished with blooming maids all round.

Up came a clever tall young man all in his youthful bloom,
And at the parting his sweetheart had cast him all in gloom;
He stepped up to his beloved, gave her to understand
That he for life must leave her and seek some foreign land.

'Oh, stay at home, dearest Willie, and be advised by me,
And never venture your sweet life all on yon stormy sea,
And never venture your sweet life all on yon stormy shore,
Where thousands of our young men lie drownd-ed there before.'

'Oh, the king he wants young men, my love, and
   for one I must go,
And for my very life, my dear, I dare not answer
   no,
And if you love me, Annie, you must love me all
   the more
That for my king and country I will leave my
   native shore.'

'Oh, it's I'll cut off my yellow locks, men's
   clothing I'll put on,
And I'll pass for your comrade as we do sail
   along.'
'Oh, your waist it is too slender, love, and your
   fingers are too small,
I'm afraid you would not answer me when on you I
   would call.

'Where the cannons loudly rattle and the balls like
   hail do fly,
And the silv'ry trumpets sound aloud to drown
   the mournful cry,
And if I was to meet a bonny wee lass, both
   lively, brisk and free,
And me to fall in love with her, what would my
   Annie say?'

'If you were to meet a bonny wee lass, both
   lively, brisk and free,
And you to fall in love with her, what would your
   Annie say?
What would I say, dearest Willie, but I would
   love her too,
And I would step aside, my love, till she would
   talk with you.'

'Oh Annie, lovely Annie, those words have broke
   my heart,
And we shall have a wedding, love, and that
   before we start.'
So this couple they've got married and they're
   sailing o'er the main:
Here's a health to all true lovers till they return
   again.

I'm from over the Mountain (a)

[H61a: "A song of an elopement," 10 Jan 1925]

k: "Trip over the Mountain." Other titles: "Come
With Me over ...," "I'll Follow You over ...,"
"The Trip We Took over ...(s)," "The True Lov-
ers' Trip over ...."

Source not given.

Key G.

It happened to be on a moonshiny night that I
   took a notion to marry,
I drew to my hat, took my staff in my hand,
   just as I had been in a hurry.
I urged along where I oftimes had been, my
   heart it rejoiced when my charmer was seen,
I lifted the latch and I bade her 'Good e'en';
   says I, 'I'm from over the mountain.'

'What notion of jesting came into your head? I'm
   glad for to meet you so merry.
It's twelve by the clock and the old folk in bed;
   speak low or you'll waken my mammy.'
'If that be a jest, then it's jesting that's true;
   I've courted a year and I think that'll do,
So this very nicht I will marry wi' you, if you
   venture wi' me o'er the mountain.'

'Oh no, my wee laddie, I'll stay as I am, I think
   it is fitter and better.'
I drew to my hat, took my staff in my hand,
   saying, 'I'll soon put an end to the matter.'
'Oh wait, my wee laddie, till I get my shoes.'
   My heart it rejoiced when I heard the glad news;
I drew to the door saying, 'I hope you'll excuse
   my simplicity frae over the mountain.'

The moon and the stars luminated the sky, the
   morning star was brightly shining
As me and my darling our journey pursued till
   we came to the altar of Hymen;
Wi' fiddling and dancing we spent the whole day,
   and the anger of marriage it soon rolled away,
And I unto my wee lassie did say, 'Do you rue
   coming over the mountain?'

'Oh no, my wee laddie, it's I dinna rue, I ta'en
   the advice of my laddie,
And when I am over the mountain wi' you, I
   regard not the friends o' my daddy.'
Let that be a warning to every fair maid: Slip
   out in the dark when the old folks in bed,
And ne'er be afraid wi' her laddie to wed or to
   venture with him o'er the mountain.

I'm from over the Mountain (b) [H61b: Dt]

Source: John Marshall (Carngad Hill, Glasgow)
from his mother (Ireland), c. 1900.

When the bright sun had sunk in the west, I
   then took a notion to marry,
I put on my hat and away I did go, I seemed to
   be in a great hurry;
When I came to the dwelling where oftimes I'd
   been, my heart gave a leap when my darling I
   seen:
She opened the door, saying, 'Won't you come
   in?' Says I, 'Will you go o'er the mountain?'

Sam Henry's Songs of the People

'O, what foolish notions come into your head?
  I'm glad for to meet you so merry,
It's just twelve o'clock and the old folk in bed,
  speak low or my daddy will hear you.'
'Now, if it be jesting, you know it is true, we
  have courted a year and I think that should do,
So this very night I'll get married to you, if
  you'll take a trip over the mountain.'

'Now if I would make an elopement with you, it
  might be attended with danger;
The people would titter and censor away and my
  parents would both frown and wonder.'
'Well, just let them tittle and censor away;
  consult with yourself, for it's wearing near day.
I don't give a fig what the lot of them say, if I
  had you once over the mountain.'

So when she saw that I was going away, her
  heart it began for to flutter,
She stepped up to me and this she did say, 'I
  will soon put an end to the matter.
Stop, stop, my own darling, till I get my shoes.'
  My heart gave a leap when I heard the glad
  news,
I ran to the door, saying, 'I hope you'll excuse
  my simplicity over the mountain.'

When the bright moon had sunk in the west and
  the morning star was brightly shining,
With a long journey pursuing great haste, we
  were joined at the altar that morning.
With peace and contentment we have spent our
  long days, the anger of marriage it soon wore
  away,
And often to my wee lassie I say, 'Do you rue
  coming over the mountain?'

'Oh no, my dear jewel, I do not rue that I took
  the advice of my laddie,
Now that I'm safe o'er the mountain with you, I
  fear not the frown of my daddy.'
Let this be a warning to every young maid:
  Just slip out at night, leave your daddy in bed,
And not be afraid with your lover to wed; think
  on the wee girl over the mountain.

The Bann Water Side [H685: 9 Jan 1937]

Source: (Dunloy district).

Key G.

One evening fair to take the air down by a shady
  grove,
  I little thought I would be caught all in the chains
  of love;

Returning to my dwelling place, a charming girl I
  spied,
She's the blooming rose of Banbridge town and the
  sweet Bann water side.

I stood awhile her to beguile, not knowing what to
  do,
Still thinking on some remedy, my pain for to
  subdue,
Saying, 'You'll have cows, horses and ploughs and
  all your wants supplied
If you'll agree to come with me from the sweet Bann
  water side.'

'If you with snares of Cupid would my happiness
  destroy,
And with your art would steal my heart, I pray
  you pass me by;
Though I have neither cows nor lands, yet God
  will be my guide,
And a servant plain I will remain on the Bann
  water side.'

'If you be poor, do not endure to live in poverty,
For I have money plenty to support both you and
  me,
And while I'm worth one shilling, love, with you I
  will divide,
So rise up now and come away from the sweet Bann
  water side.'

It's to conclude and finish and to let all lovers see
She now is mistress of my heart and all my
  property,
She has both lands and houses and money to
  divide,
And I bless the day I chanced to stray by the
  sweet Bann water side.

Beardiville Planting [H718: 28 Aug 1937]

Source: (m, w) (Bushmills).

Key G.

As I was walking up Coleraine Street,
I spied a fair damsel, both neat and complete;
Says I, 'Pretty fair maid, it's where dost thou
  dwell?'
And she answered, 'Kind sir, near to Beardiville.'

Says I, 'Pretty fair maid, your enchanting smile
And comely fine features do my heart beguile.

If I could get you with me to agree,
You would go to the sweet County Derry with me.'

Says she, 'Dearest kind sir, I think you're in
  jest,
If I thought you in earnest, I'd count myself
  blest;
I pray you consent and stop here a while,
And view those fine plantings near to Beardiville.'

It's then to her father we hastened away,
And as we drew near, the music it did play --
The pipe, flute and clarionet, and also the viol,
Did echo those plantings near to Beardville.

And as we drew near to that beautiful place,
Her father and mother did us fondly embrace,
They embraced us kindly with compliments mild,
Saying, 'You're welcome, kind sir, to sweet
  Beardiville.'

It's now to conclude and to finish my theme,
The young man has gained this beautiful dame,
He says he will love her while life doth remain,
And they bless the glad hour they met in
  Coleraine.

Bess of Ballymoney [H133: 29 May 1926]

s: (m) "The Girl I Left Behind Me"; g: "The
Star of ...."

Source: Ann McAleese (Altdorragh, Glenbush,
Armoy).

s: Mrs M'Aleese['s] ... grandmother was a servant in the house of Phil Beckett, father of
Bess, the heroine of the song. The song was
composed about a century ago.

[Bp] Key F. [Dt] Key C.

You muses nine, with me combine and lend me
  your attention,
The praises of a maid divine I now intend to
  mention;
Her radiance bright bedimmed my sight when I
  approached my honey,
With flaming breast I then addressed the star of
  Ballymoney.

Said I, 'Sweet jewel of my heart, although you
  are a stranger,
My life and fortune I could part to save you from
  all danger;

If you'll agree to come with me, no danger shall
  come on you,
Your joy I'll crown in Coleraine town, sweet star
  of Ballymoney.'

'Would you have me leave my home, these woods
  and plantings bonny,
And bid adieu to all my friends that dwell in
  Ballymoney?
Besides, my age is not seventeen, I never wooed
  with any,
And a maid awhile I will remain with my friends in
  Ballymoney.'

Then into Ballymoney town so lovingly we walk-ed,
And in a tavern we sat down where love is oftimes
  talk-ed;
Love it sparkled in our cup as sweet as sugar
  candy,
Cupid fluttered in our jug, we wet his wings with
  brandy.

So now she's bound to Coleraine town to try her
  fate with Johnny,
She bids adieu to every view around sweet
  Ballymoney.
Now she is bound for Coleraine town to try her
  fate with Johnny,
And she bids adieu to all her friends that dwell in
  Ballymoney.

The Blackwaterside [H811: 10 Jun 1939; Laws O1]

Source: Anne Toner (Straw, Draperstown) from
her mother, born 1818, who in turn learned it
from her mother.

s: ... The song is therefore about 150 years old.
The Black Water is a small tributary of the
Moyola. Its course after it issues from Lough
Fea is through a wildly romantic deep glen.

m: There is a Blackwater River in almost every
County of Ireland [1979:21].

Key C.

You maids of this nation of high and low station,
I pray pay attention and listen to me
Concerning a couple I overheard talking
As I went a-walking some friends for to see.
It happened to be on a fine summer's morning,
When viewing the streams as they gently did
  glide,

Sam Henry's Songs of the People

The rays of bright Phoebus the hills were
  adorning
Around the green banks of the Blackwaterside.

He says, 'My wee darling, we're long enough
  courting,
We're both fit for marriage, I solemnly vow,
If you are inclining sweet wedlock to join in,
Say Yes or say No, you must answer me now.
No more hesitating, but come without waiting,
I'm ready and willing to make you my bride,
You know I adore you, I praise none before you,
You're the blooming sweet maid of the
  Blackwaterside.'

She says, 'Dearest Johnny, it's too soon to
  marry,
I mean to live single a while longer yet,
My fortune is low as you very well know,
And to make you a bride I think I'm not fit;
My clothing is bare, I have nothing to spare,
I worked very hard since the time father died,
Wait a year or two more and I'll go with you sure
And forsake all my friends round the
  Blackwaterside.

He says, 'My wee dear, the Shrovetime is near,
I'm straight going to marry some blooming young
  fair,
A maid of sixteen, if she's handsome and clean,
And as for her fortune, not a traneen I care,
Nor yet for your clothing, for that I care
  nothing,
With you I could ramble this old world so wide.
Grant me my desire, you're the maid I require
From the lovely sweet banks of the Blackwaterside.'

This fair maid arose, to her mother she goes
And told her the story as plain as you see;
They both got consent, to get married they went,
They were soon joined in wedlock in sweet unity.
May their wealth still increase and their sorrow
  grow less,
In the greatest of love may they always confide;
The truth I am telling, you'll find their snug
  dwelling
On the lovely sweet banks of the Blackwaterside.

Cashel Green (I)   [H647: 18 Apr 1936]

[cf. H154 " (II)]

g: "The River Roe."

Source: Mrs Frank Kealey (Ballysally, Coleraine;
native of Dungiven).

Key G.

One evening fine in summertime, down by the Roe
  I chanced to roam;
The cooing dove my heart did move as I was
  walking all alone,
Where frisked the lambs around their dams and
  little trout did sport and play,
The thrushes song sweet echoes rung, which
  passed some pleasant hours away.

As I tripped along, my mind did throng as
  nature's aspect I did view,
Small streamlets glide in silver pride, the Roe's
  clear water to renew.
I spied a lass did far surpass all nature's objects
  I have seen,
Her charming smile did me beguile as she
  traversed sweet Cashel Green.

She was so complete with looks so sweet, her
  cheeks they were a rosy red,
Her golden hair did me ensnare that in flowing
  ringlets decked her head.
As I drew nigh I heaved a sigh, she asked me why
  I did deplore,
Said I, 'Fair maid, I'm much afraid the heart you
  from my bosom tore.'

'Why should a lad for me be sad? I had no intent
  for to ensnare,
I often go along the Roe in summer time to take
  the air,
But to mollify you seem to try, but your love for
  me might be disdain,
Young men like you oft bid adieu, which leaves
  fair maidens to complain.'

'Oh, but I'll comply, love, don't deny; unite and
  join and be my bride,
And I'll prove kind, and that you'll find, as the
  Roe waters gently glide.'
She gave consent and off we went, in wedlock's
  bands the knot did tie,
As the Roe stream glides, sure we abide, while
  scenes of nature hover by.

My Charming Coleraine Lass

[H616: 21 Sep 1935]

Other title: "The ...."

Source: (w) coll. William James Fisher (Ballygawley), from John Burgess, sr (Ballygawley); (m)
Andrew Allen (Bann Bridge Cottages, Coleraine).

s: This beautiful song has been supplied, in response to our request....
  The air [is] an exceptionally sweet melody....
It is noteworthy that all the songs about Coleraine are of special merit. In music, as in most
things, Coleraine has always been "a lady of quality."

Key C.

C24 / To Hymen's car

It being on an evening clear
As I roved down by the Bann side
To view the swan in plumage gay
A-floating on the silvery tide,
To my surprise, who did I spy,
As near to me she deigned to pass --
I knew it was no deity,
But a handsome charming Coleraine lass.

I step-ped up to this fair maid
And unto her these words did say:
'Fair maid, you have my heart betrayed,
You're fairer than the queen of May.
Will you go to yon rural plain,
Where you and I the time will pass,
While I reveal my love-sick tale
To you, my charming Coleraine lass?'

She gave consent and away we went
Unto that river that runs clear,
We both sat down upon the ground,
Where no one but ourselves could hear.
Unto my breast this fair I pressed,
As we lay on the flowery grass,
No queen could be more blessed than we,
Me and my charming Coleraine lass.

I wiped the teardrops from her eyes,
I wondered would she say me nay,
She looked at me in glad surprise,
And so we named our wedding day.
To Hymen's car we did prepare
Unto a clergy of our class
To join our hands in wedlock's bands,
Me and my charming Coleraine lass.

The Star of Donegal [H555: 21 Jul 1934]

s: (m) "Bold Jack Donahoe."

Source: native (Stranocum district).

Key E flat.

One evening fair to take the air alone, as I chanced to stray
Down by yon silv'ry stream that ran along my way,
I spied two lovers seated by an ancient ruined hall,
This fair maid's name was Mary, or the star of Donegal.

He pressed her hand and softly said, 'My darling, I must go
Unto the land of stars and stripes where peace and plenty flow,
But give me your faithful promise that you'll wed none at all
Until I do return to you, bright star of Donegal.'

She blushed and sighed and thus she cried: 'It grieves my heart full sore
To think that you're compelled to go and leave your native shore;
Here is my hand, you have my heart; I own the gift is small,
So stay at home and do not roam from matchless Donegal.'

The young man said, 'My charming maid, at home I cannot stay.
To California gold fields I'm bound to cross the sea,
To accumulate a fortune to build a splendid hall
To elevate to rank and state the star of Donegal.'

She raised her lily-white hand and said, 'The castle in its day,
With all its plains and large demesnes, from Lifford to the sea,
Belonged to my ancestors with many a stately hall,
And if my father had his rights, he'd be lord of Donegal.'

The young man said, 'My charming maid, the time is drawing near
When the Irish will return again, after their long career;
Our loving land by God's command, the fairest of them all,
And heaven will see old Ireland free, bright star of Donegal.'

He pressed her in his arms and 'My darling,' he did say,
'You know I love you dearly, although I'm going away,
Let us get wed without fear or dread and put an end to all,
And then I'll have my charming maid, bright star of Donegal.'

She gave consent, so off they went to the house of the Reverend Hugh,
They joined their hands in wedlock's bands without any more to do,
They sailed away from Derry Quay and they bid farewell to all,
And now they're in America, far, far from Donegal.

Sam Henry's Songs of the People

Glenarm Bay [H102: 24 Oct 1925]

Source: (w, m) W. L. (Landhead, Ballymoney) "who gives his address as 'a Citizen of the World.'" [Dt: (? Willie Lynn)]

[Bp] s: ... He describes the song as "very old." [Dt] Glenarm pronounced "Glen-aram." Last three words of last verse are spoken.

Key G.

Being on a mild September morn, the weather it being warm,
It was my lot to stray along the bay of sweet Glenarm,
The yellow corn was waving ripe and every field looked gay,
And the blue sea washed the pebbles white along Glenarm Bay.

'Twas there I spied a charming maid, a maid both young and gay,
The sun arose, nor brighter shone than she appeared that day.
I stepped up to this fair maid and unto her did say,
'What brings you here so early, dear, along Glenarm Bay?'

She answered me right modestly, 'What makes you ask me so?
There's nothing brings young women here but what all young men know,
It's the love that stirs a maiden young,' she modestly did say,
'And a manly man must prove himself along Glenarm Bay.'

Says I, 'My dear, you need not fear, all flattery I deny;
If you but felt the pain of love doth in my bosom lie,
You would surely pity me, my love, and name the happy day,
And cure these wounds that you gave me along Glenarm Bay.'

'I won't be your companion, sir, I'm but a maiden young,
I'm free as yet from Cupid's darts, from young men's flattering tongue,
I'm scarce eighteen, plain to be seen; oh leave me here, I pray,
For I would be a maiden still, along Glenarm Bay.'

Says I, 'My dear, if you're sincere, here is my heart and hand,
Young women's frames at first were formed to pierce the heart of man;
It was the case with you, my love, you did my heart betray,
Your killing glances wounded me along Glenarm Bay.'

She says, 'My dear, if you're sincere, here is my heart and hand.'
We'll ne'er forget the happy morn we met along the strand,
And when old age comes creeping on and our locks are getting grey,
We'll always mind the happy morn we met along the bay.

7.4: ... morn along the bay. [Dt]

Greenmount Smiling Ann [H182: 7 May 1927]

Source: (w) Lizzie Campbell (Carn, Dungiven); (m) William Devine (Cross Lane, Coleraine; [Dt: native of Foreglen, Dungiven]).

s: Words contributed, in response to our published request....

Key G.

In summertime when flowers were fine I rambled o'er the green,
The small fish they did sport and play beneath yon silvery stream,
Nigh to a grove where lovers rove, right nimbly there I ran,
While walking there, I spied that fair called Greenmount smiling Ann.

Her hair so fine waved in the wind like ringlets of pure gold,
Her snow-white breast I do protest was glorious to behold,
Her comely size it would entize the heart of any man,
Could he but see that matchless she called Greenmount smiling Ann.

A lad was seen dressed all in green as I walked towards the fair,
He bowed so low, respect to show, I solemnly declare,

This charmer sweet, so mild and meek, she gave
   to him her hand,
You may be sure the lad was pure that spoke to
   Greenmount Ann.

She sang so rare, I do declare, as she tripped
   o'er the green,
The song she sang, I mind it well, was 'Shield's
   Fair Maid of Screen,'
The small birds they did sweetly sing to chorus
   her along,
The swan did glide along the tide to welcome
   Greenmount Ann.

Through a lonesome grove this couple strode for
   an hour or something more,
In smiles and tears, in hopes and fears, to part
   was sad and sore,
I heard the people say, 'My dear, they're joined
   in Hymen's ban','
She gave consent and off they went, both he and
   Greenmount Ann.

2.3: ... would entice ... [Dt]
5.3: ... in Homen's ban', [Dt]

Gruig Hill [H626: 30 Nov 1935]

Source: (Dunloy district).

s: ... Gruig Hill lies eastward of the hamlet of
Lislaban, near Cloughmills.

Key C.

As I walked out one evening to take the caller
   air,
I spied a handsome fair maid, she did my heart
   ensnare;
Her looks divine and features fine would any
   young man kill,
And her rural habitation lies convenient to Gruig
   Hill.

I stood in consternation, not knowing what to
   say,
And looks of admiration in emotion died away;
To gain that maiden's company, I used my artful
   skill,
With right content she gave consent to walk
   round Gruig Hill.

With my loving conversation I did her entertain,
Right well she knew I'd be her slave, bound fast
   in Cupid's chain;

Her heaving breast to mine I pressed and she did
   not take it ill,
The sylvan gods had seemed to smile that day on
   Gruig Hill.

Her skin was like the driven snow and her
   cheeks a crimson hue,
The velvet turf beneath her feet was clad with
   violets blue;
Were I possessed of genius blest, could handle
   Homer's quill,
The praises great I would relate of the maid of
   sweet Gruig Hill.

Unto her father's dwelling away we did repair,
With a 'cead mile failte' we were kindly welcomed
   there;
Her parents they seemed well content and a glass
   to me did fill,
And with courage bold I drunk a health to the
   maid of sweet Gruig Hill.

I bid my love good evening and homewards bent
   my way,
Bright Venus['] beams were shining, nor longer
   could I stay,
And as I jogged along the road I thought upon
   her still,
To join our hands in wedlock's bands with the
   maid of sweet Gruig Hill.

1.1: caller = fresh and cool.
5.2: cead mile failte = 'a thousand welcomes,' traditional Gaelic greeting.

Innishowen [H209: 12 Nov 1927]

Source: (Magilligan district).

s: ... The hero of the song was John Smith, a
tailor, of Margymonaghan, Magilligan.

Key G.

'Twas on a Monday morning, the weather being
   calm and clear,
I crossed Greencastle ferry in the springtime of
   the year,
I crossed Greencastle ferry, being free from
   care and toil,
To view the hills and valleys down by the river
   Foyle.

Sam Henry's Songs of the People

Magilligan's a purty place, and that full well is
   known,
But I intend to leave it and live in Innishowen,
Where the purty girls go neat and trim in every
   degree,
And above all parts in Ireland, sweet
   Innishowen for me.

The road to Glenagivney is above Greencastle
   town,
There lives a handsome fair maid of honour and
   renown,
The smiles of her bright countenance have so
   enticed me,
By Cupid's dart I've found the smart, I'm
   wounded quite by she.

'I'm sorry, miss, you slight me, and I your
   wounded slave;
I never will deny you till I go to my grave.
Perhaps you'll rue't when I'm far off, when
   Cupid sets me free,
So take kind fortune to be your guide and come
   along with me.'

'The character that I got of you, it pleases me
   right well,
And let them all say as they will, I will go
   please mysel';
Perhaps by your industry we'll lead a happy
   life,
So I have no objections, kind sir, to be your
   wife.'

Kellswaterside [H802: 8 Apr 1939]

Other title: "By Kells Waters."

Source: (m) Jim Carmichael, fiddle (Waring St, Ballymena) from David [? Ealer ? Eaton ? Esker] (Whaupstown, Glenwherry); (w) William Moore (Tullaghans, Dunloy).

s: ... Special attention is drawn to the beauty and simplicity of the air and the sincere naturalness of the words.

Key F.

I mounted on horseback with five miles to ride
Till I came to a cottage near Kellswaterside;
Said I to myself, in this country might be
A maid young and handsome and she might fit
   me.

I dismounted my horse and went in and sat down;
A maid in the corner I viewed all around,
Her cheeks blushed like roses, her curved lips
   were red,
And her eyes were like diamonds that shone in her
   head.

'O,' said I, 'my wee lassie, will you come wi' me
To the sweet town of Antrim, where married we'll
   be?
In the sweet town of Antrim we'll get the words
   said,
And you ne'er will return to your mother a maid.'

'Your offer is good, sir, I cannot deny,
But to make your acquaintance I ne'er will comply;
To go with a stranger would grudge me in mind
At leaving Kellswater and sweethearts behind.
'My friends and my parents would all on me frown
At leaving Kellswater and fair Randalstown.'
'Your friends and your parents will not on you
   frown
For leaving Kellswater and fair Randalstown.

'For in sweet Ballybogey, where I will you bring,
You'll hear the birds whistle and nightingales
   sing;
Your heart will be glad and no tears need you
   weep,
And the birds in the evening will sing you to
   sleep.'

'Come back, my wee laddie, I'm changing my
   mind,
And now to get married my heart feels inclined;
I bid my old sweethearts a last fond adieu,
And I'll leave my old parents and follow with
   you.'

The Banks of Kilrea (I) [H150a: 25 Sep 1926]

[The first of two versions printed, in Bp to the same tune; in Dt, H150 is supplied with a second melody.]
[This is the definitely happy-ending version.]

s: (m) "A Young Sailor Bold"; o: (m) "Aghalee Heroes"; h: "Drumreagh."

Source: 2: John Mullan (Brockagh Mountain, Garvagh), learned from Pat Maguire, 60 (Philadelphia), c. 1905; Mrs Neil Dickey (Carrowreagh, Finvoy, Ballymoney); (m) Rose E. Hassan (Ballymonie, Altmover P.O., Dungiven).

Key E.

One evening for my recreation, kind fortune did
    cause me to stray
Where I met a lass in great splendure all alone by
    the banks of Kilrea.
I enfolded her into my arms, her bosom to mine I
    did press,
I asked her what fate had befelt her or chang-ed
    her colour o' dress.

'It's the cold hand of death,' she made answer,
    'has cut both my parents away,
And left me alone for to wandure all alone by the
    banks of Kilrea.'
'Since fate has decreed what has happened, pray
    tell me your sorrowful news,
I promise to be your protector and for to step
    into their shoes.

'The highest o' coternal protection this day I will
    freely repay,
Come with me to the mountains o' Swateragh and
    leave the low banks of Kilrea,
For I do not mean to deceive you, a traitor I
    highly disdain,
I'll endeavour through life to maintain you as long
    as young Friel is my name.'

We walked into town both together, her scruples
    at length she gave o'er;
We went into Boyle's at the corner and ordered
    the best in the store,
With the landlady we spent all the evening, I am
    sure it was gallant and gay,
And when we got behopes to be married, we made
    up the match in Kilrea.

The night I came down through Rasharkin, I'll
    mind it as long as I live,
I called for a five-gallon keg of the best that
    M'Cracken could give
For to treat all my friends and relations and
    everyone comes in my way
The night I bring home Nancy Hunter, she's the
    flower of the banks of Kilrea.

5.1: ... I will mind ... [Dt]

3.1: coternal = "improvised word including paternal
and maternal." [s]

The Largy Line   [H781: 12 Nov 1938]

s: (m) "original form" of "The Maid of the Sweet
Brown Knowe."

Source: Jock Smylie (Leggyfat, Limavallaghan,
Clough, Co. Antrim).

s: ... The events in the song took place about
60 years ago....

Key G.

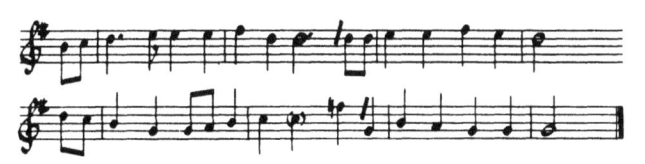

My name is George M'Caughey, I'm a shoemaker to
    trade,
I ran through Ahoghill courting all the pretty
    maids,
But I'll leave them all, both great and small,
    for they do not please my mind,
And I'll go and wed Miss Baxter along the Largy
    line.

The first place that I saw my love, I mean to let
    you know,
It being to teach the Tully band that evening I did
    go,
When the practice it was over, I loudly then did
    say,
'Is there any male or female here that goes along
    my way?'

Young A. M'Neice, he then spoke out and thus to
    me did say,
'Here is Miss Maggie Baxter, I know she goes your
    way.'
'Yes,' says Miss Baxter, 'I will go, if you just take
    your time,'
So we both jogged on together along the Largy
    line.

Now when I came up to her house, I mean to let
    you know,
My love she would not part with me, for in I had
    to go;
The treatment that she gave me, I'll keep it in my
    mind,
I could court away both night and day along the
    Largy line.

Her father he is willing and her mother, she's the
    same,
Her brother he is on for me and so's Eliza Jane;
My love she does stick close to me, for it still runs
    in her mind,
If she's spared her life, she'll be my wife along the
    Largy line.

Now here's long life to Mr Fyffe, he well deserves
    the name,
He was the man first raised the band, caused me
    to get this dame,
And if he lives to my wedding day we'd have a
    regular shine,
For I'll make him fu' and happy too, along the
    Largy line.

Sam Henry's Songs of the People

Sweet Londonderry [H813: 24 Jun 1939]

Other titles: "Londonderry (Lovely Derry) on the Banks of the Foyle."

Source: Mary Harte (Benone), daughter of Richard Butler (native, Derry).

Key D.

There's an ancient walled city, a place of great
   fame,
It lies in the north and the world knows its name;
It was there I was born and it's built on good
   soil,
It is sweet Londonderry on the banks of the
   Foyle.

My parents they left me when I was a boy,
And I took a notion the seas to enjoy;
I work hard for my living, light-hearted I toil
Far away from Londonderry and the banks of the
   Foyle.

I courted a wee girl, her age was nineteen,
And a prettier wee girl you never have seen,
For her eyes are like diamonds, her waist round
   and small,
She's the pride of Londonderry and the banks of
   the Foyle.

Well, it's now I'm contented, I'll finish my song,
Though whiles for my wee girl I sit and think
   long,
And when we get married, I'll think it no toil
To work for my wee girl by the banks of the
   Foyle.

The Lovely Banks of Mourne

[H595: 27 Apr 1935]

Other title: "The Banks ...."

Source: (Ballycastle district).

Key G.

It being on the lovely banks of Mourne
Where a farmer's son did gaze,
He was viewing his barley, lint and corn
Where sheep and kye did graze,
Where there he spied a braw wee lass,
To bathe she did prepare,
Which garred him stand behind a bush
To view this charming fair.

She jumped into the river Mourne
Where oftimes she had been,
And when she came to herself again,
Appeared like a morning queen,
Then peeping round a hazel bush,
She spied the farmer's son,
Which garred her rosy cheeks to blush,
And ower the moor she run.

With her braw white limbs and tartan plaid,
Quick ower the moor she run,
But the farmer's son followed after her,
Saying, 'Lass, what have I done?
Sure, I have barley, lint and corn,
And the owner I'll make thee,
If you'll consent, my braw wee lass,
To share your love wi' me.'

Now ne'er a word this young thing spoke,
But laughed at his fond care,
Now she's gane hame to her father's house,
And the dear be wi' her there.
To tell her name I am ashamed,
To vex her I am loth,
But with an M her name begins --
Her name and surname both.

The next time that I saw my love,
She was not half so shy,
Sure, she was fond of the farmer's son
When she thought on his land and kye.
It was in a month I made her my bride
And so for evermore,
All on the lovely banks of Mourne,
Long may the ring be wore.

4.4: the dear = [circumlocution for] the deity.

Wild Slieve Gallon Brae[s]

[H540: 7 Apr 1934]

o: (m) "The Winding Banks of Erne."

Source not given.

Key G.

It's once I loved a damsel, alas, she proved
  untrue,
I thought to climb those mountains high, her
  cottage for to view,
But whether it was magic or enchantment led my
  way,
Soon I reached the Tummock on wild Slieve Gallon
  brae.

I viewed its land and gorges along its rugged side,
And likewise Stoneybatter where the timid rabbits
  hide,
The moorcock he kept crowing the pleasure of the
  day
All along the moor and heather on wild Slieve
  Gallon brae.

Oh, just as I was musing and thinking on the
  past,
I saw a sight before my eyes which touched my
  mind at last,
For over in the heather and not too far away,
I spied a lovely damsel on wild Slieve Gallon brae.

She seemed of me unconscious, but soon her tale
  began,
Saying, 'Once I was deluded by a very false
  young man,
He promised he would marry me, but he did sail
  the seas
And left me here alone to mourn on wild Slieve
  Gallon braes.'

Now, since she lost her sweetheart as likewise I
  had mine,
Then why should two young lovers for ever more
  repine?
We made it up then and there upon that day of
  days,
And now we live contented on wild Slieve Gallon
  braes.

Sandy's Wooing [H239: 9 Jun 1928]

[Dt] Source: Sally Doherty, 95 (Oughtymoyle, Bellarena).

Key G.

'Oh, lassie, will ye come wi' me
To yonder hill beyond the lea,
And spend your days in mirth and glee
And joy that's never weary?

'For since I met you on the plain
My hert it ne'er has been my ain,
But torn in love baith fierce and keen,
And a' for you, my dearie.'

'Oh, Sandy, lad, I dinna ken,
It's hard for us to trust the men,
For aft they'll make their game o' them
Wha they dae ca' their dearie.

'Nae farther off than neighbour Kate,
See hoo she has been served wi' Pete,
Who o'er the hill has ta'en the gate
Wi' humpy-back-ed Mary.

'Wha knows but you might do the same,
Soon as you get anither dame
Wi' bags o' siller, bring her hame
And lea me dull and oorie.'

'Oh Jenny, lass, for this ne'er fear,
I hae a mealin' an' no that dear,
I'll ask nae ither worldly gear
But you to keep me cheery.

But yet when done I'll cross the plain,
If you be shy, I'll be the same,
If you be shy, I'll be the same,
If I gang tae Jean the morra.'

'Oh Sandy, lad, just stop a wee,
We'll no' cast oot 'gin we can 'gree,
It's here's my han', your ain I'll be
If that would ease your sorrow.'

He kissed her cheek, he preed her mou',
And s'ore for aye he would be true.
'This very night I will go through
To see auld Tam your daddy.'

The auld man shane gied his consent,
And for the perrish clerk they went,
Who ca'd them thrice with his intent
To marry them on Friday.

3.4: When they ... [Dt]
7.3: ... shy, you canna blame [Dt]
  .4: ... the morrow. [Dt]
8.3: It's here my hand, ... [Dt]
10.2: ... the parish clerk ... [Dt]

5.4: oorie = dismal, sad, lonely; apprehensive.
9.1: preed = sampled, tasted.

"Thank You, Ma'am," Says Dan

[H184: 21 May 1927, H689: Dp, 6 Feb 1937]

Other title: "I ...."

Source: (w) ? Gerald Crofts (Dublin); (m) Joseph M. Crofts.

s: By special permission from Mr Gerald Crofts, of Dublin, the distinguished Irish tenor, whose broadcast recitals from Dublin Station are well known.
  This droll folk song is believed to emanate from County Tipperary. The present setting is by Mr Joseph M. Crofts....
  The words "Thank you" in each verse may be spoken. In the first verse, eagerly; in the second verse, happily; in the third verse, resignedly; in the last verse, tragically. The last two notes of the last verse to be sung an octave higher.

Sam Henry's Songs of the People

[Dt, Wt] This song has been excluded as the copyright belongs to Mr Gerard Crofts, Dublin, by whose permission it was published on payment of the appropriate fee. [Dt, written] See No. 689.

Key G.

'What brought you into my house, to my house, to my house?
What brought you into my house?' said herself to Master Dan.
'I came to coort your daughter, ma'am; I thought it no great har-m, ma'am.'
'Och Dan, my dear, you're welcome here.'
'Thank you, ma'am,' says Dan.

'How came you to know my daughter, my daughter, my daughter?
How came you to know my daughter?' says herself to Master Dan.
'Goin' to the well for wather, ma'am; to raise the can I taught her, ma'am.'
Och Dan, my dear, you're welcome here.'
'Thank you, ma'am,' says Dan.

'Now I'll let you take my daughter, my daughter, my daughter,
I'll let you take my daughter,' says herself to Master Dan.
'And when you take my daughter, Dan, of course you'll take me also, Dan;
Och Dan, you are the lucky man.' 'Thank you, ma'am,' says Dan.

Now this couple they got married, got married, got married,
This couple they got married, Miss M'Dade and Master Dan,
And he supports her father, mother, brothers, aunts and sisters all!
'Och Dan, 'tis you're the lucky man.' 'Thank you, ma'am,' says Dan.

The Yowe Lamb [H175: 19 Mar 1927]

k: "Ca' the Yowes to the Knowes." Other titles: "As Johnny Walked Out," "As Molly Was Milking," "Lovely Mollie(y)," "The True Lovers."

Source: (w, m) James Stirling (Gorticloughan, Ballyrashane).

s: ... A version, quite different as to air and varying considerably in words, has been published in Robert Ford's *Vagabond Songs and Ballads of Scotland* [1,1899].

g: Some of the following items, which vary greatly, may be only "related."

Key E flat.

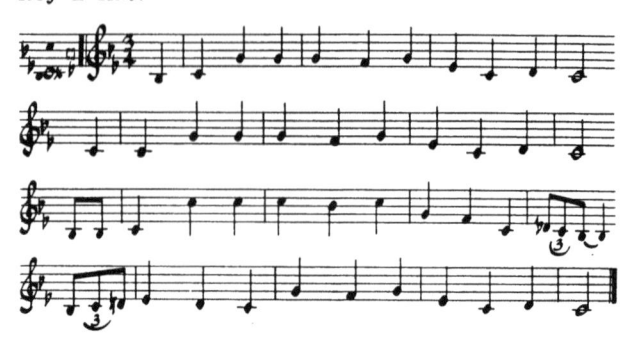

As Molly was milking her yowes one day,
Willie came to her and thus he did say,
'As your fingers go nimble, will you gang wi' me?'
 And we'll ca' the yowes ower the knowes, Molly and me.

'Gang doon tae my faither and ask his guid will,
Dae your best endeavours and try your best skill,
And if he be willing, sure I'll gang wi' thee.'
 And we'll ca' ...

'Good morrow, auld man, are you feeding your flock?
Would you gie me a yowe lamb to rear up a stock?
And she will be weel fed doon by yon green lea.'
 And we'll ca' ...

Gang doon tae my sheepfold and choose a yowe lamb,
You're as welcome tae her as any young man,
And see that she's weel fed doon by yon green lea.'
 And we'll ca' ...

He took his young Molly all by the right hand,
Saying, 'This is the yowe lamb that I do demand,
And she will be weel fed doon by yon green lea.'
 And we'll ca' ...

'Oh, faux, take you Willie, you did me beguile,
Instead of a yowe lamb it was my ae child,
But since I hae said it, sae lane let it be.'
 And we'll ca' ...

'Was there ever an aul' man bewitched as I am,
Tae gie his ae daughter instead o' a lamb?
As her fingers go nimble, I'll let her go free.'
 And we'll ca' ...

4.2: ... as ony young ... [Dt]

Petie Cam' ower the Glen [H200: 10 Sep 1927]

Other titles: "Patie's Waddin' (Wedding)."

Source: Sally Doherty, 93 (Oughtymoyle, Bellarena).

s: ... Sally Doherty ... [is] a veteran singer whose memory in her 93rd year is stored with excellent old songs which she has retained since girlhood, true to ai[r] and word-perfect, and which she sings with much enthusiasm and life-like interpretation.

[Dt] A version of this song is in Herd's *Ancient and Modern Scottish Songs*, Vol. 2 [1776] ... where it is called "Patie's Wedding." It is also included in Whitelaw's *Book of Scottish Song* [1844?:336].

Key B flat. [Bp] Quick time.

Oh, Petie cam' ower the glen,
An' a' his gay wathers before him,
He spied purty Meg on the moor,
Her beauty had like for to smoor him.

'It's didna ye hear, bonny Meg,
That you and me's gaun tae be merried?
I wad rather hae broken my leg
As that sic a bargain miscarried.

'Oh Meg, what makes ye sae nice,
Is't because I hae ne'er a maelin?
A lad that has plenty o' gear
Has neither a faut nor failin'.

'It's I hae baith yern and clews
Tae mak' ye a coat an' a slippie,
A bunch o' green ribbons tae tie
The bab on the neck o' your coatie.'

'Very weel,' quo' Meg,
But first you maun speir at my deddy,
Gin a' be bit or be bore,
There's things'll shane be ready.'

Oh, Petie cam' tottering in
Saying, 'Peace be inunder the biggin'.'
'Amen,' then quo' the auld man,
'An' I wish it may rise tae the riggin'.'

'My erran' it was to you,
For Maggie tae help me to labour,
Indeed you maun gie the best coo,
For our maelin' it is but sober.'

'Very weel,' quo' Jack,
'An' I'll be at the cost o' the merriage,
An' I'll cut the craig o' the oul' yowe,
Fo[r] I'm feared that she'll die with the sowder.

'An' that'll mak' bree enough
An' we'll gie them a ragh o' mulreestie,
An' a' the guid nibors an ye
I think they'll no be ill-feasted.'

'Very weel then,' quo Jack,
'An I'll gie them a brose in the mornin'
O' cail that was boiled yestreen,
For I like them best in the forenane.

'It's I'll hae a piper tae play
And they may a' dance that is willin',
And them that'll no' dance may sing
It's aye the wee stoupie's a fillin'.'

1.2: wathers = ?waters.
1.4: smoor = smother. [s]
2.2: merried = married.
3.1: sweer = lazy. [s: Dt]
3.4: faut = fault.
4.1: clews = balls, especially of yarn.
4.4: bab = posy, nosegay, bunch of colored ribbons.
5.2: speir = inquire, ask; deddy = father.
6.2: biggin' = building. [s]
6.4: riggin' = roof. [s]
8.3: craig [crag] = throat. [s]
10.2: brose = dish (mush) of oatmeal or peasemeal.
10.4: forenane = forenoon, morning.
11.4: stoupie = whiskey jug. [s]

The Navvy Boy [H760: 18 Jun 1938]

Source: Robert J. Lyons (Greenhill, Blackhill, Coleraine).

s: The tunes must be adapted to the words by the duplication of a note where necessary.

Key D.

When I was young and tender, I left my native home
And often to old Scotland I started out to roam;
As I walked down through Bishoptown a-seeking for employ,
The ganger he knew by me, I was a navvy boy.

As soon as I did get employ, for lodgings I did seek,
It happened to be that very night with the ganger I did sleep;
He had one only daughter and I became her joy,
For she longed to go and tramp with her own dear navvy boy.

Says the mother to the daughter, 'I think it very strange
That you would wed a navvy boy, this wide world for to range,

Sam Henry's Songs of the People

For navvies they are rambling boys and have but
  little pay,
How could a man maintain a wife with
  fourteenpence a day?'

Says the daughter to the mother, 'You shall not
  run them down.
My father was a navvy boy when he came to this
  town;
He roamed about from town to town just seeking
  for employ.
Go where he will, he's my love still, he's my own
  dear navvy boy.'

Now just a short time after this, her father died,
  I'm told,
And left unto his daughter five hundred pounds in
  gold,
And when she got the money, soon I became her
  joy,
For she longed to go and tramp with her own dear
  navvy boy.

1.4: ganger = foreman in charge of a gang of workmen.
navvy = laborer in heavy construction or excavation.

One Penny Portion

[H634: 18 Jan 1936; Laws O41]

Other titles: "The Constant Lovers," "A Sailor
Courted (Loved) (Married) (Wooed) a Farmer's
Daughter."

Source: resident (Bushmills), learned from Pat
Callaghan (Cork) in Philadelphia c. 1930.

Key G.

A sailor courted a farmer's daughter
Who lived contagious to the Isle of Man.
Take heed, good people, what followed after;
They long had courted, but underhand.

One day at parting, after discoursing
Some time concerning the ocean wide,
He said, 'My dear, at our next meeting,
If you'll consent, I'll make you my bride.'

Said she, 'For sailors, we don't admire them
Because they sail to so many parts,
The more we love them, the more they slight us
And leave us after them with broken hearts.'

'Oh no, my dear, my dearest dear,
I don't intend to serve you so,
I have got once more to cross the ocean
And you know, my darling, that I must go.'

The news was carried to his mother,
Before he put his foot on board,
That he was courting a farmer's daughter,
One penny portion could not afford.

One penny portion and to cross the ocean!
Like one distracted his mother run,
'If you don't forsake her, your bride not make he
I will disown you to be my son.'

'Oh, mother dear, you're in a passion,
And I'm very sorry for what you said;
Do you remember at your first meeting,
My father married you, a servant maid?

'Now don't dispraise her, I mean to raise her
Just as my father to you has done,
It's now I'll take her, my bride to make her,
Should you disown me to be your son.'

This fair one heard his loving story,
It's off to sea with her lover she would go,
She says, 'It's all about my fortune,
I may have money and no one know.'

'Money or not, love, you are my lot, love,
You have my heart and affection still,
It's now I'll take you, my bride sure make you,
Let my scolding mother say what she will.'

The Inniskilling Dragoon

[H98b: "Two regimental songs," 26 Sep 1925]

[cf. H631 "Fare Ye Well, Enniskillen"]

s: (m) "The Strands of Magilligan"; g: "Enniskillen Dragoon," "Fare Ye (Thee) Well, Enniskillen." Other titles: "The Inniskillin ...."

Source: Harry Evans (Coleraine).

s: ... This version is more complete than that
published by Joyce, or by "Impartial Reporter,"
Enniskillen. It is to be noted that the name of
the regiment and that of the town are differently
spelt. The air is older than the song. A local
song called "The Strands of Magilligan" [Bp: (of
no value as to words)] is sung to this air.

Key D.

A beautiful damsel of fame and renown,
A gentleman's daughter of Monaghan town,
As she rode by the barracks, this beautiful maid,
She watched from her carriage the dragoons on
    parade.

> Farewell Enniskillen, farewell for a while,
> Farewell to the borders of Erin's green isle,
> When the war is all over, we'll return in full
>   bloom,
> And you'll all welcome home your Inniskilling
>   dragoon.

They were all neatly dressed up like gentlemen's
    sons,
With bright shining swords and carabine guns;
With a silver-mounted pistol she observed him
    full soon,
Because that she loved her Inniskilling dragoon.

She looked on the bright sons of Mars on the
    right
With their armour outshining the stars of the
    night,
Saying, 'Willie, dearest Willie, you have 'listed
    full soon
To serve as a Royal Inniskilling dragoon.'

'O Flora, dear Flora, your pardon I crave,
Now and forever I will be your slave,
Your parents often slighted me both morning and
    noon,
All because that you loved an Inniskilling
    dragoon.'

'O Willie, dear Willie, do not mind what they say,
For children are duty bound their parents to
    obey,
But now you're leaving Ireland they'll all change
    their tune
And say, 'The Lord be with you, Inniskilling
    dragoon.'

Now the war it is over with Willie home at last,
His regiment lay in Dublin, but Willie got a pass;
On Sunday they were married with Flora in full
    bloom,
So now she enjoys her Inniskilling dragoon.

The Gallant Soldier [H782: 19 Nov 1938]

Other titles: "The Highland ...," "The Lovely
Maiden."

Source: Dick Gilloway, learned in Magilligan.

s: ... Magilligan, a land full of melody, traceable
in part to the influence of its great harper -- Denis Hempson (born 1695, died 1812).

Key G.

On the lofty mountains far away
There dwells a comely maiden,
And she roved out on a summer's day
For to view the soldiers parading;
They marched so bold and they looked so gay,
Their colours flying, and their bands did play,
It caused young Mary for to say,
'I'll wed you, my gallant soldier.'

She viewed the soldiers on parade
As they stood at their leisure,
And Mary to herself did say,
'At length I've found my treasure,
But oh, how cruel my parents must be
To banish my darling so far from me,
I'll part them all and go with thee,
My bold undaunted soldier.'

'Oh Mary dear, your parents love;
I pray don't be unruly,
For when I'm in a foreign land,
Believe me, you'll rue it surely;
Perhaps in battle I might fall
By a shot from an angry cannon ball,
And you so far from your daddy's hall,
Be advised by a gallant soldier.'

'Oh, don't say so, but let me go,
And I will face the daring foe,
And wander with you, to and fro,
And wed you, my gallant soldier;
I have fifty guineas of bright gold,
Besides a heart that's bolder;
I'll part it all and go with thee,
My bold undaunted soldier.'

Now when he saw her loyalty,
And Mary so true-hearted,
He says, 'My darling, married we will be,
And nothing but death will part us,
And when I'm in a foreign land,
I'll guard you, darling, with my right hand
In hopes that God may stand a friend
To Mary and her gallant soldier.'

Young Edward the Gallant Hussar

[H243a: BLp, 7 Jul 1928]

Other titles: "The Gallant ...(s)."

Source not given.

[BLp, Bt typed in 8-line stanzas, but tune fits 4
lines.]

Key C.

Sam Henry's Songs of the People

[H243b: Dt]

[Dt, Wt] Source: (m) John McLeese, Croaghbeg, Bushmills.

Key G.

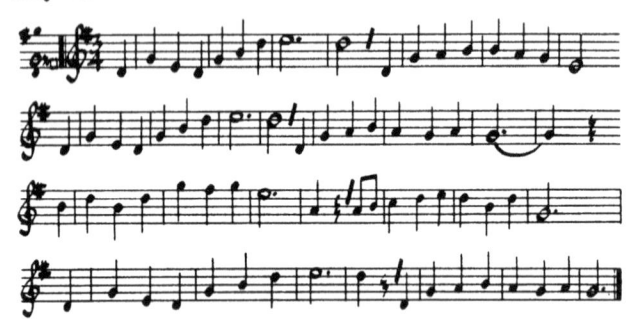

A damsel possess'd of great beauty,
She stood by her own father's gate,
The gallant hussars were on duty,
To view them this maiden did wait.

Their horses were capering and prancing,
Their accoutrements shone like a star,
From the plains they were nearer advancing,
She espied her young gallant hussar.

Their pellices were slung o'er their shoulders,
So careless they seemed for to ride,
So warlike appeared those young soldiers,
With glittering swords by their sides.

To barrack next morning so early,
This damsel she went in her car,
Because she loved him sincerely,
Young Edward, the gallant hussar.

'Twas there she conversed with her soldier,
These words they were heard for to say:
Said Jane, 'I've a heart, none has bolder,
To follow my laddie away.'

'O fie,' said young Edward, 'be steady,
And think of the dangers of war:
When the trumpet sounds, I must be ready,
So wed not your gallant hussar.'

'For twelve months on bread and cold water
My parents confined me for you,
O, hard-hearted friends to their daughter,
Whose heart is so loyal and true.

'Unless they confine me forever
Or banish me from you afar,
I will follow my soldier so clever,
To wed with my gallant hussar.'

Said Edward, 'Your friends, you must mind them,
Or else you're forever undone,
They will leave you no portion behind them,
So pray do my company shun.'

She said, 'If you will be true-hearted,
I have gold of my uncle's in store,
From this time we'll be no more parted,
I'll wed with my gallant hussar.'

As he gazed on each beautiful feature,
The tears they did fall from each eye;
'I will wed with this beautiful creature,
To forsake cruel war,' he did cry.

So now they are united together,
Friends think of them, now they're afar,
Crying, 'Heaven bless them, now and forever,
Young Jane and her gallant hussar.'

11.3: ... creature,'
　.4: To forsake cruel war he did try. [Bt]

Green Broom [H147: 4 Sep 1926]

Other titles: "The Broom-Cutter," "Broom, ...," "... Brooms."

Source: (w, m) William Davidson (Drumnakeel, Ballyvoy, Ballycastle).

s: ... A version collected by Cecil Sharp in Somersetshire [Bp only] contains only 6 verses, and is set to a different air. The version given below, both as to words and air, is English. It is an interesting question as to how it reached Ballyvoy, a district which abounds in song, and has preserved airs that date from the time of Ossian.

Key E.

There was an old man and he lived in the east,
He lived by the cutting of broom,
　Green broom,
He had one lazy son and his name it was John,
He would lie in his bed until noon,
　Gay noon,
He would lie in his bed until noon.

The old man arose and he put on his clothes,
And he cursed and he foamed through the room,
　Gay room,

If Jack would not rise and go sharpen his knives,
And get off to the woods to cut broom,
  Green broom, ...

Then Jack he arose and he put on his clothes,
He cursed and he foamed through the room,
  Gay room,
'I'm of good noble blood and my learning is good,
And must I be a cutter of broom,
  Green broom, ...

Then Jack he arose, to the green woods he goes
And he cut a large bundle of broom,
  Green broom,
And Jack travelled on till he passed many towns,
Till he came to the castle of fame,
  Gay fame, ...

Then a lady looked out of her window so high,
Jack's beauty enticed her too soon,
  Full soon,
She called aloud unto her waiting maids
To bring in that young youth and his broom,
  Green broom, ...

Then Jack he replied, 'I am not qualified
To go where I dare not presume,
  Presume,
I am not too well dressed for to vow and confess
Or to enter a young lady's room,
  Gay room, ...

'Now Jack,' then she said, 'give over your trade,
Give over your cutting of broom,
  Green broom,'
And smiling she said as she sat in the shade,
'Would you marry a youth in her bloom,
  Gay bloom, ...

Then Jack did consent to this lady's content,
And married they were in her room,
  Gay room,
And Jack blessed the day that he travelled that way,
For he's laird of the castle of fame,
  Gay fame, ...

There's not a gay cutter that travels this way
But Jack entertains to his room,
  Gay room,
There's good meat and drink, boys, what do you think?
There's an art in the cutting of broom,
  Green broom, ...

5.5: 'Bring in that young lad ...' [Dt]

John Hunter (a)   [H125a: 3 Apr 1926]

o: "Skibereen" (should be 6/8); k: "Wheelwright's Apprentice." Other title: "The Wheelwright."

Source: sisters (Adverness, Macosquin district).

[Bp only] s: Sung to me in proper traditional style by two sisters as a duet, both of whom are past the allotted span, and recalled to them with pleasure the happy days when, as girls, this song was a favourite ....

Key E flat.

I'm a stranger in this counter-ee come here to learn my trade,
I'm a stranger in this counter-ee come here to earn my bread.
It's three long years and a half, bound to a wheelwright I became,
In Glenmanus the parish I was brought up, and John Hunter it is my name.

My master has one daughter fair, called Eleanor by name;
I was scarce a year in my 'prenticeship till her lover I became;
We spent that time in mirth and fun, all for love we daurna show,
Until the time it was drawing nigh that from her I had to go.

'O, Johnnie,' she says, 'what will I do, when you do go away?'
'I think my heart will break when farewell I must say,
But if you consent to marry me now, I can work both out and in,
And, my darling, I'll go alongst with you, this wor-ld for to begin.'

'Oh, the streams they roll without control, or without the least dislay,
Oh, the streams they roll without control, or without the least dismay;
This maid she's young, she's murmuring still, all for the loss of her 'prentice boy,
And those vows to her I will fulfil, should those murmuring streams run dry.'

'I have travelled this country o'er and o'er, I have travelled it far and near;
I have travelled this country o'er and o'er till I met with you, my dear.
The bonniest lass that ever I saw, never could my fancy please,
I'll wed this maid and bring her with me to live on the Largy braes.'

2.3: daurna = dare not.
4.1: dislay = ?delay.

Sam Henry's Songs of the People

John Hunter (b) / [Dt] The Wheelwright

[H125b: Dt]

[m = H125a]

[Dt, typed on side] From John Troland of Norwich, Conn. USA.

I'm a stranger in this count-ir-ie,
Not in it was I bred,
But I came here an apprentice boy,
All for to learn my trade.
I was seven long years an apprentice bound,
Till a wheelwright I became;
In the parish of Carnmoney was I born,
And John Hunter is my name.

Oh, my master had a charming girl,
And her age was scarce sixteen,
And I not long been apprenticed till
Her true love I had been,
The time we spent in merriment,
Ne'er thought of care or woe,
Until that year the time drew near
When from her I must go.

Says I, 'My dear, the time draws near
When you and I must part,
I've served your father many's the year,
And you are my sweetheart,
But I maun go to meet my fate
And fill a workman's place,
The world is wide and I am clate
To meet it face to face.'

'Oh John,' says she, 'you're goin' away,
Alas, what will I do?
I'm afraid my very heart will break
When I take my leave of you,
But if you'll agree to marry me
I'll work both out and in,
And, my darling, it's I'll go along with you
This wide world to begin.'

1.4: ... traid. [Dt]

3.7: clate = ?[claught, clutched firmly or eagerly].

The Journeyman Tailor

[H620: 19 Oct 1935; Laws B6]

o: (m) "Villikins"; m: (m) "Still I Love Him," (m) "Six Miles from Bangor to Donaghadee." Other titles: "Bound down to Derry," "It Is of a Rich Lady," "The Jolly Stage Driver," "The Jolly Young Sailor and the (His) Beautiful Queen," "The Sailor and the Lady."

Source not given.

Key D.

It happened to be on a midsummer day
As a journeyman tailor was walking his way,
He was braw, brisk and airy as he stepped by,
She opened the door and bid him draw nigh.

'Oh, it's where were you born, love, or where
  were you bred,
Or what is your name?' this fair lady she said,
'I was born in fair Derry, dear lady,' said he,
'And James is the name my old father gave me.'

'Then, James, in this country I'd have you to
  tarry,
And some pretty fair maid I'd have you to marry;
Your learning perhaps might add to your store,
Now, James, I would have you to ramble no more.

'Your offer's enticing, fair lady,' said he,
'For you could get one of a higher degree,
But since you've decided to take on my name,
With your presence still with me, I'll still rise to
  fame.'

Her father, being standing, heard him plead his
  cause;
He welcomed his son-in-law, gave him applause,
And such a grand wedding was scarce ever seen
As the journeyman tailor and his beautiful queen.

Lough Erne Shore

[H597: 11 May 1935]

s: (m) variant of "Lovely Armoy." Other titles: "... Erin's ...," (m) "Molly of ...," "William and Eliza."

Source not given.

Key C.

You lovers of every station, give ear to these
  lines I unfold:
I was loved by a lady of honour, more better
  than silver or gold,

She dwells near the banks of Lough Erne, still
  viewing the clear purling stream,
And it was to commence my good fortune, a
  servant to her I became.

'Now, Willie, you will roll in splendour with
  lords, dukes and earls of fame,
You will correspond with the nobles and you will
  be equal the same,
For as Cupid has me entangled, no riches, my
  dear, I adore,
I despise all the nobles of London for Willie from
  Lough Erne shore.'

'Oh, you know that I am but your servant, and
  you a rich lady of fame,
Some lord or some nobleman worthy, dearest lady,
  your honour might gain,
Besides that, I am not your equal, and your
  friends would disown me therefore,
So I'll live no longer your servant till I go to
  Lough Erne shore.'

This lady she being surprised at hearing young
  Willie reply,
She flew to her chamber distracted, saying, 'For
  this young man I will die,
For if I had Venus's charms or the music of
  Orpheus in store,
I would charm the heart of young Willie and keep
  him from Lough Erne shore.'

Now Willie embraced his love's charms in marriage
  and none to control,
He drinks to the brave sons of Erin and that
  with a full flowing bowl.
He's wed to the rich English lady, though he
  was her servant before,
And hopes for to roll in great splendour once
  more upon Lough Erne shore.

It was there I remained with great pleasure, the
  truth unto you I'll explore,
Till at length she brought me to Dublin, and to
  London from that we sailed o'er;
For three months in great consolation this lady
  she did me adore,
Saying, 'William, dear, don't be uneasy for the
  parting from Lough Erne shore.'

Belfast Town   [H45: 20 Sep 1924]

o: (m) version of [Stanford/]Petrie #693. Other
titles: "The Cavehill Diamond," "Mary of the
Lagan Side."

Source: "one who learnt it from an old hand who
is still to the fore" (Magilligan).

o: Words should be in 8-line stanzas. Verse 2 as
written should be verse 5 as written.

Key D.

Belfast town, now rich and great,
Was then a village small,
And flocks of sheep grazed on that spot
Where stands the Linen Hall.

To herd the sheep was Mary's task,
And she did not repine,
She looked so happy in her flock,
She seemed almost divine.

And at that time young Dermott lived --
The royal crown he wore,
He ruled the ground from Belfast town
To Mourne's mountain shore.

To hunt the bear and savage wolf
Was this young prince's pride,
One day of age he killed three
Beneath the Cave Hill side.

Returning from his weary chase,
To give his horse some breath,
The reins upon his neck lay loose
To give his horse some breath.

And as he rode he Mary spied,
Who rose in deep alarm,
She was sleeping on a primrose bank
With her cheek upon her arm.

And as she rose, the prince she knew
And quickly genuflexed,
She knew him by the golden star
That glittered on his breast.

'O maiden, tell me who art thou
That dazzle so my eyes?
Are you a goddess from the skies
Or princess in disguise?'

'Oh, banter not a maiden fair
Of a low and mean degree,
My sovereign prince, your pardon crave,'
With that, she bent her knee.

'For I am of a lowly birth,
And poverty beside;
My widowed mother lives with me
Upon the Lagan side.'

'Say that you are poor no more,
Since those sweet charms of yours
Are far beyond in priceless wealth,
All gold or silver store.

'Come with me and be my bride,
Here is my heart and hand,
And I will share my throne with you
As queen of Erin's land.'

Sam Henry's Songs of the People

Once more her snow-white hand he pressed
As they walked side by side,
Until they to the cottage came
Where her mother did reside.

'My worthy dame,' out spoke the prince
(The prince of Mourne's land),
'The man has blessing on his youth
That has thy daughter's hand.'

'My worthy prince,' replied the dame,
'It's seventeen years and more
Since her I found outside my door,
Half buried in the snow.

'And around her neck were jewels fine
And likewise gold in store
To meet all charges till the time
I might the child restore.'

And when the prince the necklace saw,
He started with delight,
Saying, 'Mary dear, great is thy birth
And great's thy wealth and right.

'You are my uncle's long lost child,
Which shall not be denied,
Since I have found at once this day
A cousin and a bride.'

And when this royal pair was wed,
There rose with one loud roar
A general cheer from Belfast lough
To Mourne's mountain shore.

3.1: ... Dermot ... [Dt]
16.1: Around her ... [Dt]
17.1: ... the necklet saw, [Dt]
18.3: ... found this day [Dt]

Jamie and Nancy [H738: 15 Jan 1938]

Source: Pat Kealey (Dungiven).

s: [Pat Kealey's] beautiful airs are now known to the world over the radio.

Key G.

Down in yon valley, where the flowers grow
  sweet,
There Jamie and Nancy together did meet,
He asked her the reason and what brought her
  there,
She told him her parents they had proved severe.

'If your parents prove cruel, my darling,' said
  he,
'If they turn out hard-hearted, you're welcome to
  me,
If they turn out hard-hearted or the least bit
  unkind,
Come when you will and a friend you will find.'

Her two cherry cheeks were like two roses red,
The veins of her neck were like a silk thread,
She might be an equal for a lord or a knight,
Her two diamond eyes in the dark shine so
  bright.

As she lay on her pillow, she there dreamt a
  dream
That her true lover Jamie, in war he was slain,
'But I'll take a long journey, though troubled in
  mind,
In search of some seaport till my darling I'll
  find.'

She met with her darling and great was her bliss,
In her arms she embraced him with a long loving
  kiss,
She says, 'We'll get married by the powers above,
And may every young man enjoy his true love.'

Molly, Lovely Molly [H557: 4 Aug 1934]

s: (m) "The Flower of Sweet Strabane"; g: "Who Is at My Window?" k: "Rise Up, Lovely Sally."

Source: Alexander Thompson (Bushmills; formerly Ballyhunsley).

Key C.

'Oh, who is at my window? I think I hear a voice,
Or who is at my window that's keeping such a
  noise?'
'It is your love and your old sweetheart, oh, do
  you not know me?'
'Oh, begone, sir, from my window, I disdain your
  compan-ee.'

'Oh Molly, lovely Molly, why do you slight me so?
Is it for the want of money?' She quickly
  answered, 'No,
You went and you courted other fair maids and
  you left me here behind,
You may return to them again, for you never shall
  be mine.'

'Oh Molly, lovely Molly, it's pity take on me,
You know a hired servant his master must obey;
The more my body was far away, my heart was still with thee,
Arise up, lovely Molly, and come away with me.

'Oh Molly, lovely Molly, the ship's to sail tomorrow,
And when I'm on the ocean, your heart will break with sorrow,
You'll mourn for my absence, you'll sigh when it's too late,
Arise up, lovely Molly, and your pleasure shall be great.'

Within a short time after, this fair maid she arose,
And with her slender fingers she pinn-ed on her clothes;
She lifted up the window, as you may plainly hear,
And like two loyal lovers away we both did steer.

Here's to my old father that lives in Derry town,
Likewise to my mother, at us she will not frown,
My sisters and my brothers, they will all lament for me
When we are rolling far away in lands of liberty.

When a Man's in Love

[H211: 26 Nov 1927; Laws O20]

Other titles: "... He Feels No Cold"; cf. "The Boy of (A Man in) Love."

[Bp] Source: (Ballyhackett district, near Downhill).

Key C.

When a man's in love he feels no cold, as I not long ago,
Like a hero bold, to see my girl went out through frost and snow,
The moon did gently show me light all on that dreary way
Till I arrived at that sweet spot where all my treasure lay.

I tapped at my love's window, says I, 'Let me in, my dear,'
And gently she the door unlocked and slowly I drew near.
Her hands were soft, her breath was sweet, her tongue did gently glide,
I stole a kiss, which was no harm, and all her colours died.

'Since you are cold and weary, love, there's one thing you must do,
Sit down by the fireside and I'll sit close to you.'
'To sit down by the fireside with you I'll not agree,
For your parents bear an angry mind and have tormented me.'

'The laws o' nature bid us love, and beauty whispers slow,
May the powers above look down on me, for I'm tormented so;
Many's the day and many's the night I came to visit you,
Tossed by winter's angry blast and wet with the summer's dew.

'But I am going to set off for far Columbia's shore,
Where you'll never, never see again your youthful lover more.'
'And are you going to leave me? Alas, what shall I do?
Sure I would break through every tie to go along with you.

'Perhaps my parents may forget and likely may forgive,
And from this moment I intend to be your wedded wife,
Heart and hand I would freely give since true love has begun,'
And with a kiss the bargain closed, and now they're joined in one.

4.4: ... with summer's ... [Dt]

Charming Mary O'Neill

[H55: "A song of a steadfast sweetheart," 29 Nov 1924]

s: (m) "The Blind Irish Girl," (m) "The Flower of Sweet Strabane." Other titles: "... Neill," "(The Stealing of) Mary Neal(e)."

Source: (w) R[obert] B[rownlow] (Ballylaggan, Cloyfin, Coleraine); (m) one-legged man, 36, former blacksmith, from his father, Belfast carter (district between Claudy and Strabane).

[Bp] s: A correspondent, writing of the Fermoyle district, states: "Away back in the Famine years, at a house-warming and dance, a wild, reckless youth, James Just, sang a local song that made a sensation, Mary O'Neill (pronounced O'Nale). Everybody in the Balteagh district sang it for years. The song had a good effect. There was a girl present and two rival lovers. Each of these had supporters, and a free fight was expected as to who should see the girl home. To keep down disturbance a little man worked out a plan. At the end of the dance, whilst most were engaged in comparing what they remembered of

Sam Henry's Songs of the People

the song, the young lady was inveigled away a short distance, put into a cornsack, and carried right out of the fighting zone, and everything went off peaceably."

Joyce [1909] has one verse, No. 256. There are many airs with the name of this song. I have put it to "The Blind Irish Girl," which I noted in the train between Magilligan and Castlerock, from a one-legged man, formerly a blacksmith, aged 36, who learnt it from his father (a carter in Belfast), a native of the district between Claudy and Strabane. My fellow passenger was unconsciously whistling it, as he looked out of the window at the hills of Be[*hole in paper*] bathed in sunshine. He was embarrassed that I noticed it. He had a song to it of little value called "The Flower of Sweet Strabane."

Key D.

I am a bold undaunted youth, my name is John McCann,
I'm a native of sweet Donegal, convenient to Strabane;
For the stealing of an heiress I lie in Lifford gaol,
And her father swore he would hang me for his daughter, Mary O'Neill.

Then full of wrath and anger her father then did bawl,
When my trial it was over, I crossed the garden wall,
For like a loyal lover, to appear she did not fail,
And she freed me from all danger, my charming Mary O'Neill.

Her coach it was got ready to Derry for to go,
And soon she bribed the coachman for to let no one know,
He said he would keep the secret and never would reveal,
So off to Derry then we went with charming Mary O'Neill.

It was to Captain Wilson our passage we did pay
And in the town of Derry we under cover lay,
'The *Charlotte Douglas* ready lies from Derry to set sail,
So off to Quebec, come along,' cries charming Mary O'Neill.

It was over the proud swelling waves our ship did gently glide
While on our passage to Quebec, six months on a matchless tide,
Until we came to Whitehead Reef we had no cause to wail;
On Goffard Bay I thought that day I would lose my Mary O'Neill.

On the ninth of June in the afternoon a heavy fog came on.
Our captain cries, 'Look out, my boys, I fear we are all gone!'
Our vessel on a sandbank was drifted by a gale,
And forty were washed overboard along with Mary O'Neill.

With the small boats and help of the crew, five hundred lives were saved,
And forty of them now, alas, have met a watery grave.
Her yellow locks I then espied come floating with the gale,
I jumped into the raging deep and saved my Mary O'Neill.

Her father wrote a letter, as you may understand,
He said that if we would come back, he would give me half his land;
I wrote him back an answer and told him without fail,
Five pounds a week I now receive with charming Mary O'Neill.

2.1: ... father he did ... [Dt]
6.4: ... were overboard ... [Dt]

The County Tyrone [H153a: 16 Oct 1926]

o: (m) "Eamonn Magaine" (from West of Ireland). Other titles: "Bold Maginnis of the ...," "Sweet Jane of Tyrone."

Source: ([Dt] first 2 stanzas) John J. Marshall (Ardenlee Gardens, Belfast); (remainder, m) Dick Gilloway, "the popular 'man at the wheel'" on the Anchor Line from Coleraine to Portstewart, from Alex McCorriston, "the Bat" (the Doaghs, Magilligan).

s: ... The reference in the [8th] verse to a vessel from Newry to County Tyrone is explained by the fact that the Newry and Lough Neagh Canal, constructed about 1745, was able to allow sea traffic to Tyrone of vessels of 70 tons.

Key C.

C24 / To Hymen's car

[H153b: Wt]

Source: this variant tune appears only in W as sol-fa notation typed in red on the back of the H153 leaf. It is identified as the tune #521 in Petrie/Stanford 2,1902:132, written in D (key signature, two sharps), which is very similar to H153a, but the typed sol-fa version contains minor errors, shown below.

I am a boul' weaver, I've done my endeavour
In courting pretty fair maids abroad and at
  home,
And being of such mettle I never could settle
Till I'd tried some place else than the County
  Tyrone.

My father he toul' me he'd try to controul me,
He'd make me a draper if I'd stay at home,
But I tuk a notion of higher promotion
To try farther parts than the County Tyrone.

[My parents oft told me they would try to
  control me,
They would make me a draper, would I stay at
  home,
But I took a notion for higher promotion,
I would try other parts from the County
  Tyrone.]

I came to Newry, where I fell a-courting
A bonny wee lass for a wife of my own,
But she was still asking and making inquiry,
'What is your character from the County
  Tyrone?'

'For my character you need never mind it,
For married nor promised I ne'er was to none.'
She swore by her conscience she would run all
  chances
And travel with me to the County Tyrone.

Early next morning, bright Phoebus adorning,
We straight took our way by the three-mile
  stone,
And the guards did pursue us, but they never
  came to us
Till they met with an old man was walking alone.

He told them where he met us and where they
  would get us,
Showing them the road to the County Tyrone,
They being in such trouble, their pace they did
  double,
Swearing if they would get us they'd break all
  our bones.

But we came to a quay where a vessel was lying,
And there our whole state unto them we made
  known,
So they threw a plank to us and on board they
  drew us,
And they told us their vessel was bound for
  Tyrone.

This maid she lay dying, lamenting and crying,
I offered a cordial that I brought from home,
Which she kindly did mention without a
  pretension,
'And sir, I'll do without it till I go to Tyrone.'

Now we're safe landed in our native country,
In spite of her parents, I did bring her home;
My love's name, to finish, is Miss Janie Innes,
And I bold McGuinness from the County Tyrone.

1., 2.: [Dt only]
3.: [Bp only, brackets not in original; this stanza
    appears to be equivalent to stanza 2 just above.]
4.1: I first came ... [Dt]
10.3: ... Miss Jessie Innes, [Dt]

My Father's Servant Boy

[H198: 27 Aug 1927; Laws M11]

Other titles: "Answer to the Philadelphia Lass,"
"The Servant Boy."

Source: (w) J. MacKinnon (Craignagat, Ballycastle); (m) Samuel Davison, whistler (Drumnakeel, Ballyvoy, Ballycastle).

s: ... The song has been printed as a broadside
and sold at our markets and fairs.

Key C.

Ye lovers all, both great and small, attend unto
  my theme:
There is none on earth can pity me but those that
  feels my pain;
I live between Dungannon and the town of
  Aughnacloy,
But now I'm in America with my father's servant
  boy.

Where is the man who will or can a farmer's son
  despise?
His bread to win he does begin before the sun
  does rise,
My love and I are Adam's seed, I never will deny,
There is none on earth I love as well as my
  father's servant boy.

481

Sam Henry's Songs of the People

My parents wished to have me wed unto a
  gentleman,
And in the church we were to meet and join in
  wedlock's bands.
The night before I strolled from them unto a
  village nigh,
Where there I met my own true love, my father's
  servant boy.

I took my love along with me, I could do nothing
  more,
I bid adieu to all my friends and to the shamrock
  shore.
To Belfast town we both went down where the
  Ackythere did lie
And in that ship I sailed away with my father's
  servant boy.

When we reached the other side, our money was
  all gone.
Some time we were supported by a friendly
  Irishman,
Till gentlemen from Ireland did give us both
  employ:
Two pounds a week I do receive with my father's
  servant boy.

I left my parents lonesome, in sorrow they did
  weep,
Day and night condoling without a wink of sleep
Until I sent a letter to the town of Aughnacloy
Saying, 'I am in America with my father's servant
  boy.'

They sent an answer straight to me in
  Philadelphia town,
Saying if I would come home again I would get
  five hundred pound,
But I was joined in wedlock, which crowned my
  life with joy,
And until I die I'll ne'er deceive my father's
  servant boy.

This was the news that I did send from
  Philadelphia town,
That where they were worth a shilling, I was
  worth a pound,
With pleasure and contentment I never will deny,
I am living in America with my father's servant
  boy.

1.2: ... that feel ... [Dt]
2.2: ... sun doth ... [Dt]
5.4: Two pound a ... [Dt]

Jamie, Lovely Jamie [H553: 7 Jul 1934]

o: (m) "I Wish I Was in America." Other titles:
"Baltimore," "There Was a Wealthy Farmer," "You
Lovers of Old Ireland."

Source: Alexander Thompson (Bushmills), learned
at Ballyhunsley, near Bushmills, c. 1870.

Key G.

When first in Ireland I was born, it was near
  Armagh town,
I own my parents they were poor and fortune on
  us frowned,
The farm we had was rather small, with taxes
  burdened sore,
Which now compels me for to leave my native Irish
  shore.

There was a wealthy merchant in Armagh did
  reside,
He had one only daughter, who longed to be my
  bride,
When she heard that I was going away, the tears
  her eyes did blind,
Saying, 'How can you sail across the main and
  leave your love behind?

'Oh Jamie, lovely Jamie, along with you I'll go
To the scorching sands of the burning east or
  Greenland clad with snow,
My parents they'll be angry, for they are both
  proud and high,
But I will follow my farming lad until the day I
  die.'

The morning we left Ireland the weather was calm
  and clear,
I took ship in the Immediate with my Eliza dear,
In silks my darling she was dressed, most
  glorious to behold,
And in her stays her fortune laced, five hundred
  pounds in gold.

We wrote a letter to Ireland and in it did explain.
My father-in-law was not content I'd pay him back
  again,
He wrote to me an answer and this to me did say,
'Five hundred pounds I will put down on your
  first son's birthday.

'And may you ever prosper, I hope you will do
  well,
Although you took my only child to a foreign land
  to dwell.'
We took a farm in Baltimore and the trees we
  cleared away,
And for our toil and labour it did us soon repay.

Come all ye brisk young farmer lads has got the
  heart and means
To sail unto America to Baltimore's fair plains,

For there you can drink strong brandy, come from a foreign clime,
So adieu to dear old Ireland and the girls we left behind.

You Lovers All [H525: 23 Dec 1933; Laws M11]

Other titles: "The Flowers of Enniskillen," "North America."

s: (m) "from a Manuscript Book of 1659"; o: 18th-century air.

Source not given.

g: Although the themes, metre, rhyme scheme, and half the first line are very similar, this does not seem to be a version of H198 "My Father's Servant Boy."

Key G.

You lovers all, both great and small, that dwell in Ireland,
I hope you'll pay attention while I my pen command.
It was my father's anger that drove my love away,
But I'm still in hopes we'll meet again in North America.

My love is neat and handsome, to him I give my heart,
And little was our notion that ever we would part,
It was in my father's garden this flower it did decay,
But I'm still in hope it will bloom again in North America.

I do not want for money, for fortune on me shines,
Out from my father's castle I stole five hundred pounds,
And in the town of Belfast my passage I did pay,
My mind made up to follow my love to North America.

The captain's lady was kind to me, as you may understand,
She kept me in her cabin until the ship did land,
It was in the town of Quebec she landed in the quay,
I knew not where to find my love in all America.

Being sick and sore and tired, I went into an inn,
And there I found my Willie, the lad I loved, within,

I handed him a letter and unto him did say,
'I never thought to see your face in all America.'

Now this couple they got married, as you may understand,
I hear they lived quite happy in the town they call St. John,
The money that she got from home, in gold she paid it down,
And she bid farewell to Ireland and Enniskillen town.

Mullinabrone [H242: 30 Jun 1928]

[cf. H85 "Dobbin's Flowery Vale"]

g: "Willie and Mary."

Source not given.

Key E flat.

As I walked out one evening, it being in the month of May,
Down by yon shady arbour I carelessly did stray,
I heard a couple talking; he unto her did say,
'My darling, I must leave you and go to America.'

'Oh, Willie, dearest Willie, how could you change your mind?
To one you loved most dearly, how could you prove unkind?
Oh, when you reach Columbia's shore, some pretty maids you'll see,
You will not think on the broken heart and the vows you made to me.'

They kissed, shook hands and parted, and Mary turned home,
And every night she went to bed with heavy sigh and moan,
'Because I was a servant they sent my love away,
But shortly I will follow him and go to America.'

Now Mary's going to Belfast, her passage for to pay,
She's gone on board the *Joyce* so fine as I did hear them say,
She's gone on board the *Joyce* so fine, she can no longer stay,
'Adieu, farewell to Mullinabrone, I'm bound for America.'

Sam Henry's Songs of the People

'Farewell to my old father and tender mother, too,
And likewise to my old sweethearts, I bid them all adieu,
Adieu unto the hills and glens I often loved to view,
I am bound for America, my Willie to pursue.'

Now Mary she has landed, disturbed in her mind,
And looking for her Willie dear, but him she cannot find;
As Mary being out one evening, her Willie she chanced to spy,
'You are welcome here, dear Mary, you are welcome unto I.'

He pressed her in his arms and unto her did say,
'Come, let us both get married now and with no more delay,
Our parents will not hear of this, they'll hinder us no more,
We will join our hands in wedlock's bands on fair Columbia's shore.

1.1: ... evening, being ... [Dt]

Jamie's on the Stormy Sea [H78: 9 May 1925]

Source: (w, m) (Garvagh); author Bernard Covert (American) c. 1850.

s: This simple and tender song and air ... are at least a half-century old. The air would appear to be of Scottish type; it is so sweet that it seems at once familiar, but I am not aware of it having appeared elsewhere.

[Bp includes an undated clipping, including Henry's added note about the author, also typed below the song in Dt:]
  With regard to above ballad, published in *Northern Constitution* of 9th inst., I learnt to sing this over fifty years ago at a school in County Derry (not Garvagh), and have never heard it elsewhere. The melody is exactly same as in my schooldays, but an additional verse was then taught -- it came in second, I think -- and ran: --

  Warmly shone the sunset glowing, sweetly breathed the young flowers growing,
  Earth, with beauty overflowing, seemed the home of love to be;
  Nearer as I came, and nearer, finer rose the notes and clearer,
  O! 'twas heaven itself to hear her, "Jamie's on the stormy sea."

After last verse refrain of first verse was sung, viz.:

  And ere daylight died before us, etc., etc.

But with the final sentence altered to:

  Jamie's now come back to me.
                              Nemo.

(This song, I have since discovered, was written and composed about 1850 by Bernard Covert, an American, who also wrote and composed "The Sword of Bunker Hill." S. H., Song Editor.)

Key E flat.

Ere the twilight bat was flitting, in the sunset at her knitting
Sang a lonely maiden, sitting underneath the chestnut tree,
And ere daylight died before us and the vesper star shone o'er us,
Fitful rose the tender chorus: 'Jamie's on the stormy sea.'

Curfew bells remotely ringing, mingled with that sweet voice singing,
And the last red ray seemed clinging lingeringly o'er tower and tree,
And those angel tones descending, with the scene in beauty blending,
Ever had the same sweet ending: 'Jamie's on the stormy sea.'

How could I but list, but linger, to the song and near the singer,
Gently praying heaven to bring her Jamie from the stormy sea,
And while yet her lips did name me, forth I sprang, my heart o'ercame me,
'Grieve no more, for I'm your Jamie home returned to love and thee.'

Wait till the Ship Comes Home

[H481: 18 Feb 1933]

Source: Edward Kane (Lisachrin, Garvagh).

s: ... Edward Kane ... is thanked for the complete manner in which the words and music were conveyed.

Key A flat.

Jack went away to sea one day and left his Polly
  behind,
And while away an old man to Polly proved very
  kind;
Says he, 'If Jack does not come back, perhaps
  you'll marry me,
And all through life you will be my wife.' Polly to
  him would say:

Wait till the ship comes home again,
[W]ait till the ship comes home,
Then if he's not true, sure I'll marry you;
[W]ait till the ship comes home.

Twelve months passed by, yet no reply from Jack
  did Polly receive,
The people said that he was dead, but Polly would
  not believe,
And though the old man gave her gold and
  pleased her day by day,
Whene'er he would ask her to marry him, Polly to
  him would say:

One morning in the newspaper, to Polly's
  surprise, she found
The ship that Jack had sailed in, it now was
  homeward bound,
The old man sighed and soon he died, and when
  his will was read,
'Twas found that he had left all his gold to Polly,
  the girl who said:

The Garden Gate [H770: 27 Aug 1938]

Source: Willie Logue (Carnkilly, Eglinton),
learned c. 1898 "from a travelling tailor named
James Kelly, who went on crutches"; (m) played
on melodeon by Willie Logue, contributor's
nephew.

Key G.

The day being gone and the evening spent,
And the village clock had just struck eight,
Young Mary hastened with great speed
Until she reached the garden gate.

But what was there to make Mary sad?
The gate was there, but not the lad,
Which caused young Mary to sigh and cry,
'Was there ever a girl so sad as I?'

She paced the garden here and there
Until the village clock struck nine,
When Mary said unto herself,
'He will not, and he shan't be mine,

'For he promised to meet me here at eight,
And I on him no longer will wait,
And I will let all young men see
That they will not make a fool of me.'

She walked the garden o'er and o'er
Until the village clock struck ten,
When William caught her in his arms,
No more from her to part again,

Saying, 'I was away a long, long way,
Buying the wedding ring for thee,'
And how could Mary so cruel prove
As to banish forever her loved Willie?

In the morning early, when they arose,
To the village church they went straightway,
The merry bells did ring with joy
Upon this couple's wedding day.

Now all alone by yon river side
In wedded bliss they do reside,
And she blesses the hour that she did wait
On her lover at the garden gate.

Henry, the Sailor Boy [H37: 26 Jul 1924]

s: (m, all) "The River Roe," "The Winding Banks
of Erne" (author William Allingham), "Bathing in
the Roe," "Willie Reilly," "Pat O'Brien"; m: (m)
"Tramps and Hawkers." Other titles: "Henry and
Mary Ann," "The Lovers' Parting," "My Mary
Ann," "Young Henry."

Source: Mary Getty (Long Commons, Coleraine),
from Sally McConaghy, 80, her grandmother
(Dunaghy, Ballymoney).

s: ... Joyce, in his *Old Irish Folk Music and
Songs* (No. 13), states that the air, which he
names "The River Roe," is also called "Henry the
Sailor Boy," and he is only able to quote the
last two lines of the words given below [Dt: the
song here printed].
  William Allingham, the poet, who was Controller
of Customs at the port of Coleraine in 1853, and
who went from that position to the staff of the
Spectator, must have learnt this fine air when
here, as he wrote one of his best songs to it,
viz.: "The Winding Banks of Erne." [Bp only]
A song, well known in the Limavady district, is
also sung to it, i.e., "Bathing in the Roe."
[Bp, Dt] The popular ballad "Willie Reilly" is
also sung to this air, and almost all the murder
ballads were composed [Dt: are sung] to it, as
for example, [Bp only] "Pat O'Brien," of which
the Houston collection has one verse:

My name is Pat O'Brien, my life and I must
  part;
For the murder of Ann O'Brien I am sorry to
  the heart.
I hope the Lord will pardon me before the
  judgment day,
And when I'm on the scaffolding, good
  Christians for me pray.

Of four settings of the air, I have selected the
oldest form, composed in the ancient Irish gapped
scale, which contained neither *fa* nor *ti*.

[The printed columns, Bp and Wp, have this in
4, but Wt is in 3; Moulden sets it in 6/8.]

Key F.

Sam Henry's Songs of the People

Come all ye loyal lovers, a tale I will unfold
Concerning a young maiden fair and her young sailor bold;
As they both conversed together, young Mary Ann did say,
'Oh, stay at home, dear Henry, and do not go away.

'Don't leave me broken-hearted your absence to bewail,
To think that you'll be tossed about in every wind and gale;
I'll leave my friends and parents and go dress just like a man,
With you I'll go and face the foe, your own dear Mary Ann.'

'Oh no, oh no, dear Mary Ann, to that I'll not agree,
For you to leave your parents and to go along with me,
For when on board a man-of-war perhaps some cannon ball
Might strike you as you stood by me, and at my side you'd fall.

'But stay at home, my own dear girl, and be advised by me,
And rely upon the honour of your faithful Hen-e-ree,
And when the wars are over I'll return just like a man,
And fulfil the vows and promises I made to Mary Ann.'

'Go on, go on, my sailor lad, my heart will still beat true,
And may kind Providence spare your life in the danger you go through,
But do your duty manfully, let virtue guide your hand;
Return and bless your faithful girl, your own dear Mary Ann.'

Oh, early the next morning, just by the break of day,
An order came to go on board and quickly sail away
Unto some foreign climate, far from their land to steer,
Some thinking on their sweethearts, some on their parents dear.

But each one to his purty lass does toss a flowing can.
'Hurrah, my boys,' young Henry cries, 'a health to Mary Ann.'
It was upon the ocean where the seas run mountains high,
Young Henry was the first aloft, all dangers to defy.

He was loved by all his officers and respected by the crew,
A smarter sailor never stepped nor wore the jacket blue,
It was his happy fortune his captain's life to save
All on the coasts of Africa when struggling with the waves.

He threw himself into the deep, where thereabouts was tost,
If they one moment had delayed, their lives would all been lost,
They cruised about in different parts for three long years or more,
Till at length an order came on board to sail for Erin's shore.

Unto the land which gave them birth and which they loved so dear,
All dangers past, our ship at last unto the coast did steer,
The captain gave him fifty pounds the moment they did land,
And that day young Henry married was unto his Mary Ann.

8.4: ... struggling in the ... [Dt]
9.2: If they would moment ... [Dt]

9.1: tost = tossed.

The Lass of Glenshee

[H590: 23 Mar 1935; Laws O6]

Other titles: "Glenshee," "The Hills (Maid) (Rose) of ...."

Source: (m) (Croaghmore district); (w) (Garronpoint).

s: Glenshee lies between Blairgowrie and Braemar in the heart of the Grampians.

Key G.

'Twas early one morning as the day was
  a-dawning
And the sun it got up and shone bright o'er the
  lea,
I met a wee damsel was homewards returning
From herding her flocks on the slopes of
  Glenshee.

Says I, 'Bonnie lass, why so early arising?
For the sun is scarce up, nor yet over the lea.'
'Kind sir,' she made answer, 'I am but a poor
  girl,
And I'm herding the flocks on the slopes of
  Glenshee.'

Says I then for answer, 'All the river's bright
  waters
May all change their course and flow back from
  the sea;
The sun may forget to get up in the morning
If e'er I prove false to the lass of Glenshee.'

'Don't tease me no longer,' says she, 'I might
  blunder
And cause all your gentry to all laugh at me;
I'd sooner be here in my own cot for pleasure,
Or herding my flocks on the slopes of Glenshee.'

'A fool I don't find ye, so get up behind me,
I'll see that the gentry say "Mem" unto thee,
For when you return you'll be wife of its lord,
And the lady, not lass, of the slopes of
  Glenshee.'

The Hielan's o' Scotland

[H193: 23 Jul 1927; Laws N19]

s: [Bp] Old version of "Will You Gang to the Hielans, Leezie Lindsay?" [Dt] (m) "With My Love on the Road" [Joyce 1909]; (m) "Slane" (Hymnary), also (m) hymn "Be Thou My Vision"; k: "The Blaeberries." Other titles: "The Blaeberry Courtship," "Donald of the Isles," "Liz(z)ie Lindsay."

Source: Dan Glass, 70 (Kilmahamogue, Moyarget district), sung c. 1895.

Key E flat.

In the hielan's o' Scotland a young man does dwell,
For riches and beauty few could him excel,
He's awa' to the lowlands to seek for a bride
And he dressed himself up in a braw tartan plaid.

'Will you go to the hielans, bonnie lassie, wi' me?
Will you go to the hielans, my braw flocks to
  see?'
'I love better my low valleys and braw corn fields
Than all the blaeberries your wild mountain
  yields.'

Up steps her auld father and gives his advice,
Saying, 'Do not go with him, if you will be wise,
He's a poor hielan' laddie, as bare as a crow,
He's frae the north hielans for odds as we know.'

'Father, keep what you are not willing to give,
For feth I'll go with him as sure as I live.
What value's your gold and your silver to me
With the hielan's between my own darling and me?'

But no, she's awa' in spite o' them a',
She's awa' to the place, his braw flocks for to
  see,
He had nae braw steed for to carry her on,
But he aye cried, 'Bonnie lassie, dinna think the
  road lang.'

Her stockings were torn, her shoes they were
  rent,
She travell-ed on till she like was to faint,
'If it was not, my dear, for your sweet companie,
I would go to thon valley and lie doon and dee.'

'Get up, bonnie lassie, the sun's wearin' doon,
I'm afraid she'll be set 'gin we reach the mill toon,
And we maun seek lodging for both you and I,
Or else we maun sleep inunder the sky.'

Early next morning he took [her] to the ha',
He bade her look round her as far as she could
  spy.
'These lands and possessions from debts they are
  free,
And I came, my dear jewel, to share them with
  thee.'

They travell-ed on till they came to a grove,
The flocks they were feeding in numberless
  droves;
Brave Allan stood gazing his braw flocks to see,
'Step on,' cried the lassie, 'that's nae pleasure
  tae me.'

They met a wee laddie dressed in tartan trews,
And twa bonny lassies were buchtin' their ewes;
They cried, 'Honored master, are [y]ou come
  again?
It's long we have waited on your coming hame.'

'Bucht your ewes, lasses, and rin awa' hame,
Here's a swan from the south I mean for to tame,
Her father's a farmer and where will she lie?
The best bed in the hoose we'll no her deny.'

The lasses gaed hame with a wonderfu' fame
To welcome the new bride their master fetched
  hame,
With ale and good brandy they drunk their health
  roon,
And they made for the lady a braw bed o' doon.

Sam Henry's Songs of the People

2.1,2: ... the highlands, ... [Dt]
4.: [Dt, *not in* Bp.]
8.: [Dt, *not in* Bp; *also written in pencil on reverse of* Wp, *together with more fragments:*]
  Don't you remember when at school with me
  It's often? I fed on your bread and your cheese
  Likewise when you had but a handful of peas

  They came to visit father [all?]
  old [?] man took off hat
  Keep on your hat old man and don't let it fall
  It's a pity that a peacock turned out a craw.

10.4: ... waited for your ... [Dt]

The Glove and the Lions

[H474: 31 Dec 1932; Laws O25]

s: (m) "Youghal Harbour"; k: "Bold Lieutenant."
Other titles: "Bold Sea Captain," "The Carlisle Lady," "Carolina Lady," "Down in Carlisle," "In Castyle (Roslyn Isles) (St. Charles) (There Lived a Lady)," "(The) (Lady's) Fan," "The Lady (and the Glove) (of Carlisle)," "The Lion's Den," "The Velvet Glove."

Source: composite of 3: (Ballycastle) (Ballyrisk, Limavady) (Heagles, Ballymoney).

s: ... The incident described in this ballad took place early in the 16th century, when in the presence of the French king, Francis, Count de Lorge recovered his lady love's glove from the lion's den. The occurrence has been made the subject of poems, "The Glove," by Robert Browning, and "The Glove and the Lions," by Leigh Hunt. In the latter version Count de Lorge threw the glove in his sweetheart's face, and the king applauded his action as "it was vanity and not love that set a lover such a task." The people's version, which we print, has unfailing artistry as it makes the incident end happily.

Key E flat.

In Broadson Isle there lived a lady
Who had ten thousand pounds a year,
Her lovely person was so engaging,
With her few beauties could compare.

This lady she made a resolution,
She'd wed no man excepting he
Would signalise himself by valour,
Either in the war by land or sea.

There were two brothers became her lovers,
And both admired this lady fair,
Each did endeavour to gain her favour,
And how to please her it was all their care.

The oldest brother, he was a captain
Commanded by brave Colonel Kerr,
The younger, he was a third lieutenant
On board the *Tiger*, man-of-war.

Now these brothers both were valiant
And to fight were not afraid,
To hostile danger they were no stranger
And when in battle were ne'er dismayed.

The eldest, he who was a captain,
Great protestations to her did make;
The youngest swore that he would venture
His life and fortune all for her sake.

Said she, 'I'll find out a way to try them,
To see which will from danger start,
And he that will behave the bravest
Shall be the governor of my heart.'

She told her coachman to make ready
Before it was the break of day,
And then, accompanied by those gallants,
To Tower Hill they drove away.

When she at the Tower arrived,
She threw her fan in the lions' den,
Saying, 'Which of you would win a lady
Will bring me back my fan again.'

Out bespoke the faint-hearted captain,
Being so disturbed in his mind,
'In war I never was deemed a coward,
To fight my foes I am inclined.

'But here are lions, dreadful, roaring,
And to oppose them would useless prove,
So therefore, madam, for fear of danger
Some other champion must gain your love.'

Then out bespoke the bold lieutenant
In voice like thunder, loud and high,
'To show my love, my life I'll venture,
I'll bring you back your fan or die.'

When in the lions' den he entered,
The lions they looked fierce and grim,
But with his active and bold behaviour
He looked ten times as fierce at them.

And from his sheath he drew forth his rapier
And boldly faced those lions all,

And by his active and bold behaviour,
Two of the creatures soon did fall.

With heart undaunted he stepp-ed forward,
Down at the conqueror's feet it lay;
He kneel-ed low and the fan he lifted,
His warlike courage found no dismay.

The gallant action it being over,
And to the lady he took his way;
The lady in her coach sat trembling
Lest he had fallen the lions' prey.

When she saw her bold hero coming
And that no harm to him was done,
With open arms she did enfold him,
Saying, 'Take me, darling, the prize you've won.'

The king he being soon informed
That two of his lions they were slain,
He was not angry nor the least offended,
But recommended him for the same.

He changed him from a third lieutenant
And made him an Admiral of the Blue.
That very same night these two were married:
See what the power of true love can do.

Johnny Scott [H736: 1 Jan 1938; Child #99]

Other titles: "(Young) Johnie (Johnny) Scot(t)."

Source: Alexander Crawford (Leck, Ballymoney).

s: ... The ballad is very ancient (probably 16th century). In the great work of Professor Child's, sixteen variants of it are found but this Ulster version is not recorded elsewhere than below.
  Sidgwick's collection contains a version of Johnny Scott which has 34 verses.
  Similar exploits to that of Johnny Scott and the Italian occur in other ballads, as for example in a Breton ballad where a nobleman is ordered by the French king to fight a Moor and the latter is received on the sword-point of his antagonist. In Scottish tradition James Macgill having killed Sir Robert Balfour about 1679 was offered pardon by King Charles II, on condition that he would fight an Italian gladiator, which he did with successful result, and was knighted for his prowess.

Key C.

Johnny Scott's to the hunting gane,
To the English woods so wild,
And the king of England's daughter
Made a tryst to be his bride.

The king he wrote a broad letter
And sealed it with his hand,
And sent it off to Johnny Scott
As fast as it could gang.

When Johnny read the letter,
A sorry man was he,
Saying, 'Father, dearest father,
The king has sent for me.'

'If that be so, my son,' he says,
'As I suppose it be,
I fear, I fear, my lovely son,
Your face I'll never see.'

He dressed himself in apparel fine,
As fine as fine could be,
And he's away to fair England
His lady for to see.

When he came to England,
He look-ed all around,
And there he spied his lady love
As he came riding down.

'Come down, come down, my lady,' he says,
'Come down, come down to me.'
'I can't go down, dear Johnny,' she says,
'The king has bolted me.'

And when he came before the king,
He knelt low at his knee;
The king he moved his bonnet,
Thought Johnny a king like he.

'No king, no king,' said Johnny Scott,
'No king, no king,' said he;
'I'm just one of your cottage men,
Johnny Scott, they do call me.'

'If Johnny Scott it is your name,
As I suppose it be,
Before tomorrow at twelve o'clock,
A butchered man you'll be.

'We have an Italian in the next room
This day has kill-ed three,
And before tomorrow at twelve o'clock,
Your butcher he will be.'

The Italian came out of the room,
A grimly giant he,
Yards three between his shoulders,
Spans four from e'e to e'e.

They fought about, they fought all round
With swords of tempered steel,
But on the point of Johnny's sword
The death thrust he did feel.

'Come down, come down, my lady,' he says,
'Come down, come down to me;
This night you shall be in my arms,
And tomorrow my bride you'll be.'

Sam Henry's Songs of the People

The Keeper of the Game

[H681: 12 Dec 1936; Child #46]

Other titles: "Bluff the Quilt," "Captain (Mr) Wedderburn's (Washburn's) (Woodburn's) Courtship," "The Devil and the Blessed Virgin Mary," "For My Breakfast You Must Get a Bird Without a Bone," "A Gentle Young Lady," "He Rolled Her to the Wall," "An Old Man's Courtship," "The Six Questions," "Stock and Wall," "You and I in the One Bed Lie."

Source: (m, w) John Millen, jr (Fish Loughan).

Key D.

It's of a merchant's daughter that lived down
   yonder lane,
She fell in with William Dempsey, the keeper of the
   game;
Said he unto that fair young maid, 'If it was not
   for the la',
I would steal you frae your mammy and hae you
   once for a'.'

'It's go away, young man,' said she, 'and do not
   trouble me,
Seven questions you must answer if you would
   marry me,
Before I be your lover or lea' my father's ha',
Or rin awa' frae mammy and be yours once for a'.

'What's rounder than a ring? What's higher than a
   tree?
What's worse than any woman's tongue? What's
   deeper than the sea?
What tree buds first? What bird sings best? And
   where does the dew find fa'?
Answer me, I'll go with you and lea' my father's
   ha'.'

'The globe is rounder than a ring, heaven's
   higher than the tree,
The devil's worse than a woman's tongue, hell's
   deeper than the sea,
The yew buds first, the thrush sings best, the
   dew on earth finds fa',
So you must come with me this night and lea' your
   father's ha'.'

'Go away, young man,' she said, 'and do not
   trouble me,
Unless three more you answer me, I will not marry
   thee,
Before I spend with you a night, or lea' my
   father's ha',
Or rin awa' frae mammy and be yours once for a'.

'It's for my breakfast you must get a cherry
   without a stone,
And for my dinner you must have a chicken without
   a bone,
And for my supper you must have a bird without a
   gall,
Before I am your sweetheart, or lea' my father's
   hall.'

'Oh, when the cherry's in full bloom, it really has
   no stone,
And when the chicken's in the egg, it really has
   no bone,
The dove she is a gentle bird that flies without a
   gall,
So you must come wi' me at last and lea' your
   father's ha'.'

Now this couple they've got married, I hear the
   people say,
This couple they've got married and right well
   they do agree;
He was a clever fellow and he did her heart betray,
And from her mammy this wee lass the keeper stole
   away.

1.3: la' = law.

The Rich Ship Owner's Daughter

[H221: BLp, 4 Feb 1928; Child #100]

k: "John Barbour," "Willie o' Winsbury." Other titles: "Fair Mary," "John (Tom) (o') Barbary (Barbour)," "Johnny Borden," "The King's Dochter Jean," "(Lord) Thomas of Winesber(r)y (Win(e)sbury) (and the King's Daughter)," "Tom the Barber," "Young Barbour."

Source: Harry Pollock, blacksmith (Cumber-Claudy) from Joseph Gardner, 65 (Claudy) c. 1903, from his mother, maiden name Matty Cairns (Ervey).

s: [Harry Pollock] stopped the ringing music of his anvil to whistle me the air ....

[Bt, Dt have no acknowledgments or comments; stanza 4 and subsequent stanzas in Bt are incomplete, only first lines. The last word in line 4 of each stanza is repeated as indicated.]

[BLp, Dt] Key C. [Bt] Key G.

There was a lady in the east,
She dressed herself in green,
She leaned herself on her father's castle wall
For to see the ship sail in,
    In,
    For to see the ship sail in.

'What ails my daughter?' her father did say,
She looks so pale and wan,
I'm afraid she has suffered some sore sickness
Or's in love with some young man.'

'I have suffered no sore sickness,
I'm in love with no young man,
But it's oh and alas, dear father,' she says,
'It's oh, but my love stays long.'

'Is he a man of might?' he says,
'Or is he a man of fame?
Or is he one of my little sailor boys
That is ploughing the rough main?'

'He is not a man of might,' she says,
'Nor is he a man of fame,
But he is one of your little sailor lads
That is ploughing the rough main.'

'O, call him down, the spaniel dog,
O call him down,' said he,
'Tomorrow morning at nine o'clock,
He will go up the gallows tree.'

'Do not say that, dear father,' she says,
'O, say not that to me,
For if my true love you do kill,
You'll get no good of me.'

He called down his sailor boys
By one, by two, by three,
John Barbour used to be the foremost man,
But the hindmost man came he.

'Will you marry my daughter?' he says,
'And take her by the hand?
And you'll eat and drink at my table,
And be heir of all my land.'

'I will marry your daughter,' he says,
'And take her by the hand,
But I'll neither eat nor drink at your table,
And a fig for all your land.'

'For the more John Barbour is my name,
I'm heir of west Scotland,
And where you could give your daughter ten
    pounds,
I could give her eighty-one.'

2.3: ... she's suffered ... [Bt]
3.1: 'O, I ... [Bt]
 .2: But I love a young man, [Dt] But I do love a
young man, [Bt]
 .3: And oh ... [Dt]   And O, ... [Bt]
 .4: 'It's O, ... [Bt]
4.3: ... my seven sailor ... [Dt, Bt]
 .4: ... the raging main?' [Dt, Bt]
5.3: ... your seven sailor boys [Dt, Bt]
 .4: ... the raging main.'
6.4: ... will hang on the ... [Dt, Bt]
8.1: ... sailor lads. [Bt, written]
9.1: 'O, will ... [Bt]

Lord Beichan [H470: 3 Dec 1932; Child #53]

s: "Young Bekie," "Lord Bateman." Other titles:
"Lloyd Bateman," "... Akeman (Baker) (Bate(s)-
man) (Beicham) (and the Turkish Lady)," "Susan
Pyatt," "The Turkish Lady," "Young ... (Bateman) (Beham)."

Source: old lady, 90 (Bushmills district).

s: This valuable contribution to our ballad literature was traditionally learnt.... It is a variant of
a ballad well known throughout western Europe,
and weaves a story which appealed to the imagi-
nation of the people of the Middle Ages.
 The English version calls the heroine Burd Isbel, and the romance was linked with the name of
Gilbert, father of Thomas a Beckett (Archbishop
of Canterbury in 1162), who was imprisoned by
the Saracen, Prince Admiraud. The ballad is
sometimes called "Young Bekie," and that name is
thought to be a form of Beckett. Susie Fee or
Burd Isbel (as you like) knew no English but
"London" and "Gilbert," but after much tribula-
tion found her lover and was married to him.
 The singer should get the rhythm of the music
into his head and then adapt the ballad to it as
a kind of musical monologue.

[Note to H471 "The Broken Ring," 10 Dec 1932:]
In the Broadcasting Programme from Daventry
National on Tuesday evening at 9:20, celebrating
the coming-of-age of the English Folk Song and
Dance [sic] Society, the song "Lord Bateman," as
sung by Joseph Taylor, traditional folk singer,
was an outstanding item. It will interest our
readers to know that this is an English version of
the song, "Lord Beichan," published last week in
this column and was a very close rendering. Only
five verses were given out of the thirteen contained in our version. The air was not the same.

Key A. Slow.

Lord Beichan was a noble lord,
And a noble lord of high degree,
He set sail upon a ship,
Some far-off countries for to see.

He sail-ed east and he sail-ed west
Until he came to far Turkie,
Where he was taken and put in prison,
And his fair life was in jeopardie.

Sam Henry's Songs of the People

The Turk had one only daughter,
The fairest creature your eyes did ever see,
And she stole the keys of her father's prison
And said, 'Lord Beichan, I will set you free.

'Have you houses or have you dwellings,
Or does all Northumberland belong to thee?
What would you give to a fair young lady
That out of prison would set you free?'

'I have houses and I have dwellings,
And all Northumberland belongs to me,
I would give it all to a fair young lady
That out of prison would set me free.

'Seven years I will avow
And seven years I will keep it strang,
I vow I will wed with no other woman
If you wed with no other man.'

She bundled up all her good clothing
And says, 'Lord Beichan I will go and see,'
When she came to Lord Beichan's castle,
Loud at the bellhouse door rang she.

And she cried to the bold maid, 'Tell to me,
Is this Lord Beichan's castle, and is he within?'

'Oh yes, this is Lord Beichan's castle,
And he has taken his young bride in.'

'Tell him to send me a slice of bread
And a bottle of his best wine,
And not forget the fair young lady
Who did release him when close confined.'

He gave the hall door a kick with his feet
And the table with his knee,
'I'll wager all my lands and livings
That Susie Fee has come over the sea.'

Out bespoke the young bride's mother,
She never was known to speak so free,
'Surely you will not forget my daughter
If Susie Fee is come over the sea?'

'I own I made a bride of your daughter,
She is neither the better nor the worse of me,
She came to me on her horse and saddle,
She may go home on her coach and three.'

Lord Beichan prepared for another wedding,
And both their hearts were full of glee.
'I'll roam no more to far countries
Since Susie Fee came over the sea.'

6.2: strang = resolutely, vigorously.

◆ C24 REFERENCES ◆

◆ Our Wedding Day *(H534)* 454

Brunnings 1981: "She Moved Through the Fair";
?cf. "I Once Had a True Love"

IREL   Hughes 1,1909:46-8 "She Moved thro' the Fair"
  Loesberg 1,1980:19 "She Moved through the Fair"
  Tunney 1979:154 "She Moved through the Fair"

BRS   *A Broadside* 4(10,Mar)1912: "She Moved through the Fair"
  Healy 1977:78-9 "She Moved through the Fair"
  O'Keeffe 1955(1968):61 "She Moved thro' the Fair"
  120 n.d.:114 "She Moved thro' the Fair"
  Songs and Recitations 3,1976:41 "She Moved thro' the Fair"
  Walton's New 1,1966:35

REC   Margaret Barry, *CWL* 1, Columbia AKL 4941 (A3,17) "She Moved Through the Fair"; Riverside RLP 12 602 (A1) [Bikel]; [b:] Riverside S-2 (A3); Folkways FG 3575 (A6) "She Moves through the Fair"
  m: Francis McPeake, *FSB* 1 (A3) "Our Wedding Day"
  Tommy Dempsey, Trailer LER 2096 (A6) "She Moved through the Fair"
  b: Carolyn Hester, Tradition TLP 1043 "She Moves through the Fair"
  Lori Holland, Folkways FG 3518 (A4) "She Moved through the Fair"
  Mary O'Hara, London LL 1572 [Bikel]
  b: Peg Clancy Power, Folk-Legacy FSE 8 (A1) "She Moved through the Fair" [ghostless]
  b: Pete Seeger, Folkways FA 2453 (A3) "She Moved through the Fair"

◆ The Boy That Found a Bride *(H665)* 454

BRIT   Greig 1907-11(1963): #167 "Fair Gallowa'"

◆ The Swan *(H475)* 455

? *Not*: Brunnings 1981: "... - As I Was Returning Home from Wexford"

◆ The Tossing o' the Hay *(H635)* 455

IREL   Shields 1981:147-9 (#67) "Tossing the ..."
Shields/Shields *UF* 21,1975: #409

BRIT   Cf. Palmer 1979b:157 (#92) "Raking the Hay" (see Larner rec.)
  Cf. Sharp/Karpeles 1974,1:447-8 (#112) "Raking of Hay," 2 vts.

BRS   Purslow 1968 says that a usual broadside title is "Joy after Sorrow."

REC   Cf. O. J. Abbott, Leader LEE 4057 (B3) "The Bonny Bunch of Rushes Green"
  Eddie Butcher, Leader LED 2070 (A5) "Tossing the ..."
  John Butcher, EEOT *Shamrock* 3 cass. (A2) "Tossing the ..."
  Cf. Sam Larner, Topic 12T 244 (B1) "Raking the ..."
  Cf. Phoebe Smith, Topic 12TS 304 (A7) "Raking the ..."

MEL   O'Neill 1903:31 (#179)

◆ Pining Day and Daily *(H149)* 456

? Brunnings 1981: "... (See She Moved through the Fair)"

◆ The Pretty Blue Handkerchief *(H161)* 456

Brunnings 1981: "The Bonny ..."

IREL   Graves et al. n.d.,3:7-12; this might be the parent version of the song.

BRIT   Baring-Gould/Sheppard 1892(1895):84-5 "The Blue Kerchief"
  Greig 1907-11(1963): #112 "The Hanky," very different.

Palmer 1979b:150 (#87) "Bonny Blue ..."
SR #22(Oct-Dec)1984:24 "The Bonny ..."

BRS BPL H.80 (Gilbert)
Harvard 1: 4.67 (Ross), 5.183 (Catnach), 9.90 (Bebbington), 12.15 (Such)
Harvard 3: (Walker) (Fortey)

◆ The Gentle Shepherdess *(H104)* 457

Laws 1957:230 (O8) "The Sailor and the Shepherdess"
Brunnings 1981: cf. "A Farmer's Son So Sweet"

BRIT Greig 1907-11(1963): #117 "The Handsome Shepherdess"
Sharp/Karpeles 1974,1:388-9 (#98) "The Shepherdess and the Sailor"; cf. 1:386-7 (#97) "A Farmer's Son So Sweet," the same story with the sexes reversed.
Cf. Sharp/Marson 3,1906:6-8 "A Farmer's Son So Sweet"

AMER Creighton 1971:81-2 "The Shepherdess"

BRS Harvard 1: 3.135 (Forth) "The Pretty Young Shepherdess," 4.127 (Ross), 7.205 (Catnach) "The Sailor's Courtship"
UCLA 605: 3(Henson) "The Sailor's Courtship"

◆ The Bonny Wee Lass *(H763)* 458

Brunnings 1981: "... - As I Went out One Summer's Day"

IREL Moulden 1979:25-6

b: REC Frank Ritchie, Request RLP 8060
m: Willie Scott (Berwickshire), Topic 12T 183 (A5) "... Wee Trampin' ..."

◆ Lovely Annie (I) *(H561)* 458

White/Dean-Smith 1951: "Lisbon or William and Nancy"
Laws 1957:206 (N8) "William and Nancy (Lisbon; Men's Clothing I'll Put On I)"
Brunnings 1981: "Lisbon," "Farewell My Dear Nancy," ?"Jimmy and Nancy - As Beautiful Nancy Was A-Walking One Day," ?"Farewell Nancy"; cf. "I'm Going to Join the Army"
Cazden et al. *Notes* 1982: #29 "It Was Early One Monday Morning"

Not: IREL O Lochlainn 1965:445 "Farewell, Dearest Nancy"

BRIT Greig/Duncan 1,1981:142 (#63) "The Sailor and Nancy /'Twas on a Monday Morning"
Morrison/Cologne 1981:42-3 "Lisbon"

AMER Cazden et al. 1982:124-6 "It Was Early One Monday Morning"
Cf. WPA Kentucky [1939?]:108 "Lovely Nancy"

BRS Cf. UCLA 605: 5(Haly) "William and Nancy or the Loyal Lovers' Trip to Spain"

REC The Broadside, Topic 12TS 228 "Lisbon"
? cl: Aunt Molly Jackson, AFS 3335 A "William and Nancy"
Cf. Nic Jones, Trailer LER 2027 (B1) "William and Nancy's Parting" (from Manchester brs.)
Cf. A. L. Lloyd, Topic 12T 118 (B5) "Farewell Nancy"
Cf. June Tabor, Topic 12TS 360 (B2) "Lisbon"

◆ I'm from over the Mountain *(H61)* 459

Brunnings 1981: "The Trip We Took over ..."

IREL *JIFSS* 8,1910:13 "The Trip We Took over the Mountains"; 11,1912:14 (m only); 26,1929:79-80 "I'll Follow You over the Mountain," "The True Lovers' Trip over ..."
Joyce 1909:128 (#269) "The Trip We Took over the Mountain," melody and 2 lines.

BRS BPL Irish: (n.i.)
BPL H.80: (Sanders) "Trip o'er the Mountain"
Harvard 1: 10.19 (Bebbington)
Healy 1,1967b:294-5 "The True-Lover's Trip o'er the Mountain"
Walton's 132 n.d.:63 "Come with Me over the Mountain"

REC Pete Seeger, Folkways FA 2453 (A2) "The Trip We Took over the Mountain"

◆ The Bann Water Side *(H685)* 460

IREL Moulden 1979:18 says Robert Cinnamond has recorded a version for the BBC Archive.

◆ Beardiville Planting *(H718)* 460

IREL Moulden 1979:19

◆ Bess of Ballymoney *(H133)* 461

White/Dean-Smith 1951: "... or The Bonny Broomfields; Bonny Green Woods; Broomfield Wager; Merry Broomfields; West Country Wager; The Young Squire"
Dean-Smith 1954: "... Wager"
Child 1882-98(1965),1:390-9 (#43), 6 vts.; 508; 2:506; 3:506; 4:458; 5:290
Coffin/Renwick 1950(1977):51-2, 223
Bronson 1,1959:336-47; 4,1972:460
Brunnings 1981

IREL Cf. Joyce 1909:152 (#327) "The Mermaid" [Bronson]

BRIT Dawney 1972:29 "Merry Broomfield"
Greig/Duncan 2,1983:458 (#322) "The Bonnie Broomfields," 2 vts. ("Broomfield Hills"); also cf. stanza 1 of Greig/Duncan 2,1983:392 "Jock Sheep"
MacColl/Seeger 1977:63-6 (#7) [untitled]
O'Shaughnessy 1971:4-5
Oxford Ballads 1969:72-4 (#21)
Palmer 1979b:121-3 (#65)
Palmer *FMJ* 1973:288-9
Richards/Stubbs 1979:82-3

b: REC Cyril Poacher, *FSB* 4 (A10) "... Wager," Topic 12TS 252 (A1)
Ewan MacColl, *Folkways CB*, FG 3510 (B4); *Riverside CB*, RLP 12 623 (A1)
Peggy Seeger, Ewan MacColl, *LH*, Argo ZDA 68, #3 "The Broomfield Hill," 2 versions.
Martin Carthy, Topic 12TS 340 (A6), Topic 12TS 345 (B4)
Roy Harris, Topic 12TS 217 (A2) "The Bonny Green Woods"; b: Topic TPSS 221
George Maynard, Topic 12T 286 (B7) "A Wager, A Wager"
Walter Pardon, Topic 12TS 392
b: John Roberts, Tony Barrand, Folk-Legacy FSI 65 (A2) "... Wager"

◆ The Blackwaterside *(H811)* 461

Laws 1957:227 (O1)
Brunnings 1981: "Abroad as I Was Walking"

Not the same song as Kennedy 1975:351 (#151) "Down by ...," Tunney 1979:109, nor O Canainn 1978b:80-1 ("The Lovely Irish Maid"), also not *Treoir* 6,1974, nor *Chapbook* 2(4) (a "love-and-leave" version).

Sam Henry's Songs of the People

IREL   Moulden 1979:21-2

b: AMER   E. Ives 1965:78-80; lists other occurrences in Northeastern archives.

BRS   Harvard 2: (Haly)

? REC   Clancy Brothers and Tommy Makem, CBS 83070
? Bert Jansch, Transatlantic TRA 10
? Dolly MacMahon, Claddagh CC3
? Peta Webb, Topic 12TS 223 (A5)
    Not: Paddy Tunney, Topic 12T 165

b: MEL   Louis Killen, Front Hall FHR 012

◇ **My Charming Coleraine Lass** *(H 616)* 562

m: BRS   Dublin Public Library, Dix donation 2588: Chapbook, "The Coleraine Lass, to which are added ... [etc.] Ormagh painted ... for the Flying Stationers 1827."

◇ **The Star of Donegal** *(H 555)* 463

Brunnings 1981

b: IREL   O Lochlainn 1939:164-5

AMER   Haskins n.d.:38
    Wright 1975:421 (from Henry coll., BCL)

BRS   *Derry Journal* [c. 1925],1:31
    In Dublin's 1968:94-5
    Walton's New 1,1966:62-3

REC   John McGettigan and His Irish Minstrels, Topic 12T 367 (B 9)

◇ **Glenarm Bay** *(H 102)* 464

IREL   Moulden 1979:63. "Len Graham has the song from his mother (a native of Glenarm) and his grandmother in a more localized form" (note, p. 161).
m: Shields/Shields *UF* 21,1975: #161

◇ **Greenmount Smiling Ann** *(H 182)* 464

BRS   BPL Irish: (n.i.)
    Healy 1,1967b:273-4 "... Anne"

◇ **Kellswaterside** *(H 802)* 466

Brunnings 1981: "By Kells Waters"

b: AMER   Creighton 1961:51 "By Kells Waters"

◇ **The Banks of Kilrea (I)** *(H 150a)* 466

? *Brunnings 1981*: "A Young Sailor Bold (See The Oak and the Ash)"

IREL   Moulden 1979:16-7 reports 2 Derry versions recorded by Len Graham.

m: MEL   O Lochlainn 1939:12

◇ **The Largy Line** *(H 781)* 467

Brunnings 1981: (m) "The Maid of the Sweet Brown Knowe (Tune of Roll Me from the Wall; See: The Maid of the Mountain Brow)"

IREL   Moulden 1979:84; reports 2 Antrim versions colllected by Len Graham.

m: MEL   O Lochlainn 1939:38 "The Maid of the Sweet Brown Knowe"

◇ **Sweet Londonderry** *(H 813)* 468

IREL   Shields/Shields *UF* 21,1975: #246 "Londonderry on the Banks of the Foyle"

BRS   *Walton's New* 1,1966:136-7 "Lovely Derry on the Banks of the Foyle"

◇ **The Lovely Banks of Mourne** *(H 595)* 468

IREL   Moulden 1979:94-5

m: BRS   NLI broadsheets: (Mayne, Belfast) "The Banks of Mourne"

◇ **Wild Slieve Gallon Brae[s]** *(H 540)* 468

1: Not the same song the McPeake Family sing: "Slieve Gallon Brae," nor the song in Wright 1975, from Carl Hardebeck's *Gems of Melody*, 1908.

Brunnings 1981: "Wild Slav Gallen Brae," *but not* "Wild Slieve Gallion Braes"

IREL   O Lochlainn 1965:223-4 "Wild Sliav Gallen Brae," without the happy ending.

REC   David Hammond, Greenhays/Sruthan GR 702 (A 2)

◇ **"Thank You, Ma'am," Says Dan** *(H 184, H 689)* 469

Brunnings 1981

IREL   O Lochlainn 1939:182-3 "I ..."

AMER   B. Ives 1955:5-6 "I ..."

BRS   Healy 1962(1968):97-8
b: Healy 1978b
    In Dublin's 1968:18-9
    Walton's New 1,1966:14-5

REC   Delia Murphy, EMI STAL 1055 (A 7)
b: Frank Ritchie, Request RLP 8060

◇ **The Yowe Lamb** *(H 175)* 470

Brunnings 1981: "Ca' the Yowes"

m: IREL   *JIFSS* 20,1923:59 "As Molly Was Milking"
    Moulden 1979:155 reports a version from Fermanagh in Len Graham's collection.

BRIT   Aitkin 1874:1-2 "Ca' the Yawes"
    Baring-Gould/Sheppard 1892(1895):22-3 "As Johnny Walked Out"
    Alan Bruford [*Tocher* 36-7(1982): 463] calls this "a decidedly Scottish courtship song."
    Greig 1907-11(1963): #50, ?51 "Lovely Mollie" and another untitled version.
    Johnson (1853)2:273 "Ca' the Ewes to the Knowes"
m: Kennedy 1975:300 (#124) "Ca the Yowes to the Knowes"

m: BRS   BCL Biggar J1:6
    Cf. Harvard 3: (Cadman) "The True Lovers"

b: REC   Louis Killen, Front Hall FHR 012 (A 6) "Ca' the Yowes"

◇ **Petie Cam' ower the Glen** *(H 200)* 470

BRIT   Ford 2,1901:112-6 "Patie's Waddin'"
    Johnson (1853)2:396-7 "Patie's Wedding"

◇ **The Navvy Boy** *(H 760)* 471

Brunnings 1981

C24 / To Hymen's car

BRIT Cf. Richards/Stubbs 1979:111 "The Navvie Man," said to be a remaking of "The Little Beggarman" [= H751 "The Oul' Rigadoo]

◇ One Penny Portion *(H634)* 472

White/Dean-Smith 1951: "(A) Sailor Courted a Farmer's Daughter"
Laws 1957:246 (O41) "The Constant Lovers"
Brunnings 1981: "... -- A Sailor Courted a Farmer's Daughter," "The Constant Lovers," "A Sailor Courted a Farmer's Daughter"

IREL Graves 1880:225 "A Sailor Loved a Farmer's Daughter"
Graves 1882:83 "A Sailor Wooed a Farmer's Daughter" [O Lochlainn]
b: O Lochlainn 1965:8-9 "... -- A Sailor Courted a Farmer's Daughter"

BRIT Sharp/Karpeles 1974,2:560-2 (#386) "A Sailor Courted a Farmer's Daughter," 2 vts.

AMER Creighton 1933:99

BRS Harvard 1: 5.92 (Cadman), 12.102 (Such)
Harvard 3: (Catnach)
b: Healy 1966:113-4 "Come-All-Ye (Parody of The Constant Lovers)"
617 [190-?]:75

MEL Bunting 1840:102 (#138) "A Sailor Married a Farmer's Daughter" [O Lochlainn]
JFSS 1:221

◇ The Inniskilling Dragoon *(H98b)* 472

Brunnings 1981: "Enniskillen ...," "Fare Ye Well, Enniskillen"

h: IREL Cf. Clancy Bros. 1964:58
h: Cf. Graves 1895:54(#38)
h: Hayward 1938:231
h: Joyce 1909:208-9 (#399) "... Enniskillen ..." contains elements of both Henry's versions and no refrain.
Loesberg 2,1980:53 "Fare Thee Well, Enniskillen"
Shields 1981:95, 98 (#38), "... Enniskillen ...," 2 vts.
Shields/Shields *UF* 21,1975: #200

AMER Fowke 1973:170-1 "... Enniskillen ..."
Haskins n.d.:29
Kenedy 1890:134
Shoemaker 1931:237

BRS Harvard 1: 1.130 (Spencer), 2.181 (Carbutt), 7.115 (Catnach), 9.2 (Bebbington), 11.143 (Such)
Harvard 3: (Harkness)
UCLA 605: 3(Such)
h: Healy 1,1967b:98-9 "... Enniskillen ..."
Ireland Calling n.d.:15
Ireland's Own
h: McCall 4:134
O'Conor 1901:78 "... Enniskillen ..."
617 [190-?]:33 "... Enniskillen ..."
Songs and Recitations 5,1978:11 "... Enniskillen ..." (but cf. also H631, 4 sts)
Walton's New 2,1968:188
Wehman's 1887,2:11

REC Oscar Brand, Folkways FA 2428 (B4) "The Inniskillin ..."
h: Eddie Butcher, EEOT *Adam in Paradise* cass. (A1)
Tommy Dempsey, Trailer LER 2096 (A4) "The Enniskillen ..."
Bill Meek, Folk-Legacy FSE 21 (A5) "Enniskillen"

MEL Hudson ms. 1:299
O'Neill 1903:72 (#411), not the same as Henry's.

◇ The Gallant Soldier *(H782)* 473

1: Not the same song as that by the same title in Greig/Duncan 1981:215-6; but see the other Greig/Duncan reference below.

Not = Brunnings 1981: "... (See: Bold Soldier)" or "... (See: The Bold Soldier)"

BRIT Greig 1907-11(1963): #154 (no title; should be "The Highland Soldier")
Greig/Duncan 1,1981:224-7 (#91) "The Highland Soldier" ("The Lovely Maiden")
Kilkerr *FMJ* 1977:229-30; reprint, *Treoir* 12(1) 1980:17 (both misnumbered H732).

BRS BPL H.80: (n.i.) "The Highland Soldier"
Harvard 1: 6.188 (Gilbert), 7.224 (Lyle)
Harvard 3: (Harkness)

◇ Young Edward the Gallant Hussar *(H243)* 473

Dean-Smith 1954: "(The) Gallant ..."
Brunnings 1981: "...," "The Gallant Hussar"

IREL Galwey 1910:10, 27 "The Gallant ..."

BRIT Dallas 1977:89-91
Ford 2,1901:91-3 "The Gallant ..."
Greig 1907-11(1963): #150 "The Gallant ..."

AMER Hubbard 1961:141-2 "The Gallant Hussars"
Kenedy 1890:38-9

BRS Harvard 1: 1.132 (n.i.), 2.171 (Carbutt), 3.153 (Forth), 7.28 (Catnach), 9.94 (Bebbington), 12.84 (Such)
Harvard 3: (Barr) (Keys)
UCLA 605: 3(Barr); 5(Such)

REC LaRena Clark, Topic 12T 140 (A6) "The Gallant ..."

MEL Joyce 1909:137 (#290) "The Gallant Hussar"

◇ Green Broom *(H147)* 474

White/Dean-Smith 1951
Dean-Smith 1954
Brunnings 1981

BRIT Kennedy 1975:503-4 (#223) "... Brooms"; also indicates 2 more English and 2 Irish versions recorded (see also Belton rec.).
Sharp/Karpeles 1974,1:458-63 (#116), 4 vts.
Sharp/Karpeles 1975,2:38

REC Seán McDonagh, *FSB* 3 (A6) "Green Brooms"
George Belton, EFDSS LP 1008 (A3)
Paul Clayton, Folkways FW 8708 (B7)
Burl Ives, Columbia CL 628; [lc:] Columbia CL 6144; Columbia CS 9041 (B7)
Sam Larner, Folkways FG 3507 (A2d)
Kendall Morse, Folk-Legacy FSI 57 (A2)
Derek Sarjeant, Joy Special JS 5001 (B6)

◇ John Hunter / [Dt:] The Wheelwright *(H125)* 475

IREL Bunting 1983:56-7 (#35) "An Deiladoir (The Wheelwright)"
Moulden 1979:74

495

Sam Henry's Songs of the People

MEL Bunting 1840:28 (#35) "The Wheelwright"
    Joyce 1909:376 (#767) "An Bouchailli'n Fir O'ig: The Young Boy," which Joyce says is related to Bunting's "The Wheelwright."
    O'Neill 1903:35 (#202)

◆ **The Journeyman Tailor** *(H620) 476*

Laws 1957:232 (O 13) "The Jolly Young Sailor and the Beautiful Queen"
Brunnings 1981: "The Jolly Young Sailor and the Beautiful Queen," "The Jolly Stage Driver"
Cazden et al. *Notes* 1982: #30 "The Jolly Stage Driver"

g: In Karpeles 1970, Leach 1965, and Peacock 1965 the man is a sailor, in Meredith/Anderson 1967, Moore/Moore 1964, and Shields 1981 he is a journeyman tailor. Except for the difference in occupation, all are essentially the same ballad.

h: IREL Moulden 1979:75 (#44) reports a version from Eddie Butcher collected by Len Graham.
Shields 1981:108-9

AMER Cazden et al. 1982:126-7 (#30) "The Jolly Stage Driver"

cl: REC Mrs J. U. Newman, AFS 3773 A1
m: Mrs C. D. Enright, #124 in Helen H. Flanders coll.

◆ **Lough Erne Shore** *(H597) 476*

IREL *Not*: S. O'Boyle 1977;68-9
    And not: Tunney 1979:115-6

BRS Harvard 1: 4.197 (Bebbington) "Lough Erin's Shore"
    Healy 1,1967b:274-6 "William and Eliza, or ..."

REC *Not*: Paddy Tunney, Folk-Legacy FSI 7 (A3)
    Not: Paul Brady, Green Linnet SIF 3006 (Mulligan LUN 008) (A2)
    And not: Dick Gaughan, Advent 3602 (B1)

MEL Hudson ms. 1:483 "Lough Erin's Shore"
    O'Neill 1922:27 "Molly of ..."

◆ **Belfast Town** *(H45) 477*

Brunnings 1981: "... (Tune of Gorton Town)"

m: BRS Belfast Biggar: J2:12 "The Cavehill Diamond" (Nicholson)
m: Belfast Crone: "Mary of the Lagan Side"

o: MEL Stanford/Petrie 2,1902:174 (#693) "Oh Johnny Dearest Johnny"

◆ **Molly, Lovely Molly** *(H557) 478*

l: This is not at all like the song with the same title in Shields/Shields *UF* 21,1975: #273 and Shields 1981: 121-2 (Laws P36, a murder ballad), except metrically.

Brunnings 1981: "...," ?"Lovely Molly," ?"Rise Up"

IREL Moulden 1979:106

? b: AMER Cf. Creighton 1961/40 "Lovely Molly"

? b: REC Hoyt Axton, Horizon HP 1621 "Rise Up"

m: MEL *Ireland Calling* n.d.:9

◆ **When a Man's in Love** *(H211) 479*

Laws 1957:235 (O 20)
Brunnings 1981

IREL Shields 1981:158 (#71)
    Shields/Shields *UF* 21,1975: #427
h: Cf. "Songs of the People" #329, 1 March 1930
h: Tunney 1979:96-7 "... He Feels No Cold"

AMER Cf. Dean [1922]:110-1 "The Boy of Love"

REC A. L. Lloyd, Prestige/Int. 13066
h: Paddy Tunney, FSB 1 (A4); Topic 12T 139 (B2)

o: MEL O'Neill 1903:29 (#164) "... He Feels No Cold"

◆ **Charming Mary O'Neill** *(H55) 479*

White/Dean-Smith 1951: "(The) Stealing of Mary Neale"
Laws 1957:188-9 (M17) "Mary Neal."
Brunnings 1981: "... Neal"

IREL Joyce 1909:123 (#256) different air and 1 stanza (= Wright 1975:672) [Laws]
    O Lochlainn 1939:76-7 [Peacock]
    Shields/Shields *UF* 21,1975: #266 "Mary ..."
    Sparling 1888:321-3

AMER Peacock 1965,1:216-7 "Mary Neal" (= Wright 1975:369-70)
    Wright 1975:672

BRS Healy 1967a:22-4
    Healy 1,1967b:308-10 "A Much Admired Song Called Mary Neill"

MEL O'Neill 1903:33 (#184)

◆ **The County Tyrone** *(H153) 480*

Brunnings 1981: "The County of Tyrone"

IREL Moulden 1979:37
m: Shields *UF* 1971:18, 1972:48 "Bold Maginnis of the ..."

BRS Harvard 1: 1.128 (Spencer), 7.118 (Catnach), 12.123 (Such) "Sweet Jane of Tyrone"
    Harvard 3: (Harkness) (Paul)
m: Healy 1,1967b:316 "Sweet Jane of Tyrone"

cl: REC J. W. Green, AFS 2284 B

MEL Bunting 1840:97
    Bunting 1983:186-7 (#128)

◆ **My Father's Servant Boy** *(H198) 481*

Laws 1957:185-6 (M11)

IREL Shields/Shields *UF* 21,1975: #284

BRIT MacColl/Seeger 1977:252-3 (#78)

AMER Wright 1975:395-6 "Answer to the Philadelphia Lass"

◆ **Jamie, Lovely Jamie** *(H553) 482*

? Brunnings 1981: "Baltimore"

IREL Shields/Shields *UF* 21,1975: #25 "Baltimore"

AMER *CFB* 1(6,Nov/Dec)1978:40-1 "You Lovers of Old Ireland"
    Creighton 1971:83-4 "There Was a Wealthy Farmer" shares several points of similarity with Henry's ballad.
    Warner 1984:53-4 (#5) "Plains of Baltimore"

C24 / To Hymen's car

◇ You Lovers All *(H525) 483*

AMER Wright 1975:407-8 "North America, or the Flowers of Enniskillen" (brs, Haly, Cork), 408 (from Henry coll., BCL)

◇ Mullinabrone *(H242) 483*

Brunnings 1981

b: BRIT Kilkerr *FMJ* 1977:222-3; reprint, *Treoir* 12(1)1980:14

AMER Wright 1975:391 (from Henry coll., BCL)

◇ Jamie's on the Stormy Sea *(H78) 484*

Brunnings 1981

AMER Jordan 1946:59-60 describes Oliver Ditson's agreement with the "Singing Hutchinsons" to publish this, among other songs, in 1843; he also says the music was written by Bernard Covert, who later became the Hutchinsons' agent.
  Reddall 1894:66, 2 stanzas, in 2/4 time.

REC Jessie Murray, *FSB* 7 (A2)

◇ The Garden Gate *(H770) 485*

Dean-Smith 1954
Brunnings 1981

BRIT Greig 1907-11(1963): #24 says that this "lies on the border land between folk-song and book-song."

AMER Eddy 1939:195

BRS BPL H.80: (n.i.)
  Harvard 1: 2.76 (Livsey), 4.118 (Gilbert) 5.66 (Cadman), 5.134 (Catnach), 10.47 (Bebbington)
  Harvard 3: (Fortey)
  UCLA 605: 3(Such) (Pitts)
Forget Me Not [1835]:139; followed on p. 140 by "Answer to the Garden Gate."

◇ Henry, the Sailor Boy *(H37) 485*

IREL Moulden 1979:69-70

AMER Creighton 1971:73 "My Mary Ann," a fragment.
  Peacock 1965:899-900 "Young Henry," very different.

m: BRS BL Ulster: "Henry and Mary Ann"
  Harvard 1: 5.156 (Ryle) "The Lovers' Parting"

s: MEL Joyce 1909:9-10 (#13) "The River Roe"

◇ The Lass of Glenshee *(H590) 486*

Laws 1957:229 (O6) quotes Ord 1930:75, who attributes authorship to Andrew Sharpe of Perth, about the early 19th century, and attests to its great popularity.
Brunnings 1981: "... of Glen Shee" without reference; "The Hills of Glenshee"
Cazden et al. *Notes* 1982: #28 "The Hills o' ..."

c: IREL *JIFSS* 10,1912:15
  Moulden 1979:85
m: Shields/Shields *UF* 21,1975: #163 "Glenshee"

AMER Cazden et al. 1982:120-4 "The Hills of ..."
  Leach 1967:123
  Peters 1977:167
  Warner 1984:51-3 (#4)

BRS BPL H.80: (n.i.)
  m: REC O. J. Abbott, Folkways FM 4051 (A6)
    Mrs T. Ghaney, Folkways FE 4075 (A2)
  m: Lizzie Higgins, Topic 12T 185 (B6) "The Maid of ..."
  c: Milt Okun, Stinson SLP 82 "The Hills of ..."
  c: -----, Ellen Stekert, Riverside RLP 12 634 "The Hills of ..."
c: Ellen Stekert, Folkways FA 2354 (A2) "The Hills of ..."

◇ The Hielan's o' Scotland *(H193) 487*

Dean-Smith 1954: "(The) Blaeberries"
Laws 1957:212 (N19) "The Blaeberry Courtship" says this is a modernization of the story told in Child #226 "Lizie Lindsay"
Brunnings 1981: "The Blaeberries," "Leezie Lindsay"

IREL *Ceol* 1:6-7
b: Graves 1928 "Leezie Lindsay"

BRIT Duncan 1967:24-9
  R. Ford n.d.:121-5, with a long discussion.
  Oxford Ballads 1969:258-62 (#69) "Donald of the Isles [Lizie Lindsay]"

AMER Cf. Darling 1983:78-9 "Lizzie Lindsay"

b: REC *The Music of Scotland*, National Geographic 707 "Leezie Lindsay"

MEL Joyce 1909(1965):151 (#323) "With My Love on the Road," coll. schoolteacher Mackenzie (Ballycastle)]

◇ The Glove and the Lions *(H474) 488*

White/Dean-Smith 1951: "(The) Bold Lieutenant or The Lion's Den; The Velvet Glove"
Dean-Smith 1954: "(The) Bold Lieutenant"
Laws 1957:237-8 (O25) "The Lady of Carlisle"
Brunnings 1981: "The Lady of Carlisle"

IREL Shields 1981:77-8 (#26) "The Fan," reprints a broadside ("The Bold Lieutenant") on p. 65 and gives references for the story's motif in literature.
  Shields/Shields *UF* 21,1975: #138 "(The) Fan"

BRIT Sharp/Karpeles 1974,1:313-5 (#71) "The Bold Lieutenant, or The Lion's Den"; notes (1:726) recount the literary trail of this romance.

AMER Bush 3,1975:66-8 "The Lion's Den"
  Darling 1983:132-3 "Carolina Lady" (see Chandler rec.)

BRS BPL H.80: (Sanderson)

h: REC Teresa Maguire, *FSB* 7 (B4) "The Lion's Den"; BBC LP 24842
cl: Mrs T. M. Bryant, AFS 1754 A1 "The Lady of Carlisle"
h: Eddie Butcher, Free Reed FRR 003 (A2) "The Lions Den"; Leader LED 2070 (B1) "The Fan"
  Dillard Chandler, Folkways FA 2418 (A1) "Carolina Lady"
  Logan English, Folkways FA 2136 (B5) "The Lady and the Glove"
  Roy Harris, Topic 12TS 327 (B1) "The Lady of Carlisle"
  Basil May, [cl:] AFS 1587 B "The Lady of Carlisle"; AAFS L1 (B3)
  New Lost City Ramblers, Folkways FTS 31035 (B5) "The Lady of Carlisle"
  Pete Seeger, Folkways FA 2314 (B4) "Down in Carlisle (In Castyle There Lived a Lady)"; Folkways FA 2319 "In Carlisle There Lived a Lady"

Doug Wallin, Home Made Music LP 003 "The Carlisle Lady"
cl: Clay Walters, AFS 1578, 581 A1 "The Lady of Carlisle"
Nimrod Workman, Phyllis Workman Boyens, June Appal JA 001 (A7) "Bold Sea Captain"

MEL *JFSS* 5:144

◆ **Johnny Scott** *(H 736) 489*

Child 1882-98(1965),2: 377-48 (#99) "Johnie Scot", 1 vt.; 4:486-91, 4 vts.; 5:234-5; 295-6, 1 vt.
Coffin/Renwick 1950(1977):95-6, 244-5
Bronson 2,1962:484-94
Brunnings 1981: "Lang Johnny More [Child 251]"

BRIT *Oxford Ballads* 1969:304-8 (#79) "McNaughton [...]"

REC Seán Corcoran, Green Linnet SIF 1004 (B4)
? cl: Samuel Harmon, AFS 2800 B2 "Young ... Scot"

◆ **The Keeper of the Game** *(H 681) 490*

Child 1882-98(1965),1:414-25 (#46) "Captain Wedderburn's Courtship," 3 vts.; 2:507; 3:507; 4:459; 5:216-7, 291
Coffin/Renwick 1950(1977):53-4 223-4 (with added references to riddle songs and nursery songs, pp. 54, 224)
Bronson 1,1959:362-75; 4,1972:462
Brunnings 1981: "Captain Wedderburn's Courtship [Child 46]"

IREL Shields/Shields *UF* 21,1975: #377 "Stock and Wall"

AMER Milner/Kaplan 1983:24 "Captain Wedderburn's Courtship"
Cf. Moore/Moore 1964:35-8 "An Old Man's Courtship," "The Six Questions" [Coffin/Renwick]
Silverman 1966:94 "Six Questions"

BRS Hudson ms., #701 [Bronson]

REC Seamus Ennis, *FSB* 4 (B1) "Captain Wedderburn's Courtship"
Ewan MacColl, *Folkways CB*, FG 3510 (A2) "Captain Wedderburn's Courtship"; *Riverside CB*, RLP 12 628 (A5)
Cf. Bob Coltman, Minstrel JD 200 "Captain Hanley and Sweet Mazie," a contemporary retelling.
Frank Donnelly, Mulligan A 001 (B1) "You and I in the One Bed Lie"; Green Linnet SIF 1005 (B7)
Warde H. Ford, AAFS (4196 B 1) [Bronson]
Frank Harte, Topic 12T 218 "He Rolled Her to the Wall"
b: Sandy Paton, Elektra 148 "Captain Wedderburn's Courtship"

MEL Petrie/Stanford 2,1902:194 (#777) "For My Breakfast You Must Get a Bird without a Bone" [Bronson]

◆ **The Rich Ship Owner's Daughter** *(H 221) 490*

White/Dean-Smith 1951: "Tom the Barber or John/Tom Barbary; Willie o' Winsbury"
Dean-Smith 1954: "Willie o' Winsbury; Lord Thomas of Winesberry"
Child 1882-98(1965),2:398-406 (#100) "Willie o Winsbury," 8 vts.; 514-5, 1 vt.; 3:517; 4:491; 5:296
Coffin/Renwick 1950(1977):96, 245
Bronson 2,1962:495-506; 4,1972:481
Brunnings 1981: "Willie o' Winsbury"

IREL Moulden 1979:124-5
m: Shields/Shields *UF* 21,1975: #220 "John Barbour"

BRIT Buchan 1828,2:212-5 "Lord Thomas of Winesbery and the King's Daughter"
Munnelly *FMJ* 3(1)1975:124-5
Raven 1978:27 "John o' Barbary"

AMER Darling 1983:72-3 "Willie O Winsbury"
Leach 1967:57-8 "Willie O Winsbury"
Milner/Kaplan 1983:35-6 "Thomas o' Winesberrie"

REC Peggy Seeger, Ewan MacColl, *LH*, Argo ZDA 72, #7 "Willie (Thomas) o' Winsbury," 2 versions.
Anne Briggs, Topic 12T 207 "Willie o' Winsbury"
m: Robert Cinnamond, Topic 12T 269 (A4)
Dick Gaughan, Topic 12TS 384 (B2) "Willie o' Winsbury"
Cliff Haslam, Folk-Legacy FSB 93 (B5) "Willy o' Winsbury"
m: Joe McCafferty, Leader LEA 4055 (A2) "John Barbour"; EEOT *Ceolta agus* cass. (A9) [*UF* 10,1972: 94-7]
Mary McGrath, EEOT *Irish Travellers* cass. (B2) "Johnny Borden"
Tony Rose, Dingle's DIN 324 (B4) "Tom the Barber"

◆ **Lord Beichan** *(H 470) 491*

White/Dean-Smith 1951: "... Bateman"
Dean-Smith 1954: "... Bateman"
Child 1882-98(1965),1: 454-83 (#53) "Young ...," 14 vts.; 2:508-9, 2 vts.; 3:507; 4:460-2, 1 vt.+; 5:218-20, 1 vt.+, 291
Coffin/Renwick 1950(1977):58-60, 226-7; a related broadside is Laws O26 "The Turkish Lady"
Bronson 1,1959:409-65; 4,1972:465-7
Brunnings 1981: "Young Beichan [Child 53]"

m: IREL Breathnach 1971:136-9 "... Baker"
Moulden 1979:92

BRIT MacColl/Seeger 1977:66-9 (#8)
Oxford Ballads 1969:103-12 (#31) "Young Bekie"
Palmer 1980:180-3 "... Bateman"
Shepheard n.d.:24-6

AMER Darling 1983:68-9 (see Armstrong rec.)
Leach 1967:81-6
Milner/Kaplan 1983:26-6 "... Bateman"
Randolph/Cohen (1982):25-8 "... Bateman"
Roberts 1974:89 "... Batesman"
Warner 1984:134-5 "... Bateman"

BRS *Forget Me Not* [1837?45] 171 "... Bateman"

REC "... Bateman (Young Beichan)," *FSB* 4 (B3) composite: Thomas Moran "... Bacon," Jeannie Robertson "Susan Pyatt"
Ewan MacColl, *Folkways CB*, FG 3510 (A3) "Young ..."
A. L. Lloyd, *Riverside CB*, RLP 12 624 (A4) "... Bateman"
Peggy Seeger, Ewan MacColl, *LH*, Argo ZDA 73, #8 "Young ...," 3 versions.
cl: Finley Adams, AFS 2797 B2 "... Bateman"
Frankie Armstrong, Bay 206 (B1) "... Bateman"
George, Gerry Armstrong, Folk-Legacy FSI 41 (B1) "... Bateman"
Paul Clayton, Folkways FP 2007 (A2) "... Bateman"
A. Davis, Middlebury College New England Folksong Series #1 (B1) "... Bateman"
cl: Emma Dusenbury, AFS 857 A1 "... Banyan"; AFS 858 A "... Bateman"
cl: Minnie Floyd, AFS 2692 B1 "... Bateman"
cl: Munroe Gevedon, AFS 1556 A1 "... Batesman"
lc: Shep Ginandes, Elektra JH 508 "... Bateman"

cl: George Vinton Graham, AFS 3811 A1 & 2, B1 "... Bakeman"
cl: Mrs G. A. Griffin, AFS 958 B2 "... Bateman"
cl: Sam Harmon, AFS 2881 A1 "Young Beham"
   Buna Hicks, Folk-Legacy FSA 22 (B5) "Young Beham"
   Bella Higgins, Tangent TNGM 119/D (C3b) "Young Beicham (Lord Bateman)"
   "Aunt" Molly Jackson, [cl:] AFS 822 A1 & B1 "... Bateman"; AAFS L57 (B1)
   Nic Jones, Trailer LER 2027 (B2) "... Bateman"
cl: J. C. Kennison, AFS 3752 A & B "... Bakeman"
   Campbell MacLean, Tangent TNGM 119/D (C3a) "Young Beicham (Lord Bateman)"
   Ian Manuel, Topic 12TS 301 (A3) "Young ..."
   Pleaz Mobley, AAFS L12 (A1) "... Bateman"
cl: E. H. Napier, AFS 1552 B2 "... Batesman"
   New Lost City Ramblers, Folkways FTS 31035 (A4) "... Bateman"
   Joan O'Bryant, Folkways FA 2134 (A6) "... Batesman"
   Old Reliable String Band, Folkways FA 2475 (B5) "... Bateman"
cl: Lize Pace, ARS 1439 B, "... Bateman"

   Planxty, Shanachie 79035 (A4) "... Baker," reworked by Christy Moore.
   John Reilly, Topic 12T 359 (A5) "... Baker"
m: Jean Ritchie, Folkways FA 2301 (A4) "... Bateman"
   Ritchie Family, Folkways FA 2316 (B1) "... Bateman and the Turkish Lady"
b: Peggy Seeger, Folk-Lyric FL 120 (B4) "Young Beichan"
   David Slauenwhite, Folkways FE 4307 (B9) "Young ..."
cl: Marion Stoggill, AFS 1724 B "Young ..."
   Mary Sullivan, [cl:] AFS 4109 A & B1 "Lloyd Bateman"; AAFS L57 (B2)
   Isabel Sutherland, Topic 12T 151 (B3) "... Bateman"
b: Joseph Taylor, Leader LEA 4050 (A5) "... Bateman"
   Mr Thomson, Leader LEA 4050 (B2) "... Bateman"
   Rita Weill, Takoma A 1022 (B1) "... Bateman"
   Tom Willett, Topic 12T 84 (A1) "... Bateman"
cl: Mary Young, AFS 1549 A1 "... Batesman"

m: MEL Joyce 1909:317 (#317) "... Baykim"

C25

Wedlock's soft bondage: Domesticity

C25 / Wedlock's soft bondage

The Married Man [H701: 1 May 1937]

Source: Harriet Brownlow (Ballylaggan, Cloyfin) from her mother, now aged 70, from her mother, Jane Campbell, 95 (Glenmanus, Portrush).

s: The use of the word "chocolate" in verse two is interesting. It is generally thought that this product of the cacao tree is a modern foodstuff, but it was introduced to England in 1657, and had even been brought to Europe by the Spaniards in 1519, 26 years after Columbus had discovered America, where the tree is indigenous.

Key C.

I've been a married man this seven years and more,
And blessed be the day I was married;
I never had a word between my love and I,
Though late in the ale-house we tarried.
When I come home, not a word's to be said,
She lights me a candle and puts me to bed,
And lets me lie there till I settle my head,
So, girls, mind you this when you marry.

When I rise in the morning, to scold it's no use,
For scolding it ne'er mends the matter,
She makes me some tea or some chocolate hot
Or something that I do like better.
I slip her a kiss, to my work I do go,
She never says, 'Husband, why do you do so?'
But like two doves we live and no sorrow we know,
So, girls, mind you this when you marry.

On Saturday night when the money runs short,
We make the less do upon Sunday;
He says, 'My dearest dear, I'll do better next week,
I'll go early to work upon Monday.'
So all ye young women, your husbands adore,
Be ye loving and kind, be they every so poor,
And God will be always increasing your store,
So, girls, mind you this when you marry.

The Happy Pair [H753: 30 Apr 1938]

Other titles: "... Marriage"; cf. "The Contented Wife (and) Answer."

Source: Mrs Hanna (Corkey, Loughguile) from her father, Thomas Houston Loughridge (Ballyveeley) c. 1882.

s: [Mrs Hanna's father] sang it to her mother. He brightened his home with music, both vocal and on the flute, and gave reality to the song, "The Happy Pair."

Repeat last two lines of tune for last two lines of song.

Key G.

How blest has my life been, what joys I have known,
Since wedlock's soft bondage made Jessie my own;
Over walks grown with woodbine, as often I stray,
Our boys and girls frolic round us and play.

How pleasing their sports as these wantons we see,
Who borrow their looks from sweet Jessie and me.
What though on her cheek the rose loses its hue?
Her ease and good humour bloom a' the year through.

Time still, as it flies, adds increase to her truth
And gives to her mind what he steals from her youth.
Ye shepherds so gay, who make love to ensnare
And cheat with false vows the too credulous fair
In search of true pleasure, how vainly you roam;
To hold it for life, you must find it at home.

The Day We Packed the Hamper for the Coast [H488: 8 Apr 1933]

Source not given.

Key D.

Sam Henry's Songs of the People

I'm always livin' yet, tho' I nearly had a fit
  On the day we packed the hamper for the coast,
Ye can bet your fortnight's pay I had plenty for
  tae dae
  On the day we packed the hamper for the coast.
We put in forty loaves of bread, forby a smoked
  ham,
Sausages and Irish stew and marmalade and jam,
We had twenty stone o' praties and the carcase o'
  a lamb
  On the day we packed the hamper for the coast.
    Oh, my, I felt inclined tae cry,
    Nae wunner, freens, my temper I had lost.
    Roon the house I had tae flee
    Like a monkey up a tree,
      On the day we packed the hamper for the
      coast.

My arms were bit wi' clegs and they also bit my
  legs
  On the day we packed the hamper for the coast,
I was angry indeed, but was toul' tae bail my heid
  On the day we packed the hamper for the coast.
Says my guid wife, 'Noo, Pat, listen an' I'll
  tell ye what,
We'd best put in the fryin' pan, the kettle and the
  pot.'
Says I, 'In case there's mice doon there, ye'd best
  put in the cat,'
  On the day we packed the hamper for the coast.
    Oh, my, I felt inclined tae cry,
    Nae wunner, freens, my temper I had lost,
    But the cat we couldna' fin'
    So we rammed the bulldog in
      On the day we packed the hamper for the
      coast.

When it was fu' you see, says the missus unto me,
  On the day we packed the hamper for the coast,
Says she, 'Ye'd best put in anither pair or twa o'
  shoen,'
  On the day we packed the hamper for the coast.
My face got red wi' fury and my nose got black
  and blue,
Says I, 'There's room for naethin' mair, ye see,
  the hamper's fu'.'
Says she, 'As far as I can see, I'm thinkin' so are
  you,'
  On the day we packed the hamper for the coast.
    Oh, my, I felt inclined to cry,
    Nae wunner, freens, my temper I had lost,
    So I says, 'Before we slide
    We'll put a' the weans inside,'
      On the day we packed the hamper for the
      coast.

2.1: clegs = horseflies.
r.3.3: weans = children.

The Tay

[H25a: "Two old time comic songs," 3 May 1924]

A Shuttle Hill song.

Source not given.

Key A.

All you young men that wants a wife, a warnin'
  tak' by me,
And if you want to change your life, tak' wan
  that won't drink tay,
For if that I wiz single again, the truth to you
  I'll say,
I'd niver wed wae onywan wud pledge my sark
  for tay.

Sing fiddle fal the di do, fiddle fal the dee.

I am a nailer to my trade, I work at Shuttle Hill,
An' all the money that I mak' she has it at her
  will;
My wages are a pound a week an' I can safely
  say
It tak's the half o' that an' mair to keep my wife
  in tay.

The ither day when I cam' in my dinner for to
  tak',
She had it in the hoose, but she had it for to
  mak'.

I tuck my dinner then in peace an' not a word did say,
But shane she put the kettle on to mak' hersel' the tay.

Then my temper it got up and I said I would mak' wreck;
The taypot an' the kettle I instantly did breck,
But with the tongs in her right han' without any more delay,
She struck me ower the napper an' she sed she'd tak' her tay.

And then into the cradle I instantly did fall,
The baby in the cradle, it then began to bawl,
But before she let me up again, she made me gled to say,
'You're welcome, my ain dearest wife, to mak' yersel' the tay.'

1.4: ... never wed wi' ... [Dt]
4.3: ... withoot ... [Dt]
4.4: ... she said she's ... [Dt]

The Scolding Wife [H145: 21 Aug 1926]

g: "The Married Man." Other titles: "The Bad (Wicked) Wife."

Source: John Henry Macaulay (Ballycastle, Co. Antrim).

Key C.

Come all ye sprightly sporting youths, wherever you may be,
You'll never know your misery till married that you'll be,
For if marriage be a paradise, I'm sure it's I can tell,
It is my firm opinion that I never will do well.

For she's aye, aye scowlin', an' she's aye scowlin' me,
She's for everlasting scowlin' and she canna let me be.

When neighbour Tam and I go out, our whistles for to wet,
My wife she falls a-bawling and I think I hear her yet,
There's nothing I do like so well as a bottle and a friend
But that I dar'na mention for fear I might offend.

There's nothing I do like so well as a dish o' dainty meat,
But she cooks it up sae claty that yin bite I canna eat,
And if I ever chance tae thraw my lip or gi'e my heed a nod,
She says, 'You're gettin' saucy, you may go and chew your cud.'

When that I come home at night from market or from fair,
She'll meet me at the durestep and drag me by the hair,
She sets me in the corner and she'll buff me a' aroon,
And if ever I chance to miss a clout she'll hunt me roun' the toon.

Now to conclude and finish, I've got nae mair tae add,
But I'll lave it to the company if my case it isna bad.
I trust that something it will come that parted we will be,
And I hope the divil will get her yet before she finishes me.

3.2: claty [clatty] = dirty, muddy, [m:] messily.
3.3: thraw = twist.
4.2: durestep = doorstep.

Upside Down [H694: 13 Mar 1937]

s: (m) variant of "My Love Nell"; m: (m) "Star of the County Down."

Source: John Moore (Liscolman) from Sam Lamont (Carnabuoy, Cloyfin, Coleraine).

Key G.

When I was a bachelor, airy and young, I left my work and trade,
And all the harm that ever I done was courting a pretty maid;
My comrades and I took great delight in travelling from town to town,
But to my sad grief I married a wife and the world turned upside down.

My master sent me out one day, just as I drew my pay,
And then I met with an old sweetheart who caus-ed me to stay;
We scarce had got one half pint drunk when my wife came into town,
And when she saw us, scowled and brawled, and the world turned upside down.

That very night when going home I met my sister Jane,
I told her my calamity, to her I did complain;
She turned right round all on her heel, saying 'Go home, you silly clown,

Sam Henry's Songs of the People

And hit her a smack across the back and wheel her upside down.'

That very night when I went home, my wife did brawl and scowl;
I then took heed to Jane's advice and my wife began to yowl,
And since that night I've as loving a wife as e'er a man in town,
I never heard one word from her since I wheeled her upside down.

The Single Days of Old [H659: 11 Jul 1936]

s: (m) "Auld Lang Syne."

Source not given.

Key D.

The merry days -- the days of old
Before that I knew strife,
When fortune tellers fine tales told,
And love made me a wife.
Soon I found love's but a name,
For marriage makes love cold;
How different I find wedded days
To the single days of old.

How fond and faithful he was then,
Scarce ever from my side,
In whims and pets he honoured me,
And all I did was right.
Now everything I do is wrong,
He's distant, cross and cold;
How different I find wedded days
To the single days of old.

He always has appointments,
Makes excuse to get away,
He stops out nearly all the night,
Leaves me alone all day.
His kindness now he takes from home
To another, I am told;
How different I find wedded days
To the single days of old.

My health gave way, my spirits fled,
They told him I would die --
This brought the rover back again
With a tear in every eye.
To make amends, he loves his home,
No longer is he cold;
Now wedded days I find more blest
Than the single days of old.

The Wealthy Farmer

[H702: 8 May 1937; Laws Q1]

k: "The Old Man and His Wife." Other titles: "The Drummer," "Father (Old Mr) Grumble," "John Grumlie," "Little Phoebe," "Old Crumbly Crust," "Old Grumbler," "The Old Man in the Woods."

Source not given.

g: Henry's "Wealthy Farmer" is very different from the usual forms of "Father Grumble."

Key G.

There was a wealthy farmer near Dublin town did dwell,
He had thirty acres of good land and lived exceeding well,
He had horses, cows, sheep and ploughs, and plenty of good grain,
He lived at peace without dispute; he had a handsome dame.

One morning just as usual, as he and his man John
Came in to get their breakfast, the shame a bit was on;
He cursed her for a lazy slut and thus to her he said,
'Why is it, madam lazy-bones, you've not the breakfast made?'

She says unto her guid oul' man, 'If you dae stay at hame,
I'll go oot and tak' the plough alang wi' your man John;
To watch the dairy and the pigs, and rock the cradle too,'
And believe me, my dear neighbour, he had enough to do.

The pigs being wanting servants, as you have often seen,
They went into the dairy and served themselves wi' cream;
The cheese and butter suffered much before he got them out,
And the churns and pans the pigs upset and dashed the cream about.

When he got up the churn-staff to slash among the
  pigs,
Some he hit and some he missed and others broke
  their legs,
It would make a dying man to laugh if you had
  seen the fun
When the oul' sow she turned about an' bit him on
  the thum'.

When he had got a cloth prepared for to tie up his
  thum',
The children they lie squealing and calling out for
  mum;
He said, 'Your mum's gone out to plough, an' I am
  almost mad,'
The one lay squealing on the floor, the other on
  the bed.

He jumped up like a madman -- a man was never
  worse,
He being tired of women's work, no longer would
  he nurse,
He went out to yonder plain to call his wife from
  plough,
When honest John was kissing her beneath the
  whinny knowe.

Come all ye childish husbands, a warning take by
  me:
Never frown at your own wife, though cruckle
  she may be;
This man has tried the woman's work -- he likes
  his own the best,
So never frown on your own wife and you will find
  it best.

Will the Weaver [H682: 19 Dec 1936; Laws Q9]

Other titles: "Bill(y) (the) (Wildee) (Willie(y))
...," "Billy Weever," "Johnny and Old Mr Henly";
cf. "The Butcher Boy," "Butter and Cheese (and
All)," "The Cook's Choice," "The Croppy Tailor,"
"The Trooper and the Tailor."

Source: (Tyrone Ditches, near Newry).

Key E flat.

Mother dear, I have got married,
Wishing I had longer tarried,
For my wife does curse and swear
That the breeches she will wear.

She does scold and she does riot,
She is costly in her diet,
She does to the tavern go
With Will the weaver -- that I know.

'Son, dear son, go home and love her,
Never more your mind discover,
Give your woman what's her due
And she'll never trouble you.

'Give her food and give her diet,
Give her all things if she's quiet,
If she offers to rebel,
Take a stick and bang her well.'

Away he went, a neighbour met him,
Told him all things for to fret him:
'I'll just tell you who and how
That I saw with your wife just now.

'I saw your wife and Will the weaver,
Talking free and close together
On the threshold of the door;
I stepped on, I saw no more.'

Away he went in a great wonder,
Rattling at the door like thunder;
'Who is that?' the weaver cried;
''Tis my husband, you must hide.'

Into the house the husband entered,
Up the chimney Willie ventured.
Searched the house up and down,
But not a soul was to be found.

When he was nearly tired looking,
Fortune to the chimney took him,
There he saw a wretched soul
Sitting on the chimney pole.

He put on a rousing fire
For to please his own desire,
Which made the weaver cough and sneeze
Because he sat at little ease.

You never saw a chimney sweeper
Half as black as Will the weaver,
Hands and feet, legs and thighs --
Send him home with three black eyes.

The Tailor in the Tea [Dt: Sea] Chest

[H604: 29 Jun 1935; Laws Q8]

k: "Boatswain and the Tailor." Other titles:
"The Blacksmith's Daughter," "The Boatsman and
the Chest (Tailor)," "The Bold (Jolly) Boatswain
(Boatman) (of Dover)," "The Clever Skipper,"
"The Old Bo's'n," "(A) ... (Tea) Chest," "The
Wealthy Merchant"; cf. "The (Cunning) Cobbler
(and the Butcher)," "The (Bold) Trooper," "The
Cropped Tailor," "The Game Cock," "The Sea
Captain," "Tiddy the Tailor," "The Trooper and
the Tailor."

[Dp] Source: Joe M'Conaghy (Bushmills).

Key D.   [Dp] Lively.

Sam Henry's Songs of the People

There was a tarry sailor and he in this town did dwell,
He had a handsome wife and she loved a tailor well.

*Toor an addy, fol the daddy,
Toor an addy, fol the lee.*

'Oh, I say this very night you will come and visit me,
For my husband's off to China for to buy and sell some tea.'

Oh, we weren't long a-talking by the tolling of the clock
Till a booting at the hall door came as loud as it could knock.

'Oh, where now will I run to, or where now will I hide?'
'In my husband's tea-chest close to the bedside.'

'I ran quickly down the stairs and open-ed the door,
There stands my dandy husband and nine sailors more.

I ran into his arms and I pressed him with a kiss,
Saying, 'Husband dear, oh husband, what's the meaning of all this?'

'Oh, I haven't come to rob you or disturb you of your rest,
But I can not go to China without my big tea-chest.'

So four of those brave sailors, they being stout and strong,
They pick-ed up the tea-chest and carried it along.

They hadn't got as far as a mile out of town
Till the weight of the big tea-chest, it made their sweat come down.

Oh, it's then one of the sailor lads he turned round to the rest,
Saying, 'I wonder what the devil is a-kicking in the chest?'

So they took out their key and they opened up the chest,
And there lies the dandy tailor like a pigeon in his nest.

'Will we take him out to China? Will we sell him out for tea?
Will we leave him in old Ireland to rear a family?'

So we took him out to China and we sold him out for tea,
And he made a fine supply for the whole ship's company.

Now it's all you dandy tailors, a warning take by this,
That when you go a-courting, never hide in a tea-chest.

[*Differences in Dt:*]
r.1,2: ... fol dha ...
2.1: So she said unto the tailor, 'You ...
3.1: Oh, they ...
4.2: 'Open up my husband's sea-chest and hide yourself inside.'
5.1: She ran ... and opened up ...
.2: And there stood her ...
6.1: She ran ... and she ...
7.2: ... big sea-chest.'
8.2: They lifted up the sea-chest ...
9.2: When the ... big [*crossed out*] sea-chest ...
13.1: So they ... and they ...
14.2: ... sea-chest.

I Wish That You Were Dead, Goodman

[H531: 3 Feb 1934]

Other titles: "O, An (Gin) Ye Were Dead, Gudeman," "There's a Chicken in the Pot."

Source not given.

Key G.

I wish that you were dead, goodman,
And a green sod on your head, goodman,
That I might wear my widowhood
Upon a ranting Highlandman.

There's six eggs in the pan, goodman,
There's six eggs in the pan, goodman,
There yin to you and twa to me
And three to our John Highlandman.

There's beef into the pot, goodman,
There's beef into the pot, goodman,
The banes for you and the brew for me
And the beef for our John Highlandman.

There's six horses in the stable, goodman.
There's six horses in the stable, goodman,

There's yin to you and twa to me
And three to our John Highlandman.

There's fat kye in the byre, goodman,
There's fat kye in the byre, goodman,
There's nane o' them yours, there's twa o' them mine,
And the lave is our John Highlandman's.

The Auld Man and the Churnstaff

[H174: BLp, 12 Mar 1927; Laws Q2]

o: "Marrowbones"; g: "Old Man and Old Woman," "Old Woman of Slapsadam," "Marrow Bones." Other titles: "A (The) Blind Man He Can See," "The Cruel Wife," "Eggs and Marrowbone," "Johnnie(y) Green (Sands)," "Kelso," "Love My Darlin' O," "Mercian Tittery-ary-a," "(The) Old) Lady (Woman) from Boston (Dover) (Ireland) (Wexford) (Yorkshire) (in (of) Dover) (in Slab City) (in Trenton) (of Blighter Town) (of Slapsadam)," "Once I Knew an Old Lady," "The Rich Old Lady," "She Loved Her Husband Dearly," "There Is a Lady in This Town," "There Lived a Wife in Kelmie," "There Was an Old Lady (Woman) (in London) (in Our Town)," "Tigaree Torum Orum," "Tippin' It up to Nancy," "The Town (Wife) (Woman) of Kelso," "What Ails You?" "The Wily Auld Carle (Joker)."

(m) coll. A. E. Boyd (Cullycapple P.E.S.), (w) coll. Dan Duffy "of our staff" "in shorthand as the song was being sung," from John Parker, 77, "at the hospitable hearth of Mr William Reid" (Mayoghill, Garvagh).

l: Note the parallel between this story, which has an unusual outcome, and that told in Sam Henry's equally unusual version of H163 (Child #4) "The King o' Spain's Daughter": in each case the intended victim eventually relents and saves the partner from drowning.
    Stanza 8 contains an echo of Child #10 "The Twa Sisters."

[Print kindly provided by John Moulden from British Library microfilm files.]

[BLp] Key D.

Oh, there was an aul' woman in oor toon, in oor toon did dwell,
She loved her husband dearly, but anither yin twice as well.

Wi' mi ri fo roo fa raddy, boys, mi ri fo roo fa ran,
Wi' mi ri fo roo fa raddy, may she whack for ol da dan.

She went into the doctor's shop some medicine for to find,
Sayin', 'Have you any medicine wid knock an aul' man blind?'

Oh, the doctor gave her marrow bones and bid her grind them fine,
And dust them in the aul' man's eyes and that would knock him blind.

'Oh, I am tired o' this world, I'm tired of my life,
I think I'll go and droon mysel' and that'll end the strife.'

So they both went out together till they came to the river brim,
He says, 'You'll tak' a runnin' race and you must push me in.'

So they both went out together till they came to the river brim,
But when she cam' up, he stepped aside and she went tumbling in.

So loudly did she bawl and so loudly did she call,
'Ah, houl' your tongue,' the auld man said, 'sure I can't see you at all.'

Sometimes she rose to the surface and tried to catch the brim,
But the aul' man wi' the churnstaff, he birled her farther in.

Oh, when he thought she'd got enough, he pulled her to dry lan',
Sayin' 'I think the notion's oot o' your heed o' haein' anither man.'

[*Differences in Bt and Wt = Dt(c):*]
  1.2: ... husband, but anither man ... [Bt]; ... anither man ... [Wt]
  r.1 [*and throughout* Wt]: ... wi' mae ... mae ...
    .2: ... whack fol ol ... [Wt]
  2.1: ... medicine to find, [Bt]
    .2: ... ony medicine would knock ... [Wt]
  4.1: 'Oh,' says he, 'I'm tired ... [Wt]
  5.1: ... both marched out ... the river's brim, [Bt, Wt]
    .2: Says he, ... a rinnin' race an' ... [Wt]
  6.: [*Substituted in Bt, Wt:*]
  The aul' wife took a runnin' race to shove the auld man in,
  But the canny aul' fellow he stepped aside an' she went birlin' in.
  7.: [*This stanza only in Wt; not in BLp or Bt.*]
  8.1: Sometimes she sank, sometimes she swam, till she came to the river's brim, [Bt, Wt]
    .2: ... auld boy wi' ... [Wt]; ... aul' boy wi' his long churnstaff ... [Bt]
  9.1: Oh, when she ... [Bt]; ... she'd had enough ... [Wt]
    .2: ... your heid ... [Wt]

Sam Henry's Songs of the People

The Blin' Auld Man / The Covered Cavalier
[H21ab: "An auld sang in braid Scots," 5 Apr 1924; Child #274]

k: "The Blind Man He Can See." Other titles: "As I Came Rolling Home from Sea," "The Blind (Drunken) Fool," "Cabbage Head (Song)," "Coming Home Late," "The Drunk Husband," "Drunkard Blues," "Drunkard's Special," "Four (Five) (Six) (Seven) Nights Drunk," "Four Nights' Experience," "Hame Drunk Cam' I," "The Hillman," "I Came (Went) Home (Drunk) Last (One) Night," "A Jacobite Song," "A Little before Me Time," "The Merry Cuckold," "My Old Man," "(Now It's) My (The) Old Man (Came Home Again) (One Night)," "The Old Farmer and His Young Wife," "Old Man Crip," "Old Wichet," "Th' Owd Chap (Come ower t' Bank)," "Our (The) Goodman (Gudeman) (Cam Home at E'en)," "Shickered as He Could Be," "Three Nights' Experience," "Three Nights in a Bar Room," "Whiskers on a Baby's Face"; cf. "Who Went out the Back?"

s: A song of a Jacobite in hiding when a household was divided against itself after the rebellion of 1715 or 1745 (first printed in 1776). The song was probably much older and adapted for the last occasion for flight and concealment.

(H21a) Source: (m) Sally Doherty, 89 [Dt: 88] (Oughtymoyle, Magilligan).

Key F.

(H21b) Source: (m) W. T. H., esq (Coleraine)

[Bp] ... an alternative air ... (The words to be adapted almost as in a chant.)

Key F.

Oor gudeman cam' hame at e'en and hame cam' he,
And there he saw a saddle horse where nae horse should be.
'And hoo cam' this horse here, and wha's can it be?
And hoo cam' this horse here withot the leave o' me?'
　(*spoken*) 'A horse?' quo' she. 'Aye, a horse,' quo' he.
'Silly auld cockle an' blinner may ye be;
It's but a bonny milk coo my minnie sent to me.'
　(*spoken*) 'A milk coo?' quo' he. 'Aye, a milk coo,' quo' she.
'It's far ha'e I ridden and muckle ha'e I seen,
But saddles upon milk coos sa' I never nane.'

Oor gudeman cam' hame at e'en and hame cam' he,
And there he saw a siller sword where nae sword should be.
'And hoo cam' this sword here, and wha's can it be?
And hoo cam' this sword here withoot the leave o' me?'
　'A sword?' quo' she. 'Aye, a sword,' quo' he.
'Silly auld cockle and blin' may ye be;
It's but a parridge potstick my minnie sent to me.'
　'A potstick?' quo' he. 'Aye, a potstick,' quo' she.
'It's far hae I ridden and muckle hae I seen,
But siller-handed potsticks sa' I never nane.'

Oor gudeman cam' hame at e'en, and hame cam' he,
And there he sa' a muckle coat where nae coat should be.
'And hoo cam' this coat here, and wha's can it be?
And hoo cam' this coat here withoot the leave o' me?'
　'A coat?' quo' she. 'Aye, a coat,' quo' he.
'Silly aul' cockle and blinner may ye be,
It's but a pair of blankets my minnie sent to me.'
　'Blankets?' quo' he. 'Aye, blankets,' quo' she.
'It's far hae I ridden and muckle hae I seen,
But buttons upon blankets sa' I never nane.'

Oor gudeman cam' hame at e'en and hame cam' he,
He spied a pair of jack-boots where nae boots should be.

'What's this noo, gudewife, what's this I see?
How cam' these boots here withoot the leave o'
   me?'
   'Boots?' quo' she. 'Aye, boots,' quo' he.
'Silly auld cockle and blinner may ye be;
It's but a pair of waterstowps the cooper sent to
   me.'
   'Waterstowps?' quo' he. 'Aye, waterstowps,'
      quo' she.
'It's far hae I ridden and muckle hae I seen,
But siller spurs on waterstowps sa' I never
   nane.'

Ben the hoose gaed oor gudeman and ben gaed
   he,
And there he sa' a sturdy man where nae man
   should be.
'And hoo cam' this man here, and wha can he
   be?
And hoo cam' this man here withoot the leave o'
   me?'
   'A man?' quo' she. 'Aye, a man,' quo' he.
'Tak your time, my ain gudeman, and dinna
   angered be,
It's just oor cousin M'Intosh cam frae the North
   Country.'
   'M'Intosh?' quo' he. 'Aye, M'Intosh,' quo'
      she.
'Ye'll hae us a' hang'd, gudewife, I've e'en
   enough to see,
Ye're hidin' rebels in the hoose withoot the leave
   o' me.'

1.7: minnie = mother. [s: Bp]
2.2: siller = silver.
2.7: parritch spurtle = a stick for stirring porridge.
   [Dt]
4.7: waterstowps = wooden pitchers. [s: Bp]
5.1: ben = into.

The Brown-Eyed Gypsies

[H124: 27 Mar 1926; Child #200]

s: "The Gypsy Countess," "Gypsy Davy," "Johnny Faa," "Wraggle Taggle Gypsies." Other titles: "(The) Blackjack David (Dav(e)y) (Daisy)," "Clayton Boone," "The Dark-Eyed Gipsy (O!)" "Davie Faa," "The Draggle(-)tail(ed) ...," "The Gipsies Came to Lord M--'s Gate," "Gipson Davy," "Gyps of David," "Gipsy Laddie(y) O(h)," "Gypsies-O!" "The Gypsy-o," "The Gypsy Daisy (Davy) (Laddie)," "Lord Cassilis' Lady," "(The) Raggle Taggle (Gypsies)(y)...," "Seven (Yellow) ... (on Yon Hill)," "The Three Gypsies (Gypsy Laddies)," "The Whistlin' Gypsy Rover."

Source: Alexander Thompson (Islandflackey, Portrush; native of Alla, near Cumber Claudy), from Sam Canning, shoemaker (Alla) c. 1870.

s: ... The song, to different airs, has been collected by Cecil Sharp in Somersetshire ("The Wraggle Taggle Gypsies") and in Renfrewshire by Motherwell under the title "Gypsy Davy." It is sometimes known as "Johnny Faa," because that was the name of the gypsy king, "The Lord and Earl of Little Egypt." In 1609 an act of Parliament was passed, banishing the gypsies from Scotland. In 1624 Johnny Faa and seven other gypsies were hanged for the offence described in the song.

It has been published without music as No. 148 in the *Oxford Book of Ballads* [1910], where it is called "The Gypsy Countess." The version below gives the nobleman's name as Lord Barnham; in other versions he is called Earl Cassilis, but it is stated that the Cassilis family have had no such incident in their history.

Key G.

Three gipsies came to Lord Barnham's gate
And O, but they sang bonnie-o,
They sang so sweet and so complete
That they charmed the heart of the lady-o.

The lady she came down the stairs
And all her maids before her-o,
And when they saw her bonnie face
They threw their grammerie o'er her-o.

It's she gave them of the wine to drink,
And she gave them of the brandy-o,
And she threw off her bonnie fine boots
And away with the brown-eyed gipsies-o.

Lord Barnham he came riding home
Enquiring about his lady-o,
When up then comes his servant man,
'She has followed the brown-eyed gipsies-o.'

'O come saddle to me my milk-white steed,
For the brown was ne'er so speedy-o,
And I will ride until daylight
Or I will find my lady-o.'

It's he rode east and he rode west,
And he rode from Straboggie-o,
Where there he met a little old man,
He enquired about his lady-o.

'I have travelled east, I have travelled west,
I have travelled from Straboggie-o,
And the gayest lady ever I saw,
She's away with the brown-eyed gipsies-o.'

It's he rode east and he rode west,
And he rode back to Straboggie-o,
Where there he met his gay lady,
She was walking with the brown-eyed gipsies-o.

'O,' he says, 'my gay lady,
It's get thee on behind me-o,

Sam Henry's Songs of the People

And I will swear by the handle o' my sword
That a gipsy ne'er will mind thee-o.'

'O it's I have lain on the grass so green,
And I have drank of the heather-o,
And as I brew, so will I bake,
And I'll follow my brown-eyed gipsies-o.'

'O would you forsake your houses and lands?
Or would your forsake your three babies-o?
Or would you forsake your wedded lord
That lay last night beside you-o?'

'O what care I for my house or lands,
Or what care I for my three babies-o,
Or what care I for my wedded lord
That lay last night beside me-o?'

Now Lord Barnham's gone to the mayor of the town
And he told him his story-o,
These three gipsies in strong irons are bound,
And he brought back his lady-o.

1.2: ... bonnie, O. [All even-numbered lines end similarly in Bp, Dt, W (hybrid: headnotes and m typed; text printed).]

Fair Annie [H126: 10 Apr 1926; Child #62]

Other titles: "Lady Helen," "The Sister's Husband."

Source: (w) Eliza Jane Caldwell (Derryard, Dungiven), from her mother, Mrs Martha Jane Mullan Caldwell, from her mother, Eliza Black Mullan (Bovevagh, Dungiven), from her mother, Martha Redgate Black (Magilligan) = 4 generations, c. 150 years "by verbal memory only"; (m) Joseph Reid Caldwell, contributor's brother (Derryard).

s: ... This ballad is akin to No. 42 in the *Oxford Book of Ballads* [1910], and dates from the 16th century, if not earlier.

Key G.

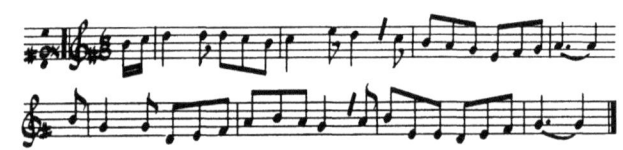

'Oh, comb your hair, fair Annie,' he said,
'And comb it down on your neck,
And try and look as maiden-like
As the day that first we met.

'Make your one bed, Annie,' he said,
'And learn to lie your lone,
For I am going across the salt sea
A new bride to bring home.'

'A brighter bride than me,' she said,
'I thought there ne'er was none,
I thought I had two of the cherriest cheeks
That e'er the sun shone on.'

He put his foot on the ship board,
The ship unto the main,
'It will be a year and a long day
Before I return again.'

A year and a long day was past,
Annie began to think long,
And stepping up to her garret so high,
She viewed her lands all round.

She looking east, she looking west,
She looking beneath the sun:
There she saw her Henry dear
And a new bride bringing home.

'I will not call him Henry dear,
For fear to harm his bride;
I shall call him Master Henry
Let the words be good or tide.'

She calling up her seven sons
By one, by two, by three,
I wish that you were seven greyhounds
This day to worry me.

She calling up her seven sons,
By one, by two, by three,
'Yonder's your own dear father,' she said,
'And a stepmother over thee.

'I will take off my purple robe
And put on a suit of pall,
I will go down to yonder sea
And drown myself withal.'

'You will not take off your purple robe
Or put on a suit of pall;
We will go down to yonder castle
And welcome the nobles all.'

She welcomed them up and she welcomed them down
With liquor and strong ale,
And she drank at the cold, cold water
To keep her colours pale.

'Oh, who will bake my wedding cake
Or who will brew my ale,
Or who will clothe my seven sons
And send them to their schale?'

'I shall bake your wedding cake,
I shall brew your ale,
And I shall clothe your seven sons
And send them to their schale.

'For to welcome a new bride home,
I doubt my heart will fail.'
She put the flute into her mouth
And she blew loud and shrill.

'What ails you, fair Annie, fair Annie,
That you make such a grievous moan?
It is like the moan of our fair Annie,
Was stolen when she was born.

'What did they call your father?' she said,
'Or what did they call your mother?
Or had you ever a sister dear,
Or had you ever a brother?'

'King Henry was my father,' she said,
'Queen Esther was my mother,
Queen Ellen was my sister,' she said,
'And King Charles was my brother.'

'If King Henry is your father,' she said,
'And Queen Esther is your mother,
And King Charles is your brother,' she said,
'Sure, I must be the other.'

'Come into your bed, fair Annie,' she said,
'You are nothing the worse of me,
Seven ships I have brought with me,
And four I am taking away,
And if ever he come to our countree,
Hanged shall he be.'

5.3: A-stepping up ... [Dt]
8.3,4 - 9.1,2: [4 lines absent from Dt.]
11.3: You will ... [Dt]
13.1: O, ... [Dt]

13.4: schale = school.

The Ship Carpenter's Wife

[H226: 10 Mar 1928]

k: "Auction of a Wife." Other titles: cf. "In Praise of John Magee," "John Hobbs," "(The) Sale of a Wife," "Wife for Sale."

Source: (w, m) William John M'Intyre (Craigtownmore, Portrush).

[Bp] s: ... William John M'Intyre, ... though over eighty, has still the heart for a song.
The last four words are spoken, not sung.

l: For the ultimate (to date) study of this curious practice, see Samuel Pyeatt Meneffee, *Wives for Sale: An ethnographic study of popular divorce* (New York: St. Martins Press, 1981).

Key G.

Pay heed to my ditty, ye frolicsome folk,
I'll tell you a story, a comical joke,
It's a positive fact I'm going to unfold
Concerning a woman by auction was sold.

There was a ship carpenter lived close to here
Who was not as fond of his wife as his beer,
He was hard up for brass, to be sure, all his life,
And so for ten shillings he auctioned his wife.

This husband and wife, they could never agree
Because he was fond of going out on the spree,
They settled the matter without more delay,
And the day of the auction they took her away.

They sent round the bellman announcing the sale
Unto the haymarket and that without fail,
The auctioneer struck with his hammer so smart,
While the carpenter's wife stood up in the cart.

Now she's put up without grumble or frown;
The first was a tailor to bid half a crown,
Who began, 'I will make her a lady so spruce,
For I'll fatten her well upon cabbage and goose.'

'Five and sixpence three farthings,' a butcher he said.
'Six and ten,' said a barber with his curly head.
Up jumps a cobbler and with a loud bawl,
'Nine shillings bid for her, bustle and all.'

'Just look at her beauty, her shape and her size,
She's mighty good-tempered and sober likewise.'
'Go on,' says a sailor, 'she's one out of four,
Ten shillings bid for her, but not a screw more.'

'Thank you sir, thank you,' says the bold auctioneer,
'She's going at ten; is there nobody here
To bid any more? Isn't this a sad job?
She's going, she's going, she's going -- at ten bob.'

The hammer came down, concluding the sale,
Poor 'Tarry' paid down then the brass on the nail,
He shook hands with Betsy and gave her a smack,
And took her away straight home on his back.

The people all relished the joke, it appears,
They gave the young sailor three hearty good cheers.
He never called 'Stop' with his darling so sweet
Till he landed with Betsy right on his own street.

They sent for the piper and fiddler to play,
And they danced and they sung until it was day,
When Jack told the company 'twas time now to go,
The piper and fiddler played 'Rosin the Bow.'

Oh, Betsy is happy at home in the croft,
Jack boxes the compass and goes up aloft,

Sam Henry's Songs of the People

While roving the ocean regardless of life,
He sings as he thinks of his ten-shilling wife.
And long may they prosper and flourish
  through life,
For Jack was well pleased with his ten-shilling
  wife.

1.3: ... fact that I now will ... [Dt]
8.4: She's going, she's going at only ten bob.' [Dt]

Whisky Is My Name (a)

[H835a: BLp, 2 Dec 1939]

Source: Mrs Strawbridge (James St, Coleraine;
native of Mallabuie, near Claudy) from James
M'Clelland, 80- (Alla) c. 1865.

s: ... This living song-link goes back, therefore,
to the year 1800.

m: The song request at the foot of the column
makes it clear that S. H. had no idea that the
end of the series was to come with the next
number....

Key C.

Whisky is my name, an' ye a' ken me weel,
An' if ye let me be, I'm a brave simple chiel,
But if ye rouse the beer, I'm as rough as the deil
When I get a clat at your noddle.

I'll tell ye a trick I played, a wee bit o' sooth:
The smith had a wife, she was kilt wi' the drouth,
She liked me that weel when she put me in her
  mooth,
She was aften carried hame in the gloamin'.

It happen'd on a day with the smith he was
  thrang,
They fetch'd tae him his wife and wi' drink she
  couldna gang,
He took her in his arms and upstairs he ran,
An' he threw her in the bed in a fury.

He lockit the door, fetch'd the key in his han',
Come runnin' doon the stair, cryin', a bewitch-ed
  man,
'Such conduct as this I'm no fit tae stan',
I'll list an' be a sodger in the mornin'.'

It happen'd as the smith he was shoeing at a
  horse,
The folk came runnin' in, saying, 'She's lyin' at
  the Cross,
If ye don't drap the shoe, yours will be the loss,
For she'll be gotten deid in the mornin'.'

'It's deil's in the folk, hae they nae wit ava?
If I hae a drunken wife, I'm no wantin' twa,'
But aye they cried, 'Smith, tak her in frae the
  sna',
Or she'll be gotten deid in the mornin'.'

He threw doon his hammer and oot then he ran;
'Oh, faith, it is hersel', but hoo got she doon?'
He took her in his arms and up the stair he ran,
Where the ither wife was aye lying snoring.

Frae the tap tae the toe, they were dressed a
  piece,
And they had such a likeness tae ither in the
  face,
That the smith couldna tell wha' was Jean in that
  case,
'Feen cares,' quo' he, 'let them sleep themselves
  sober.'

'For Jean will ken hersel as shane as she comes
  till,
For I only married yin, and that for good or ill.'
From that day tae this she ne'er tak's a gill
And she seldom wets her mooth in the mornin'.

1.4: clat at your noddle = opportunity to influence
  your head.
2.2: kilt wi' the drouth = was dreadfully thirsty.
4.1: lockit = locked.
5.3: drap = drop.
6.3: sna' = snow.
7.2: hoo = how.
8.2: tae ither = to one another.

Whiskey Is My Name (b) / The Blacksmith

[H835b: Wt≠D(c), both labeled "No. 836"]

Source: (w,m) Harriet Brownlow (Ballylagan,
Cloyfin, Coleraine); [Wt] (m) Maggie Brownlow
(Ballyagan, Cloyfin)

s: [Miss Brownlow] ... comes of a musical family.
[Wt] Noted in Pat Hackett's kitchen, 1st Dec.
1939.

l: This version is less complete and less clear
than that printed in the column.

Key C.

C25 / Wedlock's soft bondage

There was a smith and he lived a sooth,
Oh, but he had a wife and she had a drouth,
She liked it so well she put muckle in her mooth
And was often carried home in the morning.

It happened on a day when the smith he was
  thrang,
They brought to him a drunken wife, so drunk
  she couldna stan',
He took her in his arms and up the stairs he ran,
And he threw her in the bed in such a fury.

He locked up the door, brought the keys in his
  han',
And comin' doon the stairs crying, 'Ah, wretched
  man,'
And comin' doon the stairs crying, 'Ah, wretched
  man,'
Would you list me a soldier in the morning?'

The smith he went in to the shoein' of a horse,
He lifted up the hammer and he struck with such
  a force,
He lifted up the hammer and he struck with such
  a force
That he near brought doon the smiddy in a fury.

[?stanza missing]

The smith he went out and he viewed her all
  around,
'By my feth, it is her, how the divil got she
  doon?'
He took her in his arms, aye, and up the stairs
  he ran,
And he threw her in the bed where Jean was
  snoring.

'Oh, the divil's in the folk, what do they mean
  ava?'
But they cried the more, 'Take her in oot o' the
  sna'.'
'I hae yin drunken wife and I'm no needin' twa,
Or you'll get her perished lang ere mornin'.'

From the top to the toe they were dressed in linen
  space,
There was sae much likeness in yin anither's face,
There was sae much likeness in yin anither's face
That he didna ken his Jean tae the mornin'.

'By my feth,' says the smith, 'let them baith lie
  still;
When they sleep themselves sober, they will better
  ken themsel',
But frae that day tae this day, Jean widna pree a
  gill,
Nor she widna wet her lips in the mornin'.

The Wee Wifukie [H714: 31 Jul 1937]

Other titles: "... Wifikie," "There Was a Wee Bit
Wiffikie"; cf. "The Old Woman and the Peddler."

Source: R. W. Lusk (Portstewart); [o:] author
Dr. Alexander Geddes (Banff) (1737-1802) [? Alexander Watson (see Greig/Duncan note below)];
(m) Mrs Brownlow (Ballylaggan, Cloyfin).

s: This humorous Scottish song, "nane the waur
o' bein' han'led in Kilraughts," is contributed by
Mr R. W. Lusk.... It occurs in Whitelaw [1844
(1874)] without the air....
  The chorus at the end of each verse is framed
on the last two lines thereof, similarly to that set
out at the end of verse 1.

l: Concerning usage of the diminutive ending
"-ikie," cf., e.g., Moffat [1933]:19.

Key C.

There was a wee bit wifukie
And she gaed tae the fair,
She took a wee bit drapikie
That cost her muckle care,
It fell aboot the wee wife's hert
And she was like tae spue
'And oh,' quo' the wee wifukie,
'I doot I'm ower fou.'
  'I doot I'm ower fou,' quo she,
  'I doot I'm ower fou,
  And oh,' quo' the wee wifukie,
  'I doot I'm ower fou.'

'If Johnny sees me barley-sick,
I doot he'll claw my skin,
So I'll sit doon and tak' a nap
Before that I gae in.'
She laid her doon at a dyke-back
Tae tak' a wee bit nap;
By came a packy peddler
A-carrying his pack.
  A-carrying ...

He clipp-ed a' her gowden locks,
Sae bonny and sae lang,

Sam Henry's Songs of the People

He stole her pooch and pursikie,
And fast away he ran,
And when the wee wife wauken'd,
Her head was like a bee;
The wee wife cried, 'Oh Johnny lad,
I doot it's nane o' me.
   I doot it's ...

'I hae a wee bit hoosikie,
In it a kindly man,
A dog, they ca' him Doosikie,
And if it's me, he'll fa'n,
And Johnny he'll come to the door
And kindly welcome gie,
And a' the bairns aboot the hoose
Will dance if it be me.
   Will dance if ...

'I met with kindly company
And birl-ed my bawbee,
And still, if this be Bessukie,
Three placks remain wi' me,
But I will look the pursie nooks,
See gin the coinye be;
There's neither purse nor plack aboot,
So this is nane o' me.'
   So this is ...

The night was late and dang oot weet,
And oh, but it was dark,
The doggie heard a body's foot
And he began to bark.
Oh, when she heard the doggie bark
And kennin' it was he,
'Oh, weel ken ye, my Doosikie,'
Quo she, 'this isna me.'
   Quo she, this ...

When Johnny heard his Bessukie,
Fast to the door he ran;
'Is that you, my Bessukie?
Speak to your guid man.'
'Be kind tae the bairnies,
And weel mat ye be,
And farewell, Johnny,' quo she,
'This is nane o' me.'
   This is nane ...

John ran tae the minister,
His hair stood on an end,
'Pray sir, I've gotten sic a fright
I think I'll never mend,
My wife came hame withoot a heid
Crying oot maist bitterly,
"Oh farewell, Johnny," quo she,
"This is nane o' me."'
   This is nane ...

'The tale you tell seems wondrous strange,
Seems wondrous strange to me,
How that a wife withoot a heid
Could either speak or see.'
'Indeed,' said John, 'when she came hame,
The night was very dark;
When Doosikie he heard her foot,
Then he began to bark.
   Then he began ...

'"You're welcome hame," says I, "my dear,
You[']r[e] welcome hame to me."
"The divil put oot your eyes," says she,
"Don't ye see it isna me?"
And now,' says John to the minister,
'In peace that I may be,
Just tell me, is hersel' hersel',
And whose the sin may be.'
   And whose the ...

'My good man,' says the minister,
'It's plain for all to see
That sin or no, howe'er you go,
It's neither you nor she,
But things that happen hereabout
So strangely alter'd be
That I could maist with Bessie say,
'Tis neither you nor she.'
   'Tis neither ...

Now Johnny he came hame again,
And oh, but he was fain
To see his little Bessukie
Come to herself again;
He got her sitting on a stool
Wi' Tibbuck on her knee,
'Oh, come awa' Johnny,' quo she,
'Come awa' tae me.'
   Come awa' ...

1.1: wifukie = wife.
1.6: spue = spew, vomit.
3.3: pursikie = purse.
3.5: wauken'd = wakened.
4.1: hoosikie = house.
4.4: fa'n = fawn.
5.2: birled = spun (a bawbee).
5.2: bawbee = a Scottish coin of silver base, worth 3(6) pennies Scottish, or a halfpenny English.
5.4: placks = small coins; specifically, small copper coins current in 15th-16th century Scotland, worth 4 pennies in 1473.
5.6: coinye = piece of money.
6.1: dang = driven, pushed, knocked.

Johnny M' Man [H807: 13 May 1939]

Other titles: "Farewell to (Fare Ye Weel) Whiskey," "Johnnie My ...," "... My ...(, Dae Ye Nae Think o' Rising?"

Source: George Graham (Cross Lane, Coleraine) from his grandfather, Joe Wilson (Roddenfoot, Ballymoney) from his grandfather (Ballymoney).

Key D. Slow.

C25 / Wedlock's soft bondage

Johnny, m' man, dae ye naw think o' risin'?
Dae ye naw think it's time ye were gan awa'
    hame?
For ye sit up there dhrinkin' an ye keep me
    lamentin',
An' ye ne'er tak' a thocht aboot gan awa' hame.

What is that Ah dae hear at the windae?
Sure, it's jist lake the voice o' m' Jenny at hame.
Oh, come in, my dear Jenny, an' tak' a wee
    dhrapie
An' ye'll ne'er tak a thocht aboot gan awa' hame.

Dae ye min' the time when we first fell
    acquainted?
Dae ye min' the time doon in yon flowery lane,
Where we spent aal oor time in the sweet-scented
    roses,
An' ye ne'er took a thocht aboot gan awa' hame?

Richt weel Ah dae min' when we first fell
    acquainted,
Richt weel Ah dae min' doon in yon flowery lane,
But the nicht's gettin' on an' the bairns should be
    sleepin',
So rise up, m' dear Johnny, an' come awa' hame.

❖ *C25 REFERENCES* ❖

❖ **The Married Man** *(H 701) 501*

IREL Moulden 1979:104: "[Miss Brownlow] sang the song for Sam Henry forty years ago and sings it still in a small, true voice and takes great pleasure in doing so."

g: Not surely located, but a broadside, Harvard 1: 14.45 (Disley) seems to be a very closely related song.

❖ **The Happy Pair** *(H 753) 501*

BRIT Johnson (1853)1:20 "The Happy Marriage"

BRS Cf. UCLA 605: 3(Pitts) "The Contented Wife (and) Answer"

❖ **The Day We Packed the Hamper for the Coast** *(H 488) 501*

IREL Moulden 1979:41-2

❖ **The Tay** *(H 25a) 502*

BRIT Cf. also Palmer 1974a:166-7 "The Tea-Drinking Wives," with historical background.
    Williams 1923:251-2 "The Old Woman Drinking Her Tea" differs metrically.

❖ **The Scolding Wife** *(H 145) 503*

Probably not the same title in Dean-Smith 1954, which refers to George Gardiner's *Folk Songs from Hampshire* (1909).
Cf. Brunnings 1981: "The Scoldin' Wife - Instrumental," "... - When I Come Home to Supper"

IREL Cf. Joyce 1909:70-1 (#138)
    Moulden 1979:130

BRIT Ford 2,1901:88-9 "The Wicked Wife"
    Cf. Kennedy 1975:470-1 (#214): same title, metre, and message.
m: Ord 1930:151 "The Bad Wife"

BRS BPL H.80: (n.i.)

MEL Petrie/Stanford 1,1902:120 (#476)

❖ **Upside Down** *(H 694) 503*

Not = same title in Brunnings 1981.

l: This seems to have been a favored theme of broadside writers: cf. Holloway/Black 1975: #s 98, 126.

IREL Moulden 1979:150

❖ **The Wealthy Farmer** *(H 702) 504*

Laws 1957:273 (Q1) "Father Grumble" cites the article by Arthur K. Moore (*JAF* 64,1951:89-94), who in turn cites the 1842 publication of the ballad in *The Nursery Rhymes of England*, by J. O. Halliwell-Phillips.
Brunnings 1981: "John Grumlie"

IREL *JIFSS* 1(2&3):43-4 "The Old Man in the Wood" [Sharp/Karpeles]

BRIT Sharp/Karpeles 1974,2:39-40 (#205) "The Old Man and His Wife, or The Drummer"

AMER Bush 4,1977:86-7 "Father Grumble"
Randolph/Cohen (1982):124-6 "Father Grumble"

? cl: REC Mr, Mrs Jesse Aldrich, AFS 3327 A1 "Old Man Crumble"
b: Bill, Gene Bonyun, Heirloom HL 500 "The Old Man Who Lived in the Wood/s"
    Emily Budd, People's Stage Tapes cass. 04 (A5) "The Capable Wife"
    William Clauson, [b:] Victor LPM 1286 "John Grumlie"; [b:] Capitol P 8539 "The Old Man and His Wife"
b: *Everybody Sing!* Vol. 2, Wonderland RLP 1419 "Equinoxial and Phoebe"
    Bill "Pop" Hingston, People's Stage Tapes cass. 03 (A6?) "The Capable Wife"
    Margaret MacArthur, Folkways FH 5314 (B1) "Old Mr Grumble"
b: Alan Mills, Folkways FC 7009 "The Old Man in the Wood"
cl: Mrs Dizia Puckett, AFS 2983 A & B1 "Old Father Grumble"
    Sam Richards, People's Stage Tapes cass. 02 (B1) "Capable Wife"
    Edna Ritchie, Folk-Legacy FSA 3 (A5) "Old Crumley"
    Jean Ritchie, Folkways FC 7054 (B4) "The Old Man in the Woods"; AAFS L14 (B4) "Father Grumble";
[b:] Folkways FI 8352 "Old Crowley"
b: Pete Seeger, Folkways FA 2452 (A3) "Equinoxial"
b: Tom Smith, Pennywise PW 123 "The Old Man Who Lived in the Wood/s"
cl: Clyde Sturgill, AFS 3432 A "Father Grumble"
? cl: Dora Ward, AFS 1732 B "Mr Grumble"

❖ **Will the Weaver** *(H 682) 505*

Dean-Smith 1954
Laws 1957:277-8 (Q9)
Brunnings 1981: "Everyday Dirt"
Cazden et al. *Notes* 1982: #140

IREL Cf. Morton 1970:80-1 "The Wee Croppy Tailor"

Sam Henry's Songs of the People

BRIT Cf. Copper 1973:236-7 "The Cook's Choice" (a version of "Butter and Cheese and All")
  Palmer 1980:202-4 "Bill the Weaver"
  Cf. Shepheard n.d.:10-1 "The Croppy Tailor,"
which has many of the same elements, plus a last stanza:

  He said, my dear man, you have cropped me all right,
  But I've had your wife for the most of the night,
  And away run the poor croppy tailor.

Cf. also, in turn, Cazden 1958,2:14-5 "The Trooper and the Tailor.")

AMER Bush 3,1975:69-70 "Billy Weever"
  Cazden et al. 1982:516-8
  Darling 1983:147-9 (see Cansler rec.)
  Warner 1984:139-40 (#47) "Bill ..."

BRS UCLA 605: 3(Hodges); 5(Such)

REC "Rabbidy" Ernest Baxter, Topic 12T 258 (B1)
cl: Nancy Boggs, AFS 1413 B2 "Willy Weaver"
  Loman D. Cansler, Folkways FH 5330 (A10)
cl: Maude D. Clevenger, Norah de Vault, AFS 2936 A3 & B1 "Willy Weaver"
  Cf. Harry Cox, Folk-Legacy FSB 20 (B5) "The Groggy Old Tailor"
cl: Mrs M. P. Daniels, AFS 3740 A2
cl: Jennie Devlin, AFS 1845 A2
cl: Elmer George, AFS 3740 A1
cl: Nell Hampton, AFS 1585 A1
cl: Samuel Harmon, AFS 2806 A1 "Wildee Weaver"
  Cf. Sam Larner, Folkways FG 3507 (A1e) "Butter and Cheese," a similar comic situation.
cl: Huddie Ledbetter (Lead Belly), AFS 157 B2 "Billy the ..."
  Mike Seeger, Folkways FA 2325 (A8)
cl: Lena Bare Turbyfill, AFS 2847 A3 "Willy Weaver"
b: Jackie Washington, Vanguard VRS 9172 "Everyday Dirt"

◊ **The Tailor in the Tea [Dt: Sea] Chest** (H604) 505

Dean-Smith 1954: "(The) Boatsman and the Tailor (air) see (The) Green Wedding"
Laws 1957:277 (Q8) "The Boatsman and the Chest"
Brunnings 1981: "The Boatswain and the Tailor"
Cazden et al. *Notes* 1982: #138 "The Jolly Boatswain";
  cf. #139 "The Trooper and the Tailor"

IREL Morton 1970:80 "The Wee Croppy Tailor"
  Morton 1973:144-5 (#50) "The Wee Croppy Tailor"

BRIT Palmer 1979b:176-7 (#105) "The Groggy Old Tailor"
  Tocher #26(Aut)1977:94-5 "The Bold Boatswain"

AMER Cazden et al. 1982:509-13 "The Jolly Boatswain"; cf. also 513-6 "The Trooper and the Tailor"
  Cox 1939(1964):91-3 "The Wealthy Merchant"

BRS Cf. UCLA 605: 3(n.i.) "The Bold Trooper"

REC Cf. George Spicer, *FSB* 2 (A12) "The Cunning Cobbler"
  Bandoggs, Highway (Trailer) LTRA 504 (A1) "The Tailor in the Tea-Chest"
  Jumbo Brightwell, Topic 12TS 375 (A1) "The Blacksmith's Daughter"
? cl: Mrs J. A. Hart, AFS 957 B2 "The Sailor and the Tailor"
cl: Mort Montonyea, AFS 3665 A1 "Tailor and the Chest"
cl: Capt. Pearl R. Nye, AFS 1603 A "The Clever Skipper"
b: Frank Purslow, John Pearce, Folklore F-LEUT 1 "The Bosun and the Tailor"

◊ **I Wish That You Were Dead, Goodman** (H531) 506

Brunnings 1981: "O an' Ye Were Deid (Dead), Guidman," without specific reference.

IREL Joyce 1909:59 (#116) "There's a Chicken in the Pot," 1 stanza and the same melody as Henry's.

BRIT Chambers 1880:181-2 "O, An Ye Were Dead, Gudeman"
  Johnson (1853)3:421 "O Gin Ye Were Dead Gudeman"

◊ **The Auld Man and the Churnstaff** (H174) 507

Laws 1957:274 (Q2) "The Old Woman of Slapsadam [The Wily Auld Carle; The Old Woman in Dover; etc.]"
Brunnings 1981: "Eggs and Marrowbones"
Cazden et al. *Notes* 1982: #141 "The Old Woman from Boston"

c: IREL *Ceol* 1(4):8-9
c: Clancy Bros. 1964:18 "The Old Woman from Wexford"
k: Hughes 4,1936: "Tigaree Torum Orum"
  Loesberg 3,n.d.:11 "Old Woman from Wexford"
c: Morton 1973:89-90, 127 "Marrow Bones"

BRIT Greig/Duncan 2,1983:445-52 (#318) "The Wife o' Kelso," 11 vts. ("The Town of Kelso," "The Wily Auld Joker," "There Lived a Wife in Kelmie," "The Woman of Kelso," "The Wily Auld Carle," "Kelso")
  Henderson et al. 1979:84 "Marrowbones"
c: Kennedy 1975:465-6 (#208) "The Old Woman of Blighter Town"; also reports another English and 3 Irish versions (see also Connor/Doran rec.)
  Morris 1956,1:30-1 "Johnny Green," a parody with similar nonviolent ending.
  Palmer 1980:209-11 "Marrowbones"
  Richards/Stubbs 1979:85 "The Old Woman in Yorkshire"
c: Sharp/Karpeles 1974,2:43 (#207) "The Rich Old Lady, or Johnny Sands," 2 vts.

AMER Barbeau et al. 1947:13-4 "What Ails You?"
  Bush 5,n.d.:58-61 "The Old Woman of Slapsadam," "The Old Lady from Dover," "The Rich Old Lady"
  Cazden et al. 1982:18-22 "The Old Woman from Boston"
  Colorado FB 1(2,Apr)1962:7 "Old Lady in Trenton"; cf. 1(3,Nov)1962:11 "Johnnie Sands"
  Darling 1983:146 "There Was an Old Lady" (see Barker rec.)
  Jordan 1946:91-2 describes "Johnny Sands" and prints 2 stanzas.
  Peters 1977:172 "There Was an Old Woman in London"
  Silverman 1971:119 "Eggs and Marrowbones"
  Spaeth 1948:88 describes the song as written (or rewritten) by John Sinclair.
  Cf. Warner 1984:150-1 "Johnny Sands"

BRS *Songs and Recitations* 5,1978:8 "Old Woman from Wexford"

REC Mary Connors, Paddy Doran, *FSB* 7 (B6) "The Blind Man He Can See"
c: Peggy Seeger, Ewan MacColl, *LH*, Argo ZDA 71, #6 "Old Woman of Slapsadam and Johnny Sands," 3 versions.
  Horton Barker, Folkways FA 2362 (B6) "There Was an Old Lady"
c: Tom Brandon, Folk-Legacy FSC 10 (A3) "There Is a Lady in This Town"
  Cf. Grace Carr, Folkways FE 4312 (A4) "Johnny Sands"
b: Peg, Bobby Clancy, Tradition TLP 1045 (A5) "The Woman from Wexford"

b: Clancy Brothers, Tommy Makem, Columbia CL 1909 "The Old Woman from Wexford"
William Clauson, Capitol T 10158 "Johnny Sands"
c: Harry Cox, Folk-Legacy FSE 20 (B4) "Marrowbones"
? cl: Cf. Jennie Devlin, AFS 1774 A "Johnny Sands"
b: The Dubliners, Vanguard VRS 9187 "The Woman from Wexford"
lc: Richard Dyer-Bennet, Decca DL 5046 "Eggs and Marrowbones"
Seamus Ennis, Tradition TLP 1013 (B6) "Marrow Bones"; Murray Hill 920336 (2B6)
Betty Garland, Folkways FA 2307 (B1) "Love My Darlin' O"
Cf. John Kirkpatrick, Sue Harris, Topic 12TS 355 (B4) "Johnny Sands"
Jimmy Knights, Topic 12TS 375 (B8) "Marrowbones"
b: A. L. Lloyd, Prestige/Int. 13066 "Tigery Orum"
b: Alan Lomax, Tradition TLP 1029 "The Rich Old Lady"; Asch AA3 (A5) "Once I Knew an Old Lady"
John Maguire, Leader LEE 4062 (A2) "Marrowbones"
Des O'Halloran, Topic 12TS 305
Of Maids and Mistresses, Elektra 137 [Morton]
c: Lawrence Older, Folk-Legacy FSA 15 (A7) "Woman from Yorkshire"
b: *Our Singing Heritage*, Vol. 1, EKL 151 "The Rich Old Lady"
c: Maggie Hammons Parker, AAFS 66 (B3) "Mercian Tittery-ary-a"
Ken Peacock, Folkways FG 3505 (B1) "Woman from Dover"
John Reilly, Topic 12T 359 (A4) "Tippin' It up to Nancy"
b: Frank Ritchie, Request RLP 8057 "Oul' Man and the Churnstaff"
Cf. Hedy West, Topic 12T 146 "Johnny Sands"
b: Betty Vaiden Williams, Vanguard VRS 9028 "The Rich Old Lady"

For "Johnny Sands," which is usually considered to be a different ballad although derived from "Marrow Bones," see Spaeth 1948:88, Belden 1940:237-9, and Laws 1957:274-5 (Q3) for general discussion and references; cf. also Copper 1973:222-3, Pinto/Rodway 1957(1965):535-6.

◆ **The Blin' Auld Man** (*H 21*) 509

Dean-Smith 1954: "(The) Goodman; The Old Farmer and His Young Wife; Old Wichet; A Blind Man He Can See"
Child 1882-98(1965),5:88-95 (#274) "Our Goodman," 2 vts.; 281, 303-4
Coffin/Renwick 1950(1977):143-5, 272-3
Bronson 4,1972:95-129
Brunnings 1981: "Four Nights Drunk [Child 274]"

IREL Shields 1981:90-3 (#35) "The Hillman"
Shields/Shields *UF* 21,1975: #184 "(The) Hillman"

BRIT Chambers 1880:184-90 "Our Guidman Cam Home at E'en"
Chapbook 2(3):5 "Hame Drunk Cam' I"
ED&S 42(3)1980:4 "I Came Home Drunk Last Night"
Palmer 1979b:172-4 (#103) "Coming Home Late"
Richards/Stubbs 1979:143-4 "Th' Owd Chap Come ower t' Bank"
Sharp/Karpeles 1974,1:193-4 (#39) "Our Goodman," 2 vts.
Tocher #19(Aut)1975:102 "As I Came Rolling Home from Sea"

AMER Bush 4,1977:91-4 "Four Nights Drunk"
Cray 1969:6-9 "Five Nights Drunk," 2 unexpurgated versions, with [pp. 189-91] extensive notes concerning the less noble branches of this family of songs and the problems of communication encountered by collectors and editors. [Coffin/Renwick]
Darling 1983:80-1, A "Five Nights Drunk" (see Presnell rec.); 81-2, B "Our Goodman," Child #274 B
Davis 1929:493 "A Jacobite Song," similar to Henry's, but tuneless; cf. Creighton/Senior 1950:91. [Coffin/Renwick]
Cf. *JEMFQ* 65/66,1982:33 "Drunkard's Special," a blues text (see Jones rec.).
Leach 1967:28-32
Milner/Kaplan 1983:43-4 "A Little before Me Time"
Randolph/Cohen [1982]:60-3 "I Went Home One Night"
Rosenbaum 1983:98-9 "Three Nights' Experience"
Silverman 1966:84-5 "Four Nights Drunk"
Silverman 1971:140-1 "Four Nights Drunk"

REC Coley Jones, *AAFM* 1, FP 251 (A4) (from Columbia 14489-D) "Drunkard's Special"
Wade Mainer and the Mountaineers, *FMA* 2 (B8) "Three Nights in a Bar Room"
"Our Goodman," *FSB* 5 (B6) composite: Harry Cox, Mary Connors, Colm Keane
Ewan MacColl, Folkways CB, FG 3509 (A6) "Our Gudeman"; *Riverside CB*, RLP 12 621 (B1) "Our Goodman"; Folkways FW 8731 (B4) "Th' Owd Chap"
Peggy Seeger, Ewan MacColl, *LH*, Argo ZDA 68, #3 "Our Goodman," 2 versions.
Arthur Argo, Prestige-Int. 13048 (B4) "Hame Drunk Came I"
cl: Mr, Mrs E. C. Ball, AFS 1351 B1 "Three Nights Drunk"
Emmet Bankston, Red Henderson, Okeh 45292 (A, B) "Six Nights Drunk" [Bronson]
cl: H. J. Beeker, AFS 843 A2 "Our Goodman"
George Belton, EFDSS LP 1008 (A5) "My Old Man"
b: Oscar Brand, Audio Fidelity AFLP 1906 "Our Goodman"
h: Packie Manus Byrne, Davjon DJ 1020
The Dubliners, Epic BN 26337 [Milner/Kaplan]
Jack Elliott, Leader LEA 4001 (A8) "The Blind Fool"
Elliot Family, Folkways FG 3565 (= Transatlantic XTRA 1091) (B1) "The Blind Fool"
cl: Jerome Feiner, AFS 3640 B1 "Our Goodman"
cl: Mary Franklin Farmer, AFS 2861 B2, 2862 A1
h: John Fleming, Leader LEA 4055 (B2) "The Hillman"
cl: Warde H. Ford, AFS 4200 A4 "Our Goodman"
Harold Gill, Topic 12TS 349 (B5) "Seven Nights Drunk"
cl: George Vincent Graham, AFS 4217 A2 "Home Came the Good Old Man"
John Greenway, Prestige 13011 [Cray]
cl: Herbert Halpert, AFS 3640 A3 "The Other Night When I Came Home"
cl: Mrs Sabra Bare Hampton, AFS 2870 A "Three Nights Experience"
cl: Mrs M. A. Harris, AFS 1413 A4 & B1 "Our Goodman"
Clint Howard, Philo 1028 (A5) "Cabbage Head Song"
Max Hunter, Folk-Legacy FSA 75 (A3) "Five Nights Drunk"
Earl Johnson, Okeh 4509 "Three Nights Experience" [Bronson]
Jolly Boys of Lafayette, Decca DE 5431 (78 rpm) "Old Man Crip" [Bronson]
Israel Kaplan, Folkways FG 3501 (A1) [The old man came home one night ...], 1 stanza about a cuspidor.
cl: Colon Keel, AFS 2709 B1 "Three Nights Experience"
b: Douglas Kennedy, HMV B 10836 (78 rpm) "Hame Cam Oor Gudeman at E'en"
A. L. Lloyd, Topic 12T 118 (B7) "Shickered as He Could Be"
cl: Bascom Lamar Lunsford, AFS 1781 B1 "The Three Nights' Experience"
J. E. Mainer, Carolyn Mainer Helmes, Prestige-Int. DS 25003 (A1) "Three Nights Drunk"
cl: Myra Barnett Miller, AFS 842 B1 "Our Goodman"
cl: Minta Morgan, AFS 907 A1 "Home Came a Good Man"

Sam Henry's Songs of the People

Mustard and Gravy, Bluebird 7905 (78 rpm) "Five Nights Experience" [Bronson]
b: John Jacob Niles, RCA Victor Vintage Series LPV 513 "Our Goodman"
John Jacob Niles, Tradition TLP 1046 "The Good Old Man"
Hattie Presnell, Folk-Legacy FSA 22 (A3) "Five Nights Drunk"; TFS *Ballad* cass. (A1) "Six Nights Drunk"
b: The Raintree County Singers, Time S 2085 "Old Fool"
Cf. Eugene Rhodes, Folk-Legacy FSA 12 (B3) "Who Went out the Back?" a black adaptation from Blind Boy Fuller, recomposed by Rhodes.
Orrin Rice, AAFS L12 (B8) "Our Goodman"
Grant Rogers, Folk-Legacy FSA 27 (A7) "Three Nights Drunk"
cl: Simon Rolle and group, AFS 375 B2 "Our Goodman"
b: Peggy Seeger, Prestige/Int. 13029 "Five Nights Drunk"
b: Pete Seeger, Prestige 7375
George Spicer, Topic 12T 235 (B4) "Coming Home Late"
Gordon Tanner, Folkways FTS 31089 (B3) "Four Nights' Experience"
b: The Tripjacks, Squire SQ 33004 "Drunkard's Special"
Unexpurgated, Raglan R 51 (A14) "The Merry Cuckold"
Tony Wales, Folkways FG 3515 (A3) "Our Goodman"
b: The Weavers, Vanguard VRS 9024 "You Old Fool"
Charlie Wills, Leader LEA 4041 (B5) "Our Goodman"
cl: Gladys Wilder, Pauline Fanine, AFS 1564 A1 "Our Goodman"
cl: Mrs Ewart Wilson, AFS 2864 A2 "Home Came the Goodman"

◆ **The Brown-Eyed Gypsies** *(H124) 509*

White/Dean-Smith 1941: "Gipsies-o (The Wraggle Taggle Gipsies)"
Dean-Smith 1954: "(The) Gipsy Laddie; Gypsy Countess; Wraggle-Taggle Gipsies; Draggle-Tailed Gipsies; Gipsies-O; Johnny Faa"
Child 1882-98(1965),4:61-74 (#200) "The Gypsy Laddie," 11 vts.; 5:252-3, 1 vt.; 301
Coffin/Renwick 1950(1977):119-22, 254-6
Bronson 3,1966:198-250; 4,1972:494-5; cf. Svend Grundtvig, *DgF* #369
Brunnings 1981: "The Gypsy Davy [Child 200]"

h: IREL *Ceol* 1(4)1964:6-7
h: Hammond 1978:57 "The Dark-Eyed Gypsy"
h: *JIFSS* 1(2&3)1904:42 "The Dark-Eyed Gipsy O!" [Coffin/Renwick]
Loesberg 2,1980:1 "The Raggle Taggle ..."; 15 "The Whistlin' Gypsy Rover"
Munnelly *Ceol* 1972:6-8 "The Raggle-Taggle ..."
Peirce 1979:46, a 1-stanza fragment.
Planxty 1976:35 "Raggle-Taggle Gypsy" (see Planxty rec.)
Shields 1981:66-7 (#20) "The Dark-Eyed Gipsy"
Shields/Shields *UF* 21,1975: #108 "The Dark-Eyed Gypsy"
Tunney 1979:110

BRIT Dawney 1977:14 "Gipsy Laddy O"
Greig/Duncan 2,1983:331-6 (#278) "The Gypsy Laddie," 12 vts. ("Lord Cassilis' Lady," "Three Gypsy Laddies," The Three Gypsies")
Henderson et al. 1979:81-2 "The Gypsy Laddie"
Karpeles *JEFDSS* 1951:79-80 "The Gypsy Laddie"
Oxford Ballads 1969:249-50 (#66) "Johnny Faa"
Palmer 1980:117-9 "The Dragletail ..."
Richards/Stubbs 1979:135-6 "The Gypsy Laddie"
Sharp/Karpeles 1974,1:160-70 (#34) "The Gypsy Laddie, or The Wraggle-Taggle ...," 12 vts.
Shepheard n.d.:14
Spin 3(8)?1965:7 "The Gipsy Laddie"

AMER Burton 1978:46-7 "Blackjack Daisy"
Cheney et al. 1976:162-3 "The Wraggle-Taggle ..." (from Silverman 1971)
Darling 1983:75-6, A "The Gypsy Laddie," Child #200 J; 76-7, B "Gyps of David" (see Proffitt rec.); 77-3, C "Gypsy Davy" (see Older rec.); "The Gypsy Laddie," Child #200 K.
Folkways #3(Jan)1964;75 "The Gipsy Laddie" (from *Songs of All Time*)
Fowke 1973:176-7 "Seven Gypsies on Yon Hill"
Leach 1967:120-2 "The Gypsy Laddie"
Randolph/Cohen (1982):49-51
Sandburg 1950:54-5 "Raggle-Taggle"
Silverman 1971:110 "The Wraggle Taggle ...," 111 "Gypsy Davy"
SO 4(7, Fall)1954:25, 26 "The Wraggle-Taggle Gypsies," "Gypsy Davy," with article by Irwin Silber "England to America -- Transplanting a Folk Song"
Warner 1984:133-4 (#42) "Gypsy Davy"

REC "The Gypsy Laddie," FSB 5 (A8) composite: Harry Cox, Jeannie Robertson, Paddy Doran
Ewan MacColl, *Folkways CB*, FG 3510 (B3) "The Gypsy Laddie"; Riverside RLP 12 637 (A5) [Bronson]
Peggy Seeger, Ewan MacColl, *LH*, Argo ZDA 68, #3 "The Gypsy Laddie," 4 versions
A. L. Lloyd, *Riverside CB*, RLP 12 625 (A2) "Gipsies-o"
Cliff Carlisle, *Smithsonian Country* 2 (A3) "Black Jack David"; Old-Timey LP 102 (A6)
b: Tossi Aaron, Prestige/Int. 13027 "Gypsy Davy"
O. J. Abbott, Folkways FM 4051 (A2) "The Gypsy Daisy"
b: George, Gerry Armstrong, Folkways FA 2335 "Black Jack Davie/y"
John Ban, Leader LEA 4055 (A1) "The Dark-Eyed Gipsy"
cl: Mrs L. M. Bryant, AFS 1750 B1 "The Gypsy Daisy"
cl: Kate Burkett, AFS 838 B2 "Black Jack Davy"
cl: Mary Fuller Cain, AFS 2823 A3 & B1 "Gypsy Davy"
Robert J. Campbell, Leader LEE 4057 (B4) "Seven Gypsies on Yon Hill"
Isla Cameron, Prestige/Int. 13042 (B1) "Seven ..."
Martin Carthy, Topic 12TS 344 (B4) "Seven Yellow ...," a composite.
Dillard Chandler, Folkways FA 2418 (A2) "Black Jack Davy"
b: Barbara Dane, Horizon WP 1602 "Gypsy Davy"
cl: Mrs O. C. Davis, AFS 4106 A1 "Black Jack Davy"
Maire Aíne ní Dhonnchadna, Folkways FW 8781 (A5) "The Gypsy-o"
cl: Emma Dusenbury, AFS 848 A1 "Gypsy Davy"
b: *Foggy Dew-O*, Decca LK 4940 "Gypsy Rover"
b: *The Folk Scene*, Elektra SMP 6 "The Gypsy Laddie"
Dave Frederickson, Folkways FH 5259 (B3) "Gypsy Davy"
cl: Gant family, AFS 68 A1, 72 A2 "Black Jack Davy"
b: The Gateway Singers, Warner Bros. WS 1295 "Gypsy-O"
b: Terry Gilkyson, Decca DL 5457 "Gypsy Davy"
Robin Gray, Topic 12T 128 (A3) "Gypsy Laddie"
b: *Greatest Folksingers of the Sixties*, Vanguard VSD 17/18 "Whistling Gypsy"
b: Arlo Guthrie, Reprise MS 2142 "Gypsy Davy"
Woody Guthrie, AAFS L1 (A3) "The Gypsy Davy" [Bronson]; Tradition/Everest 2058 (A4)
cl: Mrs Hagie, Lena Bare Turbyfill, AFS 2846 B2 "Black Jack Davy"
David Hammond, Tradition TLP 1028 (A7) "The Dark-Eyed Gypsy"; Greenhays/Sruthan GR 702 (B6) "The Gypsy Laddie"
cl: Oscar, Sabra Bare Hampton, AFS 2873 A1 "Black Jack Davy"
cl: Samuel P. Harmon, AFS 2883 B1 "Black Jack Davy"
cl: Mrs J. A. Hart, AFS 957 B1 "Gypsy Laddie"
Lizzie Higgins, Topic 12T 185 (B3) "Davie Faa"
h: Joe Holmes, Free Reed 007 (B1) "The Dark-Eyed Gipsy"

b: *Hootenanny at the Limelight*, Somerset SF 108 (5 recs.) "The Raggle-Taggle Gypsies"
　Cisco Houston, Folkways FA 2042 (B3) "The Gypsy Dave"
cl: Joe Hubbard, AFS 2824 A2 "Gypsen Davy"
　Harry Jackson, Folkways FH 5723 (C3) "Clayton Boone"
　Buell Kazee, June Appal JA 009 (B4) "Black Jack Davy"
cl: Mrs Esco Kilgore, AFS 2823 B2 "Black Jack David"
　John Kirkpatrick, Sue Harris, Topic 12TS 355 (A2) "The Gipsy Laddie"
b: John Langstaff, HMV B.9861 (78 rpm) "The Gypsy Laddie"
b: The Limeliters, RCA Victor LPM 2393 "Whistling Gypsy"
cl: Bascom Lamar Lunsford, AFS 1782 A1 "Black Jack Davy"
　Margaret MacArthur, Folkways FH 5314 (A3) "Gypsy Davy"
b: Ed McCurdy, Elektra EKL 205 "The Gypsy Laddie"; EKL 9001 (A6)
　John MacDonald, Tangent TNGM 119/D (A2b) "The Rovin' Ploughboy"
cl: Dr. David McIntosh, AFS 3243 B1 "Black Jack Davy"
　"Tip" McKinney, Missouri Friends of the Folk Arts MFFA 1001 (B8) "Gipson Davy"
　Christy Moore, Tara 2008 (A1) "The Raggle Taggle Gipsies"
　New Lost City Ramblers, Folkways FA 2399 (A3) "Black Jack David"; Folkways FTS 31035 (B3) "Black Jack Daisy"
b: *Newport Folk Festival 1964*, Evening Concerts: Vol. 3, Vanguard VSD 9186 "Blackjack Davy"
b: John Jacob Niles, Camden CAL 245 "The Gypsy Laddie"; Tradition TLP 1046 "The Lady and the Gypsy"; RCA Victor Vintage LPV 513 "The Gypsy Laddie"
　Cathal O'Boyle, Green Linnet SIF 1005 (B5) "The Dark-Eyed ..."
　Lawrence Older, Folk-Legacy FSA 15 (A12) "Gypsy Davy"
　Old Hat Band, Voyager VRLP 3075 (A5) "Black Jack David"
b: *Our Singing Heritage*, Elektra EKL 151 "Gypsy Lover"
b: Penny Palmer, Jean Amos, RCA Victor LPM 2244 "Gypsy Davy," "Gypsy Laddio"
　Walter Pardon, Topic 12TS 392 "Raggle Taggle ..."
b: *Philadelphia Folk Festival*, Vol. 2, Prestige/Int. 13072 "The Gypsy Davy"
　Planxty, Nyon CAT 81005 (B4) "Raggle Taggle Gypsy"; Shanachie 19009 (A1)
　Frank Proffitt, Folk-Legacy FSA 1 (B5) "Gyps of David" [Bronson]
h: Tilly Quigley, Leader LEA 4055 (B6) "The Dark-Eyed Gipsy"
　Obray Ramsey, Prestige 13020 (B5) "Black Jack Davy"
　John Reilly, Topic 12T 359 (A2) "The Raggle Taggle Gypsy"
　Sam Richards, People's Stage Tapes cass. 01 (A3) "The Gipsy Laddie"
　Almeda Riddle, Vanguard VRS 9158 [Randolph/Cohen]
b: Frank Ritchie, Request RLP 8057 "The Brown-Eyed Gypsies"
　Jean Ritchie, [lc:] Elektra EKLP 2 "Gypsum Davy"; Folkways FA 2301 (A1) "Gypsy Laddie"
　Jeannie Robertson, Topic 12T 96 (A4) "The Gypsy Laddies"; Tangent TNGM 119/D (A2a)
　Pete Seeger, Folkways FA 2319 (B2) "Black Jack Davy"
cl: Mrs Alex Sing, AFS 897 A2 "Black Jack Davy"
b: *Songs of All Time*, World Around Songs N17 "The Gipsy Laddie"

　Steeleye Span, Pickwick SHM 3040 (A2) "Black Jack Davy"
　Ed Trickett, Folk-Legacy FSI 75 (A2) "Black Jack Gypsy"
　Joseph Able Trivett, Folk-Legacy FSA 2 (B6)
b: Frank Warner, Elektra EKL 153 "Blackjack Davy"
　Mike Waterson, Topic 12TS 332 (B4) "Seven Yellow ..."
　Rita Weill, Takoma A 1022 (B4) "Black-Eyed Gypsy"
b: Harry, Jeanie West, Archive of Folk Music FS 208 "Black Jack Davie/y"

h: MEL Joyce 1909:154 (#334) "The Gipsies Came to Lord M--'s Gate"

◇ Fair Annie *(H126)* 510

Child 1882-98(1965),2:63-82 (#62), 10 vts.; 2:511; 4:463; 5:220, 291
Coffin/Renwick 1950(1977):63-4, 229
Bronson 2,1962:40-43
Brunnings 1981

IREL Moulden 1979:50-1

BRIT Allingham 1865:84-9
　Henderson et al. 1979:35-7 (see Armstrong rec.)
m: Kilkerr *FMJ* 1977:215 (from Henry coll.);
reprint, *Treoir* 12(1)1980:17
　Oxford Ballads 1969:138-43 (#38)
　Raven 1978:18 "Lady Helen"

AMER Milner/Kaplan 1983:29

REC Peggy Seeger, *B&R*, Blackthorne ESB 79 (B1)
　Frankie Armstrong, Plane Label TPL 0001 (A3)
b: *Songs and Dances of Scotland*, Murray Hill 920336 "Lord Thomas and Fair Annie"

◇ The Ship Carpenter's Wife *(H226)* 511

Cf. Brunnings 1981: "Sale of a Wife (Wife Selling)"

l: For the ultimate (to date) study of this curious practice, see Samuel Pyeatt Meneffee, *Wives for Sale: An ethnographic study of popular divorce* (New York: St. Martins Press, 1981).

h: IREL Cf. Morton 1970:19-21 "In Praise of John Magee"
Shields 1981:137-9 (#62)
　Shields/Shields *UF* 21,1975: #362

BRIT Cf. *Spin* 4(2):19 "Wife for Sale (Bilston Ballad)," with article by Michael, Jon Raven.

AMER Cf. Cheney et al. 1976:138-9 "In Praise of John Magee" (from Morton 1970)

BRS Harvard 1: 11.69 (n.i.), 12.148 (n.i.)
h: NLI (Mayne, Belfast)
h: Ashton 1888:1-3 "Sale of a Wife"; he adds that such sales actually did take place, the woman with a halter to put her on the level of the cattle that were so auctioned.
　Healy 4,1969c:117-9 "A New Song Called the Sale of a Wife"

h: REC Eddie Butcher, Leader LED 2070 (B5)
h: Frank Harte, Topic 12T 218
　Cf. John Maguire, Leader LEE 4062 (B5) "In Praise of John Magee"
　Cf. Jon Raven, Broadside BRO 116 (A1) "John Hobbs"

Sam Henry's Songs of the People

◇ Whisk[e]y Is My Name / [Dt:] The Blacksmith (H604) (H835) 512

  BRIT Ford 1904:48
    Greig 1907-11(1963): #7
    Ord 1930-52

◇ The Wee Wifukie (H714) 513

  BRIT Ford 1,1899:22-5
    Greig/Duncan 2,1983:355-6 (#287) "... Wifikie," 2 vts. "In a pamphlet called 'The Wee Wifeikie and Its Authorship' (Aberdeen, 1921), William Walker discusses the various texts of the song and shows that it was written by Alexander Watson, tailor in Aberdeen, probably between 1770 and 1780" (p. 566).
    Johnson (1853)3:506-7 "There Was a Wee Bit Wiffikie"

  BRS Cf. *Songs of All Time* 1942,1957:62 "The Old Woman and the Peddler"

◇ Johnny, M' Man (H807) 514

  Brunnings 1981: "Farewell to Whiskey"

  IREL Shields/Shields *UF* 21,1975: #227 "... My ..."

  BRIT R. Ford 2,1901:254-56
    Greig 1906-7(1963):33 (no title)
    Greig 1907-11(1963): #5
    Kennedy 1975:604 (#272) "Farewell to Whiskey"; also lists another recorded Scottish version (see Murray rec.).
    Palmer 1980:215-6 "Johnnie, My ..."
    Tocher #1(Spr)1971:16-7 "Johnnie My ..."

  AMER Milner/Kaplan 1983:219 "Fare Ye Well Whiskey"

  BRS Harvard 1: 4.30 (Gilbert)

  REC Jessie Murray, *FSB* 3 (A12) "Farewell to Whiskey"
  b: The Boys of the Lough, Trailer LER 2086
    Lizzie Higgins, Topic 12T 179 (A1) "..., My ..."
    Norman Kennedy, Folk-Legacy FSS 34 (= Topic 12T 178) (A8) "..., My Man, Dae Ye Nae Think o' Rising?"
    Jean Redpath, Philo 1054 (B6) "Johnny My Man (Farewell to Whiskey)"
    Alastair Russell, Celtic Music CM 002 (B2) "Fare Thee Well, Whiskey"

  b: MEL Canterbury Country Dance Orchestra, F&W F-72-FW 3 (A1b)

Appendixes

Appendix A   Titles of songs in the original order (with dates) of their appearance in the Northern Constitution

P = printed, usually galley proof; T = typed. For other abbreviations see p. xxxix.

Date	H#	Page	Title	P	T	Notes
	0	53	The State of Arkansaw		W	[Laws H1] SH to A. Lomax, LC
17 Nov 1923	1	191	The Flower of Sweet Dunmull	B	DW	
24 Nov	2	215	Mullaghdoo	BW	D	(W is clipping)
1 Dec	3	286	The Londonderry Air	B	DW	
8 Dec	4	190	My Girl from Donegal	B	DW	
15 Dec	5	313	The Banks of Claudy			[==H693][Laws N40]
22 Dec	6	275	The Woods of Mountsandel	B	DW	[==H567]
29 Dec 1923	7	290	Bring back My Barney to Me	B	DW	
5 Jan 1924	8	311	Laurel Hill / Kyle's Flowery Braes	B	DW	
12 Jan	9	186	Lovely Armoy	B	BDW	
19 Jan	(10)	2	(Old Choir Rhymes:)			(W+article)
	10a	2	Abbey	B	DW	
	10b	2	Dublin / Coleshill	B	DW	
	10c	2	Dundee	B	DW	
	10d	2	French	B	DW	
	10e	2	Mary's	B	DW	
	10f	3	Martyrs	B	DW	
	10g	3	York	B	DW	
	10h	3	Newto[w]n	B	DW	
		3	[Additional verses]	B	DW	
26 Jan	11	110	The *Trader*	B	DW	
2 Feb	12	31	The Hare of Kilgrain	B	DW	[cf. H172]
9 Feb	13	232	The Star of Glenamoyle	W	BD	
16 Feb	14a	356	The Bonnie Wee Lass of the Glen [1st m]	B	DW	
	14b	356	The Bonnie Wee Lass of the Glen [2d m]		DW	(no B)
23 Feb	15	87	The Plains of Waterloo (I)	B	DW	[cf. H608 (II)]
1 Mar	16	392	Oh, Johnny, Johnny	BL	BDW	
8 Mar	17a	61	Fine Broom Besoms!	BL	BDW	
	17b	180	March of the Men of Garvagh	B		(no D, no W)
15 Mar	18a	358	Will Ye Pad the Road wi' Me?	B	DW	[cf. H564]
	18b	272	The Whinny Knowes	B	DW	
22 Mar	19a	194	The Glenshesk Waterside	B	DW	
	19b	196	Brow of Sweet Knocklayd	B	DW	(m=H19a)
29 Mar	20a	216	The Maid of Mullaghmore	B	DW	
	20b	245	Summer Hill	L		
5 Apr	21a	508	The Blin' Auld Man [1st m] / The Covered Cavalier	B	DW	[Child #274]
5 Apr	21b	508	The Blin' Auld Man [2d m]	B	W	(no D)
12 Apr	22a	232	The Flower of Glenleary		DW	(no B)
	22b	361	Castleroe Mill	B	DW	
19 Apr	23	307	The Banished Lover	B	DW	[see H726]
26 Apr	24a	348	The Star of Benbradden	B	DW	[see H479, H709]
	24b	217	The Banks of the Roe	B	DW	
3 May	25a	502	The Tay	W	D	(no B)
	25b	261	The Load of Kail Plants	B	DW	
10 May	26a	248	Ann o' Drumcroon	BL		[==H246]
10 May	26b	250	Mary, the Pride of Killowen	BW	D	
5 Jul	27a	371	The Maid of Mourne Shore	B	DW	[orig H34b](m=H27b)
17 May	27b	105	The Portrush Fishing Disaster (I)	BW	D	
	27c	105	The Portrush Fishing Disaster (II)	BW	D	
24 May	28a	194	Lovely Glenshesk (IIa)	B	DW	[see H547 (IIb)][cf. H544 " (I)]
	28b	158	Ballycastle, O!	B	DW	
31 May	29	53	Denny Byrne, the Piper	B	DW	
7 Jun	30a	390	My Flora and I	B	DW	
	30b	437	Young Mary of Accland	BL		[see H721][Laws M16]
14 Jun	31	411	The 'Prentice Boy	B	DW	[Laws O39]
21 Jun	32	269	Where the Moorcocks Crow	BD	W	
28 Jun	33	397	Twenty-One	B	DW	[==H611]
5 Jul	34	213	The Pretty Three-Leaved Shamrock from Glenore	B	DW	
12 Jul	35	327	The Female Highwayman	BW	D	[Laws N21]
19 Jul	36	74	Coleraine Regatta	BW	D	
26 Jul	37	485	Henry, the Sailor Boy	BW	D	
2 Aug	38	29	The Fox and His Wife	BW	D	
9 Aug 1924	39	123	Heather Jock	B	DW	

Appendix A / Original dates and order

Date	H#	Page	Title	P	T	Notes
16 Aug 1924	(40)		(Three Sleep Songs:)			
	40a	12	How Many Miles to Babyland?	B	DW	
	40b	17	A Child's Lullaby	B	DW	
	40c	20	The Lost Birdies / The Hobe and the Robin	B	DW	
23 Aug	41	231	Kate of Glenkeen	B	DW	
30 Aug	42a	148	Miss Cochrane	B	DW	
30 Aug	42b	197	The Point Maid	BW	D	
6 Sep	43	394	The Maid with the Bonny Brown Hair (a)	B		(no D, no W)[see H575]
13 Sep	44	178	The Rocky Road to Dublin	B	DW	
20 Sep	45	477	Belfast Town	BW	D	
27 Sep	46	438	Erin's Lovely Home	BW	D	[Laws M6]
3 Oct	47	236	The Valley Below	B	DW	
11 Oct	(48)		(Children's Singing Games:)			
	48a	10	I Am the Master	B	DW	
	48b	10	Green Gravel	B	DW	
	48c	10	Ring a Ring o' Roses	B	DW	
	48d	11	Water, Water, Wallflowers	B	DW	
	48e	11	I'll Tell My Ma	B	DW	
	48f	11	Here's a Poor Widow	B	DW	
	48g	11	Old Sally Walker	B	DW	
	48h	11	Broken Bridges	B	DW	
18 Oct	49	200	Knox's Farewell	BW	D	
25 Oct	50	139	The Bard of Culnady / Charles O'Neill	BW	D	
1 Nov	51	129	The Crafty Ploughboy	B	DW	[Child #283][Laws L1]
8 Nov	52a	244	Magilligan	BW	D	
8 Nov	52b	429	The Slaney Side	BW	D	[Laws M28]
15 Nov	53	96	(Sailors' Shanties:)			
	53a	97	I'm Going Home	BL	BDW	
	53b	96	It's Time for Us to Leave Her	BL	BDW	
	53c	97	Paddy Doyle	BL	BDW	
	53d	96	Tom's Gone to Ilo	BL	W	(no B, no D)
22 Nov	54	144	Mary's Dream	BW	D	[Laws K20]
29 Nov	55	479	Charming Mary O'Neill	B	DW	[Laws M17]
6 Dec	56	354	John MacAnanty's Courtship	BL	BDW	(B+sheet music)
13 Dec	57a	57	The Buttermilk Boy	BL	DW	(no B)
13 Dec	57b	228	The Maid of Erin's Isle	B	DW	
20 Dec	58	446	Eliza / When I Landed in Glasgow	B	DW	
27 Dec 1924	59	76	On the Road to Bethlehem	B	DW	
3 Jan 1925	60a	400	An Old Lover's Wedding	B	DW	[Laws P31]
	60b	401	The Laird's Wedding		D	[Laws P31](m=60a)(no B, no W)
10 Jan	61a	459	I'm from over the Mountain (a)	B	DW	
	61b	459	I'm from over the Mountain (b)		DW	(no B)(m=H61a)
17 Jan	62	148	Rachel Dear / The Maine Water Side	B	DW	
24 Jan	63	247	Rosaleen Bawn	BL	BDW	
31 Jan	64	161	The Girls from [Dt,Wt: of] Coleraine	BL	BDW	
7 Feb	65a	293	Alt[i]mover Stream	B	DW	(m=H65b)[see H229a,b]
7 Feb	65b	186	Monk McClamont's "Farewell to Articlave"	B	DW	
14 Feb	66	369	Wester Snow	B	DW	
21 Feb	67	365	Fair Maid of Ballyagan	B	DW	
28 Feb	68	276	The Star of Moville	B	DW	
7 Mar	69	201	The Happy Shamrock Shore	B	DW	
14 Mar	70a	340	I've Two or Three Strings to My Bow (a)	B	DW	
	70b	341	I've Two or Three Strings to My Bow (b)		D	(no B, no W)(m=H70a)
21 Mar	71	246	Her Bonny Blue E'e	B	DW	
28 Mar	72	374	Am I the Doctor?	B	DW	[?Child #295][Laws P9]
4 Apr	73	412	Ballindown Braes	B	DW	[Laws P28]
11 Apr	74	236	The Dear-a-Wee Lass	B	DW	
18 Apr	75a	145	The *Nightingale* (I)	B	DW	[Laws M37]
	75b	199	Bonny, Bonny	B	DW	[The *Nightingale* (II)]
25 Apr	76	314	The Mantle So Green	BD		(no W)[Laws N38]
2 May	77	418	The Silver[y] Tide	B	DW	[Laws O37]
9 May	78	484	Jamie's on the Stormy Sea	B	DW	
16 May	79	428	If I Were a Blackbird	BDW		("republished")
23 May	80	386	Phelimy Phil	B	DW	[W+staff m]
30 May	81	430	McClenahan's Jean	BW	D	
6 Jun	82	262	An Irish Serenade	BW	D	
13 Jun	83	156	The Old Stone Wall	B	DW	
20 Jun	84	364	The Maid of the Sweet Brown Knowe			[==H688][Laws P7]
27 Jun 1925	85	300	Dobbin's Flowery Vale	B	DW	[Laws O29][cf. H242]

523

Sam Henry's Songs of the People

Date	H#	Page	Title	P	T	Notes
4 Jul 1925	86	443	The Banks of the Bann	B	DW	[Laws O2][see H673]
11 Jul	87a	181	The Bright Orange Stars of Coleraine	B	DW	
11 Jul	87b	182	The Boys of Coleraine	B	DW	(m=H87a)
18 Jul	88	18	The Bonny Brown Hen	B	DW	
25 Jul	89	287	Early, Early	B	DW	
1 Aug	90	365	The Grey Mare	BW	D	[Laws P8]
8 Aug	91	156	The Little Thatched Cabin	BW	D	
15 Aug	92	86	The Hungry Army	BW	D	
22 Aug	93	72	The Wedding at Ballyporeen	BW	D	[cf. H805]
29 Aug	94	17	My Bonnie Wee Hen	B	DW	
5 Sep	95	107	The *Falcon*	BW	D	
12 Sep	96a	230	The Maid of Burndennet (a)	B	W	
	96b	231	The Maid of Burndennett (b)		D	(m=H96a)
19 Sep	97	130	Shane Crossagh	BW	D	
26 Sep	98a	64	Barossa / Oliver's Advice	B	DW	
26 Sep	98b	472	The Inniskilling Dragoon	B	DW	
3 Oct	99	89	The Three Flowers of Chivalry	BW	D	
10 Oct	100a	188	Carnanbane	L	BDW	
10 Oct	100b	193	Glenrannel's Plains	L		(?m=H100a?)
17 Oct	101	275	The Ould Lammas Fair		BDW	(B+sheet music)
24 Oct	102	464	Glenarm Bay	B	DW	
31 Oct	103	55	The Private Still	B	DW	
7 Nov	104	457	The Gentle Shepherdess	BW	D	[Laws O8]
14 Nov	105	331	The Jolly Ploughboy	BW	D	[Laws M24]
21 Nov	106	443	Johnnie Hart	B	DW	
28 Nov	107	320	Jennie of the Moor	B	DW	[Laws N34]
5 Dec	108a	329	The Rich Merchant's Daughter	BW	D	[Laws N6]
	108b	169	Mudion River	BL		
12 Dec	109	357	As I Walked Out	BW	D	
19 Dec	110	144	A Collier Lad	BW	D	
26 Dec 1925	111	229	The Holly Bough / The Pride of Altibrine	B	DW	
2 Jan 1926	112	288	A Sweetheart's Appeal to Her Lover	BW		
			/[Dt:] Oh, It's down Where the Water Runs Muddy		D	[cf. H695]
9 Jan	113	434	Young Edward Bold / The Lowlands Low	BW	D	[Laws M34]
16 Jan	114	143	Molly Bawn Lowry	BW	D	[Laws O36]
23 Jan	115a	355	Claudy Green (a)	B	DW	
	115b	241	Claudy Green (b)		DW	(m=H115a)
30 Jan	116a	201	The Brown-Haired Lass (a) [1st m]	B	DW	[1st vt]
	116b	202	The Brown-Haired Lass [2d m]		DW	
	116c	202	The Brown-Haired Lass (b)		DW	(no B)[2d vt]
6 Feb	117	44	As a King Went A-Hunting	BW	DW	[see H622]
13 Feb	118	315	Mary and Willie	BW	DW	[Laws N28]
20 Feb	119	21	The Goat's Will	B	DW	
27 Feb	120	332	Blythe and Bonny Scotland /[Dt:] India's Burning Sands	BW	D	[Laws N2]
6 Mar	121	270	Cloughmills Fair	BW	D	
13 Mar	122a	88	The Bonny Light Horseman [1st m]	BL	BDW	(B text shorter)
	122b	88	The Bonny Light Horseman [2d m]		DW	(no B)
20 Mar	123	90	The Heights of Alma	B	DW	[Laws J10]
27 Mar	124	509	The Brown-Eyed Gypsies	B	DW	[Child #200](W is hybrid)
3 Apr	125a	475	John Hunter (a)	BW		
	125b	476	/" (b) [Dt:] The Wheelwright		D	(m=H125a)
10 Apr	126	510	Fair Annie	BW	D	[Child #62]
17 Apr	127	368	The Factory Girl	BW	D	[cf. H762]
24 Apr	128	440	Henry Connor of Castledawson	BW	D	[Laws M5]
1 May	129	141	John McKeown and Margaret Deans	BW	D	
8 May	130	26	The Mayogall Asses	B	DW	
15 May	131	84	My Son Ted	B	DW	
22 May	132	398	Polly Perkins of Paddington Green	B	DW	
29 May	133	461	Bess of Ballymoney	BW	D	
5 Jun	134	168	Lochaber Shore	B	DW	
12 Jun	135	414	The Broomfield Hill	BW	D	[Child #43]
19 Jun	136	125	James Magee	B	DW	
26 Jun	137	431	Johnny Doyle	BW	D	[Laws M2](W+clipping)
3 Jul	138	256	The Black Chimney Sweeper	BL	BDW	[cf. H230](B+sheet music)
10 Jul	139	42	The Rocks of Bawn	BW	D	
17 Jul	140	30	Squire Agnew's Hunt	BW	DW	
24 Jul	141	395	Out of the Window	BW	D	[cf. H534]
31 Jul	142	294	My [Bt: The] Dear Irish Boy	W	BD	
7 Aug 1926	143	395	The Green Bushes	BW	D	[Laws P2]

Appendix A / Original dates and order

Date	H#	Page	Title	P	T	Notes
14 Aug 1926	144	270	The Maid of Seventeen	BW	D	
21 Aug	145	503	The Scolding Wife	B	DW	
28 Aug	146	180	The Knights of Malta	BW	D	
4 Sep	147	474	Green Broom	BW	D	
11 Sep	148	411	Blooming Caroline of Edinburgh Town	BW	D	[Laws P27]
18 Sep	149	456	Pining Day and Daily	BW	D	
25 Sep	150a	466	The Banks of Kilrea (I)	BW	D	
25 Sep	150b	361	The Banks of Kilrea (II)	B	DW	
2 Oct	151	124	Jamie Raeburn's Farewell	BW	D	
9 Oct	152	266	I'm Seventeen 'gin Sunday	BW	D	[Laws O17][see H793, cf. H785]
16 Oct	153a	480	The County Tyrone [1st m]	BW	D	
	153b	481	The County Tyrone [2d m]		W	(no B, D)(typed in red on back of page)
23 Oct	154	33	Cashel Green (II)	BW	D	[cf. H647 " (I)]
30 Oct	155	366	I'll Hang My Harp on a Willow Tree	BW	D	
6 Nov	156	315	Johnny Jarmin / The Rainbow	BW	D	[Laws N43]
13 Nov	157	207	Norah McShane	B	DW	
20 Nov	158	295	The Banks of Sweet Lough Neagh	BW	D	
27 Nov	159a	396	The Slighted Suitor (a)	B		[?Laws P10]
	159b	397	The Slighted Suitor (b)		DW	[?Laws P10]
4 Dec	160	292	My True Love's Gone A-Sailing	BW	D	
11 Dec	161a	456	The Pretty Blue Handkerchief (I)	B	DW	(m=H161c)
	161b	456	The Pretty Blue Handkerchief (II)		DW	(no B)(m=H161c)
11 Dec	161c	32	A Ballad of Master M'Gra[th]	B	DW	
18 Dec	162	333	Canada[,] Hi! Ho!	B	DW	[cf. Laws C17a-c]
25 Dec 1926	163	413	The King o' Spain's Daughter	DW	B	[Child #4]
1 Jan 1927	164	362	The True Lovers' Discussion	B	DW	(Dt is hybrid)
8 Jan	165a	260	Green Grow the Rashes (a)	BW	D	
	165b	260	" (b) [...s the Laurel]	BW	D	
15 Jan	166	328	Lovely Annie (II)	B	DW	[Laws N14, Polly Oliver][cf. H561 " (I)]
22 Jan	167	369	The Maid of Faughan Vale	B	DW	
29 Jan	168	399	My Bonnie Irish Boy	BW	D	[Laws P26]
5 Feb	169	298	The Maid of Carrowclare	BW	D	
12 Feb	170	299	The Blooming Star of Eglintown	BDW		(D is proof)
19 Feb	171	40	Jim, the Carman Lad	BW	D	
26 Feb	172	31	The Hare's Dream	BW	D	[cf. H12]
5 Mar	173	250	Moorlough Mary	B	DW	
12 Mar	174	507	The Auld Man and the Churnstaff	BL	BDW	[Laws Q2]
19 Mar	175	470	The Yowe Lamb	BW	D	(W is clipping)
26 Mar	176	146	Willie Lennox	BW	D	[Laws Q33]
2 Apr	177	271	O'er the Moor amang the Heather	BW	D	
9 Apr	178	233	The Flower of Gortade	BW	D	
16 Apr	179a	125	John Mitchel's Farewell to His Countrymen (a)	BL	B	
	179b	126	John Mitchell (b)		DW	
23 Apr	180	149	Holland Is a Fine Place	BW	D	[Child #92a]
30 Apr	181	131	The Breaking of Omagh Jail	BW	D	
7 May	182	464	Greenmount Smiling Ann	B	DW	
14 May	183	268	The Rambling Suiler	B	DW	
21 May	184	469	"Thank You, Ma'am," Says Dan	B		(no D, no W)[==H689]
28 May	185	128	The Three Huntsmen / Wilson, Gilmore and Johnson	B	DW	[Laws L4]
4 Jun	186	46	The Thatchers of Glenree	BW	D	
11 Jun	187	162	Dungiven Priory Church	BW	D	
18 Jun	188	401	The Girl I Left Behind	BW	D	[Laws P1b]
25 Jun	189	173	Fair Tyrone	BL	DBW	
2 Jul	190	420	Killeavy's Pride	B	DW	[see H798]
9 Jul	191	142	Annie Moore	BW	D	
16 Jul	192	101	The Shamrock Shore	BW	D	
23 Jul	193	487	The Hielan's o' Scotland	BW	D	[Laws N19]
30 Jul	194	99	The Zared	BW	D	[Laws D13]
6 Aug	195	234	A Kintyre Love Song	B		(no D, no W)
13 Aug	196	210	The Hills of Donegal	B		(no D, no W)
20 Aug	197a	247	The Blazing Star of Drim (a)	BW		
	197b	248	The Blazing Star of Drung (b)		D	
27 Aug	198	481	My Father's Servant Boy	B	DW	[Laws M11][cf. H525]
3 Sep	199	39	The Tailor Boy	BW	D	
10 Sep	200	470	Petie Cam' ower the Glen	B	DW	
17 Sep	201	265	The Ride in the Creel	BW	D	[Child #281]
24 Sep	202	119	The Boston Burglar	BW	D	[Laws L16b][cf. H691]
1 Oct	203	330	The Sailor on the Sea	BW	D	
8 Oct	204	388	Gramachree	BW	D	
15 Oct	205	319	The Banks of the River Ness	BW	D	
22 Oct 1927	206	289	The Drinaun D[h]un	BW	D	

525

Sam Henry's Songs of the People

Date	H#	Page	Title	P	T	Notes
29 Oct 1927	207	417	The Old Oak Tree	BW	D	[Laws P37]
5 Nov	208	258	Grandma's Advice	B	DW	
12 Nov	209	465	Innishowen	BW	D	
19 Nov	210	188	Farewell, Ballycastle	BL	BDW	
26 Nov	211	479	When a Man's in Love	BW	D	[Laws O20]
3 Dec	212	370	Drummond's Land	B	DW	
10 Dec	213	334	Willie Taylor (a)	BW	D	[Laws N11][see H757 "(b)]
17 Dec	214	445	The *Lady Leroy*	BW	D	[Laws N5]
24 Dec	215	393	The Bonny, Bonny Boy	B	DW	
31 Dec 1927	216	265	The Feckless Lover	B	DW	
7 Jan 1928	217	432	The Lover's Ghost	B	DW	[Child #272]
14 Jan	218a	386	Must I Go Bound? (a)	BW	D	
14 Jan	218b	386	Must I Go Bound? (b)	BW	D	(m=H218a)
21 Jan	219	177	The Connaught Man	BW	D	
28 Jan	220	243	The Flower of Magherally, O!	D	BW	
4 Feb	221	490	The Rich Ship Owner's Daughter	BL	BDW	[Child #100]
11 Feb	222	29	The Hunting Priest	BW	D	
18 Feb	223	83	The Deserter	BW	D	
25 Feb	224a	390	The Flower of Sweet Strabane [1st m]	B	DW	
	224b	391	The Flower of Sweet Strabane [2d m]		DW	(no B)
3 Mar	225	196	Owenreagh's Banks	B	DW	
10 Mar	226	511	The Ship Carpenter's Wife	BW	D	
17 Mar	227	47	The Dandy Chignon	B	DW	
24 Mar	228a	19	The Duck from Drummuck	BW	D	
24 Mar	228b	18	Nell Flaherty's Drake	BW	D	(m=H228a)
31 Mar	229a	360	Lurgan Stream (a)	B		[see H65a]
	229b	360	Lurgan Stream (b)		DW	[see H65a]
7 Apr	230	255	Nae Bonnie Laddie tae Tak' Me Awa'	B	DW	[cf. H138]
14 Apr	231a	28	The Crocodile [1st m]	BW	DW	
	231b	28	The Crocodile [2d m]		DW	
21 Apr	232	318	The Dark-Eyed Sailor	B	DW	[Laws N35]
28 Apr	233	287	The Green Banks of Banna	BW	D	
5 May	234	436	Willy Reilly	BW	D	[Laws M10]
12 May	235	203	The Shamrock Sod No More	BW	D	
19 May	236	375	Barbara Allen	BW	D	[Child #84]
26 May	237	189	Carntogher's Braes	BW	D	
2 Jun	238a	296	The Banks of the Nile [1st m]	BW	D	[Laws N9]
	238b	296	The Banks of the Nile [2d m]		DW	(no B)
9 Jun	239	469	Sandy's Wooing	BW	D	
16 Jun	240	192	Finn Waterside	BW	D	
23 Jun	241	346	The Blackbird and Thrush	BW	D	
30 Jun	242	483	Mullinabrone	BW	D	[cf. H85]
7 Jul	243a	473	Young Edward the Gallant Hussar [1st m]	BL	BDW	
	243b	474	Young Edward the Gallant Hussar [2d m]		DW	(no B)
14 Jul	244	295	The Soldier Boy	B	DW	[Laws O31][cf. H543, H678]
21 Jul	245	197	Adieu to the Banks of the Roe	B	BWD	(Bt 2 copies, 4 sts)
28 Jul 1928	246	249	Ann o' Drumcroon	B	DW	[==H26a]
22 Oct 1932	464	167	The Braes of Sweet Kilhoyle		DW	(no B)
29 Oct	465	49	The Wee Cutty Pipe		DW	(no B)
5 Nov	466	79	My Parents Reared Me Tenderly		BDW	
12 Nov	467	428	Hibernia's Lovely Jane		BDW	
19 Nov	468	441	John Reilly the Sailor Lad		BDW	[Laws M8]
26 Nov	469	144	My Lowlands, Away		BDW	
3 Dec	470	491	Lord Beichan		BDW	[Child #53]
10 Dec	471	317	The Broken Ring		BDW	[Laws N42][see H818]
17 Dec	472	258	The Nonsense o' Men		BDW	[cf. H532, H641]
24 Dec	473	354	Paddy's Land		BDW	
31 Dec 1932	474	488	The Glove and the Lions		BDW	[Laws O25]
7 Jan 1933	475	455	The Swan		BDW	
14 Jan	476	84	Bonny Woodha'		BDW	
21 Jan	477	140	Hielan' Jane		BDW	
28 Jan	478	176	Erin, My Country		BDW	
4 Feb	479	347	The Cuckoo		BDW	[see H24a, H709]
11 Feb	480a	52	Bryan O'Lynn [1st m]		BDW	
	480b	52	Bryan O'Lynn [2d m]		DWB	[mimeographed]
18 Feb	481	484	Wait till the Ship Comes Home		BDW	
25 Feb	482	391	Bring Me Back the Boy I Love (a)		BDW	[see H692 " (b)]
4 Mar	483	427	The Maid of Ballyhaunis		BDW	
11 Mar	484	177	The Mac's and the O's		BDW	
18 Mar	485	308	Mary Machree		BDW	
25 Mar	486	121	Eight Mile Bridge		BDW	
1 Apr	487	43	The Lint Pullin'		BDW	
8 Apr 1933	488	501	The Day We Packed the Hamper for the Coast		BDW	

526

Appendix A / Original dates and order

Date	H#	Page	Title	P	T	Notes
15 Apr 1933	489	48	A Cup o' Tay	BDW		
22 Apr	490	48	The Jug of Punch	BDW		
29 Apr	491	225	Happy 'Tis, Thou Blind, for Thee	BDW		
6 May	492	238	The Old Dun Cow	BDW		
13 May	493	237	Braiding Her Glossy Black Hair	BDW		
20 May	494	127	Hugh Hill, the Ramoan Smuggler	BDW		
27 May	495	227	Nancy, the Pride of the West	BDW		
3 Jun	496	96	Santy Anna	BDW		
10 Jun	497	326	The Drummer Maid	BDW		
17 Jun	498	211	Oul' Dunloy	BDW		
24 Jun	499	387	The Broken-Hearted Gardener	BDW		
1 Jul	500	359	The Maid of Craigienorn	BDW		
8 Jul	501	25	The "Crummy" Cow	BDW		
15 Jul	502	98	The Cruise of the *Calabar*	BDW		
22 Jul	503	273	Youghall Harbour	BDW		
29 Jul	504	157	Farewell He	BDW		
5 Aug	505	347	Old Arboe	BDW		
12 Aug	506	214	Sweet Loughgiel	BDW		
19 Aug	507	213	Juberlane	BDW		
26 Aug	508	226	So Like Your Song and You	BDW		(D: m only)
2 Sep	509	168	Knocklayde	BDW		
9 Sep	510	17	The Little White Cat	BDW		
16 Sep	511	157	The Hills o' Ballyboley	BDW		
23 Sep	512	225	My Bonny Breeden	BDW		
30 Sep	513	75	The Lammas Fair in Cargan	BDW		
7 Oct	514	297	The *Bold Privateer*	BDW		[Laws O32]
14 Oct	515	274	The Mountain Road	D	BW	
21 Oct	516	35	Spanking Maggie from the Ross	BDW		
28 Oct	517	7	Lullaby for a Sailor's Child	BD	W	
4 Nov	518	301	A Londonderry Love Song	BDW		
11 Nov	519	389	Belfast Mountains	BDW		
18 Nov	520	259	The Strands of Magilligan	BDW		
25 Nov	521	372	The Girl from Turfahun	BDW		
2 Dec	522	355	The Maid of Croaghmore	BDW		
9 Dec	523	63	Dun Ceithern	BDW		
16 Dec	524	328	The Squire's Bride	BDW		[Laws N20]
23 Dec	525	483	You Lovers All	BDW		[cf. H198][Laws M11]
30 Dec 1933	526	182	Neuve Chappelle	BDW		
6 Jan 1934	527	20	Robin Redbreast's Testament	BDW		
13 Jan	528	246	The Maid from the County Tyrone	BDW		
20 Jan	529	320	Bordon's Grove	BDW		
27 Jan	530	298	The Maid of Dunysheil	BDW		
3 Feb	531	506	I Wish That You Were Dead, Goodman	BDW		
10 Feb	532	367	Tarry Trousers	BDW		[see H641; cf. H472]
17 Feb	533	292	So Dear Is My Charlie to Me	BDW		
24 Feb	534	454	Our Wedding Day	BDW		[cf. H141]
3 Mar	535a	39	Waulking Song	BDW	B	
	[535b]	96	Kishmul's Galley		B	(no D, no W)
10 Mar	536	209	Oh, Derry, Derry, Dearie Me	BDW		(D, W truncated)
17 Mar	537	239	The Flower of Benbrada	BDW		
24 Mar	538	364	Cahan's Shaden Glen	BDW		
31 Mar	539	97	The Girls of Valparaiso	BDW		
7 Apr	540	468	Wild Slieve Gallon Brae[s]	BDW		
14 Apr	541	207	The Old Blacksmith's Shop	BDW		
21 Apr	542	217	Owenreagh	BDW		
28 Apr	543	103	The Sailor Boy	BDW		[Laws K13][cf. H678]
5 May	544	165	Lovely Glenshesk (I)	BDW		[cf. H28a, H547 " (IIa,b)]
12 May	545	225	O, Jeanie Dear	BDW		
19 May	546	273	The Cup of Gold	BDW		
26 May	547	195	In Praise of the Glen	BDW		[Lovely Glenshesk (IIb)]
2 Jun	548	34	One Morning Clear	BDW		[see H28a; cf. H544]
9 Jun	549	81	You Broken-Hearted Heroes	BDW		[see H724]
16 Jun	550	176	The Enchanted Isle	BDW		
23 Jun	551	40	The Cobbler	BDW		
30 Jun	552	102	Patrick O'Neal	BDW		
7 Jul	553	482	Jamie, Lovely Jamie	BDW		
14 Jul	554	400	Sweet Clonalee	BDW		
21 Jul	555	463	The Star of Donegal	BDW		
28 Jul	556	326	On Board of a Man-of-War	BDW		
4 Aug	557	478	Molly, Lovely Molly	BDW		
11 Aug	558	106	The Wreck of the *Enterprise*	BDW		
18 Aug	559	237	The Dark-Haired Girl	BDW		
25 Aug	560	112	The French Privateer	BDW		
1 Sep	561	458	Lovely Annie (I)	BDW		[Laws N8][cf. H166 " (II)]
8 Sep	562	113	Captain Coulston	BDW		
15 Sep	563	316	Lurgan Town	BDW		
22 Sep 1934	564	344	The Banks of Mourne Strand	BDW		[cf. H18a]

527

Sam Henry's Songs of the People

Date	H#	Page	Title	P	T	Notes
29 May 1937	705a	132	The Dreary Gallows [1st m]	BDW		[Laws L11]
	705b	132	The Dreary Gallows [2d m]	BDW		
5 Jun	706	180	Ta Ra, Limavady	BDW		
12 Jun	707	227	Not the Swan on the Lake	BDW		
19 Jun	708	174	Among the Green Bushes [Bp,Dp: in Sweet Tyrone]	BD	W	
26 Jun	709	348	If I Were a Fisher	BDW		[see H24a, H479]
3 Jul	710	264	The Whistling Thief	BDW		
10 Jul	711	234	The Manchester Angel	BDW		
17 Jul	712	221	The Irishman	BDW		
24 Jul	713	27	Seal Song	BDW		
31 Jul	714	513	The Wee Wifukie	BDW		[cf. H835]
7 Aug	715	166	Kearney's Glen	BDW		
14 Aug	716	218	A Shamrock from Tiree	BDW		
21 Aug	717	108	The Wreck of the *Nimrod*	BDW		
28 Aug	718	460	Beardiville Planting	BDW		
4 Sep	719	63	The Leaves So Green	BDW		
11 Sep	720	165	Glenelly	BDW		
18 Sep	721	438	Young Mary of Accland	BDW		[Laws M16][see H30b]
25 Sep	722	343	The Sweet Bann Water	BDW		[?Child #248][Laws M4]
2 Oct	723	240	The Beauty of the Braid	BDW		
9 Oct	724	82	Lovely Sally	BDW		[see H549]
16 Oct	725	278	The Basket of Oysters	BDW		[Laws Q13][cf. H700]
23 Oct	726	307	Learmount Grove	BDW		[see H23]
30 Oct	727	193	Farewell to Sweet Glenravel	BDW		
6 Nov	728	88	Drummer Boy at Waterloo	BDW		[Laws J1]
13 Nov	729	446	The Apprentice Boy / Covent Garden	BDW		[Laws M12]
20 Nov	730	190	The Hills of Tandragee	BDW		
27 Nov	731	22	The Moneygran Pig Hunt	BDW		[+NC 17 May 1924]
4 Dec	732	57	My Grandfather Died	BDW		
11 Dec	733	342	The Maid of Tardree	BDW		
18 Dec	734	149	Polly Primrose	B	DW	
25 Dec 1937	735	133	Lambkin	BDW		[Child #93]
1 Jan 1938	736	489	Johnny Scott	BDW		[Child #99]
8 Jan	737	309	Skerry's Blue-Eyed Jane	BDW		
15 Jan	738	478	Jamie and Nancy	BDW		
22 Jan	739	291	The Sea-Apprentice	BDW		
29 Jan	740	56	Mick Magee	BDW		
5 Feb	741	50	The Rakes of Poverty	BDW		
12 Feb	742	104	Loss of Seven Clergymen	BDW		
19 Feb	743	200	Emigrant's Farewell	BDW		
26 Feb	744	12	Cricketty Wee	BDW		
5 Mar	745	47	Long Cookstown / Nancy Whiskey	BDW		
12 Mar	746	62	Gaol Song	BDW		
19 Mar	747	214	Maguire's Brae	BDW		
26 Mar	748	263	Magherafelt Hiring Fair	BDW		
2 Apr	749	189	The Flower of Craiganee	BDW		
9 Apr	750	120	The Wild Colonial Boy	BDW		[Laws L20]
16 Apr	751	50	The Oul' Rigadoo	BDW		[cf. H832a]
23 Apr	752	245	The Valleys of Screen	BDW		
30 Apr	753	501	The Happy Pair	BDW		
7 May	754	111	The Good Ship *Mary Cochrane*	BDW		[see also H565]
14 May	755	297	Johnnie and Molly	BDW		
21 May	756	60	The Salutation	BDW		
28 May	757	334	Willie Taylor (b)	BDW		[see H213 " (a)][Laws N11]
4 Jun	758	23	Bellaghy Fair	BDW		
11 Jun	759	288	My Sailor Boy	BDW		
18 Jun	760	471	Navvy Boy	BDW		
25 Jun	761	228	Peggy of the Moor	BDW		
2 Jul	762	368	Campbell's Mill	BDW		[cf. H127]
9 Jul	763	458	The Bonny Wee Lass	BDW		
16 Jul	764	32	The Clady River Water Bailiffs	BDW		
23 Jul	765	312	The *Lady of the Lake*	BDW		[Laws N41]
30 Jul	766	43	The Charity Seed / We Never Died in the Winter Yet	BDW		
6 Jul	767	370	My Charming Kate O'Neill	BDW		
13 Jul	768	59	Songs of Old Ireland	BDW		
20 Jul	769	65	The Parting Glass	BDW		
27 Jul	770	485	The Garden Gate	BDW		
3 Sep	771	415	Susan Brown	BDW		
10 Sep	772	23	Sport's Lament	BDW		
17 Sep	773	229	Mary M'Veagh	BDW		
24 Sep	774	150	Susan on the Beach	BDW		[Laws K19]
1 Oct	775	171	Bonny Portrush	BDW		
8 Oct	776	261	The Young Farmer's Offer	BDW		
15 Oct 1938	777	427	The Banks of [Wt: the] Cloughwater	BD	W	

Appendix A / Original dates and order

Date	H#	Page	Title	P	T	Notes
22 Oct 1938	778	387	Norah Magee	BDW		
29 Oct	779	54	The Sailor in the Alehouse	BDW		[Laws K36]
5 Nov	780	345	The Ploughboy	BDW		
12 Nov	781	467	The Largy Line	BDW		
19 Nov	782	473	The Gallant Soldier	BDW		
26 Nov	783	34	Arthur Bond	BDW		
3 Dec	784	172	Slieve Gallen Brae	BDW		
10 Dec	785	399	My Darling Blue-Eyed Mary	BDW		[cf. H152, H793]
17 Dec	786	139	Finvola, the Gem of the Roe	BDW		
24 Dec	787	215	Where Moyola Waters Flow	BDW		
31 Dec 1938	788	300	Love's Parting / Jamie and Mary	BDW		[see H825]
7 Jan 1939	789	419	The Willow Tree	BDW		
14 Jan	790	383	The False Lover	BDW		
21 Jan	791	218	Farewell to the Banks of the Roe	BDW		
28 Jan	792	122	Whiskey in the Jar	BDW		[Laws L13a]
4 Feb	793	267	As I Gaed ower a Whinny Knowe	BDW		[Laws O17][see H152, cf. H785]
11 Feb	794	385	Under the Shade of a Bonny Green Tree	BDW		[Laws P19]
18 Feb	795	198	Farewell to Slieve Gallen	BDW		
25 Feb	796	163	Faughanvale	BDW		
4 Mar	797	327	The Drum Major	BDW		
11 Mar	798	421	The Pride of Newry Town	BDW		[see H190]
18 Mar	799	221	Charlie Jack's Dream	BDW		
25 Mar	800	164	Bonny Garrydoo	BDW		
1 Apr	801	164	Glenariffe	BDW		
8 Apr	802	466	Kellswaterside	BDW		
15 Apr	803	79	The Shepherd Boy	BDW		(W is a clipping)
22 Apr	804	262	You're Welcome as the Flowers in May	BDW		
29 Apr	805ab	73	The Ballinderry Marriage [2 m]	BDW		[cf. H93]
6 May	806	434	The Constant Farmer's Son	BDW		[Laws M33]
13 May	807	514	Johnny M' Man	BDW		
20 May	808	98	The S[team]s[hip] *Leinster Lass*	BDW		
27 May	809	162	The Maids of Downhill	BDW		
3 Jun	810	269	The Beggarman Cam' ower the Lea	BDW		[Child #279]
10 Jun	811	461	The Blackwaterside	BDW		[Laws O1]
17 Jun	812	310	The Banks of the Clyde / One Fine Summer's Morning	BDW		
24 Jun	813	468	Sweet Londonderry	BDW		
1 Jul	814	415	Lord Ronald	BDW		[Child #92]
8 Jul	815	103	Franklin the Brave	BDW		[Laws K9]
15 Jul	816	92	Old Ireland Far Away	BDW		[Laws J7]
22 Jul	817	169	Mountsandel	BDW		
29 Jul	818	317	Green Garden	BDW		[Laws N42][see H471]
5 Aug	819	219	Och, Och, Eire, O!	BDW		
12 Aug	820	257	Roger's Courtship	BDW		
19 Aug	821	220	There's a Dear Spot in Ireland	BDW		
26 Aug	822	239	Jean of Ballinagarvey	BDW		
2 Sep	823	59	O'Ryan	BDW		
9 Sep	824	166	Old Inishowen	BDW		
16 Sep	825	299	The Faithful Rambler	BDW		[see H788]
23 Sep	826	309	James Reilly	BDW		[Laws N37]
30 Sep	827	100	Yellow Meal	BDW		
7 Oct	828	286	Down in My Sally's Garden	BDW		
14 Oct	829	91	Balaclava	BDW		
21 Oct	830	64	The Yellow Bittern / An Bunnan Buidhe	BDW		
28 Oct	831	235	Autumn Dusk / Coimfeasgar Fogmair	BDW		
4 Nov	832a	49	The Black Pipe	BDW		[cf. H751]
	832b	81	Pat Muldoney	BL		[+*NC* 14 Oct 1939]
11 Nov	833	257	The Wee Article	BDW		
18 Nov	834	289	The Boatman / Fear a Bhata	BDW		
2 Dec	835a	512	Whisky Is My Name (a)	BL		[cf. H714]
	835b	512	Whiskey Is My Name (b) / The Blacksmith		DW	[DW "No. 836"]
9 Dec 1939	836	372	The Lass of Mohee	BL	BDW	[BDW "No. 835"]

531

Appendix B Additional text, mainly by Sam Henry, from the original columns

The numbers in brackets following the queries represent the columns where the songs requested were contributed and published, or are references to other printed sources.

[*Pages prefacing Bp (including quotation marks):*]

"Inserted ink amendments in the songs were variations received after publication. In some instances verses are cancelled by lines drawn across. These verses are proper to the song and the lines merely indicate that when broadcast in the series 'Ulster's Heritage of Song,' only the uncancelled verses were sung."

All rights reserved by Sam Henry, Sandelford, Coleraine.

Collection of folk songs taken down from the people by Sam Henry, Sandelford, Coleraine, Co. Londonderry, between the years 1923 and 1938, and first published in the *Northern Constitution*, Coleraine. The songs appeared in two series viz: Nos 1 to 246, and No 466 to 766 (the series continuing).

To ensure their preservation, a copy of each song has been presented to the Belfast Free Library (Reference Department).

H1 The Flower of Sweet Dunmull

[*For text, see introduction, p. xxiv.*]

H3 The Londonderry Air

This very ancient "air" was collected by Miss J. Ross, of New Town, Limavady, and sent to Mr George Petrie, in whose collection of old Irish melodies it appears (p. 57). As far as she could ascertain, it had neither name nor words. It has since been used by Elgar and other famous composers in their Irish symphonies, C. Villiers Stanford in *Songs of Old Ireland*, and, most noted of all, Mr Percy Aldridge Grainger in *British Folk Music Settings*, where one of our most modern of composers gives one of our most ancient of airs a setting of the newest and most advanced kind.

How popular the air has become may be judged by the fact that when the enclosed words were submitted to Messrs. Schott & Co., Music Publishers, London, they told me that over 80 sets of words were in use, many of the popular song kind, such as "Danny Boy."

In an endeavour to find the original words, I had a long talk with and enlisted the help of Mr Frank Kidson, of Leeds, the foremost authority on Folk Song in the North of Great Britain. He told me that he could find none. Mr Graves and Katherine Tynan have both written words, but in his opinion they were not very suitable for the old tune, in which, especially in the last verse, there is such a wonderful blend of sadness and triumph. The enclosed words were written at his request, in an attempt to capture the spirit of the air.

Sir H. Parry, in his work, "The Evolution of the Art of Music," refers to the "Londonderry Air" as the example of the finest melody in existence.

It should be a source of pride to us that from the hidden treasures of our local song this air of rarest beauty has been brought to light. An eminent continental authority once proclaimed that gem of Moore's melodies, "Oft in the Stilly Night," as the finest folk song in Europe. Probably he had not heard our "Londonderry Air."

It was not by chance that such a pearl of song as this was picked up by the banks of the Roe -- a little river that runs deeper than through Carrick Gorge, for it runs through the hearts of men. This air, that has reached us nameless and wordless, has found a tender, wistful, and triumphant response from myriads who have heard it. The Inniskillings, with that inevitable taste which men show in the presence of destiny, have chosen it as their funeral march.

What a pity that the air is chiefly linked in the popular mind with the words of "Danny Boy," a song of such unreal sentiment that our credulity is overtaxed by its improbability.

One modern setting of the air is called "Emer's Farewell to Cuchulain," and it may be that this wedded dirge of sadness and crescendos of hope was never meant for words, but for the harp that had hung too long on the willows, silent at the passing of the great hero "The Hound of Ulster."

Cecil Sharp, in his folk song investigations, found many of the English tunes in greatest perfection among the settlers of the Appalachian hills in America, where for six generations these songs of the heart had been handed down in purity from their English ancestors. Likewise we find in O'Neill's Chicago collection of Irish music [1903] the "Londonderry Air," #188. It has the following slight differences from the tune as shown above:

1st line, last note l instead of f.
4th line, $d:t_1 / l_1$ instead of $d\ r\ /\ d$.
6th line, l instead of r.
last line, $t_1\ d_1 / l_1$ instead [of] $l_1\ t_1 / d$.

In C. Villiers Stanford's setting in *Songs of Old Ireland* the 4th and last lines add the characteristic Irish ending, the 3d bars in each becoming $d:d.d$.

A beautiful setting of the "Londonderry Air" has been arranged by our former townsman, Mr W. B. Reynolds, now musical critic of the Belfast *Evening Telegraph*. The song was entitled "Far Away," and wove into beauty of sound the melodious place names of our country.

> Oh, fair the founts of Farranfore,
> And bright is billowy Ballintrae,
> But sweet as honey running o'er
> The golden shore of Far Away.

The "Londonderry Air" is accessible on the gramophone, in a fine presentation arranged by O'Connor Morris, in which the air is played on the violin by Miss Mary [*blank: name illegible. Hole punched in Bp, space in Dt*], accompanied by English string quartet and piano (Zonophone G. O. 35).

Of all the versions, the above words, written by Mr Milnes, are the most beautifully appropriate. The last lines of the verses, having a syllable for each note, avoid the awkward and unnatural slurs in other compositions.

This series of Songs for [*sic*] the People will render a signal service to the musical world if it elicits

Appendix B / Additional text by Sam Henry

from our readers some old words of titles for this air, which surely can not, with its arresting beauty, have come down nameless and wordless through the ages.

H6 The Woods of Mountsandel

"The mind of man is a door, and a song shall open or close it."

H8 Laurel Hill / Kyle's Flowery Braes

Thanks are hereby expressed to the contributors who have sent interesting songs from Carnmoon, Balleregagh, Drumafivey, and Breen, in the Bushmills, Stranocum and Armoy districts. Can any reader supply the words that are sung to the tune "Lovely Glenshesk"?

[H28a]

H15 The Plains of Waterloo

Can any reader supply the words of a ballad describing the loss of a Portrush fishing boat which refers to the brothers John and James Gillespie?

[H27c "The Portrush Fishing Disaster"]

H20b Summer Hill

Can any reader supply the words of a song beginning --

'Oor John's in America, shane will we a',
Oor John's in America, big heid an' a'.'

H43 The Maid with the Bonny Brown Hair

"Bel-Farset" writes: "Could anyone give any information or the words of a song current in the Glens (Cushendall, etc.) about the end of the 18th century, called "The Pretty Girls of Ballymedoo." [There is a beautiful air called "The Pretty Girls of Ballymena" in several of the published collections. -- Ed.]

H47 The Valley Below

Will any reader who knows the airs of the following songs kindly communicate with S.H.: -- (1) "The Yorkshire Boy" (a song of a highway robber); (2) "Knox's Farewell" (a Boveedy song).

[H51 "The Crafty Ploughboy"; H49]

H50 The Bard of Culnady / Charles O'Neill

Can Culnady readers supply any poems by Charles O'Neill?

H52a,b Magilligan / The Slaney Side

Can any reader from Dungiven district supply the words of a song called "The Brown-Haired Lad"?

[?H116 "... Lass"]

H63 Rosaleen Bawn

Can any reader supply the version of the song, "The Banks of the Bann," which contains the verse: --

You may work both late and early,
From daylight till dawn,
But you never will be able
To plough the Banks of Bann.

[H139 "The Rocks of Bawn"]

H64 The Girls from [Dt,Wt: of] Coleraine

Can any Ballycastle reader supply the full song, beginning: --

Bonny, bonny was my seat in yon red rosy yard,
And bonny was my portion in the town of Ballynagard.

[H75b "Bonny, Bonny"]

H66 Wester Snow

The reader "C" (Garvagh postmark) is thanked for sweet old song, "The Banks of the Bann." Is the air available for this old version? The more modern version of this song is of no value although the air is excellent.

[H86]

H72 Am I the Doctor?

Will any reader who knows the song and air of "M'Clenahan's Jean" kindly communicate with S.H.

[H81]

H85 Dobbin's Flowery Vale

Can any Dungiven or Feeny reader supply the words of old songs about Shane Crossagh, the famous highwayman?

[H97]

H89 Early, Early

Can any reader supply the full words of a song containing the verse: --

Broken-hearted I'll wander,
Broken-hearted I'll remain,
Since my bonny light horseman
In the war he was slain.

[H122 "The Bonny Light Horseman"]

H90 The Grey Mare

Sing you a song in the garden of life,
If only you gather a thistle;
Sing you a song as you travel along,
And if you can't sing, why, just whistle!

H91 The Little Thatched Cabin

I breathed a song into the air;
It fell to earth I know not where;
For who has sight so keen and strong,
That it can follow the flight of a song.

H98a Barossa / Oliver's Advice

[Article announcing the song competition; see introduction, p. xxv.]

Sam Henry's Songs of the People

H108a **The Rich Merchant's Daughter**

[*Repeat of article announcing song competition.*]

H109 **As I Walked Out**

[*m: The Linen Hall Library set has another note of the song competition (see H98a) and other prize winners.*]

H113 **Young Edward Bold / The Lowlands Low**

[*Another repeat of article announcing song competition.*]

The weekly prize is awarded to Mrs E. Glenn, of Mulkeragh South, Limavady, [for] a song of unusual excellence, "Polly Perkins of Paddington Green."

[H132]

H122 **The Bonny Light Horseman**

Song Competition.
The prize-winner is Mr Frank Mullin, Draperstown, for the song "The Wee Derry Pipe."

[?H465 "The Wee Cutty Pipe"]

H127 **The Factory Girl**

I do not claim to be a "poet," I don't pretend that my songs are "literary," but they are "songs of the people," and that is enough for me. Longfellow expresses better than I can what I mean: --

> Long, long afterwards in an oak
> I found the arrow still unbroke
> And the song from beginning to end
> I found again in the heart of a friend.

(Fred E. C. Weatherly, K.C., author of "Friend of Mine," "The Holy City," etc.)

H151 **Jamie Raeburn's Farewell**

Can any reader supply the song of which the following is a verse?: --

> Calm and easy I got rid of her, nice and easy
>   'deed I got rid of her,
> Calm and easy I got rid of her, just in time for
>   Lannigan's Ball.
> She stepped out and I stepped in again, I stepped
>   out and said nothing at all,
> Five long weeks I lay at Magilligan learning the
>   steps for Lannigan's Ball.

[*Another, different version is in Songs and Recitations 4:26-7; In Dublin's p. 58-60; and Loesberg 3:36-7, with added chorus.*]

H162 **Canada[,] Hi! Ho!**

Can any reader supply the words of an old song beginning: --

> Green grow the rashes and the tops of them sma',
> And love is a killing thing over us a'.

[H165a,b]

H166 **Lovely Annie (II)**

Can any reader supply the words of the song, "The Battle of Garvagh"?

H174 **The Auld Man and the Churnstaff**

Can any reader supply the words of a song, beginning: --

> The cuckoo is a bonny bird, she sings as she flies;
> She brings us glad tidings, she tells us no lies;
> She sucks the small birds' eggs to keep her voice
>   clear,
> ... "Cuckoo" till the Summer does ...

[*Last line not fully legible; off edge of print.*]

[H479]

H175 **The Yowe Lamb**

Can any reader supply the full song by blind "Zozimus" (Michael Moran), street-minstrel of Dublin, of which the following is the first verse: --

> In Egypt's land, upon the banks of Nile,
> King Pharaoh's daughter went to bathe in style;
> She tuk her dip, then walked into the land,
> And to dry her royal pelt she run along the
>   strand.
> A bulrush tripped her, whereupon she saw
> A smiling babby in a wad of straw.
> She tuk it up, and said, with accents mild,
> Tare and agers, girls, which av yez owns the
>   child?

H189 **Fair Tyrone**

"Songs that are perfectly decent, that have some Scope and Design, and that tend either to improve the Mind, mend the Manners, or make the Heart merry."

-- from the title page of an old song book.

Can any reader supply the words of a song beginning: --

> When first I saw my Glasgow lassie,
> 'Twas in the fair of sweet Strauraer.

H211 **When a Man's in Love**

Can any reader supply the complete words of a song of which the following is the first verse:

> My love is like a lozenger,
> He's small but very sweet,
> And if I had a crock of gold
> I'd plant it at his feet.

H220 **The Flower of Magherally, O!**

The request in last week's issue for songs 1 and 3 was for printed copies of the same cut out of our paper, and not for manuscript copies.

[*The request itself apparently was not preserved in any of the copies.*]

H221 **The Rich Ship Owner's Daughter**

Can any reader supply the words of the following songs: -- "The Braes of Kilhoyle," "The Mowing of the Hay," "Macaulay's Heifer," and a song about Cruckanim (near Ashlamaduff)?

[H464 "The Braes of Sweet Kilhoyle," ?H635 "The Tossing of the Hay"; *the latter two remain unidentified and presumably unpublished in Henry's column.*]

H240 Finn Waterside

[*For text, see introduction, p. xxvi.*]

H470 Lord Beichan

Mr Frank O'Kane of Gortinure, Maghera, is thanked for his offer of songs. We are pleased to know that he is still actively interested in the "Songs of the People."

H472 The Nonsense o' Men

Can any reader supply the words of a song called "Hielan' Jane"?

[H477]

H473 Paddy's Land

Can any reader in the district between Dungiven and Sperrin supply the words of a song called "The Maid of the County Tyrone"?

H475 The Swan

They sing like the nightingale, because their hearts are like his. They sing an old song their grandmothers sang when they were little girls; a song their children's children will sing one day; for songs are tender flowers that never die; they fly from lip to lip down the ages. The lips fade and fall silent one after the other, but the song lives on for ever.

Anatole France

H477 Hielan' Jane

Can any reader supply an old song written about a ploughing match at Coolhill in the Garvagh district?

H478 Erin, My Country

Can any reader supply the words or air of an old ballad of a lovely damsel and her cousin Gregor, in which the following lines occur:

"You know, cousin Gregor, with courtiers I'm plagued to the heart,
But you are the object that makes my heart smart."

"Cousin Gregor came to me all shining in blood,
And his body lies murdered in a far and green wood,
With three wounds in his body and three in his side,
With hatchets and arrows they're both deep and wide."

[*Another request for the same song at H579, but evidently also without response. See Greig/Duncan 2, 1983:497-9 (#340) "Grigor's Ghost," 2 vts.*]

H479 The Cuckoo

Can any reader in Ballycastle district supply a smuggling song about Hugh Hill, a famous brandyrunner, beginning "Ye Ballycastles now give ear"?

[H494 "Hugh Hill, the Ramoan Smuggler"]

Appendix B / Additional text by Sam Henry

H489 The Cup o' Tay

Can any reader supply the complete song, of which the following is the first verse:

My love's she's goin' away,
I hear the people say;
Her passage is paid and I'm afraid
She's gone to Americay.
It's not the money I care about,
But the way she took me in,
And when I go out, the little boys shout:
"Did iver she come back wi' the ring?"

H491 Happy 'Tis, Thou Blind, for Thee

Shakespeare and Irish Music.

"What hast here? Ballads?"

Mopsa (a shepherdess): "Pray now, buy some; I love a ballad in print, o' life, for then we are sure they are true."

-- *The Winter's Tale*, Act 4, scene 3, line 261.

It is fitting that in the week of celebrations of the memory of the bard of Avon reference should be made to the intimate knowledge shown by the world's master-poet of the old airs which were the fashion of his time and which he learnt from John Dowland (see "The Passionate Pilgrim," verse 8, line 5), the incomparable Irish lute-player, and from Edmund Spenser and others.

No less than 10 Irish airs are mentioned by Shakespeare. Words, which long puzzled his critics, have now been identified as phrases out of the Irish songs current in his day. For example, in *Henry V*, Act 4, scene 4, line 3, Pistol exclaims: "Quality? Calen O custure me!" a thinly veiled reference to the air "Colleen Oge Asthore," to which the well-known songs "The Croppy Boy" and "Happy 'Tis, Thou Blind, for Thee" are sung. In *As You Like It*, Act 2, scene 5, line 54, a curious word "Ducdame" is used, which has been found to be from the third verse of the original song, "Eileen Aroon," composed in 1380 by Carol O' Daly, and now well known as "Robin Adair." In *The Merry Wives of Windsor*, Act 3, scene 3, line 69, "if fortune they foe were not" refers to the Irish tune, "Fortune My Foe." We are told that this tune was often used for songs about criminals and may possibly be the tune known to us as "The River Roe." In *Twelfth Night*, Act 2, scene 3, line 84, "Peg-a-Ramsey," there mentioned, was from an Irish song of that name. In *The Winter's Tale*, Act 4, scene 3, line 199, the lines "Whoop, do me no harm, good man," are from an Irish tune, now commonly called "Paddy Whack" (see *Kerr's First Series of Merry Melodies*, page 40). The Irish air "Light o' Love" is mentioned in *Much Ado about Nothing*, Act 3, scene 4, line 44, and also in *The Two Gentlemen of Verona*, Act 1, scene 2, line 80. In *King Lear*, Act 3, scene 6, line 28, an old Irish song, "Come o'er the bourn, Bessy, to me" is referred to. It is also believed that there are veiled references to the Irish tunes "Bonny Sweet Robin," "Well-a-day; or Essex's Last Good-Night," "The Fading" and "Yellow Stockings."

We print the tune which Shakespeare called "Calen O Custure Me."

H501 The "Crummy" Cow

The air is a "stock" Irish air to which many old songs were sung, and, in particular, a song of the Great Lakes, about the sailing qualities of a timber

Sam Henry's Songs of the People

drogher, called "The Bigler." Can any American reader supply the words of it?

[See, e.g., Colcord 1938:200 "The Cruise of the *Bigler*"; Lomax/Lomax 1947(1966):194.]

H509 Knocklayde

"For the olden memories fast are flying from us;
Oh, that some kind hand would come
And bind them in a garland ere the present hardens
And the past grows cold and dumb."

H510 The Little White Cat

[B includes a copy of the sheet music, Curwen edition 71954 "The Wee White Cat," Irish Folk Song / collected by Sam Henry / arranged by Margaret Lyell / copyright 1937.]

H526 Neuve Chappelle

"There's no songs like the old songs. There's no tunes like the old tunes. They do go to the heart like, in particular if you've a-heard 'em when you were young. The songs you do hear now be silly, I do call. An' the tunes be but a tinpot rattle.... 'There's nothin' so good as used to be when I were a boy,' gasped Old Hezekiah. 'An' really if things hadn' changed so much I don't believe I should be so old as I be. I do feel my cough better already for the thought of old times, I do.'"

-- from the *Book of Simple Delights*, Walter Raymond.

Can any reader supply the words of a County Down song, "The Boys of Carrowdore," or "Benbradagh Hill" -- a County Derry song?

[?see H169, "The Maid of Carrowclare"; ?H572 "Benbradagh Brae"]

H529 Bordon's Grove

Can any reader send the words of an old song which contains the verse:

My love wears the tarry trousers,
My love wears the jacket blue,
My love ploughs the deep blue ocean,
So young man be off with you.

[H532 "Tarry Trousers"]

H533 So Dear Is My Charlie to Me

Can any reader supply an old Portglenone song containing the words:

I ne'er loved another nor any so well,
As Annie M'Cartney in Mooney's Hotel.

Annie was a famous beauty 100 years ago.

H548 One Morning Clear

Songs of our land, ye have followed the stranger,
With power over ocean and desert afar;
Ye have gone with our wand'rers through distance and danger,
And gladden'd their path like a home-guiding star.

Can any reader supply the words of a song which begins:

Come all ye water-bailiffs round Clady banks that lie,

and each verse ends:

For the night's too dark and stormy for to face the Inverue.

[H764 "The Clady River Water Bailiffs"]

H555 The Star of Donegal

"The world will come to an end,
But love and music can never die."

Gaelic proverb

H556 On Board of a Man-of-War

For doth not song
To the whole world belong?
Is it not given wherever tears can fall,
Wherever hearts can melt or bushes glow,
Or mirth or sadness mingle as they flow,
A heritage to all?

Can any reader supply the words of a song called "The Mowing of the Hay"?

[?H635 "The Tossing of the Hay"]

H573 Sweet Glenbush

Any little old song
Will do for me,
Tell it of joys gone long,
Or joys to be,
Or friendly faces best
Loved to see.

Thomas Hardy

H574 Pat Reilly

Can any reader supply the words of a song beginning:

Farewell, Ballymoney, and adieu to the Bann,
For the sweet County Antrim is my native land.

[?H643 "Ballymonan Brae"]

H575 The Maid with the Bonny Brown Hair (b)

Can any reader suply the words of a song beginning:

Down by a riverside a fair maid I espied,
Lamenting for her own true love;
Lamenting, crying, sighing, dying,
Dying for her own true love.

Or a song approximating it in words or meaning.

H579 Fair Maid of Glasgow Town

"Give me the making of a people's ballads,
And I care not who makes their laws."

Fletcher of Saltoun

Can any reader supply the complete song from which the following lines are taken:

She says, "Cousin Gregor, with courtiers I'm plagued to the heart;
But you are the object that makes my heart smart."
With Latin and Greek she taught him also,
That through this wide world he was fit for to go.

The lady that loved you I pity her case,
That lost such a blooming and beautiful face.
Love Gregor, love Gregor, came to me shining in
  blood,
And his body lies murdered in a far and green
  wood; ... wounds on each side,
With hatchets and arrows, the[y]'re both deep and
  wide.

[See note to H479 above.]

H585 Sloan Wellesley

Can any reader supply the words of a song about the wreck of the *George A. Hopeley* at Portstewart?

H607 The Pride of Glenelly

Can any reader supply the poems of James Devine, published about 1858?

H613 My Bonny Brown Jane

Can any reader supply the words of a song beginning: --

"I'll tell you a story that has come to pass,
Of a mare and a foal that were put out to grass."

H614 Willie Angler / The Banks of the Bann

Can any reader supply the words of the song "The Charming Coleraine Lass"?

[H616]

H616 My Charming Coleraine Lass

Can any reader supply the words of a song called "Bantry Bay" and also of a song beginning:

In the County Antrim I was born,
Near to the river Bann;
It's the prettiest little river
That runs through Ireland.
It's the nicest little river
That e'er my eyes did see,
But my mind was bent on rambling
Far from Paddy's green countrie.

[*The latter is* H632 "Paddy's Green Countrie."]

H619 The Lakes of Ponchartrain

Can any reader supply the complete words of the song beginning:

Och, as I roved out on a bright summer's morning,
Down by the banks of a clear purling stream,
It's who should I spy but my own dearest darling,
Lamenting the loss of her own darling swain;
And the song she did sing made the valleys to
  ring,
And the small feathered songsters around her they
  flew,
Saying, "The war is all over and peace is
  proclaimed,
But Johnny's not returned home from famed
  Waterloo."

[*This is Laws N32, "The Plains of Waterloo I," never printed in Henry's column.*]

Appendix B / Additional text by Sam Henry

H622 The Jolly Thresher

Can any reader supply the air of a song called "Shanty Boy," which begins:

As I walked out one evening just as the sun went
  down,
So carelessly I wandered to a place called Trenton
  town;
There I heard two maids conversing as slowly I
  passed by,
One said she loved her farmer's son and the other
  her shanty boy.

[H662]

H624 I Am a Wee Laddie, Hard, Hard Is My Fate

Can any reader supply words of song beginning:

If you meet a bonny lass wi' a dark and rolling
  eye,
Kiss her and embrace her and tell her the raison
  why;
Kiss her and embrace her till you cause her heart
  to yield,
For a faint-hearted soldier never gained the field.

H634 One Penny Portion

Can any reader supply the words of a song about a Coleraine girl, containing the lines:

Roving down Mountsandy braes,
She made the valleys ring.

[H646 "The Coleraine Girl"]

H636 Mary Smith, the Maid of Mountain Plain

Can any reader supply the air and words of a song beginning "We met 'twas in a crowd," and the chorus of which contains the words, "For thou hast been the cause of this anguish, my mother"?

[H638]

H655 The Pride of Glencoe

Can any reader supply a song of which the following is a fragment:

The first time that I met my love,
Down by yon willow tree,
He thought that I would speak to him
As I was passing by;
But afore that I would speak to him,
I would lie down and die;
Since he's gone let him go --
Farewell unto he.

Now all ye pretty fair maids,
A warning take by me,
And don't place your true love
On the top of a greenwood tree;
For the leaves they will wither,
And the branches will decay,
And the beauty of a false young man
Will soon fade away.

[*Cf.* H504 "Farewell He"]

Also a song containing the verse:

Maggie, dear Maggie, when soft dews were falling,
I chanced in its splendour to view the proud main;
The pride of the north and the beauty of Erin,
Is Maggie, who dwells near the town of Coleraine.

[H657 "Maggie of Coleraine"]

Sam Henry's Songs of the People

H666 Oville

Can any reader supply a song containing the words:
   In Dublin city there's a clock and a bell.

H668 Love Laughs at Locksmiths

Can any reader supply a song beginning --
   As I went up to Bellaghy,
   I met a wee lump of a pig,
   I got it inunder my arm
   And danced the swaggering jig.
      The[n] hi! for the cups and the saucers,
      And hi! for the butter and bread,
      And hi! for the bonny wee lassie
      That can dance the swaggering jig.

   [H758 "Bellaghy Fair"]

H669 Dungiven Cricket Match

The best music in the world is the simplest. As a woman who was rearing her family close to the foaming river replied, when we remarked, "You have always the music of the water here," "Aye, and of the childher."

H670 The Jolly Roving Tar

Answer to correspondent. -- "M. W." -- The song "Henry Connor of Castledawson" was published as No. 128 in this series.

H673 The Maid of Aghadowey

The world will come an an [sic] end, but love and song will never die.

   -- Epitaph on Marjory Kennedy-Fraser's grave in Iona. Born 1857, died 1930.

H693 The Banks of Claudy

The natural power of music is most evident when it is extremely simple and inartificial, when the sound is an echo to the sense, when the composer has attended to melody, not harmony.

-- from "The Power of Music" (1779) by John Wesley.

H698 Old Rosin the Bow

Can any reader supply the words of "The Dreary Gallows," beginning: "As I was walking the streets of Derry, my own true loved one I did spy"; or the song, "The Irish Young Lady," beginning: "An Irish young lady from old Ireland came, a most beautiful damsel, fair Sally by name"?

   [H705; H72 "Am I the Doctor?"]

H699 The Bonny Bushes Bright

[*For text, see introduction, p. xxv.*]

H704 The Maid from the Carn Brae

Can any reader in Crebilly district, Ballymena, supply the words of two songs written by a very able bard named "Tailor" Murray, about a century ago. They are entitled "Roger the Donkey" and "The Great Thimble War." A verse of the second song runs:

   The sun rose like blood and the dread thunder broke;
   O'er Crebilly wood there were vast clouds of smoke;
   While the Sons of the Patch, high and low, near and far,
   Crippled up to the scratch for the great Thimble War.

In "Roger the Donkey" a tailor is turned into a donkey and ridden all over the country by a rival.

H706 Ta Ra, Limavady

If any reader is in possession of a copy of *Poems* by a Mr Troland, of Norwich, Connecticut, U.S.A., who retired from the plumbing business there but was originally a native of mid-Antrim, the loan of the volume would be greatly appreciated by the Song Editor. It is a pity that his writings, which were published in the best American magazines, should be unknown in his own land.

H709 If I Were a Fisher

Mr Seamus MacManus, the Irish author, lecturer, and humorist, known on both sides of the Atlantic, in a letter to our Song Editor, says: "I wish every big country town in Ireland had as fine, good and interesting high-class weekly as the *Northern Constitution*. It is nearly a model for country weeklies."

H717 The Wreck of the Nimrod

And can any reader in Killagan district supply the words of a song which contains the lines:
   I am on the rakes of poverty,
   The son of a gamb-a-leer.

   [H741 "The Rakes of Poverty"]

H735 Lambkin

Note. -- Song No. 731, Polly Primrose, second to last line of refrain, bars 5 and 6 were superfluous.
   Can any reader supply a song called "The Wild Colonial Boy"?

   [H750]

H747 Maguire's Brae

Will the contributor who sent the fine song, "Mary M'Veagh," kindly state the origin of the song and whether it has been published before.

   [H773]

H750 The Wild Colonial Boy

[This column quotes a letter from an "esteemed correspondent, a native of County Derry," writing from North Auckland, New Zealand, and enclosing a text to H750. He also mentions the "famous Sayers and Heenan fight."]

H752 The Valleys of Screen

Can any reader supply a song which contains the lines:
   And farewell to the banks of the Roe,
   Adieu to thee, white-bosomed Mary.

   [H791 "Farewell to the Banks of the Roe"]

H 755 Johnnie and Molly

Can any reader supply Mr Johnston with the words of a song called "Deep Sheep Haven Bay"?

Can any reader supply the words of the song "Willie Taylor," beginning:

> Willie Taylor courted Nancy,
> All alone by the shady grove;
> All his courtship to her was love;
> Willie was pressed and sent away.

[H213, H757]

H 760 The Navvy Boy

Can any reader in Claudy district supply the words of a ballad (or the story) concerning a highwayman named Mitchell who lived in Toneduff? The ballad mentions a Captain Evans, and the refrain:

> Musha-rig-do-a-da,
> There's whiskey in the jar.

[H792 "Whiskey in the Jar"]

Can any reader supply the words of a ballad beginning:

> The Lord, in his mercy, be good to Belfast.

["Ballad to a Traditional Refrain," by Maurice James Craig (Hammond 1978:63).]

H 764 The Clady River Water Bailiffs

California Appreciates Our Songs.

The Song Editor has received the following letter from Shan Mor, who is a well-known platform artist in Los Angeles, California:

"I am returning your ballads which Seumas MacManus so kindly lent me. I have taken the liberty of copying a number of them, and when I sing them I will tell where I got them.

"Irish folk songs are great favourites here and I never sing anything else. I have several hundred letters received from radio listeners of every nationality, race and colour. I always sing without accompaniment and usually tell the story with which the song is connected.

"I think you are doing a grand job in collecting these old songs, and I would very much like to see it done in every district.

"The country folk really know and love good music and have not much use for modern jingles, so I don't think there is much danger of these songs dying out.

"With best wishes to you in your work."

Can any reader supply the words of a song containing the verse:

> My first penchant was one whose face was a
>   fortune, it was so fair;
> She walked with an air of enchanting grace but a
>   man cannot live upon air,
> For when poverty enters the door, young love will
>   out of the window fly;
> The truth of the proverb I'd no wish to try:
> "There'll be time enough for that," says I,
> "There'll be time enough for that," says I.

H 769 The Parting Glass

"The Flowers of the Forest." -- In reply to anonymous correspondent, this song, without music, can be had through any bookseller. It is published by Messrs. Curwen & Sons, Ltd., London, in *The Fellowship Song Book*, price 6d, or with historical notes, ninepence.

H 770 The Garden Gate

Can any reader supply a song containing the lines:
> And like Erin's son, I'll carry a gun
> For my lovely Cluntyfinnan maid.

H 775 Bonny Portrush

Can any reader supply the words of a ballad beginning:

> God bless Captain Nevin,
> His sweet and lovely eyes;
> It was at Derrykeighan
> He his men did exercise.

H 777 The Banks of [Wt: the] Cloughwater

Can any reader supply words of a ballad containing:

> Finn MacCool, he went to school
> With the prophet Jeremiah.

H 778 Norah Magee

> The old, old songs and the dear dead songs,
> And the songs that we hear no more,
> Like a phantom ace they haunt the place
> And the scenes that were loved of yore;
> Oh, the dear old songs I can hear them yet,
> When the weary world's asleep,
> 'Neath its comfort gray, with the stars alway
> Their wards o'er its dreams to keep.

H 794 Under the Shade of a Bonny Green Tree

Can any reader supply a song containing the lines:
> It's not for your gold, sir, that I listed here;
> But for the sake of young Shirlton, the bold
>   grenadier.

[H797 "The Drum Major"]

H 800 Bonny Garrydoo

Can any reader supply a song which contains the words:

> Happy is the ploughboy who furrows and sows;
> When he rises in the morning, to his horses he
>   goes;
> When he stables his horses, his day's labour's o'er,
> But the soldier must fight while the loud cannons
>   roar.

H 803 The Shepherd Boy

Can any reader supply the tune of a song known as "The Constant Farmer's Son."

[H806]

H 804 You're Welcome as the Flowers in May

Can any reader supply words of a song called "The Banks of Bolea."

Appendix B / Additional text by Sam Henry

Sam Henry's Songs of the People

H 809 The Maids of Downhill

Can any reader supply a song entitled "M'Clurg's Potato Digging," which was popular in Templemore district, near Eglinton in the last century.

H 812 The Banks of the Clyde / One Fine Summer's Morning

Can any reader in the Braid district, near Ballymena, supply a song called "The Loughdoo Poachers," which is wanted by a reader in New Zealand.

H 813 Sweet Londonderry

One of his majesty's lads in navy blue, who is off to Chinese waters next week, is anxious to get the words of the following song:

> It's of a damsel, both neat and handsome,
> These lines are true that I'm going to tell,
> On the Isle of Ara there's a lofty mountain
> Where this noble princess was known to dwell.

H 825 The Faithful Rambler

"Reader" (Belfast postmark) who asks that the song "Castleblayney Besoms" be published, will find it under the title "Fine Broom Besoms" as No. 17 in this series. A North-England version, "Buy Broom Besoms," may be found in Sir W. G. Whittaker's *Songs of the North*.

H 835a Whisky Is My Name

Can any reader supply the words of the song called the "Cumber Claudy Band," the first verse of which is as follows:--

> In Cumber-Claudy town we've a band of great renown,
> With drums and fifes and piccolos galore,
> When we march around at night sure the girls we do delight,
> We're the band of Cumber-Claudy to the fore.

"Ballymena Reader" is thanked for his appreciation of "Songs of the People." We regret that we cannot republish "The True Lover's Discussion" as he requests. As this song contains 176 lines, limitations of space, therefore, forbid.

Appendix C   Other relevant text, not by Sam Henry, but included by him in library copies of the columns

H2 Mullaghdoo

[*Clipping with Bp:*]

From the *Northern Whig* of 1826.
Thursday, March 2.

Masonic. -- The members of the following Masonic Lodges in the vicinity of Armoy, for the purpose of expressing their kind feelings towards their friend and neighbour, Mr Hugh Fulton, of Mullaghduff, assembled in a large field which he had intended to plough and in a few hours dug it over ready for the seed, and, after regaling themselves a little with the mountain dew, returned quietly and peaceably to their respective homes. The Lodges were: -- No. 152, Chatham Hall, No. 197, Culbane; Nos. 186 and 365, Armoy.

[*Bp typed*] Copy of note on verso of No. 2. "From copy in possession of Rev. D. B. Knox. (words identical.) Mr Robert Adams of Ballymoney writing in *Whig* says: -- I have been asked by a Mullaghdoo man to correct several opinions that have been published in your columns about the origin of the brave McKay. This Dan McKay, mentioned in the Masonic song, lived in Turnarobert and is buried in the parish church burying ground. He has a son living in Armoy at the present time. The Lodge mentioned in the song is Chatham Hall Masonic Lodge, No. 152 and is a prosperous lodge still. Hugh Fulton, Dan McKay and John Kerrechar, the poet, were all members of this lodge."

H10 Old Choir Rhymes

[*Clipping of article, publication not identified, included with W:*]

Collection of Rhymes
by Classes when practising Presbyterian
Psalmody in former days.

By John J. Marshall, M.A., M.R.S.A.I.

Some time in the early part of the 18th century, ere ever the use of hymns or instrumental music had been even imagined as a part of public worship in Presbyterian services, some progressive clergyman, or more than usually far-seeing and tolerant layman, may have first had the idea of holding singing classes for the improvement of congregational psalmody. These classes formed an event in what we, today, would consider the rather drab life of those days. Small wonder, then, that they were taken up enthusiastically by the younger members of the congregations, affording as they did an opportunity for social intercouse as well as the culture of their musical talents.

Whether the movement originated in Scotland or in Ireland, it was common to both countries, and lasted until superseded by more modern methods during the nineteenth century.

The more strict members of the Presbyterian faith had an objection to the use of the sacred psalms for the mere worldly purpose of improving their [?music]. However, difficulties arise but to be overcome, and a compromise was elected by using for the purpose a suitable verse taken from a secular poem, but more often some member of the community, gifted with a poetic faculty, composed rhymes which could be used in practice to the tunes instead of the psalms. In many cases these rhymes contain personal or local allusions and some of the more popular had circulation far beyond the congregation for the use of whose class they had originally been composed.

A number of tune books are in existence having the rhymes written by the side or underneath the tunes to which they belong. It is greatly to be desired that these interesting relics of a bygone day should be placed for permanent preservation in the collection of the Presbyterian Historical Society, which exists for the safekeeping and conservation of everything concerning the past history of the Presbyterian Church of Ireland.

[*The specimen verses are printed here.*]

(To be continued in October number.)

H137 Johnny Doyle

[*Clipping included with W:*]

Worth of an Old Song.

There were notices in the newspapers recently about a couple of humble folk in County Down who had come in for a large fortune which had been left by an American dollar millionaire, Mr Jefferson Doyle. An interesting little story is told of the way in which the recipients were traced as the nearest relatives of the rich man. There is a well-known Irish song -- known as well to the Irish in America as to the Irish at home -- which begins "I'd range the world over with you, Johnny Doyle." The millionaire died without anyone to inherit his money, and it occurred to his lawyer that perhaps there might be a clue in the "Johnny Doyle" of the song. He accordingly wrote to Dr. Grattan Flood, the well-known Irish musician, for the text and information about the origin of the song. Dr. Flood was able to supply exactly what he wanted, and this was particularly valuable, because the Johnny Doyle in the ballad was not merely a real person but the father of Mr Jefferson Doyle. The song perpetuated the memory of the elopement of Johnny Doyle about a century ago from Rathfriland, in County Down, to the United States, and there are still Doyles of the family in this place, and they have now come into a goodly heritage through the words of the song.

Indexes and reference aids

Glossary

Abbreviations

A R C O Associate of the Royal College of Organists.
L R A M Licenciate of the Royal Academy of Music.
F R S A I Fellow of the Royal Society of Antiquarians (Ireland).
M P S I Member of the Pharmaceutical Society of Ireland.
M S (N C) London Midland and Scottish (Northern Counties) Railway.

a I.
a' all.
a glee (adgee) crooked, to one side.
a gramachree ... ref.1,2 translated means 'Love of my heart, my little girl, Molly is my treasure.' [s]
aboot about.
abune [aboon] above, overhead.
ae one, only.
aff off.
aft, aften oft(en)
agin against.
agra my love.
'gree agree.
Ah I.
ain own.
airt quarter of the compass, direction.
airy sprightly, vivacious; proud, lofty, buoyant.
aisy [aizee] easy, comfortable, unstrained.
alang along.
alood aloud.
altar of Hymen marriage.
A'm I'm.
amang, 'mang among
an' and.
ance once.
ane one; own.
anither another
Aperile April.
aquail equal.
astore [a stor] my treasure.
ate eaten.
attind attend.
aul', auld old.
ava at all.
avick Irish *a mhic*, my son (term of ..endearment, ironic).
awa' away.
ax(ed) ask(ed).
aye ever, always, still, constantly, on all occasions.
bab posy, nosegay; bunch of ribbons.
babbie baby.
bairns children.
baith both.
banes bones. [s]
bannocks flat bread cakes.
banter challenge.
banyan day a nautical expression for a day without meat ration. [s]
bann[s] proclamation, especially in church, of a proposed marriage.
bap roll of bread.
bate beat[en].
bawbee a Scottish coin of silver base, worth 3(6) pennies Scottish, or a halfpenny English.
befel happened, befell.
ben in, into; inside a house.
bide stay.
biggin' building. [s]
bilabong (Australian) an arm of the river which rises and falls according to the water in the river.
billy (Australian) a can with a lid used for boiling water to make tea, etc.
bird alone forlorn, without company. (h 1981:181)
birled spun (a bawbee).
birlin' spin; carouse.
bit tiny, small (insignificant).
bizzin' buzzing.
blaeberry bilberry, whortleberry, in America called blueberry, the fruit of a dwarf hardy shrub, genus Vaccinium.
blaguard blackguard.
blate pale, void of feeling.
blaw blow.
blin', blinner blind.
blow(n) blossom(ed).
boady body.
bodilie bodily.
bonny fine, handsome, attractive.
boreen byroad.
bore crevice, opening in wall.
bould bold.
bracken coarse fern.
brae slope, hillside (especially along a river).
braid broad.
brairds sprouts, shoots.
bra', braw good, fine; well dressed, splendid.
Breeden little Bridget or Bridie. [s]
breeks britches.
brenth breadth.
brig bridge.
brislocks toasted potatoes.
brissle toast, scorch.
broon brown.
brose dish (mush) of oatmeal or peasemeal.
bucht pen.
bulldogs guns. [s]
burnie diminutive of burn, brook.
bums bailiffs (of the meanest kind).
burgoo a kind of gruel made on board ship; in army parlance, porridge and treacle. [s]
byre cow barn.
ca, ca' call
caller fresh and cool.
cam' came.
cancer the constellation of the Crab. [s]
canna(e), canna', canny cannot
cannie, cannily careful, safe; carefully.
canted turned.
cantle corner.
carle a man; also a clown, boor, person of mean family.
cat a whip for flogging sailors. [s]
cathead a timber projecting from the bow of a ship through which the ropes pass by which the anchor is raised. [s]
cauld cold.
cead mile failte 'a thousand welcomes, traditional Gaelic greeting.
ceol music. [s]
chape cheap, inexpensive.
chap(ping) rap(ping).
charmer seductive girl. [h 1981:182]
chaw chew.
chiel fellow, lad, young man.
child[h]er children.
chimley chimney.
chist chest.
clachan hamlet, village, inn.
clat at your noddle opportunity to influence your head.
clate ?[claught clutched firmly or eagerly]
claty [clatty] dirty, muddy.
claes, cleading clothing.
claw scratch, break. [g/d 2,1983:xiii]
clegs horseflies.
clever well proportioned [h 1981:182]
clew ?[from ball of thread: tight coil, knot].
clews balls, especially of yarn.
cliddery ba' a slippery ball. [s]
clock-ed hatched.
clockin' sitting, hatching.
clods heaves.
cockle a common European edible bivalve.
coft bought (g/d 2,1983:xiii).
coinye piece of money.
colcannon a dish of meal and cabbage. [s]
convanient near at hand, handy.
convoy escort, accompany (for honor, guard, or protection; hence, giving or attending a going-away party).
coo(s) cow(s).
coolibah (Australian) coonibark, a tree.
coort court.
corn dodgers cornmeal cakes.
coternal "improvised word including paternal and maternal." [s]
couldna, couldna' could not.
counthry country.
coutered accoutered, furnished, equipped.
couthie kind, agreeable.
cove fellow, chap.
craig [crag] throat. [s]
craobhin little branch. [s]
crap gizzard, throat.
crature creature.
craw crow.
cromlech prehistoric stone structure, dolmen.
croonyawn cronan, Irish for humming, a song.
crously proudly, arrogantly, boldly; cheerfully, confidently. [g/d 2,1983:xiii]
cud could.
cuilin ban flaxen hair. [s]
cutty stumpy, short.
cutty quean an ill-tempered woman. [Moffat [1933]:32].
cutty-peip short, stumpy pipe.
da father.
dacent decent.
dae do.
dang driven, pushed, knocked.
dar'na, daurna dare not.
dauchter daughter.
the dear [circumlocution for] the deity.
decripted decrepit.
dee die.
deid dead.
deil, divil devil.
derned concealed, hidden.
desaver deceiver.
deuch an dhurrus "Gaelic phrase for a parting glass, spelt here phonetically, literally means 'the drink of the door.'" [s]
dhraple small drop, sip.
didna did not.
dinna do not.
dirl vibrate, tingle.
disloadened unloaded.
divarsion diversion.
divertments diversions (of path or way).

543

Sam Henry's Songs of the People

divil a [expression of strong negation].
doatin' doting, weak-minded from old age.
dochter daughter.
doon, doun down.
doot doubt.
drap(s) drop(s).
dree suffer. [s]
drookit drenched, soaked, wet.
droon drown.
dub pool, puddle.
dudeens short clay pipes for tobacco.
dulse a red edible seaweed (*Rhodymenia palmata*).
dun ancient hill fortress or fortified eminence.
dunner thunder.
dure door.
durestep doorstep.
durstna dares not.
dyke sheugh ditch. [m]
edified (verified?). [s: Dt]
e'e, e'en eye(s)
Egmont a mountain in New Zealand. [s:Bp]
eneu ?enough.
enloping eloping.
Eochaill, probably Aughill in Magilligan, means a yew wood. [s:Bp]
ettle [ettel] plan, endeavor.
extrolinger astrologer. [s]
fa' fall.
fa'n fawn.
faha the exercise green outside the royal dun. [s]
fahan bosom. [s]
faither, fether father.
faucht fought.
Faugh-a-ballagh Clear the way! [m]
faut fault.
fecht fight.
feth faith.
flure floor.
forby(e) besides, moreover.
fornenst opposite.
fou, fu' full, replete; drunk, intoxicated.
frae from.
freens friends.
fun' found.
fussee [fusil] light musket or firelock.
gaberlunzie man beggarman, tinker, itinerant. [m/s 1977:365]
gae, gie go.
gaed gave.
gaed, gied, gaen, gan(e) went.
gale rent (periodical payment).
Gallawa' Galloway.
gang go.
ganger foreman in charge of a gang of workmen.
garding garden.
garran bawn white horse. [s]
gar(s) make(s), cause(s).
gaun going.
gave leg bail ran away.
gear goods, property.
gee (gie) give.
geen given.
gets the rout receives marching orders. [m]
gey, gye remarkably, very. [m]
gie; gied go; went.
gill measure of volume: 4 ounces.
gillstoup container for a gill.
gin if.
'gin by [a certain time].
gintale genteel.
glaur mud.
gled glad.
Go Caiseal na mioga to Cashelnamega, may be an error for Cashelnavella, a village in Co. Leitrim. [s]
gommagh [gomach] fool, simpleton.

goose a tailor's smoothing iron with a gooseneck handle.
goun gown.
gowden golden
gra love.
graip a 3- or 4-pronged fork.
gramachree her heart's love [s: Dt]; darling.
grah me [ma] chree dear of my heart.
grammerie [gramarye] magic.
greed of gear desire for wealth or goods.
green table(s) Ulster phrase for the Court of Justice [s]; witness box. [h 1981:185]
greet cry, weep.
gub [gob] beak, mouth.
gude, guid good.
gudeman goodman; husband.
gudewife goodwife; mistress of a household.
ha' hall.
hae, ha'e have.
hadnae had no(t).
hae'in having.
hairst harvest.
haithin heathen.
a half one a measure of whiskey, in Ireland a quarter gill.
haliday a festive occasion.
hame home.
han' hand.
happer hopper.
haud old.
heckler operator of thread guides in a cloth mill.
head rig the first or head row.
heed(s), heid(s) head(s).
heez hoist, lift up.
hersel' herself.
hert heart.
het hot.
hied hastened.
hielan's highlands.
himsel' himself.
hinches haunches, hips.
hing, hingin' hang(ing).
hob or nob give or take. [s]
hoo how.
hoose house.
hoosikie house.
houl', houldin' hold(ing).
howm holm.
Hymen's bonds marriage.
i' in.
ilka each, every.
ill aff badly off.
illegant elegant.
isna is not.
ither other.
iver, ivir ever.
ja's jaws.
jaist, jist just.
jeopardie danger, jeopardy.
jolly fine, handsome. [h 1981:183]
kail kale.
kame comb.
keekt peeped, glimpsed.
kemp to compete in labor. [s]
ken know.
kent knew.
kill overwhelm by a strong impression on the mind.
killing glances looks that leave impressions.
kilt wi' the drouth was dreadfully thirsty.
kine cows.
kirk church.
kirn churn.
kist chest.
knowe(s) small hill(s).
kye cows.

la' law.
lag term of transportation, penal servitude; hence, a person serving such a term.
laird lord.
laith loath.
lak', lake like.
lammies lambs.
Land League (1879-81) national Irish organization for agrarian reform, tenant protection, and famine relief. [s]
lane alone.
lang(er) long(er).
langest longest.
laste least.
lave, lea' rest, remainder, residue; leave.
laverock (sky)lark.
leal loyal, true.
lee live
lee-lang, leelong livelong.
leeved lived.
lether ladder.
light a can'le at Dymond's [Hymen's] lamp marry.
limmer jade, hussy, minx.
list enlist.
lo'e love.
loadened loaded.
lockit locked.
loo'd loved.
loon boy, lad, fellow.
losh, guid [probably a circumlocution for "Lord, God"].
luck penny portion of a price given back for luck.
luckin' looking.
luk roon look around.
mae my.
maelin' meals [s:Bp], farm [written on Bp].
mair more.
maist most.
mak's makes.
maun must.
mauna must not.
mealin' farm.
merried married.
Milesian Irishman.
min' mind.
minnie mother. [s: Bp]
misca'in' miscalling.
mither mother.
mo leanibh dhu [leanibh pronounced in two syllables, lyaniv] my dark-haired baby. [s]
moidherin' murdering.
mony many.
mooth, mou' mouth.
mounseer monsieur. [s]
mountain dew moonshine, poteen.
muckle big, large, much.
muircock moorcock.
na baclish dry up your tears. [s]
nae no, not.
naethin, naethin' nothing.
nane none.
napping stone a stone on which whins were pounded [Bp] [Dt: as food for horses].
nate neat.
navvy laborer in heavy construction or excavation.
naw no, not.
neb beak, bill, nose.
needna need not.
Ni racaid-se (pronounced "Nyee-raugha-sha") I will not go. [s]
nicht night.
nieve fist, clenched hand.
nixt next.
niver never.
no' not.
noddle head, pate.
noo now.
nor than.

Glossary

o' of
och [interjection].
O'Cahan [O Cathain], land of O'Cahan North Derry. [h 1981:6]
O'Ryan the constellation of Orion or the Hunter. His belt and his spear are easily distinguishable. [s]
Ogam writing in an ancient 20-character alphabet used by the British and Irish.
on the square without deceit, directly, openly.
ony any.
oorie dismal, sad, lonely, apprehensive; eerie.
oor our.
oot out.
or before, until.
orra, arrah [interjection].
oul', ould old.
ower, owre over.
oxters armpits.
parritch spurtle [Dt] a stick for stirring porridge.
plack small copper coin current in 15th and 16th century Scotland, worth 4 pennies.
plaised pleased.
ploo plow.
poke, pyock bag.
pooch pouch.
poteen Irish moonshine (distilled liquor, usually illicit).
praich preach.
pratie potato.
preed sampled, tasted.
puir poor.
pun' pounds.
pursikie purse.
purty pretty.
quare queer, odd.
quate quiet.
quean a young woman.
quo, quo' quoth, says.
rape rope.
reek smoke.
Ribbonmen members of a 19th-century Irish Roman catholic secret society.
rid-sprickled red-speckled.
rig ridge in a field.
end rig untilled land at the end of a plowed field. [h 1981:184]
riggin' roof. [s]
rinnin' running.
roon aboot round about.
roon around.
row(l) roll, wrap.
rugwuddie the rope or chain over the saddle of the horse that bears the weight of the cart on its back.
rung a stout rounded stick, staff.
sa' saw.
sae say, so.
saftly softly.
St. Patrick 4th-century apostle, patron saint of Ireland.
sair sore.
saison season.
sarch search.
sartin certain.
ssie saucy.
sate seat.
sated seated.
saut salt.
say, says sea(s)
schale school.
scons scones.
scoured moved about hastily or energetically.
scrip(t) shepherd's pouch.
scroogs ?[scrogs stunted bushes].
shin-a-dhoy a Gaelic phrase equivalent to the English "that's the style." [s]

shoen, shoon shoes.
sic such.
siccan such. [s]
siccar [sicker] secure, assured, confident.
sicht sight.
sidhe fairies. [s]
siller silver.
skelington skeleton.
skeps beehives.
slae sloe.
Slieve-an-Orra "the mountain of gold." [s]
sma' small.
small-clothes knee-breeches. [s]
smiddy smithy.
smoor smother. [s]
sna' snow.
snash impertinent or abusive language.
sna', snaw snow.
snow from the Dutch *snaauw*, a boat.
sodger soldier
soo sow.
soople supple.
sooth south.
s'ore swore.
soul' sold.
sowl soul.
spak spoke.
spaking speaking.
spalpeen [Irish *spalpin*] a low or mean fellow, migratory laborer, rascal.
speir, spier inquire, ask.
Sperrins "the little sky." [s]
spoiled despoiled, stripped.
spree frolic, drinking bout.
spue spew, vomit.
stane stone.
staps stops.
stoun [stound] pang, throb, pain. [m]
stoupie whiskey jug. [s]
strame stream.
strang resolutely, vigorously; strong.
Strephon a fond lover. [s]
styin' staying.
suller beggarman.
swaggie (or swagman or sundowner) a man who tramps the country in Australia.
sweer lazy. [s:Dt]
swiper [swipe drink hastily and copiously, at one gulp].
swith quickly.
syne ago, since, then.
tae in (at), to.
ta'en, taen taken.
tae ither to one another.
ta'k talk.
tak, tak' take.
tap top.
tawnie tawny.
tay tea.
taypot teapot.
tear spree.
that day month the same day a month later.
theek thatch.
thegither together.
thim them.
thocht thought.
thole pin, peg.
thon that one; yonder.
thraw(ed) twist(ed).
threed thread.
tig a light but significant touch, a tap or pat.
till to.
tint lost. [s]
tirl rattle.
tirling at the pin rattling at the door latch.
toon town.
tost tossed.
toul told.
toun town.

tousie rumpled, disheveled, shaggy.
Tower the Martello Tower at Magilligan Pont. [s:Wp]
trate treat.
tricker trigger.
trig trim or tight in dress; neat, tidy, spruce, smart.
trinklin trickling.
trowed trusted, believed in.
tuk took.
twa two.
twarthree two or three.
twarthree hunner two or three hundred.
unco unusual, strange, extraordinary.
varmint noxious, objectionable animal, pest.
wadna would not.
wake ?weak.
waltzing Matilda a name for a commercial traveller's bag of samples.
wan one.
wasna, wasny was not.
waterstowps wooden pitchers. [s:Bp]
wauken'd wakened.
wean(s) young child(ren).
wee very small, tiny.
wee bit diminutive.
weel well.
weemen women.
wellow "a derivative from the same root word as willow, meaning bending or drooping" [s: Bp]
wha('s) who(se).
whaur where.
wi, wi', wid, wid' with.
widna, widna' would not.
wifukie wife.
windae window.
win' wind.
winna will not.
winnock window.
wist knew.
withoot without.
wounded suffering from love.
wud would.
wud hae would have.
wudnae would not.
wunner wonder.
'yellow man' [m:] a golden yellow homemade toffee, made in slabs and made amenable with a hammer.
yet(t) gate.
yin one.
yis yes.
yokin' subjugation, whipping into line.
yowes ewes
yt that.

Bibliography

Major bibliographical references

Bronson 1,1959; 2,1962; 3,1966; 4,1972
Bronson, Bertrand H. *The Traditional Tunes of the Child Ballads*. 4 vols. Princeton: Princeton Univ. Press, 1959-72.

b: Brunnings 1981
Brunnings, Florence E. *Folk Song Index: A comprehensive guide to the ... collection*. New York: Garland Publishing, Inc., 1981.

c: Cazden et al. *Notes* **1982**
Cazden, Norman, Herbert Haufrecht, Norman Studer, eds. *Notes and Sources for Folk Songs of the Catskills*. Albany: State University of New York Press, 1982.

Child 1882-98(1965)
Child, Francis James. *The English and Scottish Popular Ballads*. 5 vols., 10 parts. New York: Houghton, Mifflin & Co., reprint, 5 vols., Dover Publications, 1965.

Coffin/Renwick 1950(1977)
Coffin, Tristram Potter. *The British Traditional Ballad in North America*. Philadelphia: American Folklore Society, 1950; rev. ed. 1963; [3d ed.] with a supplement by Roger deV. Renwick. Austin: Univ. of Texas Press, 1977. Bibliographical and Special Series, Vol. 2.

Coffin 1958
Coffin, Tristram Potter. *An Analytical Index to the Journal of American Folklore: Vols. 1-67, 68, 69, 70*. Philadelphia: American Folklore Society, 1958. Bibliographical and Special Series, Vol. 7.

Dean-Smith 1954
Dean-Smith, Margaret. *A Guide to English Folk Song Collections, 1822-1952: With an index to their contents, historical annotations and an introduction*. Liverpool: Univ. Press of Liverpool in association with the English Folk Dance and Song Society, 1954.

Laws 1950(1964)
Laws, G. Malcolm, Jr. *Native American Balladry: A descriptive study and a bibliographical syllabus*. Austin: Univ. of Texas Press for the American Folklore Society, 1950; rev. ed. 1964. Bibliographical Series, Vol. 1.

Laws 1957
Laws, G. Malcolm, Jr. *American Ballads from British Broadsides: A guide for students and collectors of traditional song*. Philadelphia: American Folklore Society, 1957. Bibliographical and Special Series, Vol. 8.

White/Dean-Smith 1951
White, (Rev.) E. A., comp, and Margaret Dean-Smith, ed. *An Index of English Songs: Contributed to the Journal of the Folk Song Society, 1899-1931, and its continuation the Journal of the English Folk Dance and Song Society to 1950*. London: EFDSS, 1951.

cl: AAFS Check-List 1942
Check-List of Recorded Songs in the English Language in the Archive of American Folk Song to July, 1940. Washington, DC: Library of Congress, Music Division, 1942. Mimeographed, 3 vols. (A-K, L-Z, Geographical).
[Includes Archive recording number, performer, collector, place and date, indexed alphabetically by title and by place.]

lc: AAFS Record List 1953
A List of American Folk Songs Currently Available on Records. Compiled by the Archive of American Folk Song. Washington, DC: Library of Congress, 1953.
[Includes 78-rpm and early 33-1/3 rpm long-playing phonodiscs, not limited to AAFS recordings.]

General references

Abrahams 1970
Abrahams, Roger D. *A Singer and Her Songs: Almeda Riddle's Book of Ballads*. Baton Rouge, LA: Louisiana State Univ. Press, 1970.

Aitkin 1874
Aitkin, Mary Carlyle. *Scottish Song*. London: Macmillan & Co., 1874.

Allen 1899(1976)
Allen, Rosa S., and Joseph A. Allen. *Family Songs*. Ed. Tony Saletan. Newton, MA: Newton Bicentennial Committee, The Jackson Homestead, Newton Recreation Dept., 1976.

Allen *JEFDSS* **1954**
Allen, J. W. "Some Notes on 'O Waly Waly.'" *JEFDSS* 7(3)1954:161-71.

Allingham *Ceol* **1967**
Allingham, William. "Irish Ballad Singers and Street Ballads." *Ceol* 3(1)1967:2-20.
[orig. pub. 1852; see Shields *Hermathena* 1974, n. 2].

Allingham 1865.
Allingham, William. *The Ballad Book: A selection of the choicest British ballads*. Cambridge: Sever and Francis, 1865.

Anderson, Alistair: see Handle.

Anderson 1955 (1962)
Anderson, Hugh. *Colonial Ballads*. Ferntree Gully: Ram's Skull Press, 1955; 2d ed., Melbourne: F. W. Cheshire, 1962.

Anderson, Hugh: see also Meredith.

Arnold 1950
Arnold, Byron. *Folksongs of Alabama*. Birmingham: Univ. of Alabama Press, 1950.

Asch et al. 1973
Asch, Moses, Josh Dunson, and Ethel Raim, eds. *Anthology of American Folk Music: Songs transcribed from ... recorded performances ... that appear on the renowned Folkways recording Anthology of American Folk Music; with historical*

and folkloric commentary on each song. New York: Oak Publications, 1973.

Baker/Miall 1982
Baker, Richard, and Anthony Miall. *Everyman's Book of Sea Songs.* London: J. M. Dent & Sons, 1982.

Baldwin FMJ 1969
Baldwin, John R. "Songs in the Upper Thames Valley, 1966-1969." *FMJ* 1(5)1969:315-49.

Ballard, Elizabeth Flanders: see Flanders

Barbeau et al. 1947
Barbeau, Marius, Arthur Lismer, and Arthur Bourinot. *Come A Singing! Canadian folk-songs.* Ottawa: National Museum of Canada, National Museum of Man, 1947. National Museum of Canada, Bulletin #107, Anthropological Series #26.

Baring-Gould 1905[?]
Baring-Gould, S[abine]. *A Book of Nursery Songs and Rhymes.* London: Methuen & Co., 1905[?]; reprint, Detroit: Singing Tree Press, 1969.

Baring-Gould/Hitchcock 1974
Baring-Gould, Sabine, and Gordon Hitchcock. *Folk Songs of the West Country: Annotated from the MSS at Plymouth Library and with additional material ...* London: David & Charles, 1974.

Baring-Gould/Sharp [1906]
Baring-Gould, S[abine], and Cecil J. Sharp. *English Folk Songs for Schools.* London: J. Curwen & Sons, [1906].

Baring-Gould/Sheppard 1892 (2d ed., 1895)
Baring-Gould, S[abine], and H. Fleetwood Sheppard. *Songs and Ballads of the West: A collection made from the mouths of the people.* 4 parts. London: Methuen & Co., 1892; 2d ed., 1 vol., 1895.

Baring-Gould et al. 1905
Baring-Gould, S[abine], H. Fleetwood Sheppard, and F. W. Bussell. *Songs of the West: Folksongs of Devon and Cornwall collected from the mouths of the people.* London: Methuen & Co., orig. issued in 4 parts, 1890; rev. ed., 1 vol., 1905. [Later ed. of B-G/S 1892.]

Baring-Gould/Sheppard 1895
Baring-Gould, Sabine, and H. Fleetwood Sheppard. *A Garland of Country Song.* London: Methuen & Co., 1895; reprint, Norwood, PA: Norwood Editions, 1973.

Barnes SO 1956
Barnes, Lewis L. "'Hunting the Wren' Songs in the United States." *SO* 6(1 Win)1956:16-20. [p. 19, "Billy Barlow," 8 sts. from Pete Seeger]

Barrand CD&S 1981
Barrand, Anthony G. "Songs from the Hills of Vermont." *CD&S* 11/12, 1981:20-39.

Barrett [1891]
Barrett, William Alexander. *English Folk Songs.* London: Novello Ewer & Co. [1891]; reprint, Darby, PA: Norwood Editions, 1973.

Barry 1939
Barry, Phillips. *The Maine Woods Songster.* Cambridge, MA: Powell Printing Co., 1939.

Barry, Phillips: see also Flanders.

Barry et al. 1929
Barry, Phillips, Fannie Hardy Eckstorm, and Mary Winslow Smythe. *British Ballads from Maine: The development of popular songs with texts and airs.* New Haven, CT: Yale University Press, 1929.

Bartholomew, Marshall: see Wetmore.

Baskervill PMLA 1921
Baskervill, C. R. "English Songs of the Night Visit." *PMLA* 36,1921:565-614.

Beck 1957
Beck, Horace P[almer]. *The Folklore of Maine.* Philadelphia: J. B. Lippincott Co., 1957.

Beck 1962
Beck, Horace P[almer]. *Folklore in Action: Essays in honor of MacEdward Leach.* [?Philadelphia:] American Folklore Society, 1962.

Behan 1965
Behan, Dominic. *Ireland Sings.* London: Essex Music, 1965.

Behan 1967
Behan, Dominic. *The Singing Irish.* London: Scott Solomon Productions, 1967.

Belden 1940
Belden, Henry M., ed. *Ballads and Songs Collected by the Missouri Folk-Lore Society.* Columbia, MO: Univ. of Missouri, 1 Jan 1940; 2d ed., 1955. Univ. of Missouri Studies Vol. 15(1).

Belden, Henry M.: see also Brown.

Bell, Michael: see Copper.

Bell 1861
Bell, Robert, ed. *Ancient Poems Ballads and Songs of the Peasantry of England.* London: Griffin, Bohn & Co., 1861. [Reprint, Detroit, 1968.]

Bethke 1981
Bethke, Robert D. *Adirondack Voices: Woodsmen and woods lore.* Urbana, IL: Univ. of Illinois Press, 1981.

Bikel 1960
Bikel, Theo. *Folksongs and Footnotes: An international songbook.* New York: Meridian Books, 1960.

Black, Joan: see Holloway.

Boette [1971]
Boette, Marie, ed. *Singa Hipsy Doodle: And other folk songs of West Virginia.* Parkersburg, WV, [1971].

Bok 1977
Bok, Gordon. *Time and the Flying Snow.* Sharon, CT: Folk-Legacy Records, 1977.

Botkin 1949
Botkin, B. A. *A Treasury of Southern Folklore.* New York: Crown Publishers, 1949.

Bourinot, Arthur: see Barbeau.

Brady 1975
Brady, Eilís. *All In! All In!* Dublin: Comhairle Bealoideas Eireann, 1975.

Breathnach 1971
Breathnach, Breandán. *Folk Music and Dances of Ireland.* Dublin: Talbot Press, 1971.

Breathnach, Padraig: see Walsh.

Brewster 1940
Brewster, Paul G., ed. *Ballads and Songs of Indiana.* Bloomington: Indiana Univ., 1940. Indiana Univ. Publications, Folklore Series, No. 1.

Broadwood 1908
Broadwood, Lucy E., ed. *English Traditional*

Songs and Carols. London: Boosey & Co., 1908; reprint, Tatowa, NJ, 1974.

Broadwood/Maitland [1893]
Broadwood, Lucy E., and J. A. Fuller Maitland, eds. *English County Songs: Words and music.* London: J. B. Cramer & Co. [1893].

Brockleback/Kindersley 1948
Brocklebank, Joan, and Biddie Kindersley, eds. *A Dorset Book of Folk Songs.* London: English Folk Dance and Song Society, 1948.

Brown 1952-64: 2,1952; 4,1957
Brown, Frank C. *The Frank C. Brown Collection of North Carolina Folklore.* 7 vols. General ed. Newman Ivey White. Durham, N.C.: Duke University Press, 1952-64.
Vol. 2. *Folk Ballads from North Carolina.* Ed. Henry M. Belden and Arthur Palmer Hudson. 1952.
Vol. 4. *The Music of the Ballads.* Ed. Jan Philip Schinhan. 1957.

Brown, George: see Flanders.

Bruce/Stokoe 1882(1965)
Bruce, John Collingwood, and John Stokoe, eds. *Northumbrian Minstrelsy: A collection of the ballads, melodies, and small-pipe tunes of Northumbria.* Newcastle-upon-Tyne: Society of Antiquaries, 1882; reprint, with a Foreword by A. L. Lloyd, Hatboro, PA: Folklore Associates, 1965.

Bruford *Tocher* 1982
Alan Bruford. "Bring out Your Corpus!: Definitive Collections of Scottish and Irish Folk-Songs." *Tocher*, #36-7, 1981-2:460-5.

Brumley 1970
Brumley, Albert E. *Songs of the Pioneers: A collection of songs and ballads of the romantic past.* Camdentown, MO: Pioneer Song Book, 1970.

Brune 1965
Brune, John A. *The Roving Songster.* London: Gillian Cook, 1965.

P. Buchan 1828 1,2
Buchan, Peter. *Ancient Ballads and Songs of the North of Scotland: hitherto unpublished.* 2 vols. Edinburgh: W. & D. Laing, J. Stevenson, etc., 1828.

P. Buchan 1891[?]
Buchan, Peter. *Gleanings of ... Scarce Old Ballads.* ?Peterhead: P. Buchan, 1825? Aberdeen: D. Wyllie & Son, 1891; reprint, Norwood, PA: Norwood Editions, 1974.

N. Buchan 1962
Buchan, Norman. *101 Scottish Songs.* Glasgow: Collins, Scotia Books, 1962.

Buchan/Hall 1973
Buchan, Norman, and Peter Hall. *The Scottish Folksinger.* Glasgow: Collins, 1973.

Bunting 1840
Bunting, Edward. *The Ancient Music of Ireland.* Dublin: Hodges & Smith, 1840; reprint of combined editions (with *A General Collection of the Ancient Music of Ireland....* [London: N. Clementi & Co., 1809]; *The Ancient Music of Ireland* [Dublin: W. Power & Co., 1796]); Dublin: Walton's Piano and Musical Instrument Galleries, 1969.

Bunting/O'Sullivan *JIFSS* 22-9, 1926-32
O'Sullivan, Donal, ed. "The Bunting Collection of Irish Folk Music and Songs." *JIFSS* 22-9, 1926-32 [6 parts, incl. 2 double vols., dated 1926-32 but actually published 1927-3?].
[Covers the two earlier of the three published Bunting collections: 1796 and 1809.]

Bunting/O'Sullivan/Ó Suilleabhain 1983
O'Sullivan, Donal, and Micheál Ó Suilleabhain, eds. *Bunting's Ancient Music of Ireland: Edited from the original manuscripts....* Cork: Cork Univ. Press, 1983.

Burton/Manning 1967(1970)
Burton, Thomas G., and Ambrose N. Manning. *Folksongs.* Johnson City: Research Advisory Council of East Tennessee State Univ., 1967; 2d ed., 1970. The East Tennessee State University Collection of Folklore.

Burton/Manning 1969
Burton, Thomas G., and Ambrose N. Manning. *Folksongs II.* Johnson City: Research Advisory Council of East Tennessee State Univ., 1969. The East Tennessee State University Collection of Folklore.

Burton 1978
Burton, Thomas G. *Some Ballad Folks.* Boone, NC: Appalachian Consortium Press, 1981; orig. pub. East Tennessee State University, 1978.
[Biographies of and songs from five women from Beech Mountain, NC: Rena Hicks, Buna Hicks, Hattie Presnell, Lena Harmon, Bertha Baird.] [See also cassette rec.]

Burton 1981
Burton, Thomas G., ed. *Tom Ashley, Sam McGee, Bukka White: Tennessee traditional singers.* (Tom Ashley by Ambrose N. Manning and Minnie M. Miller; Sam McGee by Charles K. Wolfe; Bukka White by F. Jack Hurley and David Evans.) Knoxville: Univ. of Tennessee Press, 1981.

Bush 1,1969; 2,1970; 3,1975; 4,1977; 5,n.d.
Bush, Michael E. *Folk Songs of Central West Virginia.* 5 vols. Glenville, WV: Michael E. Bush.

Bussell, F. W.: see Baring-Gould.

Butterworth 1974
Butterworth, George. *Folk Songs from Sussex and other songs by ...* London: Galliard / Stainer & Bell, 1974.

Butterworth, George: see also Dawney.

Calliope 1788
Calliope or, The Musical Miscellany: A select collection of the most approved English, Scots, and Irish songs set to music. London: C. Elliot & T. Kay, 1788.

Carey 1915
Carey, Clive, ed. *Ten English Folk Songs.* London: J. Curwen & Sons, 1915.

Carlton n.d.
Carlton Folk Songs. Glasgow: Mozart Allen, n.d.

Carroll *FMJ* 1975
Carroll, Jim. "Irish Travellers around London." *FMJ* 3(1)1975:31-40.

Cazden 1958 1,2
Cazden, Norman. *The Abelard Folk Song Book.* 2 parts in 1 vol. [separately paginated] New York: Abelard Schuman, 1958.

Cazden et al. 1982
Cazden, Norman, Herbert Haufrecht, and Norman

Studer, eds. *Folk Songs of the Catskills*. Albany: State University of New York [Press], 1982.

Chambers 1829
Chambers, Robert. *The Scottish Ballads*. Edinburgh: William Tait, 1829.

Chambers 1829 1,2
Chambers, Robert. *Scottish Songs*. 2 vols. Edinburgh: William Tait, 1829; reprint, 1 vol. continuously paginated, New York: AMS Press, 1975.

Chambers [1841]
Chambers, Robert. *Popular Rhymes of Scotland*. 3d ed. Edinburgh: W. & R. Chambers, [1841].

Chambers 1880
Chambers, Robert, ed. *The Songs of Scotland: Prior to Burns, with the tunes*. Edinburgh: W. & R. Chambers, 1880.

Chappell 1939
Chappell, Louis W. *Folk-Songs of Roanoke and the Albemarle*. Morgantown, WV: Ballad Press, 1939.

Chase 1956
Chase, Richard. *American Folk Tales and Songs: And other examples of English-American tradition as preserved in the Appalachian mountains and elsewhere in the United States*. New York: New American Library, Signet Key Books, 1956.

Cheney et al. 1976
Cheney, Joyce, Marcia Diehl, and Deborah Silverstein, eds. *All Our Lives: A women's songbook*. Baltimore: Diana Press, 1976.

Chickering, Geraldine Jenks: see Gardner.

Christie 1,1876; 2,1881
Christie, W[illiam], ed. *Traditional Ballad Airs*. 2 vols. Edinburgh: Edmonston & Douglas, 1876, 1881.

Clancy Bros. 1964
The Clancy Brothers and Tommy Makem Song Book. New York: Oak Publications, 1964.

Clancy Bros.: see also Graeme.

Clayre 1968
Clayre, Alasdair. *100 Folk Songs and New Songs*. London: Wolfe Publishing, 1968.

Clements 1928
Clements, Rex. *Manavilins: A muster of sea songs: As distinguished from shanties, written for the most part by seamen, and sung on board ship during the closing years of the Age of Sail, 1890-1910*. London: Heath Cranton, 1928; reprint, Norwood, PA: Norwood Editions, 1975.

Clifford 1957
Clifford, Teresa. *An Irish Folksinger's Album*. London: J. Curwen & Sons, 1957.

Cohen/Seeger 1964
Cohen, John, and Mike Seeger; Hally Wood, music editor. *The New Lost City Ramblers Song Book*. New York: Oak Publications, 1964.

Cohen, Norm: see Randolph.

Colcord 1938
Colcord, Joanna C. *Songs of American Sailormen*. Enl., rev. ed., New York: W. W. Norton & Co., 1938; reprint, New York: Oak Publications, 1964; New York: Clarkson N. Potter, Bramhall House, n.d. (Orig. pub. *Roll and Go: Songs of American Sailormen*. Indianapolis: Bobbs-Merrill Co., 1924)

Collins 1940
Collins, Fletcher, Jr. *Alamance Play-Party Songs and Singing Games*. Elon College, N.C., 1940; reprint, Norwood, PA, 1973.

Collinson/Dillon [1946]
Collinson, Francis M., and Francis Dillon. *Songs from the Countryside: As featured in Country Magazine*. Book 1. London: W. Paxton & Co. [1946].

Collinson/Dillon 1952
Collinson, Francis M., and Francis Dillon. *Folk Songs from Country Magazine*. London: W. Paxton & Co., 1952.

Combs (1925)1967
Combs, Josiah H. *Folk Songs of the Southern United States*. Austin: Univ. of Texas Press for the American Folklore Society, 1967. (Orig. pub. *Folk-Songs du Midi des Etats-Unis*. Doctoral dissertation, Univ. of Paris, 1925.)

Copper 1971
Copper, Bob. *A Song for Every Season: A hundred years of a Sussex farming family*. London: William Heinemann Ltd., 1971.

Copper 1973
Copper, Bob. *Songs and Southern Breezes: Country folk and country ways*. London: William Heinemann Ltd., 1973.

Copper/Bell JEFDSS 1961
Copper, Bob, coll.; Michael Bell, transcriber. "Five Songs from Hampshire and One from Sussex." *JEFDSS* 9(2)1961:72-80.

Costello 1923
Costello, [Eibhlin], ed. *Amhrain Mhuighe Seola: Traditional folk-songs from Galway and Mayo*. Dublin: Talbot Press, 1923.

Cox 1925
Cox, John Harrington, ed. *Folk-Songs of the South: Collected under the auspices of the West Virginia Folk-Lore Society*. Cambridge, MA: Harvard Univ. Press, 1925; reprint, New York: Dover Publications, 1967.

Cox 1939(1964)
Cox, John Harrington. *Traditional Ballads and Folk-Songs Mainly from West Virginia*. New York, 1939. Ed. George Herzog, Herbert Halpert (1939), George W. Boswell (1964). Philadelphia: American Folklore Society, 1964. Bibliographical and Special Series, Vol. 15.
[Orig. 2 mimeographed booklets, "Traditional Ballads Mainly from West Virginia" and "Folk-Songs Mainly from West Virginia" issued by the Works Progress Adminstration, Federal Theatre Project, National Service Bureau; pages renumbered.]

Crawhall 1888 (1965)
Crawhall, Joseph, coll. *A Beuk o' Newcassel Sangs* [1888]. Reprint, Newcastle-upon-Tyne: Harold Hill, 1965.

Cray 1969
Cray, Ed, ed. *The Erotic Muse*. New York: Oak Publications, 1969; reprint, New York: Pyramid Communications ("Pyramid Special"), 1972.

Creighton 1932(1966)
Creighton, Helen. *Songs and Ballads from Nova Scotia*. Toronto: J. M. Dent & Sons, 1932; corrected reprint, New York: Dover Publications, 1966.

Creighton 1961
Creighton, Helen. *Maritime Folk Songs*. Toronto: Ryerson Press, 1961; reprint, Toronto: McGraw-Hill Ryerson, 1972; reprint, Breakwater, 1979.

Creighton 1971
Creighton, Helen. *Folksongs from Southern New Brunswick*. Ottawa: National Museums of Canada, 1971. National Museum of Man, Publications in Folk Culture, No. 1.

Creighton, Helen: see also Senior.

Creighton/Senior 1950
Creighton, Helen, and Doreen H. Senior. *Traditional Songs from Nova Scotia*. Toronto: Ryerson Press, 1950.

Croker 1839
Croker, T. Clifton. *The Popular Songs of Ireland*. London: Henry Colburn, 1839.

Daiken 1949
Daiken, Leslie. *Children's Games throughout the Year*. New York: B. T. Batsford, 1945.

Dallas 1972
Dallas, Karl, comp. *The Cruel Wars: 100 soldiers' songs from Agincourt to Ulster*. London: Wolfe Publishing Ltd., 1972.

Darley/McCall 1914
Darley, Arthur, and P. J. McCall. *The Feis Ceoil Collection of Irish Airs: Hitherto Unpublished*. Dublin: Feis Ceoil Association, 1914.

Darling 1983
Darling, Charles W., ed. *The New American Songster: Traditional ballads and songs of North America*. Lanham, MD: Univ. Press of America, 1983.

Davis 1929
Davis, Arthur Kyle, Jr. *Traditional Ballads of Virginia: Collected under the auspices of the Virginia Folk-Lore Society*. Cambridge, MA: Harvard Univ. Press, 1929.

Davis 1949
Davis, Arthur Kyle, Jr. *Folk-Songs of Virginia: A descriptive index and classification of material collected under the auspices of the Virginia Folk-Lore Society*. Durham, NC: Duke Univ. Press, 1949.

Davis 1960
Davis, Arthur Kyle, Jr., ed. *More Traditional Ballads of Virginia: Collected with the cooperation of members of the Virginia Folk-Lore Society*. Chapel Hill, NC: Univ. of North Carolina Press, 1960.

Davis, Beryl: see *Spin*.

Davis/Tozer n.d.
Davis, Frederick J., and Ferris Tozer. *Fifty Sailors' Songs or Chanties*. 3d rev. ed., London: Boosey & Co., n.d.

Dawney FMJ 1976
Dawney, Michael. "George Butterworth's Folk Music Manuscripts." *FMJ* 3(2)1976:99-113.

Dawney 1977
Dawney, Michael, ed. *The Ploughboy's Glory: A selection of hitherto unpublished folk songs collected by George Butterworth*. London: EFDSS, 1977.

Dean [1922]
Dean, M[ichael] C[assius], compiler. *The Flying Cloud: And 150 other old-time songs and ballads of outdoor men, sailors, lumberjacks, soldiers, men of the Great Lakes, railroadmen, miners, etc.* Virginia, MN: The Quickprint, 1922; reprint, Norwood, PA: Norwood Editions, 1973.

DeVille/Gould n.d.
DeVille, Paul, and Maurice Gould. *The Violin Player's Pastime: A collection of 355 popular and standard airs, jigs, reels, hornpipes and miscellaneous dances for violin*. New York: Carl Fischer, n.d.

Dillon n.d. [1948?]
Dillon, Francis, ed. *Country Magazine: Book of the BBC Programme*. London: Long Acre: Odhams Press, n.d. [1948?]

Dillon, Francis: see also Collinson.

Doerflinger 1951
Doerflinger, William Main. *Shantymen and Shantyboys: Songs of the sailor and lumberman*. New York: Macmillan Co., 1951.

Duffy 1866[?]
Duffy, Charles Gavin. *The Ballad Poetry of Ireland*. Dublin: James Duffy, [1845?] 1866.

Duncan 1967
Duncan, James B. *Folk Songs of Aberdeenshire*. Ed. P. N. Shuldham-Shaw. London: EFDSS, 1967.

Duncan, (Rev.) James B.: see also Greig.

Dunn 1980
Dunn, Ginette. *The Fellowship of Song: Popular singing traditions in East Suffolk*. London: Croom Helm Ltd., 1980.

Dunson, Josh: see Raim.

Dunstan 1932 (1972)
Dunstan, Ralph. *Cornish Dialect and Folk Songs: A sequel to the Cornish Song Book*. London: As[c]herburg, Hopwood & Crew, 1932; reprint, Padstow: Lodenek Padstow, 1972.

D'Urfey 1719-20(1959)
D'Urfey, Thomas. *Wit and Mirth, or Pills to Purge Melancholy*. 6 vols. London, 1719-20; reprint, 3 vols., Hatboro, PA: Folklore Associates, 1959.

Dyer-Bennet 1971
Dyer-Bennet, Richard. *The ... Folk Song Book: 50 traditional songs & ballads with guitar accompaniments by ...* New York: Simon and Schuster, 1971.

Eckstorm, Fannie Hardy: see also Barry.

Eckstorm/Smyth 1927
Eckstorm, Fannie Hardy, and Mary Winslow Smyth. *Minstrelsy of Maine*. Boston: Houghton Mifflin Co., 1927; reprint, Ann Arbor, MI: Gryphon Books, 1971.

Eddy 1939
Eddy, Mary O. *Ballads and Songs from Ohio*. New York: J. J. Augustin, 1939; reprint, Hatboro, PA: Folklore Associates, 1964.

Edwards 1966
Edwards. Ron. *Folksong and Ballad: Part two of the Overlander Songbook*. Holloways Beach, N. Queensland, Australia: Rams Skull Press, 1966.

Fahey 1977
Warren Fahey, comp. *Pint Pot and Billy: A selection of Australian and New Zealand folksongs.*

Sydney: William Collins Publishers Pty. Ltd., 1977.

Fanning, J. Eaton: see Hutton.

Father Kemp's 1917
Father Kemp's Old Folks Concert Tunes: A collection of the most favorite tunes of Billings, Swan, Holden, Read, Kimball, Ingalls and others. To which is added a variety of anthems and choruses and divers patriotic and other songs of the greatest and best composers. Rev., enl. ed. Boston: Oliver Ditson & Co., 1889.

Firth 1908
Firth, C. H. *Naval Songs and Ballads.* London: Navy Records Society, 1908.

Fitzpatrick 1963
Fitzpatrick, W. J., ed. *An Old-Timer Talking: Reminisces and Stories Narrated by Hugh Marks of Kilkeel.* Newcastle, Co. Down: 1963.

Fitzwilliam (1963) 1, 2
Maitland, J. A. Fuller, and W. Barclay Squire, eds. *Fitzwilliam Virginal Book.* 2 vols. Reprint, New York: Dover Publications, 1963.

Flanders 1934
Flanders, Helen Hartness, ed. *A Garland of Green Mountain Song.* Boston: E. C. Schirmer Music Co., 1934. Green Mountain Pamphlets #1.

Flanders 1937
Flanders, Helen Hartness. *Country Songs of Vermont.* New York: G. Schirmer, 1937. Schirmer's American Folk-Song Series, Set 19.

Flanders 1,1960; 2,1961; 3,1963; 4,1965
Flanders, Helen Hartness, ed. *Ancient Ballads Traditionally Sung in New England.* 4 vols. Philadelphia: Univ. of Pennsylvania Press, 1961-5.
Vol. 1 (Child #s 1-53), 1960.
Vol. 2 (Child #s 53-93), 1961.
Vol. 3 (Child #s 95-243), 1963.
Vol. 4 (Child #s 250-95), 1965.

Flanders/Brown 1931
Flanders, Helen Hartness, and George Brown. *Vermont Folk-Songs and Ballads.* Brattleboro, VT: Stephen Daye Press, 1931; reprint, Hatboro, PA: Folklore Associates, 1968.

Flanders/Olney 1953
Flanders, Helen Hartness, and Margaret Olney. *Ballads Migrant in New England.* New York: Farrar, Straus & Young 1953; reprint, Freeport, N.Y.: Books for Libraries Press, 1968.

Flanders et al. 1939
Flanders, Helen Hartness, Elizabeth Flanders Ballard, George Brown, and Phillips Barry, eds. *The New Green Mountain Songster: Traditional folk songs of Vermont.* New Haven, CT: Yale Univ. Press, 1939; reprint, Hatboro, PA: Folklore Associates, 1966.

I. Ford 1940
Ford, Ira. *Traditional Music in America.* New York: E. P. Dutton & Co., 1940; reprint, Hatboro, PA: Folklore Associates, 1965.

R. Ford n.d.
Ford, Robert. *A Budget of Auld Scots Ballads.* Boston, Mass., n.p., n.d.

R. Ford 1,1899; 2,1901; 2d ed., 1904
Ford, Robert. *Vagabond Songs and Ballads of Scotland.* 2 series. Paisley: Alexander Gardner, 1899, 1901. [2d ed., 1 vol., 1904.]

R. Ford 1900
Ford, Robert. *Song Histories.* Glasgow: Wm. Hodge & Co., 1900.

Fowke 1965
Fowke, Edith. *Traditional Singers and Songs from Ontario.* Hatboro, PA: Folklore Associates, 1965; reprint, Detroit: Gale Research Co., n.d.

Fowke 1970
Fowke, Edith. *Lumbering Songs from the Northern Woods.* Austin: Univ. of Texas Press for the American Folklore Society, 1970. Memoir Series, Vol. 55.

Fowke 1973
Fowke, Edith F., comp. *The Penguin Book of Canadian Folksongs.* Baltimore: Penguin Books, 1973.

Fowke 1981
Fowke, Edith, ed. *Sea Songs and Ballads from Nineteenth Century Nova Scotia: The William H. Smith and Fenwick Hatt manuscripts.* New York: Folklorica Press, 1981.

Fowke/Glazer 1960
Fowke, Edith, and Joe Glazer. *Songs of Work and Freedom.* Chicago: Roosevelt Univ., 1960; reprint, Garden City, NY: Doubleday & Co., Dolphin Books, 1961.

Fowke/Johnston 1954
Fowke, Edith Fulton, and Richard Johnston, eds. *Folk Songs of Canada.* Waterloo, Ont.: Waterloo Music Co., 1954.

Fox 1910
Fox, C. Milligan. *Songs of the Irish Harpers.* New York: G. Schirmer, 1910.

FST 2,1969
Folk Song Today, No. 2. Ed. Tony Wales. London: EFDS Publications, 1969.

Fuld 1966
Fuld, James J. *The Book of World-Famous Music: Classical, Popular and Folk.* New York: Crown Publishers, 1966.

Fuson 1931
Fuson, Harvey H. *Ballads of the Kentucky Highlands.* London: Mitre Press, 1931.

Gainer 1975
Gainer, Patrick W. *Folk Songs from the West Virginia Hills.* Grantsville, WV: Seneca Books, 1975.

Gallagher/Peroni 1936
Gallagher, Elizabeth L., and Carlo Peroni. *Irish Songs and Airs.* Toms River, NJ, 1936.

Galvin [?1956]
Galvin, Patrick [pseud. of S. F. Hagan]. *Irish Songs of Resistance, 1169-1923.* New York: Folklore Press [?1956]; reprint, New York: Oak Publications, 1962.

Galwey 1910
Galwey, Honoria. *Old Irish Croonauns and Other Tunes.* London: Boosey & Co., 1910; reprint, Norwood, PA: Norwood Editions, 1975.

Gardner/Chickering 1939
Gardner, Emelyn Elizabeth, and Geraldine Jenks Chickering, eds. *Ballads and Songs of Southern Michigan.* Ann Arbor: Univ. of Michigan Press, 1939; reprint, Hatboro, PA: Folklore Associates, 1967.

Gems 1894
Gems of Scottish Songs. Boston: Oliver Ditson Co., 1894.

Gilchrist JEFDSS 1932
Gilchrist, Anne G. "Lambkin: A study in evolution." *JEFDSS* 1(1)1932:1-17 [reprint in Leach/Coffin 1961:204-24].

Gilchrist JEFDSS 1934
Gilchrist, Anne G. "A New Light upon the Londonderry Air." *JEFDSS* 1(3)1934:115-21.

Gilfellon, Tom: see Handle.

Glazer, Joe: see Fowke.

Glen 1900
Glen, John, ed. *Early Scottish Melodies.* Edinburgh: 1900.

Godman JEFDSS 1964
Godman, Stanley. "The 'West Sussex Gazette' Song Competition of 1904." *JEFDSS* 9(5)1964:269-73.

Gomme 1894 (1964) 1,2
Gomme, Alice Bertha, ed. *The Traditional Games of England, Scotland and Ireland: With tunes, singing-rhymes, and methods of playing according to the variants extant and recorded in different parts of the kingdom.* 2 vols. London: David Nutt, 1894; 1898; reprint, New York: Dover Publications, 1964.

Gould, Maurice: see DeVille.

Graeme 1971
Graeme, Joy, ed. *The Irish Songbook: Collected, adapted, written and sung by the Clancy Brothers and Tommy Makem.* New York: Macmillan Co. (Collier Books), 1971.

Graham EB 1929
Graham, John (L.T.S.C., Chairman of the Tonic Sol-Fa Association). "Tonic Sol-Fa." Pp. 283-4 in *The Encyclopaedia Britannica* (14th ed., New York: 1929).

Grainger 1966
Grainger, Percy. *Seven Lincolnshire Folk Songs.* Ed. Patrick O'Shaughnessy. London: Oxford Univ. Press, 1966.

Graves 1880
Graves, Alfred Perceval. *Irish Songs and Ballads.* Manchester: Alexander Ireland & Co., 1880.

Graves 1895
Graves, Alfred Perceval. *The Irish Song Book.* Dublin: Sealy, Bryers & Walker, 1895.

Graves et al. n.d.
Graves, Alfred Perceval, et al. *Irish Countryside Songs.* 3 vols. London: Stainer & Bell, n.d.

Gray 1924
Gray, Roland Palmer. *Songs and Ballads of the Maine Lumberjacks: With other songs from Maine.* Cambridge, MA: Harvard Univ. Press, 1924; reprint, Detroit, 1969.

Greenleaf/Mansfield 1933
Greenleaf, Elisabeth Bristol, and Grace Yarrow Mansfield., eds. *Ballads and Sea Songs of Newfoundland.* Cambridge, MA: Harvard Univ. Press 1933; reprint, Detroit, Gale Research Co., n.d.

Greig 1906(1963)
Greig, Gavin. *Folk-Song in Buchan.* New Deer: Buchan Field Club, 1906; reprint, 1 vol. with *Folk-Song of the North-East,* Hatboro, PA: Folklore Associates, 1963. Transactions of the Buchan Field Club, Vol. 9.

Greig 1907-11(1963)
Greig, Gavin. *Folk-Song of the North-East.* Peterhead: *Buchan Observer,* 1907-11; [m:] reprint, 2 vols., limited ed. (42 copies), Buchan Club, 1909, 1914; reprint, 1 vol. with *Folk-Song in Buchan,* Hatboro, PA: Folklore Associates, 1963.

Greig/Duncan 1,1981; 2,1983
Greig, Gavin, and (Rev.) James B. Duncan, colls. *The Greig-Duncan Folk Song Collection.* Ed. Patrick Shuldham-Shaw and Emily B. Lyle. Aberdeen: Aberdeen Univ. Press.
Vol. 1. 1981.
Vol. 2. 1983.

Greig/Keith 1925
Greig, Gavin, and Alexander Keith. *Last Leaves of Traditional Ballads.* Aberdeen: Buchan Club, 1925.

Griggs, Anne: see Grover.

Grover n.d.
Grover, Carrie B. *A Heritage of Songs.* Ed. Anne L. Griggs. Bethel, ME: Gould Academy, n.d.; reprint, Norwood, PA: Norwood Editions, [1973].

DgF
Grundtvig, Svend, Axel Olrik, H. Gruner-Nielson, and others (editors in succession). *Danmarks Gamle Folkeviser.* 10 vols., 1853-1923. Vol. 11, tunes; Vol. 12, indexes. Copenhagen: Universitets-Jubilaeets Danske Samfund, 1976.

Gundry 1966
Gundry, Inglis, ed. *Canow Kernow: Songs and dances from Cornwall.* Federation of Old Cornwall Societies, 1966.

Guthrie/Lampell 1958, 1960
Guthrie, Woody. *California to the New York Island: Being a pocketful of brags, blues, bad man ballads, love songs, Okie laments and children's catcalls* by ... woven into a script suitable for a concert, clambake, hootenanny or community sing by Millard Lampell. New York: Oak Publications for the Guthrie Children's Trust Fund, 1958, 1960.

Hagan, S. F.: see Galvin.

Hall FMJ 1975
Hall, Peter A. "Scottish Tinker Songs." *FMJ* 3(1)1975:41-62.

Hall, Peter: see also Buchan.

Hamer 1967
Hamer, Fred. *Garners Gay.* London: EFDS Publications, 1967.

Hamer 1973
Hamer, Fred. *Green Groves.* London: EFDS Press, 1973.

Hammond 1978
Hammond, David, ed. *Songs of Belfast.* Dublin: Gilbert Dalton, 1978.

Handle et al. 1972
Handle, Johnny, Colin Ross, Alistair Anderson, and Tom Gilfellon. *The High Level Ranters Song and Tune Book.* Norfolk: Galliard, 1972.

Hardebeck 1908 1,2
Hardebeck, Carl. *Gems of Melody.* 2 parts. Belfast: The Author, 1908.

Bibliography

Harlow 1962
Harlow, Frederick Pease. *Chanteying aboard American Ships.* Barre, MA: *Barre Gazette*, 1962.

Harte 1978
Harte, Frank, ed. *Songs of Dublin.* Dublin: Gilbert Dalton, 1978.

Haskins n.d.
Haskins, Mattie. *Ireland's Famous Songs.* New York, n.p., n.d.

Hatton/Fanning [189?-]
Hatton, J. L., and Eaton Fanning. *The Songs of England.* 2 vols. New York: W. A. Pond & Co. [1892?]

Haufrecht, Herbert: see Cazden.

Hayward 1925
Hayward, H. Richard. *Ulster Songs and Ballads: Of the Town and Country.* London: Duckworth, 1925.

Heart Songs 1909
Heart Songs. [Ed. Joe Mitchell Chapple] New York: World Syndicate Co., 1909.

Henderson et al. 1979
Henderson, Kathy, with Frankie Armstrong and Sandra Kerr. *My Song Is My Own: 100 Women's Songs.* London: Pluto Press, 1979.

Henry 1938
Henry, Mellinger E. *Folk-Songs from the Southern Highlands.* New York: J. J. Augustin, 1938.

Henry, Mellinger Edward: see also Matteson.

Herd 1776 1,2
Herd, David. *Ancient and Modern Scottish Songs, Heroic Ballads, etc.* 2 vols. Edinburgh: John Wotherspoon, 1776; reprint, Glasgow: Kerr & Richardson, 1869.

Herzog, George: see Hudson.

Hogg 1,1819; 2,1821
Hogg, James. *The Jacobite Relics of Scotland: Being the songs airs, and legends of the adherents to the House of Stuart.* 2 series. Edinburgh: William Blackwood, 1819, 1821.

Holloway/Black 1975
Holloway, John, and Joan Black, eds. *Later English Broadside Ballads.* London: Routledge & Kegan Paul, 1975.

Hood 1982
Hood, Mantle. *The Ethnomusicologist.* New ed., Kent, OH: Kent State Univ. Press, 1982. (1st ed., McGraw-Hill Inc., 1971.)
[Illustration 2-26, p. 80, gives "Greensleeves" in tonic sol-fa notation.]

Hubbard 1961
Hubbard, Lester A. *Ballads and Songs from Utah.* Salt Lake City: Univ. of Utah Press, 1961.

Hudson 1936
Hudson, Arthur Palmer. *Folksongs of Mississippi: And their background.* Chapel Hill, NC: Univ. of North Carolina Press, 1936.

Hudson, Arthur Palmer: see also Brown.

Hudson/Herzog 1937
Hudson, Arthur Palmer, and George Herzog. *Folk Tunes from Mississippi.* New York: National Play Bureau, Works Progress Administration, Federal Theatre Project, July 1937. National Play Bureau, Publication #25.

Hughes 1,1909; 2,1915; 3,1934; 4,1936
Hughes, Herbert. *Irish Country Songs.* 4 vols. London: Boosey & Hawkes, 1909-36.

Hughes, Robert: see Sturgis.

Hugill 1961
Hugill, Stan. *Shanties from the Seven Seas.* London: Routledge & Kegan Paul, 1961.

Hugill 1969
Hugill, Stan. *Shanties and Sailors' Songs.* New York: Frederick A. Praeger, 1969.

Hugill 1977a
Hugill, Stan. *Songs of the Sea.* Maidenhead, England: McGraw-Hill Book Co., 1977.

Hugill 1977b
Hugill, Stan. *Sea Shanties.* London: Barrie & Jenkins, 1977.

Huntington 1964
Huntington, Gale. *Songs the Whalemen Sang.* Barre, MA: Barre Publishers, 1964; reprint (with index) New York: Dover Publications, 1970.

Huntington 1966
Huntington, Gale. *Folksongs from Martha's Vineyard.* Orono, ME: Northeast Folklore Society, 1967. *NEF* 8,1966.

Hurl, Michael: see Ó Maoláin.

Hutchings 1976
Hutchings, Ashley, ed. *A Little Music: A collection of folk songs, instrumental tunes and dances.* London: Island Music, 1976.

B. Ives 1955
Ives, Burl. *Irish Songs.* New York: Duell, Sloan & Pierce, 1955.

E. Ives 1963
Ives, Edward D. *Twenty-One Folksongs from Prince Edward Island.* Orono, ME: Northeast Folklore Society, 1964. *NEF* 5,1963.

E. Ives 1965
Ives, Edward D. *Folksongs from Maine.* Orono, ME: Northeast Folklore Society, 1966. *NEF* 7,1965.

H. Johnson 1881
Johnson, Helen Kendrick. *Our Familiar Songs and Those Who Made Them.* New York: Henry Holt & Co., 1881.

J. Johnson (1853) 1-4
Johnson, James. *The Scots Musical Museum.* Ed. William Stenhouse. New ed., 4 vols. Edinburgh: William Blackwood & Sons, 1853. (Orig. pub. 6 vols. by James Johnson, Edinburgh, 1787-1803. Reprint, 2 vols., Hatboro, PA: Folklore Associates, 1962.)

Johnston, Richard: see Fowke.

Jones/Hawes 1972
Jones, Bessie, and Bess Lomax Hawes. *Step It Down: Games, plays, songs and stories from the Afro-American heritage.* New York: Harper & Row, 1972.

Jordan 1946
Jordan, Phillip D. *Singin' Yankees.* Minneapolis: Univ. of Minnesota Press, 1946.

Joyce 1873
Joyce, P[atrick] W[eston], ed. *Ancient Irish Music.* Dublin: McGlashan & Gill, 1873; reprint, M. H. Gill & Son, 1912.

Joyce 1909
Joyce, P[atrick] W[eston]. *Old Irish Folk Music and Songs.* New York: Longmans Green & Co., 1909; reprint, New York: Cooper Square Publishers, 1965.

Karpeles [1934]
Karpeles, Maud, ed. *Folk Songs from Newfoundland.* London: Oxford Univ. Press [1934].

Karpeles *JEFDSS* 1951
Karpeles, Maud. "A Return Visit to the Appalachian Mountains." *JEFDSS* 6(3)1951:77-82.

Karpeles 1970
Karpeles, Maud, ed. *Folk Songs from Newfoundland.* Hamden, CT: Archon Books, 1970. [Incorporates contents of Karpeles [1934].]

Karpeles, Maud: see also Sharp.

Keith, Alexander: see Greig.

Kelly 1964
Kelly, Stan. *Liverpool Lullabies: The Stan Kelly Song Book.* London: Heathside/*SING*, 1964.

Kenedy 1890[?]
Kenedy, J. P. *The Universal Irish Song Book.* New York: J. P. Kenedy, 1890[?].

Kennedy 1975
Kennedy, Peter. *Folksongs of Britain and Ireland.* New York: Schirmer Books, 1975.

Kerr's Cornkisters 1950
Kerr's "Cornkisters" (Bothy Ballads): As sung and recorded by Willie Kemp. Glasgow: James S. Kerr, 1950.

Kidson 1891(1970)
Kidson, Frank. *Traditional Tunes: A collection of ballad airs.* Oxford: Chas. Taphouse & Son, 1891; reprint, with a new Foreword by A. E. Green, East Ardsley (Yorkshire): SR Publishers, 1970.

Kidson 1916
Kidson, Frank. *100 Singing Games, Old, New and Adapted.* London: Bayley & Ferguson, 1916.

Kidson, Frank: see also Moffat.

Kidson/Moffat [1926]
Kidson, Frank, and Alfred Moffat. *A Garland of English Folk Songs.* London: Ascherberg, Hopwood & Crew, [1926].

Kidson/Moffat [1929]
Kidson, Ethel, and Alfred Moffat, eds. *English Peasant Songs: With their traditional airs ... from the Frank Kidson collection.* London: Ascherberg, Hopwood & Crew, [1929].

Kilkerr *FMJ* 1977
Kilkerr, Dave. "Sam Henry and 'Songs of the People.'" *FMJ* 3(3)1977:208-32. [Reprinted in *Treoir* 12(1)1980:9-18 with musical examples redrawn and in different order. Preceded by short article by Len Graham, "New Book from Blackstaff Press."]

Kincaid 1928
Kincaid, Bradley. *My Favorite Mountain Ballads and Old-Time Songs.* Chicago: Radio Station WLS, 1928.

Kincaid 1,1929; 2,1930
Kincaid, Bradley. *Favorite Old-Time Songs and Mountain Ballads.* 2 books. Chicago: Radio Station WLS, 1929, 1930.

Kindersley, Biddie: see Brocklebank.

Korson 1949
Korson, George. *Pennsylvania Songs and Legends.* Philadelphia: Univ. of Pennsylvania Press, 1949.

Lahey 1965
Lahey, John. *Australian Favorite Ballads.* New York: Oak Publications, 1965.

Lampell, Millard: see Guthrie.

LC Folk Music (1958)
Folk Music: A catalog of folk songs, ballads, dances, instrumental pieces, and folk tales of the United States and Latin America on phonograph records. Washington, DC: Library of Congress, Music Division (1958, 1964). [Includes full contents for each record, and alphabetical title, geographical indexes.]

M. Leach 1965
Leach, MacEdward. *Folk Ballads and Songs of the Lower Labrador Coast.* Ottawa: National Museum of Canada, 1965. National Museum of Canada Bulletin No. 201, Anthropological Series No. 68.

M. Leach 1967
Leach, MacEdward, ed. *The (Heritage) Book of Ballads.* New York: Heritage Press (George Macy Co.), 1967.

M. Leach/Coffin 1961
Leach, MacEdward, and Tristram P. Coffin, eds. *The Critics and the Ballad: Readings.* Carbondale: Southern Illinois Univ. Press, 1961.

R. Leach/Palmer 1978
Leach, Robert, and Roy Palmer, eds. *Folk Music in School.* Cambridge: Cambridge Univ. Press, 1978.

Linscott 1939
Linscott, Eloise Hubbard. *Folk Songs of Old New England.* New York: Macmillan Co., 1939; reprint, London: Archon Books, 1962.

Lismer, Arthur: see Barbeau.

Lloyd, A. L.: see also Vaughan Williams.

Lloyd 1952
Lloyd, A. L. *Come All Ye Bold Miners: Ballads and songs of the coalfields.* London: Lawrence & Wishart, 1952.

Lloyd 1967
Lloyd, A. L. *Folk Song in England.* New York: International Publishers, 1967. [Orig. pub.: *The Singing Englishman* (London: Workers' Music Association, 1944).]

Lloyd "Meaning" 1978
Lloyd, A. L. "The Meaning of Folk Music." Chap. 1, pp. 5-28 in Leach/Palmer 1978.

Loesberg 1,2,1980; 3,n.d.
John Loesberg, ed. *Folksongs and Ballads Popular in Ireland.* 3 vols., Cork: Ossian Publications, 1980 (vols. 1,2), n.d. (3).

A. Lomax 1960
Lomax, Alan. *The Folk Songs of North America: In the English language.* New York: Doubleday & Co., 1960.

A. Lomax 1964
Lomax, Alan. *The Penguin Book of American Folk Songs.* Baltimore: Penguin Books, 1964.

J. Lomax 1918(1938)
Lomax, John. *Cowboy Songs and Other Frontier Ballads.* New York: Macmillan Co., 1918; rev. ed., 1938.

Lomax/Lomax 1934
Lomax, John A. and Alan. *American Ballads and Folk Songs.* New York: Macmillan Co., 1934.

Lomax/Lomax 1941
Lomax, John A., and Alan Lomax. *Our Singing Country: A second volume of American ballads and folk songs.* New York: Macmillan Co., 1941.

Lyle IFMS 1974-5
Lyle, E[mily] B. "Song Chapbooks with Irish Imprints in the Lauriston Castle Collection, National Library of Scotland." *Irish Folk Music Studies,* 2,1974-5:15-30.

Lyle 1975
Lyle, E[mily] B. *Andrew Crawfurd's Collection of Ballads and Songs.* Vol. 1. Edinburgh: Scottish Text Society, 1975.

MacArthur CD&S 1981
MacArthur, Margaret C. "The Search for More Songs from the Hills of Vermont: Songs and Ballads of the Atwood Family of West Dover, Vermont." *CD&S* 11/12,1981:5-19.

McCall, P. J.: see Darley.

MacColl [?1953]
MacColl, Ewan. *Scotland Sings.* Scottish Branch of the Workers' Music Association, [?1953].

MacColl ?1956 [1962]
MacColl, Ewan. *Personal Choice: Of Scottish folksongs and ballads.* New York: Hargail Music Press, ?1956, reprint 1962.

MacColl 1965
MacColl, Ewan. *Folk Songs and Ballads of Scotland.* New York: Oak Publications, 1965.

MacColl, Ewan: see also Seeger.

MacColl/Seeger 1977
MacColl, Ewan, and Peggy Seeger, eds. *Travellers' Songs from England and Scotland.* Knoxville: Univ. of Tennessee Press, 1977.

McDonnell 1979
McDonnell, John, ed. *Songs of Struggle and Protest.* Dublin: Gilbert Dalton Ltd., 1979.

McIntosh 1974
McIntosh, David Senneff. *Folk Songs and Singing Games of the Illinois Ozarks.* Carbondale: Southern Illinois Univ. Press, 1974.

Mackenzie 1928
Mackenzie, W. Roy. *Ballads and Sea Songs from Nova Scotia.* Cambridge, MA: Harvard Univ. Press, 1928; reprint, Hatboro, PA: Folklore Associates, 1963.

M[a]cMullan, Robert: see "North Antrim."

Maguire, John: see Morton.

Maitland, J. A. Fuller: see Broadwood.

Manifold 1964
Manifold, J. S. *The Penguin Australian Song Book.* Baltimore: Penguin Books, 1964.

Manning, Ambrose: see Burton.

Manny/Wilson 1968
Manny, Louise, and James Reginald Wilson. *Songs of Miramichi.* Fredricton, N.B.: Brunswick Press, 1968.

Mansfield, Grace Yarrow: see Greenleaf.

Marshall 1931
Marshall, John. *Popular Rhymes and Sayings of Ireland.* Dungannon: Tyrone Printing Co., 1931.

Marson, Charles L.: see Sharp.

Mason [1878]
Mason, M. H. *Nursery Rhymes and Country Songs.* London: Metzler & Co. [1878]; reprint, London, 1908, and Norwood, PA: Norwood Editions, 1973.

Matteson/Henry 1936
Matteson, Maurice, and Mellinger Edward Henry, eds. *Beech Mountain Folk-Songs and Ballads.* New York: G. Schirmer, 1936 Schirmer's American Folk-Song Series, Set 15.

Meek 1978
Meek, Bill, ed. *The Land of Libertie: Songs of the Irish in America.* Dublin: Gilbert Dalton, 1978.

Meredith/Anderson 1967
Meredith, John, and Hugh Anderson. *Folk Songs of Australia: And the men and women who sang them.* Sydney: Ure Smith, 1967.

Milner/Kaplan 1983
Milner, Dan, and Paul Kaplan. *A Bonnie Bunch of Roses: Songs of England, Ireland and Scotland, 150 traditional songs from the British Isles....* New York: Oak Publications, 1983.

Minton JEMFQ 1982
Minton, John. "'Our Goodman' in Blackface and 'The Maid' at the Sookey Jump: Two Afro-American variants of Child ballads in commercial disc." *JEMFQ* #65-6(Spr-Sum)1982:31-40. [Coley Jones, "Drunkard's Special," p. 33 (3 nights); Huddie Ledbetter ("Leadbelly"), "Gallis Pole," p. 36.]

Moffat, Alfred: see also Kidson.

Moffat [1933]
Moffat, Alfred. *Fifty Traditional Scottish Nursery Rhymes: ... ballads and songs, with their traditional tunes.* London: Augener & Co. [1933].

Moffat [1897]
Moffat, Alfred. *The Minstrelsy of Ireland.* London: Augener & Co., [1897].

Moffat 1912
Moffat, Alfred. *Dances of the Olden Time.* London, 1912.

Moffat/Kidson n.d.
Moffat, Alfred, and Frank Kidson. *Seventy-five British Nursery Rhymes: And a collection of old jingles.* London: Augener & Co., n.d.

Moody/Martin 1967
Moody, T. W., and F. X. Martin, eds. *The Course of Irish History.* Cork: Mercier Press, 1967.

Moore/Moore 1964
Moore, Ethel and Chauncey O. *Ballads and Folk Songs of the Southwest: More than 600 titles, melodies, and texts collected in Oklahoma.* Norman: Univ. of Oklahoma Press, 1964.

A. Morris 1950
Morris, Alton C. *Folksongs of Florida.* Gainesville: Univ. of Florida, 1950.

G. Morris 1956,1
G. S. Morris. *Kerr's "Buchan" Bothy Ballads.* Vol. 1. Glasgow: James S. Kerr, 1956.

H. Morris ?1916
Morris, Henry [E O Muirgheasa]. *Cead de Ceoltaibh Uladh.* Dublin, ?1916 [?1935].

H. Morris 1969
Morris, Henry. *Da Cead de Ceoltaibh Uladh.* 1969.

Morrison/Cologne 1981
Morrison, Jean, ed., and Celia Cologne, arr. *Wiltshire Folk Songs.* [Wiltshire, England:] Wiltshire Folk Life Society, 1981.

Morton 1970
Morton, Robin. *Folksongs Sung in Ulster.* Cork: Mercier Press, 1970.

Morton 1973
Morton, Robin, ed. *Come Day, Go Day, God Send Sunday: The songs and life story, told in his own words, of John Maguire, traditional singer and farmer from County Fermanagh.* London: Routledge & Kegan Paul, 1973.

Motherwell 1827
Motherwell, William. *Minstrelsy Ancient and Modern.* Glasgow: Wylie, 1827.

Moulden SA 1977
Moulden, John. "The 'Songs of the People' Collection." *SA* 1(3, Mar)1977:3-6.

Moulden 1979
Moulden, John, ed. *Songs of the People: Selections from the Sam Henry collection,* Part 1. Belfast: Blackstaff Press, 1979.
[See Bruford *Tocher* 1982 for a detailed review.]

Munch 1970
Munch, Peter A. *The Song Tradition of Tristan da Cunha.* Bloomington, IN: Indiana University Research Center for the Language Sciences, 1970. Folklore Institute Monograph Series #22.

Munnelly Ceol 1972
Munnelly, Tom. "The Man and His Music: John Reilly." *Ceol* 4(1, Jan)1972:2-8

Munnelly FMJ 1975
Munnelly, Tom. "The Singing Tradition of Irish Travellers." *FMJ* 3(1)1975:3-30.

Neely/Spargo 1938
Neely, Charles, and John W. Spargo. *Tales and Songs of Southern Illinois.* Menasha, WI: George Banta Publishing Co., 1938.

Nettel 1954
Nettel, Reginald. *Sing a Song of England: A social history of traditional song.* London: Phoenix House, 1954. (Reprint of *A Social History of Traditional Song,* 1969.)

Newell 1903
Newell, William Wells. *Games and Songs of American Children.* New York: Harper & Bros., 1883; 2d ed., 1903; reprint, Dover Publications, 1963.

"North Antrim" 1933
"North Antrim" (pseudonym of Robert M[a]cMullan). *Rowlock Rhymes and Songs of Exile.* Ed. Sam Henry. Belfast: ?Quote [?Quota] Press, 1933.

Nye 1952
Nye, (Captain) Pearl R. *Scenes and Songs of the Ohio-Erie Canal.* Columbus: Ohio State Archaeological and Historical Society, 1952.

Nygard JAF 1952
Nygard, Holger Olaf. "Ballad Source Study: Child Ballad No. 4." *JAF* 65(1952):1-12.
[Reprinted in Leach/Coffin 1961:204-24.]

Nygard 1958
Nygard, Holger Olaf. *The Ballad of Heer Halewijn: Its forms and variations in western Europe, a study of the history and nature of a ballad tradition.* Helsinki: Suomalainen Tiedeakatemia, 1958. Folklore Fellows Communications, No. 169.

S. O'Boyle 1977
O'Boyle, Seán. *The Irish Song Tradition.* Dublin: Gilbert Dalton, 1977.

C. O'Boyle 1979
O'Boyle, Cathal, ed. *Songs of County Down.* Dublin: Gilbert Dalton Ltd., 1979.

O'Boyle/O'Boyle 1975
Seán Og and Manus Ó Baoill [O'Boyle]. *Ceolta Gael.* Dublin: Mercier Press, 1975.

Ó Canainn 1978a
Ó Canainn, Tomás. *Traditional Music in Ireland.* London: Routledge & Kegan Paul, 1978.

Ó Canainn 1978b
Ó Canainn, Tomás, ed. *Down Erin's Lovely Lee: Songs of Cork.* Dublin: Gilbert Dalton, 1978.

O'Kane, James: see Ó Maoláin.

Okun 1968
Okun, Milton. *Something to Sing About! The personal choices of America's folk singers.* New York: Macmillan Co., 1968.

Olney, Margaret: see Flanders.

O Lochlainn 1939
O Lochlainn, Colm. *Irish Street Ballads.* Dublin: Three Candles, 1939; [?rev. ed. 1946] reprint, New York: Citadel Press (Corinth Books), 1960.

O Lochlainn 1965
O Lochlainn, Colm. *More Irish Street Ballads.* Dublin: Three Candles, 1965.

Ó Maoláin 1982
Ó Maoláin, Ciarán, ed. *James O'Kane, the Bard of Carntogher: Poems and ballads.* Portsmouth: Broc Press, 1982.
[New ed. of Michael Hurl, ed.: *Country Poems and Ballads* by James O'Kane (London: Arthur H. Stockwell, 1938), with additions and modifications from Sam Henry's papers and "Songs of the People."]

O'Neill 1903
O'Neill, Francis. *Music of Ireland: 1850 melodies.* Chicago: Lyon & Healy, 1903; reprint, Bronx, NY: Dan Collins, 1963, 1966.

O'Neill 1907
O'Neill, Francis J. *The Dance Music of Ireland: 1001 Gems.* Chicago: Lyon & Healy, 1907; reprint, Dublin: Walton's Musical Instrument Galleries [1969?].

O'Neill 1922
O'Neill, Francis. *Waifs and Strays of Gaelic Melody.* 2d ed. Chicago: Lyon & Healy, 1922; reprint, Dublin: Mercier Press, 1980.

O Neill/MacCathmeoil 1904
O Neill, Padraig MacAodh, and Seosamh MacCathmeoil. *Songs of Uladh.* Belfast, 1904.

Opie/Opie 1951
Opie, Rona and Peter, eds. *The Oxford Dictionary of Nursery Rhymes.* Oxford: Oxford Univ. Press, 1951.

Ord 1930
Ord, John, ed. *The Bothy Songs and Ballads: Of Banff & Moray, Angus and the Mearns.* Paisley: Alexander Gardner, 1930.

Orr n.d.
Orr, Andrew. *The Feast of Reason.* Ballarat [Australia]: Baxter & Stubbs, n.d.

O'Shaughnessy 1968
O'Shaughnessy, Patrick. *21 Lincolnshire Folk Songs.* London: Oxford University Press, 1968.

O'Shaughnessy 1971
O'Shaughnessy, Patrick, ed. *More Folk Songs from Lincolnshire.* Oxford: Oxford Univ. Press, 1971.

O'Shaughnessy 1975
O'Shaughnessy, Patrick, ed. *Yellowbelly Ballads.* Lincoln: Lincolnshire & Humberside Arts, 1975.

O'Sullivan 1960
O'Sullivan, Donal. *Songs of the Irish.* Dublin: Browne & Nolan, 1960; reprint, New York: Mahony & Roese, 1967.

O'Sullivan, Donal: see Bunting.

Owens 1950
Owens, William A. *Texas Folk Songs.* Dallas: Texas Folk-Lore Society, 1950.

***Oxford Ballads* 1910**
Quiller-Couch, Arthur, ed. *The Oxford Book of Ballads.* Oxford: Clarendon Press, 1910.

***Oxford Ballads* 1969**
Kinsley, James, ed. *The Oxford Book of Ballads: Newly selected.* Oxford: Clarendon Press, 1969.

Palmer, Roy: see also Leach.

Palmer 1971
Palmer, Roy. *Room for Company.* Cambridge: Cambridge Univ. Press, 1971.

Palmer *ED&S* 1972
Palmer, Roy. "Cecilia Costello and George Dunn." *ED&S* 34(1, Spr)1972.

Palmer 1972
Palmer, Roy. *Songs of the Midlands.* East Ardley (Yorkshire): E. P. Publishers, 1972.

Palmer *FMJ* 1973
Palmer, Roy. "George Dunn: Twenty one Songs and Fragments." *FMJ* 2(4)1973:275-96.

Palmer 1973
Palmer, Roy. *The Valiant Sailor: Songs and ballads and prose passages illustrating life on the lower deck in Nelson's Navy.* London: Cambridge Univ. Press, 1973.

Palmer 1974a
Palmer, Roy. *A Touch on the Times: Songs of social change 1770 to 1914.* Baltimore: Penguin Books, 1974.

Palmer 1974b
Palmer, Roy, ed. *Love is Pleasing: Songs of courtship and marriage.* Cambridge: Cambridge Univ. Press, 1974.

Palmer 1977
Palmer, Roy. *The Rambling Soldier: Life in the lower ranks, 1750-1900; Military life through soldiers' songs and writings.* Baltimore: Penguin Books, 1977.

Palmer 1978
Palmer, Roy, ed. *Strike the Bell: Transport by road, canal, rail and sea in the nineteenth century through songs, ballads and contemporary accounts.* Cambridge: Cambridge Univ. Press, 1978.

Palmer Ballad 1979a
Palmer, Roy, ed. *A Ballad History of England: From 1588 to the present day.* London: B. H. Batsford, 1979.

Palmer Songs 1979b
Palmer, Roy, ed. *Everyman's Book of English Country Songs.* London: J. M. Dent & Sons, 1979.

Palmer 1980
Palmer, Roy, ed. *Everyman's Book of British Ballads.* London: J. M. Dent & Sons, 1980.

Palmer/Raven 1976
Palmer, Roy, and Jon Raven, eds. *The Rigs of the Fair: Popular sports and pastimes in the nineteenth century through songs, ballads and contemporary accounts.* Cambridge: Cambridge Univ. Press, 1976.

Paquin *CFMJ* 1979
Paquin, Robert. "Le Testament du Garçon Empoisonné: Un 'Lord Randal' français en Acadie." *CFMJ* 7,1979:3-17 (in French), English abstract pp. 17-8.

Peacock 1965 1-3
Peacock, Kenneth. *Songs of the Newfoundland Outports.* 3 vols. Ottawa: National Museum of Canada, 1965. National Museum of Canada Bulletin No. 197, Anthropological Series No. 65.

Peirce 1979
Peirce, Maggi Kerr. *Keep the Kettle Boiling: ... rhymes, chants, songs, etc. ... from my childhood in Northern Ireland.* [Fairhaven, MA: Maggi Kerr Peirce, 1979.]

Peroni, Carlo: see Gallagher.

Peters 1977
Peters, Harry B., ed. *Folk Songs out of Wisconsin: An illustrated compendium of words and music.* Madison: State Historical Society of Wisconsin, 1977.

Peterson 1931
Peterson, Walter. *Mountain Ballads and Old-Time Songs.* Chicago: M. M. Cole Publishing Co., 1931.

Petrie 1855
Petrie, George, ed. *The Petrie Collection of the Ancient Music of Ireland.* 2 vols. Dublin: M. H. Gill, 1855: reprint, 1 vol., Farnborough: Gregg International Publishers: 1967.

Petrie/Stanford 1,1902; 2,1902; 3,1905
Petrie, George. *The Complete Collection of Irish Music.* Ed. Charles Villiers Stanford. 3 parts. London: Boosey & Co., 1902-5.

Pickering *FMJ* 1976
Pickering, Michael. "Janet Blunt -- Folk Song Collector and Lady of the Manor." *FMJ* 3(2)1976:114-57.

Pinto/Rodway 1957
Pinto, V. de Sola, and A. E. Rodway. *The Common Muse: Popular British ballad poetry from the 15th to the 20th century.* London: Chatto & Windus Ltd., 1957; reprint, Harmondsworth, Middlesex: Penguin Books, 1965.

Planxty 1976
The Songs of Planxty. London: Mews Music Ltd., 1976.

G. Polwarth 1967
Polwarth, Gwen Marchant, ed. *Folk Songs of Northumberland: Newly collected ...* [Newcastle-upon-Tyne]: Orriel Press, 1966; rev. ed., 1967.

G. Polwarth 1972
Polwarth, Gwen. *Come You Not from Newcastle?* Newcastle-upon-Tyne: Frank Graham, 1972.

Polwarth/Polwarth 1969
Polwarth, Gwen and Mary. *North Country Songs.* Newcastle-upon-Tyne: Frank Graham, 1969.

Polwarth/Polwarth 1970
Polwarth, Gwen and Mary. *Folk Songs from the North.* Newcastle-upon-Tyne: Frank Graham, 1970.

Pound 1922
Pound, Louise. *American Ballads and Songs.* New York: Charles Scribner's Sons, 1922; reprint, 1972.

Purslow 1965
Purslow, Frank. *Marrow Bones: English folk songs from the Hammond and Gardiner mss.* London: EFDS Publications, 1965.

Purslow *FMJ* 1967
Purslow, Frank. "The George Gardiner Folk Song Collection." *FMJ* 1(3)1967:129-57.

Purslow 1968
Purslow, Frank. *The Wanton Seed: More English folk songs from the Hammond and Gardiner mss.* London: EFDS Publications, 1968

Purslow *FMJ* 1969
Purslow, Frank. "The Williams Manuscripts." *FMJ* 1(5)1969:301-14.

Purslow 1972
Purslow, Frank. *The Constant Lovers: More English folk songs from the Hammond and Gardiner mss.* London: EFDS Publications, 1972.

Purslow 1974
Purslow, Frank. *The Foggy Dew: More English folk songs from the Hammond and Gardiner mss.* London: EFDS Publications, 1974.

Raim/Dunson 1968
Raim, Ethel, and Josh Dunson. *Grass Roots Harmony.* New York: Oak Publications, 1968.

Ramsay (15 ed,1768)
Ramsay, Allan. *The Tea-Table Miscellany.* [Edinburgh, 172-] [11th ed., 1750, 4 vols.] 15th ed., Glasgow: Robert Duncan, 1768.

Randolph (1980) 1-4
Randolph, Vance. *Ozark Folksongs.* 4 vols. Columbia: State Historical Society of Missouri,1946-50; rev. ed., Columbia: Univ. of Missouri Press, 1980.

Randolph/Cohen (1982)
Randolph, Vance. *Ozark Folksongs* Ed. and abridged by Norm Cohen. Urbana: Univ. of Illinois Press, 1982.

Ranson 1948(1973)
Ranson, Joseph. *Songs of the Wexford Coast.* Enniscorthy: Godfrey's, 1948; reprint, Norwood, PA: Norwood Editions, 1973.

Raven, Jon: see Palmer.

Raven 1978
Raven, Michael, ed. *John o' Barbary: A selection of British folk music.* Derrington (Stafford): Michael Raven, 1978.

Reay, Samuel: see Stokoe.

Reddall 1894
Reddall, Henry Frederick. *Songs that Never Die.* Albany, NY: Joseph McDonough, 1894.

Reeves 1958
Reeves, James. *The Idiom of the People: English traditional verse edited with an introduction and notes from the manuscripts of Cecil J. Sharp.* New York: Macmillan Co., 1958; reprint, New York: W. W. Norton & Co., 1965.

Reeves 1960
Reeves, James. *The Everlasting Circle: English traditional verse edited with an introduction and notes from the manuscripts of S. Baring-Gould, H. E. D. Hammond, and George B. Gardiner.* London: Wm. Heinemann, 1960.

Richards/Stubbs 1979
Richards, Sam, and Tish Stubbs, colls. and eds. *The English Folksinger: 159 modern and traditional folksongs.* Glasgow: William Collins Sons & Co., 1979.

Richardson/Spaeth 1927
Richardson, Ethel Park, and Sigmund Spaeth. *American Mountain Songs.* New York: Greenberg, Publisher, 1927; reprint, 1955.

Rickaby 1926
Rickaby, Franz, ed. *Ballads and Songs of the Shanty-Boy.* Cambridge, MA: Harvard Univ. Press, 1926.

J. T. R. Ritchie 1965
Ritchie, J. T. R. *Golden City.* Edinburgh: Oliver & Boyd, 1965.

Jean Ritchie 1965
Ritchie, Jean. *Folk Songs of the Southern Appalachians.* New York: Oak Publications, 1965.

Ritson 1794
Ritson, Joseph. *Scotish Songs.* 2 vols. London, 1794; rev. ed. Glasgow: Hugh Hipkins, 1869.

Ritson 1792-1809
Ritson, Joseph. *Northern Garlands.* Newcastle: 1792-1802; reprint, Darby, PA: Norwood Editions, 1973.

Ritson 1866
Ritson, Joseph, ed. *Scottish Songs and Ballads.* Rev. ed. London: William Tegg, 1860.

Roberts 1964
Roberts, Leonard. *Sang Branch Settlers: Folksongs and tales of a Kentucky mountain family.* Austin: Univ. of Texas Press, 1974. Publications of the American Folklore Society, Memoir Series, Vol. 61.

Robinson, Earl: see Silber.

Rosenbaum 1983
Rosenbaum, Art, coll. *Folk Visions and Voices: Traditional music and song in North Georgia.* Athens: Univ. of Georgia Press, 1983.

Ross, Colin: see Handle.

Roxburghe 1871-99
The Roxburghe Ballads. Ed. William Chappell and J. Woodfall Ebsworth. 9 vols. Hertford: Ballad Society, 1871-99.

***RPSB* 1961**
Reprints from the People's Songs Bulletin: 1946-1949. Ed. Irwin Silber. New York: Oak Publications, 1961.

RSO
Reprints from Sing Out!
[Open-ended series of songs reprinted from *Sing Out!* see *SO!* under Periodicals.

Rufty, Hilton: see Smith.

Sandburg 1927
Sandburg, Carl. *The American Songbag.* New York: Harcourt Brace & Co., 1927.

Sandburg 1950
Sandburg, Carl. *Carl Sandburg's New American Songbag.* New York: Broadcast Music, 1950.

Scanlon 1923
Scanlon, Bat. *The Violin Made Easy.* San Francisco, 1923.

Scarborough 1937
Scarborough, Dorothy. *A Song Catcher in the Southern Mountains: American folk songs of British ancestry.* New York: Columbia Univ. Press, 1937; reprint, New York: AMS Press, 1966.

Schinhan, Jan Philip: see Brown.

Scofield 1981
Scofield, Twilo. *An American Sampler: The lore of the land, our traditions in song, history, foodways, and customs.* Eugene, OR: Cutthroat Press [1974 Villard St, 97403], 1981.

B. Scott 1980
Scott, Bill [William Neville], ed. *The Second Penguin Australian Songbook.* New York: Penguin Books, 1980.

J. Scott 1966
Scott, John Anthony. *The Ballad of America.* New York: Bantam Books, 1966.

Scottish Student's 1891
The Scottish Student's Song Book. Glasgow: Bayley & Ferguson, 1891; reprint, [193?].

Sedley 1967
Sedley, Stephen, comp. & ed. *The Seeds of Love.* London: Essex Music, 1967.

Seeger, Mike: see Cohen.

Seeger, Peggy: see also MacColl.

Peggy Seeger 1964
Seeger, Peggy. *Folk Songs of Peggy Seeger.* New York: Oak Publications, 1964.

Seeger/MacColl 1960
Seeger, Peggy, and Ewan MacColl, comps. *The Singing Island: A collection of English and Scots Folksongs.* London: Mills Music, 1960.

R. Seeger 1948
Seeger, Ruth Crawford. *American Folk Songs for Children.* New York: Doubleday & Co., 1948.

Senior/Creighton *JEFDSS* 1951
Senior, Doreen H., and Helen Creighton. "Folk Songs Collected in the Province of Nova Scotia, Canada." *JEFDSS* 6(3)1951:83-91.

Senior, Doreen: see also Creighton.

Sharp 1-5,1908-12(1961)
Sharp, Cecil J. *English County Folk Songs.* 5 vols. London: Novello & Co., 1908-12; reprint, 1 vol., London, 1961.

Sharp 1916
Sharp, Cecil J. *One Hundred English Folksongs.* Philadelphia: Oliver Ditson Co., 1916.

Sharp *JEFDSS* 1959
Sharp, Cecil J. "Songs, Hitherto Unpublished, from the Manuscripts of Cecil Sharp." *JEFDSS* 8(4)1959:197-9.

Sharp, Cecil J.: see also Baring-Gould.

Sharp/Karpeles 1932 1,2
Sharp, Cecil J., coll. *English Folk-Songs from the Southern Appalachians: Comprising 274 songs and ballads with 968 tunes, including 39 tunes contributed by Olive Dame Campbell.* Ed. Maud Karpeles. 2d ed., 1 vol. (2 vols. paginated separately.) London: Oxford Univ. Press, 1932. (Orig. *English Folk Songs from the Southern Appalachians*; Comprising 122 songs and ballads and 323 tunes, coll. Olive Dame Campbell and Cecil J. Sharp [New York: G. P. Putnam's Sons, 1917].)

Sharp/Karpeles 1968
Sharp, Cecil J., and Maud Karpeles. *Eighty English Folk-Songs from the Southern Appalachians.* London: Faber & Faber, 1968.

Sharp/Karpeles 1974 1,2
Sharp, Cecil J., coll. *Cecil Sharp's Collection of English Folk Songs.* Ed. Maud Karpeles. 2 vols. London: Oxford Univ. Press, 1974.

Sharp/Karpeles 1975 1,2
Sharp, Cecil J. *The Crystal Spring: English folk songs collected by Cecil Sharp.* Ed. Maud Karpeles. 2 vols. London: Oxford Univ. Press, 1975.

Sharp/Marson 1,1904; 2,3,1906; Sharp 4,1908; 5,1909
Sharp, Cecil J. [and Charles L. Marson]. *Folk Songs from Somerset.* 5 series [the 1st 3 co-edited with Marson]. London: Simpkin & Co., 1904-9.

Shay 1948
Shay, Frank. *American Sea Songs and Chanteys: From the days of iron men and wooden ships.* New York: W. W. Norton & Co., 1948. (Orig. *Iron Men and Wooden Ships*, 1924.)

Shellans 1968
Shellans, Herbert. *Folksongs of the Blue Ridge Mountains: Traditional songs as sung by the people of the Blue Ridge Mountains country.* New York: Oak Publications, 1968.

Shepheard n.d.
Shepheard, Pete, [ed.] *Folk Songs and Ballads of the Brazil Family of Gloucester.* N.p., n.d. [40 pp. printed offset from typing.]

Shields *UF* 1964
Shields, Hugh. "Some Bonny Female Sailors." *UF* 10,1964:35-45.

Shields *Ceol* 1965
Shields, Hugh. "Miscellanea from Eileen Keaney." *Ceol* 2(1)1965:6-10.

Shields *Ceol* 2(3)
Shields, Hugh. "More Female Sailors." *Ceol* 2(3):62-5.

Shields *Ceol* 1970
Shields, Hugh. "The Valley of St. Colmcille." *Ceol* 3(4,Mar)1970:104-15

Shields *UF* 1971
Shields, Hugh. "Some Songs and Ballads in Use in the Province of Ulster ... 1845?" *UF* 17,1971:3-24. [Description and index.]

Shields *YIFMC* 1971
Shields, Hugh. "Singing Traditions of a Bilingual Parish in North-West Ireland." *YIFMC* 3,1971:109-19.

Shields *UF* 1972
Shields, Hugh. "Some Songs and Ballads in Use in the Province of Ulster ... 1845: Texts." *UF* 18,1972:34-65.

Shields *Hermathena* 1974
Shields, Hugh. "William Allingham and Folk Song." *Hermathena* 117,1974:23-36.

Shields *UF* 1981
Shields, Hugh. "A Singer of Poems: Jimmy McCurry of Myroe." *UF* 27,1981:1-18.

Shields 1981
Shields, Hugh. *Shamrock, Rose and Thistle: Folk singing in North Derry.* Belfast: Blackstaff Press, 1981.
[See Bruford *Tocher* 1982 for detailed review.]

Shields/Shields *UF* 1975
Shields, Hugh, and Lisa Shields. "Irish Folk Song Recordings, 1960-1972: An index of tapes in the Ulster Folk and Transport Museum." *UF* 21,1975.

Shoemaker 1931
Shoemaker, Henry W. *Mountain Minstrelsy of Pennsylvania.* Philadelphia: Newman F. McGirr, 1931.

Shuldham-Shaw *JEFDSS* 1949
Shuldham-Shaw, Patrick. "Folk Songs Collected in the Shetland Isles." *JEFDSS* 6(1)1949:13-8.

Shuldham-Shaw *FMJ* 1966
Shuldham-Shaw, P. N. "The James Duncan Manuscript Folk Song Collection (with Ten Songs)" *FMJ* 1(2)1966:67-91. (Reprinted as "Folk Songs of Aberdeenshire," *EFDSS Journal* Reprint No. 14, 1967, repaged (1-29).

Silber/Robinson 1967
Silber, Irwin, and Earl Robinson. *Songs of the Great American West.* New York: Macmillan Co., 1967.

Silverman 1966
Silverman, Jerry. *The Panic Is On: And 62 other songs -- outrageous, irreverent, subversive, and far-out.* New York: Oak Publications, 1966.

Silverman 1971
Silverman, Jerry. *The Liberated Woman's Songbook.* New York: Collier Books (Macmillan Co.), 1971.

Slocombe *JEFDSS* 1955
Slocombe, Marie. "Some 'English' Ballads and Folk Songs Recorded in Ireland, 1952-1954." *JEFDSS* 7(4)1955:239-44.

Slocombe *JEFDSS* 1956
Slocombe, Marie. "Some 'English' Ballads and Folk Songs Recorded in Ireland, 1952-1954. Continued." *JEFDSS* 8(1)1956:16-26.

Slocombe/Shuldham-Shaw *JEFDSS* 1953
Slocombe, Marie, introduction, and Patrick Shuldham-Shaw, transcriber. "Seven Songs: Recorded by the B.B.C. from Mrs. Costello of Birmingham." *JEFDSS* 7(2)1953:96-105.

C. Smith 1927
Smith, C. Fox. *A Book of Shanties.* Boston: Houghton Mifflin Co., 1927.

L. Smith 1888
Smith, Laura Alexandrine. *The Music of the Waters.* London: Kegan, Paul, Trench & Co., 1888; reprint, Detroit, 1969.

R. Smith 1928
Smith, Reed. *South Carolina Ballads.* Cambridge, MA: Harvard Univ. Press, 1928.

Smith/Rufty ?1937
Smith, Reed, and Hilton Rufty. *American Anthology of Old World Ballads.* New York: J. Fischer & Bro., 1937.

Smythe, Mary Winslow: see Barry and Eckstorm.

Solomon 1964
Solomon, Maynard, ed. *The Joan Baez Songbook.* New York: Ryerson Music Publishers (Division of Vanguard Records), 1964.

Songster's Museum 1803
The Songster's Museum. Northampton, MA: Andrew Wright, 1803.

Spaeth 1948
Spaeth, Sigmund. *A History of Popular Music in America.* New York: Random House, 1948.

Spaeth, Sigmund: see also Richardson.

Spargo, John W.: see Neely.

Sparling 1888[?]
Sparling, H. Halleday. *Irish Minstrelsy: Being a selection of songs, lyrics and ballads.* London: Walter Scott, 1888[? White & Allen, 1890?].

Stokoe, John: see also Bruce.

Stokoe/Reay [1892?]
Stokoe, John, and Samuel Reay. *Songs and Ballads of Northern England.* Newcastle-on-Tyne: Walter Scott, [1892?]; reprint, Darby, PA, 1973.

Stout 1936
Stout, Earl J., ed. *Folklore from Iowa.* New York: American Folklore Society, 1936.

Stubbs *JEFDSS* 1968
Stubbs, Ken. "The Life and Songs of George Maynard." London: EFDSS, 1968. Journal Reprint No. 12. [*JEFDSS* 9(4)1963: 180-96.]

Stubbs 1970
Stubbs, Ken. *The Life of a Man: English folk songs from the Home Counties.* London: EFDS Publications, 1970.

Studer, Norman: see Cazden.

Sturgis/Hughes 1919
Sturgis, Edith, and Robert Hughes. *Songs from the Hills of Vermont.* New York: G. Schirmer, 1919. Schirmer's American Folk-Song Series, Set 10.
[See also reprint in Barrand *CD&S* 1981.]

Sumner 1888
Sumner, Heywood. *The Besom Maker and Other Country Folk-Songs.* London: Longmans, Green & Co., 1888; reprint, Darby, PA, 1973.

Terry 1931,1/2
Terry, [Sir] R. R. *The Shanty Book.* 2 parts. London: J. Curwen & Sons, 1931.

Thompson 1939
Thompson, Harold W. *Body, Boots and Britches: Folktales, ballads and speech from country New York.* New York: J. B. Lippincott Co., 1939; reprint, New York: Dover Publications, 1962.

Thompson 1958
Thompson, Harold W., ed. *A Pioneer Songster: Texts from the Stevens-Douglass manuscript of western New York, 1841-1856.* Ithaca, NY: Cornell Univ. Press, 1958.

Tunney 1979
Tunney, Paddy. *The Stone Fiddle: My way to traditional song.* Dublin: Gilbert Dalton, 1979.

Vallely/Vallely 1973 1-3
Vallely, Eithne and John B. *Learn to Play the Tin Whistle.* 3 vols. Belfast: Armagh Pipers Club, 1973.

Vaughan Williams [1958?]
Vaughan Williams, Ralph. *A Yacre of Land.* London: Oxford Univ. Press, [1958?].

Vaughan Williams/Lloyd 1959
Vaughan Williams, Ralph, and A. L. Lloyd. *The Penguin Book of English Folk Songs: From the Journal of the Folk Song Society and the Journal of the English Folk Dance and Song Society.* Baltimore: Penguin Books, 1959.
[See also Lloyd rec.]

Vincent 1932
Vincent, Elmore. *Lumber Jack Songs.* Chicago: M. M. Cole Publishing Co., 1932.

Walsh 1-3,1918-21
Walsh, (Father) Patrick A. [pseudonym "Padraig Breathnach"]. *Songs of the Gael.* 3 vols. Dublin: Browne & Nolan, 1918-21.

Ward 1964
Ward, Russel, ed. *The Penguin Book of Australian Folk Ballads.* New York: Penguin Books, 1964.

Warner 1984
Warner, Anne. *Traditional American Folk Songs: From the Anne and Frank Warner Collection.* Syracuse, NY: Syracuse Univ. Press, 1984.

Wells 1950
Wells, Evelyn Kendrick. *The Ballad Tree: A study of British and American ballads, their folklore, verse, and music.* New York: Ronald Press Co., 1950.

Welsh 1907
Welsh, Charles. *The Golden Treasury of Irish Songs and Lyrics.* 2 vols. New York: Dodge Publishing Co., 1907.

Wetmore/Bartholomew 1926
Wetmore, Susannah, and Marshall Bartholomew. *Mountain Songs of North Carolina.* New York: G. Schirmer, 1926.

Whall 1910(3d ed 1913)
Whall, W. B. *Sea Songs and Shanties.* Glasgow: Brown, Son & Ferguson, 1910; 3d ed., James Brown & Son, 1913. [5th ed., 1926]

Wheeler/Bridge 1937
Wheeler, Mary, and Clara Gregory Bridge. *Kentucky Mountain Folk-Songs.* Boston: Boston Music Co., 1937.

Whitelaw 1844 (1874)
Whitelaw, Alexander, ed. *The Book of Scottish Song.* London: Blackie & Son, 1844; reprint, 1874.

Wier 1929
Wier, Albert E. *Songs of the Sunny South.* New York: D. Appleton & Co., 1929.

Wilgus/Sommer 1967
Wilgus, D. K., and Carol Sommer, eds. *Folklore International: Essays in traditional literature, belief, and custom in honor of Wayland Debs Hand.* Hatboro, PA: Folklore Associates, 1967; reprint, Detroit: Gale Research Co., n.d.

Williams 1923
Williams, Alfred. *Folk-Songs of the Upper Thames.* London: Duckworth & Co., 1923.

Wilson, James Reginald: see Manny.

Winner 1885
Winner, Sep[timus]. *Winner's World of Song.* New York: Thompson Publishing Co., 1885.

WPA Kentucky [1939?]
Folk Song Project of the Federal Music Project (Kentucky), Works Progress Administration. *Folk Songs from East Kentucky.* Mimeographed. [1939?]

Wright 1975
Wright, Robert L., ed. *Irish Emigrant Songs and Ballads.* Bowling Green, OH: Bowling Green Univ. Popular Press, 1975.

Wyman/Brockway [1916]
Wyman, Loraine, and Howard Brockway. *Lonesome Tunes: Folk songs from the Kentucky mountains.* New York: H. W. Gray Co., [1916].

Wyman/Brockway [1920]
Wyman, Loraine, and Howard Brockway. *Twenty Kentucky Mountain Songs.* Boston: Oliver Ditson Co., [1920].

Yates *FMJ* 1975
Yates, Michael. "English Gypsy Songs." *FMJ* 3(1)1975:63-80.

Yates *FMJ* 1976
Yates, Michael. "Three Broadside Texts form the Press of John Pitts." *FMJ* 3(2)1976:165-9.

Yates *FMJ* 1980
Yates, Michael. "Daniel Wyatt Tate: Singer from Fancy Gap." *FMJ* 4(1)1980:3-23.

Manuscript and broadside collections

AS Thomas
The Isaiah Thomas Ballad Collection. American Antiquarian Society, Worcester, MA.

BCL Biggar
2 vols. Broadsheet slips and cuttings from broadsheet songsters. Belfast Central Library. J1, c. 1905; J2, c. 1895.

BL Ulster
"Ulster ballads." Broadsheet scrapbook C116h1 (pre-1890). British Library.

BPL H.80
Collection H.80.219. Broadsides from the British Isles. Boston Public Library.

BPL Irish
2 vol. A collection of Irish broadside songs and ballads. [Dublin, 187?] Boston Public Library.

BPL Libbie
The Libbie collection. Many Scottish broadsides. Boston Public Library.

Sam Henry's Songs of the People

BPL Partridge
4 vols. (A collection of 119 broadside songs and ballads.) The Partridge collection. Mainly Partridge and Wrigley imprints. [185?] Boston Public Library.

CUL Bradshaw
Bradshaw, Henry. *Collection of Irish broadsides.* Cambridge Univ. Library. Catalog, 1916.

CUL Madden
F. Madden collection of broadsides. 25 vols. Cambridge Univ. Library. (Vols. 24, 25 = CUL Bradshaw vols. 5, 6.)

Harvard 1
Card No. 25242.17. 14 vols. 19th-century broadsides from the British Isles, bound in 14 volumes, index in vol. 14. Harvard University Library.

Harvard 2
Card No. 25242.85F. Some 300 broadsides, mostly Irish.

Harvard 3
No card number. A very large collection of 19th-century broadsides arranged alphabetically in boxes; no index.

Henry coll.
Volumes of galley proofs and interleaved typescript contributed by Sam Henry to the Belfast Central Library (B), the National Library of Ireland, Dublin (D), and the Library of Congress, Washington, DC (W). These include only those numbers for which Sam Henry felt he was responsible. Each set includes a unique assortment of proofs/typed pages. Re other sets, see the introduction.

Houston coll.
(Manuscript?) collection, made during the late nineteenth century of songs and airs (collected around Coleraine district?) by Maud (Mrs. T. G.) Houston, whose husband was Headmaster of Coleraine Academical Institution. Some items were published in *JIFSS*, and Mrs. Houston's papers were said to have been presented to the Society, but their present location is unknown.

Hudson ms.
Hudson, Henry. *Old Irish airs.* 5 vols. [c. 1840] Boston Public Library. [Manuscript collection of Irish melodies collected in Ireland.]

NLI Broadsheets
[Broadsheets in portfolios, keyed to particular words in the titles.] National Library of Ireland, Dublin.

O'Boyle index [1954]
O'Boyle, Seán. [Indexes to the] *Sam Henry Collection* [Belfast]. Additional notes by Peter Kennedy. Prepared by direction of Sam Hanna Bell, Features Producer, BBC, Belfast. Mimeographed. British Broadcasting Corp., [1954].

UCB Brereton
A Collection of Broadside Songs. Dublin: P. Brereton [1870-80]. [M1744/C56/Case B/*P.] Morrison (music) Library, University of California, Berkeley.

UCLA 605
SC 605. Collection of English and American Broadsides. [Also includes many Irish broadsides, mainly Brereton imprints.] Special Collections, University Research Library, University of California, Los Angeles.

Broadside books and songsters

These books are popular compilations of songs whose sources are not always acknowledged in detail.

All Ireland 1950
All Ireland Song Book. Irish Songbook Co., 1950.

Ashton 1888
Ashton, John. *Modern Street Ballads.* London: Chatto and Windus, 1888; reprint, New York: Benjamin Blom, 1968.

Ashton 1891
Ashton, John. *Real Sailor Songs.* London: Leadenhall Press, 1891; reprint, New York: Benjamin Blom, 1972.

A Broadside
A Broadside. Published monthly by the Dun Emer Press, Dundrum, County Dublin [Ireland]. [Beginning with No. 2: by the Cuala Press, Churchtown, Dundrum, County Dublin. Beginning with No. 4: by E. C. Yeats at the Cuala Press....] [7 vols. in original series, 1908-15; new series, 1 vol., 1935, bound with an essay on Anglo-Irish ballads by W. B. Yeats and F. R. Higgins.] Bancroft (rare books) Library, University of California, Berkeley. [call numbers PR 1187/B8; fPR 1187/B82/1935.]

Clark n.d.
Clark, Joe. *One Hundred and Twenty Songs and Ballads of Ireland.* Dublin, n.d.

Colum 1913
Colum, Padráic. *Broad-Sheet Ballads: Being a collection of Irish popular songs.* Dublin: Maunsel & Co., 1913.

Come Let Us Sing 1974
Come Let Us Sing. Berea, KY: Christmas Country Dance School, Berea College, 1974.

Delaney's Irish 1-5 n.d.
Delaney's Irish Song Books. 5 vols. New York: William W. Delaney, n.d.

Delaney's Scotch 1910
Delaney's Scotch Song Book. New York: W. W. Delaney, 1910.

Derry Journal [c. 1925] 1,2
Old Come-All-Ye's: The finest collection of northern ballads and folk poems. 2 vols. [with some duplication; songs and ballads reprinted from] Londonderry: *Derry Journal* [c. 1925]; 2d ed. [c. 1940].

Emerald Isle 1904
The Emerald Isle Song Book. Dublin: M. H. Gill, 1904.

Forget Me Not [1835]
The Forget Me Not Songster: Containing a choice collection of old ballad songs, as sung by our grandmothers. New York: Nafis & Cornish [1835]; reprint, Norwood, PA: Norwood Editions [1974].

40 n.d.
Forty Splendid Love Songs. Dublin, n.d.

Gems n.d.
Gems of Irish Song. Glasgow: Mozart Allan, n.d.

Guinness n.d.
The Guinness Book of Irish Ballads. [Dublin?] n.p., n.d.

Hayward n.d
Hayward, Richard. Ireland Calling. Glasgow: Mozart Allan, n.d.

Healy 1962(1968)
Healy, James N. The Second Book of Irish Ballads. Cork: Mercier Press, 1962 (1968).

Healy 1965(1968)
Healy, James N. Ballads from the Pubs of Ireland. Cork: Mercier Press, 1965 (3d ed., 1968).

Healy 1967a
Healy, James N. Irish Ballads and Songs of the Sea. Cork: Mercier Press, 1967.

Healy 1,1967b; 2,3,4,1969a,b,c
Healy, James N. The Mercier Book of Old Irish Street Ballads. 4 vols. Cork: Mercier Press, 1967-9.

Healy 1977
Healy, James N., coll. & annot. Love Songs of the Irish. Dublin: Mercier Press, 1977.

Henderson 1938
Henderson, W. Victorian Street Ballads: A selection of popular ballads sold in the street in the nineteenth century. London: Charles Scribner's Sons, 1938.

In Dublin's
In Dublin's Fair City: A ballad selection with music. Dublin: Walton's Musical Instrument Galleries, 1968. Walton's Songs, Book 1.

Irish Fireside n.d.
Irish Fireside Songs. Dublin, n.d.

Irish Rover n.d.
The Irish Rover. Dublin, Walton's Piano and Musical Instrument Galleries, n.d. Walton's Song Book No. 5.

Jolliffe 1970
Jolliffe, Maureen. The Third Book of Irish Ballads. Cork: Mercier Press, 1970.

Logan 1869
Logan, W. A. A Pedlar's Pack of Ballads and Songs: With illustrative notes. Edinburgh: William Paterson, 1869.

National and Historical n.d.
The National and Historical Ballads of Ireland. Glasgow, n.d.

O'Conor 1901
O'Conor, Manus. Irish Com-All-Ye's: A Repository of ancient Irish songs and ballads comprising patriotic, descriptive, historical and humorous gems characteristic of the Irish race. New York: Popular Publishing Co., 1901.

O'Keeffe 1955(1968)
O'Keeffe, Daniel. The First Book of Irish Ballads. Cork: Mercier Press, 1955; rev. ed. 1968.

100 1857
One Hundred Songs of Ireland. London: Oliver Ditson Co., 1857.

120 n.d
One Hundred and Twenty Songs and Ballads of Ireland. Dublin: Irish Book Bureau, n.d.

Popular Songs 1860
Book of Popular Songs. 1860.

Sing an Irish n.d.
Sing an Irish Song. Dublin, n.d.

617 [190-?]
Six Hundred and Seventeen Irish Songs and Ballads. New York: Wehman Bros. [190-?]

Songs and Recitations 1,1974; 2,n.d.; 3,1976; 4,1975; 5,1978
Songs and Recitations of Ireland. 5 vols. Cork: National Publications Committee, 1974-8.

Songs of All Time 1946,1957
Songs of All Time. Delaware, OH.: Cooperative Recreation Service [now World Around Songs, Rt. 5, Box 398, Burnsville, NC 28714], 1946, 1957.

Walton's New 1,1966; 2,1968
Walton's New Treasury of Irish Songs and Ballads. 2 vols. Dublin: Walton's Piano and Musical Instrument Galleries, 1966, 1968.

Walton's 132 n.d.
Walton's 132 Best Irish Songs and Ballads. Dublin: Walton's Piano and Musical Instrument Galleries, n.d.

Walton's Treasury n.d.
Walton's Treasury of Irish Songs and Ballads. Dublin: Walton's Piano and Musical Instrument Galleries, n.d.

Wehman's Irish 1-4,1887
Wehman's Irish Song Books. 4 vols. Chicago: Wehman Bros., 1887.

Periodicals

AT
Australian Tradition. Journal of Victorian Folk Music Club and the Folk Lore Society of Victoria [Australia]. 37 issues, 1964-75.

BFSSNE
Bulletin of the Folksong Society of the Northeast. 12 numbers, 1930-37. Reprint, 1 vol. Philadelphia: American Folklore Society, 1960. Bibliographical and Special Series, Vol. 9.

CBM
Cape Breton's Magazine. Ed. Ronald Caplan. Wreck Cove, Cape Breton, N.S., Canada. Quarterly? #1, 1972? --

Ceol
Ceol: A journal of Irish music. Ed. Breandán Breathnach. Dublin. [Irregular quarterly.] 1963-85.

Ceol Tire
Ceol Tire: Newsletter of the Folk Music Society of Ireland. Dublin. [Irregular semiannual, #1(Nov) 1973--]

Sam Henry's Songs of the People

CD&S
Country Dance and Song. Country Dance and Song Society of America, 505 Eighth Ave., New York 10018, N.Y. Annual. 1, 1968--

CF
Club Folk. London: English Folk Dance and Song Society. Sporadic; bimonthly 2+ years. 1(1 May) 1967-- (17 issues).

CFB
Canada Folk Bulletin. Vancouver, B.C.: Vancouver Folk Song Society. Bimonthly. Jan-Feb 1978 -- Sept-Dec 1980 (17 issues).

CFMJ
Canadian Folk Music Journal. Toronto: Canadian Folk Music Society. Annual. 1,1973--

Chapbook
Chapbook: Scotland's Folk-Life Magazine. Aberdeen: Aberdeen Folk-Song Club; Chapbook Publications. [1, 1964 (12 issues?)]; 2,1965 (6); 3,1966 (6); 4,1967 [6?]; [?]--

Colorado FB
Colorado Folksong Bulletin. Boulder: Univ. of Colorado. Ed. Ben Gray Lumpkin; Kenneth I. Perlman. ?3 vols, Jan 1962-1964.

Davis n.d.
Folk Songs from Spin. Ed. Beryl Davis. Cheshire, England: n.d.

ED&S
English Dance and Song. London: English Folk Dance and Song Society. [More or less quarterly. For EFDSS members.]

Fabula
Fabula.

Folk
Folk: Traditional music magazine. London: EFDS Publications. 3 issues only: 1,1962; 2,Oct 1962; 3,Jan 1963.

Folkways
Folkways. Ed. John Burrison. Pennsylvania State Univ. [Sporadic.]

FMJ
Folk Music Journal. London: English Folk Dance and Song Society. Successor to JEFDSS. Annual. 1, 1965--

FR
Folk Review1. Ed. Fred Woods; Bill Caddick. Monthly, 1970?-9, to Vol. 8(7).

Hermathena
Hermathena: A Dublin Univ. review. Dublin: Dublin Univ.

IFMS
Irish Folk Music Studies / Eigse Cheol Tire. Dublin: Folk Music Society of Ireland (Cumann Cheol Tire Eireann. Nominally annual. 1,1972-3--

JAF
Journal of American Folklore. Washington, DC: American Folklore Society. Quarterly. 1(Apr) 1888-- [Index: see Coffin 1958.]

JEFDSS
Journal of the English Folk-Dance and Song Society. London: EFDSS. 9 vols., 1932-63. Succeeded by *FMJ*. [Index: see White/Dean-Smith 1951, Dean-Smith 1954.]

JEMFQ
John Edwards Memorial Foundation Quarterly. John Edwards Memorial Foundation, Folklore and Mythology Center, University of California, Los Angeles, ?1964--85[1989] (Nos. 1-76); succeeded by *American Vernacular Music*, Center for Popular Music, Middle Tennessee State Univ., Murfreesboro, TN.

JFSS
Journal of the Folk-Song Society. London, 8 vols. (35 parts), 1899-1931. Succeeded by *JEFDSS*. [Index: see White/Dean-Smith 1951, Dean-Smith 1954.]

JfV
Jahrbuch fur Volksliedforschung.

JIFSS
Journal of the Irish Folk-Song Society, London. Dublin. 27 vols., 1904-32. Vol. 16, 1923: Costello collection = Amhrá in Mhuighe Seóla; see Costello 1923. Vols. 22-29 [6 issues], 1927-32: Bunting collection; see Bunting/O'Sullivan

MT
Musical Traditions: Devoted to new perspectives on traditional music. Ed. Keith Summers. Flat 9, Westwood Lodge, Rayleigh Road, Thundersley, Essex, U.K. ?Trimestrial. #1, mid1983 --

NEF
Northeast Folklore. Orono, ME: Northeast Folklore Society. Annual. 1,1958[?]--

RSO
Reprints from Sing Out! New York: Sing Out! Magazine. More or less annual series. 1,1959--

SA
Slow Air: A traditional music broadsheet. Belfast: Arts Council of Northern Ireland. 3 Ionly: 1(1, Feb)1976; 1(2, Jun)1976; 1(3, Mar)1977.

Sing
Sing: Britain's Folk Song Magazine. Ed. Eric Winter. London, 1955?-70 (c. 11 vols, 61? issues).

SO!
Sing Out! The folk song magazine. Easton, PA (formerly New York): Sing Out! Magazine. Publication sometimes erratic; presently quarterly. 1(1, May)1950-- [Index: *The Sing Out! Song Index: A complete listing of songs printed in Sing Out! The Folk Song Magazine.* 24 pp.] See also *RSO*.

Spin
Spin: The folksong magazine. Ed. Beryl Davis. Spin Publications, Cheshire, England.

SR
The Southern Rag: The folk magazine. Ed. Ian A. Anderson. Farnham, Surrey, England. Quarterly. #1(Jul)1979--. Succeeded in July 1985 (#25) by *Folk Roots: The son of Southern Rag.* Monthly.

Tocher
Tocher: Tales, Songs, Tradition; selected from the archives of the School of Scottish Studies. Ed. Alan Bruford. Edinburgh: School of Scottish Studies. Quarterly. #1(Spr)1971 --.

Tradition
Tradition: Periodical of the University College Union Folk Song Society. London. 1966[?]--

TM
Traditional Music. Ed. Alan Ward. 90 St. Julian's Farm Rd., London SE27 ORS. 10 issues, 1975-8.

TT
Traditional Topics. Newton Abbott: Redlan Press. 4 issues: Jan-Apr 1968.

Treoir
Treoir: The magazine of traditional music, song and dance. Dublin: Comhaltas Ceoltóirí Eireann, 1969[?]--

UF
Ulster Folklife. Belfast: Ulster Folklife Committee; Ulster Folk Museum; Cultra, 1955--

WF
Western Folklore. Claremont, CA: California Folklore Society.

YIFMC
Yearbook of the International Folk Music Council.

Discography

B = (separate) booklet, L = lyrics provided.

O. J. Abbott (Ottawa).
Irish and British Songs from the Ottawa Valley. Folkways FM 4051, 1961. BL. Notes by Edith Fowke.

Derroll Adams: see Elliott.

Paul Adkins: see Philo Glee ....

Alistair Anderson: see High Level Ranters, *Bonnie Pit Laddie, Canny Newcassel.*

Ian A. Anderson: see Hot Vultures.

Arthur Argo (Scotland).
A Wee Thread o' Blue. Lyrica Erotica, Vol. 2. Prestige/Int. 13048.

Frankie Armstrong (England).
Out of Love, Hope and Suffering. Bay 206. L.

-----.
Lovely on the Water. Topic 12TS 216, 1972. Notes by A. L. Lloyd.

-----.
Songs and Ballads. Topic 12TS 273, 1975. Notes by A. L. Lloyd.

-----.
And the Music Plays So Grand. Sierra Briar SBR 4211, 1980. L.

-----: see also *My Song Is My Own.*

Dave, Toni Arthur (England).
The Lark in the Morning. Topic 12T 190, 1969. Notes by Dave, Toni Arthur, A. L. Lloyd.

Ted Ashlaw (NY).
..., Adirondack Woods Singer. Philo 1022, 1976. Notes by Robert D. Bethke.

Clarence Ashley, Tex Isley.
Folkways FA 2350, 1966. BL.

Clarence Ashley: see *Old Time Music ....*

Gary, Vera Aspey (England).
Seeing Double. Topic 12TS 407, 1979.

Bob Atcher (USA).
lc: Columbia LP HL 9006.

-----.
lc: Columbia LP HL 9013.

Ernest Austin: see *Flash Company.*

Ed Badeaux: see Tex-i-an Boys.

Joan Baez (USA).
Vanguard VRS 9078. [Solomon]

-----.
..., Vol. 2. Vanguard VSD 2097. [Solomon]

Roy Bailey (England).
Trailer LER 3021, 1971.

-----.
New Bell Wake. Fuse Records, 1976?

Brian, Valerie Bailie: see Irish Country Four.

Bandoggs (Pete, Chris Coe, Nic Jones, Tony Rose).
Highway (Trailer) LTRA 504, 1978 (1982).

Ezra "Fuzzy" Barhight: see Stekert.

Horton Barker (VA)
...: Traditional Singer. Folkways FA 2362, 1962. BL.

Tony (Anthony G.) Barrand: see John Roberts.

Margaret Barry (Ireland).
Songs of an Irish Tinker Lady. Riverside RLP 12 602. BL.

-----.
Ireland's Own ..., Street Singer. Outlet SOLP 1029.

-----, Michael Gorman (Ireland).
The Blarney Stone. Prestige/Irish 15001. Notes by Ewan MacColl.

-----, -----.
Her Mantle So Green. Topic 12T 123, 1965. Notes by A. L. Lloyd.

-----, -----.
Folkways FA 8729, 1975. BL.

Battlefield Band (Brian McNeill, Jamie McMenemy, Alan Reid, Pat Kilbride) (Scotland).
At the Front. Topic 12TS 38.

E. C. Beck: see AAFS series L56.

Bob "Fiddler" Beers, Evelyne Beers (USA).
Walkie in the Parlor: Songs with ancient psaltery. Folkways FS 2376, 1960. BL.

Dominic Behan: see MacColl.

Peter Bellamy (England).
The Fox Jumps over the Parson's Gate: English folk songs and ballads. Topic 12T 200, 1970.

-----.
Tell It Like It Was. Trailer LER 2089, 1975.

-----.
Both Sides Then. Topic 12TS 400, 1979.

-----: see also Young Tradition.

George Belton (Sussex).
All Jolly Fellows ... EFDSS LP 1008, 1967. BL.

Billy Bennington: see *English Country Music.*

Roy Berkeley: see Old Reliable ....

Mike Billington: see Raven.

Shirley Bland: see Galliards.

Harry Boardman: see *Bonny Pit Laddie.*

Dock Boggs (VA).
..., Vol. 3. Asch AH 3903, 1970.

Gordon Bok (USA).
Tune for November. Folk-Legacy FSI 40, 1970. BL.

-----.
Bay of Fundy. Folk-Legacy FSI 54, 1975. BL.

-----, Ann Mayo Muir, Ed Trickett (USA).
All Shall Be Well Again. Folk-Legacy FSI 96, 1983. BL.

The Bothy Band (Paddy Keenan, Matt Molloy, Kevin Burke, Tríona Ní Dhomhnaill, Dónal Lunny, Mícheál Ó Domhnaill) (Ireland).
Old Hag, You Have Killed Me. Green Linnet SIF 3005, 1982 (orig. Mulligan 1976).

Discography

-----.
Out of the Wind into the Sun. Mulligan LUN 013, 1977.
B. A. Botkin: see AAFS series L7.
Phyllis Workman Boyens: see Workman.
Paul Brady (Ireland).
Mulligan LUN 024.
-----.
The Barleycorn. Transatlantic TRA 185.
-----: see also Irvine; Gathering.
Sam Bracken: see Five Hand Reel.
Oscar Brand: see *Badman ..., Folk Concert ....*
Tom Brandon (Ontario).
The Rambling Irishman. Folk-Legacy FSC 10, 1963. BL. Notes by Edith Fowke.
Fred Breuning: see Roberts.
"Jumbo" Brightwell: see *Sing, Say and Play.*
Martin Brinsford: see Old Swan Band.
The Broadside (John Conolly, Brian Dawson, Mike Lee, Bill Meek, Tom Smith) (Lincolnshire).
The Moon Shone Bright. Topic 12TS 228.
h: **Anne, Francie Brolly.**
Beautiful Ireland. Homespun HRL 116, 1976.
Bertrand H. Bronson: see AAFS series L57, 58.
Fleming Brown (USA).
Folk-Legacy FSI 4, 1962. BL. Notes by Sandy Paton.
Percy Brown: see *English Country Music.*
Peter Browne: see Gathering.
Bruce Buckley (USA).
Ohio Valley Ballads. 10" Folkways FA 2025, 1955. BL. Notes by Charles Edward Smith.
John Burke: see Old Hat Band.
Thomas G. Burton (ed.).
Some Ballad Folks. Cassette recording, companion to the book. Boone, NC: Appalachian Consortium Press, 1981. [Orig. pub. 1978 by East Tennessee State Univ. Press.]
Kevin Burke: see also Bothy Band.
-----, **Mícheál Ó Domhnaill** (Ireland).
Promenade. Green Linnet SIF 3010, 1981 (orig. Mulligan 1979).
Howard Bursen (USA).
Cider in the Kitchen. Folk-Legacy FSI 74, 1980. BL.
Ellen Bush: see Old Hat Band.
Eddie Butcher (Derry).
Adam in Paradise: Traditional songs of courtship. Ulster Folk Museum EP 1969, cass. 1982. BL. Ed., notes by Hugh Shields.
-----.
I Once Was a Daysman. Free Reed FRR 003, 1976. B.
-----.
Shamrock, Rose and Thistle [1]. Leader LED 2070, 1976. L. Notes by Hugh Shields.
-----.
... Sings The Titanic and Other Traditional Folk Songs. Outlet OAS 3007, 1978.
Packie Manus Byrne (Donegal).
EFDSS LP 1009, 1969. BL.

-----.
h: Davjon Records DJ 1020, 1969.
-----.
Songs of a Donegal Man. Topic 12TS 257, 1974. Notes by Mike Yates.

Fergus Cahill: see *Ballads from the Pubs....*
Dick Cameron (USA).
Irish Folk Songs and Ballads. Folkways FG 3516, 1961. BL.
Isla Cameron (Scotland).
The Best of .... Prestige/Int. 13042, 195?
-----, Lou Killen (Northumberland).
The Waters of Tyne. Prestige/Int. 13059.
Bobby Campbell: see Exiles.
Campbell Family (Ian, Lorna, Dave, Betty, Winnie) (Scotland).
The Singing Campbells. Topic 12T 120.
Barry Canham: see *Canny Newcassel.*
Loman D. Cansler (USA).
Missouri Folk Songs. Folkways FH 5324, 1959. BL.
-----.
Folksongs of the Midwest. Folkways FH 5330, 1973. BL.
Jean Carignan: see Mills.
Richard Carlin (USA).
In Come a Bumblebee: Traditional songs and tunes on the English concertina. Folkways FW 8846, 1977. B.
Mary Ann Carolan (Drogheda, Louth).
Songs from the Irish Tradition. Topic 12TS 362, 1982. Notes by Sean Corcoran.
Jean, Elaine Carruthers: see Valley Folk.
Carter Family (A. P., Maybelle, Sara) (USA).
... on Border Radio. John Edwards Memorial Foundation JEMF 101, rev. 1977. BL, discog.
Martin Carthy (England).
... with Dave Swarbrick. Topic 12TS 340, 1977 (orig. Fontana STL 5269, 1965).
-----.
Landfall. Topic 12TS 345, 1977 (orig. Phillips 6308049, 1971).
-----.
Shearwater. Mooncrest Crest 25, 1972.
-----.
Because It's There. Topic 12TS 389, 1979.
-----: see also Steeleye Span, Watersons.
-----, **Dave Swarbrick** (England).
Second Album. Topic 12TS 341, 1977 (orig. Fontana STL 5362, 1966).
-----, -----.
Byker Hill. Topic 12TS 342, 1977 (orig. Fontana STL 5434, 1967).
-----, -----.
But Two Came By. Topic 12TS 343, 1977 (orig. Fontana STL 5477, 1968).
-----, -----.
Prince Heathen. Topic 12TS 344, 1977 (orig. Fontana STL 5529, 1969).
Barbara Cass-Beggs (coll.)
Folksongs of Saskatchewan. Folkways FE 4312, 1963. BL.

Sam Henry's Songs of the People

Dillard Chandler (NC).
The End of an Old Song. Folkways FA 2418, 1975. BL. Notes by Robert Balsam.

Samuel Charters (coll.).
The Orangemen of Ulster. Folkways FW 3003, 1961. B.

----- (ed.): see *Traditional Music of Ireland.*

Richard Chase: see *American Folk Tales ....*

Margaret Christl, Ian Robb (Canada).
The Barley Grain for Me. Folk-Legacy FSC-62, 1976. BL.

Robert Cinnamond (Antrim).
You Rambling Boys of Pleasure. Topic 12T 269, 1975. Notes by Proinsias O'Conluain.

Peg Clancy (Power) (Tipperary).
Down by the Glenside. Folk-Legacy FSE 8, 1962. BL. Notes by Sean O'Boyle.

-----, **Bobby Clancy** (Tipperary).
Tradition TLP 1045, 1963? BL. Notes by Diane Hamilton.

Clancy Brothers and Tommy Makem (Ireland).
... Sing of the Sea. Columbia CS 9658.

-----.
Tradition/Everest TLP 1042, 1961.

-----.
The Best of ... Tradition/Everest TR 2050.

-----.
At Home with ... and Their Families. Tradition/Everest TR 2060.

-----.
The Rising of the Moon: Irish songs of rebellion. Tradition/Everest TLP 1006 (also *Irish Songs of Rebellion,* Tradition/Everest TR 2070).

-----.
Irish Folk Airs. Tradition/Everest TR 2083.

LaRena Clark (Ontario).
A Canadian Garland: Folksongs from the province of Ontario. Topic 12T 140, 1965.

Eddie Clarke: see *Sailing into Walpole's Marsh.*

Paul Clayton (USA).
The Folkways-Viking Book of Folk Ballads of the English-Speaking World. Folkways FA 2310, 1956. BL. Notes by Kenneth S. Goldstein.

-----.
Bay State Ballads. 10" Folkways FA 2106, 1956. BL. Notes by Kenneth S. Goldstein.

-----.
Folksongs and Ballads of Virginia. 10" Folkways FA 2110, 1956. BL. Notes by Kenneth S. Goldstein.

-----.
Cumberland Mountain Folksongs. 10" Folkways FP 2007, 1957. BL.

-----.
British Broadside Ballads in Popular Tradition. Folkways FW 8708, 1957. BL. Notes by Kenneth S. Goldstein.

-----: see also *American Folk Tales ....*

Sara Cleveland (NY).
Ballads and Songs of the Upper Hudson Valley. Folk-Legacy FSA 33, 1968. BL. Notes by Kenneth S. Goldstein.

Pete, Chris Coe: see Bandoggs.

John Cohen (coll.).
Mountain Music of Kentucky. Folkways FA 2317, 1960. BL.

----- (coll.).
High Atmosphere. Rounder 0028, 1974. BL.

-----: see also New Lost City Ramblers.

Ellen Cohn: see *Sea Chanties ....*

Shirley Collins (England).
Sweet England. Argo RG 150.

-----.
The Sweet Primroses. Topic 12T 170, 1967.

John Conolly: see Broadside.

Billy Conroy: see *Canny Newcassel.*

Audrey Coppard.
English Folk Songs. 10" Folkways FP 917, 1955. BL.

Bob Copper (coll.).
Songs and Southern Breezes: Country singers from Hampshire and Sussex. Topic 12T 317, 1977.

-----, **Ron Copper** (Sussex).
English Shepherd and Farming Songs. Folk-Legacy FSB 19, 1964. BL. Notes by Bob Copper.

-----, -----.
A Song for Every Season. Leader LEAB 404 (4 records: LEA 4046-9), 1971. [B.] also Leader LED 2067 (1 record, selections from LEAB 404).

Seán Corcoran: see *Sailing into Walpole's Marsh.*

Cecilia Costello (Birmingham).
...: Recordings from the Sound Archives of the BBC. Leader LEE 4054, 1975. BL. Notes by Roy Palmer.

Harold Courlander (compiler).
Folk Music USA. Folkways FE 4350.

Harold Covill: see *English Country Music.*

Jim Cowdery: see *How to Change ....*

Sidney Robertson Cowell (coll.).
Wolf River Songs. Folkways FE 4001, 1956. BL.

-----.
Songs of Aran: Gaelic singing from the West of Ireland. Folkways FE 4002, 1957. BL.

Terry Cox: see Pentangle.

Harry Cox (Norfolk).
Traditional English Love Songs. Folk-Legacy FSE 20, 1964. BL. Notes by Peter Kennedy, Francis Collinson.

Helen Creighton (coll.).
Folk Music from Nova Scotia. Folkways FM 4006, 1956. BL.

-----.
Maritime Folk Songs from the Collection of .... Folkways FE 4307, 1962. BL.

Slim Critchlow (USA).
Cowboy Songs: The crooked trail to Holbrook. Arhoolie 5007.

Tom, Barbara Dahill: see Dayhills.

Jackie Daly (Cork).
Music from Sliabh Luachra, Vol. 6. Topic 12TS 358, 1977.

-----: see also De Dannan.

Bob Davenport (England).
Down the Long Road. Topic 12TS 274, 1975.

-----.
Postcards Home. Topic 12TS 318, 1977.

-----.
... and the Rakes 1977. Topic 12TS 350, 1977.

Eric Davidson: see *Iron Mountain ....*

Brian Dawson: see *Broadside.*

The Dayhills Irish Band (Tom, Barbara Dahill, Chuck Heymann).
Biscuit City BC 1318, 1977.

De Danann (Ireland) (Dolores Keane, Frankie Gavin, Charlie Piggott, Alec Finn, Johnny "Ringo" McDonagh).
Boot International ITB 4018 (= Polygram) 1975.

----- (Frankie Gavin, Johnny Moynihan, Charlie Piggott, Alec Finn, "Ringo" McDonagh).
Selected Jigs, Reels & Songs, Established 1975. Shanachie 79001, ?1977, cpr. 1978.

----- (Frankie Gavin, Jackie Daly, Alec Finn, Johnny "Ringo" McDonagh, Charlie Piggott; Seán Ó Conaire, Tom Pháidín Tom).
The Mist Covered Mountain. Shanachie 79005, copyright 1980.

Mel Dean: see *Old Swan Band.*

Tommy Dempsey (Ireland/Birmingham), John Swift.
Green Grow the Laurel. Trailer LER 2096, 1978.

John Dickinson: see *Valley Folk.*

John Doherty (Donegal).
Pedlar's Pack: Songs, stories and fiddle tunes. EFDSS LP 1003, 1964. Notes by Peter Kennedy.

-----.
Gael Linn CEF 072, 073 (2 records), 1975. Notes by David Hammond, Danny O'Donnell, Padráig Ó Baoighill.

Mairéad ní Dhomnaill: see *ní Dhomnaill.*

Tríona ní Dhomnaill: see *ní Dhomnaill.*

Seán 'ac Donnċa (Connemara).
An Aill Bain: The white rock, songs in Irish and English from Connemara. Claddagh CC9, 1972. L (Irish, English). Notes by Séamus Ennis.

Maeve Donnelly: see *Sailing into Walpole's Marsh.*

Johnny Doughty (Sussex).
Round Rye Bay for More: Traditional songs from the Sussex coast. Topic 12TS 324.

The Dubliners (Ireland).
A Drop of the Hard Stuff. Epic BN 26337.

-----.
Fiesta FLBS 1627.

Mary Duffy (Stockton-on-Tees).
Looking Back. People's Stage Tapes cass. 09, 1984.

Max Dunbar (Scotland).
Songs and Ballads of the Scottish Wars, 1290-1745. Folkways FP 3006, 1956. BL.

George Dunn (Staffordshire).
Leader LEE 4042, 1973. BL. Notes by Roy Palmer, Mike Yates, Bob Thomson.

Richard Dyer-Bennet (USA).
[Ballads.] 10" Stinson SLP 35. L. Notes by Ken Goldstein.

-----.
lc: *Twentieth Century Minstrel.* Decca DL 5046.

-----.
c: Vox 632.7.691B.

-----.
lc: *Folk Songs.* Remington RLP 199-34.

Bobby Eaglesham: see *Five Hand Reel.*

SuAnne, Dave Edmundson: see *Hotmud Family.*

Alf Edwards: see *Lloyd.*

George Edworthy (Willand, Devon).
Sing up, George! People's Stage Tapes cass. 06.

Claire Egan: see *Songs of Cork and Kerry.*

Bruce, Pat, Pete Elliott: see *Canny Newcassel.*

Derek, Dorothy Elliott (Yorkshire).
Trailer LER 2033, 1972.

Jack Elliott, Derroll Adams (USA).
Roll on Buddy. Topic 12T 105.

-----: see also *Badmen ....*

Jack Elliott (Durham).
... of Birtley: The songs and stories of a Durham miner. Leader LEA 4001, 1969. [B.]

Elliot [sic] **Family** (Durham).
The Elliots of Birtley: A musical portrait of a Durham mining family. Folkways FG 3565, 1962 (also Transatlantic XTRA 1091). BL. Notes by Peggy Seeger, Ewan MacColl.

Duncan B. M. Emrich: see *AAFS* series, L7, 12, 14, 20, 21, 26.

Tony Engle: see *Oak.*

Logan English (USA).
Kentucky Folk Songs and Ballads. Folkways FA 2136, 1957. BL. Notes by Kenneth S. Goldstein.

Séamus Ennis (Ireland).
The Bonny Bunch of Roses. Tradition TLP 1013.

-----: see also *CWL* Vol. 1.

Sam Eskin (USA).
lc: *Songs of Our Times.* Songs of Our Times 1020.

-----.
lc: *Sea Shanties and Logging Songs.* 10" Folkways FP 19. [?= FA 2019, 1951: *Loggers' Songs and Sea Shanties.* 10" LP. Introduction by John Asch.]

The Exiles (Enoch Kent, Bobby Campbell, Gordon McCulloch, Tim Lyons) (Scotland).
The Hale and the Hanged. Topic 12T 164.

John Faulkner: see *Keane.*

George Faux: see *Hom Bru.*

Jim Ferguson: see *Irish Rovers.*

Ron Field: see *Old Swan Band.*

Caleb Finch: see *Iron Mountain ....*

Alec Finn: see *De Danann.*

Archie Fisher (Scotland).
The Man with a Rhyme. Folk-Legacy FSS 61, 1976. BL.

-----.
Will Ye Gang, Love. Topic 12TS 277, 1976. Notes by Arthur Argo.

Cilla Fisher, Artie Trezise (Scotland).
For Foul Day or Fair. Folk-Legacy FSS 69, 1978. BL.

Five Hand Reel (Sam Bracken, Barry Lyons, Bobby Eaglesham, Dave Tulloch, Tom Hickland) (Scotland).
A Bunch of Fives. Topic 12TS 406, 1979.

Sam Henry's Songs of the People

Joe, Mike Flanagan (Ireland).
An Irish Delight. Topic 12T 365.

Carl Fleischauer: see AAFS series L65-6.

The Flying Cloud.
Traditional Music from Ireland, England, and Scotland. Adelphi AD 1029.

Chris Foster.
Layers. Topic 12TS 329.

Edith Fowke (coll.)
Ontario Ballads and Folksongs. Prestige/Int. 25014.

-----.
Folk Songs of Ontario. Folkways FM 4005, 1958. BL.

-----.
Songs of the Great Lakes. Folkways FM 4018, 1964. BL.

-----.
Far Canadian Fields: Companion to the Penguin Book of Canadian Folk Songs (1973). Leader LEE 4057, 1974. B.

Stuart Frank (USA).
Songs of Sea and Shore. Folkways FH 5256, 1980. BL.

-----: see also *Sea Chanties* ....

Jo Fraser: see Old Swan Band.

Dave Frederickson (USA).
Songs of the West. Folkways FH 5259, 1961. BL. Notes by Roger Abrahams.

The Galliards (Robin Hall, Jimmie MacGregor, Shirley Bland, Leon Rosselson) (England).
Monitor Presents England's Great Folk Group: ... Monitor MFS 407.

Betty Garland (USA).
American Folk Ballads. Folkways FA 2307, 1964. BL.

The Gathering (Paul Brady, Peter Browne, Andy Irvine, Dónal Lunny, Matt Molloy, Tommy Potts) (Ireland).
Greenhays/Sruthán GR 705, 1981.

Dick Gaughan (Scotland).
No More Forever. Trailer LER 2072, 1972.

-----.
Gaughan. Topic 12TS 384, 1978. BL.

-----: see also *Bonny Pit Laddie.*

Frankie Gavin: see De Danann.

Sorcha ní Ghuairim (Ireland).
... Sings Traditional Irish Songs. Folkways FW 6861, 1957. BL.

Tom Gilfellon (England).
Loving Mad Tom. Trailer LER 2079, 1972.

-----: see also High Level Ranters, *Bonny Pit Laddie, Canny Newcassel.*

Stuart Gillespie: see *Sea Chanties*....

Shep Ginandes (USA).
lc: *British Traditional Ballads in America,* Vol. 1. Elektra JH 508.

Kenneth S. Goldstein: see *Riverside CB* series (among many others).

Rick Good: see Hotmud Family.

Robert Winslow Gordon: see AAFS series L56.

Michael Gorman: see Barry.

Addie Graham (KY)
Been a Long Time Traveling. June Appal JA 020, 1978. BL.

Len Graham (Antrim).
Wind and Water: Traditional songs, ballads and lilts. Topic 12TS 334, 1977.

-----: see also Joe Holmes.

Percy Grainger (coll.).
Unto Brigg Fair: Joseph Taylor and other traditional Lincolnshire singers recorded in 1908 by .... Leader LEA 4050, 1972. BL.

John Greenway (USA).
Australian Folksongs and Ballads. Folkways FW 8718, 1959. BL.

Sarah Ogan Gunning (KY).
Girl of Constant Sorrow. Folk-Legacy FSA 26, 1965. BL.

Woody Guthrie.
The Legendary ...: In Memoriam. Tradition/Everest 2058.

Peggy Haine: see Iron Mountain ....

Robin Hall: see Galliards.

Fred Hamer: see *Garners Gay.*

Diane Hamilton (coll.).
The Lark in the Morning: Songs and dances from the Irish countryside. Tradition TLP 1004.

-----: see also *Singing Men of Ulster.*

David Hammond (Belfast).
I Am the Wee Falorie Man: Folk songs of Ireland. Tradition TLP 1028, 1959.

----- (ed.).
Ulster's Flowery Vale: Traditional songs and music of the North of Ireland. BBC 28M, 1961.

-----, Dónal Lunny.
The Singer's House. Greenhays/Sruthan GR 702, 1980.

Hammons Family: see AAFS series L65-6.

Johnny Handle: see High Level Ranters, *Bonnie Pit Laddie, Canny Newcassel.*

Mick Hanly (Ireland).
A Kiss in the Morning Early. Green Linnet SIF 3017, 1982 (orig. Mulligan 1976).

-----.
As I Went over Blackwater. Green Linnet SIF 3007, 1982 (orig. Mulligan 047, 1980).

Geordie Hanna (Tyrone).
... Sings. Eagran MD 0002, 1978. Notes by Sean O Boyle.

George Hanna, Sarah Anne O'Neill (Tyrone).
On the Shores of Lough Neagh: Traditional songs of a Tyrone family. Topic 12TS 372, 1978. Notes by John Moulden.

Dave Hardy (England).
Leaving the Dales. Red Rag RRR 008.

Marie Hare (New Brunswick).
Miramichi Songs and Ballads. Folk-Legacy FSC-9, 1962. BL. Notes by Louise Manny, Edward D. Ives.

Roy Harris (England).
The Bitter and the Sweet. Topic 12TS 217, 1972. Notes by A. L. Lloyd.

Discography

—————.
Champions of Folly: Folk songs and ballads sung by .... Topic 12TS 256, 1975.

—————.
By Sandbank Fields. Topic 12TS 327, 1977.

Sue Harris (England).
Hammers and Tongues. Free Reed FRR 020, 1978.

—————: see also *Kirkpatrick.*

John Harrison: see *Watersons.*

Leslie Harpur: see *Irish Country Four.*

Bob Hart (Suffolk).
Songs from Suffolk. Topic 12TS 225, 1973.

—————: see also *Flash Company.*

Tim Hart: see *Steeleye Span.*

Frank Harte (Ireland).
Through Dublin City: Lyrical ballads and rebel songs. Topic 12TS 318, 1973.

Cliff Haslam (England).
The Clockwinder. Folk-Legacy FSB 93, 1983. BL.

—————: see also *Colonial and Revolutionary ....*

James N. Healy: see *Ballads from the Pubs ..., Songs of Cork and Kerry.*

Joe Heaney (Galway).
Irish Traditional Songs in Gaelic and English. Topic 12T 91, 1963. Notes by A. L. Lloyd.

—————.
Come All Ye Gallant Irishmen. Philo 2004, 1975.

—————.
Seosamh Ó hÉanaí. Gael-Linn CEF 028.

Stephen Heap: see *Valley Folk.*

Karen G. Helms (coll.).
Between the Sound and the Sea: Oral Traditional Music of the North Carolina Outer Banks. Folkways FS 3949, 1977. B.

—————.
Hand-Me-Down Music: Old songs, old friends, 1. Traditional Music of Union County, NC. Folkways FES 34151, 1979. BL.

—————.
Hand-Me-Down Music: Old songs, old friends, 2. Traditional Music of Union County, NC. Folkways FES 34152, 1980. BL.

Wade Hemsworth (Canada).
Folk Songs of the Canadian North Woods. 10" Folkways FW 6821, 1955. BL.

Doreen Henderson: see *Canny Newcassel.*

Kathy Henderson: see *My Song Is My Own.*

Chuck Heymann: see *Dayhills.*

Joe Hickerson (USA).
... with a Gathering of Friends. Folk-Legacy FSI-39, 1971. BL.

—————.
Drive Dull Care Away, Vol. 2. Folk-Legacy FSI 59, 1976. BL.

Tom Hickland: see *Five Hand Reel.*

The Hickory Nuts: see *Old Time Ballads ....*

Hicks Family: see *TFS* series, 104.

Bella Higgins: see *Muckle Sangs.*

Lizzie Higgins (Aberdeen).
Princess of the Thistle. Topic 12T 185, 1969. Notes by Peter Hall.

—————.
Up and awa' wi' the Laverock. Topic 12TS 260, 1975. [BL.] Notes by Peter Hall.

—————: see also *Muckle Sangs.*

The High Level Ranters (Alistair Anderson, Tom Gilfellon, Johnny Handle, Colin Ross) (Northumberland).
The Lads of Northumbria. Trailer LER 2007, 1969.

—————.
A Mile to Ride: Music and song from Northumberland and the borders. Trailer LER 2037, 1973.

—————: see also *Bonnie Pit Laddie.*

Frank Hinchcliffe (S. Yorkshire).
In Sheffield Park. Topic 12TS 308, 1977.

Bill "Pop" Hingston (Dittisham, Devon).
Hingston's Half Hour: The life and songs of "Pop" Hingston. People's Stage Tapes cass. 03.

Bo Hinrichs: see *How to Change ...*

Sam Hinton (USA).
The Wandering Folksong. Folkways FA 2401, 1966. BL.

—————.
I'll Sing You a Story: Folk ballads for young people. Folkways FC 7548, 1972. BL.

Jim Hockenhull: see *Philo Glee ....*

Roscoe Holcomb (KY).
The High Lonesome Sound. Folkways FA 2368, 1965. BL. Notes by John Cohen.

—————.
Close to Home. Folkways FA 2374, 1975. BL. Notes by John Cohen.

—————, **Wade Ward** (VA).
The Music of ... Folkways FA 2363, 1962. BL.

Floyd Holland: see *Stone County Singing.*

Lori Holland (USA).
Irish Folk Songs for Women. Folkways FG 3518, 1960. BL. Notes by Kenneth S. Goldstein.

Maggie Holland: see *Hot Vultures.*

Joe Holmes, Len Graham (Antrim).
Chaste Muses, Bards and Sages. Free Reed 007, 1976.

—————, —————.
After Dawning: Traditional Songs, Ballads and Lilts from the North of Ireland. Topic 12TS 401, 1979.

Hom Bru (Shetland) (Peter Miller, George Faux, Gary Petterson, Ivor Pottinger).
Obadeea. Celtic Music CM 009, 1982.

Gary Hopkins: see *Hotmud Family.*

Hotmud Family (USA) (SuAnne, Dave Edmundson, Rick Good, T. J. Lundy, Gary Hopkins).
Meat and Potatoes and Stuff Like That. Flying Fish FF 251, 1981. L.

Hot Vultures (England) (Ian A. Anderson, Maggie Holland).
Sierra/Briar SBR 4212, 1980 (orig. Plant Life, 1979).

Wallace House (England).
English Folk Songs. 10" Folkways FW 6823, 1952. BL.

Cisco Houston (USA).
Hard Travelin'. 10" Folkways FA 2042, 1954. BL. Notes by Kenneth S. Goldstein.

Sam Henry's Songs of the People

How to Change a Flat Tire (Bo Hinrichs, Jim Cowdery, Ginny Phelps, Jim Martin, Dean Kuth) (USA).
A Point of Departure. Front Hall FHR 09, 1977.

Max Hunter (MO).
Ozark Folksongs and Ballads. Folk-Legacy FSA 11, 1963. BL. Notes by Mary Celestia Parler, Vance Randolph.

E. G[ale] Huntington (MA).
Folksongs from Martha's Vineyard. 10" Folkways FA 2032, 1958. BL. Notes by Kenneth S. Goldstein.

Hamish Imlach (Scotland).
... Sampler. Transatlantic TRA SAM 9.

Irish Country Four (Brian, Valerie Bailie, Leslie Harpur, Trevor Stewart) (Ulster).
Songs, Ballads and Instrumental Tunes from Ulster. Topic 12TS 209.

Irish Rovers (George, Will, Joe Millar; Jim Ferguson).
The Unicorn. Decca DL 749514.

Iron Mountain String Band (USA) (Eric Davidson, Caleb Finch, Peggy Haine).
...: An old time Southern mountain string band. Folkways FA 2473, 1973. BL.

----- (Brooke Moyer, Eric Davidson, Caleb Finch).
Walkin' in the Parlor. Folkways FA 2477, 1975. BL.

Andy Irvine: see Planxty, Gathering.

-----, **Paul Brady** (Ireland).
Green Linnet SIF 3006, 1981 (orig. Mulligan LUN 008, 1976).

Elizabeth Isaac: see *Songs of Cork and Kerry*.

Tex Isley: see Ashley.

Burl Ives (USA).
Men. ?Decca DL 8125.

-----.
The Wayfaring Stranger. lc: Stinson SLP 1. ?Columbia CS 9041.

-----.
lc: Columbia CL 6058.

-----.
lc: Columbia CL 6144.

-----.
lc: *Songs of the Colonies*. Encyclopedia Britannica Films EBF 1 (78 rpm).

-----.
lc: *Songs of the Sea*. Encyclopedia Britannica Films EBF 4 (78 rpm).

-----.
lc: *Songs of Expanding America*. Encyclopedia Britannica Films EBF 6 (78 rpm).

Edward "Sandy" Ives (USA, ME).
Folksongs of Maine. Folkways FH 5323, 1959. BL. Notes by Sandy Ives, Kenneth S. Goldstein.

Alan Jabbour: see AAFS series L65-6.

Harry Jackson (USA).
The Cowboy: His Songs, Ballads and Brag Talk. Folkways FH 5723 (2 records), 1957. BL. Notes by Kenneth S. Goldstein.

Karen James (USA).
Through Streets Broad and Narrow. Folkways FG 3547.

Bert Jansch: see Pentangle.

Bob Johnson: see Steeleye Span.

Nic Jones (England).
Ballads and Songs. Trailer LER 2014, 1970.

-----.
Trailer LER 2027, 1971.

-----.
The Noah's Ark Trap. Shanachie 79003 (= Trailer LER 2091, 1977).

-----.
From the Devil to a Stranger. Highway (Trailer) LTRA 507, 1978.

-----: see also Bandoggs.

Fred Jordan (Shropshire).
Songs of a Shropshire Farm Worker. Topic 12T 150, 1966.

-----.
When the Frost Is on the Pumpkin. Topic 12TS 233, 1974. Notes by Mike Yates.

Junior Skillet Lickers: see *Down Yonder*.

Israel Kaplan (NY).
When I Was a Boy in Brooklyn: An autobiography. Folkways FG 3501, 1961. BL.

Buell Kazee (KY).
June Appal JA 009, 1978. BL. Notes by Loyal Jones, William H. Tallmadge, Norm Cohen.

Dolores Keane: see also De Danann.

-----, **John Faulkner** (Ireland).
Broken-Hearted I'll Wander. Green Linnet SIF 3004 (orig. Mulligan LUN 033, 1979).

Sarah, Rita Keane (Galway).
Once I Loved. Claddagh CC4, 1968.

Arthur Kearney: see Tunney.

Paddy Keenan (Westmeath).
Gael Linn CEF 045, 1975. Notes by Séamus Ennis.

-----: see also Bothy Band.

Gene Kelly.
lc: Columbia JL 8001.

Rick Kemp: see Steeleye Span.

Norman Kennedy (Aberdeen).
Ballads and Songs of Scotland Sung by .... Folk-Legacy FSS 34, 1968. BL. Notes by Peter Hall.

Peter Kennedy: see CWL series Vol. 3.

Enoch Kent: see Exiles.

Sandra Kerr: see *My Song Is My Own*.

Pat Kilbride: see Battlefield Band.

Louis Killen (Newcastle).
Ballads and Broadsides. Topic 12T 126, 1965.

-----.
50 South to 50 South: ... Sings on the Cape Horn Road. South Street Seaport SPT-102, 1970. South Street Seaport Museum [New York, NY].

-----.
Old Songs, Old Friends. Front Hall FHR 012, 1977. BL.

-----.
Gallant Lads Are We: Songs of the British Industrial Revolution. Collector 1932, 1980. BL.

-----, **Sally Killen**.
Bright Shining Morning. Front Hall FHR 06.

-----: see also Cameron.

Discography

Tom Kines (Canada).
Songs from Shakespeare's Plays and Popular Songs of Shakespeare's Time. Folkways VW 8767, 1961. BL.
-----.
An Irishman in North America. Folkways FG 3522, 1962. BL.
John Kirkpatrick: see also Raven, Steeleye Span.
-----, **Sue Harris** (England).
Shreds and Patches. Topic 12TS 355, 1977.
Debora G. Kodish: see AAFS series L68.
Jimmy Knights: see *Sing, Say and Play.*
Peter Knight: see Steeleye Span, *Sing, Say and Play.*
Tony Kraber (USA).
lc: *The Old Chisholm Trail.* Mercury MG 20008.
Dean Kuth: see How to Change ....

Jim Lackey (USA).
lc: *Square Dance Album.* Mercury Album A-80 (78 rpm).
Derek Lamb (England?).
She Was Poor but She Was Honest: Nice, naughty and nourishing songs of the London music hall and pubs. Folkways FW 8707, 1962. BL.
Sam Larner (Norfolk).
Now Is the Time for Fishing Folkways FG 3507, 1961. BL. Extensive notes by Ewan MacColl, Peggy Seeger.
-----.
A Garland for Sam: Songs and ballads of Sam Larner of Winterton. Topic 12T 244, 1974. Notes by A. L. Lloyd.
June Lazare (USA).
Folk Songs of New York City. Folkways FH 5276, 1966. BL.
MacEdward Leach (coll.)
Songs from the Out-Ports of Newfoundland. Folkways FE 4075, 1966. BL.
Leadbelly (Huddie Ledbetter) (USA).
lc: *Leadbelly Sings More Play Party Songs.* Stinson SLP 41.
Denis Leahy: see *Songs of Cork and Kerry.*
Mike Lee: see Broadside.
Tom Lenihan (Clare).
Paddy's Panacea: Songs traditional in West Clare. Topic 12TS 363, 1978. Notes by Tom Munnelly.
The Ling Family (Geoff, George, Percy Ling) (Suffolk).
...: Singing traditions of a Suffolk Family. Topic 12TS 292, 1977.
A. L. Lloyd (England).
A Selection from the Penguin Book of English Folk Songs, ed. Ralph Vaughan Williams, A. L. Lloyd. Alf Edwards, concertina. Folk-Lyric FL 121 (= Selection Records, 1980).
-----.
First Person. Topic 12T 118, 1966.
-----: see also *Great Australian Legend, Riverside CB* series.
-----, **Ewan MacColl** (Scotland).
Blow Boys Blow: Songs of the sea. Tradition TLP 1026.

-----, -----.
English and Scottish Folk Ballads. Topic 12T 103, 1964. BL. Notes by A. L. Lloyd.
Alan Lomax: see AAFS series L1, *CWL* series Vols. 1, 3.
John A. Lomax, Jr.: see Tex-i-an Boys.
Trevor Lucas: see *Great Australian Legend.*
T. J. Lundy: see Hotmud Family.
Dónal Lunny: see Hammond, Planxty, Bothy Band, Gathering.
Frank Luther (USA).
lc: *Get along Little Dogies and Home on the Range.* Decca DL 5035.
Barry Lyons: see Five Hand Reel.
Tim Lyons (Ireland).
Easter Snow. Green Linnet SIF 1014, 1978.
-----.
The Green Linnet. Trailer LER 3036.
-----: see also Exiles.

Margaret MacArthur (VT).
... and family of Marlboro, VT. On the Mountains High. Living Folk Records F-LFR 100, 1971. BL.
-----.
The Old Songs. Philo PH 41001, 1975.
Jimmy McBeath (Scotland).
Bound to Be a Row. Topic 12T 303, 1978. Notes by Peter Hall.
-----: see also *Muckle Sangs.*
Joe McCafferty (Donegal).
Ceolta agus Shanchas Thir Chonaill: Songs and Stories in Irish and English. European Ethnic Oral Traditions, Trinity College, Dublin. C-90 cass., 1984. BL.
Dennis McCarthy: see *Ballads from the Pubs* ....
Ewan MacColl (Scotland).
Chorus from the Gallows. Topic 12T 16.
-----.
Bothy Ballads of Scotland. Folkways FW 8759, 1961. BL.
-----.
English and Scottish Popular Ballads (Child Ballads). 3 vols. Folkways FG 3509, 1961; 3510, 3511, 1964. BL.
-----.
The Manchester Angel. Topic 12T 147 (also Tradition/Everest TR 2059).
-----: see also Lloyd, Seeger; *B&R*, Folkways *CB*, and Riverside *CB* series.
-----, **Dominic Behan** (Ireland).
The Singing Streets: Childhood Memories of Ireland and Scotland. Folkways FW 8501, 1958 (also Topic). BL.
Jim McConnell: see Tex-i-an Boys.
Mack McCormick (coll.).
The Unexpurgated Folk Songs of Men. Raglan R-51, 1960. B.
Gordeanna McCulloch (Scotland).
Topic 12TS 370.
Gordon McCulloch: see Exiles.
Ed McCurdy.
b: *A Treasure Chest of American Folk Song.* 2 recs., Elektra EKL 205.
-----: see also *Badmen* ....

Sam Henry's Songs of the People

Johnny "Ringo" McDonagh: see De Danann.
John MacDonald (Morayshire).
  The Singing Molecatcher of Morayshire. Topic 12TS 263, 1975. Notes by Hamish Henderson.
Rory, Alex McEwen (Scotland).
  Scottish Songs and Ballads. 10" Folkways FW 6930, 1957. BL. Notes by Dean Gitter.
Shanna Beth McGee (USA).
  Love Is Teasing: Scottish and English early ballads. Folkways FW 8779, 1980. B.
John McGettigan.
  ... and His Irish Minstrels. Topic 12T 367, 1979.
Jimmie MacGregor: see Galliards.
Antoinette McKenna.
  At Home. Shanachie 29016.
Campbell MacLean: see Muckle Sangs.
Dolly Mc Mahon.
  h: *Dolly*. Claddagh CC 3.
Jamie McMenemy: see Battlefield Band.
Alison McMorland: see also *My Song Is My Own*.
  -----, **Peta Webb.**
    Topic 12TS 403, 1980.
Brian McNeill: see Battlefield Band.
Flora MacNeil.
  Craobh Non Ubhall: Traditional Gaelic Songs from the Western Isles. Tangent TGS 124.
The McPeake Family (Belfast).
  Irish Traditional Songs and Music. Topic 12T 87, 1962.
Jacqui McShee: see Pentangle.
John Maguire (Fermanagh).
  Come Day, Go Day, God Send Sunday. Leader LEE 4062, 1973. Notes by Robin Morton, John Moulden.
J. E. Mainer.
  ... with Friends at Home, Vol. 2: A tribute. Old Homestead OHCS 147, 1983.
Sarah Makem (Armagh).
  Ulster Ballad Singer. Topic 12T 182, 1968. Notes by Sean O'Boyle (Ireland).
Tommy Makem (Armagh).
  Songs of .... Tradition TLP 1044, 1961.
  -----: see also Clancy.
Bill C. Malone: see Smithsonian Coll. series.
Ian Manuel (England).
  The Frosty Ploughshare: Bothy songs and ballads. Topic 12TS 220, 1972. Notes by A. L. Lloyd.
  -----.
    The Dales of Caledonia. Topic 12TS 301, 1977. Notes by A. L. Lloyd.
Jim Martin: see How to Change ....
George Maynard (Sussex).
  Ye Subjects of England: Traditional songs of Sussex. Topic 12T 286, 1976. Notes by Mike Yates, Ken Stubbs.
Bill Meek (Down).
  Traditional and Original Songs of Ireland. Folk-Legacy FSE 21, 1965. BL.
Bill Meek: see Broadside.
George, Joe, Will Millar: see Irish Rovers.
John Millar: see *Colonial and Revolutionary ....*
Peter Miller: see Hom Bru.
Smoky Joe Miller: see *Down Yonder*.
Alan Mills (Canada).
  Folk Songs of Newfoundland. 10" Folkways FW 6831, 1953. BL.

-----, **Jean Carignan** (Quebec).
  Songs, Fiddle Tunes, and a Folk-Tale from Canada. Folkways FG 3532, 1966. BL.
Bob Mills (Arlvesford, Hampshire).
  Songs of a Hampshire Man. People's Stage Tapes cass. 05.
Howie Mitchell (USA).
  Folk-Legacy FSI 5, 1963. BL.
Kevin Mitchell (Ireland).
  Free and Easy: Traditional songs mainly from northwest Ulster. Topic 12TS 314, 1977.
Matt Molloy: see Bothy Band, Gathering.
Mick Moloney (Ireland).
  ... with Eugene O'Donnell. Green Linnet SIF 1010, 1978.
Barbara Moncure, Harry Siemsen (USA).
  Folksongs of the Catskills. Folkways FH 5311, 1963. BL.
Christy Moore (Ireland).
  Prosperous. Tara 2008, 1972.
  -----: see Planxty.
Doyle Moore: see Philo Glee ....
Kendall Morse (Maine).
  Lights along the Shore. Folk-Legacy FSI 57. BL.
Robin Morton (ed.).
  Folk Songs Sung in Ulster. Mercier Irl 11, 12 (2 recs.), 1971-2.
Artus Moser (USA).
  North Carolina Ballads. 10" Folkways FA 2112, 1955. BL.
  -----.
    North Carolina Mountain Folksongs and Ballads. Folkways FD 5331, 1974. BL.
Ann Mayo Muir: see Bok.
Brooke Moyer: see Iron Mountain ....
Tom Munnelly (ed.).
  Songs of the Irish Travellers, 1967-75: Traditional ballads and lyric songs. European Ethnic Oral Traditions, Trinity College, Dublin. C-60 cass. 1983. BL.
Delia Murphy (Ireland).
  EMI (Ireland) STAL 1055.

Tom Napper, Alastair Russell.
  Tripping Upstairs. Celtic Music CM 002.
Glen Neaves and the Virginia Mountain Boys.
  Country Bluegrass from Southwest Virginia. Folkways FA 3830, 1974. BL.
The New Lost City Ramblers (Mike Seeger, Tom Paley, John Cohen) (USA).
  Old Timey Songs for Children. 10" Folkways FC 7064, 1959. BL.
  -----.
    ... , Vol. 2. Folkways FA 2397, 1960. BL.
  -----.
    ... , Vol. 4. Folkways FA 2399, 1962. BL.
  -----.
    ... with Cousin Emmy. Folkways FTS 31015, 1968.
  ----- (Mike Seeger, Tracy Schwarz, John Cohen).
    Remembrance of Things to Come. Folkways FTS 31035, 1973.
Mairéad ní Dhomhnaill (Ireland).
  Gael-Linn CEF 055, 1976.
  -----: see also *Sailing into Walpole's Marsh*.

Discography

Tríona ní Dhomhnaill (Ireland).
    Tríona. Gael-Linn CEF 043, 1975.
-----: see also Bothy Band.
John Jacob Niles (USA).
    lc: *American Folk Love Songs*. Boone-Tolliver LP.

    The Best of .... Tradition/Everest S 2055, 1967?
Hermes Nye (USA).
    Ballads of the Civil War. 10" Folkways FH 5004 (2187, 2188)(2 recs.) 1954. BL.

Seán O'Boyle: see *Singing Men of Ulster*.
Joan O'Bryant (USA).
    Folksongs and Ballads of Kansas. 10" Folkways FA 2134, 1957. BL. Notes by Kenneth S. Goldstein.
-----.
    American Ballads and Folksongs. Folkways FA 2338, 1958. BL. Notes by Kenneth S. Goldstein.
Seán Ó Conaire: see De Danann.
Mícheál Ó Domhnaill: see Burke, Bothy Band.
Eugene O'Donnell: see Moloney.
Liam O'Flynn: see Planxty.
Des, Vince O'Halloran (Connemara).
    The Men of the Island. Topic 12TS 305.
Mary O'Hara (Ireland).
    ...'s Ireland. Tradition/Everest 2115 (Emerald Gem, Belfast), 1973.
Sarah Anne O'Neill: see Hanna.
Oak (Tony Engle, Peta Webb, Rod, Danny Stradling).
    Welcome to Our Fair. Topic 12TS 212.
Glenn Ohrlin: see *Stone County Singing*.
Milt Okun (USA).
    lc: *Adirondack Songs and Ballads from the Marjorie L. Porter Collection of North Country Lore.* Stinson SLP 82.
-----, Ellen Stekert.
c: *Traditional American Love Songs.* Riverside RLP 12 634.
The Old Hat Band (John Burke, Jeffrey Thom, Ellen Bush).
    Concert. Voyager VRLP 3075.
The Old Reliable String Band (Tom Paley, Roy Berkeley, Artie Rose) (USA).
    Folkways FA 2475, 1963. BL.
The Old Swan Band (Rod, Danny Stradling, Martin Brinsford, Jo Fraser, Ron Field, Mel Dean).
    Free Reed FRR 028, 1978.
Lawrence Older (NY).
    Adirondack Songs, Ballads and Fiddle Tunes. Folk-Legacy FSA 15, 1964. Notes by Peter McElligott.
Harry Oster: see *Sampler of Louisiana Folk Songs*.
Blanton Owen: see *VT series BRI 002*.
William A. Owens (coll.).
    cass. for *Tell Me a Story, Sing Me a Song: A Texas chronicle*. Austin: Univ. of Texas Press, 1983.
Dave Oxley: see Raven.

Tom Paley: see Seeger, New Lost City Ramblers, Old Reliable ...
Estella Palmer: see *Stone County Singing*.

Walter Pardon (Norfolk).
    A Proper Sort. Leader LED 2063, 1975.

    Our Side of the Baulk. Leader LED 2111, 1977.

    A Country Life. Topic 12TS 392.
-----.
    Bright Golden Store: Songs and melodion tunes performed by ... of Knapton in Norfolk. Home Made Music LP 301, 1983.
Uncle John Patterson: see *Down Yonder*.
Ken Peacock (Canada).
    Songs and Ballads of Newfoundland. Folkways FG 3505, 1956. [BL.]
Les Pearson: see *Canny Newcassel*.
Nigel Pegrum: see Steeleye Span.
Pentangle (Jacqui McShee, Bert Jansch, John Renbourn, Terry Cox? Danny Thompson?) (England).
    Cruel Sister. Transatlantic XTRA 1172, 1966. L.
Peter, Paul and Mary (Peter Yarrow, Paul Stookey, Mary Travers).
    Moving. Warner Bros. W 1473. 1963.
Gary Petterson: see Hom Bru.
Ginny Phelps: see *How to Change ....*
Philo Glee and Mandoline Society (Doyle Moore, Jim Hockenhull, Paul Adkins) (USA).
    Puritan 5007, 1957 (= Campus Folksong Club, Univ. of Illinois CFC 101).
Ed Pickford: see *Canny Newcassel*.
George Pickow: see Ritchie.
Charlie Piggott: see De Danann.
Planxty (Christy Moore, Andy Irvine, Dónal Lunny, Liam O'Flynn) (Ireland).
    Polydor 2383 186.
-----.
    Shanachie 79009, ?1974, ?1979.
-----.
    The Well below the Valley. Shanachie 79010, 1979.
-----.
    The Woman I Loved So Well. Tara 3005, 1980.
-----.
    Words & Music. Shanachie 79035, 1983.
Cyril Poacher (Suffolk).
    The Broomfield Wager: Traditional songs from Suffolk. Topic 12TS 252, 1975. Notes by Mike Yates, Keith Summers.
Howard Porper: see Tex-i-an Boys.
Ivor Pottinger: see Hom Bru.
Tommy Potts: see Gathering.
Peg Clancy Power: see Clancy.
Maddy Prior: see Steeleye Span.
Frank Proffitt (NC).
    ... Sings Folk Songs. Folkways FA 2360, 1962. BL. Notes by Anne, Frank Warner.
-----.
    ... of Reese, North Carolina. Folk-Legacy FSA 1 (also Topic 12T 162), 1962. BL. Notes by Sandy Paton.

Evelyn Ramsay: see Appalachia (Vol. 1).

Sam Henry's Songs of the People

Obray Ramsey (NC).
Folksongs from the Three Laurels. Prestige 13020.
-----.
Folksongs from the Gateways to the Great Smokies. Prestige 13030.
Jon Raven (with Dave Oxley, John Kirkpatrick, Mike Billington) (England).
Ballad of the Black Country. Broadside BRO 116, 1975.
Jean Redpath (Fife, Scotland).
Frae My Ain Countrie. Folk-Legacy FSS 49, 1973. BL.
-----.
Song of the Seals. Philo 1054, 1978.
-----: see also *Ballad Folk.*
Ola Belle Reed.
... and Family. Rounder 0077, 1977. B.
Ray Reed (NM).
... Sings Traditional Frontier and Cowboy Songs. Folkways FD 5329, 1977. BL.
Alan Reid: see Battlefield Band.
John Reilly (Ireland).
The Bonny Green Tree: Songs of an Irish traveller. Topic 12T 359, 1978. BL. Notes by Tom Munnelly.
John Renbourn: see Pentangle.
Eugene Rhodes (USA).
Talkin' about My Time. Folk-Legacy FSA 12, 1963. BL. Notes by Bruce Jackson.
Sam Richards: see *Songs of a Devon Farmer.*
Vivien Richman (USA).
... Sings! Folkways FG 3568, 1959. BL.
Almeda Riddle (AR).
Granny Riddle's Songs and Ballads. Minstrel JD 203, 1977.
Jim Ringer (USA).
Waiting for the Hard Times to Go. Folk-Legacy FSI 47, 1972. BL.
Edna Ritchie (KY).
Folk-Legacy FSA 3, 1962. BL. Notes by D. K. Wilgus.
Jean Ritchie (KY).
lc: *Kentucky Mountain Songs.* Elektra EKLP 2.
-----.
The Best of .... Prestige/Folklore 13003.
-----.
Children's Songs and Games from the Southern Mountains. 10" Folkways FC 7054, 1957. BL. Notes by Kenneth S. Goldstein.
-----.
British Traditional Ballads (Child Ballads) in the Southern Mountains.
   Vol. 1. Folkways FA 2301, 1961. BL.
   Vol. 2. Folkways FA 2302, 1961. BL.
Notes by Kenneth S. Goldstein.
[Title on both booklets is "Child Ballads in America."]
-----.
High Hills and Mountains. Greenhays GR 701, 1979. L.
-----: see also *American Folk Tales ..., Folk Concert ....*

-----, George Pickow (colls.).
As I Roved Out (Field Trip -- Ireland). Folkways FW 8872, 1960. B.
-----, -----.
Field Trip -- England. Folkways FW 8871, 1960. BL.
Ritchie Family (KY).
The Ritchies of Kentucky: Jean Ritchie interviews her family, with documentary recordings. Folkways FA 2316, 1959. BL. Notes by Kenneth S. Goldstein.
Tex Ritter.
lc: Capitol 112 (78 rpm) 1629.
Ian Robb: see Christl.
Bob Roberts (Suffolk).
Songs from the Sailing Barges. Topic 12TS 361, 1978. Notes by A. L. Lloyd.
John Roberts, Tony Barrand (England).
Mellow with Ale from the Horn. Front Hall FHR 04, 1975. BL.
-----, -----.
Dark Ships in the Forest: Ballads of the supernatural. Folk-Legacy FSI 65, 1977. BL.
-----, -----, Fred Breunig, Steve Woodruff.
The Second Nowell: A pageant of mid-winter carols. (*Nowell Sing We Clear*, Vol. 2.) Front Hall FHR 020, 1981. BL.
Jeannie Robertson (Scotland).
Songs of a Scots Tinker Lady. Riverside RLP 12 633.
-----.
The Cuckoo's Nest and Other Scottish Folk Songs. Prestige/Int. 13075.
-----.
...: The great Scots traditional ballad singer. Topic 12T 96, 1959. Notes by Hamish Henderson.
-----: see also *Muckle Sangs.*
Paul Robeson.
c: Vanguard VSD 57.
Grant Rogers (NY).
Songmaker of the Catskills. Folk-Legacy FSA 27, 1965. BL. Notes by Sandy Paton.
Sally Rogers (USA).
The Unclaimed Pint. Thrushwood 001, 1982.
Artie Rose: see *Old Reliable ...*
Pete Rose: see *Tex-i-an Boys.*
Tony Rose (England).
Under the Greenwood Tree: Some songs of Wessex. Trailer LER 2024, 1971.
-----.
On Banks of Green Willow. Trailer LER 2101, 1976.
-----.
Poor Fellows. Dingle's DIN 324, 1982.
-----: see also Bandoggs.
Neil V. Rosenberg: see AAFS series L68.
Colin Ross: see High Level Ranters, *Bonny Pit Laddie, Canny Newcassel.*
Leon Rosselson: see Galliards.
Alastair Russell: see Napper.

Discography

Hjalmar Rutzebeck.
Leave Her Johnnie, Leave Her: The stories and shanties of .... Folkways FSS 38554 (2 records) 1981. BL.

Derek Serjeant (England).
... Sings English Folk. Joy Special JS 5001, 1970.

Tracy Schwarz: see New Lost City Ramblers.

Willie Scott (Berwickshire).
The Shepherd's Song: Border Ballads. Topic 12T 183, 1968.

Dave Sear: see *Folk Concert* ....

Seeger Family (Peggy, Penny, Barbara, Michael).
American Folk Songs Sung by the Seegers. 10" Folkways FA 2005, 1957. BL. Notes by Charles Seeger, Sr.

Charles Seeger: see AAFS series L54.

Mike Seeger (USA).
Old Time Country Music. Folkways FA 2325, 1962. B (preliminary).

-----: see also New Lost City Ramblers.

-----, Peggy Seeger.
American Folk Songs for Children: 94 songs sung and played by ... from Ruth Crawford Seeger's American Folk Songs for Children (Doubleday, 1948). Rounder 8001-3 (3 records) 1977. B.

Peggy Seeger (USA).
... Sings and Plays American Folksongs for Banjo. Folk-Lyric FL 114. B.

-----.
Folk Songs of Courting and Complaint. Folkways FA 2049 [c: ?= FL 5401], 1955. BL.

-----.
A Song for You and Me. Prestige INT 13050.

-----: see also *B&R, LH* series, MacColl.

-----, **Ewan MacColl** (Scotland).
Two-Way Trip: American, Scots and English folksongs sung by ... Folkways FW 8755, 1961. BL.

-----, -----.
Saturday Night at the 'Bull and Mouth.' Folkways FW 8731, 1978. BL.

Peggy Seeger, Tom Paley (USA).
Who's Going to Shoe Your Pretty Little Foot? Topic 12T 113 (= Elektra EKL 295/EKS 7295).

Pete Seeger (USA).
Darling Corey. Folkways FA 2003 (= FP 3), 1950.

-----.
American Folk Songs for Children: Selections from American Folk Songs for Children, by Ruth Crawford Seeger. Folkways FC 7601 (FTS 31501), 1953 (1954). BL.

-----.
... Sings American Ballads. Folkways FA 2319. BL.

-----.
American Favorite Ballads, Vol. 2. Folkways FA 2321, 1958. BL.

-----.
Love Songs for Friends and Foes. Folkways FA 2453, 1958. BL.

-----.
Birds, Beast, Bugs and Bigger Fishes. Folkways FC 7611, 1954, 1960. BL.

-----.
With Voices Together We Sing. Folkways FA 2452, 1956, 1961. BL. Notes by Pete Seeger, Harold Thompson.

-----.
... At the Village Gate, with Memphis Slim and Willie Dixon. Folkways FA 2451, 1962. BL.

-----.
Song and Play Time. Folkways FC 7526, 1960, 1963. BL.

-----.
Wimoweh and Other Songs of Freedom and Protest. Folkways FTS 31018 (formerly FA 2455, FA 5233), 1968.

Shaun Cross Players: see *Songs of Cork and Kerry.*

Hugh Shields (ed.).
Folk Ballads from Donegal and Derry. Leader LEA 4055, 1972. BL.

----- (ed.).
Shamrock, Rose and Thistle. Leader LED 2070, 1976. BL.

----- (ed.).
Shamrock, Rose and Thistle 2: Folk singing in North Derry by Eddie Butcher, his friends and neighbours. European Ethnic Oral Traditions, Trinity College, Dublin. C-60 cass. 1982.

----- (ed.).
Shamrock, Rose and Thistle 3. European Ethnic Oral Traditions, Trinity College, Dublin. C-60 cass., 1982.

Martin Simpson: see Tabor.

Betty Smith (NC).
Songs Traditionally Sung in North Carolina. Folk-Legacy FSA 53, 1975. BL.

Harry Smith: see Folkways *AAFM* series.

Hobart Smith (VA).
America's Greatest Folk Instrumentalist. Folk-Legacy FSA 17, 1964. BL. Notes by George Armstrong.

Phoebe Smith (Suffolk).
Once I Had a True Love. Topic 12T 193, 1970. Notes by Frank Purslow.

Ralph Lee Smith.
More Dulcimer: Old time and traditional music ... with Pat Kuchwara. Troubador TR 3, 1975, 1977. BL.

Tom Smith: see Broadside.

Rosalie Sorrels (USA).
Folk Songs of Idaho and Utah. Folkways FH 5343, 1961. BL. Notes by Kenneth S. Goldstein.

-----.
The Lonesome Roving Wolves: Songs and ballads of the West. Green Linnet SIF 1024, 1980. B. Notes by Hedy West.

George Spicer (Sussex).
Blackberry Fold: Traditional songs and ballads.... Topic 12T 235, 1974.

Richard K. Spottswood: see *FMA* series.

Jo Stafford.
lc: Capitol LP H75.

Pete Steele (OH).
Folkways FS 3828, 1958. BL. Notes by Ed Kahn.

Sam Henry's Songs of the People

Steeleye Span (England) (Martin Carthy, Tim Hart, Rick Kemp, John Kirkpatrick, Nigel Pegrum, Maddy Prior).
Storm Force Ten. Chrysalis CHR 1151, 1977.

----- (Maddy Prior, Tim Hart, Rick Kemp, Bob Johnson, Peter Knight, Nigel Pegrum).
Pickwick SHM 3040, 1980 (licensed from Chrysalis).

-----.
Below the Salt. Shanachie 79039, ?1984. L.

Isla St. Clair (Scotland).
The Song and the Story. Clare Isla 1.

Ellen Stekert (USA).
Songs of a New York Lumberjack. Folkways FA 2354, 1958. BL.
[Songs from Ezra "Fuzzy" Barhight (Great Neck, L.I., NY).]

-----: see also Okun.

Belle Stewart (Scotland).
Queen among the Heather: Scots traditional songs and ballads. Topic 12TS 307, 1977. Notes by Geordie McIntyre.

Davie Stewart (Scotland).
Topic 12T 293, 1978. B. Notes by Hamish Henderson.

Lucy Stewart (Aberdeenshire).
Traditional Singer from Aberdeenshire, Scotland: Vol. 1, Child Ballads. Folkways FG 3519, 1961. B. Notes by Kenneth S. Goldstein.

The Stewart Family (Scotland).
The Stewarts of Blair (Belle, Cathie, Sheila, Alex Stewart). Topic 12T 138.

-----.
The Travelling Stewarts. Topic 12T 179, 1968.

Trevor Stewart: see Irish Country Four.
Helene Strathman-Thomas: see AAFS series L55.
Don Stokoe: see *Canny Newcassel*.

Stoneman Family (USA).
Old-Time Tunes of the South (Sutphin, Foreacre and Dickens). Folkways FA 2315, 1957. BL. Notes by Ralph Rinzler.

Danny, Rod Stradling: see Oak, Old Swan Band.
Tish Stubbs: see *Songs of a Devon Farmer*.

Tom Sullivan (USA).
On Deck and Below: The Irish at sea, music of the western ocean packet, with fiddle, banjo, Anglo concertina, pennywhistle and vocals by .... Folkways FS 3566, 1979. BL.

-----.
Salt Atlantic Chanties. Folkways FSS 37301, 1980. BL.

Andrew Rowan Summers.
lc: *Seeds of Love.* Folkways FP 21.

Isabel Sutherland (Scotland).
Vagrant Songs of Scotland. Topic 12T 151, 1966.

Dave Swarbrick: see Carthy.

June Tabor (England).
Airs and Graces. Topic 12TS 298, 1976.

-----.
Ashes and Diamonds. Topic 12TS 360, 1977.

-----, Martin Simpson.
A Cut Above. Topic 12TS 410, 1980.

Gordon Tanner: see *Down Yonder*.

Phil Tanner (Wales).
EFDSS LP 1005, 1968. BL.

-----: see also *Down Yonder*.

Dan Tate: see *Appalachia*, Vol. 2.

Cyril Tawney (England).
I Will Give My Love. Argo ZFB 87, 1973.

Joseph Taylor: see Grainger.

Tex-i-an Boys (John A. Lomax, Jr., Pete Rose, Ed Badeaux, Jim McConnell, Howard Porper) (USA).
Songs of Texas. Folkways FH 5328, 1962. BL.

Jeffrey Thom: see Old Hat Band.
Danny Thompson: ?see Pentangle.

Tom Pháidín Tom (Connemara).
Comhaltas Ceoltóirí Éireann CL 15, 1977. Notes by Séamus Mac Mathúna, Máire Aine Ní Dhonchadda, John Lewis.

-----: see also De Danann.

Artie Trezise: see Fisher.
Ed Trickett: see Bok.

Joseph Able Trivett (TN).
... of Butler, Tennessee. Folk-Legacy FSA 2, 1962. BL. Notes by Sandy Paton.

Dave Tulloch: see Five Hand Reel.

Paddy Tunney (Donegal).
The Man of Songs. Folk-Legacy FSI 7, 1962. Notes by Diane Hamilton, Seán O'Boyle.

-----.
A Wild Bees' Nest. Topic 12T 139, 1965. Notes by Seán O'Boyle.

-----.
The Irish Edge. Topic 12T 165, 1966. Notes by Seán O'Boyle.

-----.
The Mountain Streams Where the Moorcocks Crow. Topic 12TS 264, 1975. Notes by Cathal O'Baoill.

-----.
The Flowery Vale. Topic 12TS 289, 1976. Notes by Cathal O'Baoill.

-----.
The Stone Fiddle. Green Linnet SIF 1037, 1982.

-----, Arthur Kearney (Tyrone).
Ireland Her Own: A history in song of Ireland's fight for independence from the sixteenth to the twentieth century. Topic 12T 153, 1966.

Joe Val (USA).
... and the New England Bluegrass Boys. Live in Holland. Strictly Country Records [Holland] SCR 4.

The Valley Folk (Jean, Elaine Carruthers, John Dickinson, Stephen Heap) (Lancashire) .
All Bells in Paradise: Carols for all seasons.... Topic 12T 192, 1968. Notes by A. L. Lloyd.

Tony Wales (Sussex).
Sussex Folk Songs and Ballads. Folkways FG 3515, 1957. B. Notes by Kenneth S. Goldstein.

Doug Wallin.
Appalachian Ballad Singer (with Berzilla, Cas Wallin). Home Made Music LHMM 003 (forthcoming)

Virgie Wallin: see *Appalachia*, Vol. 2.

Wade Ward: see Holcomb.
Frank Warner (USA).
lc: ... *Sings American Folk Songs and Ballads.*
Elektra JH 504.
Lal, Norma Waterson (England).
A True Hearted Girl. Topic 12TS 331, 1977.
Notes by Bob Davenport.
Mike Waterson (England).
Topic 12TS 332, 1977. Notes by A. L. Lloyd.
The Watersons (Michael, Norma, Elaine, and John Harrison) (England).
Topic 12T 142, 1966.
-----.
A Yorkshire Garland. Topic 12T 167, 1966.
----- (Mike, Lal, Norma Waterson, Martin Carthy)
Green Fields. Topic 12TS 415, 1981. Notes by A. L. Lloyd.
Peta Webb (England).
I Have Wandered in Exile. Topic 12TS 233.
-----: see McMorland, Oak.
Percy Webb: see *Flash Company.*
Rita Weill (USA).
... *Sings Ballads and Folksongs.* Takoma A1022.
Roger Welsch (USA).
Sweet Nebraska Land. Folkways FH 5337, 1965. BL.
Harry, Jeanie West (USA).
Southern Mountain Folk Songs. 10" Stinson SLP 36. Notes by Harry West, Kenneth S. Goldstein.
Hedy West (GA).
Old Times and Hard Times. Folk-Legacy FSA 32, 1968 (also Topic 12T 117). BL. Notes by Hedy West, A. L. Lloyd.
-----.
Ballads. Topic 12T 163.
-----.
Serves 'Em Fine. Fontana STL 5432.
Bob White (USA).
Collector's Series. Front Hall FHR 011, 1977.
Dick Wilder: see *Badmen ....*
Josh White (USA).
lc: *Ballads and Blues*, Vol. 2. Decca DL 5247.
The Willet Family (Tom, Chris, Ben Willet) (England).
The Roving Journeymen: English traditional songs. Topic 12T 84, 1964. [BL.]
Charlie Wills (Dorset).
Leader LEA 4041, 1972. B.
Hally Wood (USA).
c: *Texas Folk Songs.* Stinson SLP 73.
Heather, Royston Wood: see Young Tradition.
Oscar Woods: see *English Country Music ....*
Steve Woodruff: see Roberts.
Nimrod Workman, Phyllis Workman Boyens (WV).
Passing through the Garden. June Appal JA 001, 1974. BL. Notes by Rich Kirby.
John Wright (Leicester).
Unaccompanied. Topic 12TS 348, 1978.
Bernard Wrigley (England).
The Phenomenal.... Topic 12TS 211, 1971. Notes by A. L. Lloyd
Martin Wyndham-Read: see *Great Australian Legend.*

The Young Tradition (Heather Wood, Royston Wood, Peter Bellamy) (England).
Galleries Revisited. Transatlantic TRA SAM 30, 1973 (orig. *Galleries*, TRA 172, 1969).

Anthologies

American Folk Tales and Songs.
Told by Richard Chase and sung by Jean Ritchie and Paul Clayton. Tradition TLP 1011, 1956.
American History in Ballad and Song, Vol. 1.
Folkways FH 5801 (3 records), 1960. BL. Ed. Albert Barouh, Theodore O. Cron.
-----, Vol. 2.
Folkways FH 5802 (3 records) 1962. BL. Ed. Albert Barouh, Theodore O. Cron.
"... And Not One Police": Fox Hollow 1969, Vol. 4.
Fox Hollow Festival (Petersburg, NY), private release.
Appalachia -- The Old Traditions: Blue Ridge Mountain Music from Virginia and North Carolina.
[Vol. 1.] Home Made Music LP 001, 1982. BL. Notes by coll. Mike Yates.
-----, Vol. 2.
Home Made Music LP 002, 1983.
The Asch Recordings: 1939-1945.
Asch AA 1/2, 3/4 (4 records), 1967. BL. Notes by Charles Edward Smith.

Badmen and Heroes and Pirate Songs and Ballads.
Ed McCurdy, Jack Elliott, Oscar Brand, Dick Wilder. Elektra EKL 129, 1957.
Back o' Benachie: Songs and ballads from the lowland East of Scotland.
Topic 12T 180, 1968. Notes by Peter Hall.
Ballad Folk: Jean Redpath with guests.
BBC 22293, 1977.
Ballads and Songs of the Blue Ridge Mountains: Persistence and Change.
Asch 3831, 1968.
Ballads from the Pubs of Ireland (James N. Healy, Fergus Cahill, Denis McCarthy).
Mercier Irl 1, 1968.
Beech Mountain, NC. The Traditional Music of ....
1: *The older ballads and sacred songs.*
2: *The later songs and hymns.*
Folk-Legacy FSA 22, 23, 1964. BL. Notes by Sandy Paton.
Berryfields of Blair, Folksongs and Music from the.
Prestige/Int. 25016. Notes by Hamish Henderson.
Bonny Lass Come o'er the Burn.
Topic 12T 128, 1962. Notes by Norman Buchan, Robin Gray.
The Bonny Pit Laddie: A miner's life in music and song.
The High Level Ranters (Alistair Anderson, Johnny Handle, Tommy Gilfellon, Colin Ross), Harry Boardman, Dick Gaughan. Topic 2-12TS 271/272 (2 records) 1975. Notes by Dr. Raymond Challinor, Tommy Gilfellon, Johnny Handle.
The Borders: Songs and dances of the English-Scottish border, recorded in Roxburghshire and Fifeshire, Scotland, and Northumberland, England.
Folkways FW 8776, 1960. BL. Notes by Samuel Charters.

Sam Henry's Songs of the People

Brave Boys: New England Traditions in Folk Music.
   Ed. Sandy Paton. New World NW 239, 1977. BL.

Canny Newcassel: Ballads and songs from Newcastle and thereabouts.
   Alistair Anderson, Barry Canham, Billy Conroy, Bruce, Pat, Pete Elliott, Tommy Gilfellon, Johnny Handle, Doreen Henderson, Les Pearson, Ed Pickford, Colin Ross, Don Stokoe. Topic 12TS 219.

Chicago Mob Scene: A folk song jam session.
   Riverside RLP12 641.

Colonial and Revolutionary War Sea Songs and Chanteys: Sung at Seaport '76.
   Cliff Haslam, John Millar. Folkways FH 5275, 1975. BL.

The Continuing Tradition, Vol. 1: Ballads.
   A Folk-Legacy Sampler. Folk-Legacy FSI 75, 1981. BL.

Devon Tradition: An anthology from traditional singers.
   Topic 12TS 349, 1979.

Devonshire Capers: Yarns, songs and music recorded in Devon.
   George Keene, Jack Rice, Mrs Dowrick, Albert Weekes, Emily Budd, Cyril Blackford, Charlie Hill, George Keene, Les Rice, Pop Hingston, Jack Gard, Dick French, Mrs Hawkins, Hartland Villagers, Aylesbeare Brownies, Jack Rice, Ruby Beer, Bill Hannaford, Lillian Lugg, Ivan Westaway, Digger Ford, Dan Chapple. People's Stage Tapes cass. 04.

Devonshire Garland.
   Sam Richards, Martin Scroggs, Tish Stubbs. People's Stage Tapes cass. 02.

Down Yonder: Old Time String Band Music from Georgia.
   Gordon Tanner, Smoky Joe Miller, Uncle John Patterson, Phil Tanner, The Junior Skillet Lickers. Folkways FTS 31089, 1982. BL. Notes by Art Rosenbaum.

Eight Traditional British-American Ballads (from the Flanders collection).
   New England Folksong Series, No. 1, 1953. B. The Helen Hartness Flanders Collection of Balladry and Folk Music. Middlebury College, VT.

English Country Music from East Anglia.
   Billy Bennington, Percy Brown, Harold Covill, Oscar Woods. Topic 12TS 229.

An English Folk Music Anthology.
   Folkways FE 38553, 1981 (2 records). BL. Recorded by Sam Richards, Tish Stubbs.

Field Trip.
   Collector Limited Edition 1201. Recorded by Jean Ritchie.

A Fine Hunting Day: Songs of the Holme Valley Beagles.
   Leader LEE 4058, 1975. BL.

Flash Company.
   Ernest Austin, Bob Hart, Percy Webb. Topic 12TS 243.

The Folk Box.
   Elektra EKL 9001, 1964. 4 records.

Folk Concert in Town Hall, NY.
   Jean Ritchie, Oscar Brand, Dave Sear. Folkways FA 2428, 1959. BL.

Folksongs and Music from the Berryfields of Blair. see *Berryfields ....*

Folksongs of the Miramichi: Lumber and river songs from the Miramichi Folk Festival, Newcastle, New Brunswick.
   Folkways FM 4053, 1962. B. Notes by Louise Manny.

40 Folk Favourites.
   Pickwick PLD 8013 (2 records).

Fylde Acoustic.
   Trailer LER 2105, 1977.
   [Anthology of British musicians playing instruments made by Roger Bucknell of Fylde Instruments.]

Garners Gay: English folk songs recorded by Fred Hamer.
   EFDSS LP 1006, 1971.

Golden Ring: A gathering of friends for making music.
   Folk-Legacy FSI 16, 1964. BL. Notes by Sandy Paton.

Golden Ring, The New
   Five Days Singing. 2 records. Folk-Legacy FSI 41, 42, 1971. BL.

The Good Old Way: British folk music today.
   Topic 412, 1980. [Sampler].

Good Time Music: National Folk Festival.
   Philo 1028, 1975.

The Great Australian Legend.
   A. L. Lloyd, Martin Wyndham-Read, Trevor Lucas. Topic 12TS 203.

The Great Scots Sampler.
   Transatlantic TRA SAM 17, 1970.

Green Grow the Laurels: Country singers from the south (England).
   Topic 12TS 285, 1976. BL. Notes by Mike Yates.

I'm Old but I'm Awfully Tough: Traditional music of the Ozark region.
   Missouri Friends of the Folk Arts MFFA 101 (2 records), 1980. BL.

I'm on My Journey Home: Vocal styles and resources in folk music.
   Ed. Charles Wolfe. New World NW 223, 1978. BL.

In an Arizona Town (Clay Springs, AZ)
   Van Holyoak, Bunk Pettyjohn, Lois "Granny" Thomas, Tim Kizzar, Ralph Rogers, Don Goodman. Arizona Friends of Folklore AFF 33-3, n.d. BL.

Interfolk Collections: A compendium of today's folkscene.
   Vol. 5. Autogram ALLP 198. [Notes in German.]

Irish Music in London Pubs.
   Folkways FG 2575, 1965. BL. Notes by Ralph Rinzler, Séamus Ennis, Mary Vernon.

Irish Rebellion Album.
   Folkways FH 5415, 1975. BL.

The Irish Tradition: The corner house.
   Green Linnet SIF 1016, 1979.

The Lambs on the Green Hills: Songs from County Clare.
    Topic 12TS 369, 1978.

More Grand Airs from Connemara.
    Topic 12T 202, 1971.

Mountain Music of Kentucky.
    Folkways FA 2317, 1960. BL. Notes by John Cohen.

The Mountain Top: Comhaltas Tour '76.
    Comhaltas Ceoltóirí Éireann CL 14.

The Muckle Sangs: Classic Scots Ballads.
    2 recs. Tangent TNGM 119/D, 1975, rev. 1979. DL.

Music of Kentucky '76: Third Annual Brandywine Mountain Music Convention.
    Brandywine Tradition Series Vol. 3. Heritage Records 18, 1977.

My Song Is My Own: Songs from women.
    Frankie Armstrong, Kathy Henderson, Sandra Kerr, Alison McMorland. Plane Label TPL 001, 1980.

The New Golden Ring: see *Golden Ring.*

Native American Ballads.
    RCA Victor (Vintage Series) LPV 58.

Negro Folk Music of Alabama.
    Vol. 1. Folkways FE 4417, 1956, 1960. Recorded, with notes and texts, by Harold Courlander.

Nyon Folk Festival 1979.
    CAT 81004/5 (2 records) 1979.

Of Maids and Mistresses. [Morton 1975]
    Elektra 137.

Old Love Songs and Ballads from the Big Laurel, NC.
    Folkways FA 2309, 1964. BL. Notes by Peter Gott, John Cohen.

Old Mother Hippletoe: Rural and urban children's songs.
    New World NW 291, 1978. BL.

Old Time Ballads from the Southern Mountains.
    County 522.

Old Time Music at Clarence Ashley's [Vol. 1].
    Folkways FA 2355, 1961. BL. Notes by Ralph and Richard Rinzler.

Old Time Music at Clarence Ashley's, Vol. 2.
    Folkways FA 2359, 1963. BL. Notes by Ralph Rinzler, extensive discography for each item.

Old Time Southern Dance Music: Ballads and songs.
    Old-Timey LP 102.

Oriel: Songs and tunes of south east Ulster.
    Eagran MD 0001, 1978. B. Notes by Mánus Ó Boyle.

Sailing into Walpole's Marsh.
    Sean Corcoran, Eddie Clarke, Mairéad ní Dhomnaill, Maeve Donnelly. Green Linnet SIF 1004, 1977.

A Sampler of Louisiana Folk Songs.
    Louisiana Folklore Society LSF 201. Collected by Harry Oster.

Sea Chanties and Forecastle Songs at Mystic Seaport.
    Stuart M. Frank, Stuart Gillespie, Ellen Cohn. Folkways FTS 37300, 1978. BL.

Sea Music of Many Lands: The Pacific heritage ... National Maritime Museum, San Francisco, Festival of the Sea 1980.
    Folkways FSS 38405, 1981. BL.

Sea Songs Seattle: Hearty renditions of traditional songs and chanteys sung at the Seattle Chantey Festival.
    Folkways FTS 37311, 1979.

Sharon Mountain Harmony: A Golden Ring of Gospel.
    Folk-Legacy FSI 86, 1982. BL.

Sing, Say and Play: Traditional songs and music from Suffolk.
    Topic 12TS 375, 1978.

Singing Men of Ulster: Irish traditional songs from the collection of Diane Hamilton and Seán O'Boyle.
    Green Linnet SIF 1005, 1977. B. Notes by Seán O'Boyle. [?= *Songs from Ulster,* Mulligan LUN A001, 1977]

So Early in the Morning: Irish children's traditional songs and games.
    Tradition TLP 1034.

lc: *Sod Buster Ballads and Deep Sea Chanteys.*
    Commodore FL 30,002.

Songs of Cork and Kerry.
    James N. Healy, Claire Egan, Denis Leahy, Elizabeth Isaac and Choir, the Shaun Cross Players. Mercier.

Songs of a Devon Farmer: Folk songs from the repertoire of William Nott, tenant farmer of Mexhaw, North Devon, ed. Cecil Sharp, 1906, performed by Sam Richards and Tish Stubbs, spoken commentary by Martin Scraggs. People's Stage Tapes cass. 01.

Songs of the Open Road: Gypsies, travellers and country singers.
    Topic 12T 253, 1975. Notes by Mike Yates.

Songs of Rebels and Redcoats.
    National Geographic Society 00788. BL.

Songs of the Sea: Maritime Museum Festival of the Sea, San Francisco, 1979.
    Folkways FSS 37315, 1980. BL.

The Southeast Alaska Folk Tradition, Vol. 1: Exploration and discovery, 1786-1897.
    Folkways FES 34031, 1980 (1981?). BL. Notes by John Ingalls, Barry Roderick.

Stone County Singing.
    Estella Palmer, Floyd Holland, Glenn Ohrlin. Shoestring Tape SGB 1.

Sussex Harvest: A Collection of traditional songs from Sussex.
    Topic 12T 258, 1975. Notes by Mike Yates.

The Traditional Music of Beech Mountain, NC: see *Beech Mountain.*

Traditional Music of Ireland.
    Ed. Samuel B. Charters.
    Vol. 1. *The older traditions of Connemara and Clare.*
    Vol. 2. *Songs and dances from Down, Kerry, and Clare.*
    Folkways FW 8781, 8782, 1963.

Sam Henry's Songs of the People

The Travelling Songster: An anthology from gypsy singers.
    Topic 12TS 304, 1977. BL. Notes by Mike Yates.

The Unfortunate Rake: A study in the evolution of a ballad.
    Folkways FA 3805, 1960. BL. Notes by Kenneth S. Goldstein.

Virginia Mountain Boys: Old time bluegrass from Grayson and Carroll Counties, VA., Vol. 3.
    Folkways FS 3839, 1980. Notes by Eric Davidson, Jane Rigg, Brooke Moyer.

When Sheepshearing's Done: Countryside songs from southern England.
    Topic 12T 254, 1975. Notes by Mike Yates.

lc: *Who Built America.*
    Folkways FP 2.

Series and sets

AAFS (AFS)
Archive of American Folk Song. (Continuing series of 12" LP records, mainly from field recordings in the Archive. Issued by the Recording Laboratory, Music Division, Library of Congress, Washington, DC 20540.)

  L 1. *Folk Music of the US.* BL. Ed. Alan Lomax.
  L 7. *Anglo-American Ballads.* BL. Ed. B. A. Botkin.
  L 12. *Anglo-American Songs and Ballads.* BL. Ed. Duncan Emrich.
  L 14. *Anglo-American Songs and Ballads.* BL. Ed. Duncan Emrich.
  L 20. *Anglo-American Songs and Ballads.* BL. Ed. Duncan B. M. Emrich.
  L 21. *Anglo-American Songs and Ballads.* BL. Ed. Duncan B. M. Emrich.
  L 26. *American Sea Songs and Shanties*, 1. BL. Ed. Duncan B. M. Emrich.
  L 28. *Cowboy Songs, Ballads and Cattle Calls from Texas.* BL. Ed. Duncan Emrich.
  L 54. *Versions and Variants of "Barbara Allen."* BL. Ed. Charles Seeger.
  L 55. *Folk Music from Wisconsin.* BL. Ed. Helene Strathman-Thomas.
  L 56. *Songs of the Michigan Lumberjacks.* BL. Ed. E. C. Beck.
  L 57. *Child Ballads Traditional in the US*, 1. BL. Ed. Bertrand H. Bronson.
  L 58. *Child Ballads Traditional in the US*, 2. BL. Ed. Bertrand H. Bronson.
  L 61. *Railroad Songs and Ballads.* BL. Ed. Archie Green.
  L 65-66. *The Hammons Family: A study of a West Virginia Family's Traditions.* BL. Ed. Carl Fleischauer, Alan Jabbour.
  L 67. *Afro-American Folk Music from Tate and Panola Counties, MS.* BL. Ed. David Evans.
  L 68. *Folk-Songs of America: The Robert Winslow Gordon collection, 1922-1932.* BL. Ed. Neil V. Rosenberg, Debora G. Kodish.

B&R
Blood and Roses: Traditional ballads from Scotland and North America. Peggy Seeger, Ewan MacColl. Blackthorne Records, 35 Stanley Ave., Beckenham, Kent, BR3 2PU England.
  Vol. 1. ESB 79, 1979. BL.
  Vol. 3. ESB 81, 1981. BL.

CWL
Columbia Records, *Columbia World Library of Folk and Primitive Music.*
  Vol. 1. *Ireland: Irish folk song from the western counties of Eire.* Ed. Séamus Ennis, Alan Lomax. Columbia AKL 4941.
  Vol. 3. *England: English folk songs.* Ed. Peter Kennedy, Alan Lomax. Columbia AKL 4943.

FMA
Folk Music in America. Ed. Richard K. Spottswood. 15 records. Music Division, Recorded Sound Section, Library of Congress, 1976.
  Vol. 2. *Songs of Love, Courtship and Marriage.*
  Vol. 6. *Songs of Migration and Immigration.*
  Vol. 12. *Songs of Local History and Events.*

Folkways AAFM
Anthology of American Folk Music. Ed. Harry Smith. B (notes, bibliography, discography).
  Vol. 1. *Ballads.* Folkways FP 251 (2 records).
  Vol. 3. *Songs.* Folkways FP 253 (2 records).

Folkways CB
The English and Scottish Popular Ballads (Child Ballads). Sung by Ewan MacColl.
  Folkways FG 3509 (#1). BL.
  Folkways FG 3510 (#2). BL.

FSB 1-10
The Folksongs of Britain. 10 vols. New York: Caedmon Records TC 1142-6, 1162-4, 1224-5, 1961--; London: Topic Records 12T 157-61, 194-8, 1971--. BL.
  Vol. 1. *Songs of Courtship* (TC 1142 / 12T 157).
  Vol. 3. *Jack of All Trades* (TC 1144 / 12T 159).
  Vol. 4. *Child Ballads 1* (TC 1145 / 12T 160).
  Vol. 5. *Child Ballads 2* (TC 1146 / 12T 161).
  Vol. 6. *Sailormen and Servingmaids* (TC 1162 / 12T 1
  Vol. 7. *Fair Game and Foul* (TC 1163 / 12T 195).
  Vol. 8. *A Soldier's Life for Me* (TC 1164 / 12T 196).
  Vol. 9. *Songs of Ceremony* (TC 1224 / 12T 197).
  Vol. 10. *Animal Songs* (TC 1225 / 12T 198).

LH
The Long Harvest: Traditional ballads in their English, Scots and North American variants. Sung by Peggy Seeger and Ewan MacColl.
  Argo (Z)DA66 (#1). BL.
  Argo (Z)DA68 (#3). BL.
  Argo (Z)DA69 (#4). BL.
  Argo (Z)DA70 (#5). BL.
  Argo (Z)DA71 (#6). BL.
  Argo (Z)DA72 (#7). BL.
  Argo (Z)DA73 (#8). BL.
  Argo (Z)DA75 (#10). BL.

Discography

Riverside CB

The English and Scottish Popular Ballads (The Child Ballads). Sung by Ewan MacColl and A. L. Lloyd. Ed. Kenneth S. Goldstein. New York: Riverside Records (Bill Grauer Productions) in association with the Folklore Press.

   Vol. 1. RLP 12-621,2, 1956. BL.
   Vol. 2. RLP 12-623,4, 1956. BL.
   Vol. 3. RLP 12-625,6, 1956. BL.
   Vol. 4. RLP 12-627,8, 1956. BL.

Great British Ballads: Not included in the Child collection.
   RLP 12-629, 1956. BL.

Smithsonian Country

The Smithsonian Collection of Classic Country Music. Selected and annotated by Bill C. Malone. Washington, D.C.: Division of Performing Arts, Smithsonian Institution.

   Side 1.5: Vernon Dalhart, "The Prisoner's Song"
   Side 2.4: Bradley Kincaid, "The Fatal Wedding"
   Side 3.3: Cliff Carlisle, "Black Jack David"

TFS

Tennessee Folklore Society, Box 512, Middle Tennessee State University, Murfreesboro, TN 37132.

   TFS 103. *Tennessee, The Folk Heritage:* Vol. 2, The Mountains. 1980? B. Notes by Charles Wolfe.
   TFS 104. *The Hicks Family: A Cumberland Singing Tradition.* 1982. [BL.]

VT

Virginia Traditions. Blue Ridge Institute, Ferrum College, Ferrum, VA.

   BRI 002. *Ballads from British Tradition.* 1981. Ed., notes by Blanton Owen. BL.

Index of titles, including alternative titles, and first lines

Alternative titles are enclosed in brackets.

[A-Begging Buttermilk I Will Go] (H57a) 57
Abbey (H10a) 2
'Abbey' tune is easy sung, The (H10a) 2
Above all the lands upon this earth there's none so dear to me (H237) 189
Above yon green mountains (H609) 199
[Abroad as I Was Walking] (H180) 149
Accland, Young Mary of [Laws M16] (a) (H30b) 437, (b) (H721) 438
Across the foaming ocean far o'er the rolling sea (H674) 219
[Across the Western Ocean] (H53b) 96
[Actual Song of the Seal] (cf. H713) 27
Adieu ...
 [..., Londonderry] (H518) 301
 ..., lovely Erin of sweet delectation (H656) 187
 [... to Cold (Dark) Weather] (H504) 347
 ... to the Banks of the Roe (H245) 197
[Affectionate Lover, The] (H668) 444
[Aghadowey, The Maid of] (H86) 436, (?Laws O2] (H673) 429
[Aghalee Heroes] (m) (H14a) 356, (H41) 231, (H87) 181, (H150a) 466, (H752) 245
Ah, gramachree ma colleen oge (H204) 388
[Airy Bachelor, The] (H586) 80
Ale House, The Sailor in the [Laws K36] (H779) 54
[Alehouse, The] (H683) 393
[Alexander] (H589) 344
[All (a)round My Hat] (H60a) 400
[All Frolicking I'll Give Over] (H188) 401
[All of Her Answers to Me Were No] (H532) 367
[All You Boys Who Go A-Courting] (cf. H532) 367
All you young men ...
 ... a warning, a warning take by me (H691) 119
 ... I pray draw near that have your liberty (H46) 438
 ... that wants a wife, a warnin' take by me (H25a) 502
[Allan Water, Banks of] (m) (cf. H204) 388
Allen, Barbara [Child #84] (H236) 375
Alma, The Heights of (H123) 90
Altaveedan, The Maid of (H603) 238
Altibrine, The Pride of (H111) 229
Alt[i]mover Stream (H65a) 293; (m) (H65b) 187
Am I the Doctor? [?Child #295] [Laws P9] (H72) 374
[Am I the Doctor You Wished for to See?] (H72) 374
[Amber, The Colour of] (cf. H16) 392
Among the Green Bushes in Sweet Tyrone (H708) 174
Among the green bushes in sweet Tyrone (H708) 174
[Among the Moor] (H177) 271
[An Dra(o)ighnean Donn] (H206) 289
[Anach Chuain] (m) (H173) 250
And ...
 ... *fine broom besoms, besoms fine and new* (H17a) 61
 ... *she lives in the valley* (H47) 236
 ... *she's only a farmer's daughter, she is only a country maid* (H528) 246
 ... *still she sang, while caverns rang* (H737) 309
 ... *you're welcome, all of you, heartily welcome* (H805a,b) 73
Ann, Greenmount Smiling (H182) 464
Ann o' Drumcroon (H26a, H246) 248

Annie ...
 ... Moore (H191) 142
 ..., Fair (H126) 510
 ..., Lovely (II) [Laws N14] (H166) 328
[Another Man's Wedding] (H60a) 400
[Answer to Betsy of Ballentine Bray] (cf. H73) 412
[Answer to the Philadelphia Lass] (H198) 481
[Antrim, The Blooming Rose of] (H612) 242
Antrim, The Green Hills of (H606) 208
Appeal to Her Lover, A Sweetheart's (H112) 288
Apprentice Boy, The [Laws M12] (H729) 446; (H31) 411, (H739) 291
[Apprentice Sailor, The] (H739) 291
Apron of Flowers, The [Laws P25] (H683) 393
[Aran's Lonely Home] (H46) 438
[Archer, Willie] (H614) 384
[Arise, Arise (Awake, Awake) (Wake, O Wake), You Drowsy Maiden (Sleeper)] (H722) 343
[Arkansas Traveller, An] (H0) 53
[Arkansaw Navvy, The] (H0) 53
Armoy, Lovely (H9) 186
Army, The Hungry (H92) 86
[Around Cape Horn] (H539) 97
Aroun' Pat Murphy's hearth there was music, song and mirth (H756) 60
Arthur Bond (H783) 34
Artikelly, The Pride of (H656) 187
As ...
 ... a King Went A-Hunting (H117) 44
 ... a king went a-hunting, a-hunting one day (H117) 44
 [... (So) (A)broad as I Was Walking] (cf. H16) 392
 ... daylight was appearing and the cloudy skies were clearing (H583) 314
 ... down by Banna's banks I strayed (H204) 388
 ... down by yonder harbour I carelessly did stray (H670) 293
 [... I Came Rolling Home from Sea] (H21) 508
 ... I Gaed ower a Whinny Knowe [Laws O17] (H793) 267
 ... I gaed oot one summer day tae tak' a wee bit stroll (H763) 458
 ... I Go I Sing (H661) 259
 ... I rode o'er by Skerry Tap (H737) 309
As I rode out ...
 ... one bright May morning (H593) 388
 ... very early (H43) 394
 ... very early to view the green meadows in spring (H575) 394
[As I Roved (Walked) Out] (H152) 266
As I roved out ...
 ..., for recreation down by the seaside (H107) 320
 [... from the County Cavan] (cf. H826) 309
 ... one evening (H662) 45
 ... one evening, all in the blooming spring (H676) 435
 ... one evening, being in the month of May (H224a,b) 390, 391
 ... one evening, being in the summer time (H240) 192
 ... one evening down by a riverside (H468) 441, (H796) 163
 ... one evening down by the banks of Clyde (H579) 345
 ... one evening in the month of sweet July (H191) 142
 ... one evening in the springtime of the year (H556) 376
 ... one evening in the sweet month of June (H518) 301
 [... One Morning] (H468) 441

 ... one morning, being in the month of May (H693) 313
 ... one morning clear, being in the pleasant month of June (H477) 140
 ... one morning to view the pleasant strand (H167) 369
 ... one summer's morning (H580) 357
 ... the other day (H762) 368
As I stood by my cabin door (H482) 391
As I traversed Benbradden hill as Zephyr's breeze blew far (H572) 159
As I walk the hills my heart is light, and as I go I sing (H661) 259
As I walk-ed out one fine evening, bright Phoebus was just looking down (H563) 3
As I walked ...
 ... down by Dublin town to hear some pleasant news (H156) 315
 ... down by the side of a bush (H241) 346
 [... down the Road to Sligo] (m) (H123) 90
 ... Out (H109) 357; (H593) 389, (H711) 234
 ... out on an evening so clear (H109) 357
 ... out on the streets of Loreto (H680) 141
 ... out one evening, being in the month of May (H242) 483
 ... out one evening down by yon shady grove (H199) 39
 ... out one evening in the springtime of the year (H244) 295
 ... out one evening to take the caller air (H626) 465
 ... out one morning down by the Sligo dock (H827) 100
 ... out one summer day (H785) 399
 [... out One Summer's Morning] (H471) 317
 ... over Mulberry Mountain (H792) 122
 ... up Manchester Street (H725) 278
As I was ...
 ... a-walking one morning in May (H161b) 456, (H836) 372
 ... sitting in my room (H490) 48
 ... walking up Coleraine Street (H718) 460
As I went ...
 ... a-walking on last Lammas Day (H22b) 361
 ... a-walking one evening in June (H214) 445
 ... a-walking one evening in May (H143) 395
 ... a-walking one fine summer morning (H794) 385
 ... a-walking one morning in June (H76) 314, (H542) 217
 ... a-walking one morning in May (H161a) 456, (H622) 44, (H655) 319
 [... out ae (One May) Morning] (H794) 385
 ... out on a morning in May (H676) 41
 ... out one morning being on the dewy grass (H650b) 264
 ... ower a whinny knowe I met a bonny lassie (H793) 267
 ... roving through the County Cavan (H826) 309
 ... up the mountain road (H515) 274
 ...walking in yon green garden (H818) 317
[As Jack the Ploughboy] (H105) 331
[As Jimmie Went A-Hunting] (H114) 143
[As Johnny Walked Out] (H175) 470
[As Molly Was Milking] (H175) 470
As Molly was milking her yowes one day (H175) 470

584

As oft I ponder, my thoughts do wander (H189) 173
[(As) Susan Strayed the Briny Beach] (H774) 150
As the sun went down o'er that eager sky and the terrible war was o'er (H816) 92
As Willie and Mary stood by the seaside (H118) 315
[As Willie and Mary Strolled by the Seashore] (H118) 315
Assist me, ye muses, and lend me your aid (H733) 342
At a cottage door one winter night as the snow lay on the ground (H678) 89
At the Eight-Mile Bridge in County Down (H486) 121
At the foot of Benbradden clear waters do flow (H24a) 348
[(At) The Foot (Maid) of the Mountain('s) Brow (Logan Bough)] (H688) 364
At the foot of Newry Mountain there runs a clear stream (H582) 238
At the Ould Lammas Fair, boys, were you ever there (H101) 275
At the Ould Lammas Fair in Ballycastle long ago (H101) 275
[At the Setting of the Sun] (H114) 143
At twenty-one I first begun to court a neighbour's child (H33, H611) 397
Attention pay, my countrymen, and hear my native news (H672) 212
[Auction of a Wife] (H226) 511
Aul', Auld [see also Old]
[Auld (Dirty) (Ragged) Beggarman (Gaberlunzie), The] (H810) 269
[Auld Lang Syne] (m) (H659) 504
[Aul' Maid, The] (H230) 255
[Auld (Old) Maid in a (the) Garret, (An)] (H138) 256
Aul' Man and the Churnstaff, The [Laws Q2] (H174) 507
[(Auld) Wife and the (Peat) Creel, The] (H201) 265
Autumn Dusk (H831) 235
[Avenging and Bright] (m) (H512) 225
[Awake, Arise (Wake up), You Drowsy Sleeper(s)] (H722) 343
[Awake, Awake, My Old True Lover] (H722) 343
[Awful Wedding] (H60a) 400

Babyland?, How Many Miles to (H40a) 12
[Bad Girl('s Lament), The] (cf. H680) 141
[Bad (Wicked) Wife, The] (H145) 503
[Baker of Milngavie, The Roving] (m) (H11) 110
Balaclava (H829) 91
[Balinderry] (H80) 386
[Balinderry and Cronan] (H80) 386
Ballad of Master M'Grath, A (H161c) 32
[Ballentown Brae] (H73) 412
Ballinagarvey, Jean of (H822) 239
Ballinderry Marriage, The (H805) 73
[Ballindown Braes [Laws P28] (H73) 412
Ballyagan, Fair Maid of (H67) 365
Ballyboley, The Hills o' (H511) 157
Ballycastle, O! (H28b) 158
Ballycastle; Farewell, (H210) 188
Ballyeamon Cradle Song (H596) 6
Ballyhaunis, The Maid of (H483) 427
Ballymonan Brae (H643) 159
Ballymoney, Bess of (H133) 461
Ballymoney, Farewell (H615) 343
Ballyporeen, The Wedding at (H93) 72
[Ballyshanny] (H672) 212
[Baltimore] (H553) 482
Bang, bang, bang goes the hammer on the anvil (H541) 207
Banished Lover, The (H23) 307
Banks of ...
[... Allan Water] (m) (cf. H204) 388
[... Champlain, The] (cf. H583) 314
[... Clady (Claudie) (Florida), The] (H693) 313
... Claudy, The [Laws N40] (H5, 693) 313
... Cloughwater, The (H777) 427

[... Clyde, The] (H765) 312
... (the) Dee, The (H583) 314
[... Glenco, The] (H655) 319
... Kilrea, The (I) (H150a) 466; (II) (H150b) 361
[... Lough Foyle, The] (m) (H2) 215, (H11) 110, (H651) 160
[(...) Moorlough Shore, The] (H27a [orig. H34b]) 371
[... Mourne, The] (H595) 468
... Mourne Strand, The (H564) 344
[(...) Moyola, (The)] (H752) 245
[... Newfoundland, The] (H194) 99, (H569) 112
[... Shannon, The] (H668) 444
... Sweet Lough Neagh, The (H158) 295
[... Sweet Lough Rae (Ray) (Rea), (On) the] (H158) 295
... the Band, The] (H86) 436
... the Bann, The [Laws O2] (H86) 436; (H614) 384
... the Clyde, The (H812) 310
... (the) Dee, The (H583) 314
[... the Inverness, The] (H205) 319
... the Nile, The [Laws N9] (H238) 296
... the River Ness, The (H205) 319
... the Roe, The (H24b) 217
Bann ...
... Water Side, The (H685) 460
..., The Banks of the [Laws O2] (H86) 436; (H614) 384
... Water, The Sweet [Laws M4] (H722) 343
[Banna's Banks] (H204) 388
Banna, The Green Banks of (H233) 287
Barbara Allen [Child #84] (H236) 375
[Barbary (Barbour), John (Tom) (o')] (H221) 490
[Barbro (Barb(a)ry) (Bav'ry) Allen (Ellen)] (H236) 375
Bard of Culnady, The (H50) 139
[Bargain with Me] (H748) 263
[Barley Straw, The] (H810) 269
[Barney, Sanford] (H0) 53
[Barnyards o' Delgaty, The] (m) (H640) 291
Barossa: The Regimental March Past of the Royal Irish Fusiliers (H98a) 64
[Barossa's Plains] (H98a)
[Basket of Eggs, The] (cf. H700) 277
Basket of Oysters, The [Laws Q13] (H725) 278
[Bathing in the Roe] (m) (H37) 485, (H65a) 293, (H65b) 187
Battle of ...
[... Alma, The] (H123) 90
... Barossa (Trafalgar), The] (cf. H98a)
... King's Mountain, The] (H185) 129
... the Nile] (H238) 296
Bawn Lowry, Molly (H114) 143
Bawn, The Rocks of (H139) 42
[Be Thou My Vision] (m) (H193) 487
Beardiville Planting (H718) 460
[Beaulampkin (Bolamkin) (Bolakin(s)) (Bolankin)] (H735) 133
Beautiful Churchill (H627) 161
Beautiful damsel of fame and renown, A (H98b) 472
[Beautiful Queen, The Jolly Young Sailor and the (His)] (H620) 476
Beauty of the Braid, The (H723) 240
[Bedroom Window] (H722) 343
[Beggar Laddie (Man), The] (H810) 269
Beggarman ...
[..., The] (H118) 315, (H810) 269
... Cam' ower the Lea, A [Child #279] (H810)
[...'s Song, The] (H751) 50
[A-Begging Buttermilk I Will Go] (H57a) 57
[Behind Yon Blue Mountain] (H609) 199
[Beichan (Bateman) (Beham), Young] (H470) 491
Being on a mild September morn, the weather it being warm (H102) 464
Being on the banks of Claudy, I heard a maid complain (H519) 389

Belfast ...
... Mountains (H519) 389
... Town (H45) 477
... town, now rich and great (H45) 477
Bellaghy Fair (H758) 23
Benbrada, The Flower of (H537) 239
Benbradden Brae (H572) 159
Benbradden, The Star of (H24a) 348
[Benone, The Shores of Sweet] (H52a) 244
[Besom Maker, The] (H17a) 61
Besoms!, Fine Broom (H17a) 61
[Bess of Ballymoney (H133) 461
Bessie ...
... (belled) and Mary (gray), or Larry's Old Goat (H119)
[... (Jessie) of Ballington Brae] (H73) 412
[... of Ballydubray] (H73) 412
Betsy ...
[... of Ballantown Brae] (H73) 412
[... Watson] (H683) 393
[..., Squire Nathaniel and] (H207) 417
Better Bide a Wee (H598) 61
[*Bigler*, The] (m) (H501) 25
[Bill Stafford (Staples)] (H0) 53
Billy ...
[... Barlow] (cf. H744) 12
[... Boy] (cf. H814) 415
[... Henry] (H176) 146
[... (John)(ny) (Willie) (O')Reilly (Rally) (Riley) (Rylie)] (H468) 441
[... (Polly) Oliver's Rambles, (Pretty)] (H166) 328
[(...) (Sailsworth), Sally (and)] (H72) 374
[... the Bob] (H744) 12
[... (Wildee) (Willie(y)) Weaver] (H682) 505
[... Weever] (H682) 505
Birdeens sing a fluting song, The (H596) 6
[Biscayo] (H699) 383
[Bite, The Yorkshire] (H51) 129
Bittern, The Yellow (H830) 64
Black ...
... Chimney Sweeper, The (H138) 256
... Duck, The] (H38) 29
[...-Eyed (Handsome) (Lovely) Molly] (H625) 342
[... Frost] (H504) 347
... Horse, The (H586) 80
... Pipe, The (H832a) 49
[Blackbird, The] (H79) 428
Blackbird and Thrush, The (H241) 346
[Blackjack David (Dav(e)y) (Daisy), (The)] (H124) 509
Blacksmith ...
..., The (H835b) 512
[...'s Daughter, The] (H604) 505
...'s Shop, The Old (H541) 207
[Blackthorn (Tree), The] (H206) 289
Blackwaterside, The [Laws O1] (H811) 461
[Blaeberries, The] (H193) 487
[Blaeberry Courtship, The] (H193) 487
Blazing Star of ...
... Drim, The (a) (H197a) 248
[... Drum] (H197a) 248, The
... Drung, The (b) (H197b) 248
Blin' Auld Man, The [Child #274] (H21) 508
Blind ...
[... (Drunken) Fool, The] (H21) 508
[... Irish Girl, The] (m) (H55) 479
[.. Man (He Can See), (A) The] (H21) 508, (H174) 507
[Bloody Alma] (H123) 90
Blooming ...
[... Caroline of Edinborough Town] (H148) 411
[... Caroline from Edinboro' Town] (H148) 411
... Caroline of Edinburgh Town [Laws P27] (H148) 411
[... Heather, The] (H177) 271
[... Rose of Antrim, The] (H612) 242
... Star of Eglintown, The (H170) 299

585

Blue ...
[... -Eyed Boy, (Go Bring Me Back) My] (H218a) 386
[... Eyed Mary] (H785) 399
[... Kerchief, The] (H161a,b) 456
Blue ...
..., The Bonnet sae (H644) 367
Bluebell's sweet that grows upon the hill, The (H511) 157
[Bluebells, Dusty] (H48a) 10
[Bluff the Quilt] (H681) 490
Blythe and Bonny Scotland (H120) 332
Boatman, The (H834) 289
[Boatsman and the Chest, The (Tailor)] (H604) 505
[Boatswain and the Tailor] (H604) 505
[(Bolamkin) (Bolakin(s)) (Bolankin) Beaulampkin] (H735) 133
Bold ...
[(...) B(W)illy (William) Taylor] (H213) 334
[... (Jolly) Boatswain (Boatman) (of Dover), The] (H604) 505
[... (Brave) Johnston] (H185) 129
[... Jack Donaho(ue)] (m) (H202) 119, (H466) 79, (H555) 463, (H750) 120, (H765) 312
[... (Bo) (Bow) (Proud) (Young) Lamkin (Lankon)] (H735) 133
[... Lieutenant] (H474) 488
[... Maginnis of the County Tyrone] (H153) 480
... *Privateer, The* [Laws O32] (H514) 297
[... Sea Captain] (H474) 488
[... Thrasher, The] (H622) 44
[(...) Trooper, The] (cf. H604) 505
[... (Brisk) Young Cropper (Farmer) (Lover) (Sailor) (Courted Me), A (The)] (H683) 393
[Bolyn, Tom] (H480) 52
[Bond, Fair Julian] (H234) 436
Bonnet (o') sae Blue, The (H644) 367
[Bonnets o' Bonnie Dundee, The] (m) (H731) 22
Bonny [or Bonnie] ...
[...y Anne] (H739) 291
[...ie Banks o' Loch Lomond, The] (m) (H511) 157
[(...y) (Cruel) Barbara Allan (Ellen)] (H236) 375
[...y Blue Handkerchief] (H161a,b) 456
...y, Bonny (H75b) 187
...y, Bonny Boy, The (H215) 393
...y, bonny was my seat in yon red rosy yard (H75b) 199
[...y Boy, The] (H168) 399, (H215) 393
[...y (Merry) Broomfields, The] (H135) 414
[(...y) Brown Girl, The] (H72) 374, (H86) 436
...y Brown Hair, The Maid with the (b) (H575) 394; (m) (H14a) 356
...y Brown Hen, The (H88) 18
...y Brown Jane, My (H613) 396
[...y Bunch of Rushes Green, The] (cf. H635) 455
...y Bushes Bright, The [Child #248] (H699) 383
[...ie Doon] (m) (H2) 215
...y Garrydoo (H800) 164
[...y Green Tree, (The)] (H794) 385
[...y Green Woods, The] (H135) 414
[...y Irish Boy, The] (H168) 399; (m) (H674) 219
[...ie Kellswater] (H695) 442
...y Labouring Boy, The [Laws M14] (H576) 435
[...ie Lassie amang the Heather] (H177) 271
...y Light Horseman, The (H122) 88
...y Mary Hay (H568) 226
...y Mary Hay, I will lo'e thee yet (H568) 226
[...y Portmore] (m) (H775) 171
...y Portrush (H775) 171
[...y Sailor Lad, The] (H644) 367

[...y Scottish Mary] (H120) 332
[...y Udny] (H775) 171
...ie Wee Hen, My (H94) 17
...y Wee Lass, The (H763) 458
...ie Wee Lass of the Glen, The (H14a,b) 356
[...y Wee Trampin' Lass, The] (H763) 458
[...ie Wee Widow] (m) (H227) 47
...y Woodha' (H476) 84
[...y Young Irish Boy, The] (H168) 399
Boone, Clayton (H124) 509
[Border Ruffian, The] (H735) 133
[Bordon's Grove] (H529) 320
[Borland's Groves] (H529) 320
[Boston Burglar, The [Laws L16B] (H202) 119
[Boston Burgular (City) (Smuggler), The] (H202) 119; (cf. H691) 119
Botany Bay [Laws L16A] (H691) 119; (H202) 119
[Bound down to Derry] (H620) 476
[Bound for Charlers (Sydney) Town] (H202) 119
Boy ...
[... and the Cow (Coo) (Highwayman), The] (H51) 129
[... of (A Man in) Love, The] (cf. H211) 479
... that Found a Bride, The (H665) 454
... I Love, Bring Me Back the (a) (H482) 391
Boys of Coleraine, The (H87b) 182
[Boyne Water, The] (m) (H785) 399
Braes of ...
[... Balquhidder] (m) (H22a) 232
... Carnanbane, The (H651) 160
[... Faughan Vale] (H167) 369
[... Glenbraon, The] (m) (H817) 169
... Sweet Kilhoyle, The (H464) 167
Braid, The Beauty of the (H723) 240
Braiding Her Glossy Black Hair (H493) 237
Bramble, The (H628) 62
[Bramble Briar, The] (cf. H806) 434
Brave ...
[... (Sweet) Ann O'Neill] (H705) 132
[... Annie and Her Young Sailor Boy] (H214) 445
[... Irish Lady, A (The)] (H72) 374
Breaking of Omagh Jail, The (H181) 131
Breeden, My Bonnie (H512) 225
[Brian (Tommy) O'(A')Lin(n)] (H480) 52
Bride, The Squire's [Laws N20] (H524) 328
[Bride's Death, The] (H60a) 400
Bright ...
[... (and) Morning Star] (H146) 180
... April sun was adorning, A (H493) 237
... Orange Stars of Coleraine, The (H87a) 181
[Brigg Fair] (H479) 347
Bring ...
... back My Barney to Me (H7) 290
[... back My Johnny to Me] (H7) 290
... Me Back the Boy I Love (a) (H482) 391
Brisk Young ...
[... Sailor, The] (H232) 318, (H471) 317; (cf. H16) 392
[... Sailor Lad, The] (H779) 54
[... Seamen] (H213) 334
[British Man-of-War, The] (cf. H556) 326
Broken ...
... Bridges (H48h) 11
... bridges falling down (H48h) 11
... Ring, The [Laws N42] (H471) 317
[... Ring Song] (H471) 317
[... Token, (The)] (H232) 318, (H471) 317
Broken-Hearted ...
[... Fish Fag, The] (cf. H499) 387
... Gardener, The (H499) 387
... Heroes, You (H549) 81
[... I Wander] (H122a,b) 88

... I'll wander for the loss of my lover (H122a,b) 88
Broom ...
... Besoms!, Fine (H17a) 61
... bloomed so fresh and fair, The (H47) 236
[...-Cutter, The] (H147) 474
[..., Green Broom] (H147) 474
Broomfield Hill, The [Child #43] (H135) 414
[Broomfield Wager] (H135) 414
Broon's Soo, Matty (H671) 22
Brow of Sweet Knocklayd (H19b) 196
Brown ...
... -Eyed Gypsies, The (H124) 509
[... Girl, The (Bonny)] (H72) 374, (H86) 436
...-Haired Lass, The (a,b) (H116a,b,c) 201
... Hen, The Bonny (H88) 18
... Jane, My Bonny (H613) 396
... Knowe, The Maid of the Sweet [Laws P7] (H84, 688) 364
[... Thorn (Bush), The] (H206) 289
[Bruton Town] (H806) 434
Bryan O'Lynn (H480a,b) 52
Bryan O'Lynn was a gentleman born (H480a,b) 52
[Bugle Played for Me, The] (H732) 57
[Buinnean (Bunnean) Bui (Buidhe), (An)] (H830) 64
[Bunclody (, and the Lad She Loves So Dear), (The) (Maid of) (Streams of)] (H479) 347
[Bung Your Eye] (H700) 277
[Bungereye] (H700) 277
Bunnan Buidhe, An (H830) 64
[Burber Helen] (H236) 375
[Buren's Grove] (H529) 320
Burglar, The Boston [Laws L16B] (H202) 119
Burndennet(t), The Maid of (H96) 230
[Burns and His Highland Mary] (m) (H8) 311
Bushes, The Green [Laws P2] (H143) 395
[Butcher('s) Boy, The] (cf. H218a) 386; (cf. H682) 505; (cf. H683) 393
[Butchers Three, The] (H185) 129
Buttermilk Boy, The (H57a) 57
[Butter and Cheese (and All)] (cf. H682) 505
[Buy Broom Besoms] (H17a) 61
[(Buy) Broom Buzzems] (H17a) 61
[Buzzems, (Buy) Broom] (H17a) 61
[By Kells Waters] (H802) 466
[By My Indenture] (H739) 291
By swamps and alligators (H619) 373
By the ...
... banks of the Barrow residing (H41) 231
... bonny bushes bright on a dark winter's night (H699) 383
... green banks of Banna I wander alone (H233) 287
... twilight of the morning, as I roved out upon the dew (H66) 369
Byrne, the Piper; Denny (H29) 53

[Ca' the Yowes to the Knowes] (H175) 470
[Cabbage Head (Song)] (H21) 508
Cabin on the Hill, The Little Old Mud (H642) 207
Cabin, The Little Thatched (H91) 156
Cahan's Shaden Glen (H538) 364
[Cailin deas Cruidthe na mbo] ("The Pretty Milking Girl") (m) (H499) 387
[Cailin O Chois tSlure] (H491) 225
[Caitin Ban, An] (H510) 17
Calabar, The Cruise of the (H502) 98
[Caledonia] (m) (H162) 333
[Caledonian Hunt's Delight] (m) (H2) 215, (H11) 110
[Calen O Custure me (Colleen Oge Asthore)] (m) (H491) 225
[Caleno Custure Me] [Callino Casturame] (m) (H491) 225
[Calton Weaver, The] (H745) 47

Call of Home, The (H674) 219
[Ca' the Yowes to the Knowes] (H175) 470
[Cameron's Got His Wife Again] (m) (H39) 123
Campbell's Mill (H762) 368
Canada[,] Hi! Ho! (H162) 333
[Canada(y)-i-o (I.O.)] (cf. H162) 333
[Canadee-i-o (-I-O)] (cf. H162) 333
[Cape Horn, The Gals (Girls) around] (H539) 97
Captain ...
[... Black] (m) (H41) 231
[... Colstein (Colston) (Coulson) (and the Pirate Ship)] (H562) 113
[... Coulston (H562) 113
[... Devin (Kelly)] (H792) 122
[... (Mr) Wedderburn's (Washburn's) (Woodburn's) Courtship] (H681) 490
[... with His Whiskers, The] (H660) 273
[Cardigan the Fearless] (H829) 91
Cargan, The Lammas Fair in (H513) 75
Carnanbane (H100a) 188
Carnanbane, The Braes of (H651) 160
Carnlough Shore (H686) 160
Carntogher's Braes (H237) 189
[Carolina Lady] (H474) 488
Caroline of Edinburgh Town, Blooming [Laws P27] (H148) 411
Carr, Susan (?Laws P33) (H690) 416
[Carrowclare] (H169) 298
[Carter's Lad] (H171) 40
[Carver's Choice, The] (m) (H101) 275
[Cashelnagleanna] (Hebridean) (m) (H586) 80
Cashel Green (I) (H647) 462
Cashel Green (II) (H154) 33
[Cashlan Ui Neill] (m) (H629) 171
[Castle by the Sea, The] (H163) 413
[Castle Hill Anthem] (cf. H514) 297
Castleroe Mill (H22b) 361
[Castles in the Air] (m) (H171) 40
[Cavehill Diamond, The] (H45) 477
[Cetch in the Creel, The] (H201) 265
[Charge of the Light Brigade, The] (H829) 91
Charity Seed, The (H766) 43
Charles O'Neill (H50) 139
[Charlestown] (H202) 119
Charlie Jack's Dream (H799) 221
Charlie to Me, So Dear Is My (H533) 292
Charming ...
[... Coleraine Lass, The] (H616) 462
[... Mary Neill] (H55) 479
... Kate O'Neill, My (H767) 370
... Mary O'Neill [Laws M17] (H55) 479
Chest, The Tailor in the Sea [Laws Q8] (H604) 505
Chignon, The Dandy (H227) 47
Child's Lullaby, A (H40b) 17
[Chile Girls, The] (H539) 97
[Chimney Sweepers Wedding] (H138) 256
Chivalry, The Three Flowers of (H99) 89
Christ-Child, Irish Lullaby for the (H630) 7
Churchill, Beautiful (H627) 161
Churnstaff, The Aul' Man and the [Laws Q2] (H174) 507
Clady River Water Bailiffs, The (H764) 32
Claudy ...
[... Banks, (The)] (H693) 313
... Green (a) (H115a) 355
... Green (b) (H115b) 241
..., Banks of [Laws N40] (H5) 313
[Clayton Boone] (H124) 509
[Clever Skipper, The] (H604) 505
[(Clipper Ship) Dreadnaught (Dreadnought), The] (H194) 99
Clonalee, Sweet (H554) 400
Cloughmills Fair (H121) 270
Cloughwater (H610) 208
Clyde, The Banks of the (H812) 310
Cobbler, The (H551) 40
[Cobbler's Boy, The] (H551) 40
Cochrane, Miss (H42a) 147

[Cockleshells] (cf. H16) 392
[Cocks Are (Is) Crowing, The] (H722) 343
Coimfeasgar Fogmair (H831) 235
[Cold (Dark) (Gonesome) (Lonesome) (Stormy) Scenes (Hours) (Winds) of Winter, The] (H637) 385
[Colehill, The Maid of the] (H612) 242
Coleraine ...
... Girl, The (H646) 209
... is a pretty place (H646) 209
[... Lass, The] (m) (H54) 144
... Lass, My Charming (H616) 462
... Regatta (H36) 74
..., The Boys of (H87b) 182
..., The Bright Orange Stars of (H87a) 181
..., The Girls from [Dt, Wt: of] (H64) 161
..., Kate of (H684)
..., Maggie of (H657) 242
Coleshill (H10b) 2
[Colinband, (William) Riley and] (H234) 436
[Colleen Dhas Rue, The] (cf. H751) 50
[Colleen Og a Store] (H491) 225
[Collen (Colvin) (Colyean) (and the Knight), May] (H163) 413
[Colley's Run-i-o] (cf. H162) 333
Collier Lad, A (H148) 144
[Collishaw (Coughlin) (Golicher) (Gallac(g)her), John(nie)(y)] (H574) 80
Colonial Boy, The Wild [Laws L20] (H750) 120
[Colour of Amber, The] (cf. H16) 392
[Colton Boy, The] (cf. H202) 119
Come all ye ...
... airy bachelors, a warning take by me (H586) 80
... brisk young fellows, wherever that you be (H151) 124
... dry-land sailors and listen to my song (H502) 98
... gentle muses, combine and lend an ear (H594) 430
... loyal lovers, a tale I will unfold (H37) 485
... maidens now that pass (H573) 212
... pretty fair maids, I hope you'll lend an ear (H110) 144
... pretty fair maids, so brisk and so merry (H138) 256
... seamen bold, I pray, and listen here awhile to me (H11) 110
... sporting young men and listen unto me (H761) 228
... sprightly sporting youths, wherever you may be (H145) 503
... tender fair maids, give ear unto my rhyme (H148) 411
... true-bred Irishmen and listen to my chant (H0) 53
... water-bailiffs that round the Clady lie (H764) 32
... young fellows and bachelors too (H797) 327
... young men inclined to ramble (H673) 429
... young sports, for the muse I will court (H516) 35
... young sportsmen, far off and near hand (H783) 34
Come all you ...
... bold sportsmen of honour and fame (H12) 31
... craftsmen that do wish (H146) 180
... good people, I pray lend an ear (H51) 129
... jolly mariners and listen unto me (H618) 85
... jolly seamen bold who plough the raging main (H27c) 105
... jovial seamen bold, of high and low degree (H717) 108
... lads and lasses and listen to me a while (H688) 364
[... Little Streamers] (cf. H520) 259
[... True Lovers] (H138) 256

Titles and first lines Cal - Crac

... loyal heroes, wherever that you be (H139) 42
... loyal lovers, I pray you to draw near (H15) 87
... loyal lovers that's locked in Cupid's chain (H584) 331
... tender-hearted chaps, I hope you'll lend an ear (H612) 242
... young fair maids, I pray lend an ear (H73) 412
Come ...
[... All Young Men and Maidens] (H113) 434
... *back to old Ireland, the land of our childhood* (H778) 387
... draw your chair up to my loom and tell to me the time (H18a) 358
... hear the last words of young Susan Brown (H771) 415
... join in lamentation, ye queens and ye princes (H533) 292
... let us all begin to 'French' (H10d) 2
[... along, Bonny Lassie, and Give Me a Waltz] (H230) 255
[... My Little Roving Sailor] (H532) 367
[... With Me over the Mountain] (H61a,b) 459
[Comical Dialogue between an Honest Sailor and a Deluding Landlady, etc., A] (H779) 54
[Coming Home Late] (H21) 508
[Company of Boatmen, A] (H644) 367
Connaught Man, The (H219) 177
Connor of Castledawson, Henry (H128) 440
Constant ...
[... Damsel, The] (cf. H16) 392
... Farmer's Son, The [Laws M33] (H806) 434
[... Lovers, The] (H108a) 329, (H634) 472
[Contented Farmer's Son], The (H806) 434
[Contented Wife (and) Answer, The] (cf. H753) 501
[Coo Coo (Cuckoo) Bird, The] (H479) 347
[Cook's Choice, The] (cf. H682) 505
[Cool Finn, The Lake of] (H176) 146
[Corncraik (Corncrake) amang the Whinny Knowes, The] (H18b) 272
Corby Mill, The Flower of (H612) 242
[Cot in the Corner, The] (m) (H8) 311
Cot where I was born in, it stands upon a hill, The (H666) 170
[Cottage[?r] D[?P]oor, The] (H593) 389
[Cottager's Daughter, The] (m) (H607) 250
[Country Carrier, The] (H664) 41; (cf. H171) 40
[Country Girl, The] (H7h) 234
County ...
[... Antrim Air] (m) (H505) 157
[... Down, Star of the] (m) (H19a) 194, 196, (H49) 200, (H100a) 188, (H694) 503, (H747) 214; (cf. H207) 417, (cf. H791) 218
[... Tyrone] (H609) 199
... Tyrone, The (H153a,b) 480
Courting ...
[... Case, The] (cf. H532) 367
[... is a Pleasure] (H625) 342
[(... My) (Her) Father's Grey Mare] (H90) 365
Covent Garden (H729) 446
[Covent's Garden] (H729) 446
Covered Cavalier, The (H21) 508
[Coverin Blue, The] (H201) 265
[Cow (That) Ate the Piper, The] (H29) 54
[Cow, Well Sold the] (H51) 129
Cowboy ...
... of Loreto, The [Laws B1] (H680) 141
[... of Loreto Song, The] (H680) 141
[...'s Lament] (H680) 141, The
Crack, crack, goes my whip, I whistle as I sing (H171) 40

587

Craf - Du Sam Henry's Songs of the People

[Crafty Farmer, The] (H51) 129
Crafty Ploughboy, The [Child #283] [Laws L1] (H51) 129
[Craiganee] (H749) 189
Craigienorn, The Maid of (H500) 359
[Creel(ie) (Girlie) and the Oysters, The] (H725) 278
[Creole Girl, The] (H619) 373
Cricketty Wee (H744) 12
Croaghmore, The Maid of (H522) 355
Crocodile ...
..., The (H231) 28
[... Song, The] (H231) 28
[...'s Mouth, The] (H231) 28
[Croodlin Dow] (cf. H814) 415
[Crook and Plaid, The] (H617) 45
[Cropped Tailor, The] (cf. H604) 505
[Croppy Tailor, The] (cf. H682) 505
Crossagh, Shane (H97) 130
Crowd; We Met, 'Twas in a (H638) 431
[Cruchan na Feinne] (m) (H512) 225
Cruel ...
[(...) Barbara Allan (Ellen), (Bonny)] (H236) 375
[... Father (and Affectionate Lover(s)), The] (H668) 444
[(...) Lake(s) (Loch) of Col Fin (Col Flynn) (Cold Finn) (Cold Stream) (?Colefaine) (Cool Flynn) (Coolfin) (Colephin) (Coulfin) (Shallin) (Shellin) (Shilin) (Shillin) (Wolfrinn), The] (H176) 146
[... Lincoln] (H735) 133
[... Wife, The] (H174) 507
[... Youth, The] (cf. H163) 413
Cruise of the Calabar, The (H502) 98
[Cruise of the Calibar, The] (H502) 98
"Crummy" Cow, The (H501) 25
[Cuckold, The Merry] (H21) 508
Cuckoo ...
..., The (H479) 347
... is a purty bird, she sings as she flies, The (H479) 347
[...'s Nest, The] (m) (H130) 26, (H675) 24
Culmore, The Maids of (H687) 302
Culnady, The Bard of (H50) 139
[Cunning Clerk, The] (H201) 265
[(Cunning) Cobbler (and the Butcher), The] (cf. H604) 505
Cup of Gold, The (H546) 273; (m) (H546) 273
Cup o' Tay, A (H489) 48
Cupid's ...
[... Garden] (H31) 411
[... Trappan or the Green Forest] (m) (H168) 399
[... Trepan] (H215) 393
[Cushendall] (m) (H111) 229
[Cushleake] (m) (H661) 259
[Cutty Wren, The] (H744) 12

Damsel ...
[..., The Constant] (cf. H16) 392
... possessed of great beauty, A (H243a,b) 473, 474
[... Disguised, The] (H584) 331
Dan Murphy's Convoy (H663) 72
Dandy Chignon, The (H227) 47
[Danny Boy] (m) (H3) 286
[Dapple(dy) (Dapherd) Grey, The] (H163) 413
Dark ...
[... and Stormy Night] (H693) 313
[...-Eyed Gipsy (O!), The] (H124) 509
...-Eyed Molly (H625) 342
...-Eyed Sailor, The [Laws N35] (H232) 318; (cf. H471) 317
...-Haired Girl, The (H559) 237
... was her hair as the dark raven's wing (H631) 294
... was the night, cold blew the wind and thickly fell the rain (H207) 417
[Daughter in the Dungeon] (H668) 444
David ...
[... and Goliath] (H803) 79
[... (Dav(e)y) (Daisy), (The) Blackjack] (H124) 509

[...'s Flowery Vale] (H212) 370
[Davie Faa] (H124) 509
Day ...
... being gone and the evening spent, The (H770) 485
... was appointed, the knot to be tied, The (H524) 328
... We Packed the Hamper for the Coast, The (H488) 501
Deans, John McKeown and Margaret (H129) 141
Dear ...
... Irish Boy, My [Bt: The] (H142) 294
[... Irish Maid, The] (H142) 294
[... Old Derry Quay] (m) (H235) 203
...-a-Wee Lass, The (H74) 236
[...; Oh, Molly] (H722) 343
[Dearest Billie] (H683) 393
[Death of Queen Jane] (H72) 374
[Death of William and Mary] (H722) 343
[Deceased Maiden Lover, The] (H683) 393
Dee, The Banks of [the] (H583) 314
[Dee, Mary o' the] (H54) 144
[Deep in Love] (H218a) 386; (cf. H683) 393
[Deep in Love, (So)] (cf. H16) 392
[Deil's Courtship, The] (cf. H532) 367
[Delgaty, The Barnyards o'] (m) (H640) 291
Denny Byrne, the Piper (H29) 53
Derry ...
..., Derry, Dearie Me; Oh, (H536) 209
[..., The Diamonds of] (H519) 389
[... Gaol] (H705) 132
[... Pipe, The] (H465) 49
[... Quay, Dear Old] (m) (H235) 203
Descend, ye chaste muses, ye bards and ye sages (H178) 233
Descend, you chaste nine, to a true Irish bard (H93) 72
Deserter, The (H223) 83
[Devil and the Blessed Virgin Mary, The] (H681) 490
[Diamonds of Derry, The] (H519) 389
[Die a(n Old) Maid, Don't Let Me] (H138) 256
[Died for (of) Love] (H89) 287, (H683) 393; (cf. H482) 931
[Dirandel] (H814) 415
[Disguised Sailor] (H108a) 329
[Dixie's (Texas) Isle] (H238) 296
[Dixon and (Said to) Johnson] (H185) 129
Dobbin's Flowery Vale [Laws O29] (H85) 300
Doctor?, Am I the [?Child #295] [Laws P9] (H72) 374
Doctor's merit no more employs the burden of my song, sir, A (H222) 29
[Dog and the Gun, The] (H585) 147
[Don't Let Me Die a(n Old) Maid] (H138) 256
[Don't Prittle Nor Prattle] (H163) 413
[Donahoe, Bold Jack] (m) (H202) 119, (H555) 463
Donald ...
[... of Glencoe] (H655) 319
[... of the Isles] (H193) 487
[...'s Return to Glencoe, (Mac)] (H655) 319
Donegal, The Star of (H555) 463
[Doolan, Larry] (H592) 41
[Doon (Down) the Moor] (H177) 271
Doon the moor, roun' amang the heather (H177) 271
[Doran's Ass] (m) (H766) 43
[Douglas, Jamie] (cf. H16) 392
[Dover Sailor, The] (H72) 374
Down by the ...
[... Fair River] (cf. H582) 238
[... Green Bushes] (H143) 395
[... Sally Gardens] (m) (H27a [orig. H34b]) 371
[(...) Sally('s) Gardens] (H828) 286
[... Seaside] (H581) 318
... seaside I spied a ship sailing (H581) 318

[(...) Tan-Yard Side] (H52b) 429
[... Woods and Shady Green Trees] (H794) 385
Down by yon ...
... green bushes, near Calder's clear stream (H476) 84
... harbour, near sweet Coleraine town (H614) 384
... shady arbour I spied a handsome maid (H144) 270
Down in ...
[... Carlisle] (H474) 488
[... Cupid's Garden] (H729) 446
... Dublin City there lives a merchant's daughter (H159a) 396
... my Sally's garden (H747) 214
... My Sally's Garden (H828) 286
[(...) ... the Town of Marlborough] (cf. H668) 444
[... Yon Meadows] (H218a) 386, (H683) 393
... yon valley, where the flowers grow sweet (H738) 478
[... Yonder Valley] (H625) 342
[(Down) the Moor; Doon] (H177) 271
Downhill, The Maids of (H809) 162
Doyle ...
..., Johnny [Laws M2] (H137) 431
..., Mary (H570) 310
... Paddy (H53c) 97
[Dragletail Gypsies, The] (H124) 509
Dragoon, The Inniskilling (H98b) 472
[Dra(o)ighnean Donn, An] (H206) 289
Drake, Nell Flaherty's (H228b) 18
Dram-a-da, toor-an-addy, toor al-oor-an-andy O (H650b) 264
[Dra(o)ighnean Donn, An] (H206) 289
Draw near me, kind friends and relations (H9) 186
[Dreadnaught (Dreadnought), The (Clipper Ship)] (H194) 99
Dreary Gallows, The [Laws L11] (H705) 132
[(Drian Naun) (Dri(y)naun) (Drinan(e)) D(h)un (Donn), The] (H206) 289
[Drim (Drum) (Drung), The Blazing Star of (a,b)] (H197a,b) 248
Drinaun Dhun, The (H206) 289
[Drowning of Young Robinson, The] (H585) 147
[Drowsy Sleeper, The] (H722) 343
Drum Major, The (H797) 327
Drumcroon, Ann o' (H26a, H246) 248
Drumglassa Hill (H703) 210
Drummer ...
[..., The] (H702) 504
... Boy at Waterloo, The [Laws J1] (H728) 88
[... Boy Edwin of Waterloo], The (H728) 88
[... Boy of Waterloo], The (H728) 88
... Maid, The (H497) 326
Drummond's Land (H212)
Drummuck, The Duck from (H228a) 19
[Drumreagh] (H150a) 466
[Drunk Husband, The] (H21) 508
[Drunkard Blues] (H21) 508
[Drunkard's Special] (H21) 508
[Du, Du,] or [The Lincolnshire Poachers] (m) (H527) 20
[Dublin (now called Coleshill)] (H10b) 2
[Dublin Weaver, The] (H745) 47
Duck from Drummuck, The (H228a) 19
[Duck, The Black] (H38) 29
Dun Ceithern (H523) 63
[Dunboe, The Parish of] (H23) 307
Dundee (H10c) 2
Dundee it is a pretty place (H10c) 2
Duneane, The Happy Green Shades of (H653) 211
Dungiven Cricket Match (H669) 179
Dungiven Priory Church (H187) 162
Dunloy, Sweet (H577) 439
Dunysheil, The Maid of (H530) 298
[Dusty Bluebells] (H48a) 10

Titles and first lines Dy – For

Dying ...
[... Cowboy (Ranger), The] (H680) 141
[... Soldier, The] (H816) 92
[... Stockman, The] (cf. H680) 141

[Eamonn Magaine] (m) (H153) 480
Early one morning as the sun was adorning (H127) 368
Early, Early (H89) 287
[Easter Snow] (H66) 369
[Echo Mocks the Corncrake, The] (H18b) 272
Edinburgh Town, Blooming Caroline of [Laws P27] (H148) 411
[Eggs and Marrowbone] (H174) 507
[Eggs in Her Basket] (cf. H700) 277
Eglintown, The Blooming Star of (H170) 299
Eight Mile Bridge (H486) 121
Eighteen sixty-nine being the date of the year (H161c) 456
[Eirigh Suas a Stoirin] (m) (H42a) 147
[Elfin Knight] (H163) 413
Eliza ...
... (H58) 446
[..., William and] (H597) 476
[... Long] (H207) 417
[Ellender, Young] (cf. H668) 444
Emigrant's ...
... Farewell, The (H743) 200
[... Farewell to Ireland, The] (H743) 200
[... Love for His Native Land, The] (H743) 200
[Enchanted Isle, The (H550) 176
[Ennery My Son] (cf. H814) 415
Enniskillen ...
[... Dragoon] (H98b) 472
[..., Fare Ye Well, (H631) 294
[..., Lovely Jane from] (cf. H471) 317
Enterprise, The Wreck of the (H558) 106
[Eochaill] (m) (H189) 173
Ere the twilight bat was flitting, in the sunset at her knitting (H78) 484
Erin ...
..., my country, although thy harp slumbers (H478) 176
..., My Country (H478) 176
[...'s Flowery Vale] (H85) 300
...'s Lovely Home [Laws M6] (H46) 438
[Estersnowe] (H66) 369

[Faa, Johnny] (H124) 509
Factory Girl, The (H127) 368
Fair ...
... Annie (H126) 510
[... Caroline (Blooming Caroline)] (H148) 411
[... Damsel (Rich Lady) from London, The] (H72) 374
[... (Fine) (Pretty) (Queen) Sally (of London)] (H72) 374
[... Gallowa'] (H665) 454
[... Julian Bond] (H234) 436
... Maid of Ballyagan (H67) 365; (m) (H108b) 169, (H164) 362
... Maid of Glasgow Town (H579) 345
[... Mary] (H221) 490
[(...) Phoebe (Phoeby) and Her (the) Dark-Eyed Sailor] (H232) 318
... Rosa (H599) 12
... Rosa was a lovely child (H599) 12
[... (Fine) (Pretty) (Queen) Sally (of London)] (H72) 374
... Tyrone (H189) 173
... (Young) Maid (Miss) (Walking) (All) in (a) (Her) (the) Garden, A] (H471) 31
..., The Ould Lammas (H101) 275
[..., She Moved through the] (H141) 395
[Fairy King's Courtship, The] (H56) 354
[Faithful Emma] (H520) 259
Faithful Rambler, The (H825) 299
Fal da dee, fal da daddy (H51) 129
Falcon, The (H95) 107

False ...
...-Hearted Johnny came to court (H163) 413
[...-Hearted Knight (and Pretty Carol Lynn), The] (H163) 413
[... (Long) Lankin (Lankum) (Lanky)] (H735) 133
[... Love] (cf. H16) 392
... Lover, The (H790) 383
... Lovers, The (H143) 395
[... Sir John] (H163) 413
[... Young Man, The] (H593) 389
[Famed Waterloo] (H76) 314
[Famous Wedding, The] (H60a) 400
[Famous Woman Drummer, The] (H797) 327
Fare ...
[... Thee Well Cold Winter] (H504) 347
[... Ye (Thee) Well, Enniskillen] (H98b) 472
... Ye Well, Enniskillen (H631) 294
[... Ye Well, My Darlin'] (H98a)
... you well, lovely Ellen, it is now we must part (H514) 297
Farewell ...
..., Ballycastle (H210) 188
... Ballycastle, farewell to thy bowers (H210) 188
... Ballymena, farewell darling swain (H58) 446
... Ballymoney (H615) 343
[... Charming Nancy] (H561) 458
..., Darling (H580) 357
[... Enniskillen] (m) (H520) 259
..., Enniskillen, fare ye well for a while (H631) 294
... *Enniskillen, farewell for a while* (H98b) 472
... He (H504) 347; (H241) 346
[... Lovely Polly] (H31) 411
[... My Dear(est) Nancy] (H561) 458
[... Nancy] (cf. H514) 297
[... She] (H504) 347
"... to Articlave", Monk McClamont's (H65b) 187
[... to Articlave] (m) (H65a) 293
[... to Ballymonan, where oftimes I have been (H643) 159
[... to Caledonia] (H151) 124
[... to Enniskillen] (m) (H137) 431
[... to Ireland] (H235) 203
[... to (Here's Adieu to All) Judges and Juries] (H746) 62
... to old Ireland, the land of my childhood (H743) 200
... to Slieve Gallen (H795) 198
... to Sweet Glenravel (H727) 193
... to Sweet Glenravel, its flowery banks and braes (H727) 193
... to Sweet Glenrannel's plains and streamlets winding clear (H100b) 193
... *to sweet Glenrannel's plains, a long farewell to thee* (H100b) 193
... to sweet Owenreagh's banks and streamlets winding clear (H225) 196
... to the Banks of the Roe (H791) 218
... to (Fare Ye Weel) Whiskey] (H807) 514
... unto old Ireland's isle since I left you behind (H632) 203
Farmer ...
..., The (H676) 42
[... and His Bride, The] (H524) 328
[... in Leicester, The] (H51) 129
[..., There Was a Wealthy] (H553) 482
Farmer's ...
[... Daughter, The] (H108a) 329, (H217) 432
[... Daughter, A Sailor Courted (Loved) (Married) a] (H634) 472
[... Son) and the Shanty Boy, The] (H662) 45
[... Son So Sweet, A] (H104) 457
... Son, The Constant [Laws M33] (H806) 434
[... Son, Wounded] (cf. H105) 331

[Fate of Young Henry in Answer to Caroline of Edinboro Town, The] (cf. H148) 411
Father ...
[... and Daughter] (H722) 343
[... (Old Mr) Grumble] (H702) 504
[... in Ambush, The] (H587) 433
Faughan Side, The (H621) 191
Faughanvale (H796) 163
Faughanvale, The Maid of (H167) 369
[Faultless (Penitent) Bride, The] (H60a) 400
[Far ower the Forth] (m) (H8) 311
Fear a Bhata (H834) 289
Feckless Lover, The (H216)
[Felix the Soldier] (cf. H131) 84
[Female Drummer (Soldier) (Warrior), The] (H497) 326
Female Highwayman, The [Laws N21] (H35) 327
[Ferguson, Janie(ey) (Jennie)] (H188) 401
Few lines on my native place with pleasure I enclose, A (H801) 164
Fhir a bhata na horo eile (H834) 289
Fine ...
... broom besoms, besoms fine and new (H17a) 61
... Broom Besoms! (H17a) 61
[... Old Irish Gentleman, The] (m) (H552) 102
Finn Waterside (H240) 192
Finvola, the Gem of the Roe (H786) 139
First ...
... of my late rambling I mean to let you know, The (H726) 307
... place that I saw my love was Ballymoney town, The (H822) 239
... time I came to the shire of Argyle, The (H186) 46
... time that I saw my love, the stormy winds did blow, The (H197a,b) 248
... time that I saw my love, 'twas on a summer's day, The (H767) 370
[Flash (Fancy) Frigate, The] (H194) 99
Flood tide that ebbs (H3) 286
Flora ...
[...] (H578) 416, (H637) 385
..., the Lily of the West [Laws P29] (H578) 416
[... MacDonald's Lament] (H533) 292
... and I, My (H30a) 390
Flower of ...
... Benbrada, The (H537) 239
... Corby Mill, The (H612) 242
... Craiganee, The (H749) 189
... Glenleary, The (H22a) 232
... Gortade, The (H178) 233
... Magherally, O!, The (H220) 243
[... Sweet Ballinascreen, The] (H752) 245
... Sweet Dunmull, The (H1) 191
... Sweet Strabane, The (H224) 390; (m) (H55) 479, (H148) 411, (H557) 478
... the valley was Mary Machree, The (H485) 308
Flowers of Chivalry, The Three (H99) 89
[Flowers of Enniskillen, The] (H525) 483
Flowery ...
[... Garden, The] (H471) 317
[... Vale, David's] (H621) 370
...Vale, Dobbin's [Laws O29] (H85) 300
[Fly up, My Cock] (H699) 383
Fol da deedle, lairo lairo lairo (H213) 334
[Foolish Boy, The] (H732) 57
[Foot (Maid) of the Mountain('s) Brow (Logan Bough), (At) The] (H688) 364
For ...
... I'd roam many a mile over hedge and stile to covet that girl, I vow (H492) 238
[... My Breakfast You Must Get a Bird Without a Bone] (H681) 490
... *she has eyes like summer skies* (H4) 190
... *she's aye, aye scowlin', an' she's aye scowlin' me* (H145) 503

589

For ...
... *the roof was thatched with straw and the walls as white as snow* (H642) 207
... *want of fine expressions to set forth my love's praise* (H589) 344
... *we are the true-born sons of Levi* (H146) 180
... *when we landed in Belgium, the girls all danced with joy* (H526) 182
[Forsaken Lover, A] (H479) 347
[Four (Five) (Six) (Seven) Nights Drunk] (H21) 508
[Four Nights' Experience] (H21) 508
[Fowler, The] (H114) 143
Fox ...
[..., The] (H38) 29
... and His Wife, The (H38) 29
[... and (the) (Grey) Goose (Geese), (The)] (H38) 29
... and his wife they lived at great strife, The (H38) 29
[... Traveled (Walked) Out, The] (H38) 29
[... Went out in Hungry Plight, A] (H38) 29
[Frank James] (cf. H691) 119
[Frank James, the Roving Gambler] (cf. H202) 119
Franklin ...
[... Expedition, The] (H815) 103
...the Brave [Laws K9] (H815) 103
[...'s Crew] (H815) 103
French (H10d) 2
French Privateer, The (H560) 112
[Frenchman's Ball, The] (cf. H131) 84
From ...
... Greenock to Darry, with hearts light and merry (H95) 107
... Londonderry we set sail all on the eighth of May (H192) 101
... old Carntogher's towering top (H49) 200
... sweet Londonderry to fair London town (H687) 302
[Frugal Maid, The] (H70) 340

[Gaberlunzie Man, The] (H183) 268, (H810) 269
[Gabhaid Sinn an Rathad Mor] (Gaelic) (m) (H48h) 11
[Gal I Left Behind, The] (H188) 401
Gallant ...
[... Highland Soldier, The] (H782) 473
[... Hussar(s)] (H243a,b) 473
... Soldier, The (H782) 473
[Galloway', Fair] (H665) 454
Gallows, The Dreary [Laws L11] (H705) 132
[Gals (Girls) around Cape Horn, The] (H539) 97
[Galway City] (cf. H532) 367
[Galway Shawl, The] (H652) 269
[Game Cock, The] (cf. H604) 505
Gaol Song (H746) 62
[Garden, A Fair (Young) Maid (Miss) (Walking) (All) in (a) (Her) (the)] (H471) 3
Garden Gate, The (H770) 485
Garrydoo, Bonny (H800) 164
Garvagh, March of the Men of (H17b) 180
[Gates (Doors) of Ivory, The] (H163) 413
Gauger ...
... once in Dublin town, the time that I was there, A (H103) 55
[..., The] (cf. H183) 268
[...'s Song, The] (H103) 56
[Gay Girl Marie] (cf. H582) 238
Gelvin Burn (H667) 192
Gentle ...
[... Maiden] (m) (H698) 51
... Shepherdess, The (H104) 457
... Young Lady, A (H681) 490
[(George) Riley, Young] (cf. H16) 392
[Gibb and the Soo, Tam] (H671) 22
[Gilgar(r)y Mountain] (H792) 122

Gilmore and Johnson; Wilson, (H185) 129
[Gipsies Came to Lord M--'s Gate, The] (H124) 509
[Gipson Davy] (H124) 509
[Gipsy Laddie(y) O(h)] (H124) 509
Girl ...
[... from Donegal] (H4) 190
... from Turfahun, The (H521) 372
... I Left Behind, The [Laws P1a] (H188) 401
[... I Left Behind Me, The] (H133) 461, (H513) 75, (H823) 58
[... I Love, The] (H482) 391
[(...) Maid I Left Behind, (The)] (H188) 401
[... of the Golden Tresses, The] (m) (H603) 238
Girls ...
... from [Dt, Wt: of] Coleraine, The (H64) 161
[... of Coleraine, The] (m) (H657) 242
... of Valparaiso, The (H539) 97
Give me Coleraine where the lovely Bann river (H657) 242
Glasgow Town, Fair Maid of (H579) 345
Glenamoyle, The Star of (H13) 232
Glenariffe (H801) 164
Glenarm Bay (H102) 464
Glenbush, Sweet (H573) 212
[Glencoe] (H655) 319
Glenelly ...
... (H720) 165
..., *Glenelly, how lovely thou art* (H720) 165
..., The Pride of (H607) 250
Glenkeen, Kate of (H41) 231
Glenleary, The Flower of (H22a) 232
Glenore, The Pretty Three-Leaved Shamrock from (H34) 213
Glenrannel's Plains (H100b) 193
Glenravel, Farewell to Sweet (H727) 193
Glenrea, The Thatchers of (H186) 46
[Glenshee] (H590) 486
Glenshesk ...
... Waterside, The (H19a) 194; (m) (H19b) 196
..., Lovely (I) (H544) 165
..., Lovely (IIa) (H28a) 194
Glen O'Lee (H672) 212
Glen, The Bonnie Wee Lass of the (H14a,b) 356
Glossy Black Hair, Braiding Her (H493) 237
Glove and the Lions, The [Laws O25] (H474) 488
[Go away from Me, Young Man] (H479) 347
[(Go Bring Me Back) My Blue-Eyed Boy] (H218a) 386
Goat's Will, The (H119) 22
God save all here,' her salutation (H756) 60
[Goddon, Maggie] (cf. H16) 392
[Going to Mass Last Sunday] (H625) 342
[Gold Watch and Chain] (H35) 327
[Golden Glove, The] (H524) 328
[(Golicher) (Gallac(g)her), John(nie)(y) Collishaw (Coughlin)] (H574) 80
Good ...
[... bye, Fare Ye Well] (cf. H194) 99
... folks, I'll tell you true, now my song commences (H36) 74
[... Night and Joy Be with You All] (H769) 65
... people, pay attention, give ear unto my song (H119) 21
... Ship *Calibar*, The (H502) 98
... Ship *Mary Cochrane*, The (H754) 111
[Goodbye, Fare You (Ye) Well] (H53a) 97
[Goodbye to Old Winter and Adieu to Its Frost] (cf. H504) 347
[Goodman (Gudeman) (Cam Home at E'en), Our (The)] (H21) 508
[Goose (Geese), (The) Fox and (the) (Grey)] (H38) 29
[Gordon, (?Sweet) Peggy] (cf. H16) 392
Gortade, The Flower of (H178) 233

Gorteen, The Maid of Sweet (H594) 430
[Gra' Mo Croi] (cf. H582) 238
[Gradh Geal mo Croidhe] (cf. H582) 238
Gragalmachree (H582) 238; (cf. H520) 259
Gramachree ...
... (H204) 388
[..., Molly] (H204) 388
[..., Sweet] (cf. H582) 238
Grandfather Died, My (H732) 57
[Grandma Would Have Died an Old Maid] (H208) 258
Grandma's Advice (H208) 258
[Grandmother Adder-cook] (H814) 415
[Granemore Hare, The] (cf. H12) 31
Gravel, Green (H48b) 10
[Great (Rummy) (Wonderful) Crocodile, The] (H231) 28
Green ...
[... and Yellow] (cf. H814) 415
... Banks of Banna, The (H233) 287
[... Bed Empty, The] (H779) 54
[... Beds, The] (H779) 54
[... Besoms] (H17a) 61
... Broom (H147) 474
[... Broom Besoms] (H17a) 61
[... Brooms] (H147) 474
... Bushes, The [Laws P2] (H143) 395; (m) (H476) 84, (H542) 217, (H821) 220
... Bushes in Sweet Tyrone, Among the (H708) 174
[... Fields of (to) America(y) (Canada), The] (H743) 200
... Garden (H818) 317
... Gravel (H48b) 10
... *gravel, green gravel, your grass is so green* (H48b) 10
[... Gravels] (H48b) 10
[... Grow the Laurel(s) (Lilacs) (Rushes (-o)(O))] (H165a) 260
... Grow the Rashes (a,b) (H165a,b) 260
[... Grows the Laurel] (H165a) 260
... *grows the laurel and so does the rue* (H165b) 260
[... Grows the Laurels (Wild Isle)] (H165a) 260
... Hills of Antrim, The (H606) 208
[... Laurel(s), (The)] (H165a) 260
[... Mountain] (H520) 259
... Tree, Under the Shade of a Bonny [Laws P19] (H794) 385
... *were the fields where I sported in childhood* (H716) 218
[..., Little Johnny] (H208) 258
[Greencastle Shore] (H192) 101
Greenmount Smiling Ann (H182) 464
Grey ...
[... Cock] (H699) 383, (H722) 343
[... Hawk, The] (cf. H215) 393
... Mare, The [Laws P8] (H90) 365
... Mare, My Rattlin' Oul' (H664) 41
[Griogal Cridhe] (cf. H582) 238
[Grogal McCree] (cf. H582) 238
[Groyle Machree] (cf. H582) 238
Gruig Hill (H626) 465
[Grumble, Father (Old Mr)] (H702) 504
Gude day, now, bonny Robin (H527) 20
[Guid-Day Now, Bonnie Robin Lad] (H527) 20
[Gyps of David] (H124) 509
Gypsy ...
[... Countess, The] (H124) 509
[... Daisy, The (Dave) (Laddie)] (H124) 509
[... Davy] (H124) 509
[...-o] (H124) 509
[Gypsies-O!] (H124) 509
Gypsies, The Brown-Eyed (H124) 509

Hair, Braiding Her Glossy Black (H493) 237
Hair, The Maid with the Bonny Brown (b) (H575) 394
Hamper for the Coast, The Day We Packed the (H488) 501
[Hame Drunk Cam' I] (H21) 508

[(Hampshire) (Lincolnshire) (Wise) Farmer (Bite), The Yorkshire] (H51) 129
Handsome ...
[... Collier Lad, The] (H110) 144
[... Shepherdess, The] (H104) 457
[... Young Servantman, The] (cf. H668) 444
[Hanky, The] (H161a,b) 456
[Hannah, Lovin'] (cf. H625) 342
Hannah M'Kay (H656) 187
Happy ...
... Green Shades of Duneane, The (H653) 211; (m) (H150b) 361
... 'Tis, Thou Blind, for Thee (H491) 225
[... Marriage] (H753) 501, The
... Pair, The (H753) 501
[... (Pleasant) and Delightful] (cf. H514) 297
... Shamrock Shore, The (H69) 201
... 'Tis, Thou Blind, for Thee (H491) 225
Hare ...
... of Kilgrain, The (H12) 31
...'s Dream, The (H172) 31
[...'s Lament, The] (H12) 31, (H172) 31
Hark how the cock with sprightly note (H10b) 2
[Harp of Erin, The] (H478) 176
Harp on a Willow Tree, I'll Hang My (H155) 366
Hart, Johnnie (H106) 443
Have you ...
'... any tobacco?' says Sam unto Bill (H465) 49
... ever been to Ireland where Derry meets Tyrone? (H601) 174
... ever stood on the Carn crest (H828) 286
Hay ...
..., Bonny Mary (H568) 226
..., The Tossing o' the (H635) 455
..., Tumbling through the (H697) 278
[Haymakers, The] (H697) 278
[Haymaking Courtship] (cf. H635) 455
[Hayraking] (H697) 278
He is gone, and I'm now sad and lonely (H7) 290
[He Rolled Her to the Wall] (H681) 490
[He Wadna Lie in Barn] (H810) 269
Heather ...
... Jock (H39) 123
... *Jock's noo awa'* (H39) 123
... Jock was stark and grim (H39) 123
[... on the Moor] (H177) 271
[Heave Away (, My Johnny)] cf. (H827) 100
Heezh Ba (H591a) 6
Heifer, The (H675) 24
Heights of Alma, The (H123) 90
[(S)Helg Yn Dreean] (H744) 12
Hen, The Bonny Brown (H88) 18
Hen, My Bonnie Wee (H94) 17
Henry ...
[... and Mary Ann] (m) (H37) 485
... Connor of Castledawson (H128) 440
[... Connors] (H128) 440
[... Joy] (m) (H136) 125
[... (Willy) My Son] (H814) 415
..., the Sailor Boy (H37) 485
Her ...
... Bonny Blue E'e (H71) 246
[(...) Father's Grey Mare, (Courting My)] (H90) 365
[... Mantle of (So) Green] (H76) 314
[... Sailor Boy] (H471) 317
[Herding Lambs amongst the Heather] (H177) 271
Here, boys, we are banded together, determined to drain our last vein (H87a) 181
Here's ...
[(...) (A Health) to All True Lovers] (H722) 343
... a health unto bonnie Kellswater (H695) 442

... a Poor Widow (H48f) 11
... a poor widow, she lies her lone (H48f) 11
Hey rick a doo, rick a daddy (H515) 274
[Hi Rinky Dum] (H152) 266
Hibernia's Lovely Jane [Jean] (H467) 428
Hielan' Jane (H477) 140
Hielans o' Scotland, The [Laws N19] (H193) 487
[Highway Robber, The] (H51) 129
[Highwayman, The] (H792) 122
Highwayman, The Female [Laws N21] (H35) 327
[Hillman, The] (H21) 508
Hills ...
[... (Maid) (Rose) of Glenshee, The] (H590) 486
... o' Ballyboley, The (H511) 157
... of Donegal, The (H196) 210
[... of Glenswilly, The] (H672) 212
[... of Mexico] (cf. H0) 53
... of Tandragee, The (H730) 190
... of Tyrone, The (H609) 199
[Hippletoe, Old Mother] (H38) 29
His Heart's Delight] (H217) 432
[His Jacket of (Was) Blue] (H644) 367
[Hobbs, John] (cf. H226) 511
Hobe and the Robin, The (H40c) 20
[Hogg, Parson] (cf. H222) 29
Holland ...
[... Handkerchief, The] (H217) 432
... Is a Fine Place [Child #92A] (H180) 149
[... Song, The] (H31) 411
Holly Bough, The (H111) 229
[Homeward Bound] (H53a) 97
[Honest Labourer, The] (H622) 44
Hooray Santy Anna! (H496) 96
Horo, mo leanibh dhu, horo, mo leanibh dhu (H645) 7
Horse, The Black (H586) 80
How ...
... beautiful young Mary looked, she was Killeavy's pride (H190) 420
... beautiful young Mary looked, she was young Flemming's pride (H798) 421
... blest has my life been, what joys have I known (H753) 501
... Many Miles to Babyland? (H40a) 12
[... Many Miles to Babylon (Bethlehem)?] (H40a) 12
... often have I wandered forth along yon river side (H19a) 194
[... Old Are You?] (H152) 266
Hugh ...
... Fulton, once my comrade dear (H2) 215
[... Fulton of) Mullaghdoo] (m) (H506) 214
... Hill, the Ramoan Smuggler (H494) 127
Hungry Army, The (H92) 86
[Hunt(ing of) the Wren, (The)] (H744) 12
Hunter, John (H125a,b) 475, 476
Hunting ...
... Priest, The (H222) 29
[... Song] (H117) 44
..., As a King Went A- (H117) 44
[Huroo-i-ah] (H201) 265
Hush Alee (H591b) 6

I am a bold undaunted youth ...
... from the county of Tyrone (H181) 131
..., I live in sweet Rarawn (H522) 355
..., I mean to let you know (H23) 307
..., my name is John McCann (H55) 479
I am a ...
... boul' weaver, I've done my endeavour (H153a,b) 480, 481
... brisk young sailor lad, just lately come on shore (H205) 465
... cobbler airy (H551) 40
... fair maiden forsaken, but I have a contented mind (H70a) 340

... jolly carter and a jolly good soul am I (H664) 41
... jolly fisherman, I catch what I can get (H639) 59
... little beggarman, a-begging I have been (H751) 50
... poor forlorn dog and Sport it is my name (H772) 23
[... Poor Stranger] (H780) 345
... rambling hero, by love I am ensnared (H52b) 429
... rambling young man, I rambled up and down (H564) 344
... *rambling young man, from town to town I steer* (H741) 50
... rover that roves strange nations (H723) 240
... roving bachelor and have been all my life (H650a) 263
... true-born Irishman, John Mitchel is my name (H179a) 125
... true-born Irishman, John Mitchell is my name (H179b) 126
... Wee Laddie, Hard, Hard Is My Fate (H624) 349
... woeful beggar as I go from door to door (H832a) 49
[... Young Maiden] (H79) 428
... young man delights in sport (H825) 299
... youth that's inclined to ramble (H788) 300
I am pining day and daily this twelve months and above (H149) 456
I Am the Master (H48a) 10
I being invited to a laird's wedding (H60b) 401
[I Built a Bower in My Breast] (H215) 393
I came from the west, from the province of Connaught (H219) 177
[I Came (Went) Home (Drunk) Last (One) Night] (H21) 508
I care not wherever through life I may wander (H91) 156
I climb the mountain, my heart is yearning (H834) 289
I courted a wee lassie when I was but young (H613) 396
I dreamt I saw my own dear bride (H469) 144
[I Drew My Ship into a Harbour] (cf. H641) 383
I hate to be teased by the nonsense o' men (H472) 258
I left Ballymoney a long way behind me (H157) 207
[I Long to be Wedding] (H138) 256
I loved a young man, I loved him well (H683) 393
[I Maun Gang tae the Garret] (H230) 255
I met her on the brow of Altaveedan Hill (H603) 239
I mounted on horseback with five miles to ride (H802) 466
[I Must Away] (H699) 383
I must away, I'll no longer tarry (H722) 343
I never will forget the sorrows of that day (H235) 203
I once ...
... had a duck when I lived in Drummuck (H228a) 19
[... Had a True-Love] (H479) 347; (cf. H141) 395
... had a wee lass and I loved her well (H141) 395
[... Loved a Boy (Girl)] (H215) 393
... loved a boy, and a bonny, bonny boy (H215) 393
[... Loved a Lass] (H165a) 260
[... Was a Guest at a Nobleman's Wedding] (H60a) 400
[... Was a Ploughboy] (H780) 345
... was a ploughboy, but a soldier I'm now (H780) 345

I s – It was Sam Henry's Songs of the People

I sit up all night with the fire burning bright (H591b) 6
[I Thank You, Ma'am, Says Dan] (H184, H689) 469
I tint my heart ae morn in May (H640) 291
I wandered in the radiant dawn (H508) 226
I was ...
[... Born in Boston] (H202) 119
... born in Boston, a place you all know well (H202) 119
... brought up in Connaught, not of a low degree (H31) 411
[... Told by My Aunt] (H138) 256
I went ...
[... to Mass on Sunday] (H625) 342
[... to See My Suzie] (cf. H532) 367
... to the fair in Bellaghy (H758) 23
[... to the Fair at Bonlaghy] (H758) 23
I will ...
[... Put My Ship in Order] (H722) 343
... tell you a story that happened of late (H114) 143
[... Walk with My Love] (H215) 393
I wish ...
... I was a fish with a long, long tail (H734) 149
[... I Was in America] (m) (H553) 482
... I was in Manchester a-sitting on the grass (H711) 234
[..., I Wish] (H683) 393
[...(, I Wish) (I Was a Maid Again)] (cf. H16) 392
[... My Love Was a Red, Red Rose] (cf. H711) 234
... That You Were Dead, Goodman (H531) 505
[I'd Cross the World for (over with) You, Johnny Doyle] (H137) 431
I'll ...
[... Beat the Drum Again] (H497) 326
[... Be Seventeen Come Sunday] (H152) 266
[... Follow You over the Mountain] (H61a,b) 459
[... Go See My Love] (H699) 383, (H722) 343
... Hang My Harp on a Willow Tree (H155) 366
... marble wall thee round about (H10f) 3
... sell the pig and cow, agra, to send you far away (H642) 207
... sing of a mountain, the pride of the north (H509) 168
... sing you of three huntsmen brave, as brave as e'er you knew (H185) 128
... Tell My Ma (H48e) 11
... tell my ma when I go home (H48e) 11
... tell you of a lady fair (H232) 318
[... Tell You of a Story] (H779) 54
[... Travel to Mt. Nebo] (m) (H589) 344
... wager, I'll wager, I'll wager wi' you (H135) 414
I'm a ...
... broken-hearted gardener and don't know what to do (H499) 387
... broken-hearted milkman, in grief I'm arrayed (H132) 398
... jolly servant lass, my name is Mary Ann (H833) 257
[... Rover and Seldom Sober] (H722) 343
... stranger in this counter-ee come here to learn my trade (H125a) 475
... stranger in this count-ir-ie, not in it was I bred (H125b) 476
... stranger in this country, from America I came (H520) 259
[... Young Bonnie Lassie] (H79) 428
I'm always livin' yet, tho' I nearly had a fit (H488) 501
[I'm an Irish Boy] (H592) 41
I'm from over the Mountain (H61a,b) 459
[I'm Goin' to the Woods] (H744) 12
... Home (H53a) 97
... home, no more to roam (H53a) 97

[... to Get Married] (H152) 266
[... to Join the Army] (cf. H561) 458
I'm Larry M'Hugh, a boy so true, I belong to the Emerald Isle (H592) 41
[I'm off to Philadelphia in the Morning] (m) (H832b) 81
[I'm Often Drunk and Seldom Sober] (cf. H722) 343
I'm Seventeen 'gin Sunday [Laws O17] (H152) 266
I'm sick o' the brick-built city (H498) 211
[If I Was a Blackbird] (H79) 428, (H479) 347
If I were ...
... a Blackbird (H79) 428
[... a Blackbird] (m) (H518) 310
... *a blackbird, I'd whistle and sing* (H79) 428
... a Fisher (H709) 348
[If One Won't, Another One Will] (cf. H159) 396, 397
Ilo, Tom's Gone to (H53d) 96
In Aghadowey there stands a village (H67) 365
In Altibrine there lives a maid, a maid of beauty rare (H111) 229
In and out those dusty bluebells (H48a) 10
In blythe and bonny Scotland, where the bluebells sweetly grow (H120) 332
[In Bonny Scotland] (H120) 332
[In Castyle (Roslyn Isles) (St. Charles) (There Lived a Lady)] (H474) 488
In Coleraine town resided (H159b) 397
[In Connaught I Was Reared] (H31) 411
[In Courtship There Lies (Meeting Is a) Pleasure] (H625) 342
[In Fair London City] (H105) 331, (H108a) 329
[In Jessie's City (Tarrytown)] (H683) 393
In Kingstown and Warwick and bonny Yorkshire (H644) 367
[In London Fair City] (H108a) 329
[In London so Fair] (H203) 330
[In Praise of John Magee] (cf. H226) 511
In Praise of the Glen [Lovely Glenshesk (IIb)] (H547)
[(In) Sheffield (Yorkshire) Park] (H683) 393
In summertime when flowers were fine I rambled o'er the green (H182) 464
[In the County of Innocent] (H585) 147
In the hielans o' Scotland a young man does dwell (H193) 487
In the land of O'Cahan where bleak mountains rise (H786) 139
In the land of O'Cahan, as I wandered at will (H538) 364
In the merry month of June, boys, from my home I started (H44) 178
In the parish of Seagoe, near the town of Armagh (H585) 147
[In the Town of Marlborough, (Down)] (cf. H668) 444
[In the Town of Oxford] (H31) 411
In the year ninety-eight, when the troubles were great (H29) 53
In the year seventy-eight, on a Monday serene (H154) 33
[In Zepo Town] (H806) 434
[Inconstant Lover, The] (H30a) 390, (H58) 446
[Independent Girl, The] (H504) 347
India's Burning Sands (H120) 332
[Indian War, The] (cf. H120) 332
[Indian (Young Spanish) Lass] (H836) 372
Innishowen (H209) 465
[Inniskillin(g) Dragoon, The] (H98b) 472
[Inniskilling Dragoon] (m) (H509) 168
Ireland Far Away, Old [Laws J7] (H816) 92
Irish ...
[... Emigrant's Lament, The] (H235) 203
[... Girl, The] (H711) 234; cf. H625) 342
[... Girl's Lament, The] (H85) 300
[... Jaunting Car, The] (H592) 41

... Jaunting Car, My (H592) 41
[... Lady, A (The) Rich (Proud)] (H72) 374
... Lullaby for the Christ-Child (H630) 7
[... Maid, The] (H85) 300
... Mother's Lament, An (H600) 140
[... Robber, The] (H792) 122
... Serenade, An (H82) 262
... Soldier Boy, The (H678) 89
[... Soldier Boy, The] (H244) 295
[... Wash-Woman, The] (H711) 234
Irishman, The (H712) 222
[Irishman's Farewell to His Country, The] (H69) 201
[Iron Door, The] (H668) 444
It being down by Bordon's Grove, as I carelessly had strayed (H529) 320
It bein' on the eighth of June, brave boys, eighteen hundred and fifteen (H608)
It being on ...
... a fine summer's morning (H14a,b) 356
... a Monday, before the cock crew day (H561) 458
... a Monday morning, it being on a pay day (H574) 80
... a pleasant morning in the cheerful month of June (H121) 270
... a summer evening, abroad as I did rove (H635) 455
... an evening clear (H616) 462
... the fourth of March, brave boys, in the year of thirty-seven (H558)
... the lovely banks of Mourne (H595) 468
It happened ...
... on a midsummer day (H620) 476
... to be at an old lover's wedding (H60a) 400
... to be on a moonshiny night that I took a notion to marry (H61a) 459
It is: see also It's, 'Tis
It is fare thee well, cold winter, it is fare thee well, cold frost (H504) 157
[It Is of a Rich Lady] (H620) 476
It's ...
... down Where the Water Runs Muddy, Oh, (H112) 288
... early one morning Willie Lennox arose (H176) 146
... in my native country, old Ireland, I do dwell (H1) 191
... now I'm going to take my leave (H651) 160
... of a damsel both neat and handsome (H668) 444
... of a farmer's daughter lived near the town of Ross (H106) 443
... of a merchant's daughter that lived down yonder lane (H681) 490
[... of a Tender Maiden] (H137) 431
... of a wild colonial boy, Jack Doolan was his name (H750) 120
[... of an Old Lord] (H108a) 329
... once I loved a damsel, alas, she proved untrue (H540) 468
... *the king of all the flowers from Killarney* (H34) 213
... three long quarters I spent a-weaving (H745) 47
... Time for Us to Leave Her (H53b) 96
... up the heathery mountain and down the rush glen (H97) 130
['Tis ('Twas) Pretty to Be in Balinderry] (H80) 386
[('Tis) Youth and Folly (Make Young Men Merry)] (cf. H16) 392
It was down ...
... by Covent Garden as I one day did walk (H729) 446
... by David's fountain where yon water does run calm (H212) 370
... by the banks of a large murmuring river (H649) 171
['Twas down in the Valley] (H479) 347
It was early, early in the spring (H236) 375

Titles and first lines It was – Ky

[It Was Early One ('Twas on a) Monday Morning] (H561) 458
['Twas Early One Morning] (H176) 146
'Twas early one morning as the day was a-dawning (H590) 486
It was in ...
... Balinderry near Ballinascreen (H805a) 73
[... Dublin City] (H168) 399
... London fair that a lady, she lived there (H203) 330
... our native country we might have liv-ed well (H69) 201
'Twas in the month of August, when yellow waved the corn (H665) 454
'Twas in the year of forty, and the year of forty, too (H65b) 186
It was on a bright and clear St. Patrick's morning (H34) 213
'Twas on a bright May morning when first I saw my darling (H74) 236
'Twas on a Monday morning, the weather being calm and clear (H209) 465
It was on a pleasant evening for pleasure as I strayed (H19b) 196
It was on a summer's evening, when my love did chance to meet (H65a) 293
'Twas on a summer's morning, /The flowers were a-blooming-o (H220) 243
It was on an Easter Monday which happened of late (H42a) 148
It was on an autumn twilight (H831) 235
'Twas on the black Crimean shore, when midnight shadows met (H99) 89
'Twas on the eighth of August (H602) 107
I've been a married man this seven years and more (H701) 501
I've had a grand experience I'm going to tell you now (H605) 340
I've travelled this wide world over (H698) 51
I've Two or Three Strings to My Bow (H70) 340
I've two or three strings to my bow (H70a) 340

Jack ...
[... Munro (Went a-Sailing)] (cf. H561) 458
[... Tar] (H779) 54
[... the Cowboy (and the Robber)] (H51) 129
[... the German] (H156) 315
[... the Ploughboy, As] (H105) 331
... went away to sea one day and left his Polly behind (H481) 484
Jacket ...
[... Green, The] (H644) 367
[... So Blue, The] (H644) 367
[...s Green] (m) (H240) 192
[Jacobite Song, A] (H21) 508
James ...
... Kennedy (H633) 147
[... Maclean] (H136) 125
[... McKee] (H136) 125
... Magee (H136) 125
... Reilly [Laws N37] (H826) 309
[..., the Roving Gambler; Frank] (cf. H202) 119
Jamie ...
... and Mary (H788) 300
... and Nancy (H738) 478
..., Lovely Jamie (H553) 482
[... (Jimmy) (John) Raeburn] (H151) 124
[... Douglas] (cf. H16) 392
... Raeburn's Farewell (H151) 124
..., Lovely (H618) 85
...'s on the Stormy Sea (H78) 484
[Jan's Courtship] (H820) 257
Jane ...
[... Innis; My Song I Will Finish, Her Name's Miss] (H153b) 481
[... from Enniskillen, Lovely] (cf. H471) 317

[... on the Banks of the Clyde, William and] (H812) 310
..., Hielan' (H477) 140
[..., Death of Queen] (H72) 374
[Janie(ey) (Jennie) Ferguson] (H188) 401
Jarmin, Johnny [Laws N43] (H156) 315
Jaunting Car, My Irish (H592) 41
[Jealous Brothers, The] (H806) 434
Jean ...
... of Ballinagarvey (H822) 239
[..., Lovely] (H822) 239
..., McClenahan's (H81) 430
[Jenny Dear] (cf. H159) 396, 397
Jennie of the Moor (H107) 320
[(Jessie) of Ballington Brae, Bessie] (H73) 412
[Jessie Walker, The] (m) (H827) 100
[Jilted Lover, The] (cf. H589) 344
Jim, the Carman Lad (H171) 40
[Jim(my) (Joe) the Carter('s) (Carrier's) Lad] (H171) 40
Jimmy [or Jimmie] ...
[...y] (H479) 347
[...y and Nancy (H755) 297
[...y and Nancy (the departure)] (H581) 318; cf. H514) 297
[...y (William) (The Sailor) and Nancy (Polly) (on the Sea)] (H561) 458
[...ie(y), Lovely] (H587) 433
[...y Ranvul] (H114) 143
[...ie(y) (Johnny) Random (Ransom) (Randal)(l)(, My Son)] (H814) 415
[(...y) (Johnny) the Miller, (Young) Roger(s)] (H90) 365
[Jock Sheep] (cf. H135) 414
Jock, Heather (H39) 123
[Johanna, John] (cf. H0) 53
John ...
[... and the Farmer] (H51) 129
[... (Tom) (o') Barbary (Barbour)] (H221) 490
[... Barbour] (H221) 490
[... Grumlie] (H702) 504
[... Hobbs] (cf. H226) 511
... Hunter (H125a,b) 475, 476
[... Johanna] (cf. H0) 53
... Magee, In Praise of] (cf. H226) 511
... McAnanty's Courtship (H56) 354; (m) (H524) 328
... McKeown and Margaret Deans (H129) 141
... McKeown and Margaret Deans, they were a matchless pair (H129) 141
... Mitchel's Farewell to His Countrymen (a) (H179a) 125
... Mitchell (H179a) 125
... Mitchell (b) (H179b) 126
...; My Love (H593) 389
... Reilly, the Sailor Lad [Laws M8] (H468) 441
... (George) (Young) Reily (Riley) (Rylie)] (H826) 309
[... Riley II] (H693) 313
[John(nie)(y) Collishaw (Coughlin) (Golicher) Gallac(g)her)] (H574) 80
[Johney Doyle] (H137) 431
Johnnie [or Johnny] ...
[...ie] (H561) 458
[...ie and Mollie] (cf. H755) 297
[...ie(y) and Molly (H755) 297
[...y and Old Mr Henly] (H682) 505
[...y Borden] (H221) 490
[...y Dial] (H137) 431
...y Doyle [Laws M2] (H137) 431
[...y Faa] (H124) 509
[...y German] (H156) 315
[...y Jarmanie] (H156) 315
[...y Jarmer] (H156) 315
...y Jarmin [Laws N43] (H156) 315
[...y, Lovely Johnny] (H637) 385, (H780) 345
[...ie My Man] (H807) 514

[...y My Man(, Dae Ye Nae Think o' Rising?] (H807) 514
...y M' Man (H807) 514
...y, m' man, dae ye naw think o' risin'? (H807) 514
[(...ie)(...y) (Willie) (O')Reilly (Rally) (Riley) (Rylie), Billy] (H468) 441
...y Scott [Child #99] (H736) 489
...y Scott's to the hunting gane (H736) 489
[...y Siddon] (H110) 144
[...ie Taylor] (cf. H213) 334
[...y the Sailor] (H779) 54
[Johnson] (H185) 129
Jolly ...
[... Beggar, The] (H183) 268, (H810) 269
[... Butchermen, The] (H185) 129
... Fisherman, The (H639) 59
[... Lumbermen, The] (cf. H162) 333
... Ploughboy, The (H105) 331
[... Reapers (Thrasher), The] (H622) 44
[... Roving Sailor, The] (cf. H670) 293
... Roving Tar, The [Laws O27] (H670) 293
[... Stage Driver, The] (H620) 476
... Thresher, The (H622) 44
[... Thresherman, The] (H622) 44
[... Young Sailor and the (His) Beautiful Queen, The] (H620) 476
Journeyman Tailor, The [Laws B6] (H620) 476
[Joy after Sorrow] (cf. H635) 455
Juberlane (H507) 213
Jug of Punch, The (H490) 48
[Julian Bond, Fair] (H234) 436
[Just in the Height of Her Bloom] (m) (H758) 23

Kail Plants, The Load of (H25b) 261
[Katie Dear] (H722) 343
Kate ...
[... of Ballinamore] (m) (H521) 372
... of Coleraine (H684)
... of Glenkeen (H41) 231
[... O'Neill] (H767) 370
[Keach in the Creel] (H201) 265
Kearney's Glen (H715) 166
Keep single and free, light-hearted like me (H70b) 341
Keeper of the Game, The [Child #46] (H681) 490
Kellswater (H695) 442
Kellswaterside (H802) 466
[Kelly's Lamentation] (H223) 83
[Kelso] (H174) 507
Kenbane, The Shores of Sweet (H648) 168
Kennedy, James (H633) 147
[(Kerry), (O')Reil(l)y from the Co. Leitrim] (H580) 357
[Keys of Canterbury (of Heaven), The] (cf. H532) 367
Kilgrain, The Hare of (H12) 31
Killeavy's Pride (H190) 420
Killowen; Mary, the Pride of (H26b) 250
[Killyclare] (H169) 298
Kilrea, The Banks of (I) (H150a) 466; (II) (H150b) 361
[Kind Miss] (H532) 367
King ...
[... Henry, My Son] (H814) 415
... o' Spain's Daughter, The [Child #4] (H163) 413
... Went A-Hunting, As a (H117) 44
[...'s (Seven) Daughter(s), The] (H163) 413
[...'s Dochter Jean, The] (H221) 490
Kintyre Love Song, A (H195) 234
Kishmul's Galley (H535b) 96
[Kitty of Coleraine] (m) (H684) 231
Knights of Malta, The (H146) 180
Knocklayd, Brow of Sweet (H19b) 196
Knocklayde (H509) 168
Knowe, The Maid of the Sweet Brown [Laws P7] (H84, 688) 364
Knox's Farewell (H49) 200
Kyle's Flowery Braes (H8) 311

[Labourer, The] (H622) 44
Labouring Boy, The Bonny [Laws M14] (H576) 435
[Lacky Bill] (H188) 401
Laddie toor an ti a (H797) 327
Ladie fol dha da and ladie fol dha dee (H697) 278
[Ladies' Bonnets and Chignons, The] (m) (H227) 47
Ladly fol ol dha dee (H486) 121
Lady ...
... and the Apprentice Boy, The] (H729) 446
[... (and the Glove) (of Carlisle), The] (H474) 488
[... (Fair Maid) Walked (There Was a Lady) in Her Father's Garden, A] (H471) 317
[... Fair, A] (H471) 317
[(...) Franklin's Lament] (H815) 103
[... Helen] (H126) 510
[... Isabel(le) (and the Elf Knight)] (H163) 413
[... *LeRoy* (*Url*), The] (H214) 445
... *Leroy*, The [Laws N5] (H214) 445
[... near New York Town, The] (H217) 432
[... of Lak] (H765) 312, The
[... of Riches, The] (H108a) 329
... *of the Lake*, The [Laws N41] (H765) 312
... *Shearbrooke*, The Wreck of the (H570) 310
...standing in her father's garden, A (H471) 317
[(...)'s Fan, (The)] (H474) 488
[Laird o' Cockpen] (m) (H480) 52
Laird's Wedding, The [Laws P31] (H60b) 401
Lake ...
[... Chemo] (cf. H157) 207
[... of Cool Finn, The] (H176) 146
...s of Ponchartrain, The [Laws H9] (H619) 373
[Lambert (Lambertkin) (Lammakin)] (H735) 133
[Lambert Linkin] (H735) 133
Lambkin [Child #93] (H735) 133
[Lambkin the (Wronged) Mason] (H735) 133
Lambkin, the finest mason that ever laid a stone (H735) 133
[Lambs, Searching for] (H548) 341
Lament ...
[... for Lord Franklin] (H815) 103
[... for Willie] (H587) 433
[... of Flora Macdonald, The] (H533) 292
[(... for) Willie(y) Leonard] (H176) 146
..., An Irish Mother's (H600) 140
..., Flora McDonald's] (H533) 292
[Lamentation Air] (m) (H772) 23
Lammas Fair in Cargan, The (H513) 75
Lammas Fair, The Ould (H101) 275
Land of the West, The (H677) 175
Largy Line, The (H781) 467
[Largy (Leargaidh) Stream] (H229) 360
[Larry Doolan] (H592) 41
Larry's Old Goat, or Bessie (belled) and Mary (gray) (H119)
Lass ...
[... amang the Heather, The] (H177) 271
[... o' Glencoe, The] (cf. H655) 319
... of Glenshee, The [Laws O6] (H590) 486
[... of Mohea (Mowee), The] (H836) 372
... of Mohee, The [DW "No. 835"] [Laws H8] (H836) 372
... of the Glen, The Bonnie Wee (H14a,b) 356
[... with the Bonny Brown Hair, The] (H43, H575) 394
[Last Night as I Lay on My Bed] (H722) 343
Last week as I sat wi' my wheel by the fire (H216) 265
[Late(ly) Last Night] (H60a) 400
[Late One Evening] (H806) 434

Laurel Hill (H8) 311
[Laurel, Green Grows the] (H165a) 260
Learmount Grove [Banished Lover (b)] (H726) 307
[Leave Her, Johnnie(y)(, Leave Her)] (H53b) 96
Leave her, Johnny, leave her (H53b) 96
Leaves So Green, The (H719) 63
Leinster Lass, The S[team]s[hip] (H808) 98
[Leitrim (Kerry), (O')Reil(l)y from the Co.] (H580) 357
Lennox, Willie [Laws Q33] (H176) 146
Let ...
... Derry boast her prentice boys (H706) 180
[... Her Go, Let Her Go, God Bless Her] (cf. H680) 141
[... Him Go(, Let Him Tarry)] (H504) 347
[... the Wind Blow High or Low] (H711) 234
[... Us Go to the Woods] (H744) 12
['Let's Go A-Hunting,' (Says Richard to Robert)] (H744) 12
[Letcher County Burglar] (cf. H202) 119
[Levi, Sons of] 180
[Liam O' Raghallaigh] (H234) 436
Light ...
[... of the Moon, The] (H699) 383
[... Brigade, The Charge of the] (H829) 91
... Horseman, The Bonny (H122) 88
Like the vi'lets in spring, like the lark on the wing (H195) 234
Lily ...
[..., Lily, Oh] (cf. H561) 458
[... of Arkansas, The] (H180) 149
[... of the West, (The)] (H578) 416
[Limerick Is Beautiful] (m) (H116a) 201, (H188) 401
[Limerick, When First I Came to County] (H580) 357
[(Lincolnshire) (Wise) Farmer (Bite), The Yorkshire (Hampshire)] (H51) 129
[Lindsay, Liz(z)ie] (H193) 487
Lint Pullin', The (H487) 43
Linton Lowrie (H640) 291
[Lion's Den, The] (H474) 488
[Lisbon] (H561) 458
Little ...
[... before Me Time, A] (H21) 508
[... Beggarman, The] (H751) 50
[... Fishes, The] (H699) 383
[... Jim, the Carter Lad] (H171) 40
[... Johnny Green] (H208) 258
[... Log Cabin by the Stream, The] (cf. H642) 207
[... Mary(, the Sailor's Bride)] (H118) 315
[... Old Log Cabin in (down) the Lane, The] (cf. H642) 207
[... Old Mud Cabin on the Hill, The] (H642) 207
[... Old Sod Shanty on the Claim, The] (cf. H642) 207
[... Phoebe] (H702) 504
[... Ploughing Boy] (H105) 331
[... Red Lark, The] (m) (H550) 176
[(...) Sally Walker (Saucer) (Water)(s)] (H48g) 11
[... Scotch Girl (?Scotchee), The] (H201) 265
[... Sparrow] (cf. H16) 392
[... Thatched Cabin, The (H91) 156
... White Cat, The (H510) 17
... white cat was walking along, The (H510) 17
[Liverpool Landlady, The] (H779) 54
[Liverpool Packet] (H194) 99
[Liza Gray] (H765) 312
[Liz(z)ie Lindsay] (H193) 487
[Lloyd Bateman] (H470) 491
[Load of Kail Plants, The (H25b) 261
Lochaber Shore (H134) 168
Locksmiths, Love Laughs at [Laws M15] (H668) 444
Lol di dary hi ho, lol di dary hi ho (H12) 31

[London Bridge (Is Broken Down) (Is Falling Down)] (H48h) 11
Londonderry ...
[... Air, The (H3) 286
[... Air], (Rory's Lament) (m) (H545) 225
... Love Song, A (H518) 301
... Love Song] (m) (H3) 286
[... (Lovely Derry) on the Banks of the Foyle] (H813) 468
... Sweet (H813) 468
[(Lonesome) (Stormy) Scenes (Hours) (Winds) of Winter, The Cold (Dark) (Gonesome)] (H637) 385
Long ...
... ago, when my hair was all curly (H773) 229
... Cookstown (H745) 47
... time since, I bid adieu, A (H506) 214
[..., Eliza] (H207) 417
Lord ...
[... Akeman (Baker) (Bate(s)man) (Beicham) (and the Turkish Lady)] (H470) 491
... Beichan was a noble lord (H470) 491
[... Donald (Randal)(l) (Rendal) (Ronald) (, My Son)] (H814) 415
[... Bateman] (H470) 491
... Beichan [Child #53] (H470) 491
[... Cassilis' Lady] (H124) 509
[(...) Franklin (and His Bold [Ship's] Crew)] (H815) 103
[... from the West, The] (H163) 413
[... Meanwell] (H735) 133
[... Ronald [Child #92] (H814) 415
[(...) Thomas of Winesber(r)y (Win(e)sbury) (and the King's Daughter)] (H221) 4
Loreto, The Cowboy of [Laws B1] (H680) 141
Loss ...
... of Seven Clergymen (H742) 105
[... of the *Lady of the Lake*] (H765) 312
[... of the *Nightingale*, The] (H75a) 145
[... of the *Royal Charter*, The (H623) 109
Lost Birdies, The (H40c) 20
[Lothian Lassie, The] (m) (H216) 265
Lough ...
[... Erin's Shore] (H597) 476
... Erne Shore (H597) 476
[... Erne's Shore] (m) (H43) 394
[... Foyle, Banks of] (m) (H11) 110
[... Foyle] (m) (H2) 215
... Neagh, The Banks of Sweet (H158) 295
Loughgiel, Sweet (H506) 214
[Loughinsholin] (H176) 146
[Louisville Burglar] (H202) 119
Love ...
[... and Porter] (cf. H16) 392
[... Has Brought Me to Despair] (H683) 393
[... is Pleasing] (H683) 393
[... I(t')s Pleasing] (H790) 383
[... Is Hot and Love Is Cold] (H16) 392
[... Is Pleasing] (cf. H641) 383
[... It Is a Killing Thing] (cf. H711) 234
... Laughs at Locksmiths [Laws M15] (H668) 444
[... My Darlin' O] (H174) 507
... Song] (O'Friel's Suite) (m) (H495) 227
[... Song] (m) (cf. H809) 162
[... Token, The] (H60a) 400
... Token, The [Laws N29] (H581) 318
[... Will Find a Way] (H201) 265
...'s Parting (H788) 300
Lovely ...
[... Armoy] (m) (H721) 438
... Annie (I) [Laws N8] (H561) 458
... Annie (II) [Laws N14] (H166) 328
... Armoy (H9) 186; (m) (H112) 288, (H597) 476
[... Banks of Mourne, The] (H595) 468
[... Bann Water] (H86) 436
[... Caroline] (H148) 411
... Glenshesk (I) (H544) 165
... Glenshesk (IIa) (H28a) 194
... Jamie (H618) 85

Titles and first lines Lov - Mol

[... Jane from Enniskillen] (cf. H471) 317
[... Jean] (H822) 239
[... Jimmie(y)] (H687) 433
[(...) Jimmie(y) (and I Will Get Married)] (H695) 442
[... Johnny] (H637) 385
[... Maiden, The] (H782) 473
[... Mollie(y)] (H175) 470, (H755) 297
[... Molly] (H149) 456, (H534) 454, (H615) 343, (H780) 345
... Nancy (H637) 385
[... Nancy] (cf. H159) 396, 397
[... Nancy (Nant-si-an), The Streams of] (H520) 259
... Sally (H724) 82
[... Willie] (H58) 446, (H479) 347, (H587) 433
[... Willie] (m) (H613) 396, (H733) 342
... Annie, Lovely (I) [Laws N8] (H561) 458
Lover ...
[... Proved False, The] (H593) 389
[...'s Curse, The] (H112) 288
[...'s Curse, The] (m) (H9) 186, (H547) 195, (H695) 442
...'s Ghost, The [Child #272] (H217) 432
...'s Ghost, The] (H699) 383, (H722) 343
[...'s Lament, The] (H637) 385
[...'s Return] (H471) 317
[...s' Parting, The] (m) ?? (H37) 485
[Lovesick Maid, The] (H138) 256
[Lovin' Hannah] (cf. H625) 342
[Loving Reilly] (H234) 436
[Low-Backed Car, The] (m) (H669) 179
[Low, Low Lands of Holland, The] (H180) 149
Lowlands ...
[...] (H469) 144
..., lowlands away, my John (H469) 144
..., *lowlands away, my John* (H469) 144
[... of Holland (Germany), The] (H180) 149
[... (So) Low] (H113) 434
[... Away] (H469) 144
Lowry, Molly Bawn (H114) 143
[Lucan Dairy, The] (cf. H732) 57
Lullaby for a Sailor's Child (H517) 7
Lullaby, A Child's (H40b) 17
Lurgan Stream (H229) 360
Lurgan Town (H563)
[Lurgy Stream(s), (The)] (H229) 360

[Ma Dimigh Tu] (H206) 289
[Madam, I Have Gold and Silver] (H532) 367
[Madam I Am Come to Court You] (H532) 367
[Magee, In Praise of John] (cf. H226) 511
Magee, James (H136) 125
Magee, Mick (H740) 56
Maggie ...
[... Goddon] (cf. H16) 392
[... Walker (Blues) (, the Girl I Left Behind)] (H188) 401
... of Coleraine (H657) 242
Magherafelt Hiring Fair (H748) 263
Magherally, O!, The Flower of (H220) 243
Magilligan (H52a) 244
Magilligan, The Strands of (H520) 259
Maguire's Brae (H747) 214
Maid ...
[... and the Soldier, The] (H152) 266
... from the Carn Brae, The (H704) 241
... from the County Tyrone, The (H528) 246
... of Aghadowey, The (?Laws O2] (H673) 429; (H86) 436
[... of Altaveedan, The (H603) 238
... of Ballyhaunis, The (H483) 427
[(... of) (Streams of) Bunclody (, and the Lad She Loves So Dear) (, The)] (H479)

... of Burndennet, The (a) (H96a) 230
... of Burndennett, The (b) (H96b) 231
... of Carrowclare, The (H169) 298
... of Craigienorn, The (H500) 359
... of Croaghmore, The (H522) 355
[... of Culmore] (H687) 302, The
... of Dunyshell, The (H530) 298; (m) (H822) 239
... of Erin's Isle, The (H57b) 228
... of Faughan Vale, The (H167) 369
[... of Island Moore, The] (cf. H500) 359
... of Mourne Shore, The (H27a [orig. H34b]) 371
... of Mullaghmore, The (H20a) 216
... of Seventeen, The (H144) 270
[(... of) (Streams of) Bunclody (, and the Lad She Loves So Dear), (The)] (H479)
[... of Sweet Gartheen (Gartine) (Gurteen), The] (H594) 430
... of Sweet Gorteen, The (H594) 430
... of Tardree, The (H733) 342
[... of the Colehill, The] (H612) 242
... of the Sweet Brown Knowe, The [Laws P7] (H84, 688) 364; (m) (H781) 467
[... on Shore, The] (H160) 292
... with the Bonny Brown Hair, The (H43, H575) 394; (m) (H14a) 356
Maids ...
... of Culmore, The (H687) 302
... of Downhill, The (H809) 162
[(... of the) Mourne Shore, The] (H27a [orig. H34b]) 371
[... Resolution to Follow Her Love, The] (H166) 328
Maiden ...
[... in the Garden, The] (H471) 317
[...'s Lament, The] (H180) 149, (H683) 393
...s of France may be graceful and merry, The (H684) 231
...s of Sixty-Three (H679) 255
[Mailigh Mo Store] (H204) 388
Maine Water Side, The (H62) 148
Man may drink and not be drunk, A (H769) 65
Man-of-War, On Board of a (H556) 326
[Manchester Angel, The (H711) 234
[Manchester 'Angel', The] ?(H502) 98
Mantle So Green, The [Laws N38] (H76) 314
Many miles away in the country in a farmer's ancient home (H528) 246
March of the Men of Garvagh (H17b) 180
Margaret Deans, John McKeown and (H129) 141
[Market Square] (cf. H202) 119
[Marlborough, (Down) in the Town of] (cf. H668) 444
Married Man, The (H701) 501
[Marrow Bones] (H174) 507
[Marrowbones] (H174) 507
[(Marry) (Maids) (Some) at Eighteen] (H138) 256
[Martha, the Flower of Sweet Strabane] (H224) 390
Martyrs (H10f) 3
Mare, My Rattlin' Oul' Grey (H664) 41
Mare, The Grey [Laws P8] (H90) 365
Mary ...
[... Acklin] (H30b, H721) 438
[... Alling] (H236) 375
[... and Sandy] (H54) 144
... and Willie (H118) 315
[... Ann and Her Servant Man] (H668) 444
... *Cochrane*, The Good Ship (H754) 111
... Doyle (H570) 310
... Hay, Bonny (H568) 226
... M'Veagh (H773) 229
... Machree (H485) 308
[... o' the Dee] (H54) 144
[... of the Lagan Side] (H45) 477
... of the Silvery Tide (H77) 418
... O'Neill, Charming [Laws M17] (H55) 479

[... Riley] (H30b, H721) 438
... Smith, the Maid of Mountain Plain (H636) 235
..., the Pride of Killowen (H26b) 250
[... Ann, Henry and] (?m) (H37) 485
[..., Fair] (H221) 490
..., Moorlough (H173) 250
Mary's ...
... (H10e) 2
... Dream [Laws K20] (H54) 144
[... Vision] (H54) 144
Master M'Grath, A Ballad of (H161c) 32
[Master McGra[th]] (m) (H161a,b) 456, (H783) 34
Matty Broon's Soo (H671) 22
[Maumee Maid, The] (H836) 372
[May Collen (Colvin) (Colyean) (and the Knight)] (H163) 413
Mayogall Asses, The (H130) 26
Mac's and the O's, The (H484) 177
McAnanty's Courtship, John (H56) 354
[McAnanty's Welcome] (H56) 354
McClamont's 'Farewell to Articlave', Monk (H65b) 187
McClenahan's Jean (H81) 430
[McCorley, Roddy] (m) (H62) 148
Machree, Mary (H485) 308
[Machrihanish Bay] (H558) 106
[(Mac)Donald's Return to Glencoe] (H655) 319
M'Grath, A Ballad of Master (H161c) 32
M'Kay, Hannah (H656) 187
McKeown and Margaret Deans, John (H129) 141
McShane, Norah (H157) 207
[Me Grandfather Died] (cf. H732) 57
[Meet Me Tonight (by the Moonlight), (Please)] (H746) 62
[Men's Clothing I'll (Clothes I Will) Put On] (H238) 296, (H561) 458
[Meeting of the Waters, The] (m) (H824) 166
[Merchant's Daughter, The] (H108a) 329, (H159) 396, 397, (H806) 434
[Merchant's Daughter and Her Sailor, The] (H108a) 329
[Mercian Tittery-ary-a] (H174) 507
Merry ...
[... Cuckold, The] (H21) 508
... days -- the days of old, The (H659) 504
[... Haymakers, The] (H697) 278
[... (Pleasant) Month of May, (The)] (H697) 278
[Michigan-i-o] (cf. H162) 333
Mick Magee [Mick McGee] (H740) 56
Midnight moon is beaming mild, The (H63) 247
[Mill Doffin' Mistress, The] (m) (H739) 291
[Miller, Young Roger the] (H90) 365
[Milngavie, The Roving Baker of] (m) (H11) 110
Mind Your Eye (H700) 277
[Mind Your Eye, Laddie] (H700) 277
[Miracle Flower, The] (H120) 332
[Miser, The (Rich) Old] (H108a) 329
Miss Cochrane (H42a) 147
Mitchell, John (b) (H179b) 126
Moan low, wild wave (H713) 27
[Modesty Answer, The] (H152) 266
Mohee, The Lass of [DW "No. 835"] [Laws H8] (H836) 372
Molly ...
[... and William] (H561) 458
[... Asthore] (H204) 388
[... (Molley) Bann (Baun) Lavery] (H114) 143
[... Bawn] (H711) 234
[... Bawn Aroo] (H114) 143
... Bawn Lowry (H114) 143; (cf. stanza 4 of H637) 385
..., Lovely Molly (H557) 478
[... My Treasure] (H204) 388
[... of Lough Erne Shore] (H597) 476
[... Was Milking, As] (H175) 470
..., Dark-Eyed (H625) 342

595

Molly ...
[Mollie (...) Lovely] (H175) 470
[..., Lovely] (H149) 456
Moneygran Pig Hunt, The (H731) 22
Monk McClamont's "Farewell to Articlave" (H65b) 187
Moon had climbed the highest hill, The (H54) 144
[Moon Shined on My Bed Last Night, The] (cf. H777) 427
Moor amang the Heather, O'er the (H177) 271
Moorcocks Crow, Where the (H32) 269
Moore, Annie (H191) 142
Moorlough Mary [Moorlug Mary] (H173) 250
[Moorlough Shore, The (Banks of)] (H27a [orig. H34b]) 371
[Morning Fair] (cf. H683) 393
Morning Clear, One (H548) 341
Mother, dear, I have got married (H682) 505
Mountain ...
... Plain; Mary Smith, the Maid of (H636) 235
... Road, The (H515) 273
[... Stream(s) Where the Moorcock(s) Crow(s), The] (H32) 269
[... Streams] (H32) 269
[...s High, The] (m) (H167) 369, (m) (H601) 174
[...s of Mourne, The] (m) (H606) 208
Mountsandel ...
... (H817) 169
..., Mountsandel, I think long to be (H817) 169
..., The Woods of (H6, H567) 275
Mourne ...
..., The Lovely Banks of (H595) 468
... Shore, The Maid of (H27a [orig. H34b]) 371
... Strand, The Banks of (H564) 344
Moville, The Star of (H68) 276
[Moyola, (The Banks of)] (H752) 245
[Mrs McGra[th]] (H131) 84; (m) (H208) 258
Mudion River (H108b) 169
[Mullagh Lovers, The] (H33, 611) 397
Mullaghdoo (H2) 215
Mullaghmore, The Maid of (H20a) 216
Mullinabrone (H242) 483
[Munro (Went a-Sailing), Jack] (cf. H561) 458
Munro, Sally [Laws K11] (H571) 441
[Murlough Shore] (m) (H134) 168
[Muntagh Wedding, The] (H93) 72
Murphy's Convoy, Dan (H663) 72
Musha, rigga-do-a-da (H792) 122
Musha ring do a da, ring do a daddy (H138) 256
[Muskoka] (H0) 53
[Musselburgh Fair] (m) cf. (H827) 100
Must I Go Bound? (a,b) (H218a,b) 386
Must I go bound and you go free? (H218a,b) 386
[My Blue-Eyed Boy, (Go Bring Me Back)] (H218a) 386
[(My) Blue-Eyed Boy, The] (H482) 391
My Bonny [or Bonnie] ...
[(...y Blooming) Highland Jane] (H477) 140
[...y, Bonny Boy] (H215) 393
...y Brown Jane (H613) 396
...ie Breeden (H512) 225
[...(...y Brown [Bon]) (Own Darling) Boy] (H814) 415
...ie Irish Boy [Laws P26] (H168) 399
[...y Labouring Boy] (H576) 435
[...y Tammy] (H814) 415
...ie Wee Hen (H94) 17
My boy he is a sailor (H759) 288
[My Boy Tommy] (cf. H814) 415
My Charming ...
... Coleraine Lass (H616) 462
... Kate O'Neill (H767) 370
[... Molly] (H625) 342

My Connor, his cheeks are as ruddy as morning (H142) 294
[My Conor His Cheeks are Like Roses] (m) (H142) 294
My Darling Blue-Eyed Mary (H785) 399
[My Dear, If You Left Me] (H206) 289
My [Bt: The] Dear Irish Boy (H142) 294
[(My) Dog and the (My) Gun] (H524) 328
My father ...
... is a farmer, his name is Edward Conn (H42b) 197
[... (He) Died (a Month Ago)] (H732) 57
[... Keeps a Public House] (H113) 434
...'s Servant Boy [Laws M11] (H198) 481
My Flora and I (H30a) 390
[(My) Flora (and Me)] (H30a) 390
My friends and comrades, pray pay attention (H610) 208
My friends, I've just come here tonight to sing a song to all of you (H52a) 244
[My Girl from Donegal] (H4) 190
My Grandfather Died (H732) 57
My grandfather died and I don't know how (H732) 57
[(My) Grandma (Grandmother) (Lives on Winson) (Green) (Lived on Yonder Green)] (H208) 258
My grandma lived in yonder village green (H208) 258
[My Grandmother Green] (H732) 57
[(My) Granny's (Grandma(w)'s) (Grandmother's) Advice] (H208) 258
My heart it is a-breaking (H759) 288
[My He'rt It Is Sair] (H683) 393
[My (The New) Irish Girl (Polly)] (H711) 234
My Irish Jaunting Car (H592) 41
[My Johnny] (H7) 290
[My Little Four-Leaf Shamrock from Glenore] (H34) 213
[(My) (The) Little (Indian) (Pretty) Mohea (Mahmee) (Maumee) (Mawhee) (Mohee)(s) (Momie)] (H836) 372
My love ...
... and I together lay (H546) 273
... he's but a sailor lad (H692) 392
[(... Is Like a) Dewdrop] (H504) 347
[... is on the Ocean] (H504) 347
... is one of the finest young men (H705a,b) 132
... John (H593) 389
..., my dove, my undefiled (H10g) 3
[...(ly) Nell] (m) (H49) 200, (H694) 503; (m) (cf. H207) 417
My Lowlands, Away (H469) 144
[My Man (Oh No,) John!] (H532) 367
[My Mary Ann] (m) ?? (H37) 485
My Mary dear, for thee I'd die (H483) 427
My name ...
... is George M'Caughey, I'm a shoemaker to trade (H781) 467
... is Jim, the carman lad, a jolly chap am I (H171) 40
[... Is John Johanna] (cf. H0) 53
... is Pat Muldoney from a place called Munterloney (H832b) 81
... it is James Dickson, a blacksmith to trade (H571) 441
... it is Jean and my age is fifteen (H230) 255
... it is Nell, right candid I tell (H228b) 18
...'s Henry Connor from sweet Castledawson (H128) 440
[My Own Bonny Boy] (m) (H168) 399
My own sweet Rosaleen Bawn (H63) 247
My parents ...
... and me could not agree (H223) 83
[... Raised Me Tenderly] (H188) 401
... Reared Me Tenderly (H466) 79
[... Reared Me Tenderly] (H188) 401
... reared me tenderly, had ne'er a child but me (H188) 401
... reared me tenderly, I being their only son (H466) 79

[My Rambloing Son] (H814) 415
My Rattlin' Oul' Grey Mare (H664) 41
My Sailor Boy (H759) 288
[My Singing Bird] (m) (H508) 226
[My Son Ted] (H131) 84
[My Son Tim] (H131) 84
[My Sunday Morning Maiden] (H503) 273
My True Love's Gone A-Sailing (H160) 292
My true love's gone a-sailing right o'er yon western main (H160) 292
[My Willie-o] (H699) 383
My young love said to me, 'My mother won't min' (H534) 454
Nancy ...
[... and William] (H479) 347
[... Bell] (H514) 297
... Whiskey (H745) 47
..., Jamie and (H738) 478
[... (the departure), Jimmy and] (H581) 318
[... (Polly) (on the Sea), Jimmy (William) (The Sailor) and] (H561) 458
..., Lovely (H637) 385
[..., Farewell Charming] (H561) 458
[..., Proud] (H72) 374
..., the Pride of the West (H495) 227
[...'s Parting, William and] (cf. H561) 458
[...'s Whiskey] (H745) 47
Nae Bonnie Laddie tae [Wad] Tak' [Her] Me Awa' (H230) 255
Near Broadson Isle there lived a lady (H474) 488
Near Oranmore in the County Galway (H652) 269
[Ned Flaherty's Drake] (H228b) 18
[Ned of the Hill] (m) (H195) 234
Nell Fla[ugh]herty's Drake (H228b) 18
[Nell, My Love] (m) (cf. H207) 417
[Nellie] (H520) 259
[Nelly Ray] (H35) 327
Neuve Chappelle (H526) 182
Never Change the Old Love for the New (H692) 392
[New Broom Sweeps Clean, A] (cf. H109) 357
Newfoundland, The Banks of (H569) 112
[Newfoundland, The Banks of] (H194) 99
[Newry Maid (Town), (The)] (H201) 265
[Newry Mountain] (cf. H520) 259, (cf. H582) 238
Newto[w]n (H10h) 3
Night ...
... is gathering gloomily, the day is closing fast (H98a) 64
... that I was married and brought home my bonny bride, The (H180) 149
[... Visit(ing) Song] (H699) 383
... was dark and the hour late, The (H789) 419
Nile, The Banks of the [Laws N9] (H238) 296
Nimrod, The Wreck of the (H717) 108
[No, Sir! (No!)] (H532) 367
[Nobleman (Squire) and the Thra(e)sher(man), (The)] (H622) 44
[Nora McShane] (H157) 207
Norah Magee (H778) 387
Norah McShane (H157) 207
[North America] (H525) 483
Not the Swan on the Lake (H707) 227
Not the swan on the lake or the foam on the shore (H707) 227
Now ...
... come all you good people and I hope you'll lend an ear (H501) 25
..., Derry boys, I wish you joys (H4) 190
..., friends, my heart is fu' o' glee (H776) 261
[(... It's) My (The) Old Man (Came Home Again) (One Night)] (H21) 508
... Roger, my son, since thou art a man (H820) 257
... one and all, both great and small, I hope you will incline (H464) 167
... the Hielan Watch is come to town (H183) 268

Titles and first lines O - On t

[O'Brien, Pat] (m) (H37) 485
O'Lynn, Bryan (H480) 52
O'Neal, Patrick (H552) 102
[O'Neale, Taddy] (m) (H64) 161
O'Neill, Charles (H50) 139
O'Neill, Charming Mary [Laws M17] (H55) 479
[(O')Reil(l)y from the Co. Leitrim (Kerry)] (H580) 357
[(O')Reilly, (Young) Willie] (H76) 314
[(O')Reilly (Riley) (the Fisherman), (Young)] (H468) 441
O'Ryan (H823) 58
O'Ryan was a man of might when Ireland was a nation (H823) 59
Oh, a beggarman cam' ower the lea (H810) 269
[O' A' the Airts the Win' Can Blaw] (m) (cf. H467) 428
[O, An (Gin) Ye Were Dead, Gudeman] (H531) 505
Oh, be kind to old Bellman (H703) 210
O, blow gentle, sweet breeze of the ocean (H7) 290
Oh, bonny Portrush, you shine where you stand (H775) 171
Oh, bring me back the boy I love (H482) 391, (H692) 392
O Bunnan Buidhe, 'tis my woe to see (H830) 64
'Oh, comb your hair, fair Annie,' he said (H126) 510
Oh, come all ye sacred muses from high Knocksoghey hill (H749) 189
Oh come to the west, love, oh come there with me (H677) 175
Oh, come with me, my city friend (H784) 172
Oh, Crossgar's sunny hills are bespangled with flowers (H22a) 232
O, dark was the day when I sailed from Cushleake (H606) 208
[Oh Dear Oh! If I Had a Sailor] (H532) 367
Oh, dearie me, in Derry all (H536) 209
Oh, Derry, Derry, Dearie Me (H536) 209
Oh! Donegal, the pride of all (H196) 210
O, Dunysheil, it is the place where my true love does dwell (H530) 298
[Oh Erin, My Country] (H478) 176
[O Faer Ye Gaun Will Boy?] (H748) 263
Oh, fair all ye vales of our own native soil (H96a,b) 230, 231
Oh, farewell to my native country (H116a,b) 201, 202
Oh friends, pay attention to what I will mention (H663) 72
[O, An (Gin) Ye Were Dead, Gudeman] (H531) 505
Oh, hark, the drums are beating, love, no longer can I stay (H238a,b) 296
[O, I Was in a Hurry] (m) (H6) 275
Oh, I wish I had someone to love me (H746) 62
Oh, if I were a clerk and could handle the pen (H165a) 260
Oh, I'll no hae the laddie (H617) 45
Oh, I'm a forsaken wee lassie, but ever contented in mind (H70b) 341
Oh, It's down Where the Water Runs Muddy (H112) 288
Oh it's early, early by the break of day (H89) 287
O, it's James Magee, it is my name, the same I will never deny (H136) 125
'O, it's oysters, oysters, oysters,' quo' she (H725) 278
Oh, it's pretty to be in the bonny Church Island (H80) 386
Oh, 'tis a famous story, proclaim it far and wide (H829) 91
O, Jeanie, Dear (H545)
O, Jeanie dear, the flow'rs, the flow'rs are springing (H545) 225
Oh Johnny ...
[... Dearest Johnny ...] (m) (H45) 477

..., ... is a sailor, just newly come ashore (H779) 54
..., ..., Johnny (H16) 392
..., Johnny, but love is bonny (H16) 392
'Oh, lassie, will ye come wi' me (H239) 469
[(O) Love Is Pleasing (a Sin) (Teasin')] (cf. H16) 392
[(Oh,) Madam, (Madam) (I'm (I Have) Come) (You Came) (A-)(Courting)] (H532) 367
[Oh, Mak' My Bed Easy] (H814) 415
Oh, meeting is a pleasure betwixt my love and I (H615) 342, (H625) 343
[Oh, Miss, I Have a Very Fine Farm] (cf. H532) 367
Oh Molly ...
[..., ... Dear] (H722) 343
[..., ... I Can't Say That You're Honest] (H82) 262
..., I can't say you're honest (H82) 262
Oh, my, I felt inclined tae cry (H488) 501
O, 'Newtown' you are hard to sing (H10h) 3
Oh, nigh to Ardee lived Mick Magee (H740) 56
Oh, Norah, dear Norah, I can't live without you (H778) 387
Oh, oh! She's as fickle as any wild rose (H499) 387
Oh, of all the queer fashions you ever did see (H227) 47
[O Once I Loved a Lass] (H699) 383
Oh, once I was courted by a bonnie Irish boy (H168) 392
Oh, Petie cam' ower the glen (H200) 470
Oh, Phelimy, Phelimy, why did you leave me? (H80) 386
O, proudly, proudly the drums will beat (H17b) 180
'O rise up, Willy Reilly, and come along with me (H234) 436
O, sweet Ballymoney, of fame and renown (H25b) 261
Oh, the lass I had the first of all was handsome, young and fair (H18b) 272
O, the ripest of apples, they soon must grow rotten (H641) 383
Oh, the sun does set down in the west when his daily journey's o'er (H57b) 228
[(O) the Sweet Dreams (Streams) of Nancy] (cf. H520) 259
O, the times are hard and the wages low (H53b) 96
Oh, there's no place so sweet, you may search where you can (H6=H567) 275
Oh, 'tis a famous story, proclaim it far and wide (H829) 91
O Tom is gone, what shall I do? (H53d) 96
[O Waly, Waly] (cf. H683) 393
[(O) Waly Waly(, gin Love Be Bonny) (up the Bank)] (cf. H16) 392
Oh, we'll never leave such scenery, my Mary dear and I (H52a) 244
Oh, were I again on my native bay (H819) 219
[O Where Are We Gannin?] (H744) 12
Oh, where is the man with a heart in his bosom (H708) 174
'Oh, who is at my window? I think I hear a voice (H557) 478
O, who is so happy, so happy am I (H30a) 390
O, ye tender lovers, I pray draw near (H20b) 245
Oh, you heroes bold of Ireland that does intend to roam (H562) 113
Oh, you may bless your happy lot, that lies secure on shore (H569) 112
Oh, Zachary Taylor was his name (H496) 96
[O]ch, och, Eire, O! (H819) 219
'Och, Missus Magra,' the sergeant said (H131) 84

Och, prate about your wine (H489) 48
O'er the Moor amang the Heather (H177) 271
[O'er the Muir] (H177) 271
[O' A' the Airts the Win' Can Blaw] (m) (cf. H467) 428
Of fondest affection and sweet recollection (H768) 59
Of late I'm captivated by a handsome young boy (H206) 289
[Off She Went Hunting] (H524) 328
Old ...
... Arboe (H505) 157
[... Ardboe] (H505) 157
[... Arkansas] (H0) 53
... Choir Rhymes (H10) 2
[... Crumbly Crust] (H702) 504
[... Daddy Fox] (H38) 29
[... Dan Tucker] (m) (cf. H706) 180
Oul' Dunloy (H498) 211
[... Erin Far Away] (H816) 92
[... Erin's Lovely Vale] (H46) 438
[... Farmer's Lover, An (The)] (H60a) 400
[... George's Square] (H188) 401
[... Grumbler] (H702) 504
... Inishowen (H824) 166
Old ...
... Ireland (H658) 175
... Ireland Far Away [Laws J7] (H816) 92
[(...) Lady (Woman) from Boston (Ireland) (Wexford) (Yorkshire) (in (of) Dover) (in Slab City) (in Trenton) (of Blighter Town) (of Slapsadam), (The)] (H174) 507
[... Laredo] (H680) 141
[... Lover's Wedding, An [Laws P31] (H60a) 400
[(...) Maid in a (the) Garret, (An) Auld] (H138) 508
[... Man Crip] (H21) 508
[... Man's Courtship, An] (H681) 490
[... Mother Hippletoe] (H38) 29
[... Mud Cabin by the Stream] (cf. H642) 207
[... Notchy Road] (H163) 413
[(...) Prisoner's Song, (The)] (H746) 62
... Rosin the Bow (H698) 51
... Sally Walker (H48g) 11
... Sally Walker, old Sally Glenn (H48g) 11
[... Smokey] (H836) 372
[... Tombolin] (H480) 52
[... Wichet] (H21) 508
[... Woman of Slapsadam] (H174) 507
Oliver's Advice (H98a)
[Oliver, Polly] (H166) 328
On a bitter cold, wild winter night (H543) 103
[On a May Morning So Early] (H152) 266
On April the first I set off like a fool (H552) 102
On Board of a Man-of-War (H556) 326
On March the first in forty-five I took my last adieu (H800) 164
[(On) the Banks of Sweet Lough Rae (Ray)] (H158) 295
On the ...
... banks of the Cloughwater, where the streams do gently glide (H777) 427
... eighteenth day of Aperile as we lay bound for sea (H560) 112
... first day of May at the close of the day (H56) 354
... glorious twelfth of July our music it sweetly did play (H87a) 181
[... Lakes of Ponchartrain] (H619) 373
[... Lakes of the Poncho Plains (Ponsreetain)] (H619) 373
... lofty mountains far away (H782) 473
... lovely banks of Bann as we watched the gliding swan (H475) 455
[... Mountain Stands a Lady] (H532) 367
[(...) (...) Plains of Mexico] (H496) 96
... Road to Bethlehem (H59) 76
... ship *Lady Shearbrooke* we left Londonderry (H570) 310

597

On the ...
... sixteenth of March in the year eighteen-nine (H140) 30
... twelfth day of November last, I hope you'll bear in mind (H577) 439
... twelfth of July in the rosy time of year (H697) 278
... twentieth of July in the year thirty-nine (H559) 237
... twentieth of October last, that dark and dismal day (H62) 148
... twenty-sixth of January, and in the seventieth year (H172) 31
[On Yonder Green Mountain] (cf. H520) 259
Once a jolly swaggie came to a billabong (H566) 122
Once I ...
[... Courted a Bonny Little Girl] (cf. H215) 393
[... Had a Love] (cf. H159) 396, 397
... had a wee hen and broon it was her tap (H94) 17
[... Knew an Old Lady] (H174) 507
[... Was (Invited to) (at) a Noble(man)'s Wedding] (H60a) 400
Once in old England lovely Annie did dwell (H166) 328
One day as I was walking along a London street (H700) 227
One early Sunday morning James Kennedy arose (H633) 147
One evening ...
... as I chanced for to roam (H809) 162
... as I chanced to stray down by the banks of Clyde (H654) 170
... as Zephyr was fanning (H654) 170
... clear, for my amusement (H115a) 355
[... Fair] (H468) 441
... fair, for my recreation (H115b) 241
... fair, to take the air (H537) 239
... fair, to take the air alone I chanced to stray (H648) 167
... fair to take the air down by a shady grove (H685) 460
... fair to take the air down by the banks o' Clyde (H808) 98
... fair to take the air, alone as I chanced to stray (H555) 463
... fine in the summertime, down by the Roe I chanced to roam (H647) 462
... for my recreation (H150b) 361
... for my recreation, kind fortune did cause me to stray (H150a) 466
One fine harvest day as I happened to stray (H513) 75
One fine summer's ...
... evening as Flora was flinging (H187) 162
... evening at the playing of ball (H587) 433
... evening I was forced to my pen (H544) 165
... Morning (H812) 310
... morning as I went out walking (H812) 310
[One Harvest Morning] (m) (H164) 362
One morning ...
... as I went to walk, to take farewell of famed Salthill (H170) 299
... Clear (H548) 341
... clear to meet my dear before the sun would rise (H548) 341
... fair, when Phoebus bright his radiant smiles displayed (H85) 300
[... in May] (cf. H680) 141
... in May when fields were gay (H177) 271
One night as I lay ...
[... on my Bed] (cf. H722) 343
... on my bed I fell into a dream (H803) 79
... slumbering in Philadelphia town (H799) 221
One Penny Portion [Laws O41] (H634) 472

One pleasant evening, as pinks and daisies (H164) 362
One Sunday morning, into Youghall walking (H503) 273
[Oor Cat's Deid] (cf. H40b) 17
[Orange] (H735) 133
[Orange and Blue, (The)] (H60a) 400
Orra, go wa' you daft wee article, you're nothing but a sham (H833) 257
Oul' Dunloy (H498) 211
[Our Captain Calls All Hands] (H514) 297
[Oor Cat's Deid] (cf. H40b) 17
Our good ship's name's the Hero, the Hero of renown (H539) 97
[Our (The) Goodman (Gudeman) (Cam Home at E'en)] (H21) 508
Our gudeman cam' hame at e'en and hame cam' he (H21a,b) 508
[Our Ship She Lies in Harbour] (H722) 343
Our Wedding Day (H534) 454
[Our Wedding Day] (H141) 395
Out of the Window (H141) 395
Outside Casey's cabin there is an old stone wall (H83) 156
O'er the Moor amang the Heather (H177) 271
Over the Mountain, I'm from (H61a,b) 459
[O'er the Muir] (H177) 271
[Overn's Flowery Vale] (H85) 300
Oville (H666) 170
Owenreagh (H542) 217
Owenreagh's Banks (H225) 196; (m) (H667) 192
[Oxford, In the Town of] (H31) 411
Oyster ...
[... Girl, (The)] (H725) 278
[... Shell Bonnet and Dandy (Chignauns)] (H227) 47
[...s] (H725) 278

Pad the Road wi' Me?, Will Ye (H18a) 358
Paddington Green, Polly Perkins of (H132) 398
Paddy ...
... Doyle (H53c) 97
[... Doyle's Boots] (H53c) 97
[... Kane] (m) (H832a) 49
...'s Green Countrie (H692) 203
[...'s Green Country] (H615) 343
[...'s Green Shamrock Shore] (H192) 101
...'s Land (H473) 354
[Paisley Officer, The] (H120) 332
[Paper of Pins] (cf. H532) 367
[Parents, Warning] (H722) 343
[Parish of Dunboe, The] (H23) 307
[Parrot Song, The] (H163) 413
[Parson Hogg] (cf. H222) 29
Parting Glass, The (H769) 65
[Parting Glass, The] (m) (H28b) 158, (H170) 299, (H494) 127, (H712) 222
Pat ...
... Muldoney (H832b) 81
[... O'Brien] (m) (H37) 485
... Reilly (H574) 80
[... Reilly] (H586) 80
[Patie's Waddin' (Wedding)] (H200) 470
Patrick O'Neal (H552) 102
Pay heed to my ditty, ye frolicsome folk (H226) 511
[Peacock, The] (m) (H28b) 158
Peggy ...
[... Gordon, (?Sweet)] (cf. H16) 392
... of the Moor (H761) 228
[... Walker] (H188) 401
Peistie Glen, The (H654) 170
Perkins of Paddington Green, Polly (H132) 398
Petie Cam' ower the Glen (H200) 470
Phelimy Phil (H80) 386
Philaloo, wirrasthru, but I'm kilt (H82) 262
[Phoebe (Phoeby) and Her (the) Dark-Eyed Sailor, (Fair)] (H232) 318

[Phoenix of Erin's Green Isle, The] (H580) 357
Pining Day and Daily (H149) 456
Pipe, The Black (H832a) 49
Pipe, The Wee Cutty (H465) 49
Piper; Denny Byrne, the (H29) 53
[Pique, La] (H194) 99
Plains of Waterloo (I), The (H15) 87
Plains of Waterloo (II), The (H608) 87
Pleasant Pastime between the Young-Men and Maids, in the Pleasant Meadows] (H697) 278
[(Please) Meet Me Tonight (by the Moonlight)] (H746) 62
Ploughboy ...
..., The (H780) 345
[..., The] (cf. H520) 259
[..., (The) Pretty] (H584) 331
[... of the Lowlands, The] (cf. H113) 434
..., The Crafty [Child #283] [Laws L1] (H51) 129
[...s' Song] (H105) 331
[Ploughman Boy] (H113) 434
[Poacher, The] (H823) 58
Point Maid, The (H42b) 197
Polly ...
[... Oliver] (H166) 328
[... Perkins] (m) (H499) 387
... Perkins of Paddington Green (H132) 398
[... Perkins of Paddington's Green] (H132) 398
... Primrose (H734) 149
[... Privateer, The] (H560) 112
[(...) (on the Sea), Jimmy (William) (The Sailor) and Nancy] (H561) 458
[..., Farewell Lovely] (H31) 411
[..., Pretty] (H479) 347
[Ponchartrain] (H619) 373
Poor ...
... aul' folks at hame, ye min', are frail and ailin' sair, The (H598) 61
[... Bob] (H820) 257
... distressed fair maid as ever you did know, A (H158) 295
[... Greeting Wilsie] (cf. H744) 12
[... (Young) Leonard] (H176) 146
[... Mary in the Silvery Tide] (H77) 418
[... Murdered Woman] (cf. H207) 417
[(...) (Pretty) (Simple) Ploughboy (Ploughing Boy) (Plowboy), The] (H105) 331
... Susan walked along the beach that skirted Sligo shore (H774) 150
[... Widow] (H48f) 11
[... (Young) Leonard] (H176) 146
Portion, One Penny [Laws O41] (H634) 472
Portrush ...
[... Fishermen, The] (H27b) 105
... Fishing Disaster (I), The (H27b) 105
... Fishing Disaster (II), The (H27c) 105
..., Bonny (H775) 171
[Port [Jig] Gordon] (m) (H483) 427
[Posey (Swappin') Boy] (H732) 57
Prentice Boy ...
[..., The] (H729) 446
[... (in Love), A (The)] (H739) 291
'..., The [Laws O39] (H31) 411
[Press Gang, The] (H108a) 329, (cf. H552) 102
Pretty ...
[(...) Billy (Polly) Oliver's Rambles] (H166) 328
... Blue Handkerchief, The (H161a,b) 456
[... Crowin(g) Chicken(s)] (H699) 383
... Drummer Boy, The] (H497) 326
[(...) Drummer-Boy, (The)] (H797) 327
[... Factory Boy, The] (cf. H105) 331
[... Fair (Little) Maid (Damsel) (Miss) (out) (in the Garden), (A)] (H471) 317
[... Four-Leaved Shamrock from Glenore, The] (H34) 213
[... Girl Milking Her Cow, The] (m) (H654) 170

Titles and first lines   Pret – Sanf

[... Ploughboy, The] (H105) (H584) 331;
  (cf. H514) 297
[... Polly] (H479) 347, (H711) 234
[... Polly (Ann) (and False William)]
  (H163) 413
[... Polly (Like a Trooper Did Ride)]
  (H166) 328
[... Polly Perkins] (H132) 398
[... Sally] (H72) 374
[(...) Sylvia (Rode out One Day)] (H35)
  327
... Three-Leaved Shamrock from Glenore,
  The (H34) 213
[... Young Shepherdess, The] (H104) 457
Pride of ...
  ... Altibrine, The (H111) 229
  ... Artikelly, The (H656) 187
  ... Glencoe, The [Laws N39] (H655) 319
  ... Glenelly, The (H607) 250
  ... Newry Town, The (H798) 421
Priest of the parish rode his garran
  bawn, The (H805b) 73
[Prince Charlie Stuart] (H533) 292
[Princess Royal] (H140) 30
[Prisoner's Song, (The) (Old)] (H746) 62
Private Still, The (H103) 55
Privateer, The French (H560) 112
Proud Nancy (H72) 374
[Puisin Ban, An] (H510) 17
Punch, The Jug of (H490) 48
[Purple Man's Dream, The] (m) (H65a)
  293, (H65b) 187

[Quaker's Courtship (Wooing), The] (cf.
  H532) 367
[(Quare) (Queer) Bungle (Bungo) Rye]
  (H700) 277
Queen ...
  [... amang the Heather] (H177) 271
  [... Jane, Death of] (H72) 374
  [... Mary(, Queen Mary)] (H230) 255
Quo' Nell, my wife, the tither night
  (H671) 22

Rachel Dear (H62) 148
Rad le whack, fol ol the dol (H92) 86
Raeburn's Farewell, Jamie (H151) 124
[Raggle Taggle (Gypsies)(y), (The)]
  (H124) 509
[Railroad Boy, The] (cf. H683) 393, (cf.
  H576) 435
Rainbow, The (H156) 315
Rakes of Poverty, The (H741) 50
[Raking the (of) Hay] (H635) 455, (H697)
  278
[Ramble-eer, The] (cf. H741) 50
Rambling ...
  [... (Roving) Cowboy (Lover), (The)]
    (H188) 401
  [... Irishman, The] (m) (H526) 182
  [... Sailor, The] (cf. H183) 268
  [... Shuler (Soldier), The] (H183) 268
  ... Suiler, The (H183) 268
Ramoan Smuggler, Hugh Hill, the (H494)
  127
[(Randal)(l) (Rendal) (Ronald)(, My Son),
  Lord Donald] (H814) 415
[Ranvul, Jimmy] (H114) 143
[Rasharkin Fair] (H530) 298
Rathlin Song, A (H696) 290
[Rattle on the Stovepipe] (cf. H641) 383
[Rattling Irish Boy] (cf. H171) 40
Rattlin' Oul' Grey Mare, My (H664) 41
Raven-Locks (H645) 7
[Ray, Nelly] (H35) 327
Rebecca, The Wreck of the (H565) 111
[Reid-cnoc mna Duibe] (m) (H485) 308
Reilly ...
  ..., James [Laws N37] (H826) 309
  ..., the Sailor Lad; John [Laws M8] (H468)
    441
  ..., Pat (H574) 80, (H586) 80
  [..., Willie] (m) (H37) 485
  ..., Willy [Laws M10] (H234) 436
  ..., (Young) Willie (O') [H76] 314
[Reilly's Jailed] (H234) 436

Rejected Lover, The (H589) 344
[Rejected Lover, The] (cf. H159) 396, 397
Rest tired eyes awhile (H596) 6
[Return, Lover's] (H471) 317
[Returning Soldier] (H471) 317
[Reynard the Fox] (cf. H172) 31
[Rhynie] (m) (H640) 291
Rich ...
  [... Farmer's Daughter, The] (cf. H51)
    129
  [... (Proud) Irish Lady, A (The)] (H72)
    374
  ... Merchant's Daughter, The (H108a) 329
  [... Nobleman] (H163) 413
  [... Old Lady, The] (H174) 507
  [(...) Old Miser, The] (H108a) 329
  ... Ship Owner's Daughter, The [Child
    #100] (H221) 490
[Richat and Robet] (H744) 12
Ride in the Creel, The [Child #281]
  (H201) 265
Riding Herd at Night (H588) 220
Riding herd at night, a lonely exile
  singing (H588) 220
Rigadoo, The Oul' (H751) 50
Right well I remember that little
  thatched cabin (H91·) 156
[Rigwiddy Carlin, The] (H748) 263
Riley ...
  [... (Sent) to America] (H468) 441
  [..., Young (George)] (cf. H16) 392
  [(...) (the Fisherman), (Young) (O')Reilly]
    (H468) 441
  [...'s Farewell] (H468) 441
  [...'s Trial] (H234) 436
Ring ...
  ... a Ring o' Roses (H48c) 10
  ..., a ring o' roses, A (H48c) 10
  [... around o' (the) Rosie(s)] (H48c) 10
[Ripest Apples] (H532) 367
Ripest of Apples, The (H641) 383
[Rise Up, Lovely Sally] (H557) 478
River ...
  ... Ness, The Banks of the (H205) 319
  [... Roe, The] (m in 4) (H774) 150
  ... Roe (I), The (H649) 171
  ... Roe (II), The (H629) 171
Roar, roar, thunder of the sea (H517) 7
Robin ...
  ... Redbreast's Testament (H527) 20
  [...'s Courtship] (H820) 257
  [...'s Testament] (H527) 20
  ..., The Hobe and the (H40c) 20
[Robinson, The Drowning of Young] (H585)
  147
Rock ...
  [... in the Same Auld Creel, The] (H201)
    265
  [... Island Line, The] (H0) 53
  [...s of Baun (Bourne), The] (H139) 42
  ...s of Bawn, The (H139) 42
  [...s of Bawn, The] (m) (H199) 39
  [...s of Gibraltar, The] (H180) 149
  ...y Road to Dublin, The (H44) 178
[Roddy McCorley] (m) (H62) 148
Roger ...
  [...] (H820) 257
  ...'s Courtship (H820) 257
  [...'s Grey Mare] (H90) 365
[Roisin Dubh] (m) (H4) 190
Ronald, Lord [Child #92] (H814) 415
(Rory's Lament) [Londonderry Air] (m)
  (H545) 225
Rosaleen Bawn (H63) 247; (H784)
  172
Rose ...
  [... in the Garden, A] (H593) 389
  [... of Tralee, The] (m) (H26b) 250; (H716)
    218
  [... Tree, The] (m) (cf. H740) 56
  [... Tree in Full Bearing, The] (m) (H551)
    40
Roses, Ring a Ring o' (H48c) 10

Rosin ...
  [... a-Beau] (H698) 51
  [... the Beau] (H698) 51
  [... the Bow] (m) (H528) 246
Rosa, Fair (H599) 12
Ross, Spanking Maggie from the (H516)
  35
[Round her Mantle So Green] (H76) 314
[Rounding the (of Cape) Horn, (The)]
  (H539) 97
[Roveing (Roaming) Boy, The] (H188) 401
Roving ...
  ... Bachelor (a), The (H650a) 263
  ... Bachelor (b), The (H650b) 264
  [... Baker of Milngavie, The] (m) (H11)
    110
  [... Gambler; Frank James, the] (cf. H202)
    119
  [... Journeyman, The] (H650) 263, (H751)
    50
Royal ...
  [... Charter] (H623) 109
  [... Comrade] (H176) 146
  [... Fair Damsel, A] (H72) 374
Roe ...
  ..., Farewell to the Banks of the (H791)
    218
  ..., The Banks of the (H24b) 217
  ..., The River (II) (H629) 171
[Rude and Rambling Boy, A] (cf. H683)
  393
[(Rummy) (Wonderful) Crocodile, The
  Great] (H231) 28

Sable curtains of the night were drawn
  up to the eastern sky, The (H27b) 105
[Saighdeur Treighthe, An] (H112) 288
Sailor ...
  [... and His (True) Love, A (The)] (H75a)
    145, (H232) 318; (cf. H514) 297
  [... and the Lady, The] (H620) 476
  [... (and the Landlady), The] (H779) 54
  [... and the Maid, The] (H471) 317
  [(... and the) Shepherdess, The] (H104)
    457
  [... Boy] (H214) 445, (H739) 291; (cf.
    H520) 259
  ... Boy, The [Laws K13] (H543) 103
  [... Boy's Farewell, The] (H543) 103
  [... Coming Home on Leave, A] (cf. H683)
    393
  [... Courted (Loved) (Married) a Farmer's
    Daughter, A] (H634) 472
  ... courted a farmer's daughter, A (H634)
    472
  [... from Dover] (H72) 374
  ... from Dover, from Dover he came, A
    (H72) 374
  ... in the Ale House, The [Laws K36]
    (H779) 54
  ... on the Sea, The (H203) 330
  [..., The Brisk Young] (cf. H16) 392
  ... Boy, My (H759) 288
Sailor's ...
  [... Courtship, The] (H104) 457
  [... Dream, The] (H815) 103
  [... (Misfortune and) Happy Marriage,
    The] (H108a) 329
  [... Return, The] (H471) 317, (H532) 367
[St. James Hospital] (H680) 141
[Sale of a Wife, (The)] (cf. H226) 511
Sally ...
  [... (and Billy) (Sailsworth)] (H72) 374
  [... and Her Lover] (H214) 445
  [... Gardens, Down by the] (m) (H27a,
    orig. H34b) 371
  ... Munro [Laws K11] (H571) 441
  ..., Lovely (H724) 82
  [..., Pretty] (H72) 374
  ... Walker, Old (H48g) 11
  ...'s Garden, Down in My (H828) 286
  ...('s) Gardens, (Down by the)] (H828)
    286
Salutation, The (H756) 60
Sandy's Wooing (H239) 469
[Sandy, Mary and] (H54) 144
[Sanford Barney] (H0) 53

599

Sant - Sto *Sam Henry's Songs of the People*

[Santa Anna (Anno)] (H496) 96
[Santianna] (H496) 96
Santy Anna (H496) 96
[Saucy Dolphin, The] (H560) 112
[Savourneen Deelish] (m) (H50) 139, (H187) 162
Says Johnnie to Molly, 'Do not mourn for me (H755) 297
[Saw You My Father (True Love John?)] (H699) 383
[Scenes (Hours) (Winds) of Winter, The Cold (Dark) (Gonesome) (Lonesome) (Stormy)] (H637) 385
Scolding Wife, The (H145) 503
[Scotch Fisherman's Song for Attracting the Seals] (cf. H713) 27
[Scotch Lassie, The] (H230) 255
Scotland, Blythe and Bonny (H120) 332
Scotland, The Hielans o' [Laws N19] (H193) 487
Scott, Johnny [Child #99] (H736) 489
Screen, The Valleys of (H752) 245
Sea ...
    ...-Apprentice, The (H739) 291
    [... Captain, The] (cf. H135) 414; (cf. H604) 505
    ... Chest, The Tailor in the [Laws Q8] (H604) 505
[Seaman('s Happy Return to) (and) His Love, A] (H581) 318
Search oul' Ireland through and through, search it near and far (H592) 41
[Searching for Lambs] (H548) 341
Seated upon an irish sward by a rustic grave in an old kirkyard (H600) 140
Seal Song (H713) 27
[Send back My Johnny to Me] (H7) 290
[Sergeant Said, The] (H131) 84
[Servant Boy, The] (H198) 481
[Servant Maid in Her Father's Garden, The] (H471) 317
[Setting of the Sun, At the] (H114) 143
Seven ...
    [... (Yellow) Gypsies (on Yon Hill)] (H124) 509
    [... Links on My Chain] (H46) 438
    [... Priests] (cf. H742) 105
    [... (Long) Years (I Loved a Sailor) (Since I Had a Sweetheart)] (H471) 317
    [... (Yellow) Gypsies (on Yon Hill)] (H124) 509
[Seventeen Come (Cum) Sunday] (H152) 266, (H785) 399, (H793) 267
Shamrock ...
    ... from Tiree, A (H716) 218
    [... Shore, The] (H20a) 216, (H69) 201, (H192) 101
    ... Shore, The (H610) 208
    ... Sod No More, The (H235) 203
    ... from Glenore, The Pretty Three-Leaved (H34) 213
Shane Crossagh (H97) 130
Shanty ...
    ... Boy (H662) 45
    [... Boy and the Farmer's Son, The] (H662) 45
    [... Boys, The] (cf. H171) 40
    [...-Girl, The] (H662) 45
She ...
    [... Lives in the Valley Below] (H47) 236
    [... Loved Her Husband Dearly] (H174) 507
    [... Moved through the Fair] (H141) 395, (H534) 454
    ... was born 'mong the wild flowers that bloom in our valley (H512) 225
She's ...
    ... *as pretty as a butterfly, she's as proud as a queen* (H132) 398
    [... Like a (the) Swallow] (H683) 393
    [... a Daughter of Daniel O'Connell] (m) (H41) 231
[Sheep, Jock] (cf. H135) 414
[Sheepcrook and Black Dog] (H30a) 390
Sheffield ...
    [... Apprentice] (H31) 411
    [... (Yorkshire) Park, (In)] (H683) 393

[(...) Prentice (Boy), The (New York)] (H31) 411
[(S)Helg Yn Dreean] (H744) 12
Shepherd ...
    ... Boy, The (H803) 79
    ... Laddie, The (H617) 45
    [...'s Boy, The] (m) (H65a) 293, (H65b) 187
[Shepherdess and the Sailor, The] (H104) 457
[Shepherdess, The Unkind] (H30a) 390
[Shickered as He Could Be] (H21) 508
[Shining (Silver) Dagger, (The)] (H722) 343
Ship ...
    [... Came Sailing, A] (cf. H16) 392
    ... Carpenter's Wife, The (H226) 511
    [... That I Command, The] (H203) 330
[Shipwreck] (H95)
[Shipwrecked] (H231) 28
[Shoemaker, The] (H551) 40
Shoheen, shoho, my child is my treasure (H630) 7
[Shooting of His Dear, The] (H114) 143
[Shores of Sweet Benone, The] (H52a) 244
Shores of Sweet Kenbane, The (H648) 168
[Shule Agra] (m) (H517) 7
[Siddon, Johnny] (H110) 144
Silly Old Man, The (H51) 129
[Silver Dagger] (cf. H699) 383
Silver[y] Tide, The [Laws O37] (H77) 418
[Silvy] (H35) 327
Silvy, Silvy, all on a day (H35) 327
Simple Ploughboy, The (H584) 331
[Since Love Can Enter an Iron Door] (H668) 444
Sing fiddle fal the di do (H25a) 502
?[Sing Tally Ho!] (H222) 29
Singing Erin-go-bragh, tourin-in-a (H6 = H567) 275
Singing, Down, down, a dumps, the darry dee (H700) 277
Single ...
    [... and Free] (H241) 346
    ... Days of Old, The (H659) 504
    [... Sailor, The] (H118) 315
[Sister Sally] (H138) 256
[Sister's Husband, The] (H126) 510
Six ...
    [... Girls] (H605) 340
    ... hundred stalwart warriors, of England's pride the best (H829) 91
    [... King's Daughters (Pretty Maids)] (H163) 413
    [... Miles from Bangor to Donaghadee] (m) (H620) 476
    [... Questions, The] (H681) 490
    ... Sweethearts, The (H605) 340
    [Sixteen Come (Next) Sunday] (H152) 266
Skerry's Blue-Eyed Jane (H737) 309
[Skibereen] (H125a) 475
[Skib(b)ereen] (m) (H162) 333, (H190) 420, (H238) 296
[Slane] (m) (H193) 487
Slaney Side, The [Laws M28] (H52b) 429
[Slapsadam, Old Woman] (H174) 507
Sleeping Beauty, The (H599) 12
Slieve ...
    ... Gallen Brae (H784) 172
    ... Gallen, Farewell to (H795) 198
    ... Gallon Brae[s], Wild (H540) 468
[Slighted Love] (H683) 393
Slighted Suitor, The (H159) 396, 397
[Sligo Shore] (H774) 150
Sloan Wellesley (H585) 147
Smiling, beguiling, cheering, endearing (H142) 294
So Dear Is My Charlie to Me (H533) 292
[(So) Deep in Love] (cf. H16) 392
So I fell in love with Mary Ann and then with Mary Jane (H605) 340
'So, Katie dear, you've told your mother (H804) 262
So Like Your Song and You (H508) 226

So now away, my hearties, that roam the mountain side (H750) 120
So twig your proud lasses as they walk along (H227) 47
[Soefield] (H31) 411
[Soft shades of evening o'er Coleraine were falling, The (H26b) 250
Soldier ...
    [... Boy, The] (H466) 79, [Laws O31] (H244) 295
    ... Boy, The Irish (H678) 89
    [... Bride's Lament, The] (H180) 149
    [... Maid, The] (H497) 326
    [...'s Farewell to Manchester, The] (cf. H520) 259
Some ...
    ... miles from here in the County Clare there stands an old farm-house (H492) 2
    ... people ramble to lands far away (H541) 207
    ... poets sing of beauties rare that strew the verdant shore (H715) 166
[Son of a Gambolier, The] (cf. H741) 50
[Sons of Fingal, The] (H478) 176
[Sons of Levi] (H146) 180
Song ...
    [... of the Ghost] (m) (H699) 383
    [... on Courtship] (H532) 367
    [..., to Curb Rising Thoughts, A] (H57a) 57
    ... of Old Ireland (H768) 59
[Sovay(, Sovay) the Female Highwayman] (H35) 327
[Sovie, Sovie] (H35) 327
Spanish ...
    [... Lady, The] (m) (H146) 180, (H766) 43
    [(... Lady in) Dublin City, (The)] (cf. H532) 367
    [... Lady (Merchant's Daughter), The] (H532) 367
    [... Privateer, The] (H560) 112
Spanking Maggie from the Ross (H516) 35
[Spinster's Lament, The] (H138) 256
[Sport Song, A] (cf. H532) 367
Sport's Lament (H772) 23
[Sporting Hero] (H792) 122
Squire ...
    ... Agnew's Hunt (H140) 30
    [(...) and the Thra(e)sher(man), (The) Nobleman] (H622) 44
    [... Hall's Watery Park] (H140) 30
    ... Nathaniel and Betsy (H207) 417
    [... of Tamworth, The] (H524) 328
    ...'s Bride, The [Laws N20] (H524) 328
    ...'s Daughter, The (H30b, H721) 437
    [...'s Young Daughter, The] (H30b, H721) 438
[Stafford (Staples), Bill] (H0) 53
[Stage Coach Driver's Lad, The] (H171) 40
Standing by the margin of the northern sea (H523) 63
Star ...
    ... of Benbradden, The (H24a) 348
    ... of Donegal, The (H555) 463
    ... of Glenamoyle, The (H13) 232
    [... of Glenamoyle, The] (m) (H108b) 169, (H164) 362
    ... of Moville, The (H68) 276
    ... of the County Down] (m) (H19a,b) 194, 196, (H49) 200, (H100a) 188, (H694) 503, (H747) 214; (cf. H207) 417, (cf. H791) 218
[State of Arkansas, The] (H0) 53
State of Arkansaw, The [Laws H1] (H0) 53
[(Stealing of) Mary Neal(e), (The)] (H55) 479
S[team]s[hip] *Leinster Lass*, The (H808) 98
[Still I Love Him] (m) (H620) 476
[Stock and Wall] (H681) 490
[(Stormy) Scenes (Hours) (Winds) of Winter, The Cold (Dark) (Gonesome) (Lonesome)] (H637) 385

[Strabane Fleet, The] (H502) 98
Strabane, The Flower of Sweet, (H224) 390
Strands of Magilligan, The (H520) 259; (m) (H98b) 472
Stream like crystal, it runs down, A (H621) 191
[Streams of Lovely Nancy (Nant-si-an), The] (H520) 259
[Streets of Derry, (The)] (H705) 132
[Streets of La(o)redo, The] (H680) 141
Strings to My Bow, I've Two or Three (H70) 340
[St. James Hospital] (H680) 141
[Suffolk Miracle, The] (H217) 432
Suiler, The Rambling (H183) 268
Summer Hill (H20b) 245
Sure Fahy sung of the Galway maid (H704) 241
Susan ...
  ... Brown (H771) 415
  ... Carr (?Laws P33) (H690) 416
  ... on the Beach [Laws K19] (H774) 150
  [... Pyatt] (H470) 491
  [... Strayed the Briny Beach, (As)] (H774) 150
  [..., Young] (cf. H556) 326
  [Susannah Clargy] (cf. H690) 416
[Swaggering Jig, The] (m) (H758) 23
Swan, The (H475) 455
[Swansea Barracks] (cf. H612) 242
[Swansea Gaol] (H746) 62
[Swapping Song] (H732) 57
Sweet ...
  [... Ballenden Braes] (H73) 412
  ... Bann Water [Laws M4] (H722) 343
  [... Calder Burn] (H476) 84
  ... Clonalee (H554) 400
  [... Cootehill Town] (m) (H494) 127
  ... Dreams (Streams) of Nancy, (O) the] (cf. H520) 259
  ... Dunloy (H577) 439
  ... Glenbush (H573) 212
  ... Gramachree] (cf. H682) 238
  ... Jane of Tyrone] (H153) 480
  [(...) Janie(ey) (Jenny) (Ginny) of the Moor] (H107) 320
  ... Londonderry (H813) 468
  [... Loughgiel (H506) 214
  [... Lurgan Town] (H563) 316
  [... Mary Ackland] (H30b, H721) 438
  [(...) Peggy Gordon] (cf. H16) 392
  [... Polly Perkins] (H132) 398
  ... Polly Primrose, a girl of nineteen summers-o (H734) 149
  [... (Queen) Mary] (H230) 255
  [... Straeban] (H224) 390
  [... Swansea (Jail)] (H746) 62
  [... William] (H163) 413
  ... William [Laws M35] (H587) 433
[Sweetheart in the Army, (A)] (H471) 317
Sweetheart's Appeal to Her Lover, A (H112) 288
[Sylvia's Request and William's Denial] (H35) 327

[T for Thomas] (H593) 389
Ta Ra, Limavady (H706) 180
Ta ra Limavady, ta ra Limavady (H706) 180
[Tab Scott] (H827) 100
[Taddy O'Neale] (m) (H64) 161
Tailor ...
  ... Boy, The (H199) 39
  ... in the Sea Chest, The [Laws Q8] (H604) 505
  [... in the (Tea) Chest, (A)] (H604) 505
  ..., The Journeyman [Laws B6] (H620) 476
  [..., The Weaver and the] (H199) 39
[Tally Ho the Hounds] (H222) 29
Tally ho, tally ho, tally ho the hounds, sir (H222) 29
Tam ...
  [... Bo (Buie)] (H748) 263

[... Gibb and the Soo] (H671) 22
[... o' the Lynn] (H480) 52
[Tammy, My Bonny] (H814) 415
[Tan-Yard Side, (Down by) the] (H52b) 429
[Tanderagee] (m) (H71) 246
Tandragee, The Hills of (H730) 190
[Tapscott] (H827) 100
Tar, The Jolly Roving [Laws O27] (H670) 293
Tardree, The Maid of (H733)
Tarry ...
  [... Sailor, The] (cf. H183) 268
  ... Trousers (H532) 367
  [... Trousers] (H641) 383
[Tavern in the Town, (There Is a) (The)] (cf. H16) 392, (cf. H683) 393
Tay, The (H25a) 502
Taylor, Willie (a) [Laws N11] (H213) 334
[Teddy McGraw] (H131) 84
[Teddy O'Neill] (m) (H657) 242
[Testament du Garcon Empoisonne, Le] (H814) 415
Testament, Robin Redbreast's (H527) 20
"Thank You, Ma'am," Says Dan (H184, H689) 469
[That Fatal Courtship] (cf. H218a) 386
Thatchers of Glenrea, The (H186) 46
Then here's good luck to the Rifles, the Inniskillings too (H526) 182
Then praise the jolly fisherman who takes what he can get (H639) 59
There ...
  [... Is an Alehouse in This Town] (H683) 393
  [... Is a Lady in This Town] (H174) 507
  [(... Is a) Tavern in the Town] (cf. H16) 392
  ... is no other spot in the land of the Gael (H720) 165
  ... is not in our island a vale or a lawn (H824) 166
  [... Lived a Wife in Kelmie] (H174) 507
  [... She Stands a Lovely (Once I Loved a Charming) Creature] (H532) 367
There was ...
  ... a gentle shepherdess was herding her flock (H104) 457
  ... a jolly ploughboy was ploughing up his land (H105) 331
  ... a lady in the east (H221) 490
  ... a lovely lady that lived near the seaside (H77) 418
  ... a merchant's daughter, being in her prime of years (H162) 333
  [... a Rich Merchant] (H108a) 329
  ... a rich merchant in London did dwell (H108a) 329
  ... a smith and he lived a sooth (H835b) 512
  ... a squire lived in this town (H217) 432
  ... a tarry sailor, and he in this town did dwell (H604) 505
  ... a wealthy farmer near Dublin town did dwell (H702) 504
  [... a Wealthy (The Rich Old) Farmer] (H188) 401, (H553) 482
  [... a Wee Bit Wiffikie] (H714) 513
  ... a wee bit wifukie (H714) 513
  ... a wee crow bigg-ed down in yon bog (H40c) 20
  [... an Old and Wealthy Man] (H217) 432
  ... an auld woman in oor toon, in oor toon did dwell (H174) 507
  [... an Old Lady (Woman) (in London) (in Our Town)] (H174) 507
  ... an old man and he lived in the east (H147) 474
  [... an Old Man Lived in Yorkshire] (H51) 129
  ... an old woman and her son (H57a) 57
  ... once a farmer's daughter near Limerick town did dwell (H806) 434
  ... racing and chasing in old Moneygran (H731) 22
There went a merry company (H59) 76

Titles and first lines Str – To c

There's ...
  [... a Chicken in the Pot] (H531) 505
  ... a Dear Spot in Ireland (H821) 220
  ... a dear spot in Ireland I'm longing to see (H821) 220
  ... a little whitewashed cabin (H787) 215
  ... a spot in dear old Donegal is very full of cheer (H627) 161
  ... a sweet little spot in the county of Derry (H64) 161
  ... an ancient walled city, a place of great fame (H813) 468
  ... an isle on the verge of the ocean (H791) 218
  ... few but has heard of McClenahan's dochter (H81) 430
  ... lots of food and prospects good (H766) 43
  ... one thing that grieves me that I will confess (H124) 509
  [... Whiskey in (a) (the) Jar (Bar)] (H792) 122
They marched through the town with their banners so gay (H660) 273
[They Say He Courts Another] (H504) 347
Thief, The Whistling (H710) 264
[Thing, The] (m) (cf. H527) 20
This evening I take my departure (H547) 195
This evening I take my departure from the lovely town where I was bred (H28a) 19
[This Fair Maid to the Meadow's Gone] (H683) 393
[Thorn Rosa] (H599) 12
Three ...
  [... Boocher Lads, The] (H185) 129
  [... Butchers (of England), The] (H185) 129
  ... Flowers of Chivalry, The (H99) 89
  ... gipsies came to Lord Barnham's gate (H137) 431
  [... Gypsies (Gypsy Laddies), The] (H124) 509
  ... Huntsmen, The [Laws L4] (H185) 129
  [... Huntsmen's Tragedy, The] (H185) 129
  [... Jolly Butchers (Sportsmen), The] (H185) 129
  [... Merry Butchers and Ten Highwaymen, The] (H185) 129
  [... Nights' Experience (in a Bar Room)] (H21) 508
  [... Quarters of the Year] (H593) 389
  [... Worthy Butchers of the North, The] (H185) 129
Thresher, The Jolly (H622) 44
[Thresher, The Nobleman and the] (H117) 44
[Thresherman (and the Squire), The] (H622) 44
[Through Lonesome Woods] (cf. H683) 393
Through the land of O'Cahan a river in beauty doth flow (H629) 171
Thrush, The Blackbird and (H241) 346
Thy fruit full well the schoolboy knows (H628) 62
[Tiarna (Tighearna) Randall, An] (H814) 415
[Tiddy the Tailor] (cf. H604) 505
[Tigaree Torum Orum] (H174) 507
[Till I Be Full] (H489) 48
[Time to be Made a Wife] (cf. H138) 256
[Time to Leave Her] (H53b) 96
[Tip, the Gray] (H90) 365
[Tippin' It up to Nancy] (H174) 507
[Tippling (Tripping) over the Lea (Plains)] (H794) 385
Tiree, A Shamrock from (H716) 218
'Tis ..., see also It is ..., It's ...
['Tis ('Twas) Pretty to Be in Balinderry] (H80) 386
[('Tis) Youth and Folly (Make Young Men Merry)] (cf. H16) 392
To all intending emigrants I pen this simple lay (H795) 198
[To Cheer the Heart] (H504) 347

601

To m – When Sam Henry's Songs of the People

To me way ay ah (H53c) 97
To my ...
... *right fol ol da daddy* (H201) 265
... *right fol-la, to my right fol-lay* (H739) 291
... *ring dou daw, fond the deedle day* (H618) 85
... *tit falairo raddle diddle airo, tit falairo whack* (H231a,b) 28
[To Pad the Road] (H18a) 358
To Rathlin's Isle I chanced to sail (H550) 176
To Strabane last Thursday I was walking (H766) 43
To the northwest of Europe there lies a green isle (H658) 175
[(To Wear a) Green Willow (Tree), The] (H60a) 400
[Tod, The] (H38) 29
Tom's Gone to Ilo (H53d) 96
Too long have I travelled the land of the stranger (H24b) 217
Too-ra-loo, too-ra-loo, too-ra-loo, too-ra-loo (H490) 48
Too-ri-ay, fol-the-diddle-day (H223) 83
Toor an addy, fol dha daddy, toor an addy, fol dha lee (H604) 505
Tossing (o') the Hay, (The) (H635) 455
Tom ...
[... Bolyn] (H480) 52
[... Sherman's Barroom] (H680) 141
[... the Barber] (H221) 490
[Top of Sweet Dunmul(l)] (m) (H1) 191
[Town of Antrim, The] (H632) 203
[Town (Wife) (Woman) of Kelso, The] (H174) 507
Trader, The (H11) 110
[Tramp, Tramp, Tramp, the Boys Are Marching] (m) (H756) 60
[Tramps and Hawkers] (m) (H37) 485
[Transport('s) Farewell, The] (H691) 119
[(Trial of) Willy Reil(l)y] (H234) 436
Trip ...
[... over the Mountain] (H61a,b) 459
[... We Took over the Mountain(s), The] (H61a,b) 459
[... with the Roving Shooler] (H183) 268
[Trooper and the Tailor, The] (cf. H604) 505, (cf. H682) 505
True ...
[... Born Sons of Levi] (H146) 180
[... Lover John] (H722) 343
[... Lovers] (cf. H699) 383
... Lover's Discussion, The (H164) 362
[... Lovers, The] (H175) 470
... Lovers' Departure, The [Laws N15] (H584) 331
[... Lovers' Trip over the Mountain, The] (H61a,b) 459
[Tuirne Mhaire] (m) (H222) 29
Tumbling through (thru') the Hay (H697) 278
Turfahun, The Girl from (H521) 372
[Turkish Lady, The] (H470) 491
'Twas ... *[see also It was ...]*
[... down in the Valley] (H479) 347
[... Early One Morning] (H176) 146
... early one morning as the day was a-dawning (H690) 486
... in the month of August, when yellow waved the corn (H665) 454
... in the year of forty, and the year of forty, too (H65b) 186
... on a bright May morning when first I saw my darling (H74) 236
... on a Monday morning, the weather being calm and clear (H209) 465
... on a summer's morning, / The flowers were a-blooming-o (H220) 243
... on the black Crimean shore, when midnight shadows met (H99) 89
... on the eighth of August (H602) 107
Twenty-One (H33, 611) 397
[Twenty Eighteen] (H532) 367

Two ...
[... Affectionate Lovers, The] (H668) 444
[... Lovers' Discussion] (H164) 362
[... (Three) (Jolly) (Jovial) Butchers (Huntsmen), The] (H185) 129
Tyrone ...
[... Ballad, A] (H173) 250
..., Among the Green Bushes in Sweet (H708) 174
..., The County (H153a,b) 480
..., Fair (H189) 173
..., The Hills of (H609) 199
..., The Maid from the County (H528) 246
..., Where Derry Meets (H601) 174

[Unconstant Lover, (The)] (H479) 347
[Undaunted Female, The] (cf. H213) 334
Under the Shade of a Bonny Green Tree [Laws P19] (H794) 385
[Unfortunate Lass (Rake), The] (cf. H680) 141
[Unkind Shepherdess, The] (H30a) 390
[Unmarried Maiden's Lament, The] (cf. H138) 256
Upside Down (H694) 503
[Up in London Fair] (H203) 330
Up the Green ...
... Forest] (H215) 393
[... Meadow] (cf. H683) 393
[... Meadows] (cf. H16) 392

Valley Below, The (H47) 236
Valleys of Screen, The (H752) 245
Valparaiso, The Girls of (H539) 97
[Verdant Braes of Skreen, The] (cf. H593) 389
[Village Maid, The] (H120) 332
[Village Pride, The] (H120) 332
[Villikins] (m) (H620) 476
[Villikins (and His Dinah)] (m) (H814) 415

Wae m' nantanoora-noora-nee (H810) 269
[Wager, A Wager; A] (H135) 414
[Wagoner, The] (H644) 367
[Wagoner's Lad, The] (cf. H479) 347
[Waillie] (cf. H16) 392
[Waistcoat and Britches] (H524) 328
Wait till the Ship Comes Home (H481) 484
Wait till the ship comes home again (H481) 484
[Walker (Blues) (, the Girl I Left Behind); Maggie] (H188) 401
Walker, Old Sally (H48g) 11
[Walkin' and A-Talkin', A-] (H479) 347
[Wallflowers] (H48d) 11
Waltzing Matilda (H566) 122
Waltzing Matilda, waltzing Matilda (H566) 122
[Wanton Widow, The] (H748) 263
[(Washburn's) (Woodburn's) Courtship, Captain (Mr) Wedderburn's] (H681) 490
Water ...
[... Is Wide, The] (cf. H16) 392
..., Water, Wallflowers (H48d) 11
..., water, wallflowers, growing up so high (H48d) 11
[..., Water, Wild Flower] (H48d) 11
Waterloo ...
[...] (H15) 87
..., The Drummer Boy at [Laws J1] (H728) 88
..., The Plains of (I) (H15) 87
..., The Plains of (II) (H608) 87
[Waukrife Minnie, The] (H152) 266
Waulking Song (H535a) 39
[Way up in Sofield] (H31) 411
We have dark lovely looks on the shores where the Spanish (H495) 227
We Met, 'Twas in a Crowd (H638) 431
We met, 'twas in a crowd, and I thought he would shun me (H638) 431

We Never Died in the Winter Yet (H766) 43
We parted from the Scottish shores, those high and mossy banks (H467) 428
We were homeward bound all in the deep (H815) 103
[We'd Better Bide a Wee] (H598) 61
[We'll Pay Paddy Doyle for His Boots] (H53c) 97
We're ...
[... All away to Sea] (H827) 100
[... All Bound to Go] (H827) 100
...marching, marching thro' Garvagh town (H17b) 180
Wealthy ...
... Farmer, The [Laws Q1] (H702) 504
[... Farmer, There Was a] (H553) 482
... Merchant, The (H604) 505
... Squire, The (H188) 401, (H524) 328
[Wearing of the Blue, (The)] (H162) 333
[Wearing of the Green, The] (m) (H52a) 244
[(Weary) Gallows, (The)] (H705) 132
[Weaver and the Tailor, The] (H199) 39
[Weaver Lad, The] (H199) 39
[Wedderburn's (Washburn's) (Woodburn's) Courtship, Captain (Mr)] (H681) 490
Wedding ...
[..., The] (H60a) 400
... at Ballyporeen, The (H93) 72
[... of Ballyporeen] (H93) 72, The
..., An Old Lover's [Laws P31] (H60a) 400
... Day, Our (H534) 454
Wee ...
... Article, The (H833) 257
... *bit awa' doon by the burn brae, A* (H71) 246
... Cutty Pipe, The (H465) 49
[... Daft Article] (H833) 257
[... Duck, The] (H228b) 18
[... Toun Clerk] (H201) 265
... *white cat, the wee white cat; The* (H510) 17
[... Wifikie, The] (H714) 513
... Wifukie, The (H714) 513
[... (Wonderful) Duck, The] (H228a) 19
Weep, weep, all who love the songs of dear Erin (H50) 139
[Welcome Sailor, The] (H581) 318
[Well Sold the Cow] (H51) 129
Wellesley, Sloan (H585) 147
[West Country Wager] (H135) 414
Wester Snow (H66) 369
[Wexford City] (H35) 327
Whack ...
... *de doo de dum* (H551) 40
... *fill ol da day* (H44) 178
... *fol ol di da, whack fol ol di daddy* (H36) 74
What ...
[... a Voice] (H89) 287; (cf. H16) 392
[... Ails You?] (H174) 507
'... brought you into my house, to my house, to my house? (H184=H68) 469
[Wheel of Fortune, (The)] (H790) 383, (cf. H532) 367
Wheelwright, The (H125a,b) 475, 476
[Wheelwright's Apprentice] (H125a) 475
When ...
... a Man's in Love [Laws O20] (H211) 479
.... *a man's in love he feels no cold, as I not long ago* (H211) 479
... Billy Green was but a boy (H690) 416
[... Cockle Shells Make Silver Bells] (H152) 266
... England calls her warlike band (H728) 88
... first from my country a stranger I went (H554) 400
[... first I Came to County Limerick] (H580) 357; (m) (H503) 273
... first I came to Ireland, some pleasures for to find (H578) 418

Titles and first lines When - Wrag

[... first I Came to the County Limerick] (H826) 309
... first I Landed in Glasgow (H58) 446
... first I saw you, sweet Moorlough Mary (H173) 250
... first I thought on Americay (H565, H754) 111
... first in Ireland I was born, it was near Armagh town (H553) 482
... first to this counteree a stranger I came (H86) 443
... first unto this country a stranger I came (H637) 385
... Flora is decked in her roses and fields are arrayed in their bloom (H87b) 1
... I first went a sea apprentice bound (H739) 291
... I rise in the morning, to my garden I'll go (H709) 348
[(... I Struck) Muskoka] (H0) 53
... I was a bachelor, airy and young, I left my work and trade (H694) 503
[... I was a Fair Maid] (H497) 326
... I was a girl of eighteen years old (H679) 255
... I was a maid about the age of sixteen (H497) 326
... I was a young maid, my fortune was told (H79) 428
[... I was Young] (H790) 383
... I was young and foolish still (H100a) 188
... I was young and in my prime, from care and trouble I was free (H473) 354
... I was young and pulled at lint I was handsome, spry and trig (H487) 43
... I was young and tender, I left my native home (H760) 471
... I was young I was airy and handsome (H591a) 6
... I was young, I was well beloved (H790) 383
... into this country first I came, my mind from love being free (H229a) 360
... Ireland was founded by Mac's and by O's (H484) 177
... Irish Eyes Are Smiling] (m) (H507) 213; cf. (H787) 215
... life has left the senseless clay (H719) 63
... morning dawns on the pleasant country round (H511) 157
... my love wakes in the morning, she oils and combs her hair (H730) 190
[... Pat Came over the Hill] (H710) 264
... Pat came o'er the hill, his colleen fair to see (H710) 264
... the bright sun had sunk in the west, I then took a notion to marry (H61b) 4
... the fulmar flies on Rathlin Head (H696) 290
... *the nights would begin to fall, all the boys would assemble* (H83) 156
... the shade of eve are falling (H507) 213
... wandering o'er the woodlands wild (H712) 221
... war had oppressed every nation with horror (H8) 311
... wintry winds are o'er and fled and Flora does her mantle spread (H28b) 158
Where ...
'... are ye goin'? How are ye doin'? Give me your hand,' sez I (H763) 458
'... are you going, my bonnie wee lass? (H152) 266
[(... Are You Going,) My Pretty (Fair) Maid?] (H152) 266
... are ye goin'? says Arty Art (H744) 12
... Derry Meets Tyrone (H601) 174
... have you been, Lord Ronald, my son (H814) 415

... Luna spreads her silver rays disclosing many's the scene (H169) 298
... Moyola Waters Flow (H787) 215
... *Moyola's gently flowing* (H787) 215
... the Moorcocks Crow (H32) 269
Whinny ...
... Knowe, As I Gaed ower a [Laws O17] (H793) 267
... Knowes, The (H18b) 272
[... Knowes, The Corncraik (Corncrake) amang the] (H18b) 272
Whirry, whirra, the cat she's deid (H40b) 17
[Whiskers on a Baby's Face] (H21) 508
Whiskers, The Captain with the (H660) 273
Whiskey [sic] Is My Name (b) [DW "No. 836"] (H835b) 512
Whiskey in the Jar [Laws L13A] (H792) 122
Whisky Is My Name (a) (H835a) 512
Whisky is my name, an' ye a' ken me weel (H835a) 512
[Whiskey Nancy] (H745) 47
[Whistlin' Gypsy Rover, The] (H124) 509
Whistling Thief, The (H710) 264
[Whitby Lad, The] (cf. H691) 119
[White Hare of Creggan, The] (m) (H154) 33
White the sheep that gave the wool (H535a) 39
Who ...
[... Comes Tapping to (Who's Taps at) (Who's That Knocking at [under]) (My Bedroom)) Window?] (H722) 343
[... Is at My Window?] (H557) 478
[... Is at My Window Weeping] (cf. H722) 343
[... Went out the Back?] (cf. H21) 508
[Whore's Lament, The] (cf. H680) 141
Why did you die, oh why did you die (H600) 140
Wi' mae ri fo ro fa raddy, boys, mae ri fo roo fa ran (H174) 507
[Widow Magra] (H131) 84
Widow, Here's a Poor (H48f) 11
Wifukie, The Wee (H714) 513
[Wife for Sale] (cf. H226) 511
Wild ...
... Colonial Boy, The [Laws L20] (H750) 120
[... Montana Boy, The] (cf. H750) 120
[... Rover (No More), (The)] (H779) 54
[... Slieve Gallion Braes] (H795) 198
... Slieve Gallion Brae[s] (H540) 468
Will you muses nine with me combine, assist me with my song (H686) 160
Will ...
... the Weaver [Laws Q9] (H682) 505
[... Ye Gang, Love] (cf. H16) 392
... Ye Pad the Road wi' Me? (H18a) 358
... You Gang to the Hielans, Leezie Lindsay? (H193) 487
[...(ie) (O')Riley] (H234) 436
William ...
[... and Eliza] (H597) 476
[... and Jane on the Banks of the Clyde] (H812) 310
[... and Nancy] (H89) 287
[... and Nancy's Parting] (cf. H561) 458
[(...) (The Sailor) and Nancy (Polly) (on the Sea), Jimmy] (H561) 458
[... (Willy) Reilly (and His Dear Colleen Bawn)] (H234) 436
[(...) Riley and Colinband] (H234) 436
[... the Rose] (H820) 257
[..., Molly and] (H561) 458
[..., Nancy and] (H479) 347
..., Sweet [Laws M35] (H587) 433
[..., Sweet] (H163) 413
[..., Young] (H166) 328
[Will(ie) (O')Riley] (H234) 436
Willie [or Willy] ...
[...ie and Mary] (H242) 483
[...ie and Minnie] (H722) 343
[...ie (William) and Mary] (H118) 315

...ie Angler (H614) 384
[...ie Archer] (H614) 384
[...ie Doo] (cf. H814) 415
...ie Lennox [Laws Q33] (H176) 146
[...ie Leonard] (H176) 146
...ie o' Winsbury] (H221) 490
[...(ie) (O')Riley] (H234) 436
[...(y) Reilly] (m) (H37) 485, (H468) 441
...y Reilly [Laws M10] (H234) 436
[...ie Returned from Waterloo] (m) (H466) 79
...ie Taylor (a,b) [Laws N11] (H213, H757) 334
...ie Taylor, a brisk young sailor (H213, H757) 334
[...ie, Lament for] (H587) 433
[...ie, Lovely] (H58) 446, (H587) 433
...ie, Mary and (H118) 315
[...ie (O')Reilly, (Young)] (H76) 314
[...ie's Ghost] (H699) 383
Willow Tree, The (H789) 419
Willow Tree, I'll Hang My Harp on a (H155) 366
Wilson, Gilmore and Johnson (H185) 129
[Wily Auld Carle (Joker), The] (H174) 507
[Wim-wam-waddles] (H732) 57
Wind in thundering gales did blow, The (H92) 86
[Winding Banks of Erne, (The)] (m) (H18a) 358, (H37) 485, (H540) 468, (H549) 81, (H612) 242, (H741) 50
Wing, Wang, Waddle-O (Wobble-O)] (H732) 57
[Winsbury, Willie o'] (H221) 490
[Wise Willie] (H744) 12
With [or Wi'] ...
... a fal lal la, fal lal la / With me ran-tan-ah, toor-an-ah (H131) 84
... a quing quang quaddle-um, jing jack traddle-um (H732) 57
... a winkletum, twinkletum, toor-ra-ra-a (H465) 49
... bat and ball we'll conquer all (H669) 179
... her apron pinned around her, I took her for a swan (H114) 143
[... Her (My) Dog and (Her) (My) Gun] (H524) 328
[... Kitty I'll Go for a Ramble] (m) (H468) 441
Wi' mae ri fo ro fa raddy, boys, mae ri fo roo fa ran (H174) 507
... me rum-rum-row, a raddy rum-rum-row (H650a) 263
... my dog and gun o'er yon blooming heather (H32) 269
... my fol ol the di do, fol ol dtha dee (H103) 55
... *my hark, tally ho! hark over yon brow* (H172) 31
[... My Love on the Road] (m) (H193) 487
Wi' mae ri fo ro fa raddy, boys, mae ri fo roo fa ran (H174) 507
... *my rifle o'er my shoulder, sure there's no boy could be bolder* (H832b) 81
... *my roor-ri-ra, fond a doo a da* (H152) 266
... my ru rum ra, far an ta a na (H793) 267
... me rum-rum-row, a raddy rum-rum-row (H650a) 263
Woman was taken out of man (H10e) 2
[(Wonderful) Crocodile, The Great (Rummy)] (H231) 28
[(Woodburn's) Courtship, Captain (Mr) Wedderburn's (Washburn's)] (H681) 490
Woodha', Bonny (H476) 84
Woods of Mountsandel, The (H6, H567) 275
[Worrysome Woman, The] (H699) 383
Would you hire with me, Tam Bo, Tam Bo? (H748) 263
Wounded Farmer's Son] (cf. H105) 331
[Wraggle Taggle Gypsies] (H124) 509

603

Wran – Z Sam Henry's Songs of the People

[Wran, The] (H744) 12
Wreck of the ...
... *Enterprise*, The (H558) 106
... *Fanad Boat*, The (H602) 107
... *Lady Shearbrooke*, The (H570) 310
... *Mary Jane*, The] (cf. H502) 98
... *Nimrod*, The (H717) 108
... *Rebecca*, The (H565) 111

[Yankee Boys, The] (cf. H532) 367
Ye ...
... Ballycastles, now give ear (H494) 127
... Christians all, where'er you be (H75a) 145
... Banks and Braes (of Bonnie Doon)] (m) (H2) 215, (H11) 110, (H506) 214
... banks and braes of Gelvin Burn, where oftimes I have roved (H667) 192
... bards may sing your sweetest lays (H521) 372
... gentle muses, it's pay attention (H108b) 169
... gods, assist my poor wearied notion (H505) 347
... hills and dales and flowery vales that lie round Mourne shore (H27a, orig. H34b) 371
... inhabitants of Ireland, attention pay to me (H623) 109
... lovers all, both great and small, attend unto my theme (H198) 481
... loyal Britons, pray give ear (H123) 90
... maidens around me are lightsome and bonny (H246) 249
... muses, I hope you'll assist me (H653) 211
... muses nine, with me combine and grant me some relief (H20a) 216
... muses nine with me combine, assist me with your aid (H500) 359
... people all, both great and small, give ear unto my song (H134) 168
... wise maids and widows pray listen to me (H122a,b) 88
Yellow ...
... Bittern, The (H830) 64
[(...) Gypsies (on Yon Hill), Seven] (H124) 509
... Meal (H827) 100
Yes, I sigh for the grove that encircles my Mary (H22a) 232
[(Yon) Green Valley] (H218a) 386
[Yon High High Hill] (H152) 266
[Yonder Hill There Is a Widow] (H532) 367
Yonder stands a pretty maiden (H532) 367
York (H10g) 3
[Yorkshire Bite, The] (H51) 129

You ...
[... and I in the One Bed Lie] (H681) 490
... Broken-Hearted Heroes (H549) 81
... broken-hearted heroes that love your liberty (H549, H724) 81,82
... feeling-hearted Christians, I pray you lend an ear (H742) 104
... folk of this nation that hear my oration (H68) 276
... followers of the nine, Apollo's tuneful line (H607) 250
... gentle muse that will ne'er refuse (H13) 232
[... Go to Old Harry!] (cf. H532) 367
... have heard of Tam O'Shanter, of Bobby Burns and all (H675) 24
... landsmen all, on you I call, to tell the truth I'm bound (H231a,b) 28
... Lovers All (H525) 483
... lovers all, both great and small, that dwell in Ireland (H525) 483
... lovers of every station, give ear to these lines I unfold (H597) 476
[... Lovers of Old Ireland] (H553) 482
... maids of Columbia, wherever you be (H636) 235
... maids of this nation of high and low station (H811) 461
... muses nine, with me combine and lend me your attention (H133) 461
... people of every station (H752) 245
... people so witty through country and city (H88) 18
[(...) Rambling Boys of Pleasure, The] (cf. H828) 286
... rantin' team of Derry boys (H669) 179
... talk of your packets, fast packets of fame (H194) 99
... tender young lovers, draw near me (H721) 438
You're Welcome as the Flowers in May (H804) 262
[(You're Welcome Home,) Young Johnny] (H779) 54
You've heard tell of the camels in the Asiatic land (H130) 26
Youghal(l) Harbour (H503) 273
[Youghal Harbour] (m) (H67) 365, (H108b) 169, (H164) 362, (H189) 173, (H474) 488, (H673) 429, (H745) 47
Young ...
[... Amy (Emma) (Emily) (Emly)] (H113) 434
... and Single Sailor, The] (H471) 317, (H818) 317
[... Barbour] (H221) 490
[... Beichan (Bateman) (Beham)] (H470) 491
[... Bekie] (H470) 491
[... Bung-'er-Eye] (H700) 277

[... Butcher Boy] (H185) 129
[... Edmund (Edmondale) (Edward) (Emsley) (Was a Sailor Boy)] (H113) 434
... Edward Bold (H113) 434
... Edward the Gallant Hussar (H243a,b) 473
... Edwin] (H113) 434
[(...) Edwin (Edmund) (Edward) in (of) the Lowlands (Low)] (H113) 434
... Ellender] (cf. H668) 444
... Emily was a servant maid, her love a sailor bold (H113) 434
... Farmer's Offer, The (H776) 261
[(...) Floro] (H30a) 390
[... (George) Riley] (cf. H16) 392
[... Henry] (m) (H37) 485
[... Johnnie] (H137) 431
[(...) John(ny) Riley] (H471) 317
[(...) Johnie (Johnny) Scot(t)] (H736) 489
[... Ladies] (cf. H16) 392
[... Maid (Stood in Her Father's) (in the) Garden, A] (H471) 317
[... Maid's Love, The] (H58) 446
... Mary of Accland [Laws M16] (H30b, H721) 437
[... Men, Come Marry Me] (cf. H138) 256
... Men and Maids] (cf. H722) 343
[(...) Mollie(y) (Peggy) (Polly) Ban (Ban) (Bann) (Baum) (Bawn) (Bond) (Bonder) (Van) (Vaughan) (Whan)] (H114) 143
... Molly she went up the street (H201) 265
[... (O')R(e)ll(l)y] (H580) 357
[(...) (O')Reilly (Riley) (the Fisherman)] (H468) 441
[... Officer, The] (H163) 413
[... Roger, Esq.] (H90) 365
[... Roger the Miller] (H90) 365
... Roger, the miller, came courting of late (H90) 365
[(...) Roger(s) (Jimmy) (Johnny) the Miller] (H90) 365
[... Sailor Bold, A] (m) (H150a) 466
[... Sailor (Trooper) Cut down (in His Prime), (The)] (cf. H680) 141
[(...) Sally Munro(e)] (H571) 441
[... (...) (Her) Servant-Man, The] (H668) 444
... Shepherd, The] (H30a) 390
[... Squire, The] (H135) 414
[... Susan] (cf. H556) 326
[... William] (H166) 328
[... William's Denial (Return)] (H205) 319
[... Willie (O')Reilly] (H76) 314
[(Your) Faithful Sailor Boy, The] (H543) 103
[Youth and Folly] (cf. H580) 357
[Youth and Folly (Make Young Men Merry), ('Tis)] (cf. H16) 392
[Youthful Damsel, The] (H561) 458
Yowe Lamb, The (H175) 470

Zared, The [Laws D13] (H194) 99

Original sources of items in the columns as given by Sam Henry

Sources: w, of text; m, of melody; a, author; c, composer; 2,w = two sources of text given; m2 = secondary source of tune (from whom a primary source learned it).

Printed and manuscript sources

book on Scottish humor w2 (H39) 123
[O'Neill 1903] m (H52a) 244
Henry Morris, *Cead de Ceoltaibh Uladh*, 1915[?1916] c· (H834) 289
American coll. 'Come-All-Ye's' [probably O'Conor 1901], remainder of w (H827) 100
The Flying Cloud [?Dean 1922] [B,W:]the balance of w (H836) 372
3d textbook, National Schools, 1865 w (H99) 89
Kennedy-Fraser and MacLeod's *Songs of the Hebrides*, 1909 w (H535b) 96
Kinloch, *Ancient Ballads*, ?1827 m (H679) 255
Petrie 1855:57 m (H3) 286
Oxford Book of Ballads [1910] #24 2,w (H135) 414
Whitelaw ?1857 w only (H707) 227
Whitelaw ?1857 ?w (H714) 513

library, Royal Irish Academy w (H582) 238
?broadsheet w (H11) 110
broadside (J Nicholson, Cheapside Song House, Castle Lane, Belfast) w (H146) 180
from the *Northern Minstrel*, broadside (Hugh Clark, Pottinger's Entry, Belfast) 1829 w (H552) 102
broadside c. 1890 ?w (H803) 79
(mimeographed) Coleraine Musical Festival, 1939, Class 29: Junior Folk Song c (H480b) 52
Gaelic Journal 6(7)1895:108 (H819) 219
published in *Northern Constitution* 17 May 1924, -m, signed Robert Stuart ?a (H731) 22
published -m, *Northern Constitution* 14 Oct 1939 w (H832b) 81

William Robb ms. c (H10a) 2; c (H10b) 2; c (H10c) 2; c (H10d) 2; c (H10e) 2; c (H10f) 3; c (H10g) 3; c (H10h) 3
found in a waste-paper basket, Trinity College (Dublin) m (H523) 63
ms. book, 1659 m (H525) 483

Sources vaguely identified

compilation of best 5,c (H750) 120
based on 3 renderings 3,w (H12) 31
best of 8 versions sent 8,w (H179a) 125
rest reconstructed from other sources w (H180) 149
best of 3 versions received w (H230) 255
known locally w (H827) 100

children of Irish Society's school, infant dept. ?w,?m (H48a) 10
old Mail Car driver [B:]w (H28b) 158
farmer w,m (H715) 166
lady c:m (H713) 27
old man, 80, corroborated 2,m (H11) 110
reader, from her mother c (H598) 61
plowman, whistler m (H190) 420
police member c. 1885 a,?m (H764) 32
"old salt" w (H539) 97
old schoolmate of SH's "en route to Magilligan, accompanist 'Tin Lizzie'" 2,m (H11) 110
woman who learned it from a "basket woman," c. 1865 w,?m (H107) 320

s: basis for Down by the Sally Gardens m (H27b) 105
traditional, based on tune from Bangor monastery, 6th century [D:]m (H80) 386
stock Irish air m (H501) 25
well-known folk air m (H508) 226
old Irish air m (H546) 273
traditional Gaelic m (H645) 7
s: resembles Lamentation Air used by Alfred Percival Graves to set Song of an Island Fisherman by Katherine Tynan [Hinkson] m (H772) 23

Unnamed sources in named places

remainder coll. (upper valley Thames [England]) ?Alfred Williams w (H698) 51
(Aberdeenshire [Scotland]) w,?m (H568) 226
native (Island of Jura [m: Scotland]) m (H713) 27
company of Australian Boy Scouts (camp, Ganavan Sands, Oban [Scotland]) w,?m (H566) 122
(Uig, Loch Snizort, Isle of Skye) (H535a) 39
second cousin of the author (Brooklyn, NY [USA]) c:w,?m (H501) 25
esteemed correspondent (native, Co. Derry; now resident, New Zealand) ?6,c (H750) 120
from a soldier pal c. 1865 (Bombay, India) w2,?m2 (H798) 421

native, 70 (Aghadowey), from his mother w,m (H24a) 348
old lady (Altibrian) c:w (H32) 269
from native (Alla, near Park, Co. Derry) 2,w (H562) 113
local singer (Arboe) m (H505) 157
(Ards, Co. Down) w (H650a) 263
native (Ardverness, Macosquin), from her father c. 1850 w,m (H58) 446
sisters (Adverness, Macosquin dist.) w,m (H125a) 475
(orig. Co. Armagh) w,?m (H732) 57
(Armagh) ?m (H744) 12
(Articlave) 3,c (H137) 431
(Articlave dist.) sung 1827 by Inishowen plowman 2,w (H192) 101; one version c (H551) 40

(Ballaghbeddy, Ballymoney) w (H232) 318
(Ballinascreen) w,?m (H833) 257
native, 82 (Ballinrees, Macosquin) w,m (H76) 314
(Ballycastle dist.) "English" w,?m (H152) 266; c (H467) 428
(Ballycastle) 8,w (H179a) 125; 3,c (H474) 488; w (H595) 468; esteemed contributor c (H732) 57
(Ballyhackett dist. near Downhill) w,m (H211) 479
(Ballyhome dist.) w,m (H94) 17
(Ballymacaldrick, Dunloy) c (H530) 298
(Ballymacaldrick dist., Co. Antrim) w,?m (H563) 316
(Ballymena) 8,w (H179a) 125; from [Sam Lamont]'s mother w2,?m2 (H789) 419
veteran singer (Burnquarter, Ballymoney) w,?m (H737) 309
anonymous (Ballymoney) c (H554) 400; from his grandfather w3,?m3 (H807) 514
(Ballymulderg, Magherafelt) 3,w;?3,m (H576) 435
native, 75 (Ballyportery, Loughguile), from her mother c. 1850 w,m (H164) 362
(Ballyrashane) w,?m (H725) 278
(Ballyrisk, Limavady) 3,c (H474) 488
(Ballyvoy, Co. Antrim) at smiddy w,m (H556) 376
(Ballywillan dist.) m (H81) 430

(Ballywindland) c (H241) 346
medical student c. 1876 (Belfast) [D:]w (H131) 84
(Bellarena) 3,c (H137) 431
(Blackhill dist., Coleraine) c:w (H81) 430
(Bond's Glen, Cumber parish [m: Co. Londonderry, near Claudy]) m (H601) 174
veteran singer (Burnquarter, Ballymoney) w,?m (H737) 309
old lady, 90 (Bushmills dist.) w (H470) 491
(Bushmills) w (H579) 345; w,?m (H580) 357; an old favorite w (H586) 80; c (H634) 472; man w,?m (H636) 235; man w,?m (H680) w,m (H718) 460; w,?m (H728) 88; 141; man c (H816) 92

(slopes of Carntogher) 2,w (H77) 418
native (Castleroe dist.) c:w (H71) 246
native (Castlewellan dist., Co. Down) w (H183) 268
one-legged man, 36, former blacksmith, from his father (district between Claudy and Strabane) "The Flower of Sweet Strabane" m (H55) 479
from fragment (Cloyfin) w (H39) 123
(Coleraine) 3,c (H137) 431; itinerant flute-player, ex-bandsman of 88th Connaught Rangers m (H179a) 125; street singer, ex-private, Royal Inniskilling Fusiliers w,?m (H526) 182; Park St children w,?m (H599) 12; w (H650b) 264
(Croaghmore dist.) [m: Ballintoy] (H590) 486
(Cool, Cumber-Claudy) [m: possibly Coolnacolpagh (Cumber Upper)] w (H13) 232
(Cushendall dist.) w (H188) 401

(Doagh dist.) c (H733) 342
(Downhill) 3,w;?3,m (H576) 435
(Drumavalley, Bellarena) m (H128) 440
from young woman (Drumrammer) w2,m2 (H76) 314
(Drumsurn dist.) w (H234) 436
(Drumtullagh dist., Mosside, Co. Antrim) w (H662) 45
(Dungiven) 8,w (H179a) 125
(Dunloy dist.) w (H533) 292; w (H626) 465
(Dunloy) w,?m (H509) 168; w (H618) 85; w (H685) 460; w (H686) 160

(Fermoyle dist.) w (H54) 144
grandnephew of Moorlough Mary (Foreglen, near Dungiven) m (H173) 250
native (Foreglen, near Claudy) w[part],m (H698) 51

from old travelling woman (Garry Bog) c. 1885 w2,?m2 (H735) 133
(Garronpoint) w (H590) 486
(Garvagh) c (H78) 484; 8,w (H179a) 125
old man, 80+ (native, glens above Garvagh) w (H38) 29
(Glenariffe) 8,w (H179a) 125
(Glenelly valley, Co. Tyrone) w (H720) 165
(Gortcorbries, Limavady) 2,c (H468) 441
old worthy (Gortinmayoghill, Aghadowey) "who has since bade farewell to all" m (H504) 157

(Heagles, Ballymoney) 3,c (H474) 488

old man (Killowen) from his mother w,?m (H40b) 17; native, while weaving at the loom c. 1875 3,w (H72) 374
(Knockloughrim) 8c:w (H179a) 125
(Knockaduff dist.) 2,w (H90) 365

605

A - S Cr Sam Henry's Songs of the People

(Lifford, Stranocum) c:w (H116a) 201
from a worker (Liscolman mill) c. 1905 w2,?m2 (H691) 119
(Lisnagunogue dist.) w (H549) 81

(Maghera) w (H707) 227
(Tyrone Ditches, near Newry) w,?m (H682) 505
resident (Magilligan) learned c. 1875 2,w (H27a) 371; (former) resident, 70 w,m (H42b) 197; learned from an "old hand who is still to the fore" w (H45) 477; [D:]w,?m (H88) 18; w,m (H95) 107; octogenarian w,m (H108a) 329; octogenarian, learned c. 1855 m (H146) 180; w, ?m (H209) 465
(Moneycannon, Ballymoney) 2,c (H468) 441
old worthy (Moneysharvin; native Aghadowey), lately gone to his rest w,?m (H820) 257
(Moyarget district) w,?m (H193) 487
man (Moyarget, Ballycastle), in his family 3 generations c:w (H524) 328
"stove" girls at Mullaghmore Bleach Green (Barklie's) w,?m (H163) 413

(Newtowncrommelin) 8,w (H179a) 125

(Oughtymoyle, Bellarena) w,m (H129) 141

(Portrush) 8,w (H179a) 125
native (Portstewart) 3,w (H72) 374
native (Proluski, near Straid) at Bushmills w,?m (H587) 433; native, in Bushmills w (H589) 344

old salt (Quay Head, Portrush) w,?m (H815) 103

(Ramelton dist.) m (H196) 210
(Raphoe, Co. Donegal) w (H208) 258
(Mt. Sawell, slopes of) w,?m (H528) 246
Skerry glen w,?m (H241) 346
(Strabane district) w,?m (H151) 124
(Stranocum dist.) c;?m (H46) 438
native (Stranocum) w (H555) 463

(Tobermore) w,?m (H748) 263
native (Tyrone border) 3,m (H8) 311; native m (H13) 232
(Tyrone Ditches, near Newry) w,?m (H682) 505

reader (Upperlands) c:w,m (H532) 367

(Vow dist.) w (H238a,b) 296

Named sources

James Adams (Woodlands, Castlerock) learned in Eglinton district c:m (H116a) 201
Andrew (Andy) Allen (Coleraine) [D: some vts.] 2,w;2,m (H34) 213; [D:]5,c (H150b) 361; w,m (H613) 396; w,?m (H614) 384; m (H616) 462; w,?m (H635) 455; c (H653) 211; w,?m (H793) 267; m (H803) 79
Joe Allen (Coleraine) [D:]w,m (H60a) 400
Joseph Allen (Drumavalley, Bellarena) w,m (H169) 298
John Anderson (Blenheim, Ontario, Canada) 6,w (H758) 120
late Canon Armstrong (Castlerock) c:m (H523) 63
Edward Armstrong (Slaughtmanus, Cross P O, Co. Derry) 2,c (H477) 140

M B (Antrim) c:m (H187) 162
Robert Bacon [D:Coleraine] w,?m (H18b) 272
from John Bailey, itinerant shoemaker, former soldier (Bog of Allen) w3,m3 (H92) 86
late Canon Barnes (Ballycastle) a (H606) 208

Louie Barnes, Miss, L R A M (Ballycastle) [D,W:]m (H28b) 158; c;?a,?mc (H661) 259; for notation class, Coleraine Musical Festival mc (H696) 290
George Barnett (Owenreagh, Sixtowns, Draperstown) a (H542) 217
Jim Baxter, leader (Coleraine Fife and Drum Band) m (H98a) 64
Mary Beckett, Mrs (Crocnamac, Portrush) c:w (H168) 399
E J Bennett (Coleraine) [B:native of Adare, Co. Limerick] c (H56) 354
from [E J Bennett]'s mother (Adare, Co. Limerick) w,m (H56) 354
late Robert Hugh Benson [D:]a (H59) 76
from Martha (Redgate) Black (Magilligan), [Eliza Mullen]'s mother w3 (H126) 510
Tom Black, fiddle (Croaghan, Macosquin) m (H172) 31; w[st. 1] (H224) 391
from Willie Black, many trades, ship's steward (Aughless, Cookstown) large repertoire of songs from sea w2,?m2 (H734) 149
William Blacker, Lt.-Col., 1777-1855 (Carrickblacker, Co. Armagh) a (H98a) 64
J Fairfax Blakeborough, Maj., folklorist coll. (Yorkshire) 2,w (H51) 129
James Bond (Termaquin, Limavady) ?w,m (H669) 179; w,?m (H670) 293; w,?m (H671) 22; w,?m (H675) 24; w,?m (H676) 41
from William Bond (Terrydoo Clyde, Limavady), [James Bond]'s father w2,?m2 (H670) 293; d. 1913 age 103 w2,?m2 (H676) 41
A E Boyd, esq [D: principal teacher] (Cullycapple [P E] School, Aghadowey) m (H99) 89; c (H165a) 260; c:m (H171) 40; c:m (H174) 507; c:m (H227) 47
Alexander Boyd (Lismoyle, Swateragh) 7,c:w (H757) 334
Mary Boyd, Miss (Aghadowey) c:w,m (H67) 365
Mrs Thomas Boyd (Ballyhamage, Doagh, Co. Antrim) w,m (H638) 431
states Robert Boyle (Agivey, Aghadowey) [B,D:]a (H63) 247
Hubert Bradley, esq, customs officer c (H151) 124
John J Bradley (Aughacarnaghan, Toomebridge) 11,c:w (H625) 342
John Bradley (Garvagh) w,?m (H799) 221
William Bradley (Tobermore) w,?m (H752) 245
Willie Bradley (Coleraine) w,?m (H798) 421; w,?m (H821) 220
John Brennan (Kilfennan, Waterside, Londonderry) w corroborated (H778) 387
James Brogan, whistler (Anticur [m: Rasharkin, Co. Antrim] m (H493) 237
Patrick Brolly (Drum, Dungiven) 5,c (H150b) 361
Mrs David Brown (Lachute Mills, Quebec, Canada) 5,c (H750) 120
Henry R Browning (Redford, Moy, Co. Tyrone) c (H131) 84
Mrs Brownlow (Ballylagan, Cloyfin [Coleraine] 3,w;?3,m (H576) 435; c (H591a) 6; c:m (H714) 513
Harriet Brownlow [Miss] [Ballylaggan, Cloyfin, Coleraine) from her mother, now 70 c (H701) 501; w (H835b) 512
Maggie Brownlow, Miss (Ballylag[g]an, Cloyfin) w,?m (H578) 418; w,m (H581) 318; w,m (H583) 314; [W:]m (H835b) 512
R R B[rownlow[?]], tinwhistle (Ballylag[g]an, Cloyfin [Coleraine) 3,m (H8) 311; m (H15) 87; [D:] Robert Brownlow w (H55) 479
John Burgess, sen (Ballygawley [Aghadowey]) w (H616) 462
Richard Butler (Derry): see Mary Harte (H813) 468

from Matty Cairns (Ervey), [Joseph Gardner]'s mother w3,?m3 (H221) 490

James Cairnes, c. 1820 teacher (Moortown School) supposed a (H505) 157
Eliza Jane Caldwell (Derryard, Dungiven) c:w (H126) 510
Joseph Reid Caldwell, whistler (Derryard), [Eliza Jane Caldwell]'s brother m (H126) 510
Martha Jane (Mullen) Caldwell, [Eliza Jane Caldwell]'s mother w (H126) 510
Pat Callaghan (Philadelphia; from Co. Cork) c. 1930 w,?m (H634) 472
Thomas Cameron, coachman (from childhood, Ballinteer) w,?m (H33) 397
Mrs Campbell (Kilrea) 3,w (H213) 334
A A Campbell [F R S A] (Belfast) w (H224a,b) 390; c (H607) 250
Anthony Campbell (Levenside, Barrhead, Scotland) c (H657) 242
from Jane Campbell, 95, [Harriet Brownlow's mother]'s mother (Glenmanus, Portrush) w2,3,?m2,3 (H701) 501
Lizzie Campbell, Miss (Carn, Dungiven) c:w (H182) 464
Mrs Thomas H Campbell (Drumlee, Finvoy) 6,c (H120) 332
John Canavan (Lower Back, Stewartstown, Co. Tyrone) a (H795) 198
from Sam Canning, shoemaker (Alla) c. 1870 w2,?m2 (H124) 509
from Edward Carlin (Killywill, Greysteel) 2,w2 (H190) 420
J[ames][Jim] Carmichael (Ballymena) c (H695) 442; c (H727) 193; c (H730) 190; c (H788) 300; c (H794) 385; 2,c (H797) 327; fiddle m (H802) 466; m (H804) 262
Mrs Tom Carmichael (Polintamney, Ballymoney) c:w (H106) 443; 6,c (H120) 332
J E Carpenter, c. 1890 a (H804) 262
from John Carr (Co. Derry), [Pat M'Loone]'s wife's uncle w3,?m3 (H635) 455
William Carton, retired schoolteacher (Garryduff, Ballymoney) c (H103) 55; c (H104) 457; c (H109) 357; c (H121) 270
from [William Carton]'s father, c. 1875 w,m (H104) 457
from [William Carton]'s mother c. 1875 w,m (H109) 357
Denis Cassidy (Fallalea, Maghera) m (H465) 49
William Cassidy (Vow, Bendooragh) 6,c (H120) 332
from James Catherwood (Carclinty, Cullybackey) when young 2,w2;?m2 (H214) 445
Hugh Clarke (Croaghan, Macosquin, Coleraine) w (H114) 143
from Mary Clarke w[later vt.] (H25b) 261
Mrs Clarke (Coleraine) "and others" 4+,c (H638) 431
Rev J R Clinton w,m (H27b) 105
Kennedy Clinton (Coolderry, Coleraine) w,?m (H608) 87
Robert Clyde (Lenamore, Bellarena) [D:]2,c (H197b) 248
Mrs D Cochrane (Dunseverick, Bushmills) 7,c:w (H757) 334
Albert Cole (Upperlands, Co. Derry) 5,c (H750) 120
Rev Luke Aylmer Conolly (Ballycastle) a (H550) 176
John Corscadden (Bushmills) 11,c:w (H625) 342
Tom Courtney (Drumcan, Cookstown) w,?m (H734) 149
Bernard Covert, c. 1850 (American) a,mc (H78) 484
noted by Maurice Craig (Belfast) c:m (H705a) 132
Alex[ander] Crawford (Leck, Ballymoney) w,?m (H735) 133; w,?m (H736) 489; w [sts 2,5] (H739) 291
Sarah Crawford, Mrs (Thorndale [Cottages] [Coleraine]) c:w (H108b) 169; c (H138) 256

Original sources V Cr - S He

Valentine Crawford (Bushmills) m (H122b) 88; fiddle m (H625) 342; whistler m (H711) 234; w,?m (H721) 438; w,?m (H722) 343; w,?m (H741) 50
from Valentine Crawford]'s father (Garry Bog, Ballymoney) c. 1875 m2 (H711) 234
Gerard Crofts (Dublin) by special permission c (H184 = H689) 469
Joseph M Crofts w,m (H184 = H689) 469
Nellie Crowley (Mrs Corrigan), teacher (Knockera, Killimer, Co. Clare, native of Kilrush, Co. Clare) a (H507) 213
Herbert Cunningham (Mullagh, Maghera) w,m (H710) 264; c (H790) 383
[Herbert Cunningham]'s mother w,?m (H790) 383
James Currie (Balnamore) c:w (H711) 234; w[slight variation] (H825) 299
from Margaret Curry, Miss (Islandtown, Clough) m2 (H780) 345
late John Dallas (Honourable the Irish Society's Boys School, Coleraine) 1880 w,?m (H628) 62
Samuel Davidson, whistler (Drumnakeel, Ballyvoy, Ballycastle) m (H198) 481
William Davidson (Drumnakeel, Ballyvoy, Ballycastle [Co. Antrim]) w,m (H147) 474; w,m (H217) 432
[De Largy: see Delarg[e]y]
[De Vine: see Devine]
Johnnie Deeney (Aughill, Magilligan, Co. Derry) c (H672) 212
Joseph Deery (Salowilly, Claudy, Co. Derry) c:w (H818) 317
from James Delaney, blind piper (Ballinasloe [Co. Galway]) m2 (H179a) 125
Margaret De Largy, Mrs (Waterfoot, Glenariff) m (H739) 291
Mrs [P] Delargey, fiddle (Waterfoot, Glenariff) w,?m (H759) 288; [James M'Dade]'s sister, from her mother, d. 1932 aged 80 m (H767) 370
Charles Dempsey, [rural] postman (Coleraine) w,m (H7) 290; w,?m (H42a) 148; m (H113) 434; from women working for his mother, fowl merchant w,?m (H136) 125
Dempsey (Drumail) 1825 a (H25b) 261
Frank Devine (Dunnaboe, Donemana) c (H96a,b) 230, 231; c:w (H173) 250
James Devine (Lough Ash [Loughash], Donemana) a (H96a,b) 230, 231; c. 1885 a (H100b) 193; c. 1876 a (H173) 250; a (H607) 250
Mrs James De Vine (Belfast) c:w (H705a,b) 132
native [D:William Devine] (Foreglen [Dungiven] Co. Derry) c:w,m (H52b) 429; W D [D:William Devine] m (H97) 131; (Coleraine; native of Foreglen ...) m (H182) 464; m (H202) 119; 3,w (H213) 334; m (H219) 177; (Coleraine) m (H228b) 18
Anna Devlin, Miss, fiddle (Kilhoyle, Drumsurn, Co. Derry) m (H225) 196
Catherine Devlin, domestic servant (Cookstown) 1827 w,m (H117) 44
from John Devlin, [Anna Devlin]'s father, from his father John Devlin, from his father Edward Devlin (all Kilhoyle) m2+ (H225) 196
Edward Devlin (Drumsurn, Co. Derry) c:w (H225) 196
Mrs Neil Dickey (Carrowreagh, Finvoy, Ballymoney) 2,c (H150a) 466
Mrs H Dinsmore (Coleraine) c (H617) 45
Mrs H Dinsmore, sen (Coleraine) c (H683) 393
Alexander Doey (Cashel, Macosquin) c:w (H172) 31
Andrew (Andy) Doey [?Dooey] (Ballymacaldrick [Dunloy] [Co. Antrim]) a;?c:w (H493) 237; a (H498) 211; a (H508) 226; a (H512) 225; a (H545) 225; from his children c,w (H631) 294; w[transl.] (H830) 64; w[transl.]

(H831) 235; w[transl.] (H832a) 49; w[transl.] (H834) 289
William Doey (Kilmoyangie, Kilraughts, Ballymoney) c (H765) 312
Jane Doherty, Miss, "American organ" (Moneygran, Loughash, Co. Tyrone) w,?m (H768) 59
Maria Doherty, Miss (Clooney, Magilligan [D:Co. Derry]) w,m (H24b) 217; w,m (H89) 287
B:resident (Magilligan) [D:Sally Dougherty, 88 (Oughtymoyle, Magilligan)] m (H21a) 508
Sally Doherty, 93 (Oughtymoyle, Bellarena) w,m (H200) 470; 2,w;?m (H201) 265; 95 [D:]w,m (H239) 469
from Catherine Donaghy, Mrs (Lisglass, near Derry), [Jane Doherty]'s grandmother c. 1885 w2,?m2 (H768) 59
Leonard Donaghy (Limavady) c,w,m2 (H706) 180
J Keevers Douglas (Ballycastle) c (H596) 6
from John Doyle, Corp., Kildare Rifles w2,m2 (H92) 86
from James Duff (Carnrallagh, Aghadowey) w2 (H165a) 260
Dan Duffy, shorthand, chez Wm H Reid (Mayoghill, Garvagh) c:w (H174) 507
Sam Dunlop, fiddle (Bushmills) m (H489) 48

Ebenezer Elliott, "The Corn-Law Rhymer" (Sheffield iron merchant, native Yorkshire [England]) a (H628) 62
John Elliot[t], fiddle (Turfahun, Bushmills) w,m (H486) 121; w,m (H487) 43; w,m (H571) 441; w,m (H577) 439
Mr D Ellis (Crumlin, Co. Antrim) c (H621) 191
from David Esker (Whaupstown, Glenwherry) m2 (H802) 466
H[arry] Evans [Coleraine] w "through" (H8) 311; c:w [o: ?a] (H26b) 250; H E [D: Harry Evans] c (H87a) 181; c:w,m (H98b) 472; 3,w;m (H207) 417

from Robert Farren, Crimean veteran (Ballymoney) m2 (H829) 91
Constable Fennell, R I C (Bellarena) a (H52a) 244
William Ferguson (Craigbrack, Eglinton) 5,c (H150b) 361
William James Fisher (Ballygawley, Aghadowey) c:w (H616) 462
Mrs Fitzwilliam in Buckstone's drama "The Green Bushes" w,?m (H490) 48
Mrs James Fleming (Drumfin, Ballymena) 6,c (H120) 332
David A Forsythe (Balnamore, Ballymoney) 2,c (H218a,b) 386; (Seacon, Ballymoney) 7,c:w (H757) 394
Mary Forsythe, Miss (Balnamore) w,?m (H762) 368

cognate sent by James Gamble (Culmore Hill, Rasharkin) "Banks of Sweet Lough Rea" c (H158) 295
William Gamble (Park, Armoy) m (H148) 411; w,?m (H160) 292
from Joseph Gardner, 65 (Claudy) w2,?m2 (H221) 490
William Gault (Milltown, Dunseverick) w (H543) 103
Alexander Geddes, Dr (Banff [Scotland]) 1737-1802 a (H714) 513
Mary Getty (Coleraine) w (H37) 485
Dick Gilloway [bus driver] (Coleraine) 2w;m (H153a) 480; w,?m (H623) 109; w,?m (H742) 104; c (H743) 200; w,?m (H782) 473
John Gilmore (Carnrallagh, Aghadowey) w (H165a) 368
Gladys Gilmour, 11 (Gortin, Kilrea), from her daddy 7,c:w (H757) 334
Dan Glass, 70 (Kilmahamogue), sung 1895 w2,?m2 (H193) 487

Katie Glass, Mrs (Ouig, Rathlin Island) 4+,c (H638) 431
Mrs James Glass (Rathlin Island) w,?m (H834) 289
Mrs E Glenn (Mulkeragh South, Limavady) c (H132) 398
George Graham (Coleraine) w,?m (H807) 514; w,?m (H810) 269; c (H817) 169; m (H825) 299; c:m (H826) 309; m (H827) 100; w,?m (H828) 286; from his father m (H829) 91; a(English vs.) (H830) 64; a(English vs.) (H831) 235; a(English vs.) (H832a) 49; a(English vs.) (H834) 289; m (H836) 372; from his mother w[part] (H836) 372
Bob Greer (Ballinaloob, Knockahollet) w,?m (H771) 415
Cathal Buidhe MacGiolla Gunna (Tullyhaw, Co. Cavan) c. 1700 a (H830) 64
William Hugh Graham (Culnady, Upperlands) 2,w (H214) 445
from [William Hugh Graham]'s mother, 75, from her mother (Ballaghbeddy, Ballymoney) 2,w2 (H214) 445

W T H, esq (Coleraine) m (H21b) 508
Pat Hackett (Coleraine) w (H18a) 358; m (H230) 255
Mrs Pat Hackett (Coleraine) learned in childhood (Ballywillan, near Portrush) w,?m (H497) 326
Mrs A[rchie] Hamill (Kiltinney, Macosquin) c (H47) 236
from [Mrs A[rchie] Hamill]'s father, principal (St. Johnston National School, Co. Donegal) w,m (H47) 236
Mrs Hanna (Corkey, Loughguile) w,?m (H753) 501
Nancy Harbison (Ballywillan, Portrush) w,m (H1) 191
from Thomas Harkin, [John Henry Macauley]'s old friend w,?m (H648) 167
James Harper, sexton, Episcopal church (Dungiven) 2,c:w (H187) 162
Mary Harte, Mrs (Benone), daughter of Richard Butler (Derry) w,?m (H813) 468
Lizzie Hassan (Coleraine) learned in Donegal 2,w;2,m (H34) 213; from blacksmith's father w,?m (H43) 394
Patrick D Hassan (Coolnamon, Feeny [D: Co. Derry]) c (H65a) 293
Rose E Hassan, Miss (Ballymonie, Altmover P O, Dungiven) m (H150a) 466
Francis (Francey) Heaney, 81 (Magherabuoy in Benady Glen, near Dungiven) a,w,?mc (H154) 33; a (H537) 239; a,?mc (H538) 364; a (H654) 170; "late" a (H809) 162
William Hegan (Belfast) c (H500) 359; a (H511) 157
Patrick Hegarty (Faughanvale) 2,w (H190) 420
W H [D:Willie Hegarty] (Agivey [dist.]) c:m (H75a) 145; c:w,m (H144) 270; 74 (Ballydevitt, Aghadowey) from his mother m (H156) 315; (Ballydevitt) c (H163) 413; 74 (Agivey) 2,w (H214) 445
Hamilton Hemingway, from an eminent K C (Dublin) w (H29) 53; from his old schoolmaster (Kilmague, near the Curragh) m (H29) 53; ex-constable, R I C w,m (H92) 86; (Burnside, Coleraine) m (H231b) 28
William Hemphill, whistler (Coleraine) m (H168) 399
from Alex Henderson (Kippaway Lake, N. Ontario, Canada) c. 1925 w (H636) 235
Mrs Joseph Henry (Drumlee, Finvoy) from her father, linen weaver 2,c (H797) 327
Sam Henry [WB:]a;c:m (H515) 274; c;a (H645) 7; c,a (H696) 290; [B:] a ["remainder"] (H75b) 99; a (H535a) 39; a (H546) 273; a (H630) 7 from Gaelic transl.; a (H713) 27; a (H775) 171 "written by request"

607

SH (H41) 231 matched text, m; (H112) 288 pieced together

SH c:m (H81) 430 set text to m; (H98a) 64 set words to m (H224a) 390 "10 versions have reached me" c:w (H524) 328 set to this m c (H825) 299, mated tune, words ?c (H199) 39 set text to this m

SH c (H0) 53; (H1) 191; (H12) 31; (H23) 307; (H24b) 217; (H35) 327; (H37) 485; (H39) 123; (H40b) 17; (H42b) 197; (H45) 477; (H51) 129; (H53a) 97; (H53b) 96; (H53c) 97; (H54) 144; (H63) 247; (H72) 374; (H89) 287; (H90) 365; (H125a) 475; (H129) 141; (H135) 414; (H147) 474; (H149) 456; (H153a) 480; (H155) 366; (H159a) 396; (H160) 292; (H161a) 456; (H164) 362; (H166) 328; (H169) 298; (H175) 470; c (H183) 268; (H185) 128; (H201) 265; (H205) 465; (H206) 289; (H209) 465; (H211) 479; (H214) 445; (H215) 393; (H217) 432; (H219) 177; (H221) 490; (H226) 511; (H231a,b) 28; (H232) 318; [D:] (H236) 375; (H535b) 96; (H571) 441; (H602) 107; (H640) 291; (H723) 240; (H742) 104; (H775) 171; (H778) 387; (H796) 163; (H805a,b) 73; (H819) 219; (H820) 257; (H835a) 512

SH c[B:m][D:w,m] (H162) 333

SH c:m (H8) 311; (H11) 110; (H28a) 194; (H65) 479; (H66) 369; (H106) 443; (H126) 510; (H128) 440; (H134) 168; (H139) 42; (H148) 411; (H156) 315; (H168) 399; (H172) 31; (H173) 250; (H179a) 125; (H181) 131; (H182) 464; (H188) 401; (H190) 420; (H198) 481; (H202) 119; (H225) 196; (H493) 237; (H503) 273; (H616) 462; (H715) 166; (H802) 466; (H803) 79; (H809) 162; (H818) 317; (H824) 166; (H827) 100

SH c:w (H38) 29; w (H114) 143

SH ?a (H523) 63

SH ?c (H13) 232; (H18b) 272; (H21a) 508; (H21b) 508; (H24a) 348; (H29) 53; (H31) 411; (H48a) 10; (H57a) 57; (H57b) 228; (H58) 446; (H62) 148; (H68) 276; (H73) 412; (H76) 314; (H77) 418; (H83) 156; (H85) 300; (H88) 18; (H91) 156; (H92) 86; (H93) 72; (H94) 17; (H95) 107; (H100a) 188; (H105) 331; (H108a) 329; (H116b,c) 202; (H124) 509; (H127) 368; (H154) 33; (H176) 146; (H177) 271; (H194) 99; (H200) 470; (H203) 330; (H207) 417; (H208) 258; [D:](H210) 188; (H212) 370; (H213) 334; [D:] (H222) 29; (H230) 255; [D:] (H236) 375; (H238a) 296; (H238b) 296; (H239) 469; (H240) 192; (H466) 79; (H470) 491; (H473) 354; (H486) 121; (H487) 43; (H492) 238; (H497) 326; (H498) 211; (H508) 226; (H509) 168; (H521) 372; (H526) 182; (H528) 246; (H530) 298; (H533) 292; (H539) 71; (H541) 207; (H543) 103; (H549) 81; (H552) 102; (H553) 482; (H555) 463; (H556) 376; (H557) 478; (H558) 106; (H559) 237; (H560) 112; (H561) 458; (H562) 113; (H563) 316; (H564) 344; (H565) 111; (H566) 122; (H572) 159; (H575) 394; (H576) 435; (H577) 439; (H578) 418; (H579) 345; (H580) 357; (H581) 318; (H582) 238; (H583) 314; (H584) 331; (H585) 147; (H586) 80; (H587) 433; (H589) 344; (H590) 486; (H591b) 6; (H593) 388; (H595) 468; (H599) 12; (H606) 208; (H608) 87; (H609) 199; (H613) 396; (H614) 384; (H618) 85; (H619) 373; (H622) 44; (H623) 109; (H624) 349; (H626) 465; (H628) 62; (H635) 455; (H636) 235; (H642) 207; (H650b) 264; (H651) 160; (H656) 187; (H662) 45; (H666) 170; (H669) 179; (H670) 293; (H671) 22; (H675) 24; (H676) 41; (H677) 175; (H678) 89; (H680) 141; (H682) 505; (H685) 460; (H686) 160; (H687) 302; (H691) 119; (H694) 503; (H698) 51; (H707) 227; (H709) 348; (H710) 264; (H718) 460; (H720) 165; (H721) 438; (H722) 343; (H725) 278; (H728) 88; (H729) 446; (H734) 149; (H735) 133; (H736) 489; (H737) 309; (H739) 291; (H741) 50; (H744) 12; (H746) 62; (H748) 263; (H751) 50; (H752) 245; (H753) 501; (H754) 111; (H759) 288; (H761) 228; (H762) 368; (H768) 59; (H771) 415; (H776) 261; (H777) 427; (H779) 54; (H780) 345; (H781) 467; (H782) 473; (H784) 172; (H786) 399; (H787) 215; (H789) 419; (H792) 122; (H793) 267; (H798) 421; (H799) 221; (H807) 514; (H810) 269; (H811) 461; (H813) 468; (H814) 415; (H815) 103; (H821) 220; (H828) 286; (H833) 257; (H835b) 512 [W:] "noted in Pat Hackett's kitchen..1st Dec 1939"; (H836) 372

SH ?c:m (H14a) 356; (H15) 87; (H27c) 105; (H49) 200; (H97) 130; (H99) 89; (H142) 294; (H146) 180; (H170) 299; (H224b) 391; [m:] (H228b) 18; (H235) 203; (H489) 48; (H504) 157; (H537) 239; (H674) 219; (H711) 234; (H770) 485; (H829) 91

SH ?c:w (H18a) 358; (H111) 229; (H113) 434; (H227) 47

SH ?m (H14a) 356; (H49) 200; (H629) 171 "remodelled"

[Sam Henry]'s mother w,?m c (H640) 291

Teresa A Henry, Miss (Ballynure, Draperstown) 11,c:w (H625) 342

David Herbison [pencilled on W] ?a (H81) 430
Mrs Herd (Drumlee, Ballymoney) m (H134) 168
Alexander Horner, sr (Moycraig, Stranocum) alt. m (H238b) 296; (Moycraig Hamilton, Mosside) w,?m (H565) 111
from Alexander [Horner], [Alexander Horner]'s father w2,m2 (H558) 106
Alexander (Alex) Horner (Moycraig Hamilton, Mosside [Co. Antrim]; formerly Carnbore, Liscolman) w (H558) 106; w,m (H560) 112; w (H561) 458; 2,w;2,m (H562) 113
from John Horner, [Alexander Horner]'s father's father, fisherman (Portballintrae) w3,m3 (H558) 106

Maud Houston [Coleraine] c;a "completed" (H80) 386; a (H233) 287

Houston coll. c (H6 = H567) 275; (H7) 290; (H17b) 180; (H20b) 245; (H30a) 390; (H33) 397; (H34) 213; (H40c) 20; (H42a) 148; (H43) 394; (H75b) 199; c:w[st. 1, cho.], m (H80) 386; 3w,m (H112) 288; c:m,w ["about half the ballad"] (H114) 143; (H117) 44; (H136) 125; (H158) 295; (H191) 142; (H233) 287

Houston coll. c:m (H16) 392; (H32) 269; (H41) 231; (H71) 246; (H111) 229; (H113) 434; (H118) 315; (H165b) 260; (H234) 436

Maud Houston's mother w[st. 1, cho.],m (H80) 386; m (H233) 287

Joseph Hughes (Coleraine) w,?m (H653) 211
Eleanor Hull a[transl. from Gaelic] (H819) 219
George Hutchinson (Ringsend, Garvagh) 11,c:w (H625) 342
Randal Hutchinson (the Aird, Giant's Causeway) w,?m (H678) 89

sung by William Irvine, Scottish traveller (Bellshill, Lanarkshire [Scotland]) w2,?m2 (H771) 415
respected resident [D:Archie Irwin], 96 (Coleraine), from his father 2,w (H51) 129

Bobbie Johnston (Aughgash P E S, Glenarm) c:w,m (H70b) 341
Samuel Johnston (Moneysharvin, Maghera) 7,c:w (H757) 334
William Johnston c (H755) 297
[William Johnston]'s grandmother (Carnkirk, near Bushmills) w,?m (H755) 297
Johnstone, c. 1835 a (H632) 203

Alex Kane (Carnkirk Mtn, Bushmills) c (H646) 209
Edward Kane (Lisachrin, Garvagh) c (H481) 484
late James Kane (Gortinure) a (H465) 49
James Kane (Clooney, Magilligan) c. 1895 w,?m (H657) 242
from James (Jim) Kane (Aughill, Magilligan [Co. Derry]) in boyhood m (H623) 109; w2,?m2 (H742) 104; w,?m (H743) 200
Kate Kane, Miss (Dreen, Park, near Mt Sawell) informant (H43) 394; w,m (H149) 456
Roddy Kane (Glack, near Limavady) m (H224a) 390
from Mrs Kealey (Teeavin, Dungiven), [James M'Closkey]'s aunt w2,?m2 (H666) 170
Bridget Kealey [Mrs] (Tirmeil [?Termeil Cottages] Dungiven) m (H14b) 356; c (H652) 175
Frank Kealey [fiddle] (Ballysally, Coleraine) w,?m (H656) 187; 3,c;m (H806) 434; m (H809) 162; (H812) 310
Mrs Frank Kealey (Ballysally, Coleraine [native of Dungiven]) c:w (H537) 239; w,m (H572) 159; c (H643) 159; c (H644) 367; c (H647) 462; c (H649) 171; c (H655) 319; c:w (H658) 175
James Kealey [fiddle] (Ballymoney), [Mrs Frank Kealey]'s son (H537) 239; learned in Dungiven m (H582) 238; c:m (H658) 175; m (H766) 43
Pat Keal[ely], fiddle (Dungiven) w,?m (H651) 160; c (H654) 170; c (H738) 478; c:w (H809) 162
Hugh Kearney (Eden, Portglenone) ?c,?m (H632) 203
according to James Kelly (Glasgow) (H632) 203
James Kelly, crippled traveling tailor c. 1895 w2 (H770) 485
James Kelly (Aneetermore, Clontoe Richardson) w,?m (H709) 348
from Thomas Kelly (Knockaduff) w2 (H677) 175
James Kennedy (formerly Ratheane [Coleraine), from an old man in a quarry w,m (H30a) 390; w,?m (H40c) 20
Maggie Kennedy, Miss (Blagh [D:Cloyfin, Coleraine]) c (H216) 265
William Kennedy, retired (L M S (N C)) railway guard (Coleraine) w,?m (H155) 366
from George Kielty, 80 (the Braid) c. 1905 w2,?m2 (H723) 240
Betty Kirkpatrick, Miss (Magherafelt) c (H237) 189

Mrs R Kirkpatrick (Maddykeel, Bendooragh), [Mrs Morrison]'s mother w (H121) 270
James H. Knox, author's brother (Belfast) c:2,w (H49) 200
Samuel Knox (Boveedy, Co. Derry) a (H49) 200

(James) Jim Lafferty (Doaghs, Magilligan) m (H139) 42; c:w,m (H141) 395; m (H235) 203
from Patrick "Paddy the Poet" Lafferty (Myroe) 1886 w2,?m2 (H206) 289
Patrick Lagan (Coleraine) c:w (H139) 42
from Sam Lamont (Carnabuoy, Cloyfin, Coleraine) w2,?m2 (H694) 503; from his mother (Ballymena) w,?m (H789) 419
John Laughlin, gardener (Cumber-Claudy [m: Cumber Lower], native Ervey) w,?m (H792) 122
from Sam Laverty (Dunaghy, Ballymoney), [William Laverty]'s brother m2 (H116b) 2
William Laverty (Drumafivey, Stranocum) w,m (H100a) 188; m (H116b) 202; ?w,m (H116c) 202
John Leighton (Ballyhome [m: Dunluce, Co. Antrim]) w,?m (H575) 394
Mrs John Leighton (Ballyhome [m: Dunluce, Co. Antrim]) w (H585) 147
Samuel Leighton (Islandmore) w,m (H185) 128
May Logan, Miss (Drumrammer, Limavady) 3,c (H806) 434
Bernard Logue, whistler, tea merchant (Eglinton, Craigbrack) m (H170) 299
Willie Logue (Carnkilly, Eglinton) c:w (H770) 485
Willie Logue, [Willie Logue]'s nephew, mandolin m (H770) 485
Tommy Long (Brockagh) c:w (H171) 40
from John Loughrey, servant (Kilgrain, Cloyfin) w2,?m2 (H205) 465
George Loughrey (Gortnamoyagh, Garvagh) 2,w (H118) 315
from Thomas Houston Loughridge (Ballyveely), [Mrs Hanna]'s father w2,?m2 (H753) 501
John Love (formerly Limavady), from his brother c. 1890 c (H808) 98; c:w (H829) 91
Samuel Lover a (H82) 262
John Lowe, gardener's son at Kenmure Castle (Galloway) [D:]a (H54) 144
R W Lusk (Portstewart) c:w (H714) 513
Patrick Lynagh (Ballinashannagh, Fanad, Co. Donegal) w,?m (H602) 107
W L "a citizen of the world (? Willie Lynn)" (Landhead, Ballymoney) c (H102) 464
'Klondyke' Lyons, traveling showman (Portstewart) w,m (H83) 156
Robert J Lyons (Greenhill, Blackhill, Coleraine [m: Aghadowey]) c (H760) 471
W J Lyons (Ballygan [sic], Macfin, Ballymoney) 1st prize, Folk Song class, Coleraine Musical Festival w,?m (H751) 50
William Lyons, [former] customs collector (Newcastle, later Dhu Varren, Portrush) (learned in Ballyrashane) w,m (H57a) 57; w,m (H57b) 228

H M learned 1860 3,w (H112) 288
John McAfee, fiddle (North Antrim) m (H466) 79
Lizzie McAfee, Miss (Gartcosh, Lanarkshire [Scotland] 2,c:w (H157) 207
Violet M'Afee, Miss (Ballybogey, Dervock) 7,c:w (H757) 334
Ann McAleese, Mrs (Altdorragh, Glenbush, Armoy) c (H133) 461
Dan[iel] M'Aleese (Gortmacrane, Kilrea) 11,c;2,m (H625) 342; c (H719) 63
from Frank M'Allister (Carnagall, Corkey) c. 1905, learned when a woodsman in America w2,?m2 (H619) 373

M'Ambrois [M'Cambridge], emigrant a (H819) 219
Harry M'Anally (Clooney, Magilligan) m (H824) 166
"more ornate" vt. from John Henry Macauley (Ballycastle) in JIFSS Vol. 2 (H14a) 356
John Henry Macauley (Ballycastle [Co. Antrim]) c:w (H14b) 356; c:w,m (H19a) 194; m (H28a) 194; [B:]c:w (H28b) 158; w,m (H31) 411; c:w (H75a) 145; c:a,mc (H101) 275; c (H107) 320; m (H140) 30; m (H142) 294; c (H145) 503; c:w ("principally"),m (H180) 149; m (H188) 401; 2,w (H190) 420; [BLp:]c (H210) 188; ?c (H478) 176; c (H569) 112; a (H588) 220; c (H592) 41; c (H648) 167; c (H660) 273; "late" c:w (H826) 309
from Pat Macauley, tailor (Greenans, Glenshesk), [John Henry Macauley]'s uncle m2 (H188) 401
P C J McAuley (Glenshesk teacher, emigrant to America) m (H19a) 194
James M'Auley (Glenariff) (Gaelic Journal) 2,w (H819) 219
from Francis McBride, sailor, then teacher (Glenshesk) 2,w2 (H190) 420
Jack McBride (Kilmore, Glenariff[e], Co. Antrim) w,m (H0) 53; c (H801) 164
Michael M'Bride, 87 (East Torr) w,m (H559) 237
brothers M'Bride, fiddle (the Smiddy, Ballycastle, Ballycastle) m (H552) 102
from Hammy McCafferty (ex-cowboy, Saskatchewan, Canada) w2,?m2 (H680) 141
from Tom McCafferty, 83 in 1920, ex-cowboy (Stitchfield, Ottawa, Canada) [Hammy McCafferty]'s uncle w3,?m3 (H680) 141
Joseph M'Callis[ter] (Broan, Killykergan, Coleraine) 2,c (H218a,b) 386
from Eileen M'Camphill (Mrs Henry Scully) (Cairney Hill, Dervock) c. 1895 w2,m2 (H577) 439
from David M'Candless (Derrykeighan) on ship off Newfoundland c. 1875 w2 (H561) 458
Hugh McCann, old mason, c. 1869 (Gulladuff) a (H119) 21
James McCaughan, carpenter (native, Lochaber, Giant's Causeway; now Bushmills) c:w (H134) 168
'Monk' McClamont (emigrant to America c. 1860, returned poorer) w (H65b) 186
from James M'Clelland, 80+ (Alla) c. 1865 w2,?m2 (H835a) 512
James M'Closkey (Hass, Dungiven) w,?m (H666) 170
John McCloskey (Dunboe) [o:?]a (H23) 307
John M'Closkey (Tyanee) w,m (H805a,b) 73
Michael McCloskey ("Paul Beg") (Cluntygeragh, Dungiven) [D:]w,?m (H222) 29
Paddy M'Closkey (Carnamenagh, Corkey, Co. Antrim) w,?m (H619) 373
Patrick McCloskey (Sawell) a (H43) 394
Pat M'Closkey (Agivey) w,?m (H740) 56
John M'Cluskey w (H766) 43
Mrs M'Cluskey (Minnegallagher) w (H796) 163
Joe McConaghy (Bushmills) w,?m (H604) 505; w,?m (H691) 119; m (H757) 334
from Sally McConaghy, 80 (Dunaghy, Ballymoney) [Mary Getty]'s grandmother w2 (H37) 485
John McCormick (Greenan, Culfeightrin) a (H28a) 194
from Alex McCorriston "the Bat" (Doaghs, Magilligan) 2,w2;m2 (H153a) 480
James McCurry, blind fiddler (Myroe) a,?mc (H36) 74; a,mc (H68) 276; a,mc (H169) 298
James M'Dade, Lieut. (New York Police Dept., USA) c:w (H767) 370
from Margaret Macaulay M'Dade (Titruan, Glenariff), [Mrs Delargey]'s mother w2,?m2 (H759) 288; [m (H767) 370]

Henry M'Daid (Toronto, Canada) c (H795) 198
Hugh McDaid (Shrove, Greencastle, Co. Donegal) w,m (H194) 99
Lawrence McDermott (Brooklyn, NY, USA), [Joseph F McGinnis]'s cousin m (H223) 83
from Lawrence McDermott's grandfather (W. Bars, Co. Leitrim) c. 1858 2,w (H223) 83
from John McDonnell, fiddle (Kilrea) w2,?m2 (H473) 354
Archie MacEachran (Kilblaan, Southend, Argyleshire [Scotland]) c (H186) 46; m (H195) 234; c (H197a,b) 247
Mrs M'Elhinney (Dungiven) w,?m (H609) 199
Alexander M'Elmoyle (Terrydoo Walker, Limavady) 5,c (H750) 120
Teady M'Erlean (Clady, Portglenone) w,m (H473) 354; c (H766) 43
John McFadden (Portrush) c:w (H140) 30; "and others" 2+c,w (H181) 131
Peggy McGarry, 85 [Ballycastle, Co. Antrim] w[sts 1 2], (H75b) 99; m (H114) 143; w (H165b) 260
Denis M'Gaughey (Aghafad, Ballinamallaght, Donemana) c (H726) 307
James M'Gilligan (Cluntygeeragh, Dungiven) 2,c:w (H187) 162
Joseph F McGinnis (Brooklyn, NY, USA) c (H223) 83; native (West Bars, Co. Leitrim) [m: J F McGinnis] a (H501) 25
Dan M'Glarry, stonecutter (Carey), best man at Dan O'Hara's wedding a (H559) 237
from Feddy M'Gonigal (Benady Glen, Dungiven) c. 1900 w2,?m2 (H752) 245
Andy M'Googan (Castlecatt) w,m (H529) 320
David J McGoogan (Balnamore, Ballymoney) 2,w("a few emendations") (H201) 265
McGowan, shoemaker (Armagh) w,?m (H85) 300
Denis McGreer, fiddle (Cushendun) m (H66) 369
Paddy M'Guckin (Coleraine) c (H745) 47
Mary M'Guigan (Newlands, Glasgow, Scotland) 3,c:w (H806) 434
Mary McHugh, Mrs, 96 (Ballytunn, Rasharkin) 5,c (H150b) 361
from [Mary McHugh]'s friend c. 1845 (Cushendall) 5,c2 (H150b) 361
Hector (Hecky) McIlfatrick, thatcher, (Ballycastle) died c. 1896 (H186) 46
Alexander McIlmoyle (Ballymully, Limavady) w,m (H236) 375
Charles M'Ilreavy, (Coleraine) w,?m (H729) 446
Daniel McIlreavy, carpenter (Portstewart, emigrant to Australia) c. 1826 a (H27c) 105
from Ruth M'Ilreavy (Loughan Hill, Coleraine), [Charles M'Ilreavy]'s grandmother w2,?m2 (H729) 446
W M'Ilreavy (Damhead) 11,c:w (H625) 342
Nellie McIntyre, Miss (Mulkeragh South, Limavady) 2,c (H229a) 360
William John McIntyre, 80+ (Craigtownmore, Portrush) w,m (H226) 511; w,?m (H231a) 28
J McK (Ballyveely, Pharis P.O., Ballymoney) 2,c (H477) 140
George M'Kay (Ballycastle) c (H627) 161
from late Willie M'Kay (Coleraine), learned in Toronto [Canada] w2,?m2 (H828) 286
Mrs M C McKeague (Tullaghans) 2,w;2,m (H212) 193
Mary M'Keever,. Mrs (Balnamore) w,?m (H761) 228
Mary McKendry, Miss (Carrowreagh, Mosside), learned in Glendun w (H66) 369
Daniel M'Kenna (Coolnasillagh, Maghera) 11,c:w (H625) 342

Francis McKenna (Ballymacpeake, Co. Derry) 5,c (H150b) 361
sung by Michael M'Kernan, 90, last native Gaelic singer in Glens (Straid, Knocknacarry) m (H819) 219
Mrs J W M'Kierahan (Home Bank, Portstewart) 4+,c(similar, more ornate m) (H638) 4
M'Kinley, blind fiddler (Swateragh) m (H187) 162
J MacKinnon (Craignagat, Ballycastle) c:w (H198) 481
M'Kittrick, schoolteacher (Magheratimpan, near Ballynahinch, Co. Down) a (H164) 362
Ewen MacLachlen, M A (Aberdeen [Scotland]) a(+transl. from Erse [Scots Gaelic]) (H707) 227
from John MacLarnon (Staffordstown [m: Randalstown, Co. Antrim]) w2,?m2 (H653) 211
D[D:aniel] MacLaughlin, esq ([D:Breezemount] Coleraine) c (H82) 262
James M'Laughlin c (H740) 56
John M'Laughlin (Ballycastle [Co. Antrim]), from his mother 2,w;m (H135) 414; from his mother w,?m (H159a) 396
sung by late John F M'Laughlin (Glenleary) w2,?m2 (H814) 415
man named M'Laughlin (Ballykelly) a (H192) 101
John M'Leese (Croaghbeg, Bushmills) m (H243b) 474
from Pat M'Loone (Coleraine; native of Dungiven) w2,?mc (H635) 455
Hugh McMillan, 79 (Kilbride, Southend, Argyleshire, Scotland), [Archie MacEachran]'s neighbor, from author w,m (H186) 46
Master M'Mullan ("the Big Master") (reared at Castlerock) a (H108b) 169
from James M'Mullan, itinerant farm laborer (Co. Derry) w2,?m2 (H687) 302
Lizzie MacMullan, Miss (the Station, Rathlin Island) 2,w (H77) 418
Robert MacMullan ("North Antrim") (Portballintrae) c (H74) 236
Sarah M'Mullan, Mrs (Articlave Upper) m (H674) 219
Patrick McMullen (Tullybane, Cloughmills) 3,w (H207) 417
James M'Naughten (Cushendall) 2,w (H819) 219
Agnes McNeill, Miss (Letterloan, Macosquin) 6,c (H120) 332
from John McNeill, sailor (The Point, Carnlough, Co. Antrim) w2,m2 (H0) 53
John M'Neill w,?m (H785) 399
John M'Neill (Coleraine), from his mother w,?m (H814) 399
Patrick McNicholl (Cashel, Dungiven) c:w (H97) 130
James McNickle (Portstewart) c:w (H189) 173
John M'Quillan (Turfahun, Bushmills), from a songsheet (Scotland) c. 1885 w,?m (H541) 207
James "Hamish Dall" Mactaggart, A R C O (Dalintober, Campbelltown, Argyleshire, Scotland) c,a (H195) 234
M'Williams, teacher (Loughgiel School) a (H506) 214
Frank Magill (Mayogall, Knockloughrim, Co. Derry) c (H119) 243
Dominick Maguire, principal (St Malachy's Schools, Coleraine) c,?m (H220) 243
Pat Maguire, 60, c. 1905 (Philadelphia [PA, USA]) w (H150a) 466
from Hugh Malone, orange seller, 70 (Ballycastle dist.) w (H142) 294
John Marshall (Carngad Hill, Glasgow), from his mother (Ireland) w (H61b) 459
John J Marshall (Belfast) [D:]w[2 sts] (H153a) 480
James Martin (Shell Hill, Coleraine) 2+,c:w (H181) 131

[Bw:](James) Maxwell [Armagh] [D:]schoolteacher (Dungiven) (H123) 90; a (H187) 162; a (H245) 195
William Meighan (Drumneech, Dungiven) c:?w (H165b) 260
John Millen (Fish Loughan, Coleraine) w,?m (H622) 44; ... Millan, jr w,?m (H624) 349; ... Millen, jr c (H681) 490
George Milliken (Co. Derry; now Clonbullogue, Co. Kildare) c:w,m (H130) 26
T Wray Milnes (Beestown, Leeds, England) a (H3) 286
Allan Mitchell (Coleraine) m (H32) 269; "late" w (H111) 229
Brieny Molloy, 80, fiddle (Meenaharvey, Glencolumbkille, Co. Donegal) m (H503) 273
Edward Montgomery (Bushmills) 11,c:w (H625) 342
Gladys Moon, Miss (Ballydevitt, Aghadowey) c (H204) 388
Lady Moore (Ballygawley Castle, Co. Antrim) m (H224b) 391
Mrs Charles Moore (Ballymacfin, Stranocum) 2,w;2,m (H212) 370; [D:] Annie White (Ballymacfin, Dervock) c (H228a) 19
Daniel Moore c. 1885 w,m (H103) 55
James Moore, A R C O (Bushmills, Co. Antrim) (copyright) (H196) 210; c (H529) 320; c:m (H532) 367
from James Moore, travelling man, old Waterloo soldier, nicknamed "Cuckoo" or "Three Wee Dears," c. 1875 w2,?m2 (H622) 44
John Moore (Cloyfin) w,?m (H687) 302
John Moore (Liscolman) w,?m (H694) 503
William Moore (Tullaghans, Dunloy) c:w (H802) 466
William Moran (Bellarena) "and others" 3+,c:w (H128) 440
Henry Morris (Ministry of Education, Eire) c (H830) 64; c (H831) 235; c (H834) 289
Mrs Morrison (Drumlee, Ballymoney) m (H121) 270; (Moneycannon, Ballymoney) m (H232) 318
Mrs Morrison (Inchmearing, Coleraine) 11,c:w (H625) 342
Margaret Morrow's (86) daughter and granddaughter (at Park, Priestland) m (H106) 443
Sara[D:h] Morrow, Mrs (Drumcrow, Carnalbana, Broughshane, Co. Antrim) c:w,m (H110) 144
Robert Morton (Ballytober, Priestland) c (H44) 178; 3,w (H112) 288
Paul Mulholland, fiddle (Coleraine; formerly Tamneyrankin, Swateragh) [BLp:]w,m (H63) 247
Master Mullan ("The Big Master"), itinerant schoolteacher (reared at Castlerock) c. 1925 a (H108b) 169
Mrs James Mullan (Draperstown) w,?m (H91) 156
John Mullan (Brockagh Mt, Garvagh 2,c (H150a) 466
from Eliza (Black) Mullen (Bovevagh, Dungiven), [Martha Jane Caldwell]'s mother m (H126) 510
William Murdoch (Coleraine; native of Dunminning, Culleybackey) learned c. 1865 w,m (H62) 148
James Murphy (Creagh, Toomebridge) 3+,c:w (H128) 440
J M [D:John Murphy] [Coleraine] former schoolmate of Sam Henry's m (H14a) 356; m (H54) 144; ... jr c:w,m (H64) 161
[D:]Hugh Murray (Managher, Culcrow, Co. Derry), from his mother c. 1865 [B:]w (H73) 412; (Managher, Drumcroon, Coleraine) (B:w;D:w,m) (H162) 333; from his mother 2,w["completion"] (H223) 83; [?] H M 3,w (H112) 288

G B Newe, esq (Cushendall) c:w (H188) 401

Margaret Noble, Miss (Cloughey, Co. Down) c (H650a) 263
Mrs M S Norris (Ballyboley, Greyabbey, Co. Down) a (H601) 174
D Nutt, sen (Feeny, Co. Derry) c (H667) 192

from Dan O'Hara, [Michael M'Bride]'s uncle w2,?m2 (H559) 237
James O'Hara (Killywill) m (H796) 163
John O'Hara (Shuttle Hill, Coleraine) 7,c:w (H757) 334
courtesy Frank O'Kane [Gortinure, Maghera] [Co. Derry], author [James O'Kane]'s son c (H704) 241; c (H712) 221; ?c (H747) 214; c (H756) 60; w (H784) 172; a (H832b) 81
James O'Kane (Gortinure, Maghera) a (H130) 26; "late" a (H465) 49; c;?a (H704) 241; a (H712) 221; a (H716) 218; "late" c;a (H747) 214; a (H756) 60; a (H784) 172; a (H787) 215
John M O'Keenan (Tulnaveagh, Leitrim Nursery, Castledawson) 3+c:w (H128) 440
Andrew Orr, linen lapper (Mullaghmore Beach Green, emigrant to Australia) [B,D:]a (H63) 247; (Derrydoragh; "The Ploughman Poet") a (H67) 365; a (H246) 249
from Robert Orr (Novally, Ballycastle) learned c. 1915 [W:]w2,?m2 (H777) 427

John Parker, 77 w,m (H174) 507; (Mayoghill [Moneydig] Garvagh) 2,w;m (H176) 146; w,?m (H177) 271; 3,w (H207) 417; "late" (Mayoghill, Aghadowey) m (H585) 147
John Parkhill (Coleraine) from his father c:m (H122a) 88
Annie Patterson, Miss, from her mother (Loughan, Coleraine) w,?m (H591b) 6
Mary Patton, Mrs (Ballylough, Bushmills) 2,c;c (H143) 395
Oliver Paul, J. P. (Coleraine) w,?m (H492) 238
Rev Walter Pitchford (Northampton, England) alt. m (H705b) 132
Harry Pollock, blacksmith (Cumber-Claudy) w,?m (H221) 490
Mrs Purcell (Dartries) 11,c:w (H625) 342

M Q [D:Matthew Quinn] 84, fiddle (Bellarena) w,m (H68) 276

from William John Rankin (Knockmult), [John McNeil]'s grandfather w2,?m2 (H785) 399
aided by Gerard Reed (Swateragh) c:m (H715) 166
William Reid (Mayoughill, Garvagh) m (H171) 40; ?w,?m (H227) 47
Joseph Reilly (Moneycannon, Ballymoney) [D:]3,w (H72) 374; 2,w (H176) 146; c:w (H235) 203
from Lizzie Reynolds, Miss (Carnkirn, Armoy) w2,?m2 (H160) 292
from Alex Riddles (Cashel, Ringsend, Co. Derry) 3,w2 (H72) 374
J Ross, Miss (New Town, Limavady) c:m (H3) 286
late Joseph Russell (Priestland) [W:]"a version" w,?m (H777) 427
William Russell (Bushmills) w,m (H74) 236
Mrs Rutherford (the Rectory, Carrickfergus) c (H763) 458

Mrs Scally (Town Head, Ballycastle) learned c. 1865 w (H113) 434
Mrs Henry Scully: see Eileen M'Camphill
late William Shaw, 80, bathing attendant (Herring Pond, Portstewart) w (H161a) 456
Matilda Shirley (R[h]ee, Agivey, Co. Derry), [Sarah Crawford]'s mother w,m (H138) 256

Original sources Si - Y

Mrs Simpson (Dervock) 4+,c (H638) 431
from late David Simpson (Edinburgh [Scotland]) w,m (H204) 388
David Simpson (the Old Manse, Ballygrainey, Co. Down) m (H818) 317
from [David Simpson]'s mother (Ballydevitt) m2 (H204) 388
James Sloan (Topland, Ballyrock) c. 1770 a (H12) 31
William Sloan (Ballyrock) 2,w;m (H90) 365; from his grandfather c. 1865 w,m (H93) 72
William Sloan (Boghill) w[st 1] (H75a) 145
William Sloan (Dundooan [Coleraine]; formerly Bushmills) m (H12) 31; m (H27c) 105
D E M Smith, esq (Belfast) c:m (H535a) 39; m (H586) 80
Frank Smith (Stitchville, near Ottawa, Canada) w,?m (H816) 92
Joseph Smith (Knockaduff, Drumcroon) w (H677) 175
Tom Smith, melodeon, from his father [Joseph Smith] m (H677) 175
John (Jock) Smylie ([Leggyfat] Limavallaghan, Clough, Co. Antrim) c,?m (H612) 242; w,?m (H723) 240; w,m (H777) 427; w,?m (H778) 387; w,m (H779) 54; w,m (H780) 345; m (H781) 467
Martin Smylie, itinerant (Carnside, Giant's Causeway) w,m (H44) 178
from Private Sam Smyrrel, companion-in-arms (Yorkshire Light Infantry, stationed in Bombay, India) w,?m (H821) 220
Henry Smyth (Mulkeragh South, Limavady) c (H192) 101
James Smyth, 80 ([Buckie Knowe] Knockmult, Macosquin) c (H717) 108; w,?m (H754) 111
from Margaret Smyth (Ballyhargin, Dungiven), [Mrs E Glenn]'s mother w,?m (H132) 398
Robert Smyth, 80, sung c. 1875, from author w,?m (H192) 101
James Spence (Portstewart) 6,c (H120) 332
Johnny Spence (Castleroe) c. 1865 a (H614) 384
James Steele (Carrichue) 11,c:w (H625) 342
late James Stewart, 80 w,?m (H776) 261
James Stewart, M P S I (Ballymoney) w,?m (H642) 207
from John Stewart, c. 1875 (Kilmandel, Culcrum, Co. Antrim) 3,w2 (H207) 417
Thomas H Stewart, fiddle (Mayoghill, Garvagh) c (H178) 233
William Stewart (Coleraine) c:w,m (H20a) 216
James Stirling (Gorticloughan, Ballyrashane) w,m (H175) 470
Mrs Strawbridge (Coleraine; native of Mallabuie, near Claudy) w,?m (H835a) 512
from Jane Steele, Mrs (Garvagh), [Mary M'Keever]'s mother, c. 1885 w2,?m2 (H761) 228
late James Stewart, 80 (Ballywatt) w,?m (H776) 261
Robert Stuart signed clipping, -m, from *Northern Constitution* 17 May 1924 ?a (H731) 22

John Sweeney (Benarees [D:Magilligan]) w,m (H23) 307
arr. E K Sweeting, sung at Coleraine Musical Festival c(D:"English version") (H161b) 456

Jackson Taggart (Carnalridge, Portrush) c:[D:w] (H22a) 232
Nancy Tassie, Mrs (Arboe) c:w (H505) 157
John Taylor (Coleraine) m (H706) 180
R R Terry, Sir (England) mc (H59) 76

Kid Thomas (Eastern Penitentiary, Philadelphia [PA, USA]) a (H746) 62
Alexander Thompson (native of Alla, near Cumber-Claudy; now Islandflackey, Portrush) w,m (H124) 509
late Alexander Thompson (Park dist., near Dungiven) w (H219) 177; (Alla, near Park) 2,c (H229) 360; [D:] [Co. Derry] w (H240) 192
Alexander Thompson (Bushmills) w,m (H521) 372; (Ballyhunsley, near Bushmills) w,?m (H553) 482; w,?m (H557) 478; w,m (H564) 344
Frank Thompson (Priestland, Bushmills) ?c (H699) 383; learned in Ballywatt c (H700) 277
John Thompson (Portstewart) 2+,c:w (H148) 41; m (H181) 131; w,m (H203) 330; w,m (H205) 465; w,?m (H206) 289; 3,w (H213) 334
Robert Thompson (Coleraine) a (H87a) 181
Thomas Thompson (Cappaghbeg, Portstewart) w,m (H215) 393
from [Thomas Thompson]'s mother (Fox Dartries, Articlave) w2,m2 (H215) 393
Tilda Thorpe (Altibrian, Articlave) c (H100b) 193
Edward Toal (Glascar, near Rathfriland) w (H593) 388
Mr Tobin, principal (Moortown P E S, Drumaney, Coagh) c (H708) 174
Anne Toner, Mrs (Straw, Draperstown) from her mother, born 1818, from her mother w,?m (H811) 461
Nancy Tracey [?sp.] (Greencastle, Co. Tyrone) in Gaelic w,?m (H830) 64
Anne Tracy (Greencastle, Co. Tyrone) in Gaelic w,?m (H831) 235
John Troland [Rev] (Norwich, CT, USA) c (H125b) 476; heard in Ireland c:w (H142) 294
W J Tweed, sung over telephone (Bushmills) 3,m (H8) 311

R O W [D:Corndale, Limavady] [B:]c:w,m (H157) 207
T W, old sailor w,?m (H53a) 97; w,m (H53b) 96; w,m (H53c) 97
Alexander Wallace (Moneycannon, Ballymoney), from his brother William w,m (H166) 328
from William "Dancing" Wallace (Slaveney), [Alexander Wallace]'s grandfather w3,m3 (H166) 328
Bernard Walls (Annagh, Desertmartin) 5,c (H750) 120
James Warnock (Knockantern, Coleraine) mc (H536) 209
Mrs S Warnock (Ballymoney) 2,w (H118) 315
daughter of late Daniel Watton (Ballyhome, Ballywillan) w,m (H35) 7
Annie White (Mrs Charles Moore) (Ballymacfin, Dervock) [D:]c (H228a) 19
Annie White, Miss (Drumafivey, Stranocum) "Murlough Shore" corroborated 2,w (H27a) 371; w,m (H105) 331; 2,c;?m (H143) 395
Dan White a (H648) 167
James Wilkinson, fiddle (Milltown, Dunseverick) m (H543) 103
John Wilkinson, employee Old Bushmills Distillery (native Liscolman) w,m (H584) 331
Lily Williamson, Miss (Ballytunn, Rasharkin) "and others" 2+,w (H148) 411
Annie Wilson (Moneycannon, Ballymoney) from her mother w,m (H127) 368
Annie Wilson, Miss (Beagh, Maghera) c:w (H156) 315
[Annie Wilson]'s grandfather, 85, from his mother w,w2 (H156) 315
from (Joseph) Joe Wilson (Roddenfoot, Ballymoney), [George Graham]'s grandfather w2,?m2 (H807) 514; w2,?m2 (H810) 269; "The Jessie Walker" m (H826) 309; m2 (H827) 100

from [Joe Wilson]'s grandfather (Ballymoney) w3,?m3 (H807) 514; w3,?m3 (H810) 269
Mary Ann Wilson, Mrs, old age pensioner (Loguestown), learned when little girl (Bovevagh, Limavady, Co. Derry) m (H162) 333; c (H167) 369
from [Mary Ann Wilson]'s mother (?Bovevagh, Dungiven) w,?m (H167) 369

from James Young (Drum, Dungiven) c. 1885 w2,m2 (H100a) 188
from Mary Ann Young (Liscolman) c. 1885 w2,?m2 (H762) 368
Thomas Young (Killywill) a (H796) 163

Collector/contributor not named

(H25b) 261; (H26a = H246) 249; (H27b) 105; (H36) 74; (H52a) 244; (H69) 76; (H60a) 400; (H61b) 459; (H65b) 186; (H122b) 88; (H123) 90; (H152) 266; (H193) 487; (H243b) 474; (H245) 195; (H246) 249; (H465) 49; (H490) 48; (H506) 214; (H507) 213; (H511) 157; (H512) 225; (H525) 483; (H536) 209; (H538) 364; (H542) 217; (H545) 225; (H550) 176; (H568) 226; (H588) 220; (H601) 174; (H604) 505; (H629) 171; (H630) 7; (H679) 255; (H716) 218; (H764) 32; (H804) 262; (H832a) 49; (H832b) 81

Source of music not named

(H18a) 358; (H22a) 232; (H25b) 261; (H26b) 250; (H27a) 371; (H37) 485; (H39) 123; (H45) 477; (H72) 374; (H73) 412; (H77) 418; (H82) 262; (H87a) 181; (H96a) 230; (H119) 21; (H120) 332; (H130) 26; (H131) 84; (H137) 431; (H155) 366; (H165a) 260; (H183) 268; (H208) 258; (H238a) 296; (H240) 192; (H470) 491; (H498) 211; (H507) 213; (H511) 157; (H512) 225; (H533) 292; (H538) 364; (H539) 97; (H542) 217; (H545) 225; (H588) 220; (H589) 344; (H591a) 6; (H592) 41; (H593) 388; (H595) 468; (H596) 6; (H598) 61; (H599) 12; (H606) 208; (H626) 465; (H627) 161; (H628) 62; (H630) 7; (H650a) 263; (H654) 170; (H662) 45; (H685) 460; (H686) 160; (H701) 501; (H707) 227; (H712) 221; (H716) 218; (H728) 88; (H744) 12; (H746) 62; (H747) 214; (H775) 171; (H784) 172; (H787) 215; (H795) 198; (H832a) 49

Source of lyrics not named

(H15) 87; (H16) 392; (H21a) 508; (H21b) 508; (H25b) 261; (H27c) 105; (H28a) 194; (H41) 231; (H98a) 64; (H116b) 202; (H122a) 88; (H170) 299; (H202) 119; (H228b) 18; (H466) 79; (H489) 48; (H503) 273; (H504) 157; (H506) 214; (H511) 157; (H512) 225; (H525) 483; (H536) 209; (H629) 171; (H674) 219; (H824) 166

No source named

(H2) 215; (H4) 190; (H9) 186; (H17a) 61; (H19b) 196; (H22b) 361; (H26a) 502; (H40a) 12; (H48b) 10; (H48c) 10; (H48d) 11; (H48e) 11; (H48f) 11; (H48g) 11; (H48h) 11; (H50) 139; (H53d) 96; (H60b) 401; (H61a) 459; (H69) 201; (H70a) 340; (H79) 428; (H84 = H688) 364; (H86) 443; (H87b) 182; (H115a) 355; (H115b) 241; (H153b) 481; (H159b) 397; (H161c) 32; (H179b) 126; (H199) 39; (H229b) 360; (H242) 483; (H243a) 473; (H244) 295; (H464) 167; (H467) 428; (H469) 144; (H471) 317; (H472) 258; (H475) 455; (H476) 84; (H479) 347; (H480a) 5; (H482) 391; (H483) 427; (H484) 177; (H485) 308; (H488) 501; (H491) 225; (H494) 127; (H495) 227; (H496) 96; (H499) 387; (H502) 98; (H510) 17; (H513)

611

Aus - A Bal *Sam Henry's Songs of the People*

(No source named)
75; (H514) 297; (H516) 35; (H517) 7; (H518) 301; (H519) 389; (H520) 259; (H522) 355; (H527) 20; (H531) 506; (H534) 454; (H540) 468; (H544) 165; (H547) 195; (H548) 341; (H570) 310; (H573) 212; (H574) 80; (H594) 430; (H597) 476; (H600) 140; (H603) 239;

(H605) 340; (H610) 208; (H611) 397; (H615) 343; (H620) 476; (H633) 147; (H637) 385; (H639) 59; (H641) 383; (H659) 504; (H663) 72; (H664) 41; (H665) 454; (H668) 444; (H673) 429; (H684) 231; (H690) 416; (H692) 392; (H693) 313; (H697) 278; (H702) 504; (H703) 210; (H724) 82; (H731) 22; (H749) 189; (H758)

23; (H769) 65; (H772) 23; (H773) 229; (H774) 150; (H783) 34; (H786) 139; (H791) 218; (H800) 164; (H822) 239; (H823) 59

Never printed in the *Northern Constitution*. Sole copy in Bt on same page as H535. (H535b) 96

Geographical index of sources

A = Co. Antrim, L = Co. Londonderry; c = city, g = glen, h = hill, i = island, p = parish, t = town, tl = townland, v = village.

Australia a (H27c) 105; w,?m (H566) 122

Canada:
  Lachute Mills, Quebec ?6,c (H750) 120
  North Ontario: Kippaway Lake w (H636) 235
  Ontario: Blenheim ?6,c (H750) 120
  Ottawa: Stitchfield w (H680) 141
  ": Stitchville, near, w,?m (H816) 92
  Saskatchewan w (H680) 141
  Toronto c (H795) 198; w2,?m2 (H828) 286

England mc (H59) 76
  Beeston, Leeds a (H3) 286
  Northampton m (H705b) 132
  Sheffield a (H628) 62
  Upper Thames valley w[remainder] (H698) 51
  Yorkshire 2,w (H51) 129; a (H628) 62
  " Light Infantry w2,?m2 (H821) 220

India:
  Bombay w2,?m2 (H798) 421; w2,?m2 (H821) 220

New Zealand ?6,c (H750) 120

Scotland w,?m (H541) 207
  Aberdeen a (H707) 227
  Aberdeenshire w,?m (H568) 226
  Argyleshire: Kilblaan, Southend [Kintyre] w (H186) 46; m (H195) 234; c (H197a) 248; 2,c (H197b) 248; [K..., S..., Campbelltown] [WB:] m (H515) 274
  ": Kilbride, Southend w,m (H186) 46
  Banff a (H714) 513
  Campbelltown: Dalintober c (H195) 234
  Edinburgh c (H204) 388
  Galloway [D:]a (H54) 144
  Ganavan Sands, Oban w,?m (H566) 122
  Glasgow, informant in, m (H632) 203
  ": Carngad Hill w (H61b) 459
  ": Newlands 3,c:w (H806) 434
  Greenock c (H755) 297
  Jura, Island of m (H713) 27
  Lanarkshire: Bellshill w2,?m2 (H771) 415
  ": Gartcosh (2)c:w (H157) 207
  Levenside, Barrhead c (H657) 242
  Uig, Loch Snizort, Isle of Skye m (H535a) 39

U S A a,mc (H78) 484
  New York: Brooklyn c;m (H223) 83; c:w,m (H501) 25
  ": Police Dept c:w (H767) 370
  Connecticut: Norwich c (H125b) 476; c:w (H142) 294
  Pennsylvania: Philadelphia w.(H150a) 466; w,?m (H634) 472
  ": Eastern Penitentiary a (H746) 62

Ireland w2 (H61b) 459; c:w (H142) 294
Eire [Republic of Ireland] c (H830) 64; c (H831) 235; [c (H834) 289]

Dublin w2 (H29) 53; c (H184 = H689) 469; m (H523) 63; w (H552) 102

Co. Cavan:
  Tullyhaw a (H830) 64

Co. Clare:
  Kilrush a (H507) 213
  Knockera, Killimer a (H507) 213

Co. Cork w,?m (H634) 472

Co. Donegal 2,w;2,m (H34) 213; w,m (H47) 236
  Ballnashannagh, Fanad w,?m (H602) 107
  Meenaharvey, Glencolumbkille m (H503) 273
  Ramelton dist. m (H196) 210
  Raphoe w (H208) 258
  Shrove, Greencastle w,m (H194) 99

Co. Galway:
  Ballinasloe m2 (H179a,b) 125, 126

Co. Kildare:
  Allen, Bog of, w (H92) 86 [? also Co. Meath]
  Clonbullogue c:w,m (H130) 26
  Kilmague: near the Curragh m (H29) 53

Co. Leitrim:
  West Bars 2,w (H223) 83; a (H501) 25

Co. Limerick:
  Adare c;w,m (H56) 354

Northern Ireland:

Co. Antrim:
  t Antrim c:m (H187) 162
  North Antrim m (H466) 79

  t Ballymena 8,w (H179a) 125; c (H695) 442; c (H727) 193; c (H730) 190; c (H788) 300; w2,?m2 (H789) 419; c (H794) 385; 2,c (H797) 327; m (H802) 466; m (H804) 262
  ": Braid river w2,?m2 (H723) 240
  t Carrickfergus c (H763) 458
  v Crumlin c (H621) 191
  g Glenshesk a (H19a) 194; 2,w2 (H190) 420
  i Rathlin Island 2,w (H77) 418; 4+,c (H638) 431; w,?m (H834) 289

A Ardclinis parish:
  Craignagat [s: Ballycastle] c:w (H198) 481 [m: not near Ballycastle]
  ?v Carnlough: The Point [m: most likely Straidkilly Point] w2,m2 (H0) 53
  Garronpoint w (H590) 486
  Glenariffe 8,w (H819) 219; [Glenariff] 2,w (H819) 219 [see also Layde p.]

  ": Titruan [o.s. Titruhan] w2,?m2 (H759) 288
  v ": Waterfoot w,?m (H739) 291; w,?m (H759) 288; m (H767) 370

A Armoy parish:
  v? Park m (H148) 411

A Ballintoy parish:
  Croaghbeg [Croagh Beg] [s: Bushmills] m (H243b) 474
  Croaghmore [Croagh More] dist. m (H590) 486
  Kilmahamogue w2,?m2 (H193) 487
  Prolusk, near Straid [Layde p.] w,?m (H587) 433; w (H589) 344

A,L Ballymoney parish:
  t Ballymoney m (H537) 239; c (H554) 400; m (H582) 238; w,?m (H642) 207; c:m (H658) 175; m (H766) 43; w3,?m3 (H807) 514; w3,?m3 (H810) 269; m3 (H829) 91
  " dist. c[incomplete] (H215) 393
  v ": Balnamore 2,w (H201) 265; 2,c (H218a,b) 386; w,?m (H761) 228; w,?m (H762) 368
  ": Pigtail Hill c:w (H711) 234; (Pig Tail ...) w[slight variation] (H825) 299
  tls Ballygan, Macfin [Macfinn] w (H751) 50
  tl Bendooragh, Maddykeel [Finvoy p.] w (H121) 270 [m: townlands 3 mi. apart]
  Burnquarter w,?m (H737) 309
  tl Drumreagh 2,w (H118) 315
  Dunaghy w2 (H37) 485; m2 (H116b) 2
  tl Garry Bog m2 (H711) 234; w2,?m2 (H735) 133
  Garryduff c (H103) 55; c (H104) 457; c (H109) 357; c (H121) 270
  Landhead m (H102) 464
  Leck w,?m (H735) 133; w,?m (H736) 489; w[sts. 2,5] (H739) 291
  Newhill w (H740) 56
  Polintamney c:w (H106) 443; 6,c (H120) 332
  Roddenfoot w2,?m2 (H807) 514; w2,?m2 (H810) 269; m (H826) 309; m2 (H827) 100
  Seacon 7,c:w (H757) 334
  Stranocum w (H555) 463 [see also Billy p.]
  " dist. c;?m (H46) 438
  ? ": Lifford c:w (H116a) 201
  ": Moycraig m (H238b) 296
  A,L: Heagles 3,c (H474) 488

A,L Ballyrashane parish: w,m (H57a,b) 57
  ? Ballyhome [s: Ballywillan] [sic] w,m (H35) 327 [see also Dunluce]
  Ballyrock 2,w;m (H90) 365; w,m (H93) 72
  ": Topland [m: presumably a local name] a (H12) 31
  Ballywatt c (H700) 277; w,?m (H776) 261

612

Geographical index A Bal - A Ram

A,L Ballywillin parish:
tl Ballywillan [Ballywillin] [s: Portrush]
  w,m (H1) 191; w,?m (H497) 326
" dist. m (H81) 430
  Portrush c:w (H140) 30; 8,w (H179a)
  125; 2+,c:w (H181) 131
t ": Crocnamac c:w (H168) 399
 ": Dhu Varren w,m (H57a,b) 57
 ": Quay Head w,?m (H815) 103

A Billy parish:
  Ballymacfin [s: Stranocum] 2,w (H212)
  370; [D: Dervock] c (H228a) 19 [see
  also Ballymoney p.]
  Ballylough [s: Bushmills] 2,c:?2,m
  (H143) 395 [see also Dunluce p.]
  Carnbore [s: Liscolman] w,m (H558) 106
  [see also Billy p.]
  Carnkirk, near Bushmills w,?m (H755)
  297 [see also Dunluce p.]
" Mt [s: Bushmills] c (H646) 209 [see
  also Dunluce p.]
  Castlecatt [Castlecat] w,m (H529) 320
  Dunseverick [s: Bushmills] 7,c:w
  (H757) 334 [see also Dunluce p.]
" ": Milltown [m: group of houses] w;m
  (H543) 103
tl Giant's Causeway: Aird w,?m (H678) 89
 ": Carnside w,m (H44) 178
 ": Lochaber [m: local name] c:w
  (H134) 168
  Liscolman m,w (H584) 331; w,?m (H694)
  503; w2,?m2 (H762) 368
" mill w2,?m2 (H691) 119
  Lishnagunogue [Lisnagogue] dist. w,?m
  (H549) 81
tl Moycraig Hamilton, Mosside [Moss-
  side] w,m (H558); w,m (H560) 112; w
  (H561) 460; 2,w;2,m (H562) 113;
  w,?m (H565) 111 [see also Drumtul-
  lagh g.]
  Turfahun [s: Bushmills] w,m (H486)
  121; w,m (H487) 43; w,?m (H541)
  207; w,m (H571) 441; w,m (H577)
  439 [see also Dunluce p.]

A Carncastle parish:
  Ballygawley Castle m (H224b) 391

A Connor parish:
  Whaupstown [Whappstown] [s: Glen-
  wherry] m2 (H802) 466 [? or Glenwhirry p.]

A Craigs parish:
?v,tl Dunminning, Culleybackey w,m
  (H62) 148 [? or Rasharkin p.]

A Culfeightrim parish:
  Ballyvoy w,m (H556) 376
 ": Drumnakeel [s: Ballycastle] w,m
  (H147) 474; m (H198) 481; w,m
  (H217) 432
 ": Smiddy, the m (H552) 102
  Carey [m: ? Carey Mill (tl) or Carey
  River, Ballyvoy] a (H559) 237
  Cushendun m (H66) 369
  East Torr w,?m (H559) 237
? Glendun w (H66) 369
  Greenan a (H28a) 194; (Greenans) [s:
  Glensheskl m (H188) 401

A Derrykeighan parish:
tl Derrykeighan w2 (H561) 458
? Cairney Hill [o.s. Carney Hill] [s:
  Dervock] c (H638) 431 [see also
  Dunluce p.]

A Doagh Grange:
  Ballyhamage [s: Doagh] [m: Kilbride
  p.] w,m (H638) 431 [? see also Kilbride p.]
" dist. c (H733) 342

A [Drummaul parish]

Drumtullagh, Grange of:
  Drumtullagh dist. [s: Mosside] w
  (H662) 45
  Carnkirn [s: Armoy] w2,?m2 (H160) 292
tl Carrowreagh [s: Mosside] w (H66) 369
  (see also Billy, Finvoy p.)

A Dunaghy parish:
  Tullybane [Tullaghbane], Cloughmills
  3,w (H207) 417
tl Limavallaghan, Clough c,?m (H612)
  242; [Leggyfat (local name), ...] w
  (H723) 240; w,m (H777) 427; w,m
  (H778) 387; w,m (H779) 54; w,m
  (H780) 345; w,m (H781) 467 [see
  also Skerry p.]

A Duneane parish:
  Staffordstown, Randalstown w2,?m2
  (H653) 211
  Aughacarnaghan [Aghacarnaghan], Toome-
  bridge 11,c:w (H625) 342

A Dunluce parish:
  Ballybogey, Dervock 7,c:w (H757) 334
  [see also Derrykeighan p.]
v Bushmills 3,m (H8) 311; m (H12) 31;
  w,m (H74) 236; m (H122b) 88; c:w
  (H134) 168; c (H196) 210; m (H489)
  48; w,m (H521) 372; c (H529) 320;
  [2,c] (H532) 367; w,?m (H553) 482;
  w,?m (H557) 478; [w,m (H564) 344];
  w (H579) 345; w,?m (H580) 357; w,m
  (H584) 331; w (H586) 80; w (H589)
  344; w,?m (H604) 505; 11,c:w;2,m
  (H625) 342; c (H634) 472; w,m
  (H636) 235; w,?m (H680) 141; w,?m
  (H691) 119; m (H711) 234; w,m
  (H718) 463; w,m (H721) 438; w,?m
  (H722) 343; w (H728) 88; w,?m
  (H741) 50; m (H757) 334; c (H816)
  92
" dist.: w (H470) 491 [see also Billy
  p.]
tl Ballyhome [s: Cloyfin] w,?m (H575)
  394; [..., Coleraine] w (H585) 147
  [see also Ballyrashane, Coleraine p.]
" dist. w,m (H94) 17
  Ballyhunsley, near Bushmills w,m
  (H521) 372; w (H553) 482; w,?m
  (H557) 478; w,m (H564) 344
  Portballintrae c (H74) 236; w3,?m3
  (H558) 106
  Priestland [s: Bushmills] ?c (H699)
  383; c (H700) 277
 ": Ballytober c (H44) 178; 3,w (H112)
  288
 ": Park, at, m (H160) 443

A Finvoy parish:
  Ballaghbeddy [s: Ballymoney] 2,w3
  (H214) 445; w (H232) 318
  Carrowreagh [s: Ballymoney] 2,c
  (H150a) 466 [see also Drumtullagh
  p.]
tl Drumlee 6,c (H120) 332; m (H121) 270;
  [..., Ballymoney] m (H134) 168; 2,c
  (H797) 327
v Dunloy w,?m (H509) 168; w (H618) 85;
  w (H685) 460; w (H686) 160
" dist. w (H533) 292; w (H626) 465
 ": Ballymacaldrick [Ballymacaldrack]
  a (H493) 237; a (H498) 211; a
  (H508) 226; a (H512) 225; c[chez]
  (H530) 298; [w (H545) 225]; c,w
  (H631) 294; w[transl.] (H830) 64;
  w[transl.] (H832a) 49; w[transl.]
  (H834) 289
" dist. w,?m (H563) 316
  Tullaghans 2,w;2,m (H212) 370; [...,
  Dunloy] c:w (H802) 466
tl Maddykeel, Bendooragh [Ballymoney p.]
  ?w (H121) 270 [m: townlands, 3
  miles apart]
  Moneycannon [Moneycanon] [s: Bally-
  money] [D:]3,w (H72) 374; w,m (H127)
  368; w,m (H166) 328; 2,w (H176)

146; m (H232) 318; c:w (H235)
203; 2,c (H468) 441
  Ballytunn [Ballytun] [s: Rasharkin]
  2+,w (H148) 411; 5,c (H150b) 361
  Vow [s: Bendooragh] 6,c (H120) 332
" dist. w (H238a,b) 296

A Glenwhirry parish:
  Whaupstown [m: Whappstown, Connor
  p.], Glenwherry [sic] m2 (H802) 466
  [? or Connor p.]

A Kilbride parish:
  Ballyhamage [s: Doagh] w,m (H638) 431
  [? see Doagh Grange]

A Killagan parish:
  Kilmandel, Culcrum 3,w2 (H207) 417
  Ballinaloob [Ballynaloob], Knockahollet [Loughguile p.] w,?m (H771)
  415 [? see Loughguile p.]

A Kilraghts parish:
  Kilmoyangie [Kilmoangey] [s: Kilraughts, Ballymoney] c (H765) 312

A Kirkinriola parish:
  Drumfin [s: Ballymena] 6,c (H120) 332

A Layde parish:
  Cushendall 5,c2 (H150b) 361; c:w
  (H188) 401; (2)w (H819) 219
  Kilmore [s: Glenariffe] w,m (H0) 53;
  c (H801) 164
  Straid, Knocknacarry [both Layde p.]
  m (H819) 219

A Loughguile parish:
  Altdorragh [Aldoragh], Glenbush [s:
  Armoy] c (H133) 461
  Ballyportery w,m (H164) 362
?tl Ballyveely w2,?m2 (H753) 501 [? or
  Ramoan p.]
tl ": Pharis 2,c (H477) 140
tl Corkey w,?m (H753) 501
 ": Carnagall w2,?m2 (H619) 373
tl ": Carnamenagh w,?m (H619) 373
  Drumafivey [Drumnafivey] [s: Strano-
  cum] 2,w (H27a) 371; w,m (H100a)
  188; w,m (H105) 331; 2,c;?2,m
  (H143) 395 [see also Ballymoney p.]
  Knockahollett; Ballinaloob [Ballyna-
  loob; Killagan p.] w,?m (H771) 415
  [? see Killagan p.]
  Loughgiel [sic] School a (H506) 214
  Moycraig [s: Stranocum] m (H238b) 296
  [see also Ballymoney p.]

A Newtown Crommelin parish:
v Newtowncrommelin 8,w (H179a) 125

A Rasharkin parish:
  Anticur m (H493) 237
  Carclinty [Carclunty] [s: Culley-
  backey] 2,w (H214) 445 [? see
  Craigs p.]
? Dunminning [s: Culleybackey] w,m
  (H62) 148 [? or Craigs p.]
  Slaveney [m: probably Slievenaghy]
  w3,m3 (H166) 328
  Culmore Hill c["cognate"] (H158) 295

A Ramoan parish:
t Ballycastle 2,c:w,m [more ornate]
  (H14a) 356; c:w (H14b) 356; c;w,m
  (H19a) 194; m (H28a) 194; [B:lc:w;
  [D,W:]m (H28b) 158; w,m (H31) 411;
  c:w (H75a) 145; w[sts. 1,2],m
  (H75b) 199; c;a,mc (H101) 275; c
  (H107) 320; m (H114) 143; (2)w;m
  (H135) 414; m (H140) 30; m (H142)
  294; c (H145) 503; w,?m (H159a)
  396; m (H165b) 260; 8,w (H179a)
  125; [BLp:] c:w[principally],m
  (H180) 149; a (H186) 46; m (H188)
  401; 2,w (H190) 420; [BLp:]c (H210)
  188; 3,c (H474) 488; c (H478) 176;

613

A Ram - L Col *Sam Henry's Songs of the People*

(*Ramoan parish*)
   a (H550) 176; c (H569) 112; a (H588) 220; [c (H592) 41]; w (H595) 468; c (H596) 6; a (H606) 208; c (H627) 161; c (H648) 167; c (H660) 273; c;?a (H661) 259; [mc (H696) 290]; c (H732) 57; c:w (H826) 309
" dist. m2 (H142) 294; w,?m (H152) 266; c (H467) 428
": Moyarget [s: Ballycastle] c:w (H524) 328
" dist. w,?m (H193) 487
t Town Head w (H113) 434
? Ballyveely w2,?m2 (H753) 501 [? or Loughguile p.]

A Skerry parish:
v Islandstown, Clough [v, Dunaghy p.] m (H780) 345 [see also Dunaghy p.]
? Skerry glen w,?m (H241) 346

A Tickmacreevan parish:
tls Drumcrow, Carnalbana, Broughshane c (H110) 144
v,g Glenarm c (H70b) 341

Co. Armagh w,?m (H732) 57; w,?m (H744) 12
c Armagh w,?m (H85) 300; [a (H123) 90]; a (H187) 162; a (H245) 195
   Carrickblacker a (H98a) 64

c *Belfast* c;2,w (H49) 200; [D:]w (H131) 84; w (H146) 180; [D:]w[2 sts.] (H153a) 480; c:w (H224a,b) 390, 391; c (H500) 359; c:m (H535a) 39; m (H586) 80; c (H607) 250; m (H705a) 132; c:w (H705a,b) 132

Co. Derry [Londonderry] c:w,m (H130) 26; w3 (H635) 455; w2,?m2 (H687) 302; ?6,c (H750) 120

c Derry [Londonderry] (H813) 468

L Dungiven, Maghera p.: Carntogher Mt. 2,w (H77) 418
L,T district between Claudy and Strabane m (H55) 479
L,T slopes of Mt. Sawell w,?m (H528) 246

L Aghadowey parish:
tl Aghadowey w,m (H24a) 348; c:m,w (H67) 365; c:m (H171) 40; a (H246) 249; w,?m (H820) 257
. Ballydevitt m (H156) 315; c (H163) 413; c (H204) 388
? tl Ballygawley [Ballygalley] c;w (H616) 462 [? see Carncastle p.]
tls Broan [o.s. Brone], Killykergan 2,c (H218a,b) 386
tl Carnrallagh w (H165a) 260
   Cullycapple c (H165a) 260
" School m (H99) 89; w (H174) 507; c:m (H227) 47
   Drumail [Drumell] a (H25b) 261
   Gleneary w,?m (H814) 415
? Gortin [s: Kilrea] [m: ?Gortin Coolhill: doubtful, but no other possible] 7,w (H757) 334
tl Gortinmayoghill m (H504) 157
   Greenhill [s: Blackhill, Coleraine] c (H760) 471 [see Coleraine p.: Blackhill]
   Knockaduff dist. 2,w (H90) 365; [see also Macosquin p.]
   Managher [s: Coleraine] w (H73) 412; [M..., Drumcroon, Coleraine] c:[B:]w;[D:]w,m (H162) 333; [M...] 2,w["completion"] (H223) 83
tl Mayoghill [s: Garvagh] m (H171) 40; [Mayoghill, G...] c[chez] (H174) 507; 2,w;m (H176) 146; w,?m (H177) 271; c (H178) 233; [M..., Moneydig

[D:]Garvagh] 3,w (H207) 417; [Mayoghill, near G...]?w,?m (H227) 47; [M..., Aghadowey] m (H585) 147 [see also Macosquin p.]
v Ringsend [s: Garvagh] 11,c:w (H625) 342

L Agivey parish:
   Agivey [s: Aghadowey] informant in (H63) 247; m (H75a) 145; 2,w (H214) 445; w,?m (H740) 56
" dist. c (H144) 270
tl ": R[h]ee, the, w,m (H138) 256
   Mullaghmore Bleach Green [B,D:] a (H63) 247; w,?m (H163) 41

L Artrea parish:
   Ballymulderg [s: Magherafelt] 3,w; ?3,m (H576) 435
   Creagh [s: Toomebridge] 3+,w (H128) 440

L Ballyaghran parish:
   Cappaghbeg [Cappagh Beg] [s: Portstewart] w,m (H215) 393
   Craigtownmore [s: Portrush] w,m (H226) 511; w,?m (H231a) 28; w (H231b) 28
   Portstewart a (H27c) 105; 3,w (H72) 374; w,m (H83) 156; 6,c (H120) 332; 2+,c:w (H148) 411; w (H161a) 456; m (H181) 131; c:w (H189) 173; w,m (H203) 330; w,m (H205) 465; w,?m (H206) 289; 3,w (H213) 334; 4+,c (H638) 431; c:w (H714) 513

A,L Ballymoney parish:
   Ballywindland [Ballywindelland] c (H241) 346

L Ballynascreen parish:
t,tl Draperstown w,?m (H91) 156 [m:==]
   Ballinascreen w (H833) 257
   Ballynure 11,c:w (H625) 342
   Owenreagh, Sixtowns a (H542) 217
   Straw w,?m (H811) 461

A,L Ballyrashane parish:
   Ballyrashane w,m (H57b) 228; w,?m (H725) 278
? Cloyfin (South) w[fragment] (H39) 123; c[incomplete] (H215) 393; w,?m (H687) 302 [? or Ballywillin p.: Cloyfin North]
   Gorticloughan w,m (H175) 470

A,L Ballywillin parish:
tl Ballywillan [Ballywillin] dist. m (H81) 430
   Ballylag[g]an (North or South) [s: Cloyfin, Coleraine] 3,m (H8) 311; m (H15) 87; w (H55) 479; 3,w;?3,m (H576) 435; w,?m (H578) 418; w,m (H581) 318; w,m (H583) 314; c (H591a) 6; c (H701) 501; c:m (H714) 513; w,[W:]m (H835b) 512
   Carnalridge [s: Portrush] [D:]c:w (H22a) 232
? Cloyfin (North) w[fragment] (H39) 123; c[incomplete] (H215) 393; w,?m (H687) 302 [? or Ballyrashane p.: Cloyfin South]
   Glenmearns [s: Portrush] w2 (H701) 501
   Inchmearing [s: Coleraine] 11,c:w (H625) 342
   Islandflackey [Island Flackey] [s: Portrush] w (H124) 509
   Islandmore, w,m (H185) 128
   Kilgrain [Killygreen] [s: Cloyfin] w2,m2 (H205) 465

L Balteagh parish:
   Ballymully [s: Limavady] w,m (H236) 375 [see also Bovevagh, Drumachose p.]
   Drumsurn (Upper and Lower) c:w (H225) 196

" dist. w (H234) 436
": Kilhoyle m,m2,m3,m4 (H225) 196
? Terrydoo w2,?m2 (H676) 41 [see also Bovevagh, Drumachose p.]
   Terrydoo Clyde [s: Limavady] w,?m (H670) 293
   Terrydoo Walker [s: Limavady] 5,c (H750) 120 [see also Bovevagh, Drumachose p.]

L Banagher parish:
v,tl Feeny c (H667) 192
": Coolnamonan w (H65a) 293
   Teeavin [Teeavan] [s: Dungiven] w2,?m2 (H666) 170

L Bovevagh parish:
tl Bovevagh [s: Dungiven] w2 (H126) 510; c (H167) 369
" [s: Limavady] m (H162) 333 [see also Balteagh, Drumachose p.]
   Ballyhargin [Ballyharigan] [s: Dungiven] w,?m (H132) 398
   Ballymonie [Ballymoney], Altmover m (H150a) 466
   Derryard [s: Dungiven] c:w;m (H126) 510
   Drum [s: Dungiven] w2,m2 (H100a) 188; 5,c (H150b) 361

L Clondermot parish:
   Lisglass, near Derry w2,?m2 (H768) 59
   Kilfennan [Kilfinnan], Waterside w[corroborated] (H778) 387

L Coleraine parish:
t Coleraine: Houston Collection c (H6 = H567) 275; c (H7) 290; c:m (H16) 392; c (H17b) 180; c (H20b) 245; c (H30a) 390; c:m (H32) 269; c (H33) 397; c (H34) 213; c (H40c) 20; c:m (H41) 231; c (H42a) 148; c (H43) 394; c:m (H71) 246; c:w[2 sts.],m (H75b) 199; c:w[st. 1, cho],m (H80) 386; c:m (H111) 229; 3,w[3 sts.],m (H112) 288; c:m (H113) 434; w2 [about half the ballad] (H114) 143; c:m (H118) 315; c (H136) 125; c:m (H165b) 260; c (H191) 142; c:m (H234) 436

t Coleraine w,m (H7) 290; [m (H14a) 356]; w (H18a) 358; w,?m (H18b) 272; c:w,m (H20a) 216; m (H21b) 508; c:w[o:?a] (H26b) 250; 2,w;2,m (H34) 213; w (H37) 485); w,?m (H42a) 148; w,?m (H43) 249; 2,w (H51) 129; [c:w;mc (H52b) 429]; m (H54) 144; [D:]w,m (H60a) 400; w,m (H62) 148; [BLp:] w,m (H63) 247; w (H64) 161; c (H82) 262; a;c:w (H87a) 181; [m (H97) 130]; m (H98a) 64; c (H98b) 472; w (H113) 434; m (H122a) 88; w (H136) 125; m (H137) 431; c:w (H139) 42; 5,w (H150b) 361; 2,w;m (H153a) 480; w,?m (H155) 366; m (H168) 399; m (H179a,b) 125, 126; m (H182) 464; m (H202) 119; 3,w;m (H207) 417; 3,w (H213) 334; [m (H219) 177]; c (H220) 243; m (H228b) 18; m (H230) 255; w,?m (H492) 238; w,?m (H497) 326; w,?m (H526) 182; w,?m (H599) 12; w,m (H613) 396; w,?m (H614) 384; m (H616) 462; c (H617) 45; [w,?m (H623) 109]; w,?m (H628) 62; w,m (H635) 455; 4+,c (H638) 431; w (H650b) 264; c;w,?m (H653) 211; c (H683) 393; m (H706) 180; w,?m (H729) 446; w,?m (H742) 104; [c (H743) 200]; 7,c:w (H757) 334; [w,?m (H782) 473]; w,?m (H793) 267; w,?m (H798) 421; m (H803) 79; w,?m (H807) 514; w,?m (H810) 269; w,?m (H814) 415; c (H817) 169; w,?m (H821) 220; m (H825) 299; c:m (H826) 309; m (H827) 100; w,w2,

614

?m,?m2 (H828) 286; m (H829) 91; a[English] (H830) 64; a[English] (H831) 235; a[English] (H832a) 49; a[English] (H834) 289; w,?m (H835a) 512; m (H836) 372

Ballysally c:w (H537) 239; w,m (H572) 159; c (H643) 159; c (H644) 367; c (H647) 462; c (H649) 171; c (H655) 319; w,?m (H656) 187; c:w (H658) 175; 3,c:m (H806) 434; m (H809) 162; c (H812) 310
Blackhill dist. c:w (H81) 430 [m: not otherwise traced; see note below.]
": Greenhill c (H760) 471 [m: ? or Aghadowey p. There is a Black Hill between Coleraine and Aghadowey.]
Boghill w[st. 1] (H75a) 145
Burnside w,m (H29) 53; [w (H92) 86]; m (H231b) 28
Blagh [D: Cloyfin] c (H216) 265 [? see also A Dunluce p.]
Carnabuoy [Carnaboy], Cloyfin w,?m (H694) 503
Dundooan m (H12) 31; m (H27c) 105
Knockantern mc (H536) 209
Loguestown m (H162) 333; [?c (H167) 369]
Loughan w2,?m2 (H591b) 6
h " Hill w2,?m2 (H729) 446
Ratheane w,m (H30a) 390; w,?m (H40c) 20
h Shell Hill 2+c:w (H181) 131
t Thorndale c (H108b) 169; c (H138) 256

L Cumber Upper parish:
tl Alla w2,?m2 (H124) 509; w,?m (H835a) 512
": near Park 2,c (H229a) 360; w (H240) 192; 2,w (H562) 113
": near Cumber-Claudy w (H124) 509
Claudy w,?m (H221) 490
": Salowilly [Sallowilly] w (H818) 317
Cumber-Claudy w,?m (H221) 490
": Cool [m: possibly Coonacolpagh] w (H13) 232
? Mallabuie, near Claudy w,?m (H835a) 512

L Cumber Lower parish:
Bond's Glen [m: near Claudy] m (H601) 174
Cumber-Claudy w,?m (H792) 122
Ervey w3,?m3 (H221) 490; w,?m (H792) 122
Slaughtmanus [Slaghtmanus], Cross 2,c (H477) 140

L Desertmartin parish:
v Annagh [m: and Moneysterlin] 5,c (H750) 120

L Desert-Oghill parish:
Lisachrin [s: Garvagh] c (H481) 484

L Drumachose parish:
Drumrammer [Drumramer] w2,m2 (H76) 314; [s: D..., Limavady] 3,c (H806) 434
Limavady c:w;2 (H706) 180; c (H808) 98; c:w (H829) 91 [see also Balteagh, Bovevagh p.]
": New Town [m: Newtownlimavady = Limavady] c:m (H3) 286
" dist.: Ballyrisk 3,c (H474) 488
": Gortcorbries 2,c (H468) 441
": Termaquin [Tirmaquin] ?w,?m (H669) 179; w,?m (H670) 293; w,?m (H671) 22; w,?m (H675) 24; w,?m (H676) 41

L Dunboe parish: [o:]?a (H23) 307
tl Articlave Upper m (H674) 219
v Articlave 3,c (H137) 31
" dist. ?c (H551) 40; 2,w (H192) 101
": Fox Dartries [Fox Dartress] w2,m2 (H215) 393

? Ballyhackett dist., near Downhill w,m (H211) 479
Benarees [D: Magilligan] w,m (H23) 307
v Castlerock a (H108b) 169; c:m (H523) 63
? ": Woodlands c:m (H116a) 201
Dartries [Dartress] 1c:w (H625) 342
Downhill 3,w;?3,m (H576) 435

L Dungiven parish:
t,tl Dungiven a (H123) 90; 8,w (H179a) 125; a;2,c:w (H187) 162; a (H245) 195; m (H582) 238; w,?m (H609) 199; w2,?m2 (H635) 455; c (H647) 462; c (H649) 171; w,?m (H651) 160; c (H652) 269; c (H654) 170; c (H738) 478; w;m (H809) 162
g Benady Glen w2,?m2 (H752) 245
Carn w (H182) 464
Cashel w (H97) 130 [see also Macosquin p.]
Cluntygeeragh 2,c:w (H187) 162; [D:] w,?m (H222) 29
? Drumneechy ?c:w (H666) 260
Hass, the w,?m (H666) 170
Magherabuoy [Magheraboy] [s: in Benady Glen, near] Dungiven a,w,?mc (H154) 33; a (H537) 239; a,?mc,?m (H538) 364; c (H654) 170; "late" a (H809) 162
Tirmeil [Turmeel] m (H14b) 356; [Termeil] [sic] c (H652) 269

L Errigal parish:
t Garvagh c (H78) 484; 8,w (H179a) 125; w2,?m2 (H761) 228; w,?m (H799) 221
": glens above w (H38) 29
tl ": Brockagh c:w (H171) 40
" Mt. 2,c (H150a) 466
": Gortnamoyagh 2,w (H118) 315
Coolnasillagh [s: Maghera] 11,c:w (H625) 342

L Faughanvale parish:
tl Faughanvale 2,c:w (H190) 420
Carrichue [m: presumably Carrickhugh] 11,c:w (H625) 342
Craigbrack [s: Eglinton] 5,c (H150b) 361; m (H170) 299
Eglinton [m: ? or Muff] dist. c:m (H116a) 201
": Carnkilly [Carnakilly] c:w (H770) 485
Foreglen c:w,m (H52b) 429; [F..., Dungiven] m (H97) 130; w (H173) 250; m (H182) 4; [m (H202) 119]; 3,w (H213) 334; m (H219) 177; [m (H228b) 18]; [F..., near Claudy] w[part],[m (H698) 51
v,tls Killywill, Greysteel [Gresteel] w (H190) 420; a,m (H796) 163
Minnegallagher w (H796) 163

L Formoyle parish:
tl Fermoyle [Formoyle] dist. w (H54) 144
tl Altibrian c:w (H32) 269; [A..., Articlave] c (H100b) 193
Ballinrees [s: Macosquin] w,m (H76) 314
Knockmult [s: Macosquin] c (H717) 108; w2,?m2 (H785) 399
": Buckie Knowe w,?m (H754) 111

L Kilcronaghan parish:
v,tl Tobermore w,?m (H748) 263; w,?m (H752) 245

L Kildollagh parish:
Coolderry (North or South) [s: Coleraine] w,?m (H608) 87
Damhead [Dam Head] 11,c:w (H625) 342
Fish Loughan [s: Coleraine] w,?m (H622) 44; w,?m (H624) 349; c (H681) 490

L Kilrea parish:
tl,t Kilrea 3,w (H213) 334; w2,?m2 (H473) 354

L Learmount parish:
Cross Roads, Dreen, informant in (H43) 394; [s: ..., Park, near Mt Sawell] w,m (H149) 456
Mt Sawell, slopes of w,?m (H528) 246
Park dist. near Dungiven w (H219) 177

L Macosquin parish:
Ardverness [Ardvarness] w,m (H58) 446; [Adverness] [sic] w (H125a) 475
tl Ballinteer w,?m (H33) 397
Cashel c:w (H172) 31 [see also Dungiven p.]
": Ringsend 3,w (H72) 374 [see also Aghadowey]
Castleroe a (H614) 384
": dist. c:w (H71) 246
Croaghan [s: Coleraine] w (H114) 143; [Croaghan, Macosquin] m (H172) 31; w[st. 1] (H224a,b) 390, 391
Derrydoragh a (H67) 3
Knockaduff, Drumcroon w,w2 (H677) 175 [see also Aghadowey p.]
Glenleary w2,?m2 (H814) 415
Kiltinney c:w,m (H47) 236
Letterloan 6,c (H120) 332

L Maghera parish:
t Maghera w (H707) 227
? Ballymacpeake (Upper) 5,c (H150b) 361 [? or Tamlaght O'Crilly p: Ballymacpeake (Lower)]
Beagh c:w (H156) 315
Fallalea m (H465) 49
Gulladuff a (H119) 21
h Knockloughrim (hill) 8,c:w (H179a) 125
": Mayogall [Moyagall] c (H119) 21
Upperlands [Upperland] 2,c:w (H532) 367; ?6,c (H750) 120
": Culnady 2,w (H214) 445

L Magherafelt parish:
t,tl Magherafelt c (H237) 189
t Castledawson: Tulnaveagh, Leitrim Nursery 3+,;w (H128) 440

L Magilligan parish (or Tamlaght-Ard):
Magilligan, 2,w (H27a) 371; w,m (H42b) 197; w (H45) 477; [D:]w,?m (H88) 18; w (H95) 107; w,m (H108a) 329; w3 (H126) 510; m (H146) 180; w,?m (H209) 465; w,?m (H782) 473
Aughill [Augill] w (H623) 109; c (H672) 212; w,?m (H742) 104; m (H743) 200
tl Ballyleighery, met at m (H170) 299
Bellarena (H52a) 244; w,m (H68) 276; 3+,w (H128) 440; 3,w (H137) 431
": Drumavalley m (H128) 440; w,m (H169) 298

615

(97b) 248
(H21a) 508; w (H129)
00) 470; 2,w;?m (H201)
(H239) 469
(H813) 468
(H24b) 217; w,m (H89)
,?m (H657) 242; m (H824) 166
m (H139) 42; c:w,m (H141) 395;
w2;m2 (H153a) 480; m (H235) 203

amlaght-Finlagan parish:
  Ballykelly a (H192) 101
  Corndale [s: Limavady] [B:] c:(2)w,m
    (H157) 207
  Glack [s: near Limavady] m (H224a)
    390
  Mulkeragh South [s: Limavady] c
    (H132) 398; c (H192) 101; 2,c
    (H229a) 360
  Myroe a,?mc (H36) 74; a,mc (H68) 276;
    a,mc (H169) 298; w2,?m2 (H206) 289

L Tamlaght-O'Crilly parish:
? Ballymacpeake (Lower) 5,c (H150b) 361
    [? see also Maghera p.]
  Boveedy [Bovedy] a (H49) 200
  Gortmacrane [s: Kilrea] 11,c;2,m (H625)
    342; c (H719) 63

Portglenone: Clady [Claudy], Glenone,
  w,m (473) 354; [P..., C...] c (H766)
  43
tl ": Eden ?c,?m (H632) 203
  Lismoyle, Swateragh 7,w (H757) 334
    [see also Killelagh p.]
  Tyanee w,m (H805a,b) 73

L Termoneeny parish:
  Mullagh [s: Maghera] w,m (H710) 264;
    c (H790) 383

Co. Down:

  Ards [peninsula] w (H650a) 263
  Ballyboley, Greyabbey a (H601) 174
  Ballygrainey m (H818) 317
  Castlewellan dist. w (H183) 268
  Cloughey c (H650a) 263
  Magheratimpan, near Ballynahinch a
    (H164) 362
  Glascar, near Rathfriland w (H593) 388
  Poyntz Pass: Tyrone Ditches [Tyrone's
    Ditches], near Newry w,?m (H682) 505

Co. Tyrone: c (H745) 47

  Coagh: Arboe [Ardboe] c:w;m (H505)
    157

": Aneetermore, Clontoe Richardson,
  Moneymore w,?m (H709) 348
": Drumaney c:m;a (H505) 157; c
  (H708) 174
Cookstown w,m (H117) 44; c (H745) 47
tl ": Aughless w2,?m2 (H734) 149
tl ": Drumcan w,?m (H734) 149
Donemana [Dunnamanagh]: Aghafad
  [m: not traced], Ballinamallaght c
  (H726) 307
": Dunnaboe [Dunnyboe] c (H96a,b)
  230, 231; c:w (H173) 250
": Lough Ash [or Loughash] a (H96a,b)
  230; a (H100b) 193; a (H173) 250;
  a (H607) 250
": Moneygran w,?m (H768) 59
Glenelly valley w (H720) 165
Greencastle w,?m (H830) 64; w,?m
  (H831) 235
Lower Back, Stewartstown a (H795)
  198
Redford, Moy c (H131) 84
Sawell a (H43) 394
Strabane dist. w (H151) 124
Tyrone border [m:presumably between
  Tyrone and Londonderry] 3,m (H8) 311;
  m (H13) 232

Irish place names

Place names in Ireland can be townlands, parishes, baronies (or half baronies) or counties (these signify rural areas); while villages, towns, and cities are centers of population (sometimes these have a name distinct from the rural area which contains them, sometimes they bear the same name as the surrounding townland, parish, barony, or county -- these terms are given in ascending order of hierarchy). All official records such as censuses have, until recently, been made according to this peculiar structure.

Townlands are given a fair definition in E. E. Evans, *Irish Heritage* (Dundalk, 1945, pp. 47-8). He traces the term to the "towns" or clusters of houses, elsewhere known as "clachans," often occupied by members of a single extended family which farmed in common the land surrounding the "town."

Townlands mainly lie wholly within one parish (the area within which particular clergymen of the episcopalian [established] church held the cure of souls) but may overlap parish or even county boundaries. This arises from the overlay of a civil organization upon an organic one. Parishes too can overlap counties.

[Because of] their origination in the Irish language, the spelling of townland names can vary. I have accepted Henry's spelling, but where the spelling on maps ... does not agree with Alfred Moore Munn, *Notes on the Place Names of the Parishes and Townlands of the County of Londonderry* (The Author, 1925) or Samuel Trimble, *County of Antrim: Schedule of the Townlands of Said County* (Belfast, 1886), I have entered the difference [parenthetically]. Because the townland names often derive from the names of the family which once lived there or because of some topographical feature, they often replicate one another although differently located.... the townlands and parishes have only limited correspondence with the towns and villages.

John Moulden

Melodic index

This tune index is based on the assumption that the melodies in the Henry collection, presumably mostly Irish, have the same general tendencies as do the English, Scottish, and American ballad tunes studied by Bertrand H. Bronson and can fairly be represented by standard Western staff notation (or equivalents) and in a modal system such as Bronson's.[1] This index is simpler than Bronson's much more refined treatment: only the first phrase of each tune is used as an indexing key.[2]

Each tune is represented by several entries on a line:

> The last columns (7, 8, 9) identify the tune by its Henry number, page location, and title (which may be truncated).
> Col. 2 gives the number and arrangement of musical phrases in the tune. (A colon : represents a major division of phrases, as between stanza and refrain portions of the tune; phrases between colons are repeated.)

[The following entries are based on determination of a "home note" or "do" = "1," from which the other notes (nearly three octaves) are numbered in ascending order from the octave below: L1, L2, ..., L7, 1, 2, ..., 7, to the octave above: U1, U2, ..., U7.]

> Col. 5: the final note, usually (but not always) "1."
> Col. 6: the "key," either that given by Sam Henry or one corrected for the actual mode.
> Col. 3: the range: named according to the lowest and highest notes in the tune, relative to "1":
> 　　a = authentic (from 1 on up).
> 　　p = plagal (from about L5 to about 5 or more).
> 　　m = mixed (from about L5 to U1 or more).
> Col. 4: the mode: a characteristic pattern of intervals in the tune. (Bronson's nomenclature represents both the pattern and the number of tones; see the "Mode identification list" which follows.) ? indicates a tune whose mode is uncertain; * marks an alternate choice of mode for the same tune.
> Col. 1: A representation of the accented notes ("formula") in the first phrase of the tune. These formulas are arranged in the index by notes in ascending order:
> 　　L1 L1 ... precedes L5 L1 ... and so on.

---

[1] Prof. Bronson elegantly and persuasively recapitulates the thoughtful development of his theory and practice in his introduction to his one-volume abridgment of Bronson 1-4(1959-72), *The Singing Tradition of Child's Popular Ballads* (Princeton, N.J.: Princeton Univ. Press, 1976), esp. sections 6-11 (pp. xxix-xliv). For further information see Bronson's "Mechanical help in the study of folk song" (JAF 62(#244)Apr-Jun 1949:84-6; his collected papers on folk music in *The Ballad as Song* (Berkeley and Los Angeles: Univ. of California Press, 1969); and his 1981 final grant report to the National Endowment for the Humanities, "Comparative Melodic Analysis of Traditional British-American Folk Ballad Tunes: User's Guide for the Bronson Database."

Breandán Breathnach justifies the assumption: "... English folk music, by and large, falls into the same modal divisions [Doh, ionian; Soh, mixolydian; Ray, dorian; and Lah, aeolian] ... and the proportion of airs in each division is surprisingly close to the Irish figures" (1971:11).

[2] In his article "Between the jigs and the reels" (Ceol 5(2)Mar 1982:43-8) Breathnach describes a similar indexing system he developed for Irish dance tunes, but he does not list the mode as a *primary* factor for indexing.

For other different practical approaches to the question of finding tunes see: the classic pair, Howard Barlow and Harold Morgenstern, *A Dictionary of Musical Themes* (1948) and *A Dictionary of Vocal Themes* (1950) (both published by Crown Publishers, New York); Denys Parsons, *The Directory of Tunes and Musical Themes* (Cambridge: Spencer Brown & Co., 1975); Kate Van Winkle Keller and Carolyn Rabson, *The National Tune Index* (microfiche; New York: University Music Editions [Box 192, Ft. George Station, New York, NY 10040], 1980), especially the descriptive booklet; and Anne Dhu Shapiro's current project, funded by the NEH in 1985-6, based on her dissertation, "The Concept of Tune-Families in British-American Folksong Scholarship" (Harvard Univ., 1975).

Sam Henry's Songs of the People

To see if a given tune may have relatives in the index:
1. Determine "1" or "do" (usually the final note, or that on which the tune seems to come to rest).
2. Determine the index formula (first-phrase accented notes) of the tune, and place the tune in formula order in the index.
3. Determine the mode from the pattern of intervals and gaps between notes in the tune. Matching this and the other index indicators for the tune may suggest whether it is similar to or different from its neighbors in the melodic index.

For example, the well-known Irish air "The Star of the County Down" has as its formula of accents 1 1 3 4 and is pi4 in mode; it has several apparent relatives in our index. In fact, all the tunes with the same first-phrase formula, in this case, resemble "The Star of the County Down."

Mode identification list[°]

Code	Mode Name	No. of Tones in the Scale	Half Steps Between	3 Half Steps Between
lyd	lydian	7	4 & 5, 7 & U1	---
l/i	lydian/ionian	6	7 & U1	3 & 5
pi1	pentatonic 1	5	---	3 & 5, 6 & U1
ion	ionian	7	3 & 4, 7 & U1	---
i/m	ionian/mixolydian	6	3 & 4	6 & U1
pi2	pentatonic 2	5	---	2 & 4, 6 & U1
mix	mixolydian	7	3 & 4, 6 & 7	---
m/d	mixolydian/dorian	6	6 & 7	2 & 4
pi3	pentatonic 3	5	---	2 & 4, 5 & 7
dor	dorian	7	2 & 3, 6 & 7	---
d/a	dorian/aeolian	6	2 & 3	5 & 7
pi4	pentatonic 4	5	---	1 & 3, 5 & 7
aeo	aeolian	7	2 & 3, 5 & 6	---
a/p	aeolian/phrygian	6	5 & 6	1 & 3
pi5	pentatonic 5	5	---	1 & 3, 4 & 6
phr	phrygian	7	1 & 2, 5 & 6	---
p/l	phrygian/locrian	6	1 & 2	4 & 6
loc	locrian	7	1 & 2, 4 & 5	---
mel	melodic minor	7	2 & 3, 7 & U1	---
har	harmonic minor	7	2 & 3, 5 & 6	6 & 7
min	minor			

Bimodal (on one tonal center)

i&m	ionian and mixolydian	d&a	dorian and aeolian
i&a	ionian and aeolian	a&p	aeolian and phrygian
m&d	mixolydian and dorian		

dim dimodal *(on different tonal centers)*

Other hexatonal

i-2	ionian minus 2nd	d-7	dorian minus 7th
i-3	ionian minus 3rd	a-2	aeolian minus 2nd
i-6	ionian minus 6th	a-3	aeolian minus 3rd
m-2	mixolydian minus 2nd	a-4	aeolian minus 4th
m-4	mixolydian minus 4th	a-5	aeolian minus 5th
m-6	mixolydian minus 6th	a-7	aeolian minus 7th
d-2	dorian minus 2nd	p-7	phrygian minus 7th

Irregular

5xx	pentatonal	3xx	tritonal
4xx	tetratonal	???	anomalous (unclassifiable)

[°]From Bronson, "User's Guide ...," 1981. Most (about 95 per cent) of the 4217 tunes in his database fit in the categories in the first half of the table; the remaining 5 per cent fall in the second half, unusual modal patterns.

Melodic index L3 L5 - L5 U1

Printed without tunes:

Glenrannel's Plains (H100b) 193
Magilligan (H52a) 244
Mudion River (H108b) 169
Young Mary of Accland (a) (H30b) 437

First-phrase Accents	Number of Phrases	Range	Mode	Final	Key	Henry Number	Page	Title
L3 L5 1 1	(8:4)	p:	ion	L5	G	(H766)	43	Charity Seed
L3 L6 3 L6/L5	(4:4)	p:	ion	1	G	(H778)	387	Norah Magee
L3 1 L6 L6	(4:4)	p:	i/m	L6	G	(H146)	180	Knights of Malta
L5 L3 1 1	(6:5)	p:	ion	1	G	(H756)	60	Salutation
L5 L3 2 L5	(4:2)	p:	ion	1	E	(H499)	387	Broken-Hearted Gardener
L5 L5 L5 7 -	(4)	p:	pi3	1	A	(H239)	469	Sandy's Wooing
L5 L5 1 3	(8)	p:	l/i	1	A	(H155)	366	I'll Hang My Harp ...
L5 L5 2 L5	(4:2)	p:	ion	1	E	(H132)	398	Polly Perkins ...
L5 L5 4 L6/L5	(4)	p:	ion	1	G	(H570)	310	Mary Doyle
L5 L5 4 L6/L5	(4)	p:	i/m	1	G	(H768)	59	Songs of Old Ireland
L5 L5 5 5	(4)	p:	*i/m	L5	G	(H186)	46	Thatchers of Glenrea
L5 L6 L5 L6	(4:4:)	p:	i/m	1	Af	(H763)	458	Bonny Wee Lass
L5 L6 1 3	(8:8)	m:	ion	1	D	(H605)	340	Six Sweethearts
L5 1 L6 L5	(4)	p:	ion	L5	G	(H137)	431	Johnny Doyle
L5 1 L7 L5	(4)	p:	?ion	L5	G	(H230)	255	Nae Bonnie Laddie ...
L5 1 L7 2	(8:10)	p:	ion	1	F	(H21a)	508	Blin' Auld Man
L5 1 1 L7	(8:3)	p:	ion	1	D	(H617)	45	Shepherd Laddie
L5 1 1 3 2 L5	(4)	p:	ion	1	F	(H16)	392	Oh, Johnny, Johnny
L5 1 - 4 2 -	(12:2)	p:	?i/m	L5	G	(H508)	226	So Like Your Song and You
L5 1 1 7	(8)	m:	m/d	1	E	(H603)	239	Maid of Altaveedan
L5 1 2 L6 1	(4)	m:	ion	1	D	(H807)	514	Johnny, M' Man
L5 1 2 1	(4)	p:	pi1	1	G	(H622)	44	Jolly Thresher
L5 1 2 1	(8)	p:	ion	1	G	(H684)	231	Kate of Coleraine
L5 1 2 -	(8)	m:	pi3	1	D	(H489)	48	Cup o' Tay
L5 1 2 3 L6	(6)	p:	ion	1	G	(H677)	175	Land of the West
L5 1 3	(6:2)	p:	ion	1	G	(H70b)	341	I've Two or Three Strings ... (b)
L5 1 3 L5	(8)	p:	i/m	1	G	(H525)	483	You Lovers All
L5 1 3 L5 L5	(4)	p:	?i/m	L5	G	(H565)	111	Wreck of the Rebecca
L5 1 3 2	(8)	p:	ion	L5	G	(H182)	464	Greenmount Smiling Ann
L5 1 3 2 -	(4:4)	p:	i-6	1	G	(H810)	269	Beggarman Cam' ower the Lea
L5 1 3 3	(4)	p:	ion	1	G	(H753)	501	Happy Pair
L5 1 3 5	(4)	p:	ion	1	F	(H40a)	12	How Many Miles to Babyland?
L5 1 3 6	(7)	m:	ion	1	D	(H90)	365	Grey Mare
L5 1 4 2	(4:2)	p:	ion	1	G	(H12)	31	Hare of Kilgrain
L5 1 4 2	(8:4)	p:	m-6	1	G	(H222)	29	Hunting Priest
L5 1 4 2 1 L5	(4)	p:	ion	1	F	(H790)	383	False Lover
L5 1 4 3	(8)	p:	*i/m	L5	G	(H97)	130	Shane Crossagh
L5 1 4 3	(8)	m:	i/m	L5	F	(H136)	125	James Magee
L5 1 5 3	(8)	p:	i/m	L5	G	(H561)	458	As I Go I Sing
L5 1 5 3	(8)	p:	?i/m	L5	G	(H661)	259	Lovely Annie (I)
L5 1 5 4	(8)	p:	?i/m	L5	Af	(H197a)	248	Blazing Star of Drim (a)
L5 1 5 4	(8)	p:	?i/m	L5	Af	(H197b)	248	Blazing Star of Drung (b)
L5 1 5 5	(4)	p:	i/m	1	A	(H835b)	512	Whiskey Is My Name
L5 1 5 U1/5	(11)	m:	ion	1	G	(H649)	171	River Roe (I)
L5 2 3 L5	(4)	p:	?pi1	L5	F	(H56)	354	John McAnanty's Courtship
L5 2 3 L5	(4)	p:	i/m	L5	G	(H524)	328	Squire's Bride
L5 2/1 4 3/1	(4)	p:	ion	L5	G	(H153b)	481	County Tyrone
L5 3 L7 L7	(4)	p:	aeo	1	A	(H835a)	512	Whisky Is My Name (a)
L5 3 L7 3	(4:4)	m:	dor	1	Ef	(H510)	17	Little White Cat
L5 3 1 L6/L5	(8)	p:	ion	1	Af	(H26b)	250	Mary, the Pride of Killowen
L5 3 1 L6/L5	(8)	p:	ion	1	G	(H716)	218	Shamrock from Tiree
L5 3 2 L5	(4)	m:	aeo	1	E	(H233)	287	Green Banks of Banna
L5 3 2 1	(8)	p:	ion	1	G	(H606)	208	Green Hills of Antrim
L5 3 3 3	(8)	p:	pi4	L4	A	(H811)	461	Blackwaterside
L5 5 6 2/1	(8:4)	p:	ion	1	F	(H708)	174	Among the Green Bushes ...
L5 U1 U1 U3	(8)	a:	ion	1	C	(H832a)	49	Black Pipe

619

L6 L6 - 1 1 2 1 Sam Henry's Songs of the People

First-phrase Accents	Number of Phrases	Range	Mode	Final	Key	Henry Number	Page	Title
L6 L6 1 2	(8)	p:	*pi1	L6	F	(H100a)	188	Carnanbane
L6 1 L5 L3	(8)	p:	ion	1	G	(H62)	148	Rachel Dear
L6 1 3 4	(4)	p:	i/m	1	F	(H568)	226	Bonny Mary Hay
L6 2 5 1	(4:2)	a:	ion	1	D	(H172)	31	Hare's Dream
L6 3 L7 L3	(4:4)	p:	?ion	1	G	(H34)	213	Pretty Three-Leaved Shamrock ...
L6 4 3 L5	(8)	p:	m-2	1	G	(H808)	98	Steamship Leinster Lass
L7 3 4 L7	(4)	a:	?d/a	1	E	(H119)	21	Goat's Will
L7 4 5 4 3	(4:6)	a:	?pi4	1	E	(H591a)	6	Heezh Ba
1 L3 1 L5	(4)	p:	*d/a	1	A	(H10b)	2	Dublin
1 L5 L4 L3	(8)	p:	a/p	1	A	(H578)	418	Flora, the Lily of the West
1 L5 L5 L2	(8)	m:	ion	1	Ef	(H789)	419	Willow Tree
1 L5 1 1	(8:8)	p:	l/i	1	G	(H528)	246	Maid from the County Tyrone
1 L5 1 2	(8:4)	p:	ion	1	G	(H833)	257	Wee Article
1 L5 1 3	(4)	m:	i/m	1	Ef	(H193)	487	Hielans o' Scotland
1 L5 2 L6	(8)	p:	ion	1	G	(H523)	63	Dun Ceithern
1 L5 3 1	(4)	p:	i/m	1	G	(H140)	30	Squire Agnew's Hunt
1 L6 L5 L3	(8:2)	p:	ion	1	A	(H231a)	28	Crocodile
1 L6 L5 L5	(8:2)	p:	ion	3	G	(H231b)	28	Crocodile
1 L6 L5 L5	(4:1)	p:	pi1	1	G	(H105)	331	Jolly Ploughboy
1 L6 L5 L5	(8)	p:	ion	1	G	(H595)	468	Lovely Banks of Mourne
1 L6 L5 L5	(4)	p:	pi1	1	G	(H740)	56	Mick Magee
1 L6 L5 L5 -	(4:4)	p:	pi1	1	G	(H208)	258	Grandma's Advice
1 L6 L5 L7 3	(8)	p:	ion	1	G	(H830)	64	Yellow Bittern
1 L6 - 1 3/5 -	(8)	p:	ion	1	G	(H652)	269	Galway Shawl
1 L6 1 2	(8)	p:	i/m	L6	G	(H769)	65	Parting Glass
1 L6 1 6/5	(8)	m:	pi1	1	D	(H219)	177	Connaught Man
1 L6 2 L5	(4)	p:	ion	1	G	(H163)	413	King o' Spain's Daughter
1 L6 2 2	(4)	p:	ion	1	F	(H75a)	145	Nightingale (I)
1 L6 3 5	(8)	p:	*lyd	L5	G	(H69)	201	Happy Shamrock Shore
1 L6/L5 6 5	(4:2)	p:	pi1	L6	G	(H122a)	88	Bonny Light Horseman
1 L6 6 5	(4)	p:	pi1	L6	F	(H574)	80	Pat Reilly
1 L7 2 L6/L5	(4)	p:	ion	1	G	(H478)	176	Erin, My Country
1 1 L5 L3	(8)	p:	pi1	1	G	(H23)	307	Banished Lover (a)
1 1 L5 L3	(8)	p:	pi1	1	G	(H522)	355	Maid of Croaghmore
1 1 L5 L3	(4:4)	p:	ion	1	G	(H527)	20	Robin Redbreast's Testament
1 1 L5 L3	(8)	p:	pi1	1	G	(H615)	343	Farewell Ballymoney
1 1 L5 L3	(8)	p:	pi1	1	G	(H632)	203	Paddy's Green Countrie
1 1 L5 L3	(8)	p:	pi1	1	G	(H685)	460	Bann Water Side
1 1 L5 L3	(8)	p:	pi1	1	G	(H726)	307	Learmount Grove
1 1 L5 L5	(8:8)	m:	i/m	1	D	(H171)	40	Jim, the Carman Lad
1 1 L5 L5	(4:2)	p:	i/m	1	A	(H465)	49	Wee Cutty Pipe
1 1 L5 1 3 2 1	(4)	p:	i/m	1	G	(H644)	367	Bonnet Sae Blue
1 1 L5 3	(8)	p:	m-6	1	G	(H178)	233	Flower of Gortade
1 1 L6 L4	(4:2)	a:	m&i	1	G	(H805a)	73	Balinderry Marriage (a)
1 1 L6 L6	(4)	p:	ion	1	G	(H718)	460	Beardiville Planting
1 1 L6 1	(8)	m:	i/m	1	G	(H467)	428	Hibernia's Lovely Jane
1 1 1 L5	(4:4)	p:	mix	1	E	(H174)	507	Auld Man and the Churnstaff
1 1 1 L6	(8:4)	p:	ion	1	C	(H145)	503	Scolding Wife
1 1 1 L7 L5	(4)	p:	ion	1	C	(H815)	103	Franklin the Brave
1 1 1 1	(8:10)	p:	i/m	1	F	(H21b)	508	Blin' Auld Man
1 1 - 2 1 L5	(4)	p:	ion	1	G	(H471)	317	Broken Ring
1 1 1 3	(8:8)	a:	aeo	1	E	(H751)	50	Oul' Rigadoo
1 1 1 3 5 5	(8)	m:	l/i	1	F	(H13)	232	Star of Glenamoyle
1 1 1 3 5 5	(8)	m:	l/i	1	C	(H723)	240	Beauty of the Braid
1 1 1 3/U1	(8)	m:	l/i	1	Ef	(H550)	176	Enchanted Isle
1 1 1 5	(8)	m:	?i-4	L6	D	(H801)	164	Glenariffe
1 1 1 U1	(13:5)	a:	l/i	1	D	(H488)	501	Day We Packed the Hamper ...
1 1 2 L6/L5	(4)	p:	pi1	1	G	(H535a)	39	Waulking Song
1 1 2 1	(4)	p:	6xx	1	F	(H53d)	96	Tom's Gone to Ilo
1 1 2 1	(8)	p:	l/i	1	G	(H61a)	459	I'm from over the Mountain ... (a)
1 1 2 1	(8)	p:	l/i	1	G	(H61b)	459	I'm from over the Mountain ... (b)

Melodic index 1 1 2 2 - 1 2 5 5

First-phrase Accents	Number of Phrases	Range	Mode	Final	Key	Henry Number	Page	Title
1 1 2 2	(8)	p:	i-6	1	G	(H628)	62	Bramble
1 1 2 2	(4:2)	p:	i-6	1	F	(H131)	84	My Son Ted
1 1 2 2	(8)	m:	l/i	1	D	(H659)	504	Single Days of Old
1 1 2 2 -	(2)	p:	ion	1	G	(H48b)	10	Green Gravel
1 1 2 7	(8)	a:	ion	1	Ef	(H717)	108	Wreck of the Nimrod
1 1 3 1	(8:2)	a:	ion	1	E	(H25a)	502	Tay
1 1 3 1	(4)	p:	pi1	L6	G	(H40b)	17	Child's Lullaby
1 1 3 1	(4)	a:	ion	1	D	(H194)	99	Zared
1 1 3 2	(8)	p:	mix	L5	G	(H162)	333	Canada Hi! Ho!
1 1 3 2	(8)	m:	ion	1	C	(H224a)	390	Flower of Sweet Strabane
1 1 3 3	(8)	m:	ion	5	Af	(H504)	157	Farewell He
1 1 3 3	(8)	m:	pi1	1	F	(H773)	229	Mary M'Veagh
1 1 3 3	(6:6)	a:	ion	1	C	(H832b)	81	Pat Muldoney
1 1 3 3/5	(8)	a:	pi1	1	Ef	(H78)	484	Jamie's on the Stormy Sea
1 1 3/4	(6:2)	a:	aeo	1	D	(H7)	290	Bring back My Barney to Me
1 1 3/4 -	(8)	a:	pi4	1	E	(H575)	394	Maid with Bonny Brown Hair
1 1 3/4 -	(8)	p:	pi4	1	E	(H791)	218	Farewell to the Banks of the Roe
1 1 3 4	(8)	a:	?pi4	1	D	(H100a)	188	Carnanbane
1 1 3 4	(8)	m:	d-2	1	D	(H537)	239	Flower of Benbrada
1 1 3 4	(8)	p:	pi4	1	Fs	(H704)	241	Maid from the Carn Brae
1 1 3 4	(8)	p:	pi4	1	Fs	(H747)	214	Maguire's Brae
1 1 3 4 -	(8)	m:	pi4	1	E	(H49)	200	Knox's Farewell
1 1 3 5	(8)	p:	pi4	1	Fs	(H207)	417	Old Oak Tree
1 1 3 6	(8)	a:	ion	1	D	(H195)	234	Kintyre Love Song
1 1 3 6 6/U1	(8)	p:	l/i	1	D	(H189)	173	Fair Tyrone
1 1 3 6 6/U1	(8)	m:	l/i	1	Ef	(H474)	488	Glove and the Lions
1 1 3 6 6/U1	(8)	m:	l/i	1	D	(H610)	208	Cloughwater
1 1 3 6 6/U1	(8)	m:	l/i	1	D	(H668)	444	Love Laughs at Locksmiths
1 1 3 6 6/U1	(8)	m:	l/i	1	D	(H673)	429	Maid of Aghadowey
1 1 3 6 6/U1	(4)	m:	pi1	1	G	(H745)	47	Long Cookstown
1 1 4 3	(4)	p:	ion	1	G	(H14b)	356	Bonnie Wee Lass of the Glen
1 1 4 3	(4:4)	p:	ion	1	G	(H493)	237	Braiding Her Glossy Black Hair
1 1 4 5 5 1	(4)	a:	mix	1	C	(H203)	330	Sailor on the Sea
1 1 5 1	(4)	p:	l/i	1	G	(H48f)	11	Here's a Poor Widow
1 1 5 1	(8)	p:	dor	1	F	(H169)	298	Maid of Carrowclare
1 1 5 2 1 L6	(6)	p:	pi1	1	G	(H40c)	20	Lost Birdies
1 1 5 4	(8)	m:	m/d	1	E	(H625)	342	Dark-Eyed Molly
1 1 5 5	(8)	p:	pi1	1	G	(H621)	191	Faughan Side
1 1 5 5	(8)	a:	ion	1	G	(H643)	159	Ballymonan Brae
1 1 6 5/5	(4:1)	p:	ion	1	G	(H138)	256	Black Chimney Sweeper
1 1 6 6/7	(4)	m:	ion	1	G	(H503)	273	Youghall Harbour
1 1 6 5	(8)	m:	ion	1	G	(H243b)	474	Young Edward the Gallant Hussar
1 1 U1 6	(4)	a:	l/i	1	D	(H813)	468	Sweet Londonderry
1 1 U1 U1	(4)	a:	?i-3	1	D	(H186)	46	Thatchers of Glenrea
1 2	(4:4)	p:	ion	1	G	(H490)	48	Jug of Punch
1 2 L5 L5	(8)	p:	ion	L5	G	(H719)	63	Leaves So Green
1 2 L5 1	(4)	p:	i/m	1	G	(H30a)	390	My Flora and I
1 2 L7 2	(4)	p:	ion	1	G	(H670)	293	Jolly Roving Tar
1 2 1 1	(4)	m:	l/i	1	D	(H754)	111	Good Ship Mary Cochrane (a)
1 2 1 2	(4)	p:	l/i	1	G	(H48g)	11	Old Sally Walker
1 2 1 5	(8)	m:	p-6	1	A	(H676)	41	Farmer
1 2 1 L5	(8:2)	p:	ion	1	G	(H700)	227	Mind Your Eye
1 2 2 1	(4)	p:	ion	1	G	(H10a)	2	Abbey
1 2 3 L5	(2)	p:	5xx	1	F	(H53c)	97	Paddy Doyle
1 2 3 L7/L5	(4:4)	p:	aeo	1	C	(H512)	225	My Bonnie Breeden
1 2 4 6	(8)	a:	ion	1	D	(H464)	167	Braes of Sweet Kilhoyle
1 2 4 7	(8)	a:	dor	1	F	(H242)	483	Mullinabrone
1 2 5 1	(8)	p:	i/m	1	G	(H2)	215	Mullaghdoo
1 2 5 1	(8)	p:	ion	1	G	(H11)	110	Trader
1 2 5 1	(8)	p:	i/m	1	G	(H506)	214	Sweet Loughgiel
1 2 5 1	(8)	p:	ion	1	G	(H651)	160	Braes of Carnanbane
1 2 5 5/4	(4)	p:	?i-3	1	G	(H817)	169	Mountsandel
1 2 5 5	(4)	a:	i/m	L6	C	(H735)	133	Lambkin

1 2 5 7 - 1 4 *Sam Henry's Songs of the People*

First-phrase Accents	Number of Phrases	Range	Mode	Final	Key	Henry Number	Page	Title
1 2 5 7	(8)	a:	dor	1	D	(H626)	465	Gruig Hill
1 2 5 7	(8)	a:	m/d	1	D	(H703)	210	Drumglassa Hill
1 2 6 3	(8)	m:	pl1	L6	D	(H584)	331	True Lovers' Departure
1 3 L5 -	(8)	p:	aeo	1	F	(H609)	199	Hills of Tyrone
1 3 L6 L5	(7:2)	p:	ion	1	G	(H47)	236	Valley Below
1 3 L6 L5	(4)	p:	?l/m	L5	G	(H124)	509	Brown-Eyed Gypsies
1 3 L6 L5	(8)	p:	ion	1	G	(H711)	234	Manchester Angel
1 3 L6 L6	(8)	m:	l/i	1	D	(H559)	237	Dark-Haired Girl
1 3 L7 1	(8)	p:	a/p	1	G	(H158)	295	Banks of Sweet Lough Neagh
1 3 1 L5	(4)	p:	pl1	L5	G	(H42a)	148	Miss Cochrane
1 3 1 L5	(8)	p:	d/a	1	A	(H220)	243	Flower of Magherally, O!
1 3 1 L5	(4)	p:	pl1	L6	G	(H762)	368	Campbell's Mill
1 3 1 L6 1	(8)	p:	ion	1	G	(H477)	140	Hielan' Jane
1 3 1 L7	(4)	a:	h-6	1	A	(H10c)	2	Dundee
1 3 1 1	(5)	m:	ion	1	F	(H216)	265	Feckless Lover
1 3 1 1 -	(4:2)	p:	i/m	1	G	(H472)	258	Nonsense o' Men
1 3 1 U1	(8)	m:	ion	1	C	(H118)	315	Mary and Willie
1 3 2 L5	(8)	p:	ion	1	G	(H728)	88	Drummer Boy at Waterloo
1 3 2 L6	(4:2)	p:	l/i	L5	G	(H223)	83	Deserter
1 3 2 L6	(4:4)	p:	i/m	1	G	(H511)	157	Hills o' Ballyboley
1 3 2 L7	(4)	a:	dor	1	Af	(H480a)	52	Bryan O'Lynn
1 3 2 1 (phr.1 spoken)	(1:4)	p:	pl1	L5	G	(H748)	263	Magherafelt Hiring Fair
1 3 2 1 L5	(6:2)	p:	ion	1	F	(H204)	388	Gramachree
1 3 2 2/L6	(4)	p:	*pl1	L6	G	(H60a)	400	Old Lover's Wedding
1 3 2 2/L6	(4)	p:	*pl1	L6	G	(H60b)	401	Laird's Wedding
1 3 2 7	(8)	a:	ion	1	Ef	(H202)	119	Boston Burglar
1 3 2 7	(8)	a:	ion	1	Ef	(H555)	463	Star of Donegal
1 3 2 7	(8)	a:	ion	1	Ef	(H750)	120	Wild Colonial Boy
1 3 2 7	(8)	a:	ion	1	Ef	(H765)	312	Lady of the Lake
1 3 3 1	(4:4)	m:	mix	L6	Ef	(H482)	391	Bring Me Back the Boy ... (a)
1 3 3 1	(4:4)	m:	mix	L6	Ef	(H692)	392	Never Change the Old Love ...
1 3 3 2	(4)	m:	ion	L6	G	(H531)	506	I Wish that You Were Dead ...
1 3 3 2/4	(4:4)	m:	d/a	1	F	(H834)	289	Boatman
1 3 3 U1	(8)	a:	i/m	1	D	(H183)	268	Rambling Suiler
1 3 4	(8)	a:	ion	1	D	(H664)	41	My Rattlin' Oul' Grey Mare
1 3 4 1	(4)	m:	ion	1	D	(H168)	399	My Bonnie Irish Boy
1 3 4 6	(8)	m:	mix	1	D	(H594)	430	Maid of Sweet Gorteen
1 3 5	(8)	m:	ion	1	G	(H139)	42	Rocks of Bawn
1 3 5 3	(4:2)	p:	l/i	1	G	(H122b)	88	Bonny Light Horseman
1 3 5 3	(4:2)	p:	pl1	1	G	(H515)	274	Mountain Road
1 3 5 4	(4)	p:	i-6	1	D	(H496)	96	Santy Anna
1 3 5 4 2 L5	(4)	p:	ion	1	G	(H818)	317	Green Garden
1 3/5 5 L7	(4:2)	a:	?ion	L6	F	(H17a)	61	Fine Broom Besoms
1 3 5 5	(4:4)	m:	ion	1	Ef	(H17b)	180	March of the Men of Garvagh
1 3 5 5	(8)	p:	ion	L5	G	(H156)	315	Johnny Jarmin
1 3 5 5	(6)	a:	ion	1	C	(H699)	383	Bonny Bushes Bright
1 3 5 5	(8)	a:	ion	1	C	(H804)	262	You're Welcome as the Flowers ...
1 3 5 6 U1 U1 -	(8)	a:	ion	1	C	(H616)	462	My Charming Coleraine Lass
1 3 5/U1	(8)	a:	ion	1	C	(H184=H68)	469	"Thank You, Ma'am" ...
1 3 5 U1	(8)	m:	ion	1	C	(H583)	314	Banks of [the] Dee
1 3 6	(8)	p:	pl1	1	G	(H563)	316	Lurgan Town
1 3 6 U1	(4:4)	m:	l/i	1	D	(H698)	51	Old 'Rosin the Bow'
1 3 7 2	(4:4)	p:	mix	1	G	(H209)	465	Innishowen
1 3 U1	(8)	m:	l/i	1	G	(H164)	362	True Lover's Discussion
1 3 U1 U1	(8)	m:	ion	1	C	(H54)	144	Mary's Dream
1 3 U1 U1	(8)	a:	i/m	1	C	(H571)	441	Sally Munro
1 4 1 7	(8)	a:	pl3	1	D	(H192)	101	Shamrock Shore
1 4 2 1	(4:4)	a:	ion	1	D	(H98b)	472	Inniskilling Dragoon
1 4 2 1	(4)	a:	?mix	1	G	(H497)	326	Drummer Maid
1 4 2 1	(4)	a:	ion	1	C	(H509)	168	Knocklayde
1 4 2 1	(4)	a:	ion	1	D	(H520)	259	Strands of Magilligan
1 4 2 1	(4:4)	a:	ion	1	D	(H631)	294	Fare Ye Well, Enniskillen

Melodic index 1 4 - 1 6 6

First-phrase Accents	Number of Phrases	Range	Mode	Final	Key	Henry Number	Page	Title
1 4 2 1	(8)	m:	ion	L5	D	(H662)	45	Shanty Boy
1 4 2 1	(8)	m:	?ion	L5	D	(H681)	490	Keeper of the Game
1 4 2 1	(4)	p:	ion	L5	G	(H663)	72	Dan Murphy's Convoy
1 4 2 1	(4)	a:	mix	1	D	(H771)	415	Susan Brown
1 4 2 1	(4:1)	a:	mix	1	D	(H797)	327	Drum Major
1 4 3 3	(8)	a:	mix	1	C	(H228a)	19	Duck from Drummuck
1 4 3 3	(8)	a:	mix	1	C	(H228b)	18	Nell Flaherty's Drake
1 4 - 7 5 -	(12:2)	a:	*m/d	1	D	(H508)	226	So Like Your Song and You
1 4 5 1	(4)	a:	*i/m	2	D	(H119)	21	Goat's Will
1 4 5 1	(13:8)	p:	ion	1	G	(H639)	59	Jolly Fisherman
1 4 5 1 L5	(4)	p:	ion	1	G	(H722)	343	Sweet Bann Water
1 4 5 5	(8)	a:	aeo	1	D	(H229a)	360	Lurgan Stream (a)
1 4 5 5	(8)	a:	aeo	1	D	(H229b)	360	Lurgan Stream (b)
1 4 5 6	(8)	m:	mix	1	G	(H1)	191	Flower of Sweet Dunmull
1 4 5 7	(8)	a:	m/d	1	D	(H180)	149	Holland Is a Fine Place
1 4 7 6	(8)	a:	?l/i	1	D	(H97)	130	Shane Crossagh
1 4 U1 6	(8)	a:	m/d	1	D	(H212)	370	Drummond's Land
1 4 U1 6	(8)	a:	m/d	1	D	(H561)	458	Lovely Annie (I)
1 4 U1 6	(8)	a:	?i-3	1	D	(H569)	112	Banks of Newfoundland
1 4 U1 7	(8)	a:	*m/d	1	Ef	(H197a)	248	Blazing Star of Drim (a)
1 4 U1 7	(8)	a:	*m/d	1	Ef	(H197b)	248	Blazing Star of Drung (b)
1 5 1 1	(4)	a:	ion	1	C	(H538)	364	Cahan's Shaden Glen
1 5 2 L5	(4:4)	p:	*aeo	3	E	(H34)	213	Pretty Three-Leaved Shamrock ...
1 5 2 L5	(4)	p:	l/i	1	G	(H641)	383	Ripest of Apples
1 5 2 1	(4)	a:	ion	1	D	(H161a)	456	Pretty Blue Handkerchief (I)
1 5 2 1	(4)	a:	ion	1	D	(H161b)	456	Pretty Blue Handkerchief (II)
1 5 2 1	(4)	a:	ion	1	D	(H161c)	456	Ballad of Master McGra[th]
1 5 2 1	(4)	a:	ion	1	D	(H620)	476	Journeyman Tailor
1 5 2 1	(4)	a:	ion	1	D	(H783)	34	Arthur Bond34
1 5 2 3/1	(4:2)	p:	ion	1	G	(H805b)	73	Balinderry Marriage (b)
1 5 2 4	(8)	a:	d/a	1	D	(H656)	187	Hannah M'Kay
1 5 3 1	(4)	m:	l/i	1	D	(H166)	328	Lovely Annie (II)
1 5 3 1	(4)	a:	d/a	1	C	(H175)	470	Yowe Lamb
1 5 3 1	(8)	a:	l/i	1	D	(H799)	221	Charlie Jack's Dream
1 5 3 2	(4)	a:	i/m	1	C	(H825)	299	Faithful Rambler
1 5 4 2	(8:4)	a:	ion	1	C	(H669)	179	Dungiven Cricket Match
1 5 4 4	(8)	a:	mix	1	D	(H26a=H246)	249	Ann o' Drumcroon
1 5 4 6/U1	(4)	a:	i/m	1	D	(H680)	141	Cowboy of Loreto
1 5 4 7	(4)	a:	m/d	1	E	(H109)	357	As I Walked Out
1 5 5 7	(8)	a:	mix	1	C	(H211)	479	When a Man's in Love
1 5 6 1	(4)	a:	*pi2	1	C	(H56)	354	John McAnanty's Courtship
1 5 6 1	(8)	a:	4xx	1	G	(H94)	17	My Bonnie Wee Hen
1 5 6 1	(4)	a:	pi2	1	D	(H516)	35	Spanking Maggie from the Ross
1 5 6 2	(8)	a:	ion	1	C	(H556)	376	On Board of a Man-of-War
1 5 6 2	(8)	m:	i/m	1	E	(H696)	290	Rathlin Song
1 5 6 3	(8)	a:	l/i	1	Ef	(H225)	196	Owenreagh's Banks
1 5 6 3	(8)	a:	ion	1	Ef	(H667)	192	Gelvin Burn
1 5 6 3	(8)	a:	l/i	1	D	(H816)	92	Old Ireland Far Away
1 5 6 5	(4:3)	p:	l/i	1	F	(H53a)	97	I'm Going Home
1 5 6 5	(8)	a:	ion	1	C	(H191)	142	Annie Moore
1 5 6 5	(8)	a:	l/i	1	D	(H678)	89	Irish Soldier Boy
1 5 6 6/5	(8:4)	a:	ion	1	C	(H600)	140	Irish Mother's Lament
1 5 6 U1	(8)	a:	ion	1	C	(H701)	501	Married Man
1 5/4 7 1	(4)	a:	mix	1	D	(H153a)	480	County Tyrone
1 5 7 2/1	(4)	a:	ion	1	D	(H755)	297	Johnnie and Molly
1 5 7 7 1 L7	(8)	a:	dor	1	C	(H505)	347	Old Arboe
1 5 U1 3	(8)	m:	ion	1	C	(H190)	420	Killeavy's Pride
1 5 U1 3	(4:4)	a:	pi1	1	C	(H513)	75	Lammas Fair in Cargan
1 5 U1 -7	(4)	a:	mix	1	D	(H104)	457	Gentle Shepherdess
1 5 U1 U1	(4)	a:	ion	1	G	(H573)	212	Sweet Glenbush
1 6 3 1	(4)	a:	ion	1	E	(H35)	327	Female Highwayman
1 6 3 1	(4)	m:	ion	1	D	(H614)	384	Willie Angler
1 6 6/1	(8)	p:	pi1	1	G	(H235)	203	Shamrock Sod No More

1 U1 - 3 1 3 2 *Sam Henry's Songs of the People*

First-phrase Accents	Number of Phrases	Range	Mode	Final	Key	Henry Number	Page	Title
1 U1 1 L5	(8)	m:	pi4	1	E	(H633)	147	James Kennedy
1 U1 5 3	(8)	a:	l/i	1	C	(H141)	395	Out of the Window
1 U1 6 6	(4:2)	a:	ion	1	C	(H792)	122	Whiskey in the Jar
1 U1 6 6/5	(4)	a:	l/i	1	D	(H794)	385	Under the Shade of a Bonny ...
1 U1 U2 5	(4)	a:	?ion	2	C	(H785)	399	My Darling Blue-Eyed Mary
2 L5 L5 L4	(4:4)	p:	mix	1	A	(H201)	265	Ride in the Creel
2 L7 2 4	(8)	p:	m-6	L5	G	(H106)	443	Johnnie Hart
2 L7 4 3	(8)	p:	ion	L5	G	(H521)	372	Girl from Turfahun
2 1 L6 1	(4)	p:	i/m	1	F	(H22b)	361	Castleroe Mill
2 1 4 3	(4)	a:	*ion	L6	D	(H585)	147	Sloan Wellesley
2 2 1 L5	(8)	p:	i/m	1	G	(H65a)	293	Alt[i]mover Stream
2 2 1 L5	(8)	p:	i/m	1	G	(H65b)	186	Farewell to Articlave
2 2/5 2 1	(4)	a:	*m/d	1	F	(H58)	446	Eliza
2 2 6 3	(8)	a:	pi1	L6	Ef	(H238a)	296	Banks of the Nile
2 3 3 1	(8)	p:	ion	1	G	(H767)	370	My Charming Kate O'Neill
2 5 1 1	(8)	m:	ion	1	Ef	(H179a)	12	John Mitchel's Farewell ... (a)
2 5 1 1	(8)	m:	ion	1	Ef	(H179b)	126	John Mitchell (b)
2 5 1 2	(8)	p:	ion	1	Af	(H199)	39	Tailor Boy
2 6 6	(8)	m:	mix	6	F	(H14a)	356	Bonnie Wee Lass of the Glen
3 L5 1 3	(8)	p:	i/m	1	G	(H741)	50	Rakes of Poverty
3 L5 3	(8)	p:	ion	1	G	(H638)	431	We Met, 'Twas in a Crowd
3 L5 3 1	(8)	p:	pi1	1	G	(H102)	464	Glenarm Bay
3 L5 3 4	(4:4)	p:	ion	1	Fs	(H79)	428	If I Were a Blackbird
3 L5 3 4	(4)	p:	ion	1	Ef	(H518)	301	Londonderry Love Song
3 L5 5	(8)	m:	ion	1	E	(H495)	227	Nancy, the Pride of the West
3 L6 L6	(8)	a:	?aeo	1	C	(H758)	23	Bellaghy Fair
3 L6 L6 L5	(8)	p:	ion	1	G	(H782)	473	Gallant Soldier
3 L6 L6 1	(4:1)	p:	i/m	1	G	(H824)	166	Old Inishowen
3 L6 L6 3 6	(4)	p:	l/i	1	G	(H634)	472	One Penny Portion
3 L6 2	(8)	m:	pi1	1	G	(H809)	162	Maids of Downhill
3 L6 3 5	(4)	p:	*lyd	1	F	(H159a)	396	Slighted Suitor (a)
3 L7 3 5	(4:2)	m:	d/a	1	G	(H73)	412	Ballindown Brae[s]
3 L7 4 1	(4)	a:	pi4	1	D	(H802)	466	Kellswaterside
3 L7 5 1	(4)	a:	ion	1	G	(H658)	175	Old Ireland
3 1 L5 1	(4)	p:	pi1	1	F	(H542)	217	Owenreagh
3 1 L5 1	(4)	p:	pi1	1	G	(H821)	220	There's a Dear Spot in Ireland
3 1 L6 L3 L3	(4:4)	p:	pi1	1	Af	(H551)	40	Cobbler
3 1 L6 L5	(8)	p:	ion	1	Bf	(H536)	209	Oh, Derry, Derry, Dearie Me
3 1 L6 1	(4:4)	p:	pi1	1	G	(H720)	165	Glenelly
3 1 L6 2 2 L6	(4)	m:	ion	1	Ef	(H629)	171	River Roe (II)
3 1 L7 L6	(8)	a:	m-4	6	Bf	(H640)	291	Linton Lowrie
3 1 1	(4)	p:	i-6	1	G	(H619)	373	Lakes of Ponchartrain
3 1 1 L5	(8)	p:	i/m	1	G	(H800)	164	Bonny Garrydoo
3 1 1 L5	(8)	p:	i/m	1	G	(H803)	79	Shepherd Boy
3 1/L6 1 L5 1	(4)	p:	i/m	1	G	(H143)	395	Green Bushes
3 1 1 L5 1	(4)	p:	i/m	1	G	(H476)	84	Bonny Woodha'
3 1 1 L6	(5)	p:	ion	1	F	(H232)	318	Dark-Eyed Sailor
3 1 1 1 3	(8:8)	p:	i/m	1	F	(H618)	85	Lovely Jamie
3 1 1 3 1 L5 -	(4)	p:	ion	1	G	(H826)	309	James Reilly
3 1 2 L5	(8)	p:	ion	L5	G	(H715)	166	Kearney's Glen
3 1 2 1	(8)	p:	pi1	1	F	(H37)	485	Henry, the Sailor Boy
3 1 2 1	(8)	p:	i/m	1	G	(H540)	468	Wild Slievegallon Brae[s]
3 1 2 1	(8)	p:	i/m	1	G	(H549)	81	You Broken-Hearted Heroes
3 1 2 1	(8)	p:	i/m	1	G	(H612)	242	Flower of Corby Mill
3 1 2 1	(8)	p:	i/m	1	G	(H665)	454	Boy That Found a Bride
3 1 2 1	(8)	p:	i/m	1	G	(H672)	212	Glen O'Lee
3 1 3 1	(4)	a:	m-4	1	G	(H76)	314	Mantle So Green
3 1 3 1	(4:2)	a:	a-7	1	E	(H820)	257	Roger's Courtship
3 1 3 2	(8)	m:	aeo	1	E	(H234)	436	Willy Reilly

Melodic index 3134 - 3344

First-phrase Accents	Number of Phrases	Range	Mode	Final	Key	Henry Number	Page	Title
3 1 3 4	(8)	a:	aeo	1	E	(H28b)	158	Ballycastle, O!
3 1 3 4	(8)	m:	pi4	1	E	(H494)	127	Hugh Hill, the Ramoan Smuggler
3 1 3 4	(8)	a:	aeo	1	E	(H712)	221	Irishman
3 1 3 4 -	(8)	a:	d/a	1	D	(H170)	299	Blooming Star of Eglintown
3 1 3 5	(4:1)	a:	ion	1	C	(H103)	55	Private Still
3 1 4 L7	(8)	a:	ion	1	D	(H688)	364	Maid of the Sweet Brown
3 1 4 L7	(8)	a:	ion	1	D	(H749)	189	Flower of Craiganee (a)
3 1 4 -7	(8)	a:	ion	1	G	(H781)	467	Largy Line
3 1 5	(8)	a:	i/m	1	D	(H798)	421	Pride of Newry Town
3 1 5 3	(5)	p:	l/i	1	G	(H645)	7	Raven-Locks
3 1 5 3	(8)	a:	ion	1	C	(H779)	54	Sailor in the Ale House
3 1 7 5	(4)	a:	ion	1	Ef	(H10e)	2	Mary's
3 1 U1 7	(8)	a:	i-6	1	C	(H764)	32	Clady River Water Bailiffs
3 2 L7 L5	(4)	p:	?d/a	L4	G	(H709)	348	If I Were a Fisher
3 2 1 L5	(8)	p:	ion	1	F	(H18a)	358	Will Ye Pad the Road wi' Me?
3 2 1 L5	(8)	p:	i/m	1	Af	(H18b)	272	Whinny Knowes
3 2 1 L5	(8:4)	p:	i/m	1	Af	(H481)	484	Wait till the Ship Comes Home
3 2 1 L5	(4)	p:	d/a	1	B	(H517)	7	Lullaby for a Sailor's Child
3 2 1 L6	(4)	p:	i/m	1	G	(H543)	103	Sailor Boy
3 2 1/L7	(8)	m:	aeo	1	E	(H498)	211	Oul' Dunloy
3 2 1 1	(4:2)	a:	ion	1	D	(H38)	29	Fox and His Wife
3 2 1 1	(8)	p:	'ion	L6	G	(H46)	438	Erin's Lovely Home
3 2 1 1	(4:4)	a:	pi1	1	D	(H80)	386	Phelimy Phil
3 2 1 1	(4:4)	a:	ion	1	Ef	(H236)	375	Barbara Allen
3 2 1 1	(4:4)	m:	ion	1	D	(H566)	122	Waltzing Matilda
3 2 2/L7	(8)	m:	dor	1	E	(H654)	170	Peistie Glen
3 2 2 1	(8)	p:	ion	1	G	(H727)	193	Farewell to Sweet Glenravel
3 2 2 1	(8)	p:	i/m	1	G	(H774)	150	Susan on the Beach
3 2 2 3	(8)	m:	pi4	1	E	(H648)	167	Shores of Sweet Kenbane
3 2 3 3 3 6/5	(4:4)	a:	l/i	1	C	(H588)	220	Riding Herd at Night
3 2 6 5	(8:4)	m:	pi1	1	D	(H63)	247	Rosaleen Bawn
3 2 6 5	(8)	a:	l/i	1	Ef	(H188)	401	Girl I Left Behind
3 2 6 5	(8)	m:	l/i	1	Ef	(H784)	172	Slieve Gallen Brae
3 2 L5 L4	(4:2)	a:	ion	U1	Bf	(H227)	47	Dandy Chignon
3 3 L5 7	(8)	m:	aeo	1	E	(H480b)	52	Bryan O'Lynn
3 3 L6 L5	(8)	p:	ion	1	C	(H591b)	6	Hush Alee
3 3 L6 L7	(4)	p:	ion	1	Bf	(H157)	207	Norah McShane
3 3 L7 1	(4)	p:	d/a	1	Fs	(H214)	445	Lady Leroy
3 3 1 L6	(4:4)	p:	pi1	1	Af	(H706)	180	Ta Ra, Limavady
3 - 1 1	(6:8)	m:	i/m	1	E	(H596)	6	Ballyeamon Cradle Song
3 3 1 5	(8)	m:	aeo	1	E	(H483)	427	Maid of Ballyhaunis
3 3 2/L6	(8)	m:	l/i	L6	C	(H545)	225	O, Jeanie, Dear
3 3 2 L6	(9)	m:	ion	1	C	(H546)	273	Cup of Gold
3 3 2/1	(8)	a:	ion	1	C	(H507)	213	Juberlane
3 3 2/1	(8:8)	a:	ion	1	D	(H787)	215	Where Moyola Waters Flow
3 3 2 1	(8:8)	m:	ion	1	D	(H83)	156	Old Stone Wall
3 3 2 1	(8)	p:	pi1	1	F	(H577)	439	Sweet Dunloy
3 3 3 L6 L6	(4)	a:	?pi1	L6	Ef	(H20b)	245	Summer Hill
3 3 3 1	(8)	p:	i/m	1	Ef	(H31)	411	'Prentice Boy
3 3 3 1	(4)	p:	i/m	1	G	(H53b)	96	It's Time for Us to Leave Her
3 3 3 1	(8)	p:	ion	1	G	(H237)	189	Carntogher's Braes
3 3 3 1	(8:4)	m:	pi1	1	D	(H592)	41	My Irish Jaunting Car
3 3 3 1	(8)	a:	ion	1	F	(H772)	23	Sport's Lament
3 3 3 2	(4)	p:	i/m	1	G	(H48e)	11	I'll Tell My Ma
3 3 3 2/1	(8)	a:	i/m	1	D	(H630)	7I	Irish Lullaby for the Christ Child
3 3/6 3 2	(4)	a:	?l/i	2	Ef	(H58)	446	Eliza
3 3 3 3	(4)	a:	d/a	1	E	(H757)	334	Willie Taylor (b)
3 3 3 5	(4)	p:	?pi1	2	G	(H116b)	202	Brown-Haired Lass
3 - 3 5 2 L6 -	(8)	m:	ion	1	D	(H3)	286	Londonderry Air
3 3 4 1/L7	(4)	p:	ion	1	G	(H64)	161	Girls of Coleraine
3 3 4 1/L7	(8)	p:	ion	1	G	(H657)	242	Maggie of Coleraine
3 3 4 3	(4)	p:	i-6	1	Bf	(H491)	225	Happy 'Tis, Thou Blind ...
3 3 4 4	(10)	a:	i/m	1	G	(H671)	22	Matty Broon's Soo

3 3 4 7 - 3 U1 Sam Henry's Songs of the People

First-phrase Accents	Number of Phrases	Range	Mode	Final	Key	Henry Number	Page	Title
3 3 4 7	(8)	a:	ion	1	D	(H466)	79	My Parents Reared Me Tenderly
3 3 5 1	(8)	m:	1/i	1	C	(H502)	98	Cruise of the Calabar
3 3 5 3	(4)	a:	aeo	1	B	(H135)	414	Broomfield Hill
3 3 5 3	(4)	a:	d/a	1	E	(H159b)	397	Slighted Suitor (b)
3 3 5 4	(8)	a:	ion	1	G	(H85)	300	Dobbin's Flowery Vale
3 3 5 4	(8)	a:	ion	1	C	(H647)	462	Cashel Green (I)
3 3 5 5	(8)	a:	mix	1	C	(H57b)	228	Maid of Erin's Isle
3 3 5 5	(8)	m:	1/i	1	D	(H116a)	201	Brown-Haired Lass
3 3/1 5 6/5 -	(4)	a:	mix	1	D	(H24b)	217	Banks of the Roe
3 3 5 U1	(4)	a:	ion	1	D	(H836)	372	Lass of Mohee
3 3 6 3 2 1	(4)	a:	1/i	1	C	(H206)	289	Drinaun D[h]un
3 3 6/5	(4)	p:	pi1	1	G	(H828)	286	Down in My Sally's Garden
3 3 6 5	(8)	a:	ion	1	C	(H586)	80	Black Horse
3 3 7 7 3	(8)	m:	pi4	1	E	(H579)	345	Fair Maid of Glasgow Town
3 4 L6 2	(8)	p:	ion	1	F	(H42b)	197	Point Maid
3/1 4 2 1	(4)	a:	mix	1	C	(H544)	165	Lovely Glenshesk (I)
3 4 2 1	(4)	a:	ion	1	C	(H814	415	Lord Ronald
3 4 3 2	(4)	a:	i/m	1	G	(H10g)	3	York
3 4 3 4	(8)	m:	i-2	1	C	(H110)	144	Collier Lad
3 4 3 4	(8)	a:	pi4	1	E	(H611)	397	Twenty-One
3 4 5 3	(8)	m:	ion	1	Ef	(H244)	295	Soldier Boy
3 4 5 5	(4)	a:	ion	1	D	(H655)	319	Pride of Glencoe
3 4 6 5	(8)	a:	ion	1	C	(H598)	61	Better Bide a Wee
3 4 U1 5	(8)	a:	?pi4	1	B	(H584)	331	True Lovers' Departure
3 4 U1 5	(8)	a:	mix	1	C	(H674)	219	Call of Home
3 5 L6	(4)	a:	1/i	1	Ef	(H245)	195	Adieu to the Banks of the Roe
3 5 L7 1	(4)	a:	mix	1	C	(H534)	454	Our Wedding Day
3 5 1 L5	(8:8)	p:	ion	1	G	(H526)	182	Neuve Chappelle
3 5 1/L6	(8)	a:	1/i	1	C	(H597)	476	Lough Erne Shore
3 5 1/L6	(4)	a:	pi1	1	C	(H112)	288	Oh, It's down Where the Water ...
3 5 1 L6/1	(4)	m:	pi1	1	Ef	(H682)	505	Will the Weaver
3 5 1 1	(4)	a:	1/i	L6	G	(H226)	511	Ship Carpenter's Wife
3 5 2 1	(8)	a:	1/i	1	D	(H210)	188	Farewell Ballycastle
3 5 2 1	(4:1)	m:	ion	1	D	(H786)	139	Finvola, the Gem of the Roe
3 5 2 4	(4)	a:	ion	1	F	(H10d)	2	French
3 5 2 5	(4)	a:	ion	1	G	(H10f)	3	Martyrs
3 5 4 1	(4)	a:	i-6	1	C	(H469)	144	My Lowlands, Away
3 5 4 1	(4)	a:	pi4	1	E	(H738)	478	Jamie and Nancy
3 5 4 2	(4:4)	p:	m-6	1	A	(H213)	334	Willie Taylor (a)
3 5 4 4/1	(4)	a:	?pi4	1	E	(H60a)	400	Old Lover's Wedding
3 5 4 4/1	(4)	a:	?pi4	1	E	(H60b)	401	Laird's Wedding
3 5 5 2	(8:2)	a:	ion	1	D	(H660)	273	Captain with the Whiskers
3 5 6 5	(8:2)	p:	i/m	1	Eb	(H92)	86	Hungry Army
3 5 6 U1	(4:2)	a:	ion	1	D	(H604)	505	Tailor in the Sea Chest
3 5 7 4/1	(8)	a:	d/a	5	G	(H679)	255	Maidens of Sixty-Three
3 5/7 7 2	(4:2)	a:	*aeo	1	D	(H17a)	61	Fine Broom Besoms
3 6 6 U1 6 5	(4)	m:	1/i	1	Ef	(H67)	365	Fair Maid of Ballyagan
3 U1 3 1/L7	(4:4)	a:	d/a	1	D	(H142)	294	My Dear Irish Boy
3 U1 5 U1	(8)	a:	ion	1	C	(H93)	72	Wedding at Ballyporeen
3 U1 7 6 2	(4)	a:	1/i	1	D	(H217)	432	Lover's Ghost
3 U1 7 6 5 -	(4)	a:	ion	1	Ef	(H218a)	386	Must I Go Bound? (I)
3 U1 7 6 5 -	(4)	a:	ion	1	Ef	(H218b)	386	Must I Go Bound? (II)
3 U1 7 6 5 -	(4)	a:	ion	1	D	(H683)	393	Apron of Flowers
3 U1 7 7 5 -	(4)	a:	1/i	1	D	(H690)	416	Susan Carr
3 U1 U1 - U3 U1 5	(4)	a:	mix	1	C	(H705b)	132	Dreary Gallows [2d tune]
3 U1 U2 5	(8)	a:	ion	1	D	(H130)	26	Mayogall Asses
3 U1 U2 5	(8)	a:	ion	1	D	(H675)	24	Heifer
3 U1 U3 2	(4)	a:	ion	U1	A	(H475)	455	Swan

Melodic index 4 - 5 3 4

First-phrase Accents	Number of Phrases	Range	Mode	Final	Key	Henry Number	Page	Title
4 L6 L7 1	(8)	p:	mix	1	G	(H608)	87	Plains of Waterloo (II)
4 1 1 4	(8)	a:	i-m	1	G	(H590)	486	Lass of Glenshee
4 1 1 7	(8)	m:	i&m	1	F	(H607)	250	Pride of Glenelly
4 1 3 5	(6)	a:	ion	1	D	(H96a)	230	Maid of Burndennet (a)
4 1 3 5	(6)	a:	ion	1	D	(H96b)	231	Maid of Burndennett (b)
4 1 3 7	(8)	a:	pi4	1	E	(H796)	163	Faughanvale
4 2 1 L7	(4)	a:	?m/d	1	D	(H57a)	57	Buttermilk Boy
4 2 3 1	(4)	a:	i-6	1	G	(H48c)	10	Ring a Ring o' Roses
4 2 3 U1	(8)	a:	ion	1	C	(H530)	298	Maid of Dunysheil
4 2 3 U1	(8)	a:	ion	1	C	(H822)	239	Jean of Ballinagarvey
4 2 6 U1	(8)	a:	?ion	1	D	(H69)	201	Happy Shamrock Shore
4 3 2 1	(4)	a:	ion	1	Ef	(H72)	374	Am I the Doctor?
4 3 6 5	(4)	a:	?aeo	1	B	(H585)	147	Sloan Wellesley
4 4 4 4	(8)	a:	dor	1	D	(H827)	100	Yellow Meal
4 4 5 1	(4)	a:	aeo	1	E	(H624)	349	I Am a Wee Laddie ...
4 4 U1 5	(8)	a:	ion	1	D	(H0)	53	State of Arkansaw
4 4 U1 5	(8)	a:	m-6	1	C	(H238b)	296	Banks of the Nile
4 5 1 5 U1	(4:2)	a:	aeo	1	C	(H176)	146	Willie Lennox
4 5 1 U1	(8)	a:	ion	1	Ef	(H27a)	371	Maid of Mourne Shore
4 5 1 U1	(8)	a:	ion	1	Ef	(H27b)	105	Portrush Fishing Disaster (I)
4 5 3 L5	(4:1)	p:	ion	1	E	(H147)	474	Green Broom
4 6 2 1	(4)	a:	*m/d	1	D	(H124)	509	Brown-Eyed Gypsies
4 6 3 2	(16)	a:	ion	1	D	(H533)	292	So Dear Is My Charlie to Me
4 7 5 4	(8)	a:	*mix	1	A	(H681)	490	Keeper of the Game
4 U1 5 2 L7 -	(8)	a:	dor	1	C	(H788)	300	Love's Parting
4 U1 U1 U1	(4)	a:	dor	1	D	(H580)	357	Farewell, Darling
5 1 L5 1	(4:2)	m:	aeo	4	E	(H793)	267	As I Gaed ower a Whinny Knowe
5 1 L6 L5	(5)	p:	ion	1	Af	(H215)	393	Bonny, Bonny Boy
5 1 L7 L7	(4:2)	m:	a/p	1	E	(H6=H567)	275	Woods of Mountsandel
5 1 L7/1	(8)	p:	mix	1	G	(H752)	245	Valleys of Screen
5 1 L7 1	(8)	m:	mix	1	E	(H150a)	466	Banks of Kilrea (I)
5 1 L7 4	(8)	a:	pi3	1	D	(H205)	465	Banks of the River Ness
5 1 1 L7	(8)	a:	pi3	1	D	(H28a)	194	Lovely Glenshesk (IIa)
5 1 1 5	(4;1)	p:	i/m	1	E	(H51)	129	Crafty Ploughboy
5 1 4 1	(8)	a:	dor	1	D	(H564)	344	Banks of Mourne Strand
5 1 4 3	(8)	p:	*i/m	L5	F	(H15)	87	Plains of Waterloo (I)
5 1 5 1	(8:4)	a:	ion	1	C	(H737)	309	Skerry's Blue-Eyed Jane
5 1 5 4	(2)	a:	4xx	1	F	(H713)	27	Seal Song
5 1 5 6	(8)	p:	i/m	1	G	(H151)	124	Jamie Raeburn's Farewell
5 1 5 7	(4)	a:	m/d	1	D	(H25b)	261	Load of Kail Plants
5 1 5 7	(8)	a:	dor	1	Bf	(H71)	246	Her Bonny Blue E'e
5 1 5 7	(4)	a:	?mix	3	D	(H159a)	396	Slighted Suitor (a)
5 1 6 U1	(8)	a:	ion	1	C	(H160)	292	My True Love's Gone A-Sailing
5 1 U1 5	(4)	a:	l/i	2	C	(H554)	400	Sweet Clonalee
5 2 L7/1	(8)	m:	m/d	1	D	(H41)	231	Kate of Glenkeen
5 2 1 1 -	(4)	a:	m/d	1	D	(H776)	261	Young Farmer's Offer
5 2 3 6	(8)	m:	pi4	1	E	(H691)	119	Botany Bay
5 2 5 2/1	(4:2)	a:	*m/d	2	E	(H22a)	232	Flower of Glenleary
5 2 5 2	(8)	p:	i/m	L5	G	(H702)	504	Wealthy Farmer
5 3 1 L5	(8)	a:	mix	1	G	(H635)	455	Tossing o' the Hay
5 3 1 3	(12)	m:	ion	1	G	(H601)	174	Where Derry Meets Tyrone
5 3 2/1	(4)	p:	?pi1	L6	F	(H43)	394	Maid with the Bonny Brown Hair
5 3 2 1	(4)	a:	*l/i	2	C	(H57a)	57	Buttermilk Boy
5 3 2 1 7 U1	(8)	a:	d/a	1	C	(H173)	250	Moorlough Mary
5 3 3 1	(8:4)	a:	l/i	1	C	(H714)	513	Wee Wifukie
5 3 3 U2	(8)	a:	d/a	1	E	(H589)	344	Rejected Lover
5 3 4 L7	(8)	a:	d/a	1	B	(H240)	192	Finn Waterside
5 3 4 1	(8)	a:	d/a	1	E	(H120)	332	Blythe and Bonny Scotland
5 3 4 1	(8)	a:	m-6	1	E	(H185)	128	Three Huntsmen
5 3 4 1	(8)	a:	aeo	1	E	(H623)	109	Loss of the Royal Charter
5 3 4 1	(4)	a:	aeo	1	E	(H806)	434	Constant Farmer's Son
5 3 4 2	(4)	p:	ion	1	G	(H770)	485	Garden Gate

5 3 5 - 5 U1 6   *Sam Henry's Songs of the People*

First-phrase Accents	Number of Phrases	Range	Mode	Final	Key	Henry Number	Page	Title
5 3 5 1	(4)	a:	dor	1	G	(H733)	342	Maid of Tardree
5 3 5 U1	(8)	a:	d/a	1	A	(H113)	434	Young Edward Bold
5 3 6 2	(8)	m:	ion	1	D	(H576)	435	Bonny Labouring Boy
5 3 U1 7/5	(8)	a:	d/a	1	E	(H129)	141	John McKeown and Margaret Deans
5 4 1 -	(8:4)	a:	?pi3	4	D	(H36)	74	Coleraine Regatta
5 4 1 1	(4:3)	m:	pi4	1	E	(H819)	219	Och, Och, Eire, O!
5 4 1 4/L7	(8)	a:	ion	1	F	(H8)	311	Laurel Hill
5 4 1 4/L7	(8)	a:	aeo	1	G	(H743)	200	Emigrant's Farewell
5 4 1 4 1	(4:4)	a:	i&m	1	Ef	(H91)	156	Little Thatched Cabin
5 4 1 U1	(4)	a:	d/a	1	D	(H705a)	132	Dreary Gallows [1st tune]
5 4 2/1 1	(8:8)	a:	ion	1	D	(H829)	91	Balaclava
5 4 3 2 1	(8)	p:	ion	1	Bf	(H562)	113	Captain Coulston
5 4 3 3 1	(8)	a:	?aeo	1	E	(H46)	438	Erin's Lovely Home
5 4 3 4	(8)	a:	pi4	1	D	(H33)	397	Twenty-One
5 4 4 1	(4)	a:	pi3	1	D	(H165b)	260	Green Grow the Rashes
5 4 4 1	(4)	a:	m/d	1	D	(H241)	346	Blackbird and Thrush
5 4 4 5	(8)	m:	pi4	1	D	(H20a)	216	Maid of Mullaghmore
5 4 4 5	(8)	m:	pi4	1	D	(H500)	359	Maid of Craiglenorn
5 4 4 5	(8)	m:	pi4	1	D	(H548)	341	One Morning Clear
5 4 5 L7 -	(4:4)	p:	ion	1	G	(H725)	278	Basket of Oysters
5 4 5 1	(4)	m:	m-6	1	D	(H613)	396	My Bonny Brown Jane
5 4 5 1 1	(4)	a:	*pi4	1	C	(H20b)	245	Summer Hill
5 4 5 4	(8)	a:	aeo	1	E	(H77)	418	Silvery Tide
5 4 5 5	(8)	a:	d/a	1	C	(H742)	104	Loss of Seven Clergymen
5 4 7 1	(8)	a:	m/d	1	D	(H148)	411	Blooming Caroline ...
5 4 7 L7	(8)	a:	dor	1	D	(H196)	210	Hills of Donegal
5 5 L7 5	(8)	a:	d/a	1	D	(H68)	276	Star of Moville
5 5 1 L5	(6:4)	p:	ion	1	Af	(H101)	275	Ould Lammas Fair
5 5 1 L5	(4:1)	p:	d/a	1	C	(H221)	490	Rich Ship Owner's Daughter
5 5 1 L5	(8:4)	p:	ion	1	F	(H541)	207	Old Blacksmith's Shop
5 5 1 L5	(8)	p:	i/m	1	G	(H593)	388	My Love John
5 5 1 L5	(8)	p:	a/p	1	G	(H724)	82	Lovely Sally (a)
5 5 1 L6	(8)	p:	d/a	1	E	(H553)	482	Jamie, Lovely Jamie
5 5 1 L6/L5	(4)	p:	i/m	1	A	(H128)	440	Henry Connor of Castledawson
5 5 1 1	(4)	a:	aeo	1	D	(H89)	287	Early, Early
5 5 1 1	(8)	m:	i/m	1	Ef	(H167)	369	Maid of Faughanvale
5 5 2 1	(4)	a:	m-6	1	G	(H154)	33	Cashel Green (II)
5 5/3 3 6/5	(4)	p:	ion	1	G	(H95)	107	Falcon
5 5 3 5	(4)	a:	5xx	1	Ef	(H48h)	11	Broken Bridges
5 5 3 5 3 L7	(8)	m:	d/a	1	E	(H115a)	355	Claudy Green (a)
5 5 3 5 3 L7	(8)	m:	d/a	1	E	(H115b)	241	Claudy Green (b)
5 5 4 L7	(8)	a:	d/a	1	D	(H637)	385	Lovely Nancy
5 5 4 5	(4)	p:	ion	1	G	(H126)	510	Fair Annie
5 5 4 7	(8:4)	m:	dor	1	C	(H473)	354	Paddy's Land
5 5 5 1	(8)	p:	ion	1	F	(H74)	236	Dear-a-Wee Lass
5 5 5 1	(8)	a:	m/d	1	D	(H123)	90	Heights of Alma
5 5 5 2	(4)	a:	i/m	1	F	(H48d)	11	Water, Water, Wallflowers
5 5 5 3	(8)	a:	aeo	1	C	(H501)	25	"Crummy" Cow
5 5 5 4	(8)	a:	a/p	1	E	(H149)	456	Pining Day and Daily
5 5 5 -	(4:1)	p:	i/m	1	G	(H710)	264	Whistling Thief
5 5 5 5	(4)	a:	i/m	1	E	(H48a)	10	I Am the Master
5 5 U1 4 1	(4)	a:	ion	1	C	(H86)	443	Banks of the Bann
5 5 U1 5	(8)	m:	ion	1	F	(H731)	22	Moneygran Pig Hunt
5 5 U1 U1	(8)	a:	l/i	1	C	(H539)	97	Girls of Valparaiso
5 6 4 3	(8)	a:	ion	1	D	(H729)	446	Apprentice Boy
5 6 5 1	(8)	p:	l/i	1	G	(H627)	161	Beautiful Churchill
5 6 6 2/6	(4)	m:	pi1	1	G	(H775)	171	Bonny Portrush
5 7 4 1	(4)	a:	dor	1	D	(H587)	433	Sweet William
5 U1 3 1	(4)	a:	pi1	1	C	(H636)	235	Mary Smith, the Maid ...
5 U1 6/2	(4)	m:	i/m	1	C	(H243a)	473	Young Edward the Gallant ...
5 U1 6/4	(8:4)	p:	ion	1	D	(H70a)	340	I've Two or Three Strings ... (a)
5 U1 6 5	(4)	a:	l-2	1	D	(H744)	12	Cricketty Wee
5 U1 6 7	(4)	a:	l/i	1	F	(H10h)	3	Newto[w]n

Melodic index 5 U1 U1 - 7 5

First-phrase Accents	Number of Phrases	Range	Mode	Final	Key	Henry Number	Page	Title
5 U1 U1 5	(8)	a:	mix	1	Ef	(H121)	270	Cloughmills Fair
5 U1 U2 U1	(4:1)	a:	ion	U1	C	(H514)	297	Bold Privateer
5 U2 U2 6	(8)	a:	l/i	5	C	(H519)	389	Belfast Mountains
5 U3 U3 6	(8)	a:	i/m	5	C	(H144)	270	Maid of Seventeen
6 L5 1 4 4 L7	(4:2)	m:	ion	1	D	(H87a)	181	Bright Orange Stars of Coleraine
6 L5 1 4 4 L7	(4)	m:	ion	1	D	(H87b)	182	Boys of Coleraine
6 1 3 2	(8)	m:	pi1	L6	Ef	(H125a)	475	John Hunter (a)
6 1 6 U3	(4)	a:	?l/i-2	6	C	(H10b)	2	Dublin
6 2 1 1	(4:1)	a:	l/i	1	C	(H486)	121	Eight-Mile Bridge
6 2 2 1	(4)	a:	l/i	1	D	(H485)	308	Mary Machree
6 3 L6 1	(4)	a:	l/i	1	C	(H108a)	329	Rich Merchant's Daughter
6 3 L6 1 5 -	(8)	p:	pi1	1	G	(H646)	209	Coleraine Girl
6 3 1 1 3	(8)	m:	pi1	1	C	(H32)	269	Where the Moorcocks Crow
6 3 1 3	(4)	a:	i/m	1	G	(H599)	12	Fair Rosa
6 3 3 L6	(8)	p:	ion	1	C	(H133)	461	Bess of Ballymoney
6 3 3 L6	(8)	m:	ion	1	D	(H823)	59	O'Ryan
6 3 3/1 -	(8)	a:	?pi1	2	C	(H780)	345	Ploughboy
6 3 3 1	(4)	a:	l/i	1	D	(H165a)	260	Green Grow the Rashes
6 3 4 1	(4)	a:	aeo	1	B	(H117)	44	As a King Went A-Hunting
6 3 6 2	(8)	p:	ion	1	G	(H134)	168	Lochaber Shore
6 3 6 3/2	(4:2)	a:	?l/i	3	D	(H22a)	232	Flower of Glenleary
6 4 4 1	(6:4)	p:	aeo	1	C	(H59)	76	On the Road to Bethlehem
6 5 1 -	(12:6)	p:	ion	1	G	(H642)	207	Little Old Mud Cabin on the Hill
6 5 1/L6	(4)	m:	l/i	1	C	(H9)	186	Lovely Armoy
6 5 1/L6 -	(4)	a:	5xx	1	C	(H547)	195	In Praise of the Glen
6 5 1 1	(4)	m:	l/i	1	D	(H24a)	348	Star of Benbradden
6 5 2 -	(8:4)	a:	*pi1	5	C	(H36)	74	Coleraine Regatta
6 5 2 1/L6	(4)	p:	pi1	1	G	(H127)	368	Factory Girl
6 5 2 1	(8:8)	m:	ion	1	F	(H4)	190	My Girl from Donegal
6 5 3 L5	(8)	m:	l/i	1	C	(H529)	320	Bordon's Grove
6 5 3 1	(4)	m:	pi1	1	D	(H602)	107	Wreck of the Fanad Boat
6 5 3 1	(8)	m:	i/m	1	D	(H760)	471	Navvy Boy
6 5 6 2	(8)	a:	l/i	1	D	(H66)	369	Wester Snow
6 5 U1	(8)	a:	pi1	1	C	(H581)	318	Love Token
6 6 1 6	(8)	a:	l/i	1	C	(H693)	313	Banks of Claudy
6 6 2 2	(8)	p:	i/m	1	G	(H107)	320	Jennie of the Moor
6 6 4 4	(8)	a:	ion	1	C	(H198)	481	My Father's Servant Boy
6 6 5 1	(8)	a:	ion	2	F	(H666)	170	Oville
6 6 5 2 1/L5	(8)	m:	ion	1	D	(H686)	160	Carnlough Shore
6 6 5 3	(8)	a:	l/i	1	C	(H111)	229	Holly Bough
6 6 6 3	(4:2)	a:	ion	L2	F	(H152)	266	I'm Seventeen 'Gin Sunday
6 U1 1	(4)	m:	ion	1	D	(H831)	235	Autumn Dusk
6 U1 3 1	(8)	a:	ion	1	C	(H88)	18	Bonny Brown Hen
6 U1 3 2	(4)	a:	l/i	1	D	(H81)	430	McClenahan's Jean
6 U1 4 5	(8)	a:	ion	1	D	(H181)	131	Breaking of Omagh Jail
6 U1 5 2	(8)	a:	ion	1	C	(H479)	347	Cuckoo
7 4 1 L7	(8)	a:	?m/d	1	D	(H557)	478	Molly, Lovely Molly
7 4 7 L7	(8)	a:	m/d	1	E	(H55)	479	Charming Mary O'Neill
7 5 1 L5 5 1	(4)	m:	d/a	1	D	(H582)	238	Gragalmachree
7 5 4/3	(4)	a:	*pi4	1	D	(H43)	394	Maid with the Bonny Brown Hair
7 5 4/3	(4)	a:	pi4	1	D	(H150b)	361	Banks of Kilrea (II)
7 5 4/3	(8)	m:	pi4	1	D	(H653)	211	Happy Green Shades of Duneane
7 5 4 4	(8)	a:	pi4	1	D	(H19b)	196	Brow of Sweet Knocklayd
7 5 4 4	(8)	a:	pi4	1	D	(H19a)	194	Glenshesk Waterside
7 5 7 5	(8)	a:	d/a	1	A	(H484)	177	Mac's and the O's
7 5 U2 5	(4)	a:	m/d	1	D	(H707)	227	Not the Swan on the Lake

629

U1 1 - U4 U1 *Sam Henry's Songs of the People*

First-phrase Accents	Number of Phrases	Range	Mode	Final	Key	Henry Number	Page	Title
U1 1 5 2	(8)	a:	ion	1	D	(H29)	53	Denny Byrne, the Piper
U1 3 1/L6 -	(8)	a:	ion	1	C	(H777)	427	Banks of Cloughwater
U1 3 1 L6	(8)	a:	l/i	1	C	(H795)	198	Farewell to Slieve Gallen
U1 3 3 1	(9)	m:	ion	1	C	(H177)	271	O'er the Moor amang the Heather
U1 3 3 3	(4)	a:	i/m	1	D	(H746)	62	Gaol Song
U1 3 3 U3	(8)	a:	i-6	1	Af	(H552)	102	Patrick O'Neal
U1 3 5 4	(8)	a:	?pi4	1	C	(H125a)	475	John Hunter (a)
U1 3 5 4	(8)	a:	?pi4	1	C	(H125b)	476	Wheelwright
U1 4 1 1 1 -	(4)	a:	dor	1	E	(H470)	491	Lord Beichan
U1 4 7 6	(8)	a:	?m/d	1	C	(H15)	87	Plains of Waterloo (I)
U1 5 1/L6	(8)	a:	l/i	1	Ef	(H695)	442	Kellswater
U1 5 2 3 6 5	(4:3)	a:	ion	1	C	(H82)	262	Irish Serenade
U1 5 3 1	(4)	a:	d/a	1	E	(H687)	302	Maids of Culmore
U1 5 3 5	(4)	a:	pi1	1	D	(H45)	477	Belfast Town
U1 5 4 4	(8)	a:	pi4	1	E	(H694)	503	Upside Down
U1 5 4 7 L7	(8)	a:	m/d	1	D	(H224b)	391	Flower of Sweet Strabane
U1 5 5 2	(8)	a:	ion	1	C	(H761)	228	Peggy of the Moor
U1 5 5 5	(8:4)	a:	i/m	1	C	(H39)	123	Heather Jock
U1 5 6 5	(2:2)	a:	i/m	1	D	(H732)	57	My Grandfather Died
U1 5 7 3	(8)	a:	mix	1	C	(H558)	106	Wreck of the Enterprise
U1 5 7 3	(8)	a:	mix	1	C	(H560)	112	French Privateer
U1 5 7 7	(8)	a:	pi3	1	C	(H572)	159	Benbradden Brae
U1 6 2 3	(8)	a:	l/i	1	C	(H487)	43	Lint Pullin'
U1 6 2 5 1	(8)	a:	ion	1	C	(H730)	190	Hills of Tandragee
U1 6/5	(4)	a:	ion	1	C	(H532)	367	Tarry Trousers
U1 6 5 5	(4)	p:	l/i	1	C	(H736)	489	Johnny Scott
U1 6 U1 3	(8:1)	a:	ion	1	C	(H44)	178	Rocky Road to Dublin
U1 6 U1 5 3 1 L6 -	(8)	a:	l/i	1	C	(H721)	438	Young Mary of Accland
U1 7 3 4	(8)	a:	d/a	1	C	(H99)	89	Three Flowers of Chivalry
U1 7 3 4	(8)	a:	mix	1	D	(H468)	441	John Reilly, the Sailor Lad
U1 7 4 4/1	(8)	a:	i-6	U1	Af	(H812)	310	Banks of the Clyde
U1 7 6 5	(8:4)	a:	ion	1	D	(H492)	238	Old Dun Cow
U1 7 6 5 9	(4:2)	a:	ion	U1	C	(H650a)	263	Roving Bachelor (a)
U1 7 6 5	(4:2)	a:	ion	U1	C	(H650b)	264	Roving Bachelor (b)
U1 U1 3 1	(8)	a:	ion	1	D	(H52b)	429	Slaney Side
U1 U1 3 7	(8)	a:	pi4	1	A	(H75b)	199	Bonny, Bonny
U1 U1 4 6	(8)	a:	mix	1	C	(H27c)	105	Portrush Fishing Disaster (II)
U1 U1 6 5/3	(8)	a:	ion	U1	Bf	(H187)	162	Dungiven Priory Church
U1 U1 6 6/3	(4:4)	a:	ion	U1	C	(H50)	139	Bard of Culnady
U1 U1/7 5 5	(4:2)	a:	pi4	1	A	(H114)	143	Molly Bawn Lowry
U1 U1 U1 5	(8)	m:	i&m	1	D	(H98a)	64	Barossa
U1 U1 U1 5	(8:8)	a:	ion	1	C	(H734)	149	Polly Primrose
U3 U1 5 1	(8:8)	a:	ion	U1	C	(H759)	288	My Sailor Boy
U4 U1 5 -	(4)	a:	ion	U1	Bf	(H200)	470	Petie Cam' ower the Glen

Sources of illustrations

All the illustrations used in this book appear on old broadsheets, most of which appear to be of Irish origin. Some are lumped together with English broadsides located in the rare-book facility in the University Research Library at the University of California, Los Angeles, and some are in the Morrison music library at Berkeley, specifically identified as Brereton broadsheets. Special thanks are due to the research librarians who made it easy to find and copy the sheets.

The following list details the sheets on which the original pictures appear by the title of the song, the library practice.

- p. v THE MARINER'S GRAVE / P. Brereton Printer 1 Lr Exchange St Dublin
- 1 CAVAN VICTORY. / A NEW SONG, [n.i.]
- 5 A New Song Call'd / GROGA'NS GROVE / P. Brereton, Printer [as p. v above]
- 9 ERIN'S LOVELY HOME / [?], Birmingham, [?]2, Thomas-st
- 16 GRANDFATHER'S / BIRD. [parody of American "Grandfather's Clock"] / [with] Stick It Up / OR WAIT TILL MY SHIP / COMES HOME. [n.i.]
- 28 Parody on / PADDLE YOUR OWN / CANOE / Brereto 1 Lr Exchange St Dub
- 30 A new song on the / Sporting Races of Kanturk / P Brereton 56 COOKE St Dublin
- 31 A new song on the / GENERAL TAXATION OF OUR DAYS. / P Brereton. Printer 55 Cooke Street
- 35 [see note above, p. 30]
- 38 The Potato and Corn Meet / ing about Tithes. [n.i.]
- 51 A much admired song called / THE / LOVERS OF DERRY / P BRERETON. Printer [as p. v above]
- 53 The / Bag of Nails / HALY, Printer, Hanover-Street, CORK.
- 58 THE IRISH TENANT FARMERS LAMENT / FROM / EVICTION FROM HIS NATIVE HOME [n.i.]
- 60 [see note above, p. 51]
- 71 HAGERTY'S BALL / P. BRERETON, Printer [as p. v above] [same cut on A New song Call'd / THE HIREING DAY / P Brereton Printer [as p. v above]]
- 76 AN ELEGY ON THE / DEATH OF THE MUCH LAMENTED / DOCTOR D M OBRIEN / P Brereton [as p. v above]
- 78 A New Song / CALL'D / WHEN THIS CRUEL WAR IS OVER / P. Brereton [as p. v above]
- 95 THE / BOATMAN OF THE OHIO. / 3. / [with] HARK AWAY / BESS. / London:-- H Such, Printer & Publisher, 177, Union Street, Borough.--S.E.
- 118 A Lamentation On / ALLEN LARKIN AND OBRIEN / WHO WERE EXECUTED AT MANCHESTER / ON THE 23th OF NOVEMBER 1867 / P. Brereton Printer 1 Lr Exch[?] St Dubli
- 133 THE SORROWFUL LAMENTATION OF ANDREW CARR / Who Was Executed on the 28 of July at Richmond Jail / FOR THE MURDER OF MARGRET MURPHY / P Brereton Printer 55 COOKE St Dublin
- 138 A DEVINE POME WRITTEN ON / SAINT FRANCIS FOUNDER / OF THE ORDER OF THE CORD / P. Brereton, Printer [as p. v above]
- 146 A new song on the birth and suffering of / OUR LORD & SAVIOUR JSUS CHRIST / P. BRERETON, Printer [as p. v above] [same cut on ON THE LOVE OF JESUS [n.i.]]
- 147 [see above, p. 51]
- 155 The Revolt of F. Hannon [n.i.]
- 173 THE ADVENTURE'S / OF / ROGER O'HARE / P. Brereton [as p. v above]

631

185	A new song on the / RELEASEMENT OF THE / POLITICAL PRIS- / ONERS [n.i.]
206	My Native Land So / Green [n.i.]
224	REILY FROM THE / Co KERRY / P Brereton COOKE St D...
254	A / MOST ADMIRE'D / PARRIDY ON / SHULEAGRA / P. BRERE- TON, Printer [as p. v above] [same cut on A new song call'd the / GAY OLD HAG [n.i.]]
285	A new song in praise of / Mr TAIT AND TEH HARBOUR / BOM- MISSIONERS [n.i.]
291	A new song on / O'CONNELL AND THE TINKERS / P BRERET N PRINTER, [?]5 CO KE ,S , DUBLIN
306	They All do it. [n.i.]
325	He Died like a true Irish Soldier / J. NICHOLSON, Printer, CHEAPSIDE SONG HOUSE 25, Church Lane, Belfast
339	The / IRISMANS FROLICKS / IN LONDON / P. Brereton [as p. v above]
353	THERE'S BOUND / TO BE A ROW. [n.i.] [with] THE MAN / AT / THE NORE. [n.i.]
366	A new song on the / SPORTING RACES / OF CAVAN / P BRE- RETON PRINTER [as p. v above]
382	The Thrashing Machine. [with] FARMERS DON'T YOU CRY. / WILLIAMSON, PRINTER, NEWCASTLE
410	[see note, p. 206 above]
426	A new and much admire'd song / Call'd the three / LOVERS TRIP TO CARRICKMAGAT / BY MICHEAL DAILY / P BRE- RETON, Printer [as p. v above]
453	The Rambling Boys / of Pleasure [n.i.]
500	O'REILLY / FROM THE CO CAVAN / Or The Phoenix of Erins Green Isle / P. Brereton Printer [as p. v above]
502	WHERE THE GRASS GROWS / GREEN / P B ereton 1 nr Ex- change St dublin
507	A new song call'd the / EMEGRANTS FAREWELL TO / DONE- GALL / P. Brereton, 1, Lr. Exchange, Strt, Dublin
521	A new song call'd / BROTHER BILL AND JAMIMA BROWN / P, BRERETON, PRINTER [as p. v above] [same cut on A new song call'd the / CONVICT ON THE ISLE OF / FRANCE / P BRERETON 56 COOKE St DUBLIN]
545	OYSTER-SHELL BONNET / AND / DANDY CHIGNAUNs / P [up- side down: Brereton] [as p. v above]
632	A new Song cal.'d the / POOR WANDERRER SIGHS / AND GRIEF ON PARTING HIS / NATIVE LAND / P Brereton [as p. v above]

Lightning Source UK Ltd.
Milton Keynes UK
UKHW051214060519
342176UK00006B/1/P